# The Cambridge Handbook of Metaphor and Thought

*The Cambridge Handbook of Metaphor and Thought* offers the most comprehensive collection of essays in multidisciplinary metaphor scholarship that has ever been published. These essays explore the significance of metaphor in language, thought, culture, and artistic expression. There are five main themes of the book: the roots of metaphor, metaphor understanding, metaphor in language and culture, metaphor in reasoning and feeling, and metaphor in nonverbal expression. Contributors come from a variety of academic disciplines, including psychology, linguistics, philosophy, cognitive science, literature, education, music, and law.

Raymond W. Gibbs, Jr., is Professor of Psychology at the University of California, Santa Cruz. He is author of *The Poetics of the Mind: Figurative Thought, Language, and Understanding; Intentions in the Experience of Meaning;* and *Embodiment and Cognitive Science.* He is co-editor of *Metaphor in Cognitive Linguistics* and of *Irony in Language and Thought: A Cognitive Science Reader* and is editor of the journal *Metaphor and Symbol.* His research interests include psycholinguistics, figurative language, and pragmatics.

# The Cambridge Handbook of Metaphor and Thought

*Edited by*

RAYMOND W. GIBBS, JR.
*University of California, Santa Cruz*

CAMBRIDGE
UNIVERSITY PRESS

CAMBRIDGE UNIVERSITY PRESS
Cambridge, New York, Melbourne, Madrid, Cape Town, Singapore, São Paulo, Delhi

Cambridge University Press
32 Avenue of the Americas, New York, NY 10013-2473, USA

www.cambridge.org
Information on this title: www.cambridge.org/9780521600866



First published 2008

Printed in the United States of America

*A catalog record for this publication is available from the British Library.*

*Library of Congress Cataloging in Publication Data*

The Cambridge handbook of metaphor and thought / edited by Raymond W. Gibbs, Jr.
p. cm.
Includes bibliographical references and index.
ISBN 978-0-521-84106-1 (hardback) – ISBN 978-0-521-60086-6 (pbk.)
1. Metaphor. 2. Psycholinguistics. 3. Language and culture. 4. Nonverbal communication. I. Gibbs, Raymond W. II. Title.
P301.5.M48C35 2008
121′.68–dc22 2007041275

ISBN 978-0-521-84106-1 hardback
ISBN 978-0-521-60086-6 paperback

# Contents

*Contributors* *page* ix

PART I: INTRODUCTION

Metaphor and thought: The state of the art 3
*Raymond W. Gibbs, Jr.*

PART II: THE ROOTS OF METAPHOR

1 The neural theory of metaphor 17
*George Lakoff*

2 Philosophy's debt to metaphor 39
*Mark Johnson*

3 Rethinking metaphor 53
*Gilles Fauconnier and Mark Turner*

4 How metaphors create categories – quickly 67
*Sam Glucksberg*

5 A deflationary account of metaphors 84
*Dan Sperber and Deirdre Wilson*

PART III: METAPHOR UNDERSTANDING

6 Metaphor as structure-mapping 109
*Dedre Gentner and Brian Bowdle*

7 How the mind computes the meaning of metaphor: A simulation based on LSA 129
*Walter Kintsch*

8 Is metaphor unique? 143
*Rachel Giora*

9 Metaphor, imagination, and simulation: Psycholinguistic evidence 161
*Raymond W. Gibbs, Jr., and Teenie Matlock*

10 Metaphor comprehension and the brain 177
*Seana Coulson*

PART IV: METAPHOR IN LANGUAGE AND CULTURE

11 Metaphor and talk 197
*Lynne Cameron*

12 Metaphor and education 212
*Graham Low*

13 Metaphor in literature 232
*Elena Semino and Gerard Steen*

14 Metaphor from body and culture 247
*Ning Yu*

15 Metaphor, semantics, and context 262
*Josef Stern*

16 Corpus linguistics and metaphor 280
*Alice Deignan*

17 Metaphor and poetic figures 295
*Yeshayahu Shen*

PART V: METAPHOR IN REASONING AND FEELING

18 Metaphor and artificial intelligence: Why they matter to each other 311
*John A. Barnden*

19 Conceptual metaphor, human cognition, and the nature of mathematics 339
*Rafael Núñez*

20 What is the "color" of law? 363
*Steven L. Winter*

21 Metaphor and emotion 380
*Zoltán Kövecses*

22 Putting it in context: Metaphor and psychotherapy 397
*Linda M. McMullen*

23 Metaphor and psychoanalysis 412
*Antal F. Borbely*

24 Crossing the senses in metaphorical language 425
*Cristina Cacciari*

PART VI: METAPHOR IN NONVERBAL EXPRESSION

**25** Metaphor and art 447
*John M. Kennedy*

**26** Metaphor in pictures and multimodal representations 462
*Charles Forceville*

**27** Metaphor, gesture, and thought 483
*Alan Cienki and Cornelia Müller*

**28** Metaphor and music 502
*Lawrence M. Zbikowski*

*Author index* 525

*Subject index* 537

# Contributors

John A. Barnden
School of Computer Science
The University of Birmingham
Birmingham, United Kingdom

Antal F. Borbely
New York Psychoanalytic Institute
New York, NY, USA

Brian Bowdle
Department of Psychology
Grand Valley State University
Allendale, MI, USA

Cristina Cacciari
Department of Biomedical Sciences
University of Modena
Modena, Italy

Lynne Cameron
Centre for Language and Communication
The Open University
Milton Keynes, United Kingdom

Alan Cienki
Department of Language and Communication
Vrije Universiteit
Amsterdam, The Netherlands

Seana Coulson
Department of Cognitive Science
University of California, San Diego
La Jolla, CA, USA

Alice Deignan
School of Education
University of Leeds
Leeds, United Kingdom

Gilles Fauconnier
Department of Cognitive Science
University of California, San Diego
La Jolla, CA, USA

Charles Forceville
Department of Media Studies
University of Amsterdam
Amsterdam, The Netherlands

Dedre Gentner
Department of Psychology
Northwestern University
Evanston, IL, USA

Raymond W. Gibbs, Jr.
Department of Psychology
University of California, Santa Cruz
Santa Cruz, CA, USA

Rachel Giora
Department of Linguistics
Tel Aviv University
Tel Aviv, Israel

Sam Glucksberg
Department of Psychology
Princeton University
Princeton, NJ, USA

Mark Johnson
Department of Philosophy
University of Oregon
Eugene, OR, USA

John M. Kennedy
Department of Psychology
University of Toronto at Scarborough
Toronto, ON, Canada

Walter Kintsch
Institute of Cognitive Science
University of Colorado
Boulder, CO, USA

Zoltán Kövecses
Department of American Studies
Eötvös Loránd University
Budapest, Hungary

George Lakoff
Department of Linguistics
University of California, Berkeley
Berkeley, CA, USA

Graham Low
Department of Educational Studies
University of York
York, United Kingdom

Teenie Matlock
Cognitive Science Program
University of California, Merced
Merced, CA, USA

Linda M. McMullen
Department of Psychology
University of Saskatchewan
Saskatoon, SK, Canada

Cornelia Müller
Department of Cultural Studies
European University Viadrina Frankfurt
Oder, Germany

Rafael Núñez
Department of Cognitive Science
University of California, San Diego
La Jolla, CA, USA

Elena Semino
Department of Linguistics and English Language
Bowland College
Lancaster University
Lancaster, United Kingdom

Yeshayahu Shen
Department of Poetics and Comparative Literature
Tel Aviv University
Tel Aviv, Israel

Dan Sperber
Institut Jean Nicod
(EHESS/ ENS/ CNRS)
Paris, France

Gerard Steen
Department of English Language and Culture
Vrije Universiteit Amsterdam
Amsterdam, The Netherlands

Josef Stern
Department of Philosophy
University of Chicago
Chicago, IL, USA

Mark Turner
Department of Cognitive Science
Case Western University
Cleveland, OH, USA

Deirdre Wilson
University College London
London, United Kingdom
and
CSMN, University of Oslo
Oslo, Norway

Steven L. Winter
Wayne State University Law School
Detroit, MI, USA

Ning Yu
Department of Modern Languages, Literatures, and Linguistics
University of Oklahoma
Norman, OK, USA

Lawrence M. Zbikowski
Department of Music
University of Chicago
Chicago, IL, USA

# The Cambridge Handbook of Metaphor and Thought

# Part I

# INTRODUCTION

# Metaphor and Thought

## The State of the Art

*Raymond W. Gibbs, Jr.*

### Metaphor and Thought: The State of the Art

The publications of the first and second editions of *Metaphor and Thought* (Cambridge University Press) in 1979 and 1993, respectively, under the editorship of Andrew Ortony, were monumental events in the world of metaphor research. The 1979 edition was the first interdisciplinary volume devoted to metaphor that included contributions from notable scholars in philosophy, linguistics, psychology, and political science. Many of the articles in that volume are now classics and continue to be frequently cited among active metaphor researchers. Several other articles from scholars in linguistics and psychology were added to the 1993 edition, which too has been widely read and discussed.

But much has changed in the world of metaphor since 1993. There is now a huge body of empirical work from many academic disciplines that clearly demonstrates the ubiquity in metaphor in both everyday and specialized language. Most importantly, there is also significant research indicating the prominence of metaphor in many areas of abstract thought and in people's emotional and aesthetic experiences. Metaphor is not simply an ornamental aspect of language, but a fundamental scheme by which people conceptualize the world and their own activities. The primary purpose of the *Cambridge Handbook of Metaphor and Thought* is to describe some of the key developments in contemporary metaphor research that detail the contribution of metaphor to human cognition, communication, and culture.

There are several distinguishing features of this handbook. First, metaphor scholarship has significantly advanced from purely speculative accounts of how metaphor works and is understood, primarily based on the analysis of a few, isolated linguistic examples. There is now much greater attention to the ways that context shapes metaphor use and understanding. Much of this work comes from experimental studies, but an increasing number of corpus studies, both small and large scaled, demonstrate some of the complexities associated with making general claims about the structure and function of metaphors in language and thought. Indeed, many of the chapters in this volume address the benefits and limitations of different methods for doing metaphor analysis, both at a local level for identifying individual instances of metaphor in language and nonverbal expression and at a global level for reliably inferring larger-scale patterns of metaphorical thought from public manifestations of metaphor. More generally, the vast literature on metaphor has used a variety of analytic techniques to investigate empirically the broad extent of metaphor in human life.

Second, there is now a greater emphasis on situating metaphor studies within broad, comprehensive models of human cognition, communication, and culture. Although metaphor is clearly an important topic in its own right, the empirical study of metaphor has broader implications for theories of mind and meaning, especially in showing the prominence of metaphorical thought in everyday life. But theories of metaphor are now, more than ever, linked to detailed theoretical frameworks that aim to describe the underlying nature of language, thought, and communication. Many of the authors in this volume view metaphor as part of a larger system of human cognition and communicative practices and consequently do not believe that verbal and nonverbal metaphor requires extraordinary human effort to be produced and understood. Moreover, seeing metaphor as a natural outcome of human minds also points to new ways in which metaphor is related to a variety of other linguistic forms and cognitive activities.

Third, and related to the previous point, metaphor scholarship now focuses greater attention to how metaphor comes into being in both thought and communication. The traditional interest in metaphor centered on the question of how people understand novel metaphorical language, with the implicit assumption that the creation of these poetic figures was attributed to special individuals with significant artistic talents. But the articles in this collection place greater emphasis on where metaphors come from (e.g., brains, bodies, and culture), why metaphor is so prominent in language and thought, and how public manifestations of metaphor (e.g., language, art, music) are specifically constrained by different communicative and emotional forces. In this way, the scope of metaphor studies has expanded enormously in recent years to cover the spectrums from brains to culture and from language and gesture to art and music.

Fourth, the incredible rise in the sheer number of scholarly works on metaphor in different academic fields illustrates a heightened sensitivity to metaphor. This increased attention demonstrates how scholars in virtually every discipline (e.g., mathematics, law, music, art) can contribute to understanding the functions and meanings of metaphor. Thus, research on metaphor is now as multidisciplinary, and interdisciplinary, as perhaps any topic being studied in contemporary academia. One result of this explosion of research on metaphor is a marvelous interaction between basic and applied scholarship, such that findings on the ways that metaphors are employed in real-world contexts offer important constraints on general theories of metaphor. Metaphor does not always appear in nice, neat packages that can be easily plucked out from some context for analysis. Speakers use metaphorical language, and engage in metaphorical thought, in complex, often contradictory patterns that make simple conclusions about both the ubiquity and structure of metaphor difficult to make. Rather than retreat back to made-up, isolated examples, many contemporary scholars exhibit great enthusiasm for uncovering the messy reality of metaphor use and the implications of such findings for comprehensive theories of metaphor.

Fifth, the interdisciplinary nature of metaphor studies now allows for greater recognition of the complex ways that metaphor arises from the interaction of brains, bodies, languages, and culture. Most earlier work conducted within traditional disciplinary frameworks aims to singularly locate metaphor as part of, for example, language (linguistics), mind (psychology), or culture (anthropology), with few scholars ever acknowledging the ubiquity of metaphor in other domains of experience such as gesture, art, and music. This often created unproductive tension between metaphor scholars as individuals defended their own "turf" and methods as being the best way to understand the essence of metaphor and its interpretation. Contemporary metaphor scholarship, as seen in many of the present chapters, has properly shown how the analysis of specific metaphoric language in context, for instance, reveals the simultaneous presence of neural, linguistic, psychological, and cultural forces. This complexity, again, makes it difficult to offer sweeping, simplistic conclusions about metaphor, where it comes from and how it is used by real human beings in naturalistic contexts. But this trend to seek out language–mind–culture interactions in metaphor studies offers the best hope for understanding the prominence of metaphor in human understanding, yet one that appreciates the subtleties of human meaning-making practices shaped by a variety of linguistic and nonlinguistic sources.

Finally, several chapters in this volume give witness to the struggle that I refer to as the "paradox of metaphor," in which metaphor is creative, novel, culturally sensitive, and allows us to transcend the mundane while also being rooted in pervasive patterns of bodily experience common to all people. Traditional metaphor scholars, and metaphor enthusiasts, typically resist arguments, and empirical findings, either suggesting the conceptual roots or embodied foundation for metaphorical thought and language. These critics see metaphor as a special rhetorical device that enables us to transcend momentarily above the ordinary literal world. Linking metaphor to the body, or entrenched conceptual thought, as in the idea of "conceptual metaphor," seems to some as far too reductive and dismissive of the power of metaphoric language to reshape our imagination.

Yet advocates of entrenched patterns of metaphorical thought readily acknowledge metaphor's ability in both verbal and nonverbal forms to create new modes of understanding often accompanied by special aesthetic pleasures. In many instances, however, creative, poetic metaphors are extensions of enduring schemes of metaphorical thought and not necessarily created de novo. Understanding how metaphor is both fundamental to many aspects of thought and yet special for creative language and artworks is a challenge taken up by several authors in this volume. My hope is that readers interested in the aesthetic qualities of metaphor will take the time to explore some of the proposals on the conceptual and embodied grounding for metaphorical thought and will see how this research draws connections between what is simultaneously ordinary and spectacular about metaphor.

All of the authors contributing to this volume are distinguished scholars from different academic fields who have done important work on metaphor and related poetic figures. The interdisciplinary world of metaphor scholarship is so large, with literally hundreds of excellent researchers making new discoveries all the time. A handbook like this one can only provide a forum for a small subset of this outstanding group of researchers, but I am pleased to present the new thoughts of the present contributors because their work is among the most widely recognized and discussed within the field. Not surprisingly, there are many areas of disagreement among the present contributors both in terms of the methods employed to do metaphor analysis and the resulting theories proposed to account for different aspects of metaphor in language, thought, and culture. Yet I am happy with this diversity of methods and theories because the topic of metaphor and thought is not one that is likely to be comprehensively characterized by any one perspective.

Contributors to this handbook were encouraged to write about their latest ideas but to do so in a way that readers new to the topic, or less familiar with the research on some facet of metaphor, will be readily able to recognize the significance of these ideas and proposals for ongoing thinking and research on metaphor. The handbook is divided into five general sections: (1) the roots of metaphor, (2) metaphor understanding, (3) metaphor in language and culture, (4) metaphor in reasoning and understanding, and (5) metaphor in nonverbal expression. I hasten to note, however, that each chapter in the volume addresses major foundational themes on the relations between metaphor, thought, and understanding. A brief overview of each contribution is presented.

## The Roots of Metaphor

The first section offers several contrasting visions on where metaphor comes from and how metaphor serves as the often unknowing foundation for human thought.

George Lakoff's chapter describes new advances in the brain sciences and neural computation relevant to metaphor ("The Neural Theory of Metaphor"). Links between brain and body are central to understanding the nature of thought, and metaphor is no exception. The neural theory follows developments in simulation semantics in which the neural circuitry characterizing the meanings of words, like "grasp," is also activated when one imagines or perceives grasping. This sense of meaning as mental stimulation is applied to the creation and use of metaphorical patterns such as those associated with "grasping concepts." The neural theory therefore offers a coherent set of explanations for why there should be conceptual metaphors in the first place, how metaphorical inferences work, how metaphors differ from blends, and how primary and complex metaphors contribute to our understanding of abstract concepts and the meanings of words, complex expressions, and grammatical constructions. Metaphor scholars need not conduct neural computational work themselves, and Lakoff offers insights on how to apply the broad scope of the neural theory to address fundamental issues on metaphorical thought and language.

Mark Johnson's chapter describes the importance of metaphor for the study of philosophy ("Philosophy's Debt to Metaphor"). Not only is metaphor a topic that has long interested philosophers, but philosophers use the same conceptual resources of metaphor as do any human being, often without any awareness, and indeed outright rejection, of the fact that they are doing so. Johnson shows how perennial questions in philosophy – What is mind and how does it work? What does it mean to be a person? What is the nature of reality? Is there such a thing as free will? What things or actions are morally good? – are all dependent on metaphor for their answers. Philosophical reasoning and theories often rest on a foundation of simple and complex metaphors. Johnson concludes that giving proper acknowledgment to metaphor, and metaphoric thinking, is essential to future progress in philosophy.

Gilles Fauconnier and Mark Turner's chapter outlines recent theoretical advances on metaphor within conceptual blending theory ("Rethinking Metaphor"). Through a detailed analysis of the TIME IS SPACE metaphor, they demonstrate how metaphor interpretation requires elaborate integration networks and various techniques for building particular networks such as cobbling and sampling, compression, emergent structure, and overarching goals. These permanent features of cognition are not special to metaphor but can give rise to counterfactuals, analogies, categorizations, and metonymies. Nonetheless, the general framework of conceptual blending theory is capable of explicating various complexities of metaphorical thought and meaning that are difficult to describe within more traditional theories.

Sam Glucksberg's chapter describes empirical research in favor of the idea that metaphors are comprehended through both categorization and comparison processes ("How Metaphors Create Categories – Quickly"). He first rejects the traditional assumptions that literal meanings are necessarily processed either before or in parallel to nonliteral meanings given experimental findings that when available, metaphorical meanings are automatically determined. Glucksberg then considers the idea that metaphors are understood entirely by comparison processes but claims instead that both literal and figurative comparison statements, including some similes, can be understood as implicit categorizations. Metaphors and similes are not identical because these two forms often communicate very different meanings for the same topic and vehicle terms. From this evidence, Glucksberg concludes that both categorization and comparison processes are used in metaphor and simile understanding, with apt metaphors working best as categorizations because the vehicle concept is an ideal example of the category it represents.

Dan Sperber and Deirdre Wilson outline their "relevance theory" perspective on metaphor in their chapter ("A Deflationary Account of Metaphors"). Under this view, speaking metaphorically is an example of "loose talk" that often is the best way to achieve optimal relevance. Even though verbal metaphors do not represent a completely accurate state of affairs, listeners are able to infer efficiently the appropriate contextual meanings of metaphors by creating ad hoc concepts following the principle of optimal relevance. Ad hoc concept construction is a process that is typical of metaphorical interpretations, but it is not exclusive to metaphors. In general, relevance theory maintains that metaphors are nothing special in terms of their processing, even if metaphors often convey special cognitive effects or meanings not easily communicated by more direct speech.

## Metaphor Understanding

The second group of chapters presents various theories of how metaphors are understood based on different computational, behavioral, and neuroscience research.

Dedre Gentner and Brian Bowdle argue in their chapter that metaphors and similes are understood with processes of similarity and analogy ("Metaphor as Structure-Mapping"). They describe how processes of structural alignment, inference projection, progressive abstraction, and re-representation of different domains are critical to immediate processing of both metaphors and similes. Moreover, widespread conceptual metaphors may be best characterized as extended structure-mappings between domains. Gentner and Bowdle then present their "career of metaphor" theory which claims that metaphors and similes typically evolve from being understood as novel comparison statements to being interpreted as category-inclusion statements in which the vehicle terms serve as the best instances of ad hoc categories. The "career of metaphor" hypothesis aims to offer a unified framework for understanding metaphor, analogy, and similarity.

Walter Kintsch's chapter offers a computational theory of metaphor understanding based on the technique of "latent semantic analysis," or LSA ("How the Mind Computes the Meaning of Metaphor: A Simulation Based on Latent Semantic Analysis"). LSA operationalizes meaning in terms of high-dimensional semantic space, measured in terms of word co-occurrence, irrespective of their symbolic relationships, and is based on a corpus of 11 million words. Word senses within LSA are not fixed but emergent from both the context-free vector that represents a word in LSA space and the context in which a word is used. This model allows Kintsch to predict the metaphorical or literal meanings of various noun-is-a-noun phrases that accord with human participants' interpretations and aptness judgments. Simple metaphorical and literal language is therefore not understood by different processes as both can be comprehended by a model of human knowledge based on how word meanings are represented that is objective and comprehensive.

Rachel Giora's chapter explores psycholinguistic studies on whether people engage in different psychological processes understanding literal and nonliteral language use ("Is Metaphor Unique?"). Her discussion analyzes various theoretical models of figurative language interpretation, with special attention to metaphor, which make different predictions on both the early processes and late products of understanding.

Giora forcefully argues that metaphor does not require distinct psychological processes to understand but that the salience of an utterance's meaning primarily determines the speed with which it is understood, not whether it is literal or figurative. She goes on to suggest how the salient–nonsalient continuum accounts for many empirical findings in the experimental literature not explainable by alternative theories and provides insights into the aesthetic appreciation of poetic metaphor.

Raymond W. Gibbs, Jr., and Teenie Matlock's chapter argues that part of our ability to make sense of metaphorical language, both individual utterances and extended narratives, resides in the automatic construction of a simulation, whereby we imagine performing the bodily actions referred to in the language ("Metaphor, Imagination, and Simulation: Psycholinguistic Evidence"). They describe empirical evidence from cognitive science showing the importance of embodied simulations in different cognitive activities and discuss very recent findings from psycholinguistics on metaphoric language interpretation that is consistent with the idea that our bodily imaginations are actively recruited in metaphor use. This process of building a simulation, one that is fundamentally embodied in being constrained by past and present bodily experiences, has specific consequences for how verbal metaphors are understood and how cognitive scientists, more generally, characterize the nature of metaphorical language and thought.

Seana Coulson reviews the major empirical findings on the neurological substrate of metaphor comprehension ("Metaphor Comprehension and the Brain"). Her discussion suggests that too much of this research assumes metaphor to be a homogenous category (e.g., metaphor and idioms are often grouped together), and that, somewhat surprisingly, there has been no empirical study of the effect of conceptual metaphors on the neurological processes involved in metaphoric language understanding. Coulson urges scientists to not simply seek the neural substrates of metaphor in traditional language areas of the brain. Much recent research and theory points to how metaphor relies on interactions between auditory, visual, kinesthetic areas of the brain, and the entire human body in the physical–cultural world more generally.

## Metaphor in Language and Culture

The third group of chapters examines the prominence and functions of metaphor in different contexts, including different languages and cultures.

Lynne Cameron explores the ways that metaphor shapes, and is shaped by, ongoing talk ("Metaphor and Talk"). Her analysis reveals that metaphors are sporadic in discourse, sometimes appearing in thick clusters and sometimes absent altogether. Cameron discusses some of the ways that metaphor is signaled in talk and allows conversational participants to manage their interactions and come to joint understandings of various ideas, while in other instances, people's talk suggests their entirely different metaphoric understandings of ideas and events. She also strongly argues that claims about conceptual metaphor are too often divorced from real language use, and that each individual may have different versions of conceptual metaphors given their respective culturally contextualized experiences and interactions.

Graham Low's chapter considers the impact of metaphor on teaching and learning, as well as on concepts of educational change ("Metaphor and Education"). He criticizes some notable past theories of educational concepts and processes, such as the idea of "generative metaphor," for failing to empirically demonstrate that people actually conceptualize situations in metaphoric, as opposed to metonymic, terms. Theoretical proposals about metaphor in education must not, therefore, be made apart from rigorous empirical analyses that are sensitive to context-sensitive differences between metaphor and metonymy. Low then examines the role of metaphor in foreign-language teaching and raises some critical questions about the indiscriminate application of cognitive theories of metaphor to classroom situations. He urges that educators pay greater attention to how metaphor is used at a discourse, and not just vocabulary, level, and that more discussion should be given to exactly what teachers want students to learn through their exposure to metaphor.

Elena Semino and Gerard Steen consider in their chapter the ubiquity and functions of metaphor in literature ("Metaphor in Literature"). They note the paradox of metaphor in literature being both continuous and discontinuous with metaphorical language use in non-literary contexts. On the one hand, many literary metaphors are based in common metaphorical schemes of thought seen in non-literary discourse (e.g., political speeches and scientific writings), while, on the other hand, some literary metaphors are unique to their specific contexts in both form and functions. Semino and Steen explain how both points of view have validity and that understanding the distribution, function, and effects of metaphor in literature will require supplementary information from both corpus-linguistic and psycholinguistic studies.

Ning Yu describes how metaphor emerges from the interaction between body and culture in his chapter ("Metaphor from Body and Culture"). He provides a detailed analysis of body-part terms for "face" in Chinese and English to show how metaphors are typically grounded in bodily experiences that are shaped by cultural understandings. Yu also shows how a decompositional analysis based on the distinction between primary and complex metaphors allows us to determine which aspects of metaphor are bodily or culturally based. Primary metaphors, derived from bodily experience, are likely to be widespread and universal, while complex metaphors, based on basic metaphoric and metonymic mappings and cultural beliefs, are likely to be more culturally specific.

Josef Stern's chapter considers whether and how a semantic theory can account for the meanings of metaphors ("Metaphor, Semantics, and Context"). Stern responds to two skeptical challenges to a semantic theory of metaphor regarding the difference between what words literally mean and can be used to say and the context-dependence of metaphorical meaning. He advances a semantic theory that elaborates how metaphor depends on the literal and how context has different roles in the communication of metaphorical meaning. More generally, Stern offers a philosophical account of how the semantic structures of metaphor help us understand its cognitive significance beyond its propositional content in context.

Alice Deignan introduces the important advances on metaphor in corpus research ("Corpus Linguistics and Metaphor"). She presents detailed analyses showing how many classic cases of both linguistic and conceptual metaphor, often arising from consideration of single texts or analysts' own intuitions, are not exhibited in the same patterns when viewed from the perspective of large corpora studies. In some instances, data from experimental psycholinguistics on metaphor understanding may not accurately reflect what people ordinarily do because the metaphors studied do not follow typical collocational and syntactic patterns. Deignan argues that metaphor scholars must therefore be more sensitive to naturalistic language patterns in constructing experimental tests and broader theories of metaphor and suggests ways that corpora linguistics can aid researchers in achieving this goal.

Yeshayahu Shen describes the relation of metaphor to several other poetic figures, notably, simile, zeugma, and synaesthetic metaphors, in his chapter ("Metaphor and Poetic Figures"). He aims to answer the difficult question – how can many novel figurative expressions whose meanings are difficult to describe often be so easy to understand? Shen argues that the cognitive "directionality" principle (i.e., metaphorical source domains tend to represent conceptually more accessible, concrete, and salient concepts than do target domains) accounts for various empirical findings on the distribution and comprehension of poetic figures.

This work complements research on conceptual metaphor theory and experimental psycholinguistic studies of figurative language by demonstrating how the meanings and systematicity of many novel, poetic figures arise from the interaction of different linguistic conventions and fundamental cognitive principles.

## Metaphor in Reasoning and Feeling

The fourth section of chapters highlights the role of metaphor in different forms of reasoning and in human feeling and expression.

John A. Barnden's chapter offers an overview of why metaphor is central to many applications of work in artificial intelligence (AI) ("Metaphor and Artificial Intelligence: Why They Matter to Each Other"). He argues that metaphorical mappings can best be described in computational terms that concretely outline what gets mapped, the effects these mappings achieve, and how to avoid unwanted side effects of these mappings. Moreover, AI work shows the importance of reasoning about beliefs and uncertainty in metaphorical thinking and verbal metaphor interpretation, and how metaphor is integrated with metonymy in much inferential understanding. AI provides an excellent set of tools for doing metaphor research that requires scholars to be explicit about underlying mechanisms of thought and language central to metaphor theory.

Rafael Núñez's chapter presents the case for an embodied, metaphorical understanding of many mathematical concepts ("Conceptual Metaphor, Human Cognition, and the Nature of Mathematics"). He offers an analysis of how various mathematical ideas are described in terms of metaphorical language and argues that such talks reflect metaphorically alive structuring of abstract concepts and thus are not dead metaphors. Núñez goes on to show how metaphoric gestures employed when people talk about mathematics provides important evidence on the psychological reality of metaphorical mathematics. Overall, mathematics arises naturally from the interactions of our brains, bodies, and experiences with the world, and conceptual metaphor has a big part in the creation and maintaining of abstract mathematical ideas.

Steven L. Winter's chapter ("What Is the 'Color' of Law?") presents an in-depth analysis of the metaphor "color of law" (i.e., referring to official misconduct or the way the trappings of office provide individuals with the power and prestige of the state) to show how both historical and contemporary legal theory is guided by metaphoric conceptualizations. Contrary to the widely held belief in legal circles that metaphors are to be avoided, with legal reasoning being best served by ideas that are propositional and defined by necessary and sufficient criteria, Winter argues that the cognitive theory of metaphor challenges the beliefs that linguistic meaning is arbitrary and a matter of speakers' self-consciously held intentions. Meaning is configured by embodied and social experiences that are framed and constrained by metaphoric processes. Recognition of metaphorical thought, and the methods of conceptual metaphor analysis, demonstrates how legislative statutes express significant aspects of our social reality that cannot be devalued by reductive approaches to legal reasoning.

Zoltán Kövecses's chapter examines the questions of whether emotion metaphors are unique to emotions and whether emotion metaphors are universal ("Metaphor and Emotion"). Based on detailed, cross-linguistic analyses, he claims that emotion metaphors primarily arise from the generic-level metaphor CAUSES ARE FORCES, and that certain specific source domains (e.g., OPPONENT, NATURAL FORCE, HEAT), apply to a wide range of target concepts other than emotion. Furthermore, even though many emotion metaphors are grounded in universal bodily experiences, there is significant cultural framing of these experiences that lead to variation in the kinds of source domains in emotion metaphors across different cultures.

Linda M. McMullen writes on the role that metaphor plays in psychotherapy

("Putting It in Context: Metaphor and Psychotherapy"). She argues that most claims about the effect of metaphorical language in psychotherapeutic outcomes ignore the contextualized nature of metaphor in client and therapist talk. Isolating specific metaphors for analysis has made metaphor seem too powerful in some cases and benign in other situations. McMullen calls for empirical investigations of metaphor that properly acknowledge the conversational exchanges and cultural contexts in which they are part. Only by putting metaphor in context can we fully understand what metaphors do for us in psychotherapy and other situations.

Antal F. Borbely's chapter describes the importance of metaphor in the concepts and practice of psychoanalysis ("Metaphor and Psychoanalysis"). Although psychoanalysts have long debated the role of metaphor in psychoanalysis, Borbely offers a new understanding of metaphor and its interaction with metonymy within psychoanalysis by situating his overview in terms of contemporary advances in metaphor research over the past two decades. By demonstrating how key psychodynamic concepts such as trauma, defense, transference, and interpretation are grounded in fundamental metaphoric and metonymic principles, this chapter provides for new links between psychoanalysis and research from cognitive science.

Cristina Cacciari's chapter addresses the topic of synaesthetic metaphor, where it comes from, and how it is understood ("Crossing the Senses in Metaphorical Language"). She argues that perceptually based metaphorical expressions (e.g., "cold silence") are grounded in the structure of perceptual experiences and the human sensory system. Contemporary research in cognitive and neuropsychology lends support to this idea, with most people being able to use synaesthetic metaphors quite easily. However, some individuals have special abilities to create and exploit cross-sensory mappings (i.e., blending sounds with colors), which also provide extraordinary evidence for how sensory experiences, supported by neural mechanisms, are fundamental to metaphorical mappings in thought and language.

## Metaphor in Nonverbal Expression

The final section describes several important research trends on metaphor in different forms of nonverbal expression.

John M. Kennedy's chapter discusses how metaphor, and other related tropes, can be realized in art objects, such as paintings ("Metaphor and Art"). He first notes that metaphors are abundant in art with metaphoric pictures often playing on the activity of picturing as a way of using a pictorial device to make a point about the topic. Metaphoric pictures are especially notable because, as Kennedy claims, the mind does not use images that most directly illustrate the thought. Kennedy introduces some contrasts between verbal and pictorial metaphors, describing, for example, how some successful verbal metaphors can make poor pictorial ones and vice versa. This chapter generally celebrates the perceptual nature of metaphoric thought and the ways that art allows people to play with metaphoric possibilities.

Charles Forceville's chapter discusses the meanings and functions of metaphor in pictures and other multimodal forums ("Metaphor in Pictures and Multimodal Representations"). He describes how metaphors in pictures, advertisements, and films share many of the same qualities observed in linguistic metaphor, including how conceptual metaphors appear to motivate many aspects of nonlinguistic metaphor. However, the study of pictorial and multimodal metaphor also raises important questions about the identification of source and target domains in all metaphorical mappings. Forceville aptly considers some of the communicative purposes of multimodal metaphors and suggests they may have more emotional impact than linguistic metaphors, and aid both local and global narrative coherence, even in cases where the creator of a picture or film, for instance, did not consciously intend these metaphors to be understood as such.

Alan Cienki and Cornelia Müller argue in their chapter that gestures offer important insights into the metaphorical nature of language, thought, and cultural ideas ("Metaphor, Gesture, and Thought"). They describe a variety of linguistic, psychological, and anthropological evidence showing how detailed analyses of gesture offer support for the claim that metaphor is a general, pervasive cognitive principle, and that many metaphoric mappings, such as those evident in metaphoric gestures, are processed online during face-to-face talk. Cienki and Müller discuss some methodological issues related to studying metaphoric gestures in naturalistic settings, including the problem of correctly identifying and labeling underlying conceptual metaphors. Their chapter emphasizes that metaphor is best conceived of as a cognitive activity that occurs online in the process of speaking and is therefore clearly an example of dynamic embodied cognition.

Lawrence M. Zbikowski's chapter provides a historical and conceptual survey of metaphor and music ("Metaphor and Music"). He argues that music is a manifestation of human cognitive capacities and tied to other aspects of human experience, such as the expression of emotion. Through his analysis of various musical compositions, Zbikowski proposes that even if music and language have different cultural functions, they both rely on embodied image-schematic structures for the expression of meaning. Musical events correlate with bodily experiences associated with many other modalities, such as vision, taste, and proprioception. In general, this chapter illustrates how the study of music, as a distinct nonlinguistic medium, provides important insights into metaphorical thinking processes.

## The Future

The state of the art in metaphor studies is a rich, colorful mosaic of ideas and research activities. Predicting the future of metaphor studies is clearly a risky business given the tremendous diversity of work now being done and as evidenced in this collection. But there are several themes that are touched on in this volume which are likely to become of even greater interest as topics of discussion and debate in the future. Let me briefly mention a few of these and their implications for metaphor research.

One issue that often arises in informal discussions of metaphor studies has to do with the reliability and generality of individual scholars' analyses of metaphor. First, how representative are particular isolated examples of verbal metaphor, for instance, of the ways people ordinarily speak of the topic/concept? Second, how reliable are analyses of individual linguistic metaphors in terms of whether they are really metaphoric as opposed to metonymic, for instance? Third, exactly how did an analyst of metaphor draw the inference that a particular pattern of metaphorical thought exists from the examination of several or many instances of individual verbal metaphors? Scholars' intuitions are clearly relevant for making claims about the nature of metaphor, what it means, and how they are possibly understood. But some metaphor scholars express concern about the variability of analysts' intuitions in making judgments about linguistic and even nonlinguistic (e.g., gesture, music, art) matters. Many metaphor scholars now seek to establish more objective criteria for determining instances of metaphor and for drawing links between patterns of metaphoric language use and metaphorical thought. Establishing reliable, and replicable, criteria for identifying metaphor in behavior and for drawing links between metaphorical language/behavior and metaphorical thought is likely to be a major focus of concern in future metaphor studies.

A related emerging concern for empirical studies of metaphor focuses on the true frequency of metaphors in language and other media. Claims about the importance or ubiquity of particular metaphorical patterns, in either language or thought, are often made without adequate empirical support, such as reporting the frequencies with which different metaphors are found in particular texts, or comparing the findings from one's own textual analysis of metaphor with those seen in large corpora.

In general, there is likely to be a heightened interest in methodological questions for defining the existence of metaphor in language and thought. My hunch is that resolutions to some of the theoretical debates about metaphor and thought will partly depend on the way scholars respond to these methodological concerns.

Finally, the chapters in this handbook speak loudly about the problems associated with making claims about the existence of metaphor in brains, minds, and culture from the analysis of metaphoric language. Does the analysis of metaphoric language, gesture, or artwork indicate that some metaphorical schemes of thought exist within idealized speaker-hearers, the conscious minds of real speakers, or the subpersonal unconscious minds, even their brains, of people as they speak, gesture, and create artworks? To what extent does the existence of a particular metaphorical way of thinking necessarily relate to brains, minds, and cultures? As mentioned earlier, many articles in this volume acknowledge the importance of brains, minds, language, and culture in both enduring and novel patterns of metaphorical thought. But teasing apart these various influences, and seeing more precisely how they interact, is likely to be a major theme of future metaphor research. Once more, much attention must be given to the exact methods metaphor scholars employ to analyze public manifestations of metaphor and infer patterns of metaphorical thought. We now know enough to feel confident in asserting that metaphor is a major player in human cognition, communication, and culture. But a future challenge for all metaphor scholars is to have greater clarity about what kinds of empirical evidence is needed, and how it is to be obtained and analyzed, to properly characterize the reach and limits of the metaphorical mind.

# Part II

# THE ROOTS OF METAPHOR

CHAPTER 1

# The Neural Theory of Metaphor

*George Lakoff*

The neural revolution is changing our understanding of the brain and the mind in radical ways, and that is no less true in the theory of metaphor. It is more than 27 years since Mark Johnson and I wrote *Metaphors We Live By* in 1979. Though the fundamental outlines of what we discovered remain as valid today as they were then, developments in brain science and neural computation have vastly enriched our understanding of how conceptual metaphor works. This is an intermediate report, as of November 2006.

You may well ask why anyone interested in metaphor should care about the brain and neural computation. The reason is that what we have learned about the brain explains an awful lot about the properties of metaphor. For example, have you ever asked why conceptual metaphor exists at all, why we should think metaphorically, why metaphors should take the form of cross-domain mappings? Have you thought about how our metaphor system is grounded in experience or about why certain conceptual metaphors are widespread around the world or even universal? Have you wondered about how complex poetic metaphors are built up out of simpler metaphors? Have you wondered about how whole systems of philosophical or mathematical thought can be built up out of conceptual metaphors? The neural theory explains all this.

It explains more as well: Why metaphorical language should take no longer to process than nonmetaphorical language. Why some sentences of the form *X is Y*, make sense as metaphors and why others fail. How conceptual metaphors can play a role in abstract concepts. These and other wondrous properties of conceptual metaphors fall out once one considers metaphor theory from the perspective of the brain.

In 1988, Jerome Feldman came to the University of California, Berkeley, as director of the International Computer Science Institute, and he and I formed the NTL (Neural Theory of Language) group. Feldman is one of the founders of the theory of neural computation, and we have been working together since then. Feldman's landmark book *From Molecules to Metaphors* surveys much of the work of our group, and is a must-read for metaphor theorists. As a background both to reading that book and to our discussion of metaphor, I offer a brief and overly simple introduction to NTL.

## A Brief Introduction to NTL

Every action our body performs is controlled by our brains, and every input from the external world is made sense of by our brains. We think with our brains. There is no other choice. Thought is physical. Ideas and the concepts that make them up are physically "computed" by brain structures. Reasoning is the activation of certain neuronal groups in the brain given prior activation of other neuronal groups. Everything we know, we know by virtue of our brains. Our physical brains make possible our concepts and ideas; everything we can possibly think is made possible and greatly limited by the nature of our brains. There is still a great deal to be learned about how the brain computes the mind. NTL combines what is known scientifically with linking hypotheses based on neural computation.

### *The Shaping of the Brain*

We are born with an enormously complex brain with hundreds of precisely and beautifully structured regions and highly specific connectivity from every region to many other regions.

Each neuron has connections to between 1,000 and 10,000 other neurons. Between birth and age five, roughly half of the neural connections we are born with die off. The ones that are used stay; the others die. That is how the brain is shaped, and such a shaping is necessary if the brain is to learn to do the huge number of things it does.

The flow of neural activity is a flow of ions that occurs across synapses – tiny gaps between neurons. Those synapses where there is a lot of activity are "strengthened" – both the transmitting and receiving side of active synapses become more efficient.

Flow across the synapses is relatively slow compared to the speed of computers: about five one-thousandths of a second (5 milliseconds) per synapse. A word recognition task – Is the following word a word of English? – takes about half a second (500 milliseconds). This means that word recognition must be done in about 100 sequential steps. Since so much goes into word recognition, it is clear that much of the brain's processing must be in parallel, not in sequence. This timing result also shows that well-learned tasks are carried out by direct connections. There is no intervening mentalese.

### *Neuronal Groups*

Jerome Feldman and colleagues, in the 1970s, developed an account of "structured connectionism" – *not* PDP connectionism! In PDP connectionism, all computation is distributed over an entire network and nothing is "localized"; that is, no meaning for function can be assigned to any single neuron or any small collection of neurons in the network. Only very restricted parts of the brain work that way.

On the other hand, structured connectionism takes into account the local structure that exists in the brain. Neuronal groups (of size, say, between, 10 and 100 neurons) are modeled as "nodes" which are meaningful and which enter into neural computation. Since each neuron can have between 1,000 and 10,000 neural connections, nodes can "overlap." That is, the same neuron can be functioning in different neuronal groups, or "nodes." The firing of that neuron contributes to the activation of each node it is functioning in. Though single neurons either fire or not, neuronal groups contain neurons that fire at different times, making the group active to a degree, depending on the proportion firing at a given time.

The modeling of neural computation is done over networks with nodes, connections, degrees of synaptic strength, and time lapses at synapses.

### *Embodiment and Simulation Semantics*

The link between body and brain is central to the concept of semantics-as-simulation in NTL. Suppose you imagine, remember, or dream of performing certain movements. Many of the same neurons are firing as when you actually perform that movement. And suppose you imagine, remember, or dream of seeing or hearing something. Many of the same neurons are firing as when you actually see or hear that thing.

*Mirror neurons* occur in fiber bundles connecting premotor/SMA cortex (which choreographs actions) with the parietal cortex (which integrates perceptions). The same mirror neurons fire when you perform an action or you see someone else performing that action. The mirror neurons are thus "multimodal"; that is, they are active not only when acting or perceiving the same action but also when imagining that you are perceiving or performing an action. Now a word like "grasp," applies both to performing and perceiving grasping; that is, it is multimodal.

Simulation semantics is based on a simple observation of Feldman's: if you cannot imagine someone picking up a glass, you can't understand the meaning of "Someone picked up a glass." Feldman argues that, for meanings of physical concepts, *meaning is mental simulation*, that is, the activation of the neurons needed to imagine perceiving or performing an action. One thing we know is that not all imagination or memory is conscious, and so not all mental simulations are. That is why we typically have no conscious awareness of most such simulations.

A *meaningful node* is a node that when activated results in the activation of a whole neural simulation and when inhibited inhibits that simulation. *Inferences* occur when the activation of one meaningful node or more results in the activation of another meaningful node.

NTL, following the theory of simulation semantics, suggests that the neural circuitry characterizing the meaning of "grasp" is the neural circuitry in the mirror neurons that are activated when imagining either performing or perceiving grasping.

The meaning of concrete concepts is directly embodied in this manner. There is now considerable evidence that perceiving language activates corresponding motor or perceptual areas. For example, *He kicked the ball* activates the foot area of the primary motor cortex.

### *Activation and Inhibition*

A flow of ions across a synapse may either contribute to the firing of the postsynaptic neuron or may help to inhibit such firing, depending on whether the charges of the ions are positive or negative. The activation of neural simulations constitutes meaningful thought.

We obviously don't think all possible thoughts at once. Indeed, most possible thoughts are either unactivated or *positively inhibited* most of the time.

### *Mutual Inhibition*

Two neuronal groups can be connected so that each inhibits the activation of the other when there is an active flow of ions of the opposite charge. This is called "mutual inhibition" This occurs, for example, when there are two inconsistent, but equally available, ways of looking at a situation.

This is common in politics, where a strict conservative worldview is typically inconsistent with a nurturant progressive worldview. That is, they are mutually inhibitory. But many people have both worldviews active in different areas of their lives and can think of a given situation first from one worldview and then from the other. When one is activated, the other is inhibited.

### *Spreading Activation: Neurons That Fire Together Wire Together*

Spreading activation at the behavioral level has been the mainstay of psycholinguistics for decades – NTL models link this behavior to neural structure. When two neuronal groups, A and B, fire at the same time, activation spreads outward along the network links connecting them, which we experience as a chain of thought.

During learning, spreading activation strengthens synapses along the way. When the activation spreading from A meets the activation spreading from B, a link is formed, and the link gets stronger the more A and B fire together. This is a basic mechanism by which the brain is shaped through experience.

### *Neural Maps*

We are born with neural circuitry that effectively activates a "map" of one part of the brain in another part of the brain. For example, the 100 million neurons coming out of the retina grow connections before birth from the retina to other areas, including the primary visual cortex at the back of the brain. These connections form a "topographic map" of the retina in V1. That is, the connections preserve topology (relative nearness), though not absolute orientation or absolute distance. When neurons next to each other coming from the retina fire, the corresponding neurons fire in V1 and are next to each other in V1.

Len Talmy (2000) has observed that spatial relations in human languages preserve topology as well. For example, containers remain containers no matter how their boundaries are stretched or contracted, and paths remain paths, no matter how they wind around. Terry Regier (1997) has constructed computational neural models of topographical maps of the visual field that can compute image-schemas with topological properties and accurately learn the words for a nontrivial range of spatial relations in a variety of languages.

### *Neural Binding*

Imagine a blue square. We know that color and shape are not computed in the same place in the brain: they are computed in quite different areas. Yet the blue square appears to us as a single whole, not as separate squareness and blueness. The name given to this phenomenon is "neural binding." Neural binding is responsible for two or more different conceptual or perceptual entities being considered a single entity.

There are three types of neural bindings:

1. Permanent obligatory bindings, for example, in your stored mental image of a parrot, the feathers are green. There is a permanent obligatory binding in the neural representation for the parrot image, between the neuronal groups that characterize feather shapes and those, elsewhere in the brain, that characterize the green color.
2. Permanently-ready-but-conditional bindings, like the bindings in the neural structure for an election-night map on which any given state can be either red or blue depending on the outcome of the vote.
3. Nonce bindings that occur on the fly as they happen to arise in context.

It is not known just how neural binding operates in the brain. One hypothesis is that neural binding is the synchronous firing of nodes. Lokendra Shastri has modeled the computational structure necessary to carry out binding in such a theory.

### *Neural Choreography*

In general, the premotor cortex and supplementary motor area (SMA) choreograph specific actions, like grasping. Grasping has a neural structure of its own. There are, in addition, neural connections between the premotor/SMA and the primary motor cortex – M1. M1 is laid out topographically according to the neurons as they are connected to the body. For example, neurons connected to the hand are in the same region of M1, with neurons connected to the index finger next to neurons connected to the middle finger. The whole body is topographically connected to the neurons in M1.

Each M1 neuronal group can perform only a simple action, like opening the elbow or pointing the index finger. To pick up a bottle, those simple M1 actions must be sequenced and choreographed. The premotor cortex/SMA does the choreography, having learned neural circuits that fire in complex sequential patterns. As each premotor/SMA neuron fires, a connection to M1 makes the right M1 neurons fire, which in turn moves certain muscle groups in the body. Picking up a bottle is like an exquisite ballet with choreographic instructions being carried by the connections to the neurons in M1, which individually control each little movement.

When the bindings are in place, the premotor/SMA circuitry + bindings + primary motor circuitry acts seamlessly like a single simple circuit.

### *Circuit Types*

NTL modeling assumes that, as our neural circuitry is being shaped by experience, certain relatively simple basic types of neural circuits emerge, as follows. The research includes ways in which circuits with these properties can be formed.

What is important for the study of thought is not the study of precise neural circuitry but rather the study of *the kinds of computations* that neural circuitry can carry out. An important topic in the neural theory of language is exactly what kinds of circuit types are necessary for human thought – for frames, image-schemas, conceptual metaphor, lexical items, grammatical constructions, and so on.

Neural bindings play a crucial role, forming complex circuits by binding nodes in one circuit type to nodes in another circuit type.

**The winner-take-all circuit:**

- Two or more subcircuits, say A and B, with mutually inhibiting connections between them.
- When A is firing B cannot fire, and conversely.

*Winner take all* circuits apply, for example, to high-level "worldview" circuits that make sense in a single way of a wide range of experiences – in politics, these might be conservative and progressive worldviews. You might understand a range of experiences using one worldview or the other, but not both at once.

**A gestalt circuit:**

- A collection of nodes, say, A, B, C, and D and a "gestalt node" G.
- When G is firing, all of A, B, C, and D fire.
- When a sufficient set of A, B, C, or D is firing, G fires, which results in all other nodes firing. One especially salient node can be sufficient in some cases, or there can be a threshold and any total activation summed over all the nodes above the threshold results in G firing.
- When G is inhibited, at least one of the other nodes is inhibited.

*Gestalt circuits* characterize the structure of frames, where the semantic roles and the scenarios are gestalt elements.

In a gestalt, the whole is more than just the sum of its parts. Accordingly, in a gestalt circuit, the whole – G – cannot be inhibited and all of its parts activated. The activation of even some of the salient parts activates the whole, and the activation of the whole activates all the parts.

**Linking circuit:**

- Two nodes, A1 and A2, a linking node L, and an activating connection C from A1 to A2.
- When A1 and L are firing, A2 is firing. But when A2 is firing, A1 need not be firing. Thus, linking is asymmetric.
- When A1 is firing and L is not, the connection C is not active. (That is, L "gates" the connection C.)
- When A1 and A2 are both firing, L is firing and the connection C is active.

Note: A1 can fire without A2 firing (if L is not firing), and A2 can fire independently of A1.

*Linking circuits* are used in metonymy: within a frame F, one semantic role A may "stand for" another B. A metonymy is characterized by (1) a linking circuit, with nodes A, B, and X a connection C linking A to B asymmetrically, and a linking node L gating the connection C from A to B, and a context X gating the L and (2) a gestalt consisting of gestalt node G and nodes F, A, B, X, and L. For example, in *The ham sandwich wants his check*, the frame F is the restaurant frame, *the ham sandwich* plays the role Dish, *his* refers to the entity that plays the role Customer, and L characterizes the metonymic link from the Dish to the Customer, and X is the condition that the waiter/waitress identifies the Customer B primarily in terms of the Dish B.

**Two-way linking circuits:**

A two-way circuit linking nodes A1 and A2 is composed of two opposite one-way linking circuits, with a gestalt node forming a gestalt of the two linking circuits.

- Nodes A1 and A2. Connections C1 and C2. Linking nodes L1 and L2. Gestalt node G.
- First linking circuit: From A1 to A2 via connection C1, with linking node L1.
- Second linking circuit: From A2 to A1 via connection C2, with linking node L2.
- Gestalt circuit: Nodes L1 and L2 with gestalt node G.
- When G is activated, both links are activated. When G is inhibited, both links are inhibited.

*Two-way linking circuits* provide the kinds of connectivity used in grammatical constructions and lexical items, where there is a two-way connection between a lexical meaning and a lexical form. In a two-way linking circuit, a gestalt node plays traffic cop, directing activation and inhibition.

**Mapping circuit:**

- Two groups of nodes: A1, B1, C1, D1, E1 and A2, B2, C2, D2, E2.
- Linking nodes LA, LB, LC, LD, LE in linking circuits that, respectively, link A1 to A2, B1 to B2, and so on.
- A gestalt circuit with nodes LA, LB, LC, LD, and LE with M as the gestalt node.
- When M is inhibited, the linking circuits are all inhibited.
- When M is activated, all the linking circuits from A1 to A2, B1 to B2, and so on are activated.

Note: The mapping is asymmetric.

*Mapping circuits* characterize conceptual metaphors. *Two-way mapping circuits* (maps with two-way linking circuits) characterize the structure of grammatical constructions.

*Mapping circuits* are also used as part of the asymmetric connections across mental spaces. A *mental space* is a neural simulation S that can be activated by a single gestalt node G with semantic roles A, B, . . . in the simulation.

A cross-space map has two mental spaces: G1 consisting of simulation S1 with semantic roles (or referents) A1, B1, . . . , and G2 consisting of simulation S2 with semantic roles (or referents) A2, B2, . . . .

G1 and G2 are linked by a *cross-space connection* made up of (1) a gestalt node G, consisting of a space-builder B, (2) a linking circuit L with a connection C from G1 to G2, and (3) a *mapping circuit* M mapping semantic roles (or referents) A1, B1, . . . in simulation S1 to semantic roles (or referents) A2, B2, . . . in simulation S2.

For example, take the sentence *If Clinton had been president of France, there would have been no scandal over his affair*. The mental spaces are G1 = The U.S. during Clinton's presidency with A1 = Clinton and S1 = his affair in the U.S., and G2 = France at that time, A2 = A Clinton-correlate and S2 = A2 is president of France who has an affair in France with no scandal; L1 is the circuit that links A1 (the real Clinton) with A2 (the Clinton correlate ≠ Clinton).

Neural binding may be added to linking in such cases to provide a cross-space identity instead of merely a cross-space correlate. For example, consider *If Clinton campaigns for his wife, she will win*. Here Clinton in the conditional space is the same as Clinton in the reality space. There is not only a Clinton-to-Clinton link defining a cross-space correlate, there is also a binding, making the correlate the same person.

In this description, the neural binding is "extra," in addition to the linking. But the binding actually makes the case cognitively simpler in that there are fewer distinct entities to keep track of. Complexity in the formal description of circuits can often correspond to simplicity in the way the brain works.

**Extension circuit:**

- A group of connected nodes, A, B, C, D, and E.
- Nodes D′ and E′, which are mutually inhibitory with D and E, respectively.
- An extension node, X.
- When either D or E is firing, X is not.
- When X is firing, both D′ and E′ are firing, and consequently D and E are not. This results in two circuit-alternatives: A, B, C, D, E, not X or A, B, C, D′, E′, X.

*Extension circuits* characterize radial categories (see Lakoff, 1993, case study 3).

**X-schema circuit:**

- A gestalt node
- State nodes
- Action nodes
- Connections, both activating and inhibiting
- Timing nodes

*X-schemas*, or "executing schemas," do things via bindings that activate other circuits. Every action node is preceded and followed by a state node, with activation spreading from states to actions to states. Timing nodes coordinate the lengths of states and actions (which may be instantaneous or elongated). Iterated actions are formed by loops from the state following an action to the state preceding the action. Conditional actions are formed by gatings – cases where activations from both nodes A and A′ are needed to activate node B.

The gestalt node activates the initial state and the final state inhibits the gestalt node. Actions typically have initial and final states, initiating and concluding actions, central actions, and may have purposes. A purposive action is one with a desired state. The purpose is met if the desired state is active after the central action, and if so, the action is concluded. Each action can be neurally bound to the gestalt node of another complex X-schema to produce quite complex actions.

X-schemas characterize the structures of states and actions, referred to as "aspect" in linguistics. Aspects can be durative or instantaneous, stative or active, completive or open-ended, iterative or noniterative.

When connected to the body via the primary motor cortex, premotor/SMA X-schemas can carry out actions. X-schemas can also define scenarios within frames or narratives and carry out chains of reasoning, by sequentially activating mental simulations.

### *Conceptual Blends*

*Conceptual blends* are neural bindings across distinct structures. We will discuss this further later.

The point of these characterizations of circuit types is that, in NTL, one has to be explicit about the computational properties of neural circuitry. Any cognitive analysis must be able to be carried out by the brain and by the relatively simple circuit types of this sort, or complex circuits formed by bindings. As we shall see, different mental operations require different types of neural circuitry that perform very specific neural computations.

### *Neural Systems Are Best-Fit Systems*

It is a common cognitive phenomenon that a fact that fits an overall conceptual organization is remembered better than a fact in isolation or one that contradicts an overall conceptual organization. Ideas make sense when they fit a whole system of ideas.

Similarly, a linguistic compound makes sense when it fits into a coherent context. Take the classic example of "pumpkin bus" – coined on a school outing. There were two buses and the road home passed a pumpkin patch. One of the buses was designated to stop there for students who wanted to buy a pumpkin. It was called the "pumpkin bus," and the compound was instantly understandable because it fit the context.

Compare two sentences: "Bill drank a soda" and "Bill drank an elephant." To get the meaning of the sentences, you need to do a mental simulation, in which Bill is drinking and a frame is activated in which a soda is bound to the patient role in the frame of drinking, which requires that it be a liquid and consumable, which it is. In "Bill drank an elephant," again the drink frame requires a consumable liquid. Since an elephant is neither – binding the concept of an elephant to the patient's role in the drink scenarios runs up against neural inhibition. However, context may change things. *Elephant* is a brand of Danish beer, and so the sentence may refer to Danish drinking experience. Or second, one could imagine a context in which an elephant was sacrificed by being cut up and put in a blender and liquefied so that one could drink it.

What determines "fit"? Maximizing the number of overall neural bindings, including context and overall knowledge, without contradiction, that is, without encountering any mutual inhibition.

A node A fits a complex network B better than complex network B′ if the strength of neural bindings one can create between A and B without mutual inhibition is greater than with B′.

### *Image-Schemas and Cogs*

Terry Regier (1997) has constructed a neural computational model for how a range of spatial relations concepts could be computed by the brain. Narayanan (1997) has constructed a neural computational model of the structure of events, that is, X-schemas. Dodge and Lakoff (2006) have speculated on many of the details involved. Gallese and Lakoff (2005) have shown that certain action circuitry has the structure of frames. They have further speculated that the meanings of grammatical elements and constructions are characterized by "Cogs," that is, secondary neural structures (e.g., premotor/SMA cortex) that bind to structures in primary cortex (e.g., motor and visual). This would explain why grammatical meanings are "abstract" in the sense that they have a very general structure but lack specific details.

We are now ready to discuss how all of this changes old metaphor theory into the neural theory of metaphor: NTM.

#### THE OLD THEORY

*Metaphors We Live By* was written in 1979, before the era of brain science and neural computation (also see Lakoff, 1993). Nonetheless, certain results from that era have stood the test of time:

- Metaphors are conceptual mappings; they are part of the conceptual system and not mere linguistic expressions.
- There is a huge system of fixed, conventional metaphorical mappings.
- The system exists physically in our brains.
- Certain metaphors are grounded via correlations in embodied experience (e.g., *More Is Up* is grounded via the correlation between quantity and verticality – you pour more water in the glass and the level goes up).
- Metaphorical mappings are typically across conceptual domains (as in *Affection Is Warmth*).
- Mappings (as in *A Competition Is a Race*) may also be from a specific case (a race) to a more general case (a competition).
- Mappings operate on source domain frame and image-schema structure.
- Via metaphorical mappings, source domain structures (image-schema and frame structures) are used for reasoning about the target domain. Indeed, much of our reasoning makes use of conceptual metaphors.
- Metaphorical mappings are partial.
- Metaphorical language makes use of conceptual metaphors.
- Many different linguistic expressions can express some aspect of the same metaphor.
- A conceptual metaphor may be used in understanding a word, even if that word is not realized in the source domain of the metaphor.

- Most conceptual metaphors are part of the cognitive unconscious, and are learned and used automatically without awareness.
- Novel metaphorical language makes use of the existing system of conventional metaphors.
- We commonly take our conceptual metaphors as defining reality, and live according to them.
- Target domain entities and target domain predications can result from metaphors.
- Two of the relevant sources of data are generalizations over inference patterns (in the source and target domains) and generalizations over lexical items (that can be used of both source and target domains).

These results will be familiar to any student of conceptual metaphor.

To those who have read "The Contemporary Theory of Metaphor," another result that has stood the test of time will be familiar:

- Complex metaphors are made up of simpler metaphors and commonplace frames.

For example, Love *Is* a Journey is composed of such conceptual metaphors as

*Purposes are Destinations*
*Difficulties are Impediments to Motion*
*A Relationship is a Container*
*Intimacy is Closeness*

plus commonplace literal frame-based knowledge that:

*A Vehicle is an Instrument for Travel,*
A Vehicle is a container in which the travelers are close together,
People are expected to have life goals,
*Lovers ideally have compatible life goals.*

These are put together in such a way that:

The life goals are destinations;
The lovers are travelers trying to reach those destinations;
Their relationship is a vehicle such that the lovers are *in* the relationship
They are *close*; and
The relationship (when working) helps them achieve life goals; and
The relationship difficulties are impediments to motion (e.g., a long, dusty road; being on the rocks or off the track).

Such compositional structures were noticed during the 1980s. It was also noticed that such structural composition was accomplished through "bindings" – identifications of one element with another. Thus, the life goals of the ideal lovers are "bound" to the life goals that are understood as destinations. A vehicle used for travel is typically a container, which is bound to the container in the metaphor that *A Relationship is A Container.*

It was also noticed that an optimization principle was at work in forming such composite metaphors:

- Maximize the overall strength of bindings.

*Destinations* occur in a travel frame. There are *Travelers* in that frame. Given that the *Life Goals* of the *Lovers* are bound to the *Life Goals* understood as *Destinations*, the optimization principle leads to the binding of the *Lovers* with *Life Goals* to the *Travelers* going to *Destinations*, to yield the metaphorical mapping that *Lovers Are Travelers*.

Those bindings make possible certain metaphorical inferences: source domain inferences that are mapped combine with target domain knowledge via binding to produce new inferences: If lovers are "stuck" in relationship, if the relationship isn't "going anywhere," then they are not making progress toward common life goals. If the lovers are "going in different directions," then they may not be able get to the same destinations, which means metaphorically that their common life goals may be inconsistent.

The NTL perspective provides a very different way of thinking about such complex metaphors. The "maximize bindings" principle is simply a consequence of the fact that the brain is a best-fit system. Inferences are new activations that arise when bindings occur. We can now explain *why* the *Love Is a Journey* metaphor exists, *why* Lovers should be Travelers, *why* Relationships are Vehicles, and *why* the Lovers' common life goals are Destinations.

In a system where *Lovers ideally have compatible Life Goals*, and *Goals (that is, Purposes) are Destinations*, then (binding Life Goals and Goals) Lovers ideally have compatible destinations, which induces (via best fit) the metaphors that *Lovers are Travelers* and Lovers ideally have compatible Destinations.

Consider our existing conceptual system where *A Relationship is a Container*, A Vehicle is a Container in which the Travelers are close together, Intimacy is Closeness, Lovers are intimate, *A Vehicle is an Instrument for Travel*, and Lovers are Travelers. Binding containers to containers, vehicles to vehicles, and travelers to travelers and bringing those bindings together with the metaphorical mapping that Lovers are Travelers yields (by best fit) A Relationship is a Vehicle that Lovers are in.

In short, the Love is a Journey metaphor arises naturally via best fit from the rest of the system.

To see the real importance of such an observation, let us look at primary metaphors and how they are acquired.

### *Primary Metaphors*

The neural theory of metaphor got its real impetus from three Berkeley dissertations done in 1997 – by Srini Narayanan, Joe Grady, and Christopher Johnson. Narayanan's dissertation was key. He modeled metaphors as neural mappings and formulated certain metaphors for international economics. He then showed that the results of source domain inferences from the domain of physical motion and action are mapped onto the international economics target domain, interact with the logic of the target domain, and produce metaphorical inferences.

Johnson studied metaphor acquisition in young children and found three stages: (1) source domain only; (2) in domains where the source and target domains were both active ("conflated"), children learned to use source domain words with target domain meanings and grammar, then later (3) used the words metaphorically.

Putting together the Johnson and Narayanan results yields the following hypothesis: in situations where the source and target domains are both active simultaneously, the two areas of the brain for the source and target domains will both be active. Via the Hebbian principle that *Neurons that fire together wire together*, neural mapping circuits linking the two domains will be learned. Those circuits constitute the metaphor.

Grady called such metaphors "primary metaphors" and observed that they are learned by the hundreds the same way all over the world because people have the same bodies and basically the same relevant environments. Therefore, we will have very much the same experiences in childhood in which two domains are simultaneously active, and so we will learn neural metaphorical mappings linking those domains naturally, just by functioning in the world. Just living an everyday life gives you the experience and suitable brain activations to give rise to a huge system of the same primary metaphorical mappings that are learned around the world without any awareness.

By best fit, different cultural frames will combine with those primary metaphors and give rise to different metaphor systems. The Love Is a Journey metaphor is a good example. The primary metaphors that ground the Love Is a Journey metaphor are

- Purposes are Destinations: Every day there is a correlation between achieving a purpose and reaching a destination, as when you have to go to the refrigerator to get a piece of fruit or a cold beer.
- Difficulties are Impediments to Motion: A difficulty is something that inhibits your achievement of some purpose,

which is metaphorically reaching a destination. Hence, difficulties are conceptualized metaphorically as impediments to motion to a destination.

- A Relationship is a Container (a Bounded Region of Space): People who are closely related tend to live, work, or otherwise spend time in the same enclosed space – your family in your home, your co-workers at the office, and so on.
- Intimacy is Closeness: The people you are most intimate with are typically the people you have spent time physically close to: your family, spouse, lover, and so on.

In each case, a correlation in experience is realized in the brain as the co-activation of distinct neural areas, which leads to the formation of circuits linking those areas.

*A Structural Prediction.* The neural theory says that complex metaphors that are extensions of existing primary metaphors bound together should be easier to learn and understand than conceptual metaphors that are totally new – since they just involve new binding and other connecting circuitry over existing conceptual metaphors. They should also seem more natural.

Take, for example, the sentence *My job is a jail.*

1. A jail restricts someone's freedom of motion to desired external destinations, thus producing frustration and other negative emotions.
2. The metaphors that *Achieving a Purpose is Reaching a Destination* and *Actions are Motions* exist in our conceptual system.
3. Binding the *restriction on freedom of motion* to *Actions are Motions*, we infer a restriction on freedom of action.
4. Binding *desired external destinations* to *Achieving a Purpose is Reaching a Destination*, we infer *achieving external purposes*.
5. *My Job is a jail* metaphorically infers that my job restricts my freedom of action in achieving external purposes, thus producing frustration and other emotions.

Thus, given the existing system, maximization of binding produces the meaning of the sentence. We predict that this should be easy to understand and to process.

Compare this sentence with a sentence like *My job is an aardvark.* An aardvark is an African animal with a long proboscis that eats ants by sticking its proboscis in anthills. There are no primary metaphors in our normal conceptual systems that provide a natural metaphorical interpretation for this sentence. However, that sentence can be metonymic, say, when said by a zookeeper whose job is taking care of an aardvark. The metonymy is In the Animal Keeper Frame, The Animal stands for The Job of Taking care of that Animal.

The neural theory in general predicts that the most immediate component metaphors for a complex metaphor will be activated and used in the mapping. In short, in most cases, new conceptual metaphors that are easy to learn and make sense of are using conceptual mappings that preexist, frame-based knowledge that preexists, and adding connections in the form of circuitry that binds, links, maps, extends, and forms gestalts.

*A Processing Prediction.* The neural theory of metaphor makes an important prediction in the case of conventional conceptual metaphorical mappings that are realized by fixed brain circuitry. When you hear a metaphorical expression, the literal meanings of the words should activate the source domain circuitry and the context should activate the target domain circuitry, and together they should activate the mapping circuit. The result is an integrated circuit, with activation of both source and target domains and processing over both at once. Thus, understanding language that makes use of a conventional conceptual metaphor should take no longer than normal frame-based nonmetaphorical processing. This result has been shown repeatedly, as in the example, *My job is a jail.*

The neural theory thus contradicts old two-step theories (before conceptual metaphor theory) that claim that the source domain is processed first and then the mapping operates to process the target domain.

Time of processing studies contradict this view.

*Asymmetry.* Each neuron fires asymmetrically, with the flow of ions from the cell body down the axon, spreading out from there. Different neurons have different firing capacities, depending on the receptors at the synapses that regulate ion flow. Those neurons that fire more tend to develop greater firing capacities. And those involved in physical bodily functioning tend to fire more. For this reason, the metaphorical maps learned are asymmetric and tend to have physical source domains (though some have social source domains).

The literature abounds with obvious examples.

- More Is Up: Our bodies are constantly monitoring physical height more than computing abstract quantity.
- Affection Is Warmth: Temperature is always there to be monitored; affection isn't.
- Intimacy Is Closeness: We constantly monitor how close we are to objects, more than we judge intimacy.

The preponderance of our system of primary metaphors is acquired in childhood, and childhood experience has an important influence on the system of primary metaphors that we learn. Consider the following important examples:

- Governing Institutions are Families: Our first experience with being governed is in our family. Thus, the social domain of the family will be used more when the metaphor is learned.
- Speech Act Force is Physical Force: Parents teach their young children by manipulating their bodies as they give directives. Thus, verbal directives are learned as having a "force."
- Arguments are Struggles: All small children struggle with their parents when their parents guide them physically in teaching them how to behave. Early verbal arguments are commonly about meeting behavioral expectations. As we grow up and learn about wars and battles, the source domain of struggle is specialized and expanded to battles and wars.

During learning, much of the abstract domain is structured by fixed projections from the embodied domain. When processing source domain words in the context of a target domain subject matter, the fixed connections result in co-activation of the two domains. Thus, source domain activations arising from inferences are projected onto the target domain via the preestablished mapping.

### *The Use of Conceptual Metaphors*

The preneural theory of conceptual metaphor was vague on a number of details. Metaphors were cross-domain mappings – from a frame in one domain to another domain, also structured by frames. Such mappings were seen as applied to target domain situations as understood in the context of commonplace information. Inferences were mapped from the source to target situation, with as much as possible frame and image-schema structure "preserved" from the source domain. Thus, in use, you had:

- The metaphorical mapping (from source domain frame to target domain frame).
- The specific situation being discussed, fitting the target domain.
- Target domain commonplace information.
- Source domain commonplace information.

Metaphorical inferences took (1) source domain inferences, (2) mappings of the results of such inferences to the target domain frames; (3) combining of those mapped inferences with target domain information to give new "metaphorical" inferences.

The neural theory of metaphor provides an explanatory mechanism for metaphorical inferences that can be modeled precisely (Narayanan, 1997) using neural computational modeling. At the heart of the modeling of metaphorical inferences is the notion of mental simulation, which represents specific situations. Let us look first at inferences in NTL, and then at metaphorical inferences.

### *Inferences*

A meaningful node in a neural circuit is a node that can activate a mental simulation.

An inference occurs when:

- the activation of a collection of meaningful nodes (the antecedent situation) in a neural circuit leads to the activation of one or more other meaningful nodes (the consequence);
- when the activation of the antecedent nodes is necessary for the consequence;
- and when the inhibition of one or more consequence nodes results in the inhibition of one or more antecedent nodes.

Inferences are simply consequences of the meaningfulness of nodes in simulation semantics, the spreading of activation, and best-fit constraints (the consequences fit the antecedents best). Recall that the maximization of binding is one of the characteristics of the best-fit property of any neural system. In short, maximizing binding can lead to inferences.

### *Metaphorical Inferences*

A metaphorical inference occurs when:

- a metaphorical mapping is activated in a neural circuit,
- there is an inference in the source domain of the mapping,
- and a consequence of the source domain inference is mapped to the target domain, activating a meaningful node.

For example, suppose the sentence is *We're driving in the fast lane on the freeway of love*. In the travel domain, driving in the fast lane on the freeway activates the inferences that

1. the vehicle the travelers are in is going a lot faster than usual,
2. the driving is exciting, and
3. it can be dangerous (the travelers can suffer physical harm).

"Freeway of love" activates the target domain of love and source domain of travel, resulting in the activation of the Love Is a Journey metaphorical mapping. The metaphorical inferences are that:

M1. the relationship the lovers are in is developing a lot faster than usual,
M2. the development of the relationship is exciting, and
M3. it can be dangerous (the lovers can suffer psychological harm).

These inferences are activated when the circuitry is activated in the processing of the sentence. The totality of source domain inferences does *not* have to proceed before any of the target domain inferences.

### *Mapping "Gaps"*

A mapping gap occurs when there is a metaphorical mapping, but part of the source domain frame has no correlate in the target domain. For example, take the sentence *I gave Sam that idea*. In this metaphor, the communication of an idea is the transfer of an object from the speaker to the hearer.

A. Source domain knowledge: the giver loses the object when he gives it to the recipient.
B. Target domain knowledge: the speaker does *not* lose the idea when he gives it to the listener.

Because we know (B) about the target domain, no mapping from (A) to (B) can be learned. Thus, what appears to be a "gap" is not a gap; it is just that an impossible mapping does not take place in the learning of the metaphor. Recall that the learning of the metaphor involves repeated co-activation of the corresponding source and target nodes, and the absence of such co-activation implies that no such maps are learned.

### *Image-Schema "Preservation"*

As Regier (1995, 1997) and Dodge and Lakoff (2006) have argued, primitive image-schemas (e.g., container, source-path-goal, degree of closeness, direction, and amount of force) are computed by brain structures that are either innate or form early. Action schemas and frames are structured using such primitive image-schemas. For example, *putting in* makes use of the container schema, the source-path-goal schema, a force schema, a direction schema, and an aspectual schema.

Metaphorical *putting in* – as in *The Founding Fathers put freedom of speech into the Constitution* – uses physical putting-in as a source domain. The inference patterns of those schemas as bound together in the source domain are then used in metaphorical inferences. For example, if you put something into a physical container, it isn't there before you put it in and it is there afterward and it remains there until something happens to remove it. That is also true of the freedoms the Founding Fathers put into the Constitution.

In preneural theories of conceptual metaphor, we spoke of "preservation" of source domain image-schemas. In the neural theory, it is the *use* of source domain image-schemas in inferences about target domain situations.

### *Mental Spaces*

A "mental space" from an NTL perspective is a mental simulation characterizing an understanding of a situation, real or imagined. The entire space is governed by a gestalt node, which makes the mental space an "entity" which, when activated, activates all the elements of the mental space.

### *Blending*

What is called "blending" is a matter of neural binding. Consider the monk blend. There are two mental spaces each structured by frames. In each, there is a mountain and a path. On day 1, the monk walks up the path to the top of the mountain, sleeps overnight there, and on day 2, the monk walks down the same path to the bottom

Day 1 is one mental space; day 2 is another. The blend consists of bindings and a gestalt circuit. The mountain on day 1 is bound to the mountain on day 2, the path on day 1 to the path on day 2, the monk on day 1 to the monk on day 2. A gestalt node forms a single blend out of the two spaces with the bindings.

Question: Is there a single place on the path where the monk is located at the same time on both days?

Answer: Yes. Where he meets himself.

We have formed a single integrated circuit containing both mental spaces, with two instances of the monk, one going up and the other coming down the mountain. Being on the same path, the up-going monk will "meet" the down-going monk in the simulation created by the bindings at some place and time. Note that there is no metaphor here.

### *Metaphors versus Blends*

A metaphor is a mapping. A blend is an instance of one or more neural bindings.

Metaphors don't occur in isolation nor do bindings. A contextual interpretation of an utterance includes both general knowledge and target domain knowledge. The overall use of metaphor involves some bindings and inferences in the source domain, bindings and inferences in the target domain, activation of metaphoric maps, and the activation of other connected nodes that characterize related knowledge (Fauconnier & Turner, 2002; Grady et al., 1999). What is called the "blend" is other overall set of bindings in the simulation that characterizes the meaning of the sentence.

To see the difference between metaphors and blends, consider the metaphor More Is Up. In a sentence like *The temperature went up*, we are understanding quantity in terms of verticality. But they are different things. Amount of heat in itself is not vertical.

But in a thermometer oriented vertically, the mercury goes up physically as the temperature increases (metaphorically goes up). The thermometer is an object that, in its very physical construction, is intended to be understood in terms of both a binding and a metaphor. The metaphor, but not the blend, is in the sentence *The temperature went up*.

Thus, metaphors exist separate from blends. Such metaphoric blends are formed when a source and a target element of a metaphor are bound together via neural binding.

Let's consider another contrast. Suppose you are explaining arithmetic to a child. You draw a line. And you say, "Think of a number as being a point on this line. Say this is zero. And to get to one you take a step from 0 to 1, located here on the line. To add 3 to 1 you take three steps from 1, like this, and you get to 4. To subtract 1 from 4, you take a step backward, and you get to 3." And so on. Here, you are just using the metaphor that numbers are points on a line. It is just a metaphor. No blending.

But if you go to the Cartesian plane where you have a number line, then you not only have the metaphor of numbers as points on a line, but you have a binding as well: the number and the point on the line are *identical* – the same entity! This metaphorical blend is actually in the mathematics of the Cartesian plane.

Again, a mere metaphor (understanding the target in terms of the source) is crucially different from that metaphor plus a binding of source entities to target entities.

### *Optimality in Blending*

A great deal follows from the understanding of blending as neural binding, given that neural systems work by spreading activation and best-fit principles. Best-fit principles include the maximization of binding, and the maximal use of conventional frames, metaphors, commonplace knowledge, and context. Maximizing neural binding means a maximal integration of all these elements and "emergent" inferences resulting from the "mixing" of inference-determining elements (e.g., from source and target domains).

The result is a set of predictions about blends – exactly the well-known properties of optimal blends:

- **Integration:** The scenario in the blended space should be a well-integrated scene.

Each neural binding across conceptual structures serves to "integrate" those conceptual structures.

- **Web:** Tight connections between the blend and the inputs should be maintained, so that an event in one of the input spaces, for instance, is construed as implying a corresponding event in the blend.

Such correspondences are given by maps, either metaphorical maps or maps connecting mental spaces (that is, simulations).

- **Unpacking:** It should be easy to reconstruct the inputs and the network of connections, given the blend.

Neural bindings have the property that they can be "relaxed"; that is, the bound structures can be conceptualized without the binding, as when you can separate off the blueness of a blue square and think of it as red.

- **Topology:** Elements in the blend should participate in the same sorts of relations as their counterparts in the inputs.

This follows immediately since a structure with an added neural binding has all the relations as the structure without that neural binding.

- **Good Reason:** If an element appears in the blend, it should have meaning. And if it arises by inference, it will be tied into the logic of the blend.

Since blends apply to simulations, and simulations have meaning, this follows immediately.

- **Metonymic Tightening:** Relationships between elements from the same input should become as close as possible within the blend. For instance, western images of personified Death often depict the figure as a skeleton, thus closely associating the event of death with an object that, in our more literal understandings, is indirectly but saliently associated with it.

These are simply cases of a metonymy plus a neural binding of the source with the target of the metonymy.

Thus, all of the optimality properties producing "good" blends are explained by simulation semantics, spreading activation, and best fit, which governs optimality in biological neural networks.

### *Emergence*

Emergence is the occurrence in a blend of an entity or proposition that does not exist in any of the blend "inputs." Emergence is explained by inference in neural systems. Maps and blends across conceptual structures can give rise to inferences not present in any "input."

Consider the example, *In France, Clinton's affair wouldn't have mattered*. In the blend, Clinton, the American chief executive, is bound to the position of the French chief executive in France. Since the French don't care about politicians' sexual liaisons, we get the inference that "In France, Clinton's affair wouldn't have mattered." This "emergent" inference does not occur in either of the inputs: France, where Clinton was not chief executive of France, and the United States, where Clinton's affair did matter. It arises by neural binding and inference.

#### BETTER ANALYSES WITH METAPHORIC BLENDS

Certain classic analyses in the blending literature which are seen as nonmetaphoric blends really should be seen as metaphoric blends. For example, there is a common metaphor in which Breaking a Record Is Winning a Race Against the Previous Record-holder. Thus, a few years ago when Mark McGwire and Sammy Sosa were both attempting to break Babe Ruth's home run record, the press represented the situation metaphorically as a race with Ruth – and each other. In the daily papers, McGwire and Sosa were represented by how many games they were "behind" or "ahead" of Ruth's 60 homerun performance. They were spoken of as "catching up" or "falling behind." The classic blending analysis misses this metaphor.

The same metaphor occurred in the situation many years back when the yacht Great America tried to break the San Francisco to Boston record through the Northwest Passage set 100 years before by the yacht Northern Light. Accordingly, the metaphor had the Great America in a "race" with the Northern Light, even though they sailed 100 years apart. The newspapers daily reported how many days "ahead" of the Northern Light the Great America was. Again, the classic blending analysis misses the metaphor.

The moral: A neural theory analysis forces us to notice analyses we might otherwise miss.

Let's consider another class of cases with the same moral. There are two widely used metaphors rarely analyzed as such.

- A Person who performs actions with certain characteristics is a Member of a Profession known for those characteristics.

Here, the mapping is from the frame of a member of a profession, with the characteristics that members of a profession are known by. Special cases, for example, a surgeon frame expands the general frame with the values filled in one way, while a butcher frame expands the general frame with the values filled in another way.

In each case, the source domain of the metaphor is a stereotype, represented as a frame whose semantic roles include kinds of characteristics. For example, a *surgeon* is known for being precise with beneficial results, while a *butcher* is known for being sloppy and acting more with force than with care, with messy results. Thus, we can say

- My lawyer presented my case with surgical skill.
- My lawyer butchered my case.

In the first, the lawyer was careful and skillful, with beneficial results. In the second, the lawyer was careless, sloppy, and heavy-handed, with messy results. Other examples can be quite diverse:

- Ichiro slices singles through the infield like a surgeon.
- Frank Thomas hacks at the ball like a butcher.

This very general metaphor accounts for the classical examples:

- My butcher is a surgeon.
- My surgeon was a butcher.

The first case says the butcher cuts meat with the care of a surgeon, while the second says that my surgeon handled my surgery in a careless, sloppy, and heavy-handed way.

A second example like this is the commonplace metaphor:

- A Person with characteristic properties is an Animal known for those properties.

Classic cases include *Man is a wolf*, *Our new salesman is a tiger*, *Harry's a pig*, and *You're trying to weasel out of this*. All examples use a stereotype of an animal, and we understand the person in terms of the characteristics of the animal stereotype.

There have been attempts to understand such cases nonmetaphorically, just in terms of bindings based on similarity. Such an approach would claim that there is no conventional metaphor at all and that all such cases are literal blends based on similar properties. We can see what is wrong with this approach by looking at cases outside the proposed conventional metaphors we just discussed. Consider sentences such as

- My surgeon is a Russian.
- My butcher is a Russian.
- My lawyer is a Russian.

There are common stereotypes of Russians, say, that they are very sentimental and emotional, sometimes to the point of losing control. If the blending approach were correct, we would expect these sentences to act like *The butcher is a surgeon* and *The surgeon is a butcher*. Just as the butcher isn't literally a surgeon by profession, nor is the surgeon literally a butcher by profession, so you would expect these sentences to be saying that the surgeon, butcher, and lawyer were not literally Russian by nationality; but they do say that. In addition, you would expect them to say that the surgery, butchering, and law practice are carried out in an overly sentimental, emotional, almost out-of-control way. But the sentences do not say that. The "Russian" sentences are literal and work just as you would expect literal sentences to work. The surgeon-butcher sentences are metaphorical, using conventional conceptual metaphors, and they work accordingly.

I conclude that the metaphor approach is accurate for cases like the surgeon-butcher and animal examples and the blending approach is not. Blends are real and result from neural bindings, mental spaces, and metaphors. But there is no reason to believe that there is a neural operation of "blending" in addition.

## THE ROLE OF METAPHOR IN ABSTRACT CONCEPTS

In *Whose Freedom?* I argue that metaphor is central to the core concept of freedom and that this abstract concept is actually grounded in bodily experience.

Physical freedom is freedom to move – to go places, to reach for and get objects, and to perform actions. Physical freedom is defined in a frame in which there are potential impediments to freedom to move: blockages, being weighed down, being held back, being imprisoned, lack of energy or other resources, absence of a path providing access, being physically restrained from movement, and so on. Freedom of physical motion occurs when none of these potential impediments is present.

Various metaphors turn freedom of physical motion into freedom to achieve one's goals. The event structure metaphor, for instance, characterizes achieving a purpose as reaching a desired destination, or getting a desired object. Freedom to achieve one's purposes then becomes, via the event structure metaphor, the absence of any metaphorical impediments to motion. Other ideas, like political freedom and freedom of the will, build on that concept.

The concept of political freedom is characterized via a network of concepts that necessarily includes the event structure metaphor and the inferences that arise via that metaphor. The ultimate grounding of the concept of political freedom is visceral, arising from the experience of *not* being free to move and the frustration that engenders.

What is the role of metaphor in our concept of political freedom? Our understanding of conceptual systems in terms of neural systems shows that conceptual metaphor is used in our understanding of political freedom but indirectly.

### METAPHOR IN SYSTEMS OF THOUGHT

In *Philosophy in the Flesh*, Mark Johnson and I argue that philosophical systems of thought rest on a relatively small number of metaphors treated as ultimate truths and used constantly in reasoning. The neural theory of metaphor allows us to understand more about such systems and people who think in terms of them most of every day.

Because the fundamental metaphors are used constantly, the synaptic strengths in the metaphors become very strong and resistant to change. Second, spreading activation and best-fit properties (including maximization of binding) make such systems highly integrated, tightly connected, with many inferences. As a result, such a system will dominate your thought, your understanding of the world, and your actions.

One will tend to see the world through the system; one will tend to construct neural simulations to fit the system; one will tend to plan the future using the system; and one will define common sense through the system. The system will tend to make experiences and facts consistent with it noticeable and important, and experiences and facts inconsistent with it invisible.

This is especially true in politics, where progressive and conservative thought are each defined by a central metaphor and a system of thought that fits it (see my *Moral Politics*).

By far the most detailed study of the role of metaphor in a system of thought is Rafael Núñez's and my book, *Where Mathematics Comes From*, which shows in great detail how many branches of higher mathematics are built up via layers of metaphor from embodied concepts.

### METAPHORICAL LANGUAGE

The neural theory of language allows us to understand better why language is so powerful. Let's start with words. Every word is defined via linking circuit to an element of a frame – a semantic role. Because every frame is structured by a gestalt circuit, the activation of that frame element results in the activation of the entire frame. Now, the frame will most likely contain one or more image-schemas, a scenario containing other frames, a presupposition containing other frames, may fit into and activate a system of other frames, and each of these frames may be structured by conceptual metaphors. All of those structures could be activated simply by the activation of that one frame element that defines the meaning of the given word. In addition, the lexical frame may be in the source domain of a metaphor. In that case, the word could also activate that metaphor. In the right context, all of these activated structures can result in inferences.

Let's suppose a word activates a network of frames, images-schemas, and metaphors. The metaphors may be only indirectly linked to the frame directly activated by the word. Is that word an instance of "metaphorical language"? That is not how the term is usually used.

We usually speak of metaphorical language when

- the frame element the word designates is in the source domain frame of the given metaphor,
- the subject matter under discussion is in the target domain of that metaphor.

Thus, *up* in the sentence *Prices went up*, activates the verticality frame, *prices* activates the quantity frame, and together they activate the *More is Up* metaphor.

In addition, the word *up* – by virtue of the metaphorical mapping – acquires a link to the quantity frame, where it activates greater quantity.

Does *up* in *Prices went up* always activate the *More is Up*? It depends. In our neural systems, the *More is Up* metaphor is always present in the neural system, always physically linked to the concept of greater quantity – connected and ready to be activated. But it is possible for the metaphorical mapping to be inhibited and for *up* to be directly activated. However, when a graph of prices physically rises, then the More is Up metaphor is activated, as it is in a sentence like *Prices reached a new peak*, where *reach* and *peak* activate the concept of Motion Upward.

Grammar can also play a role in activating a metaphor, as in the expression *freeway of love*, in which the construction sanctions an interpretation in which the head noun *freeway* comes from the source domain (travel) and object of the preposition *love* comes from the target domain. Grammatical constructions come with metaphorical constraints, as Karen Sullivan has observed. Compare *bright student* versus **intelligent light*: the modifier (*bright*) is from the source domain, while the head (*student*) is from the target domain; but the reverse doesn't work – except in a special class of cases, like *emotional intelligence*, where the modifier is a nonpredicative adjective that defines a domain (emotion).

All this is natural in a neural theory because of the connectivity involved. The form elements (words and grammatical categories) are neurally linked to the elements in conceptual system, where metaphorical mappings are linked to frame elements, which are linked to words or grammatical categories.

Consider a poetic metaphor like Dylan Thomas's line, *Do not go gently into that good night*. The line does not overtly mention death as the subject matter, but the line contains three words that each evoke a source domain frame in a metaphor for death: *go* as in *Death is Departure*; *gently* as in *Life is a Struggle*; and *night* as in *A Lifetime is a Day and Death is Night*. This is natural from a neural perspective. Each word activates a frame element in a frame *go, gently, night*. The three frames are thereby activated and each provides some activation to the corresponding metaphors for Death. This is reinforced by the fact that the sentence does not have a direct literal meaning, in which each of these words is used literally. But the source domain meanings do important work in constructing a metaphorical image of a man moving into the night ready to fight. The next line, *Rage, rage against the dying of the light* uses *dying* metaphorically in the sense of light ceasing to exist. But the activation via the metaphor of source domain of death reinforces the interpretation of the first line. This use of "activation" makes sense in the neural model.

### *The Use of Metaphoric Language*

The neural theory of metaphor also makes sense of the use of metaphoric language in context. We know that metaphor does not reside in words but in ideas. This is especially clear from cases of metaphorical ambiguity, where the same words evoke different readings using different metaphors. "It's all downhill from here" may in a given situation meaning "it's getting easier" (Ease of Action Is Ease of Motion) or "it's getting worse" (Down is Bad). Either conceptual metaphor can apply to the spatial meaning of "down" in "downhill." In a neural account, both metaphors are connected to the spatial meaning of "down," but the metaphors are mutually inhibitory. Only one can be activated, depending on context.

Consider a metaphorically ambiguous sentence like "Let's move the meeting ahead two days." If uttered on a Wednesday, it could refer to either Monday or Friday, depending on which metaphor for time is used – moving-ego or moving-time. Since they are mutually contradictory, the metaphors are mutually inhibitory. The neural theory can explain Lera Boroditsky's classic experiment at San Francisco airport. She showed that, for people waiting for a plane to come in, the motion of the plane toward them primed the moving time metaphor and they gave the answer "Monday," two days ahead of the moving time. Those who were on the plane and coming off were primed by being on the moving object, and they gave the answer "Friday," two days ahead of the moving ego.

The neural theory explains the priming in these cases. The two time metaphors are mutually inhibitory. What tips the scales is the priming – the neural activation of either a moving time or moving ego in the spatial domain.

### *What Makes Metaphorical Language Meaningful?*

Language is meaningful when the ideas it expresses are meaningful. Conceptual metaphors are meaningful when they are grounded. They are grounded, first, by source domain embodiment, and second by the embodiment of the source and target domains of the primary metaphors being used.

#### SUMMARY: WHAT DOES THE NEURAL THEORY PROVIDE?

The neural theory provides a much better understanding of how thought and language work and of how metaphorical thought fits into the picture. It also provides *explanations* for a host of phenomena. And it changes how one does metaphor analysis – and redefines what metaphor analysis is.

The neural theory explains:

- Why there should be conceptual metaphor at all; what conceptual metaphors are physically; why we have the primary metaphors we have, how the system is grounded, and why certain conceptual metaphors are widespread around the world.
- How metaphorical inferences work; why they should exist; how they operate in context, and how they interact with simulations.
- All of the properties of the old metaphor theory, the theory as described by myself and Mark Johnson in *Metaphors We Live By* and by myself in the essay "The Contemporary Theory of Metaphor."
- How metaphors can function *indirectly* in the characterization of abstract concepts.
- How a small number of metaphors can organize a whole system of thought and become the principles on which one lives one's life.
- How metaphorical language works as a simple extension of non-metaphorical language.
- Why metaphors differ from blends, and why blends do not do the job of metaphors.

The neural theory also clarifies what the study of metaphor is about, namely,

- showing how metaphorical understanding is grounded in basic human experience via primary conceptual metaphors;
- showing how primary metaphors contribute to complex conceptual metaphors;
- showing how both primary and complex metaphors contribute to the meanings of words, complex expressions, and grammatical constructions;
- showing how conceptual metaphor plays a role in abstract concepts and overall conceptual systems (as in politics, philosophy, and mathematics);
- and, finally, showing how conceptual metaphors contribute to the understanding of language and other uses of symbols.

#### HOW DOES A METAPHOR ANALYST MAKE USE OF ALL THIS?

Metaphor analysts rarely know neural computation, and they shouldn't be expected to. The Neural Theory of Language Project has figured out a way to let linguists be linguists and not computer or brain scientists. We have invented a notation that correlates with circuitry with the appropriate computational properties but can be used by analysts without worrying about the computational details. Thus, consider a notation such as:

Metaphor: LoveIsAJourney
Source Domain: Journey
Target Domain: Love

Mapping:

Travelers → Lovers
Vehicle → Relationship
Destinations → LifeGoals
ImpedimentsToMotion → Difficulties

Evokes:

Purposes Are Destinations Metaphor,
with Destinations = Self.Source.Destinations
Purposes = Self.Target.LifeGoals

Difficulties Are Impediments to Motion Metaphor,
With Impediments to Motion = Self.Source.ImpedimentsToMotion
Difficulties = Self.Target.Difficulties

Intimacy Is Closeness Metaphor,
With Closeness = Self.Source.ClosenessOf TravelersInVehicle
Intimacy = Self.Target.IntimacyOfLovers

A Relationship Is A Container Metaphor,
With Container = Self.Source.Vehicle
Relationship = Self.Target.Relationship

The statement that this is a metaphor corresponds to the appropriate mapping circuit. The name of the metaphor corresponds to the appropriate gestalt node. The arrows ("→") correspond to linking circuits. The statement of the mapping specifies what maps to what. The equal signs ("=") specify the neural bindings. The "evokes" statement sets up linking circuits activating the "component" metaphors, with neural bindings between LoveIsAJourney (called "Self" in the formalism) and the various component metaphors. There can be, and often is, a chain of "evokes" statements that ultimately lead to primary metaphors that ground the metaphor system in experience.

This formalism is easy for metaphor analysts to learn and use. It can be converted by algorithm to computational neural modeling programs that, say, take a sentence as input and produce an analysis as output. There are corresponding formalisms for grammatical and lexical constructions, metonymies, frames, image-schemas, and so on. The technical term for the notational system is *Embodied Construction Grammar*.

## Conclusion

This is where we are in the neural theory of metaphor as of November 2006. We have a reasonable early approximation to the kinds of computations that neuronal groups must perform to characterize frames, metaphors, metonymies, mental spaces, and blends. A parsing program to use these kinds of computations is being constructed. Thousands of frames and hundreds of metaphors have been analyzed informally to date and can readily be converted to the notation system. And we know enough about natural metaphor learning to understand how the metaphor system gets built up just by functioning in our everyday lives.

The neural theory of metaphor changes cognitive linguistics vastly, not the analyses themselves so much, but our understanding of how metaphor systems work.

## References

Dodge, E., & Lakoff, G. (2006). Image schemas: From linguistic analysis to neural grounding. In B. Hampe (Ed.), *From perception to meaning: Image schemas in cognitive linguistics* (pp. 57–91). Berlin: Mouton de Gruyter.

Fauconnier, G., & Turner, M. Turner. (2002). *The way we think*. New York: Basic Books.

Feldman, J. (2006). *From molecule to metaphor*. Cambridge, MA: Bradford MIT Press.

Feldman, J., & Narayanan, S. (2004). Embodied meaning in a neural theory of language. *Brain and Language*, 89(2), 385–392.

Gallese, V., & Lakoff, G. (2005). The brain's concepts. *Cognitive Neuropsychology*, 22(3–4), 455–479.

Grady, J. (1997). *Foundations of meaning*. Unpublished doctoral dissertation, University of California, Berkeley.

Grady, J., Oakley, T., & Coulson, S. (1999). Blending and metaphor. In G. Steen & R. Gibbs (Eds.), *Metaphor in cognitive linguistics* (pp. 101–124). Philadelphia: John Benjamins.

Johnson, C. (1999). *Constructional grounding*. Unpublished doctoral dissertation, University of California, Berkeley.

Lakoff, G. (1993). The contemporary theory of metaphor. In A. Ortony (Ed.), *Metaphor and thought* (2nd ed., pp. 202–251). New York: Cambridge University Press.

Lakoff, G., & Johnson, M. (1980). *Metaphors we live by* (2nd ed., 2002). Chicago: University of Chicago Press.

Lakoff, G., & Johnson, M. (1999). *Philosophy in the flesh*. New York: Basic Books.

Lakoff, G., & Núñez, R. (2000). *Where mathematics comes from*. New York: Basic Books.

Narayanan, S. (1997). *Karma: Knowledge-based action representations for metaphor and aspect*. Unpublished doctoral dissertation, University of California, Berkeley.

Regier, T. (1995). A model of the human capacity for categorizing spatial relations. *Cognitive Linguistics*, 6, 63–88.

Regier, T. (1997). *The human semantic potential: Spatial language and constrained connectionism*. Cambridge, MA: MIT Press.

Sullivan, K. (2007). *Grammar in metaphor: a construction grammar account of metaphoric language*. Unpublished doctoral dissertation, University of California, Berkeley.

Talmy, L. (2000). *Toward a cognitive semantics*. Cambridge, MA: MIT Press.

CHAPTER 2

# Philosophy's Debt to Metaphor

*Mark Johnson*

## What's at Issue in the Question of Metaphor?

Philosophy's debt to metaphor is profound and immeasurable. Without metaphor, there would be no philosophy. However, philosophy's debt is no greater, nor less, than that of any other significant human intellectual field or discipline. Philosophers must use the same conceptual resources possessed by any human being, and the potential for any philosophy to make sense of a person's life depends directly on the fact that all of us are metaphoric animals.

What I have just said is not now, nor has it ever been, widely accepted by philosophers. In fact, for the major part of our philosophical history, the idea that metaphor lies at the heart of human conceptualization and reasoning has been rejected.[1] One could even make a crude distinction between two types of philosophy – objectivist/literalist philosophies that see metaphor as a dispensable linguistic appurtenance and those that see philosophies as creative elaborations of basic conceptual metaphors.

The history of western philosophy is, for the most part, one long development of the objectivist dismissal of metaphor, punctuated rarely by bold declarations of the pervasiveness of metaphor in thought, of which Nietzsche is the most famous proponent. Where a philosopher stands on this key issue can be determined by their answer to one question: are our abstract concepts defined by metaphor, or not? Once the question is formulated in this manner, it is easy to see the profound philosophical stakes at issue. If our most fundamental abstract concepts – such as those for causation, events, will, thought, reason, knowledge, mind, justice, and rights – are irreducibly metaphoric, then philosophy must consist in the analysis, criticism, and elaboration of the metaphorical concepts out of which philosophies are made. If, on the other hand, you believe that our most important philosophical concepts are, in the final analysis, literal, then you will regard metaphor as cognitively insignificant, and you will relegate it to what you disparagingly regard as some distant corner of philosophy, typically the unfairly maligned field of aesthetics.

Anyone who thinks that there is really nothing very important at stake here should consider the following. There are a number of perennial philosophical questions that arise over and over again throughout history any time you reflect on the nature of human experience. These are questions such as What is mind, and how does it work? What does it mean to be a person? Is there such a thing as human will, and is it free? What is the nature of reality? What can I know, and how can I go about gaining that knowledge? What things or states are "good" and should therefore be pursued? Are certain actions morally required of us? Does God exist (and what difference would it make)? Is there any meaning to human existence, or is life absurd? *Both the framing of these questions and the kinds of answers we give to them depend on metaphor. You cannot address any of these questions without engaging metaphor.* Consequently, an adequate philosophy must include an extensive inquiry into the workings of metaphor and how it shapes our most important philosophical ideas.

### *Philosophical Concepts Are Metaphoric*

From a practical standpoint, it is obviously not possible to make an exhaustive survey showing that *all* our philosophical concepts are defined by conceptual metaphors. Instead, I will examine one key concept – causation – to indicate its metaphorical constitution, and I will point to research suggesting that we use metaphors to define all of our abstract concepts and thus all of our philosophical concepts.

I have selected causation as the exemplary metaphorically defined concept because it is hard to imagine a metaphysical concept that is more fundamental than that of causation. It lies at the heart of all of the sciences, is pervasive in our folk theories of the world, and is a philosophical lynchpin of virtually every ontology. When the first substantial metaphor analysis of our causal concepts emerged within cognitive linguistics over a decade ago, it became clear that the implications of this research were stunning. In my own analytic philosophical training, most of the books and articles I read assumed science to be a superior form of knowledge, partly because of its ability to give causal explanations of events. In one philosophical treatise after another, I was struck by how philosophers referred to "causes" as if they were objective forces or entities and as if there existed basically one kind of natural causation (as revealed in expressions such as "X caused Y" and "The cause of Y is X"). In an attempt to explain human actions, many philosophers also spoke of "agent causality," in order to carve out a space for human "willing," but in physical nature, natural causes ruled the day. So, there seemed to be at least one type of cause (i.e., physical) but not more than two types (adding agent causation to physical causation), and both conceptions were thought to be literal, not metaphorical. Causes were alleged to be literal entities or forces in the world.

This picture, as we will see, turns out to be mistaken, and badly so. It is a mistake that has disastrous consequences. To see why this is so, let's begin with an analysis of one of our most often used concepts of causation – that of causation as a physical force. Once detailed analyses were performed on the semantics of our causal terms, the metaphorical nature of this concept became quite evident. In cognitive linguistics, the study of causal concepts emerged from the study of how people conceptualize events generally. The first prominent conceptual metaphor involved an understanding of change of state as (metaphorical) motion from one location to another, according to the following general mapping:[2]

## THE LOCATION EVENT-STRUCTURE METAPHOR

| *Source Domain* [Motion in Space] | | *Target Domain* [Events] |
|---|---|---|
| Locations in space | >>>>> | States |
| Movements from one location to another | >>>>> | Change of states |
| Physical forces | >>>>> | Causes |
| Forced movement | >>>>> | Causation |
| Self-propelled movements | >>>>> | Actions |
| Destinations | >>>>> | Purposes |
| Paths to destinations | >>>>> | Means to ends |
| Impediments to motion | >>>>> | Difficulties |

The location event-structure metaphor comprises a vast complex system of several submappings, each of which is what Grady (1997) calls a "primary" metaphor. In English, the semantics of our terms for events is given by the detailed structure of the mapping. Each submapping supports a large number of expressions whose dependence on metaphor goes largely unnoticed in our ordinary discourse. For example, the submapping Change Of State Is Movement underlies expressions such as "The water *went from* hot *to* cold," "The system is *moving toward* homeostasis," and "The pizza is *somewhere between* warm and cold." Causation Is Forced Movement is evident in "The fire *brought* the soup *to* a boil," "His treachery *pushed* the King over the edge," "The candidate's speech *threw* the crowd into a frenzy."

Notice how these submappings code various dimensions of what linguists call *aspect*, which concerns the means and manner of an action. For instance, we say, "the stove *brought* the water to a boil" but not *"the stove *threw* the water to a boil," for a very good reason. In the source domain of physical forces and motions, to "bring" something to someone is to apply continuous force to an object to move it from one location to another, causing it to end up in that person's possession. When metaphorically extended to causation in general, the semantics of *bring* thus entails continuous application of force to bring about change of state. Thus, *bringing* water to a boil entails the constant heating of the water until it boils (i.e., until it arrives at the metaphorical boiling-state location). *Throwing* a physical object, by contrast, involves an initial application of strong force with the object continuing to move to a new location, even after the force is no longer applied. Thus, "threw," according to the submapping, is not appropriate for the case of boiling water, though it is just the right term for "Babe Ruth's homerun *threw* the crowd into a frenzy."

Now, how could a literalist philosopher have any adequate account of the semantics of *throw*, as revealed in this case of Ruth's home run? Will she say that there is a purely literal way to express the type of causation involved here? But there isn't. If we say, "Babe Ruth's homerun *caused* the crowd to get emotionally excited," we lose the key semantic details expressed by "threw." "Caused to get excited" does *not* capture the *manner* of the causation, which is rapid initial "force" followed by an extended trajectory after the initial event.

The crucial moral of this example is that the precise details of the semantics of basic causation terms are determined only by the submappings of the metaphors. The inferences we make about causal situations come from the metaphorical structure of our causation concepts. *You cannot grasp the meaning of the causal terms, nor can you do appropriate causal reasoning, without the metaphors.*

Moreover, the case of causation is even more complicated than it first appears because there turn out to be many different metaphorical conceptions of types of causation. Analyses to date reveal upwards of twenty distinct metaphors that express twenty kinds of causation (Lakoff & Johnson, 1999). A brief survey of just a few of these additional metaphors is highly instructive. It smashes the illusion of core literal concepts of causation and of any objectivist philosophy that pretends to be founded on such concepts.

Consider, for instance, a second major metaphor system for certain types of causation, one that conceives of change of state or having an attribute (or property) as the acquisition of a possession.

### THE OBJECT EVENT-STRUCTURE METAPHOR

| *Source Domain [Transfer of Possessions]* | | *Target Domain [Change of State]* |
|---|---|---|
| Possession | >>>>> | Attribute |
| Movement of possession | >>>>> | Change of state |
| Transfer of possession | >>>>> | Causation |
| Desired objects | >>>>> | Purposes |

The submapping Causation Is Transfer Of Possession is evident in expressions such as "Professor Johnson's lecture on causation *gave* me a headache, but the aspirin *took it away*," "Mary *gave* her cold *to* Janice," and "Janice *caught* Mary's cold." Moreover, even our common philosophical notion of a "property" is based on this metaphorical mapping. What does it mean for an object to "possess" a property? When something *has a property*, it is in a certain state (defined by that property). When something *loses* that property, it no longer manifests the features appropriate to that property. Additionally, there are many other submappings within this causation metaphor that specify various ways of acquiring a desired object, which equates metaphorically with acquiring a certain property or attribute and thus achieving a purpose. For example, there is the submapping Achieving A Purpose Is Getting Food, as in "I'm *hungry* for advancement," "All the best jobs were *gobbled up* early on," and "It was a *mouthwatering* opportunity." Each of the various ways we acquire food, such as hunting, fishing, and agriculture, show up in the language of our purposeful action, as in

- Trying To Achieve A Purpose Is Hunting

"I'm still job *hunting*." "She is *aiming* for rapid advancement in the firm." "Larry *bagged* a promotion." "That idea *won't hunt*."

- Trying To Achieve A Purpose Is Fishing

"Ann *landed* a big promotion." "Before that, she *had a line out* for a new job." "My boss is always *fishing* for compliments." "Every night he's out *trolling* for a date."

- Trying To Achieve A Purpose Is Agriculture

"Every worker should *reap the fruits* of his or her labor." "That promotion is *ripe for the picking*." "Harry's been *cultivating* several job prospects."

Metaphorically based expressions like these are not just colloquialisms, used loosely in ordinary talk. Once again, the submappings of the metaphor specify the precise details of the semantics of causation and determine what types of inferences we will make. Some people harbor the illusion that good science would merely avoid such expressions in causal explanations. But, as it turns out, there is *no way* to avoid the use of one or another basic causal metaphor in science, and scientists reason on the basis of the entailments of the submappings of these metaphors.

In the social sciences, for example, there are a number of quite specific metaphors that can be used for the types of causal explanation appropriate for the science of those fields. One especially common case is the causal path metaphor.

### THE CAUSAL PATH METAPHOR

| | | |
|---|---|---|
| Self-propelled motion | >>>>> | Action |
| Traveler | >>>>> | Actor |
| Locations | >>>>> | States |
| A Lone path | >>>>> | A natural course of action |
| Being on the path | >>>>> | Natural causation |
| Leading to | >>>>> | Results in |
| End of the path | >>>>> | Resulting final state |

Examples:
"Pot smoking *leads to* drug addiction." "As a nation, we're *careening* wildly *down* the *road to destruction*." "That *path* will get you nowhere, man." "You're *heading for* catastrophe."

The causal path metaphor plays a key role in certain types of causal explanation for human actions. It utilizes our common knowledge about motion through space to some destination: if you start down a certain path, you will naturally end up where that path leads you, unless something intervenes to retard or block your progress. Metaphorically, then, if you start down a certain "path" of action, it will typically lead you to a certain destination (end), unless something intervenes to retard or block your metaphorical movement. This argument is used by those who believe that certain actions or behaviors will necessitate a certain specific outcome in the ordinary course of events (as in the 1950s song lyric, "I'll tell you son, you're gonna drive me to drinkin', if you don't stop drivin' that hot rod Lincoln"). In politics, the causal path metaphor can be even more decisive. One often hears the argument that a certain third-world country is "on the road to democracy (read, capitalism)," so that, if we (the United States) will just eliminate any potential obstacles (i.e., we intervene politically, economically, militarily, or covertly), then that country will naturally and inevitably continue along the path to the desired end-state (namely, *democracy!*). Millions of dollars and sometimes even the lives of citizens are sacrificed to supposedly ensure the smooth unrestricted motion of some metaphorical entity (a country, an economy, or a political institution) along a metaphorical causal path to a metaphorically defined destination.

Another important metaphor in political and economic debate is the plate tectonics metaphor for social/political/economic change, which is appropriated from the geology of plate tectonics. According to the logic of the metaphor, continual, long-term application of "pressure" to a system, institution, or state will eventually result in a rapid, massive causal consequence. The rapid, surprising disintegration of the Soviet Union is supposed by some to be a classic example of this process. Often, when large sustained infusions of funds or manpower do not appear to be producing the desired change in a government or economy (usually both), the plate tectonics metaphor is frequently invoked to argue for the continued commitment of resources by Congress, on the assumption that we need just a little bit more pressure to produce an eventual massive transformation.

The analysis of the full range of metaphors could be continued along similar lines. In *Philosophy in the Flesh* (1999), George Lakoff and I summarized the mappings and entailments of nearly 20 different causal metaphors, showing how several of them are employed within various sciences. A number of key philosophical points emerge from these analyses:

1. An adequate conceptual analysis (in this case, of causation concepts) must provide generalizations that explain the precise details of the semantics of the terms and must explain the inferences we make concerning those concepts. The details of the semantics and inference structure of each causal concept are provided by the submappings that jointly constitute the metaphor.
2. Almost all of the basic causation concepts we studied are metaphoric.
3. There appears to be what we called a "literal skeleton" shared by all causation concepts, namely, that a cause is a determining factor in a situation. However, this bare skeleton is far too underspecified to generate any serious causal reasoning in the sciences. It is the metaphors that give rise to the relevant conceptual structure and that constrain the appropriate causal inferences.
4. Several of the main causation metaphors are mutually inconsistent. In other words, there are significant metaphors that have incompatible ontologies. For example, in the location event-structure metaphor, states are (stationary)

locations, and the object or agent changes by moving to a particular (metaphorical) location. In contrast, in the object event-structure metaphor, a state is an object that moves, rather than being a stationary location. Consequently, these two metaphors cannot be reduced to a consistent literal concept.

5. *Causation* is thus a massive radial category. At the center of the category is the closest thing to a literal conception – something like the application of physical force to an object that results in a change in its state or location. One example of this is what we call "billiard-ball causation." Other less prototypical kinds of causation are metaphorically defined.

If we take stock of the argument so far, the results are devastating for any literalist/objectivist philosophy. At least with respect to causation, there is no single literal concept of *cause*, nor are there even two or three basic literal concepts. There is no set of necessary and sufficient conditions that define all causes. Instead, there are 20 or more metaphorical concepts used by ordinary people, scientists, and philosophers in their reasoning about causation. This conclusion does not undermine science at all. It only reminds us that different scientific approaches rely on different metaphorical concepts, which can be more or less appropriate in different situations and that dictate what counts as evidence and argument within a given science. What these analyses do undermine are objectivist philosophies that accept a classical theory of literal meaning, a classical objectivist metaphysics, and a classical correspondence theory of truth.

Moreover, it appears that what is true of our causal concepts holds for all of our most important abstract philosophical concepts. The current evidence for this is inductive, but it is very impressive. Many studies have now shown the metaphorical constitution of basic concepts in the sciences (Magnani & Nersessian, 2002), law (Winter, 2001), mathematics (Lakoff & Núñez, 2000), ethics (Fesmire, 2003; Johnson, 1993), medicine (Wright, 2007), politics (Lakoff, 1996), psychology (Fernandez-Duque & Johnson, 2002; Gibbs, 1994), music (Johnson & Larson, 2003), and many other fields. In light of this metaphorical constitution of our abstract concepts, we need to rethink what we are about as philosophers. There does not now exist, and probably never will exist, an exhaustive metaphorical analysis of the full range of philosophical concepts and arguments. That would be a daunting, unending task. However, a surprisingly large number of philosophical concepts have already been subjected to conceptual metaphor analysis over the past decade and a half. Here is a partial list of some of the more prominent concepts for which we have at least a preliminary metaphorical analysis:

> *Event, Cause, Action, State, Property, Purpose, Mind, Thought, Concepts, Reason, Emotions, Knowledge, Attention, Communication, Self, Will, Moral Rule, Rights, Justice, Duty, Good, Happiness, Society, Democracy, Love, Marriage, Being, Number, Set, Infinity, Addition (Subtraction, Multiplication, etc.), the Cartesian Plane, and a host of other mathematical concepts.*

The number of key concepts analyzed so far, and the depth of those analyses, strongly support the prospect that our abstract concepts are defined by conceptual metaphor and metonymy. If this is so, then philosophical analysis is primarily metaphor analysis – working out the logic and inferential structure of the metaphors that ground our basic philosophical understanding of experience. Philosophical theories, like all theoretical constructions, are elaborations of conceptual metaphors. In a very strong sense, philosophy *is* metaphor.

## *Metaphor and Contemporary Philosophy of Language*

The reality of conceptual metaphor and its central role in abstract conceptualization and reasoning calls into question large parts of traditional western views of meaning and truth, and it also challenges most of contemporary philosophy of language. If our abstract concepts are metaphorically structured, then the classic objectivist/literalist view must be false. According to objectivist metaphysics and theory of knowledge, the world consists of objects, properties, and relations that exist in themselves, independent of human conceptual systems and human agency. Meaning is a matter of how our concepts map onto or pick out aspects of this mind-independent objective reality. Literal concepts are the direct connection between what we think (or what's in our mind) and how the world is, and this connection (sometimes called "intentionality") is the basis for the possibility of truth, which is taken to be a correspondence relation between propositions and states of affairs in the world. There cannot be any significant role for metaphor in this picture of mind and world because the cognitive content of a metaphor would need to be reducible to some set of literal concepts or propositions, if it is to have any meaning and play a role in truth claims.

Quite obviously, if conceptual metaphor is essential for abstract thought, then the classic objectivist/literalist picture cannot be correct. Conceptual metaphor is a structure of human understanding, and the source domains of the metaphors come from our bodily, sensory-motor experience, which becomes the basis for abstract conceptualization and reasoning. From this perspective, truth is a matter of how our body-based understanding of a sentence fits, or fails to fit, our body-based understanding of a situation. And when we are thinking with abstract concepts, that understanding involves conceptual metaphor. There is a form of "correspondence" here – a fitting of our understanding of a statement and our understanding of a situation. But this is not the classic correspondence of literal propositions to objective states of affairs in the world. Instead, the correspondence is mediated by embodied understanding of both the sentence and the situation.

In spite of the growing body of empirical research on conceptual metaphor that has emerged over the past two decades, contemporary analytic philosophy of language has refused to recognize the existence of conceptual metaphor. This is not surprising, considering that to do so would undermine certain fundamental assumptions of analytic philosophy. I want to examine briefly two of the most popular contemporary views of metaphor within analytic philosophy – that of John Searle and the view shared by Donald Davidson and Richard Rorty – in order to show why they cannot accept the reality of conceptual metaphor and how they are done in by its existence.

Searle (1979) approaches metaphor from a speech-act perspective, and he regards the activity of speaking a language as a highly conventionalized rule-governed form of behavior. Searle is also a literalist. He believes that the possibility of truth claims and a robust realism requires that all meaning be reducible to literal concepts and propositions that can, in the last analysis, correspond to states of affairs in the world. Various types of illocutionary speech acts would, according to Searle's account, be rule-governed functions on these basic propositional contents. So, the problem of metaphor within Searle's philosophy of language is to state the rules by which the literal sentence meaning ("S is P") used for a metaphorical utterance can come to be interpreted by a hearer as a different literal utterance meaning ("S is R") (Searle, 1979). On Searle's view, the hearer must recognize that the speaker cannot be intending to convey the literal meaning of her utterance, must then calculate the possible alternate meanings she might possibly be intending, and must finally determine which is the most appropriate literal meaning in the present context.

The problem with this literalist/objectivist version of the speech-act approach is that it simply cannot explain how metaphors actually work. Searle correctly sees that most metaphors are *not* based on an underlying set of literal similarities that might explain how P (in "S is P") calls up R (in "S is R") when we hear the metaphorical utterance. But Searle has no alternative specification of the rules for cases that cannot be based on similarities.

He must surely recognize that his final attempt to formulate a rule for certain types of metaphors *is no explanation at all!*

> *Things which are P are not R, nor are they like R things, nor are they believed to be R; nonetheless it is a fact about our sensibility, whether culturally or naturally determined, that we just do perceive a connection. (Searle, 1979, p. 108)*

Saying that it just "is a fact about our sensibility" that we do make certain connections does not explain anything. When a literalist is forced to admit that certain metaphors are not based on any literal similarities between the source and target domains, then his literalism leaves him without resources to explain where the meaning comes from or how it is possible.

Conceptual metaphor theory solves this problem by rejecting literalism and by recognizing the pervasive structuring of our abstract concepts by metaphor. On this view, metaphors are based on experiential correlations and not on similarities. Joe Grady (1997) has analyzed the experiential grounding of a large number of what he calls "primary metaphors" that are sometimes combined into larger metaphor systems. Consider, for example, the primary metaphor Affection Is Warmth. Grady hypothesizes that this metaphor is based, not on similarities between warmth and affection, but rather on our experience, from infancy, of being held affectionately and feeling warmth. Multiple experiences of this sort in childhood would involve a neuronal co-activation of brain areas tied to the experience of bodily warmth and those tied to the subjective experience of affection and nurturance. This co-activation later becomes the basis for a primary metaphor, Affection Is Warmth. One of Searle's well-known arguments against the similarity theory of metaphor is that there are no relevant literal similarities between a person named Sally and a block of ice that could explain the meaning of the metaphorical expression, "Sally is a block of ice." Quite so, for this expression is not based on similarities. Rather, it is an instance of the primary metaphor Affection Is Warmth, and so it is based on experiential correlations (of affection and warmth), rather than on similarities. If anything, the similarities are a result of the experienced correlation. However, Searle cannot accept this alternative theory because his literalism does not permit him to recognize that metaphoric source-to-target mappings could be equally as basic to our thought as are literal concepts. Searle's theory is constrained by his traditional objectivist views of meaning, knowledge, and truth.

Another extremely popular view of metaphor is Donald Davidson's deflationary rejection of metaphoric meaning. In his 1978 article, "What Metaphors Mean," Davidson provocatively answers that they do not *mean* anything at all or at least nothing beyond the ordinary literal meaning of the utterance. In short, Davidson simply denies that metaphor is a semantic phenomenon, and he thus denies that metaphor has anything to do with making truth-claims: "We must give up the idea that a metaphor carries a message, that it has a content or meaning (except, of course, its literal meaning)" (Davidson, 1978, p. 45). Metaphor is only a pragmatic effect achieved by using a certain literal utterance to induce the hearer to notice something. Davidson says that a metaphorical utterance uses its literal meaning to "intimate" or "suggest" some nonpropositional insight: "Seeing as is not seeing that. Metaphor makes us see one thing as another by making some literal statement that inspires or prompts the insight." (Davidson, 1978, p. 47).

Richard Rorty has become the flamboyant spokesman for Davidson's nonsemantic theory of metaphor. Seizing on Davidson's claim that metaphor is not about propositional content or meaning of any kind, Rorty describes metaphors as linguistic flares that catch and redirect the hearer's attention:

> *Tossing a metaphor into a conversation is like suddenly breaking off the conversation long enough to make a face, or pulling a photograph out of your pocket and displaying it, or pointing at a feature of the surroundings, or slapping your interlocutor's face, or kissing him. Tossing a metaphor*

*into a text is like using italics, or illustrations, or odd punctuation or formats. All these are ways of producing effects on your interlocutor or your reader but not ways of conveying a message. (Rorty, 1989, p. 18)*

This view of metaphor as a nonsemantic use of language for certain attention-getting purposes has an important implication that Rorty is quick to note. The distinction between the "literal" and the "metaphorical" is seen, not as one "between two sorts of meaning, nor a distinction between two sorts of interpretation, but as a distinction between familiar and unfamiliar uses of noises and marks" (Rorty, 1989, p. 17). According to Rorty, these "unfamiliar" marks and noises *somehow* get us searching for new vocabularies in which they are no longer unfamiliar, but he has no account whatever of how this process is supposed to work.

The considerable popularity of both Searle's and Davidson-Rorty's view is easily understandable within the framework of analytic philosophy of language. As different as their two views may appear to be on the surface, they both share a set of grounding assumptions about meaning and truth that are foundational for analytic philosophy. In particular, they agree (1) that meaning is conceptual and propositional in nature, (2) that meaning is truth-conditional, and (3) that only literal concepts can be the bearers of meaning. Searle thinks that metaphors can have a semantic content of sorts, but he is at a loss as to how to explain that possibility, since he sees that they are not based on literal similarities and don't seem to be literal propositions. Davidson and Rorty think that metaphors have no semantic content, are not propositional, and so cannot be bearers of truth.

Both theories are badly mistaken. Both theories ignore the growing body of empirical research on conceptual metaphor as a basic operation of abstract thinking. It should come as no surprise that neither Searle nor Davidson pays any serious attention to the work of cognitive linguists on the semantics of natural languages. If they did, they would acknowledge the pervasive role of conceptual metaphor in abstract conceptualization and reasoning. How could Searle, or especially Davidson, explain our previous analysis of the semantics and inference structure of our metaphors for causation? Their literalist views have no resources whatever to explain the polysemy and inference generalizations that are explained in cognitive linguistics by the source-to-target mappings. Rorty sees quite clearly that his view has nothing whatsoever to say about the meaning and motivation for basic metaphors in science and philosophy:

*For all we know, or should care, Aristotle's metaphorical use of* ousia, *Saint Paul's metaphorical use of* agapé, *and Newton's metaphorical use of* gravitas, *were the results of cosmic rays scrambling the fine structure of some crucial neurons in their respective brains. Or, more plausibly, they were the result of some odd episodes in infancy – some obsessional kinks left in these brains by idiosyncratic traumata. It hardly matters how the trick was done. The results were marvelous. (Rorty, 1989, p. 17)*

This is extremely clever, and beautifully expressed, but it is quite wrongheaded. For it *does* matter "how the trick was done." It does matter where these metaphors come from – that is, why we have the ones we do, how they are grounded experientially, and how they shape our thought. Moreover, there are (at least partial) answers to such questions, answers provided by conceptual metaphor theory, that challenge the basic assumptions of contemporary analytic philosophy of language.

Rorty is probably right that we aren't going to explain precisely why St. Paul came up with the metaphor for love that he did. But that does not mean that his metaphor was an irrational, unmotivated miracle, or a chance occurrence! Our inability to predict what novel metaphors will emerge does not entail the opposite extreme that metaphors just happen, irrationally. On the contrary, there is a great deal that we can say about what St. Paul's metaphor means, about how it connects up with the other conceptual metaphors for love that were common in his time (and in ours), and about how his metaphor extends or creatively blends aspects of these other metaphors. Conceptual metaphor theory can explain how this new metaphor could possibly make any sense to people and how they could draw inferences about its implications for how they should live their lives. Within cognitive linguistics, there already exist extensive analyses of the mappings for the key metaphors for love in our culture (Kövecses, 1988, 2000; Lakoff & Johnson, 1980). Nor did the Aristotlean conception of *ousia* spring fully armed from the head of Aristotle. Lakoff and Johnson (1999) have traced some of the main steps in the development of the metaphorical understanding of Being that begins with the pre-Socratic philosophers, blossoms in Plato, and is transformed in Aristotle. The idea of Being is a construction from various folk theories and conceptual metaphors concerning the nature of categories and entities in the world. Aristotle's *ousia* is a remarkable achievement, but it is not a miracle.

If, like Davidson and Rorty, you don't see that metaphor is a semantic phenomenon, then it should come as no surprise that, like them, you will regard metaphor merely as a nonrational rupture in a conceptual system (or, to use Rorty's favorite term, a "vocabulary") that inexplicably gives rise to a new way of talking. If you miss the experiential grounding of primary metaphors, you will, like Rorty, think that metaphor change is relatively arbitrary and not rationally motivated. Moreover, you will not recognize the crucial role of metaphor in shaping and constraining inference in ordinary mundane thinking, scientific research, and philosophical theorizing. In other words, Davidson and Rorty are literalists. Because they are oblivious to the pervasive workings of conceptual metaphor in shaping our conceptual systems, they cannot see that or how metaphor lies at the heart of human understanding and reasoning.

### *Philosophy as Metaphor*

Virtually all of our abstract concepts appear to be structured by multiple, typically inconsistent conceptual metaphors. If this is true, then philosophical theories are not systems of foundational literal truths about reality but rather elaborations of particular complex intertwining sets of metaphors that support inferences and forms of reasoning. Humanizing and embodying philosophy in this manner does not devalue it in any way. On the contrary, it reveals why we have the philosophies we do, explains why and how they can make sense of our experience, and traces out their implications for our lives.

In *Philosophy in the Flesh* (1999), Lakoff and Johnson analyzed several philosophical orientations to reveal their underlying metaphors. That analysis included pre-Socratic metaphysics, Platonic and Aristotelian doctrines of Being, Cartesian views of mind and thought, and some of the founding assumptions of analytic philosophy of mind and language. As an example of how a metaphorical analysis of this kind might proceed, I want to consider Jerry Fodor's "Language of Thought" metaphor for mind, since it has been so influential in recent philosophy of mind. Fodor wants to defend what he regards as a scientifically sophisticated version of the widespread folk theory that to have a mind is to have mental states (e.g., beliefs, wants, fears, hopes) that purport to be "about" aspects of our world. Thinking, as he sees it, must consist of chains of inner mental states that are somehow connected to each other (i.e., one thought leads to another) and that are also somehow connected to aspects of our experience (i.e., things in the world "cause" us to have these specific mental representations that we have). There are thus two major parts to Fodor's theory: (1) how the mental states are related and (2) how those mental states are connected to the world (or how they are caused).

The first part of his theory consists of the claim that these mental states form a "language of thought": "A train of thoughts . . . is a causal sequence of tokenings of mental representations which express propositions that are the objects of the thoughts" (Fodor, 1987, p. 17). The language of thought is purely computational:

> *Mental states are relations between organisms and internal representations, and causally interrelated mental states succeed one another according to computational principles which apply formally* to the representations. *This is the sense in which internal representations provide the domains for such data processes as inform the mental life. It is, in short, of the essence of cognitive theories that they seek to interpret physical (causal) transformations as transformations of information, with the effect of exhibiting the rationality of mental processes. (Fodor, 1975, p. 198)*

Fodor's language of thought (sometimes called "mentalese"), consists of symbols that in themselves are completely meaningless but that can be given meaning by the ways in which they are caused, or "tokened," by certain events in the world. The mental representations in this language of thought are precisely like the arbitrary, meaningless symbols in computer programs. Within a computational program, operations are performed entirely on the formal (syntactic) features of the symbols, and Fodor believes that such features can "mimic" what we think of as semantic relations between our various mental representations:

> *Within certain famous limits, the semantic relation that holds between two symbols when the proposition expressed by the one is entailed by the proposition expressed by the other can be mimicked by syntactic relations in virtue of which one of the symbols is derivable from the other. (Fodor, 1987, p. 19)*

The second key part of Fodor's theory concerns the causal grounding of the internal representations. His claim is that these symbols are mental *representations* because they are caused by aspects of the world. Fodor summarizes this aspect of his theory:

> *I want a* naturalized *theory of meaning: a theory that articulates, in nonsemantic and nonintentional terms, sufficient conditions for one bit of the world to* be about *(to express, represent, or be true of) another bit. (Fodor, 1987, p. 98)*

Fodor and his followers believe that the language of thought hypothesis expresses literal truths about the nature of mind, namely, that the mind is a computational functional program, that thinking is governed by syntactic rules, and that the meaningless symbols of mentalese are given meaning through their relation to aspects of our experience that cause them to be tokened in our minds. A large body of empirical research in the cognitive sciences shows why this view of mind cannot be correct, but that is not my focus here. Rather, my point is to show that Fodor's entire model is composed of a series of interwoven complex metaphors that give rise to specific entailments about the nature of mind and the operations of thought.

Fodor's key claim that all human thinking has the form of a language is an idea (a false idea) deeply rooted in our ordinary and philosophical ways of thinking. Because we so often express our thoughts in language, we are easily seduced into believing that human thinking has the form of a language. In other words, we presuppose the Thought As Language metaphor.

## THE THOUGHT AS LANGUAGE METAPHOR

| *Source Domain [Linguistic Acts]* | | *Target Domain [Thinking]* |
|---|---|---|
| Linguistic activity (speaking/ writing) | >>>> | Thinking |
| Words | >>>>> | Ideas |
| Sentences | >>>>> | Complex ideas |
| Spelling | >>>>> | Communicating a sequence of thoughts |
| Writing | >>>>> | Memorization |

Our ordinary ways of thinking about the operations of mind and thought draw massively on our conception of written and spoken language. The idea that thoughts are linguistic forms written in the mind is the basis for expressions such as, "Let me make a *mental note* of that," "She's an *open book* to me – I can *read* her every thought," "The public *misread* the President's intentions," and "Do you think I'm some kind of mind*reader*?" Spoken language also provides a rich source domain for our conception of thinking as speaking, as in, "She doesn't *listen to* her conscience," "I *hear* what you mean," "I can barely *hear* myself think," and "That *sounds* like a good idea." The Thought As Language metaphor covers all types of intellectual activity, as in, "Liberals and conservatives *don't speak the same language*," "He can't *translate* his good ideas into practice," "What is the *vocabulary* of basic philosophical ideas?" and "I wouldn't *read too much* into what he's saying." Notice also that, according to this mapping, careful step-by-step thinking is conceived as careful spelling, as when we say, "Our theory of embodied meaning is *spelled out* in Chapter 3," "Do I have to *spell it out* for you?" and "He always *follows the letter* of the law."

Fodor's language of thought metaphor makes intuitive sense to many people precisely because most of us assume that a purely formal language can be meaningful in the same way that a natural language is meaningful. That is, we assume the formal language metaphor.

### THE FORMAL LANGUAGE METAPHOR

| *Source Domain [Natural Language]* | | *Target Domain [Formal Language]* |
|---|---|---|
| Written signs | >>>>> | Abstract formal symbols |
| A natural language | >>>>> | A Formal language |
| Sentences | >>>>> | Well-formed symbol sequences |
| Syntax | >>>> | Principles for combining formal symbols |

Fodor correctly understands that a truly computational theory of mind requires that the language of thought be a formal language (akin to a computer language), and that a formal language cannot be modeled on a natural language. A "formal" language is an artificial language that, unlike natural languages, consists entirely of arbitrary meaningless symbols, each of which has specific formal (syntactic) features that play a role in formal operations specified for the language.

The key problem with this formal language metaphor is that actual formal languages do not and cannot possess the key features that make it possible for natural languages to be meaningful. Consequently, if Mind Is A Computational Program (i.e., the Mind As Computer metaphor), then the Language of Thought will not, in itself, be meaningful in any way. As a result, Fodor must officially reject the formal language metaphor. But then he is left with the problem of how an intrinsically meaningless Language of Thought can somehow acquire meaning.

Fodor's answer is that "tokenings" of particular mental symbols must become "representations" by being "caused" by objects and events that we experience. In other words, the "inner" mental symbols must be causally connected to things outside the mind. In his book *Psychosemantics* (1987), Fodor tries to develop a causal theory of how the symbols in mentalese can become meaningful, that is, how the symbols can come to be related to things "outside" the mind. Although I cannot argue this here, Fodor is ultimately unable to explain how there is a determinate connection between being in a certain situation and having certain specific symbols tokened in the mind. He cannot establish such relations for the reasons that Quine earlier articulated; namely, the "input" is always subject to multiple interpretations, so there is seldom or never a one-to-one correspondence between a mental symbol and an aspect of the "world."

### *Philosophy's Debt to Metaphor*

My interest here is not to evaluate the adequacy of Fodor's theory of mind and language. It is, rather, to show that his theory is based on a set of intertwined conceptual metaphors that operate, mostly unconsciously, in our culture. It is no criticism of a philosophical or scientific theory to show the underlying metaphors on which it rests. Indeed, it is the metaphors that make it possible for the theories to make sense of our experience. *All* theories are based on metaphors because all our abstract concepts are metaphorically defined. Understanding the constitutive metaphors allows you to grasp the logic and entailments of the theory. Thus, we will discover various common metaphors underpinning our philosophical theories, ranging from the pre-Socratics' notions of Being and *physis*, to ideas about God in medieval theology, to Cartesian doctrines of mind, and up to 21st-century neurocomputational theories of cognition.

It would be impractical to try to survey the metaphorical foundations of all our philosophical theories. But it is a task that can and should be undertaken if we want to understand the inner workings of any particular theory in philosophy or science. This task will always include a metaphorical analysis of concepts such as cause, being, reality, and event but also of all aspects of mind and thought themselves, such as the grounding metaphors for concepts, reason, mind, thought, knowledge, logical relations, and values that lie at the heart of a specific theory. Even the theories of metaphor themselves must be analyzed. The theory of conceptual metaphor, for example, employs metaphors of "mapping" and "projection" to conceptualize the nature of metaphor itself. Such a conception could never be absolute – could never tell the whole story or cover all of the data – and so we must always be self-reflectively aware of our own metaphorical assumptions and their limitations.

I have argued that the single biggest reason that most traditional and contemporary philosophy cannot recognize the pervasive, theory-constituting role of metaphor in philosophy is the failure of philosophers to acknowledge the existence of deep systematic conceptual metaphor. They cannot recognize it because to do so would require a fairly substantial revision of some of the founding assumptions of their philosophies. It would require them to abandon some of their founding metaphorical conceptions in favor of other metaphors. If you acknowledge conceptual metaphor, then you have to give up literalism. If you give up literalism, you must abandon objectivist theories of knowledge. If you reject objectivist metaphysics and epistemology, you must abandon the classical correspondence theory of truth. Eventually, you will have to rethink even your most basic conception of what cognition consists in.

The hold on us of objectivist and literalist views is so strong that we are sorely tempted to go to great lengths to salvage our traditional theories of mind, thought, and language. Searle ultimately falls back on a form of literalism. Davidson retains his literalism by denying that metaphors have meaning beyond their literal sense. Rorty doesn't appear to be a literalist since he sees that metaphors are terribly important in the history of philosophy, but he has no theoretical resources to explain the phenomena as anything more than contingent, irrational, inexplicable random events.

In sharp contrast, once you understand how conceptual metaphors lie at the heart of our abstract conceptualization and reasoning, you acquire a new set of tools for analyzing, explaining, and criticizing philosophical theories. Philosophies are built out of conceptual metaphors. We need not be slaves operating blindly under the harsh influence of our metaphors. We can learn what our founding metaphors are and how they work. We can analyze the metaphors underlying other cultures and philosophical systems, too. Our ability to do this type of analysis is, admittedly, always itself shaped by metaphorical conceptions of which we are hardly ever aware. However, we *can* become aware of those metaphors, we can subject them to critical evaluation, and we can creatively elaborate them in developing new philosophies to help us deal with the problems that confront us in our daily lives.

## Notes

1 In *Philosophical Perspectives on Metaphor* (1981), I have surveyed some of the more influential expressions in Western philosophy

of the denial of a serious cognitive role for metaphor.

2 The analysis of causal concepts that follows, along with their role in shaping philosophy, is adapted, with minor changes, from Lakoff and Johnson (1999), chapter 11, which is an extensive survey of the several metaphors that define our multiple concepts of events and causes.

## References

Davidson, D. (1978). What metaphors mean. *Critical Inquiry*, 5(1), 31–47.

Fernandez-Duque, D., & Johnson, M. (2002). Cause and effect theories of attention: The role of conceptual metaphor. *Review of General Psychology*, 6(2), 153–165.

Fesmire, S. (2003). *John Dewey and moral imagination*. Bloomington: Indiana University Press.

Fodor, J. (1975). *The language of thought*. New York: Thomas Y. Crowell Company, Inc.

Fodor, J. (1987). *Psychosemantics: The problem of meaning in the philosophy of mind*. Cambridge, MA: MIT Press.

Gibbs, R. (1994). *The poetics of mind: Figurative thought, language, and understanding*. Cambridge: Cambridge University Press.

Grady, J. (1997). *Foundations of meaning: Primary metaphors and primary scenes*. Unpublished PhD dissertation, University of California, Berkeley.

Johnson, M. (1981). Metaphor in the philosophical tradition. In M. Johnson (Ed.), *Philosophical perspectives on metaphor* (pp. 3–47). Minneapolis: University of Minnesota Press.

Johnson, M. (1993). *Moral imagination: Implications of cognitive science for ethics*. Chicago: University of Chicago Press.

Johnson, M., & Larson, S. (2003). Something in the way she moves – metaphors of musical motion. *Metaphor and Symbol*, 18(2), 63–84.

Kövecses, Z. (1988). *The language of love: The semantics of passion in conversational English*. Lewisburg, PA: Bucknell University Press.

Kövecses, Z. (2000). *Metaphor and emotion: Language, culture, and body in human feeling*. Cambridge: Cambridge University Press.

Lakoff, G. (1996). *Moral politics: What conservatives know that liberals don't*. Chicago: University of Chicago Press.

Lakoff, G., & Johnson, M. (1980). *Metaphors we live by*. Chicago: University of Chicago Press.

Lakoff, G., & Johnson, M. (1999). *Philosophy in the flesh: The embodied mind and its challenge to western thought*. New York: Basic Books.

Lakoff, G., & Núñez, R. (2000). *Where mathematics comes from: How the embodied mind brings mathematics into being*. New York: Basic Books.

Magnani, L., & Nersessian, N. (Eds.). (2002). *Model-based reasoning: Science, technology, values*. New York: Kluwer Academic/Plenum Publishers.

Rorty, R. (1989). The contingency of language. In R. Rorty (Ed.), *Contingency, irony, and solidarity* (pp. 3–22). Cambridge: Cambridge University Press.

Searle, J. (1979). Metaphor. In J. Searle (Ed.), *Expression and meaning: Studies in the theory of speech acts* (pp. 76–116). Cambridge: Cambridge University Press.

Winter, S. (2001). *A clearing in the forest: Law, life, and mind*. Chicago: University of Chicago Press.

Wright, H. G. (2007). *Means, ends, and medical care*. Dordrecht: Springer.

CHAPTER 3

# Rethinking Metaphor

*Gilles Fauconnier and Mark Turner*

## 1. Conceptual Mappings

The study of conceptual mappings, including metaphoric mappings, has produced great insights over the past several decades, not only for the study of language but also for the study of such subjects as scientific discovery, design, mathematical thinking, and computer interfaces. This tradition of inquiry is fulfilling its promises, with new findings and new applications all the time. Looking for conceptual mappings and their properties proves to be a rich method for discovery.[1] To the initial studies that focused on cross-domain mappings and their most visible products have now been added many additional dimensions. Detailed studies have been carried out on topics such as compression, integration networks, and the principles and constraints that govern them.[2]

This blooming field of research has as one consequence the rethinking of metaphor. We have a richer and deeper understanding of the processes underlying metaphor than we did previously. In this article, we will illustrate the central areas of theoretical advance by looking in some detail at the often-studied metaphor of TIME AS SPACE. The points we shall emphasize are the following:

- Integration networks. Conceptual products are never the result of a single mapping. What we have come to call "conceptual metaphors," like TIME IS MONEY or TIME IS SPACE, turn out to be mental constructions involving many spaces and many mappings in elaborate integration networks constructed by means of overarching general principles. These integration networks are far richer than the bundles of pairwise bindings considered in recent theories of metaphor.
- Cobbling and sculpting. Such integration networks are never built entirely on the fly nor are they preexisting conventional structures. Integration networks underlying thought and action are always a mix. On the one hand, cultures build networks over long periods of time that get transmitted over generations. Techniques for building particular networks are also transmitted. People are capable of innovating in any particular context.

The result is integration networks consisting of conventional parts, conventionally structured parts, and novel mappings and compressions. This very general point is illustrated in section 5 of our paper, with the passage "Emily's diary."

- Compression. A remarkable conclusion of recent work which was overlooked by both early metaphor theory and early blending theory is that integration networks achieve systematic compressions. The ability to use standard techniques and patterns of compression and decompression enables us to work at once over elaborate integration networks. For example, a cause–effect relation connecting different mental spaces in the network may be compressed into a representation relation or an identity relation within the integration network. Well-known examples often discussed in the blending literature include *The Grim Reaper, Digging one's own grave, Clinton and the Titanic*.[3] For TIME AS SPACE, watches, clocks, and other time-telling devices anchor *timepiece* blends with powerful built-in compressions.
- Inference. Inference transfer is not in itself the driving force behind metaphor. In fact, it is typical for "source-domain" inferences to be violated in the emergent blended space. This is because topologies in the multiple inputs may clash, so that not everything will project to the blended spaces.
- Emergent structure. The focus on single mapping and inference transfer in early metaphor theory left out many of the powers of integration networks, in particular the ability to develop emergent structure based on preexisting conceptual structures and to achieve compressions across them. In fact, as we shall see, the metaphorical mappings that seem most fundamental and observable, such as SPACE → TIME, can themselves be emergent in elaborate networks with successive blending.
- Various species of conceptual integration. What were previously regarded as separate phenomena and even separate mental operations – counterfactuals, framings, categorizations, metonymies, metaphors, and so on – are consequences of the same basic human ability for double-scope blending. More specifically, these phenomena are all the product of integration networks under the same general principles and overarching goals. They are separable neither in theory nor in practice: the majority of cases involve more than one kind of integration. The resulting products can belong simultaneously to any (or none) of the surface types "metaphors," "counterfactuals," "analogies," "framings," "categorizations," or "metonymies." The networks discussed below for the conception of time are a case in point. As shown below, they yield surface metaphors, counterfactuals, metonymies, and frames.

## 2. Time Is Space, and Then Some

To illustrate how metaphor has been rethought within the broader perspective of integration networks and compression, we will revisit the classic metaphor of time as space and show in some detail that much of what is going on in this metaphor has gone unnoticed and therefore unexplained.[4]

Time as space is a deep metaphor for all human beings. It is common across cultures, psychologically real, productive, and profoundly entrenched in thought and language.

Once recognized, the mapping seems nonproblematic: the ordering of space is projected to the ordering of time, and inferences are obtained straightforwardly for the source domain and projected to the target domain. As established by metaphor theory, the new conceptualization of the domain of time is obtained through projection from space. For example, the fact that time is measurable and stable – inferences for which we do not have independent evidence – comes from the domain of space.[5]

But metaphors, this one included, involve more than mappings or bindings between two spaces. They involve many spaces, and they involve emergent structure in the network. The apparently unproblematic mapping by itself will not account for the complex emergent structure of the network and the data that express it.

To see this, let us start by looking informally at the full emergent structure that comes with this metaphor. Consider the following examples:

1. Three hours went by, and then he had dinner.
2. *Three feet went by, and he was at the door.
3. Minutes are quick but hours are slow.
4. *Inches go by faster than feet.
5. Those three hours went by slowly for me, but the same three hours went by quickly for him.
6. For me, the hours were minutes, but for her, the minutes were hours.
7. At the end of the three hours, you will have solved the problem, but at the end of the same three hours, he will have solved it and five more.
8. Time came to a halt.
9. Sure, it's Friday afternoon, but Monday morning is already staring us in the face.
10. Next week was an eternity away.
11. For me, the three hours were forever, but for her, they did not exist.
12. It'll go by faster if you stop thinking about it.
13. Our wedding was just yesterday.
14. Where have all those years disappeared?
15. Next week was an eternity away.
16. I didn't see those years go by.

Example 1 shows that we have not merely projected units of measurement onto time but also turned those units into moving objects. This does not come from projecting units of measurement onto time. In the domain of space, a unit of measurement is not a moving object. These are incompatible sorts of elements. But in the blend, we project onto a temporal experience both unit of measurement *and* moving object from the domain of space. Incompatible elements in the domain for space are thus fused to identity for time in the blend. The notion of hours as simultaneously moving objects and units of measurement is emergent in the blended space.

Example 3 shows two things: that the emergent, moving temporal units have speed *and* that some have greater speed than others. But how could this be? The constituent parts of a moving object in space must all move at the same speed. Hours are composed of minutes. A straightforward "metaphoric" projection would require that minutes, hours, centuries, eons would all have the same speed. What has happened is that uncoupled objects that move at different speeds in space are projected onto constituent parts of a temporal interval in the blend.

There is a paradox in the standard metaphor analysis of time as space in having a source domain of moving objects that includes speed, since speed already seems to require time. This paradox is resolved in the standard analysis by assuming that motion is uniform, so that speed is irrelevant. But as we see, speed is relevant in the emergent conception of time. In fact, example 5 shows that not only can speed be different for different moving objects, but the same moving object can have different speeds. This is because we are also projecting to the temporal units in the blend our subjective experience of time and events. In our subjective, conscious experience, we have no reliable measure of time, but we do have strong feelings about the pace of events. In the blended structure, a "slow hour" is an hour to which we project our subjective experience of the events of that hour. That is why we can say, "For me, the hours were minutes, but for her, the minutes were hours." Some exceptionally fast hours can have the speed of "normal" minutes. Some very slow minutes can have the speed of "normal" hours.

And it is not just as if units of time can go fast or slowly; they can also stop altogether, as in "Time came to a halt."

And it's not just as if units of time can have variable speed. They can also have variable existence, as in, "For me, the three hours were forever, but for her, they did not exist."

In the topology of the domain of objects moving in space, all moving objects must be in different locations, and it is unusual (except, e.g., in the case of trains) that they follow the identical path. But in the blend for time, we are all in the same spot, and the very same times are moving past us on the same path.

In the topology of the domain of objects moving in space, the observers are typically at different locations, which is why they may experience the speed of the objects differently. But in the blend for time, all the observers are at the identical location. It is not their relative locations that account for the variation in perceived speed, but their attitudes toward the events that account for the variation in the speeds. The variation of speed for time is coming from the input mental space of felt experience, not from the domain of objects moving in space. The resulting emergent structure is actually incompatible with the physical space input.

In the topology of the domain of objects moving in space, distance is well ordered. Space is continuous and objects have permanence, and neither stretches of space nor objects in them vanish. But salience of times can be blended with temporal units to such an extent that, in the blend, salient times whose onset we fear can be closer and move faster. If Monday is all-important and we are anxious about what happens on Monday, we can say, "Monday is staring me in the face," even if there are several days between now and Monday. In the blend, salient times whose onset we welcome can be farther away and move more slowly, as in, "It's eons until my birthday," or "My birthday never gets any closer."

To summarize, the topology of the blend for time is incompatible with the domain of objects moving in space in many fundamental ways:

- In the domain of space, units of measurement are not moving objects. In the blend, they are.
- In the domain of space, observers are not at the same location and are not looking in the same direction. In the blend, they are. Accordingly, in the blend, everyone sees the same moving objects (that is, sees the same temporal units).
- In the domain of space, not all moving objects are on the same path. In the blend, they are.
- In the domain of space, observers in the same location looking in the same direction would see not only the same moving objects but also the same speeds for those objects. But in the blend, observers are in the same location and looking in the same direction and seeing the same moving objects, but they perceive (in principle) different speeds for those objects.
- In the domain of space, all the objects moving along a path exist, and the closer ones are perceived as closer. But in the blend, one more distant can seem closer, and some of the objects can be nonexistent.
- In the domain of space, you cannot speed up or slow down the speed of the moving object by the quality of your attention. But in the blend, varying your attention can change the speed of the moving object.

These various linguistic examples and the emergent structures that make them possible derive from a systematic but elaborate integration network that involves a number of input spaces, blended spaces, vital relations, and compressions. We will go through the relevant input spaces and intermediate blends.

**E:** E is the input of Events. Human beings are expert at parsing the world into events (selling shoes, solving math problems, dining) and objects. Here we take as given that people can think of events and objects and refer to them. This expertise includes understanding event shape, including ordering and event type, and categorizing different events as belonging to the same type or to different types. Event spaces can include subjective experience of those events. Under this parsing, a lecture is an event with many participants – the lecturer, the audience, the support staff – and each participant experiences the same event in a variety of different possible ways. So the lecture can be painful for me, pleasant for you, difficult for the lecturer, easy for the technician, challenging for the interpreter.

**X:** An important kind of event for human beings is motion through physical space from point A to point B, with corresponding objective and subjective experiences. We call this subset of E the input of experienced motion through physical space. Within X, we have a number of existing correlations. If we travel from A to B and then B to C, we know that the event of traveling from A to B is over before the event of traveling from A to C is over. This comes from our ability to order events. So, all else being equal, relative length corresponds to ordering of events. AB is shorter than AC; the event <AB> is over before the event <AC>. In this space, the use of the notion of fast versus slow is not the one used in physics but correlates with the duration of events. So, in English, we say that going from A to B is "faster" than going from A to C, even if our speed in the technical sense is the same. In X, the event of traversing the path is connected with the path.

**E/X:** E and X are blended in routine ways to yield emergent structure. One consequence of this blending is to create the common notion that has sometimes been called the Event Structure Metaphor.[6] According to this notion, we can "go through the lecture" just as we can "go through the park" because in the blend the event is motion from one point to another. In the blend E/X, any event has length and experienced motion (including speed, in the everyday sense of fast and slow rather than in the technical sense of physics). In E/X, the traveler of input X is fused with the experiencer of input E. The event in E is fused with the event of traversing the path in X and with the path in X. By this means, in the blend, an event becomes a path, and completing the event is traversing the path. As we can say that one stretch of road is faster than another because the event of traveling the first is over before the event of traveling the other, just so, we can say that one event is faster than another. E/X is a blend of a quite diffuse domain of events with a rather specific human-scale subcase of traversing a path, so that in the blend the perhaps diffuse event can be transformed to human scale. In fact, it seems from the data we have collected so far that however complicated our understanding of the domain of traversing paths (involving different terrain, vehicles, etc.), X takes into account only the lengths of the paths, so that for a given traveler, relative lengths of paths determines relative durations of traversal.

In the blended space, an event is an origin and a destination. Two travelers may begin at the same origin and arrive at the same destination; yet, they might traverse different paths, so the event can be long for one but short for the other and can be slow for one and fast for the other.

**M:** The socially (and technologically) constructed notion of time is then brought in independently as the blended domain **M** studied in *The Way We Think* (Fauconnier & Turner 2002). For starters, analogous days that we experience through observation – of, say, sun, stars, color variation, and so on – are compressed under blending into a single cyclic day (see Figure 3.1).

This blended cyclic day, C, serves as one input to yet another blended space, M. The other input to M is a natural or technical dynamic mechanism with structure that gets partially and systematically mapped onto the cyclic day. To give one example of the mapping between the "mechanism" input space and the "cyclic day" input space, we map the situation in which both rotating rods on the face of a "clock" point to 12 in the "mechanism" space onto the sun's being at its zenith in the cyclic day. In the blend, M, the cyclic day is integrated with the motion of the mechanism and we have additional shared events such as hours, minutes, seconds, years.

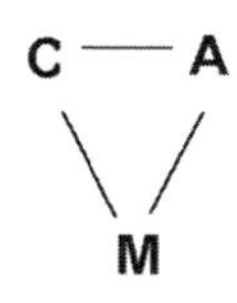

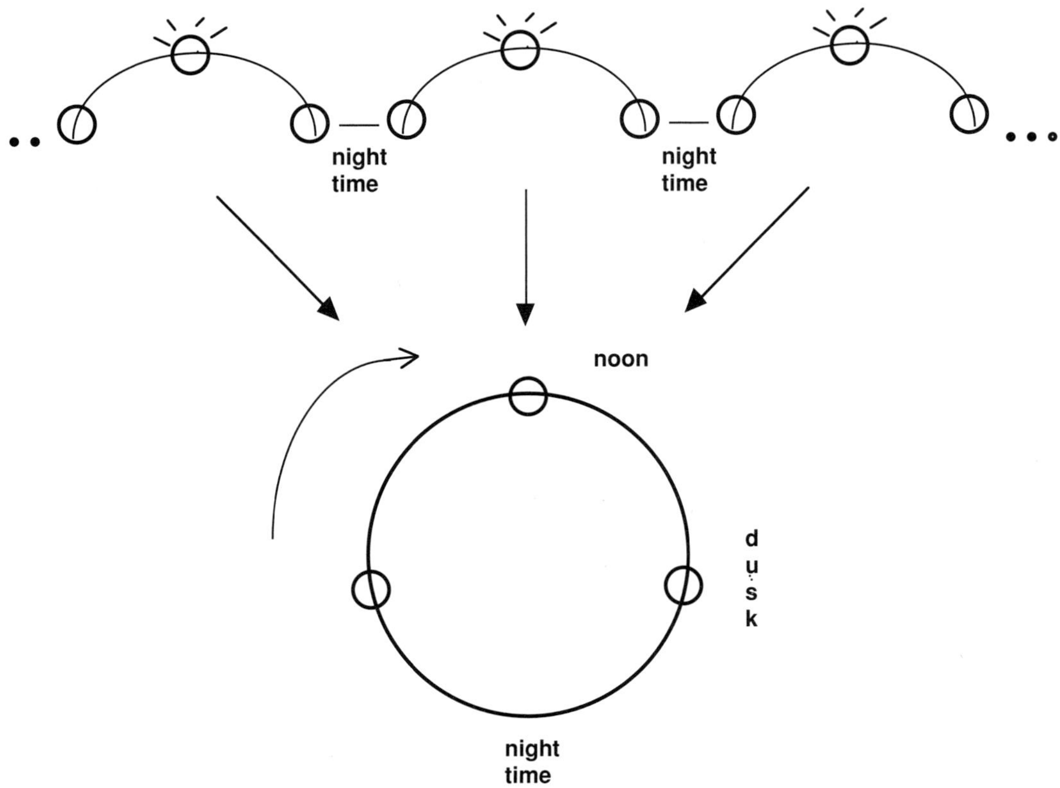


**Figure 3.1.** The blended cyclic day (C).

**M** is built on the basis of standard, normed, shared events such as "hands going around the clock." It yields emergent structure of *hours, minutes, seconds, years*, . . . , which do not exist before the creation of these compressions to ideal events. These are now, in **M**, standard shared events. The culturally constructed domain, **M**, is thus a subset of the general domain of events, **E**, and some inputs to the blend **M** may have motion in space, for technological or natural reason (hands on the clock, sand in the hourglass, sun across the sky, . . .).

The crucial feature of these material timepieces is that they have, within tolerance, matching onset and termination for the same constructed events (minute, hour, day, . . .). How they operate between onset and termination is unimportant for the mapping, as is how they mark onset and termination, so long as onset and termination stay invariant across timepieces. If they match, then, for purposes of the M network, we can compress various timepieces to one ideal timepiece because the particular onsets compress to the ideal onset and the particular terminations compress to the ideal termination. An analog clock works one way, with rods sweeping out circles past numbers, while a digital clock works another way, flashing numbers on its screen, but we do not care: each indicates the onset and termination of the hour, and these indications are simultaneous when we set them side by side. The universal idealized timepiece defines universal events in which everything in the universe participates. The change from onset to termination defines, for example, an "hour." We conceive of everything in the universe as going through that hour. How do we in practice relate to this idealized universal event? We relate to it because the compression guarantees that any local event involving motion of a tolerably accurate timepiece (watch, hourglass, sun) maps on consistently to the universal idealized event.

Notice that emergent in M we have universal events, but neither time nor measure.

Since time is a measure of duration of events in general, M cannot give us time. It is instead a sophisticated system of emergent universal events. These universal events now have universal names – hour, minute, second.

**E/X/M:** Because M is a subset of E, it maps naturally onto E/X. This is the basis for an integration with inputs E/X on the one hand and M on the other, yielding the blended space E/X/M. In that blended space, universal events in M become particular local events in E/X. They are constrained to contain local events within their span, and any local event is contained in universal events projected from M. This gives any local event an additional dimension. Inescapably, you cannot go through the local event without going through the universal event that has the same beginning and end. In the emergent structure of the blended space, the universal event becomes a universal spatial length, and therefore a measure, analogous to yards, meters, and so on.[7] This is why any event has a length – it is an hour long, a minute long, and so on. But, because of this containment, subjective experience of the local event is also for the experiencer experience of the projected universal event. So we can "go through an hour" just as we can go "through a lecture," and the hour can be painful just as the lecture can be painful. Because subjective experience varies, and going through the lecture can be pleasant for you but painful for me, so now, in E/X/M, going through the hour can be pleasant for you but painful for me, or fast for you but slow for me because of the containment of the local event in the projected universal event. In M, the universal events are invariant. Their duration cannot vary, nor can they be painful or pleasant. But in E/X/M, those universal events become local events subjectively experienced, so they can vary according to the experience, not only for different experiencers but also for the same experiencer, depending on circumstances: "I went through the first hour much more quickly than the second hour." Mastery of the full network allows simultaneous access to objective length and subjective length. "It's amazing how the eight-hour work day is longer on Monday than it is on Friday." We understand "the eight hours" as lying in M, where the duration is invariant but "longer" as lying in E/X/M, where it does vary; and so the statement is not self-contradictory.

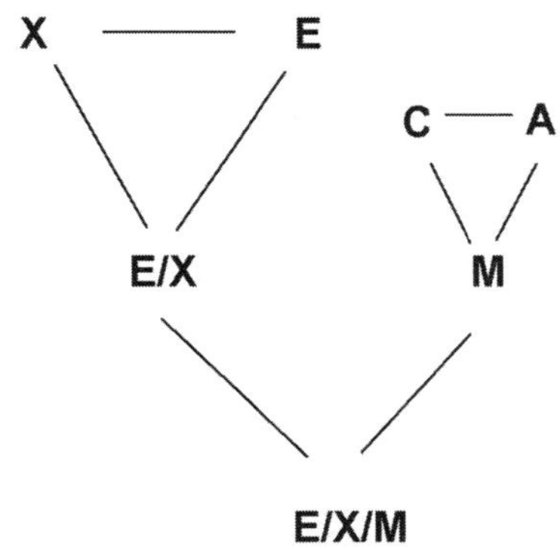


Crucially, blending is not algorithmic, and there are two different conventional ways to blend E/X and M. M has events (rotating rods for the clock) that we are all, within significant tolerance, supposed to agree about. Subjective experience does not differ for the special kinds of events in M, and that is the main reason that they are chosen to serve in M. But in general, duration can vary in E. There is a mapping between the events in E/X and the events in M, and when we blend them, we can preserve the topology of M or the topology of E/X. If we preserve the topology of M in the blended space E/X/M, then we are all agreeing about the duration of the events that are correlated with the universal events. So, you ask how long it took me to go through the lecture, and I say, "It went on too long; it was an hour and five minutes long." I am using a compressed blend E/X/M in which M topology has been projected. But I can also use the topology of duration from E/X and then in the second conventional blend, the duration can vary, depending on subjective experience. I can say, "Centuries." There is hyperbole being added, but now you know we are in the E/X/M blend dominated by the topology from E/X.

Hereafter, we will label the blend dominated by E topology E̲/X/M and the blend dominated by M topology E/X/M̲. The full network at this point contains two crucial blended spaces, E̲/X/M and E/X/M̲, with different emergent notions of time. But conceptually, we have the ability to manipulate the full network with no contradiction, choosing to operate in one blend when we need subjective time and choosing to operate in the other when we need objective time. The rich conceptual notion of time as having both objective and subjective dimensions is emergent in the entire network. E/X/M has uniform durations for all experiencers: they are all on the same path because of the universal event with invariant durations. But in E/X/M blends, the separate experiencers can be on different paths, with different durations of traversal, as in, "Remember that visiting your parents goes faster for me than it does for you."

The network we just described has many spaces, multiple projections, and hyperblends. Time in this network is not a primitive input but rather a notion that emerges from the full network. Once the entire network is achieved, it automatically contains as a by-product correspondences between time and physical space that previous analyses had to postulate: time and the time–space conceptual mapping are emergent in the network.

## 3. Duals

Metaphor theory recognizes that motion of an ego through time as space has a dual, namely, time as objects moving along a path past a stationary observer. This is a valid insight, but it, too, is a consequence of emergence in a full integration network that we will call the dual of E/X/M.

X has motion along a path. But motion is relative. Even though we know we are moving relative to the sun, it looks to us as if the sun is moving relative to us. When two trains are moving side-by-side, we can easily be in one and not know which one is moving. For any scene we inhabit, we can take ourselves as a point of reference, or something else as a point of reference. If we are in fact moving down the road, and take the tree as a point of reference, then we are going by the tree. But if we are in fact moving down the road and take ourselves as the point of reference, then, relative to us, the tree is going by us. We will call the scene in which we take ourselves as the stationary point of reference "the relative motion scene." In it, the tree is moving by us. We are not deluded by this framing. Relative motion is reflected straightforwardly in well-known examples such as

> The old tollhouse went by.
> The rough stretch of road went by.
> The forest went by.

In relative motion, the path and all the things along it move, relative to you. X has its relative motion counterpart, call it X'. X' is accurately described with expressions like:

> That stretch of road went by effortlessly.
> The first five miles went by effortlessly.

By projection, the blended space E/X has its relative motion counterpart, (E/X)'. In (E/X)', path/events move relative to the experiencer, as in:

- The lecture went by effortlessly.
- The party went by pleasantly.

By projection, the blended space E/X/M has its relative motion counterpart, (E/X/M)'. In (E/X/M)', the event paths also move relative to the experiencer, as in:

> The first two hours went by effortlessly.

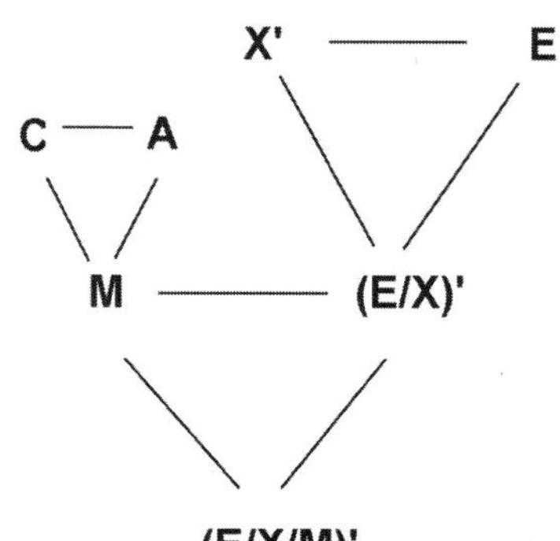

In the relative motion counterparts, relative speed is preserved. If you moved slowly through an event, then in the relative motion counterpart, the event moves slowly by you.

As the E/X/M blended space can be dominated by the topology of E or M, giving us alternatively E̲/X/M or E/X/M̲, so (E/X/M)' can be dominated by the topology of E or M, giving alternatively (E̲/X/M)' or (E/X/M̲)'. In (E/X/M̲)', all the universal events go by the same for all the experiencers. But in (E̲/X/M)', they can go by differently for different experiencers or even for the same experiencer. So, with respect to (E̲/X/M)':

- Friday always goes by faster than Monday.
- The hours sped by for him but dragged by for me.
- It took centuries for the hour to pass.
- Those three hours went by slowly for me, but the same three hours went by quickly for him.

With respect to (E/X/M̲)', we have expressions such as

- Minutes go by faster than hours.
- The same hour will go by whether you are suffering or having fun.

In (E/X/M̲)', the same hour has the same durational properties for everyone, regardless of the events the hour contains. But in (E̲/X/M)', the "same" hour can have different properties depending on the particular experiencer.

Subjective experience can vary quickly for a single experiencer, vary depending on the focus, and even toggle back and forth like a Necker cube, as in the following attested piece of data:

- *"Time goes by really slowly. At the same time, it goes by really fast."* (CNN, said by a man waiting for word on an American named "Michael" missing in the bomb detonations in London in July 2005.)

There are many ways to take this. In one, time is going by too slowly because Michael is not showing up, but time is going by too fast because the likelihood that Michael is dead increases with every passing minute.

Finally, it must be mentioned, although that is not the main focus of the present analysis, that the motion of events and times can be framed independently of an observer. This is especially true of universal times and planned events: *Tuesday follows Monday. The lecture will be followed by a reception.* Moore (2007) discusses such framing in detail. Núñez et al. (2006) demonstrate its psychological reality.

## 4. More Networks

We have seen so far that analysis of metaphor requires analysis of elaborate integration networks producing what can seem like straightforward mappings between two domains taken as primitives. The ultimate conceptual correspondence between time (itself emergent) and physical space is real and especially visible, but it is a final product of emergent structure in the elaborate integration network, not something to postulate as a basic primitive of human understanding.

Conceptual work is never-ending, and we can continue to bring more spaces and even networks into play with the elaborate integration network E/X/M. We can also use general conceptual techniques on that existing network.

One standard conceptual technique is to project agency into the occurrence of events, according to which, in the blend, the event is caused by the agent. In the blend with objective time (i.e., shared universal events, such as hours and minutes), all egos are constrained to move at the same rate. If we project agency to that causal constraint, all egos are moved through the shared universal events at the same rate by an agent, in this case often referred to as "Time," or, historically, "the hour." In this new blend, the emergent entity "Time" derives its motion from the network in which times move but derives its landmark from the network in which Ego moves. Importantly, this new agent is not a projection from the network of moving shared events (hours, etc.). It is not a particular hour that drives us along, but the movement of Time: "Time marches on,"

"Time waits for no man," "Never fear: time will carry us along," and, from Macbeth:

> Come what come may
> Time and the hour runs through the roughest day
> (Act one, scene three)

Provisioned with the blend in which Time the agent moves forward through objective universal events, we can make an additional blend in which Time moving through universal events is also moving through specific events that are scheduled for those universal events. To say that your tooth extraction was scheduled from 3 p.m. to 4 p.m. is to say that Time moved through a universal event (a particular hour) and the scheduled event simultaneously.

Additionally, we can construct the blend in which Ego moves not only through universal events (hours, etc.) but also actual events that correspond to the scheduled events in the schedule blend. Your actual tooth extraction corresponds to the scheduled tooth extraction, but might actually be a shorter or a longer or an interrupted event relative to the scheduled event. Actual and scheduled event need not coincide. Accordingly, Time may reach the end of the scheduled event before Ego reaches the end of the actual event. Moreover, Time may be closer to the end of the scheduled event than Ego is to the end of the actual event. In either case, Ego has fallen behind Time, when the comparison is between corresponding locations on the two paths. This makes other frames, such as racing, available, as in the examples from Chapter 1 of *More Than Cool Reason* (Lakoff & Turner 1989) such as "We are ahead of time" and "We are racing against time." Expressions like "Time flies" or "Time stands still" can also be construed with respect to this blend, if the scheduled or expected events differ from the actual ones.

Consider as an additional network that can come into play our independent integration network involving memory and physical space. In memory, events can be "close" or "distant," "far apart," "hard to access." Relevant linguistic data indicating blends of memory and physical distance include "Calling up things from the depths of your memory," "Bringing a forgotten event to the surface." These blends of memory and physical distance can be blended with the E/X/M networks, to produce items such as

- Our wedding was just yesterday.
- Where have all those years disappeared?
- The days of my youth are so close yet so far away.

For purposes of terminology, we will refer to the blend of memory and physical space as R/S (for Recall/Space). When we blend E/X/M with R/S, we get a new integration E/X/M/R/S, which puts a metric on memory that uses the notion of time that is emergent in the E/X/M networks. The subjective feeling in R/S that the wedding is very accessible, very close, is mapped onto the subjective feeling about the events of yesterday. So the blend endows R/S with a metric using the notion of time. Accordingly, in the E/X/M/R/S blend, the word "yesterday" provides an adequate indication of distance in memory. So in E/X/M, our wedding was not yesterday (assuming it was 18 years ago). But the memory of the wedding as experienced in R projects to yesterday in E/X/M/R/S, where the wedding of 18 years ago can now be "yesterday." In this case, the ordering topology of R/S dominates over the ordering topology in any version of E/X/M.

Now consider "Where have all those years disappeared?" Consider the reading in which this means that the speaker cannot remember the events over several years. The events in memory are gone, they map to corresponding years in E/X/M, and, accordingly, the years themselves are gone. But consider the alternative reading in which the speaker says, "My wedding was just yesterday. Where have all those years disappeared?" It is independently acknowledged that the objective distance of the wedding in E/X/M is 18 years. There is a clash between the configuration in E/X/M and the configuration in E/X/M/R/S. If the wedding was just yesterday in E/X/M/R/S (subjective memory with a time–space–motion structure), then there is no space for the 18 years that are right there in E/X/M (objective event reality with a time–space–motion structure), and those years must have disappeared. In this integration, subjective memory wins out over objective reality. Instead of objective reality's indicating that your memory is faulty, memory shows that the years must be missing. If the reasoning is carried out in objective reality, then we have examples such as "My wedding seems like just yesterday. I must be losing it (on drugs, have Alzheimer's)." In that case, objective reality wins over subjective memory. Examples such as "Where have all those years disappeared?" and others below show that when different mental spaces are built in which there are clashes, then reasoning can follow about that clash. Reasoning can be conducted in one or another of the mental spaces.

Take the variant, "My wedding seems like yesterday. The years have really gone by fast." Again, the clash is between distance in subjective memory and objective reality. The reasoning is a very standard pattern imported from ordinary motion and speed in physical space. If the train departs city A and you are in city B before you know it, you can conclude either that B is close to A or that the train travels very fast. Then if you thought that A was close to B, and you are told that in reality it is far from B, you are forced to conclude that the train traveled fast. So in the same way, if your subjective memory tells you that your wedding and today are close, but reality informs you that they are in fact far apart, then you can resolve the clash by concluding that moving objects (here, times) have traveled fast.

But notice that variable speed of time is not a property within (E/X/M)' (invariant universal time events) or within (E/X/M/R/S)' (relative distance of events in memory). Variable speed of time is a property within (E/X/M)', the subjective construction of time. The reasoning that years must have gone by fast resolves the clash between subjective memory and objective reality by inferring a greater speed in (E/X/M)'.

Time can fly, race, drag, or come to a complete halt, as in "time stands still" or "time froze." In all these cases, we need to be operating in more than one mental space, and there is some kind of clash between subjective experience and objective reality. For all of them, we can focus on (E/X/M)' in order to resolve the clash. For example, if I think it is Saturday, and I realize that it is really Monday, then the clash is resolved in (E/X/M)' by assuming that the days must have traveled fast, and I can say, "Time flies."

Other domains are covertly involved in such networks. Expectations are run parallel to experience, and they can clash for all kinds of reasons. An extreme case is when we say, "Time has frozen" or "come to a halt." We expected or desired events to be taking place, but their onset has not occurred. In (E/X/M)', times and events are blended and move together. Events not happening is the same as events not moving, and accordingly subjective time is not moving. The feeling can have many different causes. Suppose we are watching a play whose script we know well. At one point, an actor fails to deliver his line, either because he has forgotten or tripped and needs to regain balance. Of course, events are going on, but not the expected events, and the expected events will take place, just not when we expected them. The delay between expectation and reality can be solved by recruiting from (E/X/M)' a variable speed for time of zero. "Time froze while he tried to remember his line."

## 5. Cobbling and Sculpting

Nathaniel Smith notes the following passage in a novel:

*Remarkable – when I am sitting on a cushion on the floor, busy with*
*scissors and glue pot, the time just vanishes. Before I know it the*
*latticed rectangle of pale autumn sunlight has moved from the left*
*wall across the floor to the other wall and Mrs. O'Carolan is calling*

*me for supper. Perhaps time is flowing faster up there in the attic.*
*Perhaps the accumulated mass of the past gathered there is pulling*
*time out of the future faster, like a weight on a line. Or perhaps,*
*more mundanely, it is only that I am getting older every year and that*
*it is the accumulated weight of time behind me that is unreeling the*
*years with ever-increasing speed. What a horrible thing it must be to*
*grow older and find that ever-decreasing number of years hurrying you*
*faster, faster toward your grave, as if time were impatient to be rid*
*of you.*
(Ian McDonald, "Emily's Diary, November 5, 1913," in *King of Morning, Queen of Day*, pp. 82–83.)

Although this may seem fanciful, it is easily understood exactly because it is exploiting the network for time that we have discussed. A phrase such as "time just vanishes" is standard and idiomatic, and, as we saw, a result of resolving a clash between subjective experience and shared universal events. The pale autumn sunlight's moving across the room is a local timepiece that can be put into registration with other timepieces. As in the general case, subjective feelings of duration are blended with speed of motion. But now, the question arises, why would time be operating this way? The answer, again a standard derivative of the standard network, is that time has a variable speed, and now a new blend is constructed according to which that motion is induced by standard physics. Weight is pulling the timeline along. Interestingly, this still preserves the registration of the timepieces. Even though the subjective speed of time when you are doing certain things in the attic is much greater than the subjective speed of time in the kitchen, the time in the attic will match the time in the kitchen whenever you go to the bother of checking because that is a property of E/X/M̲. This network allows us to get to a point with different speeds at different spots in the network, but the points will match with M̲. The additional blending of "pulling time" is simply opportunistically exploiting a connection between objects and weight and the fact that if you have more objects, you have more weight. The mass in the past is picking out events in the subjective space. This subjective space is much fuller of events from the past when you are in the attic, among all those souvenirs, than it is in the kitchen, where you are engaged in cooking sausage to eat immediately. So when you go down to the kitchen, your subjective space changes, and the weight of the past diminishes with each step as you go down, so by the time you get to the kitchen, time is running at its usual pace, no longer being pulled precipitously along.

The variant of years being pulled faster for older people because of the greater time behind them is another way of resolving the clash by blending the subjective space in (E̲/X/M)' with a concrete frame of the pull of gravity. In the new blend, the "time objects" are linked and the increasing weight of those behind pulls the present and future ones ever faster. It exploits the fact that in (E̲/X/M)', we know that the objects move differently for different experiencers.

Spectacularly, in fact, in the last variant, it follows that a small number of years is now moving ever faster past you. In the relative motion dual of this scene, you are therefore moving faster toward the end, the grave. At this point, there is a blend with intentionality. How does this feel? Now subjective experience is restructured again to include desire for the speed on the part of time, and the cause of Time's increasing the speed is its impatience to get rid of you, that is, to bring you to your end.

## Conclusion

Metaphoric mappings, theory of metaphor, and metaphor analysis need to be revised to include permanent features of cognition:

- Integration networks
- Cobbling and sculpting
- Emergent structure

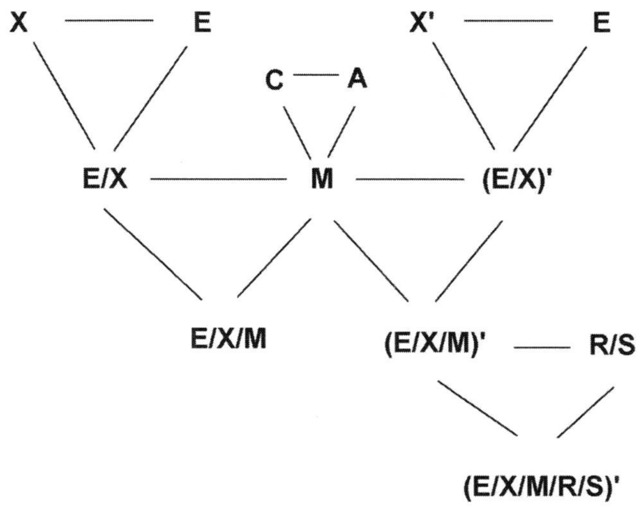


**Figure 3.2.** Integration network for time as space, including dual.

- Compression
- Overarching goals other than projection of inference.

We have shown in some detail, with TIME AS SPACE, how to go about this revised and deeper form of metaphorical analysis, taking into account the aforementioned properties of cognition. As far as we can tell, the considerations we adduced apply quite generally to any metaphorical analysis. The message for all of us metaphor theorists is that we need to go far beyond the usual focus on cross-domain mapping and inference transfer. We need to face squarely the far greater complexity of integrations that lie behind observable metaphorical conceptual systems. We need to take into account their cultural history, and we need to account explicitly for the emergent structures they produce, both over cultural time and over individual time (a child's learning of the elaborate interconnected integration networks). In the early days of contemporary linguistics, the realization that children mastered stunningly complex syntactic and phonological structures was often met with disbelief: how could toddlers possibly know so much? We know better today: the child's cognitive brain leaves in the dust our most powerful computers. So there is nothing surprising in the discovery that meaning construction is also supported and effected by highly elaborate dynamic systems. The challenge for the analyst is to delve rigorously into these remarkable constructions of the mind.

The permanent features of cognition that we have drawn attention to in the present work are part of metaphor because metaphor itself is one particularly important and salient manifestation of conceptual integration. Double-scope integration, which typically exploits clashes, is the hallmark of cognitively modern human beings. And metaphor is one of its most powerful products, one that often drives key aspects of art, science, religion, and technology.

## Notes

1 Lakoff and Johnson (1999), Coulson and Oakley (2000, 2005), Gentner, Holyoak, and Kokinov (2001), Hofstadter (1995).

2 http://blending.stanford.edu, Fauconnier and Turner (2002), Coulson (2001).

3 Fauconnier and Turner (2002, pp. 131–135), Coulson (2001).

4 Evans (2003) provides an insightful discussion of the conceptualization of time as revealed through linguistic usage and points out many difficulties for Lakoff and Johnson's conceptual metaphor theory and Grady's (1997) approach in terms of primary metaphors. He proposes an approach

in terms of multiple cognitive models which we believe does not capture the deeper unity of the phenomenon, explored in this chapter. Núñez and Sweetser (2006) provide important (nonlinguistic) evidence based on gesture in Aymara for space–time conceptual mappings and aspects of their cultural variation. Moore (2007) emphasizes that temporal metaphor can be perspective-specific or perspective-neutral.

5 Lakoff and Johnson (1999, pp. 130–161).

6 Espenson (1992), Lakoff and Johnson (1999, pp. 179–95).

7 This is the general feature of measure: for something to be a meter long means that extremities of the two objects map to each other preserving metric topology. This is coincidence of local events. To say that something is a meter long is to fuse the local with the universal. In the space of physical space, before you had the universal yardstick, let's say, all you could do is compare: this is longer than that. Once you have a universal yardstick, now everything has a length. There is now a universal stuff (of course, this is an emergent concept) just as there are universal events. The meter is made out of universal stuff conceptually, just as the hour is a universal event. Get rid of 5 pounds, take 10 minutes out of your lecture, how many square feet in your house? etc.

## References

Coulson, S. (2001). *Semantic leaps: Frame-shifting and conceptual blending in meaning construction*. New York: Cambridge University Press.

Coulson, S., & Oakley, T. (2000). Conceptual blending [Special Issue]. *Cognitive Linguistics*, 11, 3–4.

Coulson, S., & Oakley, T. (2005). [Special issue]. *Journal of Pragmatics*, 37(10).

Espenson, J. (1992). Event structure duality. University of California, Berkeley.

Evans, V. (2003). *The structure of time*. Amsterdam: John Benjamins.

Fauconnier, G., & Turner, M. (2002). *The way we think*. New York: Basic Books.

Gentner, D., Holyoak, K., & Kokinov, B. (Eds.). (2001). *The analogical mind: Perspectives from cognitive science*. Cambridge, MA: MIT Press.

Grady, J. (1997). Foundation of meaning: Primary metaphors and primary scences. Ph.D. dissertation at the University of California, Berkeley.

Hofstadter, D. (1995). *Fluid concepts and creative analogies*. New York: Basic Books.

Lakoff, G., & Johnson, M. (1999). *Philosophy in the flesh*. New York: Basic Books.

Lakoff, G., & Núñez, R. (2000). *Where mathematics comes from: How the embodied mind brings mathematics into being*. New York: Basic Books.

Lakoff, G., & Turner, M. (1989). *More than cool reason: A field guide to poetic metaphor*. Chicago: University of Chicago Press.

Moore, K. (2007). Space-to-time mapping and temporal concepts. Unpublished manuscript.

Núñez, R., Motz, B., & U. Teuscher, U. (2006). Time after time: The psychological reality of the Ego- and Time-Reference-Point distinction in metaphorical construals of time. *Metaphor and Symbol*, 21, 133–146.

Núñez, R., & Sweetser, E. (2006). Looking ahead to the past: Convergent evidence from Aymara language and gesture in the crosslinguistic comparison of spatial construals of time. *Cognitive Science*, 30, 401–450.

Turner, M. (1996). *The literary mind*. New York: Oxford University Press.

CHAPTER 4

# How Metaphors Create Categories – Quickly

*Sam Glucksberg*

"I find people confusing . . . [because they] . . . often talk using metaphor, such as he was the apple of her eye, we had a real pig of a day, they had a skeleton in the cupboard. I think it [metaphor] should be called a lie because a pig is not a day and people do not have skeletons in their cupboards and . . . imagining an apple in someone's eye doesn't have anything to do with liking someone a lot . . ." (Haddon, 2003, p. 15). So claims Christopher Boone, the protagonist in Haddon's perceptive and riotously funny novel about an autistic teenager trying to figure out the world around him.

Like metaphor theorists from Aristotle to contemporary philosophical, linguistic, and psycholinguistic writers (cf. Bowdle & Gentner, 2005; Fogelin, 1988; Searle, 1979), metaphors such as *Sam is a pig* are considered to be false categorical assertions, and so must be treated as similes (e.g., *Sam is like a pig*) in order to be understood. A preference for simile over metaphor is clearly endorsed by our autistic savant Christopher, who, referring to a neighbor whom he dislikes intensely, observes, "He had a very hairy nose. It looked like there were two very small mice hiding in his nostrils. This is not a metaphor, it is a simile, which means that it really did look like there were two very small mice hiding in his nostrils. And a simile is not a lie, unless it is a bad simile" (Haddon, 2003 p. 17).

In these few lines, Christopher Boone neatly captures the traditional pragmatic view of metaphor comprehension. Nominal metaphors such as *my lawyer is a shark* or *my surgeon was a butcher* are taken to be literally false. Literally false assertions are considered to be infelicitous because they violate one of Grice's (1975) conversational maxims, namely, to be truthful. As such, they are defective if taken literally because they do not make sense in the context of the utterance. Therefore, a hearer or reader must search for a nonliteral meaning that does make sense. Understanding nonliteral meanings thus requires three distinct processing stages:

1. Derive the literal meaning of the utterance.
2. Assess the interpretability of that meaning in the utterance context.

3. If the literal meaning does not make sense in context, then search for a nonliteral meaning that does.

As Searle (1979) put it, "Where an utterance is defective if taken literally, look for an utterance meaning that differs from sentence meaning" (p. 114). Applying this general model to how people understand nominal metaphors, we have the comparison model of metaphor comprehension. Nominal metaphors such as *some roads are snakes* or *my job is a jail* are "defective" in that they are literally false. One way to deal with this problem would be to convert a literally false categorical assertion into a true comparison assertion, that is, a simile. Similes are always literally true because any two things must always be alike in one way or another, indeed, in an indeterminate number of ways. This move produces the standard pragmatic model of metaphor comprehension. According to this model, metaphors are considered to be implicit similes. When a statement of the form X is a Y is literally false, then it is converted into a true simile, X is *like* a Y, and then treated exactly as any literal comparison (see Gentner, 1983).

This general comparison view has three important, testable psychological implications. First, literal meanings have unconditional processing priority. Literal meanings are always computed first and are computed unconditionally. Nonliteral meanings are never computed until literal meanings are computed and found to be "defective" – they do not make sense in context. Literally intended language should thus be easier to understand and should also take less time to compute than nonliterally intended language. In addition, nonliteral meaning computation is *optional*: nonliteral meanings are sought *only if* the literal meaning is uninterpretable. Thus, unless literal meanings won't work, nonliteral meanings are ignored.

A second implication of this view is that comparisons are easy to understand, whether they are literal or metaphorical. But, how do people solve the comparison problem? Since any two things can be alike in innumerable ways, how do we identify precisely those ways that are intended? Consider the old adage about inappropriate comparisons: they are characterized as comparing apples and oranges, reflecting a belief that one can't (or at least shouldn't) compare apples and oranges. A moment's reflection reveals that apples and oranges can indeed be compared and that they share many, many properties: both are edible, have a warm color, round shape, similar in size, contain seeds, grow on trees, good for making juice, names begin with a vowel, and they are unsuitable as balls in such games as tennis, field hockey, or baseball. Clearly, solving the comparison problem requires more than an exhaustive search for shared features or properties. Substituting a simile for a metaphor obviously doesn't automatically solve the comprehension problem.

A third implication of the comparison view is that metaphors and similes are, to all intents and purposes, interchangeable. Metaphoric assertions can be put in either of the two forms, X *is* a Y or X is *like* a Y. Are these two forms used to express the same meanings, or can their meanings differ systematically?

These three implications have been empirically tested, and all three turn out to be false. Instead, the following three generalizations characterize metaphor comprehension:

1. Literal meanings do not have unconditional priority, and so they are not necessarily easier to compute than nonliteral meanings. More importantly, metaphor comprehension is not optional; it does not depend on the defectiveness of literal meanings. Instead, metaphor comprehension is mandatory, that is, automatic. Whether or not a literal meaning makes sense in context, potential metaphorical meanings cannot be ignored.
2. Metaphors are rarely understood via comparison. Instead, they are usually understood exactly as they appear, as class-inclusion assertions. When someone says that their surgeon was a butcher, that is what they intend: that

their surgeon belongs to a category of persons who are butchers in one way or another.

3. Metaphors and similes are not interchangeable. These two forms express different meanings, sometimes subtly different, sometimes significantly so. Furthermore, the differences between similes and their corresponding metaphors are systematic and can be accounted for in a principled, theoretically coherent way.

The central idea is that metaphors are categorical, class-inclusion assertions. For conventional metaphors, the category preexists; it had been established when the metaphor was first coined. For novel metaphors, a category is created and the metaphor vehicle serves as the name of that category.[1] We will examine these ideas in detail. We turn now to the first issue: are literal meanings privileged vis-à-vis metaphorical ones?

## Priority of the Literal

The priority of the literal takes two forms: relative ease of processing and unconditional temporal-order priority. With respect to relative ease of processing, the long-standing assumption that literally intended utterances are understood more easily than those intended nonliterally can be easily rejected. At one extreme, familiar idioms are no more difficult to understand than their literal counterparts. Indeed, the idiomatic meanings of expressions such as "kick the bucket" are understood more rapidly than their literal meanings (*to die* versus *strike a pail with one's foot* (Gibbs, Nayak, & Cutting, 1989; see also Giora, 2003, on the issue of graded salience). This is not at all surprising, given that such expressions can be stored in a phrasal lexicon along with other familiar expressions such as clichés, song titles, lines of poetry, and the like (see Jackendoff, 1995). Understanding familiar idioms may thus be very much like understanding individual lexical items, via direct access. More surprising, perhaps, is that even novel metaphors can be understood as rapidly as comparable literal expressions, provided that the novel metaphors are apt (Blasko & Connine, 1993). It seems that given a linguistic input, literal and figurative meanings, where available, are computed in parallel, even in the absence of contextual supports (McElree & Nordlie, 1999). Consistent with these behavioral studies, studies using brain-recording (e.g., event-related potential patterns) and brain-imaging techniques (e.g., fMRI) find little evidence for differences in brain area activation patterns for literal versus metaphoric language processing (Ahrens, 2004; Pynte et al., 1996; Rapp et al., 2007; but see Stringaris et al., 2007).

If literal and figurative meanings are computed in parallel and engage the same brain areas for processing, then the second literal-priority assumption – that nonliteral meaning computation is optional – is also suspect. We know that people cannot refuse to understand literal language. Instead, understanding "occurs automatically without conscious control by the listener . . . loss of control over one's language comprehension device may correspond to knowing a language fluently" (Miller & Johnson-Laird, 1976, p. 166). Linguistic input automatically triggers semantic and syntactic analyses that generate literal sentence meaning (Fodor, 1983). Could those processes and analyses that generate metaphorical meanings also be automatically triggered by linguistic input?

Just as people cannot ignore literal meanings, people cannot ignore metaphorical meanings. A classic demonstration of the automaticity of literal language processing was provided by Stroop (1935), via the eponymous Stroop interference effect. Stroop had people attend to individual color words such as *red*, *yellow*, or *green*. These words were printed in various colors, and Stroop instructed his participants to ignore the words themselves, but instead to name the color of the ink that the words were printed in. When ink color and color name matched, people could respond quickly and accurately. When, however, they mismatched, as when the word "red" was printed in green ink, the response of saying "green" was significantly delayed. What has come to be known as Stroop interference demonstrated that fluent readers could not ignore word meanings.

A version of Stroop's paradigm provides an analogous demonstration that people cannot ignore metaphorical meanings. Glucksberg, Gildea, and Bookin (1982) asked people to read sentences and to judge whether they were literally true or false. Most of the sentences were nonproblematic: they were clearly either true or false; for example, "some birds are robins" is unambiguously true, "some birds are tables" is unambiguously false. However, a sentence such as "some birds are flutes," while literally false, has some metaphorical truth to it. Just as the word "red" printed in green ink produces response conflict, a literally false sentence that is metaphorically "true" should also produce response conflict if, indeed, people cannot ignore metaphors. And that is exactly what happened. People fell prey to the classic Stroop interference with literally false but metaphorically true sentences: they took significantly longer to correctly respond "false" to these kinds of sentences than to unambiguously false literal sentences (for replications and extensions of these results, see Blasko, 2004; Gildea, & Glucksberg, 1983; Keysar, 1989).

The priority of the literal also fails when people interpret noun–noun combinations such as *shark lawyer* or *steel arms*. Each of these phrases can be interpreted either literally or metaphorically. For example, *shark lawyer* can refer to a lawyer who represents an environmental group dedicated to protecting rare species of sharks from extinction or to a lawyer who is predatory and aggressive, as in "my lawyer is a shark." Similarly, steel arms can refer to arms that are made of steel (as in a machine of some sort or a robot) or to human arms that are strong (metaphorically, arms as strong and hard as steel). In neither of these two cases are literal meanings in any way "defective," and so if literal meanings do have priority, then they should be the preferred interpretations. However, if metaphorical meanings are generated as automatically as literal ones, then we would expect people to opt for metaphorical meanings at least as often as literal ones. Goldvarg and Glucksberg (1998) gave people two types of noun–noun combinations: those that could only be paraphrased literally, and those that could be paraphrased both literally and metaphorically. For the literal-only items, 82% of the interpretations were unambiguously literal. In contrast, for the items that could be paraphrased either literally or metaphorically, 75% of the interpretations were metaphorical. The overwhelming preference for metaphorical interpretation, even when the literal is perfectly acceptable, is clearly inconsistent with the assumption of literal priority. Even when metaphors are in the implicit form of a noun–noun combination, metaphorical meanings cannot be ignored.

### *Conclusions on the Priority of the Literal*

a. Speed of processing: metaphorical and literal meanings are processed equally quickly.[2]
b. Temporal priority: metaphorical and literal meanings are processed in parallel, with neither having unconditional priority.
c. Automaticity: Neither literal nor metaphorical meanings can be ignored. When either is available, then they are processed. In some circumstances, when both are available, metaphorical meanings may be preferred to literal (in Giora's terms [2003], they may be more salient than the literal).

## Understanding Metaphors: A Comparison Process?

### *Understanding Comparisons*

People can understand literal comparisons in at least two ways. One way would be via feature matching. The properties of the two terms of a comparison are extracted and are then matched with one another. Those properties that are in common to the two, as well as those that are not in common, are then used to establish the ground for the comparison, as well as the degree of similarity of the two concepts (cf. Gentner & Markman, 1994; Tversky, 1977). An alternative strategy can be used instead of property extraction and matching. Instead of matching the properties of the two concepts, one can identify the closest superordinate category that encompasses the two concepts and then use that category's properties as the ground for the comparison. This latter strategy is the one used in the similarities subscale of the Wechsler Adult Intelligence Scale (Wechsler, 1958). The similarities subscale contains items such as "How are oranges and lemons alike?" The correct answer, provided in the test manual, is "both are citrus fruits." This category's properties constitute the ways in which oranges and lemons are alike: they have the same kind of skin, seeds, acidic juice, and so on. The items increase in difficulty as the superordinate category becomes increasingly abstract, for example, "How are oranges and insects alike?" One answer: both are organic.

These two approaches to understanding literal comparisons are also applicable to understanding metaphoric comparisons, or similes. For example, one can try to understand how lawyers and sharks are alike by matching the properties of lawyers and of sharks, as proposed by comparison theorists such as Gentner and her colleagues (e.g., Gentner & Wolff, 1997). Alternatively, one can use the categorical approach and seek the closest category that encompasses the two concepts, *lawyer* and *shark*. One answer to the question of how lawyers and sharks are alike is both are "sharks." In what sense can such a category be identified as "Sharks"?

## *Understanding Metaphors: Dual Reference*

Just as any two concepts or objects can be alike in innumerable ways, so can any two concepts or objects belong to innumerable different categories. Consider three objects: Tuna, Shark, and My lawyer. Tuna and Shark are both fish, and they are also both foods. Neither of these categories seem applicable to "my lawyer," but sharks and lawyers can both belong to the category of predators, that is, creatures that are vicious, aggressive,

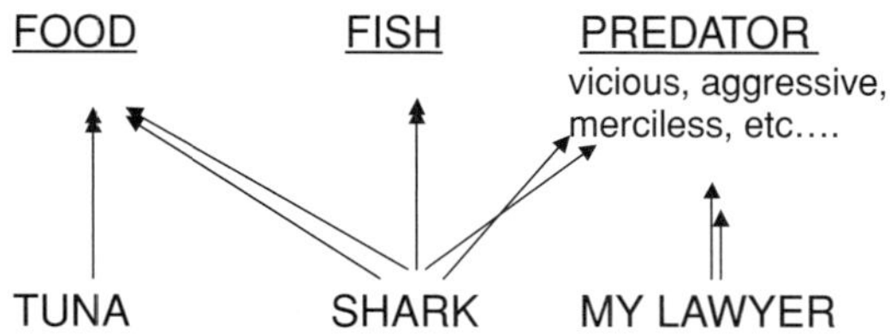


**Figure 4.1a.** Cross-categorization of Lawyer and Shark.

and merciless (see Figure 4.1a). How shall we call that category? One viable option is to use the name of a stereotypical member of the category of predators as the name of the category itself, namely, "Shark." The metaphor vehicle, "Shark," refers to a type, or category of thing. In contrast, when it is used literally, it refers to one member of that category, the marine animal "shark."

In this way, the term "shark" has dual reference. When used in metaphor form, it refers to the category of predators that we can call "Sharks." When used in simile form, it refers to the literal shark. As Roger Brown put it some years ago, "Metaphor differs from other superordinate-subordinate relations in that the superordinate is not given a name of its own. Instead, the name of one subordinate (i.e., the metaphor vehicle) is extended to the other" (Brown, 1958, p. 140). Thus, in expressions such as *My job is a jail,* the term "jail" refers to a category of unpleasant, confining, difficult to get out of, punishing situations that the literal jail exemplifies. Both *my job* and *jail* now belong to the metaphorical category "Jails."

Dual reference is not an exotic linguistic strategy that is exclusive to figurative language. Instead, it is a common,

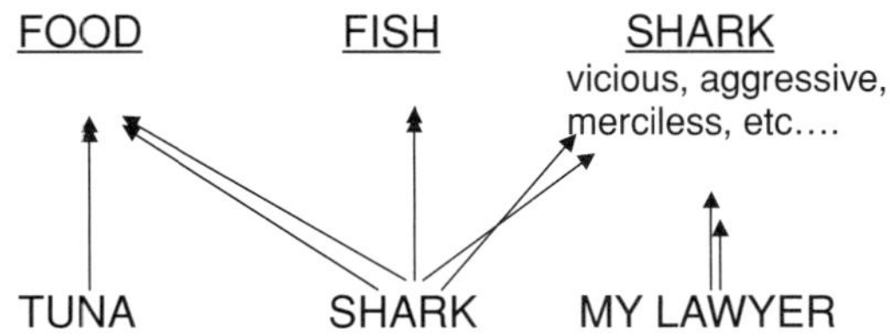


"Shark" used as a metaphor vehicle refers to a category of things, whereas used literally it refers to a specific member of that category.

**Figure 4.1b.** Cross-categorization of Lawyer and Shark.

everyday referring strategy whenever a language community lacks a name for a superordinate category, yet needs a referring expression for that category. For example, this strategy is exploited by speakers of classifier languages, languages that generally do not have names for superordinate categories. Some of the Native American languages of southwest United States are classifier languages and employ this strategy. In Hopi, for example, the most typical tree is the cottonwood, and so the name for the cottonwood tree is used to refer to trees in general (Trager, 1936–1939). When speakers wish to distinguish between cottonwood and other kinds of trees, they use *real-cottonwood* for that specific tree and *cottonwood* for the others. Similarly, Shoshoni speakers use *eagle* for all large birds of prey (Hage & Miller, 1976) unless they wish to distinguish between eagles and other large birds, in which case they use *real-eagle* for that specific bird.

In languages that generally have lexical items for superordinate categories, the same dual reference strategy can be used when a novel category is created but has yet to be named. Indeed, the use of a dual-referring expression may well create that category, as when we first use a term for a specific referent to refer generically to the category that the referent exemplifies. Examples abound: *Kleenex* for facial tissues in general, *Xerox* for dry-paper copying machines, *Jell-O* for gelatin desserts, and *Jeep* for all-purpose four-wheel drive vehicles (derived originally from the military term General Purpose, or GP, vehicle). In some cases, nouns used in this way can also be used as verbs, as in *Xeroxing* documents, or, in England, *Hoovering* to refer to the act of vacuuming with, of course, a *Hoover* vacuum cleaner.

Metaphoric categories can be named and created in precisely this way. It took less than a journalist's day for the term "Enron" to be used to refer to a newly created category, the set of *stunningly scandalous corporate accounting schemes that fraudulently enrich upper-echelon management while incurring stockholder and employee losses of unprecedented magnitude*. Is it any wonder that people latched on to a single term, "Enron," to simultaneously create and name that category, as in, "who will be the next Enron"? In most cases, the dual reference of such terms as "Kleenex" or "Enron" goes unnoticed, so natural is this discourse strategy. In some expressions, however, the dual reference function is transparent, as in "boys will be boys," where the first use of the word "boys" refers literally to young human males and the second to the category *young human males who behave in boisterous and often offensive ways*. Similarly, when Cambodia misguidedly invaded Vietnam several decades ago, the disastrous military venture was referred to as "Cambodia has become Vietnam's Vietnam." Here, the first mention of Vietnam referred, metonymically, to that country's government and military, while the second referred to the category of disastrous military ventures that Vietnam had come to symbolize to America and the rest of the world. Exactly this strategy was used when a civil-rights lawyer expressed concern for the Florida voting process in the 2004 presidential election. Voting records had disappeared after computer systems crashed after a primary election in Miami-Dade County, where votes had been disputed in the 2000 presidential election. Said the chair of the Miami-Dade Election Reform Coalition, "This shows that unless we do something now – Florida is headed toward being the next Florida" (Goodnough, 2004).

We can now understand what I like to call the paradox of unlike things compared. Literal comparison assertions compare two "like" things: two things that belong to the same taxonomic category, as in *coffee is like tea*. Such comparisons cannot be paraphrased as categorical assertions because they are inevitably false: to say that coffee IS tea doesn't make much sense (unless intended metaphorically!). In contrast, metaphoric comparisons – that is, similes – can usually be so paraphrased. Consider the simile *my lawyer is like a shark*. This assertion compares two "unlike" things, that is, two things from widely disparate categories, professional people and fish.

| Metaphorical Shark | Literal Shark |
|---|---|
| Vicious | Vicious |
| Predatory | Predatory |
| Aggressive | Aggressive |
| Tenacious | Tenacious |
| Merciless | Merciless |
| etc. | Can Swim |
| | Has Fins, |
| | Sharp teeth, |
| | Leathery skin, |
| | Gills......... |

**Figure 4.2.** Hypothetical vehicle properties.

Nevertheless, it can be paraphrased as a categorical assertion, *my lawyer IS a shark*.[3]

The property of similes and their corresponding metaphors that makes such paraphrases acceptable is the dual reference function of the metaphor vehicle. In the lawyer–shark example, the term "shark" refers at two different levels of abstraction, in the simile versus the metaphorical. In the simile, the term "shark" refers at a basic level of abstraction, the fish that lurks beneath the ocean waves. This is the literal shark, with properties such as vicious, predatory, and aggressive but also having fins, gills, and leathery skin (see Figure 4.2). In the metaphor, the term "shark" refers at a higher level of abstraction, the category of creatures that the literal shark exemplifies. Among the properties of this category are vicious, predatory, and aggressive but not properties of literal sharks such as having fins, gills, or leathery skin.[4]

### *Implications of Dual Reference for Understanding Metaphors and Similes*

Because the metaphor vehicle and the predicate of the simile refer to different entities – the categorical and the specific basic-level concept, respectively – both the process and product of comprehending the two forms should differ systematically. Three phenomena reflect the differences between understanding metaphors and understanding their corresponding similes:

1. Relative ease of understanding the two forms.
2. Effects of highlighting the literal versus metaphorical referents of the metaphor vehicle.
3. Systematic differences in how the two forms are interpreted.[5]

*Ease of understanding*. In similes, the predicate of the comparison refers directly to the literal exemplar of the metaphorical category, e.g., the fish "shark" as an exemplar of the metaphorical category of "sharks." For familiar metaphors and similes, there should be little if any difference in comprehension time because the work of sorting out the relevant from the irrelevant properties of the simile's predicate has already been done. Presumably, metaphor-irrelevant properties of sharks, such as having gills and leathery skin, can be swiftly rejected when we encounter similes such as "my lawyer was like a shark." However, for relatively unfamiliar similes and metaphors, similes should require more interpretative work because they would tend to evoke both metaphor-relevant and metaphor-irrelevant – that is literal – properties. In contrast, metaphors, because they refer directly at the categorical level, should evoke only properties of the category, not those of a category's literal exemplars. This argument applies, of course only to apt metaphors, metaphors that employ an easily recognizable prototypical exemplar of a candidate metaphorical category. Metaphors such as "Enron" and "Florida" in appropriate contexts typify such categories. Others clearly do not. For example, *their love was a filing cabinet* would not be easily and categorically understood because filing cabinets do not exemplify any readily recognizable metaphoric categories. In such cases, people might well need to resort to a comparison strategy, considering properties of filing cabinets that might plausibly apply to romantic relationships. And people often succeed, but only with effort, in this case coming up with candidate properties of filing cabinets such as *holds memories, cold and routine,* and *cluttered and old*.

For more apt metaphors, the data are sparse, but support the processing advantage of metaphors over similes. In one particularly telling study, Johnson (1996) had people read short paragraphs that ended in either a metaphor or a corresponding simile. People took less time integrating metaphors into the preceding text than their corresponding similes, suggesting that, indeed, metaphors are easier to process than similes. This is clearly inconsistent with the traditional notion that metaphors are understood by first transforming them into similes. Instead, they seem to be understood in their own right: as categorical assertions.

*Highlighting the literal versus the metaphorical.* If metaphor vehicles refer to abstract superordinate categories, then calling attention to the basic-level literal meaning of a metaphor vehicle should make comprehension more difficult. However, priming the literal meaning of a metaphor topic should have no deleterious effect because the topic is used literally. We tested this prediction by priming metaphors either with an irrelevant literal property of the topic, or an irrelevant literal property of the vehicle. People read metaphors such as *my lawyer was a shark*, preceded by (a) neutral control sentences, such as *some tables are made of wood*, (b) irrelevant topic-property sentences, such as *some lawyers are married*, and c) irrelevant vehicle-property sentences, such as *sharks can swim*. People needed more time to understand the metaphor when it was preceded by the *sharks-swim* sentence than when it was preceded by either the neutral control or the irrelevant topic-property sentences (Glucksberg, McGlone, & Manfredi 1997; McGlone & Manfredi, 2002[6]). Apparently, calling attention to the basic-level, concrete referent of a metaphor vehicle interferes with its intended function, that is, reference to the corresponding superordinate metaphorical category.

If metaphor vehicles do refer to superordinate categories and not to their basic-level exemplars, then understanding a metaphor should be comparable to understanding any ambiguous utterance. When people understand homonyms in context, such as the word *bank* in the context of money, then the contextually inappropriate meanings of the word – such as "riverbank" – are inhibited (Simpson & Kang, 1994). If understanding a metaphor also involves activating appropriate meanings and inhibiting inappropriate ones, then understanding a metaphor should involve inhibiting the basic-level, literal meaning of the metaphor vehicle. Gernsbacher, Keysar, Robertson, and Werner (2001) asked people to read either metaphors, such as *my lawyer was a shark*, or literal statements, such as *the hammerhead is a shark*, and then to verify statements related to the literal meaning of the metaphor vehicle, such as *sharks are good swimmers*. People were much slower to verify literal property statements following metaphors than following literal assertions, suggesting that literal meanings of metaphor vehicles are inhibited during metaphor comprehension. We replicated this finding and, in addition, demonstrated that the effect is due to active inhibition of irrelevant, literal meanings, not just to strategic retrieval strategies (Glucksberg, Newsome, & Goldvarg, 2001). In this respect, metaphor comprehension involves the same comprehension mechanisms that are used for literal language comprehension (see, for example, Gernsbacher & Faust, 1991).

## Metaphors Are Not Similes

### UNDERSTANDING METAPHORS VERSUS UNDERSTANDING SIMILES

A basic assumption underlying virtually all theories of metaphor is that metaphors and similes are, fundamentally, equivalent: they mean the same thing. This assumption is shared not only by comparison theorists, who hold that metaphors are fundamentally comparisons and processed as such, but also by categorization theorists. Comparison theorists such as Gentner and her colleagues, for example, argue that any given metaphor can be understood either as a simile, that is, a comparison assertion, or as a categorization, that is, a class inclusion assertion. They argue further that whether a metaphor is understood as a comparison or as a categorization assertion depends on its familiarity. Novel metaphors are invariably understood as comparisons. With repeated use, metaphors become conventionalized and can then be understood as categorization assertions and processed as such. They refer to this argument as the career-of-metaphor hypothesis. (Bowdle & Gentner, 2005). This view obviously depends critically on the assumption that metaphors and their corresponding similes mean the same thing.

Categorization theorists rely just as critically on this assumption, that metaphors and similes are virtual paraphrases of one another. Whereas comparison theorists argue that metaphors are understood as implicit similes, categorization theorists argue that the opposite is true: that similes are understood as implicit categorization assertions. Metaphors are not understood by transforming them into similes. Instead, they are intended as class-inclusion statements and are understood as such. When metaphors are expressed as comparisons, then they are interpreted as implicit category statements, rather than the other way around (Glucksberg, 2001; Glucksberg & Keysar, 1990). Recent evidence on how people understand metaphors and their corresponding similes suggest that both comparison and categorization theories are wrong in this respect. Metaphors and similes differ systematically, and so neither can be interpreted in terms of the other.

Consider, first, how people interpret metaphors and their corresponding similes. Ostensibly, metaphors and similes should yield comparable interpretations, with metaphors, perhaps, being somehow more "vivid" (Ortony, 1979). We tested this notion directly, by asking people to paraphrase either metaphors or their corresponding similes. Half the participants in this experiment paraphrased metaphors, the other half similes. For the expression *some ideas are like diamonds*, typical paraphrases included responses such as *some ideas are rare and desirable, some ideas are so interesting it is as though they shine and glitter,* and *some ideas are very valuable*. The italicized properties that were attributed to *some ideas* – rare, desirable, shine, glitter, valuable – are all properties of the literal diamond. This suggests that the predicate of a simile does indeed refer directly to the basic-level concept, in this case the literal gem, a diamond. In contrast, metaphors tended to attribute emergent properties to the topic, properties that inhere in the superordinate category of diamonds as valuable entities but not to literal diamonds. Typical paraphrases of this kind were *some ideas are brilliant and insightful* and *some ideas are fantastic and creatively very unique*. Clearly, literal diamonds cannot be insightful, and "creatively very unique" seems a stretch. Overall, metaphors tended to be interpreted in this way, with many more nonliteral, emergent attributions than literal, basic-level ones. Similes tended to attribute about an equal number of each (Hasson, Estes, & Glucksberg, 2001; see Figure 4.3). Clearly, metaphors are not just more vivid than similes. Instead, they tend to evoke more emergent properties than do similes. As Richard Russo wrote in his satirical novel of academic life, metaphors are not similes:

> *Sophomoric Student: "I like the clouds . . . They're, like, a metaphor."*
> *Sarcastic Professor: "They* are *a metaphor . . . if they were* like *a metaphor, they'd be, like, a simile." (Russo, 1997)*

Although these data clearly show that metaphors and their corresponding similes may differ in their interpretations, the case may still be made that these differences are rather subtle and could well be produced by inferences drawn after initial comprehension. If this is so, then the career-of-metaphor hypothesis might still hold. Novel metaphors would be understood via a comparison process and so would not differ in interpretations from their corresponding similes. Conventional matters might be understood via a categorization operation, and be understood slightly differently from their corresponding similes via postcomprehension inferences. In order to reject both the career-of-metaphor as well as the categorization views that treat metaphors and similes as equivalent, we

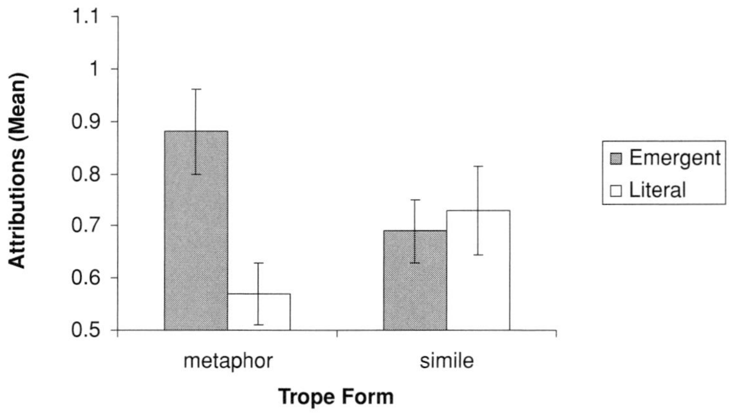


**Figure 4.3.** Mean number of emergent and literal attributions as a function of trope form.

need to show two things. First, that novel metaphors, not just conventional ones, can be privileged when in metaphor rather than in simile form. This would directly contradict the career-of-metaphor view, that novel metaphors are understood as comparisons, not as categorization assertions. Second, we need to show that novel metaphors and their corresponding similes can differ sharply in their interpretations. This would contradict the career-of-metaphor argument that novel metaphors are understood as implicit comparisons, that is, similes. On the other side of the coin, it would also contradict Glucksberg and Keysar's (1990) claim that similes are understood as implicit categorization assertions.

ARE NOVEL METAPHORS BETTER AS SIMILES?

Bowdle and Gentner (2005) asked people to judge whether novel and conventional metaphoric assertions were preferable in either metaphor or simile form. They found that novel metaphors were preferred in simile form, while conventional ones were preferred in metaphor form. More tellingly, they found that novel metaphoric assertions were understood more quickly in simile than in metaphor form, while the reverse was true for conventional metaphors. These data seem to support the career-of-metaphor argument. As a metaphor becomes more familiar, the more likely will it be treated as a categorization rather than as a comparison assertion. There may, however, be a serious problem with this conclusion. We know from earlier work that novel metaphors are processed just as quickly as comparable literal expressions, but only if the metaphors are apt, that is, if they are good metaphors (Blasko & Connine, 1993). The metaphors used by Bowdle and Gentner may have varied not only in conventionality but also in aptness. One very real possibility is that their novel metaphors, such as *A fisherman is (like) a spider*, were just not very good metaphors. Comparisons are more constrained attributive assertions than are categorizations, and so for poor or limited metaphors, comparisons may be preferred to categorical assertions. Conventional metaphors, on the other hand, would tend to be reasonably good ones; otherwise, they would not have become conventional in the first place!

To address this issue, we developed a procedure to generate apt novel metaphors to see whether they would be preferred and more easily understood in categorical rather than in comparison form (Haught & Glucksberg, 2004). We selected a set of apt and comprehensible conventional metaphorical assertions, such as *My lawyer was (like) a shark* and *Some ideas are (like) diamonds.* We then made them novel by modifying the metaphor vehicle (for metaphors) or the simile predicate term (for similes), using adjectives that are applicable to the metaphor topic, but not to the literal

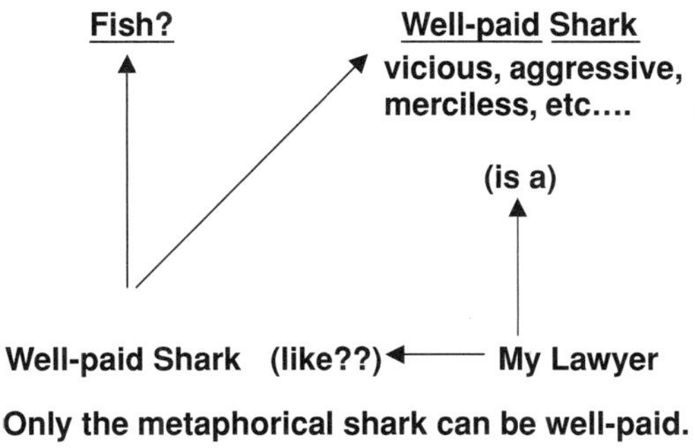


**Figure 4.4.** A conventional metaphor with no literal referent.

metaphor term, as in *My lawyer was (like) a well-paid shark* or *Some ideas are (like) theoretical diamonds*. For such constructions, we expected people to find the assertion apt and comprehensible in metaphor form because the metaphorical shark can be well paid, and the metaphorical diamond can be theoretical. However, in simile form, the predicate term refers at the literal, basic level, and so these similes should be neither apt nor comprehensible (see Figure 4.4). After all, literal sharks can't plausibly be well paid, and real, literal diamonds can't plausibly be theoretical (if they were, then they would be fake diamonds!). These metaphors and similes would provide a counterexample for the career-of-metaphor hypothesis: they would be novel expressions that work in metaphor form, but are difficult to interpret in simile form.

We gave adjectivally modified metaphorical assertions along with their original, nonmodified versions to college students in both metaphor and simile forms. One group rated each statement type in terms of how apt the expressions were, that is, how well did they communicate an idea or a characterization of the statement's topic. An independent group rated how comprehensible or easy to understand each statement was. As expected, the novel metaphors were rated as apt as their original conventional counterparts. However, in simile form, they were rated as much less apt. This finding supports the dual reference hypothesis, that the metaphor vehicle in similes refers at the literal level, but in metaphors at the superordinate metaphorical level. A metaphorical shark can plausibly be well paid, but the literal marine creature is not something that can be characterized in terms of salary or monetary income (except perhaps in fish markets or on restaurant menus). The comprehensibility ratings painted a similar picture, as did response times to judge the sensibility of each type of statement. People took about the same time to judge that the novel and original metaphors were sensible, but the novel similes took much longer to judge than did the novel metaphors. These data are clear. There is no advantage of similes over metaphors for novel metaphorical assertions, whether in terms of rated aptness, rated comprehensibility, or comprehension time. To the contrary, novel metaphors were privileged over novel similes.

But were these metaphors really novel? After all, they were all based on conventional, well-known metaphors. Can we find truly novel metaphors that are privileged in categorical over comparison form? Fortunately, Bowdle and Gentner (2005) provide the perfect source. They generated truly novel metaphors that are privileged in comparison over categorical form in two ways. First, when asked to rate these metaphors, there was a marked preference for the comparison over the categorical form. Metaphors such as *science is a glacier* were preferred in comparison form, as in *science is like a glacier*, while conventional metaphors, such as *some jobs are jail*, were preferred in categorical form. Second, their novel metaphors were understood more quickly in comparison than in categorical form, while the reverse was true for conventional metaphors. Were these results due to the novelty of the metaphors that were used, or instead to some other characteristic, such as aptness? Jones and Estes (2006) examined this question directly, and found that aptness – that is, how good a metaphor is – accounted for most of the variance in preference for trope form, as well as for differences in comprehension difficulty of comparison and categorical forms. But what accounts for relative aptness of metaphors, be they conventional or novel?

One answer to this question is suggested by the ability for most metaphors to be paraphrased quite adequately as similes and vice versa. What makes this possible is the dual reference function of metaphor vehicles, as illustrated in Figure 4.1b. In this conventional metaphor, the vehicle "shark" is polysemous. In the categorical form, it refers to the abstract metaphorical category that we call "sharks," which includes any creature that is vicious, predatory, aggressive, and which can characterize any living being from card sharks to used car salespeople to lawyers (alas). In comparison form, it refers to the literal marine creature, shark. The shark–lawyer metaphor is apt in both categorical and comparison form because both types of referents are available – the metaphorical as well as the literal. However, we can imagine metaphors for which only one type of referent is available: either for the literal for the comparison form, or for the metaphorical for the categorical form. Some adjectivally modified metaphors, such as *Many corporate lawyers are well-paid sharks*, exemplify the metaphorical referent type. Because well-paid literal sharks do not exist, this metaphor has only the one type of referent, namely, the abstract metaphorical category of predatory, aggressive creatures. Hence, it can only be understood as a categorical assertion, not as a comparison.

In this special case, the metaphor vehicle does not provide the capacity for dual reference because the literal referent – well-paid sharks – does not exist. Analogously, Bowdle and Gentner's metaphors also do not provide for dual reference. Here, the relevant abstract categories do not exist, leaving only literal referents available, as in the assertion *science is a glacier*. This assertion is difficult to interpret in categorical form because "glacier" does not call to mind any interpretable abstract metaphorical category. In contrast, the comparison *Science is like a glacier* can be interpreted by inviting the addressee to consider properties of glaciers that might be applicable to "science," perhaps cold and dispassionate, perhaps slow (or as Al Gore might remark, melting down?). How can we render such

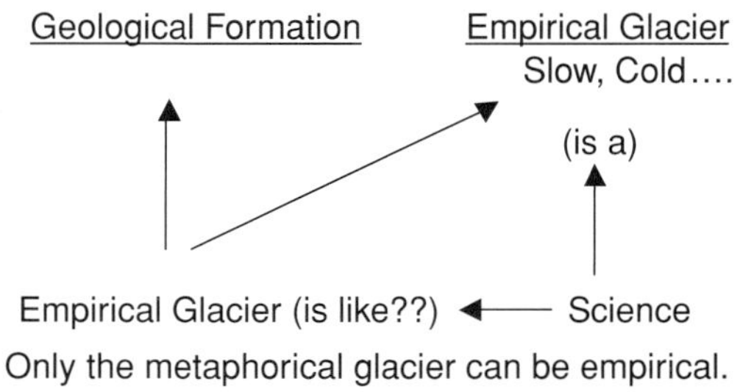


**Figure 4.5.** A novel metaphor with no literal referent.

metaphors more interpretable in categorical than in comparison form? Simply by modifying them so that instead of having no metaphorical referent, they would now have no literal referent, as in *science is (like) an empirical glacier*. Since literal glaciers cannot be empirical, science cannot be like them, as illustrated in Figure 4.5. Other examples of literal-referent metaphors that can be converted to metaphorical-referent ones include *A mind is (like) an idea-filled kitchen, A newspaper is (like) a daily telescope, A billboard is (like) an advertising wart*, and *Moon light is (like) romantic bleach*.[7]

Using Bowdle and Gentner's items and their modified versions (as above), we repeated their experiments to see (a) whether we could replicate their results when using their original items and (b) whether we could completely reverse those results when we used our modified versions of them. In brief, we replicated their findings with their original items and reversed them with the modified items. People again demonstrated a preference for comparison over categorical form for the original, literal-referent metaphors but now demonstrated a preference for categorical over comparison form for the metaphor-referent metaphors. Indeed, the preference ratings for these latter metaphor types were comparable to the ratings for conventional metaphors. More telling, we found that people understood literal-referent metaphors more quickly in comparison than categorical form but found the reverse for the metaphor-referent metaphors (Glucksberg & Haught, 2006a). Apparently, whether a metaphor is understood more easily in categorical versus comparison form does not depend on novelty or conventionality but instead on the referential and semantic properties of the metaphor. As Glucksberg and Haught (2006a) put it, "Different metaphors will have different careers" (p. 928).

CAN METAPHORS AND SIMILES HAVE DIFFERENT INTERPRETATIONS?

We turn now to a most important characteristic of metaphors and their apparent simile counterparts. We have already seen a case in which novel metaphors are far more apt and comprehensible than their simile counterparts. Can we identify a case in which a metaphor and a simile are equally apt and comprehensible but turn out to have quite different interpretations? If so, then any theory of metaphor that relies on the interpretative equivalence of metaphors and similes must be revised to account for this phenomenon.

We have already alluded to the possibility that a metaphor and its corresponding simile might have distinctly different interpretations. Consider the assertion that *my lawyer was/was like an old shark*. In the simile form, the predicate *old shark* refers to the literal marine creature. Old sharks, like old fish in general, are not particularly attractive. They tend to be past their prime, relatively weak, slow; in short, they have the properties that are stereotypically associated with old age. Accordingly, people should ascribe properties such as ineffectual, weak, and tired not only to the literal old shark but also to the topic of the simile, the lawyer who is likened to an old shark. In contrast, in the metaphor *My lawyer was an old shark*, the metaphor vehicle refers to the metaphorical shark, not the literal one. Accordingly, people should ascribe properties such as competent, aggressive, and experienced to this shark, as well as to the lawyer who is a member of the category *old sharks*. Is this difference simply attributable to comparison versus categorization in general.? Not at all. For literal statements such as *My lawyer was (was like) an old pro*, there seems to be no difference between the categorical and comparison forms. In both cases, *My lawyer* is considered to be sharp, wise, and experienced.

We gave people metaphors and their corresponding similes for which the literal and metaphorical referents of the metaphor vehicle had distinctly different properties, as in these examples, along with typical interpretations of them:

i. His job was/was like a secure jail.
   *Metaphor*: His job was very unpleasant and confining, but it was safe, like having tenure.
   *Simile*: His job was unpleasant and confining, like a high-security prison.
ii. Some ideas are/are like small diamonds.
   *Metaphor*: Some ideas are very valuable, have a lot of potential, and, if developed, they can become big diamonds.
   *Simile*: Some ideas are somewhat valuable and have some potential, but they are still small and therefore disappointing compared to bigger diamonds.

For tropes like these, people consistently provided interpretations that sharply differed between their metaphor and simile forms (Glucksberg & Haught, 2006b). The implications for theories of metaphor are as clear as they are important. Because metaphors and their corresponding similes can differ in interpretation, any theory that assumes the equivalence of metaphors and similes cannot be true. This holds for comparison theories that claim that metaphors are understood by means of a comparison process, as well as categorization theories that claim that similes are invariably understood as categorizations.

### *Comparison versus Categorization Reconsidered*

Since neither a pure comparisons nor a pure class-inclusion theory is tenable, how can we characterize these two processes for comprehending metaphors? The career-of-metaphor hypothesis seemed promising, but it ultimately failed for at least two reasons. First, novel but apt metaphors are not privileged in simile form over metaphor form. Second, and more important, similes may not have the same meaning as their corresponding metaphors, and so the theory must be able to account for any changes in meaning as a metaphor becomes more conventional.

An alternative to the career-of-metaphor hypothesis might be the quality-of-metaphor hypothesis. Really good metaphors work best as categorizations and sometimes work *only* as categorization assertions (like the well-paid shark example). In such metaphors, the vehicle concept is an ideal exemplar of the category it represents. Poor or limited metaphors might well work best as similes, even when highly conventional. Consider the familiar expression *I felt like a sardine* in the context of jam-packed, crowded situations. It has a very narrow, indeed unidimensional, predication: to be packed together like sardines in a can. In no other respect is one characterized as a sardine: not fishy, oily, small, or edible. Probably because the attribution of one, context-dependent sardine property is intended, this familiar metaphor doesn't seem to work as a categorization assertion, that is, *I felt I was a sardine* doesn't quite capture the same intention as *I felt like a sardine*.

For most metaphors, the simile and categorization forms yield the same interpretations. When they appear in metaphor form, they are understood as class-inclusion assertions. When they appear in simile form, there are two possibilities: they could be understood either as implicit categorizations or as comparisons. When, however, a metaphor and its corresponding simile yield different interpretations, then only the metaphor is understood as a categorization. The simile must be understood as a comparison. Finally, when a metaphor cannot be readily understood as a categorization, as in the sardine example or as in the science–glacier example, then it may be interpreted as a comparison but only as a narrowly constrained one. Comparison and categorization may thus be viewed as complementary strategies for understanding metaphors, with the choice of strategy dependent on the quality and aptness of the metaphor. Comparisons are resorted to when a categorization doesn't make much sense; categorizations are used when a metaphor is apt, even when it is a novel metaphor.

## Conclusions

We began our discussion of metaphor comprehension by considering three issues: The priority of literal versus figurative meanings, the role of comparison processes in metaphor comprehension, and the relation between a metaphor's and a simile's meaning. We reached three important conclusions.

1. Literal meaning does not have unconditional priority. Metaphor comprehension, like language comprehension in general, is automatic and mandatory. We cannot refuse to understand, and when metaphoric meaning is available, it will be processed (Giora, 2003; Glucksberg, 2001; Keysar, 1989).

2. Metaphors are not generally understood as comparisons, but comparisons may well be understood as categorizations, whether they are literal or figurative. Similes, in general will be understood as implicit categorizations, but only when their corresponding metaphors are apt.

3. Metaphors and similes are not always interchangeable. Because of the dual reference function of metaphor vehicles, these two forms can express different meanings, sometimes subtly different, sometimes quite sharply so. Indeed, not only can the two forms yield different interpretations, in some cases an expression may work only in metaphor form (as in the well-paid shark example) and in others only in simile form (as in the sardine example). This suggests very strongly that both comparison and categorization processes can be employed for understanding metaphors. An issue for future research to resolve is, what are the circumstances that lead to the choice of one over the other strategy for understanding both similes and metaphors?

This issue is as yet unresolved, either for literally or figuratively intended comparison assertions.

And, to return to our autistic savant Christopher Boone, we can reassure him that metaphors are not lies, and they are not similes either!

## Notes

1 For metaphors of the form X is a Y, X is the topic of the assertion, and Y the vehicle. In the surgeon–butcher example, the topic *surgeon* is assigned to the vehicle category *butchers* and inherits salient properties of that vehicle category, such as grossly incompetent. In the context of *surgeon*, incompetence is instantiated as bloody, causing bodily injury, and so. For the metaphor *my butcher is a surgeon*, topic and vehicle roles are reversed and now the topic *butcher* inherits stereotypical properties of the vehicle category *surgeons*, for example, precise, expert, skillful.

2 Some metaphorically intended utterances or expressions may well pose interpretative problems and hence take longer to understand. Indeed, some may be uninterpretable for some people in some circumstances. For a villager in Nepal who is unfamiliar with American corporate greed and practices, an expression such as "There's going to be many more Enrons down the road" would be completely opaque. Closer to home, non-apt attempts at metaphor, such as "a mind is a kitchen" or "a fisherman is a spider" (Bowdle & Gentner, 2005) are difficult to interpret and may well take a lot of time and distress. Even seasoned journalists can leave their readers hopelessly muddled in their zeal to coin novel expressions, as in this excerpt from an article on Martina Hingis's negative opinions of contemporary women's tennis: "As the cerebral point choreographer with the famous Chucky Doll grin, she used to inspire the glamour lugs on the women's tour to stretch their minds when they clomped on the court to play her" (Roberts, 2004, p. D1).

3 The interchangeability of similes and metaphors works most of the time, but as we shall see, this is not a universal property of similes and their corresponding metaphors.

4 The two levels of abstraction involved in metaphor versus simile are reflected in the definition of metaphor in the *Oxford English Dictionary* (1996): A thing considered as representative of some other (usually abstract) thing: A symbol. The literal shark is representative of the metaphorical shark category, and so can be used as a symbol of that category, as well as a referring expression for it.

5 This last phenomenon has the most critical implication for theories of metaphor comprehension. If metaphors and their corresponding similes can have quite different interpretations, then any theory that requires this last phenomenon has the most critical implication for theories of metaphor comprehension. If metaphors and their corresponding similes can have quite different interpretations, then any theory that requires metaphors and similes to "mean" the same thing, such as comparison theory, cannot be viable.

6 This finding is analogous to Klein and Murphy's (2001) demonstration that polysemous words – words that have different but related senses, such as wrapping *paper* and daily *paper* – do not prime one another. Apparently, the literal and metaphorical senses of metaphor vehicles behave much like the several senses of polysemous words.

7 Lest the reader doubt that such expressions can appear in normal text or conversation, consider this metaphor from the *New York Times* sports pages: "Coach Herman Edwards had appealed to his players' vanity leading up to the game. **Their pride was the garlic clove that Edwards waved to stave off pessimism's bloodthirsty advances**" (K. Krouse, October 25, 2005). Like our experimental items, this metaphor has no possible literal referent, and so is distinctly infelicitous in comparison form; that is, *Like* the garlic clove just doesn't work here.

## References

Ahrens, K. (2004). *Functional MRI of conventional and anomalous metaphors in Mandarin Chinese.* Paper presented at Euroconference on the Processing of Metaphor and Metonymy, Granada, Spain.

Blasko, D. (2004). *What can the study of event-related potential tell us about the understanding of nonliteral language?* Paper presented at Euroconference on the Processing of Metaphor and Metonymy, Granada, Spain.

Blasko, D. G., & Connine, C. M. (1993). Effects of familiarity and aptness on metaphor

processing. *Journal of Experimental Psychology: Learning, Memory and Cognition*, 19, 295–308.
Bowdle, B. F., & Gentner, D. (2005). The career of metaphor. *Psychological Review, 112*, 193–216.
Brown, R. (1958). *Words and things*. New York: Free Press.
Fodor, J. A. (1983). *The modularity of mind*. Cambridge, MA: Bradford Books.
Fogelin, R. (1988). *Figuratively speaking*. New Haven, CT: Yale University Press.
Gentner, D. (1983). Structure-mapping: A theoretical framework for analogy. *Cognitive Science, 7*, 155–170.
Gentner, D., & Markman, A. (1994). Structural alignment in comparison: No difference without similarity. *Psychological Science, 5*, 152–158.
Gentner, D., & Wolff, P. (1997). Alignment in the processing of metaphor. *Journal of Memory and Language, 37*, 331–355.
Gernsbacher, M. A., & Faust, M. (1991). The mechanism of suppression: A component of general comprehension skill. *Journal of Experimental Psychology: Learning, Memory, and Cognition, 17*, 245–262.
Gernsbacher, M. A., Keysar, B., Robertson, R. R. W., & Werner, N. K. (2001). The role of suppression and enhancement in understanding metaphors. *Journal of Memory and Language, 45*, 433–450.
Gibbs, R. W., Nayak, N. P., & Cutting, C. (1989). How to kick the bucket and not decompose: Analyzability and idiom processing. *Journal of Memory and Language, 28*, 576–593.
Gildea, P., & Glucksberg, S. (1983). On understanding metaphor: The role of context. *Journal of Verbal Learning and Verbal Behavior, 22*, 577–590.
Giora, R. (2003). *On our mind: Salience, context, and figurative language*. New York: Oxford University Press.
Glucksberg, S. (2001). *Understanding figurative language: From metaphors to idioms*. New York: Oxford University Press.
Glucksberg, S., Gildea, P., & Bookin, H. A. (1982). On understanding nonliteral speech: Can people ignore metaphors? *Journal of Verbal Learning and Verbal Behavior, 21*, 85–98.
Glucksberg, S., & Haught, C. (2006a). Can Florida become *like* the next Florida? When metaphoric comparisons fail. *Psychological Science, 17*, 935–938.
Glucksberg, S., & Haught, C. (2006b). On the relation between metaphor and simile: When comparison fails. *Mind & Language, 21*, 360–378.
Glucksberg, S & Keysar, B (1990) Understanding metaphorical comparisons: Beyond similarity. *Psychological Review*, 97, 3–18.
Glucksberg, S., McGlone, M. S., & Manfredi, D. (1997). Property attribution in metaphor comprehension. *Journal of Memory and Language*, 36, 50–67.
Glucksberg, S, Newsome, M. R., & Goldvarg, Y. (2001). Inhibition of the literal: Filtering metaphor-irrelevant information during metaphor comprehension. *Memory and Symbol, 16*, 277–294.
Goldvarg, Y., & Glucksberg, S. (1998). Conceptual combinations: The role of similarity. *Metaphor and Symbol, 13*, 243–255.
Goodnough, A. (2004, April 28). Lost record of vote in '02 Florida race raises '04 concerns. *New York Times*, p. B4.
Grice, H. P. (1975). Logic and conversation. In P. Cole & J. Morgan (Eds.), *Syntax and semantics: Vol. 3. Speech acts* (pp. 41–58). New York: Academic Press.
Haddon, M. (2003). *The curious incident of the dog in the night-time*. New York: Doubleday.
Hage, P., & Miller, W. R. (1976). "Eagle" = "Bird": A note on the structure and evolution of Shoshoni ethno-ornithological nomenclature. *American Ethnologist, 3*, 481–488.
Hasson, U., Estes, Z. & Glucksberg, S. (Nov. 2001). Metaphors communicate more effectively than do similes. Poster presented at the Meeting of the Psychonomic Society, Orlando, FL.
Haught, C., & Glucksberg, S. (2004). *When old sharks are not old pros: Metaphors are not similes*. Paper presented at the annual meeting of the Psychonomic Society, Minneapolis, MN.
Jackendoff, R. (1995). The boundaries of the lexicon. In M. Everaert, E van den Linden, A. Schenk, & R. Schreuder (Eds.), *Idioms: Structural and psychological perspectives* (pp. 133–166). Hillsdale, NJ: Lawrence Erlbaum Associates.
Johnson, A. T. (1996). Comprehension of metaphors and similes: A reaction time study. *Metaphor and Symbolic Activity, 11*, 145–149.
Jones, L. L. & Estes, Z. (2006). ROOSTERS, ROBINS, and ALARM CLOCKS: Aptness and conventionality in metaphor comprehension. *Journal of Memory and Language, 55*, 18–32.
Keysar, B. (1989). On the functional equivalence of literal and metaphorical interpretations in discourse. *Journal of Memory and Language*, 28, 375–385.

Klein, D. E., & Murphy, G. L. (2001). The representation of polysemous words. *Journal of Memory and Language, 45*, 259–282.

McElree, B., & Nordlie, J. (1999). Literal and figurative interpretations are computed in equal time. *Psychonomic Bulletin & Review, 6*, 486–494.

McGlone, M. S., & Manfredi, D. A. (2002). Topic-vehicle interaction in metaphor comprehension. *Memory & Cognition*, 1209–1219.

Miller, G. A., & Johnson-Laird, P. (1976). *Language and perception*. Cambridge, MA: Harvard University Press.

Ortony, A. (1979). Beyond literal similarity. *Psychological Review, 86*, 161–180.

*Oxford English Dictionary*. (1996). Oxford: Oxford University Press.

Pynte, J., Besson, M., Robichon, F. H., & Poli, J. (1996). The time-course of metaphor comprehension: An event-related potential study. *Brain & Language, 55*, 293–316.

Rapp, A. M., Leube, D. T., Erb, M., Grodd, W., & Kircher, T. T. J. (2007). Laterality in metaphor processing: Lack of evidence from functional magnetic resonance imaging for the right hemisphere theory. *Brain and Language, 100*, 142–149.

Roberts, S. (2004, June 4). Hingis makes points in a refresher course. *New York Times*, p. D1.

Russo, R. (1997). *Straight man*. New York: Random House.

Searle, J. (1979). Metaphor. In A. Ortony (Ed.), *Metaphor and thought* (pp. 92–123). New York: Cambridge University Press.

Simpson, G. B., & Kang, H. 1994. The flexible use of phonological information in word recognition in Korean. *Journal of Memory and Language* 33, 319–331.

Stringaris, A. K., Medford, N. C., Giampietro, V., Bramme, M. J., & David, A. S. (2007). Deriving meaning: Distinct neural mechanisms for metaphoric, literal, and non-meaningful sentences. *Brain and Language, 100*, 150–162.

Stroop, J. R. (1935). Studies of interference in serial verbal reactions. *Journal of Experimental Psychology, 18*, 643–662.

Trager, G. L. (1936–1939). "Cottonwood-tree": A south-western linguistic trait. *International Journal of American Linguistics, 9*, 117–118.

Tversky, A. (1977). Features of similarity. *Psychological Review, 85*, 327–352.

Wechsler, D. (1958). *The measurement and appraisal of adult intelligence* (4th ed.). Baltimore, MD: Williams and Wilkins.

CHAPTER 5

# A Deflationary Account of Metaphors*

*Dan Sperber and Deirdre Wilson*

Are metaphors departures from a norm of literalness? According to classical rhetoric and most later theories, including Gricean pragmatics, they are. No, metaphors are wholly normal, say the Romantic critics of classical rhetoric and a variety of modern scholars ranging from hard-nosed cognitive scientists to postmodern critical theorists. On the metaphor-as-normal side, there is a broad contrast between those, like the cognitive linguists Lakoff, Talmy, or Fauconnier, who see metaphor as pervasive in language because it is constitutive of human thought, and those, like the psycholinguists Glucksberg or Kintsch, or relevance theorists, who describe metaphor as emerging in the process of verbal communication.[1] While metaphor cannot be both wholly normal and a departure from normal language use, there might be distinct, though related, metaphorical phenomena at the level of thought, on the one hand, and verbal communication, on the other. This possibility is being explored in the work of Raymond Gibbs, for instance.[2] In this chapter, we focus on the relevance-theoretic approach to linguistic metaphors.

Relevance theory's approach to metaphor is deflationary. Most rhetorical, literary, and philosophical traditions emphasize both the importance and the distinctiveness of metaphor. We acknowledge its importance but dispute its distinctiveness. Certainly, metaphors are ubiquitous in language use and contribute to what Barthes called "le plaisir du texte." Specific uses of metaphors by individual authors or in given literary genres are indeed worthy of study, and so is the very idea of metaphor as a culturally salient notion with a long, rich history. Still, we see metaphors as simply a range of cases at one end of a continuum that includes literal, loose, and hyperbolic interpretations. In our view, metaphorical interpretations are arrived at in exactly the same way as these other interpretations. There is no mechanism specific to metaphor, no interesting generalisation that applies only to them. In other terms, linguistic metaphors are not a natural kind, and "metaphor" is not a

* We are grateful to Ray Gibbs, Robyn Carston, and François Recanati for valuable discussion and comments on an earlier version.

theoretically important notion in the study of verbal communication. Relevance Theory's account of metaphor is on the lean side, and is bound to disappoint those who feel that verbal metaphor deserves a full-fledged theory of its own, or should be at the centre of a wider theory of language, or even of thought.

The widely accepted view that language use is governed by a norm of literalness (which is violated by metaphor and other figurative uses – hence their distinctiveness) follows straightforwardly from the even more widely accepted view that the function of language in communication is to allow the speaker to encode her meaning and the hearer to decode it. Debunking this "code model" view of human communication is a necessary first step towards putting metaphor in a proper perspective.

## The Function of Language in Communication

A code is a systematic pairing of messages and signals. Encoding a message into a signal that a recipient can then decode is a very simple way to communicate very simple messages. Nonhuman animals do it all the time. Formally speaking, human languages are also codes: they are systems of sound-sense pairs generated by an underlying grammar. But although they are codes, human languages are vastly different from the codes of animal communication. First, and most obvious, they are incomparably richer. Languages not only contain a vast repertoire of expressive elements – the lexicon – with no counterpart in animal signalling systems, but these elements are combined by a syntax with unbounded generative capacities.

Human languages differ from animal codes in another respect that should be equally obvious but is hardly ever mentioned: they are grossly defective as codes. If communication is to be achieved purely by coding and decoding, each signal in the code must unambiguously convey exactly the same content on all occasions. Ambiguity – where the same signal is paired with several messages – will stall the decoding process. True, there are cases even in animal communication where the exact message encoded by a given signal varies with the context. In the "bee dance," for instance, the orientation of the bees' communicative movements indicates the direction in which pollen is to be found, but this indication is relative to the position of the sun at the time. Limited context-sensitivity of this type can be handled by automatic code-like rules of disambiguation and accommodated in a coding-decoding system. However, the interpretation of the linguistic utterances that humans use to communicate is far too context-sensitive to be automatically achieved in purely code-like terms. The sentences of a natural language are typically multiply ambiguous; they contain referential expressions whose values cannot be assigned by decoding alone; the senses they ambiguously encode are often elliptical or incomplete; and there are still other ways in which the encoded meaning of a sentence falls short of determining what it may be used to communicate.

So although a language is formally a code, and human communication involves linguistic coding and decoding, there is a considerable gap between the semantic structure a sentence encodes and the meaning a speaker manages to convey by uttering that sentence in a given situation. In the case of metaphors and other tropes, this gap is often acknowledged as if it were an exception, and described in terms of a distinction between literal and figurative meaning.[3] We claim that metaphors are not exceptional, and that the linguistic content of all utterances, even those that are literally understood, vastly underdetermines their interpretation.

When we say that human languages are defective as codes, we do not mean to imply that there is something wrong with them, or that we should want to improve on them (as some philosophers in the analytic tradition once proposed). On the contrary, we assume that human languages are exquisitely well suited to performing their function in communication. It is just that this function cannot be to encode speakers' intended meanings.

Humans communicate not only by using language but also by producing a variety of what we call "ostensive stimuli": that is, actions (e.g. gestures or speech) or traces of actions (e.g. writings) that are manifestly intended to attract an addressee's attention and convey some content. Many of these ostensive stimuli do not belong to a code, and so do not, properly speaking, encode anything. By using ostensive stimuli, humans are capable of communicating without language and indeed without any other code. How can a stimulus convey a meaning that it doesn't encode? By providing evidence that the communicator intends to convey this meaning.

Suppose that Mary is angry with Peter and doesn't want to talk to him. When he tries to engage her in conversation, she might

(1) stare pointedly at the ceiling
(2) open a newspaper and start reading it.

These actions do not draw on any established code. Nonetheless, what staring at the ceiling or opening a paper suggests to Peter is that Mary would rather do these things than talk to him at that time. Given that these actions are ostensive stimuli (i.e., are performed in order to attract his attention and convey some content to him), Peter understands Mary to *mean* that she doesn't want to talk to him. He interprets her in this way not because of some underlying code that systematically pairs stimuli of this type to a meaning of this type, but because her actions bring this interpretation to mind, and the best possible explanation of Mary's behaviour is to assume that this is just what it was intended to do. A stimulus can convey a meaning it does not encode by providing evidence that the communicator intends to convey this meaning. Here, the meaning is recovered not by decoding but by inference.

What is true of uncoded communicative stimuli is also true of coded stimuli used in human communication: they too convey their producer's intended meaning not by directly encoding it but by encoding some evidence of it. In the situation described, Mary might

(3) look angrily at Peter and clamp her mouth firmly shut,
(4) look angrily at Peter, put a finger to her lips, and whisper "Shhh!"

In (3) and (4), Mary makes a gesture conventionally used to convey a request for silence, from which Peter can infer that she does not want to talk to him. Unlike the actions in (1) and (2), clamping one's mouth firmly shut or whispering "Shhh" may be seen as encoding some meaning, but this encoded meaning is much vaguer than Mary's own meaning. For instance, the same gestures might be used in other situations to convey a request for secrecy. In the present situation, though, they are enough to indicate Mary's meaning.

In the same situation as before, Mary might also

(5) say, "I am deaf and dumb,"
(6) say, "I won't talk to you."

Obviously, the decoded linguistic content of Mary's utterance in (5) does not directly yield her meaning, but it provides a starting point for inferring her meaning that is not too different in effect from the gesture of clamping one's mouth shut, as in (3). In both cases, what is activated in Peter's mind is the idea of its being impossible to talk, an idea whose import is easy enough to work out in the situation.

What about Mary's utterance in (6)? Surely this, at least, encodes her exact meaning? In fact, it too falls some way short of doing so: the future tense does not indicate when Mary won't talk to Peter; the indicative form does not indicate whether she is expressing a prediction, a warning, or a threat. On another occasion, she might use the same sentence to promise Peter that she will talk to the whole group rather than just to him. Still, in the situation described, Peter can reconstruct Mary's full meaning by starting from the linguistic content of her utterance and specifying it further to reach a contextually plausible interpretation.

What these examples illustrate is the general point that, whether or not it involves the use of a language or some other code, human communication is inferential communication. The communicator provides some evidence of her meaning and the addressee infers this meaning on the basis of this evidence and the context. The evidence may or may not be coded, and if it is coded, it may or may not be linguistic, but in each case, it provides input to an inferential process whose goal is to interpret the communicator's meaning. Which raises the following question: what is the point of using a language at all if the kind of thing it can be used to achieve can also be achieved without it? The point is that a language provides an unbounded repertoire of evidence of the speaker's meaning, evidence that can be as nuanced, as complex, as richly structured as the speaker likes. Nonverbal kinds of evidence are much more limited. With language (and only with language) people can communicate about anything they can think about, whether they can point to it or not, imitate it or not, and they can do this with endless refinement. The fact that the interpretations of utterances are not encoded but merely evidenced by their linguistic meaning does not detract from the richness of linguistic communication, but, on the contrary, enhances it: every single sentence may give rise to an open array of interpretations which go well beyond the encoded senses. Some of the best illustrations of this are, of course, creative metaphors.

## How Relevance Guides Inferential Comprehension

What we have sketched so far is a view of verbal communication suggested by the work of the philosopher Paul Grice, but more radical than his. Grice characterised a speaker's meaning as an overt intention to cause a certain cognitive effect in an audience via their recognition of one's intention to cause this effect (Grice, 1989, chapters 5–6, 14, 18). A speaker's meaning, so understood, is an intention, a mental state. The mental states of others cannot be simply perceived or decoded, but must be inferred from their behaviour, together with background information. What is special about a speaker's meaning as compared with other mental states (which people usually keep to themselves) is that speakers intend their audience to discover their meaning, and provide evidence to that effect, in the form of communicative behaviour. This raises the possibility that there might be an inferential procedure uniquely adapted to comprehension.

Grice tended to take for granted – and Searle explicitly argued – that when someone uses language to communicate, she is presumed to express her meaning literally. It can then be assumed by default that the literal linguistic meaning of the utterance is *her* meaning, or at least the explicit part of her meaning (Grice's "what is said"), with only the implicit part (Grice's "implicatures") left to be inferred. This amounts, in practice, to saying that part of the speaker's meaning is decoded and part is inferred. Metaphors and other tropes, where the linguistic meaning of the utterance is not even part of the speaker's meaning, are exceptional in this respect: Grice suggested that in metaphor, the speaker is not really saying what she appears to be saying, but merely "makes as if to say" it, so that in this case, the speaker's meaning must be wholly inferred. We claim, by contrast, that verbal comprehension involves no presumption of literalness and no default interpretation, and that metaphors are in no way exceptional. All human intentional communication works in the way outlined above: the communicator produces a piece of evidence of her meaning – the ostensive stimulus – and the addressee infers her meaning from this piece of evidence and the context. Linguistic utterances are just one type of ostensive stimulus. Verbal communication is always context-sensitive and inferential.

How exactly does inferential comprehension work? Relevance theory draws on a precise characterisation of relevance and its role in human cognition to put forward a testable account of the comprehension mechanism, an account in which expectations of relevance play a crucial role.

We analyse relevance not just as a property of utterances or other ostensive stimuli, but as a property that any input to a cognitive process might possess: sights, sounds, utterances, thoughts, memories, suppositions may all be relevant to an individual at a given time. When is an input relevant? When processing it in the context of previously available information yields new cognitive effects. The input may answer a question the individual had in mind, it may raise or settle a doubt, suggest a hypothesis or a course of action, confirm or disconfirm a suspicion, correct a mistake. All these cognitive effects involve a fruitful interaction between the input and the context in which it is processed. However, the interaction may be more or less fruitful; inputs may be more or less relevant.

What makes one input more relevant than another? Suppose you are a caterer making lunch for a group of 10 people, and all you need to know is how many will want the vegetarian menu. Then the information that three of them are vegetarian would be more relevant to you than the information that three of them are Buddhists (from which it follows that they are probably, though not definitely, vegetarian). In general, it is more informative to learn that someone is a Buddhist than to learn that he is a vegetarian, but if the context is such that only his food preferences are consequential, then the less informative input is more relevant. The greater the cognitive effects produced by processing an input, the greater its relevance (to the person processing it, at the time).

However, cognitive effects are only one of two factors that affect the relevance of an input. The other is the processing effort involved in achieving these effects. Some effort of perception, memory or inference is required to represent the input, access contextual information, and derive cognitive effects. In the situation described above, suppose that the choice is between a straightforward statement that three of the guests are vegetarian and a brochure with a short biography of all 10 guests, mentioning *inter alia* whether they are vegetarian. In this case, the brochure would be less relevant than the straightforward statement: although both would contain all the information required, extracting this information from the brochure would involve more effort for the same effect, hence less relevance. In a nutshell:

**Degrees of relevance:**

(a) The greater the *cognitive effects* achieved by processing an input, the greater its relevance.
(b) The smaller the *processing effort* required to achieve these effects, the greater the relevance.

At every moment in their waking lives, humans have a huge variety of inputs competing for their attention: things and events they perceive, previous thoughts that have not been fully digested, pending goals, and so on. For contexts to use in processing these inputs, they have a vast mental encyclopaedia of accumulated knowledge on which to draw. At any given moment, most of these inputs are not worth processing, and, for any given input, most of this background information is not worth activating: the resulting process would yield too few cognitive effects to be worth the effort. Cognitive efficiency is very much a matter of selecting the most relevant inputs available at each point, and processing them in the context of background information that will most enhance their relevance. In fact, if there were not a strong tendency to select maximally relevant inputs, cognition would be an extremely wasteful activity. We assume that, among the many selective pressures that have driven the evolution of human cognitive capacities, there has been a constant pressure on the cognitive system as a whole, on its component parts, and on their articulation, towards an efficient use of brain resources. We therefore put forward the following claim:

**Cognitive Principle of Relevance:**

*Human cognition tends to be geared to the maximisation of relevance.*

We are not claiming that humans always succeed in maximising relevance, but only that they have a sufficient tendency to do so to make their massive investment in cognition evolutionarily worthwhile. More specifically, we are claiming that human perceptual mechanisms tend to pick out potentially relevant stimuli, human retrieval mechanisms tend to activate potentially relevant background assumptions, and human inferential mechanisms tend to process them in the most productive way, so that, overall, attention tends to go to the inputs with the greatest expected relevance. These claims have a variety of experimentally testable consequences (see van der Henst & Sperber, 2004). Here we are only concerned with the consequences of the cognitive principle of relevance for human communication.

Given the indefinite variety of possible objects of attention and courses of thought, it would be impossible for one person to predict what others will attend to, and what thoughts it will prompt, if their attention and thought processes were not guided by considerations of relevance. The tendency to maximise relevance is crucial to making human mental processes relatively interpretable and predictable. As a result of the same tendency, it is possible not only to interpret and predict, but also to manipulate the mental processes of others, by producing a stimulus which will predictably attract their attention and be interpreted in foreseeable ways. Jill knows it is relevant to Peter that all his guests should be happy, so she leaves her empty glass in his line of sight, anticipating that he will pay attention and conclude that she would like another drink. This is not yet a case of inferential *communication*, because, although Jill intends Peter to come to this conclusion, she provides evidence only that she is thirsty, and not that she intends to inform Peter that she is thirsty. If instead she had established eye contact with him and waved her empty glass, or said to him, "My glass is empty," then the stimulus would be ostensive, and her behaviour would be properly communicative.

Use of an ostensive stimulus as opposed to a regular non-ostensive one provides the addressee with information not only about some state of affairs (e.g., the fact that Jill would like another drink) but also about the communicator's intention to convey this information, and to do so overtly. By producing an ostensive stimulus, the communicator openly requests the addressee's attention. Since attention tends to go to the most relevant inputs available, the communicator implicitly conveys that her message is such an input. The central claim of relevance-theoretic pragmatics is that use of an ostensive stimulus raises expectations of relevance not raised by other inputs, and that these expectations guide the comprehension process. More specifically, we claim:

**Communicative Principle of Relevance:**

*Every act of inferential communication conveys a presumption of its own optimal relevance.*

The presumption of optimal relevance mentioned in the communicative principle has a precise content. The utterance (or other communicative act) is presumed to be relevant enough to be worth processing, from which it follows that it must be more relevant than other inputs competing for the addressee's attention at the time. In some conditions, it can be presumed to be even more relevant than that. Communicator and addressee have at least one common goal: that communication should succeed – that is, that the addressee should understand what the communicator meant. The more relevant the utterance, and in particular the less processing effort it requires, the more likely it is that the addressee will understand it successfully. The communicator can therefore be expected, within the limits of her expressive abilities, and without going against her own goals (and in particular the goal she is pursuing in communicating), to have aimed at maximal relevance. So when we say that every act of inferential communication conveys a presumption of its own optimal relevance, we mean something quite precise: as much relevance as is compatible with the communicator's abilities and preferences, and, in any case, enough relevance to be worth processing.

The communicative principle of relevance suggests both a path for the addressee to follow in constructing the interpretation of an utterance, and a stopping point. Since effort is one of the two factors affecting relevance, the appropriate path to follow is one of least effort. The stopping point is the point at which the current interpretation (what the speaker is taken to have conveyed, either explicitly or implicitly) satisfies the expectations of relevance raised by the utterance itself. From the speaker's point of view, the easiest way to increase the relevance of her communication, and hence the chances of being properly understood, is to express herself (within the limits of her abilities and preferences) so that the interpretation she intends to convey is the first interpretation the addressee will come across on the path of least effort that meets the expectations of relevance she herself has raised.

To illustrate, consider the following exchange:

(7) *Peter*: For Billy's birthday party, it would be nice to have some kind of show.
*Mary*: Archie is a magician. Let's ask him.

Suppose that "magician" is ambiguous for Peter, with two senses: (a) someone with supernatural powers who performs magic, and (b) someone who does magic tricks to amuse an audience. In the context of a discussion about a show for a child's birthday party, the second sense is likely to be activated first, and the information (or the reminder) that their friend Archie is a magician in this sense is likely to satisfy Peter's expectations of relevance by implying that he might perform at Billy's birthday party. In presuming that her utterance would be relevant to Peter, Mary must have expected him to derive this implication, which can therefore be seen as an implicit part of her meaning, that is, an implicature. The disambiguation of "magician" as someone who does magic tricks dovetails with this implicature, and the two confirm one another by jointly yielding an interpretation that is relevant in the expected way.

The linguistic meaning of the sentence "Let's ask him" is very schematic and gappy, leaving the second part of Mary's utterance wide open to an indefinite range of interpretations. "Him" may refer to Archie, or Billy, or someone else. "Ask" may be understood as asking for advice, help, an opinion, a favour, and so on. Thus, the whole sentence might be used to mean *Let's ask Billy whether he would like to have Archie perform magic tricks at his birthday party*. This interpretation would make sense in the situation, and would be quite compatible with Grice's maxims of conversation, or with standard theories of discourse coherence. Still, in a context where the first part of the utterance ("Archie is a magician") implicates that Archie could perform magic tricks at Billy's party, the first interpretation found by following a path of least effort will be that Peter and Mary should ask Archie to perform. Since this would satisfy Peter's expectations of relevance, he should accept it as the intended interpretation, without looking any further for alternative interpretations that might also be relevant. (None of these other potential interpretations could be optimally relevant, because extra processing effort would be required to retrieve them. They are therefore not worth considering unless there is some reason to think that Mary has failed to express herself in an optimally relevant way.)

In this example, Mary is speaking literally (which shows how far even the interpretation of an utterance that is literally understood can go beyond its linguistic meaning and is not just a simple matter of decoding). Our claim is that the very same procedure that yields a literal interpretation in this case would yield a nonliteral interpretation in others.

## Meaning Construction

The decoded senses of a word or other linguistic expression in an utterance provide a point of departure for an inferential process of meaning construction. The meaning constructed may be narrower than the decoded meaning, as in (8) or (9):

(8) I have a temperature.
(9) *Peter*: Does Gérard like eating?
*Mary*: He's French!

In (8), "temperature" would be understood as meaning a temperature above normal.[4] What the speaker is communicating would be false if her temperature were a regular 37°C/98.6°F. In (9), what Mary means is not just that Gérard is a French national but that he is what she regards as a prototypical Frenchman, and therefore someone who likes eating.

On other occasions, the meaning constructed may be broader than the decoded meaning, as in (10)–(14):

(10) Holland is flat.
(11) The stones form a circle.
(12) (*On a picnic, pointing to a flattish rock*): That's a table!
(13) (*Handing someone a tissue*): Here's a Kleenex.
(14) (*Handing someone a paper napkin*): Here's a Kleenex.

The uses of "flat" in (10) and "circle" in (11) are cases of approximation. Approximation is a variety of loose use or broadening in which a word with a relatively strict sense is extended to a penumbra of items (what Lasersohn, 1999, calls a "pragmatic halo") that strictly speaking fall outside its linguistically specified denotation. The uses of "table" in (12) and "Kleenex" in (13) and (14) are cases of category extension. Category extension, another variety of loose use or broadening, involves extending a word with a relatively precise sense to a range of items that clearly fall outside its linguistically specified denotation, but that share some contextually relevant properties with items inside the denotation. Thus, the flat rock referred to in (12) is definitely not a table, but has properties which make it a good substitute for a table on that occasion. The tissue referred to in (13) is not a Kleenex, but will do just as well. The paper napkin referred to in (14) is not even a tissue, but is the closest available thing to a tissue, and will do almost as well.

With narrowing, literalness is in some sense preserved: a high temperature is literally a temperature, and a Frenchman who likes eating is literally a Frenchman. With broadening, literalness is not preserved: Holland is not literally flat, the stones do not literally form a circle, the flattish rock is not literally a table, and neither the tissue nor the paper napkin is literally a Kleenex. However, narrowing and broadening are not two functionally distinct types of language use. They both involve the same process of meaning construction, which happens in some cases to lead to a narrowing of the encoded concept and in other cases to a broadening.

How are these narrowed or broadened lexical meanings arrived at? By following the relevance-guided comprehension procedure outlined above. With (8) ("I have a temperature"), a literal interpretation based on the decoded meaning of "temperature" would be an irrelevant truism, since anyone (or indeed anything) has a temperature, just as it has a mass or a location. In fact, there is no reason to think that the hearer constructs and entertains such a truism. Rather, what happens is that the concept TEMPERATURE is activated in the hearer's mind and points him towards a relevant interpretation. This concept has a parameter that can take a range of values, some of which would be relevant in the circumstances (by implying, for instance, that the speaker is ill and unable to work). In the process of arriving at a relevant overall interpretation of the utterance, the decoded concept TEMPERATURE provides a starting point for constructing a narrowed ad hoc concept TEMPERATURE* which ranges only over contextually relevant temperatures: that is, temperatures which depart from the human norm in a way that is easily brought to mind, with implications that are worth the hearer's processing effort.

Similarly, activation of the lexicalised concept FLAT in (10) ("Holland is flat") gives access to a range of implications that would follow from Holland's being strictly flat: that it is a good place for easy cycling or not a good place for mountaineering, for instance. These implications hold (to different degrees for different implications) even if Holland is only approximately flat. In a context where (10) is relevant, some of these implications will be immediately obvious to the hearer and will fulfil his expectations of relevance. The resulting overall interpretation (including the presumption of relevance and the implications that make the utterance relevant) will be internally consistent on the assumption that "flat" in (10) indicates the speaker's intention to convey that Holland is FLAT*, where the ad hoc concept FLAT* represents an approximation to flatness which is close enough to yield the implications that make the whole utterance contextually relevant (for a detailed discussion of this and related examples, see Wilson & Sperber, 2002).

In these two examples, the words "temperature" or "flat" are used in an utterance to evoke (or, more technically, to activate to some degree) potential implications of the encoded concepts TEMPERATURE or FLAT. More generally, we claim that ideas evoked in comprehension stand in inferential relationships to the concepts that evoke them,[5] and are not mere associations based on past co-occurrence, with no inferential status. That is, the ideas evoked by the presence of a word in an utterance are likely to be true of items in the linguistically specified denotation of the word, or, equivalently, of items in the extension of the concept encoded by the word. In the case of narrowing, the implications hold across only part of the extension of the encoded concept (e.g., only some temperatures imply illness). In the case of broadening, the implications hold not only of items in the extension of the encoded concept but also of contextually salient items which fall outside the extension, but which share with items inside the extension properties that determine these implications (e.g., cycling is easy not only in flat but also in flattish terrains).

Some of the implications evoked by the presence of a word are simultaneously evoked by the context. In (13) and (14) ("Here's a Kleenex," said of a tissue or a paper napkin), the implication *It can be used to blow one's nose* is activated in the hearer's mind not only by the word "Kleenex" but also by the fact that he has just been sneezing. Implications activated by both the utterance and the context are the first to come to mind, and are tentatively added to the interpretation until the hearer's expectations of relevance are satisfied. At that point, the explicit content of the utterance (in the case of an assertion, the propositions whose truth the speaker is committing herself to) is retroactively determined by mutually adjusting the implicit and explicit components of the interpretation. The explicit content of an utterance must be such that it contextually implies the implicit content. More technically, and in relevance-theoretic terms, the explicatures of an utterance must be such that, together with the implicit premises of the utterance, they warrant the derivation of its implicit conclusions (where both implicit premises and implicit conclusions are kinds of implicature). (On the mutual adjustment process, see Carston, 2002; Sperber & Wilson, 1998, 2005; Wilson & Sperber, 2002, 2004.)

In the case of (8) ("I have a temperature"), the result of the mutual adjustment process is a contextual construal of "temperature" as TEMPERATURE*, which is narrower than the lexicalised concept TEMPERATURE. In the case of (10) ("Holland is flat"), the result is a contextual construal of "flat" as FLAT*, which is broader than the lexicalised concept FLAT. Narrowings and broadenings of meaning are thus arrived at by exactly the same procedure of online concept construction and for the same reasons. In fact, as noted by Carston (1997), they may be combined in a single construal. Suppose that Mary in (9) says of Gérard, "He's French!" intending to implicate that he likes eating, when, in fact, she knows that Gérard happens to be a citizen of Monaco. She would then be using neither the concept FRENCH, which denotes French nationals and is encoded (let us assume) by the word "French," nor an appropriate narrowing, FRENCH*, but a concept FRENCH** which is narrower in some respects and broader in others, denoting people who fit some prototype of a French person without French nationality being either a sufficient condition or an absolutely necessary one for inclusion in its extension.

Strictly literal interpretations – those that involve neither narrowing nor broadening of the lexicalised concept – are arrived at by exactly the same process of mutually adjusting explicit content with implicit content. A literal interpretation results when the implications that make the utterance relevant in the expected way depend on the presence in the explicit content of the lexicalised concept itself (rather than some broadening or narrowing of it).[6] Literal interpretations are not default interpretations: they are not the first to be considered, and they are not necessarily easier to construct than nonliteral ones. In fact, some literal interpretations are fairly hard to get, as in (15):

(15) If Holland were flat, water would flow from the borders towards the centre.

In describing a stretch of land as "flat," we broaden the concept by ignoring not only the various types of unevenness present in any terrain, but also the curvature of the earth.[7] This second departure from the literal meaning of "flat" is not so easily corrected.

There is a continuum of cases between approximations such as (10) and (11) and hyperboles. In fact, the same utterance can be properly understood hyperbolically, loosely, or literally, depending on the facts of the matter, with no sharp dividing line between the different interpretations. Consider (16):

(16) *Mary to Peter*: The soup is boiling.

If Peter is too far away to observe the state of the soup directly, how is he to select one of these possible interpretations? On the basis of considerations of relevance, suppose he is upstairs working; when he smells the soup that Mary is making and he says he is coming down to taste it, Mary answers as in (16). Then her utterance would be relevant as a warning not to bother: "boiling" would function as a hyperbole, conveying *too hot to taste*. Or suppose that Peter is making the soup but has left the room, and Mary knows that the soup should not be allowed to boil at this stage. Then her utterance would be relevant enough if the soup were almost boiling: a loose, approximate use rather than a hyperbole. Suppose, finally, that Peter is making the soup but has left the room, and Mary knows that he wanted to skim it once it was properly boiling. Then in order to be relevant enough, her utterance would have to be interpreted literally.

## The Literal–Loose–Metaphorical Continuum

There is a continuum of cases between limited category extensions such as (12)–(14) and more creative ones such as (17) and (18):

(17) Žižek is another Derrida.

(18) For luggage, pink is the new black (*New York Times*, September 4, 2005).

In (17), "Derrida" is used as a common noun to denote a category of flamboyant and obscure philosophers à la Derrida. In (18), "black" is used to denote a category of fashionable colours. In both cases, a category is extended to include items that share with its members some properties which may or may not be essential, but are at least salient. These examples of category extension, unlike the use of "Kleenex" to refer to any tissue, are not analysable as mere loose uses. The claim in (17) is not that the differences between Žižek and Derrida are inconsequential, but that Žižek belongs to a broader category of which Derrida is the most salient member. The claim in (18) is not that pink is pretty much the same as black, but that it occupies, in the category of colours for luggage, the place previously occupied by black. Still, (17) and (18) are interpreted by the usual process: the presence of the words "Derrida" or "black" helps to activate implications about Žižek, on the one hand, and the colour pink, on the other, that make the utterance relevant in the expected way. By mutually adjusting explicit content and implicatures, the explicit content is construed as containing an ad hoc concept (DERRIDA* or BLACK*) that contextually carries these implications.

There is a continuum of cases between hyperbole and metaphor. It might seem at first blush that hyperbole involves only a quantitative difference between the concept encoded and the concept contextually constructed, as in (19) below, while metaphor also involves a qualitative difference, as in (20):[8]

(19) Joan is the kindest person on earth.
(20) Joan is an angel.

However, the quantitative/qualitative distinction is not sharp. For instance, (21) and (22) would generally be classified as hyperboles rather than metaphors, although there is both a quantitative and a qualitative difference between something that is credible and something that is not, or between a saint and an ordinary kind person:

(21) Joan is incredibly kind.
(22) Joan is a saint.

In any case, whether they are classified as hyperboles or metaphors, (21) and (22) would be interpreted in the same way: the encoded concept helps to activate contextual implications that make the utterance relevant as expected, and the concept conveyed by the hyperbole/metaphor is one of an outstanding type of kindness characterised by these implications.

There is also a continuum of cases between category extension and metaphor. It might be argued that category extension involves the projection of defining, or at least characteristic, properties of the encoded concept onto a broader category, as in (12)–(14) and (17) and (18), whereas the type of broadening involved in metaphor is based on relatively peripheral or, at least, contingent properties, as in (23) or (24):

(23) "Man is but a reed, the weakest in nature." (Blaise Pascal)
(24) My mind is cloudy.

Weakness is not a defining property of reeds (and it is only a property relative to some arbitrary comparison class); similarly, the difficulty of discerning parts is not a defining property of clouds.

However, some metaphors are based on fairly central properties of the lexicalised category. For instance, when the term for an animal body part is extended to a human body part, as in (25), the result would generally be classified as a metaphor:

(25) Henry was proud of his mane.

A category may undergo successive broadenings, with more peripheral extensions necessarily losing some of the most central features of the lexicalised category. Thus, compare (17) ("Žižek is another Derrida") with (26) and (27):

(26) Rebecca Horn is the Derrida of contemporary art.
(27) "Ferran Adria is more Derrida than Danko." (attested: http://www.egullet.org/tdg.cgi?pg=ARTICLE-tabledancingadria – Adria is the world famous chef of El Bulli, Danko is a famous San Francisco chef)

In each case, a different concept (DERRIDA*, DERRIDA**, DERRIDA***) is constructed, each marginally further away from the original concept (if we accept that there are concepts of individuals) or representation of Jacques Derrida.

Central and peripheral properties may combine, as in (28), a comment on a clip of George W. Bush allegedly wiping his glasses on an unsuspecting woman's shirt during an appearance on Jay Leno's TV show:

(28) We're all human Kleenex to him (attested: http://www.iflipflop.com/2004/10/metaphor-george-bush-uses-woman-as.html).

Here, the woman is implicitly described as a Kleenex, since she (or at least her clothes) can be used as one, and this carries the suggestion that Bush sees people as disposable artefacts with little value.

Most hyperboles involve only broadening of the encoded concept, with no narrowing. In (19), for instance, "the kindest

**Table 5.1: Inferential steps in a literal interpretation**

| | |
|---|---|
| (a) Mary has said to Peter "Archie is a magician." | *Decoding of Mary's utterance.* |
| (b) Mary's utterance is optimally relevant to Peter. | *Expectation raised by the recognition of Mary's utterance as a communicative act.* |
| (c) Mary's utterance will achieve relevance by addressing Peter's suggestion that they have a show for Billy's birthday party. | *Expectation raised by (b), given that Mary is responding to Peter's suggestion.* |
| (d) Magicians (in one lexicalised sense of the term, $\text{MAGICIAN}_2$) put on magic shows that children enjoy. | *Assumption activated both by use of the word "magician" and by Peter's wish to have a show for Billy's birthday party. Tentatively accepted as an implicit premise of Mary's utterance.* |
| (e) Archie could put on a magic show for Billy's birthday party. | *Implicit conclusion derivable from (d), together with an appropriate interpretation of Mary's utterance, which would make her utterance relevant-as-expected. Tentatively accepted as an implicit conclusion of the utterance.* |
| (f) Archie is a $\text{MAGICIAN}_2$. | *Interpretation of the explicit content of Mary's utterance as decoded in (a) which, together with (d), would imply (e). Interpretation accepted as Mary's explicit meaning.* |
| (g) Archie is a $\text{MAGICIAN}_2$ who could put on a magic show for Billy's birthday party that the children would enjoy. | *First overall interpretation of Mary's utterance (explicit content plus implicatures) to occur to Peter which would satisfy the expectation of relevance in (b). Accepted as Mary's meaning.* |

person on earth" (despite its singular form) is broadened to cover all very kind people, including Joan. By contrast, most metaphors involve both narrowing and broadening, and so cannot be seen simply as cases of category extension. In the metaphorical (20), "angel" is interpreted as ANGEL*, which is narrowed, on the one hand, to cover only prototypical kind, caring angels (excluding avenging angels, angels of wrath, or fallen angels) and broadened, on the other, to cover all very kind, caring people. However, this combination of narrowing and broadening is not a defining feature of metaphor. In the metaphorical (28), for instance, "Kleenex" is broadened to something like the category of DISPOSABLE ITEMS, and this includes not only prototypical Kleenex but all Kleenex.

## Inferential Steps

We see this continuity of cases, and the absence of any criterion for distinguishing literal, loose, and metaphorical utterances, as evidence not just that there is some degree of fuzziness or overlap among distinct categories, but that there are no genuinely distinct categories, at least from a descriptive, psycholinguistic, or pragmatic point of view.[9] Even more important than the lack of clear boundaries is the fact that the same inferential procedure is used in interpreting all these different types of utterance. Let us look in more detail at how this procedure applies to the interpretation of two examples, one at the literal end of the continuum, and the other at the metaphorical end.

At the literal end, we return to example (7):

(7) *Peter:* For Billy's birthday party, it would be nice to have some kind of show.
*Mary*: Archie is a magician. Let's ask him.

Table 5.1 shows the inferential steps that Peter goes through in interpreting the first part of Mary's utterance ("Archie is a

**Table 5.2: Inferential steps in a metaphorical interpretation**

| | |
|---|---|
| (a) Mary has said to Peter "My chiropractor is a magician." | *Decoding of Mary's utterance.* |
| (b) Mary's utterance is optimally relevant to Peter. | *Expectation raised by the recognition of Mary's utterance as a communicative act.* |
| (c) Mary's utterance will achieve relevance by addressing Peter's expressed concern about his back pain. | *Expectation raised by (b), given that Mary is responding to Peter's complaint.* |
| (d) Chiropractors are in the business of healing back pain. | *Assumption activated both by use of the word "chiropractor" and by Peter's worry about his back pain. Tentatively accepted as an implicit premise of Mary's utterance.* |
| (e) Magicians (in one lexicalised sense of the term, MAGICIAN$_1$) can achieve extraordinary things. | *Assumption activated both by the use of the word "magician" and by Peter's worry that no ordinary treatments work for him. Tentatively accepted as an implicit premise of Mary's utterance.* |
| (f) Mary's chiropractor, being in the business of healing back pain and able to achieve extraordinary things, would be able to help Peter better than others. | *Implicit conclusion derivable from (d) and (e), together with an appropriate interpretation of Mary's utterance, which would make her utterance relevant-as-expected. Tentatively accepted as an implicit conclusion of the utterance.* |
| (g) Mary's chiropractor is a MAGICIAN* (where MAGICIAN* is a meaning suggested by the use of the word "magician" in the sense of MAGICIAN$_1$ and enabling the derivation of (e)). | *Interpretation of the explicit content of Mary's utterance as decoded in (a) which, together with (d) and (e), would imply (f). Interpretation accepted as Mary's explicit meaning.* |
| (h) Mary's chiropractor is a MAGICIAN*, who would be able to help Peter better than others by achieving extraordinary things. | *First overall interpretation of Mary's utterance (explicit content plus implicatures) to occur to Peter which would satisfy the expectation of relevance in (b). Accepted as Mary's meaning.* |

magician"), with Peter's interpretive hypotheses on the left, and his basis for arriving at them on the right.

At the metaphorical end of the continuum, consider (29):

(29) *Peter*: I've had this bad back for a while now, but nobody has been able to help.
*Mary*: My chiropractor is a magician. You should go and see her.

Table 5.2 shows, again in simplified form, the inferential steps that Peter goes through in interpreting the first part of Mary's utterance ("My chiropractor is a magician").

In both cases, of course, interpretation is carried out "on line," and starts while the utterance is still in progress. We assume, then, that interpretive hypotheses about explicit content and implicatures are developed partly in parallel rather than in sequence, and stabilise when they are mutually adjusted so as to jointly confirm the hearer's expectations of relevance. And we are not, of course, suggesting that the hearer consciously goes through just the steps shown in the tables, with exactly those premises and conclusions. We are not making claims about exact sequences, consciousness, or the representational format of thought. We are making claims about factors which cause hearers to converge on an interpretation that – in the case where communication is successful – coincides with the one intended by the speaker.

Although "magician" is interpreted literally in (7) and metaphorically in (29), the same kind of process is involved in both cases. With (7), the fact that one of the lexicalised senses of "magician" is MAGICIAN$_2$, *someone who performs magic tricks to amuse an audience*, makes it particularly easy to access implications associated to this interpretation. Since these implications end up satisfying the hearer's expectations of relevance and are carried only by this precise meaning, one of the lexicalised senses of "magician" is selected by the comprehension process as the contextually indicated meaning. With (29), "magician" provides easy access to the information that if someone is a magician, they have extraordinary capacities, and this is enough to ground an optimally relevant overall interpretation. The concept used in this interpretation is substantially broader than MAGICIAN$_1$, so in this case, as a rhetorician would say, "magician" is a metaphor. However, the hearer pays no more attention to the fact that "magician" is used metaphorically in (29) than he does to the fact that it is used literally in (7).

For that matter, some people may have only a single encoded sense for "magician": *someone with supernatural powers who performs magic*. They would still have no difficulty arriving at an appropriate interpretation of (7) by extending the category of "real" magicians to include make-believe ones. For other people, the metaphorical sense may have become lexicalised, so that "magician" now has the additional encoded sense *someone who achieves extraordinary things*. They would obviously have no trouble arriving at an appropriate interpretation of (29). Mary did not intend her utterance to be understood literally in (7) and metaphorically in (29); her communicative intentions – like those of all speakers – are about content and propositional attitude, not rhetorical classification.

Relevance theory's resolutely inferential approach to comprehension suggests a solution to the "emergent property" issue raised in recent work on metaphor.[10] Consider (30):

(30) This surgeon is a butcher.

Clearly, what this utterance evokes is the idea that the surgeon in question is grossly incompetent, dangerous, and so on. The problem, at least for theories of metaphor based on associations or "connotations", is that being incompetent, dangerous, and so on are not properties particularly associated with either butchers or surgeons, so how do these properties emerge when the two categories are associated as in (30)?

If we treat the relationship between an utterance and its interpretation as inferential, then the issue is whether the properties that seem to "emerge" in the metaphorical interpretation can in fact be inferred. It should be obvious that the answer is "yes." Surgeons and butchers both characteristically cut flesh, but in quite different ways. Surgeons cut live flesh; they cut as little as possible, and with the utmost care to avoid unnecessarily severing blood vessels, nerves, or tendons, thus causing irreparable damage. Butchers cut dead flesh to produce pieces of meat for cooking; this places no principled restriction on how much should be cut (or minced, broken, pounded, etc.) and puts a premium on severing nerves, tendons, and other hard tissues. So a surgeon who treats flesh as a butcher does would indeed be grossly incompetent and dangerous. The inferential path to an adequate understanding of (30) involves an evocation of the way butchers treat flesh and the construction on that basis of an ad hoc concept BUTCHER*, denoting people who treat flesh in the way butchers do. Practically all butchers and (one hopes) very few surgeons fall within the extension of this concept. For a butcher, being a BUTCHER* is a quasi-pleonastic property. For a surgeon, on the other hand, it does imply gross incompetence – such an inconceivable degree of incompetence, in fact, that (30) must be seen not just as a metaphor but also as a hyperbole.

A meat lover who cares about precise, careful cuts might praise a butcher by saying:

(31) This butcher is a surgeon.

The interpretation of (31) is symmetrical with the one sketched above for (30), and involves the construction of an ad hoc concept SURGEON*, denoting people who cut flesh with extreme care. A butcher who is also a SURGEON* is outstandingly competent and trustworthy. The predicates BUTCHER* and SURGEON*, along with the implication of incompetence for a surgeon who is a BUTCHER* and of competence for a butcher who is a SURGEON*, emerge unproblematically in the course of an inferential comprehension process guided by the search for relevance.

Of course, examples (30) and (31) involve emergent properties that are particularly easy to analyse in inferential terms, and it remains to be seen how far the full range of cases can be dealt with along these lines. However, this account seems promising, and helps to bring out the contrast between inferential approaches to metaphor and more traditional associationist approaches. All inferential relationships are associations, but not all associations are inferential. In claiming that interpretation depends only on inferential relationships, we might have seemed to be depriving ourselves of some explanatory power. As this example suggests, just the opposite is true.[11]

## Strength of Contextual Implications, Strength of Implicatures

We maintain that metaphors are not a distinct category of language use, let alone a discrete one. Are we then denying the obvious truth that metaphors often stand out as particularly creative and powerful uses of language? If not – and indeed we are not – how are these uses of language to be explained?

Utterances achieve relevance by producing cognitive effects. An utterance may have many cognitive effects or only a few, and these effects may be stronger or weaker. To illustrate, suppose you get to the airport in time for a flight due to arrive in Atlanta at 2 p.m. Hearing an announcement that the flight may be delayed, you say to an airline employee:

(32) I have to be in Atlanta no later than 5 p.m. Will I make it?

She replies as in either (33) or (34):

(33) Well, your flight will be delayed by at least 20 minutes.

(34) Well, your flight will be delayed by at least 2 hours.

Both (33) and (34) imply (35), but only (34) implies (36):

(35) You have at least 20 minutes to do as you please before boarding.

(36) You have at least 2 hours to do as you please before boarding.

(35) in turn implies (37), while (36) implies both (37) and (38):

(37) You have time for a drink before boarding.

(38) You have time for a meal before boarding.

Clearly, (34) has more contextual implications than (33).

Both (33) and (34) also provide some evidence for the conclusion in (39):

(39) You will get to Atlanta later than 5 p.m.

Another way of putting this is to say that (33) and (34) weakly imply (39). Such weak implications (or probabilifications) are also cognitive effects, and contribute to the relevance of a cognitive input.[12] Since the probability of your arriving late is increased more by (34) than by (33), (39) is a stronger implication (and hence a stronger cognitive effect) of (34) than of (33). Still, if you were to assume on the basis of either utterance that you will indeed get to Atlanta later than 5 p.m., this assumption would depend to a considerable extent on your own background beliefs (even more so in the case of (33) than (34)), although it would of course have been encouraged by what the airline employee told you. Overall, this example shows how the contextual implications of an utterance may vary in both quantity and strength.

A competent speaker must have good reason to suppose that what she says will be relevant to the hearer. The hearer himself may have given her such a reason, in particular by asking her a question, thereby letting her know that an answer would be relevant to him. Thus, if a stranger comes up to you in the street and asks what time it is, you can feel confident that it would be relevant to tell him the time, even if you neither know nor care exactly how it would be relevant and are implicating nothing more the presumption of relevance that any utterance conveys about itself.[13]

In most conversations or discourses, the speaker cannot have good reason to think that her utterances will be relevant enough unless she has some positive idea of the cognitive effects they will achieve. From the hearer's perspective, it is quite often safe to assume that the speaker both expected and intended him to derive some of the implications that he does derive, for otherwise she could not reasonably have supposed that her utterance would be optimally relevant to him. These intended implications are implicatures of the utterance. An implicature may be more or less strongly implicated. The speaker may have in mind a specific implication on which the relevance of her utterance depends, and a strong intention that the hearer should derive it; in that case, it is strongly implicated. At the other extreme, she may have in mind a vague range of possible implications with roughly similar import, any subset of which would contribute to the relevance of her utterance, and a weak intention, for any of the implications in that range, that the hearer should derive it; these are weak implicatures. Her intentions about the implicatures of her utterance may fall anywhere between these two extremes. The strength of an implicature is determined by the manifest strength of the speaker's intention that a specific implication should be derived. It is important to distinguish the strength of an implicature from the strength of a contextual implication (whether or not it is also implicated), which is the probability that it is true, given that the premise from which it is contextually derived is true.

When the airline employee replies to your question in (32) (about whether you will get to Atlanta by 5 p.m.) as in (33) or (34), she must feel confident that, in telling you how long the delay is likely to be, she is giving you grounds for deriving a weak implication about the risk of your arriving late, thus indirectly answering your question. In other words, you can take her to be implicating that you might indeed be late, leaving it up to you to decide on the seriousness of the risk. The implication is weak – even weaker with (33) than with (34) – but it is fairly strongly implicated.

Does the airline employee also implicate (35) or (36) (that you have at least 20 minutes / 2 hours to do as you please before boarding)? Although these implications go beyond simply providing an answer to your question, they may help to make the utterance optimally relevant to you in a way the speaker might have both foreseen and intended. When a plane is delayed, people generally want to figure out how much time they will have at their disposal before boarding. To that extent, the airline employee may be seen as implicating (35) or (36). These are strong implications of her utterance – they are very probably true – but they are only weakly implicated, because they add only marginally to the relevance of the utterance, and so the speaker's intention to convey them is not strongly manifest. After all, she may have felt that her utterance was relevant enough without even considering these further implications.

What about (37) (that you have time for a drink), or (38) (that you have time for a meal)? Does the airline employee also implicate these by replying as in (33) or (34)? Again, they are strong implications, which might contribute to the relevance of her utterance in a way the speaker could possibly have foreseen, but they are even weaker implicatures, since they are among a range of implications with similar import (that you have enough time to buy a magazine, or buy and read one, that you have enough time to do your e-mail, and so on), some of which are likely to be relevant to you although the speaker is not in a position to know which. So she may be encouraging you to consider any of these implications that might be relevant to you, but not any specific one. These are very weak implicatures, if they are implicated at all. By contrast, if your question had been "Do I have time for a drink?" the reply in (33) would strongly implicate (37), and the reply in (34) would strongly implicate (37) and weakly implicate (38), whereas both replies would only weakly implicate (39) (that you will get to Atlanta later than 5 p.m.), if they implicated it at all.

## Poetic Effects

Optimal relevance may be achieved by an utterance with a few strong implications, many weak implications, or any combination of weak and strong implications. A speaker aiming at relevance may implicate (that is, anticipate and intend) a few strong implicatures or a wide range of weak implicatures (which may themselves be strong or weak implications). There are many ways of achieving relevance, which differ in both the strength of the implications conveyed and the strength with which they are implicated.[14] Here we are particularly concerned with the case where relevance is achieved through a wide array of weak implications which are themselves weakly implicated. The speaker – or writer, since this method of achieving relevance is particularly well developed in literature – has good reason to suppose that enough of a wide array of potential implications with similar import are true or probably true, although she does not know which these are (hence, they are weak implications) and is neither able to anticipate nor particularly concerned about which of them will be considered and accepted by the audience (hence, they are weakly implicated). We have argued that the cognitive effects achieved by conveying such a wide range of weak implicatures are identifiable as poetic effects (Sperber & Wilson, 1995, chap. 4, section 6; Pilkington, 2000).

The production of genuinely relevant poetic effects can be a powerfully creative form of language use (creative on the part of both communicator and audience). Effects of this type can be created by literal, loose, or metaphorical forms of expression. Thus, classical Japanese haikus, which are among the most effective forms of poetry in world literature, typically involve a literal use of language. Consider Bashō's famous haiku (written in 1680):

> On a leafless bough
> A crow is perched –
> The autumn dusk.
> (Translated by Joan Giroux, 1974)

This simple, literal description weakly implicates a wide array of implications which combine to depict a landscape, a season, a moment of the day, a mood, and so on, thereby achieving a powerful overall effect which varies to some extent from reader to reader.

By contrast, many metaphors are not particularly poetic. We are thinking here not so much of conventional metaphors which may have lost their poetic appeal, if they ever had one (was the phrase "legs of a table" ever poetic?) as of less conventional but not particularly creative metaphors used to highlight a simple idea rather than suggest a complex one. Consider (40), a political comment on the Bush administration's handling of the 2005 Katrina hurricane, compared to its handling of the 2001 terrorist attack on the United States:

(40) Well, if 9/11 is one bookend of the Bush administration, Katrina may be the other. If 9/11 put the wind at President Bush's back, Katrina's put the wind in his face. If the Bush-Cheney team seemed to be the right guys to deal with Osama, they seem exactly the wrong guys to deal with Katrina (Thomas Friedman, *New York Times*, September 7, 2005)

Here, the use of the metaphors "bookend" and "wind" to suggest opposing forces at two ends of a continuum (a case of force dynamics à la Talmy) is so flat that most readers are likely to bypass the obvious relationship between the wind and an explosion, on the one hand, and still more obviously, between the wind and a hurricane, on the other: the cognitive effects derivable from this relationship are unlikely to have been intended, and are hardly worth the effort.

Nonetheless, these metaphors serve to make the author's point, which is definitely not of a poetic nature.

Although metaphors are neither necessary nor sufficient for the creation of genuine poetic effects, they are particularly well suited to this purpose, for several reasons. Consider, first, a trivial case of metaphor such as (41):

(41) *Woman to uncouth suitor*: Keep your paws off me!

Here, "your paws" refers unproblematically to the hearer's hands. Use of the word "paws" also activates related notions, conceptions, and images having to do with animal paws, clumsiness, bestiality, and so on. From a relevance theory perspective, the fact that these ideas have been activated suggests that they may be relevant, and the effort spent in activating them, however marginal, suggests that they *should* be relevant (otherwise, the effort would have been wasted, contrary to the presumption of optimal relevance). While there is a wide range of possible implicatures which might contribute to the relevance of the utterance (that the addressee is clumsy, gross, lusting like a beast, and so on), none of them is strongly implicated by the speaker. We claim that they are weakly implicated: the hearer is indeed encouraged to consider at least some of them and see them as part of the speaker's meaning. It is these vague effects that make the use of "paws" marginally more relevant than the use of "hands."

According to classical rhetoric, the literal meaning of the word "paw" is replaced in (41) by the figurative meaning HAND. In more recent approaches based on category extension, the literal meaning of "paw" is extended to include any EXTREMITY OF A LIMB (whether animal or human). In both analyses – substitution of a figurative meaning disjoint from the literal one, or inclusion of the linguistically specified denotation in a broader "figurative" denotation – suggestions of clumsiness and bestiality are added to the figurative meaning as "connotations" of the word "paw." Here, "connotations" are associations in a strictly associationist sense: they are grounded in past co-occurrence and can go in any direction.

In fact, the word "paw" has many associations other than clumsiness and bestiality which might be activated in a metaphor, from the softness of a cat's paw to the strength of a lion's. Association of the type appealed to in associationist psychology is a process which is too vague, on the one hand, and too powerful, on the other, to account for the subtlety and directionality of weak implicatures. As noted above, we would rather appeal only to associations based on properly inferential relationships and, more generally, stick to an inferential rather than associationist account of comprehension. In (41), the alleged connotations are associated to the literal meaning of "paw" (i.e., PAW), and not to its figurative meaning HAND or EXTREMITY OF A LIMB. From an inferential point of view, the idea that the literal meaning of "paw" is discarded while its connotations remain is even more puzzling than the smile of the Cheshire cat: the cat's smile lingers at an empty location, whereas the connotations of the literal meaning of "paw" are supposed to adorn the figurative meaning that has replaced it.

The alternative analysis we favour is the one we have been defending throughout this chapter. In processing (41), the hearer develops (in parallel) tentative interpretations of the explicit and implicit components of the speaker's meaning, and stops when they fit together in the sense that the explicit content contextually implies the implicated conclusions, and the explicit content and implicit content jointly satisfy the hearer's expectations of relevance. Given that the relationship between explicit content and implicit content is properly inferential, and given the nature of the mutual adjustment process used to determine these contents, the implications evoked by the decoded senses of the words used in the utterance must be genuine implications: that is, they must hold at least part of the extension of the decoded senses. The ad hoc concepts constructed to carry these implications will then at least overlap with the concepts encoded by the utterance (otherwise, we would be dealing with purely associationist rather than inferential relations). Since the concepts PAW and HAND have disjoint extensions, we claim that "paw" in (41) could not be used to convey the meaning HAND. Nor can it be used to convey EXTREMITY OF A LIMB, since this broadened concept is not specific enough to contextually imply clumsiness, bestiality, and so on.

We assume that the ad hoc concepts built on the basis of most metaphorical terms are genuinely ad hoc: that is, they are adjusted to the precise circumstances of their use and are therefore unlikely to be paraphrasable by an ordinary language expression. This is why we resort to the "*" notation, and represent the concept pragmatically conveyed by "paw" in (41) as PAW*. PAW* is the most easily constructed concept whose extension includes the hearer's hands, and which carries the weak contextual implications generally true of prototypical paws: that they are used clumsily, grossly, and so on. These weak implications are themselves weakly implicated: that is, they are weakly intended by the speaker. The utterance on this interpretation achieves optimal relevance by making a strong explicit request that the hearer remove his PAWS* and weakly implicating that he is behaving clumsily and grossly. PAW*, so construed, involves both a broadening and a narrowing of PAW, as do most ad hoc meanings conveyed by metaphorical uses.

So even a common metaphor such as "Keep your paws off me!" achieves some of its relevance through an array of weak implicatures: a poetic touch, however modest. In more creative metaphors, relevance may depend to a much greater extent (or even entirely) on such weak implicatures, in a way that makes it quite appropriate to talk of "poetic effects." Consider the full version of Carl Sandburg's poem "Fog," whose first two lines are one of the most widely quoted examples of creative metaphor:

The fog comes
on little cat feet.

It sits looking
over harbor and city
on silent haunches
and then moves on.

"On little cat feet" evokes an array of implications having to do with silence, smoothness, stealth. Taken together with the following four lines, the phrase evokes a movement which appears both arbitrary and yet composed, so that it is tempting to see it not as random but rather as guided by mysterious dispositions. Poems are read and re-read. On a second reading, the interpretation of the whole poem provides part of the context in which the first two lines are understood. Not unlike Bashō's literal haiku, Sandburg's extended metaphor weakly implicates an ever-widening array of implications which combine to depict a place, an atmosphere, a mood, achieving a powerful overall effect that varies from reader to reader and reading to reading. It is not part of the explicit content of the poem that the fog comes silently, or smoothly, or stealthily. Rather, what is part of the explicit content is that the fog comes ON-LITTLE-CAT-FEET*. And what is this concept? It is the concept of a property that is difficult or impossible to define, a property possessed in particular by some typical movements of cats (though not all of them – little cat feet can also move in violent or playful ways) and, according to the poem, by the movement of fog. How is this ad hoc concept ON-LITTLE-CAT-FEET* arrived at? By taking the poet to be attributing to the coming of the fog that property which contextually implies the very ideas suggested by the phrase "little cat feet."

The example of Sandburg's poem should help to clarify how and why metaphors are indeed particularly likely to achieve optimal relevance through the creation of poetic effects: the effort required for ad hoc concept construction calls for matching effects, and given the freedom left to the interpreter in the construction process, these effects are unlikely to consist in just a few strongly implicated strong implications. It is not that concept construction systematically demands more effort in the case of metaphors (see Gibbs 1994a; Noveck, Bianco, & Castry, 2001). Many metaphors are very easy to process, while, as any science student knows, arriving at an adequate literal understanding of a statement may take much more effort than a loose or even a metaphorical construal. Nor is it that literal expression is intrinsically less capable than metaphor of achieving poetic effects, as the comparison between Bashō's haiku and Sandburg's haiku-like poem shows. It is just that, on the whole, the closer one gets to the metaphor end of the literal/loose/metaphorical continuum, the greater the freedom of interpretation left to hearers or readers, and the more likely it is that relevance will be achieved through a wide array of weak implicatures: that is, through poetic effects. So when you compare metaphors to other uses of words, you find a bit more of this and a bit less of that, but nothing deserving of a special theory, let alone a grand one.

## Notes

1 See, for instance, Lakoff and Johnson (1980); Lakoff (1987, 1994); Lakoff and Turner (1989); Talmy (2000); Fauconnier (1997); Fauconnier and Turner (2002); Glucksberg (2001); Kintsch (2000); Sperber and Wilson (1985/1986, 1995); Carston (1997, 2002); Wilson and Sperber (2002).

2 See Gibbs (1994a, 1994b, 1998) and also his debate with Gregory Murphy (Gibbs, 1996; Murphy, 1996, 1997).

3 Some authors (e.g. David Lewis, 1975) believe that figurative meanings are linguistically encoded rather than pragmatically inferred; however, this vastly increases both the ambiguity of language and its gross defectiveness as a code.

4 For many (perhaps most) speakers of English today, "temperature" may be ambiguous between a general sense and a narrower one equivalent to *fever*. For these speakers, "temperature" in (8) would have to be disambiguated rather than narrowed. Historically, however, this narrower linguistic meaning will have been lexicalised as a result of repeated pragmatic narrowings of a single general meaning. In this case, and in others where a narrowed or broadened meaning of a term may have undergone lexicalisation, we are discussing how it would be interpreted in dialects where it has not yet become lexicalised. In fact, far from being an objection to a pragmatic account, the frequent occurrence of lexicalised narrowings and broadenings of lexical meanings calls for a pragmatic account as a crucial component of historical lexicology.

5 Strictly speaking, only propositions have implications. When we talk (as we will) of a concept's having implications, we have in mind the implications that propositions carry in virtue of having this concept as a constituent.

6 On the notion of a literal interpretation, see Sperber and Wilson (1995, chap. 4, sections 6 and 7). On this account, when a metaphorical use becomes lexicalised, an interpretation that requires the presence of exactly this concept in the explicit content will be strictly literal.

7 It might be argued that a stretch of land is flat in a second, lexicalised sense if every point on its surface is at the same distance from the centre of the earth (rather than being on a plane), so that someone can travel across it without going upwards or downwards. A problem for this view is that the statement "If all the land on earth were at sea level, the earth would be flat" should then be true on one reading, whereas in fact it seems simply false.

8 This intuition underlies many classical rhetorical treatments and also appears to motivate Grice's account (Grice, 1989, p. 34).

9 The distinction between literal and nonliteral utterances may be relevant to normative concerns, as in law, for instance (see Wilson & Sperber, 2002, section 7).

10 See, for instance, Martinich (1984); Tourangeau and Rips (1991); Becker (1997); Gineste, Indurkhya, and Scart (2000); Carston (2002); Vega Moreno (2004, 2007); Wilson and Carston (2006).

11 For an interesting proposal to account for emergent properties by augmenting the relevance-theoretic account with the machinery of domain mappings, see Gibbs and Tendahl (2006). The relations between "domain mapping" accounts of metaphor and fully inferential accounts deserve fuller exploration than we can give them here. For now, we simply note that if emergent properties can be derived using only the independently motivated inferential mechanisms outlined above, then domain mappings may be best

seen as a result of, rather than a prerequisite to, metaphor interpretation, and as contributing to the interpretation process on the effort side, by altering the accessibility of contextual assumptions and implications, rather than playing the central role assigned to them in most cognitive linguistic accounts (see Wilson & Carston, 2006).

12 In fact, most contextual implications are typically made probable rather than certain by a premise that contextually implies them, since the implication is contingent on the truth of other contextual premises that are generally less than certain. Implying some conclusion with certainty may be seen as a limiting case of strongest possible contextual implication (see Sperber & Wilson, 1995, chap. 2).

13 Actually, even in this case, you would have to estimate how precise your answer should be in order to be optimally relevant: could you spare your hearer some processing effort without any loss on the effect side by rounding the time to the nearest multiple of five minutes, or would it be preferable in the circumstances to be accurate to the minute? And from the hearer's perspective, would it be better in the circumstances to take an answer such as "It's ten past five" as an approximation or as accurate to the minute? In most ordinary situations, mutual adjustment of the explicit content and the implicit presumption of relevance will yield an interpretation in which the response is understood as rounded (see van der Henst, Carles, & Sperber, 2002).

14 Incidentally, we believe that pragmatic approaches that idealise away differences in the strength of implicatures (as most do) are ignoring a central aspect of language use.

## References


Becker, A. (1997). Emergent and common features influence metaphor interpretation. *Metaphor and Symbol*, 12, 243–259.

Carston, R. (1997). Enrichment and loosening: Complementary processes in deriving the proposition expressed? *Linguistische Berichte*, 8, 103–127.

Carston, R. (2002). *Thoughts and utterances: The pragmatics of explicit communication*. Oxford: Blackwell.

Fauconnier, G. (1997). *Mapping in thought and language*. New York: Cambridge University Press.

Fauconnier, G., & Turner, M. (2002). *The way we think: Conceptual blending and the mind's hidden complexities*. New York: Basic Books.

Gibbs, R. (1994a). *The poetics of mind: Figurative thought, language and understanding*. Cambridge: Cambridge University Press.

Gibbs, R. (1994b). Figurative thought and figurative language. In M. A. Gernsbacher (Ed.), *Handbook of psycholinguistics* (pp. 411–446). San Diego, CA: Academic Press.

Gibbs, R. (1996). Why many concepts are metaphorical. *Cognition*, 61, 309–319.

Gibbs, R. (1998). The fight over metaphor in thought and language. In N. Katz, C. Cacciari, R. Gibbs, & M. Turner (Eds.), *Figurative language and thought* (pp. 88–118). New York: Oxford University Press.

Gibbs, R., & Tendahl, M. (2006). Cognitive effort and effects in metaphor comprehension: Relevance theory and psycholinguistics. *Mind and Language*, 21, 379–403.

Gineste, M.-D., Indurkhya, B., & Scart, V. (2000). Emergence of features in metaphor comprehension. *Metaphor and Symbol*, 15, 117–135.

Glucksberg, S. (2001). *Understanding figurative language*. Oxford: Oxford University Press.

Glucksberg, S., Manfredi, D., & McGlone, M. (1997). Metaphor comprehension: How metaphors create new categories. In T. Ward, S. Smith & J. Vald (Eds.), *Creative thought: An investigation of conceptual structures and processes* (pp. 327–350). Washington, DC: American Psychological Association.

Grice, H. P. (1989). *Studies in the way of words*. Cambridge, MA: Harvard University Press.

Kintsch, W. (2000). Metaphor comprehension: A computational theory. *Psychonomic Bulletin & Review*, 7, 257–266.

Lakoff, G. (1987). *Women, fire, and dangerous things*. Chicago: University of Chicago Press.

Lakoff, G. (1994). Conceptual metaphor home page. http://cogsci.berkeley.edu/lakoff/MetaphorHome.html.

Lakoff, G., & Johnson, M. (1980). *Metaphors we live by*. Chicago: University of Chicago Press. (New edition with Afterword, 2003)

Lakoff, G., & Turner, M. (1989). *More than cool reason: A field guide to poetic metaphors*. Chicago: University of Chicago Press.

Lasersohn, P. (1999). Pragmatic halos. *Language*, 75, 522–551.

Lewis, D. (1983). Languages and language. In D. Lewis (Ed.), *Philosophical papers* (Vol. 1, pp. 163–188). Oxford: Oxford University Press. (Original work published in *Minnesota studies in the philosophy of science*, Vol. 7, by K. Gunderson, Ed., 1975, Minnesota: University of Minnesota Press)

Martinich, A. P. (1984). A theory for metaphor. *Journal of Literary Semantics, 13*, 35–56. (Reprinted in *Pragmatics: A Reader*, pp. 507–518, by S. Davis, Ed., 1991. Oxford: Oxford University Press)

Murphy, G. (1996). On metaphoric representation. *Cognition, 60*, 173–204.

Murphy, G. (1997). Reasons to doubt the present evidence for metaphoric representation. *Cognition, 62*, 99–108.

Noveck, I., Bianco, M., & Castry, A. (2001). The costs and benefits of metaphor. *Metaphor and Symbol, 16*, 109–121.

Pilkington, A. (2000). *Poetic effects: A relevance theory perspective*. Amsterdam: John Benjamins.

Sperber, D., & Wilson, D. (1995). *Relevance: Communication and cognition* (2nd ed.). Oxford: Blackwell.

Sperber, D., & Wilson, D. (1998). The mapping between the mental and the public lexicon. In P. Carruthers & J. Boucher (Eds.), *Thought and language* (pp. 184–200). Cambridge: Cambridge University Press.

Sperber, D., & Wilson, D. (2005). Pragmatics. In F. Jackson & M. Smith (Eds.), *Oxford handbook of contemporary analytic philosophy* (pp. 468–501). Oxford: Oxford University Press.

Talmy, L. (2000). *Toward a cognitive semantics* (2 vols.). Cambridge, MA: MIT Press.

Tourangeau, R., & Rips, L. (1991). Interpreting and evaluating metaphors. *Journal of Memory and Language, 30*, 452–472.

van der Henst, J.-B., Carles, L., & Sperber, D. (2002). Truthfulness and relevance in telling the time. *Mind & Language, 17*, 457–466.

van der Henst, J.-B., & Sperber, D. (2004). Testing the cognitive and communicative principles of relevance. In I. Noveck & D. Sperber (Eds.), *Experimental pragmatics* (pp. 141–171). London: Palgrave Macmillan.

Vega Moreno, R. (2004). Metaphor interpretation and emergence. *UCL Working Papers in Linguistics, 16*, 197–322.

Vega Moreno, R. (2007). *Creativity and convention: The pragmatics of everyday figurative speech*. Amsterdam: Benjamins.

Wilson, D., & Carston, R. (2006). Metaphor, relevance and the "emergent property" issue. *Mind & Language, 21*, 404–433.

Wilson, D., & Sperber, D. (2002). Truthfulness and relevance. *Mind, 111*, 583–632.

Wilson, D., & Sperber, D. (2004). Relevance theory. In L. Horn & G. Ward (Eds.), *The handbook of pragmatics* (pp. 607–632). Oxford: Blackwell.

# Part III

# METAPHOR UNDERSTANDING

CHAPTER 6

# Metaphor as Structure-Mapping

*Dedre Gentner and Brian Bowdle*

## Introduction

Metaphor is pervasive in language and thought: in scientific discovery (Gentner, 1982; Gentner & Jeziorski, 1993; Gruber, 1995; Nersessian, 1992), in literature (Gibbs, 1994; Miller, 1993; Steen, 1989; Turner, 1987), and in everyday language (Fauconnier & Turner, 1998; Lakoff & Johnson, 1980). Not surprisingly, this richness has engendered a number of approaches to metaphor (Steen, 2007).

Our approach to metaphor centers on the question of how metaphors are processed. This approach unifies metaphor with processes of analogy and similarity. We use structure-mapping, a theory of analogy and similarity,[1] as our framework. In the first part of the chapter, we describe research that shows that the real-time processing of many metaphors and similes can be captured by detailed models from analogy. Then we turn to studies of the processing of large-scale conceptual metaphors such as *Love is a journey* and present evidence that such metaphors can be seen as extended structure-mappings between domains.

In the second part, we lay out the "career of metaphor" hypothesis, which considers the evolution of figurative statements. We review evidence in support of the claim that figurative statements begin as novel comparison statements and evolve gradually into category-inclusion statements as the base (or vehicle) terms develop an associated metaphorical abstraction.

## Metaphor Is Like Analogy

An analogy is a mapping between two represented[2] situations in which common relational structure is aligned (Gentner, 1983; Gentner & Markman, 1997; Holyoak, Gentner, & Kokinov, 2001). According to structure-mapping theory, analogical mapping is a process of establishing a *structural alignment* between two represented situations and then projecting inferences[3] (Falkenhainer, Forbus, & Gentner, 1989; Gentner & Markman, 1997; Markman & Gentner, 1993). An alignment consists of an explicit set of correspondences between the representational elements of the two situations with an emphasis on relational matches. The alignment is determined according to *structural consistency* constraints: (1) one-to-one correspondence between the mapped elements in the base and target and (2) parallel connectivity, in which the arguments of corresponding predicates also correspond. In addition, the selection of an alignment is guided by the *systematicity principle*: a matching system of relations connected by higher-order constraining relations such as causal relations is preferred over a match with an equal number of independent correspondences. Once the alignment is made, further candidate inferences are spontaneously projected from base to target (Falkenhainer et al., 1989). Systematicity also guides analogical inference: people do not import random facts from base to target but instead project inferences that complete the common system of relations (Bowdle & Gentner, 1997; Clement & Gentner, 1991).

Two analogy findings are particularly relevant for metaphor. The first is evidence demonstrating the systematicity preference: people implicitly prefer analogies that share large, deep relational structures (all else being equal) (Forbus, Gentner, & Law, 1995; Gentner, Rattermann, & Forbus, 1993); and the same is true for metaphors. A major determinant of aptness in metaphor is the presence of a substantial relational match (Gentner & Clement, 1988; Gentner & Wolff, 1997). The second is that the common system derived from a comparison becomes more salient after the comparison and more available for transfer to new contexts (Gentner, Loewenstein, & Thompson, 2003; Gick & Holyoak, 1983; Loewenstein & Gentner, 2001). Thus, the process of comparison, including metaphorical comparison, is a way of deriving new abstractions.

Of course, not all metaphors are analogies (see Gentner, 1982, for discussion). Metaphors can range from purely relational comparisons (analogies), as in (1), to purely attributional comparisons, as in (2); and some metaphors, such as (3), simply defy description in terms of alignment.

1. Patience is bitter, but its fruit is sweet.
2. His eyes were deep pools of misery.
3. The voice of your eyes is deeper than all the roses. (e. e. cummings)

Most of the metaphors studied in the psychological literature are analogies – that is, they convey chiefly relational commonalities (e.g., *Encyclopedias are gold mines*, *My job is a jail*) – though some are surface matches (e.g., *Hair is like spaghetti*). Finally, a bit of terminology: in naming the parts of a figurative statement such as "An X is (like) a Y," X is the *topic* (or *target* in the terminology of analogy), and Y is the *vehicle* (or *base*, or *source* in analogical terminology).

*Aptness and relationality.* Adults in general prefer relational metaphors, as noted in the previous section. Gentner and Clement (1988) had participants write our descriptions of objects and then interpret metaphors containing those objects (e.g., *Blood vessels are aqueducts*). Whereas the object descriptions contained both object attributes (e.g., that blood vessels are red, elastic, delicate) and relations (e.g., they carry blood through the body), the metaphor interpretations focused mainly on relations (e.g., both aqueducts and blood vessels transport something needed; they bring it to far parts of the system). More importantly, Gentner and Clement (1988) found that subjects' judgments of the aptness of metaphors were positively correlated with the relationality of their interpretations of those metaphors, and negatively correlated with the degree to which their interpretations relied on simple object properties. Thus, although relationality is not the only influence on aptness (e.g., novelty and fit with prior beliefs may enter in), still, to a large degree, people consider metaphors apt to the extent that they can find relational interpretations for them.

*The processing of metaphors.* Structure-mapping makes a number of predictions about the processing of individual metaphors that should follow if metaphors are processed like analogies. SME serves as a process model to motivate these predictions. SME, the structure-mapping engine

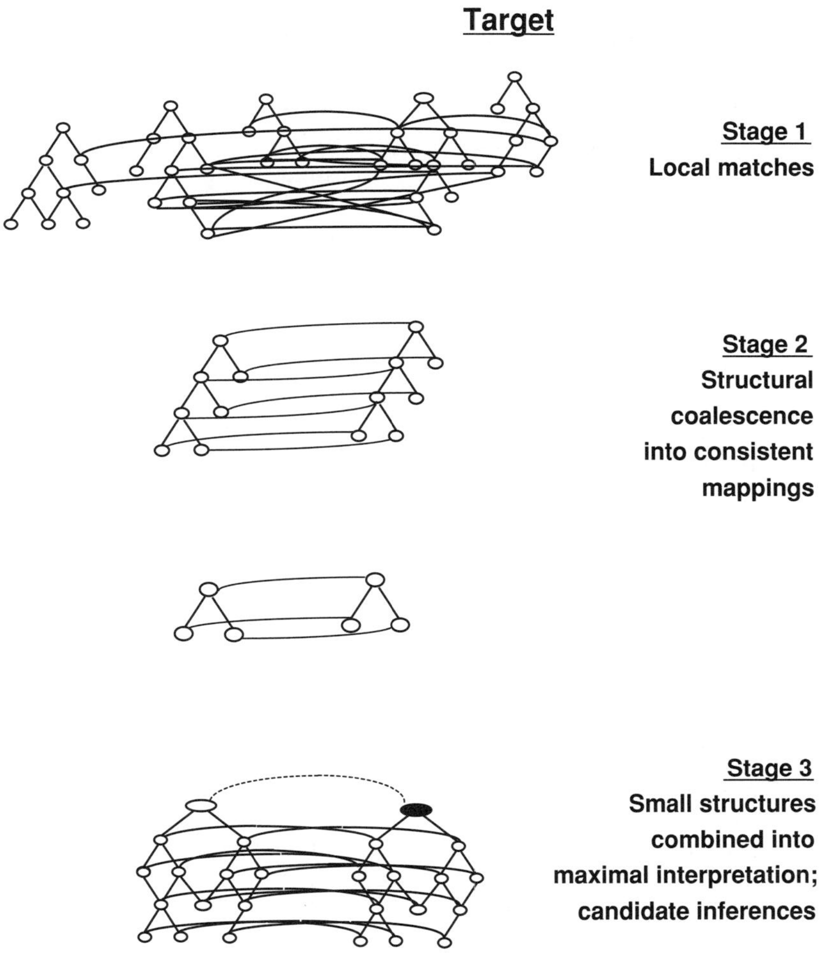


**Figure 6.1.** SME's three stages of mapping.

(Falkenhainer, Forbus, & Gentner, 1989; Forbus, Ferguson, & Gentner, 1994; Forbus, Gentner, & Law, 1995) utilizes a local-to-global[4] alignment process to arrive at a structural alignment of two representations. Figure 6.1 shows SME's three stages of mapping. In the first stage, SME begins blind and local by matching all identical predicates in the two representations. Semantic similarity is captured through partial identities: e.g., *give* and *donate* both contain the subpredicate "transfer possession" (see Gentner & Kurtz, 2006; Yan, Forbus, & Gentner, 2003). This initial mapping is typically inconsistent, containing many-to-one matches. In the second phase, these local matches are coalesced into structurally consistent connected clusters (called *kernels*). The kernels are essentially partial mappings – connected sets of structurally consistent corresponding base–target pairs. They are given structural evaluations that depend not only on the sheer number of predicates but also on the depth of the kernel's relational system (Forbus & Gentner, 1989).

In the third stage, the kernels are merged into one or a few structurally consistent global interpretations (mappings displaying *one-to-one correspondences* and *parallel connectivity*). SME does not produce all possible interpretations (a psychologically implausible process); instead, it uses a *greedy merge* algorithm (Forbus & Oblinger, 1990) that operates in linear time over the number of kernels. It begins with the maximal kernel and then adds the largest kernel that is structurally consistent with the first one, continuing until no more kernels can be added without compromising consistency. It then carries out this process beginning with the second largest kernel to produce a second interpretation.

SME then produces a structural evaluation of the interpretation(s), using a kind of cascade-like algorithm in which evidence is passed down from predicates to their arguments. This method is used – both here and for the individual kernel evaluations mentioned previously – because it favors deep systems over shallow systems, even given equal numbers of matches (Forbus & Gentner, 1989). Up to this point, the processing has been a role-neutral process of alignment. Now, however, a directional inference process takes place. Predicates connected to the common structure in the base, but not initially present in the target, are projected as *candidate inferences* in the target. Thus, structural completion can lead to spontaneous unplanned inferences.

SME has several appealing features as applied to metaphor. First, it begins blindly, without needing to know the point of the comparison in advance. Second, SME can simultaneously derive two interpretations of a comparison (e.g., a literal and a metaphorical interpretation). Because metaphor is processed in the same way as literal comparison, there is no need to initiate a special metaphoric processing routine. (Some theories implicitly postulate different processes for metaphor than for literal language, leading to a knotty problem: you have to know that a statement is a metaphor in order to process it; but you have to process it to know that it is a metaphor.) Third, inference occurs as a natural outcome of comparison, fitting the psychological intuition that inferences often arise unbidden from metaphors, and may even surprise the reasoner.

*Stages of processing.* This framework gives rise to a number of processing predictions, of which we focus on these:

- Metaphor comprehension begins with a symmetric (nondirectional) alignment process.
- If an alignment is found, then further inferences are directionally projected from base to target.
- Thus, directionality in metaphor comprehension arises *after* the initial stage of processing.

The assertion that metaphor is initially nondirectional is highly counterintuitive because, as Ortony (1979) pointed out, strong directionality is one of the hallmarks of metaphors. However, Gentner and Wolff (1997, 2000; Wolff & Gentner, 2000) have found evidence for these predictions. In one set of studies, Wolff and Gentner (2000) used the metaphor interference technique initially developed by Glucksberg, Gildea, and Bookin (1982) to investigate very early processing during metaphor comprehension. Glucksberg et al. had found that when participants made true–false judgments among statements like *Some birds are robins* and *Some birds are apples*, they took longer to reject metaphors (e.g., *Some brains are warehouses*) than to reject ordinary false statements (*Some birds are warehouses*), indicating that metaphor processing is initiated *before* literal processing has terminated.

Wolff and Gentner (2000) applied this metaphor interference technique to investigate early processing: specifically, to ask whether forward and reversed metaphors differ in the early processing stages. For forward metaphors, the results replicated Glucksberg et al.'s interference effect: forward metaphors (*Some suburbs are parasites*) took longer to reject than anomalous statements. The key question is the reversed metaphors. If metaphor is processed by a symmetric alignment, then the reversed metaphors will initially behave exactly like the forward metaphors. But if the terms of the metaphor are processed differently from the start, as in Glucksberg's attributive category theory, then reversed metaphors will not show an interference effect.[5]

Importantly, however, Wolff and Gentner found precisely the same interference effects for reversed metaphors as for forward metaphors, supporting the claim of an early nondirectional alignment process. These findings held even though the metaphors had highly conventional vehicle terms – such as *parasites*. These results are consistent with the structure-mapping claim that the initial processes in metaphor comprehension are symmetric alignment processes.

Wolff and Gentner also verified that the metaphors in the above study were strongly directional. When participants were simply asked to judge the comprehensibility of the metaphors (rather than to assess literal truth values), (1) as predicted, forward metaphors were far more likely to be judged comprehensible than reversed metaphors; and (2) as expected, response times were considerably longer than in the true–false task. These findings are consistent with the claim that even for highly directional metaphors, directionality emerges later in processing.

In a further study, Wolff and Gentner (in preparation) used a deadline task to examine stages of processing. Participants were shown forward (e.g., "A rumor is a virus") and reversed (e.g., "A virus is a rumor") metaphors and asked for comprehensibility judgments. Consistent with a symmetric early alignment process, comprehensibility judgments for forward and reversed metaphors did not differ early in processing; even though (as noted just above) forward metaphors were judged far more comprehensible than reversed metaphors later in processing. Overall, the findings suggest an early symmetric alignment process followed by a directional inference process.

*Extended mappings.* The structure-mapping view of metaphor extends naturally to extended metaphors. Structure-mapping predicts that people can process extended metaphors and can incrementally extend such mappings (Gentner, 1982; Forbus, Ferguson, & Gentner, 1994; Keane & Brayshaw, 1988). This interpretation is also consonant with domain-mapping theories such as that of Rumelhart and Abrahamson (1973) and Tourangeau and Sternberg (1981) and with theory (e.g., Kittay & Lehrer, 1981; Lakoff & Johnson, 1980) and research suggesting that metaphors are processed as large-scale conceptual systems (Gibbs, 1990, 1994; Gibbs, Nayak, & Cutting, 1989). In contrast, localist theories – such as the attributional category account (Glucksberg & Keysar, 1990; Glucksberg, McGlone, & Manfredi, 1997), which views metaphors as category inclusions – have no natural way of handling extended metaphors.

Gentner and Boronat tested whether extended metaphors are processed on-line as domain mappings (Boronat, 1990; Gentner & Boronat, 1992, Gentner, Bowdle, Wolff, & Boronat, 2001; Gentner, 1992). Specifically, our studies tested for a metaphoric consistency effect – a rise in response time when there is a shift in mapping from one base to another, even where the target and even the inferred meaning are equated. Our method was inspired by the mixed metaphors frequently captured by *The New Yorker*, for example,

> *It seems that at every turn now in my campaign, I am confronted with my fellow Republicans stabbing me in the back.*

and

> *The U.S. and the Middle East are on parallel but non-converging paths.*

If people comprehend metaphors by setting up structurally consistent, systematic domain mappings, then a shift of metaphoric base should create a disruption in the mapping process, and lead to slower processing. We used this mixed metaphor technique to test whether people can carry out an extended metaphorical mapping. All the experiments followed the same logic (see Figure 6.2). There were three kinds of passages: those with a *consistent metaphoric mapping*, those with an *inconsistent metaphoric mapping*, and a *literal control*.

The consistent passages utilized the same base throughout; for the inconsistent passages, the base was switched at the last sentence. The three passages all had the same story line, and all shared the same last sentence – the target sentence (always metaphorical), on which reading times were collected. The passages differed in the main body of the text. In the consistent passages, the same global metaphor was used in the

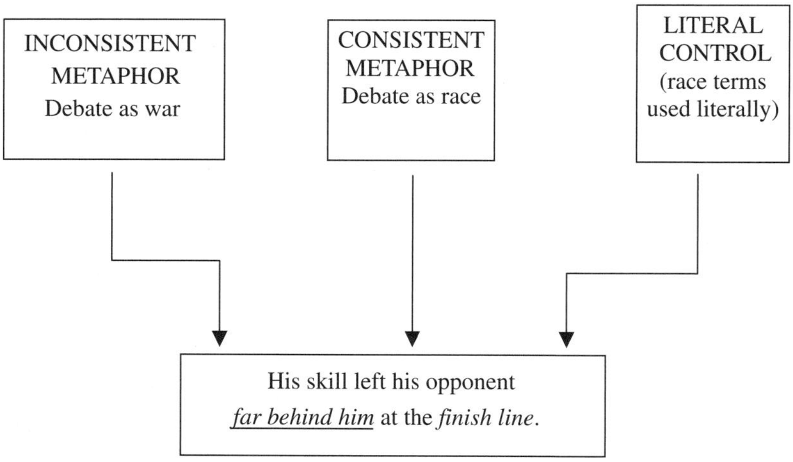


**Figure 6.2.** Design of the domain-mapping study (Boronat, 1990; Gentner & Boronat, 1992).

passage's body as in the target sentence; but in the inconsistent passages, a different global metaphor was used in the body, so that the target sentence required a switch to a new metaphor (though it expressed the same idea). In the literal controls, the body contained all of the metaphoric *terms* of the corresponding within-domain passages, but these terms were used literally.[6]

For example, there were three versions of a story about a debate (see Figure 6.2). The consistent passage used the global metaphor A DEBATE IS A RACE (e.g., *he had to steer his course carefully in the competition*). The inconsistent passage used the global metaphor A DEBATE IS A WAR (e.g., *he had to use every weapon at his command in the competition*). For both passages, the last sentence used the RACE metaphor (e.g., *His skill left his opponent far behind him at the finish line*). For the consistent passage, this represented a continuation of the global metaphor. However, for the inconsistent passage, the critical final sentence made a switch from the DEBATE AS WAR metaphor to the DEBATE AS RACE metaphor.

The domain-mapping hypothesis predicts that the last sentence will be read more quickly when it continues the same metaphoric mapping as that in the passage than when the global metaphor is changed (i.e., faster in the consistent condition than in the inconsistent condition), because the former extends an established base-to-target mapping, while the latter disrupts it. In short, the domain-mapping account predicts that the critical test metaphors will be read faster in the consistent condition than in the inconsistent condition. In contrast, localist metaphor theories, such as the class-inclusion theory of Glucksberg and Keysar (1990) and Glucksberg, McGlone, and Manfredi (1997), would predict no difference between the two metaphoric conditions, since the key (metaphoric) sentence is the same.

In the first two studies, we used novel figuratives from existing conceptual mappings. The results showed a metaphoric consistency effect, consistent with the domain-mapping account: Subjects read the critical last sentence significantly faster when it extended the existing mapping (*consistent* version) than when it switched the metaphoric mapping (*inconsistent version*). The critical last sentence was also read faster following the metaphorically consistent passage than it was following the matched literal control passage, ruling out the possibility that the reading time advantage for the metaphorically consistent passages could be attributed to mere associative priming between the words in the passage and the words in the final sentence.

The evidence thus supports the domain-mapping hypothesis for novel figuratives.

However, the results were quite different for conventional figuratives. In two further studies, Gentner and Boronat utilized passages that contained conventional figuratives, often from the same global conceptual metaphors as the novel figuratives in the earlier studies[7] – for example, DEBATE AS WAR – but here the individual metaphors were conventional.

When the individual metaphors were highly conventional, the metaphoric consistency effect disappeared (Gentner & Boronat, 1992; see also Keysar, Shen, Glucksberg, & Horton, 2000). There was no apparent cost of shifting between global metaphors. This suggests that the localist account may be correct for conventional figuratives: for highly conventional metaphors, the metaphorical interpretation becomes an alternate word sense, and the metaphor can then be processed on a lexical basis. However, one must go beyond sentence-by-sentence processing to account for the global mapping effects found for the novel figuratives.

*Directional asymmetry: How can a comparison approach account for the strong directionality of metaphors?* People show strong directional preferences in metaphor. For example, (1) seems far better as a metaphor than does (2):

1. Some jobs are jails.
2. Some jails are jobs.

The strong directionality of metaphors has been used to argue that metaphors are essentially class-inclusion statements (which are clearly asymmetric) rather than comparisons. But research on analogy shows robust asymmetries in analogy and similarity as well. In processing analogy and metaphor, the initial symmetric alignment process is followed by directional inferences. Further, because inferences are understood to flow from base to target, people prefer comparison statements that have the more informative term in the base position.

Bowdle and Gentner (1997) explored asymmetry in comparison by giving participants two brief narrative passages that were similar except that one passage (the *systematic passage*) contained a causal structure linking the events, and the other (the *nonsystematic passage*) did not. Participants preferred the direction of comparison that placed the systematic passage in the base; and when asked to generate inferences from one passage to the other, they overwhelmingly drew inferences from the more systematic passage to the less systematic one. These findings show that asymmetry in analogy follows naturally from a preference for rich inferential potential. Notably, this strong asymmetry only occurred for *alignable* pairs of passages. When the passages were unrelated, participants had no order preference, and simply drew inferences independently from within one passage or the other.

We suggest that this preference for having the more systematic representation as the base can explain the directional asymmetry of metaphor. Indeed, as Bowdle and Gentner (1997) suggested, systematicity imbalance is likely to be far stronger for metaphor than for literal similarity, with a concomitantly greater directional asymmetry. This would fit with the human predilection for metaphors that draw on highly familiar domains, such as spatial relations and bodily force dynamics – domains that are understood well enough to provide inferential structure for other domains (Fauconnier & Turner, 1998; Lakoff & Johnson, 1980).

## The Career of Metaphor

Novel and conventional figuratives differ in their behavior. Consider first a novel metaphoric base term, *snowflake*. Without being paired with a target, it is difficult to guess what meaning the term might be used to metaphorically convey. When paired with a target, however, the meaning becomes clear. For example, the metaphor *Children are snowflakes* conveys that each child is unique. Further, pairing a novel base with different targets can lead to different abstractions. For example, the metaphor *Accolades are snowflakes* conveys that praise is ephemeral. In general, novel metaphoric bases do not automatically evoke metaphoric categories in isolation. Further, the fact that they can take on radically different meanings in different contexts suggests that the comprehension of novel metaphors involves a comparison between the two terms.

Consider next a conventional metaphoric base term, *gold mine*. Even when it is not paired with a target, the hearer can already guess the metaphoric meaning of this term: *something that is a source of something valuable*. Further, pairing this base with a range of different targets (e.g., *an encyclopedia, the World Wide Web, a shopping mall,* even *the backyard)* does not substantially alter its meaning. Unlike novel bases, conventional bases can automatically evoke stable metaphoric categories.

These observations, together with Wolff and Gentner's findings, led us to propose a theoretical framework for figurative processing that takes into account the effects of conventionalization. We have called this theory *the career of metaphor* (Bowdle, 1998; Bowdle & Gentner, 1995, 1999, 2005; Gentner & Bowdle, 2001; Gentner & Wolff, 1997; Wolff & Gentner, 2000). According to the career of metaphor hypothesis, a metaphor undergoes a process of gradual abstraction and conventionalization as it evolves from its first novel use to becoming a conventional "stock" metaphor. This process results in a shift in mode of alignment. Novel metaphors are processed as comparisons, in which the target concept is structurally aligned with the literal base concept. But each such alignment makes the abstraction more salient, so if a given base is used repeatedly in a parallel way, it accrues a metaphoric abstraction as a secondary sense of the base term. When a base term reaches a level of conventionality such that its associated abstract schema becomes sufficiently accessible, the term can function as a category name.

Importantly, on our account, the basic process for understanding a figurative statement remains the same – an initial structural alignment followed by the directional projection of inferences (and sometimes by re-representation). What changes with conventionalization is not the *process* itself but the representation of the base term, whose metaphorical abstraction becomes more salient and more accessible. As the base term develops a clear metaphorical abstraction that can be accessed during comprehension, a kind of short cut becomes available. The listener can access the abstract metaphorical sense directly instead of having to derive it by aligning the two literal terms. Thus, the alignment process shifts from a horizontal alignment – that is, a comparison between two literal meanings – to a vertical alignment – that is, a comparison between a concrete literal meaning (for the target term) and an abstraction (for the base term). In general, aligning with an abstraction is easier than aligning with a more concrete representation (e.g., Ross, 1989), because there are fewer inconsistent predicates. Therefore, as conventionalization occurs there will be a corresponding decrease in comprehension time (Bowdle & Gentner, 2005).

*Metaphor and category formation.* While novel metaphors do not depend on the application of metaphoric categories, they may be used to create such categories. According to the career of metaphor hypothesis, novel and conventional metaphors draw on different representations and, hence, involve different comprehension strategies: novel metaphors are processed by direct comparison, whereas conventional metaphors are processed by accessing the metaphorical abstraction and applying it (via structural alignment) to the target – essentially treating the base term as a category of which the target is an instance. This shift from horizontal to vertical alignment is not coincidental; rather, it is a natural consequence of the structural alignment process used to interpret novel metaphors.

Consider again how novel metaphors are processed according to structure-mapping theory. First, the target and base are placed in structural correspondence. Second, further predicates connected to the aligned system in the base are mapped to the target as candidate inferences, which then count as further correspondences. One outcome of this process is that the resultant system of commonalities is highlighted.

Both the common system and the set of related inferences become more salient and more likely to be used in future situations. This process of highlighting and abstraction is also seen in studies of analogical reasoning in which learners appear to induce problem schemas as a result of structural alignment (e.g., Gentner, Loewenstein, & Thompson, 2003; Gick & Holyoak, 1983; Loewenstein & Gentner, 2001; Novick & Holyoak, 1991; Ross & Kennedy, 1990). It is also consistent with abstraction models of category learning (e.g., Elio & Anderson, 1981). Further, because structural alignment favors connected relational systems (Bowdle & Gentner, 1997; Clement & Gentner, 1991; Gentner & Medina, 1998), the abstractions that arise are often relational systems that have explanatory power.

On this view, when a given concept is encountered as the base of a metaphor for the first time, it does not evoke a metaphoric category independently of the target; rather, the category emerges from the alignment of the target and base. However, if the same abstraction is derived repeatedly in the context of the base, it may become conventionally associated with that term and may eventually be lexicalized as a secondary meaning of the base term. Only once a base term reaches this level of conventionality does it achieve dual representation of the type described by Glucksberg and Keysar (1990). This account is in line with Swinney and Cutler's (1979) lexical representation hypothesis, according to which idioms and other conventionalized "stock" expressions have stable nonliteral meanings that can be accessed directly without needing to be derived anew. This hypothesis is supported by findings indicating that the nonliteral meanings of idioms (Cacciari & Tabossi, 1988; Gibbs, 1980, 1994; Gibbs & O'Brien, 1990) and conventionalized metaphors (Blank, 1988; Blasko & Connine, 1993; Swinney & Cutler, 1979) are processed as fast, or faster, than their literal meanings. As Giora (1997) has persuasively argued, whenever a term is associated with more than one meaning, the most salient of these meanings will typically dominate during comprehension, even if this meaning is figurative rather than literal.

Evidence for the career of metaphor hypothesis has mounted over the past decade. As discussed earlier in this chapter, Gentner and Wolff (1997) found that only when the base terms of metaphors were highly conventional did they prime metaphor comprehension more effectively than the target terms. More generally, it has repeatedly been demonstrated that conventional metaphors are processed more quickly and automatically than novel metaphors (e.g., Blank, 1988; Gildea & Glucksberg, 1983; Martin, 1992). This pattern buttresses the conclusion that conventionalization results in a shift in metaphor processing from on-line active interpretation to retrieval of stored meanings (Bowdle & Gentner, 1995, 1999, 2005; Gentner et al., 2001; Gentner & Wolff, 1997; Wolff & Gentner, 2000).

An important implication of the career of metaphor framework is that metaphors can indeed give rise to new categories but only over time, as they become conventionalized. Thus, the career of metaphor view agrees in part (but not entirely) with Glucksberg and Keysar's (1990) category-inclusion model. In their original theory, the base or vehicle gives rise to a metaphoric category that is either already associated with or newly derived from the base term. Our evidence supports the first claim but not the second: a metaphor can be processed as a category statement if there is already an abstraction associated with the base; but otherwise, comparison of the two literal representations is necessary, and the abstraction emerges from the alignment process. Thus, highly conventional metaphors can indeed serve as category statements, but novel metaphors in general do not.

*Degrees of conventionalization.* This evolution can be described in terms of four stages of conventionalization, as shown in Figure 6.3. In a *novel* metaphor (as discussed earlier), the base concept has no standard metaphorical category attached to it, although the comparison between base and target will promote the formation of such a category. In a *conventional* metaphor, the

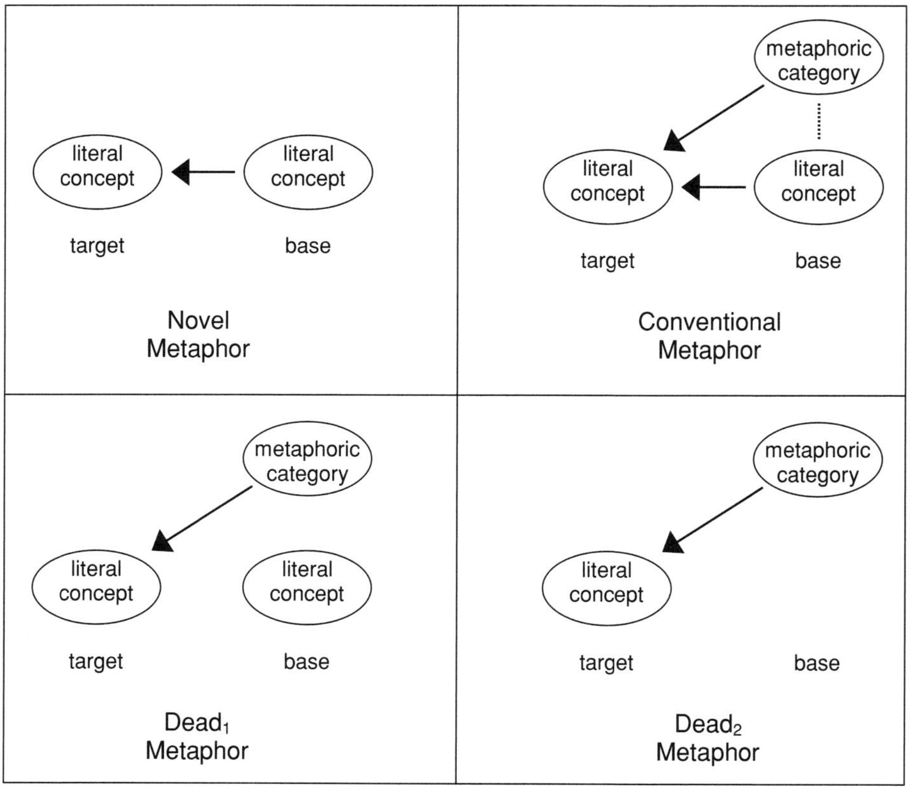


**Figure 6.3.** Living and dead metaphors.

base refers simultaneously to a literal concept and to a metaphoric category. Typically, the relationship between these senses is clearly recognizable: for example, the term *river* (as in *Time is a river*) has two associated senses: namely, *a large stream of flowing water* and *anything that moves continuously forward*. For these kinds of polysemous bases, the two senses may be processed simultaneously (Williams, 1992). However, metaphors often evolve further, to the point where the metaphoric sense seems to stand on its own, with only a tenuous relation to the literal sense. These are often called *frozen metaphors* or *dead metaphors*.

The conclusion of this evolutionary process is the death of metaphors as such (though, Phoenix-like, they often take on new life as literal category senses). Thus, in *dead*$_2$ metaphors, the base term refers *only* to the derived abstract sense, which is now taken as a literal meaning; the original specific sense no longer exists. A good example is the term *blockbuster* (as in *"Star Wars" was a blockbuster*), which roughly means *something that has a profound popular effect*. This term does not seem metaphoric; in fact, most people are unaware of the original sense of *blockbuster*, namely, *a bomb that can demolish an entire city block*.

But on the way from conventional metaphor to dead$_2$ metaphor, there is an intriguing intermediate stage, which we call *dead*$_1$ metaphors. These are similar to conventional metaphors in possessing both a literal and a metaphorical meaning, but for dead$_1$ metaphors, the relation between literal and metaphorical has become obscure. For example, temporal prepositions (e.g., *AT nine o'clock, ON Monday, IN January*) have been analyzed as metaphoric extensions of spatial prepositions (e.g., *AT the swimming pool, ON the cruise ship, IN the Pacific Ocean*; e.g., Clark, 1973; Traugott, 1978). However, a series of studies by Sandra and Rice (1995) suggests that people often do not recognize the semantic relationships between the spatial and temporal uses of prepositions.

Of course, the fact that people do not readily notice the relation does not rule out implicit connections. For example, we use two systems of space–time metaphors – ego-moving (e.g., *We are fast approaching the holidays*) and time-moving (e.g., *Exams are coming closer*). Although speakers typically appear unaware of the metaphorical nature of such usages (see McGlone & Harding, 1998), Gentner, Imai, and Boroditsky (2002) found a metaphoric consistency effect, indicating that these two systems are processed as coherent mappings. Further, Boroditsky (2000) found a priming effect from spatial sentences to temporal uses of the same metaphors. This is consistent with Gibbs's (1980) finding that $dead_1$ metaphors can be "awakened" to their metaphorical roots in some circumstances.

The career of metaphor hypothesis is consistent with the idea that metaphor is a primary source of polysemy – metaphors allow words with specific meanings to take on additional related meanings (e.g., Dirven, 1985; Lee, 1990; Lehrer, 1990; MacCormac, 1985; Miller, 1993; Nunberg, 1979; Sweetser, 1990). Over the career of a metaphor, it can move from having but a single stored (literal) meaning (the novel metaphor stage) to being polysemous (for conventional and $dead_1$ metaphors), and, sometimes, on to again having but a single meaning, namely the derived abstract sense (the $dead_2$ case).

## Metaphors and Similes

Proponents of category-based approaches to metaphor comprehension point out that nominal metaphors have the same grammatical form as literal class-inclusion statements, namely, *An X is a Y* (e.g., Glucksberg & Keysar, 1990; Kennedy, 1990; Shen, 1992). However, nominal metaphors can also be paraphrased as similes – figurative comparisons of the form *X is like Y* – which are grammatically identical to literal comparison statements. Thus, we can say both *Time is a river* and *Time is like a river*.

What is the cognitive status of metaphor–simile distinction? The dominant view is that similes are simply clearer than metaphors, explicitly inviting a figurative comparision. For example, many theorists have assumed that metaphors are understood as implicit similes (e.g., Kintsch, 1974; Miller, 1979; Ortony, 1979; Tirrell, 1991). Consistent with this view, Vosniadou and Ortony (1986) found that children were better able to understand similes than metaphors, as would follow from the idea that similes more directly invite the necessary comparison process. However, Glucksberg and Keysar (1990) have argued the reverse position: that similes are understood as implicit metaphors. This is in keeping with their class-inclusion model of figurative meaning: Metaphors directly suggest class-inclusions, and similes must be converted to metaphors in order to be processed.

We propose an integrative account of the metaphor–simile distinction – namely, *grammatical concordance* (Bowdle, 1998; Bowdle & Gentner, 1995, 1999, 2005; Gentner & Bowdle, 2001). A central intuition behind grammatical concordance is that linguistic form tells us something about function. Here we adopt Glucksberg and Keysar's (1990) insight that metaphors are seen as category statements, but we take the idea a step further, and argue that linguistic form also tells us something about similes – namely, that they are seen as comparisons.

On this view, metaphors and similes invite different comprehension strategies. Because metaphors are grammatically identical to literal class-inclusion statements, they invite categorizing the target as a member of a category named by the base. Likewise, because similes are grammatically identical to literal comparison statements, they invite comparing the target with the literal base concept. The combination of grammatical concordance with the career of metaphor hypothesis leads to a set of predictions, and thus offers a valuable route toward testing the career of metaphor hypothesis (Bowdle, 1998; Bowdle & Gentner, 1995, 1999, 2005; Gentner & Bowdle, 2001).

Consider first the case of novel figurative statements. According to the career of metaphor hypothesis, such statements are interpreted as comparisons between the two literal concepts. Thus, they should most felicitously be phrased as similes. The simile form invites comparison, which accords with the comprehension strategy required. If a novel figurative is phrased as a metaphor, the hearer is invited to access a stored metaphorical sense which does not in fact exist, so comprehension is initially thwarted. The hearer must then start over using a comparison process – a horizontal alignment with the literal concept evoked by the base.

Now consider the case of conventional figurative statements. According to the career of metaphor hypothesis, such statements may be interpreted either as comparisons or as class-inclusions, as the base term refers simultaneously to a specific literal concept and to an abstract metaphoric category. Thus, either form – simile or metaphor – can be processed directly. For conventional figurative statements, then, metaphors are interpreted as class-inclusions, whereas similes are interpreted as comparisons.

This account generates several testable predictions (see Bowdle, 1998; Bowdle & Gentner, 2005; Gentner & Bowdle, 2001). Here, we summarize some findings on grammatical form preference and comprehension time. Later, we turn to studies of the conventionalization process itself.

*Grammatical form preferences.* If conventionalization results in a processing shift from comparison to categorization, then there should be a corresponding shift in people's preference. People should prefer the comparison (simile) form for novel figuratives and the categorization (metaphor) form for conventional figuratives. Therefore, Bowdle and Gentner (2005) gave individuals novel and conventional figuratives and asked which form they preferred for each statement. To calibrate the results, we also gave participants literally similar statements (e.g., *lemon* → *orange*), for which the comparison form is most natural, and literal category statements (e.g., *robin* → *bird*), for which the categorization form is most natural.

As expected, the "X is Y" form was strongly preferred for literal categorizations and the comparison form ("X is like Y") for literal similarity. More importantly, consistent with our predictions, the preference for the metaphor form was far higher for conventional figurative statements than for novel figurative statements. Indeed, participants' preference for the comparison form was as strong for novel figuratives as it was for literal similarity statements. The conventional figuratives were more mixed, consistent with the claim that conventional figuratives may be treated either as comparisons or as categorizations.

*Processing predictions.* The career of metaphor hypothesis also makes clear predictions about the effects of conventionality on on-line comprehension. One prediction is that conventional figuratives will be faster to interpret than novel figuratives overall. This is because conventionalization results in storing a metaphorical abstraction; and, as noted earlier, vertical mappings between a target and an abstract category will tend to be computationally less costly than horizontal mappings between two concrete concepts from different domains.[8]

A more critical prediction concerns the effects of conventionality on the relative comprehension times of metaphors and similes. Because novel figuratives must be interpreted as comparisons, novel similes should be easier to comprehend than novel metaphors. This is because the simile form directly invites comparison, whereas the metaphor form prompts the expectation that an abstract metaphorical category is available – a kind of bait-and-switch, since this expectation will be unfulfilled in a novel figurative. In contrast, conventional figuratives should be easier to comprehend as metaphors than as similes. This is because the metaphor form invites categorization – a relatively simple vertical alignment between the target and the abstract metaphoric category named by the base. Here the simile form, by inviting comparison, invites a more demanding horizontal alignment between the target and the literal base concept.

We collected participants' comprehension times for novel and conventional figurative statements phrased as either metaphors or similes. The results were as predicted. First, conventional figuratives were interpreted faster than novel figuratives. And second, there was an interaction between conventionality and grammatical form, such that novel similes were faster than novel metaphors, but conventional metaphors were faster than conventional similes.

*Naturalistic evidence.* There is also indirect evidence on the real-life process of conventionalization. First, Zharikov and Gentner (2002) examined the course of development over history for a set of figuratives, based on their occurrences in the *Oxford English Dictionary*. The results showed a frequent pattern of an initial literal meaning, followed over time by figurative uses with overt comparison marking (such as simile form), followed by metaphorical uses. Table 6.1 shows the example of *sanctuary*, which initially referred to a place of worship and came over time to have a secondary reference to any safe place. As predicted by the career of metaphor account, its initial figurative uses had overt similarity markings (e.g., *She was as safe as in a Sanctuary . . .*) with the metaphoric form (e.g., *A Sanctuary was opened in his Court . . .*) occurring later, presumably as the metaphorical abstraction became conventionalized.

Second, a study of natural text by Roncero, Kennedy, and Smyth (2006) suggests that (at least for conventional target–base pairs) similes are more likely than metaphors to be accompanied by explanations. Roncero et al. searched the Internet for figurative expressions linking concepts such as *crime* and *disease* – either as similes (*crime is like a disease*) or as metaphors (*crime is a disease*). They found that similes were more likely than metaphors to be accompanied by explanations such as "Crime is like a disease because it spreads by direct personal influence." They concluded that similes may be preferred when the writer wants to express an out-of-the-ordinary relation between the target and the base. Given that a base has a conventional meaning, if the writer wants to invite going beyond that meaning, a return to the simile form is one way to invite a fresh comparison between base and target.

**Table 6.1: Timeline of occurrences of literal and figurative meanings for sanctuary**

**Initial literal meaning**

I. a holy place – a building or place set apart for the worship of God or of one or more divinities: applied, e.g., to a Christian church, the Jewish temple and the Mosaic tabernacle, a heathen temple or site of local worship, and the like; also *fig.* To the church or the body of believers

1340 . . . *in that sanctuary oure lord sall be kynge . . .*

1382 *And thei shulen make to me a seyntuarye, and Y shal dwelle in the myddil of hem.*

1530. *Sanctuarie, a place hallowed and dedicate vnto god.*

II.a – a church or other sacred place in which, by the law of the medieval church, a fugitive from justice, or a debtor, was entitled to immunity from arrest. Hence, in a wider sense, applied to any place in which by law or established custom a similar immunity is secured to fugitives.

1374 *To whiche Iugement they nolden nat obeye but defendedyn hem by the sikernesse of holy howses, that is to seyn fledden in to sentuarye.*

1463–4 *Eny persone. .that shall dwelle or inhabit within the Sayntwarie and Procyncte of the same Chapell.*

**[First figurative meaning]**

1568 *Vsing alwaise soch discrete moderation, as the scholehouse should be counted a sanctuarie against feare.*

1596 *That all the while he by his side her bore, She was as safe as in a Sanctuary.*

**[First unmarked figurative meaning]**

1700 *To form his Party, Histories report, A Sanctuary was opened in his Court, Where glad Offenders safely might resort.*

*Aptness.* Some researchers have suggested that the simile–metaphor difference is one of aptness rather than of conventionality (e.g., Chiappe, Kennedy, & Smykowski, 2003; Glucksberg, 2003; Jones & Estes, 2005). Specifically, it is claimed that the metaphor form is preferred for highly apt figuratives and the simile form for less-apt figuratives. This view is consistent with the sense that the metaphor form seems to suggest a stronger relationship between the target and base concepts than the simile form (e.g.,

Glucksberg & Keysar, 1990; Kennedy, 1990). Indeed, some studies have found a correlation between aptness and conventionality (e.g., Bowdle & Gentner, 2005; Jones & Estes, 2005).

However, there are problems with this line of argument. First, aptness is highly correlated with many other aspects of figurative statements, including relationality (Gentner & Clement, 1988), ease of interpretation, degree of metaphoricity, imagery, subjective familiarity, and the number of alternative interpretations possible (Katz, Paiio, Marschark, & Clark, 1988), as well as with ease of comprehension (Chiappe, Kennedy, & Chiappe, 2003). Thus, it's not clear whether aptness itself or one or more of these correlated dimensions is involved here. It's also not clear how aptness could play a causal role in figurative language processing, as it seems to arise as part of the process of evaluating a metaphor (e.g., Gerrig & Healy, 1983; Gibbs, 1994). Third, the empirical findings are not encouraging.[9] For example, Bowdle & Gentner (2005) found a significant *negative* correlation between rated aptness and preference for the metaphor form among novel figurative statements. That is, the more apt a novel figurative was, the more strongly the simile form was preferred over the metaphor form. For conventional figuratives, there was no difference in aptness between similes and metaphors.

In our view, the likeliest contributor to metaphor preference is relational similarity. There is evidence that relational similarity is a major determinant of aptness (Gentner & Clement, 1988) and that it can facilitate online processing (Wolff & Gentner, 2000). Indeed, Aisenman (1999) proposed that the preference for metaphor form increases with the degree of relational match. Although Aisenman found positive evidence, her study did not control conventionality. When Zharikov and Gentner (2002) orthogonally varied both base conventionality and the relationality of the figurative's interpretation[10] and elicited participants' form preferences, the results showed a strong effect of conventionality in determining a preference for metaphor form, and only a marginal main effect of relationality. In a further study, when participants were give the same figurative statements and asked to rate their agreement with either a relational or an attributional interpretation, they strongly preferred the relational interpretation for both metaphors and similes.

Aisenman's idea that relational similarity contributes to the strength and aptness of a metaphoric mapping seems correct. But the evidence to date suggests that conventionality is a far stronger determinant of preference for the metaphoric form.

*From simile to metaphor – the in vitro conventionalization of novel figuratives.* The most dramatic evidence for the career of metaphor hypothesis would be a demonstration that conventional metaphoric categories can be generated by repeated and consistent figurative comparisons involving the same base term. Therefore, we decided to test this claim directly by seeing whether we could speed up the process of conventionalization from years to minutes. The idea was to give participants multiple similes with the same base term and parallel meanings, and then test whether this shifted their preference towards the metaphor form for that base term.

There were two phases. The key manipulation occurred in the first (study) phase, in which participants were given a subset of the later test items. These items were always given in simile form in the study phase. Each subject received one-third of the items in the *multiple-similes* condition and one-third in the *multiple-literal* condition; the remaining third was not shown during study and served as the *control* condition. (Item condition was counterbalanced over subjects.) In the multiple-similes condition, the key simile (e.g., *An obsession is like a tumor*) had its base term paired with two new target terms to create new similes (e.g., *Doubt is like a tumor, A grudge is like a tumor*) with roughly parallel interpretations. In the multiple-literal condition, each base term was paired with new target terms to create two further literal comparisons (e.g., *A blister is like a tumor; An ulcer is like a tumor*).

For both these conditions, these examples were followed by an incomplete statement of the form "– *is like a tumor*." Participants were asked to complete it by writing a target term that would make it "similar in meaning to the first two."

The second (test) phase, which occurred after a 20-minute filler task, was a grammatical form preference test. Participants saw a large set of figuratives (e.g., *An obsession is (like) a tumor*). This included the figuratives they had seen in the study task, plus other figuratives (both novel and conventional), that they had not seen in the study phase. For each statement, they indicated their preference for the simile form versus the metaphor form on a sliding scale.

The key items were the figuratives used in the study task. Consistent with the career of metaphor account, participants were more likely to prefer the metaphor form (i.e., the categorization form) for items in the multiple-similes condition than for items in the multiple-literal condition, which did not differ from items not seen before. Strikingly, seeing/generating a set of novel *similes* led to a shift toward preferring the *metaphor* form. (Note that this cannot be explained in terms of a novel-form preference, for there was no such shift in the multiple-literal condition). A further striking point is that the *same figuratives* were judged in all conditions; thus, the presumed aptness of the match was held constant. Simply by varying the metaphoric conventionality of the base term – by varying participants' experience aligning parallel figurative uses, we were able to induce a shift towards the metaphoric form.

These results are evidence that aligning parallel figuratives (even in our brief *in vitro* condition) can give rise to an abstraction that becomes associated with the base; and, further, that the existence of such an abstraction leads to a preference for the metaphor form.

## Summary

We have suggested that metaphor is like analogy – that the basic processes of analogy are at work in metaphor. Specifically, we suggest that structural alignment, inference projection, progressive abstraction, and re-representation are employed in the processing of metaphor and simile. This view can help resolve some tensions in the field: for example, on this view, metaphor both reflects parallels (Murphy, 1996) and creates new similarities (Lakoff, 1990) between the domain compared, via structural alignment and candidate inferences, respectively.

We further propose that individual metaphors evolve over the course of their lives from comparison – horizontal alignment between literal meanings – in the early stages to categorization – vertical alignment between the literal target term and the base's metaphorical abstraction – as they become conventionalized. Conventionalization often results in local metaphoric categories, but it can also take the form of large-scale conventional systems of metaphors.

The career of metaphor account offers a unified theoretical framework for the study of metaphor, analogy, and similarity (see Steen [2007] for an extended discussion of these issues). It renders explicit the processing differences between metaphors at different levels of conventionality and provides a mechanism for the metaphoric generation of polysemous words. Finally, it reconciles the seemingly opposing intuitions behind traditional comparison models and more recent categorization models. Comparison is not inimical to categorization, but rather engenders it over time.

## Author's Notes

The research reported here was supported in part by NSF-ROLE grant 21002/REC-0087516 and by NSF-SLC Grant SBE 054 1957, the Spatial Intelligence and Learning Center (SILC). The development of structure-mapping theory and SME was supported by ONR Cognitive Science grant N00014-92-J-1098.

## Notes

1 Although structure-mapping is best known as a theory of analogy, metaphor has been a focus of the work from its inception (e.g., Gentner, 1982).

2 Structure-mapping theory assumes the existence of structured representations made up of entities and their attributes, functions that map entities to dimensions or to other entities, relations between objects, and higher-order relations between relations.

3 This discussion is taken chiefly from structure-mapping theory (Gentner, 1983; Gentner & Markman, 1997) and its computational model, SME, the structure-mapping engine (Falkenhainer, Forbus, & Gentner, 1989; Forbus, Gentner, & Law, 1995; Forbus & Oblinger, 1990). However, the basic tenets are accepted by most current models of analogy (e.g., Holyoak & Thagard, 1989; Hummel & Holyoak, 1997; Keane & Brayshaw, 1988; Kokinov & Petrov, 2001; Larkey & Love, 2003; Ramscar & Yarlatt, 2000).

4 Local-to-global is not the same as bottom-up, a point that occasionally engenders confusion. In SME, processing starts by identifying matching nodes at *any level* of the structure, from higher-order relations to concrete perceptual attributes. These local identities are then coalesced into global system-mappings (Falkenhainer et al., 1989; Forbus et al., 1995).

5 The attributive category theory can predict a metaphoric slowdown for forward metaphors, such as *some suburbs are parasites*, by assuming that participants implicitly experience a fit between the target, *suburbs*, and the metaphorical category associated with *parasite*, and that this spontaneous categorization temporarily overrides their ability to notice that the statement is literally false. But this explanation is highly implausible for a reversed metaphor, such as *some parasites are suburbs*. Although it might be possible to find a category associated with *suburb* that could apply to *parasite*, the search for such a match would be laborious and deliberate – hardly likely to spontaneously capture participants' attention and prevent them from noticing that the statement is literally false.

6 In this condition, participants encountered the *terms* from the metaphoric base domain in the passage but not the metaphor itself (until the final test sentence). If the facilitation for the consistent condition over the inconsistent condition were due merely to associative priming, the final sentence should not differ between the consistent condition and the literal control condition.

7 Note that in both cases, the global metaphors themselves were often familiar conceptual metaphors (e.g., *Debate as war*); the difference lay in whether the individual metaphors were novel or conventional.

8 Of course, if the two concrete concepts are literally similar to each other, the comparison will be quite fast to process, because there will be many mutually supporting matches at both the relational level and the object-attribute level (see Gentner & Kurtz, 2006, for evidence).

9 One difficulty in sorting out the evidence is that some researchers have manipulated the familiarity of the whole figurative statement (that is, the base–target pair; e.g., Blasko & Connine, 1993; Chiappe, Kennedy, & Smykowski, 2003), rather than the conventionality of the base term (the focus of the career of metaphor). These two factors are by no means identical, and sorting out the evidence is not straightforward.

10 To vary the figuratives' interpretations, each figurative was preceded by a short description of the target that focused either on object attributes or on relational structure.

## References

Aisenman, R. A. (1999). Structure-mapping and the simile-metaphor preference. *Metaphor and Symbol*, 14(1), 45–51.

Blank, G. D. (1988). Metaphors in the lexicon. *Metaphor and Symbolic Activity*, 3, 21–26.

Blasko, D. G., & Connine, C. M. (1993). Effects of familiarity and aptness on metaphor processing. *Journal of Experimental Psychology: Learning, Memory and Cognition*, 12, 205–308.

Boroditsky, L. (2000). Metaphoric structuring: Understanding time through spatial metaphors. *Cognition*, 75(1), 1–27.

Boronat, C. B. (1990). *Effects of base shift and frequency in extended metaphor processing.* Unpublished master's thesis, University of Illinois at Urbana–Champaign.

Bowdle, B. (1998). Alignment and abstraction in metaphor. In K. J. Holyoak, D. Gentner, & B. Kokinov(Eds.), *Advances in analogy research: Integration of theory and data from the cognitive, computational, and neural sciences* (pp. 300–307). Sofia, Bulgaria: New Bulgarian University.

Bowdle, B., & Gentner, D. (1995). *The career of metaphor*. Paper presented at the meeting of the Psychonomics Society, Los Angeles, CA.

Bowdle, B., & Gentner, D. (1997). Informativity and asymmetry in comparisons. *Cognitive Psychology*, 34(3), 244–286.

Bowdle, B., & Gentner, D. (1999). Metaphor comprehension: From comparison to categorization. *Proceedings of the Twenty-First Annual Conference of the Cognitive Science Society*. (pp. 90–95). Hillsdale, NJ: Lawrence Erlbaum Associates.

Bowdle, B., & Gentner, D. (2005). The career of metaphor. *Psychological Review*, *112*, 193–216.

Cacciari, C., & Tabossi, P. (1988). The comprehension of idioms. *Journal of Memory and Language*, 27, 668–683.

Chiappe, D. L., Kennedy, J. M., & Chiappe, P. (2003). Aptness is more important than comprehensibility in preference for metaphors and similes. *Poetics*, *31*, 51–68.

Chiappe, D., Kennedy, J. M., & Smykowski, T. (2003). Reversibility, aptness, and the conventionality of metaphors and similes. *Metaphor and Symbol*, *18*, 85–105.

Clark, H. H. (1973). Space, time, semantics and the child. In T. E. Moore (Ed.), *Cognitive development and the acquisition of language* (pp. 27–63). New York: Academic Press.

Clement, C. A., & Gentner, D. (1991). Systematicity as a selection constraint in analogical mapping. *Cognitive Science*, *15*, 89–132.

Dirven, R. (1985). Metaphor and polysemy. *La Polysémie: Lexicographie et Cognition* (pp. 9–27). Louvain la Neuve: Cabai.

Elio, R., & Anderson, J. R. (1981). The effect of category generalizations and instance similarity on schema abstraction. *Journal of Experimental Psychology: Human Learning and Memory*, 7, 397–417.

Falkenhainer, B., Forbus, K. D., & Gentner, D. (1989). The structure-mapping engine: Algorithm and examples. *Artificial Intelligence*, *41*, 1–63.

Fauconnier, G., & Turner, M. (1998). Conceptual integration networks. *Cognitive Science*, 22(2), 133–187.

Forbus, K. D., Ferguson, R. W., & Gentner, D. (1994). Incremental structure-mapping. *Proceedings of the Sixteenth Annual Conference of the Cognitive Science Society* (pp. 313–318).

Forbus, K. D., & Gentner, D. (1989). Structural evaluation of analogies: What counts? *Proceedings of the Eleventh Annual Conference of the Cognitive Science Society*, 34, 341–348.

Forbus, K. D., Gentner, D., & Law, K. (1995). MAC/FAC: A model of similarity-based retrieval. *Cognitive Science*, 19(2), 141–205.

Forbus, K. D., & Oblinger, D. (1990). Making SME greedy and pragmatic. *Proceedings of the Twelfth Annual Conference of the Cognitive Science Society* (pp. 61–68). Hillsdale, NJ: Erlbaum.

Gentner, D. (1982). Are scientific analogies metaphors? In D. Miall (Ed.), *Metaphor: Problems and perspectives* (pp. 106–132). Brighton: Harvester.

Gentner, D. (1983). Structure-mapping: A theoretical framework for analogy. *Cognitive Science*, 7, 155–170.

Gentner, D., & Boronat, C. B. (1992). *Metaphor as mapping*. Paper presented at the Workshop on Metaphor, Tel Aviv.

Gentner, D., & Bowdle, B. F. (2001). Convention, form, and figurative language processing. *Metaphor and Symbol*, *16*(3&4), 223–247.

Gentner, D., Bowdle, B., Wolff, P., & Boronat, C. (2001). Metaphor is like analogy. In D. Gentner, K. J. Holyoak, & B. N. Kokinov (Eds.), *The analogical mind: Perspectives from cognitive science* (pp. 199–253). Cambridge, MA: MIT Press.

Gentner, D., & Clement, C. A. (1988). Evidence for relational selectivity in the interpretation of analogy and metaphor. In G. H. Bower (Ed.), *The psychology of learning and motivation* (pp. 307–358). New York: Academic.

Gentner, D., Imai, M., & Boroditsky, L. (2002). As time goes by: Evidence for two systems in processing space-time metaphors. *Language and Cognitive Processes*, *17*(5), 537–565.

Gentner, D., & Jeziorski, M. (1993). The shift from metaphor to analogy in western science. In A. Ortony (Ed.), *Metaphor and thought* (2nd ed., pp. 447–480). England: Cambridge University Press.

Gentner, D., & Kurtz, K. (2006). Relations, objects, and the composition of analogies. *Cognitive Science*, 30, 609–642.

Gentner, D., Loewenstein, J., Thompson, L. (2003). Learning and transfer: A general role for analogical encoding. *Journal of Educational Psychology*, 95, 393–408.

Gentner, D., & Markman, A. B. (1997). Structure mapping in analogy and similarity. *American Psychologist, 52*, 45–56.

Gentner, D., & Medina, J. (1998). Similarity and the development of rules. *Cognition, 65*, 263–297.

Gentner, D., & Namy, L. (1999). Comparison in the development of categories. *Cognitive Development, 14*, 487–513.

Gentner, D., Rattermann, M. J., & Forbus, K. D. (1993). The roles of similarity in transfer: Separating retrievability from inferential soundness. *Cognitive Psychology, 25*, 524–575.

Gentner, D., & Wolff, P. (1997). Alignment in the processing of metaphor. *Journal of Memory and Language, 37*, 331–355.

Gerrig, R. J., & Healy, A. F. (1983). Dual processes in metaphor understanding: Comprehension and appreciation. *Journal of Experimental Psychology: Learning, Memory, and Cognition, 9*, 667–675.

Gibbs, R. (1980). Spilling the beans on understanding and memory for idioms in conversations. *Memory & Cognition, 8*, 449–456.

Gibbs, R. (1985). On the process of understanding idioms. *Journal of Psycholinguistic Research, 14*, 465–472.

Gibbs, R. (1990). Comprehending figurative referential descriptions. *Journal of Experimental Psychology: Learning, Memory, and Cognition, 16*, 56–66.

Gibbs, R. (1994). *The poetics of mind: Figurative thought, language, and understanding*. New York: Cambridge University Press.

Gibbs, R. W., Jr., Nayak, N. P., & Cutting, C. (1989). How to kick the bucket and not decompose: Analyzability and idiom processing. *Journal of Memory and Language, 28*, 576–593.

Gibbs, R., & O'Brien, J. E. (1990). Idioms and mental imagery: The metaphorical motivation for idiomatic meaning. *Cognition*, 36(1), 35–68.

Gick, M. L., & Holyoak, K. J. (1983). Schema induction and analogical transfer. *Cognitive Psychology, 15*, 1–38.

Gildea, P., & Glucksberg, S. (1983). On understanding metaphors: The role of context. *Journal of Verbal Learning and Verbal Behavior, 22*, 577–590.

Giora, R. (1997). Understanding figurative and literal language: The graded salience hypothesis. *Cognitive Linguistics*, 8(3), 183–206.

Glucksberg, S. (2003). The psycholinguistics of metaphor. *Trends in Cognitive Science, 7*, 92–96.

Glucksberg, S., Gildea, P., & Bookin, H. B. (1982). On understanding nonliteral speech: Can people ignore metaphors? *Journal of Verbal Learning and Verbal Behavior, 21*, 85–98.

Glucksberg, S., & Keysar, B. (1990). Understanding metaphorical comparisons: Beyond similarity. *Psychological Review, 97*, 3–18.

Glucksberg, S., McGlone, M. S., & Manfredi, D. (1997). Property attribution in metaphor comprehension. *Journal of Memory and Language, 36*, 50–67.

Gruber, H. E. (1995). Insight and affect in the history of science. In R. J. Sternberg & J. E. Davidson (Eds.), *The nature of insight* (pp. 397–432). Cambridge: MIT Press.

Holyoak, K. J., Gentner, D., & Kokinov, B. N. (2001). Introduction: The place of analogy in cognition. In D. Gentner, K. J. Holyoak, & B. N. Kokinov (Eds.), *The analogical mind: Perspectives from cognitive science* (pp. 1–20). Cambridge, MA: MIT Press.

Holyoak, K. J., & Thagard, P. (1989). Analogical mapping by constraint satisfaction. *Cognitive Science*, 13(3) 295–355.

Hummel, J. E., & Holyoak, K. J. (1997). Distributed representations of structure: A theory of analogical access and mapping. *Psychological Review*, 104(3), 427–466.

Jones, L. L., & Estes, Z. (2005). Metaphor comprehension as attributive categorization. *Journal of Memory and Language, 53*, 110–124.

Katz, A. N., Paivio, A., Marschark, M., & Clark, J. M. (1988). Norms for 204 literary and 260 nonliterary metaphors on 10 psychological dimensions. *Metaphor and Symbolic Activity, 3*, 191–214.

Keane, M. T., & Brayshaw, M. (1988). The incremental analogical machine: A computational model of analogy. In D. Sleeman (Ed.), *Third European Working Session on Machine Learning* (pp. 53–62). San Mateo, CA: Kaufmann.

Kennedy, J. M. (1982). Metaphor in pictures. *Perception, 11*, 589–605.

Kennedy, J. M. (1990). Metaphor – its intellectual basis. *Metaphor and Symbolic Activity, 5*, 115–123.

Keysar, B., Shen, Y., Glucksberg, S., & Horton, W. S. (2000). Conventional language: How metaphorical is it? *Journal of Memory and Language*, 43(4), 576–593.

Kintsch, W. (1974). *The representation of meaning in memory*. Hillsdale, NJ: Lawrence Erlbaum Associates.

Kittay, E. F., & Lehrer, A. (1981). Semantic fields and the structure of metaphor. *Studies in language*, 5(1), 31–63.
Kokinov, B. N., & Petrov, A. A. (2001). Integrating memory and reasoning in analogy-making: The AMBR model. In D. Gentner, K. J. Holyoak, & B. N. Kokinov (Eds.), *The analogical mind: Perspectives from cognitive science* (pp. 161–196). Cambridge, MA: MIT Press.
Lakoff, G. (1990). The invariance hypothesis: Is abstract reason based on image-schemas? *Cognitive Linguistics*, 1(1), 39–74.
Lakoff, G., & Johnson, M. (1980). *Metaphors we live by*. Chicago: University of Chicago Press.
Lakoff, G., & Turner, M. (1989). *More than cool reason: A field guide to poetic metaphor*. Chicago: University of Chicago Press.
Larkey, L. B., & Love, B. C. (2003). CAB: Connectionist Analogy Builder. *Cognitive Science*, 27, 781–794.
Lee, C. J. (1990). Some hypotheses concerning the evolution of polysemous words. *Journal of Psycholinguistic Research*, 19, 211–219.
Lehrer, A. (1990). Polysemy, conventionality, and the structure of the lexicon. *Cognitive Linguistics*, 1(2), 207–246.
Loewenstein, J., & Gentner, D. (2001). Spatial mapping in preschoolers: Close comparisons facilitate far mappings. *Journal of Cognition and Development*, 2, 189–219.
MacCormac, E. (1985). *A cognitive theory of metaphor*. Cambridge, MA: Bradford Books.
Markman, A. B., & Gentner, D. (1993). Structural alignment during similarity comparisons. *Cognitive Psychology*, 25, 431–467.
Martin, J. H. (1992). Computer understanding of conventional metaphoric language. *Cognitive Science*, 16, 233–270.
McGlone, M. S., & Harding, J. L. (1998). Back (or forward?) to the future: The role of perspective in temporal language comprehension. *Journal of Experimental Psychology: Learning, Memory, & Cognition*, 24, 1211–1223.
Miller, G. A. (1979). Images and models, similes and metaphors. In A. Ortony (Ed.), *Metaphor and thought* (1st ed., pp. 202–250). Cambridge, England: Cambridge University Press.
Miller, G. A. (1993). Images and models, similes and metaphors. In A. Ortony (Ed.), *Metaphor and thought* (2nd ed., pp. 357–400). Cambridge, England: Cambridge University Press.
Murphy, G. L. (1996). On metaphoric representation. *Cognition*, 60(2), 173–204.
Nersessian, N. J. (1992). How do scientists think? Capturing the dynamics of conceptual change in science. In R. N. Giere & H. Feigl (Eds.), *Cognitive models of science: Minnesota studies in the philosophy of science* (pp. 3–44). Minneapolis: University of Minnesota Press.
Novick, L. R., & Holyoak, K. J. (1991). Mathematical problem solving by analogy. *Journal of Experimental Psychology: Learning, Memory, and Cognition*, 17(3), 398–415.
Nunberg, G. (1979). The non-uniqueness of semantic solutions: Polysemy. *Linguistics and Philosophy*, 3, 143–184.
Ortony, A. (1979). Beyond literal similarity. *Psychological Review*, 86, 161–180.
Ramscar, M., & Yarlett, D. (2000). The use of a high-dimensional, "environmental" context space to model retrieval in analogy and similarity-based transfer. In L. Gleitman & A. K. Joshi (Eds.), *Proceedings of the Twenty-Second Annual Conference of the Cognitive Science Society* (pp. 381–386). Mahwah, NJ: Lawrence Erlbaum Associates.
Roncero, T., Kennedy, J. M., & Smyth, R. (2006). Similes on the Internet have explanations. *Psychonomic Bulletin and Review*, 13, 74–77.
Ross, B. H. (1989). Distinguishing types of superficial similarities: Different effects on the access and use of earlier problems. *Journal of Experimental Psychology: Learning, Memory and Cognition*, 15(3), 456–468.
Ross, B. H., & Kennedy, P. T. (1990). Generalizing from the use of earlier examples in problem solving. *Journal of Experimental Psychology: Learning, Memory, and Cognition*, 16, 42–55.
Rumelhart, D. E., & Abrahamson, A. A. (1973). A model for analogical reasoning. *Cognitive Psychology*, 5, 1–28.
Sandra, D., & Rice, S. (1995). Network analyses of prepositional meaning: Mirroring whose mind – the linguist's or the language user's? *Cognitive Linguistics*, 6, 89–130.
Shen, Y. (1992). Metaphors and categories. *Poetics Today*, 13, 771–794.
Steen, G. J. (1989). Metaphor and literary comprehension: Towards a discourse theory of metaphor in literature. *Poetics*, 18, 113–141.
Steen, G. J. (2007). *Finding metaphor in grammar and usage: A methodological analysis of theory and research*. Amsterdam/Philadelphia: John Benjamins.

Sweetser, E. (1990). *From etymology to pragmatics*. Cambridge: Cambridge University Press.

Swinney, D., & Cutler, A. (1979). The access and processing of idiomatic expressions. *Journal of Verbal Learning and Verbal Behavior, 18*, 523–534.

Tirrell, L. (1991). Reductive and nonreductive simile theories of metaphor. *Journal of Philosophy, 88*, 337–359.

Tourangeau, R., & Rips, L. (1991). Interpreting and evaluating metaphors. *Journal of Memory and Language, 30*, 452–472.

Tourangeau, R., & Sternberg, R. (1981). Aptness in metaphor. *Cognitive Psychology, 13*, 27–55.

Traugott, E. C. (1978). On the expression of spatio-temporal relations in language. In J. H. Greenberg (Ed.), *Universals of human language: Vol. 3. Word structure* (pp. 369–400). Stanford, CA: Stanford University Press.

Turner, M. (1987). *Death is the mother of beauty: Mind, metaphor, and criticism*. Chicago: University of Chicago Press.

Vosniadou, S., & Ortony, A. (1986). Testing the metaphoric competence of the young child: Paraphrase versus enactment. *Human Development, 29*, 226–230.

Williams, J. (1992). Processing polysemous words in context: Evidence for interrelated meanings. *Journal of Psycholinguistic Research, 21*, 193–218.

Wolff, P., & Gentner, D. (2000). Evidence for role-neutral initial processing of metaphors. *Journal of Experimental Psychology: Learning, Memory, and Cognition, 26*, 529–541.

Wolff, P., & Gentner, D. (2007). From symmetric to asymmetric processing: Two stages in the comprehension of metaphors.

Yan, J., Forbus, K., & Gentner, D. (2003). A theory of rerepresentation in analogical matching. *Proceedings of the Twenty-Fifth Annual Meeting of the Cognitive Science Society*.

Zharikov, S., & Gentner, D. (2002). Why do metaphors seem deeper than similes? *Proceedings of the Twenty-Fourth Annual Conference of the Cognitive Science Society*, 976–981.

CHAPTER 7

# How the Mind Computes the Meaning of Metaphor

## A Simulation Based on LSA

*Walter Kintsch*

The title of this chapter needs immediate expansion: "some types of metaphor" would be a more exact, if too long a title. A major claim of this chapter is that there is no single psychological process for metaphor comprehension but that the process of comprehending a metaphor depends on the type of metaphor and varies widely from simple associative mechanisms to elaborate problem solving. Metaphor as a class makes sense linguistically, but it is not meaningful from a computational standpoint to lump together the automatic, immediate comprehension of simple metaphors and the problem solving required to interpret an artful literary metaphor. It has often been recognized that conventional and novel metaphors may be processed in different ways (e.g., Bowdle & Gentner, 2005), but the claim made here goes beyond that: the simplest metaphors are processed in the same way as literal statements, while more complex metaphors require analogical reasoning.

Table 7.1 lists four classes of metaphors, without any claim that these provide an exhaustive classification or span the full range. The goal is merely to frame the present discussion. There are obvious differences in automaticity between these examples: (a) and (b) are easy and automatic; (c) and (d) require a great deal of deliberate analysis. Of course, once any metaphor has been encountered often enough, its meaning need no longer be computed but is simply recalled from memory (Gentner, Bowdle, Wolff, & Boronat, 2001). The focus here is on computation, however. I discuss a model for (a) that simulates the essential aspects of human comprehension for literal sentences as well as metaphors of this kind. I also offer half of a model for (b) but have next to nothing to say about (c) and nothing at all to say about (d). Thus, the computational approach discussed here is still restricted to relatively simple problems.

Computational models of psychological processes have several advantages over theories stated only verbally. They demonstrate that the postulated processes actually work the way they are said to and allow one to test their implications. However, it is not an easy task to model how metaphors are comprehended because that depends on

**Table 7.1: Examples of different types of metaphors**

| *Types of metaphors:* | *Examples:* |
|---|---|
| (a) Simple metaphors of the form $N_1$-is-$N_2$ | *My lawyer is a shark*<br>*My surgeon is a butcher* |
| (b) Simple analogy based metaphors | *She blew up at me*<br>*She shot down all of my arguments* |
| (c) Complex analogy-based metaphors | *The universe is a computer* |
| (d) Literary metaphors | *We are the eyelids of defeated caves* |

the knowledge the comprehender has that is relevant to the metaphor. In metaphor comprehension, we use our knowledge to create new meaning, new knowledge. Thus, before we can even start modeling comprehension, we need some way to represent human knowledge, which is a quite nontrivial requirement for there are no existing models of human knowledge that are fully adequate, comprehensive, and objective. There are two ways out of this dilemma. Instead of working with a general model of human knowledge, the theorist can feed the comprehension model whatever knowledge is required. Several existing models are discussed that take this approach. These models have made significant contributions to our understanding of comprehension, but they are incomplete because they circumvent the question how the knowledge representations relevant to understanding are constructed. Here, I propose to focus instead on the very process of constructing knowledge representations in comprehension, using latent semantic analysis, or LSA, to model human knowledge. LSA is not a fully adequate model of all of human knowledge, but it is comprehensive and objective, and it captures enough of how word meanings are represented to serve as a useful basis for modeling higher cognitive processes that are strongly knowledge dependent, including metaphor comprehension.

LSA infers meaning relations among words and texts by observing how words are used in a very large number of documents, comprising millions of word tokens (Landauer & Dumais, 1997; Landauer, McNamara, Dennis, & Kintsch, 2007). LSA constructs a semantic space that is both a generalization and an abstraction of the input data. It is a generalization because LSA fills in the gaps in the data, so that it is possible to estimate meaning relationships among words and texts that have never been directly observed in the corpus. It is an abstraction because LSA discards incidental information and focuses on the essential semantic relations. The method that is used to construct a semantic space is dimension reduction via singular value decomposition, a well-known mathematical technique. A good way to think about a semantic space is as a map of meanings: one can look up in this map the semantic distance between any items, where items may be words or sentences or whole texts. However, the map of meanings is more complicated than the familiar two-dimensional maps because about 300 dimensions are needed to adequately represent the semantic space. Items are vectors in this space, and their semantic relatedness is given by the cosine of the angle between their vectors. The cosine is a measure like the more familiar correlation coefficient, where values close to +1 indicate high levels of similarity, and 0 indicates independence, except that there are no large negative values in the semantic space because there are no real semantic opposites (antonyms are, in fact, highly related semantically). For example, *tree* and *bark* are semantically related with a cosine of .70; *tree* and *trees* are almost as highly related, with a cosine of .57 (one *tree* and many *trees* are related, but by no means the same), while *tree* and *computer* have a cosine of 0. Another concept that is made much use of in the present chapter is that of a semantic neighborhood. The semantic neighborhood of a word consists of the words that have the highest cosine with it in the semantic space. Thus, *tree* is a close neighbor of *bark*, the third closest; *dog* is also a neighbor of *bark*, but a more distant one, being the 72nd closest, reflecting the fact that the *tree*-meaning of the homonym *bark* dominates the *dog*-meaning in the corpus on which the LSA space used for these computations is based. However, in the neighborhood of *barked* (a different word than *bark* for LSA), *dog* is the closest neighbor, whereas *tree* is nowhere to be found. Readers are invited to check these examples or explore their own on the Web site http://lsa.colorado.edu.

What does this all have to do with metaphors? According to the model proposed here, simple metaphors like *My surgeon is a butcher* are understood by modifying the vector that represents the meaning of *surgeon* in LSA in such a way that those parts that are related to *butcher* become emphasized and unrelated parts are de-emphasized, that is, by creating a contextualized vector that represents *surgeon-who-is-a-butcher*. The same process underlies literal comprehension: to understand *My surgeon is skillful*, a *surgeon-who-is-skillful* vector is created in much the same way.

## Word Senses, Literal and Metaphorical

A caricature of the way most cognitive scientists currently conceive of how the meaning of words is represented in the mind might go something like this. There exists a mental lexicon that is a bit like a real lexicon in that it lists all the literal meanings and senses of all the words. There are significant controversies about various aspects of this general scheme, such as how to retrieve the right sense at the right time, or about the role of perceptual information or embodiment, but the general scheme of listing senses and meanings is widely accepted. LSA suggests a completely different approach, discarding the whole concept of a mental lexicon. What LSA does is to infer a context-free semantic representation for the meaning of each word – a vector in the semantic space. Thus, the homonym *bark* (which can refer to the sound dogs make, the surface of tree trunks, or a certain type of sailing ship) is represented by a single vector that mixes up the *dog*- and *tree*-, and *ship*- meanings of *bark*; similarly, in LSA, there is a single vector for the verb *give*, which has 44 senses in WordNet (http://wordnet.princeton.edu/). Nevertheless, when these ambiguous vectors are used in context, sensible results are obtained. Thus, *bark* is strongly related to both *tree* (cos = .70) and *dog* (cos = .34), but *dog* and *tree* are not related (cos = .06). However, people are aware of the different meanings of *bark* and the many senses of *give*, and if LSA is to mimic how people perceive meaning, it too must be capable of contextualizing the meaning of a word.

The predication model of Kintsch (2001) is an algorithm that allows word senses and meanings to emerge when an LSA vector is used in context. Thus, instead of a list of different meanings in a mental lexicon, a contextual meaning is generated from the context-free LSA vector every time a word is used. The word vector is subtly, or not so subtly, modified by the context it appears in. What a word means in this model is always different, depending on the context of its use. Word senses are not fixed but are emergent. There is no mental lexicon; instead, meaning is always generated anew from two components: the context-free vector that represents a word in the LSA space and the context in which the word is used.

In the construction-integration model of Kintsch (1998), discourse representations are built up through a spreading activation process in a network defined by the concepts and propositions in a text. Predication works the same way: a network is constructed containing the word to be modified and its semantic neighborhood and linked to the context; spreading activation in that network ensures that those elements of the neighborhood most strongly related to the context become activated and are able to modify the original word vector. Figure 7.1 shows how the meaning of *bark* is generated in the context of *dog* and in the context of *tree*. In the actual model, the semantic neighborhood of *bark* would be much larger; for simplicity, only three neighbors of *bark* are shown in Figure 7.1, linked to both *bark* and

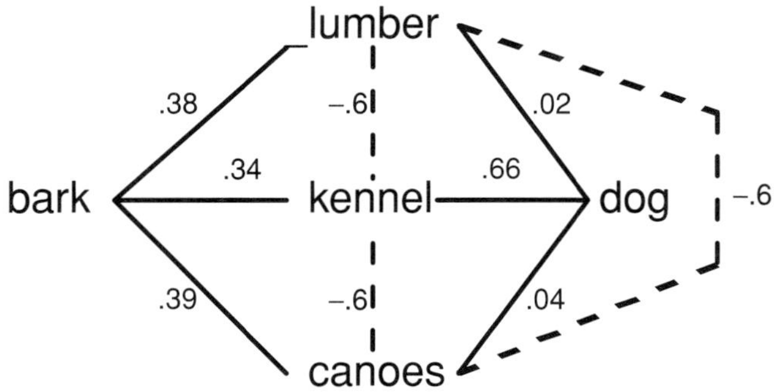


**Figure 7.1.** Spreading activation networks for the generation of the contextual meaning of *bark* in the context of *dog* and *tree*. Only three items from the neighborhood of *bark* are included. The link strengths of positive links (plain lines) are the cosines between words; the total strengths of negative links (dashed lines) are chosen to equal the sum of the positive links.

the context word (either *dog* or *tree*) by their cosine values. The three neighbors themselves inhibit each other in such a way that the total positive and negative link strength balance. As a result of spreading activation in these networks, words in the semantic neighborhood of *bark* that are related to the context become activated, and words that are unrelated become deactivated. Thus, in the context of *dog*, the activation of *kennel* becomes 1 and the activation of the other two words becomes 0; in the context of *tree*, the activation values for *lumber, kennel,* and *canoes* become 1, 0, and .02, respectively. The contextual meaning of $bark_{dog}$ is then the centroid of the *bark* and *kennel* vectors; that of $bark_{tree}$ is the (weighted) centroid of *bark, lumber,* and *canoes*. $Bark_{dog}$ becomes more *dog*-like and less *tree*-like; the opposite happens for $bark_{tree}$. If we had considered more than just three neighbors and selected a larger set of context-relevant neighbors to modify the *bark* vector two distinct meanings of *bark* would have emerged: selecting the six most highly activated neighbors to modify *bark* from a neighborhood of 500, the cosine between $bark_{tree}$ and $bark_{dog}$ is only .03. Furthermore, $bark_{dog}$ is no longer related to *tree*, cos = −.04, and $bark_{tree}$ is no longer related to *dog*, cos = .02.

The effect of predication on homonyms that have unrelated meanings is quite dramatic. That is not always the case. Words have different senses. In the present view, they have infinitely many senses, a new one in every context the word is used, but these senses need not differ much from each other. For instance, if the adjective *long* is used in the context of *time*, its vector is hardly modified at all, for *time* selects neighbors of *long* that are already very close to it (and hence have little effect when combined with the original vector); when *long* is used in the context *yard*, its meaning is changed a little more because slightly different neighbors are emphasized in the context of *yard* than in the context of *time*; however, when we talk about *a long story*, the sense of *long* is noticeably different than in *a yard long*: it moves away from *measure* and *distance* and comes closer to *book* and *read* (for more detail, see Kintsch, in press). Similarly, the *house* vector in the context of *yard* is not much modified, but the context *House of Representatives* quite changes the *house* vector, de-emphasizing the *house–yard* relation and moving it closer to *Congress* and *Senate*. In general, one can say that when words are used in the way they are normally used, context will have little effect on their meaning because high-frequency contexts are already well reflected by their LSA vector. However, if a word is used in an unexpected way, context affects its meaning a great deal, modifying its vector to reflect the unusual (or less usual) context.

The model of a generative lexicon sketched here (also Kintsch, 2001, 2007) sidesteps many of the problems encountered by the conventional view of the mental lexicon. (Klein & Murphy, 2001, although adopting that view, provide an excellent discussion of the serious difficulties faced by models of the mental lexicon). But the mental lexicon is not the primary concern of this chapter; the point here is, rather, that metaphor comprehension comes for free with the predication model. More specifically, the comprehension of metaphors of type (a) in Table 7.1 may involve no more than the same sort of sense generation that is needed every time a word is employed when it is used literally. Literal comprehension and metaphor comprehension, at least for the simplest kind of metaphors, involve the same psychological process, except that there is more of it in the metaphor case. Predication often does not do much when words are used in their canonical sense; when they are used metaphorically, the effects of predication are always pronounced, in contrast.

## The Predication Model for Simple Metaphors

Three lines of argumentation will be used here to evaluate the claim that (simple) metaphors and literal comprehension are the same in terms of the psychological processes involved. First, it will be shown that the predication algorithm yields intuitively sensible interpretations of metaphors. Second, the algorithm will be used to simulate some experimental results from the psycholinguistic literature. Finally, an attempt will be made to situate the present model in the context of the literature on metaphor and metaphor comprehension.

To show that predication generates sensible interpretations of metaphors is not a very strong argument, but it is a necessary precondition. Predication generates a vector, that is, a list of 300 numbers that by itself is totally uninterpretable. Kintsch (2000, 2001) demonstrated that this vector moves in the direction it is supposed to when compared with intuitively compelling semantic landmarks. Thus, *shark* alone is strongly related to *swim* and *fins* and only moderately related to *viciousness* and *bloodthirsty*; however, the *sharklawyer* that is generated from *My lawyer is a shark* is less related to the *fish* and more strongly to *viciousness* and *bloodthirsty*. Thus, what we say about *lawyer* is not that he is a *fish* (though residual *fish*-meanings are still there, too!) but that he is *vicious* and *dangerous*. Consider the reversible metaphor *My surgeon is a butcher – My butcher is a surgeon* with respect to the landmarks *scalpel* and *axe*. *Surgeon* is related to *scalpel*, cos = .29, but not to *axe*, cos = .05. *Butcher* is related to *axe*, cos = .37, but not to *scalpel*, cos = .01. *Surgeon* in the *butcher* context, however, is more strongly related to *axe*, cos = .42, than to *scalpel*, cos = .10. Conversely, *butcher* in the *surgeon* context has a cos = .25 with *scalpel* and cos = .26 with *axe*. According to this model, not even a surgeon-like butcher quite sheds his image.

A somewhat stronger test of the model involves its ability to simulate experimental results reported in the literature on metaphor comprehension. Kintsch (2000) has shown that the model can account for the qualitative results of two priming studies. In the first of these studies, by Glucksberg, McGlone, and Manfredi (1997), the time readers took to comprehend metaphors was measured as well as the interpretation that they generated. The metaphors were presented in two experimental conditions, with a literal prime and alone. For instance, if the metaphor to be comprehended was *My lawyer is a shark*, the literal prime would be *Sharks can swim*. Glucksberg et al. found that readers interpreted the metaphors as intended in both conditions, but that they took significantly longer when literal primes preceded them. Simulations with the predication model yield just this pattern: the final outcome is the same in the model, with and without prime, but a literal prime activates all the literal links in the semantic neighborhood and it takes several cycles of spreading activation before that activation is overcome and the appropriate metaphorical links begin to dominate. Without the literal prime, the metaphorical links are strong from the very beginning. The final state is the same, however, with and without a prime: the model settles on the intended metaphorical interpretation.

Another experiment that was simulated in Kintsch (2000) is just the reverse of the study just described: at issue is the comprehension of a simple literal statement (such as *Sharks are good swimmers*), with either a literal prime (*The hammerhead is a shark*) or a metaphorical prime (*My lawyer is a shark*). Gernsbacher and Keysar (1995) have shown that people have no problem verifying the target statement in either case, but the metaphorical prime slows them down. In the model, the literal prime activates all the right links in the semantic neighborhood, so that they have an advantage when the target statement is presented for verification; the metaphorical prime, however, gives an initial advantage to all the wrong links when the literal target has to be verified; it takes several cycles of a spreading activation to overcome that advantage, but overcome it will be, as both people and the model understand the target statement correctly.

Kintsch and Bowles (2002) have used the predication model to explore the differences between easy to understand and difficult to understand metaphors. Subjects rated a large number of metaphors of the form $N_1$ *is* $N_2$ for ease of comprehension on a scale of 1 to 5. For instance, *The mosquito is a vampire* was rated easy (1.29), while *Happiness is a ditch* was rated difficult (4.20). Subjects also completed sentence frames of the form $N_1$ *is* – with what they thought each metaphor was supposed to mean. For example, in response to *Some jobs are jails*, the 30 subjects gave the following responses: *confining* (six times), *dead ends* (twice), *hell* (twice), *prisons with no escape* (twice), and 18 answers given only by one person, such as *endless* and *hard to get out of*. The average cosine between pairs of responses in this set is .37.

Easy and difficult metaphors differed greatly in the responses they elicited. First, almost half of the subjects gave the same response (or paraphrases) when the interpretation was easy, versus only 21% for difficult metaphors. For difficult metaphors, subjects often did not come up with a response at all, which never happened for easy metaphors. Also, responses were more coherent for easy metaphors (the average cosine among responses was .64) than for difficult metaphors (cos = .55). All of these differences were statistically significant. What is surprising here is not that subjects are more consistent when they interpret easy metaphors, but how consistent their responses still are even to metaphors whose interpretation is far from obvious. The model simulations help us to understand why.

The first question Kintsch and Bowles asked was whether the model generates interpretations of metaphors that are like the ones people generate. To answer this question, the cosine was computed between the metaphor vector the model generated (i.e., the centroid of $N_1$, $N_2$, and four of its neighbors that are most strongly related to $N_1$) and the total set of responses produced by the subjects. This cosine turned out to be cos = .51 on the average, which is a sizeable value, hugely above the cosine between the metaphor vector and a random set of words of equal size. Interestingly, this value was the same for easy and difficult metaphors. In one case, there are a few strong responses given by most subjects; in the other, there is a more widely distributed response set, but the model accounts for both. Closer inspection of what the model does may help us understand what people do. For easy metaphors, such as *Happiness is gold*, the model does not have to look far among the close neighbors of *gold* to find ones that are related to *happiness*; for instance, *precious* is a very close neighbor of *gold* with a cosine of .67, and it is also strongly related to *happiness*, cos = .30. Thus, the model will zero in on a few strong responses, as people do. One might think that with difficult metaphors what happens is that the model has to search for neighbors much farther down the list to find something appropriate. Thus, for *Happiness is a ditch*, anything *happiness*-related in the neighborhood of *ditch* is very far away from *ditch*. But at that point, the spreading activation process does not activate that item strongly enough because the cosine with *ditch* is too low. Thus, no strongly activated item related to both words is found, and the most strongly activated words happen to be spurious items that are related only to one or the other of the words in the metaphor, not both. Thus, for *Happiness is a ditch*, whatever commonality there is in the subjects responses are either words related to *ditch* only (*deep*) or words related to *happiness* only (*precious*) – subjects respond with something, and the model computes something, but in either case, it is not really an interpretation of the metaphor but a stopgap.

Kintsch and Bowles (2002) conclude, albeit tentatively, that the predication model can predict the aptness of a metaphor: if the model finds a close neighbor of the predicate that is at all related to the argument, readers will consider it an apt metaphor, much as envisaged in the salience imbalance theory of Ortony (1979). However, generating a metaphorical meaning is not a matter of feature transfer: the neighbors that are selected by the predication model to create a metaphorical interpretation of a word do not simply become attributes of that word but rather, by being merged into the word vector, change its relation to the whole semantic space, with possibly wide-ranging effects throughout that space.

Many questions about metaphor comprehension remain to be answered, however. If literal statements and metaphors are processed the same way, how is it possible that people have no trouble saying that *My lawyer is a shark* is a metaphor and *Sharks can swim* is not? Of course, human judgment is not always as reliable – it may take some convincing before the linguistically untrained undergraduate accepts that *The stock market went down* involves a metaphor, but in general, there is a real distinction there. An explanation may involve the notion of embodiment: for literal statements, the nonverbal representation maps directly into the verbal one, whereas this may not be the case for metaphorical statements. Another distinction that needs to be made is that between metaphors and similes (e.g., Glucksberg, 2001). The predication model creates contextualized representations in the same way for both. It may be the case, however, that the linguistic cues *is-a* versus *like* are instructions to treat these representations differently: for an *is-a* metaphor to be apt, all that is required is that there are one or a few links between the near neighborhood of the predicate and the argument; the *like* in a simile, however, requires that most or at least many of the neighbors of the predicate are appropriate for the argument. Thus, *He eats like a pig* implies that his eating was like that of a pig in most respects, while *He is a pig* may say something about his behavior, character, even appearance, without disputing the obvious difference in many other respects between man and pig. However, these questions deserve more systematic research before these speculations can be considered as more than tentative.

The most important claim made by the present model is that literal and metaphoric comprehension are the same. Historically, a sharp distinction has been made between literal and figurative language. Metaphor was considered a way to express literal semantics indirectly: if a statement does not make sense literally, it must be reinterpreted metaphorically (e.g., Searle, 1979). A series of psychological experiments in the 1970s and 1980s has provided conclusive evidence against this sequential view, however (for a review, see Gibbs, 1994). Currently, two classes of theories of metaphor dominate the discussion in cognitive science and compete with each other. Literal and figurative comprehension are thought to involve either parallel processes or are considered essentially the same. According to Lakoff and Johnson (1980) and Gibbs (1994) metaphor comprehension occurs in parallel with literal comprehension, but it is special because metaphors are understood with reference to a set of conceptual metaphors, which are organizing principles in long-term memory. According to Glucksberg and his collaborators (for a review, see Glucksberg, 1998), metaphor and literal comprehension are the same: metaphors are understood not by accessing conceptual metaphors from long-term memory but by creating an ad hoc category in working memory. The present model is closely related to Glucksberg's class-inclusion model. The main difference is that it spells out exactly how that new category is generated in context.

But the predication model is not necessarily in conflict with the Lakoff–Gibbs approach either. Predication works by selecting context appropriate information from the semantic neighborhood of words, which contains information about the conceptual schemata that are claimed to be essential for metaphor comprehension. Thus, the neighborhood of *love* must contain items relevant to the various *love*-schemata, such as *love is a journey, love is insanity, love is a battle*, and so on. A particular metaphor about *love* would pick out items relevant to one of these schemata to construct a unique and novel concept in working memory, thereby creating a new class in the Glucksberg sense, or accessing a Lakoffian knowledge schema. The difference between a literal statement like *Love is an emotion* and a metaphor like *Love is madness* might simply be that a different body of knowledge becomes relevant – what we know about emotions in one case, and what we have learned about how people behave when they are in love. One might argue, then, about whether human knowledge is indeed organized in terms of metaphorical knowledge schemata as posited by Lakoff, but the difference between parallel and same processing of metaphors disappears in the present model. Thus, expressing a theory in computational terms, in this case, does not help us to distinguish between alternatives, but questions whether these theories are in fact alternatives as far as processing is concerned. In the present framework, literal and metaphorical statements are processed the same way but might very well depend on distinct bodies of knowledge.

## Metaphor and Analogy

So far, we have restricted ourselves to metaphors of type (a) in Table 7.1, simple $N_1$-*is*-$N_2$ constructions. Metaphors of type (b) are considerably more complicated from a processing standpoint because of a shift in emphasis from semantic content to semantic relations. It no longer suffices to look at how the meaning of a word, its semantic content, is modified when it is used metaphorically, but what matters is the semantic relationship between words. To understand *She blew up at me*, it is not sufficient to let *she* select the items it likes out of the neighborhood of *blew up*; understanding requires a deeper analysis in this case. Many authors (e.g., Gentner & Markman, 1997; Gentner et al., 2001; Lakoff & Johnson, 1980) have pointed out that such metaphors are based on an underlying analogy, and that understanding requires that the unexpressed implied elements of that analogy must in some way be reconstructed. To understand what *she* did, we must note that *she* corresponds to some object that can *blow-up* – a *kettle*, a *bomb*, or even a *volcano*, whatever happens to be most salient in one's personal experience – and that *blow-up* corresponds to something like *become-angry*. The analogy problem that needs to be solved in this case is (*volcano*) : *blow-up* : *she* : (*become-angry*). *Volcano* and *become-angry* are enclosed with brackets, because the whole point of a metaphor is that these can be left vague and underspecified; it is some container that blows up, and she acts in a violent and destructive manner. What is important is that the relation between *volcano* : *blow-up* and *person* : *become-angry* is preserved. In LSA terms, we generate a vector in the semantic space that is related to "person" in the same way that blow-up is related to "volcano" – naming it *become-angry* is only for our convenience and a little misleading, for the whole point is that we have created a vector in the semantic space that does not correspond to an existing literal expression in our language, thereby extending the expressivity of language.

**Table 7.2: Sample analogy problems (after Mangalath, Quesada, & Kintsch, 2004)**

| *scissors : cut* | *diversion : boredom* |
|---|---|
| knife : cut | assurance : uncertainty |
| clamp : sharpen | enmity : hatred |
| pen : write | secrecy : curiosity |
| chair : sing | reward : deed |
| | sluggishness : fatigue |

A complete computational model of how people understand metaphors like *She blew up at me* does not yet exist. However, to understand such metaphors, an underlying analogy problem must be solved, and the predication model has been extended to solving analogy problems.

A set of 374 analogy problems from old versions of the Scholastic Aptitude Test (SAT) collected by Turney and Littman (2005) was used as a test bed. These problems are all of the same form as the examples shown in Table 7.2, with answers to be selected from a set of multiple-choice alternatives. Intuitively, people solve these problems by considering the meaning of each of the word pairs to determine the nature of the semantic relations that exist between the words. Are they related as an instance to a class, or a part to a whole, or as opposites – or in some other way? If one or more prominent semantic relations are detected between the words of the source pair, people analyze the relations between the words in the target pairs and look for the alternative that most closely matches the source pair in terms of the semantic relationship between the words.

In the case of the *scissors* : *cut* example, the most obvious semantic relation that links these two words is "is-used-to" which matches the relation in two of the target pairs, (a) *knife* : *cut* as well as (c) *pen* : *write*. These are said to be the structurally related target pairs, and both would be correct answers in an analogy test. Alternative (b) is semantically similar to the source pair but is not structurally related because *clamps* are not used to *sharpen*.

Mangalath, Quesada, and Kintsch (2004) have proposed a model of analogical problem solving that mimics the way people solve such problems. First, the meaning of the source words is contextually elaborated. This is done with the predication algorithm in exactly the same way as for metaphors. Specifically, the contextualized meaning of each word in the context of the other is generated, yielding a vector composed of the two words themselves and whatever semantic neighbors are most relevant to each in the context of the other. Second, this vector representing the contextualized meaning of a word pair is compared with a number of prominent semantic relations that have been identified in the linguistic literature, specifically, 10 between-word relations that have been identified in WordNet (Fellbaum, 1998). Each relation is characterized for this purpose by a set of words commonly used to express this relation. Table 7.3 shows the semantic relations and their corresponding words that have been employed in the analyses reported by Mangalath et al.

The cosines between the *scissors-cut* vector and hyponymy or antonymy words, for example, will be relatively low (*kind-of* or *opposite-of* do not fit in well with *scissors-cut*), whereas the cosines between the use and entailment words will be higher (*scissors* have the purpose of *cutting*, *cut* may imply *scissors*, etc.). To determine which multiple-choice alternative is most like the source pair in terms of semantic relations, the model computes the correlation between the cosines of the source pair and the 10 relations and the cosines of each alternative pair and the 10 relations. In the present example, these correlations are $r = .99$ for *knife-cut* (i.e., the semantic relations between *scissors-cut* and *knife cut* are identical), and $r = .86$ for *pen-write*, also very high. The semantically similar (*scissors* and *clamp* are related, as are *cut* and *sharpen*) but structurally unrelated (*clamps* are not used to *sharpen*) distracter *clamp-sharpen* correlates less highly than the semantically dissimilar but structurally related *pen-write*, $r = .79$. The unrelated alternative *chair-sing*, does not

**Table 7.3: Ten semantic relations and the words used to express these relations (after Mangalath, Quesada, & Kintsch, 2004)**

| | |
|---|---|
| (i). | Hyponymy – X is a type of Y (for example – *Maple:Tree*) {Subordinate of, superordinate to, rank, class, category, family, genus, variety, type of, kind of, hyponym} |
| (ii). | Degree – X means extremely Y (*Pour:Drip*) {level, stage, point, magnitude, extent, greater, lesser, intensity, severity, extreme, degree} |
| (iii). | Meronymy – The parts of X include the Ys (*Body:Arm*) {part, whole, component, made up of, portion, contains, constituent, segment, piece of, composite, meronym} |
| (iv). | Taxonomy – X is an item in the category Y (*Milk:Beverage*) {classification, containing, structure, relationship, hierarchy, system, framework, taxonym} |
| (v). | Synonymy – X is the same as Y (*Work:Labor*) {equivalent, equal, likeness, match, interchangeable, alike, same as, similar, close to, like, synonym} |
| (vi). | Antonymy – X is the opposite of Y (*Find:Hide*) {opposite, unlike, different, antithesis, opposed, contradiction, contrast, reverse, anti, not the same as, antonym} |
| (vii). | Characteristic – X is a characteristic of Y (*Dishonesty:Liar*) {indicative, representative of, typical of, feature, attribute, trait, property, mannerism, facet, quality, characteristic} |
| (viii). | (Plurality – X is many Ys (*Throng:People*) {mass, bulk, several, many, lots of, numerous, crowd, group, more, number, plural} |
| (ix). | Endonymy – X entails Y (*Coop:Poultry*) {entails, require, evoke, involve, suggest, imply, presuppose, mean} |
| (x). | Instrument – X is used to Y (*Scissors:Cut*) {do with, manipulate, operate, function, purpose, role, action, utilize, employ, use} |

correlate at all, $r = .22$. Figure 7.2 shows the pattern of results obtained for the second example shown in Table 7.2. The pattern of cosines between the source pair *boredom-diversion* and the semantic relations correlates most highly with the correct choice *assurance-uncertainty*, $r = .96$. The two alternatives that share some relational similarity with the correct choice, *enmity-hatred* and *secrecy-curiosity*, yield high correlations, $r = .55$ and $r = .61$, respectively. The alternatives that are clearly different structurally yielded low correlations, $r = .29$ for *reward-deed*, and $r = .15$ for *sluggishness-fatigue*.

The Mangalath et al. model was evaluated against the whole set of 374 analogy problems from old SAT tests collected by Turney and Littman (2005). The model chose the correct response on 48% of the problems and erred on 34%. For the remaining 18%, the model failed to produce an answer because one or more words in the problem did not appear in the corpus on which LSA was based. That corpus was the General Reading Space (available at lsa.colorado.edu) that estimates the total reading material that a typical high school graduate might have read, amounting to about 11 million words. Thus, the model's performance should be compared to the performance of students taking the SAT, not to highly educated people who would get most of these SAT problems correct. In fact, Mangalath et al. estimated that their model performed at a level corresponding to the 41st percentile of college-bound seniors. They also reported an experiment in which the solution rates of college freshmen for various analogy problems were compared with each other and the model. The model's solution rates on different problems were just as similar to that of the college freshman as one student to another. Thus, the model's performance does not appear to be discernibly different from that of the students who might be expected to take the SAT.

Turney and Littman (2005) achieve a comparable performance rate, with 47% correct solutions, which improved to 56% in a newer version of their model (Turney, 2004). Their system is an artificial intelligence system, not a model of human

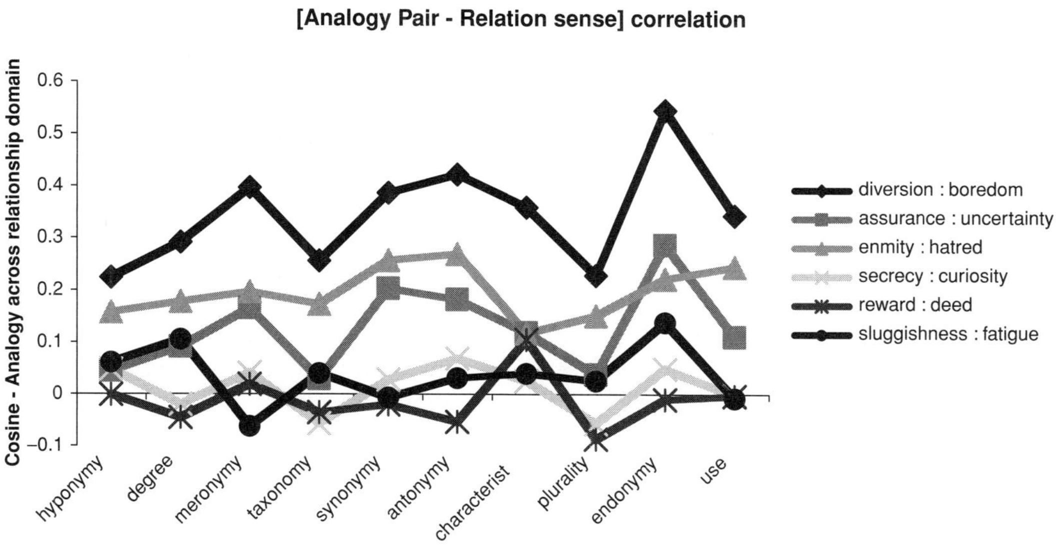


**Figure 7.2.** The cosines between 10 semantic relations and the analogy *diversion* : *boredom* and five alternatives.

problem solving and involves searching a very large database for the relations that exist between the various word pairs. There are other psychological models of analogy making and several well-developed theories. The present model is quite compatible with the theoretical thinking on analogy (e.g., Gentner, 1983; Holyoak & Thagard, 1989). Its main contribution is that it is a computational model that, unlike other computational models, builds its own problem representation in an automatic way and does not have to rely on hand-coded representations. There are computational models that can handle more difficult analogy problems (French, 2002, provides a review), but they bypass the crucial initial step of generating the knowledge representation for a problem.

The model of analogy so far developed is a building block for a complete computational model of metaphor understanding for metaphors of type (b) in Table 7.1. What is missing is a component that generates the terms for the analogy from memory. The existing model demonstrates, however, that a system based on associative knowledge like LSA can be extended to model analytical reasoning and hence may someday be capable of modeling comprehension for more complex metaphors.

## Metaphors as Expressions of Similarity, Category Membership, and Analogies

At various points in this chapter, comparisons were made between the present model and the rich psycholinguistic literature on metaphor. A recent paper by Bowdle and Gentner (2005) provides a convenient framework to make these comparisons more systematic, thus placing the present model more precisely within the existing literature.

Bowdle and Gentner (2005) have compared and contrasted three different views of metaphoric mapping: the classical theory that metaphors express similarities (of which Aristotle and Ortony, 1979, are representative); the view of Glucksberg and others that metaphors express category memberships (e.g., Glucksberg & Keysar, 1990); and their own model, which regards metaphors as analogies. They discuss a number of problems of the first two approaches. Since the present model is clearly related to both of these approaches, it is instructive to see how it fares with respect to these criticisms. Bowdle & Gentner find four problems with similarity models.

1. Similarity models beg the question, which properties are selected for the comparison. Thus, in *Dew is a veil,* there are numerous properties of *dew* and *veil* (e.g., *silent*) that are irrelevant to the meaning of the metaphor. The present model never selects properties but adds word vectors. Since both *dew* and *veil* are related to *silent* in more or less the same way, their vector sum will have the same relation to *silent* as either term alone. Hence, irrelevant properties are not (or only minimally) affected by the predication algorithm.
2. Similarity models have problems with the asymmetry of metaphors. The predication procedure is essentially asymmetric.
3. Features can mean something different in different contexts, for example, both *men* and *wolves* are *predatory,* but what that means is quite different. In the predication model, when *predatory* is predicated about *wolves* its vector representation is different than when it is predicated about *men*.
4. Metaphors may transfer whole knowledge systems from one domain to another, as in *The mind is a computer,* or the example shown in Table 7.1 (c). This is a criticism of the present model, too, which has not been extended to complex system analogies.
5. Thus, the first three criticisms that Bowdle and Gentner have about similarity-based models of metaphor are no problem for the present model. They also make two criticisms of the category-based models.
6. It is not clear how category membership models arrive at the appropriate category. In their example, *A child is a snowflake* elicits the category *uniqueness,* while *Youth is a snowflake* requires the category *transience*. In the present model, all categories are constructed interactively from topic and vehicle as the metaphor is comprehended, so no preexisting categories have to be selected (as in the interactive property attribution model of Glucksberg et al., 1997).
7. Bowdle and Gentner object to the computational complexity of category-based models because it would "place unreasonable demands on a hearer's mental capacity" (p. 195). As the present model shows, that is not necessarily a problem: the predication algorithm is a simple spreading activation process in an already established semantic network, no more complex than many existing models of human performance. Spreading activation is presumably a parallel process in the brain and makes only small demands on its resources.

The model proposed here combines aspects of similarity comparisons and category classification, but it does not suffer from most of the limitations that Bowdle and Gentner noted for these types of models. Furthermore, it includes an analogy component. It is, however, limited to rather simple forms of metaphor and analogy. In its present form, it cannot deal with complex, system-based analogies that are central to some of the most interesting types of metaphor.

## The Creativity of Language

Metaphor researchers typically are not satisfied with studying comprehension in the laboratory under controlled and hence unnatural conditions, or with computer simulations of simple examples. The work reported here has been restricted to a limited range of metaphors – type (a) in Table 7.1, with a partial exploration of type (b). Both of these are simple metaphors whose comprehension is typically automatic and effortless. Indeed, one might complain that neither really involves what makes metaphors so interesting for most people – the creative aspect of cognition. Suppose we grant that people really understand simple, conventional metaphors in the manner sketched here. Some researchers who believe that metaphor is essential to creative thought might not find this work relevant to their concerns. That would be a mistake, however, and a fundamental misunderstanding of the creativity of language. What this chapter demonstrates is that human thought is creative even in its simplest forms, that meanings are never fixed, to be picked out ready-made from the right drawer when needed but are emergent, to be generated in the context of use. This is true for literal word senses as well as for metaphor, where the contextual effects are particularly noticeable. Creative thought is found not only in deep, literary metaphors or complex, scientific analogies but is pervasive in language, even if we can only model it explicitly in its simplest forms.

It has often been argued that metaphor represents an extension of the range of what language can express. People are simply unwilling to be silent about what they cannot talk about – they use metaphor instead. However, metaphor and literal comprehension are still considered by most authors to be different processes. The present work suggests that, while they clearly differ in linguistic analysis, in terms of psychological processes their underlying continuity should be emphasized.

The kind of computational model presented here is at present unable to cope with complex metaphors. Type (c) is well beyond its scope. To understand such metaphors, we need to compute not merely a single analogy as in the previous examples. Instead, a whole analogical structure must be generated that may have many different correspondences and alignments.[1] There are models of analogy making that can deal with complex structures, for example, like mapping the solar system into atomic structure. Such models (e.g., Forbus, Gentner, & Law, 1995; Hummel & Holyoak, 1997) can perform more complex mappings than the present model. However, because they rely on hand-coded propositional knowledge representations, they circumvent an essential component of the comprehension process, the construction of the problem-relevant knowledge representation, which is the focus of the present approach.

Writers have often reported that the very act of writing down an idea helped them to clarify it. Ideas in the head sometimes appear brilliant, only to be unmasked as unformed and incoherent when we try to put them down on paper. The virtue of computational modeling is much like that of writing down our thoughts: it forces us to think through a problem and face its implications. This chapter demonstrates how this approach, which has been successful in many areas of research, can also be effective in the study of metaphor.

## Note

1 Furthermore, this example (*The universe is a computer*) is an empty metaphor for most of us because understanding it requires a great deal of technical knowledge about quantum mechanics that we don't have.

## References

Bowdle, B. F., & Gentner, D. (2005). The career of metaphor. *Psychological Review, 112*, 193–216.

Fellbaum, C. (Ed.). (1998). *WordNet: An electronic lexical database*. Cambridge, England: Cambridge University Press.

Forbus, K. D., Gentner, D., & Law, K. (1995). MAC/FAC: A model of similarity based retrieval. *Cognitive Science, 19*, 141–205.

French, R. M. (2002). The computational modeling of analogy-making. *Trends in Cognitive Sciences, 6*, 200–205.

Gentner, D. (1983). Structure mapping: A theoretical framework for analogy. *Cognitive Science, 7*, 155–170.

Gentner, D., Bowdle, B., Wolff, P., & Boronat, C. (2001). Metaphor is like analogy. In D. Gentner, K. J. Holyoak, & B. N. Kokinov (Eds.), *The analogical mind: Perspectives from Cognitive Science* (pp. 199–253). Cambridge, MA: MIT Press.

Gentner, D., & Markman, A. B. (1997). Structure mapping in analogy and similarity. *American Psychologist, 52*, 45–56.

Gernsbacher, M. A., & Keysar, B. (1995). *The role of suppression in metaphor interpretation.*

Paper presented at the Psychonomic Society, Los Angeles.

Gibbs, R. W. (1994). Figurative thought and figurative language. In M. A. Gernsbacher (Ed.), *Handbook of psycholinguistics* (pp. 411–446). San Diego, CA: Academic Press.

Glucksberg, S. (1998). Understanding metaphors. *Current Directions in Psychological Science, 7*, 39–43.

Glucksberg, S. (2001). *Understanding figurative language: From metaphors to idioms*. New York: Oxford University Press.

Glucksberg, S., & Keysar, B. (1990). Understanding metaphorical comparisons: Beyond similarity. *Psychological Review*, 97, 3–18.

Glucksberg, S., McGlone, M. S., & Manfredi, D. A. (1997). Property attribution in metaphor comprehension. *Journal of Memory and Language*, 36, 50–67.

Holyoak, K. J., & Thagard, P. (1989). Analogical mapping by constraint satisfaction. *Cognitive Science*, 13, 295–355.

Hummel, J. E., & Holyoak, K. J. (1997). Distributed representation of structure: A theory of analogical access and mapping. *Psychological Review*, 104, 427–466.

Kintsch, W. (1998). *Comprehension: A paradigm for cognition*. New York: Cambridge University Press.

Kintsch, W. (2000). Metaphor comprehension: A computational theory. *Psychonomic Bulletin & Review*, 7, 257–266.

Kintsch, W. (2001). Predication. *Cognitive Science*, 25, 173–202.

Kintsch, W., & Bowles, A. R. (2002). Metaphor comprehension: What makes metaphors difficult to understand? *Metaphor and Symbol*, 17, 249–262.

Kintsch, W. (2007). Meaning in context. In T. K. Landauer, D. McNamara, S. Dennis, & W. Kintsch (Eds.), *Handbook of latent semantic analysis* (pp. 89–106). Mahwah, NJ: Erlbaum.

Klein, D. E., & Murphy, G. L. (2001). The representation of polysemous words. *Journal of Memory and Language*, 45, 259–282.

Lakoff, G., & Johnson, M. (1980). *Metaphors we live by*. Chicago: University of Chicago Press.

Landauer, T. K., & Dumais, S. T. (1997). A solution to Plato's problem: The latent semantic analysis theory of acquisition, induction and representation of knowledge. *Psychological Review*, 104, 211–240.

Landauer, T. K., McNamara, D., Dennis, S., & Kintsch, W. (Eds.). (2007). *Handbook of latent semantic analysis*. Mahwah, NJ: Erlbaum.

Ortony, A. (1979). Beyond literal similarity. *Psychological Review*, 86, 161–180.

Mangalath, P., Quesada, J., & Kintsch, W. (2004) *Analogy-making: A computational model based on LSA*. Paper presented at the Cognitive Science Society, Chicago.

Searle, J. (1979). Metaphor. In A. Ortony (Ed.), *Metaphor and thought*. New York: Cambridge University Press.

Turney, P. D. (2004). *Human-level performance on word analogy questions by Latent Relational Analysis*. National Research Council Canada.

Turney, P. D., & Littman, M. L. (2005). Corpus based learning of analogies and semantic relations. *Machine Learning*, 60, 251–278.

CHAPTER 8

# Is Metaphor Unique?

*Rachel Giora*

## Introduction

Is metaphor unique as assumed by Aristotle (350 BCE-a, b) and more recently by Grice (1975) and Searle (1979)? Is metaphor more creative than literal language? Are the processes involved in making sense of nonliteral language different from those involved in interpreting literal utterances? The following literal pun (1) and the (originally Hebrew) metaphors in (2) and (3) (in italics for convenience) might help illustrate these questions. The first example appeared in *Haaretz in English*; the second example appeared in an editorial of the far-left Israeli magazine *Etgar*; the third example projects the attitude of a rightwing Israeli journalist toward the prospective Road Map Agreement between the Palestinians and the Israelis:

(1) Till barriers do them part

Together, the separation fence, the Law of Citizenship, and the curfew are breaking down and restructuring marriages in Arab society. (Ettinger, 2004)

(2) The anti globalization movement . . . refused to point an accusing finger at the political address responsible for the economic chaos – the White House and its satellites. Bin Laden made concrete, even if lunatic, the insubstantial slogan of the [anti globalization] movement. ("Smash Capitalism," 2003, p. 3)

(3) Yeah, during two years they [the Palestinians] are *to pay lip service* {Hebrew: 'lip tax'} to democracy. But they are not required *to pay hard cash* – to truly and sincerely accept the existence of a Jewish state. (Shavit, 2003)

The first example is a literal pun. It gives rise to two literal meanings: a novel one, which is made explicit (*Till barriers do them part*) and a salient one, which is evoked by the explicit and which is associated with the marriage vows (*Till death do us part*). The interplay between these two meanings, allowed by the activation and retention of both, makes up the message of the utterance. It alludes to the damage inflicted on Palestinian families by the Israeli brutal occupation. The second example seems to invite activation and retention of the salient, nonliteral sense of a conventional metaphor – the anticapitalism sense of *Smash Capitalism* – alongside its less salient, somewhat literal meaning which evokes the sense of real smashing of some of the symbols of capitalism (on meaning salience, see Giora, 1997, 2003; see also section on "Models of Metaphor Processing," this chapter). The third example features a (Hebrew) conventional idiomatic phrase – *pay lip service* – which is suggestive of an apparent, insincere commitment. In addition, it features a novel metaphor – *pay hard cash* – which, in the given context, is an extension of both the literal and nonliteral senses of the previous idiom, alluding to the opposite of that idiom, that is, to some substantial, binding commitment.

Do we engage in different processes, then, when trying to make sense of such literal and nonliteral uses? Admittedly, in all the examples, the salient sense of the expressions cannot escape our mind even when apparently inappropriate: The novel literal use of *Till barriers do them part* activates the salient literal vow *Till death do us part*. The novel literal use of *Smash Capitalism* allows an insight into the salient nonliteral sense of the metaphor – the anticapitalism protest – on top of the novel literal interpretation of the collocation alluding to the physical destruction of trade center buildings, which is now brought to the fore (see also Giora, Fein, Kronrod, et al., 2004). Similarly, the novel metaphor in (3) – *pay hard cash* – draws on the conventionalized nonliteral use of *pay lip service* intending, however, to get across its opposite – a binding commitment, while echoing the literal monetary sense.

The third example is particularly interesting because it also resonates[1] with metaphors, appearing earlier in the text (see 4). These also include a negative metaphor (*does not include such an obvious barter*) whose salient literal meaning derives from the same semantic field (of financial or monetary exchanges) as the metaphors that follow it:

(4) The road map does not include such an obvious *barter*. Instead it goes back to the old mistake of giving a huge *credit* to a suspicious *loaner*. It gets back to the belying medicine of postponing the *pay* day. (Shavit, 2003)

Such extensions (as seen in both 3 and 4) suggest that the literal meaning of the negated metaphor has been activated (via intra-lexical priming; see Fodor, 1983, p. 81) and has not been suppressed automatically even in the presence of a contextual cue to the contrary. Instead, it has been retained for future purposes. Thus, even when a local contextual cue such as negation alerts the comprehender to the contrary, suppression is kept on hold until late context either invites it or not (see, Giora, Fein, Aschkenazi, & Alkabets-Zlozover, 2007).

These literal and metaphoric examples help shed light on an enduring question in the pragmatics and psycholinguistics of metaphor. They suggest that, contra the traditional view, which assumes the uniqueness of metaphor (Grice, 1975; Searle, 1979), metaphors and literals need not differ but instead may involve similar processes and products. In what follows, I will adduce evidence that argues against the uniqueness hypothesis.

Apparently, some of the issues to be discussed here belong in the early stages of comprehension, disclosing early processes, while others belong in the later interpretation processes, disclosing utterance products (on the time course of metaphor interpretation involving early *processes* and late *products*, see Gibbs, 1993, 1994, pp. 115–119; see also section on "Models of Metaphor Processing"). Early stages pertain to bottom-up, automatic, and stimulus-driven processes such as lexical access; later processes pertain to the products of these processes, which involve top-down procedures such as inferencing, loosening or narrowing of initial outputs, and suppression or even retention of inappropriate outputs. The various models of figurative language have different assumptions and predictions concerning the time course of metaphor understanding in as far as early *processes* and late *products* are concerned.

## Models of Metaphor Processing

Metaphor theories can be viewed as either advocating the supremacy of context effects or subscribing to the priority of lexical effects. Though they all acknowledge the effects of context on the products of metaphor, they disagree as to the size of the effect and its time course. The various assumptions have different implications with regard to the issue of metaphor uniqueness.

### *On the Temporal Priority of Context Effects*

#### THE DIRECT ACCESS VIEW

Most contemporary theorists advocate the superiority of contextual over lexical processes. They assume a single mechanism that is sensitive to both linguistic and nonlinguistic information. On this view, contextual information interacts with lexical processes very early on, and when context is sufficiently rich and supportive, it allows comprehension to proceed smoothly and seamlessly, selectively accessing appropriate meanings while blocking incompatible albeit salient ones. Consequently, early processes should involve no contextually inappropriate phase (Ortony, Schallert, Reynolds, & Antos, 1978). This should be particularly true of meanings of complete phrases or sentences (Gibbs, 1994).

Given that a strong prior context allows early processes to involve no inappropriate outputs, no suppression or retention of such outputs is anticipated when later interpretation processes take place. That is, a view that attributes to (rich) contextual information a major role in the early stages of comprehension, predicts no differences between metaphors and literals embedded in such a context (see Ortony et al., 1978). This view, however, will find it difficult to account for the involvement of "inappropriate" literal meanings in metaphor comprehension and interpretation (examples 2–4; though one could argue they might be reactivated).

#### THE CONSTRAINT-BASED SATISFACTION MODEL

A more recent version of the direct access view is the constraint-based satisfaction model. According to this view, comprehension is achieved through parallel satisfaction of multiple probabilistic constraints, including constraints from lexical representations. According to constraint-based models, if contextual constraints outnumber lexical constraints, they will win over, and comprehension will proceed seamlessly, tapping only appropriate meanings (Katz & Ferretti, 2001, 2003; Pexman, Ferretti, & Katz, 2000). According to this version of the direct access view, differences in processes would be a result of difference in the amount of constraints biased in favor of one interpretation rather than between literals and metaphors.

### *On the Temporal Priority of Lexical Meanings*

#### THE STANDARD PRAGMATIC MODEL

The direct access view argues against the standard pragmatic model (Grice, 1975; Searle, 1979), which posits the priority of *literal* meanings. This view, which assumes that literal meanings of both words and sentences should be accessed initially, regardless of contextual information, concedes that the consequences of initial input analyses are accidental. While they may result in contextual fit, they might just as well lead to mismatch with prior context, which would then have to be redressed. Alleviating such dissonances would, in many cases, invite suppression of contextually inappropriate outputs. The standard pragmatic model, then, predicts initial literally oriented processes for both literals and metaphors, with a second stage of adjustment in the case of metaphors only. According to this model, somewhat downstream, literal meanings of metaphors will have to be suppressed. Much like the direct access view, this view will find it difficult to account for the involvement of 'inappropriate' literal meanings in metaphor comprehension and interpretation as shown by examples 2–4, though, again, one could argue that these meanings might be reactivated.

THE UNDERSPECIFICATION VIEW

The underspecification model of metaphor comprehension (Frisson & Pickering, 2001; Pickering & Frisson, 2001) also posits the priority of lexical effects. It assumes that lexical entries are stored as highly abstract, underspecified entities. Initially, metaphors (and other polysemies) are accessed via a single, abstract core. Context effects should occur following lexical access and determine the contextually appropriate, specific meaning of the metaphor. Results indeed show that only when resolution is required, comprehenders use contextual information to home in on the more specific, contextually appropriate sense.

Somewhat similar views are entertained by relevance-oriented theoreticians (Carston, 2002; Sperber & Wilson, 1986/1995, this volume). Though there is no commitment to an underspecification view, metaphor interpretation is taken to be fully shaped by context only following initial access of minimal output – logical forms and linguistic meanings. The final interpretation is achieved via loosening and narrowing down of these initial outputs (Carston, 2002, pp. 323–359). Narrowing down involves the extension of conceptual material and is thus consistent with an underspecification view of the lexicon. Loosening, which involves the subtraction of conceptual material, seems less so. Discarding features of a concept that has already been accessed, however, is in line with the view that metaphor interpretation involves suppression of inappropriate features. But this might just as well be true of literals as well. On this view, then, literals and metaphors need not differ.

THE GRADED SALIENCE HYPOTHESIS

Following the modular view (Fodor, 1983), the graded salience hypothesis (Giora, 1997, 1999, 2003; Peleg, Giora, & Fein, 2001, 2004) assumes two distinct mechanisms that run parallel. One is bottom-up, stimulus driven, and sensitive only to linguistic stimuli; another is top-down, predictive and integrative, and sensitive to both linguistic and extra-linguistic knowledge. Unlike the traditional modular assumption (Fodor, 1983), however, the graded salience hypothesis assumes that the bottom-up, modular mechanism is salience sensitive: more salient responses – responses coded in the mental lexicon and foremost on our mind due to, for example, conventionality, frequency, familiarity, or prototypicality – are accessed faster than and reach sufficient levels of activation before less salient ones. Accordingly, such responses would be accessed upon encounter, regardless of contextual information or authorial intent. Low salience responses, however, may not reach a threshold and may not be visible in a context biased toward the more salient meaning of the stimulus. Nonsalient meanings are not coded. They are constructed on the fly as a result of top-down processes.

Though this model seems to argue in favor of the temporal priority of salient responses, it does not discard the possibility of the temporal priority of nonsalient meanings. Rather, a highly predictive context may facilitate responses on its own accord very early on. Still, it would not interfere with automatic, stimulus-driven lexical processes and would not block activation of salient responses. Though the contextual mechanism has a predictive role that may speed up derivation of the appropriate responses, it would not obstruct inappropriate, coded responses upon encounter of the stimulus. Indeed, contextual information may be strong and even faster than lexical processes, so that it may evoke appropriate meanings even before the linguistic stimulus is encountered. This may be particularly true when the stimulus is placed at the end of a strong sentential context, after most information has been accumulated and integrated, allowing effective guessing and inferential processes. However, it does not interact with lexical processes but runs parallel (Peleg et al., 2001, 2004). Unlike the modular view (Fodor, 1983), then, the graded salience hypothesis does not always predict slower contextual effects and resultant sequential processes. Neither does it assume that activation of a whole linguistic unit should be accomplished before contextual information comes into play. Rather, across the communication route, context and linguistic processes run parallel, with contextual information evoking meanings on its own accord, yet affecting only the end product of the linguistic process.

Additionally, the graded salience hypothesis does not assume that contextually inappropriate meanings should be discarded unconditionally on account of their local contextual misfit (for a different view, see Gernsbacher, Keysar, Robertson, & Werner, 2001; Swinney, 1979). Instead, it views late processes such as retention of relevant and irrelevant information and suppression of contextually inappropriate outputs as more attentive to global discourse considerations, such as global coherence, than to local ones, such as local coherence (Giora, 2003; Giora, Fein, Aschkenazi, et al., 2007). Thus, even if the literal meaning of metaphors seems irrelevant in a given context (local coherence; negation), it might be retained because it is perceived as instrumental in constructing the appropriate metaphoric interpretation or as conducive to the interpretation of the next expression in line (global coherence). This might explain the availability of the apparently inappropriate literal meaning of *pay lip service* in the extended novel metaphor *pay hard cash* (3) which follows it (global resonance). This may also account for the availability of this literal meaning in the metaphors (*credit*; *loaner*; *pay day*) that follow the negated metaphor (*do not include such an obvious barter*) in (4). This might also explain the availability of an inappropriate, metaphorically related meaning (*fast*) in the following (originally Hebrew) negated metaphor (in bold for convenience), which was retained in the mind of the producer echoing his interlocutor's thought, in spite of a local cue to the contrary:

(5) A: Listen, with your car, you are there, maximally, in 5 minutes . . .
B: Come on . . . *My Daihatsu is not a jet*. A **fast** car . . . superb car . . . But there's a limit . . . (Cited in Altiti & Arvatz, 2005; Giora, 2006)

This view of suppression and retention, then, runs counter to the assumptions of the alternative models and suggests that both retention and suppression are not automatic but attentive to global discourse considerations.

According to the graded salience hypothesis, then, the relevant distinction is not between metaphors and literals but between salient and less salient meanings. Salient meanings will always be accessed, which explains the involvement of such meanings in examples 1–5, regardless of figurativeness or literality. Less salient meanings will lag behind. Retention and suppression will affect salient and less salient meanings alike, whether or not they are "appropriate," depending on their discourse role.

## Context Effects: Inhibition/Suppression/Retention

Although the direct access models and the standard pragmatic approach disagree as to whether early processes are sensitive to prior contextual information, they agree that later processes are. This is also true of the relevance theoretic account and the underspecification model. On these views, the output of later integration processes involves only contextually appropriate meanings. Even if inappropriate senses have infiltrated early processes, they would later be subdued by a rich and supportive context and be replaced with contextually appropriate alternatives. Thus, if *My surgeon is a butcher* involves reference to a literal "butcher" whose salient property is "using knives to chop messily or clumsily," this literal property would be discarded once the abstract metaphoric sense of "messiness and clumsiness" is constructed (Glucksberg, Newsome, & Goldvarg, 2001). In contrast, according to the suppression/retention hypothesis supplementing the graded salience hypothesis (Giora, 2003; Giora & Fein, 1999b), suppression of salient, "inappropriate" meanings is not automatic. It would take effect only if meanings interfere with constructing the appropriate interpretation. However, if these meanings are not detrimental to comprehension or if they are conducive to the appropriate interpretation (e.g., the literal meaning of metaphors and ironies), suppression would not be triggered (see Giora, Fein, Laadan, Wolfson, Zeituny, Kidron, Kaufman, and Shaham, 2007). Indeed, at times, salient meanings would not be suppressed even when they interfere with contextually appropriate interpretations, because they would be too hard to quench on account of their high salience (e.g., the idiomatic meanings of familiar idioms, see example 9). Theories, then, that do not subscribe to early inhibition processes, acknowledge later suppression effects whether automatic or pragmatically oriented.

According to the direct access view and the constraints-based model, however, one could, in fact, expect early inhibition of inappropriate meanings. Thus, when context is strong and supportive, initial activation of inappropriate word and sentence meanings will be aborted. Such processing should result in exclusive activation of contextually appropriate products. Inhibition, then, relates to early context effects, which should be able to monitor initial activation of responses.

## Findings

### *Inhibition of Contextually Inappropriate Properties*

Is there support for the view that context penetrates lexical processes and selects contextually appropriate meanings exclusively while inhibiting incompatible ones? In Peleg et al. (2001), we argued against the inhibition hypothesis. Using lexical decision tasks, we demonstrated that even a strong and supportive (Hebrew) context (*Sarit's sons and mine went on fighting continuously. Sarit said to me: These delinquents won't let us have a moment of peace*) did not inhibit salient but contextually incompatible meanings ("criminal") of targets (*delinquent*) which were as available as contextually compatible meanings ("kids."). This was true even where contextual information should have been highly effective, as when target words were placed at the end of sentences and probed immediately afterward (*Sarit's sons and mine went on fighting continuously. Sarit said to me: A moment of peace won't let us have these delinquents*).

Similarly, in Rubio Fernández (2007), following figuratively biasing contexts, such as *John doesn't like physical contact. Even his girl friend finds it difficult to come close to him. John is a cactus.*, salient, literal meanings, whether directly relevant to the (novel) metaphor ("spike") or not ("plant"), were accessed immediately at 0 msec delay and retained even at a 400 msec delay.

Likewise, in Hasson and Glucksberg (2006), "inappropriate" figurative meanings ("fast") of negated metaphors (*The train to Boston was **no rocket***) related to the metaphoric target (*rocket*) were accessed initially in spite of a contextual cue (negation) to the contrary. They were accessible at short and medium delays of 150 and 500 msec.

Note that even when, due to a strong context, reading times of literal and nonliteral interpretations of whole sentences did not differ significantly (Inhoff, Lima, & Carroll, 1984; Ortony et al., 1978), incompatible (literal) meanings of metaphors were nonetheless accessed on account of their salience (Brisard, Frisson, & Sandra, 2001; Janus & Bever, 1985). In all, such findings argue against the inhibition hypothesis. They show that salient meanings were always accessed, regardless of context.

Will contextually incompatible meanings of whole sentences, rather than just their constituents, be activated, regardless of context? According to the graded salience hypothesis (Giora, 1997, 1999, 2003), they will if they are highly salient. Indeed, reading times of whole sentences whose sentential meaning is salient (e.g., familiar idioms) were slower when rich prior context biased them towards their less salient, literal interpretation (Gibbs, 1980; Giora, Fein, Kronrod, et al., 2004). There is then no evidence for inhibition of highly salient but incompatible meanings when the literal–nonliteral issue is considered.

### *Suppression of Contextually Incompatible Properties*

Will incompatible meanings activated initially be discarded as inappropriate following lexical processes? A number of studies have attempted to test suppression of contextually inappropriate, particularly literal meanings of metaphors. An outstanding study in this respect is Keysar's (1994), which showed that suppression of inappropriate meanings of whole sentences does not distinguish literal from metaphorical interpretations. If context falsifies the literal interpretation or renders it implausible, comprehenders opt for the metaphorical one; if context renders the metaphorical interpretation implausible, readers opt for the literal one. If both are acceptable, comprehension is seamless; if both are unacceptable, comprehension runs into difficulty (Keysar, 1989). Context effects thus apply to literal and metaphorical interpretations in a similar fashion.

Some theories assume suppression of metaphor "inappropriate" (literal) properties even in the absence of prior context. One such example is the class inclusion view (Cacciari & Glucksberg, 1994; Glucksberg & Keysar, 1990; Shen, 1992). According to this view, metaphors of the form X is a Y (*That defense lawyer is a shark*) involve a dual reference to both a basic-level (literal) concept (the literal "shark") and to an ad hoc, superordinate category constructed on the basis of the basic-level concept (the metaphorical "tenacity"). This dual reference, however, is momentary. Once the superordinate category has been constructed, basic-level information is discarded, enabling a straightforward, frictionless understanding of the metaphor. Suppression of basic-level information thus allows for the metaphor vehicle to uniquely refer to the superordinate category.

To test this suppression hypothesis, Gernsbacher et al. (2001) presented participants with either a metaphoric (*That defense lawyer is a shark*) or a literal (*That large hammerhead is a shark*) class inclusion statement as primes, followed by basic-level target statements (*Sharks are good swimmers*). Reading times of basic-level targets were slower following a metaphoric than following a literal prime. Given that suppression comes with a cost (Gernsbacher, 1990), such findings are consistent with the view that basic-level meanings are suppressed during metaphor interpretation.

However, it is possible that these basic-level (literal) meanings have been rejected on account of their irrelevance to the metaphor interpretation rather than on account of their basic-level abstraction. Had basic-level, metaphor relevant alternatives tested (such as "teeth" or "jaws" when "shark" is at stake), findings might have been different.

Indeed, in Rubio Fernández (2007), following a metaphor (*John is a cactus*), only relevant basic-level meanings ("spike") were accessible both at short (0, 400 msec) and long (1000 msec) delays. In contrast, irrelevant superordinate meanings ("plant") were accessible only at the short delays. Such findings demonstrate that basic-level meanings need not be discarded on account of their basic-level abstraction. Instead, when relevant, they are retainable and partake in the construction of the contextually appropriate metaphoric interpretation despite their contextual misfit.

Hasson and Glucksberg's (2006) study demonstrates reduced levels of activation of irrelevant metaphoric meanings ("fast") of negated metaphors (*The train to Boston was no rocket*) presented out of a specific discourse context. Recall that in their study Hasson and Glucksberg showed that at short delays, incompatible concepts ("fast") were accessible, despite a contextual (negation) cue to the contrary. However, 1000 msec after offset of the negative statements, no facilitation of incompatible meanings ("fast") was observed. Following negation, then, and in the absence of a specific context, metaphor incompatible meanings were reduced to baseline levels. In a follow-up on Hasson and Glucksberg, however, Giora, Fein, Aschkenazi, et al. (2007) showed that once these items were furnished with late relevant contexts (*The train to Boston was* ***no rocket. The trip to the city was *fast*, though.***), negated metaphors ("rocket") facilitated related concepts (*fast*) even as long as 1000 msec following their offset. Such results demonstrate that, in the presence of a context motivating retention, suppression was not triggered.

Note, further, that, as predicted by the retention hypothesis (Giora & Fein, 1999a, 1999b) studies investigating affirmative metaphors demonstrated that only inappropriate meanings that interfered with the final interpretation of the utterances were suppressed. In contrast, incompatible meanings (e.g., literal meanings of metaphors) conducive to the final interpretation of nonliteral utterance were retained. Thus, in Williams (1992), salient meanings ("strict") of familiar metaphors (*firm*) were shown to be activated initially, regardless of context (about "teacher," "bed"). They were however suppressed only in a context (about "bed") in which they were disruptive. In contrast, salient meanings ("solid") conducive to the utterance interpretation (*firm teacher*) retained their initial levels of activation even after a long delay, despite their apparent inappropriateness.

Complementarily, findings obtained from word-fragment completion tasks, which tap later processes, showed that salient (literal) meanings of low familiar idioms were retained in idiomatically biasing contexts, suggesting that their apparent inappropriateness or "irrelevance" in that context did not trigger their suppression (Giora & Fein, 1999b). Indeed, as assumed by the suppression/retention hypothesis (Giora, 2003; Giora & Fein, 1999b), since metaphoric and idiomatic interpretations of such strings rely on their literal interpretation for their final output, there is no need for these irrelevant interpretations to be discarded, as they are not disruptive (see also Cacciari & Glucksberg, 1995).

Additional support for this pragmatic view of suppression comes from findings that in literally biasing contexts, retention of the literal interpretations of idioms superceded that of the idiomatic meanings of idioms. In these contexts, where in fact the idiomatic meanings had no role in constructing the final literal interpretation of the utterance, they were not retained. The same pattern was found for high and low familiar metaphors (though not for unfamiliar metaphors; Giora & Fein, 1999b). Interestingly the opposite was found for familiar proverbs and their familiar literal interpretation (Ferretti, Schwint, & Katz, 2007). In an ERP study, Ferretti et al. found that, although reading times did not distinguish figurative from literal targets, brain waves indicated ease of processing in literally rather than in figuratively biasing contexts. It might be the case that the familiar proverbial meaning of proverbs does not interfere with its literal interpretation. In all, such findings support the view that metaphors and literals are processed along the same lines. When the literal interpretation is disruptive to metaphoric interpretation it is discarded (Giora & Fein, 1999b; Rubio Fernández, 2007; Williams, 1992); when the metaphoric interpretation interferes with making sense of figurative items biased towards their literal interpretations, these interpretations are discarded (Giora & Fein, 1999b). When it is not, it is retained (Ferretti et al., 2007).

Is suppression triggered when no specific context is mentioned? Not really. Indeed, when tested out of a given context, familiar metaphoric words seemed to discard their metaphoric meaning in the left hemisphere. However, these meanings were retained in the right hemisphere. For instance, in Anaki, Faust, and Kravetz (1998), word primes (*stinging*), having salient metaphoric and literal meanings, were shown to be accessed both literally and metaphorically in the left hemisphere but only metaphorically in the right hemisphere. However, after a delay, the metaphoric meaning was retained only in the right hemisphere, while in the left hemisphere, it was suppressed, retaining only the literal meaning. The left hemisphere, then, discarded the metaphoric information, which was, however, retained in the right hemisphere.

### *Retention of Contextually Incompatible Properties*

According to the retention hypothesis (Giora, 2003; Giora & Fein, 1999b), meanings made available by lexical processes would be retained even when contextually incompatible provided they are conducive, or, at least, not detrimental to the final representation of the output. Evidence of retention of such incompatible meanings was found in the lab as well as in naturally occurring discourses. Recall that in Williams (1992) and Rubio Fernández (2007), salient, literal meanings of metaphors, which were shown to be activated initially regardless of contextual fit, were retained when they contributed to the final interpretation of the utterance. However, meanings, which were disruptive to the metaphor representation, were not preserved (see previous section). Similar findings were also demonstrated by Allbritton (1992, as reported in Gibbs, 1994; see also Allbritton, McKoon, & Gerrig, 1995). In this study, recognition of incompatible, literally related probes ("boiling") was facilitated following a paragraph that instantiated a conventional metaphor involving this meaning both in the outset (*Edward was boiling with anger*) and at the end – at the priming sentence position (*Hoping to prevent a scene, she tried to lower his thermostat*). Such facilitation was not observed following a similar paragraph whose final priming sentence was unrelated to that metaphor. In addition, people showed preference for metaphor resonance. They preferred metaphorical text progression, instantiating the same literal source domain, over one that did not. Thus, *blow your stack* was preferred over *bite your head off* (both alluding to anger) as a continuation of a description of anger, which was put in terms of heated fluid in a container (Gibbs, 1994, p. 163; Nayak & Gibbs, 1990). This suggests that so-called metaphor irrelevant meanings might be retained for discoursal purposes such as maintenance of metaphor resonance. (For evidence demonstrating lack of metaphorical resonance, see Shen & Balaban, 1999). These findings, then, suggest that, instead of suppressing locally incompatible meanings (e.g., literal meanings of metaphors), context might affect their retention because they might become instrumental in future processes (see Giora, Fein, Aschkenazi, et al., 2007).

Instances of natural discourses, which elaborate on early mention of metaphor irrelevant meanings, also support the retention hypothesis (see examples 2 and 3 above). For example, a recent ad promoting an Israeli daily (*Haaretz*) abounds in references to the literal, irrelevant meaning of the metaphor used. The slogan – *Haaretz. Food for thought* – is placed against a background image of a jam jar whose label resonates with the literal meaning of the slogan: *Haaretz – without a populist sweetener*. In addition, there is a text extending this metaphor, elaborating on its literal meaning: "Haaretz is inviting you to entertain and digest new insights. Haaretz is feeding you with a variety of ideas and opinions. Some of them might even be different from yours. So What? They are only an appetizer". All these form an array of conventional metaphors whose literal meanings, even those within the scope of negation, are retained and resonate with each other.[2]

Indeed, a survey of some spoken American discourses reveals that the incompatible literal meanings of both conventional and novel metaphors are echoed and resonated with in late contexts by both the producer of the speech and her or his interlocutor (Giora, 2003).

Consider, for instance, the elaboration on the literal meaning of the "death" metaphor (*gone*) in *where did they go to* (Du Bois, Chafe, Meyer, & Thompson, 2000, SBC: 005):

(6) PAMELA: . . . (H) I just think it's so wei = rd, that they're *go = ne*. . . . and where did they *go* to.

This is also true of written discourses as shown by Giora and Balaban (2001). Giora and Balaban collected 60 metaphors from the op-ed section of *Haaretz*, half of which were literally resonated with by their late context. Findings showed that novel and familiar metaphors were equally likely to be followed by a reference to their literal meaning (see 7 below for a recent example). That is, the metaphors, whose literal meaning was resonated with and elaborated on in the immediate or next context, were not evaluated as more or less familiar than those that received no literal extension. Importantly, half of the metaphors that received the highest familiarity ratings had literal extensions. These findings suggest that meanings made available to the producer herself were not discarded automatically, even when contextually incompatible. They were also not retained automatically. Instead, both their suppression and preservation seemed attentive to global discourse consideration rather than to local cues such as local irrelevance.

(7) The billionaires' racehorses

Fifteen years ago, in an interview with *Hadashot*, the late Swiss millionaire Gabai Maimon called Benjamin Netanyahu "*my racehorse*." Netanyahu's friends in the Likud were scandalized by the blunt language, but ever since, it has been clear that every primary *race* to elect the party's candidates for Knesset brings out new *racehorses* from the *stables* of the wealthy. In effect, any self-respecting businessman now keeps at least one such racehorse in his stable (Kim, 2004).

This is also true of contrastive metaphors, which resonate with the opposite of the literal meaning of a prior metaphoric occurrence:

(8) A war in Iraq will soon break out, and with it a great *darkness* will descend on events in the territories . . . This is the time to caution us all that under the cover of that darkness, grave things may come to pass.

Not that there is much *light* there now, either. (Levy, 2003)

This last metaphor (*Not that there is much light there now, either*) is particularly illustrative because it has an ironic reading. As shown in Giora, Fein, Ganzi, and Alkeslassy Levi (2005), negation of an overstatement (*much light*) results in an ironic reading. This was also true of negated metaphoric overstatements (Giora, Fein, & Aschkenazi, 2004). In Giora, Fein, and Aschkenazi, (2004), the negative metaphors used in Hasson and Glucksberg (2006), which contained top-of-the-scale expressions (*The train to Boston was no rocket*), were rated as more ironic than literal equivalents that did not make up an overstatement (*The train to Boston was not fast*). Clearly, to be read as such, these ironies must have retained their salient but "irrelevant" metaphoric meaning. Indeed, in Pexman et al. (2000), ironic metaphors took longer to read than baseline literals, suggesting that more than one interpretation was involved in the final representation (see also Colston & Gibbs, 2002).

At times, contextually incompatible meanings are retained because they are too salient to be quenched. Consider the joke Iddo cracks in the following example (9, cited in Giora, 2003, p. 19). The episode took place at Iddo's home while he and Omri (native speakers of Hebrew, aged 7 years and 8 months) were eating supper and Iddo had just fetched himself a glass of juice out of the refrigerator:

(9) Omri: I want to drink too.
Iddo's mother: Iddo, *totci lo et ha-mic* ("take the juice out [of the refrigerator] for him").
Iddo (laughingly) ha . . . ha . . . *lehotci lo et ha-mic* ("to take/squeeze the juice out of him" –a Hebrew idiom meaning "drive him crazy").

While the contextually compatible interpretation of this idiom is literal, the salient idiomatic meaning could not escape the addressee's mind. Though disruptive, it was difficult to suppress and was therefore retained for humorous purposes.

Findings, then, demonstrating retention of contextually incompatible meanings, irrespective of figurativeness or literalness, are explainable only by the graded salience hypothesis and the suppression/retention hypothesis (Giora, 1997, 1999, 2003; Giora & Fein, 1999b). They are not accountable by the alternative models.[3]

## Metaphor and Discourse Coherence

Would metaphors and literals affect discourse coherence differently? Are metaphors unique in this sense? According to the standard pragmatic model (Grice, 1975; Searle, 1979) they are: metaphors but not their literal interpretations involve an overt breach of a coherence norm to be alleviated by inferential processes of adjustment to contextual information. On this view, metaphors should take longer to read than literals and should score lower on coherence ratings. The direct access view anticipates no processing difficulties for metaphors relative to their literal interpretation when prior context is rich and supportive (Gibbs, 1994; Ortony et al., 1978). It therefore predicts similar reading times for metaphors and their literal counterparts and similar coherence ratings for the two interpretations. The underspecification view also predicts similar coherence ratings. According to the graded salience hypothesis (Giora, 1997, 1999, 2003), the relevant distinction is not between literals and metaphors but between various degrees of meaning salience. Thus, contextually compatible but less or nonsalient meanings would often take longer to activate (depending on their sentential position, see Peleg et al., 2001, 2004) and would be rated as less coherent than contextually compatible but salient meanings, regardless of metaphoricity. This predicts that utterances whose less or nonsalient interpretation is contextually compatible (novel metaphors intended figuratively; highly familiar metaphors and idioms intended literally) would take longer to read and would be rated as less coherent than their more accessible counterparts (literal meanings of novel metaphors intended literally; figurative meanings of highly familiar metaphors and idioms intended figuratively). However, similarly familiar utterances (familiar metaphors intended figuratively and their familiar literal interpretations intended literally) would take equally long to read and would be rated as similarly coherent. Coherence, then, is not a matter of literality or figurativeness but a function of the salience of the intended interpretations.

Indeed, as predicted by the graded salience hypothesis, idioms (*spill the beans*) took longer to read in a context inviting their less salient, literal interpretation than in a context inviting their more salient idiomatic meaning (Gibbs, 1980; Giora, Fein, Kronrod, et al., 2004). Novel metaphors (*their bone density is not like ours*) took longer to read in a context inviting their nonsalient, figurative interpretation than in a context inviting their more accessible, literal interpretation (Giora & Fein, 1999b, see also Brisard et al., 2001; for different findings see Ortony et al., 1978); familiar metaphors (*wake up*) did not take longer to read than their familiar literal interpretations (Giora & Fein, 1999b).

Similarly, as predicted by the graded salience hypothesis, contextually compatible familiar metaphors and their literal interpretation did not vary in terms of coherence. In contrast, contextually compatible novel metaphors were rated as less fitting with prior context than their literal equivalents. In addition, most highly familiar metaphors (*big eyes*) were rated as less coherent when embedded in a context inviting their less salient literal interpretation than in a context inviting their highly salient figurative meaning (Giora, Fein, Kronrod, et al., 2004; Shuval & Giora, 2005). Coherence then is sensitive to degree of salience rather than to literality or metaphoricity.

## Metaphor and Aesthetics

Is figurativeness unique in that it is more pleasing or aesthetic or more creative than literal language, as assumed by the classical view of metaphor (Aristotle, 350 BCE-a, b; see also Sopory & Dillard, 2002)? According to the optimal innovation hypothesis (Giora, 2003; Giora, Fein, Kronrod, et al., 2004), it is not. Instead, it is optimal innovativeness that is aesthetic. An optimally innovative stimulus is one that evokes a novel response while allowing for the recovery of a salient one from which it differs qualitatively. *Smash Capitalism* in the context of example (2) constitutes an optimal innovation. While activating the salient nonliteral sense of the expression, it also allows an insight into its more concrete, less salient, literal interpretation from which it differs significantly. Optimal innovation would thus be more pleasing than either a more or a less familiar stimulus, regardless of figurativeness.

Findings indeed showed that metaphoric interpretations of novel metaphors, which, by definition, are optimally innovative, were rated as more pleasing than their more familiar, literal counterparts. In contrast, no such difference was found for familiar metaphors and their literal interpretations, which were rated as similarly pleasing. Given that both their literal and nonliteral meanings enjoy similar salience, they do not involve optimal novelty and were therefore indistinguishable from each other. In contrast, since the less salient, literal interpretations of highly familiar metaphors constitute optimal innovations, they were rated as more pleasing than their salient, metaphoric meanings (Giora, Fein, Kronrod, et al., 2004; Shuval & Giora, 2005). These studies support the view that it is not figurativeness that accounts for aesthetic judgments but optimal innovativeness.

## Neurological Correlates and Processing Mechanisms

The bulk of evidence adduced so far argues against the literal/nonliteral divide. Would more direct evidence such as neural correlates support this lack of distinction? Recent findings from brain research and brain imaging indeed support the view that the crucial distinction is not between literals and nonliterals but between salient and less or nonsalient meanings (Giora, 2007). While the left hemisphere was found to specialize in processing salient meanings of familiar stimuli, the right hemisphere was found to specialize in processing less or unfamiliar stimuli, regardless of metaphoricity (Arzouan, Goldstein, & Faust, 2007; Eviatar & Just, 2006; Giora & Stringaris, in press; Giora, Zaidel, Soroker, Batori, & Kasher, 2000; Mashal & Faust, 2008; Mashal, Faust, & Hendler, 2005; Mashal, Faust, Hendler, & Jung-Beeman 2007; Papagno, Oliveri, & Romero, 2002; Schmidt, DeBuse, & Seger, 2007; Sotillo et al., 2005; Sundermeier, Virtue, Marsolek, & van den Broek, 2005). Such studies corroborate earlier results showing that the left hemisphere is engaged in processing conventional verbal metaphors (Winner & Gardner, 1977) while the right hemisphere is engaged in processing novel metaphors (Bottini et al., 1994).

An exception in this respect is a study by Rapp, Leube, Erb, Grodd, & Kircher (2004), who found activation in the left hemisphere for novel metaphors. It is possible, however, that this was affected by a nonlinguistic task, which involved judging whether the targets had a positive or negative connotation (p. 401).

But even utterances having similarly familiar interpretations such as literal (*Some men are soldiers*) and metaphoric (*Some men are lions*) class inclusion statements, taking similarly long to read, might involve some different underlying processes. Using brain imaging, Stringaris, Medford, Brammer, Giampietro, and David (2007) showed that while these similarly accessible targets were largely processed in the left hemisphere, they engaged different areas in that part of the brain. Specifically, they showed that, in addition to increased involvement of areas classically associated with linguistic processing, the left thalamus was recruited for the processing of metaphors but not of literals (see also Mashal et al., in press. For somewhat conflicting findings, see Mashal et al., 2007, in which not just two-word metaphoric expressions but also such literal expressions activated the left thalamus compared to meaningless expressions). Stringaris et al. suggest that this might highlight some difference between metaphoric and literal class inclusion statements. In the former, but not in the latter, processing involves the identification of shared properties resulting in the construction of a novel and emergent ad hoc concept. Such findings might allude to metaphors' open-endedness, they argue. Indeed, such findings tie up with studies demonstrating that figurative expressions such as idioms, while being understood more quickly than literal paraphrases, convey a wider range of entailments (Gibbs, 1992). They further agree with the assumption that figurative language may be more poetic in that it allows for a wider range of weak implicatures than literals (Sperber & Wilson, 1986/1995). These claims, however, will have to be tested against studies of literal puns of various degrees of salience and literal optimal innovations, which seem to make up a more appropriate literal counterpart for metaphors than the literals examined (see Coulson & Severens, 2007; Mashal et al., in press, for an initiation). In any event, such studies suggest that the time it takes to process an utterance is not necessarily a good indicator of the underlying processes involved.

Is metaphor processing different from irony interpretation? Colston and Gibbs (2002) embedded metaphoric utterances (*This one's really sharp*) in irony and metaphor inducing contexts. They showed that targets took longer to read when intended ironically than when intended metaphorically. However, a close look at the items used suggests that, while most of the targets had a salient metaphoric sense, their ironic interpretation was novel, which might explain the different reading times found.

A similar attempt to compare metaphors and ironies was made by Pexman et al. (2000). Using moving windows, Pexman et al. embedded familiar (*Children are precious gems*) and less familiar metaphors (*Her mind is an active volcano*) in irony inducing contexts. They found that reading times of less familiar (metaphoric and ironic) targets, measured at the figurative key word (*volcano*) of the statement, at the space following that word, and at the first word of the next sentence, increased relative to familiar items (embedded in metaphor inviting contexts). Such findings do not attest to differences involved in irony and metaphor processing. Rather, they contrast *familiar* and *unfamiliar* metaphors but equate *unfamiliar* instances of both irony and metaphor. They thus disclose differences involved in processing items of different salience. Indeed, neural correlates of the processes involved in making sense of conventional metaphors versus nonconventional ironies reveal specialization of the left hemisphere in processing metaphors and selective right hemisphere involvement in comprehension of nonsalient ironic language (Eviatar & Just, 2006; Giora et al., 2000). Although metaphor and irony involve different comparison processes (similarity vs. contrast), there is not enough evidence yet to suggest that they are processed differently.

## Counterexamples?

On the view that, unlike literals, many metaphors involve conceptual mappings from source to target domain (notably Lakoff, this volume; Lakoff & Johnson, 1980; Lakoff & Turner, 1989), metaphor might indeed be unique. But is it really the case that source to target domain mappings are different for metaphors than for literal expressions? According to Coulson (Coulson, this volume; Coulson & Van Petten, 2002) it is not. Rather, some literals involve literal mappings comparable to metaphors. For instance, in *That stone we saw in the natural history museum is a gem*, the literal sense of the target word (*gem*) conveys its conventional, literal meaning and should involve simple processes. However, *The ring was made of tin, with a pebble instead of a gem* invites literal mappings – mappings of conceptual structure from a different domain. It should therefore require more complex processes. In contrast, processing the target in

*After giving it some thought, I realized the new idea is a gem* should induce most complex processes, because the speaker's idea should induce metaphorical mapping – it should be metaphorically linked to a gemstone to evoke properties such as brightness and clarity.

Findings indeed show that metaphors elicited the largest N400s (N400 brain waves' amplitude is largest for contextually incompatible or surprising items). Next came the literal mappings, eliciting larger N400s than the literals. These results, thus, establish a complexity continuum in place of the literal/nonliteral divide (for a salience-based analysis of these findings, see Giora, 2003, p. 120). In addition, evidence from research into optimal innovations (Giora, Fein, Kronrod, et al., 2004) allows us to suspect that literal (*Till barriers do them part*, see 1) and metaphorical optimal innovations might involve similar mapping processes.

## Conclusions

Is metaphor unique in any sense then? Although we might have entertained the thought that metaphor is special, most of the evidence adduced so far offers but limited support of it (see also Giora, 2002). Rather, the bulk of evidence presented here argues against the literal/nonliteral distinction. Instead, it proposes the salient–nonsalient continuum. Thus, there is ample evidence suggesting that meanings are accessed in order of their salience rather than in relation to their literality or nonliterality. Similarly, there is also enough evidence showing that it is not the incompatible literal meaning of metaphors that is always suppressed. Suppression might discard irrelevant meanings regardless of figurativeness or literality. Similarly, it is not only the irrelevant literal meaning that is retained. Once contextual processes invite retention of irrelevant meanings, they are retained regardless of literalness or nonliteralness. Similarly, it is not metaphor that is incoherent; it is less and at times nonsalient meanings that are difficult to integrate into recently constructed representations. Likewise, it is not metaphor that is pleasing; it is optimal innovation that is aesthetic, whether literal or nonliteral (for more research on the non-uniqueness issue, see also Giora, 2002, 2003, 2007; Giora & Stringaris, in press).

Is metaphor unique in that it is, at least, the only source of metaphoric or poetic effects? The following poem (10) by Aharon Shabtai (2005: 8; my translation) might disabuse us even of this belief. Although the poem is entirely literal, involving literal similes, it results in metaphorical implicatures. Thus, "Sharon is like a man" implies that the Israeli Prime Minister is not human – not a "man" in the metaphoric sense:

(10) Sharon is like a man

> Sharon is like a man,
> And the dawning peace is like peace
> And the newspaper trumpeting it
> Is like a newspaper,
> The teachers are like teachers,
> And education is like education.
> Out of the window of bus number 5
> I look at the people on the sidewalks,
> Following them in my thought,
> And it all confirms
> They are like people,
> The shoes, the bitten falafel, etc.
> At the grocery,
> In nervous hands
> I test the potatoes
> And they too, they too
> Are like potatoes.

Metaphor, then, is not the only source of poetics or even of metaphorical interpretations. It seems that notions such as "resonance" (Du Bois, 1998) and "optimal innovation" (Giora, Fein, Kronrod, et al., 2004) can be considered as additional sources for poetic effects.

## Author Note

The research reported here was supported by grants by Tel Aviv University Adams Super Center for Brain Studies, and by Tel Aviv University Basic Research Fund. I thank

Daphna Barnai for examples 2 and 3 and Cristina Cacciari, Seana Coulson, Ray Gibbs, Sam Glucksberg, Uri Hasson, Arnon Kehat, Orna Peleg, and Argyris Stringaris for comments on an earlier draft.

Correspondence concerning this article should be addressed to Rachel Giora, Department of Linguistics, Tel Aviv University, Tel Aviv 69978, Israel. E-mail: giorar@post.tau.ac.il; http://www.tau.ac.il/~giorar.

## Notes

1 In Du Bois (1998), resonance is defined as "the catalytic activation of potential affinities across utterances," which while activating affinities may also induce change.

2 For the view suggesting that these meanings might emanate from their "root metaphor," that is, from preexisting conceptual mappings between conceptual domains, see Lakoff (this volume) and Lakoff and Johnson (1980).

3 Retention of meanings made available by interlocutors during conversation or during writing might originate in and allow for a more comprehensive communicative machinery titled "dialogic syntax" (Du Bois, 1998, 2001), whose verbal manifestation results in a vast amount of resonance of speakers' utterances with their own and others' utterances.

## References

Allbritton, D. (1992). *The use of metaphor to construct text representations: Evidence for metaphor-based schemas*. Unpublished doctoral dissertation, Yale University.

Allbritton, D. W., McKoon, G., & Gerrig, R. J. (1995). Metaphor-based schemas and text representations: Making connections through conceptual metaphors. *Journal of Experimental Psychology: Learning, Memory and Cognition*, 612–625.

Altiti, A., & Arvatz, S. (2005). *Negative metaphors*. Unpublished manuscript, Tel Aviv University.

Anaki, D., Faust, M., & Kravetz, S. (1998). Cerebral hemispheric asymmetries in processing lexical metaphors. *Neuropsychologia*, 36, 691–700.

Aristotle. (350 BCE-a). *Poetics*. (H. S. Butcher, Trans.). The Internet classic archive. http://classics.mit.edu/Aristotle/poetics.html.

Aristotle. (350 BCE-b). *Rhetoric* (R. W. Roberts, Trans.). http://libertyonline.hypermall.com/Aristotle/Rhetoric/Rhetoric.html.

Arzouan, Y., Goldstein, A., & Faust, M. (2007). "Brain waves are stethoscopes": ERP correlates of novel metaphor comprehension. *Brain Research*, 1160, 69–81.

Bottini, G., Corcoran, R., Sterzi, R., Paulesu, E., Schenone, P., Scarpa, P., et al. (1994). The role of the right hemisphere in the interpretation of figurative aspects of language: A positron emission tomography activation study. *Brain*, 117, 1241–1253.

Brisard, F., Frisson, S., & Sandra, D. (2001). Processing unfamiliar metaphors in a self-paced reading task. *Metaphor and Symbol*, 16, 87–108.

Cacciari, C., & Glucksberg, S. (1994). Understanding figurative language. In M. A. Gernsbacher (Ed.), *Handbook of psycholinguistics* (pp. 447–477). San Diego, CA: Academic Press.

Cacciari, C., & Glucksberg, S. (1995). Understanding idioms: Do visual images reflect figurative meanings. *European Journal of Cognitive Psychology*, 7, 283–305.

Carston, R. (2002). *Thoughts and utterances*. Oxford: Blackwell.

Colston, H. L., & Gibbs, R. W., Jr. (2002). Are irony and metaphor understood differently? *Metaphor and Symbol*, 17, 57–80.

Coulson, S., & Van Petten, C. (2002). Conceptual integration and metaphor comprehension: An ERP Study. *Memory & Cognition*, 30, 958–968.

Coulson, S., & Van Petten, C. (2007). A special role for the right hemisphere in metaphor comprehension? ERP evidence from hemifield presentation. *Brain Research*, 1146, 128–145.

Coulson, S., & Severens, E. (2007). Hemispheric asymmetry and pun comprehension: When cowboys have sore calves. *Brain and Language*, 100, 172–187.

Du Bois, J. W. (1998, January). *Dialogic syntax*. Paper presented at the Cognitive Theories of Intertextuality Meeting, Tel Aviv University.

Du Bois, J. W. (2001). Towards a dialogic syntax. Unpublished manuscript, University of California, Santa Barbara.

Du Bois, J. W., Chafe, W. L, Meyer, C., Thompson, S. A. (2000). *Santa Barbara corpus of spoken American English* [CD-ROM].

Philadelphia: Linguistic Data Consortium. www.ldc.upenn.edu/Publications/SBC/.

Ettinger, Y. (2004, July). Till barriers do them part. http://www.haaretz.com/hasen/pages/ShArt.jhtml?itemNo=449462&contrassID=2&subContrassID=1&sbSubContrassID=0&listSrc=Y.

Eviatar, Z., & Just, M. A. (2006). Brain correlates of discourse processing: an fMRI investigation of irony and metaphor comprehension. *Neuropsychologia*, 44, 2348–2359.

Ferretti, T. R., Schwint, C. A., & Katz, A. N. (2007). Electrophysiological and behavioral measures of the influence of literal and figurative contextual constraints on proverb comprehension. *Brain and Language*, 101, 38–49.

Fodor, J. (1983). *The modularity of mind*. Cambridge, MA: MIT Press.

Frisson, S., & Pickering, M. (2001). Obtaining a figurative interpretation of a word: Support for underspecification. *Metaphor and Symbol*, 16, 149–172.

Gernsbacher, M. A. (1990). *Language comprehension as structure building*. Hillsdale NJ: Lawrence Erlbaum.

Gernsbacher, M. A., Keysar, B., Robertson, R. W., & Werner N. K. (2001). The role of suppression and enhancement in understanding metaphors. *Journal of Memory and Language*, 45, 433–450.

Gibbs, R. W., Jr. (1980). Spilling the beans on understanding and memory for idioms in conversation. *Memory & Cognition*, 8, 449–456.

Gibbs, R. W., Jr. (1992). What do idioms really mean? *Journal of Memory and Language*, 31, 485–506.

Gibbs, R. W., Jr. (1993). Processes and products in making sense of tropes. In A. Ortony (Ed.), *Metaphor and thought* (2nd ed., pp. 252–276). Cambridge: Cambridge University Press.

Gibbs, R. W., Jr. (1994). *The poetics of mind*. Cambridge: Cambridge University Press.

Giora, R. (1997). Understanding figurative and literal language: The graded salience hypothesis. *Cognitive Linguistics*, 7, 183–206.

Giora, R. (1999). On the priority of salient meanings: Studies of literal and figurative language. *Journal of Pragmatics*, 31, 919–929.

Giora, R. (2002). Literal vs. figurative language: Different or equal? *Journal of Pragmatics*, 34, 487–506.

Giora, R. (2003). *On our mind: Salience, context, and figurative language*. New York: Oxford University Press.

Giora, R. (2006). Anything negatives can do affirmatives can do just as well, except for some metaphors. *Journal of Pragmatics*, 38, 981–1014.

Giora, R. (2007). Is metaphor special? *Brain and Language*, 100, 111–114

Giora, R., & Balaban, N. (2001). Lexical access in text production: On the role of salience in metaphor resonance. In T. Sanders, J. Schilperoord, & W. Spooren (Eds.), *Text representation* (pp. 111–124). Amsterdam: John Benjamins.

Giora, R., & Fein, O. (1999a). Irony: Context and salience. *Metaphor and Symbol*, 14, 241–257.

Giora, R., & Fein, O. (1999b). On understanding familiar and less-familiar figurative language. *Journal of Pragmatics*, 31, 1601–1618.

Giora, R., Fein, O., & Aschkenazi, K. (2004). *A functional approach to suppression: the case of negative metaphors*. Paper presented at the Euroconference on Computational and Neuropsychological Approaches to Metaphor and Metonymy, Granada.

Giora, R., Fein, O., Aschkenazi, K., & Alkabets-Zlozover, I. (2007). Negation in context: A functional approach to suppression. *Discourse Processes*, 43, 153–172.

Giora, R., Fein, O., Ganzi, J., & Alkeslassy Levi, N. (2005). On negation as mitigation: The case of irony. *Discourse Processes*, 39, 81–100.

Giora, R., Fein, O., Kronrod, A., Elnatan, I., Shuval, N., & Zur, A. (2004). Weapons of mass distraction: Optimal innovation and pleasure ratings. *Metaphor and Symbol*, 19, 115–141.

Giora, R., Fein, O., Laadan, D., Wolfson, J., Zeituny, M., Kidron, R., Kaufman, R., & Shaham, R. (2007). Irony processing: Expectation versus salience-based inferences. *Metaphor and Symbol*, 22, 119–146.

Giora, R., & Stringaris, K. A. (In press). Neural substrates of metaphor. In P. Hogan (Ed.), *The Cambridge Encyclopedia of the Language Sciences*. Cambridge: Cambridge University Press.

Giora, R., Zaidel, E., Soroker, N., Batori, G., & Kasher, A. (2000). Differential effects of right and left hemispheric damage on understanding sarcasm and metaphor. *Metaphor and Symbol*, 15, 63–83.

Glucksberg, S., & Keysar, B. (1990). Understanding metaphorical comparisons: Beyond similarity. *Psychological Review*, 97, 3–18.

Glucksberg, S., Newsome, M. R., & Goldvarg, Y. (2001). Inhibition of the literal: Filtering metaphor-irrelevant information during metaphor comprehension. *Metaphor and Symbol, 16*, 277–294.

Grice, H. P. (1975). Logic and conversation. In P. Cole & J. Morgan (Eds.), *Speech acts: Syntax and semantics* (Vol. 3, pp. 41–58). New York: Academic Press.

Hasson, U., & Glucksberg, S. (2006). Does understanding negation entail affirmation? *Journal of Pragmatics, 38*, 1015–1032.

Inhoff, A. W., Lima, S. D., & Carroll, P. J. (1984). Contextual effects on metaphor comprehension in reading. *Memory & Cognition, 12*, 558–567.

Janus, R. A., & Bever, T. G. (1985). Processing of metaphoric language: An investigation of the three stage model of metaphor comprehension. *Journal of Psycholinguistic Research, 14*, 473–487.

Katz, A, N., & Ferretti, T. R. (2001). Moment-by-moment reading of proverbs in literal and nonliteral contexts. *Metaphor and Symbol, 16*, 193–221.

Katz, A. N., & Ferretti, T. R. (2003). Reading proverbs in context: The role of explicit markers. *Discourse Process* 36, 19–46.

Keysar, B. (1989). On the functional equivalence of literal and metaphorical interpretations in discourse. *Journal of Memory and Language*, 28, 375–385.

Keysar, B. (1994). Discourse context effects: Metaphorical and literal interpretations. *Discourse Processes, 18*, 247–269.

Kim, H. (2004, July). The billionaires' racehorses. Haaretz.com.

Lakoff, G., & Johnson, M. (1980). *Metaphors we live by*. Chicago: University of Chicago Press.

Lakoff, G., & Turner, M. (1989). *More than cool reason: A field guide to poetic metaphor*. Chicago: Chicago University Press.

Levy, G. (2003, September). *The IDF's "permissiveness" in the territories*. http://www.zmag.org/content/showarticle.cfm?SectionID=22&ItemID=3007.

Mashal, N., & Faust, M. (2008). Right hemisphere sensitivity to novel metaphoric relations: Application of the Signal Detection Theory. *Brain and Language, 104*, 103–112.

Mashal, N., Faust, M., & Hendler, T. (2005). The role of the right hemisphere in processing nonsalient metaphorical meanings: Application of Principal Components Analysis to fMRI Data. *Neuropsychologia, 43*, 2084–2100.

Mashal, N., Faust, M., Hendler, T., & Jung-Beeman, M. (2007). An fMRI investigation of the neural correlates underlying the processing of novel metaphoric expressions. *Brain and Language, 100*, 115–126.

Mashal, N., Faust, M., Hendler, T. & Jung-Beeman, M. (In press). Processing salient and less-salient meanings of idioms: an fMRI investigation. *Cortex*.

Nayak, N. P., & Gibbs, R. W., Jr. (1990). Conceptual knowledge in the interpretation of idioms. *Journal of Experimental Psychology: General*, 119(3), 315–30.

Ortony, A., Schallert, D. L., Reynolds, R. E., & Antos, S. J. (1978). Interpreting metaphors and idioms: Some effects of context on comprehension. *Journal of Verbal Learning and Verbal Behavior, 17*, 465–477.

Papagno, C., Oliveri, M., & Romero, L. (2002). Neural correlates of idiom interpretation. *Cortex, 38*, 895–898.

Peleg, O., Giora, R., & Fein, O. (2001). Salience and context effects: Two are better than one. *Metaphor and Symbol, 16*, 173–192.

Peleg, O., Giora, R., & Fein, O. (2004). Contextual strength: The whens and hows of context effects. In I. Noveck & D. Sperber (Eds.), *Experimental pragmatics* (pp. 172–186). Basingstoke: Palgrave.

Pexman, P. M., Ferretti, T. R., & Katz, A. (2000). Discourse factors that influence irony detection during on-line reading. *Discourse Processes, 29*, 201–222.

Pickering, M., & Frisson, S. (2001). Processing of verbs: Evidence from eye movements. *Journal of Experimental Psychology: Learning, Memory, and Cognition, 27*, 556–573.

Rapp, A. M., Leube, D. T., Erb, M., Grodd, W., & Kircher, T. T. J. (2004). Neural correlates of metaphor processing. *Cognitive Brain Research, 20*, 395–402.

Rubio Fernández, P. (2007). Suppression in metaphor interpretation: Differences between meaning selection and meaning construction. *Journal of Semantics*, 1–27.

Schmidt, G. L., DeBuse, C. J., & Seger, C. J. (2007). Right hemisphere metaphor processing? Characterizing the lateralization of semantic processes. *Brain and Language, 100*, 127–141.

Searle, J. (1979). *Expression and meaning*. Cambridge: Cambridge University Press.

Shabtai, A. (2005). *SUN OH SUN*. Tel Aviv: Xargol (in Hebrew).

Shavit, A. (2003, May). 1967 for 1948. *Haaretz*, B1.

Shen, Y. (1992). Metaphors and categories. *Poetics Today*, 13, 771–794.

Shen, Y., & Balaban, N. (1999). Metaphorical (in)coherence in discourse. *Discourse Processes*, 28, 139–153.

Shuval, N., & Giora, R. (2005). Beyond figurativeness: Optimal innovation and pleasure. In S. Coulson & B. Lewandowska-Tomaszczyk (Eds.), *The literal and nonliteral in language and thought* (pp. 239–254). Frankfurt am Main: Peter Lang.

Smash capitalism [editorial]. (2003). *Etgar*, 9, 3.

Sopory, P., & Dillard, J. P. (2002). The persuasive effects of metaphor. *Human Communication Research*, 28(3), 382–319.

Sotillo, M., Carretíe, L., Hinojosa, J. A., Tapia, M., Mercado, F., López-Martýn, S., et al. (2005). Neural activity associated with metaphor comprehension: spatial analysis. *Neuroscience Letters*, 373, 5–9.

Sperber, D., & Wilson, D. (1986/1995). *Relevance: Communication and cognition*. Oxford: Blackwell.

Stringaris, A. K., Medford, N. C., Brammer, M. J., Giampietro, V., & David, A. S. (2007). Deriving meaning: Distinct neural mechanisms for metaphoric, literal, and non-meaningful sentences. *Brain and Language*, 100, 150–162.

Sundermeier, B. A., Virtue, S. M., Marsolek, C. J., & van den Broek, P. (2005). Evidence for dissociable neural mechanisms underlying inference generation in familiar and less-familiar scenarios. *Brain and Language*, 95, 402–413.

Swinney, D. A. (1979). Lexical access during sentence comprehension: (Re)consideration of context effects. *Journal of Verbal Learning and Verbal Behavior*, 18, 645–659.

Williams, J. N. (1992). Processing polysemous words in context. Evidence from interrelated meanings. *Journal of Psycholinguistic Research*, 21, 193–218.

Winner E., & Gardner, H. (1977). The comprehension of metaphor in brain-damaged patients. *Brain*, 100, 717–729.

CHAPTER 9

# Metaphor, Imagination, and Simulation

## Psycholinguistic Evidence

*Raymond W. Gibbs, Jr., and Teenie Matlock*

### Metaphor, Imagination, and Simulation: Psycholinguistic Evidence

A person with a sharp eye can find metaphors almost anywhere. A public bulletin board on the University of California, Santa Cruz, campus once had a flyer with a picture of a large black boot, typical of those worn by students, with the words *You have feet. Stomp out racism in your scene*, followed by an invitation to attend a campus meeting on the topic. This flyer was notable with the contrast between the picture and the caption, because, after all, one cannot physically stomp out an abstract idea or concept like racism. Of course, racism is manifested in concrete behavior such as language and other acts. But the concept of racism also refers to certain beliefs and attitudes that are distinctly immaterial and cannot be stomped out, regardless of what sort of fashionable boot one is wearing.

When students were asked about their reactions to the flyer and their understanding of *stomp out racism*, they all observed the humor in the juxtaposition of the picture and caption; yet, none thought that there was anything unusual about the idea of stomping out an abstract idea such as racism. "It's sort of a metaphor," as one woman said, because "you can't really stomp out racism with your feet, but you can use your efforts to stop racism by finding and killing it, as if stomping out a nasty insect crawling on the ground." Another student said that he could "think of racism as if it were some object, or a living thing, that does terrible damage and needs to be stopped or squashed, before it hurts other people." A third student explained, "Racist people have to be stopped. As horrible as it sounds, these people need to be controlled, and destroyed, or at least the beliefs they have. Racism needs to be stopped dead in its tracks."

These students' comments reflect their immediate, off-the-cuff imaginative understandings of the phrase *stomp out racism* by conceiving racism as if it was a physical being or object with the ability to hurt others that must be eradicated by those with the power to do so. Consistent with this figurative reading, people envisioned *stomp out racism* by imagining their bodies in action against the metaphorical object or living entity of racism, which is a specific instantiation of the more general conceptual metaphor AN IDEA IS AN OBJECT OR LIVING ENTITY. We maintain that students' impressions of *stomp out racism* illustrate a fundamental process by which metaphorical language is interpreted. People understand metaphors by creating an imaginative simulation of their bodies in action that mimics the events alluded to by the metaphor. Understanding the word *stomp* in *stomp out racism* is not done by accessing some highly abstract meaning that captures something of all physical and nonphysical uses of *stomp*. Interpreting the metaphorical meaning of *stomp out racism* also does not require that the concrete, physical features of *stomp* be completely inhibited or ignored. However, under our view, the physical, embodied meaning of *stomp* makes perfect sense in combination with *racism* when this abstract concept is conceptualized metaphorically.

Much research in cognitive linguistics suggests that many abstract concepts, such as racism, are understood, at least partly, in embodied metaphorical terms (Gibbs, 1994, 2006; Lakoff & Johnson, 1999). For example, understanding the conventional phrase *Our relationship is at a crossroad* is partly accomplished through the activation of the conceptual metaphor ROMANTIC RELATIONSHIP IS A JOURNEY. This enduring chunk of metaphorical thought has a source domain (e.g., JOURNEY) that is grounded in the pervasive bodily experience, or image-schema, of SOURCE-PATH-GOAL, which together give the idea RELATIONSHIP its embodied character. Psycholinguistic research shows that people appear to access embodied conceptual metaphors in some form when interpreting why many words and phrases have the metaphorical meanings they do, as well as when they immediately comprehend many verbal metaphors (Gibbs, 1994, 2006a).

We claim in this chapter that the recruitment of embodied metaphors in some aspects of verbal metaphor understanding is done imaginatively as people re-create what it must be like to engage in similar actions. The key to this imaginative process is simulation, in this case the mental enactment of the very action referred to in the metaphor. For example, abstract concepts are often understood as physical objects that can be touched, held on to, dropped, and, indeed, stomped on. When hearing *stomp out racism*, listeners imagine engaging in a relevant body action, such as stomping with their feet, that facilitates metaphorical construal of the abstract notion of racism as a physical entity. Although there is no physical action performed, the mental simulation created has embodied elements as people imagine themselves performing the relevant action. In this way, simulating what it must be like to engage in similar actions facilitates the recruitment of embodied metaphors in some aspects of verbal metaphor understanding. Our purpose in this chapter is to make the case for embodied simulation in a theory of metaphor understanding. We do this by describing relevant research from cognitive science on the importance of embodied simulation in cognition and language use. We then discuss current experimental work from psycholinguistics that is consistent with the claim that embodied simulations are created during metaphor understanding.

## Embodied Simulation

People simulate all sorts of things in all sorts of ways. Some simulations are physical and serve a communicative function. Imagine, for instance, that you are sitting in a restaurant in a foreign country. You have long finished your meal and want to pay the bill. Eventually, you manage to catch your waiter's attention and pretend to scribble something in the air. In doing so, you are replacing the word *bill*, or its appropriate equivalent, with an iconic gesture that you assume will be familiar to him. The waiter understands and brings you the bill. Imagine next that you have just gotten on a crowded bus and see an old friend outside on the street. She waves and you then hold your hand up to your ear as if you are holding a cell phone. As the bus is pulling away, your friend nods and does the same in return. In both the restaurant and on the bus, you do a physical action that communicates something clear and unambiguous to your interlocutor. You simulate physical actions (signing a bill, making a phone call) that are familiar and grounded in shared knowledge. Such actions are common in everyday situations in which speech may not suffice on its own, or in which speech is not possible (Bavelas, Kenwood, Johnson, & Phillips, 2002; Clark & Krych, 2004). People typically simulate actions or objects in these situations that are familiar and can readily be understood.

Other physical simulations are not communicative but are useful to performing various cognitive tasks such as problem solving. Imagine you are learning to play Tetris, a popular video game. In this game, two-dimensional shapes fall one at a time from the top of the screen, landing on the bottom or on top of shapes that have already landed. The object of the game is to fill rows of squares all the way across. Filled rows dissolve and move down, and unfilled rows stack up. The game ends when incomplete rows stack up and reach the top of the playing field. As you decide where to place pieces, you press keys on a keypad to move them right or left, spin them clockwise or counterclockwise, or suddenly drop them to the bottom. Counter to what would be expected, as you become better at the game, you do more and more seemingly superfluous actions. For instance, you rapidly spin a piece to the right position before dropping it. Such actions might not seem useful while you are playing the game because they are not always necessary and take extra time. Yet they are useful because they allow you to simulate many possible placements before you move a piece to its final location (see Kirsh & Maglio, 1994). Or imagine you are playing the word game Scrabble. As you wait for your turn, you move your tiles around before placing them on the board. In doing so, you simulate words to be played by activating new letter configurations that would not be available without moving them around (Maglio, Matlock, Raphaely, Chernicky, & Kirsh, 1999). Using physical actions to simulate future actions or states is not limited to playing games. It's part of everyday reasoning. Imagine that you are presented with two glasses of water. Both glasses are the same height and both are half full, but one is thin and one is wide. You are asked whether water will pour from the thin glass or the wide glass first if the glasses are tilted at the same rate. Like most people, you are likely to give an incorrect answer if you make this judgment on the fly. However, if you are asked to pretend that you are tilting the glass, you are more likely to provide a correct answer (that the wide glass will pour the water first) (Schwartz & Black, 1999). The role of physical actions or imagined physical actions in all these cases is important. In reasoning about everyday events and actions, people frequently engage in physical simulations as a way of "offloading" mental computation into the world, which makes problem solving much easier (Clark, 1997).

Other simulations are purely mental. If you close your eyes and imagine your house right now, you can "see" various objects and rooms. You can visually scan from one object to another, or "walk" from one part of the house to another. You are constructing a spatial mental model from your memory of a place that shares certain attributes with that actual physical space (Bower & Morrow, 1990). As you "go" through the house, you can imagine moving quickly or slowly (Morrow & Clark, 1988). You can keep track of where objects are or where they once were by anchoring them to other objects (Morrow, Bower, & Greenspan, 1989). You can change your perspective from a subjective viewpoint to a more objective one, such as from your own perspective as the mover to a bird's-eye perspective (Tversky, 1996). You can also construct a spatial mental model when reading a description of a scene or seeing a graphical depiction, such as a map (Denis & Cocude, 1989). In all cases, when you imagine yourself or another person going through a house or any other spatial environment, you are simulating motion, and to some extent, that motion shares properties with actual movement in the world, either perceived or enacted (Tversky, 2000; Zwaan & Radvansky, 1998).

One of the interesting elements of embodied simulations is that people engage in these processes not only when motion is explicitly mentioned (e.g., when imagining stomping out something or moving through a house) but also when motion is to some degree implicit. For example, studies show that people infer the presence of motion when they read handwriting (Babcock & Freyd, 1988) or view a series of photographs where motion between the events depicted is implied (Freyd, 1983). Thus, people perceive handwriting displays based on the gestures that produced them and not just the static features of the letters. Neuroscience research reveals that brain areas associated with visual processing of motion are active when people see both pictures depicting real and implied motion (Kourtzi & Kanwisher, 2000). These findings suggest that processing implied motion in static scenes is very similar to perception of real motion.

All of these different studies suggest that people can readily, and mostly unconsciously, create simulations of real-world events as they communicate with others, hear stories, solve problems, and even perceive motionless displays. Psycholinguistic studies also demonstrate the importance of embodied simulations in ordinary language understanding. For instance, reading sentences with visual semantic components can selectively interfere with visual processing. Thus, participants in one study took longer to perform a visual categorization task in the upper part of their visual field when they heard sentences depicting upward motion, such as *The ant climbed* (Richardson, Spivey, Barsalou, & McRae, 2003). When people perform physical actions, such as forming a fist or moving a lever toward the body, they were slower to verify as meaningful sentences that described unrelated actions, such as *aim a dart* (Klatzky, Pelligrino, McCloskey, & Doherty, 1989), and *close the drawer* (Glenberg & Kaschak, 2002). Moreover, performing a simple physical action, such as rotating a knob in a clockwise direction, can interfere with people's speed comprehension of statements like *Eric turned down the volume*, which describes a scenario where a person moves his or her wrist in a counterclockwise manner (Zwaan & Taylor, 2006). In general, these psycholinguistic studies demonstrate that people's understanding of linguistic descriptions of action mentally simulate the action. As such, there is significant psycholinguistic evidence consistent with the broad claim that language use is closely tied to embodied imagination.

Many cognitive scientists, especially philosophers, describe cognitive simulations as conscious, deliberative acts of pretense (Goldman, 2006; Gordon, 1986; Harris, 1992). But simulation processes that are critical to language processing are different from engaging in pretense (Currie & Ravenscroft, 2002) and are likely automatic, unconscious, and prereflexive (Gallese, 2000). Thus, one pretends to do something (e.g., talking on a telephone) by performing some other, somewhat analogous, action (e.g., holding your hand in a particular shape by your ear). On the other hand, most imaginative simulations are mental actions where one is not doing one thing to stand for another but where one mentally engages in actions similar to those overtly referred to. For instance, when Ray imagines what it feels like to kick a football, he does not engage in some other action, such as kicking a cantaloupe. Instead, he mentally constructs a scenario of his own body kicking a football. This simulation is not abstract in the way, for example, that a computer simulation of a hurricane mimics abstract elements of how a hurricane moves. Embodied simulations often have a bodily feel to them, in the way that a person may experience sensations of movement when flying an aircraft simulator (Gibbs, 2006a). People may not necessarily be aware of these sensations, as demonstrated by research on ideomotor actions, indicating that people often unconsciously move in similar patterns to others around them (Knuf, Aschersleben, & Prinz, 2001). Embodied simulations are imaginative acts that are intimately involved with subpersonal processes (Currie & Ravenscroft, 2002) and, in most cases, are performed automatically without significant conscious reflection.

## Studies on Metaphorical Simulation

The research from cognitive psychology and psycholinguistics suggests that people can easily simulate motion, especially relevant to bodily movement, when they were engaged in various cognitive tasks, including nonmetaphorical language understanding. But do people simulate motion in situations that are physically impossible to do, such as those represented by metaphorical phrases like *grasp a concept* and *stomp out racism*? The studies described next asked people to do different things in experimental situations that tap into various conscious and unconscious mental processes, such as imagining metaphorical actions and answering questions about their images, draw maps depicting metaphorical events, making appropriate responses to metaphorical statements, reading metaphorical phrases after performing, or imagine performing, different bodily movements, and walk while thinking about the meaning of metaphorical narratives.

Some of these experiments examined the products of metaphor understanding (i.e., the meanings people inferred), while others investigated the processes by which people construct these products. One must be careful to not draw unwarranted conclusions about the processes of linguistic understanding from an examination of products alone or assume that fast-occurring mental processes necessarily reflect much about the eventual products of those interpretation processes (Gibbs, 1994). Yet the experimental examination of both the processes and product of understanding are useful to demonstrate different aspects of how people automatically construct imaginative understandings of metaphors that are closely tied to their mental simulating the actions referred to by these expressions. Metaphorical simulations are not abstract, or amodal, but are created in terms of "as if" bodily action, where people imagine moving their bodies in ways specific to their metaphorical understandings of the abstract concepts noted in metaphorical statements, such as *grasp a concept*.

Many psycholinguists studying metaphor use do not endorse our claim that metaphors are understood in terms of embodied simulations. These scholars suggest that many of the types of metaphorical expressions studied in the research described below are not actually metaphors, or understood by processes linked to bodily processes related to mental simulations. Although it is quite possible that different theoretical accounts may be needed to explain various kinds of metaphorical language (e.g., "A is B" metaphors vs. metaphors arising from correlations in experience), we will argue later on that embodied simulations may be required to understand even classic "A is B," or resemblance, metaphors. For the moment, the research described examines different aspects of how embodied simulations enable people to make sense of various metaphorical expressions, draw specific inferences about their meanings, and immediately comprehend these expressions in certain experimental situations. We suggest as a methodological imperative that one cannot dismiss the idea of embodied simulations as being critical to metaphor interpretation unless one has explicitly looked for such evidence and failed to find it. However, much current psycholinguistic research indicates that positive evidence in favor of the simulation account can be readily observed as we now report.

### *Imagining Impossible Actions*

Asking people to describe their understanding of *stomp out racism* reveals that people can easily imagine ways that an abstract idea like racism can be physically stomped out. For some, this ability to imagine concretely physically impossible events may seem odd. But people's pervasive schemes of metaphorical thought, in which abstract concepts are often metaphorically understood in concrete ways, enables them to imagine the impossible and makes it seem quite plausible.

There have been many experimental studies investigating people's abilities to form mental images for metaphorical phrases (Gibbs & O'Brien, 1990; Gibbs, Strom, & Spivey-Knowlton, 1997), which reveal that conceptual metaphors constrain the kinds of images people have for expressions like *spill the beans* and *don't put all your eggs in one basket*. These metaphorical expressions, however, may be easy to imagine because they are sensible when used concretely, because one can, for instance, literally spill the beans in some situations. But can people form mental images for physically impossible actions that express metaphorical meaning, such as *stomp out racism* or *grasp the concept*? If so, might these imaginative creations arise as a result of embodied simulations?

One set of experiments explored these questions by comparing people's mental images for concrete (e.g., *chew on the gum*) and metaphorical (e.g., *chew on the idea*) phrases (Gibbs, Gould, & Andric, 2006). Unlike imagining nonmetaphoriocal action statements (e.g., *chew on the gum*), where people's images should focus on the procedural characteristics of the concrete actions (i.e., moving their mouths as they chew the gum), people's mental images for metaphorical phrases should show an analogical understanding of how abstract domains, such as ideas or concepts, can be actively structured in terms of embodied source domains (i.e., chewing on something to get more out of it).

Participants were first presented specific phrases that were either metaphorical or nonmetaphorical, given 10 seconds to form a mental image of that action, and asked, "What is particularly noticeable in your image?" People's responses could be roughly divided into two groups. The first set of answers made some specific reference to the participants actually participating in the action mentioned in the statement. For example, "My jaw goes up and down as I chew," was one response given to "chew on the idea." People gave far more of these specific references to participating in the action responses for the nonmetaphors (63%) than to the metaphors (29%).

But for the metaphors, people gave significantly more conceptualized descriptions of the action (71%) than they did for the nonmetaphors (37%). For instance, for the metaphor *stretch for understanding*, one person said that the most noticeable thing in his image was "there is much stretching going in both in terms of the ideas being stretched out to see if they are true and me stretching to better see of examine the idea." The participant essentially noted that IDEAS ARE OBJECTS which can be physically inspected by stretching them out to more effectively examine them, and that UNDERSTANDING IS GRASPING enables the person to extend his or her body to better control the object, and thus better understand it. This response concretely illustrates how embodied metaphors constrain the mental images people construct when interpreting metaphorical action statements.

Participants were also asked, "Why is this concept (e.g., idea) sometimes associated with this action (e.g., chewing)?" Once more, people could give a concrete explanation of the relevant process or action, such as, "That is what you do with gum – chew on it" for *chew on the gum*. But for the metaphors, people specifically provided analogous, conceptual explanations as to why some concept was sometimes associated with some action or process. For example, for the metaphorical phrase *chew on the idea*, one person said, "Chewing is related to a slow methodological activity and it could be related to turning something over in your mind to better understand it." Overall, people gave analogous, conceptual explanations far more often to the metaphors (77%) than to the nonmetaphors (36%), showing that people's mental images for metaphorical action phrases are constrained by their embodied, metaphorical understandings of the target domains referred to in these expressions (e.g., ideas, concepts, feelings).

If people understood metaphors by engaging in embodied simulations, then moving their bodies in ways relevant to the actions mentioned should enhance the creation of these simulations. A second study again presented people with different metaphorical and nonmetaphorical expressions, formed mental images for these phrases, and then answered a series of questions about their images. In Experiment 2, however, people also participated in one of three enactment conditions in which they first did one of three things: (a) watched the experimenter make a bodily action relevant to the main verb in each statement (e.g., making a stretching motion before forming a mental image for the phrase *stretch for understanding*), (b) watched the experimenter make a relevant bodily action, which they then imitated, before being given 10 seconds to form their mental image for a phrase, or (c) watched the experimenter make a relevant bodily action, then imagined themselves doing the same action, before forming a mental image for the phrase. These three experimental treatments were referred to as the watching, imitating, and imagining conditions, respectively.

This study showed, once more, that across all three enactment conditions, 78% of these referred to additional bodily actions and consequences of these actions related to the main verb in each metaphorical phrase. For example, when one participant was given the phrase *put your finger on the truth* (in the imagine condition), she replied, "I guess being able to touch the truth is an important thing, being able to relate to it, being able to actually see that it is a physical thing and can be examined." This evidence shows how moving the body in relevant ways enhances the creation of embodied simulations, compared to Experiment 1 where no movement was performed. These actions enabled people to construct more easily embodied simulation that made these impossible actions, like *grasping the concept*, plausible and meaningful.

### *Real and Imagined Bodily Movement Enhances Simulations during Immediate Metaphor Comprehension*

The extent to which people ordinarily engage in imagistic processes during immediate metaphor processing that they can consciously reflect on is unclear. But one possibility is that moving the body, or overtly imagining moving the body, in relevant ways facilitates immediate metaphor comprehension. If abstract concepts are indeed understood as items that can be acted upon by the body, then performing a related action should facilitate sensibility judgments for a figurative phrase that mentions this action. For example, if participants first move their arms and hands as if to grasp something and then read *grasp the concept*, they should verify that this phrase is meaningful faster than when they first performed an unrelated body action. Engaging in body movements associated with these phrases should enhance the online simulations that people create to form a metaphorical understanding of abstract notions, such as *concept*, even if a *concept* is not something that can be physically grasped.

In fact, a computerized reading-time study showed that participants responded more quickly to the metaphorical phrases that matched the preceding action (e.g., the motor action grasp was followed by *grasp the concept*), than to the phrases that did not match the earlier movement (e.g., the motor action kick was followed by *grasp the concept*) (Wilson & Gibbs, 2007). People were also faster in responding to the metaphor phrases having performed a relevant body movement than when they did not move at all. In short, performing an action facilitates understanding of a metaphoric phrase containing that action word. One possibility is that people's bodily action prompted them to think of the verb in the subsequently presented phrase (e.g., a grasping action led people to think of the word *grasp*). But a control study showed that people were not especially good at thinking of the exact word in the phrase when they just performed the bodily action, and that there was no correlation between successful identification of the actual word and priming effects for that item in the reading time experiment. It appears, then, that moving in an appropriate manner does not activate a lexical item but enhances how people create a relevant embodied simulation to understand a metaphorical phrase.

A second study asked people to imagine specific bodily actions before they made their speeded responses to word strings. Once again, participants were faster to process the metaphors when the act imagined was consistent with the meaning of the phrase than when the imagined act was inconsistent. This result reveals that real movement is not required to facilitate metaphor comprehension, only that people mentally simulate such action. Once again, a control study demonstrated that this finding was not due to simple lexical associations created from doing or imagining the actions and seeing specific words in the phrases.

Most theories of metaphor understanding assume that people must inhibit the physical meaning of a word like *grasp* in *grasp the concept* to properly infer its abstract, metaphoric meaning (Glucksberg, 2001). This view suggests that having people make a grasping motion before reading *grasp the concept* should interfere with their immediate processing of the phrase. Yet the present studies show this is not the case. Real and imagined body movement helps people create embodied simulations of metaphorical meanings that involve "what it must be like" processes that make use of tactile-kinesthetic experiences. People may not create a complete literal interpretation for a phrase like *grasp the concept*, and reject that in favor of a metaphorical reading. But they do use their embodied understanding of various action verbs to construct metaphorical interpretations of abstract concepts to make meaningful combinations of the physical with the abstract. Of course, the studies discussed here did not examine normal metaphor comprehension in context, and seeing how appropriate discourse situations, where various bodily actions are also performed, affect metaphor understanding. But this is an exciting topic for future psycholinguistic research.

### *Bodily Imagination in Thinking about Time*

Imagine that you have a meeting scheduled for this coming Wednesday when a colleague approaches you and says, *Next Wednesday's meeting has been moved forward two days.* Would the meeting now be held on Monday or Friday of that week? Your answer to this question depends on your interpretation of *moved forward*, which alludes to the fact that people often conceptualize time in terms of physical space. But do people ordinarily simulate actual movement forward as part of their understanding of time statements such that referring to next Wednesday's meeting? One possibility is that many people's embodied simulations for time concepts depend on their current bodily movements.

Many studies have examined people's experience of time, including the way they talk about time metaphorically. In a series of studies by Boroditsky and Ramscar (2002), students waiting in line at a café were given the statement *Next Wednesday's meeting has been moved forward two days* and then asked *What day is the meeting that has been rescheduled*? (The question was adapted from McGlone & Harding, 1998.) Students who were farther along in the line (i.e., who had thus very recently experienced more forward spatial motion) were more likely to say that the meeting had been moved to Friday. Similarly, people riding a train were presented the same ambiguous statement and question about the rescheduled meeting. Passengers who were at the end of their journeys reported that the meeting was moved to Friday significantly more than did people in the middle of their journeys. Although both groups of passengers were experiencing the same physical experience of sitting in a moving train, they thought differently about their journey and consequently responded differently to the rescheduled meeting question. These results demonstrate how ongoing sensorimotor experience has an influence on people's comprehension of metaphorical statements about time. As seen in the studies on imagining and understanding *grasp the concept*, moving the body in particular ways can facilitate people's creation of simulations of action relevant to the actions referred to by metaphoric language that alters the way these metaphors are interpreted.

Having people perform different types of movement can also affect their understanding of time metaphors. Participants in another experiment were asked to study a drawing that depicted a chair with a rope attached (Boroditsky & Ramscar, 2002). Half of the participants imagined that they were pulling the chair toward them with the rope. The other half imagined being seated in the chair, pulling themselves forward along the rope. Following the imagination activity, the participants were asked the same question about the meeting being moved forward two days. Participants who imagined pulling the chair toward their bodies were more likely to answer that the meeting had been moved to Monday, consistent with the metaphorical idea that time is an object moving toward them. Conversely, the participants who imagined pulling themselves along the rope more often answered that the meeting had been rescheduled for Friday, consistent with the idea that time is a stationary object with the person moving toward it. Once again, ongoing body movement shapes online metaphor understanding, suggesting that people simulate what time, in this case, is like in relation to their bodies, which affects the way we respond to the metaphorical time question (see also Gentner, Imai, & Boroditsky, 2002; McGlone & Harding, 1998; Núñez, Motz, & Teuscher, 2006).

### *Fictive Motion and Embodied Simulation*

Suppose a Realtor is talking to you on the phone about a piece of property. He uses descriptions such as *There's an apple orchard that runs along the hillside* and *A dirt road goes across a creek*. How do you make sense of his descriptions given that he is using motion verbs (*runs, goes*) but there is no actual motion? Such sentences are common in English, and you readily generate an image of an elongated orchard that "goes" from one point on a hillside to another. In processing the sentence, you understand that no *actual* motion transpires because you know that things like orchards and dirt roads can't move and you are used to hearing sentences that have inanimate subjects; yet, in scanning from one part of the image to another, you experience a fleeting sense of motion. This subjective sense of motion is what Talmy (1996) and others have called *fictive motion* (see also Langacker, 1987; Matsumoto, 1996).

Some language theorists have questioned whether any sort of motion imagery is involved in processing fictive motion sentences (Jackendoff, 2002). But several psycholinguistic experiments have provided evidence to support the idea that people do simulate motion in processing these sentences. Participants in one set of experiments were timed as they read fictive motion target sentences, such as *The road goes through the desert*, at the end of stories about protagonists traveling through physical space (Matlock, 2004). Overall, people took less time to read and make a decision about these fictive motion sentences after they had read about travel that was fast (versus slow), over a short distance (versus long), or through an easy terrain (versus difficult). But critically, people did not differ in the time it took them to read nonfictive motion sentences (e.g., *The road is in the desert*) under the same conditions. The results of these studies indicate that thought about actual movement can influence the time it takes to process fictive motion sentences. For instance, when people think about slow motion, they simulate more slowly when thinking about fictive motion. The results suggest that embodied simulation is part of understanding a common form of figurative language.

Other research supports the idea that fictive motion includes simulated motion. Matlock, Ramscar, and Boroditsky (2005) tested whether *fictive motion* would influence people's understanding of time because relatively abstract ideas about time and the understanding of fictive motion both involve a shared underlying representational format extracted from our concrete experience with actual moving objects. In one experiment, participants first read sentences with or without fictive motion, such as *The tattoo runs along his spine* or *The tattoo is next to his spine*, and then drew the meaning conveyed by the sentence. Next, they answered the ambiguous question adapted from McGlone and Harding (1998) and used in Boroditsky and Ramscar (2002), *Next Wednesday's meeting has been moved forward two days. What day is the meeting now that it has been rescheduled?* People were more likely to respond Friday (versus Monday) if they had read and drawn a fictive motion sentence but were evenly divided in their answers if they had read and drawn a nonfictive motion sentence. Fictive motion depictions included more motion elements (e.g., cars, bikes) than did nonfictive motion sentences (see Matlock, Ramscar, & Boroditsky, 2004).

In a second experiment, participants read one of four fictive motion sentences that varied according to magnitude of fictive motion, defined as the number of scan points along a path (i.e., *Four / 8 / 20 / over 80 pine trees run along the driveway*). The question was whether more scan points would encourage more movement through time, and hence, more Fridays. Participants were more likely to say *Friday* than *Monday* overall. However, the difference was enhanced for people who had read sentences with 8 and 20 scan points (pine trees) and nonexistent for people who had read sentences with very few (4) or very many (over 80) scan points, suggesting that number of scan points (and hence, more fictive motion simulation) promoted more motion through time.

In a third experiment, people read and drew fictive motion sentences with motion "going away" from or "coming" toward the individual (e.g., *The road goes/comes all the way to/from New York*). The goal was to investigate whether fictive motion simulation included a diffuse, undirected type of motion or a more directed type of motion. The results showed that participants were more likely to say *Friday* when the direction was going away from them, and more likely to say *Monday* when the direction was coming toward them, suggesting that fictive motion simulation includes direction.

This set of studies shows that people engage in thought about motion when thinking about fictive motion and when they are thinking about time. So, for instance, when people have done a fictive motion simulation, they imagine forward motion, and this encourages them to take a forward moving perspective and move forward through time. And when the path they have thought about is long, they are even more likely to think about forward movement through time. Last, when people simulate motion along a path as they read *The road goes all the way to New York*, they are predisposed to then move forward through time, specifically, to Friday.

Follow-up studies with the same ambiguous time question provide further evidence that fictive motion can influence the understanding of time metaphors (see Ramscar, Matlock, & Boroditsky, in progress). Even when participants draw *no* picture to convey the meaning of a fictive or a nonfictive motion sentence, they are more likely to say *Friday* than *Monday* with fictive motion. They are also more likely to say Friday with a "just right" number of scan points and with fictive motion "going away" from them. The results of this control study are important because they demonstrate that the effect was not due to hand movements while drawing the meaning conveyed by the sentence. Other work shows that counting direction can influence the understanding of time (see Matlock, Ramscar, & Srinivasan, 2006). People are more likely to respond *Friday* to the ambiguous time question after counting from 5 to 17, and more likely to say *Monday* after counting from 17 to 5. The results indicate that "going" from number to number either away from zero or toward zero, the default position of the speaker or listener (see Lakoff & Núñez, 2001), encourages people to conceptually move forward through time or back through time. The results provide further evidence that people simulate motion even when there is no explicit mover to imagine, and novel evidence that they do so even when there is no physical space to imagine.

Other psycholinguistic research has explored whether fictive motion language affects people's visual processing of spatial scenes (Matlock & Richardson, 2004). Participants' eye movements were tracked as they were presented with simple drawings of trajectories, such as roads, rivers, and pipelines, while they passively heard either fictive motion or nonfictive motion descriptions such as *The road goes through the valley*, *The road is in the valley*. When people heard fictive motion descriptions they spent more time inspecting the trajectory region of the scene than when they heard nonfictive motion descriptions. Follow-up work ruled out the possibility that fictive motion descriptions were simply more interesting, and that alone attracted more visual attention to trajectory region versus other parts of the picture (Richardson & Matlock, 2007). Together these eye-tracking studies provide additional evidence that people engage in embodied simulation when they are processing fictive motion sentences.

Finally, data from a map task provide further evidence that fictive motion includes mentally simulated motion. Pairs of participants were asked to put landmarks on a blank map where a director told a mapmaker what to do (Matlock & Clark, 2006). All pairs drew the same map with the same lines. Some participants drew lines that represented roads, while others drew lines that represented pipelines. Overall, participants who depicted roads used more motion verbs and produced more path gesture (sweeping gestures that go from one point in space to another) than those who produced identical lines for pipelines. These results suggest that in giving directions about how to draw a system of roads the director was drawing on knowledge about what roads are ordinarily used for, in particular, for travel through space. Drawing on that knowledge and putting it into verbal or visual form allows the director to simulate motion and invite the listener to simulate motion.

Together these psycholinguistic studies on fictive motion demonstrate that people naturally and tacitly simulate motion in understanding everyday spatial descriptions such as *The road goes through the park* or *A fence runs along the coastline*. The results show that figurative language understanding included embodied simulation that draws on what is known about motion through perception and action.

### *Walking the Walk While Thinking about Metaphorical Talk*

Many of the psycholinguistic studies described in this chapter illustrate how bodily action, and imagining specific bodily acts, constrains, and often facilitates people's interpretation of verbal metaphor. These real and imaginative bodily reenactments had specific consequences for how people interpreted the meanings of various metaphors. We now discuss a novel situation in which the embodied simulation created to understand metaphor affects how people move their whole bodies as they continue to think about what they have heard. Consider the following two brief narratives about the development of two different romantic relationships.

STORY A

Imagine that you are a single person. A friend sets you up on a blind date. You really like this person and start dating a lot. Your relationship was moving along in a good direction. But then it got even better. The relationship felt like it was the best you ever had. This continues to this day. No matter what happens, the two of you are quite happy together.

STORY B

Imagine that you are a single person. A friend sets you up on a blind date. You really like this person and start dating a lot. Your relationship was moving along in a good direction. But then you encountered some difficulties. The relationship did not feel the same as before. This lasted for some time. No matter how hard you two tried, the two of you were not getting along.

Story A describes a successful relationship, while B describes a relationship that appears to be in trouble. Both stories are similar, however, in conceiving of the relationships as entities that can move along some sort of path (RELATIONSHIPS ARE JOURNEYS), as indicated in the fourth line *Your relationship was moving along in a good direction*. Although no other part of the two stories explicitly refers to journeys, the two stories provide different impressions of the "relationship journey." Thus, Story A suggests a smooth, uninterrupted journey that is still progressing, while Story B implies a more difficult, perhaps interrupted, journey that may no longer be progressing.

Do people actually draw different inferences when reading these two stories? To what extent are the different meanings inferred based on the embodied metaphor RELATIONSHIPS ARE JOURNEYS? One study examined people's metaphorical interpretations of these two stories by asking them to make judgments about different aspects of the relationships depicted (Gibbs, 2006b). College students specifically judged the successful metaphorical relationships (Story A) to be progressing further, moving along in a straighter line and the story participants to be heading more in the same direction than was the case for the unsuccessful metaphorical story (Story B). Of course, there is nothing in these two stories that directly asserts anything about the distance, speed, extent, and direction of the relationship "journeys" traveled. All of these inferences were drawn on the basis of people's metaphorical understandings of the stories as referring to RELATIONSHIPS ARE JOURNEYS, as suggested by the *Your relationship was moving along in a good direction* statement. Might these inferences be based on people's embodied simulation of the relationships, in which readers imagine moving along in a good direction that is then affected by the subsequent positive and negative character of the relationships?

One new set of studies used a new methodology to examine whether people's interpretations of simple narratives, like the above stories, partly rely on their embodied simulations of the metaphors involved (Gibbs, 2006b). People infer the detailed meanings of simple narratives involving conceptual metaphors by imagining their participation in the metaphorical actions explicitly mentioned in these stories. For example, when hearing *moving along in a good direction,* listeners imagine engaging in a body action, such as traveling along some path, which facilitates their metaphoric understanding of the abstract, and physically impossible, idea that romantic relationships can move along a path toward some goal. If people imaginatively simulate themselves in the journey, then listening to these different renditions of the RELATIONSHIPS ARE JOURNEYS conceptual metaphor should have different real-world embodied effects. To assess this idea, people listened to one of the two above stories, were blindfolded, and then walked along a path toward an object while they thought about the story. People should walk differently when hearing successful and unsuccessful metaphor stories, while these effects should be greatly attenuated after hearing nonmetaphorical narratives that did not suggest a conceptualization of the relationship as a kind of physical journey.

This hypothesis was tested in a novel by having participants physically walk toward an object, 40 feet away, after hearing either a successful or unsuccessful story in either the metaphorical or nonmetaphorical condition. Another experimental condition asked participants to simply imagine walking to the object after hearing one of the stories. Analysis of the walking times generally showed that people walked significantly longer for the successful metaphorical stories (15.7 seconds) than for the unsuccessful metaphorical stories (12.8 seconds), but that this difference was not reliable in the nonmetaphorical condition (14.8 and 14.6 seconds). Analysis of the length of walking (in vertical relationship to the target) again showed that people walked farther for the successful stories (2.4 feet beyond the object) than for the unsuccessful ones (2.3 feet below the object).

Another experimental condition asked participants to simply imagine walking to the object after hearing one of the stories. For the imagined condition, participants were blindfolded, heard a story, but were then instructed to only imagine walking out to the yellow ball as they thought about the story and to press a stopwatch as soon as they imagined arriving at the ball. The results of the imagine condition showed that people imagined walking longer for the successful metaphor stories (11.4 seconds) than for the unsuccessful metaphoric narratives (9.5 seconds). Unlike the data for the walking condition, where no difference was obtained, people imagined walking longer in the unsuccessful condition (12.5 seconds) than in the successful one (9.5 seconds). The reason for this latter finding is not clear.

These studies suggest that people's interpretation of the stories partly involved creating an embodied simulation, or a reenactment, of the relationship journey alluded to in the different metaphorical narratives. Even though relationships are not physical entities that literally travel along physical paths, people nonetheless conceive of relationships in metaphorical ways, especially when prompted to do so by statements like *Your relationship was moving along in a good direction*. This metaphorical conceptualization is not purely abstract but embodied in the sense that participants imagine themselves moving in the different relationship journeys which subsequently affected their walking, and imagining of walking, as they thought about the stories.

We recognize that an experiment where people hear stories and then walk blindfolded toward an object is not a traditional method to assess immediate understanding of verbal metaphors. Unlike many of the other studies described in this chapter that examine the processes by which metaphors are understood, the walking experiment looks at the products of people's interpretations. People may have walked differently in the various conditions of the walking experiment because of imaginative processes that occurred after they had originally heard and understood the metaphorical and nonmetaphorical stories. More experimental work is necessary to test for this and other alternative explanations of these findings. But the results are still intriguing, and indeed consistent with the embodied simulation view advocated for in this chapter.

## Conclusion

Metaphor is closely allied to human imagination. Our claim in this chapter has been that significant aspects of metaphor use involve people simulating what it must be like to engage in specific bodily actions referred to in metaphorical expressions. These mental reenactments first demonstrate how the imagination is tied to bodily action and more specifically suggest the ongoing role that imaginative processes play in verbal metaphor understanding.

The vast body of work in cognitive science showing that simulations are critical to many aspects of cognition and nonmetaphorical language use is certainly consistent with our arguments about embodied simulations in understanding metaphor. Yet the surprising part of the psycholinguistic research described previously is that people engage in embodied simulations for actions that in many cases are not physically possible to do in the real world, precisely because they involve abstract entities. One may argue, once more, that physical aspects of grasping or moving forward must be ignored or inhibited to understand properly metaphorical expressions such as *grasp the concept* or *the relationship was moving forward in a good direction*. But imagining one engaging in these actions is quite sensible given that many abstract concepts are at least partly understood in metaphoric terms. These embodied metaphorical conceptions mesh perfectly with bodily actions, such as when one thinks of concepts or racism as a concrete entity, sometimes animate, that can be touched, held on to, controlled, and stomped on. The psycholinguistic evidence presented here provides different glimpses into how embodied simulations shape people's immediate interpretation and conscious reflection of different kinds of metaphorical language that is rooted in correlations in bodily experience (e.g., GRASPING IS UNDERSTANDING). We also contend that the empirical findings reviewed here are inconsistent with claims that (a) people do not understand conventional statements such as *The road runs along the coastline* and *He finally grasped the concept* in metaphorical terms, or that (b) people access these figurative meanings by simply accessing a preestablished sense from a mental lexicon without engaging in any imaginative bodily activities.

One of the peculiar aspects of metaphor scholarship is the degree to which the field is split between people studying classic A is B metaphors (e.g., *My lawyer is a shark*), and those studying metaphors arising from correlations in experience (e.g., *I can see the point you are making*). Not surprisingly perhaps, people studying these different aspects of metaphor tend to adopt very different theoretical perspectives to explain metaphor in language and thought. Classic or resemblance metaphors are typically viewed as having little to do with embodied action and are understood through comparison or categorization processes (Gentner and Bowdle, this volume; Glucksberg, this volume). But it may be the case that people construct embodied simulations when they infer the metaphorical meanings of resemblance metaphors. Consider, for example, some metaphors for teachers: *teachers are tour guides, teachers are fishermen*, or *teachers are astronauts*. Each of these seems to contrast dissimilar domains where the goal is to understand which aspects of the source domain (e.g., tour guides) gets mapped onto the target domain (e.g., teachers).

Yet people are not simply mapping static or relational features of source domains and not just creating some superordinate category of which the target domain is a prototypical member. Instead, people understanding a statement like *teachers are tour guides* are constructing an embodied simulation of what it must be like to be a tour guide, and using that information to further constrain what the metaphor implies. One Web site (AnnenbergMediaLearner.org) has an interactive workshop for teachers titled, "What's your metaphor," where teachers write in answers to "What metaphor describes you as a teacher?" and asks participants to then "explain how this metaphor characterizes you as a teacher." The remarkable thing about people's metaphors is that they are the entire "A is B" form, but then describe the metaphor in terms of bodily action. For instance, one person claimed that their metaphor was *A teacher is a fisherman*, and wrote, "Standing by the river, putting the hook into the water (no barbs on the hook). Constantly guiding the rod down the river, toward the sea of self-fulfillment. There are rapids that can cause the fish to experience a sense of confusion, but the tension from the rod is a constant, guiding them toward calmer waters. This journey cannot be completed by one fisher, the rod is passed to the next fisher (teacher)."

This example is representative of how all these teachers interpreted their metaphors. People simulated what it must be like to be a fisherman, tour guide, astronaut and described in detail the actions they would take that may be similar to those done when teaching and what impact they had on their students. Thus, the new category of *A teacher is a fisherman*, for example, is created and appreciated by running the simulation, or engaging in an "as if" scenario where bodily action and its effects are critical to the metaphor's meaning. In fact, simulating embodied experiences may be critical to many aspects of categorization, not just those having to do with metaphor. One study supporting this idea asked people to generate exemplars from both common taxonomic categories, such as furniture and fruits, and ad hoc categories, such as things dogs chase or reasons for going on a holiday (Vallee-Tourangeau, Anthony, & Austin, 1998). When people were then asked to describe their strategies for generating the exemplars, participants in both the taxonomic and ad hoc groups often reported using "experiential mediation." Thus, when generating exemplars of "fruit," people did not read off some list in their heads but imagined themselves in a familiar grocery store walking in the produce section noting individual types of fruit as they were encountered. These findings show that embodied simulation may not be something restricted to creating and understanding ad hoc categories, which include novel metaphors but are applied when common taxonomic categories are accessed as well (see Barsalou, 2003).

## References

Babcock, M., & Freyd, J. (1988). Perception of dynamic information in static handwritten forms. *American Journal of Psychology, 101*, 111–130.

Barsalou, L. W. (2003). Situated simulation in the human conceptual system. *Language and Cognitive Processes, 18*, 513–562.

Bavelas, J. B., Kenwood, C., Johnson, T., & Phillips, B. (2002). An experimental study of when and how speakers use gestures to communicate. *Gesture, 2*, 1–17.

Boroditsky, L., & Ramscar, M. (2002). The roles of body and mind in abstract thought. *Psychological Science, 13*, 185–189.

Bower, G. H., & Morrow, D. G. (1990). Mental models in narrative comprehension. *Science, 47*, 44–48.

Clark, A. (1997). *Being there: Putting brain, body, and world together again.* Cambridge, MA: MIT Press.

Clark, H. H., & Krych, M. A. (2004). Speaking while monitoring addressees for understanding. *Journal of Memory and Language*, (1), 62–81.

Currie, G., & Ravenscroft, I. (2002). *Recreative minds.* Oxford: Clarendon Press.

Denis, M., & Cocude, M. (1989). Scanning visual images generated from verbal descriptions. *European Journal of Cognitive Psychology, 1*, 293–307.

Freyd, J. J. (1983). The mental representation of movement when static stimuli are viewed. *Perception & Psychophysics, 33*, 575–581.

Gallese, V. (2000). The inner sense of action: Agency and motor representations. *Journal of Consciousness Studies, 7*, 23–40.

Gentner, D., Imai, M., & Boroditsky, L. (2002). As time goes by: Evidence for two systems in processing space-time metaphors. *Language and Cognitive Processes, 17*, 537–565.

Gibbs, R. (1994). The poetics of mind: Figurative thought, language, and understanding. New York: Cambridge University Press.

Gibbs, R. (2006a). *Embodiment and cognitive science.* New York: Cambridge University Press.

Gibbs, R. (2006b). *Walking the talk while thinking about the talk: Embodied interpretation of metaphorical narratives.* Manuscript submitted for publication.

Gibbs, R., Gould, J., & Andric, M. (2006). Imagining metaphorical actions: Embodied simulations make the impossible plausible. *Imagination, Cognition, & Personality.* 25, 221–238.

Gibbs, R., & O'Brien, J. (1990). Idioms and mental imagery: The metaphorical motivation for idiomatic meaning. *Cognition, 36*, 35–68.

Gibbs, R., Strom, L., & Spivey-Knowlton, M. (1997). Conceptual metaphors in mental imagery for proverbs. *Journal of Mental Imagery, 21*, 83–110.

Glenberg, A. M. (1999). Why mental models must be embodied. In G. Rickheit & C. Habel (Eds.), *Mental models in discourse processing and reasoning* (pp. 77–90). New York: North-Holland.

Glenberg, A., & Kaschak, M. (2002). Grounding language in action. *Psychonomic Bulletin & Review, 9*, 558–565.

Glucksberg, S. (2001). *Understanding figurative language: From metaphors to idioms.* New York: Oxford University Press.

Goldman, A. (2006). Simulating minds: The philosophy, psychology, and neuroscience of mind reading. New York: Oxford University Press.

Gordon, R. (1986). Folk psychology as simulation. *Mind & Language, 1*, 158–171.

Harris, P. (1992). From simulation to folk psychology: The case for development. *Mind & Language, 7*, 120–144.

Jackendoff, R. (2002). *Foundations of language.* New York: Oxford University Press.

Kirsh, D., & Maglio, P. (1994). On distinguishing epistemic from pragmatic action. *Cognitive Science, 18*, 513–549.

Klatzky, R. L., Pellegrino, J. W., McCloskey, B. P., & Doherty, S. (1989). Can you squeeze a tomato? The role of motor representations in semantic sensibility judgments. *Journal of Memory and Language, 28*, 56–77.

Knuf, G., Aschersleben, G., & Prinz, W. (2001). An analysis of ideomotor action. *Journal of Experimental Psychology: General, 130*, 779–798.

Kourtzi, Z., & Kanwisher, N. (2000). Activation in human MT/MST by static images with implied motion. *Journal of Cognitive Neuroscience, 12*, 48–55.

Langacker, R. W. (1987). *Foundations of cognitive grammar: Vol. 1. Theoretical prerequisites.* Stanford, CA: Stanford University Press.

Lakoff, G., & Johnson, M. (1999). *Philosophy in the flesh: The embodied mind and its challenge to western thought.* New York: Basic Books.

Lakoff, G., & Núñez, R. E. (2001). Where mathematics comes from: How the embodied mind brings mathematics into being. New York: Basic Books.

Maglio, P. P., Matlock, T., Raphaely, D., Chernicky, B., & Kirsh, D. (1999). Interactive skill in Scrabble. In *Proceedings of the Twenty-first Annual Meeting of the Cognitive Science Society*. Mahwah, NJ: Erlbaum.

Matlock, T. (2004). Fictive motion as cognitive simulation. *Memory & Cognition, 32*, 1389–1400.

Matlock, T., & Clark, H. H. (2006). *Joint spatial mental models*. Manuscript in preparation.

Matlock, T., Ramscar, M., & Boroditsky, L. (2004). The experiential basis of motion language. In A. Soares da Silva, A. Torres, & M. Goncalves (Eds.), *Linguagem, cultura e cognicao: Estudo de linguistica cognitiva* (pp. 43–57). Coimbra: Almedina.

Matlock, T., Ramscar, M., & Boroditsky, L. (2005). The experiential link between spatial and temporal language. *Cognitive Science, 29*, 655–664.

Matlock, T., Ramscar, M., & Srinivasan, M. (2006). *Even the most abstract motion influences the understanding of time*. Manuscript in preparation.

Matlock, T., & Richardson, D. C. (2004). *Do eye movements go with fictive motion?* Proceedings of the 26th Annual Conference of the Cognitive Science Society., Mahwah, NJ: Erlbaum.

Matsumoto, Y. (1996). Subjective motion and English and Japanese verbs. *Cognitive Linguistics, 7*, 183–226.

McGlone, M. S., & Harding, J. L. (1998). Back (or forward?) to the future: The role of perspective in temporal language comprehension. *Journal of Experimental Psychology: Learning, Memory, & Cognition, 24*, 1211–1223.

Morrow, D. G., Bower, G. H., & Greenspan, S. L. (1989). Updating situation models during narrative comprehension. *Journal of Memory and Language, 28*, 292–312.

Morrow, D. G., & Clark, H. H. (1988). Interpreting words in spatial descriptions. *Language and Cognitive Processes, 3*, 275–291.

Núñez, R. E., Motz, B. A., & Teuscher, U. (2006). Time after time: The psychological reality of the ego- and time-reference-point distinction in metaphorical construals of time. *Metaphor and Symbol, 21*, 133–146.

Ramscar, M., Matlock, T., & Boroditsky, L. (2007). *The experiential basis of abstract language comprehension*. Manuscript in preparation.

Richardson, D. C., & Matlock, T. (2007). The integration of figurative language and static depictions: An eye movement study of fictive motion, *Cognition, 102*, 129–138.

Richardson, D. C., Spivey, M. J., Barsalou, L. W., & McRae, K. (2003). Spatial representations activated during real time comprehension of verbs. *Cognitive Science, 27*, 767–780.

Schwartz, D. L., & Black, T. (1999). Inferences through imagined actions: Knowing by simulated doing. *Journal of Experimental Psychology: Learning, Memory, and Cognition, 25*, 116–136.

Talmy, L. (2000). *Toward a cognitive semantics: Vol. 1. Conceptual structuring systems*. Cambridge, MA: MIT Press.

Tversky, B. (1996). Spatial perspective in descriptions. In P. Bloom, M. A. Peterson, L. Nadel, & M. F. Garrett (Eds.), *Language and space* (pp. 463–491). Cambridge, MA: MIT Press.

Tversky, B. (2000). Remembering spaces. In E. Tulving & F. Craik (Eds.), *The Oxford handbook of memory* (pp. 363–378). New York: Oxford University Press.

Vallee-Tourangeau, F., Anthony, S., & Austin, N. (1998). Strategies for generating multiple instances of common and ad hoc categories. *Memory, 5*, 555–592.

Wilson, N., & Gibbs, R. (2007). *Real and imagined body movement primes metaphor comprehension. Cognitive Science*, 31, 721–731.

Zwaan, R. A., & Radvansky, G. A. (1998). Situation models in language comprehension and memory. *Psychological Bulletin, 123*, 162–185.

Zwaan, R. A., & Taylor, L. (2006). Seeing, acting, understanding: Motor resonance in language comprehension. *Journal of Experimental Psychology: General, 135*, 1–11.

CHAPTER 10

# Metaphor Comprehension and the Brain

*Seana Coulson*

*Don't know what you've got 'till it's gone; they've paved paradise, and put up a parking lot. – Joni Mitchell*

During lunch one afternoon in the fall of 1990, retired *New York Times* reporter A. H. Raskin felt a strange sensation in his right arm and slowly slipped out of consciousness. When he awoke again in New York Hospital, his world would never be the same. Raskin had suffered a stroke that resulted in damage to the front portion of his left hemisphere. As a result, he was unable to move his right arm and leg, unable to speak, and unable to understand even the simplest language. Eventually, Raskin regained the ability to walk, to move his arm, and to understand what was said to him. Though he did his best to produce nouns and verbs together in an order that others might make sense of, fluent speech remained a challenge for him the rest of his life (Raskin, 1992).

Raskin suffered from Broca's aphasia, a language disorder often accompanied by weakness or paralysis of the right side of the body. Broca's aphasics have largely intact comprehension abilities but can speak only with effort, typically producing short, telegraphic phrases. The condition is named after 19th-century neurologist Paul Broca who prompted scientific discussion as to whether language ability could be localized in the brain with his classic report of two patients with profound communicative deficits following large left frontal lobe lesions (Broca, 1865). Localization received further support from Broca's contemporary, Wernicke (1874), who reported two patients with severe language comprehension deficits, apparently due to the presence of a lesion in the posterior portion of the left temporal lobe. Although Wernicke's aphasics can speak fluently, their speech includes made-up words known as paraphasias (e.g., *treen* for *train*), and their sentences are often incoherent. In contrast, the incidence of aphasic deficits in patients with lesions in the right hemisphere is far less common (Hécaen & Consoli, 1973).

Cognitive neuroscientists' understanding of the relationship between brain activity and language ability derives largely from the study of brain injured patients. Since damage to the front portion of the brain is associated with difficulty speaking, it is assumed that left frontal areas play a crucial role in language production. Similarly, since damage to the posterior portion of the brain is associated with difficulty understanding language, it is assumed that left posterior temporal areas play a crucial role in language comprehension. The logic is that the damaged area plays a critical role in the compromised function. Consequently, the left hemisphere (LH) is considered the language hemisphere, while the right hemisphere (RH) is the "minor" hemisphere.

However, language deficits have also been associated with damage to the RH. In contrast to the severe language impairment in patients with left hemisphere damage (LHD), patients with RHD exhibit more subtle deficits involving the relationship between an utterance and its context. RHD production, for example, is marked by socially inappropriate remarks, tangential speech, digressions of topic, combined with a failure to utilize nonverbal cues (Joanette, Goulet, & Hannequin, 1990). In experimental studies of their comprehension, RHD patients have been shown to have difficulty understanding jokes (Bihrle, Brownell, & Gardner, 1986; Brownell, Michel, Powelson, & Gardner, 1983), interpreting sarcastic utterances (Giora, Zaidel, Soroker, Batori, & Kasher, 2002; Rehak, Kaplan, & Gardner, 1992), and have been characterized as deriving overly literal interpretations of metaphoric language (Winner & Gardner, 1977). Thus, the left hemisphere is associated with language processing traditionally construed as linguistic, that is, phonological, syntactic, and semantic analysis, while the right hemisphere has been associated with processing typically construed as pragmatic, or extra-linguistic.

The role of the two hemispheres in metaphor comprehension thus has potential implications for the dispute in cognitive science as to whether metaphor should be considered the province of semantics or pragmatics. According to traditional views, metaphor represents a departure from normal, that is, literal, language use and thus falls within the province of pragmatics (Grice, 1975; Searle, 1979). However, others have argued that metaphoric meanings undermine the very distinction under dispute, that between linguistic and nonlinguistic meanings. Ordinary language is replete with metaphors of varying degrees of entrenchment (Gibbs, 1994; Lakoff & Johnson, 1999; Sweetser, 1990; Turner, 1991). Moreover, the recruitment of real-world knowledge and local contextual information is necessary for the comprehension of both literal and metaphorical meanings (Coulson, 2001; Gibbs, 1994; Gibbs & Gerrig, 1989).

The relationship between the cognitive and neural processes underlying the comprehension of literal versus metaphorical language has thus been a key research issue. Though much research on this topic has utilized various behavioral measures of processing, cognitive neuroscientists have increasingly used measures of brain function to address the validity of particular models of metaphor comprehension. In section 1, we review the use of electrophysiological measures to assess the real-time processing of metaphors. These findings suggest that while metaphor comprehension often recruits increased processing resources, it is influenced by many of the same variables as is the comprehension of literal language. The commonality between the processing of literal and metaphorical language suggested by electrophysiological measures is somewhat puzzling in view of the suggestion that metaphor comprehension recruits right hemisphere brain areas not utilized in the processing of literal language.

This puzzle is addressed in section 2 as we review the original evidence for the right hemisphere theory of metaphor and counter with more recent evidence that argues against it. This section involves discussion of a number of the different sorts of methods used in cognitive neuroscience, including the study of patients with brain damage as well as methods such as repetitive transcranial magnetic stimulation (rTMS) that lead to transient damage in otherwise normal people. We discuss experiments that use the divided visual field priming paradigm that is particularly helpful in drawing inferences about hemispheric differences, along with neuroimaging studies of metaphor comprehension in healthy adults. These different methodologies provide convergent evidence that the recruitment of right hemisphere areas depends not on the figurativity of the materials, but on their complexity.

Finally, in section 3 we speculate about how the study of the brain might enhance our understanding of metaphor comprehension. We briefly discuss evidence for the sensorimotor grounding of concepts in general, and metaphor in particular. In keeping with conceptual metaphor theory, we suggest that metaphor involves the utilization of brain areas implicated in concrete concepts for use in the construal of abstract domains.

## 1. Real-Time Comprehension of Metaphors

The neurophysiology of language processes can be investigated in healthy people via the non-invasive recording of event-related brain potentials (ERPs). ERPs are small voltage fluctuations in the electroencephalogram (EEG) that are time-locked to perceptual, motor, or cognitive events collected by recording EEG while participants perform a cognitive task such as reading (Rugg & Coles, 1995). By averaging the EEG time-locked to multiple tokens of a given type (e.g., the onset of a word used metaphorically), it is possible to isolate aspects of the electrical signal that are temporally associated with the processing of that type of event (such as understanding a metaphoric meaning). The result of averaging is a waveform with a series of positive and negative peaks, known as components, and labeled by reference to their polarity ("P" for positive-going and "N" for negative-going), and when they occur relative to the onset of the stimulus event, or relative to other ERP components.

Over the past 25 years, cognitive neuroscientists have identified ERP components associated with processing different sorts of linguistic information, such as the link between the N400 and semantic integration processes. The N400 component of the ERPs was first noted in experiments contrasting sentences that ended sensibly and predictably with others that ended with an incongruous word. Congruous words elicited a late positive wave, while incongruous endings elicited a negative wave beginning about 200 ms after word onset and peaking at 400 ms (Kutas & Hillyard, 1980). Subsequent experiments have shown that finer gradations of semantic context also modulate N400 amplitude. For example, amplitude shows a strong inverse correlation with the predictability of the eliciting word within a given sentence context (Kutas, Lindamood, & Hillyard, 1984). In general, experimental manipulations that make semantic integration more difficult result in larger amplitude N400, while those that facilitate it result in smaller N400.

Because ERPs provide an online index of brain activity related to language comprehension, they have been used to test various models of metaphor comprehension. Pynte, Besson, Robichon, and Poli (1996), for example, used ERPs to address the validity of three hypotheses about metaphor comprehension: the standard model, the parallel hypothesis, and the context-dependent hypothesis. First, the *standard pragmatic model* posits two discrete stages of metaphor processing, as metaphorical meanings are accessed only after the literal meaning has been rejected. This model predicts an initial effect of metaphoricity on the N400, reflecting the literal incongruity, followed by a later ERP effect, reflecting the access of the metaphorical meaning. However, although metaphors (*Those fighters are* LIONS) elicited slightly larger N400s than literal controls (*Those animals are* LIONS), there were no reliable ERP effects after the N400, namely, between 600 and 1200 ms after the onset of the sentence's final word. Pynte and colleagues (1996) thus suggested that the enhanced N400 to the metaphors reflected participants' apprehension of the literal incongruity of these sentences, as predicted by the model. However, the absence of late ERP effects is contrary to the predictions of the standard model.

In contrast to the standard model, the *parallel hypothesis* is that literal and metaphorical meanings are processed in parallel. According to the parallel model, if N400 amplitude reflects the difficulty of comprehending literal meanings, it should also reflect the difficulty of comprehending metaphorical meanings. The parallel model thus entails that differences in the comprehensibility of familiar versus unfamiliar metaphors should be reflected in N400 amplitude. However, when presented out of context, Pynte et al. (1996) found no differences in ERPs elicited by familiar metaphors such as "*Those fighters are* LIONS," and unfamiliar metaphors such as "*Those apprentices are* LIONS."

The *context-dependent hypothesis* is the idea that the metaphorical meaning is directly accessed when it is relevant to the preceding context. To test this hypothesis, Pynte and colleagues (1996) recorded ERPs as participants read sentences with familiar and unfamiliar metaphors placed in either relevant (e.g., for the lion example, "*They are not cowardly*") or irrelevant (e.g., "*They are not idiotic*") contexts. The context-dependent hypothesis predicts that regardless of the familiarity of the metaphor, the relevance of the context should modulate N400 amplitude. Accordingly, Pynte et al. (1996) found that while metaphor familiarity did not affect the ERPs, the relevance of the context did. Compared to the relevant contexts, metaphors in irrelevant contexts elicited more negative ERPs in both the N400 window and the subsequent 600–1000 ms interval, suggesting irrelevant metaphors were more difficult to process.

Further evidence that metaphorical meanings are activated very early in the processing stream comes from an ERP study of the metaphor interference effect (MIE). The MIE is elicited in a sentence verification paradigm in which the subject is given literally true, literally false, and metaphorically true (but literally false) sentences. The MIE refers to the increased response times to reject metaphorically true sentences such as, "*The divorce is a nightmare*," compared to literally false sentences such as "*The divorce is a table*" (Glucksberg, Gildea, & Bookin, 1982). Because the task demands that the participant attend only to the literal meaning of these sentences, the MIE is interpreted as reflecting the automatic activation of metaphoric meanings.

Kazmerski and colleagues recorded ERPs as healthy participants judged the literal truth of sentences such as "*Tulips grow from a bulb*," "*The beaver is a lumberjack*," and "*The rumor is a lumberjack*." They observed an MIE in participants' reaction times, as it took participants longer to respond "no" to the metaphorical sentences than their literal counterparts (Kazmerski, Blasko, & Dessalegn, 2003). Interestingly, the MIE was only 11 ms in participants with low IQ (<100), but was 35 ms in participants with high IQ (>115). The ERP correlates of the MIE included a smaller N400 for the metaphorically true sentences than the literally false sentences, suggesting participants found metaphorical words easier to process than the anomalous endings, as well as a larger late positivity for the metaphors, perhaps reflecting the greater difficulty in responding "no" to these items. Moreover, these ERP effects were marked and robust in the high IQ group, but largely absent in the low IQ group whose behavioral MIE was also negligible.

Research to date thus suggests that, contrary to the Standard Model of metaphor comprehension, metaphoric meanings are available quite early in processing, affecting the ERPs beginning 250–300 ms after the onset of a metaphorical word (Kazmerski et al., 2003; Pynte et al., 1996). Decontextualized metaphors elicit slightly larger N400s than plausible literal controls such as "*Those animals are lions*" (Pynte et al., 1996), suggesting they place more demands on semantic integration processes. However, metaphors elicit smaller N400s than implausible literal controls such as "*The rumor is a lumberjack*" (Kazmerski et al., 2003), suggesting they are easier to process than incongruous sentence completions. This latter finding casts doubt on the suggestion that the enhanced N400 (relative to plausible literal endings) elicited by metaphors indexes their literal incongruity.

Coulson and Van Petten (2002) have suggested that N400 amplitude to metaphors is driven by the complexity of mapping and blending operations involved in the comprehension of metaphors but also in the comprehension of literal language. In our model, metaphor comprehension involves coordinating various conceptual domains in a *blend*, a hybrid model that consists of structure from multiple conceptual domains, and that often develops emergent structure of its own. Metaphor comprehension involves the temporary construction of simple cognitive models along with the establishment of mappings, or systematic correspondences among objects and relationships represented in various models. Mappings are based on relationships such as identity, similarity, or analogy. Consequently, metaphoric meanings – that use analogy to link objects in different spaces – do not fundamentally differ from meanings that employ other sorts of mappings.

For instance, understanding the metaphor in "*All the nurses at the hospital say that surgeon is a butcher,*" requires coordinating conceptual structure associated with surgery, butchery, and a blend of the two. To understand this metaphor it is necessary to apprehend mappings between surgeon and butcher, patient and dead animal (e.g., cow), as well as scalpel and cleaver. However, it also involves construction of a blended model that integrates some information from each of the two domains. In this example, the blend inherits the goals of the surgeon, and the means and manner of the butcher. The inference that the surgeon is incompetent arises when these structures are integrated to create a hypothetical agent with both characteristics.

Similar conceptual operations are involved in understanding literal language. For example, understanding butcher in "*During the war, that surgeon had to work as a butcher,*" also requires the comprehender to establish mappings and integrate information about a surgeon's training and skill with general information about butchers, and other aspects of the context (Coulson & Matlock, 2001). One might for instance, infer that the surgeon in question was overqualified for his job, or that he was forced to work as a butcher in a labor camp. Differences in the comprehensibility of these *butcher* sentences, then, might be less a matter of their figurativity than the extent to which they require the comprehender to activate additional information to establish mappings and elaborate the blend.

To test these ideas, Coulson and Van Petten (2002) compared ERPs elicited by words in three different contexts on a continuum from literal to figurative, as suggested by conceptual integration theory (Fauconnier & Turner, 1998). For the literal end of the continuum, they used sentences that prompted a literal reading of the last term, as in "*He knows that whiskey is a strong intoxicant.*" At the metaphoric end of the continuum, they used sentences such as "*He knows that power is a strong intoxicant.*" The literal mapping condition, hypothesized to fall somewhere between the literal and the metaphoric uses, involved sentences such as, "*He has used cough syrup as an intoxicant.*" Literal mapping stimuli employed fully literal uses of words in ways that were hypothesized to include some of the same conceptual operations as in metaphor comprehension. These sentences described cases where one object was substituted for another, one object was mistaken for another, or one object was used to represent another – all contexts that require the comprehender to set up a mapping, that is, understand a correspondence, between the two objects in question and the domains in which they typically occur.

In the time window in which the N400 is observed (300–500 ms post-onset), ERPs in all three conditions were qualitatively similar, displaying similar waveshape and scalp topography, suggesting that processing was similar for all three sorts of contexts. Moreover, as predicted, N400 amplitude differed as a function of the metaphoricity, with literals eliciting the least N400, literal mappings the next-most, and metaphors the most N400, suggesting a concomitant gradient of processing difficulty. The graded N400 difference argues against the literal/figurative dichotomy inherent in the standard model, and suggests processing difficulty associated with figurative language is related to the complexity of mapping and conceptual integration.

Although the comprehension of metaphoric meanings poses a challenge that is greater than that associated with literal language of comparable syntactic complexity, there does not seem to be much evidence to support a view of metaphor comprehension as involving a qualitatively distinct processing mode. ERP studies of metaphor comprehension suggest metaphoric meanings are active during the same temporal interval as literal meanings (Kazmerski et al., 2003). As in the case of literal language, semantic integration difficulty of metaphoric language is largely a function of contextual support (Pynte et al., 1996), and may also be attributable to demands of conceptual mapping and blending operations (Coulson & Van Petten, 2002).

## 2. RH Role in Metaphor Comprehension

Results reviewed above thus suggest that qualitatively similar processing mechanisms underlie the comprehension of literal and metaphorical meanings. These, however, stand in opposition to the argument from neuropsychology that the right hemisphere (RH) is crucial for metaphor comprehension. If metaphorical meanings can be construed as "residing" in the RH, metaphor could be considered pragmatic, extra-linguistic knowledge distinct from literal language. Perhaps because of its theoretical implications, this issue has received by far the most attention from cognitive neuroscientists.

However, the exclusive association between RH damage and metaphor comprehension deficits is in fact rather equivocal. We review evidence both for (2.1.1) and against (2.1.2) the right hemisphere theory of metaphor from the study of patients with neurological deficits. We follow with a discussion of evidence from techniques used on healthy adults, such as rTMS (2.2), visual half-field priming (2.3), and neuroimaging (2.4), all of which argue against the claim that the RH is the exclusive province of metaphoric meanings.

### 2.1 *Patient Studies*

#### 2.1.1. EVIDENCE FOR THE RH THEORY

The characterization of RHD patients as being overly literal in metaphor interpretation originates in a study done by Winner and Gardner (1977) in which they asked RHD patients to match sentences such as "*He had a heavy heart*," to a pictorial depiction from an array that included an illustration of the literal meaning of the phrase (a man lifting an oversized heart), the metaphoric meaning (a man crying), and different aspects of the literal meaning (a picture of a large weight, a picture of a heart). While RHD and LHD patients were both impaired relative to healthy controls, the RHD patients were more likely to err by choosing the literal foils, that is, the man stumbling under the weight of the massive heart. In a similar task, LHD aphasic patients were better able to match words such as *wealth* with connotative pictorial representations, such as an arrow pointed up or down, than were RHD patients (Gardner & Denes, 1973).

RHD patients have also been shown to have problems with metaphoric meanings in purely verbal paradigms. For example, Brownell and colleagues gave participants word triads, such as *cold-hateful-warm*, and asked them to pick the two words that had the same meaning, or that went together better (Brownell, 1984; Brownell, Simpson, Bihrle, Potter, & Gardner, 1990). Semantic relationships between the words were based on either denotative relationships, such as the antonymy between *cold* and *warm*, connotative relationships, such as that between *cold* and *foolish*, metaphoric relationships as in *cold* and *hateful*, or were unrelated as in *cold* and *wise*. RHD patients showed normal use of antonym association, but less than normal use of metaphoric equivalence;

LHD patients showed the opposite pattern (Brownell, 1984).

Further, in a comparison of RHD and LHD patients' language abilities, Van Lacker and Kemplar (1987) found that while both groups performed well in the comprehension of single words, and RHD patients were better able to comprehend novel sentences, the LHD patients were better able to comprehend familiar idiomatic phrases. Given that LHD patients tend to have more obvious language deficits than their RHD counterparts, the finding that LHD patients actually perform better than those with RHD on figurative language comprehension tasks points toward a special role for the RH in figurative language comprehension.

An alternative explanation, however, is that the RHD deficit lies in appreciating the less frequent meaning of an ambiguous word, rather than the appreciation of metaphoric meanings, *per se*. To address whether the RHD deficit could be attributed to the appreciation of the less frequent meaning of an ambiguous word, Gagnon and colleagues tested metaphoric adjectives as well as non-metaphoric, but ambiguous, nouns (cf. Brownell et al., 1990). Relative to normal controls, both RHD and LHD patients' performance was impaired. Although performance of both groups was comparable on the metaphoric adjectives, RHD patients outperformed the LHD patients on the non-metaphoric nouns (Gagnon, Goulet, Giroux, & Joanette, 2003). While the LHD patients' deficits argue against the idea that metaphor comprehension is the exclusive province of the RH, these data suggest that metaphoric meanings pose a particular problem for RHD patients.

#### 2.1.2. EVIDENCE AGAINST THE RH THEORY

The original studies reporting impaired metaphor comprehension in RHD patients have been criticized for several methodological shortcomings (see e.g., (Joanette et al., 1990). For example, in their landmark "heavy heart" study, Winner and Gardner (1977) did not assess whether perceptual deficits often associated with RHD affected patients' task performance. Indeed, in many such studies, perceptual deficits are not assessed, and even the language abilities of the patients are not studied in detail (see Oliveri, Romero, & Papagno, 2004, for critique). The number of subjects is typically quite small, as is the number of stimuli. Further, because many of the studies that support the view of RHD metaphor comprehension deficits have used forced choice paradigms, some researchers have suggested the RHD deficit lies not in comprehension, per se, but in rejecting the alternative meanings of the experimental stimuli.

RHD metaphor comprehension impairments are most evident in tasks that require controlled strategic processing. For example, Tompkins used an auditory word priming paradigm to test both automatic and controlled aspects of word processing (Tompkins, 1990). As is customary, this was achieved by varying the amount of time between the onset of the prime and the target words (known as stimulus onset asynchrony, or SOA). When SOA is short, performance reflects fast-acting automatic processes; when SOA is longer, performance reflects slower controlled processes. At the short, but not the long, SOA, ambiguous primes facilitated performance for both literally and metaphorically related targets, suggesting RHD patients can access the metaphoric meanings of words, but are impaired in the strategic use of semantic knowledge (Tompkins, 1990; Tompkins, Boada, & McGarry, 1992). These findings suggest that while both hemispheres are sensitive to word-level metaphoric meaning, task demands can impact performance due to limited attentional and memory resources in these patients.

Working memory limitations may particularly affect performance on picture matching as there is considerable evidence that these tasks underestimate patients' metaphor comprehension abilities. A test of a large number of RHD participants' metaphor comprehension abilities showed that although RHD patients were significantly impaired on both a picture-matching and a verbal task, their impairment on the picture-matching task was more severe (Rinaldi, Marangolo, & Baldassarri, 2002). As in Winner and Gardner (1977), RHD participants were able to verbally explain the meaning of statements for which they had chosen the incorrect literal picture (Rinaldi et al., 2002). Other investigators have found that even neurologically intact participants perform better on verbal tests of figurative language comprehension than on tests that involve picture matching (Papagno, Tabossi, Colombo, & Zampetti, 2004). Further, in a test of both LHD and RHD patients, while LHD performance on verbal and pictorial subtests was correlated, RHD performance was not, suggesting non-linguistic factors may contribute to this dissociation (Zaidel, Kasher, Soroker, & Baroti, 2002).

Indeed the ability to understand figurative language is compromised not only by unilateral lesions in the RH, but also by other neurological conditions. As noted above, both LHD and RHD individuals are impaired on tests of figurative language comprehension (Gagnon et al., 2003; Papagno et al., 2004). Unlike their RHD counterparts, LHD patients have been shown to be impaired both on picture matching tasks and on a task that requires them to give a verbal explanation of idiom meaning (Papagno et al., 2004). Giora and colleagues (Giora et al., 2002) found that RHD patients performed better than LHD patients on a test of the comprehension of highly conventional metaphors – though not on a test of sarcasm comprehension. Moreover, these investigators found that metaphor comprehension was negatively correlated with lesion extent not in the right hemisphere, but, rather, in the left middle temporal gyrus and the area surrounding the left supramarginal and superior temporal gyri (also known as Wernicke's area).

Impaired idiom comprehension in the face of largely intact literal language comprehension has also been observed in individuals with conditions that compromise executive functions, such as Down's syndrome (Papagno & Vallar, 2001), and Alzheimer's disease (Papagno, 2001). To address the relationship between executive functions and idiom comprehension, Papagno, Lucchelli, Muggia, & Rizzo (2003) gave patients with Alzheimer's disease (AD) a wide battery of tests that assessed their language abilities, executive function (via a dual task performance paradigm), and idiom comprehension using a picture matching task. As a group, AD patients performed similarly to healthy controls on the literal language tests, but worse than controls on the idiom task. Although literal sentence comprehension scores were not correlated with performance on any other tests, idiom comprehension scores correlated with performance on the dual task. The detrimental effect of AD on central executive functions can negatively affect figurative language comprehension by impairing the ability to suppress literal meaning.

In fact, the study of patients with agenesis of the corpus callosum (ACC), has shown that metaphor comprehension can be impaired even in individuals with damage to neither side of the brain (Paul, Van Lancker-Sidtis, Schieffer, Dietrich, & Brown, 2003). In this condition, the corpus callosum, the fiber tract that connects the two hemispheres, does not develop, but brain maturation is otherwise relatively normal. In a study of a large sample of these patients with normal IQ stores, individuals with ACC performed normally on tests of literal language comprehension, but were impaired on tests of formulaic, non-literal language (Paul et al., 2003). Moreover, as in the idiom comprehension deficits of RHD patients, the ACC patients tended to err by picking a literal depiction of the idiomatic phrase. The similarity between performance of RHD patients and ACC patients with intact RHs indicates a crucial role for interhemispheric interaction in idiom comprehension.

### 2.2 *Repetitive Transcranial Magnetic Stimulation*

Although the study of brain injured patients has been an invaluable source of information for cognitive neuroscientists, there are some inherent limitations to this method. Lesion size and location can vary drastically among the members of a patient group, complicating inferences about the cause of any observed deficits. People also differ in their degree of neural plasticity, or the extent to which the brain can "rewire" itself to compensate for the damaged tissue. Indeed, plasticity makes it difficult to infer whether preserved language function reflects activity in the reorganized brain, or the normal ability of the spared tissue. However, these limitations are much less of a factor in rTMS.

Used on neurologically intact adults, rTMS involves transmitting a series of magnetic pulses to the scalp in order to disrupt the underlying brain activity. In these experiments, participants undergo stimulation to particular scalp regions (either with a real series of magnetic pulses, or a "sham" series), and subsequently perform a cognitive or language task. Although the disruption is transient and fully reversible, its effect on cognitive activity can be used to infer the importance of the affected brain area for the cognitive process being tested. rTMS allows the cognitive neuroscientist to test the effects of disrupting activity in a relatively small, targeted area of an otherwise normal brain.

Oliveri and colleagues used rTMS to disrupt activity in right and left frontal and temporal brain areas while participants did a picture matching task (Oliveri et al., 2004). Sentences involved either opaque idioms (*He is in shape*) or literal controls (*He is drawing*). Pictures included either a depiction of the idiomatic interpretation (a picture of a man showing off his muscles) or a potential literal interpretation of the same sentence (a mouse embedded in a geometric wedge of cheese). Pictures for the literal sentences were either literal depictions of the sentence (a boy drawing), or an identical picture save one detail (a picture of a boy approaching a canvas). rTMS was applied over left and right temporal and frontal cortex.

Left frontal rTMS induced a small but significant impairment, but right frontal rTMS did not (Oliveri et al., 2004). Further, left temporal rTMS disrupted performance on both literal sentences and idioms, while right temporal rTMS actually facilitated performance on both idioms and literal sentences. This facilitation may result because homologous LH areas were disinhibited, suggesting a critical role for left temporal areas in performance of this task. These studies suggest LH temporal lobe activity is critical for idiom comprehension. Thus neuropsychological studies that point to the importance of the RH for idiom processing may instead reflect a generalized reduction in processing capacity (e.g., working memory and attentional resources). In the face of reduced resources, patients resort to strategies that result in their preference for literal depictions.

### 2.3 *Visual Half-Field Priming*

Another technique that has been used to investigate the role of the right hemisphere in neurologically intact individuals is the visual half-field priming paradigm. By presenting stimuli outside the center of gaze, it is possible to selectively stimulate visual cortex in the left or right hemisphere. In normal individuals, the information is rapidly transmitted to other brain regions, including those in the other hemisphere. Nonetheless, differences in the initial stages of processing can indicate hemisphere-specific computations (Chiarello, 1991). Presumably, because reading is primarily supported by LH activity, lexical decision times (the amount of time it takes a participant to judge whether or not a string of letters forms a real word) are typically shorter with presentation to the right visual field (RVF/LH). However, priming effects – the difference in response times to related and unrelated words – are sometimes larger with presentation to the left visual field (LVF/RH), depending on the sorts of materials. Larger priming effects with RVF/LH presentation are typically interpreted as indicating an LH bias for the materials, while larger LVF/RH priming effects indicate an RH bias.

Research in the visual half-field paradigm has suggested the two hemispheres play different, complementary roles in language processing (Beeman & Chiarello, 1998). Chiarello (1985), for example, has suggested that linguistic input results in automatic semantic activation in both hemispheres, but that only the LH engages in post-lexical integration processes. Moreover, semantic activations in the LH are more specific than in the RH, and subject to inhibitory processes (Chiarello, 1988). This portrait of focused semantic activation in the LH, and more disparate activations in the RH is supported by a study of semantic paralexias produced by normal participants when words were laterally presented (Rodel, Landis, & Regard, 1989). Further, whereas both hemispheres show priming for closely associated words (*sharp, knife, cut*), the RH is more likely to show priming when the relationship between words is more oblique (*glass, foot, cut*) (Beeman & Chiarello, 1998).

Beeman and colleagues explicitly link RHD patients' impaired performance on pragmatic language comprehension tasks such as metaphor comprehension to differences in semantic activations in the two hemispheres of the brain (Beeman et al., 1994). Alluding to hemispheric differences in the size of receptive fields in the visual system (Marsolek, Kosslyn, & Squire, 1992), Beeman and colleagues suggest semantic representations in the LH are fine coded, while those in the RH are coarsely coded. These investigators speculate that while information activated by the LH is usually adequate to connect discourse elements, information activated in the RH can be crucial for connecting elements that are distantly related. RHD patients' deficits in metaphor comprehension might result because the pertinent information is not activated in the RH. Similarly, Brownell suggests the RH contribution to metaphor comprehension is diffuse activation across a loosely organized semantic network that is not actively suppressed, and consequently can result in the formation of distant associations needed to understand metaphors (Brownell, 2000).

Using the visual half-field priming paradigm to examine hemispheric asymmetries in the processing of metaphoric language, Anaki and colleagues had participants read centrally presented words with literal and metaphoric meanings, and then make lexical decisions to laterally presented target words (Anaki, Faust, & Kravets, 1998). If the prime was *stinging*, for example, the target might be a word such as *bee* that related to the literal meaning of the prime, or a word such as *insult* that related to the prime's metaphorical meaning. Target words appeared either, 200 ms after the onset of the prime, thought to index automatic processing, or 800 ms after the onset of the prime, thought to index later, more controlled, stages of processing. At the short SOA, both literal and metaphorical meanings were primed with presentation to the RVF/LH, and the metaphorical meaning was primed with presentation to the LVF/RH. At the longer SOA, Anaki and colleagues found priming for the literal meaning with presentation to the RVF/LH, and priming for the metaphorical meaning with presentation to the LVF/RH. These researchers have argued that their findings suggest metaphoric meanings are initially activated in both cerebral hemispheres, and subsequently decay rapidly in the LH, while being maintained in the RH.

However, researchers using sentential stimuli found evidence that suggests metaphor comprehension involves both left and right hemisphere processing (Faust & Weisper, 2000). Faust and Weisper showed participants centrally presented sentence fragments such as "*My job is a*" followed by the lateralized presentation of a target word. Target words could make the sentence literally true, literally false, or metaphorically true. Participants were asked to judge the literal truth-value of the sentences – and thus respond "no" to the metaphoric endings. Results showed that regardless of which visual field the target was presented to, a metaphor interference effect was observed. That is, "no" responses to metaphoric endings were slower and less accurate than those to the literally false endings, suggesting the metaphoric meaning was available in both hemispheres to produce response conflict.

In fact, subsequent attempts to replicate results reported by Anaki and colleagues have failed. Using English materials, Kacinik found literal (*stinging* BEE) and metaphor (*stinging* INSULT) priming with RVF/LH presentation at short SOAs, but only literal priming with an 800 ms SOA; with LVF/RH presentation, literal priming was observed at SOAs of 100, 200, and 800 ms, while metaphor priming was evident only in accuracy scores, suggesting the activation of the metaphoric meaning in the RH was weak, at best (Kacinik, 2003).

When the adjective–noun pairs were presented in sentence contexts, RVF/LH literal and metaphor priming was observed after both ambiguous (*Andrea obviously wasn't aware of the icy* SLOPE/GLARE) and unambiguous (*I lost my balance on the icy* SLOPE/GLARE vs. *Ben turned his head only to see her icy* GLARE/SLOPE) sentence primes (Kacinik, 2003). Similarly, with LVF/RH presentation, literal and metaphor priming was observed after both sorts of sentence primes, though priming effects were larger after the unambiguous sentences (Kacinik, 2003). These results suggest metaphoric meanings are available to both the LH and the RH (see also Kacinik & Chiarello, 2007).

Kacinik also addressed hemispheric asymmetry in the processing of more complex sentential metaphors such as "*The train I take to work is a bullet*," by testing for hemifield priming of probes related to the literal (*KILLED*) and metaphorical (*FAST*) meaning of the sentence final noun (Kacinik, 2003). Probes (e.g., *JAWS*) were preceded either by a consistent sentence prime, (e.g., *The lifeguard thought he saw a shark*), or an inconsistent one (e.g., *The lawyer they've hired is a shark*).

Priming was observed bilaterally for both literal and metaphorical meanings in consistent contexts. Inconsistent probes were never primed with RVF/LH presentation. Further, while inconsistent literal probes were primed in the LVF/RH, inconsistent metaphorical probes were not. Though these data support the idea that semantic activations in the RH are somewhat less sensitive to context than in the LH, they argue against the RH as the preferred substrate of metaphor comprehension. Indeed, recent work in the visual half-field priming paradigm suggests both hemispheres have the capacity to comprehend metaphorical meanings.

## 2.4 *Neuroimaging*

Perhaps the best-known technique for assessing the functional role of various brain regions in healthy people is neuroimaging. Imaging techniques such as positron emission tomography (PET) and functional magnetic resonance imaging (fMRI) are used to detect brain regions in which different experimental conditions are associated with increased metabolic activity. Though metaphor comprehension has received little attention from neuroimagers, one widely cited PET study of metaphor comprehension supports the view of the RH as being preferentially involved in this aspect of language comprehension.

In this study, participants judged whether literal sentences were plausible (*The boy used stones as paperweights*) or implausible (*The lady has a bucket as a walking stick*). In the metaphor condition, participants judged whether metaphors were interpretable (*The old man had a head full of dead leaves*), or uninterpretable (*The investors were trams*). Both literal and metaphorical sentences activated LH areas in the prefrontal and basal frontal cortex, middle and inferior temporal gyri, temporal pole, parietal cortex, and precuneus (Bottini et al., 1994), areas often activated by sentence comprehension tasks (Bookheimer, 2002).

However, metaphor comprehension was also associated with increased RH activation in the prefrontal cortex, the middle temporal gyrus, the precuneus, and the posterior cingulate (Bottini et al., 1994). Activations in the right precuneus have previously been attributed to conscious inspection of mental images, while prefrontal activation has been argued to reflect the difficulty of a decision task (Fletcher, Shallice, Frith, & Frackowiak, 1996). Bottini and colleagues argue that the prefrontal activations reflect retrieval from episodic memory, and the precuneus activation reflects increased mental imagery associated with metaphor comprehension. They speculate that these activations result because metaphor comprehension requires the retrieval of imageable experiences from episodic memory.

In contrast, an event-related fMRI study revealed no evidence of preferential RH activation to metaphor comprehension (Rapp, Leube, Erb, Grodd, & Kircher, 2004). Rapp and colleagues asked healthy adults to read simple metaphorical statements or literal statements with the same syntactic structure. For example, the metaphor "*The lovers' words are harp sounds*," had the following literal counterpart, "*The lovers' words are lies*." Participants' task was to judge whether each sentence had a positive or negative connotation (matched across literal and metaphorical sentences). Relative to literal statements, metaphors activated left inferior frontal cortex, inferior temporal gyrus, and posterior middle temporal gyrus. No RH activation was observed.

One difference between the PET study that revealed RH activation for metaphors and the fMRI study that did not is that task difficulty in the literal and metaphorical sentences was well-matched in the latter (Rapp et al., 2004) but not the former (Bottini et al., 1994). Consequently, RH recruitment may depend on overall task difficulty, rather than the figurativity of the meanings. Other fMRI studies in healthy adults indicate that when literal sentence comprehension places increased demands upon lexical and syntactic processes it results in increased activation both in classic LH language areas and in their RH homologues (Keller, Carpenter, & Just, 2001).

In general, RH activation is associated with complex sentences and discourse level processing (Bookheimer, 2002; Kircher, Brammer, Andreu, Williams, & McGuire, 2001; St. George, Kutas, Martinez, & Sereno, 1999), suggesting it is semantic complexity that triggers the recruitment of RH areas. RH activation in metaphor comprehension tasks, then, might not reflect the retrieval of metaphoric meanings from the RH. Rather, RH activations might simply result because the semantic complexity of metaphors is greater than that of their literal controls.

### 2.5 *Summary*

Initially, the portrait of the RH as the preferred substrate of metaphor comprehension looked quite compelling. On picture-matching tasks, RHD patients are more likely than their LHD counterparts to choose literal depictions of metaphoric idioms as the best representation of their meaning (Van Lancker & Kempler, 1987; Winner & Gardner, 1977). Further, on verbal tests, while RHD patients are able to understand multiple meanings of ambiguous nouns, they have difficulty accessing the metaphoric meaning of adjectives (Brownell, 1984; Brownell et al., 1990; Gagnon et al., 2003). Visual half-field studies suggest that while metaphoric meanings are initially activated in both hemispheres, they are only sustained in the RH (Anaki et al., 1998). Finally, functional neuroimaging of healthy adults has revealed increased activation of RH brain areas during metaphor comprehension (Bottini et al., 1994).

However, in each case there is evidence against the RH metaphor proposal. Recent functional imaging results reveal that metaphor comprehension activates only LH language areas (Rapp et al., 2004). Visual half-field studies suggest that when metaphors are embedded in sentence contexts, both hemispheres have access to metaphoric meanings (Faust & Weisper, 2000; Kacinik, 2003). Both neuropsychological studies and rTMS research with normals suggests that the crucial brain areas for metaphor comprehension are left temporal lobe areas crucial for normal comprehension of literal language (Giora et al., 2002; Oliveri et al., 2004).

## 3. The Neural Substrate of Metaphor Comprehension

As we progress through the 21st century, it will be important to move beyond the traditional question of the right hemisphere's role in metaphor comprehension to address the particular cognitive and neural underpinnings of this complex process. By combining information from the study of brain injured patients with behavioral, electrophysiological, and imaging data from healthy participants, it is possible to learn a great deal about the neural substrate of particular cognitive processes. In particular, research on the sensorimotor grounding of concepts and research on the neural instantiation of cross-domain mappings are areas of great promise in the study of metaphor.

### 3.1 *Sensorimotor Grounding of Concepts*

An exciting development in neuroimaging research is the finding that the neural substrate of action and perception is often exploited in higher cognitive activities, including conceptualization that may be important for language comprehension. Sensory regions, for example, are active during sensory processing as well as during sensory imagery (Kosslyn, Thompson, Kim, & Alpert, 1995). Motor regions are active during the execution of action, but also during motor imagery, as well as during the perception of the motor actions of others (Decety et al., 1997; Deiber et al., 1998; Jeannerod & Decety, 1995; Jeannerod & Frak, 1999).

A series of studies suggest further that modality-specific areas become active in conceptual tasks, for example, color-processing regions (i.e., V4) are active for color concepts, motion processing areas (MT/MST) are active for conceptualizing motion, and shape (infero-temporal) versus motor (pre-motor cortex) processing regions for animals versus tools, respectively (Martin, 2001; Martin & Chao, 2001). One issue for future research is whether modality-specific activation occurs in the comprehension of metaphors.

Reasoning on the basis of neural learning mechanisms, Pulvermüller and colleagues have long argued that the neural representation of word meaning must differ as a function of our experience with what those words represent (Braitenberg & Pulvermuller, 1992; Pulvermüller, 1996, 1999). Hebbian learning, for example, is a mechanism by which connection strength between two neurons increases as a function of correlated firing. Because we might expect that words for objects would tend to co-occur with the visual experience of those objects, correlated firing patterns between the neural representations of the wordforms and the associated visual experiences would result in the establishment of permanent connections between their neural substrates. Similarly, because words for actions would tend to co-occur with motor activity, simple Hebbian learning would result in connections between activity in motor cortex and the neural representation of action words (Pulvermüller, 2003).

Similarly, in the neural theory of language (NTL), it has been proposed that language comprehension involves simulating the situation being described (Feldman & Narayanan, 2004). For example, the simulation semantics of NTL suggests that cortical networks that subserve the action of grasping also serve as the neural substrate of the meaning of *grasp*. Because metaphor involves exploiting concepts from a concrete domain to understand a more abstract one, this framework suggests that networks that subserve the action of grasping are also activated to understand the metaphorical meaning of *grasp*. Conceptual blending theory, which suggests that "grasping an idea" involves the parallel activation of an abstract and a concrete meaning of grasp, also makes this prediction (Coulson & Matlock, 2001).

Recent findings suggest the representation of word meaning extends beyond the classic language areas identified by neuropsychologists (Damasio, Grabowski, Tranel, Hichwa, & Damasio, 1996; Tranel, Logan, Frank, & Damasio, 1997), and raise the possibility that the neural substrate of metaphor comprehension depends on the particular source (vehicle) and target (topic) domains of the metaphor. In this framework, one would not expect metaphorical meanings to be processed in a single brain area, or even a particular network of brain areas. Rather, action metaphors would be expected to recruit brain areas underlying the comprehension of action, while spatial metaphors would be expected to recruit brain areas that subserve spatial cognition.

### 3.2 *Cross-Domain Mappings and the Mental Number Line*

The idea that conceptual knowledge is grounded in sensorimotor experience is closely related to the claim in cognitive linguistics that metaphoric understandings of abstract domains recruit concepts from more experientially basic ones (Lakoff & Núñez, 2000). One example for which there is some empirical support is that the abstract concept of numbers is understood by recruiting spatial concepts in the metaphor of numbers as points on a spatially extended line. Inherent in the concept of a number line, this metaphor posits a mapping or correspondence between particular numbers and particular regions in space, such that quantity goes from left to right, with the largest numbers mapping onto the right-most regions of the line.

This predicts that neural structures that support spatial reasoning will be systematically recruited in numerical operations, and that damage to brain structures involved in spatial reasoning will also have a detrimental effect on numerical calculations that recruit the mental number line. In fact, neuroimaging studies show that right intraparietal areas important for visuospatial processing are consistently activated by number comparison tasks (Chochon, Cohen, van de Moortele, & Dehaene, 1999; Pinel, Dehaene, Rivière, & Le Bihan, 2001). Further, the prediction that damage to the underlying substrate of visuospatial processing is borne out by the fact that *hemineglect* impacts various arithmetic tasks.

Hemineglect is a neurological condition resulting from lesions to the RH parietal lobe in which the patient has difficulty attending to objects on the left side of space. Consistent with a mapping between numbers and regions of space, hemineglect patients have been shown to be impaired when making judgments about numbers to the left of a reference number on a linear number line. For example, when asked to judge whether numeric stimuli were greater or less than 5, patients with neglect were slower to respond to 4 than to 6; when asked to judge whether numeric stimuli were greater or less than 7, patients with neglect were slower to respond to 6 than 8 (Vuilleumier, Ortigue, & Brugger, 2004).

Another task on which hemineglect is apparent is line bisection, in which the participant is asked to mark the midpoint of a line. Patients with neglect tend to place their marks slightly to the right of the midline – presumably because they are unaware of the left-most portion of the line (Bisiach & Vallar, 2000). Zorzi and colleagues tested RHD patients with and without hemineglect on a variety of arithmetic tasks (Zorzi, Priftis, & Umilta, 2002). All patients scored well on tests of subtraction and number comparison. However, only the hemineglect patients were impaired on a test on which they had to estimate the midpoint of two numbers. They tended to pick a number that was higher than the correct answer – analogous to a mark to the right of the midline on the line bisection task. These analogous patterns of deficits on the spatial and arithmetic problems points to the neurological reality of a metaphorical mapping between numbers and points on a spatially extended line ordered from left to right.

This mapping is further supported by evidence that experimental manipulations that affect the direction of attention in space affect performance on the midpoint estimation task. Rossetti and colleagues (2004) tested for the cognitive consequences of prism adaptation by having patients with hemineglect perform the midpoint estimation task before and after a session in which they wore prism glasses that shift the visual world by 10 degrees. In addition to the actual prism adaptation session, patients also underwent a sham adaptation period in which they wore goggles that had no effect on the visual world. Performance on number bisection was not impacted by wearing the sham goggles, but was reliably improved after prism adaptation, suggesting a functional link between parietal regions involved in the representation of space and numbers (Rossetti et al., 2004).

## 3.3 *Conclusions*

Overall, the investigation of the neurological substrate of metaphor comprehension has proceeded at a rather coarse level, and addressed only the most basic of issues. Indeed, most research on this topic treats metaphoric language as a single monolithic category. Metaphors and idioms are frequently lumped together into one undifferentiated category (see Gagnon et al., 2003; Oliveri et al., 2004, for critique). Further, though there are a number of reasons to expect differences in the processing of highly conventional, lexicalized, metaphors and more novel ones Giora, 1997; Giora et al., 2002, this difference has not been thoroughly tested with the methods of cognitive neuroscience. Similarly, among novel metaphors there has been no investigation of the impact of conformity to *conceptual metaphors*, abstract patterns of metaphoric mapping such as that between progress and motion along a path, or love relationships and journeys (Lakoff & Johnson, 1999; Lakoff & Turner, 1989).

However, research on how the neural substrate of perception and action can be co-opted by higher-level processes suggests new avenues for research. Rather than contrasting literal and metaphorical meanings, future researchers may investigate differences between visual, auditory, and kinesthetic metaphors. Though the mental number line may seem a far cry from the so-called dream work of language, the underlying mechanism of cross-domain mappings may ultimately help us to understand how abstract concepts can emerge in brains that evolved to propel the body through the physical, social, and cultural world.

## References

Anaki, D., Faust, M., & Kravets, S. (1998). Cerebral hemispheric asymmetries in processing lexical metaphors. *Neuropsychologia*, 36, 353–362.

Beeman, M. J., & Chiarello, C. (1998). Complementary right- and left-hemisphere language comprehension. *Current Directions in Psychological Science*, 7(1), 2–8.

Beeman, M. J., Friedman, R., Grafman, J., Perez, E., Diamond, S., & Lindsay, M. (1994). Summation priming and coarse coding in the right hemisphere. *Journal of Cognitive Neuroscience*, 6, 26–45.

Bihrle, A., Brownell, H., & Gardner, H. (1986). Comprehension of humorous and nonhumorous materials by left- and right-brain damaged patients. *Brain & Cognition*, 5, 399–411.

Bisiach, E., & Vallar, G. (2000). Unilateral neglect in humans. In F. Boller & G. Grafman (Eds.), *Handbook of neuropsychology* (pp. 459–502). Amsterdam: Elsevier.

Bookheimer, S. (2002). Functional MRI of language: new approaches to understanding the cortical organization of semantic processing. *Annual Review of Neuroscience*, 25, 151–188.

Bottini, G., Corcoran, R., Sterzi, R., Paulesu, E., Schenone, P., Scarpa, P., et al. (1994). The role of the right hemisphere in the interpretation of figurative aspects of language: A positron emission tomography activation study. *Brain*, 117, 1241–1253.

Braitenberg, V., & Pulvermüller, F. (1992). Entwurf einer neurologischen Theorie der Sprache. *Naturwissenschaften*, 79, 103–117.

Broca, P. A. (1865). Sur la faculté du language articulé. *Bulletin de la Societe Anatomie de Paris*, 6, 493–494.

Brownell, H. (1984). Sensitivity to lexical denotation and connotation in brain damaged patients. *Brain & Language*, 22, 253–265.

Brownell, H. (2000). Right hemisphere contributions to understanding lexical connotation and metaphor. In Y. Grodzinsky, L. Shapiro, & D. Swinney (Eds.), *Language and the brain: Representation and processing* (pp. 185–201). San Diego: Academic Press.

Brownell, H., Michel, D., Powelson, J., & Gardner, H. (1983). Surprise but not coherence: Sensitivity to verbal humor in right-hemisphere patients. *Brain & Language*, 18, 20–27.

Brownell, H., Simpson, T., Bihrle, A., Potter, H., & Gardner, H. (1990). Appreciation of metaphoric alternative word meanings by left and right brain-damaged patients. *Neuropsychologia*, 28(4), 375–383.

Chiarello, C. (1985). Hemisphere dynamics in lexical access: Automatic and controlled priming. *Brain & Language, 26*(1), 146–172.
Chiarello, C. (1988). *Right hemisphere contributions to lexical semantics*. New York: Springer-Verlag.
Chiarello, C. (1991). Interpretation of word meanings by the cerebral hemispheres: One is not enough. In P. Schwanenflugel (Ed.), *The psychology of word meaning*. Hillsdale, NJ: Lawrence Erlbaum Associates.
Chochon, F., Cohen, L., van de Moortele, P., & Dehaene, S. (1999). Differential contributions of the left and right inferior parietal lobules to number processing. *Journal of Cognitive Neuroscience, 11*(6), 617–630.
Coulson, S. (2001). *Semantic leaps: Frame-shifting and conceptual blending in meaning construction*. Cambridge: Cambridge University Press.
Coulson, S., & Matlock, T. (2001). Metaphor and the space structuring model. *Metaphor & Symbol, 16*, 295–316.
Coulson, S., & Van Petten, C. (2002). Conceptual integration and metaphor: An ERP study. *Memory & Cognition, 30*(6), 958–968.
Damasio, H., Grabowski, T. J., Tranel, D., Hichwa, R. D., & Damasio, A. R. (1996). A neural basis for lexical retrieval. *Nature, 380*(6574), 499–505.
Decety, J., Grezes, J., Costes, N., Parani, D., Jeannerod, M., Procyk, E., et al. (1997). Brain activity during observation of actions: Influence of action content and subject's strategy. *Brain, 120*, 1763–1777.
Deiber, M. P., Ibanez, V., Honda, M., Sadato, N., Raman, R., & Hallett, M. (1998). Cerebral processes related to visuomotor imagery and generation of simple finger movements studied with positron emission tomography. *Neuroimage, 7*(2), 73–85.
Fauconnier, G., & Turner, M. (1998). Conceptual integration networks. *Cognitive Science, 22*, 133–187.
Faust, M., & Weisper, S. (2000). Understanding metaphoric sentences in the two cerebral hemispheres. *Brain & Cognition, 43* (1–3), 186–191.
Feldman, J., & Narayanan, S. (2004). Embodied meaning in a neural theory of language. *Brain and Language, 89*(2), 385–392.
Fletcher, P., Shallice, T., Frith, C., & Frackowiak, R. (1996). Brain activity during memory retrieval: The influence of imagery and semantic cueing. *Brain, 119*(5), 1587–1596.
Gagnon, L., Goulet, P., Giroux, F., & Joanette, Y. (2003). Processing of metaphoric and non-metaphoric alternative meanings of words and right- and left- hemispheric lesion. *Brain and Language, 87*, 217–226.
Gardner, H., & Denes, G. (1973). Connotative judgments by aphasic patients on a pictorial adaptation of the semantic differential. *Cortex*, 9(2), 183–196.
Gibbs, R. (1994). *The poetics of mind: Figurative thought, language, and understanding.* Cambridge: Cambridge University Press.
Gibbs, R., & Gerrig, R. (1989). How context makes metaphor comprehension seem "special." *Metaphor & Symbolic Activity*, 4(3), 145–158.
Giora, R. (1997). Understanding figurative language: The graded salience hypothesis. *Cognitive Linguistics*, 7 (1), 183–206.
Giora, R., Zaidel, E., Soroker, N., Batori, G., & Kasher, A. (2002). Differential effects of right and left hemisphere damage on understanding sarcasm and metaphor. *Metaphor and Symbol, 15*, 63–83.
Glucksberg, S., Gildea, P., & Bookin, H. B. (1982). On understanding nonliteral speech: Can people ignore metaphors? *Journal of Verbal Learning & Verbal Behavior, 21*(1), 85–98.
Grice, H. (1975). Logic and conversation. In P. C. J. Morgan (Ed.), *Syntax and semantics: Vol. 3. Speech acts*. New York: Academic Press.
Hécaen, H., & Consoli, S. (1973). Analyse des troubles de language au cours des lesions de l'aire de Broca. *Neuropsychologia, 11*, 377–388.
Jeannerod, M., & Decety, J. (1995). Mental motor imagery: A window into the representational stages of action. *Current Opinion in Neurology*, 5(6), 727–732.
Jeannerod, M., & Frak, V. (1999). Mental imaging of motor activity in humans. *Current Opinion in Neurobiology*, 5(6), 735–739.
Joanette, Y., Goulet, P., & Hannequin, D. (1990). *Right hemisphere and verbal communication.* New York: Springer-Verlag.
Kacinik, N. A. (2003). *Hemispheric processing of literal and metaphoric language*. Unpublished PhD dissertation, University of California, Riverside.
Kacinik, N. A., & Chiarello, C. (2007). Understanding metaphors: Is the right hemisphere uniquely involved? *Brain and Language, 100*, 188–207.
Kazmerski, V., Blasko, D., & Dessalegn, B. (2003). ERP and behavioral evidence of individual

differences in metaphor comprehension. *Memory and Cognition, 31*(5), 673–689.

Keller, T. A., Carpenter, P. A., & Just, M. A. (2001). The neural bases of sentence comprehension: A fMRI examination of syntactic and lexical processing. *Cereb Cortex, 11*(3), 223–237.

Kircher, T., Brammer, M. J., Andreu, N., Williams, S., & McGuire, P. K. (2001). Engagement of right temporal cortex during processing of linguistic context. *Neuropsychologia, 39*, 798–809.

Kosslyn, S. M., Thompson, W. L., Kim, I. J., & Alpert, N. M. (1995). Topographic representations of mental images in primary visual cortex. *Nature, 378*, 6556.

Kutas, M., & Hillyard, S. A. (1980). Reading senseless sentences: Brain potentials reflect semantic incongruity. *Science, 207*, 203–205.

Kutas, M., Lindamood, T., & Hillyard, S. A. (1984). Word expectancy and event-related brain potentials during sentence processing. In S. K. J. Requin (Ed.), *Preparatory states and processes* (pp. 217–237). Hillsdale, NJ: Lawrence Erlbaum Associates.

Lakoff, G., & Johnson, M. (1999). *Philosophy in the flesh: The embodied mind and its challenge to western thought*. New York: Basic Books.

Lakoff, G., & Núñez, R. (2000). *Where mathematics comes from: How the embodied mind brings mathematics into being*. New York: Basic Books.

Lakoff, G., & Turner, M. (1989). *More than cool reason: A field guide to poetic metaphor*. Chicago: Chicago University Press.

Marsolek, C. J., Kosslyn, S. M., & Squire, L. R. (1992). Form-specific visual priming in the right cerebral hemisphere. *Journal of Experimental Psychology: Learning, Memory, and Cognition, 18*, 492–508.

Martin, A. (2001). Functional neuroimaging of semantic memory. In R. K. Cabeza, A. (Ed.), *Handbook of functional neuroimaging of cognition* (pp. 153–186). Cambridge: MIT Press.

Martin, A., & Chao, L. (2001). Semantic memory and the brain: Structure and processes. *Current Opinion in Neurobiology, 11*(2), 194–201.

Oliveri, M., Romero, L., & Papagno, C. (2004). Left but not right temporal involvement in opaque idiom comprehension: A repetitive transcranial magnetic stimulation study. *Journal of Cognitive Neuroscience, 16*(5), 848–855.

Papagno, C. (2001). Comprehension of metaphors and idioms in patients with Alzheimer's disease: A longitudinal study. *Brain, 124*, 1450–1460.

Papagno, C., Lucchelli, F., Muggia, S., & Rizzo, S. (2003). Idiom comprehension in Alzheimer's disease: The role of the central executive. *Brain, 126*, 2419–2430.

Papagno, C., Tabossi, P., Colombo, M., & Zampetti, P. (2004). Idiom comprehension in aphasic patients. *Brain and Language, 89*, 226–234.

Papagno, C., & Vallar, G. (2001). Understanding metaphors and idioms: A single-case neuropsychological study in a person with Down syndrome. *Journal of the International Neuropsychological Society, 7*(4), 516–528.

Paul, L., Van Lancker-Sidtis, D. R., Schieffer, B., Dietrich, R., & Brown, W. (2003). Communicative deficits in agenesis of the corpus callosum: Nonliteral language and affective prosody. *Brain and Language, 85*, 313–324.

Pinel, P., Dehaene, S., Rivière, D., & Le Bihan, D. (2001). Modulation of parietal activation by semantic distance in a number comparison task. *Neuroimage, 14*, 1013–1026.

Pulvermüller, F. (1996). Hebb's concept of cell assemblies and the psychophysiology of word processing. *Psychophysiology, 33*, 317–333.

Pulvermüller, F. (1999). Words in the brain's language. *Behavioral and Brain Sciences, 22*, 253–336.

Pulvermüller, F. (2003). *The neuroscience of language*. Cambridge: Cambridge University Press.

Pynte, J., Besson, M., Robichon, F., & Poli, J. (1996). The time-course of metaphor comprehension: An event-related potential study. *Brain & Language, 55*, 293–316.

Rapp, A., Leube, D., Erb, M., Grodd, W., & Kircher, T. (2004). Neural correlates of metaphor processing. *Cognitive Brain Research, 20*, 395–402.

Raskin, A. H. (1992). The words I lost. *New York Times*. September 19.

Rehak, A., Kaplan, J., & Gardner, H. (1992). Sensitivity to conversational deviance in right-hemisphere damaged patients. *Brain & Language, 42*, 203–217.

Rinaldi, M., Marangolo, P., & Baldassarri, F. (2002). Metaphor comprehension in right brain-damaged subjects with visuo-verbal and verbal material: A dissociation (re)considered. *Cortex, 38*, 903–907.

Rodel, M., Landis, T., & Regard, M. (1989). Hemispheric dissociation in semantic relation. *Journal of Clinical and Experimental Neuropsychology, 11*, 70.

Rossetti, Y., Jacquin-Courtois, S., Rode, G., Ota, H., Michel, C., & Boisson, D. (2004). Does action make the link between number and space representation? Visuo-manual adaptation improves number bisection in unilateral neglect. *Psychological Science, 15*(6), 426–430.

Rugg, M. D., & Coles, M. (Eds.). (1995). *Electrophysiology of mind: Event-related brain potentials and cognition*. Oxford: Oxford University Press.

Searle, J. (1979). *Expression and Meaning: Studies in the theory of speech acts*. Cambridge: Cambridge University Press.

St. George, M., Kutas, M., Martinez, A., & Sereno, M. I. (1999). Semantic integration in reading: Engagement of the right hemisphere during discourse processing. *Brain, 122* (Pt. 7), 1317–1325.

Sweetser, E. (1990). *From etymology to pragmatics: Metaphorical and cultural aspects of semantic structure*. Cambridge: Cambridge University Press.

Tompkins, C. (1990). Knowledge and strategies for processing lexical metaphor after right or left hemisphere brain damage. *Journal of Speech and Hearing Research, 33*(2), 307–316.

Tompkins, C., Boada, R., & McGarry, K. (1992). The access and processing of familiar idioms by brain-damaged and normally aging adults. *Journal of Speech and Hearing Research, 35*(3), 626–638.

Tranel, D., Logan, C. G., Frank, R. J., & Damasio, A. R. (1997). Explaining category-related effects in the retrieval of conceptual and lexical knowledge for concrete entities: operationalization and analysis of factors. *Neuropsychologia, 35*(10), 1329–1339.

Turner, M. (1991). *Reading minds: The study of English in the age of cognitive science*. Princeton, NJ: Princeton University Press.

Van Lacker, D., & Kemplar, D. (1987). Comprehension of familiar phrases by left- but not by right-hemisphere damaged patients. *Brain & Language, 32*, 265–277.

Vuilleumier, P., Ortigue, S., & Brugger, P. (2004). The number space and neglect. *Cortex, 40*, 399–410.

Wernicke, C. (1874). *Der Aphasische Symptomenkomplex*. Breslau: Max Cohn and Weigert.

Winner, E., & Gardner, H. (1977). The comprehension of metaphor in brain-damaged patients. *Brain, 100*, 719–727.

Zaidel, E., Kasher, A., Soroker, N., & Baroti, G. (2002). Effects of right and left hemisphere damage on performance of the "right hemisphere communication battery." *Brain & Language, 80*(3), 510–535.

Zorzi, M., Priftis, K., & Umilta, C. (2002). Brain damage: Neglect disrupts the mental number line. *Nature, 417*, 138–139.

# Part IV

# METAPHOR IN LANGUAGE AND CULTURE

CHAPTER 11

# Metaphor and Talk


*Lynne Cameron*


*I must begin, not with hypothesis, but with specific instances, no matter how minute.*

(*Paul Klee*)

When people talk to each other, they make widespread use of metaphor. In talk, metaphor is a shifting, dynamic phenomenon that spreads, connects, and disconnects with other thoughts and other speakers, starts and restarts, flows through talk developing, extending, changing. Metaphor in talk both shapes the ongoing talk and is shaped by it. The creativity of metaphor in talk appears less in the novelty of connected domains and more in the use of metaphor to shape a discourse event and in the adaptation of metaphor in the flow of talk. Metaphor in talk is not evenly spread but gathers in clusters and occasionally, and then significantly, is altogether absent. People use metaphor to think with, to explain themselves to others, to organise their talk, and their choice of metaphor often reveals – not only their conceptualisations – but also, and perhaps more importantly for human communication, their attitudes and values. Beginning with specific instances of metaphor in talk, and understanding how people use metaphor, will help us construct better hypotheses about the nature of metaphor.

This chapter reviews features of metaphor use that have been found in a range of types of spoken discourse. The first major section focuses on the 'shape' of metaphor in talk: its density and distribution, form and systematicity, conventionality and signalling. The second section describes how people use metaphor in processes of human social interaction: how metaphor carries attitudes and values, how metaphor is used in the management of talk and in the negotiation of ideas and understandings. The third section considers the connection between metaphor in talk and conceptual metaphor. Methodological issues in researching metaphor in talk are discussed in each section, with some concluding thoughts on a future research agenda.

## The 'Shape' of Metaphor in Talk

Metaphor in talk is dynamic. In even short stretches of talk, we can see metaphor in flux as speakers adjust and adapt to what the other says. When metaphor is examined over longer stretches of talk, regularities and stabilities in the dynamics of metaphor emerge, and it is these features that are described in this section.

The first extract of talk is between two people engaged in post-conflict reconciliation.[1] Pat Magee was a political activist in Ireland, and nearly 20 years earlier planted a bomb that killed Jo Berry's father. They have come together at Jo's request so that she can construct some understanding of Pat's motivation. Extract 1 comes from near the start of their second meeting at a point where they are exploring their respective reasons for talking to each other. Pat asks Jo whether she expected their meetings to lead to her understanding him as an individual person or as a member of a movement that was engaged in a political struggle. In her response, Jo explains how the personal and the political came together for her on the day of the bombing. (Micro-pauses are marked with dots inside brackets.)

Extract 1 Reconciliation talk

Pat: I suppose there's a question that *comes to* my mind from that
er I don't (.) think we've *covered* before
(.) er did you *see* it as like individuals
or did you *see* it as a sort of (.) *big political picture*
the IRA or the war
you know what I mean er
you were you were aware that there's a
er it was going to be an individual who
you'd be sitting down with
Jo: I *saw* it as both
as er
when
(. . .) on that day it was like suddenly I was *thrown into* the conflict
it was suddenly my conflict
it was suddenly my conflict
and it felt like *my heart was broken*
*through* the conflict
and (.) the suffering was my suffering
I couldn't *separate* it
I couldn't be *detached* anymore
and that that er
that *pain* that *loss* was *shared by* (.) everyone
and you know and after that
(.) the *pain on every side*
you know
I felt it
and I wanted to understand (. . .) the politics of it

In this talk, the 'specific instances' that are of interest are linguistic metaphors, indicated by underlining in Extract 1. Linguistic metaphors are expressions in language that have the potential to be understood metaphorically. Context, preceding and subsequent instances may offer evidence of speakers' intentions or interpretations, but this evidence is not required for metaphor identification. Linguistic metaphor is identified through the use of words or phrases that potentially link to a vehicle (or source) domain which is distinct from the domain of the surrounding, ongoing talk (the topic or target). An alternative to domain difference as criterion for linguistic metaphor is the use of words and phrases with some meaning other than their basic or core sense, where basic is primarily physical and concrete.

### *How Much Metaphor Is Used in Talk?*

The first question that might be asked about metaphor in talk is how frequently it is used. Anyone who has tried to answer such a question will know that it is far from straightforward. Consider Extract 1, which lasts for about 50 seconds, from a 50-minute conversation. If we are to calculate the frequency of metaphor use in the extract, we need some measure of the number of metaphors per unit of time.

The 16 metaphor *vehicles* are likely to include several controversial decisions, while there may well be other lexical items that some researchers would want included as metaphorical. For example, the inclusion

of *through* (line 20) as metaphorical relies on a series of decisions: first, to include prepositions and second, to distinguish a physical sense of *through* that might be said to be metaphorically invoked in talking about *conflict* (Cameron, 2003, p. 73). For some people, *felt* in line 30 might warrant being considered metaphorical, since it could be argued that there is a basic physical sense of *feeling* which is distinct from the emotional and cognitive sense implied here. How researchers define and identify 'metaphor' can vary enormously. What is more, borderline cases often involve very frequent lexical items and so decisions about inclusion or exclusion can make considerable differences to the overall number of metaphors identified. I have written elsewhere and at length about the difficulties involved in putting boundaries on a fuzzy category like metaphor, with its many graded dimensions (Cameron, 1999, 2003). The solution lies in explicit statements about the identification procedure, especially boundary decisions, that will enable other researchers to replicate the method.

A meta-analysis of figures reported for the number of linguistic metaphors used in talk of different types showed that metaphor density ranges from around 20 metaphors per 1,000 words for college lectures to around 50 in 'ordinary discourse' and 60 in teacher talk (Cameron, 2003, p. 57). In order to compare figures, assumptions had to be made about relations between the various units chosen by researchers to represent time. Most researchers do not in fact use temporal units, but textual units of transcribed talk, that is sentences, turns, or words. Textual units are in some ways more helpful since they allow comparison with metaphor density in written discourse, but they vary in how valid they are as temporal equivalents.

A candidate for a standard unit of transcription for spoken interaction that, being both linguistic and cognitive, may better suit metaphor research than the turn, is the intonation unit, as developed by Chafe (Chafe, 1996). The intonation unit aims to be a unit of language and thought in which a single 'idea' is voiced in a single intonation contour. Accurate transcription of full and truncated intonation units requires training and practice, and reliability checking (Stelma & Cameron, 2007). Once training is completed, the researcher has a unit that offers possibilities for analysing the interaction of talking and thinking. Over a considerable amount of transcribed data, the intonation unit also turns out to be fairly stable as a temporal unit, of nearly 2 seconds (Cameron & Stelma, 2004). Precise reporting of decisions made about categories and units is needed for replicability and for reliable or valid comparisons across studies. Without this, we will be unable to build reliable knowledge of how people use metaphor in talk.

To calculate metaphor density, we divide the number of linguistic metaphors by the number of words in the transcription, after removal of non-talk features such as pause markings and speaker names. When calculated as the number of metaphor vehicles per 1,000 words, metaphor density presents in sensibly sized numbers. The metaphor density of Extract 1 comes out at 100.6 metaphors per 1000 words, which happens to coincide with the overall figure for the conversations.

Across three types of spoken discourse that I have so far examined using the same methods of identification and measurement, there is considerable variation in metaphor density. In comparison with the high metaphor density of reconciliation talk at about 100 metaphors per 1,000 words, a doctor–patient interview used around half as many metaphors, with a density of 55 metaphors per 1,000 words. Classroom talk had the lowest metaphor density but this also varied with the type of discourse event or lesson. Overall density was around 27 metaphors per 1,000 words, with the highest density of over 40 in a lesson on apostrophes and the lowest of under 15 in a mathematics lesson. To understand why speakers in different discourse contexts make differential use of metaphor, we need more qualitative, discourse-analytic, studies of talk such as those reviewed later in this chapter.

### *The Distribution of Metaphors in Talk*

When we plot the occurrence of metaphors minute by minute across a discourse event, we find that they are not evenly distributed but tend to cluster at certain points in the talk. This tendency has been noted in psychotherapeutic talk (Pollio & Barlow, 1975), college lectures (Corts & Pollio, 1999), classroom talk (Cameron, 2003), sermons (Corts & Meyers, 2002), and is also a feature of some written texts (Koller, 2003; Low, 1997). Recent work has also found the converse, that there may be phases of talk in which metaphor is nearly absent (Cameron & Stelma, 2004); this is further discussed later in the chapter.

Clustering (or bursts, as Corts and colleagues call them) of metaphors occur on both micro and macro scales of talk. As happens in Extract 1, it is common in talk for metaphors to be used in groups of three or more (lines 1–6; 15–20; 22–28), and rare for a single, isolated metaphor to occur. Clustering also occurs on a scale of minutes, compared with the seconds covered by three or four intonation units, and, in the studies described previously, often mark points in talk where something complex or unfamiliar needs to be explained or interpreted. Part of the reason for clustering is thus topical; explanations of a topic that requires the use of metaphor are likely to produce multiple instances of the same and connected metaphors. It seems likely that processing factors also contribute to clustering. Like any lexical item, metaphors are subject to the repetition and reformulation that characterise spontaneous talk (McCarthy, 1988). Furthermore, when one speaker uses metaphor, other speakers seem more likely to adapt their own talk and become metaphorical in response.

### *The Grammar of Metaphor in Talk*

The form of linguistic metaphors in a particular language depends on the affordances offered by its vocabulary and grammar. Metaphors in English make particular use of:

- verbs: 63% of the linguistic metaphors in my educational data were verbs or verb phrases, compared to 22% for nominal metaphors. This tendency is replicated in my other data sets and is clearly evidenced in the extracts in this chapter. Brooke-Rose (1958) reported a similar phenomenon in her study of poetry.
- delexicalised verbs and prepositions, often in combination, for example *now go back to your memory (= think about it again)*
- noun phrase formulations such as '*the xxx of yyy*', for example *the blanket of gases; the overall picture of the age*
- adjective + noun for condensing comparisons into metaphors, for example *trees like little lollipops → lollipop trees*.

The tendency for English to place metaphoricity in the verb merits more attention than it has been given, since it has implications for what we take to be the very nature of metaphor. There is considerable evidence from a range of sources that nouns and verbs play different roles in language use. Sapir (1921) claimed that every language expresses a distinction between what is being talked about, usually a person or object, and what is said about that subject, usually an action or outcome of an action. The "universal lexicalisation of the prototypical discourse functions" (Hopper & Thompson, 1984, p. 703) leads to what are termed *nouns* and *verbs*. The process is replicated ontogenetically as nouns emerge from early labels for concrete objects and verbs from early labels for specific actions in first language acquisition (Brown, 1958). Cross-linguistically, nouns function referentially and are reliably acquired early and rapidly. Verbs, on the other hand, show more cross-linguistic variation. They express relations between objects or people and seem to encode slightly different conceptual relationships in different languages (Gentner, 1982, p. 325). Early vocabulary acquisition typically shows a small number of verbs that are used in a range of communicative contexts (Gentner, 1978).

This early flexibility of the verb continues (Hopper, 1997). Brooke-Rose noted the ability of verbs to shift their meaning slightly depending on their collocated nouns, and suggested that the easy extension of a verb's meaning when used with many different nouns might lead to an originally metaphoric use becoming much less striking (Brooke-Rose, 1958). The ease with which verbs can extend their meaning may also explain why verbalisation occurs less frequently than nominalisation in morphological conversion (Hopper & Thompson, 1984). In English, the two processes of nominalisation (a verb becomes a noun) and verbalisation (a noun becomes a verb) are asymmetric. Nominalisation of events is frequent and carried out through a range of affixes including *-ion, -ing, -ment*. The converse process of creating new verbs from nouns is less frequent and is conceptually loosening, in the sense that it creates an event or action that has links with an entity. Consider the examples:

he *burrowed through* the crowd (from Hopper & Thompson, 1984)
the computer *calendarises* the data (author's data)
I *video-ed* the programme
they are being *short-cutted*

In each case, the new verb has a connection with the original noun (*burrow, calendar, video, short cut*) but these connections are of very different sorts. There are implications here for metaphor, in that identifying a verbalisation like *burrowed* as a linguistic metaphor requires there to be sufficient connection to the original noun to warrant a claim of cross-domain mapping.

Corpus studies of metaphor suggest that the process of conventionalisation involves a stabilising of lexico-grammatical form. For example, the word *shoulder* appears in metaphors either as a verb (always metaphorical) or in a small number of nominal phrases such as *cold shoulder* (Deignan, 1999). A person's knowledge of conventionalised metaphors will thus be likely to include knowledge about form, which can be used to assist processing and interpretation.

The flexibility of verbs in use contributes to the difficulty that researchers face when identifying verb metaphors. Decisions about verbs need to consider both the verb and its conventional collocates, since the meaning of a verb inheres in its use with these, rather than in its referential uses as with nouns.

### *Implicit Topics*

The verbal nature of many linguistic metaphors connects with the frequent absence of explicit metaphor topics. In Extract 1, metaphor vehicles such as *see, thrown into, separate* are used without explicit reference in the topic domain; the other speaker has to make sense of the inferred meaning from the context of the ongoing discourse. The need to infer metaphor topics seldom seems to create a major problem for shared understanding, but it does open up the possibility for differences in understanding between one speaker and another. The lack of an explicit topic also creates an opportunity for more significant or intentional shifts in meaning when a speaker shifts the use or interpretation of a vehicle term. In a later section, we see how the appropriation of one speaker's metaphor vehicle by the other can help achieve interactional purposes. In educational discourse, lack of knowledge of the topic domain may lead students to misinterpret the intended reference of a metaphor vehicle (Cameron, 2003).

### *Vehicle Development and the Systematicity of Linguistic Metaphor*

The metaphor vehicles include two lexical chains across Extract 1 (line numbers in brackets):

*see* (4) – *see* (5) – *picture* (6) – *saw* (12)
*broken* (19) – *separate* (22) – *detached* (23) – *loss* (25) – *shared by* (25) – *on every side* (28)

These connected vehicle terms create the systematicity of metaphor which is found locally in specific discourse events and, more globally, across discourse communities (Cameron, 1999). It is, of course, the systematicity of linguistic metaphor that underpins many of the claims of cognitive metaphor theory, in which globally systematic metaphors are labelled 'conceptual metaphors'.

At the more local level of the extract, systematicity is created by several modes of 'vehicle development' (Cameron, 2003, p. 165; 2008). The vehicle *see* is repeated, verbatim and with change of tense, while the vehicle *separate* is relexicalised as *detached*. Repetition and relexicalisation of metaphor vehicles parallels what happens with other lexis in spontaneous talk (McCarthy, 1988). A third mechanism of vehicle development is Jo's explication of *separation* through elaboration of the idea of the coming together of the personal and the political, from line 20 on.

Vehicle development is the basis for creativity and play with metaphor in talk, through novel relexicalisations or expansions (Carter, 2004). In the following extract, a student picks up a teacher's throwaway comment by extending the vehicle of her metaphor about time. The teacher reciprocates by adding to the vehicle development in the last line with *quickly*.

Extract 2 Student play with teacher's metaphor (from Cameron, 2003, p. 141)

Teacher: (*to the class*) *where does the time go?*
(some minutes later)
yes Paul?
Paul: I know *where the times goes* (1.0)
*into the past*
Teacher: *into the past* (.)
you're right
*quickly into the past*

As we will see in the rest of this chapter, vehicle development and metaphor shifting underlie many of the phenomena observed in metaphor use in talk.

### *Conventionalized and Deliberate Linguistic Metaphors*

The two vehicle domains of *seeing* and of *separation* illustrate another dimension of metaphor: the degree to which a metaphor is conventionalised within the discourse community. Conventionalisation is a dynamic process that takes place within the talk of a discourse community and from which emerges a metaphor that can act as common currency in future talk. In talk between a particular teacher and group of children in my data, the phrase *lollipop trees* emerged as a way of describing over-simple pictures in which trees were drawn as a circle on top of a stick (Cameron, 2003, p. 117).

The metaphor UNDERSTANDING IS SEEING is conventionalised, not just in this particular discourse community but across many, and is likely to be automatically used and understood by speakers. In comparison, the metaphors of separation and bringing together of the personal and political, and of shared pain, found in Extract 1, appear to be constructed on the spot by Jo as she tries to explain herself to Pat. The metaphors that she constructs are not particularly *novel*, the usual contrast with conventional, but they are *deliberate*, meaning that the speaker searches for what she or he considers an appropriate way of expressing an idea. The result of the search is a linguistic metaphor. I suggest that for metaphor in talk, it is useful to think of deliberate metaphors in contrast to conventionalised metaphors. Novel metaphors – which seem to occur quite rarely in spontaneous talk – are deliberate, since some kind of search for an appropriate expression must have preceded production. In my classroom data, deliberate metaphors account for about 10% of the linguistic metaphors, are likely to be nominal rather than verbal, and to be signalled in some way.

### *Tuning of Linguistic Metaphors*

Signals of deliberate metaphors may include pausing, hesitation, and the use of 'tuning devices'. The metaphor of the *big political picture* in lines 5–6 is a deliberate metaphor signalled by the phrase *a sort of*. In a corpus-based study of such words and phrases, we found that *sort of* and *kind of* are widely used in front of metaphors, often in combination with each other and with *like* (Cameron & Deignan, 2003). We suggested that such phrases act as 'tuning devices' to help speakers activate metaphorical interpretation in on-line talk. What appears to govern the use of tuning devices is a speaker's judgement about the 'expectedness' of a particular metaphor in the specific discourse context (Cameron & Deignan, 2003, p. 158). They may direct listeners to one of several possible interpretations, preventing inappropriate literal interpretation, or indicate the nature of the mapping between topic and vehicle. Tuning devices can also tone down or mitigate the interpretation of a metaphor, that, without the device, might come across as overly strong (compare *it was **like** suddenly I was thrown into the conflict*, line 16, with *suddenly I was thrown into the conflict*) or face-threatening.

Tuning devices are used across genres and contexts of talk, as one of several ways in which speakers reduce the risk of ambiguity that is, in theory but seldom in practice, associated with using metaphor. They serve as an example of how metaphor in talk is shaped by the pressures and possibilities of human interaction, and it is to these pressures and possibilities that we turn next.

## How People Use Metaphor in Talk

In understanding the discourse roles and functions of metaphor, researchers combine analysis of metaphor use with various methods of discourse analysis, including conversation analysis, functional analysis and narrative theory. In this section, I describe how metaphor has been found to work in the affective dimension of human interaction, how it helps in discourse management, and how it can be used to construct discourse spaces in which speakers can negotiate new understandings.

### *The Affective Impact of Metaphor*

When speakers bring a new vehicle domain into their talk through the use of metaphor, they have the potential to adjust the semantic prosody of the ongoing discourse (Louw, 1993). Metaphors carry not only ideational content but also something of speakers' attitudes and values in respect of that content. Vehicle choice offers affective potential. Three dimensions of affect help to analyse how speakers' choices of metaphor vehicles contribute to the affective work of metaphor: alignment–distancing; positive–negative evaluation; emphasis–de-emphasis (Graumann, 1990). When the topic of talk is uncomfortable for speakers in some way, metaphor helps to distance and de-emphasise. Comparing the use of metaphor with its absence shows how this distancing works.

Absence of metaphor is not much mentioned in the literature but was a significant feature of reconciliation talk (Cameron & Stelma, 2004). Stretches of talk without metaphor were of two sorts. Talk about travel or meeting arrangements had no need of metaphor because content was literal and physical. The more interesting metaphor-free episodes were narrative accounts of extremely painful events. In a particularly key episode, Jo Berry, who we saw in Extract 1, describes her daughter asking if she could come to meet the bomber:

Extract 3 Jo tells Pat what her daughter said

Jo . . . (1.0) before I . . . left this morning,
I decided to tell my children,
. . . that I was gonna meet you.
Pat hmh
Jo . . . (1.0) and I told my seven year old.
Pat yeah
Jo . . . and she said,
I want to come.
. . . I want to tell him,
. . . that was a bad thing he did,
to kill my mum's daddy.
Pat hmh
Jo I want to tell him,
Pat hmh
Jo . . . can I come?
she said,
and I said,
well no,
. . . but you can write it *down*,
or I'll tell him,

. . . no.
she said,
I must come and tell him.
Pat hmh

The use of the child's words and simple syntax in lines 8–23 makes for a striking stretch of talk, that clearly affects Pat, who refers to it several weeks and again several years later. By using reported speech, Jo presents the human consequences of his political action to Pat in an abrupt and raw manner, *to kill my mummy's daddy*, without the distancing effect of metaphor.

Pat himself sometimes talks without metaphors, again creating raw and high-impact narratives, for example, about being imprisoned and beaten by the army. Such bare, direct talk, marked by an absence of metaphors, is rare; it seems that, although it creates a strong impact on the listener, it is probably too painful to say or to listen to more than rarely (Kirmayer, 2004). More often, as with *loss* or *separation* in Extract 1, metaphor helps speakers by enabling emotionally difficult topics to be talked about indirectly.

### Metaphor and the Management of Talk

Extract 1 begins with Pat doing some discourse management in lines 1–4, as he introduces the new topic of the personal and the political. Metaphor plays several important roles in the management of talk. Firstly, it is used in talk to describe the process of the talk:

> a question that *comes to* my mind
> (a question that) . . . we've *covered* before

and in doctor–patient talk:

> let me just say something and *put it on the table* and then we can think about this
>
> ok *let me go back one step*

In classroom talk, metaphors are frequently used in 'agenda management' at the beginning and end of lessons and tasks (Cameron, 2003). At this point in a lesson or task, the teacher summarises upcoming activity in terms of both content and procedure. In addition, however, agenda management metaphors often served affective purposes as well as transactional ones. In Extract 4, the teacher not only tells students what they are going to study but also frames this activity so that it does not seem too onerous. (Note: intonation units were not used in this transcription. Longer pauses are shown in brackets with time to the nearest second)

Extract 4 Opening a lesson on rocks (from Cameron, 2003, p. 127)

Teacher: now what I'm going to do (.) this afternoon (1.0)
because I can't think of any other way to do it (1.0)
is to *give* you *a little bit* of information (2.0)
*on* which we can *build* (.) our understanding (1.0) of (.) rocks (4.0)
and the minerals that *come out of* rocks (1.0)
and also (.) how rocks weather (2.0)
*in other words* (.) what happens to rocks (1.0)
when (.) the snow (.) and the wind
and the ice and the rain and the temperature (1.0) *acts upon* them
so there are really two things we're going to *look at* (2.0) this half term (1.0)
one is how rocks weather (1.0)
and the other is (.) about the minerals (.) that are in them (.) that we can use

In terms of content, the geological activity is talked about using personification or at least animacy, a common technique in explanations of scientific concepts (Cameron & Low, 2004): *come out of*; *acts upon*. In terms of procedures, teaching the quite difficult geological concepts set out in lines 20–24 is metaphorically referred to as *give a little bit of information* (line 5), and later (in line 18) as *look at*. In doing agenda management, the teacher uses metaphor to align herself with the students in the learning process (also through the use of *we* with the metaphor *build on* in line 7), and chooses metaphors that emphasise the ease of the process rather than its possible difficulties. Metaphors in agenda management help teachers not only to summarise content but also to motivate and engage students in the learning process.

A combined ideational and affective role for metaphors in discourse management is also found in non-classroom talk. Metaphors, and in particular metaphorical idioms, are used by speakers in spontaneous informal conversations at points of topic transition as a way of simultaneously summarising content, expressing an opinion, and closing the topic (Drew & Holt, 1988, 1995, 1998). Extract 5 is taken from Drew and Holt's collection of telephone conversations, and shows Leslie (L) telling her mother (M) about the death of someone they both knew. The metaphorical idiom occurs in line 17: *he had a good innings* (a cricketing metaphor meaning a long life).

Extract 5 Completing a topic with a metaphorical idiom (from Drew and Holt, 1995, p. 121, with some changes to the original transcription)

L: he was the vicar's ward n anyway he died suddenly this week and he was still working
(0.3)
M: good gracious
L: he was seventy nine
M: my word? (.)
L: yes he was um
M: you've got some real workers down there heh
L: he was a p
yes indeed
he was a buyer for the only horsehair factory left in England
M: good gracious
L: and he was their buyer (.)
so he *had a good innings* didn't he?
M: I should say so.
yes (.)
marvellous
L: anyway we had a very good evening on Saturday

The metaphor *had a good innings* does several discourse management tasks. It summarises the topic of the old man's life and death, with a positive evaluation. In lines 18–20, the mother accepts this summary by agreeing with her daughter, and the daughter then opens the new topic of Saturday evening. The summary clears the way for topic transition, not just in terms of content but also affectively, by providing a 'space' in which both speakers can agree and align.

### *Metaphor as Offering a Shared Discourse Space*

Drew and Holt's suggestion that metaphorical idioms offer speakers a neutral 'third space' outside of the conversation where they can align and agree (Drew & Holt, 1988) suggests a powerful way of understanding how deliberate linguistic metaphors can contribute to the dynamics of talk and thinking, beyond the mechanics of topic transition. In psychotherapeutic talk, for example, the therapist may deliberately shift to a new generative metaphor and offer it to the client as a way of thinking about the problem under discussion. Extending the metaphor through vehicle development can build a third, metaphorical, space in which therapist and client can discuss very painful topics in a more neutral or less negative way, returning later to the real world, in hopes of bringing new understandings generated by the metaphorical talk (Evans, 2003). Research into the use of metaphor by seriously ill people shows that generative metaphors are used, with and without mediation by others, to conceptualise experience and adjust behaviour (Gibbs & Franks, 2002; Gwyn, 1999). The idea of a metaphorically constructed third space can be applied to the reconciliation talk. Here metaphor offers speakers, coming from very disparate standpoints, a place in which to align or to negotiate towards deeper understanding of the other.

### *Negotiating and Appropriating Metaphors in Talk*

There are many instances, as with *see* in Extract 1, where conventionalised metaphors used by one speaker are repeated or developed by the other in a subsequent turn. However, sometimes a speaker adopts the other's metaphor over a longer period of talk, in a move that is significant for increased alignment and understanding, and that exploits the opportunities of non-explicit topic and vehicle shifting. This happened with the gradual appropriation of *healing*, a metaphor first used by Jo in a poem she read aloud to Pat to describe recovering from her father's death in the bombing and on a wider scale:

> the heat *heals* the pain
> . . .
> for the *healing* of the world
> . . .
> I feel that my heart *heals*
> As Ireland *heals*

In responding to the poem, Pat picks up this metaphor and uses it to refer to helping other victims:

> move on in their own *healing* process

Later in the same discourse event, when Pat is talking about his feelings, he uses the *healing* metaphor for the first time in reference to himself, with much hesitation, pausing, and rhetorical questions all suggesting some diffidence or unease at doing so:

> how do you put it?
> . . . maybe that's part of *healing* too
> my *healing*

After this point, the *healing* metaphor is used in the talk to refer to both Jo's recovering from grief and Pat's working through the consequences of his actions. We can see how metaphor offers affordances in spoken interaction for participants to shift their alignment and their meanings: the affective force of *healing* is intrinsically positive; in using it to refer to recovering from grief as Jo does, Pat aligns himself with her; in tentatively appropriating it to describe his own process of accepting responsibility, he moves even closer by placing their two processes in the same vehicle space. By extending and shifting the topic reference of the vehicle term *healing*, the metaphor offers an expression that can be shared, a discourse space where the distance between participants is reduced.

The property of a metaphor vehicle to be applied to different Topics has been labelled 'multivalency' (Goatly, 1997, p. 255). The action of employing a previously used vehicle with a new topic can be called 'vehicle re-deployment', and appropriation of another's metaphor is one possible outcome of vehicle re-deployment (Cameron, 2008).

Metaphors offered by one speaker can also be directly challenged, although this does not seem to happen very often. In one instance in the reconciliation talk, Jo describes the reconciliation process as *building a bridge*. Pat uses this metaphor but adjusts the vehicle slightly, suggesting that he is not ready to agree completely with Jo's perspective, and that their disparate starting points still need to be acknowledged:

> *in the journey . . . coming to a bridge . . .*
> *with two ends*

### *Negotiating Technical Language through Metaphor*

An important ideational role of metaphor in talk is making accessible the technical language of specialist groups to non-experts. Although technical language makes use of metaphor, greater use of metaphor is observed when experts from a group are required to talk with non-experts, as when a teacher talks to students or a doctor talks to a patient. In this kind of situation, technical ideas are mediated through language that is somewhere between everyday talk and the technical language. This mediating talk makes heavy use of 'sub-technical metaphor' (Cameron, 2003, p. 112).

We can see an example in the next extract, where a doctor is explaining to a patient how her urinary problem will be treated. He explains the cognitive behavioural therapy through a series of metaphors that include *recalibrate, messages, re-acclimatise, drill.*

Extract 6 Doctor explains treatment to a patient[2]

actually what's required is a behavioural approach
to try and tackle that problem
and re-*recalibrate* those messages in a way
so that actually your brain *re-acclimatises* to only *passing*
only *getting the message pass* urine
when the pressure volume is significant
so it actually is quite an *uncomfortable* process to *go through*
we call it bladder *drill*

In addition to their ideational function, the sub-technical metaphors also work on an affective plane, through empathy and through personification. In line 10, the doctor explicitly empathises with the patient with the euphemistic metaphor *uncomfortable*. In line 8, he uses personification when he speaks of the brain as *getting the message*. As in the agenda management process of Extract 4, the personification of non-human processes serves to make them less distant and threatening.

The philosopher David Cooper cites Hegel's suggestion that personification is 'an important strategy for making the world seem less alien'. He argues further that metaphor works towards the 'cultivation of intimacy' among people and socio-cultural groups, and that this affective function may be even more crucial to human beings than the ideational function of developing concepts (Cooper, 1986, p. 166). However, we might wish to argue the relative importance of the affective and the conceptual, we need to take account of the many ways in which linguistic metaphor influences the attitudes and feelings of people in interaction.

## Linguistic and Conceptual Metaphor

Having seen various features of metaphor as it is used in talk, and how speakers shape and shift metaphor as they work towards greater understanding or less distance, this section considers how linguistic metaphor in dynamic and dialogic interaction connects with conceptual metaphor as hypothesised in cognitive metaphor theory.

The connection is not straightforward. Cognitive metaphor theory is concerned with thinking or concepts abstracted across speech communities rather than with individual language use and thinking. In the other direction, instances of language use cannot give researchers direct access to thought or mental representations, but only offer traces of activity from which inferences can be made. To cross the gap between discourse evidence and cognitive metaphor theory requires theoretical and empirical work; the gap may even be epistemologically unbridgeable. Meanwhile, I suggest two important caveats for researchers in both discourse analysis and cognitive linguistics:

- The systematic metaphors that can be abstracted from discourse events are not necessarily conceptual metaphors.
- The minds of individual language users do not necessarily include conceptual metaphors as part of their cognitive resources.

Each is now discussed.

### *Systematic and Conceptual Metaphors*

When analysing metaphor in talk, it is possible to gather together semantically connected linguistic metaphors into sets. For example, the metaphor of reconciliation as *building a bridge* can be seen as linked with metaphors in Extract 1 such as *broken*, (*not*) *separate*, (*not*) *detached*, *on every side*, with the extension *a bridge with two ends*, and with many other metaphorical expressions in the data. Across all these linguistic metaphors the Vehicle domain of 'connection' is mapped on to the Topic domain of reconciliation, where the label 'connection' is chosen to capture general idea expressed by the linguistic metaphors. The participants in the reconciliation talk can then be said to use the metaphor: RECONCILIATION

IS CONNECTION. I call such generalised mappings from a particular discourse context, 'systematic metaphor'.

The use of systematic metaphors in a discourse event is significant in suggesting how participants are thinking about topics as they talk about them. However, while the systematic metaphor may well describe something of individuals' underlying conceptual knowledge, it cannot be assumed to be a 'conceptual metaphor'. Conceptual metaphors are 'enduring conceptual mappings from source to target domains that motivate a wide range of linguistic expressions' (Gibbs, 2002, p. 80), that is they are conventionalised across a speech community. Systematic linguistic metaphors are likely to be influenced by the context of discourse, by the topic, and by the nature of the discourse event. To claim RECONCILIATION IS CONNECTION as a conceptual metaphor would require additional evidence of conventionalisation from a range of reconciliation contexts and events.

The methodological problem of choosing how to label a systematic metaphor to best capture the nature of a collection of linguistic metaphors found in data (also discussed in Semino, 2005; Semino, Heywood, & Short, 2004; Vervaeke & Kennedy, 1996) can be resolved somewhat by holding on to this distinction between systematic and conceptual metaphors. While cognitive metaphor theory, because of its aims, needs to describe conceptual metaphorical mappings in the most abstract and general form possible, researchers concerned with the thinking of specific individuals are probably well advised not to generalise too far from the actual words used in the linguistic metaphors.

Generalising from linguistic metaphor to conceptual metaphor also risks hiding the finding that talk contains large proportions of verb metaphors. The high incidence of verb metaphors in empirical data contrasts with the nominalised A IS B form conventionally given to conceptual metaphors. Grouping and labelling linguistic metaphors in cognitive metaphor theory is a nominalising process: for example, when verb metaphors such as *comes to* (Extract 1, line 1) and *move on* (section on *healing* as metaphor) are grouped under the conceptual umbrella of JOURNEY metaphors.

In their 2004 paper, Semino and colleagues discuss issues in labelling the conceptualisations underlying linguistic metaphors found in a study of conversations of cancer patients. Their discussion of three metaphors – *galloping away; erupt; dormant* – is particularly relevant here. They argue that generalising up to conceptual metaphors CANCER IS A HORSE; CANCER IS A VOLCANO is not warranted, since their data includes no examples of direct reference to horses, animals, or volcanoes in relation to cancer. Their alternative analysis takes account of the conventional metaphorical collocates of the linguistic metaphor vehicle terms in other domains in order to decide on an appropriate conceptual metaphor label. Investigation of corpus data showed that only 38% of the collocates of the verb *erupt* include *volcano (es)*. The other 62% involve metaphorical collocates such as *fire or sound, war, groups of people, new situations or movements, sores or spots on the skin*. They then propose a conceptual metaphor VIOLENT NEGATIVE ACTIVITY IS OVERFLOW FROM A CONTAINER, within which *erupt* would be one kind of overflow resulting from the further metaphor BODY PARTS ARE CONTAINERS, thus avoiding the metaphor CANCER IS A VOLCANO. The use of additional corpus evidence allows them to propose a conceptual metaphor on the basis of linguistic metaphor evidence. Although this analysis still involves some nominalisation, as ACTIVITY/OVERFLOW, it produces a much more 'verbal' description of the conceptualisation underlying verbal linguistic metaphor.

An alternative to the inductive methods just described is to work deductively, searching out linguistic metaphors in talk that appear to instantiate conceptual metaphors, or to combine inductive and deductive approaches. For example, Keller-Cohen and Gordon (2003) use linguistic metaphors, including *proven guilty, innocent*, as evidence for a claim that their interviewee uses the conceptual (or more accurately, systematic) metaphor of BEING ON TRIAL to structure the narrative in her life story. The structure of the source/vehicle domain is then expanded, and other metaphorical statements are mapped onto it, thereby building up their claim. These different approaches to spoken discourse data illustrate how systematicity in linguistic metaphor can generate hypotheses about conceptual metaphor that can be tested further with different kinds of evidence.

### *Conceptual Metaphors and Individual Minds*

In the process of developing contemporary metaphor theory, claims about conceptual metaphor have abstracted away from the use of linguistic metaphor in the talk of individuals and are made about some generalised speech community. When cognitive linguists then speak of metaphors 'we' use, it is important to remember that they are (or should be) referring to 'people in general', and not to specific individual language users.

Conceptual metaphors may 'exist' in the mind of an individual, acquired and developed through culturally contextualised experience and interaction with the physical and social world. If so, each individual will have a slightly different version, since they have different minds, developed through different experiences and interactions. On the other hand, conceptual metaphors may not be in the minds of individuals at all, only 'existing' in their systematised and abstracted forms, as written down by cognitive linguists, or in distributed form across many people within a cultural context (Gibbs, 1999; Quinn, 1991).

## Conclusion

There is still much to be discovered about metaphor in talk, and I would highlight the following as needing to be placed on the research agenda:

- work with large connected data sets to understand more about the dynamics of metaphor in talk on several interconnected timescales and levels of social organisation.
- the role of personal style in metaphor use
- the interaction of genre and metaphor use
- the impact of metaphor absence in a range of discourse contexts.

The methods and categories used in investigation and description need to capture the interactional and dynamic nature of metaphor in talk.

In the building of metaphor theory, linguistic metaphor is often taken as starting point and as evidence. However, the linguistic metaphor that we see in such arguments is often stunted and impoverished in comparison with the richness and complexity observed in its use in talk. The chapter has reviewed some of what we know about how people use metaphor in their talk, the nature of linguistic metaphor, how it shifts and changes in the process of talk, and how metaphor helps speakers achieve interactional purposes. From the traces that we find in talk, we are building up a picture of metaphor as a varied and multidimensional language resource. Its nature reflects its evolution in the dynamics of situated language use, created through the constraints and affordances of the human brain/mind, with its search for coherence and desire for novelty, and through the needs and pleasures of human social interaction.

## Notes

1 This, and other reconciliation talk data in the chapter, come from the project Using Visual Display to Explore Metaphor in Conciliation Talk, funded by the UK Arts and Humanities Research Board under their Innovation Award Scheme. The author gratefully acknowledges AHRB support and the participants for generously allowing their conversations to be analysed.

2 The author would like to thank Celia Roberts of Kings College, London, and Director of the Patients with Limited English and Doctors in General Practice (PLEDGE) project, who kindly provided the data in this extract.

## References


Brooke-Rose, C. (1958). *A grammar of metaphor*. London: Secker and Warburg.

Brown, R. (1958). How shall a thing be called? *Psychological Review, 65*, 14–21.

Cameron, L. (1999). Identifying and describing metaphor in spoken discourse data. In L. Cameron & G. Low (Eds.), *Researching and applying metaphor* [pp. 105–132]. Cambridge: Cambridge University Press.

Cameron, L. (2003). *Metaphor in educational discourse*. London: Continuum.

Cameron, L. (2008). Metaphor shifting in the dynamics of talk. In M. Zanotto, L. Cameron, & M. Cavalcanti (Eds.), *Confronting metaphor in use: An applied linguistic approach* (pp. 45–62). Amsterdam: Benjamins.

Cameron, L., & Deignan, A. (2003). Using large and small corpora to investigate tuning devices around metaphor in spoken discourse. *Metaphor and Symbol, 18*(3), 149–160.

Cameron, L., & Low, G. (2004). Figurative variation in episodes of educational talk and text. *European Journal of English Studies*, 8(3), 355–373.

Cameron, L., & Stelma J. (2004). 'Metaphor clusters in discourse'. *Journal of Applied Linguistics, 1*(2), 27–36.

Carter, R. (2004). *Language and creativity: The art of common talk*. London: Routledge.

Chafe, W. (1996). *Discourse, consciousness, and time*. Chicago: University of Chicago Press.

Cooper, D. (1986). *Metaphor*. Oxford: Blackwell.

Corts, D., & Meyers, K. (2002). Conceptual clusters in figurative language production. *Journal of Psycholinguistic Research*, 31(4), 391–408.

Corts, D., & Pollio, H. (1999). Spontaneous production of figurative language and gesture in college lectures. *Metaphor and Symbol*, 14(1), 81–100.

Deignan, A. (1999). Corpus-based research into metaphor and its application to language reference materials. In L. Cameron & G. Low (Eds.), *Researching and applying metaphor* (pp. 177–199). Cambridge: Cambridge University Press.

Drew, P., & Holt, E. (1988). Complainable matters: The use of idiomatic expressions in making complaints. *Social Problems*, 35(4), 398–417.

Drew, P., & Holt, E. (1995). Idiomatic expressions and their role in the organisation of topic transition in conversation. In M. Everaert, E.-J. v. d. Linden, A. Schenk, & R. Schreuder (Eds.), *Idioms: Structural and psychological perspectives* (pp. 117–132). Hillsdale, NJ: Lawrence Erlbaum Associates.

Drew, P., & Holt, E. (1998). Figures of speech: Figurative expressions and the management of topic transition in conversation. *Language in Society*, 27, 495–522.

Evans, C. (2003, November). *Metaphor and creation of space for play*. Paper presented at Health and Discourse Seminar, Metaphors in Healthcare Communication, Cardiff University.

Gentner, D. (1978). On relational meaning: The acquisition of verb meaning. *Child Development*, 49, 988–998.

Gentner, D. (1982). Why nouns are learnt before verbs: Linguistic relativity vs. natural partitioning. In S. Kuczaj (Ed.), *Language development: Language, culture, and cognition* (pp. 301–334). Hillsdale, NJ: Lawrence Erlbaum Associates.

Gibbs, R. W. (1999). Taking metaphor out of our heads and putting it into the cultural world. In R. W. Gibbs & G. Steen (Eds.), *Metaphor in cognitive linguistics* (pp. 145–166). Amsterdam: John Benjamins.

Gibbs, R. (2002). Psycholinguistic comments on metaphor identification. *Language and Literature, 11*(1), 78–84.

Gibbs, R., & Franks, H. (2002). Embodied metaphor in women's narratives about their experiences with cancer. *Health Communication, 14*(2), 139–165.

Goatly, A. (1997). *The language of metaphors*. London: Routledge.

Graumann, C. (1990). Perspective structure and dynamics in dialogues. In I. Markova & K. Foppa (Eds.), *The Dynamics of Dialogue* (pp. 105–126). London: Harvester Wheatsheaf.

Gwyn, R. (1999). "Captain of my own ship": Metaphor and the discourse of chronic illness. In L. Cameron & G. D. Low (Eds.), *Researching and applying metaphor* (pp. 203–220). Cambridge: Cambridge University Press.

Hopper, P. J. (1997). Discourse and the category 'verb' in English. *Language and Communication, 17*(2), 93–102.

Hopper, P. J., & Thompson, S. A. (1984). The discourse basis for lexical categories in Universal Grammar. *Language*, 60, 703–752.

Keller-Cohen, D., & Gordon, C. (2003). "On trial": Metaphor in telling the life story. *Narrative Inquiry*, 13(1), 1–40.

Kirmayer, L. (2004). The cultural diversity of healing: Meaning, metaphor and mechanism. *British Medical Bulletin*, 69, 33–48.

Koller, V. (2003). Metaphor clusters, metaphor chains: Analyzing the multifunctionality of metaphor in text. *Metaphorik* (5), 115–134.

Louw, B. (1993). Irony in the text or insincerity in the writer? – The diagnostic potential of semantic prosodies. In M. Baker, G. Francis, & E. Tognini-Bonelli (Eds.), *Text and technology: In honour of John Sinclair* (pp. 157–176). Amsterdam: John Benjamins.

Low, G. (1997). *A celebration of squid sandwiches: Figurative language and the management of (non-core) academic text.* Unpublished manuscript. University of York.

McCarthy, M. (1988). Some vocabulary patterns in conversation. In R. Carter & M. McCarthy (Eds.), *Vocabulary and language teaching* (pp. 181–200). London: Longman.

Pollio, H., & Barlow, J. M. (1975). A behavioural analysis of figurative language in psychotherapy: One session in a single case study. *Language and Speech*, 18, 236–254.

Quinn, N. (1991). The cultural basis of metaphor. In J. Fernandez (Ed.), *Beyond metaphor: The theory of tropes in anthropology* (pp. 56–93). Stanford, CA: Stanford University Press.

Sapir, E. (1921). *Language*. New York: Harcourt, Brace and World.

Semino, E. (2005). The metaphorical construction of complex domains: The case of speech activity in English. *Metaphor and Symbol*, 20(1), 35–70.

Semino, E., Heywood, J., & Short, M. (2004). Methodological problems in the analysis of metaphors in a corpus of conversations about cancer. *Journal of Pragmatics*, 36(7), 1271–1294.

Stelma, J., & Cameron, L. (2007). Intonation units in spoken interaction: Developing transcriber competence. *Text & Talk*, 27(3), 361–393.

Vervaeke, J., & Kennedy, J. (1996). Metaphors in language and thought: Falsification and multiple meanings. *Metaphor and Symbolic Activity*, 11, 273–284.

CHAPTER 12

# Metaphor and Education

*Graham Low*

Metaphor makes things exciting and understandable and, as such, has been applied to education since time immemorial. However, education is now an enormous area and the number of articles and books dealing with metaphorical aspects of it is far beyond the scope of a short article.[1] What I want to do in this chapter is to select a small number of topics that I consider to be central to education, but which remain problematic in one way or another, or are simply unresearched. I shall attempt to examine why they are problematic and establish, more positively, if anything can be done to reduce the problems.

I start by considering the role of metaphor in implementing educational change. I argue that metaphor analysis does have a useful role to play, but that many of the published examples, from Schön's (1979) generative metaphor, to the semiotic analysis of Labbo (1996) and Oxford et al.'s (1998) language teacher/ing metaphors, tend to over-identify metaphor and ignore the complex and content-sensitive role of metonymy. Metaphoric modelling in education cannot be somehow outside the normal constraints and rigour of empirical academic analysis.

I then go on to look at the importance of metaphor in teaching and learning. The last half of this section concentrates on the important problem of foreign language teaching, where learning about the subject is *not* the aim of learning and indeed may have little effect on language acquisition. After a brief review of metaphoric competence, I examine three fairly practical problems: when to teach things as metaphor (and when not to), how to cope with cultural differences, and whether to teach basic senses first. Essentially, I argue that we cannot just apply recent cognitive theory indiscriminately to the classroom. We need, for example, to think carefully about how much metalanguage learners can reasonably be exposed to. We also need to consider how metaphor is used at discourse level (i.e. not just as an aspect of vocabulary), and to establish what it is that we want learners to actually do with metaphor. Lastly, we need to recognise that testing for 'metaphoric competence' in a foreign language poses particular difficulties for proficiency testing as currently conceived.

The chapter ends with some recommendations for future research.

## Metaphor and Educational Change

Educational concepts and processes are frequently described in metaphoric terms, either as single "A IS B" metaphors (e.g. EDUCATION IS PREPARING MENTAL MEALS; LEARNING IS POURING WATER INTO A JUG), or as clusters of metaphors. The reasons for creating analogies or models are generally fairly obvious; one wants to,

- find a salient, memorable label for an otherwise difficult concept;
- clarify a concept which is diffuse, abstract, or generally complex;
- extend thought; or
- locate problems with a particular conceptualisation and then bring about some sort of change.

It was this last point which led Schön (1993) to develop his influential narrative approach, which he called "generative metaphor". In most therapy or counselling sessions, the analyst lets the patient talk freely about his/her life and problems and listens for key events or key words. If key terms are identified, these can then be focused on and become the basis for further action, or treatment. In reality, things are more complicated than this and recent research (e.g. Cameron, 2003b; Cameron & Stelma, 2004) has emphasised the to-ing and fro-ing of metaphor between counsellor and "patient". However, Schön's idea was that if planners listened to the "stories" told by people affected by a situation, these people would spontaneously indicate, by their use of metaphor, what was uppermost in their minds and the way they conceptualised their problem(s). The planners thus needed to listen out for the salient metaphoric expression, establish what it showed in the speaker's mind, translate this into what it implied in the planners' conceptualisation of the situation, and then make changes. A metaphorical version, almost, of grounded theory in education. It is the fact that the metaphor, once located, leads planners to think in new ways and to implement changes they had not thought of that explains Schön's use of the label "*generative* metaphor".

The generative metaphor procedure makes two problematic assumptions. The first is that the speaker does in fact conceptualise the situation in metaphoric terms. Unfortunately, this assumption is belied by Schön's own examples of housing policy, which either show metaphor closely linked to metonymy (urban areas can show "decay" and communities need to be "healthy", p. 145), or, in the case of a locale likened to a "natural community" which needs space to interact (p. 146), are almost entirely metonymic. The second assumption is that the informant does not need metaphoric language to indicate or convey metaphor. However, if no metaphoric language is needed, it becomes virtually impossible for the researcher to validate any metaphors identified. One might argue, though Schön does not, that identification is possible if phenomena like pictures coexist with the narrative – or in the case of oral narratives, coughing, drawing pictures, or behaviourally acting out a metaphor while talking (Low, 1999, 2003). The value of this sort of secondary support is emphasised by Cortazzi and Jin (1999) in their similar, "narrative" approach to discovering teachers' conceptualisations of learning. But the point is that the images or behaviour constitute *further* evidence of metaphor, not the *only* evidence.

One might also note that neither of the planning texts cited as evidence by Schön are "stories" or "narratives" by affected users, in the sense that Cortazzi and Jin's speakers were the teachers or students who were the interested parties. Rather, the texts were by planners or by later analysts, so one might argue that context is important and that different parties will generate evidence of different types and values.

To sum up, framing problems is fine, but you cannot assume the framing is metaphoric. Indeed, metonymy may even be an inevitable aspect of generative metaphor. It is noticeable, for example, that Block's (1999) excellent attempt to apply generative metaphor to second language acquisition research situations resulted in a set of examples that were almost totally metonymic. Similarly, Sarason's (1993) use of Schön's procedure to argue the case for wholesale educational change in the United States generated (as it were) two valuable perspectives, "primary prevention" and "reform", but how far these are genuinely metaphors is highly debatable; despite the persistent use by one of the book's reviewers of "new images" and "multiple lenses" (Harrington, 1994), the concepts are better seen as metonymies, or even as quite literal activities. Lastly, both the nature and source of the data used as input are important and need to be discussed as part of the procedure.

This sort of metaphoric modelling has proved particularly attractive to language educators, who have not only constructed metaphoric models of language learning and teaching, but have often linked them to teacher development. Indeed, the implication can be that teachers found to be misconceptualising, say, language as a conduit, are in need of some sort of re-education (Block, 1992; de Guerrero & Villamil, 2002). In a short survey of such models of teaching and learning (Low, 2003), I noted four methodological problems that echo the comments above on generative metaphor.

### *Problem 1: Assuming a Priori That Metaphor Must Be Involved*

The assumption that all observed behaviour can be treated as metaphor, and that clusters of metaphors can always be given "overarching" labels goes well beyond Schön's claim and is a feature of semiotic analysis (Labbo, 1996). However, Labbo's own study of children developing aspects of literacy in their first language illustrates two of the difficulties of making this assumption. First, the author admitted to creating the metaphors to match her own interpretation ("It cannot be assumed that screenland is a metaphor the children would sanction", p. 380) and secondly, even the data cited at times failed to provide a justification for treating it as metaphoric. Simply finding children playing around in class, for example, is not by definition metaphoric, unless evidence can be found of play being treated by the children as something else (or vice versa).

### *Problem 2: Identifying an Underlying Metaphor Simply Because an Expression Is Consistent with It*

This is a frequent complaint about conceptual metaphor research in particular and can simply indicate an over-enthusiastic analyst. An example would be where Oxford et al. (1998, p. 12), conclude that reports of a teacher rushing through a syllabus "therefore led to the inescapable . . . Teacher as manufacturer metaphor". The reports are consistent with the metaphor, but no more. One cannot use them to make claims about metaphors of teaching.

### *Problem 3: Treating a Descriptive Model as a Procedural Model*

The fact that someone uses a metaphoric expression does not prove that the underlying metaphor is actively used by them as a guide to thinking or acting. Neither does the fact that an analyst finds a metaphor to be an apt way of capturing the essential details of a situation. Hence, Scribner's (1988) description of literacy as "divine grace", where above-average readers are in a "state of grace" but below-average ones have fallen from it, carries no implication whatsoever that readers themselves conceive of their skills in religious terms. In Bartelt (1997), a group of English as a foreign language (EFL) university students consistently reported translating from their first language (L1) when they spoke the target language (or L2). Bartelt interpreted the translation as a metaphor (though the evidence for this is not convincing) and noted several times that this was a description of the data. At the same time, however, he argued that the model was in effect procedural, and that it "largely determine[s] not only perceptions, but also the types of interaction selected [by the learners] to deal with in the [external] environment" (p. 34) and that the saliency of the model in the learners' brains was sufficient to necessitate a wholesale change in teaching methods (p. 33). It may well have been the case that a change would have been highly desirable, but specific evidence is needed to argue that the cause of metaphoric language or behaviour is an internalised procedural model.

### *Problem 4: Reporting Metonymic Links as If They Were Metaphor*

Oxford et al. (1998) propose, on the basis of their data, the metaphors TEACHING AS REPEATING and TEACHER AS DELEGATOR. The problem here is that teachers have to repeat and delegate many times in a quite literal fashion as part of their basic job. Focusing on the relationship between delegating and teaching at the expense of the teacher's other roles is metonymy, not metaphor. For repeating to be metaphoric, the teacher would need to appear to be repeating, while not actually repeating. A more complex example of the same confusion comes from Block (1992), who reported the student-generated metaphor A TEACHER IS A FRIEND. If a teacher acts "like a friend" without actually being one, a limited case for metaphor could be sustained. On the other hand, being friendly is simply one core aspect of being a professional teacher, so there is a strong case for metonymy. If the student feels that the friendliness is sufficient to justify seeing the teacher as a real friend (or more realistically perhaps, as a "sort of friend") then presumably the metaphor claim would become invalid. The classification "being my friend" is notoriously unstable with teenagers and so the claims for metaphor or metonymy could vary with context: both between students and within students, that is, from hour to hour.

The role of metonymy in educational models is extremely interesting from a conceptual or a discourse point of view, but one needs to ask whether it is as interesting from an educational viewpoint. In one sense, the planner or teacher trainer is simply presenting the reader with a series of characteristics of the job or task, noting that some people overemphasise one or two of the characteristics and suggesting that such an imbalance can lead to undesirable teaching or learning behaviour. On the other hand, the TEACHER AS FRIEND example shows that metaphor and metonymy can be hard to differentiate because the grounds for categorisation can vary depending on context. This context dependency can become important if the object of the analysis is, as it is with generative metaphor, to implement long-term stable social or educational change.

Just as Lakoff and Johnson (1980) explored the points where different metaphors for, say, ANGER are inconsistent or cannot be mixed, so one other important use of metaphoric models is to examine multiple metaphors for vagueness, ambiguity, or confusion within an education policy, or policy document. Thus, Goatly (2002) dissected the various metaphors of the Hong Kong government's (2000) proposal for educational reform and established that several either involved little actual reform, or else appeared to act more as a barrier to reform. Either way, they clashed with the metaphors that did appear to suggest genuine reform. Goatly concluded that the government was offering mixed messages, or simply being vague by using the same lexeme (*construction*; *building*) to mean several, often opposed, things.

In sum, then, metaphor analysis can play an important role in establishing educational problems and indicating fruitful directions for change, but only where methodological precautions are taken and the evidence is rigorously evaluated.

## Metaphor and Teaching/Learning

Metaphoric models repeatedly present the educator with metaphors in A IS B format (e.g. TEACHING IS BREADMAKING) – a format much less frequent in naturally occurring discourse than verb, or noun, phrases. One may accordingly ask whether learners too should be presented directly with metaphors or analogies in A IS B form.[2] For subjects other than language, the position seems uncontroversial and backed by a range of research studies. Using analogies is an essential aspect of academic expertise, whether one is discovering things or creating theories (Goswami, 1992; Holyoak & Thagard, 1995; Sutton, 1993); they are "an utterly essential part of theories" (Campbell, cited in Hesse, 1966, 4); they allow the teacher to communicate with learners who have not mastered a theory (Lawson, 1993); they allow learners to visualise abstract concepts (Duit, 1991); they allow learners to generate inferences and testable predictions (Dagher, 1995; Duit, 1991; Gentner & Holyoak, 1997; Holyoak & Thagard, 1995; Lawson, 1993; Sutton, 1993); they motivate learners (Duit, 1991); they allow the teacher to tailor teaching to individual needs and levels of understanding (Duit, 1991). Metaphors also affect subsequent behaviour (as where Bromme and Stahl's [1999] students created different types of hypertext documents, depending on the "hypertext is . . ." metaphor they had learned). Finally, Cameron (2003a) noted that if a metaphor is adequately salient, it can also aid recall at a later date, particularly if it is concrete rather than abstract (Harris et al., 1999, 7).

A IS B format seems particularly important where younger children are involved. Research suggests (e.g. Cameron, 2003a; Gentner & Toupin, 1986) that they cannot work with analogies and metaphors unless (a) the metaphors are presented explicitly, (b) Source–Target correspondences are given, and (c) the children have an adequate understanding of the Source domain *before* the metaphor is given. Cameron's (2003a) study showed that this latter point applied *within* a (class) discourse as well as between sessions; metaphor only really worked with 10-year-olds when the Grounds had been given by the teacher and understood earlier in the same lesson. Sequencing of metaphoric language and information within a lesson is therefore crucial.

A further constraint was noted by Spiro et al. (1989). Spiro et al. were concerned that single A IS B metaphors were leading university medical students to create oversimplified and even false models of the concepts being taught, and that the problem was exacerbated where everyday senses of terms were transferred to scientific domains. One of their suggestions was that teaching should involve multiple metaphors, where each metaphor was designed to compensate for what was being backgrounded by the others. There have been few empirical tests of such systematic convergence, but Cameron's observational study did find that successful primary teaching of science appeared to correlate with the use of more than one metaphor.

Another area that is important, but which is relatively unresearched, is the extent to which explicit training in metaphor might help learners cope with poor or misleading explanations by textbook writers or teachers. This sort of situation can occur even in quite surprising contexts; just to give one example, Low (2005) examined how an account of (Darwinian) evolution of life on earth in the leading article of a high-status science magazine was (ironically) full of animacy terms and metaphors. It is clear that humans do compensate "naturally" for rhetorical devices such as extreme case formulation in conversation (thus mothers adjust rapidly to "But *everyone's* got new trainers, Mum!"), but how far this skill extends to coping with academic explanations is unknown. We might expect the finding (above) that metaphor training leads to a greater ability to find and solve problems to extend to poor explanations, but apart from some support from a study by Littlemore (2004), again we simply do not know.

A constructivist approach to learning would predict that learning would be increased if students could engage critically with academic concepts by generating their own analogies. BouJaoude & Tamim (2000) cite a series of studies which indicate that this is (or can be) the case; students who were able to generate their own analogies demonstrated an increase in critical thinking, questioning and problem-solving skills, and an ability to apply them to scientific texts and ideas (Middleton, 1991; Wittrock & Alesandrini, 1990; Wong, 1993). They also demonstrated greater recall of subject-specific detail when reading (Glynn, 1996). The fact that this can happen does not imply that all students find analogy generation easy or helpful. Of the fifty-one 12-year-olds studying biology in BouJaude and Tamim's study, for example, all reported that analogies helped them recall concepts taught, but only 18% said they would use them without the teacher's advice and just 6% found them helpful for studying (2000, p. 62); the others preferred study methods relating to what appeared in their exams.

Learning a second language is not the same as studying science. Knowing about a language is not the same as using it, reacting to words out of context is not the same as using them in context and, most worryingly of all, it still remains singularly unclear how far direct instruction actually facilitates acquisition. Being presented with models or rules of the grammar of the target language, for example, appears to have minimal effects on language learning, particularly where the advice is intended as developmental or as corrective feedback (Norris & Ortega, 2000; Truscott, 1996, 2004). Truscott did however note that in some studies, direct presentations of grammar rules nevertheless resulted in increased learning of lexis, rather than grammar. This would seem to suggest that there is a chance that A IS B presentations might aid the acquisition of at least some lexis. Whether they will aid learners to *use* the lexis productively is entirely another matter. To date, however, the bulk of the published interventions have proposed precisely that: increased learning should result from the student being shown (or intuiting) the A IS B metaphors which underlie target language vocabulary (or grammar) items, followed by some sort of discussion with the teacher, or between the learners. It has to be said, however, that most of the studies in the literature are not randomised controlled trials, or even controlled trials, and few involve adequately delayed post-tests. Some are basic pre-/post-test studies, but others are simply suggestive or anecdotal. An example is Rich (2002), who recommended, on the basis of undisclosed experience, that EFL students may profitably generate and discuss metaphors of the classroom and learning, as a way of group bonding and of raising awareness of one's own culturally derived expectations about teaching and learning.

More weight can be put on the results of a number of small-scale empirical studies. Littlemore (2004) for example reported that a group of university EFL students of business and politics were in general more able to think critically by comparing statements in L2 academic texts with metaphors, after undergoing an intervention involving guessing, comprehending, and exploring the implications of metaphors, in "naturalistic" as well as canonical A IS B form, in subject-specific discourse. The finding agrees with those of Middleton (1991) for biology, but the sample was very small and there was no control group. At the level of lexis, Boers (2000) found that EFL university students recalled vocabulary better in the short term if the expressions had, at the time of presentation, been grouped "meaningfully" in terms of underlying metaphors. In all cases, the metaphors were conventional not innovative. In a similar vein, Csábi (2004) found secondary school students had better short-term recall of phrasal verbs and idioms based on "hold" and "keep" when the underlying metaphors were explained to them.

What evidence there is, then, suggests that A IS B presentation can be useful to develop learner motivation and act as input to small group work. It is also easy for a teacher to move discussions about A IS B metaphor structure from regular class work to language awareness sessions. Lastly, it is not hard to instigate discussions where the learners dissect say LOVE IS WAR and develop new metaphors and exponents in the L2. One might predict that A IS B type discussions meet the requirements that language learners should engage actively with the language, reflect on it, and work purposefully on tasks using it (Doughty & Long, 2003).

However, while all this seems useful in making students notice patterns in the L2 and relate those patterns to real life phenomena or social expectations, there is no reason whatsoever to assume that it will increase

(a) their ability to understand a new message, or its implied appropriateness or creativity, or (b) their skill at producing a fluent, accurate, appropriate, rich, humorous or subtle L2 utterance. And it certainly does not guarantee an ability to sustain the to-ing and fro-ing of metaphoric expressions within an interaction.

Although Niemeier (1997) suggested that conceptual metaphors like TIME IS MONEY lend themselves to a variety of classroom presentation formats, which allows teachers to appeal to different types of learner (repeating the point made by Duit 1991) and to develop holistic teaching methods which provide input visually, intellectually, and physically, the fact remains that there is a virtual absence of empirical intervention studies which systematically test and compare alternative approaches to teaching metaphor skills.[3] A number of suggestions are listed below, but most still involve ways of clarifying A IS B correspondences or making them perceptually salient.

Lindstromberg (1996) has suggested the use of conceptual diagrams when teaching prepositions and indeed trajectory lines (usually arrows) have been used for years to help learners understand time expressions. A conceptual approach to the metaphors underlying "Christmas is approaching" and "We are approaching Christmas" can certainly help the materials designer correct the directionality of the arrows relative to the referent. These are sometimes portrayed in textbooks in ways that run counter to the expressions they are illustrating; thus Hamp-Lyons and Heasley (1987, p. 57) have,

```
TIME1 --> T2 --> T3 --> T4
Past ----------> Present ---> Future
```

rather than, say,

```
TIME (past) <-- DAY1 -- D2 -- D3 -- D4 -- (future)
YOU -------------------------- ----------------->
```

but there is still no real documented evidence that this enhances the correct or more fluent use of expressions like "the day before yesterday", or "the following evening".

Again, Lindstromberg (2001) and Holme (2001), have both proposed that acquiring metaphoric items might be facilitated by acting them out, in the manner of total physical response (TPR) learning (Asher, 2000). The suggestion is based on the idea that large amounts of metaphor are embodied – in the sense that the Sources not only (a) refer to sensory experience, to the human body, or to relatively familiar actions involving it, but also (b) evoke some sort of sensory response by the listener. Holme suggested acting out tenses in English; Lindstromberg verbs of movement. There is now some preliminary evidence (Lindstromberg & Boers, in press) that advanced learners can learn verbs of movement efficiently in the short term using TPR, but more research is needed. One obvious difficulty with TPR as a generic solution is that, although some metaphors lend themselves to physical imitation, not all do. Many image schemata, for example, seem "drawable" but scarcely actable and even the primary metaphors suggested by Grady (1998), which tend to be correlations between actions and perceptions (like "Swallowing is Accepting") can be hard to act out in full. So, while the potential for acting out seems well worth exploiting (on the twin indirect justifications that multiple intelligences require multiple modes of presentation, as Neimeier and Duit argued, and that Asher produced valid evidence of learning at initial stages using TPR), it needs to be borne in mind that acting cannot account fully or at all for many metaphors.

One fairly obvious variation on acting or drawing is the provision of concrete objects. Basic objects, like containers, feature in several conventional metaphors and image schemata and group interaction with interesting objects has long been a stable part of primary level teaching. Li's (2002) use of physical containers in the classroom might therefore be expected to enhance learning the target language. Unfortunately, while the results suggest that increased lexical learning did indeed take place, individual aspects of the teaching method were not analysable as separate variables, so all that can be concluded is that, like in Boers and Dechemeleer (2001), generally relating lexis to underlying metaphor enhances short-term recall.

A further device that has been suggested (e.g. by Boers & Demecheleer, 1998) as a way of dealing with the fuzziness and subtlety of metaphoric extension is to present learners with a set of sentences organised in a cline with the literal senses first, followed by increasingly metaphorical ones. Again, however, while the technique makes considerable sense for words with complicated patterns of extension (like "off" or "over"), there is no empirical evidence suggesting that it genuinely aids performance or learning, and even at an explanatory level it hides the divergent pathways (or radial categories) needed for an adequate explanation.

One possible approach to helping learners identify and work with L2 metaphor might be to teach it initially in explicit form as simile, paralleling science teaching accounts, such as "atoms are like solar systems". There may be some limited value to this in specific contexts, but many metaphoric expressions are not easily expressible as similes, particularly where a degree of possession is asserted; "You are my life" becomes almost meaningless as "You are like my life", or again, "Honey" becomes almost insulting if full identification is not made and the addressee is simply held to resemble a thick fluid. Even where a choice of format exists between metaphor and simile, people have been found to show fairly strong preferences for one or the other, depending on whether the transfer involves simple attributes or relationships (Aisenman, 1999). At a discourse level, similes are far from straightforward, and can be seen as avoidance and obfuscation devices as much as tools for clarification. People also have a tendency to interpret them differently from metaphors, relying much more on existing (or core, or typical) semantic knowledge (Fishlov, 2003). This is even reflected in conventional expressions; "life is a joke" involves little or no humour, whereas "life is like a joke" may well do. In sum, similes have limited value as training tools for metaphor interpretation.

Before leaving this section, I would like briefly to return to the topic of primary metaphor. Grady and Johnson (2002, pp. 535–536) make the frequently observed point that conventional expressions relating to THEORIES ARE BUILDINGS, do not make use of several core characteristics of buildings, like having windows or walls. They argue however that such vocabulary "gaps" are better explained by going below the conceptual metaphor to "primary" A IS B connections such as PERSISTING IS REMAINING ERECT and ORGANISATION IS PHYSICAL STRUCTURE; a building is simply an exemplification of the primary metaphors. There is little in the way of published educational intervention studies, but intuitively, the idea of presenting language learners with primary metaphors has great appeal, especially if the learners are adult and at an advanced level. Teachers can ask, "Where exactly is the metaphor in this expression?" and answers like "intimacy is closeness" (leading to "psychological distance is real distance") may be easy to comprehend. On the other hand, it is unclear how far younger learners could understand explanations so far removed from the surface expressions and it is not at all clear whether any learners could cope with the categories of "primary scene" and "primary subscene" developed to constrain and explain the primary metaphors.

## Establishing What to Teach

Deciding what exactly to teach is far from easy in language education. At times, it is clear that an expression or structure needs to be taught, but there is no agreement about whether it is (or should be treated as) metaphor. This applies particularly to things like delexical verbs (e.g. "make a joke", "have a laugh") and to numerous fixed expressions (Grant & Bauer, 2004, have a good summary of previous arguments). At the level of discourse, identification problems can relate more to agreeing on boundaries than on word meaning; does one, for example, include the literal Target ("they") as well as the Source terms ("pigged out") as the "metaphoric expression" in a text? If a word is metaphoric, does one include all syntactically dependent expressions such as relative clauses (i.e. do they "inherit" metaphoricity?) (Steen, 1999). Staying at the level of discourse, there are further occasions when it may simply not be clear what metaphor is used for, how listeners and speakers use it, and/or whether one would wish to teach it anyway. Thus, although both Strässler (1982) and Low (1988) flagged the fact that many conventional emotion metaphors seem far more appropriate to third party reports than personal confessions in face-to-face interactions ("he hit the roof" rather than "I shall hit the roof when I see you next"), the topic remains relatively unresearched and Kövecses, making exactly the same point in 2003, is forced to rely on an anecdotal discussion with a single native speaker. A more poignant example is whether you actively teach learners to use metaphor to (verbally) attack individuals or else to operate, as politicians are often accused of doing, just this side of the edge of telling lies. The answer depends on your philosophy of language teaching. If you believe (as I do) that learners should be trained to survive in the real L2 world and actually be able to come out on top when they interact with native speakers, then the answer is a qualified yes.

A less controversial question is whether we ask learners to look for chains and clusters in discourse, and to produce them when they speak or write. There is abundant evidence that the phenomena exist in oral and written discourse. Metaphors regularly form chains through text (e.g. Garton et al., 1991; Koller, 2003), frames concurrently around whole texts, subsections and paragraphs (Low, 1997; Koller, 2003) and clusters at key points (Cameron & Low, 2004; Corts & Meyers, 2002; Koller, 2003; Low, 2005; Cameron & Stelma, 2004). People create these effects for clarity, to focus the receiver's attention, or to induce a particular type of conceptualisation of the topic. There is some suggestion that the differing reasons are more concentrated in oral text (resulting in single multifunctional expressions) and can be more spread out in written texts (Low, 1997, 2005). Possibly inadvertently, producers also often add "outliers" to their clusters. These outliers are not "regular" metaphors, but take on a degree of metaphoricity by virtue of being near clear-cut metaphors (Low, 2005), and since they can occur before as well as after the metaphors, recognition can depend in part of how often one reads the text (Sayce, 1953). There would seem to be little reason for not teaching students to work with these phenomena in the L2, at least at an advanced level.

## The Notion of Metaphoric Competence

Discussing metaphor interpretation and use in skill terms introduces the notion of metaphoric competence. At a very general level, few would deny that we want learners to develop metaphoric competence in the L2. The problem is trying to establish what that means in practice. Different approaches are possible. One could start with interactions and texts and list a number of key skills that learners need to do with them if they are to survive in an L2 environment. Examples would be "knowing where a speaker has shifted the degree of 'activeness' (or metaphoricity) of an expression" (say a technical term), or "knowing when a speaker has gone beyond conventionality and is being mildly creative – or else is operating on an *ad hoc* basis" (e.g. Carter & McCarthy, 2004; Low, 1988). Because these discourse-related skills rely so heavily on the use of social context, linguistic co-text, and one's expertise in the relevant topic, they are generally compatible with recent approaches to task-based teaching, as long as teachers bear in mind that they are relevant in one form or another to just about every real-world language-use task. People can activate and deactivate metaphor in everything from buying a loaf of bread to writing an academic journal article.

An alternative approach is to isolate a small set of psychological skills which are either held to underlie a broad range of actual metaphor performance, or which are indirectly related to performance and serve more as predictors (e.g. Littlemore, 2001a; Pollio & Smith, 1980). Unfortunately, it remains to be shown experimentally whether interventions (i.e. teaching) focusing on, say, lateral thinking skills do serve to improve the accuracy, the rhetorical/interactive power, or the appropriateness of spontaneous L2 performance – as tested by a delayed post-test comprising free construction test items.

A third approach is to formulate metaphor skills so that they fit into existing models of communicative competence. The model currently commonest among language teachers and testers treats communicative competence as comprising four orthogonal components: linguistic, sociolinguistic (meaning contextual appropriateness), discourse, and strategic. The latter is somewhat ambiguous as it can imply learning strategies, communication strategies, or both. The model has developed over a number of years, starting with Canale and Swain (1980), revised by Bachman (1990), by Bachman and Palmer (1996), and more recently by Douglas (2000). Although Skehan (1998) has criticised the general concept of a componential model of competence as being descriptive rather than explanatory, it has had the merit of helping course designers and language testers build relatively comprehensive profiles and needs analyses. This has also in practice served to limit the interest in metaphor. Bachman (1990) treated metaphor as involving oblique cultural references and an activity which only advanced learners could be expected to do. It can be shown without much difficulty (Littlemore & Low, 2006) first that metaphor skills apply to all four components (and thus need to be acquired by learners at most levels) and second that learners do in fact experience difficulty working with metaphor in all four areas.

Clearly, the way metaphoric competence is formulated will depend very much on the purpose of the formulator, and there is no one best solution. From a teaching perspective, it is important to highlight the point that learning *about* metaphor – learning, for example, that "run up a flag", "run up a bill", or "the run up to an election" are metaphoric, or knowing that LOVE IS A JOURNEY has numerous exponents in English – will not *per se* improve your ability to *use* metaphoric expressions effectively as a speaker. Nor will it necessarily help you compute implicit and explicit messages on line as a listener.

I would thus endorse the value of the first of the three approaches above and, with this in mind, I shall list some of the things language learners need to do, but which they are rarely taught or exposed to in a classroom. Productively, speakers need to know how to use non-specific metaphor to "decouple" from a narrative or conversational topic, in order to summarise it, evaluate it, withdraw gracefully from the argument, or simply change topic. Receptively, listeners need to be able to pick up on the previous speaker's metaphor, use their knowledge of the target culture and discourse practices to guess what the speaker is implying, and choose to "run with" the metaphor, extend it, or even close it down. They need moreover to be aware of the implications of the strategy they themselves adopt. They need to recognise where style jumps take place, where speakers and writers stop being metaphoric. They need to recognise where the speaker is extending or elaborating beyond conventional language and why – are they being friendly, humorous, sarcastic, or even addressing a third party? Learners need to recognise where the speaker is avoiding a topic, or refusing to take responsibility (Lerman, 1983). Lastly, they need to recognise when texts or speakers are operating simultaneously on multiple levels (as in many, possibly most, jokes, advertisements, and banter) and to establish what effects and messages are being hinted at on each level. We might also note that the effect of an advertisement may well rely on the reader slowly accessing different meanings in real time and that the sequence may well *not* be from less metaphoric to more metaphoric: much will depend on the contextual clues provided by the accompanying pictures, text, and even graphic layout.

It will be apparent that the above list emphasises receptive skills over productive skills. The reason is simply that all listeners and readers need to cope with "incoming" L2 metaphor, whereas speakers and writers can choose whether and when they use it. What will determine that choice in actual practice remains relatively unresearched, but the list may include existing L1 preferences, as well as the learner's "identity" as a second language user – whether they choose to be the sort of person that uses a lot of L2 metaphor. Although the question of L2 identity has been a topic of discussion for some years in the applied linguistic literature, little or none of the discussion has revolved around metaphor and we currently have little idea whether learners transfer metaphor preferences across languages, or construct preferences anew as they acquire an L2.

The Canale/Swain/Bachman model of communicative competence has been widely used as a basis for designing language tests and this raises the question of how metaphoric competence can best be tested. Specific teaching interventions will require tests of the content or skills involved, like any other achievement test (as in the case of Littlemore 2001). Far more interesting is how metaphoric competence could be tested as part of general L2 proficiency. I noted earlier that forced-choice and even constrained-response tests have been shown to overestimate learning in key areas of language (Norris & Ortega, 2000; Truscott, 1998), so we might assume that metaphoric competence is best tested by some form of free-response direct communicative test. There have been to date very few attempts to generate an overall measure of L2 metaphoric competence. One recent exception is Azuma (2003), who paired a test of interpreting metaphors in running text with a test which required learners to use specific target metaphors in a free writing exercise. However, even here, no attempt was made to distinguish or assess the sort of discourse control skills mentioned earlier and the primary interest was examining how the test related to vocabulary knowledge.

Accurately measuring metaphoric competence, especially productively, is not going to be easy, largely because the use of active/deliberate metaphor is usually optional, and almost every discourse task can be achieved perfectly adequately without it. On the other hand, we are now beginning to obtain reliable estimates of the average frequency of metaphor in native-speaker texts of various types (e.g. Koller, 2003; Cameron, 2003a; Cameron & Stelma, 2004), so these could perhaps be used in future to give rough estimates of over and underuse. Such estimates would however need to be judged against baseline L1 data of individual preferences. However, not only is it rare for language proficiency tests of any sort to modify their scores with reference to desired L2 identity, but we are, as I noted above, some way away from linking individual metaphor-use preferences and L2 metaphor use, so there is little in the way of precedent in the research literature.

In short, we still do not know exactly how we would expect L2 learners to differ in terms of metaphoric competence. We do, however, know that cultural background plays an important part in metaphor interpretation. Littlemore (2001) found that a group of Bangladeshi civil servants misread the evaluative content of a UK lecture on government, because they expected that "speakers in authority would not criticise their own government". She also noted (2003) that students from a culture that is less tolerant of uncertainty found it difficult to grasp a lecturer's contention that "freeing up the economy" is a good idea. It has been repeatedly found that learners interpret the L2 through the "lens" of their L1 (e.g. Kellerman, 1986, 2001;

Sakuragi & Fuller, 2003), but if this is the case, it is hard to see how one single proficiency test battery could realistically be used as a universal measure of metaphoric competence.

## If an Expression *Involves* Metaphor, Do We Teach It *as* Metaphor?

Thus far, I have noted that identifying a metaphor may not be simple or straightforward, but in general, when something has been identified as metaphoric, the assumption has been made that it should be treated as such by the teacher and the learner. It is, however, important to recognise that this is no more than an assumption and its validity is worth exploring.

Vocabulary would appear to be the area most conducive to teaching items *as* metaphor in the language classroom, but even in this context, the need for a complex metalanguage rapidly arises. The teacher needs, for example, to have some way of explaining that another item or sense is somehow "less metaphoric", or "not metaphoric at all", or even "metonymic". Metaphors are also frequently iterative, in the sense that they will use an earlier metaphor as input (i.e. as Source), so it is not enough to explain metaphor as a simple link between a literal and a figurative sense. Thus, if "in the running for president" is explained as a transfer from horse racing (Deignan, 2003), "in the running" is still not transparent, largely because it is already metaphoric (*and* metonymic) in the racing context. It is also hard in many cases to talk cross-culturally about metaphor without reference to metonymy. There are numerous examples in the literature (e.g. Yu, 2003, on differences between English and Chinese), but Charteris-Black (2003) makes the point particularly starkly in his study of figurative uses of English and Malay oral body parts where he sees the key difference between his two data sets as the "tendency in English to metonymy and hyperbole and in Malay to metaphor and euphemism" (p. 306). The question thus arises of how much metalanguage to introduce and whether all learners can cope with it.

There is some indirect evidence on the question of age. It is commonly accepted that young children demonstrate a preference for thinking metonymically before they think metaphorically (e.g. Winner, 1988) and this has recently been found to be the case for young L2 learners (Piquer, 2003, 2004), so figurative metalanguage would not seem generally usable below the age of around eight years. Even with adults, it is no easy task to arrive at a meaningful understanding of terms like "literal" with language learners who are not budding linguists. I have seen no published language teaching (or indeed science teaching, it should be added) materials that even begin to approach this topic. I conclude that it may well be desirable to avoid metalanguage unless it is clear that the learners can cope with it.

There are in fact numerous points where one has to wonder whether it is preferable to teach items "literally", as simply as "having a certain meaning". It has been argued, for example, that the "quotative" use of "like" in "I was like 'it's great'" developed with a metaphorical component (Buchstaller, 2001a, 2001b) and it could certainly be taught using a Boers-type set of sentences involving a cline of metaphoricity, starting from the "literal" comparison "A chair is like a sofa". However, the metaphoric component in quotative "like" is not transparent, the word would not be identified as metaphoric, or potentially metaphoric, using, say the Pragglejaz criteria (see Steen, 2005), and it is easy to teach it without any reference to metaphor.[4] Similar arguments may be made for teaching delexical verbs; little would seem to be gained pedagogically by hunting for metaphoric support for saying, "make an error" and "do an exam" rather than "do an error" and "make an exam".

A rather different situation is represented by the common use of the term "literally" to mean "metaphorically" (as in "She literally hit the roof when I told her"). The word is probably more obviously "metaphoric" than "like", but this time the metaphoricity is highly complex, involving an interaction between several different underlying metaphors and nonmetaphoric propositions. While intermediate learners can easily be taught to use the word accurately and effectively in their discourse, any attempt to explain the nature of the metaphoricity is likely to be met with incomprehension and confusion.

Though it is becoming popular to argue that prepositions and particles should be taught by bringing the nature or degree of the metaphoricity to the learners' attention (Boers, 2000; Dirven, 2001; Lindstromberg, 1996), I want to argue for a degree of caution and to suggest that the older, naïver direct method approach might just work more effectively in many cases. Most prepositions show very complex semantic structure, and we frequently do not understand what motivates certain senses (see Dirven, 2001). Teaching all of them cognitively becomes a highly complex and time-consuming task, with no guarantee that the learner will (a) understand the concepts involved, (b) understand the sense of the expression itself, or (c) actually use the expression in real discourse.

One particular area of interest in this connection is the language of classroom or learning management. Huge amounts of the lexis are highly metaphoric (e.g. "go through homework", "go over it", "run though a text", "run over it", "look through it", "look over it", "look at a topic", "skip over something", "skip through it", "pass over it", "home in on it", "touch on it"; "work through it"; "work on it"; "work at it, then rework it"). Classroom/learning management represents one of the few genuinely communicative uses of language in formal teaching situations and therefore large amounts of it need to be learned and used by teachers and learners. To some degree, the semantic similarity of the movement verbs and of the dynamic particles in "run over" and "go through" can be relatively easily explained using visual images of a sheet of paper and an arrow. But the complexity of distinguishing the radical difference between "pass over a topic" and "go over a topic" would appear to be far too much for young learners. Somehow, a distinction needs to be made, but as yet we have no real criteria for making that judgement.

## Should We Teach Basic Meanings First?

One might assume that metaphor would be cognitively easier to learn if the "literal" or "basic" meaning is acquired first, particularly as this is often a familiar human activity or closely connected with the human body. When applied to an instructional context, however, the argument that abstractions and extensions can best be taught by first teaching basic meanings has several practical difficulties, especially where conventional metaphor is involved.

First, the basic sense may well be a much rarer word, possibly representing archaic technology that the learner may never need to use (Low, 1988). Deignan (2003) quotes the example of horse metaphors in English; while literal "horse" occurs in contexts of leisure, metaphors involving horses refer almost totally to transport or heavy work. The rarity situation arises in several ESP contexts (e.g. to *buttress* an argument) but is also evident in general English, with words like "arrow" or "cursor".

Second, the "basic sense first" requirement assumes that we can in fact agree on what exactly is logically more basic. For example, the particle "on" is sometimes explained as having two basic senses (position and movement forward) both of which can be traced back hundreds of years (Lindstromberg, 1998). On the other hand, it is not hard to create a simple derivation of one from the other. What should the teacher do? And does it really matter?

A third difficulty is that the metaphorical expression may need to be used by the learner early on, before the literal sense. "Buttress" (above) is an example of this, but so is much classroom management language ("*skip* that bit"), or greetings ("I'm *called* Fred", "*How's* life", "*How* are you?" "*Cheers*"), or personal descriptions ("I live *in* Bristol", "Tell me *about* your brother"). The basic-first requirement is essentially unrealistic here and runs counter to communicative, or particularly task-based learning, principles.

Fourth, the basic-first requirement assumes a linear, cumulative approach to learning, which is simply not true for language, whether first or second. This is tantamount to saying: Lessons 1 to 5 use present tenses, Lessons 6 and 7 the present progressive, and Lesson 8 regular past tenses. However, we know that learners make heavy use of formulae which they analyse as learning develops and interlanguage restructures (see Wray, 2000, 2002). Thus, as Low and Lau argued strongly as far back as 1983, teaching should create unanalysed reference points or reference expressions, which represent points of known sense and use, to which learners can refer when learning becomes more complex or to which they can step back to when confused and the interlanguage is undergoing reconstruction.

## The Importance of Culture

I would like to return briefly to the notion of culture in language and language teaching. If L2 metaphor genuinely reflects L2 culture, should salient aspects of that culture be taught before the linguistic exponents, so that the words would have a genuine meaning for the learners? There are a number of problems here that researchers have raised but which are rarely considered in the educational literature. For example, if so many animal-related metaphors relate to an agricultural, pre-industrial society, where speakers might actually have some direct experience of animals (e.g. "to hare off", "an old hen", "a sow's ear"), should we initially teach a vision of Jane Austen's England? If anger metaphors show a line of technological development from "letting off steam" to "blowing a fuse" and "blowing a gasket", do we first teach the history of technology? If so many emotion metaphors in English derive from the old medical approach to the humours, do we teach that? If English is full of metaphors of the sea and naval battles, do we teach a politically right-wing vision of England as a besieged island community preserving its individual national identity? There is no clear or universal answer to this question. There is possibly a good reason to teach learners about gardening, as England is full of gardening centres, the airwaves are full of gardening programmes, and the English in general spend much time caring for minute patches of ground. On the other hand, gardening is not terribly motivating to adolescent learners even in England and, more importantly, we need to have some understanding of how contemporary native speakers feel about these metaphors – something which can in part be established, as Stubbs (2001) noted, by exploring the frequencies and collocations of literal uses of "horse", "fuse", or "garden" in contemporary corpora, but which really also needs supporting data from interviews and reaction studies.

Deignan (2003) notes that metaphors involving culture frequently involve generalised, or prototypical cultural situations. Apart from the important teaching implication that many of these can be expressed as images, or image schemata, which could be taught in terms of pictorial reference points (Constable's "Haywain" on every classroom wall?), it raises the key question of how far using a metaphor becomes a statement of "buying in" to a culture and/or belief in the patterns underlying the lexis. This was noted as a serious point where teachers are accused of being professionally incompetent if the fact of their using, say, the conduit metaphor is held to reflect a belief that this is how communication works. People use conventional expressions because they exist and are used, not because they believe them. Only when pressure is exerted to use, for example, "chair" or "chairperson" do people stop and think about possible implications of (here) "chairman". Language teachers somehow need to find a balance between teaching learners to have gut reactions about metaphor and teaching highly inaccurate models of second language culture. They also need to take on board the question of variation and limitation on productive use of prototypes; does *everyone* say, "It's not my cup of tea"? Do coffee drinkers? Younger speakers? Working class speakers? Speakers from minority communities? and when they do use it, is it used "seriously", or tongue in cheek and humorously? Moreover, can it be abbreviated? Most proverbs can, but I have seen no example of "not my cup". These considerations are central to the interpretation of a metaphor in context and to the learner's selection of a voice or persona – the L2 person that they elect to become.

## Conclusion

Metaphor has been used from time immemorial to facilitate education, and research has begun to indicate why it has proved so enduringly successful. While endorsing its usefulness in expanding the mind, developing critical thinking, encouraging problem finding, and in aiding categorisation and memorisation, I have tried in this chapter to suggest that this is a good point to stop for a moment and reflect. I have suggested, in the context of planning and evaluating educational change, that metaphoric modelling needs to be thought out carefully and the role of metonymy in particular resolved. I have also suggested that applications of cognitive theories of metaphor to language teaching should not be indiscriminate and should go hand-in-hand with research into alternative methods of teaching metaphor and more comprehensive thought about the metaphoric skills we want learners to acquire, especially at discourse level. To this end, I have tried to sound a cautionary note about using metalanguage with learners and assuming that metaphor is easily identifiable. I have also argued that testing metaphor skills within the construct of general language proficiency presents very different problems from testing metaphor for specific research projects and remains essentially unknown and unexplored territory. The potential for exciting and dynamic teaching of metaphor is enormous, but there is still a lot of development work to do.

This brings me to the final section: directions for future research and development. The impact of metaphor and analogy in science teaching has been researched for several years, but metaphor remains a relatively new topic for foreign language teaching. Developing the arguments in this chapter slightly, I want to suggest five key research directions for the start of the 21st century:

1. Much of the evidence described in this chapter for success with direct training in cognitive ideas and metalanguage remains purely suggestive, as it has come from studies involving small samples, advanced learners, and a lack of delayed post-tests. Again, while data have been analysed for significance, effect sizes have not been calculated. What is needed now are studies with larger, mixed-level samples, delayed post-tests and where effect sizes are reported.

2. It is as important that these larger-scale studies test the claim that *indirect* instruction increases learning (e.g. Littlemore's, 2004, study of the impact of metaphor training on critical thinking), as it is that they test the claim (e.g. Boers, 2000) that *direct* teaching aids retention.

3. Further research is also needed into a variety of methods and techniques of teaching metaphor: not just total physical response, but the varied application of visual, tactile, and behavioural support (possibly exploring synaesthesia), as well as the use of contextual factors like moreless metaphoric style jumps (as suggested in Low, 1988).

4. The instructional research needs to go hand-in-hand with innovative attempts to develop innovative metaphor teaching materials and to integrate metaphor teaching, at *both* semantic and pragmatic levels, into learning tasks and activities. The materials and lesson plans in Lazar (2003) and (at the time of writing) the OneStop English Internet site are a very valuable start, but they tend to focus on just semantics/lexis and to be stand-alone exercises, rather than integrated into broader instructional programmes.

5. Recent attempts to measure learner command of idiomatic and formulaic sequences (e.g. Schmitt, 2004) could be modified to test certain aspects of metaphoric competence, but innovative research is needed to establish just how metaphoric competence dovetails with general language competence and to find a way of testing proficiency, particularly with regard to the 'productive' skills of reading and writing.

## Acknowledgement

My thanks to Lynne Cameron and Jeannette Littlemore for commenting on the first draft of the chapter.

## Notes

1 Readers interested in a broad canvas can consult Ortony (1999, "Metaphor and Education" section) or Cameron and Low (1999).

2 I include extended A IS B expressions, such as "Lava is like runny butter" (from Cameron 2003a), where a third concept C is added, to denote a constraint or (as here) the Ground.

3 It is of interest to note a degree of circularity here; metaphors are suited to holistic language teaching, but holistic language teaching relies heavily on the use of metaphors. A quick check of the index to Stevick's (1980) classic *Teaching Languages: A Way and Ways* reveals 12 Sources labelled as metaphor (e.g. "ferry", "mask", "pebble", "spark plug"), three labelled as analogies ("evangelism", "music" and "swimming"), and at least nine others classable as metaphor (e.g. "mask change", "soothing syrup").

4 At the time of this writing, the initial paper describing the Pragglejaz guidelines were being constructed. Steen (2005) is simply an explanatory overview.

## References


Aisenman, R. A. (1999). Structure-mapping and the simile-metaphor preference. *Metaphor and Symbol*, 14(1), 45–52.

Asher, J. (2000). *Learning another language through actions: The complete teacher's guidebook* (6th ed.). Los Gatos, CA: Sky Oak Productions.

Azuma, M. (2003, September). *Metaphorical competence in an EFL context.* Paper presented at the 5th International Conference of Researching and Applying Metaphor (RAAM V), Paris. *Program and Abstracts*, p. 54.

Bachman, L. F. (1990). *Fundamental considerations in language testing.* Oxford: Oxford University Press.

Bachman, L. F., & Palmer, A. S. (1996). *Language testing in practice.* Oxford: Oxford University Press.

Bartelt, G. (1997). The ethnography of second language production. *IRAL*, 35,(1), 23–35.

Block, D. (1992). Metaphors we teach and learn by. *Prospect*, 7(3), 42–54.

Block, D. (1999). Who framed SLA research? Problem framing and metaphoric accounts of the SLA research process. In L. Cameron & G. D. Low (Eds.), *Researching and applying metaphor* (pp. 135–148). Cambridge: Cambridge University Press.

Boers, F. (2000). Metaphor awareness and vocabulary retention. *Applied Linguistics*, 21(4), 553–571.

Boers, F., & Demecheleer, M. (1998). A cognitive semantic approach to teaching prepositions. *English Language Teaching Journal*, 52 (3), 197–203.

Boers, F., & Dechemeleer, M. (2001). Measuring the impact of cross-cultural differences on learners' comprehension of imageable idioms. *ELT Journal*, 55, 255–262.

BouJaoude, S., & Tamim, R. (2000, December). Analogies generated by middle-school science students – types and usefulness. *School Science Review*, 82, 57–63.

Bromme, R., & Stahl, E. (1999). Spatial metaphors and writing hypertexts: A study within schools. *European Journal of Psychology of Education*, 14(2), 267–281.

Buchstaller, I. (2001a). An alternative view of like: Its grammaticalisation in conversational American English and beyond. *Edinburgh Working Papers in Applied Linguistics*, 11.

Buchstaller, I. (2001b). He goes and I'm like: The new quotatives revisited. http://www.ling.ed.ac.uk/~pgc/archive/2002/proc02/buchstaller02.pdf.

Cameron, L. (2003a). *Metaphor in educational discourse*. London: Continuum.

Cameron, L. (2003b, September). *Socio-cognitive factors affecting metaphor use in the discourse of reconciliation.* 5th International Conference of Researching and Applying Metaphor (RAAM V), Paris. *Program and Abstracts*, p. 146.

Cameron, L., & Low, G. D. (1999). Metaphor: State of the art survey. *Language Teaching*, 32(2), 77–96.

Cameron, L., & Low, G. D. (2004). Figurative variation in episodes of educational talk and text [Special issue on metaphor variation]. *European Journal of English Studies*, 8(3), 355–377.

Cameron L., & Stelma, J. (2004) Metaphor clusters in discourse. *Journal of Applied Linguistics*, 1:27–36.

Canale, M., & Swain, M. (1980). Theoretical bases of communicative approaches to second language teaching and testing. *Applied Linguistics*, 1, 1–47.

Carter, R., & McCarthy, M. (2004). Talking, creating: Interactional language, creativity and context. *Applied Linguistics*, 25(1), 62–88.

Charteris-Black, J. (2003). Speaking with forked tongue: A comparative study of metaphor and metonymy in English and Malay phraseology. *Metaphor and Symbol*, 18(4), 289–310.

Cortazzi, M., & Jin, L. (1999). Bridges to learning: Metaphors of teaching, learning and language. In L. Cameron & G. D. Low (Eds.), *Researching and applying metaphor* (pp. 149–176). Cambridge: Cambridge University Press.

Corts, D. P., & Meyers, K. (2002). Conceptual clusters in figurative language production. *Journal of Psycholinguistic Research*, 31(4), 391–408.

Csábi, S. (2004). A cognitive linguistic view of polysemy in English and its implications for teaching. In M. Achard & S. Niemeier (Eds.), *Cognitive linguistics, second language acquisition, and foreign language teaching* (pp. 233–256). Berlin: Mouton de Gruyter.

Dagher, Z. (1995). Review of studies on the effectiveness of instructional analogies in science education. *Science Education*, 79, 295–312.

de Guerrero, M. C. M., & Villamil, O. S. (2002). Metaphorical conceptualizations of ESL teaching and learning. *Language Teaching Research*, 6(2), 95–120.

Deignan, A. (2003). Metaphorical expressions and culture: An indirect link. *Metaphor and Symbol*, 18(4), 255–272.

Dirven, R. (2001). English phrasal verbs: Theory and didactic application. In M. Putz, S. Niemeeier, & R. Dirven, (Eds.), *Applied cognitive linguistics: II. Language pedagogy* (pp. 3–27). Berlin: Mouton de Gruyter.

Doughty, C. J., & Long, M. H. (2003). Optimal psycholinguistic environments for distance foreign language learning. *Language Learning and Technology*, 7(3), 50–80.

Douglas, D. (2000). *Assessing English for specific purposes*. Cambridge: Cambridge University Press.

Duit, R. (1991). On the role of analogies and metaphors in learning science. *Science Education*, 75, 649–672.

Fishlov, D. (2003, September). Shall I compare thee? Semantic categories and the interpretation of similes. Paper presented at the 5th International Conference on Researching and Applying Metaphor (RAAM V), Paris. *Program and Abstracts*, p. 76.

Garton, G., Montgomery, M., & Tolson, A. (1991) Ideology, scripts and metaphors in the public sphere of a general election. In P. Scannel (Ed.). *Broadcast talk* (pp. 100–118). London, Newbury Park, New Delhi: Sage.

Gentner, D., & Holyoak, K. (1997). Reasoning and learning by analogy. *American Psychologist*, 52, 32–34.

Gentner, D., & Toupin, C. (1986). Systematicity and surface similarity in the development of analogy. *Cognitive Science*, 10, 277–300.

Glynn, S. (1996). *Effects of instruction to generate analogies on students' recall of science text.* Reading Research Report No. 60. Athens, GA: National Reading Research Center.

Goatly, A. (2002). Conflicting metaphors in the Hong Kong SAR educational reform proposals. *Metaphor and Symbol*, 17 (4), 263–294.

Goswami, U. (1992). *Analogical reasoning in children.* Hillsdale, NJ: Lawrence Erlbaum Associates.

Grady, J. (1998). The conduit metaphor revisited: A reassessment of metaphors for communication. In J. P. Koenig (Ed.), *Conceptual structure, discourse and language* 2 (pp. 205–218). Stanford, CA: CSLI.

Grady, J., & Johnson, C. (2002). Converging evidence for the notions of *subscene and primary scene*. In R. Dirven & R. Pörings (Eds.), *Metaphor and metonymy in comparison and contrast* (pp. 533–554). Berlin: Mouton de Gruyter.

Grant, L., & Bauer, L. (2004). Criteria for redefining idioms: Are we barking up the wrong tree? *Applied Linguistics*, 25(1), 38–61.

Hamp-Lyons, L., & Heasley, B. (1987). *Study writing: A course in written English for academic and professional purposes*. Cambridge: Cambridge University Press.

Harrington, H. L. (1994). Reframing change: Generating new images through multiple lenses. *Teaching and Teacher Education*, 10(3), 355–360.

Harris, R. J., Tebbe, M. R., Leka, G. E., Garcia, R. C., & Erramouspe, R. (1999). Monolingual and bilingual memory for English and Spanish metaphors and similes. *Metaphor and Symbol*, 14(1), 1–16.

Hesse, M. (1966). *Models and analogies in science*. Notre Dame, IN: University of Notre Dame Press.

Holme, R. (2001). Metaphor, language, learning and affect. *Humanising Language Teaching* (online), 3(6), 7 pp. http://www.hltmag.co.uk/

Holyoak, K., & Thagard, P. (1995). *Mental leaps: Analogy in creative thought*. Cambridge, MA: MIT Press.

Kellerman, E. (1986). An eye for an eye: Crosslinguistic constraints on the development of the L2 lexicon. In E. Kellerman & M. Sharwood Smith (Eds.), *Crosslinguistic influence in second language acquisition* (pp. 35–48). New York: Pergamon.

Kellerman, E. (2001). New uses for old language. In J. Ceñoz, B. Hufeisen, & U. Jessner (Eds.), *Cross-linguistic influence in third language acquisition: Psycholinguistic perspectives* (pp. 170–191). Clevedon: Multilingual Matters.

Koller, V. (2003). Metaphor clusters, metaphor chains: Analysing the multifunctionality of metaphor in text. *Metaphorik*, 5, 115–134.

Kövecses, Z. (2003). Language, figurative thought and cross-cultural comparison. *Metaphor and Symbol*, 18(4), 311–320.

Labbo, L. (1996). A semiotic analysis of young children's symbol making in a classroom computer center. *Reading Research Quarterly*, 31(4), 356–385.

Lakoff, G., & Johnson, M. (1980). *Metaphors we live by*. Chicago: Chicago University Press.

Lawson, A. (1993). The importance of analogy: A prelude to the special issue. *Journal of Research in Science Teaching*, 30, 1213–1214.

Lazar, G. (2003). *Meanings and metaphors*. Cambridge: Cambridge University Press.

Lerman, C. L. (1983). *The functions of metaphor in discourse: Masking metaphor in the Nixon conversations*. Paper presented at the 1983 Whim Conference Metaphors Be With You: Humour and Metaphor [Mimeo]. English Department, Arizona State University. (Short version published in D. L. F. Nilsen (Ed.), *Whimsy*, 2, 133–148.)

Li, F.-Y. (2002). *The acquisition of metaphorical expressions, idioms, and proverbs by Chinese learners: A conceptual metaphor and image schema approach*. PhD thesis, Chinese University of Hong Kong.

Lindstromberg, S. (1996). Prepositions: Meaning and method. *ELT Journal*, 50(3), 225–236.

Lindstromberg, S. (1998). *English prepositions explained*. Amsterdam: John Benjamins.

Lindstromberg, S. (2001). (Sometimes) Against the grain: Total physical response for teaching metaphorical language. *Humanising Language Teaching*, 3(5), 5 pp. http://www.hltmag.co.uk/sep01/lind.htm (accessed 28 Dec. 2004).

Lindstromberg, S., & Boers, F. (2005). From movement to metaphor with manner-of-movement verbs. *Applied Linguistics*, 26, 241–261.

Littlemore, J. (2001). Metaphoric competence: A language learning strength of students with a holistic cognitive style? *TESOL Quarterly*, 35(3), 459–491.

Littlemore, J. (2003). The effect of cultural background on metaphor interpretation. *Metaphor and Symbol*, 18(4), 273–288.

Littlemore, J. (2004). Conceptual metaphor as a vehicle for promoting critical thinking skills amongst international students. In L. Sheldon (Ed.), *Directions for the future: Directions in English for academic purposes* (pp. 43–50). Oxford: Peter Lang.

Littlemore, J., & Low, G. (2006). *Figurative thinking and foreign language learning*. New York: Palgrave Macmillan

Low, G. D. (1988). On teaching metaphor. *Applied Linguistics*, 9(2), 125–147.

Low, G. D. (1997). *A celebration of squid sandwiches: Figurative language and the management of (non-core) academic text*. Unpublished project report, University of York.

Low, G. D. (1999). Validating metaphor research projects. In L. Cameron & G. D. Low (Eds.), *Researching and applying metaphor* (pp. 48–65). Cambridge: Cambridge University Press.

Low, G. D. (2003). Validating metaphoric models in applied linguistics. *Metaphor and Symbol*, 18(4), 239–254.

Low, G. D. (2005). Explaining evolution: The use of animacy in an example of semi-formal science writing. *Language and Literature*, 14(2), 129–148.

Low, G. D., & Lau, I. (1983). The discourse-task syllabus: a design option for high surrender value courses for adult beginners. *Language Learning and Communication*, 2(3), 295–308.

Middleton, J. (1991). Student-generated analogies in biology. *The American Biology Teacher*, 53, 42–46.

Niemeier, S. (1997, May). *A didactic view on metaphor and metonymy*. Paper presented at the Second International Conference on Researching and Applying Metaphor (RAAM II), Copenhagen.

Norris, J. M., & Ortega, L. (2000). Effectiveness of L2 instruction: A research synthesis and quantitative meta-analysis. *Language Learning*, 50(3), 417–528.

OneStop English, metaphor lessons. http://www.onestopenglish.com/english_grammar/metaphor.htm (accessed 12 Dec. 2004).

Ortony, A. (Ed.). (1999). *Metaphor and thought* (2nd ed.). Cambridge: Cambridge University Press.

Oxford, R., Tomlinson, S., Barcelos, A., Harrington, C., Lavine, R. Z., Saleh, A., et al. (1998). Clashing metaphors about classroom teachers: Toward a systematic typology for the language teaching field. *System*, 26, 3–50.

Piquer, A. M. (2003, September). *Figurative capacity in young learners of English as a foreign language*. Paper presented at the 36th Annual meeting of BAAL (British Association of Applied Linguistics), University of Leeds.

Piquer, A. M. (2004). Young EFL Learners' Understanding of Some Semantic Extensions of the Lexemes 'Hand', 'Mouth' and 'Head'. (European) PhD thesis, University of Extremadura, Spain.

Pollio, H. R., & Smith, M. K. (1980). Metaphoric competence and complex human problem solving. In R. P. Honeck & R. P. Burns (Eds.), *Cognition and figurative language* (pp. 365–392). Hillsdale, NJ: Lawrence Erlbaum Associates.

Rich, S. (2002). Problems of understanding in cross-cultural learning conversations and a way forward. In C. Lee & W. Littlewood (Eds.), *Culture, communication and language pedagogy* (pp. 65–73). Hong Kong: Hong Kong Baptist University.

Sakuragi, T., & Fuller, J. W. (2003). Body-part metaphors: A cross-cultural survey of the perception of translatability among Americans and Japanese. *Journal of Psycholinguistic Research*, 32(4), 381–395.

Sarason, S. B. (1993). *The case for change: Rethinking the preparation of educators*. San Francisco, CA: Jossey-Bass.

Sayce, R. A. (1953). *Style in French prose*. Oxford: Clarendon Press.

Schmitt, N. (Ed.). (2004). *The acquisition and use of formulaic sequences*. Amsterdam: John Benjamins.

Schön, D. A. (1979/1993). Generative metaphor: A perspective on problem-setting in social policy. In A. Ortony (Ed.), *Metaphor and thought* (pp. 137–163). Cambridge: Cambridge University Press.

Scribner, S. (1988). Literacy in three metaphors. In E. R. Kingten, B. M. Kroll, & M. Rose (Eds.), *Perspectives in literacy* (pp. 71–81). Carbondale, IL: Southern Illinois Press.

Skehan, P. (1998). *A cognitive approach to language learning*. Oxford: Oxford University Press.

Spiro, R. T., Feltovitch, P., Coulson, R., & Anderson, D. (1989). Multiple analogies for complex concepts: antidotes for analogy-induced misconceptions in advanced knowledge acquisition. In S. Vosniadou & A. Ortony (Eds.), *Similarity and analogical reasoning* (pp. 498–531). Cambridge: Cambridge University Press.

Steen, G. (1999). From linguistic to conceptual metaphor in five steps. In R. W. Gibbs & G. Steen (Eds.), *Metaphor in cognitive linguistics* (pp. 55–77). Amsterdam: John Benjamins.

Steen, G. (2005). What counts as a metaphorically used word? The Pragglejaz experience. In S. Coulson & B. Lewandowska (Eds.), *The literal-nonliteral distinction* (pp. 299–324). Berlin: Peter Lang.

Stevick, E. W. (1980). *Teaching languages: A way and ways*. Rowley, MA: Newbury House.

Strässler, J. (1982). *Idioms in English: A pragmatic analysis*. Tübingen: Gunter Narr Verlag.

Stubbs, M. (2001). *Words and phrases: Corpus studies of lexical semantics*. Oxford, UK: Blackwell.

Sutton, C. (1993). Figuring out a scientific understanding. *Journal of Research in Science Teaching*, 30, 1215–1227.

Truscott, J. (1996). The case against grammar correction in L2 writing classes. *Language Learning*, 46, 327–369.

Truscott, J. (1998). Noticing in second language acquisition: A critical review. *SLA Research*, 14, 103–135.

Truscott, J. (2004). The effectiveness of grammar instruction: Analysis of a meta-analysis.

*English Teaching & Learning,* 28(3), 17–29.

Winner, E. (1988). *The point of words: Children's understanding of metaphor.* Cambridge, MA: Harvard University Press.

Wittrock, M., & Alesandrini, K. (1990). Generation of summaries and analogies and analytic and holistic abilities. *American Educational Research Journal,* 27, 489–380.

Wong, E. (1993). Self-generated analogies as a tool for constructing and evaluating explanations of scientific phenomena. *Journal of Research in Science Teaching,* 30, 367–380.

Wray, A. (2000). Formulaic sequences in second language teaching: Principle and practice. *Applied Linguistics,* 21(4), 463–489.

Wray, A. (2002). *Formulaic language and the lexicon.* Cambridge: Cambridge University Press.

Yu, N. (2003). Metaphor, body, and culture: The Chinese understanding of gallbladder and courage. *Metaphor and Symbol,* 18(1), 13–32.

CHAPTER 13

# Metaphor in Literature

*Elena Semino and Gerard Steen*

In this chapter, we survey the main current directions and challenges in the study of metaphor in literature. We begin by discussing different approaches to the relationship between metaphor in literature and metaphor in non-literary language, including both the study of the properties of metaphorical expressions and the study of readers' responses to metaphorical expressions in different (literary and non-literary) genres. We then show how research on the uses and functions of metaphors in literature has drawn attention to the patterning of metaphors within individual texts, the works of individual authors, and the works belonging to particular literary genres. We finish by considering the implications of these different lines of investigation for future work on metaphor in literature and for metaphor studies more generally: we believe that metaphor in literature needs to be studied by combining literary approaches with discourse analytical, corpus-linguistic, and psycholinguistic techniques.

A particularly striking example of metaphor in poetry is the following two lines from Sylvia Plath's poem 'Tulips', written in March 1961. The first-person speaker in the poem is a woman who is a patient in a hospital following an operation. The poem is mostly concerned with her reaction to the arrival of a bunch of tulips at her bedside, which she perceives as an unwelcome and threatening disruption of the peaceful anonymity of the hospital environment. The (bright red) flowers are contrasted with the (white) hospital setting in a range of ways, and via a rich array of metaphors. In particular, the tulips are presented as a reminder of the responsibilities and connections of life outside the hospital, which the poetic speaker had gladly abandoned in order to become an anonymous hospital patient [according to Ted Hughes (Hughes, 1970), the poem was inspired by some tulips Plath received while recovering in hospital after an appendectomy]. In the third of the nine stanzas of the poem, the speaker says that, having now 'lost' herself, she is 'sick of baggage'. The rest of the stanza makes explicit what she means by 'baggage', and ends with the following two lines:

My husband and child smiling out of the
family photo;
Their smiles catch onto my skin, little
smiling hooks. (Plath, 1965: 20)

Although family responsibilities are amongst the aspects of one's life that can be negatively evaluated via the conventional metaphorical expression 'baggage', it is often the case that the enforced loneliness imposed by hospitalisation leads patients to view more positively their relationships in everyday life, as well as any reminders of those relationships (including floral gifts and photographs). Readers familiar with Plath's poetry, however, are unlikely to be surprised by the poetic speaker's attitude, since they will have come across similarly negative, or, minimally, ambivalent representations of the role of wife and mother in other poems (such as 'Morning Song', 'The Applicant', and so on). The second line of our quotation adds a further troubling image, which involves more novel and creative metaphorical expressions than 'lost myself', and 'sick of baggage' in the first part of the stanza. The metaphorical expressions 'catch onto' and 'hooks' construct the conventional smiles of the family photograph as objects that both force an unwelcome physical connection with the poetic speaker and cause her physical pain. The use of these metaphorical expressions potentially triggers a number of contrasts, for example between the (conventionally positive) emotional associations of family photographs and the pain caused by sharp physical objects, and between the visual image of a smile and the concrete physical characteristics of hooks. In the context of the poem, this metaphorical representation is consistent with the emotions and worldview expressed in both the previous and the following stanzas. However, this does not reduce its salience and its potentially disturbing effects.

Most scholars seem to agree that the metaphorical expressions typically found in literature are more creative, novel, original, striking, rich, interesting, complex, difficult, and interpretable than those we are likely to come across in non-literary texts. It is also often claimed that literary writers use metaphor to go beyond and extend our ordinary linguistic and/or conceptual resources, and to provide novel insights and perspectives into human experience. Plath can be said to be doing precisely this in the lines quoted earlier: she uses creative metaphorical expressions to present an unconventional and potentially disturbing perspective on a familiar object (a family photograph) and on a woman's relationship with her husband and offspring. The single major assumption that appears to be shared, implicitly or explicitly, by the vast majority of studies of metaphor in literature is that there is a difference between metaphor in literature and metaphor elsewhere.

Different approaches to metaphor in literature, however, disagree, sometimes quite dramatically, on *how* metaphor in literature differs from metaphor outside literature, or, in other words, on what the relationship is between metaphor in literature and metaphor elsewhere. For the sake of exposition, we will make a broad distinction between approaches that emphasize the *discontinuity* between metaphor in literature and metaphor in non-literary language, and approaches that emphasize the *continuity* between metaphor in literature and metaphor in non-literary language. Our own view is that both approaches are correct, and that precise details about the distribution, function, and effect of metaphor in literature versus outside literature need to be collected and examined by means of corpus-linguistic and psycholinguistic studies.

## The Discontinuity between Metaphor in Literature and Metaphor Outside Literature

An important influence on modern linguistic approaches to literary texts has been the Formalist view of literature (and poetry in particular) as characterised by 'the aesthetically intentional distortion of the linguistic components of the work, in other words the intentional violation of the norms of the standard' (Mukařovský, 1970, p. 42).

Anglo-American Stylistics in particular, has developed sophisticated linguistic accounts of the different ways in which linguistic choices in literary texts can deviate from general linguistic norms and conventions. The use of linguistic deviation, it is argued, foregrounds a particular (stretch of) text, and potentially refreshes (or de-automatizes) the reader's attitudes and worldviews (e.g. Leech, 1969; Nowottny, 1965; Short, 1996). Within this tradition, the use of metaphorical expressions is seen as a particular type of linguistic deviation involving the semantic level of language, since, it is claimed, metaphorical statements are, if taken literally, illogical, absurd, or nonsensical (e.g. Short, 1996, 43).

In the case of our quotation from Plath, the use of the verb 'catch onto' with 'smiles' as subject and the use of the noun 'hooks' with 'smiling' as pre-modifier can be described as violations of normal selection restrictions, resulting in apparently illogical, nonsensical meaning relations (i.e. between the concepts evoked by 'smiling' and 'catching onto skin', and between the concepts evoked by 'smiles' and 'hooks'). This foregrounds the relevant expressions, demands an interpretation on the part of the reader, and may lead to the de-automatization of the reader's view of the relevant aspects of reality (e.g. family relations, the experiences of hospital patients, the role of women in the family, and so on).

Scholars operating within this tradition also suggest that metaphor in literature is different from (and superior to) metaphor outside literature because of the way in which metaphorical expressions interact with one another and with other aspects of the literary text in which they occur. Nowottny (1965: 72ff.) points out that poems are more highly structured in linguistic terms than other text-types, and that metaphorical patterns in particular can contribute to the complex textual organisation that leads to a poem's overall significance and effects (see also Leech, 1985). This is the case for our example as well. Although the 'hooks' metaphor is not extended in 'Tulips' beyond the line we have quoted, it can be related to several other metaphorical expressions in the poem that evoke underwater scenarios. Earlier in stanza 3, for example, the poetic speaker describes her own body as a pebble that the nurses tend to as water gently runs over pebbles; in stanza 4 she describes herself as a sinking cargo boat; in stanza 6 she describes the tulips as 'a dozen red lead sinkers'; in stanza 8 the result of the disruption caused by the tulips is presented as follows: 'Now the air snags and eddies round them the way a river/ Snags and eddies round a sunken rust-red engine'; and in the final stanza the poetic speaker compares the water she drinks with that of the sea. Although each of these metaphors works differently from the others, cumulatively they contribute to the expression of the speaker's helplessness, (partly voluntary) loss of control, and ambivalent perception of her surrounding environment.

Although the studies we have mentioned so far often show a deep awareness of the cognitive functions of metaphor (e.g. Leech, 1969: 158; Nowottny, 1965: 60), they explicitly focus on metaphor as a *linguistic* phenomenon. Tsur's (1987, 1992) cognitive poetics, in contrast, employs cognitive theories in order to account systematically for 'the relationship between the structure of literary texts and their perceived effects' (Tsur, 1992: 1). As far as metaphor is concerned, Tsur aims to explain how the particular characteristics of individual novel metaphors in poetry lead to particular and often unique effects. He claims that metaphorical expressions involve logical contradictions which are resolved by cancelling irrelevant features of the vehicle and transferring the remaining features to the tenor (Tsur, 1987: 79ff.; 1992: 209ff.). For example, the expression 'smiling hooks' used in reference to smiles in a photograph can be said to involve a logical contradiction between the vehicle ('hooks') and the topic ('smiles'/'smiling faces'). Resolving the contradiction involves cancelling irrelevant features of the vehicle (e.g. 'made of metal') and projecting the remaining features onto the tenor (e.g. 'causing a forced and painful connection between entities').

While Leech (1969) and others are concerned with how the use of metaphor is foregrounded with respect to the use of literal language, Tsur (1987) develops an account of why some literary metaphors are perceived as 'unmarked' while others are perceived as 'marked'. More specifically, he makes a distinction between metaphors that tend to be perceived as emotive, elevated, or sublime, and those that tend to be perceived as witty, ironical, or far-fetched. The former, Tsur argues, draws attention onto the concordant, compatible elements of tenor and vehicle (they have an 'integrated focus'); the latter, in contrast, draws attention to the incongruity between the tenor and the vehicle (they have a 'split focus') (Tsur, 1987: 7). Plath's expression 'smiling hooks' comes in the latter category. The choice of 'hooks' as a vehicle for smiles emphasizes the contrast between flesh and metal, love and pain, the shape of a smile and the shape of a hook, and so on. This may account for why this metaphor, although effective, may well be perceived by some readers as disturbing and possibly rather forced.

The approaches to metaphor in literature we have discussed so far do not all belong to the same tradition, but they have a number of important similarities. Even though all recognize that metaphor is not an exclusively literary phenomenon, they emphasize the discontinuity between metaphor in literature and metaphor elsewhere by focusing on highly creative, original, and often complex literary examples. Their aim is to investigate the uses of metaphor in particular texts, genres, or authors, and to explain how particular linguistic choices in particular contexts lead to particular effects. They therefore emphasize the uniqueness of each particular use of metaphor in literature, and offer analyses and interpretations that can often be appreciated for their depth and richness regardless of whether one shares the particular scholar's theoretical assumptions. These studies also provide extensive accounts of the variety of metaphorical structures that can be found in literature, and of their potential effects. When they consider the relationship between literary and non-literary metaphors, the studies discussed in this section tend to attribute primacy to metaphor in literature, and hence to see metaphors outside literature as largely derivative, and therefore less worthy of investigation. Leech (1969) puts it thus:

> *In the dictum 'Language is fossil poetry', Emerson draws our attention to the fact that the expressive power of everyday language largely resides in countless 'dead' metaphors, which have become institutionalized in the multiple meanings of the dictionary. (Leech, 1969: 147)*

## The Continuity between Metaphor in Literature and Metaphor Outside Literature

Since the late 1970s, the 'countless "dead" metaphors' of everyday language that Leech mentions in the previous quotation have played a central role in the development of the cognitive theory of metaphor by Lakoff and his colleagues (Gibbs, 1994; Lakoff & Johnson, 1980, 1999; Lakoff & Turner, 1989). As is well known, cognitive metaphor theorists have shown that ordinary, everyday language is pervaded by patterns of conventional metaphorical expressions (e.g. 'I need a sense of direction', 'I am not getting anywhere in life'), and have proposed that these patterns reflect systematic metaphorical mappings across domains in long-term memory – known as conceptual metaphors (e.g. LIFE IS A JOURNEY). Within this theory, metaphor is a ubiquitous and indispensable linguistic and cognitive tool, which we use systematically to conceive of our more abstract, subjective experiences (e.g. the workings of our minds), in terms of concrete, physical experiences (e.g. manipulating physical objects).

The rise of cognitive metaphor theory has led to a re-evaluation of the role of metaphor in everyday, non-literary language, and to a new perspective on metaphor in literature. In their study of metaphor in poetry, Lakoff and Turner (1989) claim that the metaphorical expressions produced by prestigious poets can often be seen as novel uses of the conventional conceptual metaphors that also underlie much of our everyday metaphorical language. They argue, for example, that Bunyan's line 'As I walked through the wilderness of this world' in *The Pilgrim's Progress* (1965) is a creative realization of the same conventional conceptual metaphor (LIFE IS A JOURNEY) that gives rise to many conventional, everyday ways of talking about living one's life (Lakoff & Turner, 1989: 9–10). More specifically, they identify four main modes of metaphorical creativity in poetry, namely the extension, elaboration, questioning, or combination of conventional conceptual metaphors (Lakoff & Turner, 1989: 67–72). Their main point is that poets challenge and extend the ordinary ways in which we think and express ourselves by using creatively the same metaphorical tools that we all use in everyday language. Contrary to what we noticed in the previous section, therefore, this approach sees metaphor in everyday language as primary, and metaphor in literature as the creative exploitation of ordinary, non-literary metaphors.

In the case of our line from 'Tulips', the metaphorical expressions 'catch onto' and '(smiling) hooks', although quite novel in context, can be related to a conventional tendency to talk about social and emotional relationships between people in terms of physical connections (e.g. in the expressions 'the ties of blood relationships' and 'the mutual bond of friendship'). On the basis of conventional expressions such as these, Kövecses (2000: 94) has proposed that '[a] common way to comprehend relationships is through the source domain of PHYSICAL LINKS or CONNECTIONS'. Against this background, the expressions 'Their smiles catch onto my skin' and 'little smiling hooks' can be seen as creative exploitations of the conceptual metaphor (FAMILY) RELATIONSHIPS ARE PHYSICAL LINKS which, in Lakoff and Turner's (1989) terms, is here creatively elaborated by realizing the notion of 'physical link' via the specific concept of 'hook'. The specific choice of the image of hooks catching onto skin, however, heightens the contrast between the source and target concepts, and introduces the additional elements of compulsion and pain, which are not normally part of the general conceptual metaphor. In addition, the word 'hook' also has a number of conventional metaphorical uses that might be relevant to the genesis and understanding of Plath's specific image. As a verb, 'to hook' is often used to suggest involuntary dependence, as in the expressions 'Some drugs can hook you almost instantly', and 'People hooked on horoscopes' from the *British National Corpus*. As a noun, 'hook' is also used in the idiomatic expression 'off the hook', which indicates freedom from a particular duty, responsibility or unpleasant situation. All of this can help to explain why, although the specific metaphorical expressions are quite striking and novel, most readers are likely to agree that they represent the poetic speaker's perception of the strength and inevitability of her relationship with her family, which she is made newly aware of every time she looks at the photograph.

This kind of approach accounts primarily for the most basic (and often shared) aspects of readers' interpretations of specific literary metaphors. Lakoff and Turner (1989) repeatedly emphasize this, by referring to the relative ease with which apparently complex literary metaphors can be interpreted by readers (Lakoff & Turner, 1989: 35). Indeed, Lakoff and Turner are not primarily concerned with individual examples, texts, or authors in their own right, but with what individual instances of metaphor in literature share with many other metaphorical expressions (both literary and everyday) that can be traced back to the same conceptual metaphors. This contrasts sharply with the concern for the uniqueness of the structure and effects of each individual use of metaphor which is at the centre of the work by Tsur and others (see Swan, 2002; Tsur, 2000). While, on the one hand, this kind of cognitive approach provides profound insights into the relationship between metaphor in literature and metaphor in everyday language, it tends to underestimate the importance of totally novel metaphors, which cannot easily be accounted for in terms of conventional patterns and conceptual metaphors. This applies, for example, to the third stanza of Plath's poem 'Morning Song', where an extended metaphor is used to present motherhood in terms of the relationship between a cloud, the rain, and the wind (see Semino, 1997: 181–182, 220):

> I'm no more your mother
> Than the cloud that distils a mirror to reflect its own slow
> Effacement at the wind's hand.

It is important that cognitive metaphor theorists take proper account of cases such as this, where metaphorical creativity goes well beyond the metaphorical resources of everyday language (and thought).

Like cognitive metaphor theory, relevance theory (Sperber & Wilson, 1986, 1995) also emphasizes the continuity between metaphor in literature and metaphor in everyday language, as well as between literal and metaphorical language. As Pilkington (2000: 89) puts it, 'relevance theory holds that metaphorical utterances form a natural part of language use that do not deviate from any norm.' Within this theory, metaphorical utterances, like literal utterances, are produced and comprehended according to the principle of relevance, that is by achieving the best possible compromise between processing effort and interpretative effects. However, creative metaphors of the kind typically found in poetry require additional cognitive effort and yield a wide array of weakly communicated implicatures. This, according to relevance theorists, is what constitutes the essence of what they call 'poetic effects' (Pilkington, 2000; Sperber & Wilson, 1986, 1995: 217–223; see also the papers in *Language and Literature*, vol. 5, no. 3, 1996).

From this point of view, Plath's expression 'little smiling hooks', for example, would be interpreted by bringing together the most relevant aspects of our 'encyclopaedic entries' for 'smiling' and for 'hooks'. Because these two specific entries are not normally associated, this would not lead to a small number of 'strong' interpretative effects (as would be the case with many literal expressions as well as conventional metaphorical expressions), but to a large number of 'weak' interpretative effects. While it is problematic, in our view, to claim that expressions such as 'little smiling hooks' *only* give rise to weakly entertained interpretative conclusions, the notion of 'poetic effects' does capture the diffuseness, vagueness, and richness of the interpretations we tend to derive from poetry in particular, and explains all this both in relation to the relevant linguistic expressions themselves and to the readers' willingness to expend greater cognitive effort than usual. Relevance theorists, however, frustratingly tend to focus on individual expressions in isolation and hardly ever produce overall accounts of metaphorical patterns in whole texts (e.g. Sperber & Wilson, 1986: 237ff.; Vicente, 1996).

On the face of it, it is hard to reconcile the approaches to metaphor in literature we have discussed in this section with those we discussed in the previous section. Indeed, the mutual attacks (and partial misrepresentations) of the main proponents of the different approaches do little to promote dialogue and convergence (e.g. Lakoff & Turner, 1989: 110ff.; Tsur, 2000). However, we hope to have shown that, in spite of sometimes profound theoretical differences, each approach can contribute in significant ways to our understanding and appreciation of the workings of metaphor in literature. While it is important to recognize the different structures and potential effects of metaphor in literature and the unique characteristics of each individual example, it is also crucial to appreciate the strength of the connections between creative and conventional uses of metaphor. The short analyses of the quotation from 'Tulips' that we have carried out according to each different approach do not come to totally incompatible conclusions, but partly complement each other by elucidating different aspects of Plath's choice of metaphor.

Lakoff and Turner's approach, for example, explains the most basic, automatic, and widely shared aspects of readers' understanding of Plath's metaphorical expressions. It also explains why she might have chosen 'hooks' as a vehicle for the strength of familial relationships, rather than 'hammers', for example. On the other hand, however, the line is salient and striking precisely because of the uniqueness and originality of the choices Plath made, both within the line itself and in the rest of the poem. While the formalist view of metaphor as linguistic deviation can no longer be sustained, the idea that some metaphorical expressions are more foregrounded than others remains highly relevant, and is not at all incompatible with more recent cognitive approaches. The expressions that are linguistically conventional in the sense of Lakoff and his colleagues are less likely to be foregrounded unless they are put into deliberately metaphorical formulae, such as *A is B* simile, or analogy. Novel linguistic metaphors, by contrast, are likely to be foregrounded precisely because they are unconventional (either in purely linguistic terms or both linguistically and conceptually). In addition, Tsur's various dimensions of markedness for metaphors explain why some novel metaphors may be more foregrounded (or 'marked') than others.

Overall, therefore, we agree with Swan (2002) that the 'disciplinary commitment' of cognitive metaphor theory 'to describe what is regular, invariant, and generalizable across an open-ended sample of instances' does not necessarily have to 'prevent a cognitive approach to metaphor from joining a description of its systematic structure with accounts of particular, situated, acts of meaning' (Swan, 2002: 450–451). In our view, this actually applies to the study of metaphor generally: when investigating authentic uses of metaphor, it is always important to consider both the specificity of individual expressions in context and their relationship with large, conventional patterns in a particular genre, discourse, or language. To illustrate how this is possible, we shall now discuss a number of recent studies on the use and function of metaphor in literature.

## The Uses and Functions of Metaphor in Literature

While metaphor theorists have recently highlighted the presence of general metaphorical patterns within or even across languages, literary scholars tend to focus on the role of specific metaphorical patterns within particular literary genres or texts, or in the works of individual authors. This is an idiographic approach to metaphor which highlights the particular and the specific of a particular metaphorical use or pattern, while making a number of tacit assumptions about what is more general and normal for metaphor in and outside literature, either on the basis of the continuity or the discontinuity position discussed earlier. We shall illustrate these idiographic possibilities for research on metaphor in literature, which are mainly devoted to an explication of how metaphor in literature *can* work. We will then come back to their relation with the more general approaches to metaphor in literature in the last section.

In an influential study, Lodge (1977) attempts to demonstrate that the opposition between metaphor and metonymy (as proposed by Roman Jakobson) can account for the differences between different modes of discourse, genres, literary schools, authors, texts, and parts of texts. While there are many difficulties with Lodge's claims, he undeniably provides insightful observations on differences in the frequencies and uses of metaphor in poetry as opposed to prose, as well as, for example, modernist writing as opposed to realistic and anti-modernist writing.

More recently, a number of studies have considered the uses and functions of metaphor in specific genres. Crisp (1996), for example, argues that the prototypical property of Imagist poetry is the use of metaphorical expressions that realise what Lakoff and Turner (1989) call 'image metaphors', metaphors that involve the mapping of visual images rather than concepts. In the following lines from Hulme's well-known poem 'Autumn', a simile is used to map the visual image of a human face onto that of the moon:

> I walked abroad,
> And saw the ruddy moon lean over a hedge
> Like a red-faced farmer.

Crisp argues that the use of image metaphors such as this results from a rejection of abstract concepts and a commitment to produce poems that are focused on concrete, visually perceptible objects. More specifically, the preference for image metaphors rather than conceptual metaphors reflects the literary agenda of poets such as Ezra Pound and T. E. Hulme, for whom 'metaphor, far from being conceptual, is anti-conceptual, presenting an experience of the uniquely individual inaccessible to general concepts' (Crisp, 1996: 83). Similar studies of the uses of metaphor that are characteristic of particular literary genres have recently been conducted on Japanese haikus (Hiraga, 1999), science fiction and fantasy novels for young adults (Walsh, 2003), and fictional and non-fictional accounts of 'split self' experiences (Emmott, 2002).

Traditionally, literary scholars have been even more concerned with how individual authors use metaphor in their works, and have treated metaphorical patterns as an important part of a writer's style and literary agenda. Lodge (1977), for example, claims that Philip Larkin privileged metonymy over metaphor in his poems as a reaction to the style of poets such as Dylan Thomas – 'a metaphoric writer if ever there was one' (Lodge, 1977: 213). He also describes the development of Virginia Woolf's writing towards experimentation and modernism as a move from a metonymic to a metaphoric style.

More recently, scholars influenced by cognitive metaphor theory have started to regard metaphorical patterns not simply as part of a writer's individual style but also as a reflection of his or her individual worldview. Margaret Freeman (1995, 2000), for example, has argued that Emily Dickinson's poetry is characterised by metaphorical patterns that reflect the dominance of a set of partly idiosyncratic conceptual metaphors, such as LIFE IS A VOYAGE IN SPACE. These metaphors contrast with the culturally dominant conceptual metaphors of the time, and combine to create what Freeman calls Dickinson's 'conceptual universe'. Similar studies have been conducted on W. H. Auden's use of personification (Hamilton, 1996) and Gerald Manley Hopkin's use of metaphors to mediate between the material and the transcendent (Sobolev, 2003).

This focus on individual language use is of course characteristic of literary studies but also raises the more general issue of metaphor's role in individuals' idiolects and personal worldviews. As Kövecses (2002: 193–195; 2005: 106ff.) has pointed out, our everyday experience suggests that different people use metaphor in (partly) different ways, but this 'individual variation' has so far received little attention on the part of metaphor scholars. This is not just a problem in studies of literary metaphor but also holds for studies of the cognitive representation of metaphor in cognitive linguistics and cognitive psychology (Blasko, 1999).

The acme of the idiographic approach concerns the use of metaphor in individual literary texts, from all three main literary genres. Here scholars are primarily concerned with the text's specific effects and achievements, and particularly with the way in which metaphorical choices and patterns contribute to convey particular themes, atmospheres, and worldview(s). There are three competing and well-known analyses of Shakespeare's sonnet 73, for example, which attempt to explain the complex and ambivalent effects of Shakespeare's choice and juxtaposition of metaphors for aging and death (Lakoff & Turner, 1989: 26ff.; Nowottny, 1965: 76ff.; Tsur, 1987: 155ff.). Other notable recent studies of salient metaphorical patterns in individual poems are Deane's (1995) analysis of Yeats' 'The Second Coming' and Crisp's (2003) discussion of Lawrence's 'The Song of a Man Who Has Come Through'. In both cases, the focus is on how creative uses of conventional conceptual metaphors result in particular representations of specific situations and experiences.

Metaphorical patterns have also been shown to be significant to the interpretation of literary narratives. In his discussion of sustained metaphors (or 'megametaphors') in novels, Werth (1994, 1999: 23ff.) identifies the intricate metaphorical patterns used in Forster's *A Passage to India* to express a particular view of the different types of people living in colonial India, including their characteristics, their mutual power relationships, and their relationship with the natural world. In her study of *1984*, Simon-Vandenbergen (1993) argues that Orwell exploits conventional conceptual metaphors to create pervasive metaphorical patterns that contribute to the overall meaning of the novel and particularly to the creation of 'the image of a society which is frightening in its perfect coherence' (Simon-Vandenbergen, 1993: 181). Popova has shown the centrality of metaphorical patterns in Patrick Süskind's *Perfume* (Popova, 2002) and in Henry James's *The Figure in the Carpet* (Popova, 2003). Interestingly, her analysis of metaphors in *The Figure in the Carpet* also aims to account for how different groups of literary critics have arrived at contrasting interpretations of the novel.

The use of metaphor in individual plays has received comparatively less attention, with the notable exception of Shakespeare's works. In a series of influential studies, Donald Freeman has argued that individual plays by Shakespeare are dominated by linguistic realisations of particular sets of conventional conceptual metaphors. According to D. C. Freeman (1995), for example, *Macbeth* is pervaded by metaphorical expressions drawing from the source domains of PATH and CONTAINERS, which are central to the way in which the play's main character and plot are constructed by the writer and comprehended by readers (see also Freeman, 1999, on *Anthony and Cleopatra*). Like other scholars working within cognitive metaphor theory (e.g. Popova, 2002), Freeman presents his analyses as evidence of the validity of the theory and of its power to put literary criticism on a firmer empirical footing (but see Downes, 1993, for a critique of this approach).

Several studies have focused on how metaphorical patterns can contribute to the projection of the worldviews of individual characters in both novels and plays (e.g. Lodge, 1977; Black, 1993). Semino and Swindlehurst (1996), for example, show how the idiosyncratic 'mind style' of the protagonist (and first-person narrator) in Kesey's *One Flew Over the Cuckoo's Nest* is reflected in the consistent and creative use of conventional conceptual metaphors drawing from the source domain of MACHINERY. Similarly, Semino (2002) argues that Clegg's pathological worldview in Fowles's *The Collector* results from his unconventional metaphorical conceptualisation of women (and other aspects of reality) in terms of insects generally and butterflies in particular. In the following extract, for example, Clegg expresses his reaction to observing from a distance Miranda – the woman he has become infatuated with:

> *Seeing her always made me feel like I was catching a rarity, heart-in-mouth, as they say. A Pale Clouded Yellow, for instance. I always thought of her like that, I mean words like elusive and sporadic, and very refined – not like the other ones, even the pretty ones. More for the real connoisseur. (Fowles, 1998: 9)*

In both cases, the character's dominant source domain comes from areas of experience that they are highly familiar with (Bromden is a trained electrician; Clegg is a passionate lepidopterist). However, in the course of the novel, Bromden progressively reduces the level and nature of his dependence on the MACHINERY source domain, and experiences a dramatic life change; Clegg, in contrast, is unable to reconceptualise women in a different way after the first disastrous experience with Miranda, so that, at the end of the novel, he is about to embark on a repetition of the same experience with another woman.

A number of studies on Shakespeare's plays have similarly shown how the contrasts in different characters' worldviews can be related to their reliance on different metaphorical conceptualisations of particular domains of experience. Freeman (1993) argues that the lack of mutual understanding between Lear and Cordelia in *King Lear* is due to the fact that they view love and family ties in terms of incompatible conceptual metaphors. Barcelona (1995) shows how the language of different characters in *Romeo and Juliet* suggests that they hold different metaphorical views of romantic love. In all these studies, the focus is once again on patterns in *individual* metaphor use, and on what they may suggest about individual minds and worldviews. However, here the relevant individuals are fictional characters, and metaphor's role is to contribute to the process of literary characterisation.

Literary studies of metaphor are typically idiographic, in that they focus on the use and function of selected metaphors from specific texts. In some cases, they do not even go beyond the bounds of one text, but we have also illustrated those studies which are concerned with groups of texts, by one author or from one genre. What all of these studies share is their attention to the specific, particular, or situated meanings and potential effects of a selection of metaphorical expressions. In analyzing these metaphors, assumptions are made about more general patterns of metaphor in literature, which act as a background against which the metaphors under analysis are assumed to function and sometimes even stand out. With the accumulation of such idiographic studies, however, and with the clear presence of the two competing traditions of the continuity and discontinuity between literary and non-literary uses of metaphor, it has become increasingly important to address the general relation between metaphor and literature in a direct fashion. This is where we will now turn, in order to suggest some of the future possibilities for the study of metaphor in literature.

## Metaphor in Literature as Text versus Literature as Cognition

As we said at the beginning of this chapter, in spite of their differences, all of the approaches we have discussed so far share the assumption that metaphors in literature are more creative and novel than metaphors outside literature. Although intuitively satisfying, however, this assumption is rather hard to prove empirically. Pilkington (2000: 119–121) attempts to provide an account of aesthetic value in relation to metaphor within the context of relevance theory, but, in general, authors tend to state, rather than demonstrate, the superior creativity they attribute to literary metaphors. This is especially true since more recent work on metaphor in discourse has also emphasized the pervasive creativity of everyday, ordinary language. Most of the examples that Fauconnier and Turner (2002) use to exemplify highly complex and imaginative blends are not taken from literature. And in a corpus-based study of informal conversations, Carter (1999, 2004) has found frequent and systematic uses of original verbal play, including 'metaphor extension', that is the creative exploitation of conventional metaphorical expressions. He concludes:

> *The opposition of literary to non-literary language is an unhelpful one, and the notion of literary language as a yes/no category should be replaced by one which sees literary language as a continuum, a cline of literariness in language use with some uses of language being marked as more literary than others. (Carter, 2004: 69)*

But even this is an approach which may be too simple, since differences between registers do not appear to be mono-dimensional. Large-scale corpus work on register variation has shown that, even at a purely formal level, registers vary on many dimensions (Biber & Conrad, 2001). When semantic and other properties of metaphor in literary versus non-literary discourse are included as well, the overall picture becomes too complex for useful reduction to a single parameter (cf. Steen, 1999; Steen & Gibbs, 2004).

Answering the questions we raised above eventually requires quantitative comparison of metaphor use across different (literary and non-literary) genres. This is an area where very little work has been carried out so far, since literary scholars normally support their claims by means of general argumentation and the analysis of selected extracts (e.g. Lodge's [1977] comparison of different genres and types of writing on the basis of Jakobson's distinction between metonymic and metaphoric modes of writing). A notable exception is Goatly (1997), who has compared the use of metaphor in samples from six different genres (in English). Amongst other things, he has found that modern lyric poetry has a larger percentage of active and extended metaphors than other genres, both literary (e.g. modern novels) and non-literary (e.g. conversation and news reports). This provides some statistical support for Lodge's (1977) claims that literary language is more metaphorical than non-literary language, and that poetry is more metaphorical than prose fiction. However, much more work needs to be done in this area, both in terms of modelling the relevant dimensions of metaphor (Steen, 1999), methodology (e.g. Crisp, Heywood, & Steen, 2002; Heywood, Semino, & Short, 2002; Steen, 2002a, 2002b, 2005) and in terms of the size and variety of the data samples. Some pointers to research attempting to address these issues may be made here.

One problem with Goatly's study of metaphor in literary and non-literary texts is its reliability: he did the identification and analysis of the metaphors by himself, without testing the quality of his performance. This is a typical problem in poetic and linguistic analyses of metaphor, where analysts tend to engage on an individual basis with their object of investigation. One way to improve this aspect of the study of metaphor in literature is to carry out the analysis with more than one researcher, reporting degrees of agreement between independent analyses. For instance, Shen (1995) investigated the directionality of metaphorical mappings for similes in poetry, assuming that poetic mappings might differ from non-literary mappings in that they might also include mappings from abstract to concrete and from non-salient to salient (instead of the other way around, as is the overall tendency for metaphor). He found that, even in poetry, the more 'natural' and 'comprehensible' patterns are more frequent. What is most important about Shen's study in the present context, however, is that the data were examined for agreement between four independent analysts. Kreuz et al. (1996) adopted a similar procedure for a study of the co-occurrence between metaphor and a number of other figures of speech in literature.

An alternative approach to the comparison between metaphor in and outside literature is to make use of informants. This is an approach which is even less customary in literary studies because it leaves the object of study to people who are not literature scholars (but see Schram and Steen, 2001). However, it has been applied with some success in other approaches. Thus, Katz et al. (1988) present norms for 204 literary and 260 non-literary metaphors on 10 psychological dimensions, which are based on judgments by 634 informants regarding, for instance, their degree of ease of comprehension, metaphoricity, imageability, and so on. Their data do not indicate substantial differences between the literary and non-literary samples. Yet, even though these data are reliable, as indicated by the appropriate measure, there are various other methodological problems with the study, which led to further work reported in Steen (1994). His studies did indicate differences between literary and journalistic metaphors on various dimensions for two languages, English and Dutch. In particular, literary metaphors were found to be more difficult, more positively valued, more impolite, and more unbiased than journalistic metaphors (1994: 202).

The methodological problems previously invoked are part of an even more encompassing issue which has frustrated research on metaphor in literature, namely the distinction between doing research on metaphors in texts versus on their interpretation by readers. In literary studies, the distinction between text and interpretation is fraught with theoretical and even ideological problems (e.g. Kreuz and MacNealy, 1996; Schram & Steen, 2001). In linguistic studies of metaphor, the cognitive turn has led to an approach to metaphor and its cognitive import which has confounded use, function, and effect in ways which are unacceptable to psycholinguists and other social scientists (Steen, 1994; Steen & Gibbs, 1999). After all, metaphor in literature may be distinct because of its properties and distribution in literary versus non-literary texts, it may be distinct because of its special treatment by its authors and readers, or it may be distinct because of an interaction between these two parameters. We shall therefore conclude our discussion of challenges to the study of metaphor in literature with some brief comments about this area of research.

If the expectations that metaphors in literary texts are, on average, different than metaphors in other texts can be confirmed by more solid evidence, this leads to how these differences as well as the underlying variation are handled by readers when they process literary texts. When we adopt Gibbs's distinction between metaphor comprehension, recognition, interpretation, and appreciation (e.g. Gibbs, 1994), it is striking that not much work has been done on the first seconds of the comprehension of metaphor in literature. A study of the recognition, interpretation, and appreciation of metaphors, however, is available from Steen (1994; cf. Glicksohn, 1994; Goodblatt & Glicksohn, 2002). It generally showed that readers pay more attention to metaphors in literature than to metaphors in journalism in various ways.

One aspect of this finding concerned readers' consciously experiencing metaphors as a typically literary rather than a journalistic device, as was shown by two studies using an underlining task (Steen, 1994: 50ff.). This may be attributed to the greater attention and value which readers are expected to attach to the language of literature (e.g. Zwaan, 1993). Another aspect of this increased attention to metaphor in literature concerns the number of times readers perform particular cognitive operations in comparison with journalism. Aspects of Gibbs's processes of recognition, interpretation, and appreciation were all analyzed in the data collected by means of a think-aloud task, and the results consistently pointed to a higher incidence of these processes for the literary text than for the journalistic text. This even held across two groups of readers where one group may be designated as expert, while the other may be designated as non-expert. And metaphor difficulty and positive or negative emotive value were shown to influence the average incidence of these processes in various ways, both within and between the domains of literature and journalism.

Attention to metaphor in literature is therefore not just due to the attitude of the reader. It interacts in highly specific and diverging ways with properties of metaphor. The two variables of difficulty and value examined in Steen (1994) indicate the complexities that may be expected when we turn to the full range of 'literary' properties of metaphor traditionally invoked by scholars of metaphor in literature. In recent work, this approach has been extended beyond what is traditionally regarded as literary, to include the linguistic forms, conceptual structures, and communicative functions of metaphor in discourse (Steen, 2004). An underlining task showed that properties relating to each of these dimensions of metaphor can influence the recognition of metaphor, to the effect that, for instance, metaphorically used nouns are recognized more often than metaphorically used verbs, or that metaphorically used words at the beginning or an end of a paragraph are recognized more often than those in the middle.

## Conclusions

As we have shown, the study of metaphor in literature raises an issue that is very familiar to literary scholars: the complexity of the relationship between uses of language that are regarded as 'literary' and uses of language that are regarded as 'non-literary'. Further research is clearly needed into the differences between the use of metaphor in literature and elsewhere, and between responses to metaphor uses in literature and in non-literary genres. Importantly, however, the study of creative uses of metaphor in literature highlights the issue of metaphorical creativity more generally, which is relevant to all metaphor scholars: creative uses of metaphor are not confined to literature but can be found across many contexts and discourses, from informal conversation through political speeches to scientific articles. This leads to questions about the characteristics, triggers, and functions of metaphorical creativity in discourse generally. An analysis of what counts as metaphorical creativity cannot simply be based on a general notion of deviation, but even the four types of creativity proposed in Lakoff and Turner (1989) do not do justice to the variety and complexity of metaphorical phenomena that can be encountered in discourse, both literary and non-literary. In addition, more research is needed into the contexts in which metaphorical creativity is encountered, and into the functions that creative metaphorical expressions may perform (re-conceptualisation, humour, increased intimacy, and so on).

In the course of the chapter, we have also emphasized how the study of metaphorical uses of language, in literature and elsewhere, needs to take into account both the unique characteristics of particular uses in context, and the way in which particular uses relate to general conventional patterns, that may reflect shared cognitive structures and processes. On the other hand, the study of metaphor in literature brings to the fore the importance of studying variation in metaphor use at the level of individual speakers and writers. While cognitive metaphor theory in particular relates conventional metaphorical patterns in a language to shared cultural and cognitive models, many studies of metaphor in literature relate distinctive, idiosyncratic metaphorical patterns in a writer's works, a single text, or parts of a text to an individual's particular cognitive habits, concerns, goals, and worldview. As Kövecses (2002: 193–195; 2005: 106ff.) points out, this is an area where further research is needed, not just in relation to literature but also to real-life discourse. Only then can the special as well as the general qualities of metaphor in literature be described in contrast with the properties of metaphor in other domains of discourse. As we have shown, this needs to take into account general methodological norms of sociolinguistics (as in studies of register variation) and psycholinguistics (as in experimental studies of text processing). This is essential for the further study of metaphor in literature as an individual reading process along lines of investigation which can also do justice to research on metaphor in psychology and the other social sciences.

## References


Barcelona, A. (1995) Metaphorical models of romantic love in *Romeo and Juliet*, *Journal of Pragmatics*, 24, 667–88.

Biber, D., & Conrad, S. (2001). Register variation: A corpus approach. In D. Schiffrin, D. Tannen, & H. E. Hamilton (Eds.), *The handbook of discourse analysis* (pp. 175–196). Oxford: Blackwell.

Black, E. (1993). Metaphor, simile and cognition in Golding's *The Inheritors*. *Language and Literature*, 2, 37–48.

Blasko, D. (1999). Only the tip of the iceberg: Who understands what about metaphor? *Journal of Pragmatics*, 31, 1675–1683.

Bunyan, J. (1965). *Pilgrim's progress*. London: Penguin.

Carter, R. (1999). Common language: corpus, creativity, and cognition. *Language and Literature*, 8(3), 195–216.

Carter, R. (2004). *Language and creativity*. London: Routledge.

Crisp, P. (1996). Imagism's metaphors: A test case. *Language and Literature*, 5, 79–92.

Crisp, P. (2003). Conceptual metaphors and its expressions. In J. Gavins & G. Steen (Eds.), *Cognitive poetics in practice* (pp. 99–114). London: Routledge.

Crisp, P., Heywood, J., & Steen, G. J. (2002). Identification and analysis, classification and quantification. *Language and Literature, 11*(1), 55–69.

Deane, P. D. (1995). Metaphors of centre and periphery in Yeats' *The Second Coming. Journal of Pragmatics, 24*, 627–642.

Downes, W. (1993). Reading the language itself: Some methodological problems in D.C. Freeman's *'According to my bond': King Lear and recognition. Language & Literature, 2*, 121–128.

Emmott, C. (2002). 'Split selves' in fiction and in medical 'life stories': Cognitive linguistic theory and narrative practice. In E. Semino & J. Culpeper (Eds.), *Cognitive stylistics: Language and cognition in text analysis* (pp. 153–181). Amsterdam: John Benjamins.

Fauconnier, G., & Turner, M. (2002). *The way we think: Conceptual blendings and the mind's hidden complexities.* New York: Basic Books.

Fowles, J. (1998). *The collector.* London: Vintage.

Freeman, D. C. (1993). 'According to my bond': *King Lear* and re-cognition. *Language and Literature, 2* (1), 1–18.

Freeman, D. C. (1995). 'Catch[ing] the nearest way': *Macbeth* and cognitive metaphor. *Journal of Pragmatics, 24*, 689–708.

Freeman, D. C. (1999). 'The rack dislimns': Schema and metaphorical pattern in *Anthony and Cleopatra. Poetics Today, 20*(3), 443–460.

Freeman, M. H. (1995). Metaphor making meaning: Emily Dickinson's conceptual universe. *Journal of Pragmatics, 24*(6), 643–666.

Freeman, M. H. (2000). Poetry and the scope of metaphor: toward a cognitive theory of literature. In A. Barcelona (Ed.), *Metaphor and metonymy at the crossroads: A cognitive perspective* (pp. 253–281). Berlin: Mouton de Gruyter.

Gibbs, R. W., Jr. (1994). *The poetics of mind: Figurative thought, language, and understanding.* Cambridge: Cambridge University Press.

Glicksohn, J. (1994). Putting interaction theory to the empirical test: Some promising results. *Pragmatics & Cognition, 2* (2), 223–235.

Goatly, A. 1997. *The language of metaphors.* London: Routledge.

Goodblatt, C., & Glicksohn, J. (2002). Metaphor comprehension as problem solving: An online study of the reading process. *Style, 36*(3), 428–445.

Hamilton, C. (1996). Mapping the mind and the body: On W. H. Auden's personifications. *Style, 36*, 408–427.

Heywood, J., Semino, E., & Short, M. H. (2002). Linguistic metaphor identification in two extracts from novels. *Language and Literature, 11*(1), 35–54.

Hiraga, M. (1999). 'Blending' and an interpretation of haiku: A cognitive approach. *Poetics Today, 20*, 461–482.

Hughes, T. (1970). The chronological order to Sylvia Plath's poems. In C. Newmann (Ed.), *The art of Sylvia Plath: A symposium* (pp. 187–195). London: Faber and Faber.

Katz, A., Paivio, A., Marschark, M., & Clark, J. (1988). Norms for 204 literary and 260 nonliterary metaphors on psychological dimensions. *Metaphor and Symbolic Activity, 3* (4), 191–214.

Kövecses, Z. (2000). *Metaphor and emotion.* Cambridge: Cambridge University Press.

Kövecses, Z. (2002). *Metaphor: A practical introduction.* Oxford: Oxford University Press.

Kövecses, Z. (2005). *Metaphor in culture: Universality and variation.* Cambridge: Cambridge University Press.

Kreuz, R. J., & MacNealy, M. S. (Eds.). (1996). *Empirical approaches to literature and aesthetics.* Norwood, NJ: Ablex.

Kreuz, R. J., Roberts, R. M., Johnson, B. K., & Bertus, E. L. (1996). Figurative language occurrence and co-occurrence in contemporary literature. In R. J. Kreuz & M. S. MacNealy (Eds.), *Empirical approaches to literature and aesthetics* (pp. 83–98). Norwood, NJ: Ablex.

Lakoff, G., & Johnson, M. (1980). *Metaphors we live by.* Chicago: Chicago University Press.

Lakoff, G., & Johnson, M. (1999). *Philosophy in the flesh: The embodied mind and its challenge to western thought.* New York: Basic Books.

Lakoff, G., & Turner, M. (1989). *More than cool reason: A field guide to poetic metaphor.* Chicago: University of Chicago Press.

Leech, G. N. (1969). *A linguistic guide to English poetry.* London: Longman.

Leech, G. N. (1985). Stylistics. In T. van Dijk (Ed.), *Discourse and literature: New approaches to the analysis of literary genres* (pp. 39–57). Amsterdam: John Benjamins.

Lodge, D. (1977). *The modes of modern writing: Metaphor metonymy, and the typology of modern literature.* London: Edward Arnold.

Mukařovský, J. (1970). Standard language and poetic language. In D. C. Freeman (Ed.), *Linguistics and literary style.* New York: Holt, Rinehart and Winston, Inc.

Nowottny, W. (1965). *The language poets use.* London: The Athlone Press.

Pilkington, A. (2000). *Poetic effects: A relevance theory perspective*. Amsterdam: John Benjamins.

Plath, S. (1965). *Ariel*. London: Faber and Faber.

Popova, Y. (2002). The figure in the carpet: Discovery or re-cognition. In E. Semino & J. Culpeper (Eds.), *Cognitive stylistics: Language and cognition in text analysis* (pp. 49–71). Amsterdam: Benjamins.

Popova, Y. (2003). 'The fool sees with his nose': Metaphoric mappings in the sense of smell in Patrick Süskind's *Perfume*. *Language and Literature*, 12(2), 135–152.

Schram, D. H., & Steen, G. J. (Eds.). (2001). *The psychology and sociology of literature: In honor of Elrud Ibsch*. Amsterdam: John Benjamins.

Semino, E. (1997). *Language and world creation in poems and other texts*. London: Longman.

Semino, E. (2002). A cognitive stylistic approach to mind style in narrative fiction. In E. Semino and J. Culpeper (Eds.), *Cognitive stylistics: Language and cognition in text analysis* (pp. 95–122). Amsterdam: John Benjamins.

Semino, E., and Swindlehurst, K. (1996). Metaphor and mind style in Ken Kesey's *One Flew Over the Cuckoo's Nest*. *Style*, 30(1), 143–166.

Shen, Y. (1995). Cognitive constraints on directionality in the semantic structure of poetic vs. non-poetic metaphors. *Poetics*, 23, 255–274.

Short, M. (1996). *Exploring the language of poems, plays and prose*. London: Longman.

Simon-Vandenbergen, A.-M. (1993). Speech, music and de-humanisation in George Orwell's *Nineteen Eighty-Four*: A linguistic study of metaphors. *Language and Literature*, 2, 157–182.

Sobolev, D. (2003). Hopkin's rhetoric: Between the material and the transcendent. *Language and Literature*, 12(2), 99–115.

Sperber, D., & Wilson, D. (1986). *Relevance: Communication and cognition*. Oxford: Blackwell.

Sperber, D., & Wilson, D. (1995). *Relevance: Communication and cognition* (2nd ed.). Oxford: Blackwell.

Steen, G. J. (1994). *Understanding metaphor in literature: An empirical approach*. London: Longman.

Steen, G. J. (1999). Metaphor and discourse: Towards a linguistic checklist for metaphor analysis. In L. Cameron & G. Low (Eds.), *Researching and applying metaphor* (pp. 81–104). Cambridge: Cambridge University Press.

Steen, G. J. (2002a). Metaphor identification: A cognitive approach. *Style*, 36(3), 386–407.

Steen, G. J. (2002b). Towards a procedure for metaphor identification. *Language and Literature*, 11(1), 17–33.

Steen, G. J. (2004). Can discourse properties of metaphor affect metaphor recognition? *Journal of Pragmatics*, 36(7), 1295–1313.

Steen, G. J. (2005). What counts as a metaphorically used word? The Pragglejaz experience. In S. Coulson & B. Lewandowska (Eds.), *The literal-nonliteral distinction* (pp. 299–324) Berlin: Peter Lang.

Steen, G. J., & Gibbs, R. W., Jr. (1999). Introduction. In R. W. Gibbs, Jr., & G. J. Steen (Eds.), *Metaphor in cognitive linguistics* (pp. 1–8). Amsterdam: John Benjamins.

Steen, G. J., & Gibbs, R. W., Jr. (2004). Questions about metaphor in literature. *European Journal of English Studies*, 8(3), 337–354.

Swan, J. (2002). 'Life without parole': metaphor and discursive commitment. *Style*, 36 (3), 446–465.

Tsur, R. (1987). *On metaphoring*. Jerusalem: Israel Science Publishers.

Tsur, R. (1992). *Toward a theory of cognitive poetics*. Amsterdam: Elsevier (North Holland) Science Publishers.

Tsur, R. (2000). Lakoff's roads not taken. *Pragmatics and Cognition*, 7, 339–359.

Vicente, B. (1996). On the semantic and pragmatics interface: coming full circle. *Language and Literature*, 5 (3), 195–208.

Walsh, C. (2003). From 'capping' to intercision: Metaphors/metonyms of mind control in the young adult fiction of John Christopher and Philip Pullman. *Language and Literature*, 12(3), 233–251.

Werth, P. (1994). Extended metaphor: A text world account. *Language and Literature*, 3(2) 79–103.

Werth, P. (1999). *Text worlds: Representing conceptual space in discourse*. London: Longman.

Zwaan, R. A. (1993). *Aspects of literary comprehension: A cognitive approach*. Amsterdam: John Benjamins.

CHAPTER 14

# Metaphor from Body and Culture

*Ning Yu*

## Introduction

In this chapter, I study the thesis that conceptual metaphors emerge from the interaction between body and culture. While the body is a potentially universal source for emerging metaphors, culture functions as a filter that selects aspects of sensorimotor experience and connects them with subjective experiences and judgments for metaphorical mappings. That is, metaphors are grounded in bodily experience but shaped by cultural understanding. Put differently, metaphors are embodied in their cultural environment. To demonstrate how body and culture interact to result in the emergence of metaphors, I focus on the body-part terms for "face" in Chinese and English, which are used through metonymic and metaphoric extension to structure concepts that are more abstract. I will show that the newer version of conceptual metaphor theory, with a decompositional analysis based on the distinction between primary and complex metaphors, can help us gain insights into metaphorical compounds in terms of what components they may have and how these components are combined into more complex structures.

## Primary and Complex Metaphors

Cognitive semantics maintains that our minds are embodied in such a way that our conceptual systems draw largely upon the peculiarities of our bodies and the specifics of our physical and cultural environments (e.g., Gibbs, 1994, 2003; Johnson, 1987, 1999; Lakoff, 1987, 1993; Lakoff & Johnson, 1980, 1999). In *Metaphors We Live By* (1980), Lakoff and Johnson argue that conceptual metaphors, which structure our conceptual systems to a significant extent, are not arbitrary, but grounded in our physical and cultural experience. While they emphasize the importance of "direct physical experience," or embodied experience, as part of the experiential basis of conceptual metaphors, they also point out that such experience (Lakoff & Johnson, 1980, 57):

> *is never merely a matter of having a body of a certain sort; rather,* every *experience*

> *takes place within a vast background of cultural presuppositions. . . . Cultural assumptions, values, and attitudes are not a conceptual overlay which we may or may not place upon experience as we choose. It would be more correct to say that all experience is cultural through and through, that we experience our "world" in such a way that our culture is already present in the very experience itself.*

Empirical studies of conceptual metaphors have revealed that some of them are potentially universal, others widespread, and still others culture-specific (see Kövecses, 2005, for a detailed discussion). While conceptual metaphor theory accounts for such variations in universality and culture-specificity in general terms of interaction between body and culture (e.g., Gibbs, 1999, 2003), which constitutes the experiential basis of conceptual metaphors, the question still remains, however, as to how such experiential basis actually works. In other words, the question is how, exactly, the interplay between body and culture gives rise to conceptual metaphors that are universal, widespread, or culture-specific.

In order to answer that question, the newer version of conceptual metaphor theory puts forth a "decomposition" account based on the distinction between two kinds of conceptual metaphors: *primary metaphors* and *complex metaphors* (see Grady, 1997a, 1997b, 1998; Grady, Taub, & Morgan, 1996; see also Gibbs, Lima, & Francozo, 2004; Kövecses, 2002, 2005; Lakoff & Johnson, 1999, 2003). In short, as argued, primary metaphors derive directly from our experience and very often from our common bodily experience and therefore are more likely to be universal, whereas complex metaphors are combinations of primary metaphors and cultural beliefs and assumptions and, for that reason, tend to be culture-specific.

More specifically, the decompositional approach to the analysis of conceptual metaphors has an important implication, namely the judgment of conceptual metaphors in terms of their universality and cross-cultural variation. Primary metaphors, as primitives that "represent metaphorical conceptualization of the most fundamental sort" (Grady, 1997b, 285–286) and that compose compounds of complex metaphors, are "the metaphors with the most direct motivation, and the least arbitrary structure, and should therefore be the most common cross-linguistically" (Grady, Taub, & Morgan, 1996, 186). As Grady (1997b, 288) further points out, it is expected that primary metaphors "have the widest cross-linguistic distribution. Since they arise directly from experience – and in many cases, from the bodily experience of the world shared by all humans – they are more likely to be universal than the more complex metaphors which are combinations of them."

In their formulation of a newer version of conceptual metaphor theory, Lakoff and Johnson (1999) suggest that the decomposition account, as part of the integrated theory, has shed some new light on the question of which metaphors are universal (or at least widespread) and why. Drawing upon the distinction between primary and complex metaphors, they explain that complex metaphors are "molecular," made up of "atomic" metaphorical parts called primary metaphors (p. 46; see pp. 50–54 for a list of common primary metaphors). Primary metaphors are derived directly from experiential correlations, or "conflations in everyday experience" that "pair subjective experience and judgment with sensorimotor experience" (p. 49). For example, Lakoff and Johnson (1999, 54) suggest that the primary metaphor MORE IS UP "is embodied in three important ways. First, the correlation arises out of our embodied functioning in the world, where we regularly encounter cases in which More correlates with Up. Second, the source domain of the metaphor comes from the body's sensorimotor system. Finally, the correlation is instantiated in the body via neural connections." As they argue, primary metaphors, as conceptual mappings via neural connections,

> *are part of the cognitive unconscious. We acquire them automatically and unconsciously via the normal process of neural learning and may be unaware that we*

*have them. We have no choice in this process. When the embodied experiences in the world are universal, then the corresponding primary metaphors are universally acquired. (Lakoff & Johnson, 56)*

In contrast, complex metaphors, "formed by conceptual blending" (Lakoff & Johnson, 46), are "built out of primary metaphors plus forms of commonplace knowledge: cultural models, folk theories, or simply knowledge or beliefs that are widely accepted in a culture" (p. 60). Thus, they (Lakoff & Johnson, 2003, 257) suggest:

> *Inevitably, many primary metaphors are universal because everybody has basically the same kinds of bodies and brains and lives in basically the same kinds of environments, so far as the features relevant to metaphor are concerned.*
>
> *The complex metaphors that are composed of primary metaphors and that make use of culturally based conceptual frames are another matter. Because they make use of cultural information, they may differ significantly from culture to culture.*

For instance, Lakoff and Johnson (1999, 60–61) suggest that the complex metaphor A PURPOSEFUL LIFE IS A JOURNEY is composed of the following cultural belief (reformulated here as two propositions) and two primary metaphors:

PEOPLE SHOULD HAVE PURPOSES IN LIFE
PEOPLE SHOULD ACT SO AS TO ACHIEVE THEIR PURPOSES
PURPOSES ARE DESTINATIONS
ACTIONS ARE MOTIONS

Whereas the two primary metaphors (PURPOSES ARE DESTINATIONS and ACTIONS ARE MOTIONS), based on common bodily experience, are likely to be universal, the complex metaphor (A PURPOSEFUL LIFE IS A JOURNEY) is less so. This is because its validity in a particular culture depends on this culture's holding the combination of the two propositions (PEOPLE SHOULD HAVE PURPOSES IN LIFE and PEOPLE SHOULD ACT SO AS TO ACHIEVE THEIR PURPOSES) and the two primary metaphors, as listed above.

In what follows, I discuss how the interaction between body and culture contributes to the emergence of metaphors. I will argue that, for conceptual metaphors, body is a source, whereas culture is a filter. That is, while body is a potentially universal source domain from which bodily-based metaphors emerge, culture serves as a filter that only allows certain bodily experiences to pass through so that they can be mapped onto certain target-domain concepts. I will do so by focusing on the face, a part of the body, and outline how figurative expressions involving the body-part terms for "face" in Chinese and English emerge from the interplay between some biological facts about, and cultural understanding of, the face.

## Body as a Source for Emerging Metaphors

It needs to be pointed out that, from cognitive linguistic perspective, "the distinction between metaphor and metonymy is scalar, rather than discrete: they seem to be points on a continuum of mapping processes" (Barcelona, 2000a, 16). Metonymy may be a more fundamental cognitive phenomenon than metaphor, and, in many cases, metaphor may be motivated by metonymy (Barcelona, 2000b, 2002; Panther & Radden, 1999; Radden, 2002, 2003). To put it differently, metonymy very often is the link between bodily experience and metaphor in the mapping process from concrete experience to abstract concepts: bodily experience → metonymy → metaphor → abstract concepts. As Dirven (2002, 11) points out, the cognitive theory of metaphor is "revolutionary" in that it is intimately linked to two major claims: (i) the experientialist, bodily basis of metaphor and metonymy and (ii) the universalist basis for conceptual metaphors and metonymies. Apparently, this experientialist and universalist basis of metaphor is constructed around the core of human body.

**Table 14.1: Senses associated with the body part of face in English and Chinese**

| | English | Chinese | |
|---|---|---|---|
| *Relevant senses associated with the body part of face* | *face* | *lian* | *mian* |
| 1. front of head from forehead to chin | + | + | + |
| 2. a look on the face as expressing emotion, character, etc. | + | + | + |
| 3. front, upper, outer, or most important surface of something | + | + | + |
| 4. outward appearance or aspect; apparent state or condition | + | | + |
| 5. composure; courage; confidence; effrontery | + | + | + |
| 6. dignity; prestige | + | + | + |
| 7. have or turn the face or front towards or in a certain direction | + | | + |
| 8. meet confidently or defiantly; not shrink from; stand fronting | + | | + |

Our body plays a crucial role in our creation of meaning and its understanding, and our embodiment in and with the physical and cultural world sets out the contours of what is meaningful to us and determines the ways of our understanding (Gibbs 1994, 1999, 2003; Gibbs et al., 2004; Johnson 1987, 1999; Lakoff & Johnson, 1999). It follows that human meaning and understanding are to a considerable extent metaphorical, mapping from the concrete to the abstract and linking sensorimotor experience with subjective experience. It also follows that our body, with its experiences and functions, is a potentially universal source domain for metaphorical mappings from bodily experiences onto more abstract and subjective domains. This is because humans, despite their racial or ethnical peculiarities, all have the same basic body structure, and all share many common bodily experiences and functions, which fundamentally define us as being human (see also Yu, 1995, 1998, 2000, 2001, 2003b, 2003c, 2003d, 2004). Sharing this common cognitive foundation of embodiment, different languages should have parallel conceptual metaphors across their boundaries.

For instance, my comparative study of body-part terminology shows that the terms for the face in Chinese and English have developed figurative meanings along similar routes with similar stops, extending from literal through metonymic to metaphoric, as shown in Table 14.1 (Yu, 2001, 25). Such parallel figurative extensions of the senses of *face* in English and its two basic counterparts *lian* 'face' and *mian* 'face' in Chinese, it is suggested, reflect the metonymic and/or metaphoric understanding of the face as "highlight of appearance and look," "indicator of emotion and character," "focus of interaction and relationship," and "locus of dignity and prestige" (Yu, 2001). They are rooted, as is argued, in some biological facts and functions of the face as part of our body: namely, the face is the most distinctive part, on the interactive side, the front, of a person, which as an external body part is most suggestive and expressive of one's internal world (see Yu, 2001, for a detailed discussion).

Since the face is the most distinctive part of a person, we identify or remember people primarily by their faces. Picture IDs show people's faces. One thing that stands out in our memory of people is their face. With such a solid experiential basis, little wonder there is a common metonymy in our conceptual systems: FACE STANDS FOR PERSON. Thus, in both Chinese and English old or new members of a group are referred to as "old or new faces," as in (1).

(1) a. *Kai-xue* *women ban chuxian*
open-school our class appear
*le* *ji-zhang* *xin* *mian-kong*
PRT a few-CL new faces
'As the school opened, a few new faces appeared in our class.'

b. He put some new faces in the Cabinet.

Note that in (1a) the Chinese word *mian-kong* 'face' is a compound derived from *mian*, other such compounds including *lian-mian*, *lian-kong*, *mian-mao*, and *yan-mian*.

As the most distinctive body part that has such features as eyes, brows, nose, and mouth on it, the face is the external part that is the most suggestive or expressive of one's inner world. One's feelings can be all "written on one's face." For instance, we smile when happy and cry when sad. The reactions to emotions and feelings all show on our faces. These common bodily experiences are expressed as a common conceptual metonymy FACE STANDS FOR FEELINGS. Given in (2) are some examples.

(2) a. *Ta bao-zhe renjiade datui*
he hold-PRT others' thigh
*yao zhaogu, yinggai gandao*
ask-for favor should feel
*lian-hong*
face-red
'Holding others' thigh asking for favor, he should feel ashamed (lit. face-red).'

b. *Ta tai lian-ruan, zongshi*
he too face-soft always
*buhaoyisi jujue bieren-de*
find-it-difficult reject others'
*yaoqiu*
demands
'He's too soft-hearted (lit. face-soft), always finding it difficult to reject others' demands.'

c. He argued until he was blue in the face.

d. He'd always wanted to star in action movies but his face just didn't fit.

In (2a), a Chinese example, feeling "face-red" means "feeling ashamed," whereas in (2c), an English example, the color of "blue in the face" is conventionally associated with the feeling of anger. In both examples, one's facial expressions stand for one's feelings, while details of linguistic expressions are furnished by both physiological experiences and cultural beliefs. The examples in (2b) and (2d) are more metaphorical in nature. In both cases, the physical qualities of the face refer to the abstract qualities of the person, namely, personality and character. Hence, the metaphors are PERSONALITY IS FACE and CHARACTER IS FACE. As in (2b), a softhearted person is said to have a "soft face," whereas in (2d) the "face" that does not "fit" a particular type of role actually refers to the lack of "makings of becoming an action movie star."

By metaphorical extension from the metonymies, the "face" can also refer to the outward appearance of something or apparent state and condition of something abstract. The conceptual metaphors OUTWARD APPEARANCE IS FACE and APPARENT STATE IS FACE are extensively manifested in both Chinese and English. For example:

(3) a. *Tamen juexin gaibian*
they are-determined change
*shan-cun mian-mao.*
mountain-village's face
'They are determined to change the face of the mountain village.'

b. *Gaidui yi gai*
this team completely changed
*gong-ruo shou-qiang de*
offense-weak defense-strong MOD
*lao mian-kong, zhu-chang yi si*
old face home-field by four
*bi yi da-sheng ke-dui.*
to one rout visiting-team
'This team completely changed its old face of weak offense and strong defense, routing the visiting team four to one on its home field.'

c. The whole village presented a face of placid contentment.

d. His report put a new face on the matter.

While the "face" can metonymically stand for the physical appearance of a person, it is then metaphorically mapped onto the outward appearance of something, such as a village as in (3a) and (3c). In (3b) and (3d), the "face" is metaphorically mapped onto the apparent state of something abstract. It refers to the "characteristic playing style" of a soccer team in (3b), and to the "state of affair" of a matter in (3d).

Finally, given below are examples that have to do with the metaphorical mappings from the "face" to the feelings of dignity and prestige. It seems that conceptual metaphors DIGNITY IS FACE and PRESTIGE IS FACE exist in both Chinese and English, giving rise to corresponding linguistic expressions in these two languages. Look at the following sentences in Chinese.

(4) a. *Chuyu wunai, ta zhihao*
out-of no-choice he is-forced
*she-lian xiang ren*
sacrifice-face from others
*jie qian.*
borrow money
'With no option left, he was forced to borrow money from others at the sacrifice of his dignity (lit. his face).'

b. *Wo xiang qing ni chi wanfan,*
I want invite you eat dinner
*ni ken-bu-ken shang-lian?*
you willing-or-not grant-face
'I'd like to invite you to dinner. May I have the honor (lit. Are you willing to grant me the face)?'

c. *Wo zhidao wode lian xiao,*
I know my face small
*shuohua ye bu-dingyong.*
say-words still not-useful
'I know I'm just a nobody (lit. have a small face); my words carry no weight.'

d. *Kan zai wode bo-mian shang,*
look at my thin-face on
*yuanliang ta zhe yici.*
forgive him this time
'Looking at my humble face (i.e., for my sake), forgive him this time.'

In (4a) and (4b), "face" (i.e., dignity or prestige) can be "lost" or "gained," and it can be "transferred" from one person to another. The people who can "grant face" to others must have much prestige and command much respect, as in (4b). In (4c) and (4d), the degree of prestige is conceptualized metaphorically as dimensions of face. Little wonder it is argued that one's face, as one's social image, is measurable in terms of how much face one claims from others and how much face people give that person (Ho, 1994). If, as is said, one's face "is a function of perceived social position and prestige within one's social network" (Hwang, 1987, 961), that "position" should be capable of quantification. In (5) listed are similar examples in English.

(5) a. He refused to admit he made a mistake because he didn't want to lose face.
b. Are the ministers involved more interested in saving face than telling the truth?
f. She gained great face with the extraordinary performance.
g. He's a man of considerable face in the local community.

In reality, one's feelings, including feelings of dignity and prestige, tend to show on one's face. In other words, the conceptual metaphors DIGNITY IS FACE and PRESTIGE IS FACE have a metonymic or bodily basis and are linked with the conceptual metonymies FACE STANDS FOR FEELINGS, in general, and FACE FOR DIGNITY and PRESTIGE, in particular. The conceptual metaphors here are based on some kind of experiential correlation. The metaphorical link between the feelings of dignity and prestige on the one hand and the face on the other is not accidental or arbitrary but rooted in some common bodily experience. That is why we are more likely to see, in various cultures, the face rather than, say, hands or feet associated with feelings, even though hands and feet can still represent feelings as part of the body language through gestures.

What I presented above is a case of embodied nature of human meaning and understanding. The kind of body we have and how it functions influence and shape what and how we can mean and understand (see also Yu, 1998, 2000, 2001, 2002, 2003b, 2003c, 2003d, 2004). In both languages, the semantic extensions are structured by metonymy and metaphor, which in turn are grounded in common bodily experiences. Thus, the common bodily experiences account for the parallel meaning extensions between them. Some conventionalized expressions are even closely equivalent across the languages. Listed below are some examples.

| Chinese | English |
|---|---|
| *beng-lian* (stretch-face) | pull a long face |
| *ban-lian* (harden-face) | straighten one's face |
| *lou-mian* (show-face) | show one's face |
| *dang-mian* (to-face) | to one's face |
| *mian-dui-mian* (face-to-face) | face to face |
| *liang-mian* (two-face) | two-faced |
| *diu-lian* (lose-face) | lose face |
| *baoquan-mianzi* (keep intact-face) | save face |
| *you-lian* (have-face) | have the face/cheek |

A question to ask is: If, for instance, the conceptual metaphors DIGNITY IS FACE and PRESTIGE IS FACE are based on certain experiential correlation rooted in some common bodily experience, are they universal? My speculation is that they are not. A potential metaphor is not an actual metaphor. It will become an actual metaphor only after it passes through the filter of the culture.

## Culture as a Filter for Emerging Metaphors

While human body, with its many common bodily experiences, is a potentially universal source for emerging conceptual metaphors structuring abstract concepts, culture, however, functions as a filter that will only allow certain bodily experiences to emerge and map onto certain target concepts (see, e.g., Yu, 2000, 2003a, 2004). This means that many bodily experiences, though commonly shared by all human beings, may not pass the filter of culture for metaphorical mappings. As Lakoff and Johnson (1980, 19) state when commenting on the relationship between physical and cultural experience as experiential bases for orientational or spatialization metaphors:

- Our physical and cultural experience provides many possible bases for spatialization metaphors. Which ones are chosen, and which ones are major, may vary from culture to culture.
- It is hard to distinguish the physical from the cultural basis of a metaphor, since the choice of one physical basis from among many possible ones has to do with cultural coherence.

In arguing for the significance of cultural basis for metaphors, Gibbs (1999, 155) points out that "embodied metaphor arises not from within the body alone, and is then represented in the minds of individuals, but emerges from bodily interactions that are to a large extent defined by the cultural world," and the "bodily experiences that form the source domains for conceptual metaphors are themselves complex social and cultural constructions." Cultural models, "in shaping what people believe, how they act, and how they speak about the world and their own experiences," set up specific perspectives from which "aspects of embodied experience are viewed as particularly salient and meaningful in people's lives" (p. 154). In short, "social and cultural constructions of experience fundamentally shape embodied metaphor" (p. 155). In the past few years, therefore, the important role of culture in the emergence of conceptual metaphors and their specific linguistic realizations has attracted considerable attention from metaphor researchers (e.g., Barcelona, 2001; Barcelona & Soriano, 2004; Boers, 2003; Boers, Demecheleer, & Eyckmans, 2004; Charteris-Black, 2003; Deignan, 2003; Kimmel, 2004; Kövecses, 2001, 2003, 2004, 2005; Littlemore, 2003; Low, 2003; Maalej, 2004; Özcaliskan, 2004; Talebinejad & Dastjerdi, 2005).

In the previous section, I argued that the conceptual metaphors DIGNITY IS FACE and PRESTIGE IS FACE are not arbitrary but grounded in some common bodily experience. Their bodily basis, that is, people's feelings tend to show on their faces, explains why there are such metaphors. However, the bodily basis of metaphors is only part of the total experiential basis. It can account for the motivation of a metaphor but does not license its actual selection. The actual selection of a metaphor depends to an important extent on its cultural basis. In this section, I take a decompositional approach to the analysis of DIGNITY IS FACE and PRESTIGE IS FACE. I will demonstrate that these two, simple as they are, are indeed complex metaphors, constructed out of more complicated combinations of primary and complex metaphors and metonymies, as well as cultural beliefs and assumptions. As Lakoff and Johnson (1999, 46) suggest, "Complex metaphors are formed by conceptual blending."

At this point, I want to stress that DIGNITY IS FACE and PRESTIGE IS FACE are really the shorthand for more complicated metaphorical compounds. As such, they consist of multiple components, with each of them being a condition for their selection or realization. Only in those languages that meet all the conditions, which constitute what I call the "cultural filter," can they exist and be manifested linguistically. That is to say, embodied experience, no matter how universal it is, has to pass through the filter of culture before it can be mapped metaphorically onto abstract concepts.

In what follows, I first take on the analysis of the complex metaphor DIGNITY IS FACE. As we have seen in the previous section, DIGNITY is not understood merely as FACE. Instead, it is FACE AS A PHYSICAL OBJECT. That is, the source concept is formed by conceptual blending based on a complex metaphor. Look at the following:

(6) a. DIGNITY IS A FEELING (a proposition)
  b. A FEELING IS A PHYSICAL OBJECT (a primary metaphor)
  c. FACE STANDS FOR A FEELING (a metonymy)

As indicated in the parentheses next to it, (6a) is a proposition that represents the pre-mapping target-domain concept understood as a kind of "feeling." (6b) is a primary metaphor involving a fundamental metaphorical mapping in our conceptual systems from sensorimotor experience (of manipulating physical objects) to subjective experience (a feeling). (6c) is a metonymy that represents the bodily basis supporting the association and connection of the face with feelings. That is, while dignity is a kind of feeling, a feeling is generally conceptualized metaphorically as a physical object and the face metonymically stands for a feeling. Thus, (6b) and (6c) are combined into one complex metaphor, as in (7b):

(7) a. DIGNITY IS A FEELING (a proposition)
  b. FACE IS A PHYSICAL OBJECT (a complex metaphor)

In (7b), the target concept FACE really stands for A FEELING and the metaphor is about a feeling. For the next step, (7b), a complex metaphor, is embedded into the source-domain slot of (7a) to replace A FEELING, so that we have (8a).

(8) a. DIGNITY IS (FACE IS A PHYSICAL OBJECT)
  b. DIGNITY IS FACE AS A PHYSICAL OBJECT

As (8a) shows, the source-domain concept, placed in the parentheses, is no longer a simple one but a composite one formed by conceptual blending. It is a complex metaphor (FACE IS A PHYSICAL OBJECT) formed by combining (6b) with (6c) and is embedded into the source-domain slot. So combined, the source-domain concept is neither a simple FACE nor just A PHYSICAL OBJECT, but a blend of both, on top of A FEELING. Thus, (8a) is interpreted as the following: While dignity is a feeling (6a), the face metonymically stands for that feeling (6c), which is also understood metaphorically as a physical object (6b). For the purpose of simplicity, we can rewrite (8a) as (8b), to eliminate the parentheses.

At a higher level, (8b) is then combined with another, proposition, DIGNITY IS A

DESIRABLE FEELING, which reflects the cultural belief, and we then have a new complex metaphor as in (9a):

(9) a. DIGNITY IS FACE AS A VALUABLE POSSESSION (a complex metaphor)
  b. DIGNITY IS FACE AS A PHYSICAL OBJECT (a complex metaphor)
  c. DIGNITY IS A DESIRABLE FEELING (a proposition)

Here (9b) and (9c), which are **indented** to the right from (9a), represent the two components of (9a). Since dignity is culturally accepted as a desirable feeling, the face that stands for this feeling now turns from an ordinary physical object into a valuable possession.

In summary, what we call a conceptual metaphor, DIGNITY IS FACE, is really the shorthand for a complex metaphor (9a) combined from metaphorical, metonymic, and propositional components. Taking a decompositional approach to analysis, I list the whole metaphorical compound and its component elements below in (10):

(10) a. DIGNITY IS FACE AS A VALUABLE POSSESSION (a complex metaphor)
  b. DIGNITY IS FACE AS A PHYSICAL OBJECT (a complex metaphor)
    c. DIGNITY IS A FEELING (a proposition)
    d. FACE IS A PHYSICAL OBJECT (a complex metaphor)
      e. A FEELING IS A PHYSICAL OBJECT (a primary metaphor)
      f. FACE STANDS FOR A FEELING (a metonymy)
  g. DIGNITY IS A DESIRABLE FEELING (a proposition)

With its metaphorical, metonymic, and propositional components, (10) should represent an important part of the cultural model for the concept of DIGNITY. As a complex metaphor, (10a) is decomposed into the combination of another complex metaphor (10b) and a proposition (10g) representing the cultural belief. Then, (10b), a complex metaphor itself, is decomposed into two components: (10c) is a proposition presenting the pre-mapping target concept, whereas (10d) is another complex metaphor representing the source concept. Note that the source-domain concept itself is a complex metaphor composed of a primary metaphor (10e) and a metonymy (10f). Thus, the source concept is a blended composite FACE AS A PHYSICAL OBJECT, where the FACE stands for A FEELING, which in turn is understood as A PHYSICAL OBJECT. The metonymy in (10f) serves as the bodily basis for the whole compound.

The final complex metaphor (10a) presupposes the combination of all the components in (10b–g). Any change in the number of components and their combinations will change the outcome of the metaphorical compound. For instance, if the metonymy FACE STANDS FOR A FEELING is not selected in a culture, the final complex metaphor and its combinations would look different as below:

(11) a. DIGNITY IS A VALUABLE POSSESSION (a complex metaphor)
  b. DIGNITY IS A PHYSICAL OBJECT (a primary metaphor)
    c. DIGNITY IS A FEELING (a proposition)
    d. A FEELING IS A PHYSICAL OBJECT (a primary metaphor)
  e. DIGNITY IS A DESIRABLE FEELING (a proposition)

In this culture, then, "dignity" is conceptualized as "a valuable possession," but it has nothing to do with the "face."

To put the decompositional analysis under perspective, I summarize it as the following. The DIGNITY IS FACE metaphor is the shorthand for the complex metaphor DIGNITY IS FACE AS A VALUABLE POSSESSION (10a), which in turn is a compound of metaphorical, metonymic, and propositional components (10b–g) put together through multilevel substitutions and combinations. So constructed, this compound has a complex internal structure with multiple elements. Any change in the number or content of those elements, and in the way they are combined, will result in a different compound. Such compounds are assembled by cultures. Therefore, the sets of components (metaphorical, metonymic, and propositional) and the ways they are combined function as conditions that "shape" the final products of complex metaphors. They constitute what I mean by "cultural filters."

Now I turn to the complex metaphor PRESTIGE IS FACE. As I see it, it shares the similar components and combinations as that for DIGNITY, to an important extent. Thus, (12a–g) below are the same as (10a–g) above, except that the target-domain concept now is PRESTIGE.

(12) a. PRESTIGE IS FACE AS A VALUABLE POSSESSION (a complex metaphor)
- b. PRESTIGE IS FACE AS A PHYSICAL OBJECT (a complex metaphor)
  - c. PRESTIGE IS A FEELING (a proposition)
  - d. FACE IS A PHYSICAL OBJECT (a complex metaphor)
    - e. A FEELING IS A PHYSICAL OBJECT(a primary metaphor)
    - f. FACE STANDS FOR A FEELING (a metonymy)
- g. PRESTIGE IS A DESIRABLE FEELING (a proposition)

The concept of PRESTIGE differs, however, from DIGNITY in that it involves something more, which is expressed by the following additional metaphor in (13a):

(13) a. AMOUNT OF ONE'S PRESTIGE IS SIZE OF ONE'S FACE (a complex metaphor)
- b. PRESTIGE IS FACE AS A PHYSICAL OBJECT (a complex metaphor)
- c. PRESTIGIOUS IS BIG (a primary metaphor)

Again, (13a) is decomposed into two component parts: (13b) and (13c). As a complex metaphor itself, (13b) is the same as (12b), and therefore entails everything in (12c–f), omitted here for simplicity. (13c), PRESTIGIOUS IS BIG, is a primary metaphor, on a par with IMPORTANT IS BIG. What (13a) entails, supported by (13c), is that "having more prestige is having a bigger face" and "having less prestige is having a smaller face." Once again, what I called earlier a conceptual metaphor PRESTIGE IS FACE is only the convenient shorthand for a compound of metaphors (both complex and primary), metonymies, and propositions that combine into a significant part of the cultural model for the concept of PRESTIGE.

The complex metaphors analyzed through decomposition in this section as compounds of metaphors, metonymies, and propositions are constructed by a culture (see also Yu, 2003a). Only those cultures that have selected the same components combined in the same way will have the same complex metaphors as in (10a), (12a), and (13a). Although they contain quite strong embodied components, their embodied grounding only accounts for their motivation, whereas their actual selection and combination in a specific way depend largely on cultural factors. For instance, it is possible to find the primary metaphor A FEELING IS A PHYSICAL OBJECT common, but their specific-level instances DIGNITY IS A PHYSICAL OBJECT and PRESTIGE IS A PHYSICAL OBJECT absent, in a culture. It is possible that such concepts as DIGNITY and PRESTIGE are understood in terms of substances, forces, or locations, rather than objects. If that is the case, the complex metaphors analyzed in this section would not exist in this culture. We can also assume a situation where DIGNITY and PRESTIGE are conceptualized as objects, but not as faces, despite the fact that there exists a robust experiential link between feelings and the face. This is what I mean by saying "culture is the filter for emerging metaphors." Not everything in the source can actually emerge for metaphorical mappings.

## Further Discussion

In the previous two sections, I have outlined the bodily and cultural bases of the metaphors involving the body-part terms for the "face" in Chinese and English. The bodily basis consists of some biological facts and functions of the face as part of our body. The body-part terms referring to the "face" have developed the figurative meanings that they have because of the functions perceived of, and the values attached to, the face as part of our body. More generally, our body serves as a potentially universal source domain for metaphors. On the other hand, the cultural basis of metaphor consists in its interpretative function, thus viewing certain parts of the body or certain aspects of bodily experience as especially salient and meaningful in the understanding of certain abstract concepts. In other words, culture plays a crucial role in linking embodied experiences with subjective experiences for metaphorical mappings. Thus, for instance, in both Chinese and English the face is selected as a source-domain element to participate in the conceptual integration in the bodily based metaphors for DIGNITY and PRESTIGE. The choice of one aspect from a range of possible bodily experiences for a target concept is a matter of cultural preference. That is, cultural models function as a filter that lets certain elements from the source domain to be mapped onto the target domain while keeping others from getting through.

It is worth mentioning in passing that, while I have shown in the previous two sections that both Chinese and English share the conceptual metaphors DIGNITY IS FACE and PRESTIGE IS FACE and some other conceptual metaphors and metonymies, I have ignored here some important differences in other aspects between these two languages (see Kövecses, 2005, for dimensions of cultural variation in conceptual metaphor and its expression). For instance, Chinese and English differ in the extent to which these two conceptual metaphors are linguistically manifested or conventionalized (see Yu, 2001, for a more detailed discussion). Thus, proportionate to the fact that the English word *face* corresponds to several Chinese body-part terms for "face," some English idiomatic expressions have multiple Chinese counterparts used in different contexts with different emphases. For example, the English idiom *lose face* corresponds to several Chinese compound words: *diu-lian* (lose-face), *pao-lian* (toss-face), *qiang-lian* (scrape-face), and *sao-lian* (sweep-face). Here, the last three Chinese examples elaborate on the first one by conflating the semantic component of manner in them. The next example shows a different kind of elaboration. The English idiom *save face* basically means "save one's own dignity or self-respect." Equivalent to this meaning Chinese has *baoquan-mianzi* (keep intact-face), that is, "to save one's own face." Related to this Chinese also has compounds such as *gu-mianzi* (consider-face), *yao-mianzi* (want-face), and *ai-mianzi* (love-face), referring to people who are "keen on saving their face." Furthermore, the elaboration also takes a different direction to "saving other people's face." Therefore, in Chinese there are compounds like *guquan-mianzi* (take care to preserve-face), *jiang-mianzi* (talk-face), *ai-mianzi* (hindered by-face), *liu-mianzi* (preserve-face), *mai-mianzi* (buy-face), *gei-lian* (give-face), and *gei-mianzi* (give-face). These examples show that it is important to save not only one's own face, but also others' face. Face-saving is more reciprocal in Chinese. Apparently, Chinese is richer than English with conventional expressions involving the body part of face. This linguistic evidence seems to be linked with the fact the concept of face, or "social face," is central to the Chinese construal of their social life.

As I have demonstrated in the previous section, the decomposition account based on the distinction between primary and complex metaphors is a useful analytical tool. By decomposing more complex metaphorical compounds into their primitive components, we can gain insights into how such metaphorical compounds have come into being through a process of mapping between, and combining of, their basic components, thus gaining a better sense of their nature of complexity. The decompositonal approach also enables us to make more detailed comparisons between conceptual metaphors in and across languages. For example, as I have shown, in both Chinese and English the metaphorical compounds for DIGNITY and PRESTIGE are similar in some ways but different in others. The similarities and differences between them are displayed by (10), (12), and (13) in section 4, summarized below as three complex metaphors:

(14) a. DIGNITY IS FACE AS A VALUABLE POSSESSION (a complex metaphor)
b. PRESTIGE IS FACE AS A VALUABLE POSSESSION (a complex metaphor)
c. AMOUNT OF ONE'S PRESTIGE IS SIZE OF ONE'S FACE (a complex metaphor)

As shown in (14a) and (14b), both DIGNITY and PRESTIGE are conceptualized metaphorically in terms of a conceptual blending FACE AS A VALUABLE POSSESSION. However, PRESTIGE differs from DIGNITY in that it is also understood in terms of another complex metaphor AMOUNT OF ONE'S PRESTIGE IS SIZE OF ONE'S FACE in (14c). (14c) entails two metaphorical components: (1) PRESTIGE IS FACE AS A PHYSICAL OBJECT (a complex metaphor), and (2) PRESTIGIOUS IS BIG (a primary metaphor).

With the decomposition approach based on the distinction between primary and complex metaphors, we are able to break a metaphorical compound into its components of metaphors (complex and primary), metonymies, and propositions, and distinguish more bodily-based components from more culturally bound ones. For instance, because DIGNITY and PRESTIGE are culturally accepted as positive feelings, they are thus understood in part as "valuable possessions" rather than in more general terms of "physical objects." Also, because PRESTIGE is culturally regarded as a positive feeling, the amount of one's prestige becomes directly related to the dimension of one's "face." Thus, "larger or thicker faces" are better than "smaller or thinner faces," and vice versa. In a different case, however, the opposite could be true. Take as an example "shamelessness," which is also metaphorically understood in part in terms of the "face." Because it is negative, a "thick-face" is derogatory rather than complimentary.

While bodily based elements are more likely to be widespread or even universal, it is not necessarily true that they are universally applicable or activated. It all depends, I believe, on the level of generality at which they exist in the hierarchy of our conceptual systems. For instance, the metaphorical compounds for DIGNITY and PRESTIGE have two bodily based components: FACE STANDS FOR A FEELING (a metonymy) and A FEELING IS A PHYSICAL OBJECT (a primary metaphor). These two derive directly from our experience. Thus, while FACE FOR A FEELING as a conceptual metonymy is probably widespread or even universal, its two specific-level instances, FACE FOR DIGNITY and FACE FOR PRESTIGE, are less likely so. While they are both activated in Chinese and English, they may not be active metonymies in other languages. For a further example, look at the following metaphorical hierarchy:

| | |
|---|---|
| Level 1: | A MENTAL STATE IS A PHYSICAL OBJECT |
| Level 2: | A FEELING IS A PHYSICAL OBJECT |
| Level 3: | DIGNITY IS A PHYSICAL OBJECT<br>PRESTIGE IS A PHYSICAL OBJECT |

These four conceptual metaphors all seem to be primary metaphors, but they stay at three different levels of generality that constitute a hierarchical structure. A MENTAL STATE IS A PHYSICAL OBJECT is a generic metaphor at the higher level (Level 1). It is the object-dual in binary contrast with the location-dual A MENTAL STATE IS A LOCATION. Thus, for example, "love" as a mental state can be either a location (e.g., *to fall in love*) or a physical object (e.g., *to receive love*). An abstract state in general is also conceptualized in dual versions. For instance, we can "bring peace and stability to a country," that is, A STATE IS A PHYSICAL OBJECT, or "push that country toward peace and stability," that is, A STATE IS A LOCATION, and more specifically, A DESTINATION (see Yu,

1998, chapter 5 for relevant analyses of Chinese examples).

At the intermediate level (Level 2), a feeling inherits the properties of a mental state as its subcategory (cf. thought, will, etc.), and is also conceptualized as a physical object. At the lower level (Level 3), dignity and prestige are two kinds of feelings (cf. admiration, respect, jealousy, humiliation, etc.), and are by inheritance physical objects as well. Therefore, dignity and prestige, like discrete entities, can be "lost" or "gained" and can be "transferred" from one person to another.

The four conceptual metaphors at all three levels of hierarchy are likely to vary in terms of universality or culture-specificity although they may all be primary metaphors. At the higher level, A MENTAL STATE IS A PHYSICAL OBJECT, with its high level of abstraction, is likely to be universal (see also Yu, 1998). This is because it sits at the tip of a huge hierarchical pyramid. Linguistic instantiations of any number of possible conceptual metaphors at the levels below it can prove its existence in a language and culture. At the intermediate level, A FEELING IS A PHYSICAL OBJECT has a lower probability of being universal than A MENTAL STATE IS A PHYSICAL OBJECT, because feelings are understood metaphorically as substances, forces, temperatures, locations, and so forth, as well as objects. A culture can choose all of them, or any number of them, as the source domains for feelings. For the same reason, DIGNITY IS A PHYSICAL OBJECT and PRESTIGE IS A PHYSICAL OBJECT at the lower level have an even lower probability of being selected by a culture compared with A FEELING IS A PHYSICAL OBJECT. It seems that there is a direct relationship between the level of generality and the likelihood of universality: as the level of generality goes up, the likelihood of universality increases, and vice versa. Since DIGNITY IS A PHYSICAL OBJECT and PRESTIGE IS A PHYSICAL OBJECT exist at a more specific level, its likelihood of universality is thus much lower than A FEELING IS A PHYSICAL OBJECT, and even lower than A MENTAL STATE IS A PHYSICAL OBJECT.

## Conclusion

In sum, metaphor emerges from the interaction between body and culture. While metaphorical mappings are largely grounded in bodily experience, the choice of one from many possible options in the large pool of bodily experiences depends largely on cultural understanding and interpretation. When cultures have common understanding and make the same interpretation, constrained by common bodily experiences, they are likely to share conceptual metaphors, and vice versa. Also, primary metaphors, derived directly from embodied experience, are more likely to be widespread or even universal, whereas complex metaphors, composed of more basic metaphoric and metonymic mappings and cultural beliefs and assumptions, are more likely to be culture-specific.

A decompositional analysis based on the distinction between primary and complex metaphors, as demonstrated in this study, equips us with a fine and effective analytical tool for metaphor study. This tool enables us to see which elements of a metaphor are bodily based or culturally bound. As I have analyzed in this study, complex metaphors may be conceptual compounds with complex internal structures composed of a series of basic elements (i.e., metaphors, metonymies, and propositions) combined with one another at different levels. Only those cultures that have selected the same number of basic elements and combine them in the same way should have the same conceptual metaphors. In an important sense, the number of elements and the way they are combined, as selected by a culture, serve as conditions that constrain the construction of metaphors in that culture. It is in this sense that common bodily experiences are "filtered" by culture before they can emerge and map metaphorically onto abstract concepts. It is also in this sense that the decomposition account, as demonstrated in this study, has the potential for a "grammar of metaphors," which enables us to describe and analyze metaphors, namely, their component elements and the ways that combine them, in more subtle and systematic terms.

Since so little empirical research has been done in this area, this summary should not be taken as a conclusion but a hypothesis for future study in a new direction.

## Acknowledgment

I am heartily grateful to Ray Gibbs for his insightful comments and suggestions on early versions of this chapter, and solely responsible for deficiencies that remain.

## References

Barcelona, A. (2000a). Introduction: The cognitive theory of metaphor and metonymy. In A. Barcelona (Ed.), *Metaphor and metonymy at the crossroads: A cognitive perspective* (pp. 1–28). Berlin: Mouton de Gruyter.

Barcelona, A. (2000b). On the plausibility of claiming a metonymic motivation for conceptual metaphor. In A. Barcelona (Ed.), *Metaphor and metonymy at the crossroads: A cognitive perspective* (pp. 31–58). Berlin: Mouton de Gruyter.

Barcelona, A. (2001). On the systematic contrastive analysis of conceptual metaphors: Case studies and proposed methodology. In M. Pütz, S. Niemeier, & R. Dirven (Eds.), *Applied cognitive linguistics: II. Language pedagogy* (pp. 117–146). Berlin: Mouton de Gruyter.

Barcelona, A. (2002). On the ubiquity and multiple-level operation of metonymy. In B. Lewandowska-Tomaszczyk & K. Turewicz (Eds.), *Cognitive linguistics today* (pp. 207–224). Frankfurt: Peter Lang.

Barcelona, A., & Soriano, C. (2004). Metaphorical conceptualization in English and Spanish. *European Journal of English Studies, 8*, 295–307.

Boers, F. (2003). Applied linguistics perspectives on cross-cultural variation in conceptual metaphor. *Metaphor and Symbol, 18*, 231–238.

Boers, F., Demecheleer, M., & Eyckmans, J. (2004). Cross-cultural variation as a variable in comprehending and remembering figurative idioms. *European Journal of English Studies, 8*, 375–388.

Charteris-Black, J. (2003). Speaking with forked tongue: A comparative study of metaphor and metonymy in English and Malay phraseology. *Metaphor and Symbol, 18*, 289–310.

Deignan, A. (2003). Metaphorical expressions and culture: An indirect link. *Metaphor and Symbol, 18*, 255–271.

Dirven, R. (2002). Introduction. In R. Dirven & R. Pörings (Eds.), *Metaphor and metonymy in comparison and contrast* (pp. 1–38). Berlin: Mouton de Gruyter.

Gibbs, R. (1994). *The poetics of mind: Figurative thought, language, and understanding.* New York: Cambridge University Press.

Gibbs, R. (1999). Taking metaphor out of our heads and putting it into the cultural world. In R. Gibbs & G. Steen (Eds.), *Metaphor in cognitive linguistics* (pp. 145–166). Amsterdam: John Benjamins.

Gibbs, R. (2003). Embodied experience and linguistic meaning. *Brain and Language, 84*, 1–15.

Gibbs, R., Lima, P., & Francozo, E. (2004). Metaphor is grounded in embodied experience. In G. Steen (Ed.), special issue on "Metaphor." *Journal of Pragmatics, 36*, 1189–1210.

Grady, J. (1997a). Foundation of meaning: Primary metaphors and primary scenes. PhD dissertation, University of California, Berkeley.

Grady, J. (1997b). THEORIES ARE BUILDINGS revisited. *Cognitive Linguistics, 8*, 267–290.

Grady, J. (1998). The conduit metaphor revisited: A reassessment of metaphors for communication. In J. Koenig (Ed.), *Discourse and cognition: Bridging the gap* (pp. 205–218). Stanford, CA: CSLI Publications.

Grady, J., Taub, S., & Morgan, P. (1996). Primitive and compound metaphors. In A. Goldberg (Ed.), *Conceptual structure, discourse and language* (pp. 177–187). Stanford, CA: CSLI Publications.

Ho, D. (1994). Face dynamics: From conceptualization to measurement. In S. Ting-Toomey (Ed.), *The challenge of facework: Cross-cultural and interpersonal issues* (pp. 269–286). Albany: State University of New York Press.

Hwang, K. (1987). Face and favor: The Chinese power game. *American Journal of Sociology, 92*, 944–974.

Johnson, M. (1987). *The body in the mind: The bodily basis of meaning, imagination, and reason.* Chicago: University of Chicago Press.

Johnson, M. (1999). Embodied reason. In G. Weiss & H. Haber (Eds.), *Perspectives on embodiment: The intersections of nature and culture* (pp. 81–102). New York: Routledge.

Kimmel, M. (2004). Metaphor variation in cultural context: Perspectives from anthropology. *European Journal of English Studies, 8*, 275–294.

Kövecses, Z. (2001). Cognitive linguistic view of learning idioms in an FLT context. In M. Pütz, S. Niemeier, & R. Dirven (Eds.), *Applied cognitive linguistics: II. Language pedagogy* (pp. 87–115). Berlin: Mouton de Gruyter.

Kövecses, Z. (2002). *Metaphor: A practical introduction.* Oxford: Oxford University Press.

Kövecses, Z. (2003). Language, figurative thought, and cross-cultural comparison. *Metaphor and Symbol, 18*, 311–320.

Kövecses, Z. (2004). Introduction: Cultural variation in metaphor. *European Journal of English Studies, 8*, 263–274.

Kövecses, Z. (2005). *Metaphor in culture: Universality and variation.* Cambridge: Cambridge University Press.

Lakoff, G. (1987). *Women, fire, and dangerous things: What categories reveal about the mind.* Chicago: University of Chicago Press.

Lakoff, G. (1993). The contemporary theory of metaphor. In A. Ortony (Ed.), *Metaphor and thought* (2nd ed.; pp. 202–251). Cambridge: Cambridge University Press.

Lakoff, G., & Johnson, M. (1980). *Metaphors we live by.* Chicago: University of Chicago Press.

Lakoff, G., & Johnson, M. (1999). *Philosophy in the flesh: The embodied mind and its challenge to western thought.* New York: Basic Books.

Lakoff, G., & Johnson, M. (2003). Afterword. In G. Lakoff & M. Johnson (Ed.), *Metaphors we live by* (pp. 243–276). Chicago: University of Chicago Press.

Littlemore, J. (2003). The effect of cultural background on metaphor interpretation. *Metaphor and Symbol, 18*, 273–288.

Low, G. (2003). Validating metaphoric models in applied linguistics. *Metaphor and Symbol, 18*, 239–354.

Maalej, Z. (2004). Figurative language in anger expressions in Tunisian Arabic: An extended view of embodiment. *Metaphor and Symbol, 19*, 51–75.

Özcaliskan, S. (2004). Time can't fly, but a bird can: Learning to think and talk about time as spatial motion in English and Turkish. *European Journal of English Studies, 8*, 309–336.

Panther, K., & Radden, G. (Eds.). (1999). *Metonymy in language and thought.* Amsterdam: John Benjamins.

Radden, G. (2002). How metonymic are metaphors? In R. Dirven and R. Pörings (Eds.), *Metaphor and metonymy in comparison and contrast* (pp. 407–434). Berlin: Mouton de Gruyter.

Radden, G. (2003). The ubiquity of metonymy. CLEAR 8. Hamburg: Department of British and American Studies, University of Hamburg.

Talebinejad, M., & Dastjerdi, H. (2005). A cross-cultural study of animal metaphors: When owls are not wise! *Metaphor and Symbol, 20*, 133–150.

Yu, N. (1995). Metaphorical expressions of anger and happiness in English and Chinese. *Metaphor and Symbolic Activity, 10*, 59–92.

Yu, N. (1998). *The contemporary theory of metaphor: A perspective from Chinese.* Amsterdam: John Benjamins.

Yu, N. (2000). Figurative uses of *finger* and *palm* in Chinese and English. *Metaphor and Symbol, 15*, 159–175.

Yu, N. (2001). What does our face mean to us? *Pragmatics and Cognition, 9*, 1–36.

Yu, N. (2002). Body and emotion: Body parts in Chinese expression of emotion. In N. Enfield & A. Wierzbicka (Eds.), special issue on "The Body in Description of Emotion: Cross-linguistic Studies." *Pragmatics and Cognition, 10*, 333–358.

Yu, N. (2003a). Metaphor, body, and culture: The Chinese understanding of *gallbladder* and *courage*. *Metaphor and Symbol, 18*, 13–31.

Yu, N. (2003b). Synesthetic metaphor: A cognitive perspective. *Journal of Literary Semantics, 32*, 19–34.

Yu, N. (2003c). The bodily dimension of meaning in Chinese: What do we do and mean with "hands"? In E. Casad & G. Palmer (Eds.), *Cognitive linguistics and non-Indo-European languages* (pp. 330–354). Berlin: Mouton de Gruyter.

Yu, N. (2003d). Chinese metaphors of thinking. In G. Palmer, C. Goddard, & P. Lee (Eds.), special issue on "Talking about Thinking across Languages." *Cognitive Linguistics, 14*, 141–165.

Yu, N. (2004). The eyes for sight and mind. *Journal of Pragmatics, 36*, 663–686.

CHAPTER 15

# Metaphor, Semantics, and Context

*Josef Stern*

## 1. Why Not a Semantics for Metaphor?

Any speech act we perform using language literally we can also perform with language used, or interpreted, metaphorically. Sometimes we make metaphors simply for their poetic power, their beauty, or their aesthetic pleasure. But we also employ metaphors, just like the literal, to elucidate abstract scientific and mathematical concepts and in folk explanations of human actions. And in everyday discourse interspersed with metaphors, we make assertions, ask questions, and issue commands and requests – just as we do with literal language. Suppose Romeo actually announced, as he does in the context depicted in Shakespeare's play, that

(1) *Juliet is the sun.*

Although he is surely making us attend to a likeness between Juliet and the sun (Davidson, 1984), and possibly inviting us to view her in a certain light (Loewenberg, 1975; Moran, 1989), Romeo is also saying something true or false of Juliet, and this something he is saying – for example, that Juliet is greater than her peers, the center of his life, and the object of his adoration – is not what would be said by (1) literally, namely, that she is a body of gases in the sky. But *what* he is saying metaphorically is *said* no differently than the literal contents of other utterances. One can either understand the content of his metaphor or fail to grasp it – just as we can succeed or fail to get a literal content (Bergmann, 1982; Hills, 1997; Moran, 1989; Stern, 2000). Parties can disagree over a metaphor, either over what it says or, when they agree on its content, over its correctness. And once we understand the metaphor, we can also judge it to be successful, appropriate, forceful, or apt. This last judgment call may depend on many criteria, including noncognitive images and affects conveyed by the metaphor. But it will also depend on our grasp of when, or under what conditions, it would be true. Not that we always find its actual truth-value what is most interesting or most valuable about the metaphor. But to grasp declarative metaphors, we must know the circumstances that would render them true, circumstances that are not generally the same ones that would render the sentence, interpreted literally, true. In short, metaphorical uses, or interpretations, of sentences, no less than literal utterances, have truth-conditions, and those truth-conditions are different from those they would have were they interpreted literally. If truth-conditions are either identical with or determined by meanings, then one sentence first used literally and then metaphorically must also have different meanings.

All this talk of meaning, truth, and propositional content suggests that metaphor ought to fall within the scope of semantics or a theory of meaning. Nonetheless, philosophers, linguists, and cognitive scientists have typically been resistant to semantic treatments of metaphor. The grounds for resistance have varied over time, and they have also changed as conceptions of semantics have changed. In this chapter, I shall concentrate on two contemporary sources of skepticism. The first is based on the distinction between what words literally mean and what they can be used to say. The first is the domain of semantics, the second of pragmatics, and metaphor, it is argued, falls under the second. Here is one argument for this claim. If a metaphorical interpretation of an expression Ø were a kind of meaning, it would be additional to the literal meaning of Ø, thereby rendering Ø ambiguous. But unlike the multiple meanings of genuinely ambiguous expressions like "bank" and unlike the meaning of an idiom like "red herring" that is independent of those of its constituents "red" and "herring," the metaphorical meaning of an expression is not independent of its literal meaning – in the sense of "independent" according to which a speaker can know one without knowing the other.[1] A speaker cannot understand what is metaphorically said when Romeo utters (1) without knowing the literal meaning of "the sun" (and without a variety of beliefs about its literal referent). This dependence is not just a contingent diachronic relation about how the metaphorical historically originated from the literal. It is a constitutive claim about the way in which our understanding of a metaphorical interpretation involves our knowledge of its literal meaning. Even while used or interpreted metaphorically, the literal meaning of Ø is active (Davidson, 1984). But if what Ø metaphorically expresses depends on Ø meaning what it does literally, then what Ø metaphorically expresses cannot be something it means, a metaphorical meaning. Rather it must be a function of how the speaker *uses* Ø to say something with but beyond its literal meaning. Hence, metaphor is a matter of pragmatics rather than semantics.

A second source for skepticism about the semantic status of metaphor stems from its "context-dependence." Theorists intend either or both of two things by this slogan. First, unlike literal meaning which is individuated by linguistic type, (many) metaphorical interpretations of utterances of the same expression (type) vary widely from one occasion, or context, to another. Second, metaphorical interpretations are a function of all sorts of extra-linguistic presuppositions and skills such as the perception of similarities and salient features. For both reasons, it is concluded that metaphor does not fall under the kind of language-specific knowledge that constitutes semantic competence.

In response to these skeptical challenges, I shall argue that a semantic theory of metaphor can and indeed must take into account both its context-dependence and how metaphor depends on the literal. The crux of my explanation is to model the metaphorical interpretation, or use, of language on the demonstrative interpretation, or use, of language (Kaplan, 1989), that is, to treat metaphors, demonstratives, and indexicals (for all their differences) as one semantic kind (Stern, 2000). To show this, I argue first that metaphorical interpretations systematically depend on structured sets of contextual presuppositions, individuated by their literal vehicles.[2] Second, we need meanings for metaphors (in addition to their truth-conditional or propositional interpretations) in order to constrain the extra-linguistic contributions of the context, that is, to constrain the possible metaphorical contents we can express with given expressions. These metaphorical meanings will turn out to have the same semantic properties as the meanings of indexicals and demonstratives (or of a hybrid of them). I begin (section 2) with a brief prehistory of semantic accounts of metaphor, both to illustrate how different conceptions of the enterprise of semantics have yielded different semantic theories of metaphor and to motivate our turn to context. In section 3, I elaborate the conception of semantics that guides my own theory. In sections 4 and 5, I sketch a semantic theory of metaphor by elaborating the different roles of the context in metaphorical interpretation and its notion of literal-dependent metaphorical meaning. In the final section, I illustrate one kind of cognitive work performed by our notion of metaphorical meaning above and beyond its truth-evaluable content.

## 2. The Prehistory of Semantic Theories of Metaphor

Semantic theories of metaphor first came into vogue in the fifties and sixties in reaction to rhetoricians who demoted metaphor to mere stylistic decoration, to logical positivists who dismissed it as meaningless emotive venting, and to romanticist critics who celebrated its poetic power to create and express the nondiscursive. Analytic philosophers like Max Black (1962), Monroe Beardsley (1962, 1978), and Paul Henle (1958) sought to rehabilitate metaphor by showing that it is cognitively meaningful no less than the literal. However, in the course of their attempts, these philosophers made metaphor appear even "more" cognitive and "more" meaningful than the literal. Black's "interactionism," Beardsley's "metaphorical twist," and Henle's "iconicism" endowed metaphors with the capacity to express literally unparaphrasable and inexpressible meanings with a power to (ontologically) create novel similarities and features. The net result made metaphor sui generis, effectively insulated from the home domain of the theory of meaning (which continued to concern itself almost exclusively with the literal) and explanatorily occult, less and less distinguishable from the noncognitive and nonpropositional views of metaphor the semantic approach was proposed to counter.

With the emergence of theoretical linguistics in the sixties and seventies, semantic theories of metaphor underwent a renaissance. Two general strategies can be discerned as theorists tried to revive earlier ideas with their new formal resources. The first strategy attempted to explain both the recognition and interpretation of metaphors in terms of the then widely held doctrine that all metaphors are, taken literally, semantically anomalous or grammatically deviant (Beardsley, 1962, 1978; Goodman, 1976; Levin, 1977; Matthews, 1971; cf. now White, 2001). This fault of the sentence – the violation of co-occurrence conditions – was taken to exclude its literal interpretation, from which it was concluded that the utterance is ipso facto identified and interpreted as a metaphor. Either a new metaphorical sense emerges from secondary connotations to which the interpreter shifts when the literal meaning fails; or the metaphorical interpretation is produced as the product of cancellation-, weighting-, and transference-operations performed on components of the lexical entries of the words. On either story, the metaphorical interpretation counts as semantic because it is a function of violations of *semantic* conditions. All a speaker needs to know in order to recognize and interpret a metaphor are the linguistic or semantic rules the sentence breaks.

The fatal flaw of this strategy was its assumption that all, most, or representative metaphors *are* grammatically deviant, semantically anomalous, or even just plain false under their literal interpretation. In the mid-seventies, this dogma was decisively challenged by numerous counterexamples of "twice-true" metaphors (Binkley, 1976; Cohen, 1975, 1976 [who invented the phrase]; Reddy, 1969). Defenders of deviance then made one of two moves. Either they reverted to pragmatic explanations of the unacceptability of the literal interpretation, for example, its uninformativeness or irrelevance in its context, thereby shifting the proper locale for metaphor away from semantics and meaning to pragmatics and use. Or diehard defenders attempted to maintain that, despite appearances, all literal interpretations really are semantically deviant. The problems with this second line of defense are instructive.

For example, against purported counterexamples to the semantic anomaly theory, Eva Kittay (1987) argues that critics fail to correctly identify the literally incongruous unit. In some cases, it is an immediate constituent phrase (e.g., Eliot's "a slum of bloom"), in others the whole sentence, but in yet other cases, it is the utterance-in-its-situational-context. This prima facie pragmatic anomalousness, she in turn argues, is really indicative of an underlying semantic incongruity because all salient elements of a situational context can "be rendered linguistically" (62), thereby "placing the identification of metaphors squarely within the province of semantics" (75). Consider the *sentence* (2)

(2) The rock is becoming brittle with age (Reddy, 1969),

whose subject description is used metaphorically to refer to an aging professor. (2) contains no semantic or linguistic incongruity. But if we imagine it to be uttered in the situational context which we in turn *linguistically* represent by (3)

(3) He responds to his students' questions with none of his former subtlety.

Then in order for (2) and (3) to cohere conversationally the pronoun in (3) must be anaphorically co-referential with "the rock" in (2). But the latter is [-animate] and the verb "responds" in (3) takes only a [+animate] subject; hence, the "conversion sentence" (4) that links the antecedent in (2) with its anaphor in (3):

(4) The rock is he.

And (4) is semantically anomalous. QED

This may be a possible description of an interpreter's reasoning but it does not offer a *semantic* explanation of either the identification or interpretation of the metaphor in (2). Granting the co-reference captured in (4), it remains to be shown that the pronoun is a linguistically controlled anaphor rather than a demonstrative whose referent would be determined in part extra-linguistically. Furthermore, the conversational coherence that drives the anaphoric linking is pragmatic. Hence, there need be no semantic connection between (2) and (3). The fact that (4) involves an incongruity does nothing to explain away (2) as a counterexample to the deviance thesis. In sum, context may be crucial to both the identification and interpretation of a metaphor, but one must be cautious when incorporating it into semantics not to rob it of its explanatory power (Beardsley, 1978; Stern, 1983).

The second semantic strategy that emerged in the fifties and sixties attempted to cash out metaphorical–literal dependence by assigning to each expression a set of component features ("selectional features" or "semantical hypotheses") as its lexical entry, by identifying that set with its literal meaning, and then deriving its metaphorical interpretations by canceling or deleting one or another feature in the set, ipso facto highlighting the remaining ones. Thus, "the metaphorical meanings of a word . . . are all *contained* . . . within its literal meaning . . . reached by removing any restrictions in relation to certain variables" (Cohen, 1993; Cohen & Margalit, 1972, 735). The speaker who knows the literal, or lexical, meaning of an expression as part of his semantic competence ipso facto knows its metaphorical meaning, since the latter is nothing but a proper part of the former that results from feature-cancellation.

The virtue of this strategy was its straightforward explication of how the metaphorical "depends" on the literal in terms of *containment*. But this strength was also its defect. The strategy is plausible when the metaphorical interpretation results from dropping clear size and age variables that belong to the literal, lexical entry of a word, like those in the entry for "baby" in the metaphor "The old man is a baby." But in order to capture the full variegated range of properties that many words can express metaphorically, this approach must broaden the (literal) lexical entries for words to include almost every property "commonly known" about its referents. This descriptive desideratum conflicts, however, with the idea of lexical features as those known to a speaker in virtue of her semantic competence. Even if we grant that common knowledge is part of the "dictionary meaning" of a word – including false but stereotypical features (such as Searle's, 1993, example of the stereotypical features of "gorilla") – many metaphors express properties noticed on and restricted to their occasion of utterance rather than antecedently accepted associations. The only way to capture all such properties in a literal, lexical entry of an expression would be to make *every* property of an individual, including the merely presupposed or newly noticed in context, a lexical feature. The theory that results is hardly semantic.[3]

Again, the moral of this story is that we must take seriously context and, specifically, the contribution of extra-linguistic presuppositions and beliefs, in metaphorical interpretation. But it is as important, when we build context into semantics, that we must respect the distinction between the linguistic and extra-linguistic. How, then should we proceed? Most contemporary theorists conclude from its context-dependence that metaphor should be treated in pragmatics as a matter of use rather than in semantics as a kind of meaning. But there are two competing understandings of the use-meaning distinction in this connection. Some take what a speaker can use the word to mean to be a pragmatic notion of speaker's meaning *in addition to* semantic sentence meaning. Such a notion of meaning is rule-governed but the proposed principles or rules are pragmatic, for example, conversational maxims that generate implicatures (Grice, 1975), the mutual recognition of intentions (Fogelin, 1988), speech act illocutions or perlocutions (Cohen, 1975), principles of relevance that underlie "loose" use of language (Sperber & Wilson, 1986), or principles of recall or association ("being called to mind"; Searle, 1993). So, for all these authors, the claim that metaphor falls in pragmatics is the claim that the kind of rules and conditions that make up the theory are use-based.

For a second group, to call metaphor a matter of pragmatics or use is to oppose it to linguistic phenomena that can be explained in terms of meaning; to say that metaphor is a matter of use means that it defies theoretical, law-like explanation. The most radical exponent of this line is Richard Rorty (1987) according to whom "metaphor belongs exclusively to the domain of use," a "jungle" of irregular and unpredictable noises, in sharp contrast to the regular "literal use of language" for which "semantical notions like 'meaning' have a role" (p. 285). A more moderate but more influential proponent of more or less the same stance is Donald Davidson (1984, 1986) who makes a quartet of provocative claims: (i) that there is no metaphorical meaning in addition to or in place of the literal meaning of expressions used metaphorically; (ii) that all a metaphor is is an imaginative use of a sentence exclusively with its literal meaning, whose (non-rule-governed) *effect* is to make us notice a likeness; (iii) that what the metaphor conveys is nonpropositional, not a "definite cognitive content"; and (iv) that there can be no compositional semantic theory of metaphor that shows how the metaphorical meaning of every expressible metaphor is a function of a finite number of simple meanings and a finite number of rules of composition. Moreover, Davidson argues that those who think of the feature R expressed by a metaphorical utterance "S is P" as a metaphorical *meaning* of P in its context are just playing fast and loose with the notion of meaning. For the whole point of meaning (i.e., literal meaning) is to serve as a feature of an expression (type) that it "has prior to and independent of the context of use" (1984, 247) and hence can explain why all its tokens make the same truth-conditional contribution to the utterances in which they occur. There are no analogous cross-contextual regularities to explain for metaphor since each metaphorical utterance of P in its context appears to express a different truth-conditional feature R in that context. Hence, there is no reason to posit metaphorical meaning.

I shall not systematically evaluate these theories here (see, however, Stern, 2000), but their twofold challenge to us is clear: If we are to develop a semantic theory of metaphor, we must, first, demonstrate how we can capture its context-dependence without totally obscuring the boundary between the linguistic and extra-linguistic and, second, we must show why, given the substantial contextual input to our understanding of metaphor, a level of semantic knowledge is explanatory. This brings me to our conception of semantics and its relation to context.

## 3. Semantics versus Pragmatics of Metaphor

The first semantic theories of metaphor defended its cognitive meaningfulness in an environment that took it instead to be rhetorical, emotive, or merely stylistic. The second generation took metaphor to be semantic insofar as it could be explained in terms of violations of semantic rules for literal language. Contemporary views characterize metaphor as a semantic phenomenon in order to deny that it is a (entirely) *pragmatic* affair. However, this dispute over metaphor takes place against a rich background of controversy among philosophers, linguists, and cognitive scientists over the general character of the semantics–pragmatics distinction in the study of language. Before turning to metaphor, let me therefore say how I draw this distinction. It will be helpful to distinguish two different issues surrounding the distinction and its relation to context-dependence. The first concerns what aspects of interpretation, or what we intuitively understand by our utterances, to include in semantics and what in pragmatics. Some (Montague, 1974) take semantics to be exclusively concerned with eternal or context-independent language, pragmatics with the context-dependent, indexicals, and demonstratives as well as conversational implicatures and indirect speech acts. Others (Stalnaker, 1972) take semantics to be a theory of propositions or truth-conditions regardless of the sentences that express them. Thus, semantics will include propositions expressed by sentences containing demonstratives and indexicals, but also ones that are shaped by speakers' intentions. Pragmatics then deals with all additional implications conveyed by speech acts that bear on their appropriate use in context. Yet a third group (Stanley, 2000; Stanley & King, 2005; Stanley & Szabo, 2000) takes semantics to be a theory of the meanings, or semantic values, of simple expressions in the language and of the rules for combining them into the complex meanings, or semantic values, of more complex expressions (including sentences). Pragmatics in turn deals with all other intuitively understood or implicated propositions conveyed by the utterance.

My view of this first issue, like the third position, takes semantics to be concerned with the meanings of the parts of language and their combinatorics. But rather than being a theory of the semantic values themselves and their rules of composition, I take semantics to be a theory of the speaker's *knowledge* of meaning that underlies his ability to produce and comprehend utterances (Higginbotham, 1992). This *knowledge* of meaning does not *itself* necessarily yield understanding, or knowledge of truth-conditions, of any utterance; its point is rather to *constrain* which communicative intentions – intentions to express truth-valued claims – are expressible employing particular linguistic representations. It interfaces both with the other sub-faculties of the speaker's language faculty and with his extra-linguistic mental faculties, perceptual skills, and commonsense knowledge – which I count as the context of the interpretation. (I return to the context below.) *Only* in conjunction with these other skills, attitudes, and competences, does the speaker's semantic knowledge generate knowledge of actual truth-conditions and, hence, understanding of utterances. Nonetheless, while it is not strictly speaking semantic, I also would not say that the speaker's knowledge of propositions, or truth-conditions, is pragmatic. Let's instead distinguish among: (i) semantic knowledge proper (of the meanings of simple expressions and the rules of compositionality), (ii) semantically constrained extra-linguistic knowledge (of truth-conditions or propositional content), and (iii) semantically unconstrained knowledge (of various kinds of context-dependent implicatures, affects, illocutions, causal effects, and other information inferred from the content of utterances).

Furthermore, following Kaplan (1989), I distinguish the (propositional) *content* of a (sub-sentential) expression (in its context) from its *character*. Content is the factor corresponding to the expression relevant to evaluating the truth of its utterance (as part of a sentence) at a circumstance, or what the expression contributes to the truth-conditions of its utterances. Character is a function from contexts to contents that, in each context, determines what its content would be. For example, the character of the indexical "I" is the rule that each of its tokens refers to its speaker in its context, where that individual (in the context, say, me when I am its utterer) is the referential value or content relevant to the truth-condition of the utterances in which that token of "I" occurs.[4] All expressions (types), it should be added, have characters. However, the characters of eternal expressions are "constant," that is, they determine the same referential value (content) in all contexts; only those of demonstratives and indexicals are nonconstant – yielding different referential values (contents) in different contexts. Now, it is character, not content (or referential value) in a context (knowledge of which depends, say, for "I" on extra-linguistic knowledge of who is speaking), which is what a speaker knows when he knows the (linguistic) meaning of an expression. Character rather than content is, then, closest to our notion of (conventional) linguistic meaning, and knowledge of character constitutes the domain of semantic theory.[5]

The second issue is the question how extra-linguistic context determines or affects what is intuitively said by an utterance, its truth-conditions, or propositional content. At one extreme, what is said by some sentences (e.g., "I am happy") is sensitive to context in ways that are explicitly constrained by the meanings of their constituent expressions, for example, the rule for the first-person indexical "I" that each of its utterances (directly) refers to its speaker (who is therefore its propositional content). At a second extreme, there are utterances (e.g., "Can you shut the door?" uttered in a context in which there is a draft, meant as a request to close it, as opposed to a context in which the addressee is asked whether he is physically capable of moving a two-ton door) whose intuitive content also depends on context but is constrained by no linguistic or semantic feature, only by the speaker's extra-linguistic purposes or intentions in uttering it. With regard to these two classes of utterances, (almost) everyone agrees that what is said by utterances at the first extreme falls in semantics and that what is communicated at the second extreme does not. However, between these two extremes there is a wide range of utterances, such as

(5) It is raining (at a contextually salient location).
(6) Every student (in the course) failed the exam.
(7) I ate breakfast (this morning).

whose intuitive truth-conditions (which includes the parenthetic content) are context-dependent but do not contain a concrete linguistic element in the sentence uttered that linguistically controls the contextual contribution. About these utterances, it is an open theoretical question whether there are linguistic constraints that govern their context-dependent content. The *contextualists* argue that our intuitive understanding of utterances, including even simple expressions and even simple sentences (like (5)–(7)) is so pervasively context-sensitive that we must acknowledge truth-conditional factors contributed by and in context that are not semantically licensed or governed. All truth-conditions are at best pragmatically determined (Bach, 1994, 2002; Carston, 1988, 2002; Récanati, 2004; Sperber & Wilson, 1995; Travis, 2000).[6] A second camp, the *literalists*, argue that the intuitive truth-conditions of utterances admittedly contain factors not articulated by overt, concrete constituents, but that does not show that those contextual contributions are not semantically constrained. On the contrary, when we examine simple sentences embedded in more complex configurations (e.g., quantified conditionals or anaphoric constructions), various constraints on their contextual dependence become evident. This data shows that at a more abstract level of semantic representation of the utterance, at the level of its logical form, there do exist underlying abstract linguistic elements whose meaning constrains these additional contextual contributions to the truth-conditions (Stanley, 2000).

My own view on this second issue is aligned with the literalists. Not only are there context-dependent *expressions*; some eternal expressions admit context-dependent *interpretations* or *uses*, and these context-dependent interpretations or uses are semantically constrained no different from the context-dependent expressions themselves (Kaplan, 1989). For example, definite descriptions composed of eternal expressions can be used demonstratively to refer (at all, including counterfactual, circumstances) to the individual (uniquely) designated by them in their context of utterance. Thus, the content of these uses or interpretations is context-dependent, even though they contain no concrete demonstratives. Moreover, they are governed by the same semantic constraints that apply to explicit demonstratives. In their case, as the literalist claims, their semantic constraints are best represented by an abstract operator at the level of logical form. Indeed, David Kaplan has proposed such an operator "Dthat" for this very purpose: to take eternal (nonrigid) definite descriptions Ø and convert them into lexical representations Dthat[Ø] that represent the demonstrative (hence, rigid and context-dependent) interpretation of Ø.

Now, this general dispute over the contextual determination of truth-conditions, as in (5)–(7), has a variant for metaphor. There is in general no explicit verbal expression (e.g., an operator like "metaphorically speaking") that constrains the contextual contribution to metaphorical interpretation, that is, the truth-conditions or proposition expressed by the utterance interpreted metaphorically in a context. The contextualists (Bezuidenhout, 2001; Récanati, 2004) therefore conclude that metaphor is a product of direct, that is, semantically unconstrained, contextual enrichment. I argue, on the other hand, that the contextual contribution to the contents of metaphors is semantically constrained. And while the constraints are not realized in concrete verbal constituents of metaphorical utterances, they are borne by more abstract representations (like Kaplan's "Dthat") that occur at an underlying level of logical form. Furthermore, the constraints on metaphorical interpretations have the same formal structure as the constraints that govern the truth-conditional interpretation of demonstratives and indexicals, constraints carried by their nonconstant characters. So, if there is a semantic theory of metaphor, its domain will also be knowledge of metaphorical character, rather than of the contents, or truth-conditions, of metaphors in particular contexts.

## 4. The Context of a Metaphor

With this general conception of semantics in hand, we now have the resources to sketch a semantic theory for metaphor, a theory of metaphorical meaning, that takes into account both its context-dependence and literal-dependence. Translated into our semantic vocabulary, the different metaphorical interpretations that utterances of one expression (type) can express in different contexts and on different occasions are their (propositional) contents, the factors that bear on the truth-value of their utterances. Because the individual features (e.g., being greater than her peers for "is the sun" in (1)) expressed in these contents depend in part on the speaker's extra-linguistic skills and presuppositions, the contents of these metaphorical interpretations are not *themselves* known *solely* in virtue of semantic competence. But it does not follow that metaphor lies entirely outside semantics. What the speaker does know in virtue of his semantic knowledge is the character of the metaphor, that is, a rule or directive to map a parameter of the context into the content of the metaphor in that context. Metaphorical character constrains which contents can be metaphorically expressed by which expressions in which contexts. And insofar as the function of meaning is generally to constrain which intentions can be expressed by which linguistic items on which occasions, we can take its character to be the meaning of a metaphor. In order to work out these constraints, let's take a closer look at the context of a metaphor.

Context plays three roles in communicative exchanges involving metaphor. First, as we noted earlier, context – the speaker's intention, the topic of discourse, and other presuppositions – plays a crucial role in our identification or recognition of an utterance as a metaphor. No syntactic or semantic condition (like grammatical or semantical deviance) signals that

(8) Two roads diverged in a wood, and I – /I took the one less traveled by (Frost)

is a metaphor, only the contextual participants' presuppositions and beliefs about the author/speaker's intention. This role of context is no different for metaphor than for the literal. But because it is only *after* the assignment of a type to the sounds or words that it is possible to semantically interpret them, this role of the context is *pre-semantic*.

A second role of the context in metaphorical communication is *post-semantic*. Utterances interpreted metaphorically, no different from those used literally, can be used for an indefinite number of purposes or with various extra-linguistic intentions: to question, demand, warn, flatter, deceive, or threaten. If I ask my son

(9) Did a typhoon hit your room?

not only am I not asking him whether (literally) a typhoon struck; I am also not asking for a yes-or-no answer to the question (expressed metaphorically) whether his room is or is not a mess; I am gently *directing* him to clean it up – or else. (Compare the literal question in a similar context: "Why are all your clothes and books scattered on the floor?") His knowledge of that intention will be a function of his (and my) beliefs about my general attitudes toward neatness, authority, and so on. Likewise, suppose one of Romeo's peers believes that Juliet is the kind of woman who, like the sun, consumes those who get too close to or too intimate with her, who engage her directly in the eye. He might utter (1) to warn Romeo to cool it and keep his distance. Again, this role of context is no different for metaphor than with the literal. What is practically communicated is an inference drawn in context from a prior proposition that constitutes the base understanding of the utterance. Hence, this role of the context for a metaphor, which assumes that it already has a content, or truth-conditions, or says something, is post-semantic.

Do the pre-semantic and the post-semantic exhaust the roles of the context in communicative exchanges involving metaphor? In the literal use of certain linguistic expressions, there is also a third *semantic* role for the context. Take a sound sequence containing the sound "i." In its pre-semantic role, context enables us to assign that sound to a given linguistic type (with its conventional meaning or character): either the affirmative "aye" or the organ-term "eye" or the yelp "ai" or the first-person indexical "I." Suppose now that the token is assigned the first-person pronoun "I" as its type. And suppose I (JS) am bickering with my buddy Sam over a bill, and I tell him emphatically (with stress on "I")

(10) I am not paying

in order to bring him to understand the proposition expressed in that context by

(11) You are paying.

or perhaps:

(12) If anyone pays, it won't be me.

Here context functions in its post-semantic role, determining an implicature, the pragmatic meaning of (10). But for the first-person indexical "I," there is yet a third, semantic role for context. Given the meaning-rule or character of "I," the context and, in particular, its speaker parameter fixes the truth-conditional factor or propositional constituent for my (JS's) utterance of "I" in (10);

(10*) <Not<JS, Pays>>

This role of the context – articulated by the linguistic meaning, or character, of the indexical and by which the contribution of the context is constrained to the actual speaker – is semantic.

Is there an analogous semantic role for the context in metaphorical interpretation? We noted at the beginning of the paper that metaphorical interpretations of one expression (type) vary from occasion to occasion and from context to context. Now, in fact there are a variety of different contextual factors that feed into this variability. For example, contrast the interpretation of (1) in the context depicted in Shakespeare's play (1*)

(1*) But soft, what light through yonder window breaks?
It is the East, and Juliet *is the sun*.

Arise *fair sun* and kill the envious *moon*,
Who is already sick and *pale* with grief,
That thou her maid art far *more fair* than she . . .

Two of the *fairest stars in all the heaven*,
Having some business, do entreat her *eyes*.
*To twinkle in their spheres* till they return.
What if her *eyes* were there, they in her head?
The *brightness of her cheek* would shame those stars,
*As daylight doth a lamp*; her eyes in heaven
Would through the airy region *stream so bright*,
That birds would sing, and think it were *not night* . . .
(*Romeo and Juliet* II, ii, 2–23; my emphasis)

with the interpretation of the "sun" metaphor in Salisbury's description of the end of Richard II's reign

(13) Ah, Richard, with the eyes of heavy mind
I see thy glory like *a shooting star*
Fall to the base *earth* from the *firmament*.

*Thy sun* sets weeping in the lowly *west*,
Witness *storms* to come, woe and unrest;
Thy friends are fled to wait upon thy foes,
And crossly to thy good all fortune goes.
(*Richard II*, II, iv; my emphasis)

Here the (setting) sun exemplifies and thereby expresses (declining) glory, (lost) authority, and insecurity. And contrast also these two Shakespearean "sun" metaphors with the Spanish Hebrew poet Judah Halevi's use of "the sun" in his love poem:

(14) The *night* the girl gazelle displayed to me
*Her cheek – the sun* – beneath its *veil* of hair,
*Red as a ruby*, and beneath, a *brow*
Of moistened *marble* (color wondrous fair!)

> I fancied her *the sun*, which *rising reddens*
> Clouds of morning with its *crimson* flare.
> (Scheindlin, 1986, 119)

where it expresses the beloved's radiance but (together with the "marble" metaphor) absolute coldness and unapproachability.

In each of these contexts, the utterance of "(is) the sun" expresses a different metaphorical interpretation. In Stern (2000), I called these "exemplication metaphors" because their content consists of a set of features its literal referent *exemplifies* or of which it is a *sample* in the context (Goodman, 1976). What distinguishes this class of metaphors is that the features exemplified or sampled by the individual referred to by the literal vehicle of any single metaphorical expression in turn depend on the schema or sample set to which that literal referent belongs and on the range of features sampled by the schema as a whole. In each of these passages, or literary contexts, the author spells out in detail the appropriate schema, network, or family of expressions (marked by italics) relative to which the single metaphorical expression is interpreted. This systemic dimension of metaphorical interpretation was first pointed out by Nelson Goodman but in recent years it has become a leitmotif in the literature, due in large measure to the research on "conventional metaphors" of the linguist George Lakoff and his school (Gibbs, 1994; Lakoff, 1993; Lakoff & Johnson, 1980; Lakoff & Turner, 1989; for alternative accounts, see Glucksberg, 2001; Glucksberg & Keysar, 1990, 1993; Kittay, 1987; Thompson & Thompson, 1987; Tirrell, 1989; White, 1996). But the important point is that in these complex metaphors (1*), (13), and (14), the interpretations of "the sun" vary according to the schema of objects with which the (literal) referent or extension of the literal vehicle is classified in the context. Thus, the underlying unit for the interpretation of an individual metaphor is its whole schema, network, or family, whether or not the latter is made explicit in the context or is simply common knowledge.

Not all metaphors are exemplificational in this way. A speaker may utter (1) in a context in which he makes clear that he is drawing on stereotypical beliefs about the eternal, predictable circular motion of the sun to express the content that Juliet is utterly (and boringly) reliable, predictable, and regular in her movements, someone you can always count on to rise and set, who never surprises or inspires. With yet another class of complex metaphors, the speaker/author may build up its interpretation by drawing out the various, more or less strong inductive consequences of a root metaphor. For example, in T. S. Eliot's "The Love Song of J. Alfred Prufrock," the yellow fog is a cat that rubs its back on the window, licks its tongue, makes sudden leaps, curls about the house, and sleeps. Closer attention to these (different kinds of) systematic networks in metaphorical interpretation, and their interaction, will enable us to understand better how complex metaphors in poetry function. (On the analysis of complex metaphors, see now White, 1996.)

Now, if we take each of these different interpretations – each of the individual features expressed in the content – one by one, they look idiosyncratic and unrelated, as the use-theorists of metaphor contend. But if we look at the triples of interpretations (propositional contents), expression types (with their literal meaning), and the respective contexts, each of the different interpretations corresponds to a difference in context, either a verbally articulated (literary) context or one constituted by unarticulated beliefs or presuppositions The moral is that there may be little that is regular so long as we look only at particular metaphorical interpretations in each context in isolation. However, at one interpretative "level" more abstract – a level that *relates* each metaphorical interpretation of the same expression (type), with its constant literal meaning, to a relevant feature of its respective context of use, namely, shared presuppositions – metaphorical interpretation does follow regularities and supports predictions. Same expression (with the same literal meaning), in the same context – that is, with the same presuppositions – the result is the same interpretation. Same expression, different contexts – that is, different presuppositions – different interpretations. The structure of these variations – which may be the "transfer" of which Aristotle spoke in the *Rhetoric* – is essential to understand both the productivity and mechanism of metaphorical interpretation. And it is at this level that relates interpretation to context that we should look for the semantic constraints to be captured in a notion of metaphorical meaning.

In sum, to answer our earlier question, Is there a semantic role for the context in metaphorical interpretation? I am suggesting that the semantic context for the interpretation of a metaphor consists in a set of contextual presuppositions associated with its literal vehicle, a contextual parameter like the familiar and relatively well-defined parameters for singular demonstratives and indexicals – the speaker for "I," the time of utterance for "now," the demonstratum for "that," and so on. There remain significant differences between the context-dependence of metaphors and demonstratives and indexicals, but they are of degree rather than kind. For predicate demonstratives, such as "thus" or "is that way," the parameter is already less clear: an ostended property or manner. For metaphors, whose basic syntactic unit is the predicate, the contextual parameter is even less defined.

By "presupposition" here I mean the pragmatic notion, a species of propositional attitude (Stalnaker, 1972, 1973), a set of propositions to which a speaker, in making an utterance, commits himself in that, in their absence, his utterance would be inappropriate or (as with metaphor) uninterpretable as it is. These presuppositions constitute the context of a metaphor insofar as they define its range of possible interpretations on the occasion. As we have seen in our examples, the contents of the presuppositions can differ significantly depending on the "kind" of metaphor. For some, the presuppositions can be characterized as "common knowledge" about features or properties associated with the metaphorical expression – bearing in mind that "knowledge" here does not carry the implication that the presuppositions must be true or even believed to be true. As Black (1962) first observed, what is relevant to the metaphorical interpretation of an expression Ø is its "system of associated commonplaces," rather than its definition or the features actually true of Ø's. In other cases, the presuppositions are local to the actual context of utterance, for example, those that are taken to be exemplified, or sampled, by the referent of the literal vehicle relative to a sample schema which, in turn, depends on salience in context (see Stern, 2000). In yet other cases, the relevant presuppositions are made in accordance with a principle of accommodation (Lewis, 1979) simply in order to enable the interpretation of the metaphor. Finally, the full set of relevant presuppositions for a metaphorical interpretation includes not only those associated with the literal vehicle (e.g., "is the sun" in (1)) but also those associated with other elements in its linguistic and extra-linguistic environment (e.g., "Juliet"). However, while those associated with the metaphorical expression serve to generate potential features of content, those associated with the environment filter out the features that cannot be appropriately taken to be the content of the metaphor in the context (Reinhart, 1970; Stern, 2000).[7]

What makes something a metaphor according to this account is both narrower and wider than the received view. There is no one kind of associated property (e.g., a feature of resemblance) that serves as the ground for all metaphors; rather interpretations draw on all sorts of properties. But what is essential is that the feature be presupposed to be "associated" with the literal vehicle of the metaphor in the context. What distinguishes a metaphor is not the content of the feature that enters into its interpretation, but its context-sensitive meaning (character) that draws on the contextually presupposed feature. The semantics addresses this notion of metaphorical meaning, while the no less important (and often more interesting) characteristics of the presuppositions themselves (like those adumbrated in the previous paragraph) belong to pragmatics, the application of the speaker's semantic knowledge in and to a context to yield actual propositions and more.

## 5. Metaphorical Meaning

The role of metaphorical meaning, analyzed as character, is to specify how the interpretation of a metaphor – its content, namely, the set of features that belong to its truth-conditions – depends on and varies with a specific parameter of its context, namely, a particular set of presuppositions associated in the context with its literal vehicle. The speaker's semantic competence in metaphor, like the semantic competence that underlies her ability to use demonstratives, consists in knowledge of that meaning, or character, namely, a function from the metaphorically relevant associated properties in the context set of presuppositions to the particular subset of properties that constitute the content of the metaphor in that context. Together with its contextual presuppositions, the character yields the content of the interpretation, but the meaning is not itself part of that content. (For other accounts of the context-dependence of metaphor, see Berg, 1988; Bergmann, 1982; Bezuidenhout, 2001; Kittay, 1987; Leezenberg, 2001; Nogales, 1999; Scheffler, 1979.)

Thus far, I have emphasized parallels between demonstratives and metaphors. But there are also differences. Meanings (or characters) are meanings (or characters) of expressions; but metaphor is a kind of *use* or *interpretation* of arbitrary expressions, and uses (interpretations) don't have meanings. Furthermore, unlike semantic competence in demonstratives and indexicals that involves knowledge of the meanings of individual linguistic items, metaphorical competence involves mastery of an interpretive skill or ability one can apply to arbitrary expressions across the language. To address these two differences, I have therefore coined an operator "Mthat," modeled after David Kaplan's "Dthat" (see section 3), that both lexically realizes metaphorical interpretation (and thereby provides a bearer for its meaning) and captures its skill-like character. "Dthat" takes the description "the man in black" and produces the demonstrative-description "Dthat['the man in black']" that directly (and rigidly) refers to the individual in the context who fits the description. By analogy, "Mthat" takes a literal expression like "is the sun" and produces the "metaphorical expression" "Mthat['is the sun']" that expresses a particular subset of presupposed properties associated with the embedded literal vehicle in the context. "Mthat," like "Dthat" is not an actual expression of English; it is an abstract linguistic element, syntactically represented at the level of logical form, intended to capture the linguistic competence that underlies our ability to use or interpret expressions metaphorically. Of course, there are still differences between metaphors (or metaphorical expressions) and demonstratives (and indexicals) or Dthat-descriptions. The content of "Dthat[Ø]" in a context is an individual; the content of "Mthat[Ø]" is a set of properties. The former is the individual that fits or satisfies the description Ø; the latter is a subset of the properties that are parametrically related to Ø (like the relation of the speaker to "I"). Finally, both the characters and contents of Dthat-descriptions are arguably compositionally determined by the characters and contents, respectively, of their component descriptions. On the other hand, neither the character nor the content of a metaphorical expression Mthat[Ø] is a compositional function of the character or content, respectively, of its constituents. However, the metaphorical expression "Mthat[Ø]" is *individuated by* the linguistic type of its literal vehicle: If Ø and Ψ are of different types, then Mthat[Ø] and Mthat[Ψ] are of different types. The reason for this is that the context set of presupposed metaphorically associated properties is not associated with either the extension or intension of the literal vehicle. If it were, we ought to be able to substitute a co-extensive or co-intensional expression for Ø without affecting the metaphorical interpretation; but it is easy to see that that is not the case if you try to interchange either the co-extensional "the largest gaseous blob in the solar system" and "the sun" or the co-intensional "Tully" and "Cicero" (Stern, 2000) or "cur" and "mongrel" (Hills, 2002). Rather the contextual parameter for metaphor is a context set of metaphorically relevant presuppositions associated with the literal *word* Ø (in a sentence in a context) or (possibly) with its (literal) *character* (in *S* in *c*).[8] This, I want to propose, is the sense in which the metaphorical–the character of the metaphor – depends on the literal – on the literal vehicle itself, the word or its meaning (character). Its literal-dependence is not historical or genetic, nor does it require that the speaker *understand* what the utterance literally says. But the literal vehicle is active in the metaphorical interpretation because the relevant contextual parameter is triggered by, and individuated in accordance with, its meaning.

The function of linguistic meaning in general is to capture linguistic *constraints* that determine which of a speaker's intentions can be (literally) communicated by which expressions. Similarly, metaphorical meaning constrains the content a speaker can use an expression to express metaphorically. Let me give one example, beginning with a similar constraint that governs the interpretation of indexicals. Suppose I utter

(15) I live in Jerusalem.

If Susan reports what I said, she must say

(16) Stern says that he lives in Jerusalem,

*not*

(17) Stern says that I live in Jerusalem

because the content of the indexical "I" is *always* fixed by its actual context, the context of its speaker, not by that of the belief-worlds of the subject of (17), "Stern." Therefore, Susan *must* shift from "I" to "he" (or to another word that expresses the content of "I" in (15)). I call this condition according to which the interpretation of an indexical always cleaves to its actual context of utterance *The Actual Context Constraint* (ACC). Similarly, suppose I say:

(18) He [points at a person who in c is Al] might have been president.

Because (18) contains a modal, uttered in the context c (which includes the world w(c), the world of the context c), it is true at w(c) just in case

(19) There is some world w* (accessible to w(c)) in which Al *is* president.

It is not enough for (18) to be true at w(c) for there to be someone in w*, say, George, who is pointed at in w* and who is president in w*. Although the truth-value of (18) is determined by the *facts* at w*, its *interpretation* or *content* is fixed by its actual context c, as the ACC predicts.

A similar story holds for metaphor. Suppose Count Paris in Shakespeare's play denies (1) but concedes:

(20) Well, Juliet might have been the sun (uttered in c which includes w(c))

where "is the sun" is again interpreted metaphorically to express the proposition that Juliet is peerless. Since (20) is also a modal sentence, it is true in w(c), the world of its context of utterance, just in case

(21) There is some world w*(accessible to w(c)) in which Juliet *is* peerless.

that is, where she has the property metaphorically expressed by "is the sun" back in c. Here, again, the relevant interpretation is not the interpretation "is the sun" would be given in w* had it been uttered there. Suppose, for example, that in w* "the sun" is the paradigm example of boring regularity; it is not sufficient for (or relevant to) the truth of Paris's utterance of (20) in c, interpreted metaphorically, that Juliet in w* be tediously predictable in her actions. She must possess in w* the property expressed by the metaphor in c. Like demonstratives, metaphorical interpretation obeys the ACC. As with "I," its meaning does not determine what the metaphor *must* say, or under what conditions it is true; it only specifies what the interpretation *cannot* be. This common constraint calls for a common kind of meaning, the nonconstant character common to indexicals and metaphors.[9]

## 6. The Cognitive Significance of Metaphors

As we saw in section 2, from their beginning semantic theories of metaphor have been concerned with questions of cognitive significance. It was assumed either that the metaphorical mode of expression is merely stylistic, rhetorical, or decorative, carrying no additional cognitive value beyond what could be expressed literally, or that the cognitive significance of a metaphor is sui generis, completely unlike the information conveyed by literal language. And to decide among these alternatives, philosophers often appealed to tests of literal paraphrasability (Black, 1962; Cavell, 1967). However, these tests were severely hampered by inherently unclear criteria for success (Bergmann, 1982; Davidson, 1984; Levinson, 2001; Stern, 2000). In recent years, philosophers have turned the inquiry in new, more promising directions. Some have examined the cognitive functioning of metaphors in scientific theories, religious language, and art and ethical criticism (Alston, 1964; Boyd, 1993; Denham, 1998). Others have explored ways in which a metaphor can make us *see* something *as* something else that cannot be captured by a simple belief attitude (Black, 1993; Davidson, 1986; Davies, 1982; Moran, 1989). Yet others have looked at the role of metaphors in creating a sense of intimacy or community and their relation to jokes and riddles, an approach that promises to illuminate other cognitive aspects of metaphor such as their sense of surprise (Cohen, 1978; Stern, 2000).

I shall conclude this chapter with one example of how a metaphorical mode of expression can bear a kind of information apart from its truth-conditional content that carries explanatory power in belief-ascriptions. Marie, a young woman in her teens, suffered from the eating disorder of anorexia nervosa. In treatment, she explained to her therapist that her mother had forbade her to continue seeing her boyfriend. Angrily, she reported, she had said to herself:

(22) I won't swallow that [referring to her mother's interdiction].

Let's assume that in the context in which she uttered (22) Marie's use of the word "swallow" was metaphorical (Merleau-Ponty, cited in Danto, 1978). Let's also suppose that *what* Marie *said* by (22) interpreted metaphorically, is expressed by

(23) Marie won't obey her mother's interdiction.

Does (23) adequately express everything said by Marie's utterance of (22)? Yes and No. Yes, insofar as (22) is true, spoken by Marie referring to her mother's interdiction, just in case Marie does not obey her mother's interdiction, that is, (23). No, insofar as her utterance of (22) is meant to contribute to an *explanation* of her anorexic behavior, albeit as an irrational way of resisting her mother's command. For in order to explain why Marie stopped *eating* in terms of a belief we would ascribe to her on the evidence of her utterance of (22), we must somehow include as part of the representation of her belief the fact that what she said, namely, that she would not obey her mother, was expressed metaphorically using the verb "swallow." Only under that metaphorical mode of expression of what she said – only if we include *how* she metaphorically believed, or expressed, *what* she believed – can we see any connection, conscious or unconscious, between her belief and her subsequent anorexic behavior. To be sure, Marie's behavior and the connection she made are not rational, and no explanation should make it so. But only by acknowledging the cognitive and explanatory significance of the metaphorical meaning with which she expressed her belief can we explain her behavior at all. The metaphorical mode in which Marie expressed her belief is essential, not to determine whether what she said is true or false, but for our folk-psychological purposes of explaining her behavior.[10] But this additional information seems to be individuated by the character of the metaphorical expression underlying (22). By investigating these structures, semantic theories of metaphor can help us better understand its cognitive significance above and beyond its propositional content in context.

## Notes

1 A red herring is a fallacy of irrelevance, so-called because of the reputed practice of escaped convicts who used pickled herrings to throw bloodhounds off the scent. It is not difficult to imagine a current speaker who knows that a red herring is an irrelevant argument even if she does not know that a herring is a fish or (much less plausibly) that "red" is the name of a color.

2 The literal vehicle for a metaphor is the expression, for example, "is the sun" in (1) as it would be interpreted or (semantically) meant literally.

3 Similar objections apply to Kittay's (1987) "perspectival theory," which elaborates Black's interaction theory using semantic field theory; see Stern (2000).

4 Here I assume that indexicals (and demonstratives) are directly referential terms; the content of an utterance of "I" is the very individual who is speaking, not (even) a (rigid) conceptual representation of the individual.

5 Where the simple expression is eternal, or not-context-sensitive, the character/meaning is equivalent to the content, or referent or semantic value assigned to it; that is, two expressions will have the same character/meaning iff they have the same content iff they have the same referent. Therefore, as Kaplan (1989) notes, this semantics is not adequate to capture differences of meaning (if there are any) among co-referential proper names.

6 Among these authors, some take this to mean that a principled, explanatory pragmatic theory of truth-conditions is possible, others that sensitivity to use excludes the possibility of a theory or general explanations.

7 Here the one question whether a given feature is appropriate content should be distinguished from a second question whether the content, once fixed, is an appropriate thing to assert or utter in the context.

8 I emphasize that the presuppositions are associated with the literal *word* and only "possibly" with its character because, where we are dealing with eternal words (like the examples of co-intensional expressions cited in the text), any two co-intensional expressions will have the same character as well. This points to a general inadequacy in Kaplan's semantics to deal with context-independent expressions, an inadequacy that carries over to our application of the semantics to metaphor. For further discussion, see Stern (2000), Hills (2002), and Stern (2006).

9 Similarly, to report someone's metaphor, either the reporter can try to express only the content of the original utterance without replicating its metaphorical character or, if he wishes to preserve the metaphorical mode of expression, he must also recover the presuppositions of the original context in order to preserve the content. For discussion, see Stern (2000) and, for criticism, Bezuidenhout (2001), Camp (2005), and Stern (2006).

10 See Stern (2000) which compares "essential metaphors" of this kind to John Perry's (1979) "essential indexicals"; in both cases, it is the character of the respective expression that carries the additional information relevant to the explanation.

## References

Alston, W. P. (1964). *Philosophy of language*. Englewood Cliffs, NJ: Prentice Hall.

Bach, K. (1994). Conversational impliciture. *Mind and Language*, 2, 141–154.

Bach, K. (2002). Semantics, pragmatics. In J. Campbell, M. O'Rourke, & D. Shier (Eds.), *Meaning and truth: Investigations in philosophical semantics* (pp. 284–292). New York: Seven Bridges Press.

Beardsley, M. (1962). Metaphorical twist. *Philosophy and Phenomenological Research*, 22, 293–307.

Beardsley, M. (1978). Metaphorical senses. *Nous*, 12, 3–16.

Berg, J. (1988). Metaphor, meaning, and interpretation. *Journal of Pragmatics*, 12, 695–709.

Bergmann, M. (1982). Metaphorical assertions. *Philosophical Review*, 91, 229–242.

Bezuidenhout, A. (2001). Metaphor and what is said: A defense of a direct expression view of metaphor. In P. A. French & H. K. Wettstein (Eds.), *Midwest studies in philosophy: Vol. 25. Figurative language* (pp. 156–186). Boston, MA: Blackwell.

Binkley, T. (1976). On the truth and probity of metaphor. *Journal of Aesthetics and Art Criticism*, 33, 171–180.

Black, M. (1962). Metaphor. In M. Black, *Models and metaphors* (pp. 25–47). Ithaca, NY: Cornell University Press.

Black, M. (1993). More about metaphor. In A. Ortony (Ed.), *Metaphor and thought* (2nd ed., pp. 19–41). Cambridge: Cambridge University Press.

Boyd, R. (1993). Metaphor and theory change: What is "Metaphor" a metaphor for? In A. Ortony (Ed.), *Metaphor and thought.* (2nd ed., pp. 481–532). Cambridge: Cambridge University Press.

Camp, E. (2005). Metaphors and demonstratives: Josef Stern's *Metaphor in Context. Nous*, 39, 715–731.

Carston, R. (1988). Implicature, explicature, and truth-theoretic semantics. In R. Kempson (Ed.), *Mental representations: The interface between language and reality* (pp. 155–181). Cambridge: Cambridge University Press.

Carston, R. (2002). *Thoughts and utterances: The pragmatics of explicit communication.* London: Blackwell.

Cavell, S. (1967). Aesthetic problems of modern philosophy. In M. Black (Ed.), *Philosophy in America* (pp. 74–97). Ithaca, NY: Cornell University Press.

Cohen, L. J. (1993). The semantics of metaphor. In A. Ortony (Ed.), *Metaphor and thought* (2nd ed., pp. 58–70). Cambridge: Cambridge University Press.

Cohen, L. J., & Margalit, A. (1972). The role of inductive reasoning in the interpretation of metaphor. In D. Davidson & G. Harman (Eds.), *Semantics of natural language* (pp. 721–762). Dordrecht: Reidel.

Cohen, T. (1975). Figurative language and figurative acts. *Journal of Philosophy*, 72, 669–690.

Cohen, T. (1976). Notes on metaphor. *Journal of Aesthetics and Art Criticism*, 34, 249–259.

Cohen, T. (1978). Metaphor and the cultivation of intimacy. *Critical Inquiry*, 5, 3–12.

Danto, A. (1978). Freudian explanations and the language of the unconscious. In J. H. Smith (Ed.), *Psychoanalysis and language* (pp. 325–353). New Haven, CT: Yale University Press.

Davidson, D. (1984). What metaphors mean. In D. Davidson. *Inquiries into truth and interpretation* (pp. 245–264). Oxford: Oxford University Press.

Davidson, D. (1986). A nice derangement of epitaphs. In E. LePore, (Ed.), *Truth and interpretation: Perspectives on the philosophy of Donald Davidson* (pp. 433–446). Oxford: Basil Blackwell.

Davies, M. (1982). Idiom and metaphor. *Proceedings of the Aristotelian Society*, 83, 67–85.

Denham, A. (1998). Metaphor and judgments of experience. In R. Casati & C. Tappolet (Eds.), *European review of philosophy* (Vol. 3, pp. 225–253). Stanford, CA: CSLI Publications.

Fogelin, R. (1988). *Figuratively speaking.* New Haven, CT: Yale University Press.

Gibbs, R. W. (1994). *The poetics of mind.* New York: Cambridge University Press.

Glucksberg, S. (2001). *Understanding figurative language: From metaphors to idioms.* Oxford: Oxford University Press.

Glucksberg, S., & Keysar, B. (1990). Understanding metaphorical comparisons: Beyond similarity. *Psychological Review*, 97, 3–18.

Glucksberg, S., & Keysar, B. (1993). How metaphors work. In A. Ortony (Ed.), *Metaphor and thought.* (2nd ed., pp. 401–424). Cambridge: Cambridge University Press.

Goodman, N. (1976). *Languages of art.* (2nd ed.). Indianapolis, IN: Hackett.

Grice, H. P. (1975). Logic and conversation. In D. Davidson & G. Harman (Eds.), *The logic of grammar* (pp. 64–75). Encino, CA: Dickenson.

Henle, P. (1958). Metaphor. In P. Henle (Ed.), *Language, thought, and culture* (pp. 173–195). Ann Arbor: University of Michigan Press.

Higginbotham, J. (1992). Truth and understanding. *Philosophical Studies*, 65, 3–16.

Hills, D. (1997). Aptness and truth in verbal metaphor. *Philosophical Topics*, 25(1), 117–154.

Hills, D. (2002). Review of Josef Stern, *Metaphor in context. Philosophical Review*, 111, 473–478.

Kaplan, D. (1989). Demonstratives. In J. Almog, J. Perry, & H. Wettstein (Eds.), *Themes from Kaplan* (pp. 481–563). Oxford: Oxford University Press.

Kittay, E. F. (1987). *Metaphor: Its cognitive force and linguistic structure.* Oxford: Oxford University Press.

Lakoff, G. (1993). The contemporary theory of metaphor. In A. Ortony (Ed.), *Metaphor and thought* (2nd ed., pp. 202–251). Cambridge: Cambridge University Press.

Lakoff, G., & Johnson, M. (1980). *Metaphors we live by*. Chicago: University of Chicago Press.

Lakoff, G., & Turner, M. (1989). *More than cool reason: A field guide to poetic metaphor*. Chicago: University of Chicago Press.

Leezenberg, M. (2001). *Contexts of metaphor*. Amsterdam: Elsevier Science.

Levin, S. (1977). *The semantics of metaphor*. Baltimore: Johns Hopkins University Press.

Levinson, J. (2001). Who's afraid of a paraphrase?" *Theoria*, 67, 7–23.

Lewis, D. (1979). Scorekeeping in a language game. *Journal of Philosophical Logic*, 8, 339–359.

Loewenberg, I. (1975). Identifying metaphors. *Foundations of Language*, 12, 315–338.

Matthews, R. (1971). Concerning a "linguistic theory" of metaphor. *Foundations of Language*, 7, 413–425.

Montague, R. (1974). Pragmatics. In R. Thomason (Ed.), *Formal philosophy* (pp. 95–118). New Haven, CT: Yale University Press.

Moran, R. (1989). Seeing and believing: metaphor, image, and force. *Critical Inquiry*, 16, 87–112.

Nogales, P. (1999). *Metaphorically speaking*. Stanford, CA: CSLI Publications.

Perry, J. (1979). The problem of the essential indexical. *Nous*, 13, 3–21.

Récanati, F. (2004). *Literal meaning*. Cambridge: Cambridge University Press.

Reddy, M. (1969). A semantic approach to metaphor. *Papers from the Fifth Regional Meeting of the Chicago Linguistics Society*. University of Chicago–Linguistics Department, Chicago, pp. 240–251.

Reinhart, T. (1970). On understanding poetic metaphor. *Poetics*, 5, 383–402.

Rorty, R. (1987). Unfamiliar noises: I. Hesse and Davidson on metaphor. *Proceedings of the Aristotelian Society*, 61(Suppl.), 283–296.

Scheffler, I. (1979). *Beyond the letter*. London: Routledge & Kegan Paul.

Scheindlin, R. (1986). (Trans.). *Wine, women, and death: Medieval Hebrew poems on the good life*. Philadelphia: Jewish Publication Society.

Searle, J. (1993). Metaphor. In A. Ortony (Ed.), *Metaphor and thought* (2nd ed., pp. 83–111). Cambridge: Cambridge University Press.

Sperber, D., & Wilson, D. (1985/86). Loose talk. *Proceedings of the Aristotelian Society*, 86, 153–171.

Sperber, D., & Wilson, D. (1995). *Relevance: Communication and cognition*. (2nd ed.). Oxford: Basil Blackwell.

Stalnaker, R. (1972). Pragmatics. In D. Davidson & G. Harman (Eds.), *Semantics of natural language* (pp. 380–397). Dordrecht: Reidel.

Stalnaker, R. (1973). Presuppositions. *Journal of Philosophical Logic*, 2, 447–457.

Stanley, J. (2000). Context and logical form. *Linguistics and Philosophy*, 23, 391–434.

Stanley, J., & King, J. (2005). Semantics, pragmatics, and the role of semantic content. In Z. Szabo (Ed.), *Semantics vs. pragmatics*. (pp. 111–164). Oxford: Oxford University Press.

Stanley, J., & Szabo, Z. (2000). On quantifer domain restriction. *Mind and Language*, 15, 219–261.

Stern, J. (1983). Metaphor and grammatical deviance. *Nous*, 17, 577–599.

Stern, J. (2000). *Metaphor in context*. Cambridge, MA: MIT Press.

Stern, J. (2006). Metaphor, literal, literalism. *Mind and Language*, 21, 243–279.

Thompson, A., & Thompson, J. O. (1987). *Shakespeare, meaning, and metaphor*. Iowa City: University of Iowa Press.

Tirrell, L. (1989). Extending: The structure of metaphor. *Nous*, 23, 17–34.

Travis, C. (2000). *Unshadowed thought*. Cambridge, MA: Harvard University Press.

White, R. M. (1996). *The structure of metaphor: The way the language of metaphor works*. Oxford: Basil Blackwell.

White, R. M. (2001). Literal meaning and "figurative meaning." *Theoria*, 67, 24–59.

CHAPTER 16

# Corpus Linguistics and Metaphor

*Alice Deignan*

## Introduction

Corpus linguistic research techniques can yield facts about language use that might otherwise remain hidden. They can therefore trigger new insights into underlying patterns, and it will be shown in this chapter that together these are leading to developments in our understanding of metaphor. Findings from corpus linguistic research indicate that linguistic metaphor is determined by context as well as the speaker's or writer's intended meaning. That is, metaphor is a textual and social phenomenon as well as a cognitive one. A further contribution is to metaphor theory. Patterns of linguistic metaphor suggest that the conceptual systems that underlie them interact dynamically. Corpus research generally proceeds from the accumulation of detailed observations about language in use to theoretical questions, and this chapter begins with an example of one such observation.

In work in the cognitive school, it has been proposed that temperature is a common metaphor for feeling and that anger is often talked about as the pressure of fluid in a heated container (Gibbs, 1994; Lakoff, 1987). Research has tended to focus on how individuals experience anger. For instance, Lakoff's (1987) work describes the processes in an individual which lead to him or her becoming angry, linked to his or her physiological reactions. Gibbs (1994) reports research exploring people's reactions to sentences such as *He almost exploded with anger* and *She blew her stack when she heard about her husband's affair* (1994: 18–19), each of which describe one individual's behavior in terms of heat and pressure. However, corpus and text linguistic research into heat metaphors of anger suggest that this is not in fact the most frequent use. Heat metaphors are more often found in talk about the collective anger of a group of people and its impact, than in talk about the feelings of individuals.

Van Teeffelen's (1994) text analysis of metaphors in popular literature around the Palestinian–Israeli conflict starts with a detailed examination of the texts themselves and the identification of linguistic metaphors. He finds a number of linguistic metaphors that seem to realize a mapping of anger onto heat, including *inflamed, igniting,* and *wildfire*. In his data, these characterize not the sensations of an individual but the behavior of a large group of people. Further, and importantly for his argument that the discourse is racist, the metaphors are used only to talk about Palestinians, not about Israelis. Palestinians tend to be characterized metaphorically as a mass, "governed by the laws of nature" (p. 393), in contrast to the "rational" Israeli protagonists.

Corpus analysis of metaphors of fire and heat also suggests that they predominantly describe the behavior of people as a group rather than as individuals. For instance, the expression *fan the flames* is frequently used metaphorically, sometimes to talk about desire but more frequently to talk about anger. With this meaning, it invariably refers to the behavior of a group, in citations such as

(1) Newly empowered extremist groups in nearly every state are *fanning the flames* of intolerance and bigotry.

Other lexis that frequently realize the mapping include *ignite, spark, fires,* and *heated* (idioms like *blow your top/stack* are much rarer in the corpus). Entities that are *ignited* or *sparked* (*off*) can include an individual's actions but in the texts analyzed were more likely to be wars and other mass events. *Fires* are also more likely to refer to the behavior of a group of people than to an individual, and entities that are metaphorically *heated* are almost always speech events such as debates, discussions, and arguments rather then people or their feelings. Some of this bias toward collective experience could perhaps be accounted for by the nature of the texts studied, which include a number of newspapers and therefore reporting of collective events. However, it would not be true to say that there are few accounts of individuals' feelings in the texts. There are a number, but they do not tend to show as much use of heat and fire metaphors as do descriptions of conflict.

There are some exceptions, such as the following citation from popular literature, in which heat is used to describe an individual's feelings:

(2) She could feel the anger churning, growing, bubbling up inside her. Autumn didn't feel trapped any more, but *burning* with rage. All the hate she felt for his father she turned and directed at him.

But these are rare.

Writers in the cognitive tradition argue that the grounds for the conceptual mapping ANGER IS FIRE, or more specifically, PRESSURE OF HEATED FLUID IN A CONTAINER, lie in the bodily sensation of warmth that we experience when angry (for example, Lakoff, 1987). The evidence from text and corpus analysis points to another possible motivation. Fire has the potential to become uncontrollable and very destructive, and it can be started – *ignited* – with a small and apparently innocuous *spark*. The behavior of large groups of people can be mapped onto this behavior of fire, resulting in the conceptual metaphor AN ANGRY GROUP OF PEOPLE IS A WILDFIRE. The linguistic evidence suggests that both mappings exist, each contributing to a different set of linguistic expressions, and sometimes interacting with and reinforcing each other. The corpus analysis described here suggests that the second mapping has had a stronger influence on current language use, though that is not direct evidence of its conceptual significance. Van Teeffelen's work also suggests an important ideological aspect to this mapping.

This corpus analysis has shown an aspect of metaphorical use that had not been picked up in discussions of heat metaphors, but that, like many corpus observations, seems self-evident once made. Observations like this could be dismissed as details, having little importance for theory. Corpus linguists would not accept this, as I explain in the next section, where I outline some basic principles of corpus linguistics. In later sections, I show how corpus data can challenge intuitively derived linguistic data of the kind used in some experimental work on metaphor. I then return to the contributions of corpus work to metaphor theory.

## Corpora in Research

### *Corpora*

A "corpus" can be any collection of spoken or written texts. These could consist of the work of a single author, a number of issues of one or more newspapers, collections of transcribed spoken data, or more broadly based collections of a range of text types. The linguistic topics that can be investigated using a corpus are wide ranging.

In terms of size and construction, corpora can be divided into two main types: "ready-made" corpora and corpora compiled by the researcher. "Ready-made" corpora have been compiled by groups of academic or commercial researchers. They are often available to individual researchers, and include the Bank of English (http://www.collins.co.uk) and the British National Corpus (http://info.ox.ac.uk/bnc). Corpora of this kind are large, and in an attempt to enable judgments about the language as a whole, they usually include a wide range of text types, although it would obviously be unsafe to claim that any corpus can ever be truly representative of the language experience of all speakers. Unless otherwise indicated, the corpus referred to throughout this chapter is a 56-million-word sample of the Bank of English, and all citations are taken from it.

The second type of corpus is one which the researcher has designed him or herself, usually because they wish to study language in a specific context. Corpora of this kind that have been used for metaphor research include Cameron's corpus of educational discourse (2003), Koller's corpus of newspaper reports and journal articles on the topic of mergers and acquisitions (2003), and Santa Ana's corpus of issues of the *Los Angeles Times* (1999). These corpora tend to be much smaller than ready-made corpora and have usually been designed with the aim of representing one text-type or genre rather than the language as a whole. The researcher often has a specialized knowledge of the text type and discourse context, and an interest in associated social factors, so small corpora can allow for an in-depth analysis of metaphor in its discoursal and social contexts. This is in contrast to, and sometimes complementing, the overview of linguistic patterns of metaphor afforded by large ready-made corpora.

### *Corpus Linguistics*

"Corpus linguistics" is usually taken to refer to analysis that is conducted with the aid of specialized corpus software, but perhaps more important than the tools of the discipline is the theoretical approach which has emerged. This is manifested in two central and related characteristics. Firstly, a corpus-linguistic analysis should be *corpus-driven* as opposed to *corpus-based*, and secondly, it should take account of all the data. Tognini-Bonelli (2001) discusses the nature of corpus-driven research, writing that it does not start with preexisting theories, which are simply confirmed or illustrated with the support of corpus data, but starts with the corpus. Moon's (1998) work on fixed expressions and idioms (FEIs) is an example of corpus-driven work. Her studies begin with an examination of every FEI in her corpus, using a tight definition of FEI, and automatic identification procedures. In contrast, corpus-based work would examine preselected idioms and use the corpus to illustrate existing hypotheses. Moon's corpus-driven approach results in new insights into the role of FEIs in the organization of discourse, and into the importance of their evaluative orientation. In reality, corpus-driven research in its purest form tends to be an ideal, and many corpus studies, including most metaphor studies, of necessity start with some sort of working hypothesis, but this is explored and tested through the data rather than being preimposed on them.

The second feature of corpus linguistic research is described by Sinclair as follows:

> *It is a central part of the methodology . . . that every instance has the same weight as any other, and that selection is on the*

> *basis of the number of instances of a certain kind. No instance is ignored or overlooked.* (2004: 40)

This is seen in Deignan's analyses of metaphorically used words, which typically work with either every citation of a word or a large random sample and attempt to produce a classification that covers every citation examined. For example, Deignan (1999c) analyzed 1,000 randomly selected citations of key words from the source domain of temperature and classified the metaphorical uses by meaning. This led her to argue that the semantic relations between the metaphorical uses are not as clearly structured as is sometimes claimed. For instance, metaphorical *hot* is occasionally used antonymously to metaphorical *cold*, but in many cases, there is only a slim semantic relationship between the metaphorical uses.

### Searching Corpora

Ready-made corpora are usually far too big to read from end to end and are searched using various computer programs. Specialized corpora can be searched using corpus software but are sometimes searched by hand. Assuming that the researcher uses corpus software, as is usually the case, the first information that is often accessed is frequency: which word forms are the most frequent in the corpus. As the next step, the best-known way of studying individual words in a corpus is through the use of a program which searches for citations of particular word forms, and generally organizes them so that the search word (or *node*) is in the middle of the computer screen, in the form of a *concordance*. The following is an extract of the concordance of *drove*.

1. *called in a white Vauxhall, and drove away soon afterwards.*
2. *home as fast as possible. He seldom drove fast, and all the way home he*
3. *he considered the Jewish conspiracy drove him to repudiate the Jewish*
4. *These two today were crazy. They drove me mad." United boss Steve*
5. *the resort to overflowing, she drove out a few miles to the Eden Roc*
6. *during the Watergate scandal that drove President Richard Nixon out of*
7. *quite like that before and never drove quite like that again." It*
8. *at the university. Twice a week I drove Ted to the clinic. He*
9. *the court heard. Mcardle twice drove the lorry from Belfast to the*
10. *customer. He took his key and drove to the backside of the old*
11. *country to Michigan, rented a car, drove up to a rusting Volkswagen van*
12. *dizziness and so on which probably drove you to get the drugs in the*

Printed extracts such as this can misrepresent the process of analyzing concordance data. For reasons of space, a sample of 12 citations is shown here, whereas the corpus contains 2,161 citations of *drove*, and 16,348 citations of all the inflections of *drive*, noun and verb. In a typical analysis, these would be processed automatically for information about *collocates*, that is, the words that co-occur with the node more frequently than a chance distribution of words would predict (in the case of *drove*, collocates include *car*, *lorry*, and *fast*). A sample much larger than the above would then be examined in more detail, commonly 500 to 1,000 citations.

A central difficulty for metaphor researchers is deciding on a starting point for research. Machine techniques favor a single word or fixed multiword expression as the starting point of analysis, whereas metaphor researchers are often interested in patterns at a larger or deeper scale. Reading a corpus from beginning to end and identifying areas of interest is only a realistic possibility for small corpora. Cameron and Deignan (2003) used small and large corpora interactively, to exploit the advantages of each. Charteris-Black (2004) read a sample of each of his large corpora, and identified metaphors that he then searched for in the full corpora. Other possibilities include using thesauri to ensure that every term from a particular semantic field is searched for, or beginning with linguistic metaphors listed in the conceptual metaphor literature and searching for their collocates, techniques described by Deignan (1999a).

### Concordances and Intuition-Based Description

From a computer's point of view, a word form is simply a string of letters bounded by spaces, and in terms of the potential of modern computers, counting the frequency of a word form in a bank of texts is not a difficult task. Producing a concordance of the word form and calculating its most frequent collocates involve several more tasks, but these are nonetheless relatively straightforward. However, these very simple computational tools have proven to be tremendously powerful in generating insights about language in use. All fluent speakers of a language tend to use words in largely conventional patterns, and we therefore must have such patterns stored internally, but, for some reason, they are often not available to intuitive reflection (Sinclair, 1991, 2004). The use of automatic frequency counts and concordance programs brings patterns to the researcher's attention, so that they can be studied with the aid of his/her linguistic knowledge. When we try to access our knowledge of word use without using concordance data, metaphorical uses may not occur to us, or we may think of ones which are memorable because they are innovative, and disregard conventional but vastly more frequent uses. The heat metaphors for anger discussed in the Introduction are one example. In the following concordance of *drove*, four citations appear to be metaphorical:

1. he considered the Jewish conspiracy drove him to repudiate the Jewish
2. These two today were crazy. They drove me mad." United boss Steve
3. during the Watergate scandal that drove President Richard Nixon out
4. dizziness and so on which probably drove you to get the drugs in the

While these metaphorical uses of *drove* seem obvious with hindsight, it is difficult to be certain that they would have occurred to unaided intuition. In the following section, I give an example of a mismatch between the patterns found in the corpus and those found in intuitively derived linguistic data.

## Linguistic Data in Experimental Work

Some metaphor researchers use experiments in which informants are asked to react to texts of different kinds, often consisting of literal and metaphorical phrasings of the same idea. The informants' reaction times are measured and compared, and then discussed in the light of hypotheses about metaphor. The researchers generally invent the texts, which often contain examples of language that are rare or nonexistent in the corpus.

For a corpus linguist, one problem arises when the texts used do not display natural patterns of collocation and meaning. Current research on collocation suggests that people may process text in longer units than the single word, often in units of three or more words (for example, Erman & Warren, 2000; Wray, 2002). This phenomenon is sometimes known as "chunking", and may explain how we are able to process text as rapidly as we do (Sinclair, 1991). In order to chunk text and thus read at a normal speed, we are reliant on recognizing typical groupings of words. It follows that where words are used atypically we may be considerably slowed down. When metaphor experiments find variations in informants' reaction times, these may be due to atypical language patterns in texts, rather than to the added difficulty (or ease) of processing figurative or innovative language.

An example can be found in work by Keysar et al. (2000). In a complex series of experiments, Keysar and his co-researchers investigated the view that people use conceptual mappings to understand conventional expressions. They concluded that they probably do not, although they may use mappings in interpreting nonconventional expressions. One of their experiments investigated whether novel metaphorical expressions elicit conceptual mappings and included a comparison between reaction times to a novel metaphorical sentence, when it followed a short text consisting of "stock phrases" versus a short text consisting of "novel metaphors." Two of the texts used for the experiment were as follows:

1. As a scientist, Tina thinks of her theories as her children. She is a *prolific* researcher, *conceiving* an enormous number of new findings each year. *Tina is currently weaning her latest child.*
2. Tina thinks of her theories as her children. She is a *fertile* researcher, *giving birth* to an enormous number of new findings a year. *Tina is currently weaning her latest child.* (p. 582)

In each text, the first sentence makes the metaphorical mapping explicit. According to the researchers, the second sentence of the first text contains conventional expressions or "stock phrases", that is, *prolific* and *conceiving*, whereas the second sentence of the second text contains novel metaphors, that is, *fertile* and *giving birth*. The third sentence of each consists of the same novel metaphor *weaning her latest child*. (No items were italicized in the experiment.) Participants' reaction times to the third sentence in these and two other contexts were measured and compared. The assumption appears to be that this final sentence is ambiguous between a literal and metaphorical interpretation, and that informants may take different amounts of time to resolve the ambiguity, depending on whether a particular interpretation has been primed by the preceding context.

In order to check the researchers' judgments as to the conventionality or otherwise of each expression, 12 native speakers were asked for their views. Many corpus linguists would feel that this part of the procedure is potentially unsound because of the known unreliability of intuitive judgments in comparison to the examination of naturally occurring data (Sinclair, 1991). Corpus investigation suggests that this is indeed a problem for these texts.

The experiment makes several assumptions about usage, including the following:

1. that *fertile*, used in the second sentence of the second text, is a novel metaphor;
2. that *weaning*, in the last sentence of each text, is a novel metaphor;
3. that *latest child*, in the last sentence, is potentially ambiguous between the meanings "a child" and "a set of experimental findings."

Corpus analyses raised problems with each of the three assumptions, showing the following:

1. There are 365 citations of *fertile* in the corpus, 210 of which refer to land that can bear crops easily. Ninety-seven citations refer to people, animals, or plants. The meaning in this second group of citations is slightly different from that implied by the use of the metaphor in the previous text: *fertile* in this context tends to refer to the potential to reproduce rather than the fact of reproducing frequently. Citations include:

(3) The operation can rarely be reversed so that the man becomes *fertile* again.

More significantly, *fertile* is not a novel metaphor in the corpus. There are 61 citations in which it appears to be used metaphorically. Metaphorical meanings are linked to each of the two literal meanings. The "land" sense seems to motivate the expression *fertile ground*, which appears 20 times and is always metaphorical, in citations such as

(4) There is little doubt that growing discontent offers *fertile ground* for gains by the opposition.

The "capacity to reproduce" sense seems to motivate the use of *fertile* in citations such as

(5) For once, the artist's *fertile* imagination failed him.

2. *Wean* and its inflections occur 188 times in the corpus. There are five citations

taking the form seen in the last line of the experimental texts: that is, followed by a direct object which is clause-final. All of these are literal, for instance:

(6) She didn't imagine any trouble *weaning* her daughter.

All occur in relatively specialized texts, discussing feeding in child care, and on this limited evidence it appears that it would be unusual to use *wean* in a more general discussion about a person's children, as is suggested by the experimental texts. This in itself might affect participants' decoding time.

Although this lexico-grammatical pattern never appears with a metaphorical meaning of *wean*, other patterns are found in metaphorical uses relatively frequently, in citations such as:

(7) . . . to help fund jobs and *wean* single mums off welfare benefit and back into work.

(8) . . . *wean* people away from exclusive reliance on the automobile.

There is a further fairly frequent pattern, in which *wean* seems to mean not "take away from," but "be raised on," in metaphorical citations such as:

(9) . . . staffed by mechanics and engineers *weaned* on the local racing scene.

According to these data, Keysar et al.'s assertion that the use of *wean* in the final sentence is a novel metaphor is true in the strictest sense, in that no metaphors were found in the corpus taking this exact lexico-grammatical form. However, *wean*, like *fertile*, has several metaphorical uses which are closely related semantically to the uses given them in the texts. It seems possible that these metaphorical uses might be activated in participants during the experiments. This could lead to one of two problems: first, participants might not be processing either or both words as novel but as conventional metaphors. Second, in doing so they might be slowed down by the slightly atypical lexico-grammatical environments in which they appear in the texts.

3. Finally, the experiment appears to depend on an assumption that *latest child* is ambiguous between a literal and a metaphorical interpretation. Corpus data suggest that in fact the metaphorical interpretation is probably favored, because the collocation *latest* + *child* almost never occurs. There are 16,016 citations of *child* in the corpus; *latest* appears in the immediate left slot just twice, in the expressions "latest child rapist" and "latest child prodigy." In contrast, *youngest* appears 41 times before *child*; this would seem to be the usual way of talking about the child most recently born to someone. This impression is supported by an examination of collocates of *latest* and *youngest*: *latest* occurs 6,524 times in the corpus. The top immediate right lexical collocates, in order of frequency, are *figures*, *development*, *book*, *round*, *news*, *album*, *film*, *reports*, *edition*, and *technology*, words which seem to be in the same semantic domain as the intended metaphorical meaning of *child* in the experiment. *Youngest* occurs 883 times in the corpus, and its top right lexical collocates are *son*, *daughter*, *child*, *player*, *member*, *prime minister*, *person*, *children*, *brother*, and *boy*. It seems likely therefore that the collocation *latest child* will strongly suggest a nonconventional meaning of *child*, regardless of the preceding context, because the typical language pattern is broken.

The experimental text analyzed here is not unusual in containing instances of language that behave in different ways in the corpus from the researchers' assumptions. Corpus analyses of other experimental data, as well as elicited data, have shown similar discrepancies (Deignan, 2005a). Research involving experimental and elicited data has made many important contributions to knowledge about how metaphors work, but naturally occurring data are a necessary complement, and it is to be hoped that the insights from the study of naturally occurring language can inform and develop experimental work.

I have given two examples of corpus data adding to and raising questions about intuitively generated linguistic data, in the language about anger discussed in the Introduction, and in Keysar et al.'s data here. Examples of such discrepancies can be found easily, in virtually every corpus analysis, and researchers need to be aware of the unreliability of elicited and invented data. However, this is not by any means the most important contribution of corpus linguistics to metaphor studies. A number of significant insights into metaphor use have resulted from the accumulation of linguistic details through corpus study, and the most far-reaching of these will be described in the following sections.

## Metaphor as a Textual and Social Phenomenon

It is now widely agreed that metaphor is a cognitive phenomenon, and a mass of evidence has been accumulated to support the proposition that many linguistic metaphors, especially those that are most conventionalized and embedded in the language, are realizations of mental mappings. However, corpus linguistic research suggests that a mental mapping theory of metaphor is not in itself sufficient to account for the patterns found in language. Other factors seem to contribute to shaping the linguistic data. Charteris-Black (2004) uses corpus data to claim that metaphor use is shaped by societal and ideological factors as well as cognitive ones. In the following subsections, I draw on his and other corpus research to claim that metaphor use is influenced by linguistic, genre, cultural, and ideological factors. That is, metaphor is textual and social as well as cognitive.

### *Metaphor and Linguistic Context*

When we choose a metaphor to express an idea, we are influenced by the other words in our utterance. Corpus evidence indicates that linguistic metaphors are constrained by their co-text, in common with other features of language in use. I examined concordance data for *blow* and *price*, identified their frequent collocates, and from these identified and studied the most frequent fixed expressions containing the words (Deignan, 1999b, 2005b). I found that most fixed expressions are used with either the literal or the metaphorical meaning of *blow* or *price*, more usually the metaphorical meaning. It is much rarer for an expression to be used in both source and target domains, even when there is nothing in its intrinsic meaning that ties it to either domain. Examples include *heavy blow*, and *pay a high price*, which are commonly found with metaphorical meanings but rarely with literal ones. Typical citations are:

(10) The announcement will be a *heavy blow* to investors.

(11) Top cop Dr. Ian Oliver appears to have *paid a high price* for the scandal surrounding his police force. The under-pressure Chief Constable, 58, looks 10 years older than he should.

There are some apparent exceptions. However, in these cases, linguistic differences can generally be found at a more detailed linguistic level. For instance, *at any price* is used with both literal and metaphorical meanings of *price*, as in the following citations.

(12) All the great works of that period are either owned by museums or private collectors who won't sell *at any price*.

(13) In court she was portrayed as jealous, violent, paranoid, spiteful, bent on destroying her spouse *at any price*.

Corpus analysis shows that the metaphorical meaning of *at any price* is more usual, and where a literal meaning is intended, this is always signaled by the presence of a word from the semantic field of buying and selling, *sell* in citation (12).

Exceptions are found where a pattern is exploited for creative purposes. It might be expected that a literal expression would sometimes be used inventively with a metaphorical meaning, but in fact, the reverse seems more common. Fixed expressions associated with the target domain are used with a source domain meaning or allusion for creative or comic effect. For example, an advertisement in a British newspaper for the Edinburgh Theatre Festival Fringe events features a photograph of an acrobat performing a back somersault, with the caption, "No need to bend over backwards to get to the Fringe" (*The Independent*, March 19, 2005). Corpus data confirm that *bend over backwards* is rarely used with the literal meaning that is alluded to here.

The association of collocations and fixed expressions with a single meaning of a word is not predicted by cognitive metaphor theory. Indeed, cognitive theory could be taken to suggest the opposite: if a source domain including the logical relations between its entities is mapped onto a target domain, we would expect a replication of the logical relationships. At the linguistic level, this would imply that the same expressions would appear in both domains, realizing the underlying conceptual relationships.

Developments in linguistic theory, notably work by Sinclair (for example, 1991, 2004) provide a plausible explanation. Sinclair claims that collocation is one of the most important forces in shaping language in use (1991). The notion of "chunking," or producing and decoding text in units of several words, was described above. Work in corpus lexicography (for instance, Moon, 1987), has shown that each meaning of a word has its own distinctive sets of collocates. This implies that once a particular metaphor is chosen, its collocates will be partly predetermined. If a speaker wants to talk about the disadvantages of a situation in terms of the metaphor *pay*, other metaphors such as *high* and *price* are likely to spring to mind. Linguistic convention is thus a factor in metaphor choice and patterning.

### *Metaphor and Genre*

A second factor affecting metaphor choice is genre, specifically the topic and purpose of a text. Charteris-Black (2000) found a number of metaphors which are more frequent in a corpus of *The Economist* than in the Bank of English sub-corpus of general magazines. Quantitative data alone did not enable him to do this. For instance, the words *fat* and *diet* are more frequent in the general magazine corpus, which might suggest that the two words would have little role in conveying meanings specific to *The Economist*. However, a detailed examination shows that this is not the case. In the *Economist*, both *fat* and *diet* tend to have specialized metaphorical meanings relating to the economy. Citations include:

> *They forced importers to slash their once* fat *margins.*
> *State-owned firms surviving on a* diet *of subsidy and protection. (2000: 155)*

The differences in meanings of these words across the two corpora could be attributed to topic. Articles about literal diets would be less expected in *The Economist* than in a general interest magazine.

Corpus research by Skorczynska (2001) and Skorczynska and Deignan (2006) shows that topic is not the only aspect of genre that affects metaphor choice. Purpose is also a factor. They compared metaphor use in a corpus of popular periodicals, including *The Economist*, with a corpus of research journals on the same topic and found that there is relatively little metaphor use in common. In their sample corpus of research journals, consisting of around 30,000 words, which they searched by hand, they found 21 metaphorically used terms realizing six source domains, and two one-shot metaphors. In their sample periodicals corpus of the same size, they found 72 metaphorically used terms (types), realizing 11 source domains. Five of the six source domains found in the research corpus were also found in the periodicals corpus: HUMAN/ANIMAL LIFE, MECHANICS, JOURNEY, GAMES and HUNTING. However, only four linguistic metaphors, *grow*, *growth*, *flow*, and *game*, were common to both sample corpora. The source domains of JOURNEY and HUNTING are realized in both corpora but do not share a single linguistic realization. For example, in the research corpus, JOURNEY is realized by *free ride* and *free rider*, while in the periodicals corpus it is realized by *bump, derail, race, road, station,* and *train*. This would be unexpected if topic were the sole factor determining metaphor use, because the two corpora included texts on a number of very similar topics. The researchers analyzed the context and function of the metaphors in detail and concluded that the purpose of the text seems to be an important factor in determining choice of metaphor. For instance, different metaphors are chosen to illustrate economic concepts to a lay reader than those that are used to model theory to a co-researcher.

### *Metaphor Is Culturally Determined*

Cross-linguistic corpus work has demonstrated that sometimes different languages use different metaphors to talk about the same topic. Differences in metaphor choice have been attributed to several cultural factors: the salience of source domains and differences in attitudes toward the source or target domain. Boers and Demecheleer (1997) found evidence for the first factor. They analyzed metaphors from economics discourse, using corpora of English, French, and Dutch texts. Their corpora were small, at around 43,000 words of English and 20,000 words each of French and Dutch, but were highly comparable. They studied the linguistic realizations of metaphors from three source domains: PATHS, HEALTH, and WAR and found linguistic metaphors traceable to each of the three source domains in all three languages. The source domains were used across the three languages with different levels of frequency. Health metaphors are three times as frequent in French as in Dutch, while path metaphors are more frequent, though not as markedly so, in English than in the other two languages. English prefers path metaphors to the other two domains, while war metaphors are preferred in French and Dutch. The researchers speculate that this could be due to the British seafaring past. They also found that national stereotypes are evident in metaphor choice. For instance, the British texts used gardening metaphors more than three times as frequently as the French texts, while the French texts used nearly five times as many food metaphors as the English ones. These findings suggest that a similar range of metaphors is available in the three languages, but the salience of the source domain in the speakers' culture influences the choice they make.

Semino (2002) finds different groups of metaphors used in her corpora of English and Italian newspapers and claims that these reflect the different attitudes held by the two cultures towards the topic, and occasionally toward the source domain (2002). She analyzed data from early 1999, when the new pan-European currency, the Euro, was introduced. Britain and Italy have strikingly different attitudes toward the Euro. Britain did not join the Eurozone, and a number of British people remain strongly opposed to greater integration with the other economies of Europe. Italy, in contrast, is generally Europhile, and the Euro was adopted enthusiastically. Semino found that these different attitudes are reflected in the metaphors used in the two corpora. The corpora showed a number of shared metaphors from the source domains of BIRTH, JOURNEYS, CONTAINERS, SPORT, and DREAMS. However, these tend to be exploited differently by the media in the two countries. For instance, in Italy, the birth metaphor was accompanied by enthusiasm for the metaphorical baby's health, while in Britain the metaphor was either undeveloped or had negative overtones. In one British example, the Euro is compared to a "heavyweight" baby that is not shown in public, a reference to the three-year delay before the introduction of Euro coins and notes. As Semino points out, different uses of the "baby" metaphor may also reflect the Italians' very positive attitudes toward babies and children, so in this case, the different linguistic metaphors reflect values in the source domain as well as attitudes toward the target domain.

### *Metaphor Is Ideological*

A central claim in contemporary metaphor theory is that metaphor is ideological. Lakoff presented this argument at the start of the first Persian Gulf War in the strongest terms, claiming "Metaphors can kill" (1991). Corpus findings are completely consistent with his argument. Koller studied the ideological use of metaphor within merger and acquisition texts (2003). She built her own specialized corpus, consisting of 164,000 words of articles published between 1996 and 2000 in *Business Week, The Economist, The Financial Times,* and *Fortune*. Koller searched for metaphors from the source domains of WAR/VIOLENCE and MARRIAGE/ROMANCE, concordancing 48 lemmas from these domains and establishing which words and expressions are used frequently with metaphorical meanings. VIOLENCE metaphors in her corpus included *bruise, killer,* and *victim* as well as expressions more closely associated with war, such as *takeover battle* and *fight off corporate raiders*. MARRIAGE/ROMANCE metaphors include *woo* and *flirt*. Koller's frequency counts showed that WAR metaphors are more than three times more frequent than MARRIAGE ones. The initial, quantitative part of her study thus revealed several important facts about the metaphors of mergers and acquisition discourse which would have been difficult to retrieve in other ways. As in much corpus work, the quantitative findings formed a starting point for the qualitative study of metaphors in text. In some cases, this showed a conflation of WAR/VIOLENCE and MARRIAGE/ROMANCE metaphors in the same utterances, for example:

> *At a recent conference [he] joked that if* suitors *in the telecom industry now need fat chequebooks and a bunch of flowers. And if gallantry is rebuffed? Call in the* tanks. *(2003: 193)*

Koller concludes that the large number of metaphors from the male-oriented source domain of WAR/VIOLENCE help to construct the discourse as male and thus, in her view, as excluding of women. The male orientation is strengthened by the use of MARRIAGE/ROMANCE metaphors to talk about mergers and acquisitions. In these metaphors, the dominant company is assumed to be male, while the company in the weaker position is assumed to be female.

Charteris-Black's (2000) findings from a corpus of economics discourse are consistent with an ideological view of metaphor. He found that animate metaphors are used to talk about economies in general terms, the main source domains being sickness and health, and the human life cycle and family. The sickness and health metaphor is realized in citations such as:

> *As the bank continued to* haemorrhage *both deposits and loans. (2000: 155)*

Charteris-Black argues that such metaphors imply that the economy is animate but passive and that "this perception permits the economist to present himself as a doctor or surgeon who can take an active role in influencing economic events" (ibid.). Other typical linguistic realizations of animate metaphors include *healthy, ailing, infant,* and *parent*. However, in talking about the market and market movements more specifically, different sets of metaphors are used, and these tend to be inanimate. For instance, the market is described as a liquid, in metaphorical expressions such as *float* and *buoyant,* and as a ball, in expressions such as *bounce back* and *rebound*. In contrast to animate metaphors, which suggest an entity that has its own volition but is nonetheless subject to some control, inanimate metaphors present the markets as natural forces, beyond human control, a message which can be detected in the use of *drop* and *rebound* in the following citation:

> *After such a sharp* drop *in growth some* rebound *seems inevitable. (Charteris-Black 2000: 158)*

Charteris-Black's (2004) comparative analysis of metaphor use across corpora of a range of different genres confirms his view that metaphor is always evaluative, never neutral. He uses corpus techniques to analyze metaphor use on the Old and New

Testaments, and in the Koran, as well as in U.S. presidential speeches and British party manifestos. His comparisons reveal ways that metaphors are used to present an ideological message in different but related texts. For instance, the different focuses in the Old and New Testaments can be seen in its metaphors. The Old Testament contains many more metaphors that stress God's retribution.

The corpus studies described here present a view of metaphor that is consistent with contemporary metaphor theory but which adds to it. Much current research stresses the cognitive dimension of metaphor, and tends to explore its informational content. Corpus linguistic studies show that the informational message to be conveyed is only one of the factors that affect metaphor choice. Other factors are textual, that is, the linguistic co-text, and social, that is, the function of the text, and its cultural and ideological context.

## Metaphor as the Product of Dynamic Interactions

As well as enriching our understanding of the mechanisms generating linguistic metaphors, a corpus view of metaphor can contribute more directly to contemporary metaphor theory. In this section, two lines of research are described, both of which suggest that metaphor is a dynamic phenomenon.

### *Interaction between Source and Target Domains*

Corpus evidence points to an interaction between source and target domains, such as is proposed in the blending theory (Fauconnier & Turner, 2002). Deignan (2005a) examined the grammatical behavior of linguistic metaphors and compared this with the behavior of their literal counterparts, focusing on realizations of HUMAN BEHAVIOR IS ANIMAL BEHAVIOR. She found that there is a tendency for words that are nouns in the source domain to be used as verbs in the target domain. For instance, *horse, hound, ferret, squirrel, wolf,* and *pig* are all commonly verbs in the target domain of human behavior. This grammatical difference is probably due to the different inherent structures of the source and target domains. Animals dominate the source domain, while in the target domain, ways of behaving are more prominent than entities. The source domain is therefore predominantly realized through nouns, while the target domain requires a rich range of verbs and some adjectives. Some source domain verbs and adjectives such as *bark, growl,* and *vicious* are used to talk about human behavior, but they do not seem to be the most frequent linguistic realizations of the mapping. Lakoff's invariance hypothesis (1993) would imply that source domain entities would not form part of the mapping because they do not have direct correspondences in the target domain. Many potential target domain meanings would therefore remain unrealized through this particular conceptual metaphor. Instead, what seems to happen is that source domain nouns undergo grammatical transformation to become verbs, enabling them to be used to talk about behavior.

One result of grammatical differences between source and target domains is that the logical relationships between entities in each domain differ. For instance, the relationship between *dog* and *hunt* and between *hound* and *hunt* is between agent and verb in the source domain. The relationship is syntagmatic, as the following corpus citations show:

(14) Rabbits were *hunted* with fast mongrel *dogs*.
(15) . . . issues such as *hunting* with *hounds*.

However, in the target domain of human behavior, *dog* and *hound* are not used as nouns. Both are verbal, as in the following citations:

(16) She has been *dogged* by tragedy.
(17) He complains of being *hounded* by intolerable pressure on and off the field.

Their metaphorical meaning is hyponymous to *pursue*. Although they are not synonymous to *hunt,* as used in the following citation, they are in a paradigmatic rather than a syntagmatic relationship with it:

(18) [He] is now out of prison and thinks he will be *hunted* by the underworld because they will look on him as a grass.

Similarly, *squirrel* and *hoard* have a syntagmatic relationship in the source domain, generally subject–verb, but in the target domain of human behavior, they are almost synonymous. Corpus analysis of animal metaphors suggests that grammatical differences between domains, and corresponding differences between logical relationships are the norm for this conceptual mapping (Deignan, 2005a). Similar patterns have been observed by other corpus researchers. Koller (2003) notes differences in word class between source and target domains, while Cameron (2003) finds high levels of verbal metaphors in her corpus.

These findings have implications for a strong view of metaphorical mapping, because they suggest that a one-to-one mapping of logical correspondences between entities is less common than sometimes assumed in the theoretical literature. In particular, they challenge an interpretation of conceptual metaphor theory that suggests that the target domain is largely constructed by source domain correspondences. Corpus data suggest that the inherent structure of the target domain does not only constrain the mapping, it helps to shape it.

### *Metaphor and Metonymy*

Corpus research by Deignan (2005a, b) and Charteris-Black (2003) contributes to the discussion about the interaction between metaphor and metonymy. Corpus data suggest a very large number of linguistic expressions generated by this interaction, possibly more than generated by either pure metaphor or pure metonymy. It also seems that there are more types of interaction than in the original framework proposed by Goossens (1995).

Goossen's important insight into the interaction between metaphor and metonymy was developed from a study of dictionary data. The examples used in dictionaries tend to be simplified, meaning that important linguistic patterns may be lost. Deignan (2005b) used the Bank of English to search for lexical items from a number of source domains. She investigated Goossen's categories, finding that *metaphor from metonymy* was by far the most frequent and that within this category more detailed distinctions can be drawn. Corpus data also show that individual expressions may belong in different categories depending on how they are used. Charteris-Black demonstrates the potential ambiguity between literal and figurative readings of expressions such as *lick one's lips* (2003). The following citations of *keep an eye on* also demonstrate a range of interpretations:

(19) This means that while Julia is cooking she can still *keep an eye on* their two young children.

(20) [The job] entails collecting the rent and *keeping an eye* on some housing association flats.

(21) Often a scheme will need backing for several years. During this time, the Field Director [will] *keep an eye on* its progress.

In citation (19), the expression seems literal, because it is certainly intended to refer to the physical act of watching (though it contains a metonymical use of *eye* to denote the act of watching). However, there is more than a purely literal meaning, and the expression also connotes caring: Julia is not simply watching her children, she is doing so in order to ensure their safety. This use of *keep an eye on* is therefore metonymic, because one action is used to stand for a wider pattern of behavior. In citation (21), the expression is very unlikely to have any literal reading, because its object, *progress,* is abstract in this context, and it is therefore an instance of Goossen's *metaphor from metonymy*. In citation (20), the expression is ambiguous in that it could refer to either literal watching, or it could be nonliteral, if it refers to caring for flats in a more general sense, for instance, ensuring that repairs are carried out. The source domain of body parts and actions generates a number of expressions that are ambiguous and context-dependent in this way (Moon, 1998). As in studies described in the previous section, corpus data suggest a rich, dynamic, and context-bound view of figurative language.

## Conclusion

In this chapter, it has been shown that corpus analysis can reveal many linguistic details that could be passed over in the examination of single texts, and might not be observed at all when data are elicited rather than gathered from language in use. Even when these details are noted, it is easy to dismiss them as insignificant, especially if they interfere with apparently tidy patterns. However, patterns like differences in part of speech and ambiguity between metonymy and metaphor are so frequently found in the corpus that they should perhaps be regarded as regularities in themselves. It is unsafe to assume that these linguistic details are not manifestations of deeper level metaphorical features. At the very least, they need to be studied in their own right and the implications fed back into metaphor theory. Studying linguistic metaphors in naturally occurring data has not produced findings that contradict contemporary metaphor theory, but it has suggested that other factors affect metaphor choice. In common with other features of language in use, metaphors are shaped by their linguistic context, genre, culture, and ideology as well as their informational content.

In critiquing experimental approaches to metaphor research, I argued that the collocational and syntactic patterns in which words are found are an important cue in readers' searches for meaning. This means that reading-time data from texts which contain atypical patterns may not be an indicator of the complexity of processing figurative or literal language. It is therefore important for reading-time experiments to use naturalistic language. Because even native speakers of a language cannot reliably access collocational and syntactic patterns using unaided intuition, it is very difficult to invent naturalistic sentences and short texts. Corpus data would form a useful resource in the design of such work.

Corpus linguistics is a relatively young field and has been applied to the study of metaphor for only a decade or so; it is to be expected that the ways in which corpora can contribute to our understandings of metaphor will continue to broaden.

## References

Boers, F., & Demecheleer, M. (1997). A few metaphorical models in (western) economic discourse. In W. A. Liebert, G. Redeker, & L. Waugh, (Eds.), *Discourse and perspective in cognitive linguistics* (pp. 115–129). Amsterdam: John Benjamins.

Cameron, L. (2003). *Metaphor in educational discourse*. London: Continuum.

Cameron, L., & Deignan, A. (2003). Combining large and small corpora to investigate tuning devices around metaphor in spoken discourse. *Metaphor and Symbol*, 18, 149–160.

Charteris-Black, J. (2000). Metaphor and vocabulary teaching in ESP economics. *English for Specific Purposes*, 19, 149–165.

Charteris-Black, J. (2003). Speaking with forked tongue: A comparative study of metaphor and metonymy in English and Malay phraseology. *Metaphor and Symbol*, 18, 289–310.

Charteris-Black, J. (2004). *Corpus approaches to critical metaphor analysis*. Basingstoke, Hampshire: Palgrave Macmillan.

Deignan, A. (1999a). Corpus based research into metaphor. In L. Cameron & G. Low (Eds.), *Researching and applying metaphor* (pp. 177–199). Cambridge: Cambridge University Press.

Deignan, A. (1999b). Linguistic metaphors and collocation in non-literary corpus data. *Metaphor and Symbol*, 14, 19–38.

Deignan, A. (1999c). Metaphorical polysemy and paradigmatic relations: A corpus study. *Word*, 50, 319–338.

Deignan, A. (2005a). *Metaphor and corpus linguistics*. Amsterdam: John Benjamins.

Deignan, A. (2005b). A corpus perspective on the relationship between metaphor and metonymy. *Style*, 39, 72–91.

Erman, B., & Warren, B. (2000). The open choice principle and the idiom principle. *Text*, 20, 29–62.

Fauconnier, G., & Turner, M. (2002). *The way we think: Conceptual blending and the mind's hidden complexities*. New York: Basic Books.

Gibbs, R. W. (1994). *The poetics of mind: Figurative thought, language, and understanding*. Cambridge: Cambridge University Press.

Goossens, L. (1995). Metaphtonymy: The interaction of metaphor and metonymy in expressions of linguistics action. In L. Goossens, P. Pauwels, B. Rudzka-Ostyn, A. Simon-Vanderbergen, & J. Vanparys (Eds.), *By word of mouth: Metaphor, metonymy and linguistic action in a cognitive perspective* (pp. 59–174). Amsterdam: John Benjamins.

Keysar, B., Shen, Y., Glucksberg, S., & Horton, W. S. (2000). Conventional language: How metaphorical is it? *Journal of Memory and Language*, 43, 576–593.

Koller, V. (2003). "A shotgun wedding": Co-occurrence of war and marriage metaphors in mergers and acquisitions discourse. *Metaphor and Symbol*, 17, 179–203.

Lakoff, G. (1987). *Women, fire, and dangerous things: What categories reveal about the mind*. Chicago: Chicago University Press.

Lakoff, G. (1991). *Metaphor and war: The metaphor system used to justify war in the Gulf*. http://www.oregon.edu/~uophil/metaphor/lakoff1.htm.

Lakoff, G. (1993). The contemporary theory of metaphor. In A. Ortony (Ed.), *Metaphor and thought*. (2nd ed., pp. 202–251). Cambridge: Cambridge University Press.

Moon, R. (1987). The analysis of meaning. In J. M. Sinclair (ed.) *Looking up* (pp. 86–103). New York: HarperCollins.

Moon, R. E. (1998). *Fixed expressions and idioms in English: A corpus approach*. Oxford: Clarendon Press.

Santa Ana, O. (1999). "Like an animal I was treated": Anti-immigrant metaphor in U.S. public discourse. *Discourse and Society*, 10, 191–224.

Semino, E. (2002). A sturdy baby or a derailing train? Metaphorical representations of the euro in British and Italian newspapers. *Text*, 22, 107–139.

Sinclair, J. (1991). *Corpus, concordance, collocation*. Oxford: Oxford University Press.

Sinclair, J. (2004). *Trust the text: Language, corpus and discourse*. London: Routledge.

Skorczynska, H. (2001). Metaphor in scientific business journals and business periodicals: an example of scientific discourse popularisation. *Ibérica* 3: 43–60.

Skorczynska, H., & Deignan, A. (2006). Readership and purpose in the choice of economics metaphor. *Metaphor and Symbol*, 21(2), 87–104.

Tognini-Bonelli, E. (2001). *Corpus linguistics at work*. Amsterdam: John Benjamins.

Van Teeffelen, T. (1994). Racism and metaphor: the Palestinian-Israeli conflict in popular literature. *Discourse & Society*, 5(3), 381–405.

Wray, A. (2002). *Formulaic language and the lexicon*. Cambridge: Cambridge University Press.

CHAPTER 17

# Metaphor and Poetic Figures

*Yeshayahu Shen**

Poetic discourse poses one of the most fascinating challenges to cognitive theories of figurative language. It is commonly assumed – by literary critics, psychologists of art, and philosophers alike (e.g., Shklovsky, in Lemon & Reis, 1965; Van Peer, 1986) – that the stylistic properties of poetic language, particularly figurative expressions, deliberately pervert or flout regular cognitive principles so as to achieve the effects unique to poetic discourse – the creation of such effects being the goal of all poetic discourse. According to Shklovsky, one of the chief proponents of this view, art seeks "to make the object 'unfamiliar,' to make forms difficult, to increase the difficulty and length of perception, because the process of perception is an aesthetic end in itself and must be prolonged" (Shklovsky, in Lemon & Reis, 1965).

However, many figurative expressions that appear in poetic discourse demonstrate a puzzling phenomenon (which represents, in a nutshell, the puzzle of artistic creativity in general). On the one hand, they are novel, creative, imaginative, and aesthetically pleasing; on the other hand, taken in isolation, they are, in many cases, easily understood and comprehended, even for ordinary readers.

How can we account for the fact that these expressions succeed in communicating in spite of their novelty? The general answer I propose is that poetic figures conform to certain cognitive principles that allow their ideas to be communicated. This general statement will be illustrated by three types of figurative language, namely, simile, zeugma, and synaesthetic metaphors. My goal is to examine how and to what extent one fundamental cognitive principle, namely, the directionality principle, affects the use of these three figurative types. Another goal is to extend previous cognitive research into poetic figurative language (e.g., Lakoff & Turner 1989) in two major respects. First, to broaden the study of figurative types by including three figurative types that have received relatively little attention in the literature. Second, to examine some additional aspects of the distribution in poetic

* This research was supported by The Israel Science Foundation administered by The Israel Academy of Sciences and Humanities, no. 939/02.

discourse and the comprehension of the three poetic figurative types that have not been previously examined, and which may suggest an even greater conformity of poetic figures to cognitive constraints than has been previously acknowledged.

## The Directionality Principle

Figurative thought conforms to certain principles, such as systematicity (cf. Gentner, 1983) and global mapping (Lakoff & Johnson, 1980; Tourangeau & Sternberg, 1982), which have been explored in some depth. Of these principles, the directionality of mapping is the most fundamental principal and therefore one of the most systematically and comprehensively studied. This principle states:

> *The metaphorical source domain tends to represent a conceptually more accessible (i.e., more concrete or more salient) concept than the target.*

There have been a great many studies in both linguistics and psycholinguistics, some of which have not only substantiated this principle but taken it several steps further. It has thus been suggested that in many languages figurative expressions tend, in accordance with this principle, to become conventionalized (Lakoff & Johnson, 1980; Sweetser, 1990). It has also been claimed that it is the directionality of mapping principle that largely determines the direction of diachronic meaning extension (Sweetser, 1990; Traugott, 1982). In addition, there have been several psycholinguistic experiments, indicating that structures consistent with the directionality principle are consistently viewed as more natural and comprehensible as well as being easier to recall (Johnson & Malgady, 1979; Ortony, 1979; Ortony et al., 1985; Shen, 1992; Tversky, 1977).

This principle, then, appears to be fundamental to figurative thought and cognition in general (see, for example, Shen (1997), who views it as a special case of the "cognitive reference point" principle).

### *Compatible and Clashing Expressions*

Given this principle, we may distinguish between two types of metaphorical structures, namely, compatible and clashing ones. A compatible structure (COS) is a metaphorical expression whose linguistic structure is compatible with the cognitive principle, as in the simile "education is like a ladder." Here, the noun "education," being the grammatical subject of the comparison, represents the metaphor target, while "a ladder," being the comparison predicate, is the metaphor source. Since the target ("education") is more abstract than the source ("a ladder") this comparison is compatible with the directionality principle, which favors this direction of mapping.

A clashing structure (CLS) is a metaphorical expression whose linguistic structure clashes with the cognitive principle, for example, "a ladder is like education." Here, the target (the grammatical subject) represents a more concrete concept than the source, thus clashing with the conceptual principle.

The main question that I address is the following: To what extent does the conceptual directionality principle (DP) affect the use of metaphorical expressions of the three figurative types analyzed here? I will investigate this question with respect to two major issues, namely, the distribution and comprehension of the three figurative types. In particular, I will address the following questions:

1. *Distribution in poetic discourse*: Are COS figurative expressions used more frequently than CLS ones even in poetic discourse, an area in which figurative language is used in the most creative way possible? And, if so, does this hold true for the poetry of all languages, periods, and schools?
2. *Comprehension*. This issue is divided into two related sets of questions:
   i. Are COS figurative expressions cognitively more basic and easier to understand than CLS ones? That is, is it easier to assign meaning to COS

than to CLS expressions? Are they viewed as a more natural or more meaningful construct? Are they easier to recall?

ii. Does the DP give rise to an "inversion effect" in subjects' interpretation and recall of CLS expressions? That is, do subjects tend to invert the target and base terms in interpretation and recall of the three figurative types? (see also Chiappe et al. 2003; Glucksberg et al. 1997).

## Simile

Similes are metaphorical comparisons composed of two nominal terms, one of which belongs to the target and the other to the source domain. Accordingly, in the simile *education is like a ladder,* "education" is the target domain and "ladder" the source domain. Similes have been studied extensively in various fields, such as literary studies (e.g., Fishelov, 1996), philosophy and linguistics (e.g., Beardsley, 1981), and cognitive psychology (Glucksberg et al., 1997; Chiappe et al., 2003; Ortony et al., 1985). The issues investigated include description and interpretation of specific similes, description of the various forms similes can take in poetry (Fishelov, 1996), and attempts to describe the differences between similes and metaphors and the psychological mechanisms involved in their processing (Glucksberg & Keysar, 1990; Ortony et al., 1985).

A major observation made in many of these studies (notably, Ortony et al., 1985, elaborated by Glucksberg & Keysar, 1990; Chiappe et al., 2003; Glucksberg et al., 1997) is that similes (not necessarily as opposed to metaphors) are directional comparisons characterized (in accordance with the directionality principle) by a preference to map more accessible (salient, typical, concrete) concepts into less accessible ones rather than the other way around, as the previous example, *education is like a ladder,* illustrates. In what follows, I will elaborate on this observation with respect to the use of similes in poetic discourse (an issue that has been insufficiently discussed in the cognitive literature), as well as various comprehension issues that have not been discussed in past literature.

*Distribution of similes in poetic discourse.* While most studies in cognitive psychology and psycholinguistics have focused on nonpoetic similes (conventional ones or ones artificially constructed for experimental purposes), one question of interest in this chapter is whether similes used in poetic discourse also conform to the directionality principle. Shen (1995) investigated the frequency with which the two simile types (COS and CLS) were used in various poetic corpora. I assembled a corpus of 400 similes excerpted from the poems of four eras of periods in twentieth century Hebrew poetry, each represented by four of its most prominent poets. In order not to prejudice the analysis, not only were the 16 poets markedly different from one another in style, but the similes extracted from their poems were chosen at random. This meant that contextual factors, whether a particular poem, individual poet, or specific school of poets, would not affect the structural pattern arising from the study's results and could thus be discounted when assessing those results.

This latter point is supported by the fact that the poetic characteristics of each of the four corpora examined, representing as they did successive periods in the history of Hebrew poetry, were markedly different from, even at odds with, one another. This is a reflection of the continual struggle between the poets of different generations – a struggle, incidentally, characteristic of literary evolution in general. Accordingly, it would be reasonable to assume that the poets of one generation of Hebrew poets, while rejecting the poetic proclivities of their predecessors, would eventually find their own poetic strategies being spurned by their immediate successors. This being the case, the four corpora used in the study being poetically antithetically, should, on the face of it, have used a wide range of poetic metaphors noticeably different from one another in terms of COS and CLS dominance.

The similes taken from the poems were analyzed using two measures of accessibility: (1) abstract versus concrete and (2) salience. In terms of abstract versus concrete, a COS simile is one in which the subject, target term X, is more abstract than the predicate, source term Y, as in the simile *emptiness (X) like a weight (Y) is heavy on the heart*. A CLS simile embodies the opposite case, where the subject target terms are more concrete than the predicate source terms, as in the simile *the flowers (X) blossom like a dream (Y)*. Salience was measured only in those similes where the ground (or shared property) of the two nominal terms was explicitly stated, as in the simile *a flock of birds leaves behind it a trail like a jet plane*, where the ground (*leaves a trail behind them*) is explicitly stated. In such cases, the degree of salience of the shared property in each of the simile's terms was assessed. In COS similes, the level of salience is higher in the source term, as, in the previous simile, where *a flock of birds leaves a trail like a jet plane*, with "jets" (the source term) much more prone to leaving trails than "birds" (the target term). In CLS similes, it is the target term that is the more salient of the two. Thus, in the simile *the fire is hot like a cloud*, the shared property of "hot" is more closely associated with the target term "fire" than with the source term "cloud."

The results of the study were clear-cut: On both counts of accessibility, the number of COS similes greatly exceeded the number of CLS ones. On the abstract versus concrete scale, 95% of the similes were of the COS type and only 5% CLS, while on the salience scale, 73% were COS constructs and 27% CLS ones.

To determine whether these findings apply to the poetic corpora of other languages as well, a similar analysis was carried out on nineteenth and twentieth century Russian and Arabic poetry (see Shen, 2007). The results in both cases produced the same striking pattern, as in which COS similes by far outnumbered CLS similes. This supports the view that even the most creative use of figurative language, poetic discourse, is subject to cognitive constraints (for further details see Shen, 1997, 2002).

### COMPREHENSION

The first comprehension issue is whether the COS similes are cognitively simpler structures than the CLS ones. There is some evidence to suggest an affirmative answer to that question. Thus, Ortony et al. (1985) found that the degree of similarity between the terms used in COS similes, such as *libraries are like gold mines* or *rage is like a volcano*, was considered higher than that for CLS similes such as *gold mines are like libraries* or *a volcano is like rage*. Furthermore, COS similes were judged as being more meaningful than CLS ones. Shen (1995) pointed out that not only were COS similes thought to be more natural than CLS ones, but that it took most people longer to interpret CLS similes. In addition, the interpretations generated for CLS similes proved to be a great deal more heterogeneous than those provided for COS ones, a clear indication that CLS similes are, indeed, much harder to interpret.

Let us now consider a more radical effect the DP might have on the way people comprehend similes (see also Chiappe et al., 2003; Glucksberg et al., 1997). Arguably, if people's preference for mapping from a more accessible to a less accessible domain (as suggested by the DP principle) is a strong one, it might result in a radical inversion effect in their comprehension of CLS similes. That is, when people are asked to interpret a given CLS simile or retrieve it from memory, they might invert the target and source terms, yielding a structure compatible with the DP.

To test this possibility, two experiments, a recall and an interpretation generation experiment (Shen & Shalev, in preparation), were conducted. Both experiments employed the same stimuli: two sets of twelve similes, the first consisting of COS similes, the second of CLS similes. The COS similes included expressions such as *a friend is like an anchor* and *libraries are like gold mines*, while the CLS similes simply reversed the order of the nominals in the COS simile, as in *an anchor is like a friend* and *gold mines are like libraries*. In each of the two experiments, the subjects were read the simile in either the COS or the CLS form.

All the similes used in the experiments were the Hebrew equivalent of the ones employed by Ortony in his study of the question of directionality in metaphorical comparisons. Ortony et al. (1985) had established that COS similes (although they did not use this word for them) have the property that some of the highly salient properties of the source term match some of the less salient properties of the target term. In the case of *a friend is like an anchor*, "providing support" – the shared property – is a high-salience characteristic of the source term "anchor" and a low salience characteristic of the target term "friend" (for a more detailed argument, see Shen, 1995).

RECALL

Subjects first read a list of similes (half COS and half CLS). After an interval of a few minutes, they were asked to write down, as accurately as possible, what they could recall from the comparisons they had read. The subjects' responses were then analyzed for the number of inversions they performed on the original similes they had encountered in the initial phase. As hypothesized, the number of inversions subjects made for the CLS was significantly higher than those made for the COS similes. In fact, not even a single COS simile (out of the 12 analyzed) was inverted in recall by most subjects, whereas seven out of the 12 CLS similes had instances of inversion.

INTERPRETATION GENERATION

The aim of this experiment was to examine the effect of the DP on simile comprehension, using a different task. One might argue that even if the DP influences recall of CLS similes, it must not affect the comprehension process at its initial phases, when it is not necessary to use delayed recall. The present experiment was intended to investigate this possibility.

The subjects in this experiment were given the same set of items that had been used in the recall experiment and were asked to provide a one-sentence interpretation for each simile. Their responses were then analyzed for the number of inversions of the noun phrases in the interpretation. The responses were classified into two groups, "preserving" and "inverting" responses. Preserving responses are those in which the target and source terms of the original simile were preserved in the subject's response. For example, one preserving response for the simile *A friend is like an anchor* was "A friend helps you as an anchor helps the boat." Other examples of preserving responses included "a lecture makes you sleep like a sleeping pill," for the simile *a lecture is like a sleeping pill*; and, "the books in the library are worth as much as treasure found in a gold mine," for the simile *a library is like a gold mine*.

Inverted interpretations are those that reverse the original simile's target and source positions. For instance, the simile *an anchor is like a friend* was interpreted variously as "like the anchor that keeps a vessel from drifting away, so a friend too can act like an anchor" or "a friend can be like an anchor if you have a close friend." An instance of an inverted interpretation for the simile *a beehive is like a university* was the response "a university has a lot of departments and a lot of students, just as there are a great many compartments and bees in a beehive." For the simile *a book is like a beam* inverted interpretations included: "a book is like a beam for the soul" and "reading a good book is like a warm beam on a rainy day: pleasant, surprising and enjoyable."

We hypothesized that the number of inverting responses generated for CLS would be significantly higher than those generated for COS. This prediction was fully confirmed. Thus all 12 COS similes generated preserving responses, whereas 10 out of the 12 CLS similes generated inverting responses, in full accordance with our prediction. Another striking characteristic of the responses generated by the subjects was that only eight of the 336 responses generated for the 12 COS similes were inverting responses. These results show a very robust pattern of inverting the CLS while preserving the COS.

## Zeugma

The next figure to be addressed, namely, the zeugma, allows us to examine the effect of the DP on the structure of metaphorical sentences other than similes. A zeugma is a figure of speech in which a word is made to govern two other elements in such a way that a different sense relationship is obtained in each case. Examples are "He packed his shirts and sorrow" and "She caught an airplane and a husband." In both of these cases, one term ("packed" or "caught") stands in the same syntactical relation to two other terms ("shirt" and "sorrow" in the first instance, "airplane" and "husband" in the second), but with a different meaning in each case.

There are two ways in which such zeugmas can be presented. In one case, the more salient term is introduced first, followed by the less salient one, while in the other, the less salient term precedes the more salient one. Accordingly, *he packed his shirt and sadness* is an example of the first type, and *he packed his sadness and shirt* is an example of the second. In both cases, it is assumed that the literally used noun (*shirt*) is more salient then the metaphorical one (*sadness*), with regard to the shared predicate.

Arguably, a structure in which the more salient term occurs first is compatible with the directionality principle, while the inverted structure clashes with it. One study supporting this claim is the study of Kelly, Bock, and Keil (1986) of the relation between salience (as measured by a term's prototypicality within a given category) and sentence structure using recall and preference ratings. When presented with two sentences, such as *The man bought an orange and a lemon in the grocery store* and *The man bought a lemon and an orange in the grocery store*, most of the subjects in Kelly et al.'s study judged the first sentence, in which "orange" – the salient (prototypical) term in the category "fruit" – preceded "lemon" – the less salient term – to be the more natural one. Furthermore, Kelly et al. noted that when recalling zeugmas that reversed the "normal" order, the subjects consistently inverted the original zeugma by positioning the prototypical terms before the non-prototypical ones. According to Kelly et al., this preference arises from the greater "cognitive accessibility" of the prototypical terms. Thus, the precedence-of-the-salient-item rule is compatible with the directionality principle. This clearly shows that a COS zeugma is one in which the more salient term precedes the less salient one, while a CLS zeugma one in which the less salient term precedes the more salient one.

Having distinguished between COS and CLS zeugmas, we will now discuss the distribution of these two types in poetic discourse and how they are comprehended.

### DISTRIBUTION

Two large-scale field studies, one conducted in 1997, the other in 2002, and both analyzing various poetic corpora, supported the contention that, regardless of language, period, or school of poetry, poets use more COS than CLS zeugmas (see Shen, 1997, 2002). In 1997, Shen assembled a sample of 350 zeugmas taken from Hebrew poems written between 1900 and 1980. Each of the poems belongs to one of four defining periods in modern Hebrew poetry, which were markedly different from one another in their poetic characteristics. Nevertheless, as in the case of similes, our hypothesis was that contextual factors, such as the particular poem, poet, or school of poetry in question, would not affect the structural pattern emerging from the study's results. In addition, to establish whether the study's findings extended beyond the realm of Hebrew poetry to poetry in general, a large number of zeugmas were extracted from the poems of Allen Ginsberg, a poet famous for using zeugmas. The results in both cases were unequivocal: approximately 83% of the zeugmas of the Hebrew poets as well as of Ginsberg had literal-first order, while only 17% were of the metaphorical-first type.

Shen (2002) reported on a similar study that attempted to discover whether these structural norms were also valid across time – whether they could, for example, be applied to medieval Hebrew poetry. Using the same methodology as above, Shen extracted 55 zeugmas from the poems of 11 major medieval Hebrew poets. The results confirmed the 1997 study's findings in that out of 55 zeugmas, 43 (78%) were literal-first zeugmas, and only 11 (22%) were metaphorical-first (Shen, forthcoming).

The same pattern emerged in the literary corpora of other languages, such as Arabic and Russian, pointing to a clear preference on the part of poets in general for COS type zeugmas (Shen, in press). In sum, the poetic corpora of languages, eras, and schools of poetry employ a great many more COS than CLS zeugmas.

COMPREHENSION

Various studies have suggested that COS zeugmas are cognitively simpler and easier to comprehend than their CLS counterparts. Shen (1998) found that subjects judged COS zeugmas as more natural than COS ones. Similarly, subjects in another study (Shen & Shalev, in preparation) judged COS as easier to assign interpretations to.

More interesting findings were found in studies that examined the potential "inversion effect" on people's comprehension of CLS zeugmas. As in the case of similes, a recall and an interpretation–generation experiment were used to investigate this possibility.

In the recall experiment (Shen, 1998), subjects received a list of items, each consisting of a question (e.g., "What did the soldier pack?") and a related answer that represented a zeugma (e.g., "The soldier packed his shirt/sadness and sadness/shirt"). Half of the sentences were COS zeugmas (e.g., "The soldier packed his shirt and sadness"), while the other half had a CLS structure. The experiment was carried out in two stages. First, the subjects were asked to read a list of items such as those described above. Then the experimenter read the questions aloud and asked the subjects to provide the answers from the previous stage as accurately as possible. As hypothesized, subjects reversed significantly more noncanonical (nonliteral first) than canonical (literal first) structures that they had originally read.

The interpretation–generation study (Shen, in preparation) provides further support for the claim that inversion effects occur more frequently in CLS zeugmas than in their COS counterparts. The rationale underlying this experiment is similar to the one presented in the case of the simile. Subjects received a list of zeugmas (similar to the list that was used in the recall experiment) and were asked to provide short (single-sentence) interpretations of these expressions.

The results were then divided into preserving interpretations, which maintained the original ordering of the nouns, and inverting interpretations, which inverted the original order. For example, a typical preserving interpretation for the (COS) zeugma *The soldier packed his shirt and sorrow* was "The soldier packed his shirt while blocking his feelings"; and for the zeugma *Dana peeled the wallpaper and the memories*, "Dana peeled the wallpaper and erased the memories." Inverted responses for the CLS zeugma *The soldier packed his sorrow and shirt* included interpretations such as "while packing his shirts he thought about his sorrow" and "the soldier prepared to leave while trying to overcome his sorrow." Similarly, the CLS zeugma *The baby sipped kisses and milk* generated the response "the baby sipped milk and willingly accepted kisses." On the whole, the number of inverting responses generated by CLS zeugmas was significantly higher than those generated for COS zeugmas (Shen, in preparation).

In sum, the results of both the recall and the interpretation–generation experiments strongly suggest that the DP radically affects the comprehension of CLS versus COS zeugmas.

## Synaesthetic Metaphor

Unlike similes and zeugmas, which involve concrete-to-abstract mapping, synaesthesias (e.g., *a sweet silence*) entail the mapping of two concrete terms, belonging to two different sensory domains. Synaesthetic metaphors are expressions in which one sensory modality is described in the terms of another. Accordingly, a voice (hearing modality) can be described as sweet (taste modality) or a musical note (again hearing modality) as sharp (taste modality). Similarly, colors (sight modality) are often defined as cold or hot (touch modality; see Dann, 1999; Tsur, 1992; Ullmann, 1945).

Are certain modalities more liable to be mapped onto others or are all modalities equally prone to mapping? It had previously been suggested (e.g., Shen, 2002; Shen & Cohen, 1998; Ullmann, 1945; Tsur, 1992) that there is a graduated scale of sensory modalities ranging from sight – the "highest" modality – followed by sound, smell, taste, and, finally, touch – the "lowest" sense). This hierarchy reflects salience, as suggested by Shen and Aisenman (2008) and Shen and Gadir (2006; in press), in that "lower" sensory terms are more salient, representing more concrete or more immediate sensations. Lower sensory modalities tend to include more experienced-based sensations (i.e., those sensed as a physiological sensation of the experiencer as feeling cold or feeling the roughness of a certain texture), while higher ones tend to represent object-based sensations (attributed to the object being perceived); hence, the former are sensed as being more immediate than the latter in that they involve a direct bodily experience of the perceiver (see Shen & Aisenman 2008; Shen & Gadir, 2006; in press). Furthermore, the lower sensory modalities (touch and taste) involve direct contact between the sensory modality and the object of perception, while the higher ones (hearing and vision) do not require such a direct contact.

Taken together, these characteristics of the sensory domain suggest that the "lower" the sensory term, the more immediate and concrete is the sensation it represents.

> Applying the general DP to the case of synaesthetic metaphor yields the principle: *The low-to-high structure is cognitively a simpler structure than the high-to-low one.*

Given this principle, we can distinguish between compatible and clashing synaesthetic metaphors. Thus, a COS-type synaesthetic metaphor, such as *a sweet silence*, is one in which the target and source terms are compatible with the cognitive directionality principle. In other words, the head noun, in the target slot, represents a higher sensory modality, while the adjective, positioned in the source slot, represents a lower one. In a CLS synaesthetic metaphor, the opposite holds true. Thus, *a sweet silence*, in which the head noun ("silence") represents a higher sensory modality (hearing) than the adjective ("sweet"), which has the modality of taste, is a COS synaesthesia, while *a silent sweetness* is an example of a CLS synaesthesia, as in this case the head noun "sweetness" is of lower modality than the adjective "silent."

Having established the distinction between COS and CLS synaesthesias, we can now discuss their distribution in poetic discourse and how they are understood.

### DISTRIBUTION

There have been a large number of studies investigating the distribution of COS versus CLS synaesthesia in both poetic and nonpoetic discourse. In general, these studies have yielded the robust generalization that COS are much more frequently used than their CLS counterparts – across languages, historical periods, genres, and poetic schools. For example, Ullmann (1945) demonstrated this tendency in the English and French poetry of the nineteenth century. Other studies showed the same tendency in modern Hebrew poetry (Shen & Cohen, 1998), Serbo-Croatian poetry and modern Russian poetry (see Shen & Aisenman 2008), Biblical and post-Biblical Hebrew (Shen &

Gadir, in press), Indonesian (Shen & Gil, in press), Rumanian impressionistic and Hungarian poetry (Dombi, 1974), and Chinese (Yu, 2003).

COMPREHENSION

There is some evidence to suggest that COS synaesthesias are cognitively simpler and easier to comprehend than CLS ones. Thus, Shen and Cohen (1998) found that COS are easier to generate interpretations for than their CLS counterparts. Another study (Shen & Aisenman (2008), found that COS synaesthesias are better recalled, judged as being more natural, and judged as easier to generate a context to, than CLS ones. These findings largely substantiate the claim that COS synaesthetic metaphors are cognitively simpler than CLS metaphors.

As with the inversion effect we found for similes and zeugmas, here too there is some initial evidence suggesting that people tend to invert CLS synaesthesia much more than COS ones. Of particular interest are findings obtained in two interpretations–generation studies (Shen & Cohen, 1998) that used Hebrew noun–adjective expressions as stimuli (in Hebrew the noun precedes the adjective) while the other (Shen & Gadir, in press) used genitive (noun–noun) expressions.

### *Interpretation Generation of Noun–Adjective Constructions*

The first interpretation–generation experiment was conducted by Shen and Cohen (1998), with a design similar to that of the interpretation–generation experiments for similes and zeugmas. That experiment used as stimuli metaphorical expressions that appeared in either a comparison construction (in the case of similes) or a conjunction construction (in the case of zeugmas). To broaden our study of the scope of the linguistic forms used in metaphors, the present experiment makes use of a different linguistic form – the noun–adjective construction. This allowed us to see whether the DP also applies to metaphors with other linguistic structures.

The subjects were presented with a list of synaesthetic metaphors, half of which were COS synaesthesias (e.g., *sweet silence*), while the other half were CLS ones (e.g., *a silent sweetness*). They were asked to generate a short interpretation for each one. The responses were analyzed for the frequency of inversion effect. Almost all the inversions (24 out of 25) occurred with the CLS synaesthesias, while only one case of COS synaesthesia generated an inversion.

For example, the synaesthesias *sweet silence* and *silent sweetness* were both given the interpretation "pleasant silence," which maintained the original target–source division in the first instance (in which the mapping proceeds from the source domain of taste to the target of sound), but reversed it in the second (in which the mapping is from sound to taste). This suggests that the cognitive preference for mapping the lower onto the higher domain may, under certain conditions, override the default linguistic convention, whereby the head noun and adjective of a synaesthetic noun phrase are automatically assigned the target and source positions, respectively.

### *Generating Interpretation for Genitive (Noun–Noun) Structures*

An even more dramatic inversion effect was found in a subsequent study (Shen & Gadir, in press) that examined the interpretation generated by subjects for a totally different linguistic form – the genitive (noun–noun) construction. Using stimuli items of this type of construction (usually ignored in the psycholinguistic study of metaphoric language, which typically focused on either adjective–noun or comparison constructions) allows us to examine whether the DP's effect cuts across various types of linguistic constructions.

The genitive always involves two nouns. In Hebrew, the head noun comes first and the modifier second. The latter provides some kind of defining information (usually of ownership) about the former. Thus, in the Hebrew genitive construction, *the handbag of the teacher* "handbag" is the head noun and "teacher" is the modifier, as the latter characterizes the former (i.e., which handbag? The handbag belonging to the teacher). The linguistic rule or convention for the Hebrew genitive is that the head and modifier nouns represent the topic (target) and descriptive (source) concept, respectively (for a few exceptions, see Halevi, 1981). Hence, in the Hebrew phrase *the chair of the teacher* (again, verbatim translation) the head noun "chair" is the topic (target) concept, while the modifier "teacher" is the descriptive source concept.

In a synaesthetic genitive metaphor, each of the two nouns belongs to a different sensory modality, as in *the music* (sound) *of caressing* (touch). In terms of the abovementioned rule, the head noun, "music," is the target, and the modifier, "caressing," is the source.

We can distinguish between two types of synaesthetic genitive metaphors, those that are compatible with the DP and those that clash with it. A compatible genitive structure is one in which the target noun (the first) belongs to a higher sensory modality than the source (second) noun, as in *the music of caressing.* A clashing structure introduces the opposite ordering of the nouns, as in *the caress of music*.

The assumption is that the interpretation of a given synaesthesia should, in principle, reflect a person's initial judgment about which of the two nouns is the target and which the source concept. Accordingly, if conceptual principles have no bearing on the interpretation of genitive synaesthetic expressions, these being affected solely by default linguistic conventions, then most interpretations of genitive synaesthesias, whether compatible or clashing, will classify the head noun as the target and the modifier as the source domain. This means that the interpretations in the case of clashing synaesthesias will be compatible with the linguistic rule but not with the conceptual rule. However, if the cognitive bias is stronger than the linguistic default convention, a different pattern should emerge. In this case, the interpretations should reverse original synaesthesia's target and source domains, by identifying the head noun as the source and the modifier as the target, significantly were often greater in clashing synaesthesias than in compatible ones. This is because, the linguistic convention accords with the cognitive bias in compatible synaesthesias, while the opposite is true for clashing synaesthesias. Hence, investigating the way in which synaesthetic metaphors are interpreted, in both their compatible and clashing formats, should tell us whether cognitive bias rules as the cognitive constraints theory claims.

In the interpretation–generation experiment 80 subjects were asked to interpret a series of synaesthetic metaphors, in either compatible or clashing form. The interpretations were dividing into matching and nonmatching responses. Matching responses were those in which the noun in the target slot was of a higher modality than the noun in the source slot. Thus, the compatible synaesthesia *the aroma of caressing,* in which the topic (target) noun "aroma" is of higher sensory modality (smell) than the modifier (source) noun "caressing" (touch), produced the matching response, "the agreeable smell of the lover, who provides warmth," in which target domain noun (smell) is of a higher modality than the source domain noun (touch). Nonmatching responses were those in which topic (target) term belonged to a lower sensory modality than the modifier (source) term, as in the case of the synaesthesia *the spiciness of shouting,* which was taken to mean "a spicy taste that causes one to shout," a clearly nonmatching response, in which the target term is of a lower modality (taste) than the source term (sound). Eighty-six percent of the interpretations proved to be matching responses, and only 14% nonmatching ones. These findings showed that, as predicted, there is a distinct tendency to reconfigure the target and source concepts in accordance with the cognitive bias when deciphering clashing synaesthesias – that is, the original target–source order is inverted in line with the directionality principle.

GENERAL DISCUSSION

The main argument put forward in this chapter is that the use of various types of figurative expressions in poetry is, cross-linguistically, highly selective and systematic and that this selectiveness is to a large extent constrained by cognitive principles. This argument has some bearings on at least three lines of research on the cognitive study of poetic figures.

The first one is used primarily in the areas of cognitive poetics (e.g., Tsur, 1992) and the empirical study of literature (e.g., van-Peer, 1986). By and large, these theories assume that poetic structures (with figurative structures a central case in this respect) interfere with cognitive principles to achieve aesthetic effects. The present view complements this line of research by suggesting that, in addition to interference with cognitive principles, figurative expression in poetry also conforms with cognitive principles. This may (at least partly) account for the communicability of those poetic expressions.

A second line of research is the one associated with Lakoff's paradigm of conceptual metaphors and its elaborations, such as the cognitive theory of metaphor (e.g., Freeman, 1995; Lakoff & Turner, 1989) and blending theory (Hiraga, 1999; Turner & Fauconnier, 1995). The shared assumption of this group of theories is that figurative expressions appearing in poetic discourse, as well as entire poems, rely on and extend the basic "deep" conceptual metaphors that govern everyday figurative expressions. In this respect, the present approach shares the assumption that poetic figurative expressions conform to general cognitive principles or constraints. However, the present account extends this line of research in several major respects. It broadens the scope of figurative types traditionally studied by focusing on less studied figures in this tradition (for an exception, see Yu, 2003), such as synaesthetic metaphors and zeugmas. Furthermore, it investigates in some detail various linguistic forms that have been less studied, such as conjunctions and genitive constructions (in addition to noun–adjective and comparison constructions). The importance of including a variety of linguistic forms, is that it allows us to investigate more convincingly the claim that figuration is not merely a linguistic phenomenon but also a conceptual one. If this is indeed the case, then the effect of general cognitive mechanisms should apply to a large array of linguistic forms employed by figurative language.

The present approach also has some bearing on a third line of research – the psycholinguistic study of figurative language (e.g., Chiappe et al., 2003; Glucksberg et al., 1997; Ortony et al., 1985). These researches have studied the various cognitive mechanisms at play during the processing of figures, notably metaphors and similes (as well as the differences between their use in comprehension and production). The present chapter extended some of the conclusions reached by these researches (e.g., the asymmetries of similes and metaphors in general, as pointed out by Ortony et al., 1985, and Glucksberg & Keysar, 1990) in several respects. Typically, these researches studied the cognitive underpinnings of nonpoetic (conventional or artificially constructed) figurative expressions; the present research has extended some of their generalizations (in particular, those relevant to asymmetries in similes) to the novel and creative use of figurative expressions composed by poets for artistic purposes. Furtheremore, it has shown that these generalizations cut across not only different types of figuration but also linguistic structure (i.e., comparison, conjunction, or genitive), language boundaries, genre boundaries (poetry and prose), historical periods, and experimental tasks.

Of particular importance is the "inversion effect" finding for CLS expressions, which has not been studied very much in past psycholinguistic research on figurative language (but see Chiappe et al., 2003 and Glucksberg et al., 1997 who pointed out inversion effects in the comprehension of similes). To recapitulate, for each of the three figures we examined an inversion effect of the CLS structures was found, whereby subjects showed a tendency to change a CLS structure into a COS structure. Such inversions are not merely superficial inversions of word order but rather a radical inversion of the meaning of the expression in question. Thus, a subject who interprets the CLS simile *an anchor is like a friend* as "a friend can be like an anchor if you have a close friend" shows a radically different understanding of the simile in question (and not only a difficulty in comprehending it) from the meaning "suggested" by the linguistic form: Under this reading, the expression says something about a friend (that he resembles an anchor), rather than something about an anchor (as the linguistic form of the original simile "suggests"). This may suggest that the cognitive preference for mapping more accessible onto less accessible domains not only determines which structures are considered more natural or are easier to comprehend but that under certain conditions it may determine the very meaning of a metaphorical expression by determining which is the target concept (that is, what the expression is about) and which is the source (that is, what is being said, metaphorically, about the target). Traditionally, researchers in the field have tacitly assumed that a linguistic convention determines the target and source distinction for any metaphorical expression. Thus, it has been tacitly assumed that there is a linguistic convention that assigns the target slot to the grammatical subject of a comparison structure (that is, "A" in the "A is like B" structure), the head noun of an adjective–noun construction (e.g., "silence" in "a sweet silence"), or the head noun in a genitive (noun–noun) construction (e.g., "sunset" in "sunset of blood"). The inversion effect finding may suggest that the cognitive bias toward considering more accessible concepts as sources and less accessible ones as targets may override the relevant default convention when the two clash (that is, if the latter assigns an accessible concept the target slot and less accessible one the source slot). This far-reaching effect of the conceptual bias requires further research into the fine-grained details of the way the linguistic default conventions and the conceptual or cognitive principles interact to produce the meaning of metaphorical expressions.

## References


Beardsley, M. (1981). *Aesthetics: Problems in the philosophy of criticism* (2nd ed.). Indianapolis: Hackett Publishing Company, Inc.

Chiappe, D., Kennedy, J., & Smykowski, T. (2003). Reversibility, aptness, and the conventionality of metaphors and similes. *Metaphor and Symbol*, 18(2), 85–105.

Dann, K. T. (1999). *Bright colors falsely see: Synaesthesia and the search for transcendental knowledge*. New Haven, CT: Yale University Press.

Dombi, Erzsebet (1974). Synaesthesia and poetry. *Poetics*, 11: 23–44.

Fishelov, D. (1996). *Like a rainfall: Studies and essays on poetic simile*. Jerusalem: The Magness Press.

Freeman, D. (1995). "Catch[ing] the nearest way": *Macbeth* and cognitive metaphor. *Journal of Pragmatics*, 23(6), 689–708.

Gentner D. (1983). Structure-mapping: A theoretical framework for analogy. *Cognitive Science*, 7, 155–170.

Glucksberg, S., & Keysar, B. (1990). Understanding metaphorical comparisons: Beyond similarity. *Psychological Review*, 97, 3–18.

Glucksberg, S., McGlone, M., & Manfredi, D. (1997). Property attribution in metaphor comprehension. *Journal of Memory and Language*, 36, 50–67.

Halevi, R. (1981). Tmurot be-ma'mada shel ha-smixut ha-pruda be-ivrit shel yamenu. *Leshonenu*, 63, 61–80 (in Hebrew).

Hiraga, M. K. (1999). "Blending" and an interpretation of haiku: A cognitive approach. *Poetics Today*, 20, 461–481.

Johnson, M., & Malgady, R. G. (1979). Some cognitive aspects of figurative language association and metaphor. *Journal of Psycholinguistic Research*, 8, 249–265.

Kelly, M. H., Bock, J. K., & Keil, F. C. (1986). Prototypicality in a linguistic context: Effects on sentence structure. *Journal of Memory and Language*, 25, 59–74.

Lakoff, G., & Johnson, M. (1980). *Metaphors we live by*. Chicago: University of Chicago Press.

Lakoff, G., & Turner, M. (1989). *More than cool reason: A field guide to poetic metaphor*. Cambridge: Cambridge University Press.

Ortony, A. (1979). Beyond literal similarity. *Psychological Review*, 86, 161–180.

Ortony, A., Vondruska, R., Foss, M., & Jones, L. (1985). Salience, similes, and the asymmetry of similarity. *Journal of Memory and language*, 24, 569–594.

Shen, Y. (1989). Symmetric and asymmetric comparisons. *Poetics*, 18(6) 517–536.

Shen, Y. (1992). Metaphors and categories. *Poetics Today*, 13(4), 771–794.

Shen, Y. (1995). Constraints on directionality in poetic vs. non-poetic metaphors. *Poetics*, 23, 255–274.

Shen, Y. (1997). Cognitive constraints on poetic figures. *Cognitive Linguistics*, 8(1), 33–71.

Shen, Y. (1998). Zeugma: Prototypes, categories, and metaphors. *Metaphor and Symbol 13(1)*, 31–47.

Shen, Y. (2002). Cognitive constraints on verbal creativity. In E. Semino & J. Culpeper (Eds.), *Cognitive stylistics: Language and cognition in text analysis* (pp. 211–230). Amsterdam/Philadelphia: John Benjamins Publishing.

Shen, Y. (in press). Why do we pack the shirt before the sorrow? One aspect of the relation between poetics and cognition. In: *Balshanut Ivrit*. Bar Ilan University: Ramat Gan.

Shen, Y. (2007). Foregrounding and communication: The battlefield between deviation and cognitive constraints. To appear in: *Language and Literature*. 16:2. pp. 169–181.

Shen, Y., & Cohen, M. (1998). How come silence is sweet but sweetness is not silent: A cognitive account of directionality in poetic synaesthesia. *Language and Literature, 7(2)*, 123–140.

Shen, Y., & Aisenman, R. (forthcoming, 2008). Heard melodies are sweet, but those unheard are sweeter: Synaesthesia and cognition. To appear in: *Language and Literature* (17:2).

Shen, Y., & Gadir, O. (forthcoming). Target and source Assignment in Synaesthetic Possessive Constructions. To appear in: *Journal of Pragmatics.*

Shen, Y., & Gadir, O. (2006). How to interpret the "smelliness of noisiness": Interpretations of synaesthesia in the genitive form? In: *Balshanut Ivrit teurit, xishuvit, v-yisumit*, 58. pp. 61–82. Ramat Gan: Bar Ilan University. *(in Hebrew)*

Shen, Y., & Gadir, O. (In press). Synaesthesia, cognition and diachronic meaning extension. *Leshonenu. (in Hebrew)*

Shen, Y., & Gil, D. (In press). "Sweet Fragrances from Indonesia: A Universal Principle Governing Directionality in Synaesthetic Metaphors". In: Willie van Peer & Jan Auracher (eds). *New Beginning for the Study of Literature.* Cambridge: Cambridge Scholars Publishing, 2007.

Shen, Y., & Shalev, H. *Inversion effects in similes.* Manuscript submitted for publication.

Shklovsky, V. (1965). Art as technique. In L. T. Lemon & M. J. Reis (Eds.), *Russian formalist criticism* (3–24). Lincoln: Nebraska University Press.

Sweetser, E. (1990). *From etymology to pragmatics.* Cambridge: Cambridge University Press.

Tourangeau, R., & Sternberg, R. J. (1982). Understanding and appreciating metaphors. *Cognition*, 11, 203–244.

Traugotte, E. (1974). Explorations in linguistic elaboration: Language change, language acquisition, and the genesis of spatio-temporal terms. In John M. Anderson and Charles Jones (Eds.) *Historical Linguistics I*, New York: American Elsevier, 263–314.

Tsur, R. (1992). *Toward a theory of cognitive poetics*. Amsterdam: North Holland.

Turner, M., & Fauconnier, G. (1995). Conceptual integration and formal expression. *Metaphor and Symbolic Activity*, 10, 183–204.

Tversky, A. (1977). Features of similarity. *Psychological Review*, 84, 327–352.

Ullmann, S. (1945). Romanticism and synaesthesia. *PMLA (Publications of the Modern Language Association)*, 60, 811–845.

Yu, N. (2003). Synaesthetic metaphor: a cognitive perspective. *Journal of Literary Semantics, (32)*, 19–34.

# Part V

# METAPHOR IN REASONING AND FEELING

CHAPTER 18

# Metaphor and Artificial Intelligence

## Why They Matter to Each Other

*John A. Barnden*

### Introduction

Why is Artificial Intelligence (AI) concerned with metaphor, and what special contributions can AI offer to metaphor research? This chapter will indicate why AI needs to study metaphor and will outline what AI has been contributing to the illumination of metaphor, whether it is processed by artefacts or by the human mind.

Specific contributions of AI research on metaphor that one can already point to, and that will be addressed to varying extents in this chapter, include the following: creation of detailed mechanisms for reasoning within the terms of the source-domain in a metaphor, in order expand the relevance of known source-target mappings; increased emphasis on uncertainty and gradedness in metaphorical reasoning; a richer view of overriding (source-over-target as well as target-over-source); mechanisms for exploiting context; important steps towards integration with metonymy interpretation; some emphasis on disanalogy and a limitation of the role of parallelism between source and target; the usefulness of reversed transfers (transfers from source domain to target domain); the importance of non-assertional metaphor; increased doubt about whether the notion of a "domain" is actually important and well-founded; and clarification of ways in which literal meaning can be involved in metaphor interpretation.

The plan of the chapter is as follows. The next section will make some observations about AI, explain why metaphor is important to applications-oriented aspects of AI, and indicate why, in general terms, AI can make distinctive contributions to the study of cognition as a whole, metaphor included. Then a new section will sketch five different, relatively recent AI research works on metaphor. This is to set the scene for the following section, which will discuss specific contributions of AI to metaphor research. The issues will be summarized in a brief concluding section. The chapter does not attempt to survey AI research on metaphor completely or to provide a history of this work, despite the fact that AI has long had an interest in metaphor (cf. e.g. Carbonell, 1980, 1982; Norvig, 1989; Russell, 1976, 1985; Way, 1991; Weber, 1989; Weiner,

1984; Wilks, 1978), and also simile (e.g. Winston, 1979) and analogy (see Hall, 1989, for a review). Readers interested in AI work not covered here may also wish to look at Martin's (1996) and Russell's (1986) reviews and the extensive review in Fass (1997, chap. 11). Also, we omit description of work on theoretical approaches to metaphor that while being interesting and important in themselves do not address processing issues to any large extent, such as the approaches of Asher and Lascarides (1995), Hintikka and Sandu (1990), Indurkhya (1991, 1992), van Genabith (2001), and Vogel (2001). For reasons of space we omit description of computational study of metaphor in corpora (e.g. Mason, 2004) despite some close connections to AI. The chapter makes some mention of metonymy because of the close connection of metaphor and metonymy and because, as we will see, some major AI work on metaphor also addresses metonymy.

## Artificial Intelligence

AI has at least three separate, though interrelated, aims:

*An "engineering" aim*: To engineer, or provide computational principles and methods for engineering, *useful artefacts* that are arguably intelligent, without necessarily having any mechanistic similarity to human or animal minds/brains. The usefulness may be in an industrial domain or an everyday, practical domain, but may also be in other domains such as art or mathematical theorem proving.

*A "psychological" aim*: To devise computational principles, computationally detailed theories, or running computational systems that provide a basis for possible testable accounts of *cognition in human or animal minds/brains*.

*A "general/philosophical" aim*: To devise computational principles, computationally detailed theories, or running computational systems that serve as or suggest possible accounts of cognition *in general*, whether it be in human-made artefacts, in naturally occurring organisms, or in cognizing organisms yet to be discovered, or that illuminate *philosophical issues* such as the nature of mind, thought, intelligence, consciousness, perception, language, representation, learning, rationality, society, and so on . . . not forgetting computation itself.

On top of this multiplicity of aims, the word "intelligence" is usually taken very broadly in the field, to cover not only pure rational thought but also almost anything that could come under the heading of "cognition," "perception," "language use," "emotion" and so forth. Thus, the name "artificial intelligence" has always been something of a *nom de plume*, with both parts of the name each hinting at only one aspect of the nature of the actual endeavour.

The three aims are often inextricably combined in a given piece of research. For one thing, an individual researcher may have more than one of the aims. But also, of course, developments in pursuit of any one of the aims could happen to inspire advances towards one of the others, and endeavours towards any one of the aims can proactively look for inspiration from research towards the others.

Before going on, it is useful to explain why metaphor is important for the Engineering aim of AI. Many intelligent artefacts that need to communicate well with people using human language will need to be able to cope with metaphor. Metaphor is prevalent in human linguistic discourse, even when it is just mundane conversation. Slightly more indirectly, some intelligent artefacts need to understand linguistic communication between people, for instance for the purpose of understanding newspaper articles written by people for other people. Indeed, metaphor is becoming an increasingly looming obstacle for Engineering AI, as attempts are made to bring better automated human-language processing into commercial products, to develop ever more advanced computer interfaces and virtual reality systems, to develop automated understanding and production of emotional expression given that this is often conveyed explicitly or implicitly by metaphor (Delfino & Manea, 2005; Emanatian, 1995; Fainsilber & Ortony,

1987; Fussell & Moss, 1998; Kövecses, 2000; Thomas, 1969; Yu, 1995), and also of gesture and sign language given that these forms of communication have strong metaphorical aspects (McNeill, 1992; P. P. Wilcox, 2004; S. Wilcox, 2004; Woll, 1985).

To return to the set of aims overall: their multiplicity, and their nature taken individually, cause problems in the evaluation of developments in AI. Engineering developments can clearly be evaluated on the basis of actual usefulness or promise of such, but the nature of evaluation is more difficult for the other aims. Evaluation can be on criteria such as coherence, simplicity, computational efficiency and so forth, and on whether the development in question does in principle achieve the intended cognitive ends, but beyond that the evaluation must be in the indirect, long-term, and subjective sense of the extent to which the development contributes eventually to other fields such as Philosophy or Psychology, or is at least perceived as embodying interesting and inspiring ideas for these fields. Since Psychology is currently the locus of intensive research on metaphor, it is worth stressing that within the Psychological aim there is not necessarily any goal to produce an immediately testable psychological theory. Rather, the aim is creatively to provide computationally well-founded and well-designed bases from which psychologists or others could proceed to develop testable theories.

I hope that in the descriptions of the three aims above the reader will have observed the hedging about whether the AI developments are actually "implemented" (that is, realized in the form of computer software or hardware). Hence the mention of *computational principles, methods,* and *computationally detailed theories*, not just working computational systems. A product of AI research does not have to be a working computer program or piece of computer hardware. Rather, it can be a system description or formal logical account that is detailed and specific to the extent that software or hardware could readily if laboriously be developed. It can also be a description of new types of representation, inferencing or other processing that could form part of an AI system (implemented or otherwise).

Such products of AI may be left without implementation not through neglect but rather because they can be assessed, to a useful degree, in terms of their coherence, effectiveness, efficiency, interest, distinctiveness, and so on without being implemented. Also, the act of creating the product can uncover problems and issues that would be unlikely to arise in less detailed and specific theorizing. Much of the point of creating even a *working* AI system is not so much to use it in practice but to serve just such ends as uncovering problems and gaps, studying the relationship to other proposed systems, and so on. In short, much of the point of developing a detailed computational account, implemented or not, is aid in the development of *principles, methods,* and *theories* in more detail and with greater security than would otherwise be likely.

These explanations about AI could be paralleled to some extent by observations about Computer Science in general. Much research in Computer Science is not directly about producing working software or hardware. For example, much of the field is mathematical theory directed at the nature of computation, the complexity of algorithms, the abstract meaning of computer programs, and the well-founded design of programming languages and computer systems.

Given that the Psychological and General/Philosophical aims of AI impinge on the concerns of other disciplines, the question arises as to whether AI research has anything special to offer to such disciplines over and above what they can do by themselves. There are several reasons for a positive answer. First, AI has special expertise in a wide variety of different forms of computation, in putting them on a proper, well-thought-out foundation and, importantly, in finding complicated combinations of them or compromises between them. The hope is that a strong Computer Science background or context enables many AI researchers to come up with suggestions that are, in computational ways, more advanced, richer, more subtle, more complex, more formally coherent, and/or more extensively and securely developed than is generally possible in other disciplines, with their own demands and pressures concerning other matters.

Pressure towards developing effective compromises and combinations comes from the applications focus within the Engineering aim, and from the focus in all three aims of the production of working artefacts or at least *detailed* computational schemes and methods. These foci can also provide a useful "sanity check," helping for example to uncover unwelcome but difficult-to-discern interactions between parts of a theory, to avoid vagueness in descriptions of representations and processes, to avoid over-simplification, and to ensure greater coverage of underlying technical issues than in other fields.

## AI Research on Metaphor: An Illustrative Review of Recent Work

In outlining the nature of AI above we looked at some general reasons why it is in a position to make helpful contributions to the study of cognition, or, at least, why it is in a better position to make certain types of advance than other disciplines are. As for specific metaphor research issues on which AI is in a relatively good position to be helpful, we will examine some of them after reviewing, in this section, a handful of particular metaphor research works within AI.

### *Hobbs*

Important work on metaphor in AI was done by Hobbs (1990, 1992). The ideas do not seem to have met with a substantial implementation effort, but Hobbs has devised a detailed computational account from which implementations could be developed reasonably readily as an extension to the implemented TACITUS system (Hobbs et al., 1993). We can divide the work into the following three strands:

1. *Unmodified-property transfer*: When X is metaphorically described as Y, this method can attribute to X a property P of Y, provided P also makes sense for X without modification. A simple example is interpreting "John is an elephant" to mean that John is clumsy, given that clumsiness is (let us assume) a property of elephants, and given that it can also be applied to people.
2. *Transfer by known mappings within inference*: This method uses known mappings between aspects of the source domain and aspects of the target domain. Importantly, unmapped aspects of the source domain can be used in a metaphor by virtue of their source-domain inferential connections to the source-domain elements that *are* mapped by known mappings. Also, the mappings are themselves cast as inference rules (see below). Thus, uses of mappings are just inference steps along with any other.
3. *Mapping discovery by analogy*: hypothesizing mappings between complex situations in source and target from scratch, by means of structural matching, in order to handle metaphor that is novel to the understander.

All three strands are placed (in Hobbs, 1992) within a general inferential framework for natural language understanding, which, in particular, also handles metonymy. This framework has abduction as its guiding principle and its central means of inference. In essence, linguistic expressions are regarded as outward signs of underlying situations that are conveyed by the expressions, and the understander's task is to move abductively from the outward signs to the underlying situations. A crucial aspect of Hobbs's overall abductive approach is that it is, thereby, an approach founded on *uncertain* inference.

In the first strand, Unmodified-Property Usage, Hobbs has an appealing, context-driven view of how the properties are selected in a given case. As he says, "John is an elephant" cannot be precisely interpreted outside of context (Hobbs, 1990, 59). But he claims that, given suitable context, coherence considerations can lead to a precise interpretation. Thus, Hobbs asserts that "Mary is graceful, but John is an elephant" suggests the interpretation that John has a property that contrasts with gracefulness. If it is known that elephants are clumsy, and this is the only elephant property that contrasts with gracefulness, then the clumsiness interpretation is secured. This context-driven approach to the choice of properties to transfer contrasts with approaches that use selection principles relying on, for example, context-insensitive notions of salience of properties (as in Ortony, 1979).

In the third strand – mapping discovery by analogy – Hobbs does not differ much in broad outline from other researchers (e.g. Falkenhainer, Forbus, & Gentner, 1989; Gentner, 1983) who propose analogical structure-matching as the way to deal with (some) metaphor. Arguably the second strand, transfer by known mappings within inference, is the most interesting of the three. Hobbs provides as a prime example the use of spatial metaphor in Computer Science. One talks of a variable in a computer program as being "at", a number, say 100, as a way of saying that the variable's value is 100. Hobbs proposes therefore that a communicating agent that is familiar with this way of talking (or thinking) could have an inferential rule that can be glossed in English as

> *IF in some situation a variable's value is V THEN in that situation the variable is* [spatially-]at *V.*

Thus, this rule embodies a *known mapping link* between the source domain of space and the target domain of computer-science entities. The rule has the same status as any other inferential rule, and can be used at any convenient point during an overall process of inference-based understanding. It may look strange that the rule has the IF/THEN going from target to source rather than source to target. This is because rules are used abductively in Hobbs's approach: the variable's being spatially-at V leads to the abductive hypothesis that the variable's value is V.

The displayed rule acquires an indefinite amount of extra power in the following way. One talks of a variable "going" from say 100 to 200, as a way of stating a value change; of a variable being "between" two numbers; of a variable "keeping one step behind" another; and so forth: productively using an indefinite large part of the domain of space. Hobbs argues that such talk can be handled without the need to have separate mappings for "go," "between," and so on: rather, it suffices to use inferential connections within the source domain such as one between *going* and *being-spatially-at* and, thereby to be able to connect *going* to the mapping displayed above from being-spatially-at to having-as-value. Thus, a variable's "going" from 100 to 200 is ultimately interpreted as a change from a situation of having value 100 to a situation of having value 200.

Finally, Hobbs (1990) regards metaphor as crossing over between different domains, but fully accepts that domains have fuzzy boundaries and that the notion of domain is difficult. He therefore propounds that the exact scope of the notion of metaphor is theory-relative, in depending on decisions about what domains exist: there is no objective, theory-free fact of the matter about the boundaries of metaphor. In any case, Hobbs's actual computational approach does not impose or operationally rely upon any domain divisions at all. Therefore, mapping rules could in principle link concepts that, intuitively, are arbitrarily close.

### *Martin*

An implemented computer program, called MIDAS, for metaphor interpretation and generation was produced by James Martin (1990, 2000). The acronym MIDAS stands for Metaphor Interpretation, Denotation, and Acquisition System. MIDAS was designed in part as a supplement to the Unix Consultant system, a computer program for automatically answering users' questions about the Unix operating system.

MIDAS incorporates knowledge of a set of a roughly Lakovian conceptual metaphors. The specific set included can be changed and is not itself the interesting side of the system. We will assume here, for expositional purposes, that MIDAS knows the conceptual metaphor USING A COMPUTER PROCESS IS BEING PHYSICALLY INSIDE A REGION. The system's knowledge base consists of a network of concepts. Among the concepts are the concept of using a computer process and the concept of being inside a region. These two concepts are linked by a "metaphor map." The metaphor map will be notated here in the following way, although the real structure is much more complex:

*being-inside-a-region* ↔ *using-a-computer-process*

Also, the two concepts have roles (or "slots") within them. Correspondingly there are two additional metaphor maps, this time crossing between roles:

*the-enclosing-region* ↔ *the-used-process*
*the-thing-enclosed* ↔ *the-process-user.*

As a result of knowing the conceptual metaphor, the system can easily understand a statement such as "I am in Emacs" to mean that the speaker is using Emacs, given that the word "in" accesses the being-inside-a-region concept. The literal interpretation that the speaker is physically in Emacs is rejected, because Emacs is not represented in the system as being a region. By contrast, the metaphorical interpretation is accepted because Emacs is represented as being a computer process. Importantly, though, the literal interpretation does not need to be rejected *before* the metaphorical one is accepted. The system tries to apply the possibly relevant conceptual metaphors it knows, irrespective of whether the literal interpretation is acceptable.

MIDAS can also interpret metaphorical utterances that do not immediately fit its known mappings. The process of handling such utterances is handled by the MES (Metaphor Extension System) component of MIDAS. It uses two different techniques: *similarity-extension* and *core-extension*. Suppose the system knows that conversations are similar to computer processes, in the sense that they are both special cases of a more general concept of a process. Then the system can interpret the sentence *I am in a conversation* by using its known conceptual metaphor USING A COMPUTER PROCESS IS BEING PHYSICALLY INSIDE A REGION. Because of the known similarity between COMPUTER PROCESSES and CONVERSATIONS, the system has a mechanism for coming up with the new conceptual metaphor BEING ENGAGED IN A CONVERSATION IS BEING PHYSICALLY INSIDE A REGION.

This similarity-extension method is powerful, but core-extension is yet more so. The system can interpret the sentence "How do I get into Emacs?" just on the basis of knowing the conceptual metaphor USING A COMPUTER PROCESS IS BEING PHYSICALLY INSIDE A REGION and knowing some simple things about regions. The system is unable to find an acceptable interpretation using that conceptual metaphor directly. However, through knowing about a **result** relationship between the concept of *moving-into* (accessed by the phrase "get into") to the concept of being *physically-in*, and knowing that a usage of a process by a user is a *result* of the user invoking that process, the system can conjecture that the speaker is asking, in effect, "How do I invoke Emacs?" The system will create a new conceptual metaphor INVOKING A COMPUTER PROCESS IS PHYSICALLY MOVING INTO A REGION. The term "core-extension" is used because the concepts involved, such as moving-into and being-physically-in, must be "core-related." This somewhat complex notion covers only rather direct relationships such as the *result* relationship involved above.

Martin seeks to avoid having a literal-first account in an effort to obey the "total time constraint" (Gerrig, 1989) that conventional metaphors should take no longer to process than superficially similar literal language. MIDAS certainly avoids being literal-first in the sense that it avoids the need to *reject* literal interpretations before considering metaphorical ones. However, it does need to *construct* literal interpretations before considering metaphorical ones.

As Fass (1997, 316) points out, MIDAS is to be applauded for being able to prefer a metaphorical reading of "McEnroe killed Connors" (i.e., defeated him) to a literal reading, even though the latter is itself semantically acceptable. It turns out that the scoring mechanisms in the system, which knows that McEnroe and Connors are sportsmen, cause it to regard a SPORTIVE DEFEATING AS KILLING interpretation as more tightly fitting the sentence than a literal interpretation does, because sports-defeat requires its role-fillers to be competitors whereas killing has a much less specific requirement.

Martin does not make any use of the notion of a domain in his account of MIDAS, and there are no explicit domain divisions in MIDAS. Metaphor maps can in principle join arbitrarily close concepts, and what metaphor amounts to for the system is therefore entirely dependent on what maps happen to be included and how existing conceptual metaphors can be extended.

### *Fass*

A second major implemented AI system for metaphor processing is that of Dan Fass (1997), indirectly related to the research of Wilks (1978). Fass's system is called meta5 (punningly, a step beyond meta*phor*). The system proceeds entirely by discovering analogies between source and target structures from scratch, with the process being guided by a relevance criterion explained below. It should be mentioned at once that the analogies discovered are of a very simple sort. However, the processing needed to discover them can be complex and subtle. Also, the system is unusual in measuring the degree of *dis*analogy between source and target structures, and using this measure in rating the aptness of the metaphor.

One standard-bearing example of meta5's processing is provided by

(4) My car drinks gasoline

taken from Wilks (1978). The system can interpret this as meaning "My car uses gasoline" essentially by finding an analogical match between the prior knowledge the system has that animals drink drinkable stuff and the prior knowledge that cars in general use gasoline. As a consequence, in constructing the internal meaning representation of the sentence, a *use* word-sense is employed as the right sense for the verb "drink" in the sentence.

In somewhat more detail, we can explain the process as follows, assuming the system only has one lexical sense for the verb "drink," namely the normal sense of an animal imbibing a liquid. We notate this sense here as *drink*. That the agent must be an animal and the patient must be a liquid is encoded as "preferences" (or "selection restrictions") in the permanent representation of the lexical sense in the system. The system finds, though, that the actual agent according to the sentence, the car, is not an animal. At some point the system will therefore look for a possible metaphorical way of interpreting the car-drink relationship in the sentence. It does this by seeing whether its knowledge about animals contains an item that is *relevant* to the sentence. The approach here is simple: from the sentence it takes only the *drink* word-sense, notes this sense's preference for an animal agent, and sees whether in the knowledge about animals there is information that they take part in a relationship that is either drinking or a word-sense-wise ancestor of drinking. Indeed, the system finds the knowledge item that *animals drink drinkable-stuff*. No other knowledge item for *animal* is relevant.

The system then looks for knowledge items within its prior knowledge of cars that match that animal knowledge item. It finds that the following matching item: *cars use gasoline*. It determines that there is a match because the *use* word sense and the *drink* word-sense are "sisters": they both have the same immediate parent sense, namely *expend*. Equally, the senses *drinkable-stuff* and *gasoline* are sisters, with *liquid* as parent. Such a pair of sister relationships between two knowledge items is necessary for them to match. The system has now found a metaphorical relationship between "car" and "drinks" in the sentence, and can build a sentence meaning representation tantamount to "My car uses gasoline."

The system also looks at its non-relevant knowledge items about *animal* and *car*, in the above sense of relevance, and measures both how many other matching knowledge items there are and how many knowledge items for each of those two word-senses are not matched by a knowledge item for the other. The extra matches contribute to the strength of the metaphor, but the difference counts are inspired by the claim of Tourangeau and Sternberg (1982) that the greater the conceptual distance between source and target the more apt the metaphor. The counts can be used to choose between competing metaphorical interpretations, in other examples.

A point on which meta5 can be criticized, and is indeed criticized by Fass himself (1997, sect. 10.3.1.1), is that there is no coordination between a metaphorical relation found between the agent and verb ("car" and "drink") and a metaphorical or other relation found between verb and patient ("drink" and "gasoline"). Thus, the system does not look holistically at the sentence in determining the presence of analogies. This creates a problem with a sentence such as "My car drinks coffee," which Fass wishes his system to regard as anomalous and not metaphorical, and therefore not to settle on a metaphorical relation between the car and the drinking. Fass suggests a detailed solution to this problem, not discussed here.

The incremental semantic construction approach in the (unfixed) system is in itself interesting because it means that the system does not even *construct* a literal interpretation of the *whole sentence* before investigating metaphoricity, let alone *reject* a literal interpretation. But it is important to note that in the investigation by the system of a *part* of the sentence, such as "my car" together with "drinks," the system does adopt a fully literal-first approach: a metaphorical relation is only sought if an acceptable literal interpretation cannot be found for that part. Although it can be argued that this is a wrong approach even for sentence-parts, it does the service of showing us that the question of processing order in metaphorical sentence interpretation is much more complex than that of how literal and metaphorical interpretations of the *whole* sentence are ordered.

The system includes a complex numerical scoring mechanism to choose between competing interpretations of sentence parts as it goes along. This is largely based on lengths of paths in the semantic network. Fass (1997, sect. 10.2.2) has implemented a system extension in which the match scoring aspects of the system are enriched. The enrichment adds a diagnostic-salience measure on knowledge items that is dependent on how much inheritance was involved in finding them: for example, that a car has a definite physical boundary is inherited from further away in the semantic network than that a car has wheels, and is therefore less salient. Differences of salience could then be used to refine the comparative evaluation of discovered analogies.

On the other hand, there are major problems with the simplistic requirement that metaphorical analogies require sister relationships between cell components. For instance, it appears that the metaphorical interpretation above could not be found if, instead of *gasoline* being a direct descendant of *liquid*, there were a *liquid-fuel* sense interposed. However, given that the system already includes complex distance-based scoring, it would be straightforward to adjust the system to allow generalized cousin relationships rather than sister relationships, and to downplay or discount relationships that involved excessively long paths.

Finally, meta5 is interesting in being a fully implemented system that performs complex metonymic understanding as well as metaphorical understanding. It has knowledge of some conventional metonymic relationships such as ARTIST FOR ART PRODUCT and can therefore interpret sentences such as "John reads Shakespeare." Indeed, the system can handle arbitrarily long chains of metonymy. A limitation of the system is that metonymic interpretation is tried strictly before metaphorical, restricting the possibilities of interaction. The system can nevertheless obtain some forms of mixed metaphorical/metonymic interpretation.

There is no notion of domain in the design of the system, and word-senses are not sorted by domain. Indeed, as the sister relationship (above) is the core of analogy in meta5, metaphorical relationships can be between structures that are conceptually arbitrarily close up to sisterhood. Gasoline could have kerosene as a sister.

Finally, Iverson and Helmreich (1992) implemented a system, Metallel, that can be viewed as a substantially modified version of meta5, correcting some of its deficiencies. The system is ably summarized by Fass (1997, sect 10.1). Metallel views metonymy and metaphor as being on a par, rather than metonymy having precedence as in meta5. Once Metallel has found some potential available metonymic and metaphorical interpretations by a somewhat loose form of path search, it selects between them on the basis of a "grounding" process, which incorporates a type of analogical matching much like meta5's but that takes into account the whole sentence, not just parts of it in succession as meta5 does.

### *Barnden: ATT-Meta, Map-Transcendence and Pretence*

The present author has implemented an approach, called ATT-Meta, for performing a type of reasoning that is arguably often necessary for metaphor interpretation. The approach is described in Barnden (1998, 2001a), Barnden, Glasbey, Lee, and Wallington (2004), Barnden, Helmreich, Iverson, and Stein (1994), Barnden and Lee (1999, 2001), and Lee and Barnden (2001a). The implemented ATT-Meta program is only a reasoning system and does not take linguistic strings as input, but, rather, logical forms assumed to be derivable from sentences by initial processing. For now the reader can take these logical forms to encode the literal meanings of the sentences, but we will refine this point below.

The metaphorical utterances of main interest in the ATT-Meta project are those that are conceptually related to known conceptual metaphors but that transcend them by involving source-domain elements not directly handled by the mappings in those metaphors. In ATT-Meta parlance these utterances are *map-transcending*. For instance, going back to the Hobbs examples, the sentence "N leaps from 1 to 100" is map-transcending for an understander if he/she/it only knows a *physically-leap* lexical sense for the verb "leap" but does not know a mapping for that sense into the target domain of variables and values, even though he/she/it does know a mapping from, say, *spatially-at* to *have-as-value*. Similarly, if an understander knows a metaphorical mapping from *physically-in* to *using-a-process* (see Martin case) but has no mapping for *physically-enter*, then the sentence "How do I enter Emacs?" is map-transcending.

Clearly, map-transcendence is a fuzzy concept that is relative to particular understanders and particular conceptual metaphors the understander knows, and to our intuitive perceptions as to what is conceptually related to what (e.g. physically-leaping to being-spatially-at). Nevertheless, it is a useful intuitive characterization of a phenomenon that lies along a broad sector of the spectrum between conventional metaphor on the one hand and, on the other hand, entirely novel metaphor where no relevant mapping is known at all. Map-transcendence is strongly related to the phenomenon of unused parts of the source domain as discussed in Lakoff & Johnson (1980).

Very broadly speaking, ATT-Meta's approach is similar to Hobbs's second strand (Transfer by Known Mappings within Inference): ATT-Meta is based on rules encapsulating known metaphorical correspondences such as between *physically-at* and *has-as-value*, and on an integrated inferential framework which, in particular, allows arbitrarily rich source-domain reasoning to connect sentence components to source-domain concepts that can be mapped by known mappings. So, both systems can infer that a variable N *has value* 100 from any sentence couched in spatial terms that implies that N is *physically-at* 100, as long as the systems have the necessary knowledge about physical space to infer that N is physically-at 100 from the sentence. The inference can be arbitrarily indirect and complex in principle. To make the point, a vivid example would be a sentence such as "N started a circuitous route towards 100 but didn't complete the journey until after M fell to 0." This implies, among other things, that N (at some point) had value 100.

However, there is a fundamental difference of approach, as well as many technical differences of representation and reasoning, between ATT-Meta and Hobbs's scheme. The difference is that ATT-Meta avoids placing internal propositions such as *N is physically-at 100*, which are not statements about reality, on a par with statements such as *N has value 100*, which are. Hobbs's approach does maintain them on a par: there is nothing in his internal representation to say that the former proposition is merely a metaphorical pretence or fiction.

Instead, ATT-Meta creates a special computational "mental space" in which such propositions and inferences arising from them are kept aside from propositions and reasoning about reality. We call this space a *metaphorical pretence cocoon*. Thus, the internal proposition *N physically-leaps from 1 to 100* arising directly from the sentence "N leaps from 1 to 100" is placed in the cocoon, and the inference result that (say) *N is spatially-at 100 afterwards*, together with the inference chain itself, lies within the cocoon. A metaphorical mapping rule that takes *spatially-at* to *has-as-value* can then give the result that, in reality, N has value 100 afterwards.

By clearly marking some propositions as being pretences, the use of a cocoon ensures that the system is not misled by the propositions directly derived from metaphorical utterances, that is, propositions like *N physically-leaps from 1 to 100*. Notice that in the case of "McEnroe killed Connors," the understander needs to be clear that the directly derived proposition *McEnroe biologically killed Connors* is not a statement about reality. But, in addition, if the understander knows that McEnroe definitely did not biologically kill Connors in reality, we do not want to let that information defeat the pretend information that McEnroe did biologically kill Connors. Thus, pretence cocoons prevent pretences from infecting reality but equally protect the integrity of pretences.

The use of cocoons has another benefit. Lee and Barnden (2001a) studied mixed metaphor of various types, and showed how ATT-Meta deals with them. The main distinction studied was between serial mixing (commonly called chaining), where A is viewed as B and B is viewed as C, and parallel mixing, where A is used simultaneously as B and as C (see also Wilks, Barnden, & Wang, 1991). Serial mixing is viewed as having the B material in a cocoon that is directly embedded in the reality space, whereas the C material as in a cocoon embedded within the B cocoon. Thus, there is a pretence within a pretence. In parallel mixing, on the other hand, the B and C material is either combined in a single cocoon or is in two separate cocoons both directly embedded within the reality space. Thus, we have two pretences either side by side or blended with each other. There are unresolved issues about how to decide between these two possibilities, but in any case different dispositions of pretence cocoons allow important differences between types of mixing of metaphor to be reflected in the processing.

We have indicated that what is initially inserted in the pretence cocoon in the case of "N leaps from 1 to 100" is the proposition *N physically-leaps from 1 to 100*, and what is inserted in the case of "McEnroe killed Connors" is *McEnroe biologically killed Connors*. This reflects a general assumption in the ATT-Meta approach that what is inserted in the cocoon is a "direct" meaning of the metaphorical sentence (or of some metaphorical sentence-component such as a clause). A direct meaning is a logical form derived compositionally from the "direct" senses of lexical units in sentences. A direct sense is just any sense listed for the lexical unit in the understander's lexicon, so that it is directly accessible from the lexical unit. In particular, we have been assuming that the verbs "leap" and "kill" have as direct senses the concepts of *physically leap and biologically kill* respectively.

Clearly, a given lexical unit could actually have more than one direct sense, and indeed some of the direct senses could be metaphorical or special in some other way. We simply embrace such possibilities, saying that if, for instance, "leap" had something like *change-value* as a direct sense, then "N leaps from 1 to 100" could be understood without use of the inferential pretence mechanism outlined above, although in principle the mechanism could still be redundantly used as well. Equally, a direct sense may be figurative in some way but still lead to the construction of a proposition in the pretence cocoon. For instance, suppose the word "star" has *astronomical-star* and *prominent-movie-actor* as its only direct senses, and that we regard the latter as a figurative sense. Then "Mike is a star of the department" could be understood via the pretence mechanism using *Mike is a prominent movie actor in the department* in the cocoon. (Another option could be to use the *astronomical-star* sense.)

Thus, in the ATT-Meta approach, the pretence mechanism is potentially useful if direct meanings of sentences lead by within-pretence reasoning to within-pretence propositions that can be mapped by known mapping rules. It is irrelevant whether a direct meaning is dubbed as "literal" or not. We may or may not wish to regard *physically leap* as a literal sense of "leap" and *prominent-movie-actor* as a literal sense of "star", but such terminological decisions have no bearing in themselves on whether the pretence mechanism could be fruitful.

Another fundamental reason for not relying on a notion of literal meaning arises from serial mixing (A as B as C). In such a case, some of the phrasing in the utterance refers to the C domain, and this can cause material to arise in the B domain by C-to-B transfer. Therefore, B-to-A transfers may be working on metaphorical material derived by transfer from C. For this reason alone, it is misguided to think of metaphorical mapping as a matter of transforming literal meanings. The consequences of this point have hardly been explored in metaphor research.

Insofar as direct meanings of sentences *can* often be regarded as literal meanings, ATT-Meta is in the class of systems that rely on constructing a literal meaning first (not necessarily from a whole sentence, but perhaps from a component such as a prepositional phrase or clause). Still, there is no reliance on *rejecting* that literal meaning before proceeding to metaphorical processing.

Before continuing this description of ATT-Meta we also must explain that its reasoning is entirely query-directed. Query-directed reasoning – more usually called goal-directed reasoning – is a powerful technique much used in AI (see e.g. Russell & Norvig, 2002). In this form of reasoning, the process of reasoning starts with a query – an externally supplied or internally arising question as to whether something holds. Queries are compared to known propositions and/or used to generate further queries by some means. In a rule-based system such as ATT-Meta, queries are compared to the result parts of rules, and then new queries arise from the condition parts. For example, in the case of a rule that says if someone is a student then he or she is presumably poor, a query as to whether John is poor would give rise to a subquery as to whether John is a student.

The system's metaphor-based reasoning is thoroughly integrated into a general-purpose rule-based framework for uncertain reasoning using qualitative uncertainty measures. ATT-Meta's reasoning both in source-domain terms and in target-domain terms is generally uncertain. Rules and propositions are annotated with qualitative certainty levels. There is a heuristic conflict-resolution mechanism that attempts to adjudicate between conflicting lines of reasoning, by considering their relative specificity.

We are now ready to look in more detail at an example. Consider:

*In the far reaches of her mind, Anne believed that Kyle was having an affair.*

This is slightly adapted from a real-discourse example (Gross, 1994). We assume ATT-Meta is given knowledge of conceptual metaphors MIND AS PHYSICAL SPACE and IDEAS AS PHYSICAL OBJECTS. We also assume that "far reaches" only has a spatial sense for the system and that the notion is not mapped to the mental domain by any conceptual metaphor known to the system. The most important mapping known to ATT-Meta is the following, and is part of ATT-Meta's knowledge of IDEAS AS PHYSICAL OBJECTS:

*degree of (in)ability of an agent's conscious self to operate physically on an idea that is a physical object*, in the pretence cocoon, *corresponds to degree of (in)ability of the agent to operate in a conscious mental way on the idea*, in the reality space.

A given metaphorical mapping link such as this is implicit in a set of *transfer rules* that we will not detail here.

In the example as we run it using ATT-Meta, the system is given an initial target-domain query (IQ) that is, roughly speaking, of the form *To what exact degree is Anne able to consciously operate mentally on the idea that Kyle had an affair?* In Barnden and Lee (2001) we justify this as a reasonable query that could arise out of the surrounding context. The query is *reverse-transferred* from target terms to source terms via the above mapping to become a query of form *To what degree is Anne's conscious self able to operate physically on the idea?*

ATT-Meta can then reason that that degree of physical operability is very low, using the source-domain information gleaned from the mention of "far reaches" in the utterance and from commonsense knowledge about physical spaces and objects. Once this very low degree is established in the source domain, it is forward-transferred via the mapping to give a very low degree of conscious mental operability as the answer to the initial query (IQ). The program's reasoning for this example is treated in more detail in Barnden and Lee (2001). A variety of other examples are also computationally treated in that report and Barnden (2001c), Barnden et al. (2002), and Lee and Barnden (2001b).

We must note a largely unimplemented aspect of the ATT-Meta approach: "view-neutral mapping adjuncts" (VNMAs) (Barnden & Lee, 2001; Barnden et al., 2003). With partial inspiration from Carbonell's (1982) AI work on metaphor, we view certain aspects of source domain information such as attitudes, value judgments, beliefs, functions, rates, gradedness, uncertainty, and event structure to carry over to the target domain by default (the results can be overridden). For instance:

- We assume that the ordering of events and their qualitative rates and durations carry over by default, whatever the nature of the particular metaphorical mapping being used, thus avoiding the need for individual mapping rules to deal with them.
- If an agent A in the pretence has an attitude X (mental or emotional) to a proposition P, and A and P correspond, respectively, to an agent B and a proposition Q in reality, then B has attitude X to Q.
- As for gradedness, if a property P in a pretence corresponds to a property Q in reality, then a degree of holding of P should map to the same degree of holding of Q (unless there is additional evidence about Q).

We have produced an experimental implementation that handles rates and durations as VNMAs, but much work remains to be done on other VNMAs. In particular, gradedness is currently handled directly in individual rules – notice the degrees in the metaphorical correspondence used above. In place of this handling, we would like to have instead simpler mapping rules that do not mention degree, relying on a separate, general mechanism for the degree transfer.

Finally, the ATT-Meta approach does not rely on domain distinctions, even theoretically, let alone enshrine them in some way in the implemented system. Although in this article we generally adopt the common practice of saying that metaphor transfers information from a source domain to a target domain, the ATT-Meta approach has a different stance: metaphor is a matter of transferring from a *pretence* to *reality* (or to a surrounding pretence, in the case of serial mixing). Notice that in the mapping rule set out above, reference is made to pretence and reality, not to domains. It does not matter what domains the information used in the pretence comes from, and this means that it does not matter how we may intuitively circumscribe the source and target domains in the metaphor. In particular, it does not matter how close, difficult to distinguish, or overlapping those domains are. In practice, it will often be the case that we can theoretically identify a source domain in which the direct meaning of the sentence lies, and that inferences from this meaning also lie within that domain. However, this has no bearing on the course of processing, and the reasoning within the pretence is not limited by any consideration of domains.

### *Narayanan*

Srini Narayanan has implemented a metaphor-understanding system (Narayanan, 1997, 1999) that has mostly been applied to interpreting metaphorical statements about economic policy, where the source domain is that of everyday physical movement activities such as walking, as in the headline "Liberalization plan stumbling." However, it would appear reasonably straightforward to apply a modified version of the system to other source and target domains, and Narayanan (1999) mentions using a health-based source domain.

The system has been applied to many utterances about economics from newspaper articles, and has powerful facilities for addressing subtle aspects of such utterances. However, much as in the case of ATT-Meta, the system does not take sentences as such as input, but rather simple feature-value representations that could result from initial processing of sentences or other discourse fragments. The system is based on knowing a set of conceptual metaphor maps such as ACTING IS MOVING, OBSTACLES ARE DIFFICULTIES, and FAILING IS FALLING.

Examples of fragments successfully handled include "Liberalization plan stumbling," "European Giant falls sick," "taking a cautious step in the right direction" and "Economic reform is like crossing a river by feeling for the stones." Narayanan is especially concerned to deal with aspect, that is, the internal temporal structure of events. The system can deal with, for instance, the intermittent nature of an action such as rubbing, the aspect conveyed by the perfect form of verbs, and aspect conveyed in phrases such as "start to pull out," "on the verge of," and "back on track."

Both the source domain and the target domain are represented as fixed network structures, of rather different types. The target domain representation is a "belief network" (Pearl, 1986), in which nodes stand for economic variables needed for depicting the economic situations of interest. The variables include economic actors (example value: Indian Government), economic policy (example value: capitalism), status of a policy, gross domestic product, geographical location, rate of progress, level of difficulty (e.g. of implementing a policy), and goals of actors. Each node is repeated across a small sequence of time slices (up to four), so that for instance there is a policy node for time 1, a policy node for time 2, and so on. Nodes are linked together to represent probabilistic relationships between variables. For instance, the links state the conditional probability of policy being such-and-such at time 2 given that it is so-and-so at time 1 and a policy failure happens at time 1. When the belief network is used for inference, particular probability values at nodes are fixed on the basis of input and metaphorical transfer, and then the links cause posterior probabilities for particular variable values at nodes to be calculated. In this way, the network can probabilistically model a complex unfolding economic situation.

The source-domain representation is, roughly speaking, a type of marker passing network in which (the main type of) nodes represent states that can occur in activities such as walking, falling and getting up. Links between these nodes show how states can (stochastically) be caused by predecessor states, and markers passing along these links simulate the progress of activities.

The state nodes in the source domain include a subset that serve as the inputs to the system's metaphorical maps. For instance, the DIFFICULTIES ARE OBSTACLES map responds to the presence of a marker in the *bump* node in the source-domain network and contributes to the setting of the probability level at the *difficulty* node in the target network. One type of map, "parameter" maps, handles gradedness. For instance, velocity in the source domain is mapped to rate of progress of a policy in the target domain, or distance travelled in walking to degree of completion of an economic plan.

The processing within the source-domain network allows rich examples of map-transcendence to be handled. For instance, consider any discourse fragment that mentions an economic policy approaching a cliff edge. Recall that *falling* maps over to *failing*. Provided that the source-domain network has the right structures to predict falling from walking to the cliff's edge, the system can infer the target domain conclusion that the economic policy will fail.

Clearly, the system makes strong use of source-domain inference, if we regard the mental simulation of activities within the source domain as inference. Furthermore, it is uncertain inference, because of the stochastic nature of marker passing between state nodes. It is clear also from the above that the system places great weight on gradedness.

As for the role of literal meaning, consider the sentence "Economic reform is like crossing a river by feeling for the stones." This will be input to the sentence in the form of a setting of the source-domain network that depicts a fictional entity, corresponding to economic reform, crossing a river, and so on. In this sense, the system constructs a whole literal interpretation first. However, the system does not itself evaluate whether economic reform can itself cross a river, so, as with Hobbs's approach, MIDAS and ATT-Meta, there is no sense in which the system itself *rejects* a literal meaning before computing a metaphorical one.

The system is, clearly, strongly founded on domain distinctions, which are explicit in the structure of the system. Given the intuitive, qualitative distance between economics and bodily movement, this might not, superficially, appear to be a problem. However, various types of extension or enrichment of the system could soon run into problems. For one thing, mental processes are important both for physical activities in the world (e.g. reasoning about what to do at a crossroads) and in the economic domain, and this is already weakly evident in Narayanan's work. A more detailed treatment of mental processing in the two domains would require separate and differently organized network structures to handle mental states, whereas intuitively the two domains simply overlap on the matter of mental processes, which themselves could just as much be viewed as forming a domain.

### *Veale: The Sapper System*

Tony Veale (Veale, 1998; Veale & Keane, 1997) has constructed Sapper, an implemented hybrid symbolic/connectionist model for finding structural analogies. It is based on a semantic network framework in which nodes stand for concepts and between which activation values can flow. The work on Sapper appears to be largely separate from Veale's work on a "conceptual scaffolding" theory of metaphor (Veale & Keane, 1992).

Sapper does not take linguistic input as such, but rather attempts to find a metaphorical mapping between any two concepts S and T in its network that are from different domains, for instance *composer* and *[military] general*. In this example, the system comes up with a rich metaphorical mapping, involving component correspondences such as *orchestra* corresponding to *army*, *musician* to *soldier* and *musical-instrument* to *musket*. In this way it is similar in orientation to analogy-finding systems in Cognitive Psychology, such as SME and ACME. Indeed, Veale has shown in much detail, both theoretical and experimental, that his system can find analogies similar to those found by SME and ACME, while performing less processing.

Sapper has a long-term "bridge"-forming aspect and a short-term structure-matching aspect. The former is done in advance of any analogy-finding, and finds potential analogical correspondences between concepts. It does so by means of purely symbolic processing over the semantic network, based on certain simple heuristics (a "Triangulation" rule and a "Squaring" rule). Such a potential correspondence is called a bridge and is implemented as a special link between the nodes.

Analogy-finding per se in a particular case, such as for *composer* and *general*, consists of the short-term structure-matching aspect. This aspect exploits the long-term bridges via activation-spread in a way to be described shortly, and thereby constructs overall, coherent mappings containing component correspondences such as between *orchestra* and *army* in the example above.

Structure-matching works in outline as follows, given two nodes S and T, thought of as the source and target nodes respectively. Activation is sent out from S and T, to a prespecified distance ("horizon") in the network. If the two waves of activation meet at a bridge between two nodes S′ and T′, respectively, then the system sees if there is a chain of links from S to S′ that is isomorphic to a chain of links from T to T′. That is, the two chains consist of links of the same types in the same directions. Then for each pair of corresponding nodes on the chains the system considers them to be mapped to each other, and takes the overall mapping thus defined by the chains to be a partial interpretation of the T-is-S metaphor. Now the system takes the "richest" partial interpretation found by this method, and considers the remaining ones in descending order of richness, attempting to combine them consistently with the richest one. The final result is Sapper's overall metaphorical interpretation of T-is-S.

The theory behind Sapper places important, explicit weight on domains, and domain distinctions are used in the structure-matching process. A domain in Sapper is relative to a given "root" node. The domain for the node is the region of the semantic network that is reachable from the node via network links in a particular way. However, Veale does not appear to address the difficulties arising with source and target domains that intuitively overlap, which would require that activation flow during structure-matching not be domain-confined as he assumes it to be. For instance, drums are used in bands in armies, not just in ordinary orchestras.

It appears that the processing in Sapper is entirely symmetrical between source and target, so that for instance "a composer is a general" creates the same metaphorical correspondences as "a general is a composer." This may look as though it goes against claims in the metaphor literature (e.g. Ortony, 1979, 197) about the asymmetry of metaphor. However, it is not difficult to bias the processing in Sapper in ways that would asymmetrically affect the activation flow and thus ensure asymmetrical results. Also, Barnden (2001d) argues that asymmetry is a more subtle and delicate matter than it is usually portrayed as being; for example, the true asymmetry between S-is-T and T-is-S can reside in which particular mapping links are used in interacting with the overall discourse rather than with whether the links themselves differ between S-is-T and T-is-S. Indeed, on his website Veale describes how Sapper does structural transfer, in a way roughly similar to other analogy systems. Structure on the source side that is not paralleled on the target side can be transferred as "candidate inferences" to the target side. Structural transfer from S to T involves different pieces of domain information from those involved in transfer from T to S, even when the same metaphorical linkages are involved.

Sapper could be said to perform source-domain inference in using activation flow within that domain. Activation levels represent gradedness, for instance the degree to which the property denoted by the node holds. The levels therefore do not represent degrees of certainty, as they do in many connectionist systems.

## Discussion: Contributions of AI to Metaphor Research

Here we examine some specific issues on which AI is being helpful to metaphor research. We will draw heavily on the preceding review of particular AI approaches, but will also make additional observations.

### *Mundaneness*

Non-AI research such as that of Lakoff (Lakoff, 1993; Lakoff & Johnson, 1980) and of many researchers in Corpus Linguistics and Applied Linguistics has shown us that metaphor is an aspect of ordinary, everyday language, not just of literary or other heightened forms. AI is in a peculiar position to add both to the appreciation of the variety and complexity of metaphor as it arises in practical discourse and to the question of how to process real metaphor in practical contexts, because of the inclusion within AI of applications-oriented research. One of the AI systems reviewed above (MIDAS, by James Martin) concentrated on metaphor arising in question-and-answer sessions between users and an automated Unix help system. Narayanan's research used the domain of economics as an application area. A research project led by the present author, not reviewed above but drawing upon the ATT-Meta research, is looking at the metaphorical expression of affect (emotion, value judgments, etc.) in the context of an e-drama system that supports virtual dramatic improvisation by users sitting at computer terminals (Zhang, Barnden, & Hendley, 2005). Improvisations can be on any topic, but the system has in particular been used for improvisations concerning school bullying and embarrassing illnesses.

### *Non-Assertional Metaphor*

One consequence of looking at applications is as follows. In describing MIDAS we cited a metaphorical question as an example – "How do I get into Emacs?" It is remarkable, though not generally remarked upon, that the vast bulk of writing on metaphor has concentrated on assertions. Yet, metaphor is just as appropriate in questions, commands, and so on, as it is in assertions, and often occurs in non-assertions in real discourse. Non-assertional metaphor raises special issues. Questions and commands are usually not about conveying new information about the target or making the understander appreciate the target in a special way, yet existing theorizing on the meanings or connotations of metaphorical utterances presupposes that some new information or special view of the target is being communicated. In particular, whereas with an assertional metaphorical utterance an incompatibility between one potential interpretation and the target domain may indicate that the interpretation is incorrect, in the case of a metaphorical question the incompatibility may mean simply that a negative response is needed or the speaker has an incorrect supposition about the target domain, so that an answer could be directed at countering this. It could turn out that particular existing theories based on assertional metaphor could be smoothly generalized to deal with non-assertional metaphor, but the issue needs at least to be explicitly addressed.

### *Details of Mappings*

Much work on metaphor outside AI has specified particular mappings between sources and targets. The mappings are often backed up by discursive accounts of how they could help in the understanding of particular example utterances or types of utterance. However, without their being embedded in a detailed computational system it is difficult to determine whether, on the one hand, the mappings really do achieve all the effects they are credited with, and whether, on the other hand, they successfully avoid interacting to produce unwanted side-effects. In other words, mappings proposed in non-AI literature on metaphor are typically only vaguely evaluated as to coverage, coherence, and effectiveness. In contrast, systems such as MIDAS and ATT-Meta provide a framework within which to do extensive experimentation with alternative sets of mappings.

### *Source-Domain Reasoning and Pretence Reasoning*

Several of the reviewed AI systems (those of Hobbs, Martin, Narayanan) make crucial use of online source-domain inference: inference that is in terms of the source-domain subject matter and that is made at the time of trying to understand a metaphorical utterance. Source-domain reasoning was also briefly advocated in the work of Carbonell (1982) on metaphor in AI. The ATT-Meta system is centred on the closely related notion of within-pretence reasoning.

Now, source-domain inference has arisen quite frequently in the non-AI literature. For example, comments in Lakoff (1993) and Lakoff and Turner (1989, 62, 64, 94) suggest the use of source-domain inference. The discussion of metaphorical inference patterns in Turner (1987) appears to allow for online source-domain inference. The work of Ruiz de Mendoza Ibáñez (1999) on interactions between metonymy and metaphor includes mention of metonymy occurring within the source domain of a metaphor, and this amounts to a type of online source-domain inference. As for online within-pretence reasoning, Levin's (1988) work on metaphor in literature implies the use of it, and van Dijk (1980) provides a tentative account of metaphor in terms of counterfactuals. The "blending" ("conceptual integration" approach) in Cognitive Linguistics (Fauconnier & Turner 1998), when applied to metaphor, makes inference within the blend-space central. A blend-space is similar to a pretence cocoon in ATT-Meta, though the latter concept is more computationally specific while being unconstrained by notions of domain.

But the study of source-domain reasoning and within-pretence reasoning in AI research on metaphor has given flesh to and clarified the somewhat schematic and limited discussion of it in the non-AI literature. What AI can distinctively contribute is detailed, effective mechanisms for performing it. Complex technical matters of representation, reasoning, and evidence-comparison are involved here, especially when uncertainty and gradedness are brought in.

The reason for the intense attention to source-domain and within-pretence reasoning in AI may be that, in concentrating on real examples of metaphor in mundane contexts, the researchers concerned have been affected by the fact that truly novel metaphor is far from being predominant in metaphor in real discourse, and have concentrated on the rich, open-ended exploitation of already-known mappings. Source-domain or within-pretence inference enables the map-transcending aspects of the utterance – the aspects not directly handled by known mappings – to be linked to the aspects that are so handled. Map-transcendence is a central problem of metaphor that has not been adequately treated, although the Hobbs, Martin, Narayanan, and Barnden approaches are important developments.

### *Economizing on Parallelism, and Use of Disanalogies*

Hobbs, Narayanan, and Barnden all recognize that much or all of what one needs to get out of a map-transcending metaphorical utterance can often or perhaps usually be got *without finding target-domain correspondents for the map-transcending items*. This stance is against the idea that the fundamental task in metaphor understanding is to establish new mappings; indeed, to establish as much parallelism as possible between the two domains. Rather, the three approaches seek to exploit as far as possible the already known mappings. In particular, Barnden, Helmreich, Iverson, and

Stein (1996) explicitly championed the thesis that it is often misguided to think that map-transcending source-domain elements should be expected to have a parallel in the target, let alone to think that it is profitable to look for it. For example, it seems excessive to expect the "dim recesses" mentioned in "The idea was in the dim recesses of Tony's mind" to actually correspond to any identifiable components of the mind in reality, rather than serving *merely to connote physical inaccessibility within the metaphorical pretence*. On the other hand, there are certainly situations where one needs to find some target-domain correspondents. The question of which these situations are is an outstanding research issue, on which a start is made in Barnden and Lee (2001).

Relatedly, the benefits of attending to disanalogies between source and target in metaphor deserve more study. Fass's system (meta5) is unusual, and unique among the systems reviewed, in regarding disanalogies between source and target as a source of useful information.

### *Dissolving Metaphorical Transfers into the Overall Processing*

The Hobbs and Barnden approaches achieve great flexibility in allowing target-domain (or within-reality) reasoning steps, source-domain (or within-pretence) reasoning steps, and metaphorical transfer steps to be arbitrarily mixed together in a completely uniform and task-dependent way. This flexibility is a contribution to conceptions of how the different types of processing in metaphor can fit together. Most discussions of metaphor appear to assume that transfer steps occur in some special phase of processing.

The flexibility of mixing is aided by casting mappings as inference rules that are applied in the same way as other rules. Usually in metaphor research, whether in AI or elsewhere, mappings are a different sort of entity, which inhibits even the realization that a uniform treatment would be liberating and beneficial.

### *Context and Extent*

It is often pointed out that the information conveyed by a metaphorical utterance can be highly sensitive to context, and a considerable amount of psychological experimentation and philosophical theorizing has addressed this (e.g. Giora, 1997; Leezenberg, 1995; Stern, 2000). Context is important for the understanding of much non-metaphorical language as well, but metaphor heightens its effect.

The sentence "Mike is a rock" is highly indeterminate as to what it might convey, absent any specific context. Perhaps the speaker is intending to convey that Mike can be relied upon. However, in "Mike's friends are very upset by criticism, but he's a rock" the contribution of "rock" is much more definite. It is probably not getting at Mike's reliability: the sentence is arguably saying that Mike is highly tolerant of criticism, and if so it is presumably exploiting a correspondence between invulnerability of rocks to physical assault and tolerance of criticism by people.

In this example the disambiguating context about Mike's friends and criticism is near to the metaphorical clause, but in other cases the necessary contextual information might arise from further afield, and might have to be derived from the surrounding passage or other information by subtle or knowledge-intensive processes of inference. Thus, a full approach to metaphor must deal with possibly complex, extensive passages of discourse, and complex inference.

Although AI work on metaphor has yet to address context fully, some of the systems reviewed above give context a crucial guiding role and are at least in a position to accommodate its effects smoothly. Hobbs and Barnden place much weight on reasoning goals derived from context as a crucial driver of what metaphorical interpretations are drawn, and their approaches are unusual amongst detailed metaphor-processing schemes in this respect. Contextual-goal drivenness is a powerful tool not only against the often-noted indeterminacy of metaphorical meaning (see e.g. Stern, 2000) but also against the problem of inappropriate or irrelevant aspects of the source domain getting in the way (such as the shape of a pig's tail when classifying a person as a pig). In a contextual-goal driven approach, those irrelevant aspects will simply tend not to be queried.

As we have made clear, many authors outside AI have discussed the importance of context. What AI can contribute is detailed, computationally tested mechanisms by which it can be brought to bear.

### *Uncertainty*

The information gained from metaphor is generally uncertain. The indeterminateness of the import of "Mike is a rock" without a sufficiently specific context is itself a type of uncertainty. Even with the context shown above, we cannot be *certain* that Mike is tolerant of criticism (according to the speaker). Perhaps, after all, the speaker is intending to convey that Mike can be relied upon to give support to his colleagues when they are upset by criticism.

But even if an interpretation in terms of Mike's tolerance to criticism is correct, we cannot be certain about the degree of tolerance: perhaps the speaker is merely trying to say that Mike has a normal level of tolerance, in contrast to his colleagues' marked lack of tolerance. After all, different types of rock have different degrees of vulnerability to physical assault, and, without further information, it can merely be a presumption that a rock has a high degree of invulnerability.

Therefore as well as the uncertainty arising between there being qualitatively different possible interpretations (e.g. one appealing to reliability and one appealing to tolerance), there is also uncertainty arising from within the source domain itself. Another example of the latter phenomenon would arise from talking about someone "burying" an idea in his mind. In the physical world, once something is buried it (at best) only *normally* stays buried. There can therefore be no *certainty* that the idea will not "pop up" again.

Most work on metaphor sidesteps detailed considerations of uncertainty, although systems such as SME and ACME, where there are scoring mechanisms, do provide some support for a restricted type of uncertainty handling. Amongst our reviewed AI systems, those of Narayanan, Hobbs, and Barnden all allow the system's source-domain reasoning and target-domain reasoning to be uncertain. Uncertainty is important for making the overall processing do justice to people's use of metaphor, but greatly complicates the technical nature of the computational framework.

### *Source/Target Overrides*

The uncertainty issue also reveals the importance of often allowing information transferred from source to target *to override information about the target.* This possibility is under-studied in metaphor research, because usually the information about a target domain is cast simplistically in the form of certainties which cannot be overridden. This practice has led to researchers, outside AI and within, almost exclusively concentrating on the fact that target-domain information must sometimes override what comes from the source. Of course, this is indeed appropriate in many cases: since it is certain that France and Germany are not cognitive agents and are therefore incapable of love, metaphorically casting the relationship of those countries within the EU as a "marriage" (Musolff, 2004) should not lead to the result that they love each other in reality.

But, if a piece of target-domain knowledge is not certain, but let us say merely a default, there is no reason in principle why the information should not be overridden by transfers from the source. Thus, "SnakeByte Technologies nursed its competitor RabbitWare Inc. back to health" would override the default that competing companies do not normally deliberately help each other. The utterance "In the far reaches of her mind, Anne believed that Kyle had been unfaithful" defeats the normal presumption that people's thoughts about their spouses' possible affairs are central and conscious ones. It may even be that one important function of metaphor is to convey situations that are exceptions to target-domain defaults. The exception-expressing function of metaphor may be especially significant given that exceptional situations are less likely to be easily expressible using the resources native to the target domain.

It appears that only in the context of the ATT-Meta system has the process of source-over-target overriding been studied in computational detail, though see Indurkhya (1992, 85–86) for other comments on the importance of such overriding. In ATT-Meta, both directions of override are possible, depending on the fine detail of the reasoning lines involved in particular cases.

### *Gradedness*

The rock example above brings out the importance of matters of gradedness (degree) in metaphor. It is gradations, not black-and-white propositions, that metaphor is often getting at, a point that deserves greater emphasis in metaphor research. The interpretation suggested for "Mike's friends get very hurt by criticism, but he's a rock" was not the bald proposition that Mike is tolerant of criticism but that he is *highly* so. Equally, the sentence "The memory was hidden far back in the labyrinth of John's memory" plausibly does not convey that the memory was completely inaccessible to John but rather that it was *highly* inaccessible, or very difficult to access. A range of specific examples of gradedness in metaphor interpretation can be found in Barnden (2001b, 2001c).

Once gradedness and uncertainty are considered it also becomes evident that a metaphorical utterance may not necessarily introduce totally new information but may rather change the degree of holding, and/or the certainty, of some existing piece of information. Gibbs and Tendahl (2006) discuss this under the heading of the "strengthening" of (and the opposite: contradiction of) existing assumptions, in the light of considerations of metaphor in Relevance Theory (Carston, 2002; Sperber & Wilson, 1995). In the rock example, other evidence may already have established that Mike *may* be *somewhat* insensitive to criticism, so the sentence is both strengthening the *may* to *presumably* and strengthening the *somewhat* to *highly*. Note also that such strengthening goes beyond the notion that metaphor can draw attention to or increase the salience of (Ortony, 1979) pieces of information about the target domain. We are talking instead about adjusting pieces of information about the target domain.

It cannot be claimed that AI or any other field has developed generally accepted, comprehensive methods for handling gradedness. Nevertheless, Narayanan and Barnden place weight on the handling of gradedness and the transfer of graded information from source to target. Perhaps as important as the actual handling of gradedness in some recent AI metaphor systems is the sheer fact that the pressure in AI towards considering the details of processing practical examples in realistic contexts makes one more readily appreciate the central role that gradedness plays in metaphor (going beyond the obvious role of gradedness in scale-based conceptual metaphors such as MORE IS UP).

### *Domain Distinctions*

Metaphor is frequently characterized as a matter of mappings or transfers between different "domains," often to make a contrast with metonymy, which is often claimed to operate within a single domain. On the other hand, some authors have questioned the usefulness of the domain notion or the degree of distinctness that is required between the two domains in a metaphor (see e.g. Dirven & Pörings, 2002; Kittay, 1989). For simplicity of discussion we have sometimes used the notion of domain uncritically in this article. It is certainly true that in much metaphor there is an intuitive sense in which the source and target are qualitatively very different. The question is whether real sense can be made of this and whether it matters to metaphor processing anyway.

The present author found, in his own AI work on the ATT-Meta approach, the detail and clarity required for well-founded computational implementation to be a major factor in his coming to doubt the usefulness of the concept of "domain" in studying metaphor (and metonymy). In trying to make decisions about what domains particular pieces of knowledge should be assigned to he came to realize what a hopeless and arbitrary task it was. The resulting despair was relieved by an ultimate realization that having domain distinctions was not operationally useful in any case.

The nature of the other systems in the review above also throws doubt on the usefulness of the notion. Only Veale and Narayanan actually have domains affect how their systems are structured and how the processing works. Hobbs does believe that metaphor is a matter of mapping between qualitatively disparate domains, but this stance has no operational effect in his system. In contrast, Barnden regards this disparateness as merely being a common case and is happy for the two sides of a metaphor to be arbitrarily close in their qualitative nature. Metaphors such as "Thatcher was Britain's Reagan" are common, and have source and target domains that are broadly similar in subject matter. For an example with even less qualitative distance between the two sides, one's neighbour's teenage children can act as a metaphor for one's own: if one has a daughter Jenny and the neighbours have a son Jonathan who behaves similarly to Jenny, then one could say "Jenny is our family's Jonathan." Of course, it is open to someone to say that the Jenny family is qualitatively different from the Jonathan family, and that they are therefore different domains, but this is post hoc rationalization with no operational significance.

Despite the closeness between target and source in the Jenny/Jonathan example, the metaphorical utterance appears quite apt to the present author. If this impression is shared with others, it may appear to conflict with the evidence adduced by Tourangeau and Sternberg (1982) that the greater the conceptual distance between source and target the more apt the metaphor. However, note that the linguistic form of the metaphorical utterance and the presence of context are important factors. A bald statement that "Jenny is Jonathan" without much context might well not come over as apt.

Apart from considerations of overall qualitative closeness, there is often a considerable amount of overlap between the intuitive source and target domains in metaphor even when they otherwise differ a great deal. We noted some overlap between the economics (target) and health (source) domain in the Narayanan discussion – and we could also have pointed out that health services are part of the economy – and between the orchestra and army domains in the Veale discussion. With reference to the Fass discussion, the domain of cars involves the domain of animals because cars can carry people and other animals.

It is quite possible to maintain a fiction that domains do real work in metaphor as long as one only deals schematically with some isolated examples, and does not try to come up with a unified and processually detailed approach to metaphor that can work on a wide variety of metaphors on the basis of the same overall knowledge base.

### *Relationship to Metonymy*

The relationship of metaphor to metonymy is highly contentious and complex (Dirven & Pörings, 2002; Fass, 1997). It has proved difficult to distinguish clearly between the two phenomena, and they may be at ends of a spectrum within which many compromises are possible. Particular discourse examples are often hard to classify as to whether they exhibit metonymy or metaphor. Also, metaphor and metonymy often co-occur in richly interactive ways in discourse. However, there has been little work on processing accounts that handle both phenomena. As it happens, two of the AI approaches reviewed above – those of Hobbs and Fass – pay much attention to metonymy as well as to metaphor, and allow certain types of interaction. They complement work such as that of Ruiz de Mendoza Ibáñez (1999) and Goossens (1990) outside AI. Hobbs's approach is perhaps especially noteworthy in that, as in the case of metaphor, it embeds metonymy as just one type of inference within the system's inferencing as a whole (Hobbs et al., 1993). Therefore, in principle, arbitrarily complex and diverse mixes of metaphor and metonymy should be able to be handled, and it is likely that compromises between metaphor and metonymy are possible.

If domains are abandoned as a well-founded underpinning for metaphor, then metaphor cannot be distinguished from metonymy on the usual ground of between-domain moves versus within-domain moves. Thus, any profound effect that metaphor research in AI and other disciplines may ultimately have on the fate of domains must be matched by a profound effect on the metaphor/metonymy relationship.

### *The Literal: Its Nature and Use*

Strongly related to the domains issue is a theme that appears throughout the field of metaphor, and continues to be a matter of debate in the field (Gibbs & Tendahl, 2006): the role, if any, of the literal meaning of metaphorical utterances (or words in them) in deriving their metaphorical meaning.

Of the systems reviewed, only Fass's (meta5) has any use for the idea of having to *reject* a literal interpretation before considering a metaphorical one, and even in his case the incremental semantic processing (while problematic in itself) means that the rejection is by sentence-part rather than by whole sentence. See Lytinen, Burridge, and Kirtner (1992) for another system with a related incremental quality.

The approaches of Hobbs, Martin, and Narayanan do rely on *constructing* a literal interpretation of a metaphorical sentence, or sentence-like subunit such as a clause. Barnden's approach is similar in this respect, though there it is a "direct" meaning that is constructed, with the question of whether it is necessarily to be called the literal interpretation being left as a terminological side issue. It should not be feared that there is necessarily any conflict between these approaches and psychological experimental results about metaphor processing being about as fast as, or sometimes faster than, literal-language processing under certain conditions (see e.g. Gibbs & Tendahl, 2006, for a discussion of such results). This speediness does not of itself show that literal meanings are not being computed. The evidence on these matters from psychological experiment is mixed, because it is bound up with the nature of the context of the metaphorical utterance and the novelty or otherwise of its metaphorical elements: context could by itself suggest part or all of the meaning, and a piece of familiar metaphorical terminology could have its target-domain meaning listed in a lexicon. Also, the type of literal (or direct) meaning that is constructed in the aid of metaphor understanding is plausibly less fully fledged than that needed in cases where the linguistic string really should be interpreted literally. In the latter case, the literal meaning itself needs to involve integration with the context, whereas in the metaphor case it is instead the metaphorical meaning that needs to be fully integrated with context. It is possible that all that the metaphorical processing is adding is the occasional hop from a complex source-domain (or pretence) scenario into a target-domain (or reality) scenario, and the time for such hops could be swamped by the time needed for all the other processing going on, such as anaphor resolution and semantic/pragmatic inferencing of many other types. AI can contribute here in clarifying the overall computations needed and how they can be imaginatively structured and optimized.

Finally, note that serial mixing (chaining) of metaphor complicates the role of literal meaning in metaphor, as noted in the discussion of ATT-Meta. What is transferred online in metaphor can already be a product of online metaphorical transfer.

### *Transfer of Attitudes and Value Judgments*

A metaphorical utterance often conveys or instigates a mental or emotional attitude or a value judgment about the target subject matter. This is perhaps especially prevalent in metaphor used in political discourse (see e.g. Musolff, 2004). The attitude or judgment can be on the part of some person mentioned in the discourse, or it can be on the part of the speaker/hearer. For instance, talking about somebody's mind as if it were a "cess-pit" may be intended to make the hearer have an emotional revulsion to, or negative value judgment of, the ideas of that person. On the other hand, saying that "The problem crushed Mike into the ground" primarily conveys something about Mike's emotions, although of course it can also engender the meta-emotion of sorrow about Mike's feelings.

Although attitudes such as emotions and value judgments are of widely recognized importance for metaphor, it is important to have detailed accounts of how exactly they may be processed in metaphor understanding. The processing of attitudes interacts heavily with ordinary inferencing, rather than being an isolatable matter. In addition, emotions and value judgments are intrinsically graded, so the theme in this subsection interacts strongly with the general gradeness issue we identified above.

The description of the ATT-Meta project mentioned that mechanisms are being developed in that project for transferring attitudes and value judgments from source to target by default, whatever the particular conceptual metaphor involved, obviating the need for special mechanisms per conceptual metaphor.

### *Connections to Reasoning about Beliefs*

Little research into metaphor has taken into account the fact that if a hearer wishes to understand what a speaker means by a particular metaphorical utterance, it is the speaker's beliefs about the target and source domains, and so on, that are important, not the hearer's. In effect, the metaphorical processing should occur within the speaker's "belief space" (as perceived by the hearer). Relatedly, metaphor can occur within the complement clauses of mental state verbs, as in "Mary believes that SnakeByte nursed RabbitWare back to health." One interpretation of such a sentence is that the metaphorical conception of the target is Mary's own (or rather, Mary's own, as viewed by the speaker), not (directly) the speaker's. In this case, metaphorical processing should be embedded within a belief space for Mary (within a belief space of the speaker). Stern (2000) and van Dijk (1980) are rare in metaphor research in addressing these issues, albeit only in an abstract way.

The issues are important in the ATT-Meta project. As well as handling metaphor, the ATT-Meta system can perform reasoning about agents' beliefs and reasoning. Methods are being developed for processing metaphor within the context of a specific agent's beliefs rather than within the system's own view of reality. This involves embedding a pretence cocoon within a belief space for the agent.

Conversely, in personification metaphor, it can be necessary to reason about the beliefs and reasoning of the entity that is metaphorically viewed as a person. This involves, in ATT-Meta terms, embedding a belief space within a pretence cocoon.

### *Reversed Transfers*

The ATT-Meta approach is unusual in advocating that "reverse transfers" – transfers of information from target to source domain (more properly, reality to pretence) – are useful in metaphor understanding. One reason is the reverse transfer of reasoning queries that arise (notionally) from context. A query in target-domain terms can be reversed-transferred to become a query in source-domain terms, and an example was given in the review of ATT-Meta above. This and two other reasons for doing reverse transfers are discussed at length in Barnden et al. (2004). One of them is based on an argument that, in the case of a conceptual metaphor being used in a distributed way across multiple utterances, it may be easier and more effective to form a coherent scenario in source-domain terms than to do so directly in target-domain terms by translating each metaphorical utterance into target-domain terms. This approach can instead involve "metaphorizing" the literal sentences in the relevant discourse segment: translating the information in them into source-domain terms. We present this possibility as a potentially fruitful topic for future research into metaphor.

## Conclusion

AI is not just about the engineering of "intelligent" artefacts for useful purposes but also about mapping out the space of possible principles and mechanisms of cognition, whether artificial or natural. For the Engineering aim, metaphor is an important challenge, and AI can draw here on insights on the problem from many other disciplines. Conversely, through its non-Engineering aims, various features of AI – its partial applications focus, its input from Computer Science, its need or ambition to produce detailed processing accounts – put AI in a good position to help metaphor research. The help can consist of facilitating certain types of advance, identifying certain types of neglected problem, or effecting salutory changes of emphasis. This is not to say that these advances, problem identifications, and emphasis shifts could not arise from other disciplines, but just that AI is especially well-placed to generate them.

Specific helpful things that one can point to already as coming out of AI research on metaphor – whether they are advances, problem identifications, or emphasis shifts – include the working out of detailed mechanisms for source-domain reasoning, the detailed elaboration of the alternative notion of within-pretence reasoning for metaphor, the casting of mappings as inference rules, the emphasis on and inclusion of gradedness in metaphor interpretation, mechanisms for exploiting context, the thorough inclusion of uncertainty into metaphorical reasoning, a richer view of overriding (source-over-target as well as target-over-source), important steps towards integration with metonymy interpretation, some emphasis on disanalogy, the usefulness of reversed transfers, steps towards mechanisms for handling the default transfer of attitudes and value judgments, the importance of non-assertional metaphor, enriched doubt about domains, and clarification and specification of ways in which literal meaning can be involved in metaphor interpretation.

All these matters require much further research, within AI and outside. But let us celebrate the fact that metaphor is, *par excellence*, an area for truly interdisciplinary investigation!

## Acknowledgments

This chapter draws on research supported by grants GR/M64208 and EP/C538943/1 from the Engineering and Physical Sciences Research Council of the United Kingdom. I am indebted to members of the metaphor research group in my department – Sheila Glasbey, Mark Lee, and especially Alan Wallington – for their help with the development of this article, and to Ray Gibbs for comments and guidance.

## References

Asher, N., & Lascarides, A. (1995, March). Metaphor in discourse. In *Proceedings of the AAAI Spring Symposium Series: Representation and Acquisition of Lexical Knowledge: Polysemy, Ambiguity, and Generativity* (pp. 3–7). Stanford, CA.

Barnden, J. A. (1998). Combining uncertain belief reasoning and uncertain metaphor-based reasoning. In M. A. Gernsbacher & S. J. Derry (Eds.), *Proceedings of the Twentieth Annual Meeting of the Cognitive Science Society* (pp. 114–119). Mahwah, NJ: Lawrence Erlbaum Associates.

Barnden, J. A. (2001a). Uncertainty and conflict handling in the ATT-Meta context-based system for metaphorical reasoning. In V. Akman,

P. Bouquet, R. Thomason, & R. A. Young (Eds.), *Proceedings of the Third International Conference on Modeling and Using Context: Vol. 2116. Lecture Notes in Artificial Intelligence* (pp. 15–29). Berlin: Springer.

Barnden, J. A. (2001b). *Application of the ATT-Meta metaphor-understanding approach to selected examples from Goatly* (Technical Report CSRP-01-01). Birmingham, UK: School of Computer Science, University of Birmingham.

Barnden, J. A. (2001c). *Application of the ATT-Meta metaphor-understanding approach to various examples in the ATT-Meta project databank* (Technical Report CSRP-01-02). Birmingham, UK: School of Computer Science, University of Birmingham.

Barnden, J. A. (2001d). The utility of reversed transfers in metaphor. In J. D. Moore & K. Stenning (Eds.), *Proceedings of the Twenty-Third Annual Meeting of the Cognitive Science Society* (pp. 57–62). Mahwah, NJ: Lawrence Erlbaum Associates.

Barnden, J. A., Glasbey, S. R., Lee, M. G., & Wallington, A. M. (2002). *Application of the ATT-Meta metaphor-understanding system to examples of the metaphorical view of* TEACHERS AS MIDWIVES (Technical Report CSRP-02-10). Birmingham, UK: School of Computer Science, University of Birmingham.

Barnden, J. A., Glasbey, S. R., Lee, M. G., & Wallington, A. M. (2003). Domain-transcending mappings in a system for metaphorical reasoning. In *Conference Companion to the 10th Conference of the European Chapter of the Association for Computational Linguistics* (EACL 2003) (pp. 57–61). Association for Computational Linguistics.

Barnden, J. A., Glasbey, S. R., Lee, M. G., & Wallington, A. M. (2004). Varieties and directions of interdomain influence in metaphor. *Metaphor and Symbol*, 19(1), 1–30.

Barnden, J. A., Helmreich, S., Iverson, E., & Stein, G. C. (1994). An integrated implementation of simulative, uncertain and metaphorical reasoning about mental states. In J. Doyle, E. Sandewall, & P. Torasso (Eds.), *Principles of knowledge representation and reasoning: Proceedings of the Fourth International Conference* (pp. 27–38). San Mateo, CA: Morgan Kaufmann.

Barnden, J. A., Helmreich, S., Iverson, E., & Stein, G. C. (1996). Artificial intelligence and metaphors of mind: within-vehicle reasoning and its benefits. *Metaphor and Symbolic Activity*, 11(2), 101–123.

Barnden, J. A., & Lee, M. G. (1999). An implemented context system that combines belief reasoning, metaphor-based reasoning and uncertainty handling. In P. Bouquet, P. Brezillon, & L. Serafini (Eds.), *Second International and Interdisciplinary Conference on Modeling and Using Context: Vol. 1688 Lecture Notes in Artificial Intelligence* (pp. 28–41). Berlin: Springer.

Barnden, J. A., & Lee, M. G. (2001). *Understanding usages of conceptual metaphors: An approach and artificial intelligence system* (Technical Report CSRP-01-05). Birmingham, UK: School of Computer Science, University of Birmingham.

Carbonell, J. G. (1980). Metaphor – a key to extensible semantic analysis. In *Proceedings of the 18th Annual Meeting of the Association for Computational Linguistics* (pp. 17–21).

Carbonell, J. G. (1982). Metaphor: An inescapable phenomenon in natural-language comprehension. In W. Lehnert & M. Ringle (Eds.), *Strategies for natural language processing* (pp. 415–434). Hillsdale, NJ: Lawrence Erlbaum Associates.

Carston, R. (2002). *Thoughts and utterances: The pragmatics of explicit communication*. Oxford: Blackwell.

Delfino, M., & Manea, S. (2005, April). Figurative language expressing emotion and motivation in a web based learning environment. In *Proceedings of the Symposium on Agents That Want and Like: Motivational and Emotional Roots of Cognition and Action* (pp. 37–40), at AISB'05 Convention, University of Hertfordshire, UK. Brighton, UK: Society for the Study of Artificial Intelligence and Simulation of Behaviour.

Dirven, R., & Pörings, R. (Eds.). (2002). *Metaphor and metonymy in comparison and contrast*. Berlin: Mouton de Gruyter.

Emanatian, E. (1995). Metaphor and the experience of emotion: The value of cross-cultural perspectives. *Metaphor and Symbolic Activity*, 10(3), 163–182.

Fainsilber, L., & Ortony, A. (1987). Metaphorical uses of language in the expression of emotions. *Metaphor and Symbolic Activity*, 2(4), 239–250.

Falkenhainer, B., Forbus, K. D., & Gentner, D. (1989). The structure-mapping engine: Algorithm and examples. *Artificial Intelligence*, 41(1), 1–63.

Fass, D. (1997). *Processing metaphor and metonymy*. Greenwich, CT: Ablex.
Fauconnier, G., & Turner, M. (1998). Conceptual integration networks. *Cognitive Science, 22*(2), 133–187.
Fussell, S. R., & Moss, M. M. (1998). Figurative language in descriptions of emotional states. In S. R. Fussell & R. J. Kreuz (Eds.), *Social and Cognitive Approaches to Interpersonal Communication*. Hillsdale, NJ: Lawrence Erlbaum Associates.
Gentner, D. (1983). Structure-mapping: A theoretical framework for analogy. *Cognitive Science, 7*(2), 95–119.
Gerrig, R. J. (1989). Empirical constraints on computational theories of metaphor: Comments on Indurkhya. *Cognitive Science, 13*(2), 235–241.
Gibbs, R., & Tendahl, M. (2006). Cognitive effort and effects in metaphor comprehension: Relevance theory and psycholinguistics. *Mind & Language, 21*, 379–403.
Giora, R. (1997). Understanding figurative and literal language: The graded salience hypothesis. *Cognitive Linguistics, 8*(3), 183–206.
Goossens, L. (1990). Metaphtonymy: the interaction of metaphor and metonymy in expressions for linguistic action. *Cognitive Linguistics, 1*, 323–340.
Gross, L. (1994). Facing up to the dreadful dangers of denial [U.S. ed.]. *Cosmopolitan, 216*(3).
Hall, R. P. (1989). Computational approaches to analogical reasoning: a comparative analysis. *Artificial Intelligence, 39*, 39–120.
Hintikka, J., & Sandu, G. (1990). Metaphor and the varieties of lexical meaning. *Dialectica, 44*(1–2), 55–78.
Hobbs, J. R. (1990). *Literature and cognition* (CSLI Lecture Notes No. 21). Stanford, CA: Stanford University.
Hobbs, J. R. (1992). Metaphor and abduction. In A. Ortony, J. Slack, & O. Stock (Eds.), *Communication from an Artificial Intelligence perspective: Theoretical and applied issues* (pp. 35–58). Berlin: Springer-Verlag.
Hobbs, J. R., Stickel, M. E., Appelt, D. E., & Martin, P. (1993). Interpretation as abduction. *Artificial Intelligence, 63*, 69–142.
Indurkhya, B. (1991). Modes of metaphor. *Metaphor and Symbolic Activity, 6*(1), 1–27.
Indurkhya, B. (1992). *Metaphor and cognition: An interactionist approach*. Dordrecht: Kluwer.
Iverson, E., & Helmreich, S. (1992). Metallel: An integrated approach to non-literal phrase interpretation. *Computational Intelligence, 8*(3), 477–493.
Kittay, E. F. (1989). *Metaphor: Its cognitive force and linguistic structure* (Paperback ed.). Oxford: Clarendon Press.
Kövecses, Z. (2000). *Metaphor and emotion: Language, culture, and body in human feeling*. New York: Cambridge University Press.
Lakoff, G. (1993). The contemporary theory of metaphor. In A. Ortony (Ed.), *Metaphor and thought* (2nd ed.) (pp. 202–251). Cambridge: Cambridge University Press.
Lakoff, G., & Johnson, M. (1980). *Metaphors we live by*. Chicago: University of Chicago Press.
Lakoff, G., & Turner, M. (1989). *More than cool reason: A field guide to poetic metaphor*. Chicago: University of Chicago Press.
Lee, M. G., & Barnden, J. A. (2001a). Reasoning about mixed metaphors with an implemented AI system. *Metaphor and Symbol, 16*(1&2), 29–42.
Lee, M. G., & Barnden, J. A. (2001b). *Mental metaphors from the master metaphor list: Empirical examples and the application of the ATT-Meta system* (Technical Report CSRP-01-03). Birmingham, UK: School of Computer Science, University of Birmingham.
Leezenberg, M. (1995). *Contexts of metaphor*. ILLC Dissertation Series, 1995–17, Institute for Language, Logic and Computation, University of Amsterdam, The Netherlands.
Levin, S. R. (1988). *Metaphoric worlds*. New Haven, CT: Yale University Press.
Lytinen, S. L., Burridge, R. R., & Kirtner, J. D. (1992). The role of literal meaning in the comprehension of non-literal constructions. *Computational Intelligence, 8*(3), 416–432.
Martin, J. H. (1990). *A computational model of metaphor interpretation*. San Diego, CA: Academic Press.
Martin, J. H. (1996). Computational approaches to figurative language. *Metaphor and Symbolic Activity, 11*, 85–100.
Martin, J. H. (2000). Representing UNIX domain metaphors. *Artificial Intelligence Review, 14*(4–5), 377–401.
Mason, Z. J. (2004). CorMet: A computational, corpus-based conventional metaphor extraction system. *Computational Linguistics, 30*(1), 23–44.
McNeill, D. (1992). *Hand and mind: What gestures reveal about thought*. Chicago: University of Chicago Press.

Musolff, A. (2004). *Metaphor and political discourse: Analogical reasoning in debates about Europe*. Basingstoke, UK: Palgrave Macmillan.
Narayanan, S. (1997). *KARMA: Knowledge-based action representations for metaphor and aspect*. Unpublished PhD thesis, Computer Science Division, EECS Department, University of California, Berkeley.
Narayanan, S. (1999). Moving right along: A computational model of metaphoric reasoning about events. In *Proceedings of the National Conference on Artificial Intelligence* (AAAI '99, pp. 121–128). AAAI Press.
Norvig, P. (1989). Marker passing as a weak method of text inferencing. *Cognitive Science*, 13(4), 569–620.
Ortony, A. (1979). The role of similarity in similes and metaphors. In A. Ortony (Ed.), *Metaphor and thought* (pp. 186–201). Cambridge: Cambridge University Press.
Pearl, J. (1986). Fusion, propagation, and structuring in belief networks. *Artificial Intelligence*, 29(3), 241–288.
Ruiz de Mendoza Ibáñez, F. J. (1999). *From semantic underdetermination via metaphor and metonymy to conceptual interaction* (Series A: General & Theoretical Papers No. 492). LAUD Linguistic Agency.
Russell, S. W. (1976). Computer understanding of metaphorically used verbs. *American Journal of Computational Linguistics*, 2, 15–28.
Russell, S. W. (1985). Conceptual analysis of partial metaphor. In L. Steels & J. Campbell (Eds.), *Progress in Artificial Intelligence* (pp. 193–201). Chichester, UK: Ellis Horwood.
Russell, S. W. (1986). Information and experience in metaphor: A perspective from computer analysis. *Metaphor and Symbolic Activity*, 1(4), 227–270.
Russell, S., & Norvig, P. (2002). *Artificial Intelligence: A modern approach*. Englewood Cliffs, NJ: Prentice Hall.
Sperber, D., & Wilson, D. (1995). *Relevance: Communication and cognition* (2nd ed.). Oxford: Blackwell.
Stern, J. (2000). *Metaphor in context*. Cambridge, MA: Bradford Books/MIT Press.
Thomas, O. (1969). *Metaphor and related subjects*. New York: Random House.
Tourangeau, R., & Sternberg, R. J. (1982). Understanding and appreciating metaphors. *Cognition*, 11, 203–244.
Turner, M. (1987). *Death is the mother of beauty: Mind, metaphor, criticism*. Chicago: University of Chicago Press.
van Dijk, T. A. (1980). Formal semantics of metaphorical discourse. In M. K. L. Ching, M. C. Haley, & R. F. Lunsford (Eds.), *Linguistic perspectives on literature* (pp. 115–138). London: Routledge and Kegan Paul.
van Genabith, J. (2001). Metaphors, logic, and type theory. *Metaphor and Symbol*, 16(1&2), 43–57.
Veale, T. (1998). "Just in Time" analogical mapping, an iterative-deepening approach to structure-mapping. In *Proceedings of the Thirteenth European Conference on Artificial Intelligence* (ECAI '98). New York: John Wiley.
Veale, T., & Keane, M. T. (1992). Conceptual scaffolding: a spatially founded meaning representation for metaphor comprehension. *Computational Intelligence*, 8(3), 494–519.
Veale, T., & Keane, M. T. (1997). The competence of sub-optimal structure mapping on 'hard' analogies. In *Proceedings of the International Joint Conference on Artificial Intelligence*. Nagoya, Japan.
Vogel, C. (2001). Dynamic semantics for metaphor. *Metaphor and Symbol*, 16(1&2), 59–74.
Way, E. C. (1991). *Knowledge representation and metaphor*. Dordrecht: Kluwer.
Weber, S. H. (1989). Figurative adjective-noun interpretation in a structured connectionist network. In *Proceedings of the Eleventh Annual Conference of the Cognitive Science Society* (pp. 204–211). Hillsdale, NJ: Lawrence Erlbaum Associates.
Weiner, J. (1984). A knowledge representation approach to understanding metaphors. *Computational Linguistics*, 10(1), 1–14.
Wilcox, P. P. (2004). A cognitive key: Metonymic and metaphorical mappings in ASL. *Cognitive Linguistics*, 15(2), 197–222.
Wilcox, S. (2004). Cognitive iconicity: Conceptual spaces, meaning, and gesture in signed language. *Cognitive Linguistics*, 15(2), 119–147.
Wilks, Y. (1978). Making preferences more active. *Artificial Intelligence*, 11, 197–223.
Wilks, Y., Barnden, J., & Wang, J. (1991, August). Your metaphor or mine: Belief ascription and metaphor interpretation. In *Proceedings of the 12 th International. Joint Conference on Artificial Intelligence*, Sydney, Australia (pp. 945–950). San Mateo, CA: Morgan Kaufmann.
Winston, P. H. (1979). Learning by creating and justifying transfer frames. In P. H. Winston & D. Brown (Eds.), *Artificial Intelligence: An MIT*

*Perspective* (Vol. 1, pp. 347–374). Cambridge, MA: MIT Press.

Woll, B. (1985).Visual imagery and metaphor in British Sign Language. In W. Paprotté & R. Dirven (Eds.), *The ubiquity of metaphor: Metaphor in language and thought* (pp. 601–628). Amsterdam: John Benjamins.

Yu, N. (1995). Metaphorical expressions of anger and happiness in English and Chinese. *Metaphor and Symbolic Activity,* 10(2), 59–92.

Zhang, L., Barnden, J. A., & Hendley, R. J. (2005, July). Affect detection and metaphor in e-drama: The first stage. In *Proceedings of the Workshop on Narrative Learning Environments, 12th International Conference on Artificial Intelligence in Education* (AIED-2005), Amsterdam.

CHAPTER 19

# Conceptual Metaphor, Human Cognition, and the Nature of Mathematics

*Rafael Núñez*

## 1. Introduction

After finding "conclusive" radio proof of intelligent aliens, Dr. Ellie Arroway, an attractive, competent, and passionate scientist, finds herself discussing with high-level politicians over the urgency of understanding such extraterrestrial messages. In response to the mocking question of "why don't they [the aliens] just speak English?" she serenely and convincingly answers without the slightest hesitation: *"Mathematics is the only truly universal language, Senator."*

The line is from the movie *Contact*, written by the Pulitzer Prize–winning author Carl Sagan, in which the hero (played by Jodie Foster) brings forth a deep and widespread belief that mathematics is "out there," constituting the very fabric of the cosmos, and transcending not only the existence of human beings, but of *any* possible beings in the universe. This view is unconsciously swallowed and sustained by millions through other similar movies and pop-science books (some of them written by well-known scientists like Carl Sagan himself). But this view of mathematics doesn't only exist in Hollywood and the general media. It is also alive in many mathematics and philosophy departments, as well as in other academic institutions that endorse different forms of Platonism. The belief is deep and often unnoticed and unquestioned: mathematics, whose existence is independent of human beings, is the ultimate universal language.

But, is it? In this chapter, I want to defend a radically different view of the nature of mathematics. One that, building on findings in cognitive science – especially Conceptual Metaphor Theory, Gesture studies, and on the embodied foundations of human thinking – sees mathematics as an all too human enterprise. I will start by describing what George Lakoff and I, in our book *Where Mathematics Comes From*, called "The Romance of Mathematics" (Lakoff & Núñez, 2000). I will argue that when the understanding of the nature of mathematics is concerned, this common view is at odds with findings in the contemporary scientific study of the human mind. Then, in order to illustrate the crucial constitutive role that conceptual metaphor – along with other mechanisms of the human mind – play in the genesis of mathematical ideas, I will analyze a case study involving the elusive notions of limits and continuity in modern mathematics. Based on the work I have done with Lakoff in what we have called the *Cognitive Science of Mathematics* (Lakoff & Núñez, 1997, 1998, 2000; Núñez & Lakoff, 1998, 2005), I will eventually argue that formal definitions and formal languages in mathematics, although extremely useful in the praxis of the discipline, don't capture the full content of mathematical ideas. Formal mathematics is not all of mathematics, and cannot provide a foundational account of the nature of mathematics. I will analyze the conceptual metaphors and other everyday bodily grounded mechanisms that provide the inferential organization of such concepts as limits and continuity of real-valued functions. Then, as an extension to this work, I will address the issue of the psychological reality of such metaphorical mechanisms via the study of real time speech–gesture co-production. We'll see that the essential and constitutive meaning that these metaphors provide is not captured by the usual technical formalisms that are taken as the definition of what mathematics *really* is. Finally, I will close the chapter with an analysis of some philosophical and theoretical implications of this embodied-oriented view of the nature of mathematics, in which conceptual metaphor plays a fundamental role in making mathematics what it is. As we'll see, the ontology of mathematics is not left untouched.

## 2. The Romance of Mathematics

The idea that mathematics exists "out there," timeless and eternal, transcending human beings, and constituting the "only truly universal language," is a natural idea. After all, the reasoning goes, is it not the case that the truth of the Pythagorean Theorem is valid everywhere? Not only in Greece, but also in Easter Island, in the South Pole, at the bottom of the Pacific Ocean, on the moon, in Saturn, or anywhere in the universe? And is it not the case that the validity of that theorem transcends time, such that its truth was not only valid during the time of the Greeks, but it is still valid now, and it will continue to be valid forever? Is it not the case that the constant $\pi$ expresses a universal property, namely, the ratio between the perimeter of a circumference and its diameter? Is this not a truth that *any* intelligent being *anywhere* in the universe would be able to grasp?

Indeed, it is not easy to see that these mathematical truths are in fact the product of human imagination, very peculiar, objective, stable, effective, abstract, well-adapted, and robust ones, but human nonetheless. These extraordinary properties make mathematics a unique form of knowledge, which is gathered not through empirical evidence (as it is done in science via experimental and correlational studies) but through formal proof. A piece of mathematical knowledge is accepted by the mathematical community only if there is a proof of its absolute certainty (not just by providing statistically significant robust evidence for it, as it is done in science). These unique properties give mathematics the aura of being predominantly about timeless eternal objective truths, providing structure and order to the universe. As the great Galileo – founder of modern science – said, "The laws of the universe are written in mathematics. It is our role to learn how to read them."

In the preface of our book *Where Mathematics Comes From*, George Lakoff and I called this widespread folk and academic conception of the nature of mathematics, the *Romance of mathematics*, a kind of mythology that goes like this (Lakoff & Núñez, 2000, xv):

- Mathematics has a truly objective existence, providing structure to this universe and any possible universe, independent of and transcending the existence of human beings or any beings at all.
- Mathematics is abstract and disembodied – yet it is real.
- Human mathematics is just a part of abstract, transcendent mathematics (the concrete and mundane side of it).

- Hence, mathematical proof allows us to discover transcendent truths of the universe.
- Mathematics is part of the physical universe and provides rational structure to it. There are Fibonacci series in flowers, logarithmic spirals in snails, fractals in mountain ranges, and $\pi$ in the spherical shape of stars and planets and bubbles. Hundreds of books showing how "wonderful" and "magic" mathematics is, continuously sustain this belief.
- Mathematics even characterizes logic, and hence structures reason itself – any form of reason by any possible being.
- To teach and to learn mathematics is therefore to teach and to learn the language of nature, a mode of thought that would have to be shared by any highly intelligent beings anywhere in the universe.
- Because mathematics is disembodied and pure reason is a form of mathematical logic, pure reason itself is disembodied. Hence, machines can, in principle, think.

This view is often carried over to the practice of mathematics teaching. As a result there is an overemphasis on dogmatic oriented forms of education instantiated via formal definitions, reductionistic forms of logic, axioms, algorithms, and so forth, all of which result in forgetting the human nature of mathematics. For instance, did your high-school teacher ever really *explain* to you, in human *meaningful* terms (not in terms of formal proofs and arbitrary definitions and axioms), why the multiplication of two negative numbers yields a positive result? Or did your college mathematics professor really explain to you why the empty set is a subset of every set? And what that means? How would *you* explain such simple but profound "truths" to a student or to another colleague? Or how would you explain the *meaning* of Euler's famous formula $e^{\pi i} + 1 = 0$, that is, not by providing a proof *that* the statement is true, but by providing an explanation of *why* the statement is true by virtue of what it *means*?[1]

But despite its immediate intuitiveness, and despite the support it gets from many outstanding physicists and mathematicians, the *Romance of mathematics* is (nowadays) *scientifically* untenable. It is a mythology, and as such, arguing for or against it is a matter of faith, not a matter of scientific debate. So, moving away from this discussion, in the remainder of the chapter I will argue that addressing the question of the nature of mathematics requires an informed empirical approach: The cognitive science of mathematics, that is, the study *of* mathematics as a subject matter for cognitive science. I will claim that this question doesn't belong exclusively to philosophy or to mathematics proper (where formal proof suffices), but to the contemporary scientific study of the mind, which by gathering interdisciplinary efforts from neuroscience to linguistics to cognitive psychology can show how the human mind, with the conceptual systems it creates, makes mathematics possible. In this chapter, I'll focus on findings in cognitive linguistics – a sub-discipline of cognitive science – especially in conceptual metaphor theory.

## 3. Metaphor in Mathematics?

The idea that metaphor plays a constitutive role in mathematics seems, at a first glance, a flat contradiction. Mathematics is objective, rigorous, unambiguous, and precise. How can metaphor, which appears to lack those features, have anything to do with mathematics? The answer lies in one of the essential properties of mathematics: it is an abstract fully idealized conceptual domain.

Indeed, perhaps one of the most striking features of mathematics is that it is characterized by the fact that the very entities that constitute what the field is are idealized mental abstractions. These entities cannot be perceived directly through the senses. Even, say, a point, which is the simplest entity in Euclidean geometry, can't be actually *perceived*. A point, as defined by Euclid is a dimensionless entity, an entity that has only location but no extension. No powerful microscope will ever be able to allow us to actually perceive a point. A point, after all, with its precision and clear identity, is an idealized abstract entity. Nowhere is the imaginary nature of mathematics more evident than in the case of *infinity*. Because of the finite nature of our bodies and brains, no direct experience can exist with the infinite itself! Yet, infinity in mathematics is essential. It lies at the very core of many fundamental concepts such as limits, least upper bounds, topology, mathematical induction, infinite sets, points at infinity in projective geometry, to mention only a few. When studying the very nature of mathematics, the challenging and intriguing question that comes to mind is the following: if mathematics is the product of human ideas, how can we explain the nature of mathematics with its unique features such as precision, objectivity, rigor, generalizability, stability, and, of course, applicability to the real world?

Such a question doesn't represent a real problem for approaches inspired in platonic philosophies, which rely on the existence of transcendental worlds of ideas beyond human existence. But this view doesn't have any support based on scientific findings and doesn't provide any link to current empirical work on human ideas and conceptual systems (it may be supported, however, as a matter faith – not science, by many Platonist scientists and mathematicians). The question doesn't pose major problems to purely formalist philosophies either, because in that worldview mathematics is seen as a rule-driven manipulation of meaningless symbols. The question of the origin of the meaning of mathematical ideas doesn't even emerge in the purely formalist arena. For those studying the human mind scientifically, however (e.g., cognitive scientists), the question of the nature of mathematics is indeed a real challenge, especially for those who endorse an *embodied* oriented approach to cognition that sees mind and body as being intimately co-defined. How can an embodied view of the mind give an account of an abstract, idealized, precise, sophisticated and powerful domain of ideas if direct bodily experience with the subject matter is by definition not possible?

In *Where Mathematics Comes From*, Lakoff and I give some preliminary answers to the question of the cognitive origin of mathematical ideas (Lakoff & Núñez, 2000). Building on findings in mathematical cognition, and using mainly methods from cognitive linguistics, we suggest that most of the idealized abstract technical entities in mathematics are created via human cognitive mechanisms such as conceptual metaphor, that extend the structure of bodily experience (thermic, spatial, chromatic, acoustic, etc.) while preserving essential properties of the inferential organization of such domains of bodily experience. For example, as it is explained elsewhere in this volume, linguistic expressions such as "send her my *warm* helloes" and "the teacher was very *cold* to me" are statements that refer to the somewhat abstract domain of Affection. From a purely literal point of view, however, the language used belongs to the domain of Thermic experience, not Affection. The meaning of these statements and the inferences one is able to draw from them are structured by precise mappings from the Thermic domain to the domain of Affection: Warmth is mapped onto presence of affection, Cold is mapped onto lack of affection, X is warmer than Y is mapped onto X is more affectionate than Y, and so on. Research in cognitive linguistics has shown that these phenomena are not simply "linguistic" in nature, but rather they are about thought. In cognitive science the complexities of such abstract and non/literal phenomena have been studied through mechanisms such as conceptual metaphors (Gibbs, 1994; Lakoff, 1993; Lakoff & Johnson, 1980; Lakoff & Núñez, 1997; Núñez, 1999, 2000, 2008; Sweetser, 1990), conceptual blends (Fauconnier & Turner, 1998, 2002; Núñez, 2005), conceptual metonymy (Lakoff & Johnson, 1980), fictive motion, and dynamic schemas (Talmy, 1988, 1996, 2003). Based on these findings Lakoff and I analyzed many areas in mathematics, from set theory to infinitesimal calculus, to logic, to projective geometry, to transfinite arithmetic, by means of a technique we called

*Mathematical Idea Analysis*. We showed how, via everyday human embodied mechanisms such as conceptual metaphor and conceptual blending, the inferential patterns drawn from direct bodily experience in the real world get extended in very specific and precise ways to give rise to a new emergent inferential organization in purely imaginary domains.[2] We found that a great many cognitive mechanisms that are not specifically mathematical are used to characterize mathematical ideas. These include such ordinary cognitive mechanisms as those used for basic spatial relations, groupings, small quantities, motion, distributions of things in space, changes, bodily orientations, basic manipulations of objects (e.g., rotating and stretching), iterated actions, and so on.

Thus, for example:

- Conceptualizing the technical mathematical concept of a class makes use of the everyday concept of a collection of objects in a bounded region of space.
- Conceptualizing the technical mathematical concept of recursion makes use of the everyday concept of a repeated action.
- Conceptualizing the technical mathematical concept of complex arithmetic makes use of the everyday concept of rotation.
- Conceptualizing derivatives in calculus requires making use of such everyday concepts as motion, approaching a boundary, and so on.

From a non-technical perspective, this should be completely obvious. But from the technical perspective of cognitive science, there is a challenging question one must ask: Exactly what everyday concepts and cognitive mechanisms are used in exactly what ways in the unconscious conceptualization of technical ideas, such that they provide the precise inferential structure observed in mathematics? Mathematical Idea Analysis, depends crucially on the answers to this question. Lakoff and I have found that mathematical ideas are grounded in bodily based mechanisms and everyday experience. Many mathematical ideas are ways of mathematicizing ordinary ideas, as when the idea of subtraction mathematizes the ordinary idea of distance, or as when the idea of a derivative mathematicizes the ordinary idea of instantaneous change. As we'll see, conceptual metaphor plays a crucial role in realizing the very mathematicization process, by extending the inferential organization of everyday bodily grounded experiences to abstract domains. It is now time to analyze some of these findings in more detail by going over the case study.

## 4. A Case Study: Limits and Continuity of Functions

In the spirit of Mathematical Idea Analysis, we can start by taking a look at technical books and articles in mathematics and by carefully analyzing how these texts actually characterize ideas such as limits and continuity. Let us consider the following examples taken from some classic books and textbooks:

1) While discussing limits, we read in the Russian classic *Matematika, ee soderzhanie metody i znachenie* [Mathematics, its contents, methods and meaning] by A. Aleksandrov, A. N. Kolmogorov, and M. A. Lavrent'ev [1956/1999]:

   If a variable $x_n$ may be represented as a sum

   $x_n = a + \alpha_n,$

   where $a$ is a constant and $\alpha_n$ is an infinitesimal, then we say that the variable $x_n$, for $n$ increasing *beyond* all bounds, *approaches* the number $a$ and we write

   $\lim x_n = a$ or $x_n \to a$

   The number $a$ is called the *limit* of $x_n$. (Vol. 1, p. 82, underlined italics are ours).

   The first thing we notice is that, strictly speaking, this statement refers to a sequence of discrete and motionless values (real numbers) that a variable $x_n$ takes corresponding to increasing discrete and motionless values taken by $n$. If we examine this statement closely we can see that it describes static facts about numbers. We can observe that there is *no motion* whatsoever involved. No entity is actually *approaching* anything or moving *beyond* anywhere. So, why then did these well-respected Russian authors (or why do mathematicians in general, for that matter) use dynamic language to express static properties of static entities? And what does it mean to say that the "variable $x_n$ *approaches* a number $a$," when in fact the variable can only have a fixed and distinct value given fixed and distinct values of $n$?

2) While discussing limits of infinite series, R. Courant & H. Robbins write in their classic book *What Is Mathematics* (Courant & Robbins, 1978):

> We describe the behavior of $s_n$ by saying that the sum $s_n$ *approaches* the limit 1 as $n$ *tends* to infinity, and by writing
>
> $$1 = 1/2 + 1/2^2 + 1/2^3 + 1/2^4 + \cdots,$$
>
> where on the right we have an *infinite series*" (p. 64, underlined italics are ours).

This statement refers to a sequence of discrete and motion-less partial sums of $s_n$ (real numbers), corresponding to increasing discrete and motion-less values taken by $n$ in the expression $1/2^n$ where $n$ is a natural number. If we examine this statement closely we can observe that it describes some facts about numbers, and about the result of discrete operations with numbers. Again, *no motion* whatsoever is involved. No entity is actually *approaching* or *tending* to anything. So why then did Courant and Robbins (or why do mathematicians in general) use dynamic language to express static properties of static entities? And what does it mean to say that the "sum $s_n$ approaches," when in fact a sum is simply a fixed number, a result of an operation of addition?

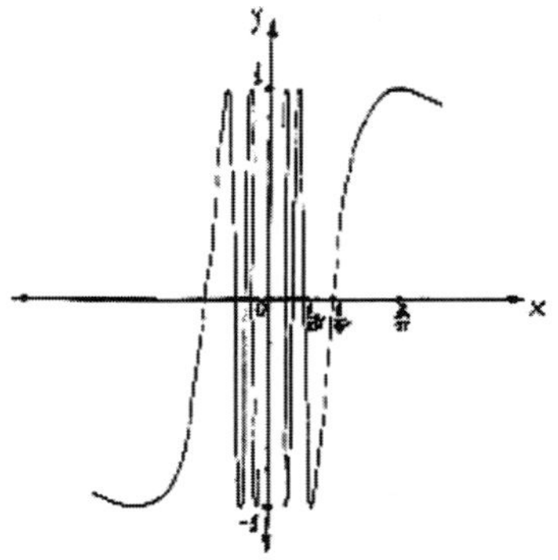


**Figure 19.1.** The graph of the function $f(x) = \sin 1/x$.

3) Later in the book, Courant and Robbins analyze cases of continuity and discontinuity of trigonometric functions in the real plane. Referring to the function $f(x) = \sin 1/x$, whose graph is shown in Figure 19.1, they say: ". . . since the denominators of these fractions increase without limit, the values of $x$ for which the function $\sin 1/x$ has the values 1, −1, 0, will cluster nearer and nearer to the point $x = 0$. Between any such point and the origin there will be still an infinite number of *oscillations* of the function" (p. 283, underlined italics are ours).

Once again, if, strictly speaking, a function is a mapping between elements of a set (coordinate values on the $x$-axis) with one and only one of the elements of another set (coordinate values on the $y$-axis), all that we have is a static correspondence between points on the $x$-axis with points on the $y$-axis. How then can the authors (or mathematicians in general) speak of "*oscillations* of the function," let alone an infinite number of them?

These three simple examples illustrate some deep and important issues regarding the semantic structure of mathematical ideas. They show how mathematical ideas and concepts are described, defined, illustrated, and analyzed in mathematics books. You can pick your favorite mathematics books and you will find similar patterns.

In all three examples above, static numerical structures are involved, such as partial sums and mappings between coordinates on one axis with coordinates on another. Strictly speaking, absolutely no motion or dynamic entities are involved in the formal definitions of these terms. So, if no entities are really moving, why do authors continue to speak of "approaching," "tending to," and "oscillating"? If mathematical definitions are indeed so precise, why is there still dynamic language when purely static entities are concerned? Where is this motion coming from? What does dynamism mean in these cases? What role is it playing (if any) in the meaning of these statements about mathematics facts?

In order to answer these questions we will first look at how pure mathematics characterizes real numbers, limits, and continuity of real-valued functions. We will eventually find that in these cases the logic of formal mathematics of set-theoretic entities and of universal and existential quantifiers is intrinsically static, and that the presence of dynamic content along with its inferential structure is a manifestation of human meaningful cognition that is not captured by mathematics formalisms.

### *Pure Mathematics and Real Numbers*

In pure mathematics, entities are brought to existence via formal definitions, formal proofs (theorems), and axiomatic methods (i.e., by declaring the existence of some entity without the need of proof. For example, in set theory the axiom of infinity assures the existence of infinite sets. Without that axiom, there are no infinite sets). In the case of real numbers, 10 axioms taken together fully characterize this number system and its inferential organization (i.e., theorems about real numbers). The following are the axioms of the real numbers.

1. Commutative laws for addition and multiplication.
2. Associative laws for addition and multiplication.
3. The distributive law.
4. The existence of identity elements for both addition and multiplication.
5. The existence of additive inverses (i.e., negatives).
6. The existence of multiplicative inverses (i.e., reciprocals).
7. Total ordering.
8. If $x$ and $y$ are positive, so is $x + y$.
9. If $x$ and $y$ are positive, so is $x \cdot y$.
10. The Least Upper Bound axiom.

The first 6 axioms provide the structure of what is called a *field* for a set of numbers and two binary operations. Axioms 7 through 9 assure ordering constraints. The first nine axioms fully characterize *ordered fields*, such as the rational numbers with the operations of addition and multiplication. Up to here we already have a lot of structure and complexity. For instance we can characterize and prove theorems about all possible numbers that can be expressed as the division of two whole numbers (i.e., rational numbers). Along a line we can also locate (according to their magnitude) any two different rational numbers and be sure (via proof) that there will always be (infinitely many) more rational numbers between them (a property referred to as density). With the rational numbers we can describe with any given (finite) degree of precision the proportion given by the perimeter of a circle and its diameter (e.g., 3.14; 3.1415; etc.). With the rational numbers, however, we cannot "complete" the points on the line, and we can not express with infinite exactitude the magnitude of the proportion mentioned above ($\pi = 3.14159\ldots$). For this, we need the full extension of the real numbers. In axiomatic terms, this is accomplished by the tenth axiom: the *Least Upper Bound axiom*. All ten axioms characterize a *complete ordered field*.

Nothing in the first nine axioms of real numbers helps us understanding the origin of motion in the above mathematical statements about infinite series, and continuity. All nine axioms simply specify the existence of static properties regarding binary operations and their results, and properties regarding ordering. There is no explicit or implicit reference to motion in these axioms. Since what makes a real number a real number (with its infinite precision) is the Least Upper Bound axiom, it is perhaps this very axiom that hides the dynamic secret we are looking for. Let's see what this axiom says:

> 10. *Least Upper Bound axiom: every nonempty set that has an upper bound has a least upper bound.*

And what exactly are an upper bound and a least upper bound? This is what pure mathematics says:

> *Upper Bound*
> $b$ is *an upper bound* for $S$ if
> $x \leq b$, for every $x$ in $S$.
>
> *Least Upper Bound*
> $b_o$ is a *least upper bound* for $S$ if
>
> - $b_o$ is an upper bound for $S$, and
> - $b_o \leq b$ for every upper bound $b$ of $S$.

But once again, all we find here are statements about motionless entities such as universal quantifiers (e.g., for every $x$; for every upper bound $b$ of $S$), membership relations (e.g., for every $x$ in $S$), greater than relationships (e.g., $x \leq b$; $b_o \leq b$), and so on. In other words, there is absolutely no indication of motion in the Least Upper Bound axiom, or in any of the other nine axioms. In short, the axioms of real numbers, which are supposed to completely characterize the "truths" (i.e., theorems) of real numbers, don't tell us anything about a sum "approaching" a number, or a number "tending to" infinity (whatever that means!).

Would the concept of continuity provide the answer?

### *What Is Continuity?*

What is, according to pure mathematics, continuity of functions? It is common to find in mathematics textbooks continuity for functions defined as follows:

- A function $f$ is continuous at a number $a$ if the following three conditions are satisfied:

1. $f$ is defined on an open interval containing $a$,
2. $\lim_{x \to a} f(x)$ exists, and
3. $\lim_{x \to a} f(x) = f(a)$.

Where by $\lim_{x \to a} f(x)$ what is meant is the following:

> Let a function $f$ be defined on an open interval containing $a$, except possibly at $a$ itself, and let $L$ be a real number. The statement
>
> $\lim_{x \to a} f(x) = L$
> means that $\forall\, \varepsilon > 0, \exists\, \delta > 0$,
> such that if $0 < |x - a| < \delta$,
> then $|f(x) - L| < \varepsilon$.

As we can see, pure formal mathematics defines continuity in terms of limits, and limits in terms of static universal and existential quantifiers applied on static numbers (e.g., $\forall\, \varepsilon > 0, \exists\, \delta > 0$), and the satisfaction of certain conditions which are described in terms of motionless arithmetic difference (e.g., $|f(x) - L|$) and static smaller than relations (e.g., $0 < |x - a| < \delta$). Once again, these formal definitions don't tell us anything about a sum "approaching" a number, or a number "tending to" infinity, or about a function "oscillating" between values (let alone doing it infinitely many times, as in the function $f(x) = \sin 1/x$).

A close inspection of mathematics textbooks reveals that often, right before giving this formal $\varepsilon$-$\delta$ definition of continuity, a paragraph or two are dedicated to the "informal" characterization of the idea of continuity, one that appeals to an "intuitive" description. Here is, for instance, the famous Russian book *Mathematics, Its Contents, Methods and Meaning* by Aleksandrov, Kolmogorov, and Lavrent'ev (1956/1999) mentioned earlier: "The general idea of a continuous function may be obtained from the fact that its graph is *continuous*: that is, its curve may be drawn without lifting the pencil from the paper." (p. 88; our emphasis).

And here is a quote from the classic textbook *Calculus* by G. Simmons (1985), while discussing the same topic: "In everyday speech a 'continuous' process is one that *proceeds without gaps* or interruptions or sudden changes. Roughly speaking, a function $y = f(x)$ is continuous if it displays similar behavior" (p. 58; our emphasis).

In both texts, we observe a characterization of continuous functions given in dynamic terms. In both cases there is something moving: the pencil drawing a curve on the paper in the former, and something unfolding without gaps in the latter. In both cases we have something moving from some position in space towards some other location in an uninterrupted manner. In both books these dynamic descriptions are given as a way of helping the reader by providing some immediate intuitive idea of what a continuous function *means*. The Russian book even characterizes the meaning of a "continuous function" *in terms of* something that *is* "continuous," whose meaning corresponds to what Simmons' Calculus textbook characterize as "everyday speech." This meaning corresponds precisely to the concept of *natural continuity* described by Núñez & Lakoff, 1998): the continuity conceived by the creators of calculus, Leibniz and Newton, in the 17th century, and in fact, all mathematicians up to the 19th century.

It is natural continuity that brought Euler to refer to a continuous curve as "a curve described by freely leading the hand" (cited in Stewart, 1995, 237), and the great Kepler to measure "an area swept out by the motion of a (celestial) point on a physical 'continuous curve'" (Kramer, 1970, 528). Natural continuity – continuity as we normally conceive it outside of mathematics – is based on a *source-path-goal schema*, a fundamental pre-conceptual *image schema* concerned with motion which has the following elements:

a. A trajector that moves
b. A source location (the starting point)
c. A goal – that is, an intended destination of the trajectory
d. A route from the source to the goal
e. The actual trajectory of motion
f. The position of the trajector at a given time
g. The direction of the trajector at that time
h. The actual final location of the trajector, which may or may not be the intended destination.

The source–path–goal schema is very general and can be extended in many ways: the speed of motion, the trail left by the thing moving, obstacles to motion, forces that move one along a trajectory, additional trajectors, and so on. The schema is topological in the sense that a path can be expanded or shrunk or deformed and still remains a path and it has an internal spatial logic and built-in inferences (see Figure 19.2). For instance, If you have traversed a route to a current location, you have been at all previous locations on that route; If you travel from $A$ to $B$ and from $B$ to C, then you have traveled from $A$ to C; If there is a direct route from $A$ to $B$ and you are moving along that route toward $B$, then you will keep getting closer to $B$; If $X$ and $Y$ are traveling along a direct route from $A$ to $B$ and $X$ passes $Y$, then $X$ is further from $A$ and closer to $B$ than $Y$ is; and so on.

Building on the source–path–goal schema, natural continuity has the following essential features in its inferential organization (Núñez & Lakoff, 1998):

a. Continuity, traced by motion, takes place over time.
b. The trace of the motion is a static holistic line with no "jumps."

None of these features are present in the $\varepsilon$-$\delta$ characterization of continuity. And the reason is simple. The $\varepsilon$-$\delta$ static characterization corresponds in fact to a radically different set of human ideas with a different inferential organization. It corresponds to the static everyday notion of *preservation of closeness near a location*: being within a given distance from a specific location.

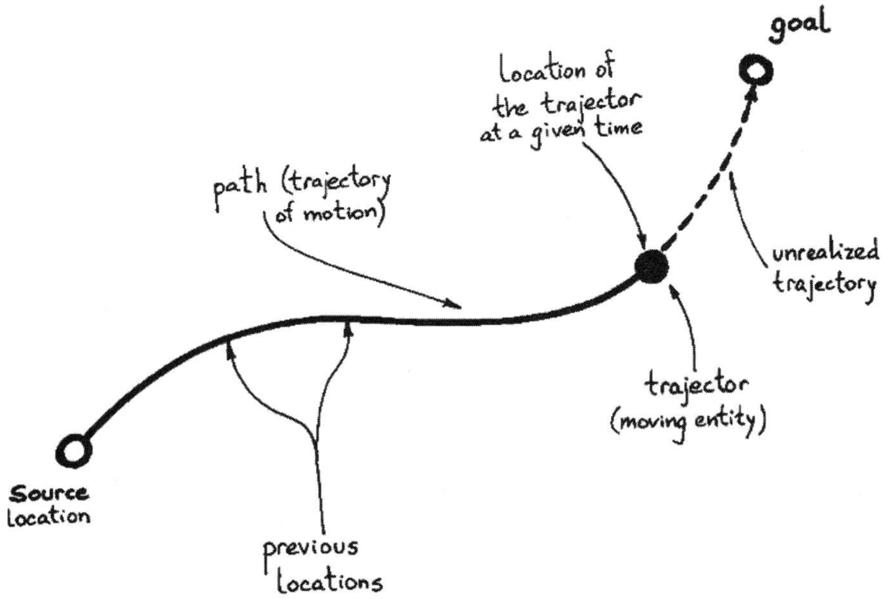


**Figure 19.2.** The source–path–goal schema (after Lakoff & Núñez, 2000, 38). We conceptualize linear motion using a conceptual schema in which there is a moving entity (called a trajector), a source of motion, a trajectory of motion (called a path), and a goal with an unrealized trajectory approaching that goal. There is a logic inherent in the structure of the schema. For example, if you are at a given location on a path, you have been at all previous locations on that path.

Preservation of closeness has static locations, landmarks, reference-points, distances, but no trajectors, no paths, no directionalities, no motion, and therefore no "jumps." As I have argued elsewhere in collaboration with G. Lakoff and other colleagues (Lakoff & Núñez, 1997, 2000; Núñez & Lakoff, 1998; Núñez, 2000; Núñez, Edwards, & Matos, 1999) "preservation of closeness" is an everyday human concept with a very precise inferential organization, recruited by Cauchy and Weierstrass in the 19th century to carry out the program of arithmetizing analysis (for details see Lakoff & Núñez, 2000, chaps. 12–14). Mathematical Idea Analysis shows that the inferential organization of the idea of preservation of closeness is not the same as the one of natural continuity. The two concepts – natural continuity and $\varepsilon$-$\delta$ continuity – simply have, cognitively, two radically different logics (Núñez & Lakoff, 1998).

The fact that the $\varepsilon$-$\delta$ definition doesn't capture the inferential structure of natural continuity shouldn't be a surprise. In *Where Mathematics Comes From*, Lakoff and I showed what well-known contemporary mathematicians had already pointed out in more general terms (Hersh, 1997; Kaput, 1979):

- The structure of human mathematical ideas, and its inferential organization, is richer and more detailed than the inferential organization provided by formal definitions and axiomatic methods. Formal definitions and axioms neither fully formalize nor generalize human concepts (Lakoff & Núñez, 2000).

We can illustrate this with a relatively simple example taken from our book. Consider the function $f(x) = x \sin 1/x$ whose graph is depicted in Figure 19.3.

$$f(x) = \begin{cases} x \sin 1/x & \text{for } x \neq 0 \\ 0 & \text{for } x = 0 \end{cases}$$

According to the $\varepsilon$-$\delta$ definition of continuity this function is continuous at every point. Indeed, for all $x$, it is always possible

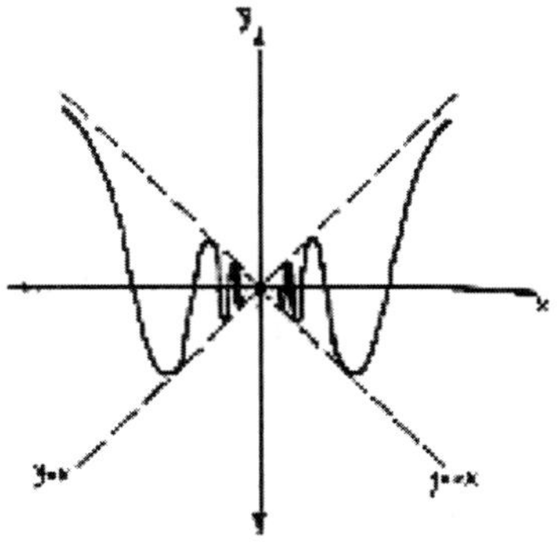

**Figure** 19.3. The graph of the function $f(x) = x \sin 1/x$.

to find the specified $\varepsilon$'s and $\delta$'s to satisfy the conditions for preservation of closeness. However, according to *natural continuity* this function is *not* continuous. The inferential organization of natural continuity requires that certain conditions have to be met. For instance, in the semantics of a naturally continuous line we should be able to tell how long the line is between two points. We should also be able to describe essential properties of the motion of a point along that line. With this function we cannot do that. Since the function "oscillates" infinitely many times as it "approaches" the point (0, 0) we cannot really tell how long the line is between two points located on the left and right sides of the plane. Moreover, as the function approaches the origin (0, 0) we cannot tell whether it will cross from the right plane to the left plane "going down" or "going up." As a result, the function violates two essential properties of natural continuity and therefore it is not continuous. Consequently, the formal $\varepsilon$-$\delta$ definition of continuity (1) simply doesn't capture the inferential organization of the human everyday notion of continuity (natural continuity), and (2) contrary to what is claimed in most mathematics books and textbooks, it *does not generalize* the notion of continuity either. The function $f(x) = x \sin 1/x$ is $\varepsilon$-$\delta$ continuous but it is not naturally continuous.

The point is that what is characterized formally in mathematics leaves out a huge amount of inferential organization of the human ideas that constitute mathematics. This is precisely what happens with the dynamic aspects of the expressions we saw before, such as "approaching," "tending to," "oscillating," and so on. Motion, in these examples, is a genuine and constitutive manifestation of the nature of these mathematical ideas. From the point of view of pure mathematics, however, the essential dynamic components of the inferential organization of these ideas are not captured by the $\varepsilon$-$\delta$ formalisms and the axiomatic system for real numbers.

### *Conceptual Metaphor and Fictive Motion*

In the case of limits of infinite series, motion in "the sum $s_n$ *approaches* the limit 1 as *n tends* to infinity" emerges *metaphorically* from the successive values taken by *n* in the sequences as a whole. It is beyond the scope of this chapter to go into the details of the mappings involved in the various underlying conceptual metaphors that provide the required dynamic inferential organization (for details see Lakoff & Núñez, 2000, chaps. 8–9). We can point out, however, that there are many conceptual metaphors and metonymies involved. There are conceptual metonymies in cases such as a partial sum *standing for* the entire infinite sum; there are conceptual metaphors in cases where we conceptualize the sequence of these metonymical sums as a *unique trajector* moving in space (as it is indicated by the third-person singular verb conjugation in "the sum $s_n$ approache<u>s</u>"); there are conceptual metaphors for conceiving infinity as a single location in space such that a metonymical *n* (standing for the entire sequence of values) can "tend to;" there are conceptual metaphors for conceiving the number "1" (not as a mere natural number but as an infinitely precise real number) as the result of the infinite sum; and so on. Notice that none of these expressions can be literal. The facts described in these sentences do not exist in any real perceivable world. They are metaphorical in nature. It is important to understand that these conceptual metaphors and metonymies are not simply concrete "representations" of the formalisms, or "noise" added on top of formalisms. Indeed, they are constitutive of the very embodied ideas that make mathematical ideas possible. It is the inferential organization provided by our embodied understanding of "approaching" and "tending to" that is at the core of these mathematical ideas.

In the case of the "oscillating" function, the moving object is one holistic object, the trigonometric function in the Real plane, constructed metaphorically from an infinite number of discrete real values for $x$, whose absolute value is progressively smaller. In this case, motion takes place in a specific manner: moving towards the origin from two opposite sides (i.e., for negative and positive values of $x$) and always between the values $y = 1$ and $y = -1$. As we saw, a variation of this function, $f(x) = x \sin(\frac{1}{x})$, reveals deep cognitive incompatibilities between the dynamic notion of continuity implicit in the example above and the static $\varepsilon$-$\delta$ definition of continuity.

But, the question that remains open is, From where do these mathematical objects get motion? What cognitive mechanism is allowing us to conceive static entities such as partial sums or values of functions in dynamic terms? The answer is *fictive motion*, a fundamental embodied cognitive mechanism through which we unconsciously (and effortlessly) conceptualize static entities in dynamic terms, as when we say *the road goes along the coast*. The road itself doesn't actually move anywhere. It is simply standing still. But we may conceive it *as moving* "along the coast." Fictive motion was first studied by Len Talmy (1988, 1996, 2003), via the analysis of linguistic expressions taken from everyday language in which static scenes are described in dynamic terms. The following are linguistic examples of fictive motion:

- The fence *stops* right after the tree.
- The border *runs along* the river.
- The US west coast *goes all the way down* to San Diego.
- After *crossing* the bridge the path *goes through* the forest and then it *reaches* the main house.
- Unlike Tokyo, in Paris there is no train line that *goes around* the city.
- The Equator *passes through* many countries.

Motion, in all these cases, is fictive, imaginary, and not real in any literal sense. Not only do these expressions use verbs of action, but they also provide precise descriptions of the quality, manner, and form of motion. In all cases of fictive motion there is a "trajector" (the moving agent) and a "landscape" (the space in which the trajector moves). Sometimes the trajector may be a real object (e.g., the *road* goes; the *fence* stops), and sometimes it is metaphorical and imaginary (e.g., the *Equator* passes through; the *border* runs). In fictive motion, real world trajectors don't move but they have the potential to move or the potential to enact or enable movement (e.g., a car moving along that road). In mathematics proper, however, the trajector has always a metaphorical component. That is, the trajector as such can't be literally capable or incapable of enacting movement, because the very nature of the trajectory is imagined via metaphor (Núñez, 2003). For example, a point in the Cartesian plane, which inherits a huge amount of its inferential structure from Euclidean geometry, is an entity that has location (determined by its coordinates) but has no extension. So when we say "point $P$ *moves* from $A$ to $B$" we are ascribing motion to a metaphorical entity that only has location. First, as we saw in earlier entities, which have only location (i.e., points) do not exist in the real world, so as such, they do not have the potential to move or not to move in any literal sense. They simply do not exist in the real world. They are metaphorical entities. Second, literally speaking, point $A$ and point $B$ are distinct locations, and in the Cartesian plane no point can change location while preserving its identity since a point's location is uniquely determined by its coordinates and vice versa. That is, the trajector (point $P$) cannot preserve its identity throughout the process of motion from $A$ to $B$, since that would mean that it is changing the very properties that are defining it, namely, its coordinates.

With this basic understanding of how conceptual metaphor and fictive motion work, we are in a position to see the embodied cognitive mechanisms underlying mathematical expressions such as:

- sin $1/x$ *oscillates* more and more as $x$ *approaches* zero
- $g(x)$ never *goes beyond* 1
- If there exists a number $L$ with the property that $f(x)$ *gets closer and closer to* $L$ as $x$ gets larger and larger; $\lim_{x\to\infty} f(x) = L$.

In these examples fictive motion operates on a network of precise *conceptual metaphors* (such as NUMBERS ARE LOCATIONS IN SPACE, which allows us to conceive numbers in terms of spatial positions) that provide the inferential structure required to conceive mathematical functions as having motion and directionality. Conceptual metaphor generates a purely imaginary entity in a metaphorical space, and fictive motion makes it a moving trajector in this metaphorical space. Thus, the progressively smaller numerical values taken by $x$ which determine numerical values of sin $1/x$, are via the conceptual metaphor NUMBERS ARE LOCATIONS IN SPACE conceptualized as spatial locations. The now metaphorical spatial locus of the function (i.e., the "line" drawn in the plane) becomes available for fictive motion to act upon. The progressively smaller numerical values taken by $x$ (now metaphorically conceptualized as locations progressively closer to the origin) determine corresponding metaphorical locations in space for sin $1/x$. In this imaginary space, via conceptual metaphor and fictive motion now sin $1/x$ can "oscillate" more and more as $x$ "approaches" zero.

In a similar way the infinite precision of real numbers themselves can be conceived as limits of sequences of rational numbers, or as limits of sequences of nested intervals. Because, as we saw, limits have conceptual metaphor and fictive motion built in, we can now see the fundamental role that these embodied mechanisms play in the constitution of the very nature of the real numbers themselves.

## 5. Are These "Dead" Metaphors? Or Are They Psychologically Real?

So far, in this case study we have analyzed some mathematical ideas like limits, continuity, and series through methods in cognitive linguistics that build models of the inferential organization involved in the semantics of *linguistic expressions* (e.g., conceptual metaphor, conceptual metonymy, and fictive motion). But because conceptual metaphor theory, based mainly on purely linguistic grounds, has made important claims *about* human cognition, abstraction, and mental phenomena, some psychologists have rightly questioned the lack of empirical evidence to support the psychological reality of conceptual metaphor. What experimental psychologists want to know is whether there is any cognitive reality in people's minds when they listen to, utter, or read such metaphorical expressions (see, for example Gibbs, 2006; Gibbs & Colston, 1995; Murphy, 1997). How do we know, for instance, that some of the metaphors we observe in linguistic expressions are not mere "dead metaphors," expressions that were metaphorical years ago but which have become "lexicalized" in nowadays language? How do we know that these metaphors are the actual result of real-time cognitive activity? Is it the case that people actually operate cognitively with these conceptual metaphors? And how can we find out the answers to such questions? Could it be the case that metaphorical expressions using terms like "approaching" or "getting closer and closer" are simply "dead metaphors," that is, expressions that once had dynamic spatial content but that now have become separate lexical items, no longer with connections with space and motion? Maybe all that we have in the mathematical expressions we have examined is simply a story of dead metaphors, with no psychological reality whatsoever.

Experimental psychologists have tried to answer similar questions regarding everyday linguistic expressions using priming techniques, a well-known experimental paradigm in which subjects are systematically biased via specific stimulation involving the source domain in order to evaluate whether they carry the corresponding inferences into the target domain. If by priming the source domain of the metaphor one gets systematic variation in the inferences made in the target domain, then one could conclude that individuals do reason metaphorically, or otherwise they would not be sensitive to the priming. In this chapter, however, in order to address the question of the psychological reality of the conceptual metaphors involved, I will use a different form of empirical analysis: real time gesture–speech–thought co-production. As we will see, the study of human *gesture* provides embodied convergent evidence of the psychological reality of many conceptual mappings, metaphorical, metonymical and others. Gesture studies, via a detailed investigation of real-time cognitive production, bodily motion (mainly hands and arms), and voice inflection, show that the conceptual metaphors and fictive motion involved in the mathematical ideas analyzed above, far from being dead, do have a real-time and very embodied psychological reality.

### *Gesture as Cognition*

In the study of the human mind, gestures have been left out of the picture for a very long time. They constitute the forgotten dimension of thought and language. In Chomskian linguistics, for instance, where language has been seen mainly in terms of abstract grammar, formalisms, and syntactic combinatorics, there was simply no room for "bodily production" such as gesture. In mainstream experimental psychology gestures were left out, among others, because being produced in a spontaneous manner, it was very hard to operationally define them, making rigorous experimental observation on them extremely difficult. In mainstream cognitive science, which in its origins was heavily influenced by classic "disembodied" artificial intelligence, there was simply no room for gestures either. Cognitive science and artificial intelligence were heavily influenced by the information-processing paradigm and what was taken to be essential in any cognitive activity was a set of bodyless abstract rules and the manipulation of physical symbols governing the processing of information. In all these cases, gestures were completely ignored and left out of the picture that defined what constituted genuine subject matters for the study of the mind. At best gestures were considered as a kind of epiphenomenon, secondary to other more important and better-defined phenomena.

But in the last decade or so, the field of gesture studies has moved forward dramatically, thanks to the work of pioneers such as Kendon (1980, 2004), McNeill (1992, in press), Goldin-Meadow (2003), and many others. Research in a variety of areas, from child development, to neuropsychology, to linguistics, and to anthropology, has shown the intimate link between oral and gestural production. Finding after finding has confirmed that gestures are often produced in synchronicity with speech, that they develop in close relation with speech, and that brain injuries affecting speech production also affect gesture production. The following is an abbreviated list of sources of evidence supporting (1) the view that speech and gesture are in reality two facets of the same cognitive linguistic reality, and (2) the embodied approach for understanding language, conceptual systems, and high-level cognition:

1. Universality: Speech-accompanying gesture is a cross-cultural universal (McNeill, 1992; Núñez & Sweetser, 2001, 2006; Iverson & Thelen, 1999; Kita & Essegbey, 2001).
2. Largely unconscious production: Gestures are less monitored than speech, and they are to a great extent unconscious. Speakers are often unaware that they are gesturing at all (McNeill, 1992).
3. Speech–gesture synchronicity: Gestures are co-produced with speech, in co-timing patterns which are specific to a given language (McNeill, 1992).

4. Gesture production with no visible interlocutor: Gestures can be produced without the presence of interlocutors, e.g., people gesture while talking on the telephone, and in monologues; congenitally blind subjects gesture as well (Iverson & Goldin-Meadow, 1998).
5. Speech–gesture co-processing: Stutterers stutter in gesture too, and impeding hand gestures interrupts speech production (Mayberry & Jaques, 2000).
6. Speech–gesture development: Gesture and speech development are closely linked (Bates & Dick, 2002; Goldin-Meadow 2003; Iverson & Thelen, 1999).
7. Speech–gesture complementarity: Gesture can provide complementary (as well as overlapping) content to speech content. Speakers synthesize and subsequently cannot distinguish information taken from the two channels (Kendon, 2000).
8. Gestures and abstract metaphorical thinking: Linguistic metaphorical mappings are paralleled systematically in gesture (Cienki, 1998; McNeill, 1992; Sweetser, 1998; Núñez, 2003; Núñez & Sweetser, 2001, 2006).

In all these studies, a careful analysis of important parameters of gestures such as hand shapes, hand and arm positions, palm orientation, type of movements, trajectories, manner, and speed, as well as a careful examination of timing, indexing properties, levels of iconicity, and the coupling with environmental features, give deep insight into human thought.[3] Among many properties, gestures usually have three well-defined phases, called preparation, stroke, and retraction (McNeill, 1992). The stroke is in general the fastest part of the gesture's motion, and it tends to be highly synchronized with speech accentuation and semantic content. The preparation phase is the motion that precedes the stroke (usually slower), and the retraction is the motion that takes place after the stroke has been produced (usually slower as well), when the hand goes back to a resting position or to whatever activity it was engaged in.

**Figure 19.4.** A professor of mathematics teaching a university level class on convergence of sequences of real numbers. Here he is referring to a case in which the numbers of a sequence "oscillate."

With these tools from gesture studies and cognition, we can now analyze mathematical expressions like the ones we saw before, but this time focusing on the gesture production of the speaker (in this case a mathematician teaching a university level mathematics course). The following gestures have been recorded during upper division mathematics classes at a major university in California. Keep in mind that these gestures are abstract (metaphorical) in nature, in the sense that the entities that are indexed with the various hand shapes – like points and numbers – are purely imaginary entities.

Figure 19.4 shows a professor of mathematics teaching theorems about convergence of sequences of real numbers. In this particular situation, he is talking about a case in which the values of an infinite sequence do not get closer and closer to a single value as $n$ increases, but "oscillate" between two fixed values. His right hand, with the palm towards his left, has a hand shape called *baby* O in American Sign Language and in gesture studies, where the index finger and the thumb are touching and are slightly bent while the other three fingers are fully bent. In this gesture the touching tip of the index and the thumb is metaphorically *indexing* a metonymical value standing for the values in the sequence as $n$ increases (it is almost

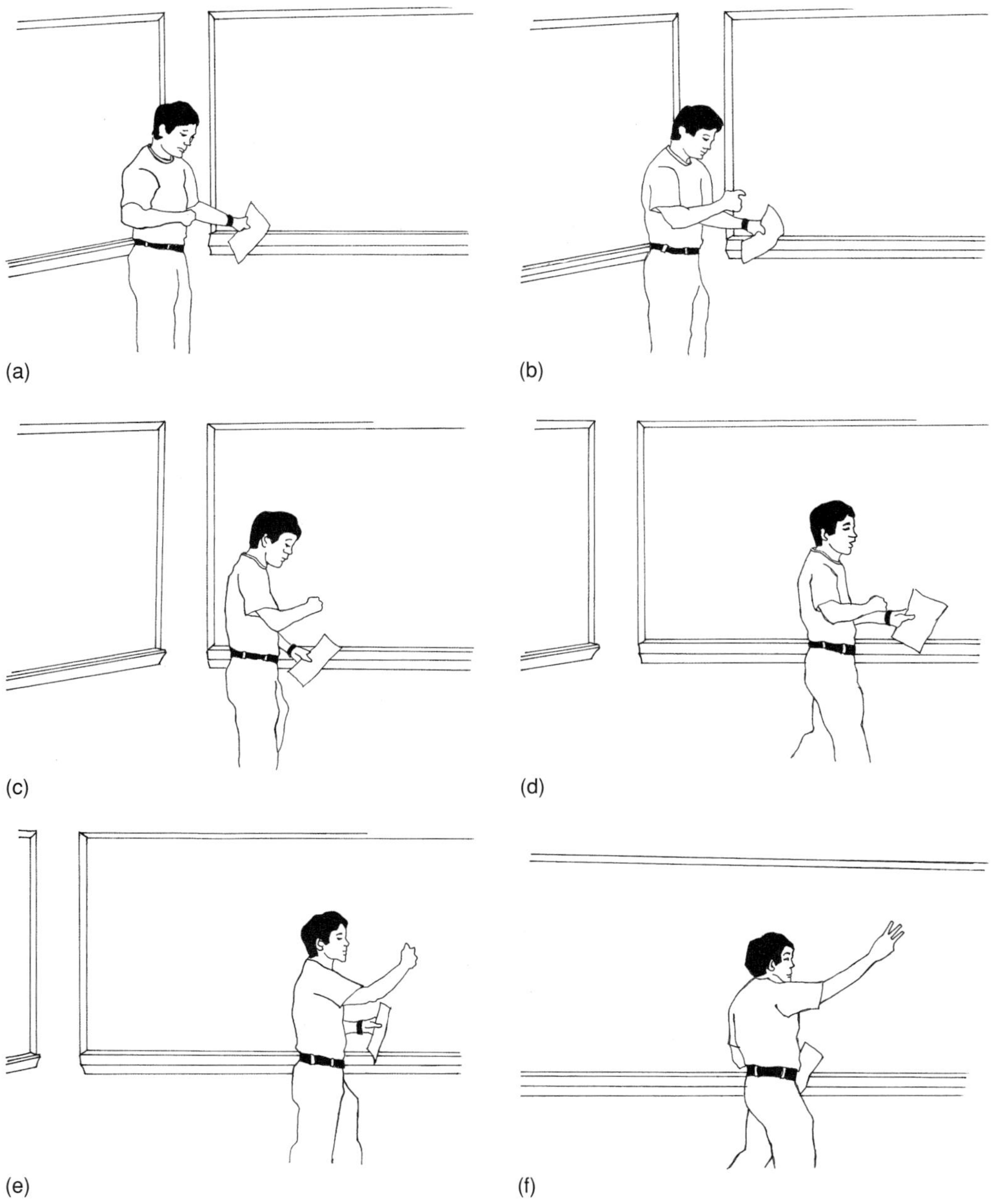


**Figure 19.5.** A professor of mathematics in a university level class talking about an unbounded monotone sequence "going in one direction" (a through e) and which "takes off to infinity" (f).

as if the subject is carefully holding a very tiny object with those two fingers). Holding that fixed hand shape, he moves his right arm horizontally back and forth while he says "oscillating."

Hands and arms are essential body parts involved in gesturing. But often it is also the entire body that participates in enacting the inferential structure of an idea. In the following example (Figure 19.5), a professor of mathematics is teaching a course involving notions of calculus. In this scene, he is talking about some particular theorems regarding monotone sequences.

As he is talking about an unbounded monotone sequence, he is referring to the important property of "going in one direction" (i.e., taking increasingly large

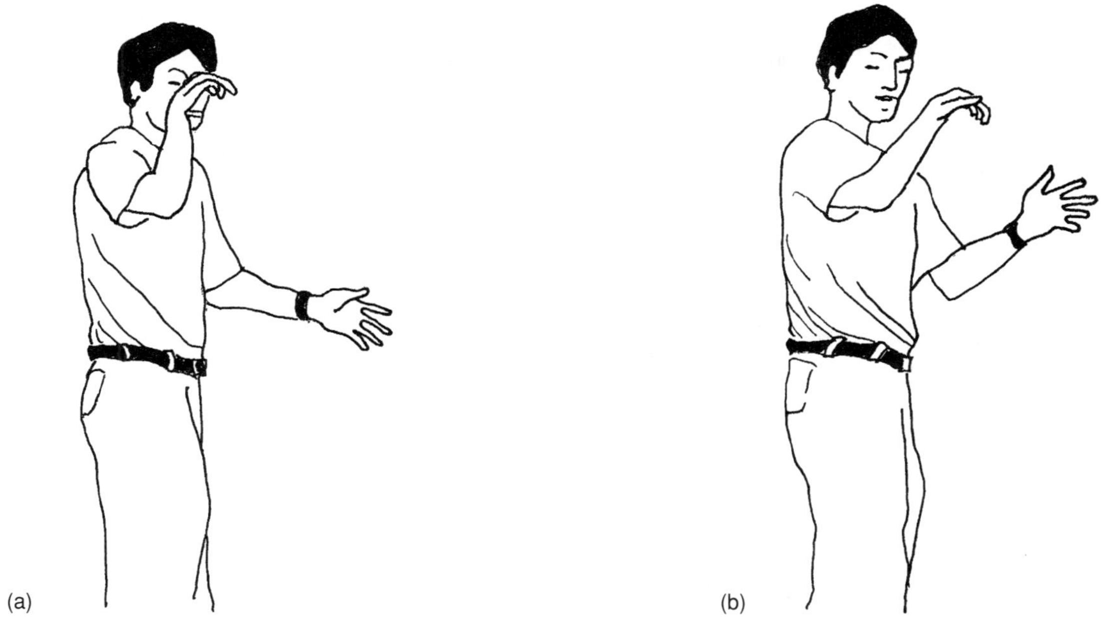

**Figure 19.6.** A professor of mathematics in a university level class talking about a constant sequence.

values). As he says this he is producing iterative unfolding circles with his right hand and at the same time he is walking frontward, accelerating at each step (Figure 19.5a through 19.5e). His right hand, with the palm toward his chest, displays a shape called *tapered* O (thumb relatively extended and touching the upper part of an extended index bent in right angle, like the other fingers), which he keeps in a relatively fixed position while doing the iteration circular movement. A few milliseconds later he completes the sentence by saying "it takes off to infinity" at the very moment when his right arm is fully extended and his hand shape has shifted to an extended shape called *B spread* with a fully (almost over) extension, and the tips of the fingers pointing frontward, slightly at eye-level.

Sometimes, when the sequence exhibits a peculiar property, hand shapes adopt specific forms that match the meaning of those properties. In Figure 19.6, we see the same professor talking this time about a situation where the sequence is constant. His dominant hand (the right one, with which he has been writing on the board) curls back, his elbow is bent in 90 degrees and his wrist is maximally bent with the palm oriented down. His fingers are also bent pointing downward (Figure 19.6a). Then while keeping that hand shape he extends his elbow (and wrist) producing a small frontward (and slightly downward) motion with his right hand. In the meantime, his left hand, with palm toward right, raises slowly, forming a *five* hand shape (Figure 19.6b). As he says the word "constant", he abruptly stops the forward motion with his right hand marking a location situated a couple of inches in front of his open five left hand (Figure 19.6c). While keeping his left hand totally fixed and holding the same "five" hand shape, he iterates a couple of times the same frontward movement with his right hand always stopping sharply at the same location, just a few inches from the open palm of his left hand. These abruptly stopped movements performed with the curled hand shape while referring to a constant sequence sharply contrast with the smooth open ended fully extended arm, hand, and fingers of the previous example produced when referring to an unbounded monotone sequence (Figure 19.5).

It is important to mention that in these three cases the blackboard is full of mathematical expressions containing formalisms like the ones we saw in section 4 (e.g., formalisms, with universal and existential quantifiers, which have no indication or reference to motion). The gestures (and the linguistic expressions used), however, tell us a very different conceptual story. In these examples, these mathematicians are referring to fundamental dynamic aspects of the mathematical ideas they are talking (and thinking) about. In the first example, the oscillating gesture match – and it is produced synchronically with – the linguistic expressions used. In the second example, the unfolding iterative circular gesture matches the inferential organization of the iteration involved in the monotone sequence, and the entire body moves forward as the sequence unfolds. Since the sequence is unbounded, it "takes off to infinity," an idea which is precisely characterized in a synchronous way with the full frontal extension of the arm and the hand. That motion contrasts with the one in the third example, where a curled shaped hand moves slightly forward but hits repeatedly the same location, never being able to go further.

We can conclude from these examples that:

- First, gestures provide converging evidence for the psychological and embodied reality of the linguistic expressions analyzed with classic techniques in cognitive linguistics, such as metaphor and fictive motion analysis. In these cases gesture analysis shows that the metaphorical expressions we saw earlier are not cases of dead metaphors. The above gestures show that the dynamism involved in these ideas has full psychological and cognitive reality, which is enacted in real time while speaking and thinking in an instructional context.
- Second, these gestures show that the fundamental dynamic contents involving infinite sequences, limits, continuity, and so on, are in fact *constitutive* of the inferential structure of these ideas. Formal language in mathematics, however, is not as rich as everyday language and cannot capture the full complexity of the inferential structure of mathematical ideas. It is the job of the cognitive science of mathematics to characterize the full richness of mathematical ideas (it is not the job of mathematics itself).

### *The Moral*

The main point of our case study was to show that even the most abstract conceptual system we can think of, mathematics(!), is ultimately embodied in the nature of our bodies, language, and cognition. Conceptual metaphor and fictive motion, being extremely fast, highly efficient, and effortless cognitive mechanisms that preserve inferences, play a fundamental role in bringing many mathematical concepts into being. We analyzed several cases involving dynamic language in mathematics, in domains in which, according to formal definitions and axioms in mathematics, no motion was supposed to exist at all. Via the study of gestures, we were able to see that the conceptual metaphors underlying the linguistic expressions were not simply cases of "dead" metaphorical expressions. Gesture studies provide real-time convergent evidence supporting the psychological and cognitive reality of the embodiment of mathematical ideas, and their inferential organization. Building on gestures studies we were able to tell that the above mathematics professors, not only were using metaphorical linguistic expressions, but that they were in fact, in real time, thinking dynamically!

## 6. Philosophical Implications

From the work in the cognitive science of mathematics that we have been analyzing throughout this chapter, it follows that mathematics is a human enterprise. Mathematics is a technical conceptual system that makes use of the same conceptual mechanisms of thought as in other intellectual domains (e.g., conceptual metaphor, fictive motion), which shows a remarkable optimal use of a human's limited and highly constrained biological resources. To understand the inferential organization that makes mathematics what it is, is to understand how the human mind uses everyday cognitive mechanisms in very special and sophisticated ways. Mathematical Idea Analysis is a tool that can serve this purpose.

Results in the cognitive science of mathematics, such as the ones analyzed here, have an immediate consequence for the philosophy of mathematics. It provides a new answer for what is perhaps the most intriguing philosophical question involving mathematics: What is the nature of mathematics? The answer can be summarized as follows:

- Mathematics, as we know it or can know it, exists by virtue of the embodied mind.
- All mathematical content resides in embodied mathematical ideas.
- A large number of the most basic, as well as the most sophisticated, mathematical ideas are metaphorical in nature.

Results in the cognitive science of mathematics also have another immediate consequence: it disconfirms the *Romance of Mathematics* mentioned at the beginning of the chapter. From a scientific perspective, there is no way to know whether there are objectively existing, external, mathematical entities or mathematical truths. Debating over such issues is a matter of faith, not science. However, we can empirically show that human mathematics is embodied, that is, that it is grounded in bodily experience in the world and that is primarily a matter of mathematical *ideas*, which are significantly metaphorical in nature. Mathematics is not purely literal; it is an imaginative, profoundly metaphorical enterprise, where the metaphorizing is, of course, generated, realized, and sustained by humans. The metaphorizing doesn't pre-exist humans and it is not independent of them. Therefore, Human mathematics is not structured after objectively pre-existing, external timeless mathematical entities or eternal mathematical truths.

These conclusions ought not to be taken as a confirmation that mathematics is then merely a matter of social conventions, as it is often argued by radical social constructivists and post-modernists. In fact, the work described in this chapter also disconfirms such views: Mathematics is not a matter of pure social conventions. Being embodied, mathematics uses general mechanisms of embodied cognition and is grounded in experience in the world, and therefore, it is not arbitrary. It is highly constrained by the peculiarities of the human brain and body, and the linguistic and cultural practices that they sustain and can afford. Mathematics, therefore, is not purely subjective; is not a matter of mere social agreement; and it is not purely historically and culturally contingent (although historical and cultural factors do enter into mathematics in many important ways. For details, see Lakoff & Núñez, 2000, chap. 15).

The crucial role that metaphor plays in making mathematics what it is, also raises issues regarding *ontology* and *truth*. Two central questions driving much of the philosophy of mathematics of the 19th and 20th centuries have been: What are mathematical objects? And, What is mathematical truth? The most common contemporary answers to these questions come from those who believe in the romance of mathematics, as well as from scholars who defend the idea that mathematics must have "secure" foundations which, in themselves, are mathematical entities (e.g., Set-theoretic entities). Adherents of the former and many defenders of the latter thus provide similar answers:

- Mathematical objects are real; they are objective entities existing independently of human beings.
- Mathematical truths are objective truths of the universe.

But, as we have seen such answers are refuted by results in the cognitive science of mathematics such as the mathematical idea analysis of limits and continuity of functions. From this work, we see that the ontology of mathematics is inseparable from the human imagination and the mechanisms – such as conceptual metaphor – that make it possible. Mathematical objects are embodied concepts – that is, they are ideas that are ultimately grounded in human experience and put together via normal human conceptual mechanisms, such as conceptual metaphors and fictive motion. And in what concerns Truth, mathematical truth is like any other truth. A statement is true if our embodied understanding of the statement accords with our embodied understanding of the subject matter and the situation at hand. Truth, including mathematical truth, is thus dependent on embodied human cognition (see Lakoff & Johnson, 1999, chaps. 6–8; Núñez, 1995, 2008; Núñez & Sweetser, 2006). It comes out of the inferential organization provided by mechanisms such as conceptual metaphor, which characterize specific entailments via precise mappings from the source domain to the target domain.

Finally, another important issue covered in this chapter is that of formalism. Formalist mathematicians often dismiss "intuition," on the grounds that it is vague and often mathematically incorrect. It is important to contrast mathematical ideas, as we have been discussing them, with "vague intuitions." The cognitive science of mathematics offers a way for studying the precise structure of mathematical ideas and their inferential organization. And, as we have seen, the "intuitively" dynamic notions associated to limits and continuity are not vague intuitions. Mathematical idea analysis studies the structure and grounding of many of the most central ideas in all mathematics. The precise characterizations given of metaphorical mappings reveal real, stable, and precise conceptual structure. They make as precise as it is possible in contemporary cognitive science what is left vague in the practice of formal mathematics.

A "formalization" of a subject matter in terms of set theory often hides the conceptual structure of that subject matter. Mathematical idea analysis begins to make that conceptual structure precise. What it does is to make explicit what is implicit in the practice of formal mathematics: It characterizes in precise cognitive terms the mathematical ideas in the cognitive unconscious that go unformalized and undescribed when a formalization of conscious mathematical ideas is done. This includes the bodily grounding of mathematical ideas and a characterization of the metaphors, blends, and other mechanisms of the mind that give mathematical thought an abstract character. What this implies is that pure formalization does not do what many scholars claim for it. It does not formulate otherwise vague ideas in a rigorous fashion. Instead, it uses metaphor to replace certain ideas with other ideas – ideas for which there is a well-understood symbolization and method of calculation. It is important to bear in mind what does and does not occur when some domain of mathematics is "formalized":

1. The original ideas are not kept; they are replaced metaphorically by other ideas: For instance, in the case of continuity of functions, metaphors involving dynamic and holistic entities (e.g., a function "oscillating") are replaced by static and discrete ones (as they are characterized by the idea of "preservation of

closeness," which is formalized through the use of universal and existential quantifiers).

2. The formalization is not an abstract generalization over the original ideas: For example, we saw that the function $f(x) = x \sin 1/x$ is $\varepsilon$-$\delta$ continuous, but NOT *naturally continuous*. The $\varepsilon$-$\delta$ formalization thus doesn't capture the full meaning of the original ideas implicit in natural continuity.
3. The original ideas receive no mathematical idea analysis under the formalization: Motion and holistic properties, for instance, are simply left out of the formalizations of limits and continuity.
4. The ideas of set theory and formal logic receive no mathematical idea analysis under the formalization: The formal language is taken for granted. For example, the $\varepsilon$-$\delta$ formalization of continuity does not provide a cognitive semantic analysis of the existential and universal quantifiers it uses. They are taken as given.

In sum, Conceptual metaphor plays a fundamental role in originating and sustaining the very mathematics we know. From the work George Lakoff and I have done in the cognitive science of mathematics and the study of conceptual metaphor underlying mathematical ideas, thus emerges a human embodied view of the nature of mathematics (Lakoff & Núñez, 2000, p. 377):

- Mathematics is a natural part of being human. It arises from our bodies, our brains, and our everyday experiences in the world. Cultures everywhere have some form of mathematics.
- There is nothing mysterious, mystical, magical, or transcendent about mathematics. It is an important subject matter for scientific study. It is a consequence of human evolutionary history, neurobiology, cognitive capacities, and culture.
- Mathematics is one of the greatest products of the collective human imagination. It has been constructed jointly by millions of dedicated people over more than two thousand years, and is maintained by hundreds of thousands of scholars, teachers, and people who use it every day.
- Mathematics is a system of human concepts that makes extraordinary use of the ordinary tools of human cognition. It is special in that it is stable, precise, generalizable, symbolizable, calculable, consistent within each of its subject matters, universally available, and effective for precisely conceptualizing a large number of aspects of the world as we experience it.
- The effectiveness of mathematics in the world is a tribute to evolution and to culture. Evolution has shaped our bodies and brains so that we have inherited neural capacities for the basics of number and for primitive spatial relations. Culture has made it possible for millions of astute observers of nature, through millennia of trial and error, to develop and pass on more and more sophisticated mathematical tools – tools shaped to describe what they have observed. There is no mystery about the effectiveness of mathematics for characterizing the world as we experience it: That effectiveness results from a combination of mathematical knowledge and connectedness to the world. The connection between mathematical ideas and the world as human beings experience it occurs within human minds. It is human beings who have created logarithmic spirals and fractals and who can "see" logarithmic spirals in snails and fractals in palm leaves.
- In the minds of those millions who have developed and sustained mathematics, conceptions of mathematics have been devised to fit the world as perceived and conceptualized. This is possible because concepts like change, proportion, size, rotation, probability, recurrence, iteration, and hundreds of others are both everyday ideas and ideas that have been mathematicized. The mathematization of ordinary human ideas is an ordinary human enterprise.
- Through the development of writing systems over millennia, culture has made

possible the notational systems of mathematics. Because human conceptual systems are capable of conceptual precision and symbolization, mathematics has been able to develop systems of precise calculation and proof. Through the use of discretization metaphors, more and more mathematical ideas become precisely symbolizable and calculable. It is the human capacity for conceptual metaphor that makes possible the precise mathematization and sometimes even the arithmetization of everyday concepts – concepts like collections, dimensions, symmetry, causal dependence and independence, and many more.

- Everything in mathematics is comprehensible – at least in principle. Since it makes use of general human conceptual capacities, its conceptual structure can be analyzed and taught in meaningful terms.
- We have learned from the study of the mind that human intelligence is multifaceted and that many forms of intelligence are vital to human culture. Mathematical intelligence is one of them – not greater or lesser than musical intelligence, artistic intelligence, literary intelligence, emotional and interpersonal intelligence, and so on.
- Mathematics is creative and open-ended. By virtue of the use of conceptual metaphors and conceptual blends, present mathematics can be extended to create new forms by importing structure from one branch to another and by fusing mathematical ideas from different branches.
- Human conceptual systems are not monolithic. They allow alternative versions of concepts and multiple metaphorical perspectives of many (though by no means all!) important aspects of our lives. Mathematics is every bit as conceptually rich as any other part of the human conceptual system. Moreover, mathematics allows for alternative visions and versions of concepts. There is not one notion of infinity but many, not one formal logic but tens of thousands, not one concept of number but a rich variety of alternatives, not one set theory or geometry or statistics but a wide range of them – all mathematics!
- Mathematics is a magnificent example of the beauty, richness, complexity, diversity, and importance of human ideas. It is a marvelous testament to what the ordinary embodied human mind is capable of – when multiplied by the creative efforts of millions over millennia.
- Human beings have been responsible for the creation of mathematics, and we remain responsible for maintaining and extending it.

## Notes

1 In *Where Mathematics Comes From*, Lakoff and I include a four-chapter case study exclusively dedicated to the analysis of the underlying conceptual metaphors and blends that make that famous formula true by virtue of what it *means*.

2 Details of how conceptual metaphor and conceptual blending work can be found elsewhere in this volume. For a general introduction to these concepts see Lakoff & Núñez (2000, chaps. 1–3), and the references given therein.

3 An analysis of the various dimensions and methodological issues regarding the scientific study of gesture studies is beyond the scope of this chapter. For details, see references mentioned above.

## References

Aleksandrov, A., Kolmogorov, A. N., & Lavrent'ev, M. A. (1956/1999). *Matematika, ee soderzhanie metody i znachenie* [Mathematics, its contents, methods and meaning]. Mineola, NY: Dover.

Bates, E., & Dick, F. (2002). Language, gesture, and the developing brain. *Developmental Psychobiology*, 40, 293–310.

Cienki, A. (1998). Metaphoric gestures and some of their relations to verbal metaphoric expressions. In J.-P. Koenig (Ed.), *Discourse and cognition* (pp. 189–204). Stanford, CA: CSLI Publications.

Courant, R., & Robbins, H. (1978). *What is mathematics?* New York: Oxford.

Fauconnier, G., & Turner, M. (1998). Conceptual integration networks. *Cognitive Science, 22* (2), 133–187.

Fauconnier, G., & Turner, M. (2002). *The way we think: Conceptual blendings and the mind's hidden complexities*. New York: Basic Books.

Gibbs, R. (1994). *The poetics of mind: Figurative thought, language, and understanding*. New York: Cambridge University Press.

Gibbs, R. (2006). Why cognitive linguists should care more about empirical methods. In M. González, I. Mittelberg, S. Coulson, & M. Spivey (Eds.), *Methods in cognitive linguistics* (pp. 2–18). Philadelphia: John Benjamins.

Gibbs, R., & Colston, H. (1995). The cognitive psychological reality of image-schemas and their transformations. *Cognitive Linguistics, 6*, 347–378.

Goldin-Meadow, S. (2003). *Hearing gesture: How our hands help us think*. Cambridge, MA: Harvard University Press.

Hersh, R. (1997). *What is mathematics, really?* New York: Oxford University Press.

Iverson, J., & S. Goldin-Meadow. (1998, November). Why people gesture when they speak. *Nature, 396*, 228.

Iverson, J., & Esther Thelen, E. (1999). Hand, mouth, and brain: The dynamic emergence of speech and gesture In R. Núñez and W. Freeman (Ed.), *Reclaiming cognition: The primacy of action, intention, and emotion* (pp. 19–40). Thorverton, UK: Imprint Academic.

Kaput, J. (1979). Mathematics and learning: Roots of epistemological status. In J. Lockhead & J. Clement (Eds.), *Cognitive process instruction* (pp. 289–303). Philadelphia: Franklin Institute Press.

Kendon, A. (1980). Gesticulation and speech: Two aspects of the process of utterance. In M. R. Key (Ed.), *The relation between verbal and nonverbal communication* (pp. 207–227). The Hague: Mouton de Gruyter.

Kendon, A. (2000). Language and gesture: unity or duality? In D. McNeill (Ed.), *Language and gesture* (pp. 47–63). Cambridge: Cambridge University Press.

Kendon, A. (2004) *Gesture: Visible action as utterance*. Cambridge: Cambridge University Press.

Kita, S., & Essegbey, J. (2001). Pointing left in Ghana: How a taboo on the use of the left hand influences gestural practice. *Gesture, 1*, 73–95.

Kramer, E. (1970). *The nature and growth of modern mathematics*. New York: Hawthorn Books.

Lakoff, G. (1993). The contemporary theory of metaphor. In A. Ortony (Ed.), *Metaphor and thought* (2nd ed., pp. 202–251). New York: Cambridge University Press.

Lakoff, G., & Johnson, M. (1980). *Metaphors we live by*. Chicago: University of Chicago Press.

Lakoff, G., & Johnson, M. (1999). *Philosophy in the flesh*. New York: Basic Books.

Lakoff, G., & Núñez, R. (1997). The metaphorical structure of mathematics: Sketching out cognitive foundations for a mind-based mathematics. In L. English (Ed.), *Mathematical reasoning: Analogies, metaphors, and images*. Mahwah, NJ: Lawrence Erlbaum Associates.

Lakoff, G., & Núñez, R. (1998). Conceptual metaphor in mathematics. In J. P. Koenig (Ed.), *Discourse and cognition: Bridging the gap*. Stanford, CA: CSLI/Cambridge.

Lakoff, G., & Núñez, R. (2000). *Where mathematics comes from: How the embodied mind brings mathematics into being*. New York: Basic Books.

Mayberry, R., & Jaques, J. (2000). Gesture production during stuttered speech: insights into the nature of gesture-speech integration. In D. McNeill (Ed.), *Language and gesture*. Cambridge: Cambridge University Press.

McNeill, D. (1992). *Hand and mind: What gestures reveal about thought*. Chicago: University of Chicago Press.

McNeill, D. (2005). *Gesture and thought*. Chicago: University of Chicago Press.

Murphy, G. (1997). Reasons to doubt the present evidence for metaphoric representation. *Cognition, 62*, 99–108.

Núñez, R. (1999). Could the future taste purple? In R. Núñez & W. Freeman (Eds.), *Reclaiming cognition: The primacy of action, intention, and emotion* (pp. 41–60). Thorverton, UK: Imprint Academic.

Núñez, R. (2000). Mathematical idea analysis: What embodied cognitive science can say about the human nature of mathematics. Opening plenary address in *Proceedings of the 24th International Conference for the Psychology of Mathematics Education, 1*, 3–22. Hiroshima, Japan.

Núñez, R. (2003, July). Fictive and metaphorical motion in technically idealized domains. *Proceedings of the 8th International Cognitive Linguistics Conference* (p. 215). Logroño, Spain.

Núñez, R. (2005). Creating mathematical infinities: The beauty of transfinite cardinals. *Journal of Pragmatics, 37*, 1717–1741.

Núñez, R. (2008). Mathematics, the ultimate challenge to embodiment: Truth and the grounding of axiomatic systems. In P. Calvo & T. Gomila (Eds.), *Elsevier Handbook of Embodied Cognitive Science*. New York: Elsevier.

Núñez, R., Edwards, L., & Matos, J. F. (1999). Embodied cognition as grounding for situatedness and context in mathematics education. *Educational Studies in Mathematics*, 39(1–3), 45–65.

Núñez, R., & Lakoff, G. (1998). What did Weierstrass really define? The cognitive structure of natural and $\varepsilon$–$\delta$ continuity. *Mathematical Cognition*, 4(2), 85–101.

Núñez, R., & Lakoff, G. (2005). The cognitive foundations of mathematics: The role of conceptual metaphor. In J. Campbell (Ed.), *Handbook of mathematical cognition* (pp. 109–124). New York: Psychology Press.

Núñez, R., & Sweetser, E. (2001, July). *Proceedings of the 7th International Cognitive Linguistics Conference* (pp. 249–250), Santa Barbara, CA.

Núñez, R., & Sweetser, E. (2006). With the future behind them: Convergent evidence from Aymara language and gesture in the cross-linguistic comparison of spatial construals of time. *Cognitive Science*. 30, 401–450.

Simmons, G. F. (1985). *Calculus with analytic geometry*. New York: McGraw Hill.

Stewart, I. (1995). *Concepts of modern mathematics*. New York: Dover.

Sweetser, E. (1990). *From etymology to pragmatics: Metaphorical and cultural aspects of semantic structure*. New York: Cambridge University Press.

Sweetser, E. (1998). Regular metaphoricity in gesture: bodily-based models of speech interaction. In *Actes du 16e Congrès International des Linguistes*. Elsevier.

Talmy, L. (1988). Force dynamics in language and cognition. *Cognitive Science*, 12, 49–100.

Talmy, L. (1996). Fictive motion in language and "ception." In P. Bloom, M. Peterson, L. Nadel, & M. Garrett (Eds.), *Language and space*. Cambridge, MA: MIT Press.

Talmy, L. (2003). *Toward a cognitive semantics: Vol. 1. Concept structuring systems*. Cambridge, MA: MIT Press.

CHAPTER 20

# What Is the "Color" of Law?

*Steven L. Winter**

## Introduction

Lawyers and mainstream legal theorists generally take a dim view of metaphor. Much of their suspicion stems from an objectivist epistemology. In the words of one recent commentator: "Metaphors are falsehoods. If they were literally true, they wouldn't be metaphors." On this view, metaphors must ultimately be translated into the facts for which they stand lest they lead to confusion and error.[1] Some mainstream legal theorists concede that metaphor is useful because it is vivid and evocative but worry that its poetic and subjective qualities will compromise clarity and comprehensibility.[2] The influential antiformalists of the early twentieth century – the Legal Realists and their predecessors – were leery of metaphor because they identified it with the misleading conceptualism of legal formalism.[3] Famously, Justice Cardozo observed that: "Metaphors in law are to be narrowly watched, for though starting as devices to liberate thought, they end often by enslaving it."[4] Conventional legal reasoning, in contrast, strives to reduce a complex problem to a policy, principle, propositional rule, or some other set of necessary and sufficient criteria. In theory, these definitional criteria will allow professionals to delineate legal categories with greater precision, draw appropriate distinctions, and then make correct decisions.

This chapter examines a particularly important and surprisingly intractable set of legal problems for which the conventional approach fails utterly: questions of governmental and official accountability. Conventional legal analysis fails here (and elsewhere, too) because it assumes that concepts are literal, that signification is arbitrary, and that meaning is intentional and truth-conditional. But this traditional methodology proves hopelessly inadequate to a social conception like "the state," which cannot be reduced to a set of objectifiable criteria. Instead, it leaves lawyers and judges struggling in vain to parse figurative language as if it were literal or to sound

* Steven L. Winter is the Walter S. Gibbs Professor of Constitutional Law at Wayne State University Law School.

the depths of an unfathomable legislative subjectivity.

For more than seven centuries, Anglo-American legislators and judges have turned to a legal metaphor – "under color of office" and its variants – to make sense of the issues raised by cases of official accountability. In this chapter, I use the cognitive theory of metaphor both to illuminate this previously neglected legal history and to uncover important aspects of legal reasoning as it has actually been performed by flesh-and-blood practitioners. But the import of this analysis is more general: It illustrates, in a real-world, high-stakes context, some of the most profound implications of the theory of metaphorical reason. Where conventional epistemologies assume either the determinacy of objectivist logic or the arbitrariness of social coherence theory, the actual, historical operations of metaphorical reason reveal the imaginative, yet systematic nature of human rationality. Where conventional theories of meaning see (or fear) unbridled subjectivity, the empirical data demonstrate the ways in which an imaginative human rationality is constrained by the embodied, socially situated nature of our cognitive processes. Metaphor is both a basic dimension of human reason and an indispensable tool of legal thought: For, as we shall see, it is only by metaphor that we are able to express significant aspects of our social reality – aspects that are otherwise devalued, distorted, or eliminated by more conventional, reductive approaches to human reasoning.

## Too Much or Too Little

All questions of governmental and official accountability presuppose that one can reliably identify when an action is that of a governmental entity or official. But this is much more difficult than it may seem. Because every official is also a private individual, it is often unclear when that person has acted *as* an official and when he or she has acted in their private capacity. Beyond this obvious problem of role ambiguity, however, lies the more profound problem that the state as an entity is an entirely conceptual construct. There are many legal contexts in which no one doubts the official character of the primary legal actors, but the question nevertheless remains whether their actions should be imputed to the governmental entity that employs them: Questions of what counts as state action subject to the proscriptions of the Fourteenth Amendment,[5] governmental immunity from suit under the Eleventh Amendment,[6] and municipal liability under the 1871 Civil Rights Act,[7] to name just a few, all turn on the theory by which one determines whether the agents' acts are considered to be those of the state.

Properly understood, the state is the amalgamation of the actions of a large number of actual human beings acting in particular social roles. But while this pragmatist understanding of the state is correct, it is – as Justice Frankfurter observed – also the source of much difficulty: "Since the state . . . can only act through functionaries, the question naturally arises what functionaries, acting under what circumstances, are to be deemed the state. . . . The problem is beset with inherent difficulties and not unnaturally has had a fluctuating history in the decisions of the Court."[8] The problem "who or what is the state?" is a problem of *social meaning*. Without the concept "state" there would only be groups of similarly clad thugs impinging on our autonomy or protecting us (at a price, no doubt) from other such groups. In this sense, the state is an imaginative social product over and above its personnel and its other material manifestations. The state exists only because we conceptualize it *as such*.[9]

For the average citizen of a modern democracy who has never experienced a radical change of regime, the state seems indisputably real. In periods of political instability, however, the imaginative, socially constructed nature of the state is cast in bas-relief. Consider, for example, the effect of the Nazi occupation of France during World War II and the formation of a collaborationist government at Vichy:

> *[It] meant that suddenly each citizen was thrust into a situation where he had to "argue within himself over the social pact and reconstitute a state by choice" . . . Where before there had been habitual allegiance, now there was necessarily a deliberate decision for or against the Vichy regime. The Occupation brought to the foreground a truth usually ignored: the state rests upon nothing other than the collective effect of choices made by individuals.*[10]

But even in more ordinary circumstances when there is only a single government widely accepted as legitimate, the socially constructed nature of the state means that there is no clear-cut way to determine whether it is a governmental entity that has acted. For just as the citizens can withhold their consent from an authority they view as illegitimate, a legal system can withhold its authorization from the acts of its officials. When it does, the resulting doctrinal difficulties are monumental: Is an illegal act by a state official state action? If the answer to that question is "yes" (as it is), is that act shielded by the state's sovereign immunity under the Eleventh Amendment? And if the answer to the latter question is "no" (as, in fact, it is), then how does one resolve the contradiction between these two inconsistent characterizations?

It might seem that the obvious solution to the problem is to identify the state with only those who act pursuant to the specific authorization of its positive law. But this position – which I refer to as "the reductive approach" – obliterates much of what is supposed to be accomplished by the commitment to governmental accountability represented by the ideal of "a government of laws and not of men."[11] In a simplistic sense, the reductive view seems to fit well with the rule-of-law ideal. A governmental officer who fails to comply with the rules specifying her official conduct is no longer viewed as acting for the state and is instead treated as any other wrongdoer. But, the reductive approach quickly proves incoherent because there *is* no government apart from the men (and women) who instantiate it. This incoherence becomes manifest under either of two circumstances: (1) when the issue is the enforcement of constitutional constraints on actions that are peculiarly governmental – the Eleventh Amendment problem, for example; or (2) when the system is designed to invoke legal constraints that are defined in terms of official action.[12]

Worse yet, the search for reliable objectified criteria either proves too much or too little.[13] If state action is identified with state permission, then every actor – public and private, official and unofficial – is always acting as the state.[14] Conversely, if state action is reduced to direct authorization by positive law, then, strictly speaking, no putatively illegal act could be attributed to the state until its highest court had upheld it against legal challenge.[15] Here, then, is a case where the rationalist tools of standard legal analysis lead to confusion rather than clarity.

It is noteworthy, therefore, that historically the Anglo-American legal tradition relied on the "color of office" metaphor to mediate the application of legal restrictions on the exercise of state power. Remarkably complex in structure, the expression is actually premised on two different metaphorical conceptions – one embodied, the other culturally contingent. Notwithstanding these differences in origin and structure, both metaphorical concepts share the connotation of action that presents a deceptive appearance. More importantly, we will see how this meaning-rich metaphor represents a sophisticated response to the conceptual problems raised by cases of official misconduct – a response that is not possible on more conventional legal reasoning.

## Sheriffs, Sureties, and the "Colour of Their Office"

Today, the difficulties caused by the constructive nature of the state arise most frequently in the context of constitutional litigation under section 1983, the 1871 Civil Rights Act that provides redress for constitutional violations committed "under color of" state law.[16] But the underlying conceptual problem was familiar to the common law, which for centuries used the "color of office" concept to mediate appropriate legal controls over sheriffs and other officers. The phrase "Colour of his Office" first appeared in an English statute of 1275 that prohibited seizures of property without a warrant or other proper authority.[17] As Sir Edward Coke explained in his annotation of the statute:

> Colore officii *is ever taken in malam partem, as* virtute officii *is taken in bonam: And therefore this implyeth a seisure unduly made against law.*
>
> *And he may doe it* colore officii *in two manner of wayes: Either when he hath no warrant, or when he hath a warrant, and doth not persue it.*[18]

A statute of 1444 prohibited sheriffs and their officers from taking "under color of their office" any "thing . . . to their use, profit, or avail, of any person by them . . . to be arrested or attached, nor of none other for them, for the omitting of any arrest or attachment" or for "mainprise, letting to bail, or eschewing any ease or favour to any such person so arrested." The statute was aimed at extortion and other abuses of the bail bond process by local sheriffs, who would release debtors upon the posting of an indemnification bond in an amount exceeding the original debt. The statute regulated who was eligible for bail and expressly excepted from bail those arrested upon execution for debt. It further specified the form for bail bonds and provided that "if any of the said sheriffs . . . take any obligation in other form by colour of their offices, that it shall be void."[19]

During the final years of the reign of Henry VIII, a yeoman by the name of Thomas Maningham fell in arrears with his fishmonger, Thomas Palley, in the amount of 200 marks sterling. On May 18, 1545, Palley sued out a writ in execution of the debt, which Maningham had previously confessed in court. The writ was addressed to the sheriff of the county of Bedford, Lewis Dive, who was directed to seize all of Maningham's property and to imprison Maningham until he had fully satisfied his debt to Palley. Dive executed the writ, seizing the property, and arresting Maningham. Maningham's brother John, however, obtained bail for him. John Maningham endorsed and gave to Dive a surety bond in the amount of £40 that agreed to indemnify and "keep, without damage, the said sheriff against our Lord the King, and one Thomas Palley."[20]

Dive later sued John Maningham on the bond. Maningham's defense was that the bond was void under the statute. In response, Dive argued that the bond was not covered by the statute and, therefore, not covered by the provision rendering void any nonconforming obligation. On this logic, the bond was like any contract enforceable at common law.* The court ruled that the statute applied, held the bond void, and rendered judgment for the defendant John Maningham.

In rejecting Dive's claim, the court made two arguments. First, it reasoned that the statute had to be interpreted in light of the mischief it sought to remedy. Accordingly, it held that the clauses which prescribed the form of all bonds and which made all nonconforming bonds void were intended to apply as well to bonds entered into for nonbailable offenses: "so that if the sheriffs or other officers will let prisoners at large, they must do it at their peril, for by this statute their safe conduct, that is to say, the obligations to save them harmless, is cut off and destroyed (pp. 107–108)." Second, and more important for our purposes, the court reasoned that:

> *[I]f the obligation is not void for this cause, it seems to me that (if it is taken in other form than the statute limits) these words, viz.* colore officii, *will make it void for it is to be considered that Thomas Maningham . . . was in execution under the custody of the plaintiff, not as Lewis Dive, but*

* Thus, Dive argued that "here Thomas Maningham was in upon execution, and was one of those contained in the exception, and the letting him go at large is an escape, and so is out of the intent of the statute and is meerly [sic] at the common law, in which case the obligation stands at common law and is good (pp. 100–101)."

> *as sheriff, for the writ to take Thomas Maningham was directed to him as sheriff, and so as officer he had the custody of him, then when he took the obligation, he took it as officer, but he took it unduly, for he was not bailable, but yet he took it as sheriff,* ergo *he took it* colore officii sui*; for this word* colore officii sui *is always taken* in malam partem, *and signifies an act badly done under countenance of an office, and it bears a dissembling visage of duty, and is properly called* extortion. *As if an officer will take more for his fees than he ought, this is done* colore officii sui, *but yet it is not part of his office, and it is called extortion, which is no other than robbery, but it is more odious than robbery, for robbery is apparent, and always hath the countenance of vice, but extortion, being equally as great a vice as robbery, carries the mask of virtue, and is more difficult to be tried or discerned, and consequently more odious than robbery. Wherefore here inasmuch as the obligation was made for the deliverance of Thomas Maningham, who was in the custody of the plaintiff as officer, it cannot be denied but that he took the obligation for his deliverance* colore officii, *although it was not* virtute officii sui. *(p. 108)*

Note the court's conspicuous difficulty with the problem of role ambiguity. It is all the more remarkable because the issue before it seems so simple and straightforward. The sheriff, after all, had done precisely what the statute prohibited. What appears to have troubled the court was the fact that, as quoted above, the clause rendering the obligation void appeared to be addressed to sheriffs acting in their official capacity.* Yet, on the reductive approach, an unauthorized or illegal act is not a genuine act of the state itself. Indeed, the statute at issue in *Dive* opened with the King's disavowal of "the great perjury, extortion, and oppression" committed by his sheriffs and their deputies.[21] Nevertheless, the court concluded that Dive had acted in his official capacity even though his actions were plainly outside his rightful authority: "[W]hen he took the obligation, he took it as officer, but he took it unduly, for he was not bailable, but yet he took it as sheriff, *ergo* he took it *colore officii sui*." In this way, the court addressed the duplicitous quality of the sheriff's actions "badly done under countenance of an office, and [bearing] a dissembling visage of duty." As Maningham's counsel argued, "*colore officii* implies that the thing is under pretence of office, but not duly, and the office is no more than a cloak to deceit, and the thing is grounded upon vice, and the office is as a shadow thereto (p. 102)."

Nineteenth-century American courts faced similar problems of role ambiguity. The issue arose with some frequency in suits alleging that, in executing a writ of attachment, the sheriff had in fact seized goods belonging to the wrong person. Because sheriffs were likely to be people of limited means, a party injured by the sheriff's unlawful act would seek recovery against the sureties on the officer's bond faithfully to perform the duties of his office. If the sheriff's act were treated as the unlawful act of a private actor, the injured party could not recover against the sureties because, as some courts reasoned, "there being no authority, there is no office, nothing official."[22]

Thus, from the sureties' perspective, a fully reductive analysis would have ensured a "heads I win, tails you lose" situation: "The argument, if sound, would preclude a recovery in any case against the sureties. If an authority could be shown, their defence would be complete; if there was none, the act would be extra official, and not within the scope of their undertaking."[23] Accordingly, most courts recognized that the bond would be forfeited and the sureties liable in cases of nonfeasance or misfeasance. Though some drew the line at cases of malfeasance, other less reductive courts recognized that wrongs committed under a claim of authority were *colore officii* and retained their official character. As one court reasoned, when a sheriff executed a writ to seize the goods from the wrong person, he

* This is what makes sense of Dive's claim that the debt was outside the statute: If the obligation was not taken in his official capacity, then it was just a contract between two private parties no different than any other obligation at common law.

nevertheless "does this in his character of sheriff, *colore officii*, and not as a naked trespasser without color of authority."[24] Accordingly, the majority rule – later adopted by the Supreme Court for federal officers – gave the injured party recourse against the sureties in cases of malfeasance such as a wrongful attachment.[25]

In the twentieth century, the Supreme Court interpreted the "under color of" law language of the Civil Rights Acts to include deprivations of constitutional rights caused by state officers acting in violation of state law or otherwise without authority: "Misuse of power, possessed by virtue of state law and made possible only because the wrongdoer is clothed with the authority of state law, is action taken 'under color of' state law."[26]

How does "under color of law" express this meaning? Why is action "under color of office" contrasted to that of "a *naked* trespasser"? And what does any of this have to do with the problem of role ambiguity?

## What Can Be Done by "Color of Law"?

A conventional legal analysis would view the phrase "color of office" as a term of art that had arbitrarily acquired its meaning through consistent historical usage. But that would miss entirely the semantic content and conceptual significance of this metaphorical expression. This single phrase actually consists of two *different* metaphors: one, a highly general set of metaphors from perceptual experience; and, the other, a metaphor and a metonymy that arose from specific social practices relating to governmental officers. Despite these differences in origin and structure, each metaphorical concept expresses in a different way the sense of deceptive appearance. While both metaphors are systematically elaborated in ordinary language, it is the second metaphorical conception that is systematic in legal reasoning. Indeed, because it plays a surprisingly important role in legal contexts where the doctrinal term "color of law" is ostensibly irrelevant, we can fairly say that this metaphor constitutes a significant, entrenched part of our conceptual system.

Metaphor, in other words, is a matter of thought and not mere language. It refers to a tightly structured set of conceptual mappings in which a target domain is understood in terms of a source domain of more readily comprehended, embodied, or social experience.[27] This conceptual mapping is conventionally represented by means of a mnemonic of the form TARGET-DOMAIN-IS-SOURCE-DOMAIN. But this is only a representation; the metaphor is the set of conceptual mappings and not the mnemonic. So, too, it is important not to confuse the metaphor, which is the conceptual mapping, with the many metaphorical expressions that are its linguistic manifestations. For example, a conceptual metaphor like CONTROL IS UP motivates many different metaphorical expressions such as "she held *up* publication until the footnotes were complete," "he's *under* my thumb," "she's *on top of* the situation," or "he's at the *height* of his power." Conversely, metaphorical expressions that use the same linguistic term can represent entirely different conceptual metaphors. Thus, metaphorical expressions such as "slow *up*!" and "he's cooking *up* a storm" are not instances of a single "up" metaphor, but rather different metaphorical expressions predicated on different conceptual metaphors – in this case CONTROL IS UP and ACTIVITY IS UP, respectively.*

Thus, the nonidentity between a metaphorical expression and its underlying conceptual mapping works both ways: not only can one conceptual mapping be productive of many metaphorical expressions, but one metaphorical expression can be composed of more than one mapping. The only

* A delightful example is the otherwise contradictory conventional expressions "slow *up*" and "slow *down*." "Slow *up*" is premised on CONTROL IS UP and connotes an exercise of mastery or control. "Slow *down*" is an instance of the ACTIVITY IS UP metaphor and connotes cessation of activity or a decrease of energy. In many contexts, both connotations will be applicable and either expression might be used. But in other cases, only one of the conceptual metaphors will make contextual sense – which is why one says "giddy *up*," but not "giddy *down*."

constraint is that the multiple mappings must be metaphorically coherent. This, as we shall see, is the case with respect to the "color office" metaphor.

1. There is a widespread, cross-cultural set of conceptual metaphors based on the MIND-AS-BODY metaphor. In this latter metaphor, the mind is conceptualized as a body moving through space and various entailments of travel are mapped onto intellectual operations. Thus: ARGUMENTS (AND OTHER LOGICAL STRUCTURES) ARE JOURNEYS, as when the professor asks "*Where* were we?" or, in questioning a student, "where is this argument *going*?"; KNOWING IS SEEING, as in a conventional phrase like "which *view* do you espouse?"; and IDEAS ARE LIGHT-SOURCES, as in familiar expressions like "his theory really *sheds some light* on our problem" or "she wrote a *brilliant* paper."[28]

The first, most general sense of the statutory expression "under color of" law derives from these metaphors. The simple phrase "under law" is predicated on the CONTROL IS UP metaphor and expresses the sense of lawful action – that is, that the person's (or institution's) actions are governed by the law. The meaning of the term "color" derives from the conceptual metaphors KNOWING IS SEEING and IDEAS ARE LIGHT-SOURCES. In its nonmetaphoric sense, color is "[t]he quality or attribute in virtue of which objects present different appearances to the eye, when considered with regard only to the kind of light reflected from their surfaces."[29] The metaphorical expression "under color of" law uses two entailments of our everyday knowledge of color. The first is that color is a quality of surfaces and, therefore, may reveal absolutely nothing about the interior or substance of the object under view. The second experiential entailment is that color perception is highly dependent upon the quality of light. Some colors are not perceptible at night, for example. Similarly, we know that if we view an object in other than white light, the color we see will not be true. Action "under color of" law is action that has only the *appearance* of being governed by law – that is, it is not action "under law," but only "under the *color* of law."[30] Thus, a deprivation of rights "under color of" law connotes an injury by an officer acting with an air of authority that is tainted or false.* Or, in the older variant "under color of office," the officer presents himself to the victim in a "false light" so that, as Manningham's counsel argued, "the thing is grounded upon vice, and the office is as a shadow thereto."

The sense of "color" as "false light," which derives from the conceptual metaphors KNOWING IS SEEING and IDEAS ARE LIGHT-SOURCES, is systematic in both ordinary English and legal discourse. The common notion that metaphor is merely "colorful" language in contradistinction to "clear" prose is, ironically, an instance of these conceptual metaphors.[31] In *Two Gentlemen of Verona* (act I, scene ii, lines 1–4), Shakespeare uses the phrase "under the color of" to connote deception.

> *Already I have been false to Valentine,*
> *And now I must be as unjust to Thurio.*
> *Under the color of commending him,*
> *I have access my own love to prefer.*

Another familiar example is the legal concept of a "colorable argument," which connotes an argument that has surface plausibility (i.e., "color") but that, when examined closely or thought through clearly, is nevertheless wrong. As one court noted: "'Colorable' is defined as 'having the appearance, especially the false appearance, of right.'"[32] Thus, "color" also signifies pretextuality, as in the following rather virulent statement during the House debate by an opponent of the 1871 Civil Rights Act:

> *Mr. Speaker, under the pretext of protecting the people, the people are enslaved; under the pretext of establishing order, lib-*

* This sense of "color" is not related to the conventional expression "true colors." (As in the sentence: "He acts like a nice guy; but when something important is at stake, he really shows his *true colors*.") As we will see in a moment, the metaphorical expression "true colors" is related to the second sense of "color of law." But both the expression "true colors" and its complement "under false colors" also take their significance from the fact that appearances can be deceiving.

*erty is being overthrown; under the pretext of securing the rights of the voter, the voter is disenfranchised; under color of maintaining the manhood of man in the political equality of the colored man, the manhood of man is denied in the political degradation of the white man.*[33]

A related usage appears in eighteenth- and nineteenth-century English law concerning contempt of Parliament, where it refers both to illegal actions and false accusations.[34]

Across the centuries, the term "color" in legal doctrine has invariably connoted some degree of falsity, ranging from fraud to pretext to mistaken appearance. In *Woolsey v. Dodge*, for example, the federal circuit court rejected the defendant's contention that "the mode of giving jurisdiction in this case is merely colorable; or in other words that it is a fraud upon the law."[35] The term had a different, but related connotation in the rather charming medieval doctrine of "colour." A "colour" was a common law pleading device, already extant by 1400, that continued in use in England until the beginning of the nineteenth century. The purpose of the device was to avoid pleading the general issue and, thus, take the case away from the jury. It allowed the defendant to convert the issue to a question of law "by giving the plaintiff a 'show' or 'colour,' i.e. by imagining a fictitious title for the plaintiff, specious, but inferior to his own, and asking the judgment of the Court upon it."[36] Another usage appears in various nineteenth-century American property law doctrines. Under many state statutes of limitation for cases of adverse possession, for example, a defendant with "color of title" who had been in possession for the requisite period could defeat a plaintiff with superior title.[37]

There is a related usage of "color of law" as "pretense or appearance of law" that is of particular interest because it was widespread in English political culture during the second half of the seventeenth century. The concept of "colour of law" was a potent political and rhetorical tool used by both sides in the political struggle between King and Parliament that culminated in the Revolution of 1688.[38]

*[T]he condemnation of legal form as a weapon of political persecution was used not only against the king but by him, as well, as an offensive device. In the* quo warranto *proceedings against the City of London, the corporation was charged with the "oppression of the Kings Subjects by Colour of Law." It was alleged that the City was pretending, and indeed seeming, to act in compliance with law but in fact was not. It is probable that the City was less guilty than the king of the pretense of legal regularity. . . . But what is more important is that these allegations were being directed from all sides (p. 65)*

In subsequent political debate, the claim that a particular procedure had "legal color" was invoked to maintain the appearance of continuity and legitimacy even in the face of substantial change:

*The argument could be completely wrong and at the same time totally convincing. All that was really required was the application of legal principle to the political problems at hand. Of little consequence was the relevance of the legal procedures employed. The 'colour of law' was usually quite enough. (p. 83)*

These seventeenth-century debates confirm that "color of law" was more than a technical legal term; by the late seventeenth century, it had become part of the larger English-speaking political culture.

In the period leading to the Revolution of 1688, the concern with oppression under pretense of law and abuse of legal form merged with the need to preserve the appearance of legality while one legal regime supplanted its predecessor.[39] During Reconstruction, the concern with oppression under pretense of law and abuse of legal form confronted the attempt to subvert the post–Civil War legal regime and to reestablish a social and political hierarchy dislodged by military defeat. In a different way in each context, "color of law" was invoked as the tool with which to restore a sense of legal order. In the former period, "by colour of law" marked Parliament's concern that its political actions be governed by the appearance of legality. In the latter period, "under color of" law signified Congress's concern with actions by Southern officials that used the appearance of legality to mask oppression.

2. The second sense of "color of law" is contingent on particular social practices relating to government officials. Perhaps for that reason, this second sense of "under color of" law seems to be primary. It is the principal sense that animates the reasoning in many of the most important cases dealing with official misconduct. Moreover, it is the sense that best captures the equivocalness caused by the conceptual opacity of the state and the ambiguous character of its agents.

One less familiar connotation of "color" comes from heraldry, where it refers concretely to the tints employed in heraldic crests. An early use of the term referred to the insignia of a knight.[40] A contemporary usage that bears much the same sense is that of "colors" as referring to the flag and, hence, the flag's bearers as the "color" guard. (It is this sense that is employed in the phrases "to show one's true colors" and "acting under false colors.") In these expressions, "color" is a metonymy where the color – which is often more striking or more easily perceived than the design – stands for the entire emblem.

The original expression "by Colour of his Office" dates from the previously noted statute of 1275, a time when many of the King's officers and agents would actually have worn the King's coat of arms. As it is used in this early statute, the metonymic expression "color of office" signified conduct that had all the trappings and indicia of an official act even though it was without sufficient warrant in law. Thus, the phrase "color of office" is a compound metonymic expression: "Color" stands for the King's coat of arms and the coat of arms stands for the office (and/or the King himself). The phrase is also a metaphorical expression once the metonymy is extended to represent the general *concept* of official misconduct (that is, without regard to the actual dress of the governmental agent). "Color of office" is a metaphor that is based on a metonymy; it signifies the appearance or guise of authority. Or, as argued by Maningham's counsel, "*colore officii* implies that the thing is under pretence of office, but not duly, and the office is no more than a *cloak* to deceit (p. 102; emphasis added)."

This metaphoric sense of "color of office" is not just some ancient relic of interest only to etymologists. There continues to be an experiential grounding for the metaphor in contemporary practices like the uniforms and insignia of the military and police. For example, in *Monroe v. Pape*, Justice Douglas observed "that Congress has power to enforce the Fourteenth Amendment against those who carry *a badge of authority of a State* . . ., whether they act in accordance with their authority or misuse it."[41] The underlying idea remains the same: The officer's attire or vestments signify the office, both in the practical sense that they indicate the wearer's position and in the symbolic sense that they represent the honor and authority of the office. Thus, to "invest" in office (from the Latin *vestire* "to dress") is "To clothe *with* or *in* the insignia of an office; hence, *with* the dignity itself."[42] It was conventional in the nineteenth century to say that one was "vested in office," and the installment of new officers is still referred to as an "investiture."

The enduring vitality of the metaphor as part of our conceptual system is conspicuous in legal doctrine. Virtually all of the modern cases dealing with the meaning of state action under the Fourteenth Amendment rely on metaphorical understandings derived from this sense of "color of office." In *Ex parte Virginia*, where the federal statute at issue did not contain the words "under color of" law, the Supreme Court first invoked the guise of authority conception to resolve the state action question:

> *Whoever, by virtue of public position under a State government, deprives another of property, life, or liberty, without due process of law, or denies or takes away the equal protection of the law violates the constitutional inhibition; and as he acts in the name and for the State, and* is clothed with the State's power, *his act is that of the State. This must be so, or the constitutional prohibition has no meaning. Then the State* has

clothed one of its agents *with power to annul or to evade it*.[43]

Similarly, though Justice Frankfurter dissented from *Monroe's* holding that "under color of" law encompassed unauthorized action by the police, he nevertheless conceded that the conduct of the police in that case was state action "because they are *clothed with an appearance of official authority* which is itself a factor of significance in dealings between individuals. . . . The *aura* of power *which a show of authority carries* with it has been created by state government."[44]

In both these quotations (as in the earlier quotes from *Monroe*), the metaphorical sense of "color of office" as guise of authority is the basis for an inference pattern in which the outward appearance of official power – a "show of authority" under state law – explains why official misconduct falls within the reach of the Fourteenth Amendment. Significantly, neither of these quotes concerns the interpretation of the statutory phrase "under color of" law; in each case, the pivotal inference that action which constitutes an abuse of state authority is nevertheless state action prohibited by the Fourteenth Amendment is supplied by the "color of office" metaphor.

We can observe the complementary metaphorical inference pattern at work in cases involving a state's immunity from suit under the Eleventh Amendment. In *Ex parte Young*,[45] the Supreme Court used the "color of office" metaphor in applying the ultra vires doctrine* to avoid the state sovereign immunity problem: "the officer proceeding under such [unconstitutional] enactment comes into conflict with the superior authority of that Constitution, and he is in that case *stripped of his official or representative character* and is subjected *in his person* to the consequences of his individual conduct."[46] Commentators criticize these "classic" doctrines of state action and ultra vires as logically inconsistent; Justices treat *Young* as an embarrassing, if necessary fiction.[47] But this inconsistency arises only on a reductive analysis that reifies the state and treats it as a "thing" separate from the actual persons who act in its name. For it is only on that reductive view that the governmental agent who acts illegally can be said to act not *qua* agent, but *qua* private person amenable to a common law action for redress.

But there is no state separate from the persons and institutions that embody it; the state exists only because the cultural meaning represented by its officials has been internalized and actualized by the society in question. Thus, as the Supreme Court pointed out in *Ex parte Virginia*, the Fourteenth Amendment "must act upon persons, not upon the abstract thing denominated a State."[48] Each of these persons is the social embodiment of the state, whether he is following its dictates or flaunting them. An official who abuses his office exploits this social meaning, in effect transforming the state into a government of men and not of laws. Thus, although *Young* remains problematic for other reasons, its doctrine makes quite good sense in the run of the mill case: An official who exploits or abuses his or her office is capitalizing on the social meaning of the state – which he or she represents, but does not fully personify. The official acts *as* the state, but only contingently so as a temporary embodiment of that construct. When called to account for his or her actions in violation of that trust, however, the official can be held liable as an individual "stripped of his official or representative character and . . . subjected in his person to the consequences of his individual conduct."

It is precisely these connotations that are captured by the "color of office" metaphor. It expresses the way in which the trappings of office provide a veneer of authority, proclaiming that the officer acts with the full power and prestige of the state. At the same time, however, the metaphor communicates the transient and provisional character of that representation – the fact that beneath the uniform and insignia of authority is a person who, in any given case, may not conform his or her behavior to the legal requirements of the office.

* At common law, an agent who acts outside his authority (ultra vires) cannot bind his principal.

The real problem with *Young* is that it conflates the *colore officii* concept with the doctrine of ultra vires. Where the common law distinguished official misconduct from the act of a "naked trespasser," *Young* treats the two as if they were the same. If *Young* has a fictive quality, it is because it fails to recognize the metaphorical quality of its own reasoning – as if the officer actually were "stripped of his official character" and reduced to a "naked trespasser." This leads to the rather bizarre bit of illogic in which the Court says that: "State officials sued for damages in their official capacity are not 'persons' for purposes of the suit because they assume the identity of the government that employs them. . . . By contrast, officers sued in their personal capacity come to court as individuals."[49] The fiction common to both these doctrines is that the officer is not sued as an individual tortfeasor at common law, but rather as a state official who has violated constitutional norms. These are not mistakes that arise under the nonreductive, metaphorical understanding expressed by the *colore officii* concept.

The "color of office" metaphor has been used by Anglo-American judges and lawyers over hundreds of years and across otherwise unrelated doctrinal categories to express the complex social meaning of official misconduct. It is the metaphoric conceptualization by which our legal–political culture historically has mediated the problems arising from the conceptual opacity of the state. As this cultural metaphor has taken shape in the case law, it has an intricate set of sophisticated entailments. At the first level, it connotes the sense in which the office may serve to camouflage or mask misbehavior. As Maningham's counsel explained, "*colore officii* implies that the thing is under pretence of office, but not duly, and the office is no more than a cloak to deceit." Accordingly, the "color of office" metaphor shares with the false light concept the metaphorical entailment of deceptive appearance. As noted in *Dive*, the metaphor conveys that the more serious evil of official misconduct is that the injury is compounded by deception: "As if an officer will take more for his fees than he ought, this is . . . robbery, but it is more odious than robbery, for robbery is apparent, and always hath the countenance of vice, but extortion, being equally as great a vice as robbery, carries the mask of virtue."

At the second level, the "color of office" metaphor expresses the sense that official misconduct does not have the same social meaning as a private wrong like robbery because, as Justice Frankfurter acknowledged, the wrongdoers "are clothed with an appearance of official authority which is itself a factor of significance in dealings between individuals." It signifies the dual character of the officer who is both a person and the provisional embodiment of the State. When an officer commits a wrong: "He does this in his character of sheriff, *colore officii*, and not as a naked trespasser without color of authority." Thus, the problem of conduct under "color of office" concerns the distinctive social meaning occasioned by abuse of official authority. When, for example, Los Angeles police officers beat Rodney King, they *were* acting *as* police and not as private individuals with a personal vendetta. They were acting as police officers and, at the same time, acting in a manner neither authorized nor approved by the city, its mayor, or most of its constituents. They were acting *officially*, but not *legally*.

At the third level, "under color of office" connotes the sense that the evil of official misconduct is not a matter of deception so much as duplicity and betrayal. In this sense, the notion of "color of office" as guise of authority is different than the sense of "under color of" law as false light. The false light metaphor implies that there is some deeper truth beneath the appearance. But the fundamental difficulty addressed by the "color of office" metaphor is that there is no other reality beneath the social meaning of the state, just as there is no other state separate from the officials who instantiate it. The problem of official misconduct is not one of deceit but of betrayal and abuse. The abusive officer is not a wolf in sheep's clothing, but a renegade who appears to be one thing *and is that thing* even as he betrays his appearance by his action. The actor *is* an officer *and* a wrongdoer. Thus, the "color of office" metaphor signifies that the fundamental problem is not a matter of truth and falsity, so much as it is a problem of integrity and treachery in the performance of a public trust. To put it another way, the concern is less a matter of truth and deception as it is a matter of virtue and vice.

This is the reason that the obverse of "under color of office" is "by virtue of office" and not simply "under law" or "by authority of law." This understanding is expressed by Coke who, echoing the earlier language of *Dive*, explained that the import of these terms is a matter of wickedness and virtue: "*Colore officii* is ever taken in malam partem, as *virtute officii* is taken in bonam." The officer who acts "under color of office" acts within his or her role as an officer, but without fidelity to that role. Which is why, even the standard definition of "under color of" law speaks in terms of: "Misuse of power, possessed *by virtue of state law*."[50] Action "under color of" law is conduct that is understood to be that of the state and, therefore, has all the affective power of an act of betrayal by those upon whom one relies for protection.

## Conclusion

The case of governmental accountability is a critical one for the legal enterprise. If the law cannot protect us from its own minions, then the ideal of a government of laws and not of men is just a cruel hoax. Faced with this acid test, law's preferred methodology comes up shockingly short. The obsession of law is definition and control. Conventional legal reasoning tries to pin things down by identifying principles, drawing distinctions, applying rules, and invoking other necessary and sufficient criteria. Yet, for all these aspirations to precision, the standard methodology of law cannot manage the complexity of the social meaning of the state without turning to the imaginative human capacity that the poet Wallace Stevens calls the "disposition to metaphor."[51]

Conventional legal method fares no better even if we de-escalate the stakes. There has long been a debate about the import of the phrase "under color of" state law as it is used in the Reconstruction Era civil rights statutes. Standard legal analysis of this question takes one of two forms. One approach, prominent in the Supreme Court opinions, is to inquire into the "plain meaning" of the statutory phrase. Thus, dissenting in Monroe, Justice Frankfurter argued that "the prior decisions . . . have given 'under color of [law]' a content that ignores the meaning fairly comported by the words of the text."[52] Yet, in an earlier case, Justice Douglas had come to just the opposite conclusion: "If, as suggested, the statute was designed to embrace only actions which the state in fact authorized, the words 'under color of state law' were hardly apt words to express the idea."[53]

The principal alternative approach is to inquire into the intent of the legislature that enacted the statute. On this approach, the argument would look something like this: When the "under color of" law phrase was incorporated into the Reconstruction civil rights statutes, it came already freighted with the historical and legal significance of six centuries of legal usage. As a matter of the canons of statutory interpretation, we should accord the provision the meaning intended by the legislators. In using the "under color of" law language, Congress adopted a common law term of art with a well-known meaning. That is why the legislative history contains little direct discussion and no explicit definition of the statutory phrase. In order to maintain fidelity to legislative intent, we must interpret the statute in light of the legal understanding of the phrase that prevailed at the time of the law's passage.[54]

One advantage of this argument, aside from its conventionality, is that it offers a coherent way of parsing a statute whose legislative history is otherwise rather opaque. But it has several weaknesses familiar to legal critics. How many of those who voted for the statute were lawyers? How many actually knew the technical legal significance of the phrase "under color of" law? And which of the divergent definitions might they have been familiar with?

The cognitive theory of metaphor makes two contributions at this juncture, and at two different levels of sophistication. First, it enables us to assess the ordinary language meaning of the "color of law" metaphor. Cognitive theory provides a methodology supported by extensive empirical evidence that makes it possible to test the competing assertions about the "plain meaning" of the phrase "under color of" law. A cognitive analysis of how the metaphor expresses the meaning that it does leads to the conclusion that, for the ordinary member of our linguistic culture, "under color of" law connotes something like "under a false or misleading appearance of lawful authority."

Second, the cognitive theory of metaphor answers the skeptical questions that trouble the conventional argument about legislative intent by undermining the fundamental assumptions that give them force. In the absence of some objectivist theory of meaning, the standard approach to statutory interpretation assumes that the historical legal usage of the phrase is relevant only if the legislators were aware of it and intended to incorporate that meaning into the statute. This understanding in turn depends on two highly conventional, but mistaken assumptions: (1) that linguistic meaning is essentially arbitrary; and (2) that, even if meaning is socially contingent, it is still largely a matter of the conscious intention of self-directing actors.

Developments in cognitive theory challenge both these assumptions. First, they present a complex picture of human rationality as an embodied process that is experientially grounded and elaborated imaginatively through conceptual operations such as metaphor, metonymy, and modeling (rather than rule-governed formulas). One implication of this understanding, however, is that questions of meaning no longer fit into the conventional epistemological categories. The recognition that meaning is grounded in experience entails a rejection of the determinacy sought by objectivist logic *and* the arbitrariness assumed by most social coherence theories. Meaning is not determinate. The import of transfigurative processes such as metaphor is that there can be no linear, algorithmic function that links experiential input to imaginative output. But neither is meaning arbitrary. Not only is meaning configured by the kinds of bodies and social experiences that we have, it is framed and constrained by the systematic nature of cognitive processes like metaphor.

To put it another way, human conceptualizations are not arbitrary in the sense that they can be *just anything*. Rather, the metaphoric nature of these conceptualizations means that they can be many things *of a specified, related type*. Thus, as we have seen, the various legal senses of "color" are organized around a central sense of "color" as "false appearance." Similarly, the second metaphorical sense of "under color of" law is grounded in socially contingent practices. Here, too, we will see that the historical meaning of the phrase is neither arbitrary nor isolated. Rather, it is related to those practices metaphorically and elaborated in legal reasoning in a systematic and coherent manner.

Second, the understanding of human rationality as grounded in experience yields the further conclusion that meaning cannot be viewed as a matter of the conscious intention of self-directing actors. Every aspect of legal reasoning occurs against the backdrop of a massive cultural tableau which provides the tacit assumptions or sedimentations that render those legal conceptions intelligible. Because these socially constructed contexts are always anterior to any of us as individuals, our very ability to have a world is already constrained by the cultural constructs in which we find ourselves. Since legislators, too, can only act in terms of the embedded cultural understandings that enable meaning, an important part of any statute is not made by the legislator but is contingent on the preexisting practices that are conventional for and constitutive of that culture. The meaning of the "color of law" metaphor is not merely a matter of consistent historical usage by judges and legislators, but a function of its continuing vitality as an embedded part of our culture's socio-linguistic system.

The meaning of "under color of" law, then, is a case where the standard legal tools lead to confusion rather than clarity. Instead of directing us to the historical usage and social meaning of this legal metaphor, conventional legal analysis has led lawyers and judges either to parse figurative language as if it were literal or to plumb in vain the depths of legislative subjectivity. The cognitive theory of metaphor, in contrast, opens a treasure trove of historical and semantic insight leading us to see how the conceptual metaphor incorporated in these statutes better expresses significant aspects of our social reality – aspects that are otherwise devalued or eliminated by more conventional, reductive approaches to legal reasoning.

So, we now know the answer: Law strives to be black and white. Yet, for all its efforts, it cannot help but express itself in all the colors of human imagination.

## Notes

1 Eugene Volokh, *Same-Sex Marriage and Slippery Slopes*, 33 HOFSTRA L. REV. 1155, 1157 (2005). This view derives from Locke. JOHN LOCKE, AN ESSAY CONCERNING HUMAN UNDERSTANDING 508 (Book 3, Chapter 10) (Peter H. Nidditch ed. 1975) (condemning metaphor and other figurative speech as "perfect cheat" and insisting upon literal prose "if we would speak of things as they are"). *Cf.* LON FULLER, LEGAL FICTIONS viii (1967) ("When all goes well and established legal rules encompass neatly the social life they are intended to regulate, there is little occasion for fictions.").

2 *See, e.g.*, David A. Anderson, *Metaphorical Scholarship*, 79 CALIF. L. REV. 1205, 1214–15 (1991) (Metaphor "is useful because it is evocative, but it may evoke different ideas in different readers. It liberates the author from some of the rigidity of exposition, but also from the demands of precision and clarity.").

3 *See* Felix Cohen, *Transcendental Nonsense and the Functional Approach*, 35 COLUM. L. REV. 809, 812 (1935) ("When the vivid fictions and metaphors of traditional jurisprudence are thought of as reasons for decisions, rather than poetical or mnemonic devices . . . , then [one] . . . is apt to forget the social forces that mold the law."); Wesley Newcomb Hohfeld, *Some Fundamental Legal Conceptions as Applied in Judicial Reasoning*, 23 YALE L. J. 16, 24 (1913) ("Much of the difficulty, as regards legal terminology, arises from the fact that many of our words were originally applicable only to physical things; so that their use in connection with legal relations is, strictly speaking, figurative or fictional.").

4 Berkey v. Third Ave. Ry. Co., 244 N.Y. 84, 94, 155 N.E.2d 58, 61 (1930). Cardozo's point is often echoed. *See, e.g.*, Eugene Volokh, *The Mechanisms of the Slippery Slope*, 116 HARV. L. REV. 1026, 1137 (2003) ("as with many metaphors, it starts by enriching our vision and ends by clouding it"); Tiller v. Atlantic Coastline R.R., 318 U.S. 54, 68 (1943) (Frankfurter, J., concurring) ("A phrase begins life as a literary expression; its felicity leads to its lazy repetition; and repetition soon establishes it as a legal formula, undiscriminately used to express different and sometimes contradictory ideas.") (referring to the use of the term "assumption of risk").

5 *Compare* Home Telephone & Telegraph Co. v. City of Los Angeles, 227 U.S. 278, 288 (1913) ("[W]here a state officer, under an assertion of power from the state, is doing an act which could only be done upon the predicate that there was such power, the inquiry as to the repugnancy of the act to the 14th Amendment cannot be avoided by insisting that there was a want of power."), *with* Barney v. City of New York, 193 U.S. 430, 437 (1904) (the complained of action of the Rapid Transit Board "was not only not authorized, but was forbidden by the legislation, and hence was not action by the State of New York").

6 *Compare* Ex parte Young, 209 U.S. 123, 159 (1908) ("[T]he use of the name of the State to enforce an unconstitutional act to the injury of complainants is a proceeding without the authority of and one which does not affect the State in its sovereign or governmental capacity."), *with* Pennhurst State School & Hospital v. Halderman, 465 U.S. 89, 107 (1984) ("[T]he general criterion for determining when in fact a suit is against the sovereign is the *effect* of the relief sought.").

7 *Compare* Monell v. Department of Social Services, 436 U.S. 658 (1978) (municipality

liable under 42 U.S.C. §1983 for unconstitutional actions pursuant to governmental "policy or custom"), *with* Oklahoma City v. Tuttle, 471 U.S. 808, 823 n.7 (1985) (plurality opinion) ("We express no opinion on whether a policy that itself is not unconstitutional . . . can ever meet the 'policy' requirement of *Monell*.").

8 *Snowden v. Hughes*, 321 U.S. 1, 16 (1944) (Frankfurter, J., concurring).

9 *Cf.* BENEDICT ANDERSON, IMAGINED COMMUNITIES: REFLECTIONS ON THE ORIGIN AND SPREAD OF NATIONALISM 6 (rev. ed. 1991) ("[T]he nation . . . is an imagined political community. . . . It is *imagined* because the members of even the smallest nation will never know most of their fellow-members, meet them, or even hear of them, yet in the minds of each lives the image of their communion.").

10 KERRY H. WHITESIDE, MERLEAU-PONTY AND THE FOUNDATION OF AN EXISTENTIAL POLITICS 185–86 (1988) (quoting MAURICE MERLEAU-PONTY, HUMANISM AND TERROR: AN ESSAY ON THE COMMUNIST PROBLEM 36–37 (John O'Neill trans. 1969)).

11 MASS. CONST., Pt. 1, Art. XXX ("A Declaration of the Rights of the Inhabitants of the Commonwealth of Massachusetts"); *see also* Marbury v. Madison, 5 U.S. (1 Cranch) 137, 163 (1803). On the origins of the phrase, see Frank M. Michelman, *The Supreme Court 1985 Term – Foreword: Traces of Self-Government*, 100 HARV. L. REV. 4, 4 n.2 (1986).

12 *See Home Telephone*, 227 U.S. at 284 (rejecting the reductive argument because "the enforcement of the doctrine would hence render impossible the performance of the duty with which the Federal courts are charged under the Constitution. Such paralysis would inevitably ensue.").

13 LARRY ALEXANDER & PAUL HORTON, WHOM DOES THE CONSTITUTION COMMAND?: A CONCEPTUAL ANALYSIS WITH PRACTICAL IMPLICATIONS 89–90 (1988) (concluding that only the "Legalist model," in which the Constitution speaks only to government officials who can meaningfully be said to be "lawmakers," and the "Naturalist model," in which the Constitution speaks to everyone, are "fully principled").

14 *See* Robert Hale, *Coercion and Distribution in a Supposedly Non-Coercive State*, 38 POL. SCI. Q. 470 (1923). *See also* Duncan Kennedy, *Form and Substance in Private Law Adjudication*, 89 HARV. L. REV. 1685, 1748–51 (1976).

15 *Home Telephone*, 227 U.S. at 283 ("Under this hypothesis . . . , it could not be assumed that the State had authorized its officers to do acts in violation of the state constitution until the court of last resort of the State had determined that such acts were authorized."). This, in effect, is the position taken by the Court in many of its recent decisions. Henry Paul Monaghan, *State Law Wrongs, State Law Remedies, and the Fourteenth Amendment*, 86 COLUM. L. REV. 979, 982 (1986); Steven L. Winter, *The Meaning of "Under Color of" Law*, 91 MICH. L. REV. 323, 328–32, 407–18 (1992).

16 42 U.S.C. § 1983 (1986). The same language appears in the criminal civil rights provision, 18 U.S.C. § 242 (1988), originally adopted in 1866, which was the model for section 1983.

17 Statute of 3 Edw. 1, ch. 24 (1275), *reprinted in* 1 STATUTES AT LARGE 92–93 (Danby Pickering ed. 1762). The appearance of the phrase in this statute is almost a hundred years earlier than any of the entries in *The Oxford English Dictionary* for legal uses of the term "colour" and 15 years earlier than the earliest example given for a nonlegal use. III THE OXFORD ENGLISH DICTIONARY 499–500 (2d ed. 1989) (definitions 2.a., 11.c. & d.) [hereinafter OED].

18 SIR EDWARD COKE, THE SECOND PART OF THE INSTITUTES OF THE LAWES OF ENGLAND 206 (facsimile ed. 1979) (originally published in 1642).

19 Statute of 23 Hen. 6, c. 10 (1444), *reprinted in* 3 STATUTES AT LARGE 269, 271–72 (Danby Pickering ed. 1762).

20 Dive v. Maningham, Mich. Term. 4 Edw. 6, 1 Plowden's Reports 60, 61–62, 75 Eng. Rep. 96, 97–99 (Common Bench 1551) (first reported in 1578). Subsequent citations are to the English Reports and are given in text.

21 3 STATUTES AT LARGE at 269–70.

22 *Ex parte* Reed, 4 Hill 572, 574 (N.Y. Sup. Ct. 1843); *see also* United States v. Cranston, 25 F. Cas. 692 (C.C.D.C. 1828) (No. 14,889) (sureties not liable for action without legal process); Governor *for the use of* Simmons v. Hancock, 2 Ala. 728 (1841) (sureties not liable for fraud). *Reed* was overruled in The People *ex rel.* Kellogg v. Schuyler, 4 N.Y. 173 (1850).

23 *Schuyler*, 4 N.Y. at 180.

24 Sangster v. Commonwealth, 58 Va. (17 Gratt.) 124, 130 (1866).

25 Lammon v. Feusier, 111 U.S. 17, 20–22 (1884) (canvassing cases); *see also* Van Pelt v. Littler, 14 Cal. 194 (1859); Commonwealth for Davy v. Stockton, 21 Ky. (5 T. B. Mon.) 192 (1827); Carmack v. Commonwealth *for the use of* Boggs, 5 Binn. 184 (Pa. 1812).

26 Monroe v. Pape, 365 U.S. 167, 184 (1961); United States v. Classic, 313 U.S. 299, 326 (1941).

27 For discussions of the empirical evidence for and neural basis of metaphor, see my A CLEARING IN THE FOREST: LAW, LIFE, AND MIND (2001); GEORGE LAKOFF & MARK JOHNSON, PHILOSOPHY IN THE FLESH: THE EMBODIED MIND AND ITS CHALLENGE TO WESTERN THOUGHT (1999); GERALD M. EDELMAN, BRIGHT AIR, BRILLIANT FIRE: ON THE MATTER OF THE MIND (1992); GERALD M. EDELMAN, THE REMEMBERED PRESENT: A BIOLOGICAL THEORY OF CONSCIOUSNESS (1989); GERALD M. EDELMAN, NEURAL DARWINISM: THE THEORY OF NEURONAL GROUP SELECTION (1988); GEORGE LAKOFF, WOMEN, FIRE, AND DANGEROUS THINGS: WHAT CATEGORIES REVEAL ABOUT THE MIND (1987); MARK JOHNSON, THE BODY IN THE MIND: THE BODILY BASIS OF MEANING, IMAGINATION, AND REASON (1987); and GEORGE LAKOFF & MARK JOHNSON, METAPHORS WE LIVE BY (1980).

28 EVE SWEETSER, FROM ETYMOLOGY TO PRAGMATICS: METAPHORICAL AND CULTURAL ASPECTS OF SEMANTIC STRUCTURE 28–32 (1990); *see also* LAKOFF & JOHNSON, *supra* note 27, at 48, 87–96.

29 OED, *supra* note 17, at 499 (definition 1).

30 There is a related sense in which the phrase connotes action that, rather than having the appearance of being governed by law, is governed by the appearance of law as in the "good faith" interpretation of the "under color of" provision of the Captured and Abandoned Property Act. Act of July 27, 1868, ch. 276, § 3, 15 Stat. 243–44, amending Act of March 3, 1863, ch. 120, 12 Stat. 820; *see* Lamar v. McCulloch, 115 U.S. 164, 186 (1885). This is the sense in which the aspiration to "legal color" dominated political debate in England during the second half of the seventeenth century. *See* discussion text accompanying notes 38–39 *infra*.

31 *See, e.g.*, THOMAS C. GREY, THE WALLACE STEVENS CASE: LAW AND THE PRACTICE OF POETRY 36 (1991) ("[T]he kind of misrepresentation most significant in law is the rhetorical *coloring* of objective reality with subjective wishes and desires. Using rhetorical tropes and figures, a speaker can project emotions to the audience in the *guise* of objective qualities.") (emphasis added). The distinction between prose and metaphor is closely related to the Enlightenment conception of Reason, which seeks transparency and strives to avoid the coloration of emotion. *See, e.g.*, LOCKE, *supra* note 1 ("But if we would speak of things as they are, we must allow that all the art of rhetoric, besides order and clearness; all the artificial and figurative applications of words eloquence hath invented, are for nothing else but to insinuate wrong ideas, move the passions, and thereby mislead the judgment.").

32 Virginia v. De Hart, 119 Fed. 626, 628 (C.C.W.D.Va. 1902).

33 Cong. Globe, 42d Cong., 1st Sess. 364 (1871) (statement of Representative Archer). The OED gives a related nonlegal usage of "colour" as "[a] show of reason, a specious or plausible reason or ground; fair pretense, pretext, cloak." OED, *supra* note 17, at 500 (definition 12.a.).

34 *See* HOMERSHAM COX, THE INSTITUTIONS OF THE ENGLISH GOVERNMENT 218 (1863).

35 30 Fed. Cas. 606, 608 (C. C. D. Ohio 1854) (Case No., 18,032), *affirmed* 59 U.S. 331 (1855). In *Woolsey*, a bank shareholder sued in equity to enjoin the collection of a state tax on the ground that the tax violated the contract clause. Federal jurisdiction was founded on diversity; the reference to "jurisdiction" is to the court's equity jurisdiction

36 EDWARD JENKS, A SHORT HISTORY OF ENGLISH LAW 163–64 (6th ed. 1949) (citing a reported case in the Year Book for the second year of the reign of Henry IV); IX SIR WILLIAM HOLDSWORTH, A HISTORY OF ENGLISH LAW 299–302 (1925).

37 Wright v. Mattison, 59 U.S. 50, 56 (1855); *see also* Beaver v. Taylor, 68 U.S. 637, 641 n.2 (1863) ("A void deed taken in good faith is a sufficient color of title."); Pillow v. Roberts, 54 U.S. 472, 477 (1851) ("One who enters upon a vacant possession, claiming for himself under any pretence or color of title, is equally

protected with the forcible disseizor."). A related usage of "color of title" in the sense of apparent authority appears in Cocke v. Halsey, 41 U.S. 71 (1842). There, the Supreme Court held that, even if the clerk's appointment had been irregular under state law, the fact that he had "color of title" meant that his acts were "colore officii" and binding on third parties. *Id.* at 86–87.

38 HOWARD NENNER, BY COLOUR OF LAW: LEGAL AND CONSTITUTIONAL POLITICS IN ENGLAND, 1660–1689 at 130 (1977) ("Legal process, or at least its appearance 'by colour of law,' would serve as the constant guide to political action from 1660 on."). Subsequent page references are given in text.

39 As Nenner observes:

> The Stuarts had exploited the law not wisely but too well. The legal past was theirs, but it was . . . jeopardized and then lost through politically insensitive, even if constitutionally proper, use. . . . Parliament opposed the king with its own interpretation of the law; and, when that failed, it assumed the burden of legal justification by recourse to the best, indeed the only, approximation of law it could find – the weapon of legal color. (p. 199)

40 OED, *supra* note 17, at 499 (definitions 2.b. & 6.a.).

41 365 U.S. 167, 171–72 (1961) (majority opinion; emphasis added).

42 VIII OED, *supra* note 17, at 46 (definition 4).

43 *Ex parte* Virginia, 100 U.S. 339, 347 (1880) (emphasis added); *accord Home Telephone*, 227 U.S. at 287 ("[T]he theory of the Amendment is that where an officer or other representative of a State in the exercise of *the authority with which he is clothed* misuses the power possessed to do a wrong forbidden by the Amendment, inquiry concerning whether the State has authorized the wrong is irrelevant.") (emphasis added).

44 *Id.* at 238 (emphasis added); *see also* Terry v. Adams, 345 U.S. 461, 475 (1953) (Frankfurter, J., concurring).

45 209 U.S. 123 (1908).

46 *Young*, 209 U.S. at 159–60 (emphasis added).

47 HOWARD P. FINK & MARK V. TUSHNET, FEDERAL JURISDICTION: POLICY AND PRACTICE 127 (2d ed. 1987) ("[T]he *Young-Home Telephone* pair retains the air of mysticism that surrounds most legal fictions."); Akhil Reed Amar, *Of Sovereignty and Federalism*, 96 YALE L.J. 1425, 1490 n. 257 (1987); Pennhurst State School & Hospital v. Halderman, 465 U.S. 89, 106–07 (1984) (describing the reductive approach of *Ex parte Young* as a necessary "fiction" and characterizing the dissent's ultra vires theory of *Young* as "out of touch with reality").

48 *Ex parte Virginia*, 100 U.S. at 347.

49 Hafer v. Mello, 502 U.S. 21, 27 (1991).

50 *Classic*, 313 U.S. at 326 (emphasis added); *Monroe*, 365 U.S. at 184; *Screws*, 325 U.S. at 109; *see also Ex parte Virginia*, 100 U.S. at 347 (referring to illegal actions made possible "by virtue of public position under a State government"); *Young*, 209 U.S. at 160–61 (referring to the Attorney General's "power by virtue of his office" even though he was "stripped of his official or representative character").

51 WALLACE STEVENS, *A Collect of Philosophy*, in OPUS POSTHUMOUS 186 (1957).

52 *Monroe*, 365 U.S. at 222 (Frankfurter, J. dissenting).

53 *Screws*, 325 U.S. at 111 (plurality opinion).

54 *See, e.g.*, Cannon v. University of Chicago, 441 U.S. 677 (1982).

CHAPTER 21

# Metaphor and Emotion

*Zoltán Kövecses*

Emotion concepts are composed of a number of parts: metaphors, metonymies, "related concepts," and cultural models (see, for example, Kövecses, 1986, 1988, 1990). Given these parts, a number of questions arise, including the following: (1) What are emotion metaphors, metonymies, related concepts, and how are they all related to each other? (2) Is there a "master metaphor" for the emotions? (3) Are emotion metaphors unique to the emotions? (4) How do emotion metaphors differ from metaphors for other related domains, such as human relationships? (5) What is the precise role of metaphors, metonymies, and related concepts in the cognitive construction of particular emotion concepts? (6) Are emotion metaphors universal?

In my view, the major finding that emerges from the study of metaphors characterizing the emotion domain is that, essentially, there are no emotion-specific metaphors. If this finding is correct and if it can be generalized to other domains, it will turn out that our metaphorical conceptual system is organized by a hierarchy of metaphors at different levels of specificity. This idea was first suggested by Kövecses (1995a, 2000a) in his study of friendship and the notion of the "scope of metaphor," and it seems that the study of emotion metaphors provides further evidence for the feasibility of such a proposal.

## (1) What Are Emotion Metaphors, Metonymies, and Related Concepts?

It is a well established feature of emotion language that it is highly figurative; that is, it is dominated by metaphorical and metonymic expressions. It is also well known that most of these expressions belong to a variety of conceptual metaphors and metonymies. Below is a selection of such conceptual metaphors and metonymies in two emotion concepts: anger and love. Each conceptual metaphor and metonymy is illustrated by at least one linguistic example.

### *Metaphors*

*Anger*:

*anger is hot fluid in a container: She is* boiling with *anger.*
*anger is fire: He's doing a* slow burn. *His anger is* smoldering.
*anger is insanity: The man was* insane with *rage.*
*anger is an opponent in a struggle: I was* struggling with *my anger.*
*anger is a captive animal: He* unleashed *his anger.*
*anger is a burden: He* carries *his anger* around *with him.*
*the cause of anger is trespassing: Here* I draw the line.
*the cause of anger is physical annoyance: He's* a pain in the neck.
*anger is a natural force: It was a* stormy *meeting.*
*anger is a social superior: His actions were completely* governed *by anger.*

*Love*:

*love is a nutrient: I am* starved for *love.*
*love is a journey: It's been* a long, bumpy road.
*love is a unity of parts: We're* as one. *They're* breaking up. *We're* inseparable. *We* fused together.
*love is a bond: There is a close* tie *between them.*
*love is a fluid in a container: She was* overflowing with *love.*
*love is fire: I am* burning *with love.*
*love is an economic exchange: I'm* putting more into *this than you are.*
*love is a natural force: She* swept *me* off my feet.
*love is a physical force: I was* magnetically drawn to *her.*
*love is an opponent: She tried to* fight *her feelings of love.*
*love is a captive animal: She* let go of *her feelings.*
*love is war: She* conquered *him.*
*love is insanity: I am* crazy about *you.*
*love is a social superior: She is completely* ruled by *love.*
*love is rapture / a high: I have been* high on *love for weeks.*
*the object of love is a small child: Well,* baby, *what are we gonna do?*
*the object of love is a deity: Don't* put *her* on a pedestal. *He* worships *her.*

In general, it can be suggested that a conceptual metaphor consists of a source and a target domain and that the source domain is, at least in the everyday cases, typically a better understood and more concrete domain than the target domain. Clearly, this generalization has certain limits, as, for instance, the conceptual metaphor THE OBJECT OF LOVE IS A DEITY indicates.

### *Metonymies*

Conceptual metonymies, unlike conceptual metaphors, involve a single domain, or concept. The purpose of metonymy is to provide mental access to a domain through a part of the same domain (or vice versa) or to a part of a domain through another part in the same domain (for more explanation of the nature of metonymy, see Kövecses & Radden, 1998). Thus, metonymy, unlike metaphor, is a "stand-for" relation (i.e., a part stands for the whole or a part stands for another part) within a single domain. Some examples follow (taken from Kövecses, 2000):

*Love*:

*increase in body heat stands for love: I* felt hot all over *when I saw her.*
*increase in heart rate stands for love: He's a* heart-throb.
*blushing stands for love: She* blushed *when she saw him.*
*dizziness stands for love: She's in a* daze *over him. I* feel dizzy *every time I see her.*
*sweaty palms stand for love:* His palms became sweaty *when he looked at her.*
*inability to breathe stands for love: You* take my breath away.
*interference with accurate perception stands for love: He* saw nothing but her.
*inability to think stands for love: He* can't think straight *when around her.*
*physical closeness stands for love: They* are always together.
*intimate sexual behavior stands for love: She* showered *him* with kisses. *He* caressed *her gently.*
*sex stands for love: They* made love.

*loving visual behavior stands for love: He* can't take his eyes off of *her. She's* starry-eyed.

In other words, emotion metaphors and metonymies can be conceptual and linguistic in Lakoff and Johnson's (1980) sense. When I talk about emotion metaphors and metonymies, I will mean conceptual metaphors and conceptual metonymies of the kind indicated in small caps above.

There is an important connection between emotion metaphors and metonymies; namely, that the metonymies can be said to motivate the metaphors. This motivation is not simply linguistic or conceptual but also physical, in the sense that the metonymies indicate certain physical aspects of the body involved in emotion. The physical aspect indicated by emotion metonymies can be factored into two types: behavioral and physiological. For example, INTIMATE SEXUAL BEHAVIOR and LOVING VISUAL BEHAVIOR are behavioral responses that metonymyically indicate love, while AN INCREASE IN HEART RATE is a physiological one. Both types can be specific or generic. LOVING VISUAL BEHAVIOR is specific to love but AN INCREASE IN HEART RATE is general, in that it characterizes both love and anger, among other emotions. Another property of such behavior- and physiology-based metonymies is that, taken jointly, they provide a specific profile for basic-level emotion concepts, such as anger, fear, and love.

### *Related Concepts*

A special case of emotion metonymies involves a situation in which an emotion concept B is part of another emotion concept A (see, for example, Kövecses 1986, 1990, 1991a, 1991b). In cases like this, B can metonymically stand for A. This can explain why for instance the word *girlfriend* can be used of one's partner in a love relationship. Since love (A), at least ideally, involves or assumes friendship (B) between the two lovers, the word *friend* (an instance of B) can be used to talk about an aspect of love (A).

There is a large range of emotion concepts that are related to love. The concepts express, and also define, the range of attitudes we have toward the beloved. We can call them "related concepts." These concepts comprise literal general knowledge based on our various conception(s) of love (see Kövecses, 1988). Some of the most important related concepts for love include liking, sexual desire, intimacy, longing, affection, caring, respect, and friendship. Related concepts can be placed along a gradient of their centrality in the definition of an emotion concept, such as love; some of them appear to be inherent parts of the conception of love (such as liking and affection), some of them are only loosely associated with it, in that they are a part of some idealized model of love (such as friendship or respect), and some fall in between (such as caring). (For the linguistic justification of these claims, see Kövecses, 1988, 1990, 1991a).

## (2) Is There a "Master Metaphor" for Emotion?

The examination of emotion metaphors, such as the ones above, raises the issue of whether the conceptual metaphors that characterize particular emotions are isolated and independent of each other, or alternatively, they form some kind of a general system in the sense that they are instantiations of a generic or high-level superordinate metaphor? To put the same question more simply, we can ask, Is there a "master metaphor" for emotion?

As can be seen from the examples above, anger and love are characterized by an overlapping set of metaphors, including FIRE, INSANITY, NATURAL FORCE, BURDEN, and others. If two very different emotions such as anger and love share so much metaphorical structure, then we can expect other emotions (at least the basic, or primary ones, like fear, joy, sadness, and lust) to share just as much or more. Indeed, the study of such emotion concepts shows that there is a great deal of overlap among the metaphors that characterize them (Kövecses, 2000b). Given this, it might be the case that there exists a master metaphor for the emotions. But if it does exist, what could it be like? Len Talmy (1988) observed that many aspects of language can be profitably described and explained by what he called "force-dynamics" (Talmy, 1988). The description of an event in terms of force dynamics involves the following parts:

Force entities:
  Agonist
  Antagonist
Intrinsic force tendency:
  toward action
  toward rest (inaction)
Resultant of the force interaction:
  action
  rest (inaction)
Balance of strengths:
  the stronger entity
  the weaker entity

Let us now examine the most basic and skeletal emotion scenario in our folk theory of emotion. In this scenario, there is a cause that induces a person (self) to have an emotion, and the emotion causes the person to produce some response. In a schematic way, this can be given as:

*(1) a cause leads to emotion and (2) emotion leads to some response.*

Since we know from the Event Structure metaphor (Lakoff, 1990) that causes are conceptualized as forces (hence, CAUSES ARE FORCES), we can regard "cause" in part one and "emotion" in part two as forces. This then allows us to apply force dynamics to the emotion domain.

Let us first look at the first part of the scenario. If we think of the agonist as an entity that has an intrinsic force tendency toward inaction, that is, to stay inactive or at rest, the corresponding entity will be the self in the emotion domain; and if we think of the antagonist as an entity that has an intrinsic force tendency toward action, that is, to overcome the inaction of the agonist, to cause it to act, the corresponding entity will be the cause of emotion in the emotion domain.

Consider now the second part of the scenario, using the same definition of agonist and antagonist as before. If we think of the agonist as an entity that has an intrinsic force tendency toward inaction, the corresponding entity will be the self again, who will produce some kind of response. And if we think of the antagonist as an entity that has an intrinsic force tendency toward action, the corresponding entity will be the emotion itself. In other words, in both cases the emotion agonist will be the self (in that it becomes emotional in part one, and it produces a response in part two) and the emotion antagonist will be the cause of emotion in the first part and the emotion itself in the second part of the scenario. These instantiations of the abstract force-dynamic schema will apply to the majority of emotion metaphors (though not to all). Source domains that tend to focus on the first part of the basic emotion scenario are mostly PHYSICAL FORCES, either MECHANICAL or MAGNETIC. By contrast, source domains that tend to focus on the second part include OPPONENT, NATURAL FORCE, SOCIAL SUPERIOR, and the like. (For a more detailed discussion, see Kövecses, 2000b, chap. 5.)

Now let us take some conceptual metaphors and see how force dynamics applies to them. We can begin with EMOTION IS AN OPPONENT (IN A STRUGGLE). Consider some examples for this metaphor:

*Emotion is an opponent.*
*He was* seized by *emotion.*
*He was* struggling with *his emotions.*
*I was* gripped by *emotion.*
*She was* overcome by *emotion.*

There are two opponents in this struggle. As the first and third examples suggest, one opponent is inactive (the one that is seized and gripped all of a sudden). This is the agonist. The other, the one who seizes and grips, is active and attempts to cause opponent one to give in to his force. This is the antagonist. There is some struggle in which opponent one tries to resist opponent two's force and opponent two tries to make him give in to his force. There is the possibility of either opponent one winning or

**Table 21.1: Emotion is an opponent**

| *Metaphorical mapping* | *Agonist's force tendency* | *Antagonist's force tendency* | *Resultant action* |
|---|---|---|---|
| *Source* | Opponent 1 opponent 1's attempt to resist opponent 2 | Opponent 2 opponent 2's attempt to cause opponent 1 to give in to his force | either opponent 2 wins or opponent 1 wins |
| *Target* | Rational self self's attempt to try to maintain control | Emotion the emotion causing the self to lose control | self either loses or maintains control |

Source: OPPONENT IN A STRUGGLE
Target: EMOTION

opponent two winning. Corresponding to opponent one in the source is the rational self in the target, while corresponding to opponent two in the source is the emotion in the target domain. Corresponding to opponent one's force tendency in the source is the rational self's force tendency to try to maintain control over the emotion, and corresponding to opponent two's force tendency is the emotion's force tendency to cause the self to lose control. This force-dynamic interpretation can be represented in Table 21.1.

Next let us take the NATURAL FORCE metaphor. When this is applied to emotion, the underlying logic is that there is an extremely forceful entity (like wind, wave, storm, etc.) that affects a physical object and this object can't help but undergo its usually disastrous effects. When people say that they are *overwhelmed* by an emotion or that they are *swept off their feet*, it is this kind of effect that they imagine. This metaphor encapsulates perhaps the most deeply seated belief about emotions; namely, that we are passive and helpless in relation to them, just as physical objects are passive and helpless in relation to powerful natural forces acting on them. Schematically again, Table 21.2 captures all this.

The OPPONENT and NATURAL FORCE metaphors both focus on the second part of the skeletal emotion scenario—"emotion → response."

The last metaphor of emotion that I use to demonstrate the workings of force dynamics in the conceptualization of emotions is the EMOTION IS A PHYSICAL FORCE metaphor. This metaphor tends to have its main focus on the first part of the emotion scenario—"cause → emotion." It comes in a variety of forms (MECHANICAL, ELECTRIC, GRAVITATIONAL, MAGNETIC), which are illustrated with some examples below:

*EMOTION IS A PHYSICAL FORCE:*
*EMOTION IS A MECHANICAL FORCE; EMOTIONAL EFFECT IS PHYSICAL CONTACT*
*When I found out, it* hit *me* hard.
*That was a terrible* blow.
*She* knocked *me* off my feet.
*EMOTION IS A MAGNETIC FORCE*
*I was* magnetically drawn to *her.*
*I am* attracted to *her.*
*She found him* irresistible.
*That* repels *me.*

In the source domain, there is a physical object with the force tendency toward inaction, that is, to continue to be as before. There is also another force-exerting entity here, a physical force that has the force tendency to produce some effect in the object.

Correspondingly, there is a rational self that has the force tendency to stay as before (that is, unemotional), and there is a cause (of emotion) that has the force tendency to cause the self to become emotional. This situation is depicted by such examples as "The news *hit* me *hard*" or "I was *attracted to* her," where a cause of emotion acts on the rational self causing it to become emotional.

**Table 21.2: Emotion is a natural force**

| *Metaphorical mapping* | *Agonist's force tendency* | *Antagonist's force tendency* | *Resultant action* |
|---|---|---|---|
| *Source* | Physical object to keep being the same | Natural force to cause an effect in physical object | physical object undergoes effect in a passive way |
| *Target* | Rational self to continue to behave as before the emotion | Emotion to cause the self to respond to emotion | self responds to the emotion in a passive way |

Source: NATURAL FORCE
Target: EMOTION

Again, Table 21.3 presents this logic in diagrammatic form.

We can represent this interplay of forces in emotion as a conceptually richer version of our initial skeletal emotion scenario:

(1) *cause of emotion – force tendency of the cause of emotion <—> rational self – force tendency of self*
→ (2) *self has emotion*
→ (3) *self's force tendency <—> force tendency of emotion*
→ (4) *self's emotional response*

In this richer schema, it becomes clear that the various components of the emotion domain are conceptualized as forces that interact with each other. The schema shows that there are two main points of tension in the experience of emotion: the first taking place between the cause of emotion and the rational self, resulting in the emergence of emotion, and the second between the self that has the emotion but who is still in control over it and the force of the emotion, resulting in the self losing control and producing an emotional response. Most (though not all) metaphors in the emotion domain can be characterized as an interaction of forces. This leads to the conclusion that there exists a single master metaphor for emotion: EMOTIONS ARE FORCES. A large number of emotion metaphors are specific-level instantiations of this superordinate-level metaphor, each playing a somewhat different role in conceptualizing the emotion domain.

## (3) Are Emotion Metaphors Unique to the Emotions?

We have seen above that emotion metaphors are largely instances of a generic-level "master metaphor" EMOTION IS FORCE. However, it is another question whether the FORCE metaphor instantiated in a variety

**Table 21.3: Emotion is a physical force**

| *Metaphorical mapping* | *Agonist's force tendency* | *Antagonist's force tendency* | *Resultant action* |
|---|---|---|---|
| *Source* | Physical object to remain unaffected by force | Physical force to produce effect in object | object undergoes effect |
| *Target* | Self to remain unemotional | Cause of emotion to cause self to become emotional | self is emotional |

Source: PHYSICAL FORCE
Target: EMOTION

of ways is *specific to* the emotion domain. Theoretically, this possibility seems like a valid option. But to decide what is actually the case is an empirical question. We have to check whether the various FORCE metaphors identified for the emotion domain, such as PRESSURIZED CONTAINER, OPPONENT, NATURAL FORCE, BURDEN, and so on, are used in the conceptualization of domains other than the emotions.

Let us begin with the PRESSURIZED CONTAINER metaphor. It is clear that it has uses outside the emotion domain, such as when we talk about "trouble *brewing*" or a "situation being *explosive*." OPPONENT metaphors are not limited to the emotions either. In addition to "*struggling with* my emotions," I may be "*struggling with* differential equations." And the same goes for NATURAL FORCE, BURDEN, and all the other FORCE metaphors discussed earlier. This situation suggests a somewhat surprising conclusion; namely, that there seem to be no emotion-specific conceptual metaphors. The various FORCE metaphors we have looked at all appear to have applications outside the emotion domain, and in this sense cannot be regarded as emotion-specific.

More generally, it could perhaps be argued that our metaphorical conceptual system does not consist of domain-specific sets of metaphors. Instead, it seems to be structured by more extensive and inclusive metaphorical source domains, such as FORCE. Elsewhere, I point out that the FORCE metaphor characterizes not only the emotion domain but also morality and rational thought (see Kövecses, 2000b).

By claiming that the source domain of FORCE functions as a master metaphor for emotion and that its application extends beyond the emotions, I do not claim that some *other* metaphors of emotion cannot be emotion-specific. They can be. There are some source domains that seem to be both specific to a particular emotion and limited to the emotion domain. These include TRESPASSING, PHYSICAL ANNOYANCE for ANGER; HIDDEN ENEMY, SUPERNATURAL BEING for FEAR; BEING OFF THE GROUND, AN ANIMAL THAT LIVES WELL, PLEASURABLE PHYSICAL SENSATION for HAPPINESS; HAVING NO CLOTHES ON, DECREASE IN SIZE, BLOCKING OUT THE WORLD for SHAME. For example, trespassing leads to anger, dancing about (in being off the ground) indicates happiness, and decrease in size shows that the person is ashamed or embarrassed. How can we account for the emotion-specificity of these source domains?

I'd like to suggest that the specificity of the source domains derives from two factors. Some of them have to do with causes of emotion, whereas some of them have to do with effects of emotion. Both the causes and the effects in question appear to be unique to a given emotion. Thus, for example, it can be suggested that given the metaphor SHAME IS HAVING NO CLOTHES ON, having no clothes on is a potential cause for shame and it is typically associated with shame. Or, to take another example, dancing and jumping up and down (but not stomping your feet) is typically associated with joy/happiness and it is seen as a result or effect of this emotion; hence the metaphor HAPPINESS IS BEING OFF THE GROUND (which, unlike the "UP" metaphor, is not an evaluative "orientational metaphor" in the Lakoff-Johnson sense).

More generally, we can say that emotions can be, and are, comprehended via both their assumed typical causes and their assumed typical effects. When this happens, we can get emotion-specific metaphorical source domains. Here are some of the emotion-specific metaphors deriving from assumed typical causes and effects of particular emotions:

*EMOTION IS A CAUSE OF THAT EMOTION:*
*ANGER IS TRESPASSING*
*ANGER IS PHYSICAL ANNOYANCE*
*FEAR IS A HIDDEN ENEMY*
*FEAR IS A SUPERNATURAL BEING*
*A HAPPY PERSON IS AN ANIMAL THAT LIVES WELL*
*HAPPINESS IS A PLEASURABLE PHYSICAL SENSATION*
*SHAME IS HAVING NO CLOTHES ON*
*EMOTION IS AN EFFECT OF THAT EMOTION:*
*happiness is being off the ground*
*shame is a decrease in size*
*to be ashamed is to block out the world*

Although the particular source domains are unique to particular emotion concepts, the cognitive mechanism of understanding a state-event (in this case, an emotion state-event) in terms of its cause or effect is fairly general (see Kövecses, 1991b, 1994). The nature of this process is essentially metonymic (see Kövecses & Radden, 1998).

In sum, it appears that the major emotion metaphors, that is, which have some kind of FORCE as their source, apply outside the emotion domain and thus in this sense they are not emotion-specific. At the same time, there are some minor metaphors that appear to be emotion-specific. The justification for the distinction between major and minor metaphors is based on the constitutive role that the "major" metaphors play in the construction of emotion concepts.

## (4) How Do Emotion Metaphors Differ from Metaphors for Relationships?

If emotion concepts are characterized by the EMOTIONS ARE FORCES superordinate metaphor, we can ask which metaphor characterizes neighboring domains. A domain that is conceptually close to that of emotion is human relationships, including love, friendship, and marriage. Kövecses (1995a) looked at the American conception of friendship on the basis of a number of interviews conducted with several Americans. The linguistic data provided by the interviews indicate that there are a large number of conceptual metaphors (such as FRIENDSHIP IS A BUILDING) that apply to the American conception of friendship. The analysis of these metaphors also showed that they come from a small number of metaphorical systems: metaphors for Communication (e.g., COMMUNICATION IN FRIENDSHIP IS SHARING OBJECTS), for Emotion (e.g., EMOTIONAL INTENSITY IS TEMPERATURE, EMOTIONAL CLOSENESS IS PHYSICAL CLOSENESS), for States and Relationships (e.g., STATES ARE OBJECTS, RELATIONSHIPS ARE BONDS, INTERACTIVE RELATIONSHIPS ARE ECONOMIC EXCHANGES), for Complex Systems (e.g., ABSTRACT COMPLEX SYSTEMS ARE BUILDINGS/ MACHINES, etc.), for Events (e.g., LIFE IS A JOURNEY), and for Positive/Negative Evaluation (e.g., DESIRABLE ENTITIES ARE VALUABLE THINGS). Moreover, it was shown that these metaphors also apply to the conceptualization of other human relationships, in particular, to love and marriage. Love is a special case here because it functions both as an emotion and a relationship.

In each of these systems, we have a complex abstract concept as target domain and a simpler, nonabstract concept as a source domain. Communication is understood as the sharing of physical objects; emotions as physical phenomena (e.g., properties of physical objects); states as physical objects and relationships as bonds; complex abstract systems as complex physical objects; events as physical motion; and the property of being positive or negative as value or lack of value.

Now we are in a position to attempt to answer the question how the metaphorical conceptualization of emotion differs from that of human relationships, like friendship, love, and marriage. The specific-level source domains that can be found in the conceptualization of most human relationships include the following:

Sharing (experience) objects
Distance (close/distant)
Warmth
Bond
Economic exchange
Building
Implement
Machine
Plant
Journey
Valuable commodity

This list and the list of emotion metaphors do not provide a complete set of specific source domains for either human relationships or emotions; nevertheless, taking the lists above as a representative set of source domains for emotions and relationships, we can make some interesting observations.

There seems to be only a minimal overlap between the two sets. Human relationships share CLOSENESS and WARMTH with emotions. BURDEN from the emotion set may perhaps also apply to relationships since it has the general meaning of indicating any difficulty or stress. When characteristic emotion metaphors, that is, the FORCE-related ones, apply to human relationships, they usually have to do with love only – a human relationship that is also an emotion. This explains why there are only marginal cases of FORCE metaphors for friendship, which is, as studies show, regarded as a poor case of emotion. (It may be that some of the debate concerning whether love is or is not an emotion, or whether it is a basic emotion, is also attributable to this "double-nature" of love.) In her study of love, Baxter (1992) found that FORCE metaphors form the third largest group of metaphors for love, following metaphors related to WORK and JOURNEY. In our terms, it is the COMPLEX SYSTEMS metaphor that involves all the work-related aspects of friendship and relationships in general.

But the really important point is that, as we saw in the previous section, the emotion metaphors are predominantly "force-related" ones organized into a coherent system by the underlying master metaphor EMOTION IS FORCE. What is obvious at first glance is that the typical relationship metaphors are *not* FORCE metaphors (with the exception of love, as we noted). The question is, Is there a master metaphor underlying the various specific-level non-force metaphors for human relationships? JOURNEY seems to be a crucially important metaphor in the conceptualization of love and marriage, as the studies by Baxter (1992) and Quinn (1991) indicate. However, it appears to play only a marginal role in the comprehension of friendship.

The source domains for friendship on the list above that belong to robust metaphorical systems in our conception of relationships are SHARING (EXPERIENCE) OBJECTS, BONDS, and ECONOMIC EXCHANGE characterizing INTERACTIVE RELATIONSHIPS, on the one hand, and BUILDING, IMPLEMENT, MACHINE, and PLANT, on the other, characterizing COMPLEX ABSTRACT SYSTEMS. The category of INTERACTIVE RELATIONSHIPS is a conflation of what I called the "communication system" and the "state" system, respectively. The "state" system, as characterized above, includes states, relationships, and interactions. The metaphors for communication as analyzed above indicate that communication is viewed as a form of interaction, and as such it fits the INTERACTIVE RELATIONSHIP group naturally. The rest of the metaphorical source domains, such as BUILDING, MACHINE, IMPLEMENT, PLANT, for example, form the COMPLEX ABSTRACT SYSTEMS group (for details see Kövecses, 1995, 2000b). In other words, these are the two metaphor systems that stand out in the materials that have been examined.

The available evidence concerning human relationships points to the conclusion that it is these two large systems that organize most of our everyday understanding of what human relationships are. The bulk of the data presented in the studies mentioned above shows that much of the content and structure of our knowledge about relationships derives from the rich set of mappings that characterize the two systems. In this sense, we seem to have two underlying generic-level metaphors for human relationships: INTERACTIVE RELATIONSHIPS ARE ECONOMIC EXCHANGES and COMPLEX ABSTRACT SYSTEMS ARE COMPLEX PHYSICAL OBJECTS. Of the two, the latter appears to be the more pervasive and dominant one in the data, and thus, again in this sense, it can be regarded as the "master metaphor" for human relationships. However, it has to be noted that, unlike emotions, human relationships do not seem to be characterized by a single and clear-cut overarching master metaphor.

## (5) What Is the Role of Metaphors in the Cognitive Construction of Particular Emotion Concepts?

In order to answer the question in the title of this subsection, we have to look at some of the details of the relationship between "dominant," or "central," metaphors for emotion concepts, on the one hand, and the cultural models, on the other, that characterize these emotion concepts. I will take the emotion concept of ANGER as an example.

Lakoff and Kövecses (1987) characterized the naive, or folk, understanding of anger in English as a prototypical cognitive, or cultural, model. They suggested the following model based on linguistic evidence in American English:

1. *Offending event*

    *Wrongdoer offends self.*
    *Wrongdoer is at fault.*
    *The offending event displeases self.*

    *The intensity of the offense outweighs the intensity of the retribution (which equals zero at this point), thus creating an imbalance.*
    *The offense causes anger to come into existence.*

2. *Anger*

    *Anger exists.*
    *Self experiences physiological effects (heat, pressure, agitation).*
    *Anger exerts force on the self to attempt an act of retribution.*

3. *Attempt to control anger*

    *Self exerts a counterforce in an attempt to control anger.*

4. *Loss of control*

    *The intensity of anger goes above the limit.*
    *Anger takes control of self.*
    *Self exhibits angry behavior (loss of judgment, aggressive actions).*
    *There is damage to self.*
    *There is danger to the target of anger, in this case, the wrongdoer.*

5. *Retribution*

    *Self performs retributive act against wrongdoer (this is usually angry behavior).*
    *The intensity of retribution balances the intensity of offense.*
    *The intensity of anger drops to zero.*
    *Anger ceases to exist.*

The main idea here was that the metaphors and metonymies associated with anger converge on and constitute the model, with the different metaphors and metonymies mapping onto different parts of the model.

Native speakers of Hungarian seem to have the same cultural model of anger (*düh*). The *but*-test that Lakoff and Kövecses (1987) used to ascertain the validity of the model for English yields the same results for speakers of Hungarian as it does for speakers of English. For example, the sentence "He was angry, but he didn't lose control" and its Hungarian equivalent sound more natural than the sentence "He was very angry, but he lost control" in both languages. This is because the conjunction "*but*" is used to counter expectations. In this case, the expectation dictated by the prototypical model would be that once we're very angry (stage 2), we tend to lose control (stage 4). In other words, the applicability of the *but*-test indicates deviation from the prototypical cultural model. Since it indicates the same kinds of deviations in the two languages, it also shows that the underlying prototypical cultural models have a similar overall structure.

In the characterization of Japanese *ikari* (and, less typically, also *hara*), Matsuki (1995) notes in connection with the model found in American English: "The scenario applies to Japanese anger, although Stage 3 is more elaborate than in English" (p. 145). In the Japanese conception, the control aspect of *ikari* is more elaborate because anger first appears in *hara*, then it goes up to *mune*, and finally to *atama*. As Matsuki points out, *hara* is a container (the stomach/bowels area) and, metonymically (CONTAINER FOR CONTENT), can also be the emotion itself. *Mune* is the chest and *atama* is the head. If anger reaches *atama*, the angry person is unable to control anger.

King (1989) suggests that there are two prototypical cognitive models operating in Chinese:

1. *Offending event*

    *Wrongdoer offends self.*
    *The offending event displeases self.*
    *The offense causes an imbalance in the body.*

2. *Anger*

*Anger exists.*
*Self experiences physiological effects (heat, pressure, agitation).*

3. *Attempt to control anger*

*Self exerts a counterforce in an attempt to control anger.*

4. *Release of anger*

*Self releases anger by exhibiting angry behavior.*

5. *Restoration of equilibrium*

*The amount of discharged anger balances the excess in the body.*
*The imbalance disappears and equilibrium is restored.*

The other model differs from the one above in stages 4 and 5:

4. *Diversion*

*The force of anger is diverted to various parts of the body.*
*Self exhibits somatic effects (headaches, stomachaches, etc.)*

5. *Compensating event*

*The compensating event pleases the self (this is usually sympathetic behavior directed at self).*
*The intensity of compensation balances the intensity of the offense.*
*The somatic effects of anger disappear.*
*Anger ceases to exist.*

In addition to the several differences, we find several things in common among these models. They all seem to be composed of several successive stages, and they all seem to have an ontological, a causal, and an expressive aspect. Based on the characterizations given earlier, the following general structure of the respective emotion concepts (*anger*, *düh*, *ikari/hara*, and *nu*) can be identified.

The prototypical cognitive models have an *ontological* part that gives us an idea of the ontological status and nature of anger, that is, the kind of thing/event it is: in all four languages anger, or its counterpart, is a force inside the person that can exert pressure on him or her. The ontological part also includes some physiological processes associated with the respective emotion. It is the ontological part of the model that constitutes the second stage of the cognitive model or scenario as a whole.

The first stage in the model corresponds to the *causal* part. This presents anger and its counterparts as an emotion that is caused, or produced, by a certain situation.

Still another part of the model is concerned with the *expressive* component; that is, the ways in which anger, or its counterpart is expressed in the different cultures. The cognitive models tell us that all four cultures conceive of anger as something that is somehow expressed.

Finally, the expressive component is preceded by a *control* component that is manifested as two separate stages of the model: attempt at controlling expression and loss of control over expression.

Thus, the resulting five-stage model for the four cultures seems to be the following:

*(1) cause → (2) existence of anger, or its counterpart (in the form of a force) → (3) attempt at control → (4) loss of control → (5) expression*

(Here, the arrow → indicates temporal succession and causal sequence). Since expression and control are closely linked with each other (i.e., at issue is the control of expression), it is possible to conceive of the two as a single aspect and refer to them as the expression part of the model, yielding the highly schematic model:

*cause → existence of emotion (as forceful entity) → expression.*

This then seems to be the *most basic structure* that all four cultures share in their folk understanding. This is the generalized model of emotions that we saw in a previous section.

But how can metaphors create such a model? My suggestion is that this happens by means of the set of mappings that characterize conceptual metaphors. Some metaphors play a central role in defining a particular model for a concept. In the case of anger, the central metaphor that "lends" structure to the model of anger in a variety of cultures is that of THE ANGRY PERSON IS A PRESSURIZED CONTAINER. The particular structure that anger and other emotion concepts share is the "cause-existence of emotion-expression" schema. This is defined, in large part, by the PRESSURIZED CONTAINER metaphor that is characterized by the following mappings. (Unlike above, here the arrow → indicates simultaneous activation of elements in the source and the target, but, in a historical perspective, I would claim that the relationship between the simultaneously activated elements was also temporal and causal):

*the container with the substance (fluid or gas) → the person who is angry*
*the heat or pressure of the substance → the intensity of anger*
*the forceful substance in the container → the anger*
*trying to keep the forceful substance inside the container → trying to control the anger*
*the substance going out of the container → the involuntary expression of the anger*

I believe that these are the mappings that play a constitutive role in the construction of the basic structure of the folk understandings of anger and its counterparts in different cultures. Without these mappings (i.e., imposing the schematic structure of how the force of a fluid or gas behaves in a container onto anger), it is difficult to see how anger and its counterparts could have acquired the structure they seem to possess: a situation producing a force inside a person, and then the force causing the person to act in certain ways that should be suppressed. The "cause-emotion force-involuntary expression" structure remains a mystery and a completely random occurrence without evoking the PRESSURIZED CONTAINER metaphor. Through its detailed mappings, the metaphor provides a coherent structure for the concepts.

In the view presented here, the conceptual metaphors and metonymies contribute actively to the structure and content of the prototypical cultural models. To illustrate this with another example, consider Zulu. In Zulu, the chief conceptual metaphor that does the job of providing the skeletal structure for anger is a version of the PRESSURIZED CONTAINER metaphor: ANGER IS IN THE HEART (Kövecses, 2000a; Taylor & Mbense, 1998). However, just like in English, additional metaphors focus on particular aspects of this generic structure. In the case of Zulu anger, two metaphors are especially important for the "expression" part of the basic model, which specifies the nature and intensity of angry behavior. Speakers of Zulu elaborate on two metaphors that speakers of English do not (or do to a much smaller degree): ANGER (DESIRE) IS HUNGER and ANGER IS A NATURAL FORCE (Taylor & Mbense, 1998). If the metaphor DESIRE IS HUNGER is elaborated as voracious appetite that devours everything indiscriminately and NATURAL FORCE as a force that destroys everything, as is the case in Zulu, then this will probably influence the cultural model of anger, as is indeed the case according to Taylor and Mbense. Instead of venting their anger on a specific target (in English, the person who offended you), Zulu people appear to respond in a less clearly directed way and behave aggressively toward everyone indiscriminately. This is not to say that English cannot have this response or that Zulu cannot have the directed response; rather, the two languages seem to differ in what they consider the prototypical cultural model for the concept.

The major claim I am making here is this: Systematic links take us from (possibly universal) actual physiology of anger through conceptualized metonymy and metaphor to cultural models. In the process, the broader cultural contexts also play a crucial role, in that they fill out the details left open in the schematic basic structure. In other words, I believe that we can offer a satisfactory explanation of the emergence of cultural models of emotions if we take into account the possibly universal experiential basis of our emotion concepts, the conceptualization of this experiential basis by means of conceptual metonymies, the conceptual metaphors that often derive from these metonymies, and the broader cultural context. The central conceptual metaphor in the case of anger is the PRESSURIZED CONTAINER metaphor (and the generic FORCE metaphor for the emotions in general; see Kövecses, 2000b), but other domains, such as human relationships, would be structured by other central or "master" metaphors.

We should of course not imagine the process of the emergence of cultural models in sequential steps, going from experiential basis to cultural model. A probably more adequate way of thinking about it would be to say that the components I outlined here are all at work at the same time, mutually influencing each other. In the course of this joint evolution, the conceptualized experiential basis (often appearing as conceptual metonymies) and the emerging conceptual metaphors contribute to the basic schematic structure of the cultural model, while the simultaneously present cultural context fleshes out the details of the schema.

## (6) Are Emotion Concepts and Emotion Metaphors Universal?

It might seem in light of what was said in the previous section that I am suggesting that emotion concepts and metaphors are in general universal. Although we find a great deal of commonality in emotion concepts and metaphors both across languages/cultures and through time (see Kövecses, 2005), we can see a great deal of variation as well. The interesting question is, How does this variation come about if emotion concepts and metaphors are embodied in universal human experience? I will discuss three possible reasons for this (based on Kövecses, 2005).

### *Variation as a result of differential framing*

Let us take lust, or sexual desire, as an example. In English, the concept is commonly conceptualized as heat (of fire) (Kövecses, 1988; Lakoff, 1987). This gives rise to such conventionalized expressions as the following:

She's *burning with* desire.
I've got the *hots* for her.
He's *on fire* for her.

The linguistic examples of the LUST IS HEAT metaphor are based on the mappings below:

*The thing that is hot (from fire) → the lustful person*
*The heat → the lust*
*The degree of the heat → the intensity of the lustful feeling*

These are the main mappings that characterize the metaphor as it is used in English. In the metaphor, both the lust of the lustful person and that of the person who is lusted after can be viewed as *hot*. The degree of the heat indicates the intensity of the sexual desire on the part of either person.

In contrast, in Chagga, an African language spoken in Tanzania, the LUST IS HEAT metaphor is understood differently (Emanatian, 1995). Consider the following examples taken from Emanatian:

*Nkeóka*
*"She roasts."*
*Nékeha*
*"She burns."*

As can be seen, all three examples are about women. The meaning of the expressions is given by Emanatian as "She is sexually desirable." This contrasts markedly with English where a similar expression involving intense heat would mean something like "She has intense feelings of lust." The next Chagga example does not indicate intense sexual desire either, as a corresponding English expression would, but again sexually desirable qualities:

*Náworé 'úshangu lo móro*
*"She has a 'heaven' of fire."*
*She has desirable sexual attributes (skills, natural endowments, interests)*
*The lack of these qualities is expressed by the notion of coldness:*
*Kyamúya rikó lilya*
*"She's cold."*
*She lacks desirable sexual attributes.*

What is particularly interesting about these examples is that the SEX IS HEAT metaphor, though it employs the same source domain as the corresponding English metaphor, provides a differential perspective on sexuality in comparison to English: The target domain to which it applies is slightly changed (it involves male sexuality only) *and* the source domain is employed differently in Chagga than in English. In other words, the domain of sexuality is framed differentially in the two languages despite the same source domain that is employed. To see the exact details of this, here are the mappings of the Chagga SEX IS HEAT metaphor:

*the thing/substance burning → the woman with the desirable sexual qualities*
*warmth or heat of the thing/substance → desirable sexual qualities of a person*
*the person who observes the burning thing → the man who finds a woman sexually desirable*

Thus, we find that differences in the English and Chagga mappings for roughly corresponding metaphors (SEXUAL DESIRE IS HEAT and SEX IS HEAT) result from differential framings in both the source and the target domains. This is remarkable because the same universal physiology seems to support roughly the same metaphor in two cultures with the source and target being framed differently in the two languages.

### *Variation as a result of differential experiential focus*

The notion of "experiential focus" is intended to be a general explanation of why even highly embodied metaphors may vary across languages and time (Kövecses, 2005). The basic idea is this: Embodiment may consist of a variety of aspects, or components, and any of these may become the preferred one in a given culture and at a given time. Which aspect(s), or component(s), of (otherwise) universal embodiment receive(s) more attention from speakers of a language largely depends on the broader cultural context.

A case in point is the conceptualization of anger in English and Chinese. As studies of the physiology of anger across several unrelated cultures show, increase in skin temperature and blood pressure are universal physiological correlates of anger. This accounts for the ANGER IS HEAT metaphor in English and in many other languages. However, King's (1989) and Yu's (1995, 1998) work suggest that the conceptualization of anger in terms of heat is much less prevalent in Chinese than it is in English. In Chinese, the major metaphors of anger seem to be based on pressure, not on pressure *and* heat. This indicates that speakers of Chinese have relied on a different aspect of their physiology in the metaphorical conceptualization of anger than speakers of English. The major point is that in many cases the universality of experiential basis does not necessarily lead to universally equivalent conceptualization—at least not at the specific level of hot fluids, in the case of anger.

Another example of how different cultures utilize a presumably universal bodily basis in anger is offered by Michelle Rosaldo in her description of Ilongot anger (Rosaldo, 1980). The Ilongot are a former headhunting tribe living in Northern Luzon, Philippines. For young Ilongot men, anger, *liget*, is a highly energized state that they need in order to successfully accomplish their headhunting raids. In Rosaldo's words: "The *liget* that Ilongots associate with youthful prowess and, for them, with the universal agitation that makes young men want to kill, takes on reality and significance because it is bound up not in mystery or cosmology, but in three forms of relation central to Ilongot social life" (Rosaldo, 1980, 138).

Indeed, Rosaldo glosses the Ilongot term for anger as "energy/anger." This suggests that for the Ilongot anger (*liget*) figures as a generalized state of arousal that can sufficiently motivate their actions. They think of their anger also as hot but, most importantly, as an agitated and energized state that makes them want to go out and take heads. Clearly, this is, for us, a surprisingly different way of building on our presumably universal bodily experience in conceptualizing anger.

Finally, there may be cultures where people clearly have a universal physiological component, and yet the conceptualization of anger or other emotion concepts is only marginally based on metaphors or metonymies. One such language is Tsou (an Austronesian language spoken in parts of Taiwan), where the emotions are primarily expressed linguistically through an elaborate prefix system attached to emotion *verbs* (not nouns). But as Shuanfan Huang (2002), the linguist who studied the language, tells us even in this language there exists the conceptual metaphor ANGER IS EXCESS AIR or FIRE IN A CONTAINER.

### *Variation as a result of differential experiential focus through time*

Let us now consider how historical change may influence which metaphors are used in a particular language. We can start the discussion of this issue with the following question: Do cognitive linguists suggest that universal embodiment necessarily leads to the same application of a source domain to a particular target through time? Work by Caroline Gevaert (2001) demonstrates that the conceptualization of anger changed considerably from the Old English to the Middle English period. On the basis of a variety of corpora, she showed that heat-related words account for only 1.59% of all the words describing anger before 850. The number of heat-related words for anger dramatically increases in the period between 850 and 950. Then the number of these words decreases between 950 and 1050 to 6.22% and then to 1.71% by around 1,200, and then to 0.27% by around 1300. After 1300, the number starts growing again, and after 1400, it becomes dominant in texts that describe anger. As has been noticed in previous work (see, e.g., Kövecses, 1986; Lakoff, 1987; Lakoff & Kövecses, 1987), heat-related words account for a large portion of all the expressions that are used to talk about anger in present-day English.

What do Gevaert's findings tell us then? Her findings indicate that the conceptualization of anger in terms of heat is not a permanent feature of the concept of anger in English, but that it can, and does, fluctuate in the course of the development of English. This is an extremely important finding because it bears directly on the issue of universality of metaphorical conceptualization across time. If the conceptualization of anger in terms of heat is a mechanical or automatic consequence of our real physiology in anger, this fluctuation should not occur. It cannot be the case that people's physiology changes in anger every one or two hundred years or so. How can we account for this fluctuation then? Is there an answer that is consistent both with the cognitive linguistic view of embodiment and with the obvious changes in conceptualization of anger through time?

I believe the answer is that universal physiology provides only a *potential* basis for metaphorical conceptualization—without mechanically constraining what the specific metaphors for anger will be. Heat was a major component in the concept of anger between 850 and 950, and then after a long decline, it began to play a key role again at around 1400—possibly as a result of the emergence of the humoral view of emotions in Europe (see Geeraerts & Grondelaers, 1995; Gevaert, 2001, 2005). We can notice the same kind of fluctuation in the use of the domain of "swell," which I take to be akin to what we call the "pressure" component in the conceptualization of anger today. Pressure was a major part of the conceptualization of anger until around 1300, but then it began to decline, only to emerge strongly again, together with heat, in the form of the HOT FLUID IN A CONTAINER metaphor centuries later. The point is that we should not expect any of the *conceptualized* responses associated with anger to remain constant in conceptualizing anger (and the emotions in general) throughout the ages. Experiential focus may change across time even within the same language.

More generally, what I would like to emphasize here is that universal embodiment associated with a target domain may consist of several distinct components, or aspects. The conceptual metaphors that emerge may be based on one component, or aspect, at a certain point of time and on another at another point of time. Which one is chosen depends on a variety of factors in the surrounding cultural context. Moreover, the conceptual metaphors may be based on one component, or aspect, in one culture, while on another component, or aspect, in another culture.

## Conclusions

There are two conclusions I wish to highlight. First, emotion metaphors largely fall under the generic-level metaphor: CAUSES ARE FORCES. The still generic-level instance of this metaphor is EMOTIONS ARE FORCES. Such generic force metaphors can be described by means of Talmy's force dynamics and apply to many domains outside emotion. In this sense, there are no emotion-specific metaphors that are of major significance in the conceptualization of emotions. The specific source domains of OPPONENT, NATURAL FORCE, CAPTIVE ANIMAL, HEAT, and so on apply to a much wider range of target concepts in the conceptual system. This suggests a hierarchical organization for how we make use of metaphorical conceptualization. Such an organization can take the form of either generic to specific within a single hierarchy (which seems to be the case for emotion) or generic to specific in a number of different hierarchies (which seems to be the case for friendship). Second, I suggest that despite the universality of bodily experience on which many of our more specific emotion metaphors (such as LUST IS HEAT and THE ANGRY PERSON IS A PRESSURIZED CONTAINER) are based, we get a large amount of nonuniversality in the metaphorical conceptualization of emotion. This is because either the framing or the experiential focus of the source domains may vary from culture to culture.

## References


Baxter, L. A. (1992). Root metaphors in accounts of developing romantic relationships. *Journal of Social and Personal Relationships*, 9, 253–275.

Emanatian, M. (1995). Metaphor and the expression of emotion: The value of cross-cultural perspectives. *Metaphor and Symbolic Activity*, 10, 163–182.

Geeraerts, D., & Grondelaers, S. (1995). Looking back at anger: Cultural traditions and metaphorical patterns. In J. Taylor & R. MacLaury (Eds.), *Language and the cognitive construal of the world* (pp. 153–179). Berlin: Gruyter.

Gevaert, C. (2001). Anger in Old and Middle English: a 'hot' topic? *Belgian Essays on Language and Literature*. pp. 89–101.

Gevaert, C. (2005). *The* ANGER IS HEAT *question: Detecting cultural influence on the conceptualization of anger through diachronic corpus analysis*. In N. Delbecque, J. van der Auwera and D. Geeraerts (Eds). *Perspectives on variation: Sociolinguistic, historical, comparative* (pp. 195–208). Berlin: Mouton de Gruyter.

Huang, S. (2002). Tsou is different: A cognitive perspective on language, emotion, and body. *Cognitive Linguistics*, 13(2), 167–186.

King, B. (1989). *The conceptual structure of emotional experience in Chinese*. PhD diss., Ohio State University.

Kövecses, Z. (1986). *Metaphors of anger, pride, and love: A lexical approach to the study of concepts*. Amsterdam: John Benjamins.

Kövecses, Z. (1988). *The language of love: The semantics of passion in conversational English*. Lewisburg, PA: Bucknell University Press.

Kövecses, Z. (1990). *Emotion concepts*. Berlin: Springer-Verlag.

Kövecses, Z. (1991). A linguist's quest for love. *Journal of Social and Personal Relationships*, 8, 77–97.

Kövecses, Z. (1994). Tocqueville's passionate "beast": A linguistic analysis of American democracy. *Metaphor and Symbolic Activity,* 9(2), 113–133.

Kövecses, Z. (1995a). American friendship and the scope of metaphor. *Cognitive Linguistics* 6, 315–346.

Kövecses, Z. (1995b). Anger: Its language, conceptualization, and physiology in the light of cross-cultural evidence. In J. R. Taylor & R. MacLaury (Eds.), *Language and the cognitive construal of the world* (pp. 181–196). Berlin: Mouton.

Kövecses, Z. (1999). Does metaphor reflect or consitute cultural models? In R. Gibbs & G. Steen, eds., *Metaphor in cognitive linguistic.* (pp. 167–188). Amsterdam: John Benjamins.

Kövecses, Z. (2000a). The scope of metaphor. In A. Barcelona (Ed.), *Metaphor and metonymy at the crossroads* (pp. 79–92). Berlin: Mouton.

Kövecses, Z. (2000b). *Metaphor and emotion.* New York: Cambridge University Press.

Kövecses, Z., & Radden, G. (1998). Metonymy: Developing a cognitive linguistic view. *Cognitive Linguistics,* 9(7), 37–77.

Lakoff, G. (1987). *Women, fire, and dangerous things: What categories reveal about the mind.* Chicago: University of Chicago Press.

Lakoff, G. (1990). The invariance hypothesis: Is abstract reason based on image schemas? *Cognitive Linguistics,* 1, 39–74.

Lakoff, G., & Johnson, J. (1980). *Metaphors we live by.* Chicago: University of Chicago Press.

Lakoff, G., & Kövecses, Z. (1987). The cognitive model of anger inherent in American English. In D. Holland and N. Quinn (Eds.), *Cultural models in language and thought* (pp. 195–221). Cambridge: Cambridge University Press.

Matsuki, K. (1995). Metaphors of anger in Japanese. In J. R. Taylor & R. MacLaury (Eds.), *Language and the cognitive construal of the world* (pp. 137–151). Berlin: Mouton.

Quinn, N. (1991). The cultural basis of metaphor. In J. Fernandez (Ed.), *Beyond metaphor. The theory of tropes in anthropology* (pp. 56–93). Stanford, CA: Stanford University Press.

Rosaldo, M. (1980). *Knowledge and passion: Ilongot notions of self and social life.* Cambridge: Cambridge University Press.

Talmy, L. (1988). Force dynamics in language and cognition. *Cognitive Science,* 12, 49–100.

Taylor, J., Mbense, T. (1998). Red dogs and rotten mealies: How Zulus talk about anger. In A. Athanasiadou & E. Tabakowska (Eds.), *Speaking of emotions: Conceptualization and expression* (pp. 191–226). Berlin: Mouton.

Yu, N. (1995). Metaphorical expression of anger and happiness in English and Chinese. *Metaphor and Symbolic Activity* 10: 223–245.

Yu, N. (1998). *The contemporary theory of metaphor: A perspective from Chinese.* Amsterdam: John Benjamins.

CHAPTER 22

# Putting It in Context

## Metaphor and Psychotherapy

*Linda M. McMullen*

### Much Is Made of Metaphor, and Little Has Been Learned

Such might be a pithy evaluation of what are, for the most part, two parallel literatures on the use of metaphor in psychotherapy. On the one hand, there is a conceptual or theory-based, practice-oriented literature directed at therapists and that is primarily focussed on articulating presumed functions of metaphor in psychotherapy and on ways for therapists to make deliberate use of metaphor. This literature is often filled with directives for therapists as to how to employ metaphors, with case examples illustrating the use of metaphors, with examples of problem-targeted metaphors that are embedded in narratives, and with bold claims as to the effectiveness of metaphors in promoting client change. In this literature, there is an assumption that the functions of metaphor are isomorphic with the goals of psychotherapy; hence, the appropriate and strategic use of metaphor is claimed to advance the aims of therapy. Much is made of metaphor.

On the other hand, there is an empirical literature that is typically focussed on either the client's use of metaphor or the joint use by client and therapist. Some of this literature is based on quantitative analyses, and some on qualitative analyses. As with the conceptual or theory-based, practice-oriented literature, the focus is on explicating how the use of metaphor in psychotherapy is related to outcome or to important aspects of the process of therapy. However, in the empirical literature, which is quite small in comparison to the conceptual or theory-based, practice-oriented literature, different questions are asked, different definitions are used, and different methods are employed across studies, and, typically, the findings are rather disappointing in the sense that predictions are not confirmed or the evidence is not particularly convincing. As there is no replication of studies or even little use of common research strategies from one study to the next, claims are sometimes contradictory or tied too specifically to the study to be of much value. It would not be unreasonable for a reader of this literature to conclude that the empirical investigation of metaphor use in psychotherapy, particularly in terms of its relation to outcome, is either too difficult or misguided. Little has been learned.

In this chapter, I consider two questions. First, what leads writers in this area to attribute such power to metaphor? Second, what is it about the empirical investigation of metaphor use in psychotherapy that has resulted in a rather limited advancement of knowledge? In addressing these two questions, I argue that the practice of isolating metaphors for special consideration, of failing to analyse the conversational exchanges and cultural discourses of which they are a part, and of ignoring the situated nature of psychotherapy has led to claims that are unwarranted or trite. I suggest that we need more seriously to take context into account in both our conceptual or theory-based writings and in our empirical investigations in order to understand more fully what participants in psychotherapy do with metaphors.

## The Power of Metaphor

Psychotherapy is considered a particularly fertile space for the study of metaphor and other forms of figurative language (e.g., simile, personification, hyperbole).[1] With its reliance on the exchange of words between a client and a therapist, this form of intervention (at least as it is typically practised in most westernized contexts) is a site that demands the use of words to accomplish various actions, usually conceptualized in terms of a facilitation of change in the client through the mutual work of the client and the therapist. Such work often involves the use of new words or the development of familiar words in new ways, and, as such, metaphors – both conventional and novel instances – typically abound in this context.

Beginning with some of the earliest writings on the functions of metaphors in psychotherapy, much has been claimed with regard to the power of metaphor in the work of psychotherapy. Lenrow (1966) outlined several functions served by metaphors, including referring to and highlighting subtle social roles that a client takes, simplifying events in a way that allows certain elements to be emphasized more than others, fostering a climate that permits therapists to communicate about intimate characteristics of the client in a non-intrusive way, and providing a model of trying out new ways of understanding that can be applied to future situations. Fine, Pollio, and Simpkinson (1973), in building on the functions articulated by Lenrow (1966), emphasized the capacity of metaphor (and other forms of figurative language) for enabling clients to express what has previously been inexpressible, to fill the gap between what they are able to communicate about how they feel and what they may be actually experiencing. To illustrate their point, Fine et al. provided the example of a client who, in trying to communicate a puzzling sensation to her therapist, said that her "heart was a basketball being bounced up and down" (p. 89). Using this metaphor elicited a response from the therapist that communicated a recognition of the fear of having something that big inside him whose movement was not under his control, a response which, according to Fine et al., was received by the client as empathic and understanding.

Going beyond the expressive and communicative functions of metaphor, Pollio, Barlow, Fine, and Pollio (1977) focussed on how employing novel metaphors to talk about problems in a new and unusual way can serve to make explicit what has previously been implicit, thereby facilitating problem description and resolution, and Barlow, Pollio, and Fine (1977) alluded to how a therapist's use of the client's metaphors can both ease the tension and anxiety common to therapy and facilitate problem solving. As support for their argument, Barlow et al. illustrated how a client and a therapist delicately embraced the difficult topic of the client's anger and impotence through a series of new and elaborated metaphors. In part of their illustrative excerpt, the client used the metaphor of wearing "a white hat," which was a reference to his self-presentation as a helper and rescuer and then subsequently elaborated this metaphor by saying that "the white hat" has "sort of turned gray" and is getting "a little dirty" (p. 216) which was understood as an acknowledgement that, at times, he is not nice. In response, the therapist introduced the notion of the client being afraid that "an angry monster" would be exposed if the "white hat" were taken off, to which the client, in turn, responded with the metaphor of "the mouse that roared," a well-formed figure that was thought to tap into a sense of his own ineffectualness. Barlow et al. interpreted this sequence as evidence of how metaphors are implicated in the disclosure of revealing material, in the articulation of problems, and in the development of insight.

This focus on the power of metaphor to facilitate the work of psychotherapy continues in the literature 25–35 years after the appearance of these early articles. In a paper published in 1995, Cirillo and Crider outlined what they considered to be four varieties of metaphorical communication: (1) making a point vividly with an implied comparison, for example, referring to a family member as "a bulldog" as a way of capturing his or her stubbornly determined behaviour; (2) accommodating disparate interests through multiple meanings, for example, describing a relationship as "a tennis match" as a way of capturing both its competitive nature and the opportunities it provides for achievement and mastery; (3) changing perspectives on a topic with borrowed terminology, for example, a therapist fashioning a metaphor from something a client previously said in order to draw an analogy about a current situation; and (4) using a novel combination to create or reveal something new, for example, imagining oneself as the various features of a rosebush as a way of exploring rejected or unknown aspects of the self. They linked these four varieties to specific therapeutic aims, such as capturing complex emotional themes in concise and memorable ways, uniting diverse intentions and bridging disparate conflicting interests of individuals or groups, reframing problems, and discovering new possibilities for feelings and behaviour.

Similarly, Lyddon, Clay, and Sparks (2001) claimed that metaphors can play a significant role in facilitating at least five developmental change processes: (1) by being sensitive to a client's metaphors, a therapist can convey understanding of the client's ways of knowing and can contribute to the development of a shared language and collaborative relationship; (2) by symbolizing emotions that have been previously unexpressed, unexplored, or unrecognized, the use of metaphors can assist clients in constructing new personal meanings of their experience; (3) because metaphors can highlight and make vivid that which has previously been unspoken and unexplored, they can assist in uncovering and challenging tacit assumptions; (4) metaphors may enable clients to access new information about themselves in indirect ways, and may assist therapists in helping clients to express and examine painful feelings and experiences in a manner that minimizes resistance; and (5) metaphors might serve as devices for discovery by facilitating the client's awareness of previously unknown aspects of the self or of the self's relationships with others, and by creating new possibilities for action.

In this literature, claims about metaphor are aligned with a common view of language and its power. Specifically, as noted by Guerin (2003), "that what language does is to refer, represent, communicate, or express and that the power of language to do these things is somehow contained in the words themselves" (p. 251). In the context of psychotherapy, metaphors are thought to *refer* to views of the self and others, to the social roles enacted by clients and others, to ways of thinking and feeling, and to the central problems in the client's life. Similarly, they are thought to *represent* or symbolize emotions, tacit assumptions, and less-than-conscious experiences. Because of their symbolic nature, metaphors are also claimed both to assist clients in being able to *express* that which is difficult to put into words and to speak, and to enable therapists to say that which might be difficult for clients to hear. The referential, representational, and expressive capacities of metaphors are thought further to promote *communication* between client and therapist as they assist in the development of a shared language over the course of therapy.

According to these claims, much can be accomplished with metaphors. In essence, metaphors can assist all of the work of psychotherapy. They can provide information about the client, can foster a collaborative relationship between the client and the therapist, and can facilitate new ways of talking, thinking, and understanding.

Similar claims are made in the practice-oriented literature, although in some instances the power of metaphor is stated even more explicitly and strongly. This literature spans a variety of theoretical perspectives, including cognitive therapy (Muran & DiGiuseppi, 1990), depth psychotherapy (particularly, Jungian and psychoanalytic perspectives; Kopp, 1995; Siegelman, 1990), strategic therapy (Haley, 1973), and Ericksonian psychotherapy (e.g., Close, 1998; Combs & Freedman, 1990; Pearce, 1996), with the bulk of the writings based in depth psychology and Ericksonian principles.

The focus on the power of metaphor in the tradition of depth psychology has typically been framed in terms of how metaphor makes possible the communication and interpretation of unconscious meaning (Arlow, 1979). In some early writings, Ekstein and colleagues (as cited in Arlow, 1979) claimed that the use of metaphor enabled patients (primarily those labelled borderline or psychotic) to maintain a distance from anxiety-provoking content, and that the therapist's subsequent use of the patient's metaphors in the interpretation of the patient's conflict would prevent the patient from experiencing severe anxiety or panic. While other writers (e.g., Forrest, 1973) also emphasized the capacity of metaphor to reveal the nature of a patient's character structure and defences as well as his or her unconscious fantasies, some (e.g., Wright, 1976) claimed that metaphor reveals the ego in its creative operations, integrates the conscious and the unconscious, and leads to a new vision.

More recent writings in this tradition have emphasized not only the capacity of metaphor both to reveal and to protect, and to join the new with the unknown, but also its unique utility for communicating emotions and other sensorimotor states and for enabling interpersonal connection. One of Siegelman's (1990) primary claims is that "affect and metaphor are closely connected" (p. 6), and that clients often make use of metaphors and other forms of figurative language when they want to convey strong affect that cannot be easily communicated in other ways. For example, in trying to capture the physical sensations and interpersonal consequences of an expression of anger, a client might say, "I stab people with my voice." If a therapist is able to stay with such metaphors and encourage the client to explore them, the client's level of experiencing and the potential for insight are believed to expand. Similarly, Kopp (1995) claimed that when therapists encourage clients to stay with their own metaphors and expand and elaborate them, clients will be moved to deeper levels of experiencing and will gain meaning and insight. Vivona (2003) added another element to this possibility by claiming that metaphors not only embrace and bridge verbal and sensorimotor experience but also allow the client and the therapist to embrace each other, thereby enabling interpersonal as well as intrapsychic connection. In a detailed account of her work with a female client in psychotherapy, Vivona (2003) illustrated how the client's metaphor that others expected her to be "a doll with no insides" provided a means for linking her bodily act of wrist-cutting with her desire to show her therapist what was inside her. Building on this metaphor, Vivona's empathic articulation of her own decision not to look at her client's wounded wrist (It's "as though I don't want to see your insides") and her subsequent expression of her client's disappointment at not being physically touched by her ("The touch of words is not the same as the touch of hands") was understood as a joint experience of the power and limitations of their relationship.

Although depth psychology theorists typically emphasize what can be learned from the content of client-generated metaphors and how the therapist's careful work within these metaphors can lead to change [see Kopp (1995) and Siegelman (1990) in particular], theorists and practitioners who base their work on the principles articulated by Milton Erickson typically emphasize the strategic use of therapist-generated metaphors. In this literature, the power of metaphor is claimed to lie in its capacity for indirect communication, or what Barker (1996) labelled "outflanking maneuvers" (p. 14). For example, Combs and Freedman (1990) maintained that interacting with clients in metaphor allows the therapist to gather information indirectly, thereby avoiding much of the awkwardness and defensiveness that can occur when information about sensitive issues is asked for directly. In addition, they claimed that the indirection of metaphor allows therapists to embed new ideas and suggestions for future action in a way that permits clients to try new patterns of thinking, feeling, and behaving without having to commit consciously or openly to them. For instance, in working toward a goal of changing a client's approach to sexuality from being a self-absorbed performance to involving sensitivity and accommodation to a partner, a therapist might intersperse suggestions about sex in discussions with the client about another "love" of his life – woodworking – that does, in fact, engender expressions of tenderness and caring.

Other writers in this tradition are more graphic and expansive in their claims of what metaphor can do. For Barker (1996), metaphor "may serve to enrich virtually any communication process" (p. 23), and, according to Pearce (1996), "is worth hours of conversation in uncovering the client's past" (p. 10), "liberates both client and therapist from preconceived notions" (p. 5), and "permeates, facilitates, and, in some ways, redefines the client-therapist relationship" (p. 6).

A large literature exists in the Ericksonian tradition in which the construction and delivery of therapeutic metaphors is detailed. In much of this literature, metaphors are situated within narratives. Some writers stop short of specifying the content of therapeutic metaphor and prefer, instead, to outline basic principles of the construction of metaphors. For example, Barker (1996) maintained that it is important to consider the social, cultural, and vocational background of the client in determining the content of a metaphor, but also claimed that in designing and using a metaphor, the therapist should take into account the language style, vocabulary, and primary sensory channels used by the client in processing information. Noting whether the client uses visual (e.g., "I see what you mean"), auditory (e.g., "That sounds pretty bad"), or kinaesthetic predicates (e.g., "That feels about right") and responding with similar language is proposed as potentially being helpful. Barker further claimed that the successful delivery of a metaphor whose content and form are designed for a particular client is dependent on such prerequisites as an adequate level of rapport between therapist and client, preparation of and agreement by the client for the use of such an approach, the establishment of agreed upon goals for therapy, confidence in the use of metaphor on the part of the therapist, and good timing and pacing.

Other writers go further and not only specify the techniques for implementing a metaphor but provide an anthology of therapeutic narratives directed at particular problems. Pearce (1996) listed several considerations that he claimed should be taken into account in the therapeutic use of metaphor, including identifying the repetitive and self-defeating nature of the client's problem, the choice of sensory modality in which the metaphor should be delivered, the cadence and tone that should be used, the deliberate interspersing of focussed words (e.g., the client's name), embedding commands in a way that focuses the client's attention, and avoiding explanation. He then provided a compendium of narratives that provides practitioners with a thematic inventory of metaphoric material to use in various situations. Similarly, Burns (2001) constructed an entire book of stories that are oriented to particular problems experienced by clients (e.g., fear, anger, uncertainty, relationship difficulties, loss, inferiority) and to particular desired outcomes (e.g., empowerment, acceptance, learning from experience, attaining goals, engaging in self-care, experiencing happiness). Although Burns (2001) cautioned against a verbatim, prescriptive, fixed, and universal use of these metaphoric stories, he nevertheless suggested that they might provide useful themes for future work with clients, and provided guidelines for therapists to employ in developing and administering their own metaphors.

Like those writers who make claims about the functions of metaphors, writers who direct their work primarily to practitioners adopt a model of language that is focussed on its referential, representational, expressive, and communicative power. Some of these writers also emphasize the determinative power of language. For example, Siegelman (1990) claimed that metaphors "not only reflect past experience but also become filters that regulate how we see our present experience and how we project our future" (p. 65). Others (e.g., Barker, 1996; Pearce, 1996) have claimed that metaphors are indirect strategies for getting clients to do things. Regardless, it is still the metaphor, itself, – its content and its production – that is a source of power.

There is much about the enterprise of psychotherapy and about metaphor that conspires to support such a position. Psychotherapy has historically been known as the "talking cure." Typically, clients are thought to reveal important aspects of themselves, and therapists are thought to be able to affect change in clients, through *what* is said and *how* something is said. The content and form or style of client and therapist language is, then, thought to be the heart of most types of psychotherapy. As Russell (1987) stated, "the identification of what is said in psychotherapy with what is done in psychotherapy" (p. 1) is commonplace.

Having established the use of language as pre-eminent in the work of psychotherapy, the question becomes, "What is it about metaphor, specifically, that enables so much to be claimed?" Consistent with theses developed by scholars of metaphor (see Tilley, 1999), writers in this area have focussed on the expressibility, vividness, and compactness of metaphor. For some (e.g., Sunderland, 1997–98), it is the symbolism and imagery of metaphor that gives it power, particularly in the sense of enabling the imagination to be put into action (Tilley, 1999). For others (e.g., Martin, Cummings, & Hallberg, 1992), it is its concrete, graphic nature, its potential to draw attention to itself, to stand out and be memorable. And for others (e.g., Pearce, 1996), it is its dual capacity for compact, concise communication and for multiple meanings and interpretations. Given the nature and scope of metaphor, it becomes possible (and perhaps even easy) to make claims about how it functions to further the work of psychotherapy, as is particularly evident in the work of Cirillo and Crider (1995) and Lyddon et al. (2001).

The weakness in these writings is not that writers have categorically extolled the power of metaphor. Indeed, many (see, for example, Burns, 2001; Siegelman, 1990) have urged psychotherapists against an overly zealous and rigid approach to working with clients' metaphors or to developing their own metaphors, and have underscored that metaphors are just one form of communication to be attended to in psychotherapy. What is problematic is that by focussing on the referential, representational, expressive, communicative, and even determinative power of metaphors, what is said and how it is said have too often not been adequately situated. In essence, a focus on words has taken precedence over a focus on talk and, in particular, on talk as a form of situated action. Not focussing on what metaphor is actually accomplishing in a particular client–therapist conversation can consequently result in claims about the functions of metaphors that are not adequately grounded in evidence.

In line with this focus on the content and form of metaphor, the evidence that is presented to support the claims about the power of metaphor often consists of a summarized account of the client's and therapist's use of a particular metaphor, coupled with brief fragments of actual client and therapist talk, or a metaphorical story that serves to illustrate how a problem might be approached. What is not adequately available and rarely, if ever, analysed are the contexts in which the use of metaphor in psychotherapy is situated.

Specifically, we typically do not ask the following kinds of questions: (1) How does the enterprise and practice of psychotherapy, as situated in a particular historical, cultural, and social context, influence a client's and a therapist's choice of and engagement with metaphors? For example, I have found that metaphors of the self as hostile and submissive (e.g., "I'm weak," "I'm down," "I caved in," "I put up walls") and of others as hostile (e.g., "He's cold," "She lashed out," "He jumped on me") are particularly prominent in psychotherapy as it is typically practised in contemporary western societies, i.e., on an outpatient basis with persons experiencing problems related to autonomy and intimacy. However, how these problems are addressed (e.g., by dream work, homework assignments, gender analysis) and how the corresponding metaphors are attended to and taken up might differ depending on the theoretical orientation of the therapist (e.g., psychoanalytic, cognitive-behavioural, feminist), the time frame of the therapy (e.g., open-ended vs. time-limited), and the participants' willingness to engage with metaphors. Who participates in which sanctioned activities for what purposes are features of context that should receive attention in our investigations. (2) When a particular metaphor is used, how is it received, and how is it further shaped by its effects on the listener? For example, does the therapist ask for elaboration of a particularly evocative metaphor produced by a client (e.g., "What do you mean when you say you put yourself out in the firing line and are shot down by people?"), or does he or she ignore the metaphor or use it as a stimulus for resisting the client's presentation (e.g., "Maybe you get a thrill by being in the firing line")? (3) How does metaphor work in conjunction with other rhetorical devices to achieve particular ends? For example, consider the potential for misunderstanding when the metaphoric phrase "My mother's a saint" is stripped of factual and intonational details and taken at face value, rather than understood as an expression of sarcasm. Without a more detailed and nuanced analysis of metaphor in context, this area of study runs the risk of being plagued by what Guerin (2003) has deemed "misleading, tautological, and vacuous theorizing" (p. 251). Having drawn attention to the use of metaphor in psychotherapy as an area worthy of study is a potentially important move on the part of past contributors. However, to move beyond the tautological stance that "metaphor is important in psychotherapy because it promotes the goals of therapy," a different position is now needed.

## The Limits of Metaphor Research

Empirical research on metaphor and psychotherapy has been guided, for the most part, by broad questions about how the content and use of metaphor facilitate the process of psychotherapy and/or are related to the eventual outcome of the therapy. Except for those studies in which data from post-session inquiry interviews were analysed (e.g., Angus & Rennie, 1988, 1989; Rasmussen, 2000; Rasmussen & Angus, 1996), this research almost exclusively entails the analysis of metaphors used in actual sessions of psychoanalytically oriented, psychodynamic, Gestalt, or process-experiential psychotherapy [see Martin et al. (1992) for an exception].

The accumulated findings of this research underscore the highly contextualized nature of metaphor use. Some studies have been based, in part, on rates of production of metaphors (and other forms of figurative language) and/or on the distinction between novel and frozen metaphors, with an assumption that novel metaphors do the work in psychotherapy. These studies have shown that overall use of metaphors varies across clients, therapists, and sessions, and is not consistently related to outcome. For example, in the analysis of a single, highly successful case of Gestalt therapy, Pollio and Barlow (1975) found that the client used more instances of figurative language than did the therapist; Hill and Regan (1991) also reported that, across eight cases of brief psychotherapy, clients used more metaphors than therapists. In a comparison of the use of novel figurative language (mainly metaphors) over the first two, middle two, and last two sessions of one successful and one unsuccessful case of psychotherapy, I found that, regardless of outcome, the therapists' use of novel figures (e.g., "You could bottle your anger forever until it becomes a fine old wine") was higher than that of the client (McMullen, 1985). Contrary to expectation, Angus (1996) reported that clients and therapists in three good outcome cases of brief dynamic psychotherapy produced proportionally fewer novel metaphors than their counterparts in poor outcome cases. In contrast, Amira (1982) found that rate of production of novel figures failed to discriminate successful from unsuccessful cases of psychodynamically oriented psychotherapy.

Research focussed on whether and how clients and therapists make use of each other's metaphors has also revealed significant variability in such usage. In addition, in many of the cases that appear in the literature, sharing or co-elaboration of a metaphor was not very common and was not necessarily found to be a marker of the kind of therapy process that is thought to produce change. For example, Hill and Regan (1991) reported that in their single-case study of a client and a therapist who used a large number of metaphors, the client repeated only 3% of therapist-introduced metaphors within the same session, while the therapist repeated 13% of client-introduced metaphors. Similarly, I found the extent to which clients in successful cases "took up" therapist-introduced instances of figurative language (e.g., "You've got yourself in an emotional stranglehold") to be minimal in an absolute sense (McMullen, 1985, 1989). In terms of outcome comparisons, I found a successful and an unsuccessful case of psychotherapy to be differentiated by the extent to which the client repeated more instances of figurative language introduced by the therapist versus self-introduced figures (McMullen, 1985). Specifically, the client with the unsuccessful outcome repeated more of her own figures (e.g., "Women can be ballsy"), while the client with the successful outcome repeated figures originally introduced by the therapist (e.g., "I don't want to be numbed"). Alternatively, I found other cases of successful and unsuccessful psychotherapy to be similar in that the clients consistently used many more of their own figures (e.g., "I've been burned by others," "I'm the trophy of the rhinoceros you put on your mantle," "I'm balking in life," "My fiancée's pulling a good-sized net around me") than therapist-introduced figures (McMullen, 1989). Typically, this way of analysing how metaphors are employed has not revealed differences in therapists' use in relation to therapy outcome. Specifically, therapists have been found to use their own and the clients' figures to roughly the same extent or to repeat and elaborate their own figures (McMullen, 1985, 1989).

Although extended bursts of the use of figurative language by clients have been found to relate to problem setting and problem solving (Pollio & Barlow, 1975), it is also clear that the repeated use and/or elaboration of a particular metaphor within a particular session does not always signal a productive process. From a study in which clients and therapists were asked to recall their thoughts and feelings during times when a metaphor was used in a recently conducted session of psychotherapy, Angus and Rennie (1988) constructed two patterns of metaphoric communication: one that was labelled "meaning conjunction" and was associated with the development of a mutually shared understanding of the meaning of metaphor, and one that was labelled "meaning disjunction" and was associated with a joint misunderstanding of the meaning of a metaphor. In the former, the therapist's figurative elaboration of a client's daydream about destroying the therapist's office (i.e., "You act like a neglected child") and his curiosity about the client's associations to it seemed to signal a mutual understanding and to open up new ways for the client to appreciate the metaphor. In the latter, the therapist's repeated engagement with a client's metaphor (e.g., "an ogre") was much like a Socratic dialogue (e.g., "Do you see how it seems to be like it's either you act [like a good guy] or you're an ogre?"), and appeared to be designed to influence the client to identify what the therapist had already decided was the "true" way to understand what was being talked about.

Similarly, Rasmussen and Angus (1996) constructed two core categories from an analysis of post-session inquiry interviews focussed on metaphor sequences in single sessions of psychoanalytically oriented psychotherapy (two with clients labelled as borderline and two with clients labelled non-borderline). One category, which was termed a "representational mode of interaction" and was characteristic of dyads with the non-borderline clients, involved the use of metaphors whose meanings were previously negotiated by the client and the therapist and contributed to a shared therapeutic vocabulary. The other category which was termed a "literal mode of interaction" and was characteristic of dyads with the clients labelled as borderline involved the use of metaphors whose meanings had not been previously negotiated and did not provide stability or reflect a shared therapeutic vocabulary. A further analysis of the data generated from the inquiry into the use of metaphoric sequences by these therapists, however, revealed mixed results in terms of the impact of these sequences on the clients and on the therapeutic process (Rasmussen, 2000). In only one case of a client labelled as non-borderline was the therapist's metaphor ("cut to the bone") interpreted as empathically resonating with the client's experience of feeling raw and exposed over the loss of a relationship and as effectively communicating a sense of attunement. In the other three cases, the therapist's metaphor was either not understood or was interpreted as failing to have the desired effect. For example, rather than leading to an examination of the client–therapist relationship, a therapist's query, "But have you ever felt kind of backed against the wall in here at all?" led the client to begin a conversation about issues of confidentiality and procedures around record-keeping.

Evidence that metaphor use is related both to what are considered productive and not-so-productive aspects of psychotherapy process is also found across other studies. For example, Pollio and Barlow (1975) and Pollio et al. (1977) reported that novel figurative language co-occurred or alternated with expressions of insight on the part of the client, and Hill and Regan (1991) reported that the therapist's use of metaphors co-occurred with his self-rated intention to encourage insight on the part of the client and to provide support to the client. Similarly, both Hill and Regan (1991) and Martin et al. (1992) found that therapists' interventions involving metaphors were rated as more helpful by the participants than were other interventions. In a cross-case analysis of metaphors thought to be related to depression, Levitt, Korman, and Angus (2000) reported that, in comparison with the client in the poor outcome case, the client in the good outcome case had higher levels of experiencing when using metaphors of being "burdened." However, Hill and Regan (1991) reported that, contrary to expectation, the client in their study was rated at a lower level of experiencing when she was using metaphors (e.g., "I feel like jumping off a roof," "I'm at rock bottom") than when she was not. In a study focussed on the use of novel figures of speech in three sessions from each of seven cases of psychodynamic therapy, Stuart (1997) found that novel figures (e.g., "This man . . . and I got along like two strange bull dogs") sometimes accompanied increased experiencing on the part of the client, but most often coincided with decreasing experiencing. Both Hill and Regan (1991) and Stuart (1997) interpreted their findings as indicating that some metaphors can be used for defensive purposes, that is, to avoid the expression of painful emotions or to "permit expression without full experiencing" (Stuart, 1997, p. 234).

In general, a shift away from a straightforward analysis of overall rates of production and shared usage, from distinctions of type (frozen versus novel) and from global predictions about metaphor use and therapy process variables in the empirical research, has been accompanied by a recognition that a focus on the analysis of therapy-relevant metaphors might be a productive line of investigation. Following from my own (McMullen, 1989) and others' (Angus & Rennie, 1989) conclusions that metaphors of the self, of others, and of interpersonal relationships are central in psychotherapeutic talk, I used the interpersonal circumplex (e.g., Kiesler, 1985; Leary, 1957) as a way of classifying clients' metaphors of the self's and others' interpersonal actions. In an analysis of 21 cases of psychodynamically oriented psychotherapy, I found that the majority of clients in good outcome cases used metaphors that presented their own actions as friendly and dominant (e.g., "I'm a social animal," "I stand up to others"), while the majority of clients in poor outcome cases used metaphors that presented their actions as submissive and hostile (e.g., "I'm a doormat," "I exploded last night") (McMullen & Conway, 1994). In addition, clients in these same outcome groupings were further differentiated on the basis of their use of what I called "metaphors of the self," specifically, metaphors of being "fragmented" versus being "together" or "whole." Although all of these clients, regardless of outcome status, used metaphors that presented the self as "fragmented" or as composed of "parts," those clients who benefited more from psychotherapy spoke of a misplaced, nascent, or wounded, but nevertheless, existing or possible self (e.g., "I feel like I've lost [a] part of me," "I think my scabs are in good order, but my scars are still sensitive"), while those clients who benefited less presented metaphoric images of not being anchored in the self and of having repudiated certain parts of themselves to the point that these parts were constructed as unknown to, or deeply separate from, other parts (e.g., "I just really don't know . . . how to find myself," "I'm a stranger to myself," "I'm incomplete . . . parts of me that would contribute a wholeness are just blocked off") (McMullen & Conway, 1996). Levitt et al. (2000) also reported that they were able to distinguish a good from a poor outcome case of process-experiential psychotherapy on the basis of how metaphors linked to depression were developed over the course of therapy. Specifically, in the good outcome case, metaphors of being "burdened" were transformed into metaphors of "unloading the burden," while no such transformation was evident in the poor outcome case.

The idea that an analysis of metaphors can capture the significant themes in a particular case of psychotherapy and can be used to chart the progress of psychotherapy has resulted in the development of new methods of analysis and in illustrative case studies. For example, Ingram (1994) developed a hierarchically structured method for analysing metaphoric content and themes and illustrated how this structure could be used to identify specific functions of metaphors, such as serving as stages that lead the client to realize a central dilemma, explicating a central dilemma, and epitomizing the nature of the client's conflict. By moving from a content area, through themes and higher-order themes, and eventually to a central theme, this hermeneutic method focuses the analysis both on what is talked about and on what the text (or psychotherapy transcript) is about. In an analysis of a single session of psychoanalytic psychotherapy in which a client's metaphors linked to being "my own prisoner" were prominent, Ingram (1994) illustrated how "significant figures are those that encompass and explicate content areas, themes, and higher order themes that contribute to the central theme" (p. 284).

In a similar but less structured way, Angus and colleagues (Angus, 1996; Angus & Korman, 2002) conducted intensive analyses of metaphors in which metaphor phrases from transcripts of psychotherapy sessions are identified and, on the basis of thematic similarities, sorted into clusters which are then organized into crosscutting thematic categories. From the analysis of a single case of good outcome, brief dynamic psychotherapy (Angus, 1996), and from two good outcome cases of brief experiential psychotherapy (Angus & Korman, 2002), they concluded that a core set of metaphor themes predominated in each case (primarily "RELATIONSHIP AS WAR OR CONFLICT"), that these themes evolved as therapy progressed, and that, in all themes, change occurred in a nonlinear, dialectical fashion in that clients tended to oscillate from one session to the next in their use of subcategories of the metaphor theme.

What seems clear from nearly 30 years of research is that researchers have moved from a highly decontextualized approach to studying the use of metaphors in psychotherapy to a recognition that both what is said using metaphors and how it is said might be a more productive focus. I want to argue, however, that this latter focus, in its present form, is also quite limiting. For example, establishing that significant or key metaphors are those that are related to, or contribute to, the development of a central theme in a particular case of psychotherapy can be reduced to tautology in that the determination of what constitutes a central theme must inevitably be based on a consideration of both the literal and the metaphoric language used by the client and the therapist. In addition, showing that the content of therapy-related or core metaphors can differentiate cases of poor outcome from those with good outcome and that this content can change over time perpetuates a narrow, decontextualized focus only on the referential and representational aspects of language. Not only is this kind of analysis based on small fragments of metaphoric phrases extracted from a stream of client and therapist talk but also meaning is overshadowed by content.

What is missing in these approaches is a recognition that content is located in particular contexts and that it can have multiple functions or meanings. As argued by Eubanks (2000), "we cannot know what a metaphor means unless we know the circumstances in which the metaphor is uttered – by whom and to whom. . . . Use . . . is precisely what we must consider in order to understand any metaphoric expression" (pp. 17–18). Although some of the work of Angus and her colleagues (specifically, Angus & Rennie, 1988, 1989; Rasmussen, 2000; Rasmussen & Angus, 1996) has focussed attention on how metaphors could be used in different ways and have different impacts, their line of work has not been pursued, in any significant or direct way, by other researchers. As such, their findings remain limited to the analysis of a small number of metaphor sequences in a small number of psychotherapy sessions.

### *The Promise and Challenges of a Contextual Approach to Metaphor and Psychotherapy*

Some scholars and researchers in this area have concluded that a contextual approach to understanding the use of metaphor in psychotherapy is needed. For example, in building on a previous call that research into the functions of metaphor take into account the context and goal of discourse (Crider & Cirillo, 1991), Cirillo and Crider (1995) stated that "the more interesting and effective future research will examine metaphors in context, delimiting them carefully in terms of structure and interpretation, and documenting patterns of relationship between specific contexts, therapeutic goals, and effects of metaphor" (p. 518). Similarly, Rasmussen (2000) concluded that "it is . . . important to emphasize that the use of metaphor is embedded in an ongoing and exceedingly complex clinical process. Consequently, the study of metaphor in the clinical situation needs to be kept in context to account for this complexity" (p. 372).

What would a contextual approach to studying metaphor in psychotherapy entail? This question is, by no means, simple, and my response will inevitably be incomplete. However, my purpose in considering it is to draw attention to the need for a more particularized and nuanced conceptualization of metaphor in psychotherapy and for a more situated empirical approach. To begin with, a different perspective on language needs to be adopted, one in which words are not taken to be a source of power to make things happen (Guerin, 2003) but in which language is understood as "[deriving] its significance in human affairs from the way in which it functions within patterns of relationship" (Gergen, 1994, p. 52), including both microsocial exchanges and broad patterns of cultural life. Viewing language not in terms of its referential, representational, expressive, or communicative functions, but rather in terms of its strategic use, requires that we focus on what talk between a speaker and a listener in a particular context is accomplishing [see Gergen (1994) for a fuller account of the correspondence versus social constructionist view of language].

One way to begin thinking about what a contextual approach would entail is to start not with a focus on metaphors, per se, but rather on events of clinical interest, for example, on identity talk, on empathic ruptures, on therapist challenges, on client sadness. Given the pervasiveness of metaphors, there is a high likelihood that these events will be constituted, in part, by metaphors; if not, the very absence of metaphors might be informative. Taking the focus off metaphors, per se, could have a dual effect of grounding our analyses in what are considered to be clinically relevant questions and of lessening the practice of analysing decontextualized fragments of talk, as is typically the case in empirical research, or of presenting summary descriptions of the use of metaphors as stand-alone interventions, as is often the case in the conceptual, or theory-based, professional literature.

After having defined and identified events of interest, one way of keeping the study of metaphor situated would be to adopt the practices used by discourse analysts. Although there is a great deal of diversity in the theoretical and ideological underpinnings of different versions of discourse analysis (e.g., conversation analysis, critical discourse analysis, discursive psychology, Foucauldian discourse analysis), what is relevant to the present discussion is that discourse analysis requires a focus on discursive practices, that is, on what people are doing with their talk, and/or on discursive resources, that is, what it is that people draw on when they talk (Willig, 2001). Exploring what people are doing with their talk and how this work is being done involves an analysis of "how the discourse is structured or organized to perform various functions and achieve various effects or consequences" (Wood & Kroger, 2000, p. 95). Identifying the interpretative repertoires (Potter, 1996, p. 116) or systematically related sets of terms that people draw on when they talk keeps a focus on the wider social and institutional frameworks within which discourse is produced. In such an approach, metaphors are understood as one of many analytical concepts that are employed by a speaker to perform certain actions. As such, any particular metaphor can have multiple meanings, perform a variety of functions, and be a defining feature of socially and culturally available resources of interpretation.

With this approach, metaphors would not be isolated and extracted for analysis. Rather, they would be considered as one of several discursive devices that are variously used and drawn upon to meet certain goals. These goals may or may not be of analytic relevance to a researcher interested in a particular set of events in psychotherapy, and any particular instance of a metaphor may or may not further these goals. However, once having determined that an event containing a metaphor sequence is of analytic interest, this sequence must be kept in context during analysis. Doing so would require that a researcher have knowledge of how the meanings of any particular metaphor have been understood and developed (perhaps over several therapy sessions), and determine through a focus on a sequence of consecutive exchanges between a client and a therapist how the metaphor functions with other discursive devices (including non-metaphoric devices) to achieve certain goals.

This kind of analysis would then need to be placed in a broader set of ethnographic observations and interpretations. Specifically, as Guerin (2003) argued, we need to document the social, economic, historical, and cultural contexts of events being studied. In this case, we need to be more explicit about the kind of social influence process that constitutes psychotherapy as practised in a particular time and place, about the circumstances under which any particular person seeks psychotherapy, and about the therapist's understanding of his or her role.

For example, applying a contextual approach to some of my recent work on the talk of depressed women in psychotherapy (McMullen, 1999) would require that I begin not with an analysis of metaphors, per se, but rather with a topic of clinical interest, such as how acts of self-condemnation and self-affirmation are constituted in the conversations between the women and their therapists. In selecting instances of such acts for analysis, I might notice that many of these instances include metaphors of "mothering" and of "being child-like." Although I might choose to limit my analysis to conversational sequences containing these metaphors, I would need to rely on entire transcripts (or audio tapes) of the course of psychotherapy to develop an understanding of what a client means, for example, when she metaphorically refers to herself as "Aunt Susan," as "a three-year-old," or as "smothering my husband with mother love." Specifically, I would need to rely on literal language as well as on entailments of these metaphors in developing my understanding.

Making an argument that metaphors of "mothering" and of "being child-like" are implicated in acts of self-condemnation and self-affirmation would require, in addition to understanding the meaning of a particular metaphor, evidence of how the metaphor is taken up and jointly developed by the client and the therapist in multiple conversations in which these acts are accomplished. Such evidence would include an analysis of how various rhetorical devices (e.g., narratives, non-verbal acknowledgements, humour) are used in conversation by the client and the therapist in the service of endorsing the metaphor, rejecting it, or negotiating its interpretation.

Understanding psychotherapy as an asymmetrical interpersonal influence process in which one person (the client) is expected to disclose personal problems to another person (the therapist) who is expected to provide expert guidance with respect to these problems would be crucial for limiting any claims I might make about how self-condemnation and self-affirmation are performed discursively. In addition, in a contextual approach, the question of what supports the availability of metaphors of "mothering" and of "being child-like" as sites for self-condemnation and self-affirmation by women in some contemporary western societies would be necessary to address. For instance, I might cite evidence of the simultaneous prizing and devaluing of mothers and children (e.g., Caplan, 1989; McMahon, 1995; Zelizer, 1985) in these societies as an interpretative framework for my analysis.

## Conclusion

All metaphors are not equal in their contribution to the work of psychotherapy. If we are to add to both our conceptual and empirical understandings of the use of metaphor in psychotherapy, we need to adopt an approach that permits an articulation of the range of such contributions. I have argued that the largely decontextualized approaches used to date have led to claims that are over-reaching or banal. In particular, claims about the power of metaphor in psychotherapy are possible precisely because metaphors have been isolated and extracted from the talk of which they are a part, and our research findings are limited because the highly contextualized nature of metaphor in client and therapist talk has not been adequately recognized. These specific outcomes reflect the fact that metaphor theory and metaphor research, in general, have largely ignored the conversations that surround and subsume metaphors (Eubanks, 2000).

The literature on metaphor and psychotherapy illustrates the pitfalls of doing decontextualized metaphor analysis.

However, it also has the potential to draw the metaphor researcher's attention to the importance of situating one's analysis. I fully acknowledge the enormous challenge and necessarily partial nature of adopting an approach that takes context seriously for, as Crider and Cirillo (1991) correctly asserted, "any context specified could itself be embedded in a context" (p. 188). Nevertheless, with a more situated analysis (both in the local and in the broader sense) might come more nuanced and mutually informing theoretical and empirically based developments.

## Note

1 Given the preponderance of the use of metaphors in psychotherapy (as opposed to other figures of speech), there is a tendency in the literature to equate metaphor with figurative language in general. In keeping with the dominant trend (and unless otherwise indicated), I use "metaphor" in an inclusive way and as interchangeable with "figurative language."

## References


Amira, S. A. (1982). Figurative language and metaphor in successful and unsuccessful psychotherapy (Doctoral dissertation, Vanderbilt University, 1982). *Dissertation Abstracts International*, 43, 1244B.

Angus, L. E. (1996). An intensive analysis of metaphor themes in psychotherapy. In J. S. Mio & A. N. Katz (Eds.), *Metaphor: Implications and applications* (pp. 73–84). Mahwah, NJ: Lawrence Erlbaum Associates.

Angus, L. E., & Korman, Y. (2002). Conflict, coherence, and change in brief psychotherapy: A metaphor theme analysis. In S. Fussell (Ed.), *The verbal communication of emotions: Interdisciplinary perspectives* (pp. 151–165). Mahwah, NJ: Lawrence Erlbaum Associates.

Angus, L. E., & Rennie, D. L. (1988). Therapist participation in metaphor generation: Collaborative and non-collaborative styles. *Psychotherapy*, 25, 552–560.

Angus, L. E., & Rennie, D. L. (1989). Envisioning the presentational world: The client's experience of metaphoric expression in psychotherapy. *Psychotherapy*, 26, 372–379.

Arlow, J. A. (1979). Metaphor and the psychoanalytic situation. *Psychoanalytic Quarterly*, 48, 363–385.

Barker, P. (1996). *Psychotherapeutic metaphors: A guide to theory and practice*. New York: Brunner/Mazel.

Barlow, J. M., Pollio, H. R., & Fine, H. J. (1977). Insight and figurative language in psychotherapy. *Psychotherapy: Theory, Research and Practice*, 14, 212–222.

Burns, G. W. (2001). *101 healing stories: Using metaphors in therapy*. New York: Wiley.

Caplan, P. J. (1989). *Don't blame mother: Mending the mother-daughter relationship*. New York: Harper and Row.

Cirillo, L., & Crider, C. (1995). Distinctive therapeutic uses of metaphor. *Psychotherapy*, 32, 511–519.

Close, H. T. (1998). *Metaphor in psychotherapy: Clinical applications of stories and allegories*. San Luis Obispo, CA: Impact.

Combs, G., & Freedman, J. (1990). *Symbol, story, and ceremony: Using metaphor in individual and family therapy*. New York: W. W. Norton & Company.

Crider, C., & Cirillo, L. (1991). Systems of interpretation and the function of metaphor. *Journal for the Theory of Social Behaviour*, 21, 171–195.

Eubanks, P. (2000). *A war of words in the discourse of trade: The rhetorical constitution of metaphor*. Carbondale: Southern Illinois University Press.

Fine, H. J., Pollio, H. R., & Simpkinson, C. (1973). Figurative language, metaphor, and psychotherapy. *Psychotherapy: Theory, Research and Practice*, 10, 87–91.

Forrest, D. V. (1973). On one's own onymy. *Psychiatry*, 36, 266–290.

Gergen, K. J. (1994). *Realities and relationships: Soundings in social construction*. Cambridge, MA: Harvard University Press.

Guerin, B. (2003). Language use as social strategy: A review and an analytic framework for the social sciences. *Review of General Psychology*, 7, 251–298.

Haley, J. (1973). *Uncommon therapy: The psychiatric techniques of Milton H. Erickson, M.D.* New York: Norton.

Hill, C. E., & Regan, A. M. (1991). The use of metaphors in one case of brief psychotherapy.

*Journal of Integrative and Eclectic Psychotherapy*, 10, 56–67.

Ingram, J. L. (1994). The role of figurative language in psychotherapy: A methodological examination. *Metaphor and Symbolic Activity*, 9, 271–288.

Kiesler, D. J. (1985). *The 1982 interpersonal circle: Acts version*. Unpublished manuscript, Virginia Commonwealth University.

Kopp, R. R. (1995). *Metaphor therapy: Using client-generated metaphors in psychotherapy*. New York: Brunner/Mazel.

Leary, T. (1957). *Interpersonal diagnosis of personality*. New York: Ronald Press Company.

Lenrow, P. B. (1966). Use of metaphor in facilitating constructive behavior change. *Psychotherapy: Theory, Research and Practice*, 3, 145–148.

Levitt, H., Korman, Y., & Angus, L. (2000). A metaphor analysis in treatments of depression: Metaphor as a marker of change. *Counselling Psychology Quarterly*, 13, 23–35.

Lyddon, W. J., Clay, A. L., & Sparks, C. L. (2001). Metaphor and change in counseling. *Journal of Counseling and Development*, 79, 269–274.

Martin, J., Cummings, A. L., & Hallberg, E. T. (1992). Therapists' intentional use of metaphor: Memorability, clinical impact, and possible epistemic/motivational functions. *Journal of Consulting and Clinical Psychology*, 60, 143–145.

McMahon, M. (1995). *Engendering motherhood: Identity and self-transformation in women's lives*. New York: Guilford.

McMullen, L. M. (1985). Methods for studying the use of novel figurative language in psychotherapy. *Psychotherapy*, 22, 610–619.

McMullen, L. M. (1989). Use of figurative language in successful and unsuccessful cases of psychotherapy: Three comparisons. *Metaphor and Symbolic Activity*, 4, 203–225.

McMullen, L. M. (1999). Metaphors in the talk of "depressed" women in psychotherapy. *Canadian Psychology*, 40, 102–111.

McMullen, L. M., & Conway, J. B. (1994). Dominance and nurturance in the figurative expressions of psychotherapy clients. *Psychotherapy Research*, 4, 43–57.

McMullen, L. M., & Conway, J. B. (1996). Conceptualizing the figurative expressions of psychotherapy clients. In J. S. Mio & A. Katz (Eds.), *Metaphor: Implications and applications* (pp. 59–71). Mahwah, NJ: Lawrence Erlbaum Associates.

Muran, J. C., & DiGiuseppe, R. A. (1990). Towards a cognitive formulation of metaphor use in psychotherapy. *Clinical Psychology Review*, 10, 69–86.

Pearce, S. S. (1996). *Flash of insight: Metaphor and narrative in therapy*. Needham Heights: MA: Allyn and Bacon.

Pollio, H. R., & Barlow, J. M. (1975). A behavioral analysis of figurative language in psychotherapy: One session in a single case study. *Language and Speech*, 18, 236–254.

Pollio, H. R., Barlow, J. M., Fine, H. J., & Pollio, M. R. (1977). *Psychology and the poetics of growth: Figurative language in psychology, psychotherapy, and education*. Hillsdale, NJ: Lawrence Erlbaum.

Potter, J. (1996). *Representing reality: Discourse, rhetoric and social construction*. London: Sage.

Rasmussen, B. (2000). Poetic truths and clinical reality: Client experiences of the use of metaphor by therapists. *Smith College Studies in Social Work*, 70, 355–373.

Rasmussen, B., & Angus, L. (1996). Metaphor in psychodynamic psychotherapy with borderline and non-borderline clients: A qualitative analysis. *Psychotherapy*, 33, 521–530.

Russell, R. L. (Ed.). (1987). *Language in psychotherapy: Strategies of discovery*. New York: Plenum Press.

Siegelman, E. Y. (1990). *Metaphor and meaning in psychotherapy*. New York: Guilford.

Stuart, J. J. (1997). Novel figurative language and patient experiencing in psychodynamic therapy. *Psychotherapy Research*, 7, 219–237.

Sunderland, C. C. (1997–98). Brief group therapy and the use of metaphor. *Groupwork*, 10, 126–141.

Tilley, C. (1999). *Metaphor and material culture*. Oxford, UK: Blackwell Publishers.

Vivona, J. M. (2003). Embracing figures of speech: The transformative potential of spoken language. *Psychoanalytic Psychology*, 20, 52–66.

Willig, C. (2001). *Introducing qualitative research in psychology: Adventures in theory and method*. Buckingham, UK: Open University Press.

Wood, L. A., & Kroger, R. O. (2000). *Doing discourse analysis*. Thousand Oaks, CA: Sage.

Wright, K. J. T. (1976). Metaphor and symptom: A study of integration and its failure. *International Review of Psychoanalysis*, 3, 97–109.

Zelizer, V. A. (1985). *Pricing the priceless child: The changing social welfare of children*. New York: Basic Books.

CHAPTER 23

# Metaphor and Psychoanalysis

*Antal F. Borbely*

## Introduction

Over the course of three decades of research, various cognitive disciplines have explored the phenomena of metaphor and metonymy, aiming at a deeper understanding of the role they play in human language, thought, and, more recently, artificial intelligence. This research has led to an increasing consensus that the mind inherently functions metaphorically (Lakoff & Johnson, 1980) and metonymically (Dirven, 1993; Gibbs, 1999). If the claim that the mind functions metaphorically turns out to be valid, it will come as no surprise that concepts, theories, and disciplines dealing with mental functioning all contain, explicitly or implicitly, a centrally important notion of metaphor. Here we shall focus on psychoanalysis and delineate the very close relationship between its key psychodynamic terms on the one hand and metaphor and metonymy on the other.

Despite cognitive scientists' recent emphasis on embodied experiential categories of thought as unconsciously established and processed (Lakoff, 1987; Lakoff & Johnson, 1980, 1999; Rosch, 1978; Varela, Thomson, & Rosch, 1991), they have paid scant attention to psychoanalytic theory. Psychoanalysts, for their part, have generally not helped matters, as their knowledge base gains expression in the idiosyncratic terminologies of rival psychoanalytic schools, making integration with cognitive science claims more difficult still. And yet, the central role of metaphor and metonymy in mental functioning is quite congenial to psychoanalytic thought in all its contemporary guises. In fact, psychoanalysis as both theory and practice exemplifies the mind's most profound metaphor theory – "by another name" – and key psychoanalytic dynamic concepts such as psychological trauma, neurotic defense, normal defense, transference, free association, and interpretation are directly related to the mind's metaphoric and metonymic functioning.

As a clinical modality, psychoanalysis exploits the metaphoric relationship between past and present conscious and unconscious mentation, including the use of unconsciously established new categories (Glucksberg & Keysar, 1993). The analyst tries to understand, and to help the analysand understand, present mentation (as expressed in free associations, dreams, transference experiences, symptoms, defenses, and enactments) as metaphorically informed by relevant past experiences. Conversely, mentation based on present inferences, which relies on the verbal input of free associations and their clinical interpretation, is used to metaphorically update past mentation and to reintegrate sequestered experiences and fantasies into a biographic narrative. Following my previous work on this topic (Borbely, 1987), I characterize all information (conscious or unconscious, healthy or neurotic) originating in the here-and-now that illuminates and reframes the then-and-there as "inferential interpretation," and all information (conscious or unconscious, healthy or neurotic) from the then-and-there that illuminates and reframes the here-and-now as "transferential interpretation." It follows that psychoanalysis by definition relates past and present metaphorically to one another, irrespective of whether or not a metaphor is linguistically expressed. For the psychoanalyst, metaphorical comprehension shifts from "seeing something in terms of something else" to "seeing something in terms of another time."

## History

Despite the relevance of psychoanalysis to a psychodynamic understanding of metonymy and metaphor, psychoanalytic theorists have traditionally restricted their purview to classically conceived notions of linguistic figures (Arlow, 1979; Freud, 1913; Levin, 1979; Loewald, 1960; Makari & Shapiro, 1993; Ogden, 1997; Reider, 1972; Rosen, 1977; Sharpe, 1940; Shengold, 1981; Wurmser, 1977). Only recently have analysts joined the discussion initiated by cognitive scientists about conceptual metaphor and metonymy (Borbely, 1995, 1998, 2004; Holland, 1999; Melnick, 1997; Modell, 1997, 2003).

Commensurate with recognition of metaphor and metonymy as phenomena of thought rather than merely of language is recognition of the difference between figurative expression of language and figurative thought using language (Gibbs, 1994a, 1994b, 1999). From this latter distinction, it follows that traditional syntactical criteria for metaphor have ceased to be definitional at the level of thought and also, as we shall see, at the psychodynamic or mental level. Unconscious categories, embodied in metaphoric experiencing, are now believed to precede, both temporally and epistemically, a purportedly more objective category-based thinking. Thus, an expression such as "UP IS MORE" (Lakoff, 1987) has come to be seen as the result of an unconsciously embodied human experience, such as the observation that filling a container with water raises the water level. And the term *embodiment* refers not only to behaviorally grounded internalizations, as in the example just given, but also to internalizations rooted in interpersonal configurations infused with the passions and conflicts denoted by psychoanalytic terms such as "id" (passions, including unacceptable and therefore repressed ideas connected with them); "ego" (reality adaptation; mediation between id and superego demands); "superego" (conscience-related demands and prohibitions); "Oedipal conflict" (triangular relationships between child, mother, and father, complicated by sexual and aggressive impulses); and the developmental anxiety series (anxiety of separation; of loss of love; of genital mutilation; guilt; and social disapproval).

It is then the psychoanalyst, so familiar with irrational aspects of mentation as they enter into psychological understanding, who is in a position to connect "UP IS MORE" to ubiquitous fantasy formations, among which may be the perception of the visible male genital, with the rising motion of the erect penis, as "more of or a better genital" than the "castrated" female one. What is at issue is not the correctness of this or any other psychoanalytic explanation in a particular context, but the mere possibility of integrating irrational fantasies with cognitive science theories.

## Defense and Figurativity

Metaphor as a set of correspondences between two distant conceptual domains (Lakoff & Johnson, 1980) is a device for seeing something, or understanding something, "*in terms of*" something else (Burke, 1945, 503; Ricoeur, 1977, 83). Consider these examples: Freud saw sexuality *in terms of* personality development and motivation *in terms of* unconscious processes. The phrase "*in terms of*" indicates that we are likely dealing with a metaphor. In addition to "in terms of," Ricoeur (1977, 6), following Aristotle (McKeon, 1941, 1459 a 3–8), invokes the notion of "tension between identity and difference" by which he means something "is the same as/is not the same as" something else. I term this latter expression a "hedging equation." In metonymy, the phrase "stands for" is used in the sense of something being substituted for something else (such as defense for defended against; see below) or belonging to something else ("hands" belongs to "sailor" in "all hands on deck"). Figures are substitutions of literal meanings by hedged meanings of the type "is/is not." Such hedged meanings are typically associated with sarcasm or irony, so that "John is such a good friend" means "John is *not* a good friend." In this example, "is not" has the sense of "is the opposite of the expected."

Among all figures, only metaphor and metonymy use, in addition to an is/is not hedging, a hedgingly *equated* meaning of the form "[the target] is the same/is not the same as [the source]." Thus in the metaphor "my job is a jail," "my job" is the same and is not the same as "a jail," and in the metonymy "the crown is the king," "the crown" is the same and is not the same as "the king." In mentation as biographic narrative, the hedging part of the metaphoric hedging equation can be seen as an expression of temporal and semantic transition ("is/is not anymore") and the equation itself functions as an expression of continuity ("is still the same/is not the same"). Taken together, hedging and equation provide the necessary narrative coherence that mediates between diachronic meaningfulness and synchronic, socially participatory relevance throughout psychological development. As we shall see later, metaphor is in an ongoing way involved in re-conceptualizations, re-categorization of concepts, and re-classification of categories and domains. The metonymic hedging equation, while conservative with respect to direct re-categorization, is nevertheless involved in change. To be specific, a metonymic extension can be used to emphasize elements of frames, scenes, and scenarios for refocusing purposes or open-endedly to allude to, illuminate, activate (Kövecses & Radden, 1998, 39), or provide access to mentational entities (Langacker, 1993).

Figurative expressions are usually conscious and directed to others, whereas neurotic defenses are usually unconscious and self-directed. In neurotic defenses, a mentation is employed to ward off some other mentation that would be anxiety provoking if allowed into consciousness. What Anna Freud (1936) termed "defense mechanisms" (repression, reaction formation, idealization, identification, projection, and the like) signify neurosis only if they are used for situationally inappropriate purposes and result in symptom formation or pathological character formation. Whether normal or neurotic, defenses are metaphorically or metonymically structured source/target relations between mental entities connected to each other along synchronic and diachronic temporal dimensions (see below). At the mental level, normal and neurotic defenses alike correspond to what Johnson (1987, 29) calls "image-schemas" on the cognitive level: "I conceive of them as structures for organizing our experience and comprehension." Defenses, thus understood, comprise in their ensemble not only an individual's epistemic instrument but an ongoing manner of experiencing life, relating to others, recasting one's priorities, and designing new enterprises. As such, changes in one's structure of defenses, occurring typically during a psychoanalysis, lead to a different way of experiencing life. In what follows, I focus on the diachronic dimension of defense in relation to metaphor and metonymy.

Let us consider the specifically psychoanalytic meaning of a figurative utterance consisting of the speaker saying something while meaning something else, for example, "you are a nice friend!" meaning "you are a disappointing friend." A neurotically defensive person who makes such an utterance is saying (or experiencing) something with the unconscious aim of warding off, that is, remaining unaware of, a related aspect of mentation that consciously would be anxiety provoking. "I love my brother so much" is emphasized; "I also hate him quite a bit" is warded off. The person in the grip of a neurotic defense is inadvertently saying something so as not to own up to something else. If figures are illocutionary in that they aim at an effect (for the addressee) beyond what is said, defenses are illocutionary in that they aim to prevent an effect (for the speaker and possibly for the addressee) beyond what is said. In this sense, defenses function as "negative" or "denying" figures, and they may be contrasted with conventionally "positive" or "assertive" figures (Bloom, 1976, 293f).

Metonymy shares with neurotic defense the internal structure of a "stands for" relationship between two parts located within the same domain (crown "stands for" king). But while metonymy allows one mental entity to gain access to, activate, or highlight another conceptual or mental entity (Bartsch, 2002; Langacker, 1993, 30; Radden & Kövecses, 1999; Sweetser & Fauconnier, 1996, 13), neurotic defense is a device barring access to a conceptual or mental entity. The neurotic defense stands with its defending mentation for something defended against, but that "something" is as yet undefined and sequestered in an inaccessible mentational system. Thus, neurotic defense, with its two poles, has the structure of a negative, access-barring metonymy, and it may be usefully juxtaposed to positive, access enabling forms of metonymy.

Psychodynamically speaking, there is contiguity between a defending part of mentation, the anxiety mobilized by warded-off fantasies approaching consciousness, and the warded-off fantasies themselves. Gradually, with mounting awareness, the warded-off "something" will be discovered and, once accessible (now in the form of a positive metonymy), it can be more deeply explored in terms of related experiences (metaphor). Let us illustrate this claim with the following: A six-year-old girl, whose infant brother was recently born, shows some of the ambivalent reactions usually seen on such occasions. Instead of talking about her joy and anger, she exclaims: "I love my brother so much!" She defensively uses her positive feeling to cover up (i.e., to defend against) aggressive fantasies. Each time the latter threaten to erupt into consciousness, she unconsciously mobilizes opposite feelings to ward them off and to avoid anxiety.

Both conceptually and experientially, the little girl's overcompensatory love and repressed aggression are bound together; like source and target in a metonymy, they are contiguous and therefore part of the same domain. Love comes to *stand for* hate. The experienced child analyst senses in this child's productions a compulsive avoidance, a "stands for" or "stands instead" metonymy, and understands that the underlying defensive structure may eventually give way to an "in terms of" metaphor. The clinical task consists of helping the unconsciously conflicted child transform in as nontraumatic a manner as possible the negative, access-barring metonymy (i.e., the neurotic defense) into a positive, access-providing form of metonymy (i.e., the defense allows a first, acceptable view of the defended against mentation). If the clinical work is successful, the child will eventually understand her death wishes toward her brother metaphorically, whether *in terms of* her reaction to feeling displaced by the brother, her fantasy of having been a bad child who was never good enough for her parents, or her immaturity-based, culturally reinforced assumption that a boy is "better" than a girl, specifically regarding the respective genital (see above). In the process, her feared aggression will come to lose its compulsive character and be understood as a reaction to trauma-based unconscious fantasies which, previously disguised, are now metaphorically understandable and acceptable. As the child becomes aware of her conflicting feelings, which can be progressively tolerated without undue anxiety, the defense of reaction formation becomes less and less necessary and may vanish completely.

## The Linguistic, Conceptual, and Mental Levels of Metaphor and Metonymy

Figurativity has been defined in multiple and often confusing ways that correspond to the various disciplinary contexts in which it is invoked (Fahnestock, 1999). Thus, we have figurativity as ornamentation and persuasion in discourse (rhetoric); figurativity as syntactic/semantic relations (linguistics); figurativity as conceptual/semantic relations of thought (cognitive sciences); and, finally, and most germanely to my thesis, figurativity as dynamic relations of mentation (psychoanalysis). It is convenient to assign these definitions to one of three explanatory levels: the linguistic, the cognitive, and the mental.

Each level of figurativity entails a different notion of metaphor and metonymy, and each level works with distinct entities as sources and targets: words, concepts, and psychodynamics. Thus, each level has a different basis for the metaphoric incongruence criteria: syntax, semantics, and temporality. The basic similarity of these three levels resides in the nature of the source–target relationship. In all three levels, that is, "*stands for*" is emblematic of metonymy with same domain mapping, whereas "*in terms of*" is emblematic of metaphor with inter-domain mapping. The mental level includes not merely thoughts but also emotions (Johnson, 1987) and drive-related motivations (Brenner, 1982; Laplanche & Pontalis, 1973; Freud, 1905, 1915a, 1915b, 1933, 1940) along with various amalgams of these three conceptually separate components. If, cognitively speaking, imagination, using metaphor and metonymy as its devices, has the ability to "project concepts onto other concepts" (Barcelona, 2000, 2; Jackendoff, 1992, 198), then, mentally speaking, it similarly has the ability to project psychodynamics onto other psychodynamics.

The term "psychodynamics" is used here in the specifically psychoanalytic sense of a mental organization that encompasses contradictory motivational psychological forces (e.g., thoughts, urges, wishes, impulses, desires, fears, emotions, moods) in dynamic and fluid tension (Moore & Fine, 1990). Such forces encompass the conscious and unconscious, symbolic and subsymbolic, and rational and irrational psychological aspects of all semiotic entities, states, and processes that enter into an individual's life. This psychodynamic perspective on imagination opposes the common assumption that thoughts are symbolically organized, whereas emotions and desires are organized only subsymbolically (Dennett, 1991; Smolensky, 1987).

Psychodynamic forces are simultaneously influenced by many processes, among them genetic information; neuro-endocrine physiology; and new and previous experiences, including traumatic ones. These influences are mentally processed in terms of dispositions, desires, fears, moods, thoughts, and fantasies. Clinical observations and the theoretical inferences to which they give rise sustain the hypothesis that the aforementioned components are in constant interaction; that they are not always sharply delineated among themselves; that they change over time; and that they are context and task dependent. In view of this combinatorial explosion of interactions and transformations, our designating entities, states and processes as "thoughts," "emotions," and "passions" (desires, aggression) is little more than an attempt to comprehend complexly interwoven processes that are codified symbolically and subsymbolically. Metaphor and metonymy are informational and organizational devices that allow complex mentation to "move in realms that lie outside the range of concepts, where thought [better: 'mentation'] has not hardened into concepts" (Bredin, 1984, 56–57, my bracketed phrase). Psychoanalytic terms, for example "defense," "impulse," "transference," "unconscious conflict," and "anxiety," aim at capturing the grammar underlying the psychodynamic entities of the mind's language.

## Metaphor, the Structure of Normal Defense

Metaphoricity has been defined by Kittay (1987, 69) as a conceptual incongruity. On the linguistic level, such incongruity is expressed as a hedging equation of syntactic selection restricted words (in "JULIET IS THE SUN," a living entity is equated with a lifeless one). On the conceptual level, the incongruity is between different semantic contents hedgingly equated with each other ("UP IS MORE"). On the mental level, the incongruity is between hedgingly equated psychodynamically reverberating issues belonging to different developmental stages, different times ("THE SUPERVISOR IS THE FATHER").

In normal defense, what is experienced today is metaphorically evaluated *in terms of* previous experiences without being rigidly determined by the latter. It is this metaphoric tension between the here-and-now and the then-and-there that lends depth and authenticity to our experiencing. This tension arises precisely because source and target in metaphor relate in a manner whereby engendered meaning still has to be specified without ever achieving final state status (Rohrer, 1995). To put the matter prosaically: Experiences change their meaning based on other experiences.

Let us now turn to psychoanalytic practice, which makes full use, albeit implicitly, of the metaphoric dialectic between past and present.

## Trauma as Loss of Metaphoricity

Under nontraumatic conditions, experiences are mentally registered with an optimal vagueness as to their present, past, and future meaning. Such vagueness (Tuggy, 1993) is a manifestation of the metaphoric hedging equation on the mental level. This necessary vagueness or openness, this nonfinite state status of an experience in being registered, will be referred to as an experience's "metaphoric potential," or its "metaphoricity." Such metaphoricity, in its clinically relevant sense, allows future and past chains of experiences to be meaningfully conveyed to each other (Katz, 1998, 22), accommodating ever-changing perspectives, contexts, and points of view. Without metaphoricity's hypothetical and provisional vagueness, expressed in a hedging equation, experiences are not assimilable, that is, their meaning cannot be shaped from the vantage point of other experiences. Psychological trauma, which leads to severe anxiety, impairs or destroys the possibility of registering an experience with appropriate ambiguity. It thus diminishes an experience's metaphoric potential regarding the formation of, and inclusion by, new perspectives (Bartsch, 2002, 49).

Trauma leads to rigidly accepting the meaning of an experience as frozen and therefore as conclusively valid in all contexts and for all times. This reliance on a fixed meaning contrasts with the ability to comprehend an experience more flexibly, with any single meaning understood as hypothetical as to content and context, provisional as to time, and so existing outside finite state phenomena. That is, trauma tends to a "literality" divorced from metaphoric process, a literality in which the overly specific meaning of an experience is unambiguous, inflexible, and even axiomatic. Thus sequestered from modifying outside experience, trauma must be defended against to avoid anxiety and the subjective feeling of meaninglessness threatened by its eruption into consciousness. On this account, a traumatic experience collapses the present domain and the past domain into a single, namely, a pseudo-present, one. This temporal domain coalescence leads the individual to experience what belongs to the past falsely as of present origin. Past and present domains are now prevented to metaphorically communicate with each other. The pseudo-present *stands for* the past rather than being informed *in terms of* the past. Neurosis can be seen as a confusion of times. To the extent of our neurotic impairments we live in the past (or in the future) rather than in the present.

Consider this clinically salient fact: A father beats his son. For the son, the domains "father" and "painful, anxiety-provoking mistreatment causing intolerable fantasies," are experientially fused together as metonymic source and target of one domain. The sequestrations are kept from consciousness by an access-barring structure, that is, by a neurotic defense. The defense consigns the sequestrations to an unconscious status in order to protect the son from re-experiencing massive anxiety. The neurotic defense wards off the anxiety-provoking meaning of the beating experience, as exemplified in fantasies of homicide, castration, or homosexual seduction involving the father as perpetrator or victim, which in their ensemble we characterize as "the defended against."

What does this neurotic defense look like clinically? It may take a variety of forms. For example, the son may succeed in keeping these anxiety-provoking fantasies unconscious by erecting the defenses of repression and idealization. The father's positive attributes will then be exaggerated, whereas his shortcomings, together with the painful and dangerous fantasies connected to them, will be scotomized, that is, barred from consciousness. Metaphoricity is thereby replaced by a compulsively functioning, access-barring, metonymic defense. Such defensiveness is itself typically hidden from awareness by another metonymically functioning defense termed "rationalization." Taken together, the neurotic defenses of repression, idealization, and rationalization drain the father-beating-his-son experience of the optimal vagueness associated with metaphoricity. The meaning of the experience is not subject to interpretation by other "non-beating" experiences that may be adaptively useful in various contexts. The experience of a father beating his son is not provisional as to its openly evolving "ultimate" meaning; it is not context-dependent. Trauma, by short-circuiting the metaphoricity that allows, as mentioned previously, future and past chains of experiences to be meaningfully conveyed to each other, precludes an optimally resilient, autopoetic self-organization. Absent such resilience, the individual's responsiveness to the present and openness to the future are severely restricted. Psychoanalysis, when it is successful, restores this resilience through metaphorizing interpretation that leads to a reconceptualization of previously established concepts and their recategorization (Glucksberg & Keysar, 1993) along new dimensions of relevance and meaningfulness (Borbely, 1998).

To summarize, the defense against a sequestered part of mentation, which is activated each time a warded-off impulse threatens to become conscious, metonymically stands for the defended against. Trauma, as we have seen, transforms a two-domain metaphoric experience into a one-domain metonymic one. What are the special attributes of this kind of metonymy? As mentioned above, while metonymy is usually defined as a mental access providing device, in neurotic defense it is access barring: Since the defense bars access to the defended against, we use the term "negative metonymy." We may define normal defense as having a metaphoric structure and neurotic defense as having a negative metonymic one.

## The Negative Metonymic Structure of Neurotic Defense and Its Interpretation

According to Taylor (1995, 83ff, see also Croft, 1993), the essence of metonymy "resides in the possibility of establishing connections between entities which co-occur within a given conceptual structure." One of these co-occurring mental entities, the source, can provide access to another mental entity, the target. In the psychoanalytic resolution of neurotic defense, a negative metonymic, access baring, mental constellation is gradually transformed via a positive metonymic into a metaphoric one, where access is provided and awareness can be increased.

As an example of clinically impaired metaphoricity and its therapeutic transformation, consider the following: An analyst tells the analysand, who is inappropriately fearful of his superior in the workplace, "You treat your supervisor as if he were your father." He points out that the analysand symptomatically experiences the relationship to the supervisor as "standing for" the relationship to his father. It is as if the domain pertaining to "supervisor" were the same as the domain originally pertaining to "father." (It is assumed, of course, that the father was feared.) The original experience with father, an authority, has been unconsciously displaced onto the supervisor, another authority, since the original constellation has been registered axiomatically rather than with provisional vagueness. "Supervisor" now metonymically stands for "father." Conceptually, an obsolete "father constellation" has been extended through time to the present situation and is falsely experienced as pertaining to the "here and now" rather than only to the "then and there."

With successful analytic work, the supervisor's and father's roles as authority figures will come to be metaphorically equated. "Stands for" will yield to "identity in difference" or "in terms of," a precondition of the ability to differentiate between past and present. Sameness will be understood as metaphoric similarity rather than as metonymic contiguity. The social constellations pertaining to "supervisor" and "father" will simultaneously be appreciated as identical and yet as vastly different, that is, as belonging to the separate domains of work and family. With the restoration of metaphoricity, the previous temporal/semantic conflation, which yielded a symptomatic conflation of "supervisor" and "father," gives way to temporal bi-directionality (from past to present and from present to past) with a domain tension appropriate to different events from different times, biographically understood.

Negative metonymy, then, is tantamount to a faulty time tagging that derives from the sequestration of past experiences. This temporal conflation is closely connected with the following: the axiomatization of past experiences (with its pseudo-relevance for the present), the isolation of such experiences from an updating process by subsequent experiences, and the loss of context sensitivity. The negative metonymic structure of neurosis thereby becomes a confusion of times. The past, rather than being held in abeyance to inform the present (normal defense), collapses with the present to (partly or entirely) determine it as a mere extension of the past. The resulting psychopathological formation collapses two domains into a single functional domain. Within this domain, defense and defended against relate metonymically to each other, which is to say they rigidly belong to each other. Metaphoric transparency has given way to metonymic opaqueness.

## Transference, Metonymically and Metaphorically Conceived

Figurativity, which provides a conceptual handle for comprehending the nature and treatment of neurotic defenses, is no less essential for understanding the clinical transference. Through his invention of the psychoanalytic method, the application of which required a special psychoanalytic setting, Freud created an intimate environment that elicited unconscious and conscious experiences from the analysand's past. Transference, in its specifically psychoanalytic sense, refers to the displacement onto the analyst of attitudes, feelings, and expectations originally experienced in relation to the analysand's significant childhood figures, as these attitudes, feelings, and expectations have been mobilized by the psychoanalytic treatment setting (see Moore & Fine, 1990). The analysand, it should be stressed, transfers these childhood feeling states onto the analyst even though they have no substantive connection to his or her here-and-now relationship to the analyst.

The transference, thus understood, has a simultaneously metonymic and metaphoric structure: The analyst, as presently experienced, "stands for" real or imagined figures and experiences of the past. In neurotic transference as in neurotic defense, a time confusion takes place. What is experienced in the here-and-now really belongs to the then-and-there. The analyst is experienced as if he or she metonymically stands for a (usually parental) childhood figure. With repeated interpretation of neurotic transference, the analyst will come to be experienced metaphorically "in terms of" a childhood figure. Metonymic certainty will give way to optimal metaphoric vagueness as the transference experience is integrated into the mainstream of biographic narrativity. This resolution of metonymic into metaphoric transference will be accompanied by increased awareness as metonymic perplexity yields to metaphoric insight. On this view, Freud's emblematic statement regarding the goals of psychoanalytic treatment, "Where Id was Ego shall be," is transformed into, "Where metonymy was, metaphor shall be."

The transformation of metonymic into metaphoric transference has several aspects, all of which aid in reversing traumatic experience. Traumatically sequestered experiences may be re-experienced in the transference simultaneously in four different ways: as current, because it is presently occurring; as of experiential relevance and poignancy, because it is occurring in a relationship with the analyst; as confusing, because the analyst is experienced as a childhood figure; and as obsolete in the present, because successful interpretations have restored metaphoricity and ended (or at least significantly attenuated) the initial temporal conflation.

The therapeutic action of analytic treatment resides in the fact that the current reliving of the sequelae of earlier trauma occurs with a different protagonist who seeks to metaphorize through interpretation what was originally and traumatically metonymized.

As in neurotic defense, the set of issues implicated in the transference may at first be experienced with metonymic unease. This time, however, unease is experienced within a benign therapeutic relationship and optimally gives way to the relief of restored relevance, poignancy, and ambiguity afforded by this relationship. Interpretations unavailable in the past provide new – and newly assimilable – insights. The latter serve to forestall "mindless" repetition of the traumatic insults of the past. The awareness of the obsoleteness of relational dynamics that had for many years appeared to be of great, even overwhelming, relevance to the present is a surprising and liberating experience for the analysand. Psychoanalytic interpretation is a (re)-metaphorization of damaged or lost metaphoricity. On this view, interpretation is not only an integral part of the psychoanalytic enterprise, but is an intrinsic part of the mind's metaphoric functioning. Normal defense can now be understood as a successful self-interpretation, neurotic defense as an unsuccessful one. By interpreting, the analyst metaphorizes the analysand's metonymic stagnations.

## The Primary, Secondary, and Metaphoric Processes

Having conceptualized the metaphoric process as constitutive of normal mental functioning, its relationship to what psychoanalytic theory designates "primary process" and "secondary process" remains to be discussed. The primary process is unconscious, follows the pleasure principle, and uses displacement and condensation to allow ideas to attach themselves to unconscious wishes. The secondary process is used when explicit explanatory demands impinge on the individual. A property of consciousness, it adheres to the reality principle and is associated with propositional and logical thought, reasoning, and judgment (Laplanche & Pontalis, 1973).

Most psychological change occurs unconsciously, via the primary process, involving the secondary process only peripherally. It is here proposed that the processes involved in psychological growth be assigned to the metaphoric process, as this process operates at the mental level set forth above. Intuitively, the metaphoric process occupies an intermediate position between the primary process and secondary process. It shares with the primary process the following connecting devices for associations: Displacement (positive metonymy; a constituent of metaphor) and condensation (a constituent of metaphor). Conversely, it shares with the secondary process the governance of the reality principle and the advanced cognitive and judgmental capabilities associated with the reality-governed maturational process. To summarize, primary process captures irrational mentation, secondary process rational mentation, and the metaphoric process imaginative rationality. Since the latter is closely associated with psychological growth, a disturbance in the capacity to metaphorize typically leads to neurotic conflict and impaired creativity.

Alternatively, the metaphoric process may be integrating most features of both the primary and secondary process. Only the chaos associated with the primary process and the rigidities of thought and behavior associated with the secondary process stand outside the integration. That is, the metaphoric process represents an integration of primary process and secondary process as they coalesce in the optimal functioning of the mind. The unintegrated aspects of primary process and secondary process are manifestations of the mind's suboptimal, negative metonymic functioning.

The metaphoric process is nonlinear, vaguely determined by temporal informedness, and yet unpredictable; its suspended pertinence never reaches final state status. Borrowing from the terminology of complexity theory, we may associate primary process with chaos or turbulence; secondary process with order or quiescence; and metaphoric process with an intermediate position at the 'edge of chaos' (Kauffman, 2000). The process of free association, the linchpin of the psychoanalytic method, brings the metaphoric process closer still to the edge of chaos – for the purpose of optimizing creative risk taking.

With its intermediate position between primary and secondary process, the metaphoric process is linked to the realm of connotations as opposed to the realm of denotations (secondary process) or chaotic associations (primary process). In the realm of connotations, old meanings are preserved in metaphoric tension with new meanings (Radman, 1997, 83). The imaginative rationality operative within the metaphoric process has a heuristic function: It anticipates and searches by guessing, by playful trial actions, and by developing new insights and meanings that are appropriately agnostic or open ended in terms of their value. In the process old rules are discarded and new ones created as the individual embraces changing notions of relevance and meaningfulness, an integral aspect of creatively recasting the world and the self (Ricoeur, 1977).

## The Metaphor Languages of Different Psychoanalytic Schools

Neurosis has been conceptualized as the individual's damaged ability to metaphorize owing especially to psychological trauma usually occurring in childhood. The therapeutic action of psychoanalytic treatment, on the other hand, has been equated with the analyst's interpretative (re)-metaphorizations of neurotic defenses and symptoms. The additive effect of such interpretations over the course of a treatment is to help the analysand to recover his or her instances of lost metaphoricity. As an aspect of this interpretive task, the analyst must relate clinical experiences occurring in the here-and-now of the transference to childhood occurrences that are either released from childhood amnesia or reconstructed through the joint efforts of analysand and analyst. The analyst brings the transference and the childhood events into metaphoric alignment.

All psychoanalytic schools that analyze transferences are necessarily concerned with connecting transference experiences with developmental childhood constellations. To this end, different types of analysts employ their own metaphor languages. Thus, analysts identified with psychoanalytic self psychology will connect lapses in empathy occurring in the transference/counter-transference with lapses among the caregivers of early childhood; Kleinian psychoanalysts will observe elements of the paranoid and depressive positions in the transference and trace them back to corresponding childhood events; and classical Freudian analysts will discern incestuous and aggressive fantasies in the transference and attempt to link them, whether explicitly or implicitly, to childhood events. It may be hoped that the metaphor theory of psychoanalysis, which provides a conceptual umbrella that subsumes these and other interpretive emphases, will promote more fruitful collaboration among analysts of different theoretical persuasions.

## Summary and Outlook

The key terms of psychoanalysis may be taken to designate aspects of the mind's metaphoric functioning, including its negative metonymic impairment when functioning suboptimally. This understanding is premised on the elaboration of a temporal metaphor concept, which is located at the very center of psychoanalytic theory. A temporal metaphor is conceived as connecting temporal domains rather than syntactically or semantically defined domains. As such, a temporal metaphor does not take words, sentences, or texts as the units to be connected but rather psychodynamic constellations occurring at different points in a person's narrative life history. Within the temporal domain, psychodynamics manifest themselves as structures (defense, defended against), forces (repression, impulse), or nonspecified influences (inference, transference). Such varied psychodynamic entities may denote, variously, different states of aggregation and mobility, different rates of change over time, and different functional aspects of mentation. What unites these psychodynamic configurations is their temporal bi-directionality (from past to present and from present to past) and the domain tension maintained between differing times (metaphoric relationship) or, suboptimally, the collapse of these times into a single domain (negative metonymic relationship). This approach encourages the development of a psychodynamic metaphor theory applicable to the traditional setting of clinical psychoanalysis. Equally important, it permits a deeper understanding of normal personality development, especially in its psychodynamic aspects, beyond the clinical setting. By showing how psychodynamic terms like trauma, defense, transference, and interpretation denote different aspects of the mind's metaphoric and metonymic functioning a common language between psychoanalysis and other cognitive sciences can be envisaged, facilitating an interdisciplinary dialogue.

## References

Arlow, J. (1979). Metaphor and the psychoanalytic situation. *Psychoanalytic Quarterly, 48*, 363–385.

Barcelona, A. (2000). Introduction: The cognitive theory of metaphor and metonymy. In A. Barcelona (Ed.), *Metaphor and metonymy at the crossroads* (pp. 1–30). New York: Mouton de Gruyter.

Bartsch, R. (2002). Generating polysemy: Metaphor and metonymy. In R. Dirven & R. Porings (Eds.), *Metaphor and metonymy in comparison and contrast* (pp. 49–74). New York: Mouton de Gruyter.

Bloom, H. (1976). *Revisionism from Blake to Stevens.* New Haven: Yale University Press.

Borbely, A. (1987). Towards a temporal theory of the mind. *Psychoanalysis and Contemporary Thought*, 10, 923–936.

Borbely, A. (1995). Marx and Freud, a reassessment: From the industrial age to the information age. *Nature, Society, and Thought*, 8, 55–77.

Borbely, A. (1998). A psychoanalytic concept of metaphor. *International Journal of Psychoanalysis*, 79, 459–487.

Borbely, A. (2004). Toward a psychodynamic understanding of metaphor and metonymy: Their role in awareness and defense. *Metaphor and Symbol*, 19(2), 91–114.

Borbely, A. (in press). The centrality of metaphor and metonymy in psychoanalytic theory and practice. *Psychoanalytic Inquiry*.

Bredin, H. (1984). Metonymy. *Poetics Today*, 5, 45–58.
Brenner, C. (1982). *The mind in conflict*. New York: International University Press.
Burke, K. (1945). *A grammar of motives*. New York: Prentice Hall.
Croft, W. (1993). The role of domains in the interpretation of metaphors and metonymies. *Cognitive Linguistics*, 4, 335–370.
Dennett, D. (1991). Mother nature versus the walking encyclopedia: A western drama. In W. Ramsey, S. Stich, & D. Rumelhardt (Eds.), *Philosophy and connectionist theory*. Hillsdale, NJ: Lawrence Erlbaum Associates.
Dirven, R. (1993). Metonymy and metaphor: Different mental strategies of conceptualization. *Leuvense Bijdragen*, 80, 1–28.
Fahnestock, J. (1999). *Rhetorical figures in science*. Oxford: Oxford University Press.
Freud, A. (1936). *The ego and the mechanisms of defense*. New York: International University Press.
Freud, S. (1905). Three essays on the theory of sexuality. In *S.E.*, 7.
Freud, S. (1915a). The unconscious. *S.E.* 4.
Freud, S. (1915b). Repression. *S.E.* 14.
Freud, S. (1915c). Instincts and their vicissitudes. *S.E.* 14.
Freud, S. (1933). New introductory lectures on psycho-analysis. *S.E.* 22.
Freud, S. (1940). An outline of psychoanalysis. *S.E.* 23.
Freud, S. (1985/1974). The neuro-psychosis of defense. In James Strachey (Ed.), *S.E. (Standard Edition of the Complete Psychological Works of Sigmund Freud)*, 3. London: Hogarth Press and the Institute of Psychoanalysis.
Gibbs, R. (1994a). Figurative thought and figurative language. In M. Gernsbacher (Ed.), *Handbook of psycholinguistics* (pp. 411–466). New York: Academic Press.
Gibbs, R. (1994b). *The poetics of mind*. Cambridge: Cambridge University Press.
Gibbs, R. (1999). Speaking and thinking with metonymy. In K.-U. Panther & G. Radden (Eds.), *Metonymy in language and thought* (pp. 61–76). Amsterdam: John Benjamins.
Glucksberg, S., & Keysar, B. (1993). How metaphors work. In A. Ortony (Ed.), *Metaphor and thought* (pp. 401–424). Cambridge: Cambridge University Press.
Holland, N. (1999). Cognitive linguistics. *International Journal of Psychoanalysis*, 80, 357–363.
Jackendoff, R. (1992). What is a concept? In A. Lehrer & E. F. Kittay (Eds.), *Frames, fields, and contrasts* (pp. 191–208). Hillsdale, NJ: Lawrence Erlbaum Associates.
Johnson, M. (1987). *The body in the mind: The bodily basis of meaning, imagination, and reason*. Chicago: University of Chicago Press.
Katz, A. (1998). Figurative language and figurative thought. A review. In A. Katz, C. Cacciari, R. Gibbs, Jr., & M. Turner (Eds.), *Figurative language and thought* (pp. 3–43). New York: Oxford University Press.
Kauffman, S. (2000). *Investigations*. Oxford University Press.
Kittay, E. (1987). *Metaphor: Its cognitive force and linguistic structure*. Oxford: Clarendon Press.
Kövecses, Z., & Radden, G. (Eds.). (1998). Metonymy: Developing a cognitive linguistic view. *Cognitive Linguistics*, 9, 37–77.
Lakoff, G. (1987). *Women, fire, and dangerous things: What categories reveal about the mind*. Chicago: University of Chicago Press.
Lakoff, G., & Johnson, M. (1980). *Metaphors we live by*. Chicago: University of Chicago Press.
Lakoff, G., & Johnson, M. (1999). *Philosophy in the flesh: The embodied mind and its challenge to western thought*. New York: Basic Books.
Langacker, R. (1993). Reference-point constructions. *Cognitive linguistics*, 4, 1–38.
Laplanche, J., & Pontalis, J.-B. (1973). *The language of psycho-analysis*. New York: Hogarth Press.
Levin, F. (1979). Metaphor, affect and arousal: How interpretation might work. *Psychoanalytic Quarterly*, 48, 231–243.
Loewald, H. (1960). On the therapeutic action of psychoanalysis. *International Journal of Psychoanalysis*, 41, 16–32.
Makari, G., & Shapiro, T. (1993). On psychoanalytic listening: Language and unconscious communication. *Journal of the American Psychoanalytic Association*, 41, 991–1020.
McKeon, R. (1941). *The basic works of Aristotle*. New York: Random House.
Melnick, B. (1997). Metaphor and the theory of libidinal development. *International Journal of Psychoanalysis*, 78, 997–1016.
Modell, A. (1997). Reflections on metaphor and affects. *Annual of Psychoanalysis* 25, 219–234.
Modell, A. (2003). *Imagination and the meaningful brain*. Cambridge, MA: MIT Press.
Moore, B., & Fine, B. (1990). *Psychoanalytic terms and concepts*. New Haven, CT: Yale University Press.
Ogden, T. (1997). Some thoughts on the use of language in psychoanalysis. *Psychoanalytic Dialogues*, 7, 1–21.

Radden, G., & Kövecses, Z. (1999). Towards a theory of metonymy. In K.-U. Panther & G. Radden (Eds.), *Metonymy in language and thought* (pp. 17–60). Amsterdam: John Benjamins.

Radman, Z. (1997). *Metaphors: Figures of the mind*. London: Kluwer Academic.

Reider, N. (1972). Metaphor as interpretation. *International Journal of Psychoanalysis, 53*, 463–469.

Ricoeur, P. (1977). *The rule of metaphor: Multidisciplinary studies of the creation of meaning in language*. Toronto: University of Toronto Press.

Rohrer, T. (1995). *The cognitive science of metaphor from philosophy to neuropsychology* [Draft]. http://philosophy.uoregon.edu/metaphor/neurophl.htm.

Rosch, E. (1978). Principles of categorization. In E. Rosch & B. Lloyd (Eds.), *Cognition and categorization*. Hillsdale, NJ: Lawrence Erlbaum Associates.

Rosen, V. (1977). Sign phenomena and unconscious meaning. In *Style, character and language* (pp. 171–193). New York: Jason Aronson.

Sharpe, E. (1940). Psychophysical problems revealed in language. *International Journal of Psychoanalysis, 21*, 201–213.

Shengold, L. (1981). Insight as metaphor. *Psychoanalytic Study of the Child, 36*, 289–305.

Smolensky, P. (1987). Connectionist AI, symbolic AI, and the brain. *AI Review, 1*, 95–110.

Sweetser, E., & Fauconnier, G. (1996). Cognitive links and domains: Basic aspects of mental space theory. In G. Fauconnier & E. Sweetser (Eds.), *Spaces, words, and grammar*. Chicago: University of Chicago Press.

Taylor, J. (1995). *Linguistic categorization. Prototypes in linguistic theory*. Oxford: Clarendon Press.

Tuggy, D. (1993). Ambiguity, polysemy, and vagueness. *Cognitive Linguistics, 4*, 273–290.

Varela, F., Thomson, E., & Rosch, E. (1991). *The embodied mind: Cognitive science and human experience*. Cambridge: MIT Press.

Wurmser, L. (1977). A defense of the use of metaphor in analytic theory formation. *Psychoanalytic Quarterly, 46*, 466–498.

CHAPTER 24

# Crossing the Senses in Metaphorical Language[1]

*Cristina Cacciari*

## Introduction

Metaphor and perceptual experience are tied together in the history of epistemology (Cazeaux, 2002) and narrative literature (Ackerman, 1990). Although we rarely, as experimental psychologists, take advantage of literary sources, undeniably novelists and poets had provided us with wonderful examples of linguistic metaphors based on sensory experiences.[2] Not only Proust, Poe, Baudelaire, to cite some, but also contemporary novelists help us in reflecting on the language with which we name perceptual experiences. This happens to be the case in *Smell*, a novel by the Indian writer Radhika Jha, that offers an extremely rich repertoire of perceptual metaphors. *Smell* describes the young protagonist Leela Patel's efforts to find her way in Paris after escaping from the anti-Indian riots in Nairobi. Leela Patel has an instinctive knowing of how to blend spices with food for maximizing their flavors, a natural sense for cooking driven by an implicit dialogue with the flavors and scents of Indian spices. The clash between the French and the Indian cultures is translated into a sense-based conflict, as shown by the opening of the novel that describes a metaphorical battle among culturally bound smells and aromas: the scent of freshly baked baguettes, driven by the spring Parisian breezes, does battle with the smells emanating from cardamom, masala, turmeric, cinnamon, and coriander stored in the *Epicerie Madras* of Leela's uncle. Like an unwelcome army, the aroma of French bread captures Leela's nostrils reminding her of being parted from home, in a foreign distant culture that even perceptually invades her life. In Jha's novel, smell and taste metaphorically and perceptually go hand in hand, just as in *La physiologie du goût. Or méditations de gastronomie trascendente*[3] written almost two centuries ago (1825) by the gastronome Jean Anthelme Brillat-Savarin.

As we will see in this chapter, the metaphorical use of sensory language is rather unbalanced across modalities. This in part reflects the fact that the informational richness of perceptual experiences is hardly rendered by linguistic expressions. As an example, consider the case of chromatic experience and color names: in Italian, we often describe both the sky and the sea with the same adjective "azzurro" ("blue"): we use this "stereotype" of color,[4] even though we are well aware that it does not capture at all the chromatic characteristics of the two percepts. Another example comes from the descriptions of smells, perfumes, and aromas: we often name them borrowing words from other sensory experiences (e.g., taste: sweet, bitter) or using the source name (as in the smell of jasmin):[5] "the words we apply to smells represent either the objects that produce them metonymically, as in *rose*, or their qualities through analogues derived from other modalities, as in *bitter*" (Marks, 1996, 40). Unsurprisingly, smell is defined as a speechless sense (Ackerman, 1990).

More generally, what constitutes a "veridical label" for a smell or for other perceptual experience? In many cases, there is no one-to-one correspondence between a smell and its name, and participants asked to name a smell end up naming it with labels that do not match either the odorant's chemical name nor that of the source (e.g., the smell of my grandmother's kitchen; Boisson, 1997; David et al., 1997; Schab, 1990).[6] A question addressed further on in this chapter is whether this language imbalance is culturally bound, or it also reflects adaptive aspects and neuro-cognitive underpinnings: as noted by Williams in his work on synaesthetic adjectives, "connections might exist among ontogeny, phylogeny, the neurophysiology of sensation, cognition, and naming" (1976, 473) that suggest a point of interaction between mind and brain.

## The Aim of the Chapter

Years ago the anthropologist Brenda Beck (1978, 1987) defined metaphors as "bridges." She argued, "If forced to delimit the concept of metaphor I would insist on the experiential, body-linked, physical core of metaphorical reasoning abilities" (Beck, 1987, 11). The aim of this chapter is to dig into the "physical" core of the metaphorical language used to name sensory experiences. The working hypothesis that drives this chapter is that most perceptually based metaphorical expressions (e.g., a cold silence, a stony flavor)[7] are motivated and rooted in the structure of perceptual experiences and sensory systems. Metaphors do not reflect an abstract–amodal combination of word senses, but rather constitute the linguistic expression of the neural endowment necessary for treating sensory information. This hypothesis is not entirely new, in a sense. Marks (1982, 1996) partly anticipated it with his work on perceptual metaphors. He argued, "Even if some perceptual metaphors end up being mediated linguistically, their origins appear to be wholly in perception itself, starting within perceptual processes before being overlaid and dominated by linguistic ones" (1996, 59). Consistently, recent work in the neurosciences (e.g., Arbib & Rizzolatti, 1996; Ramachandran & Hubbard, 2001a, 2001b; Rizzolatti & Arbib, 1998) suggests that the semantic motivation for many metaphors is rooted in, and reflects, the structure of the neural architecture that subserves sensory and motor experiences. Perceptually based theories of knowledge also propose that conceptual and perceptual knowledge share a common neural substrate and a format. For instance, according to the Perceptual Symbol System model (Barsalou, 1999), conceptual knowledge is grounded in sensorimotor systems, a viewpoint shared by Embodied Cognition theories (e.g., Gibbs, 2003) as well. Whereas amodal theories of knowledge do not assume activation of perceptual information whenever a linguistic label of a percept is encountered, perceptual theories claim that people represent and process concepts activating and using perceptual simulations or re-enactments (Barsalou et al., 2003).

A brief outline of the chapter: first, I consider synaesthetic metaphors, the most investigated case of linguistic bridge across the senses. Then I examine the psychophysical properties underling cross-sensory similarities in figurative language. This introduces the third part of the chapter centered on the neuro-cognitive basis of synaesthesia

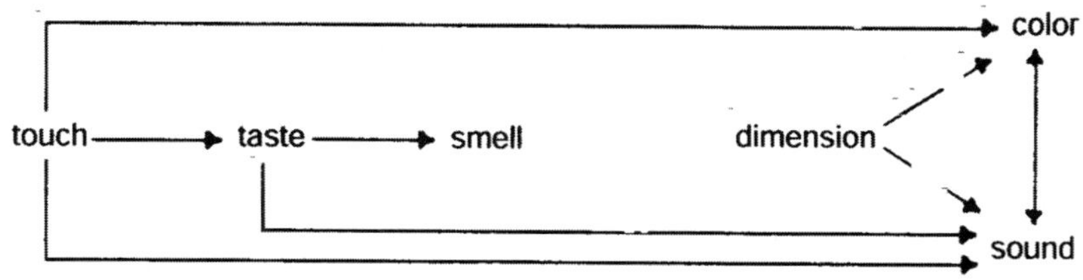


**Figure 24.1.** The direction of metaphorical transfer across sensory modalities (Williams, 1976).

where it is not a linguistic statement but a perceptual experience to cross sensory boundaries (e.g., between number and colors, or vision and touch). Then other cases of multimodality are discussed before driving some tentative conclusions about the relationships between metaphorical language and sensory experience.

## Linguistic Synaesthesia: Crossing the Senses Metaphorically

In synaesthetic metaphors, words that pertain to one sensory modality (e.g., vision) are extended to express another sensory modality (e.g., audition), as exemplified by Kandinskij who named one of his drawings as follows: "Double sound, cold tension of the straight lines, warm tension of the curved lines, the rigid to the infinity, the flexible to the compact." Two main approaches investigated the psychological dimensions underlying sensory metaphors:

1. A taxonomic approach that identified the directions of the metaphorical borrowings trying to establish a hierarchy among the sensory modalities acting as "donors" and "recipients," respectively.
2. A psychophysical approach that analyzed the physical characteristics of the signals and events that enter into linguistic synaesthetic metaphors (e.g., the pitch of a sound, the brightness of a light). We start by examining the first approach that identified the senses acting as metaphorizers (the donors) and metaphorized (the recipients).

## Directions of Metaphorical Mapping across the Senses

Williams (1976) proposed a model of metaphorical transfer across modalities (the five senses, plus color and dimension) based on the analysis of the semantic change over time of more than 100 English synaesthetic adjectives (see also Classen, 1993; Day, 1996; Derrig, 1978; Howes, 2002; Pelamatti & Savardi, 2003; Ullman, 1945, 1962). To Williams, a systematic sequence exists in the application of sensory terms from a modality to another based on a hierarchy among the senses relative to the order in which they give or receive a semantic sense from other modalities (see Figure 24.1). Touch is at one extreme as the more common donor, and color and sound at the opposite extreme, as the most common recipients. In Williams's corpus, references to smell do not contribute to denote other modalities (but see Callejas, 2001, for counterexamples extracted from Hearney's poetry), taste is only used to refer to smell and sound, and dimension only to color and sound. Williams exemplifies the main "first-order" types of metaphorical transfer as follows:

1. Touch words: they are generally transferred to taste (e.g., "sharp taste"), color (e.g., "dull color"), and sound (e.g., "soft sounds"). Touch words are rarely shifted to denote vision or smell.
2. Taste words: they are transferred to smell (e.g., "sour smell") and sound (e.g., "sweet music") but not back to tactile experience or forward to dimension or color.

3. Olfactory words: they are not transferred to other senses.
4. Dimension words: they are transferred to color (e.g., "flat gray") or sound (e.g., "deep sound").
5. Color words: they are shifted only to sounds (e.g., "bright sound").
6. Sound words: they are transferred only to color (e.g., "quiet green").

Sensory words in English transferred "from the physiologically least differentiating, most evolutionary primitive sensory modalities to the most differentiating, most advanced, but not vice versa" (Williams, 1976, 464–465). Although one can imagine possible counterexamples (Callejas, 2001), or look into natural corpora for finding some, other evidence suggests that the senses and features considered by Williams are not equally distributed in the donor or recipient positions (see below).

The problem of directionality in synaesthetic language had been previously raised by Ullmann (1945) who examined 2000 synaesthetic metaphors extracted from English, French, and Hungarian poetry. His directionality scale went from the "highest" modality (sight) to the "lowest" one (touch): the metaphor's topic usually represented a term belonging to the highest point in the scale and the metaphor's modifier (or vehicle) to the lowest point (e.g., "a cold light" is much more frequent than "a lighted coldness"). Recently, Shen (1997, 1998) investigated a contemporary corpus of Hebrew poetry finding analogous mappings from low values onto high ones that would reflect a mapping "from more accessible or basic concepts onto less accessible or less basic ones /that/ seems more natural and is preferred over the opposite mapping" (Shen, 1997, 51). Hence, "a sweet silence," where the mapping proceeds from taste (a highest point) to sounds (a lower point), would be preferred and more frequent in poetry than the reverse, "a silent sweetness" (Shen, 1998).

Interestingly, some authors recently claimed that the directionality of synaesthetic metaphors mirrors that observed in real synaesthesia, as exemplified by the higher frequency of induction from hearing to vision than of the reverse (e.g., Cytowic, 1989; Day, 1996; Ramachandran & Hubbard, 2001b). The directionality would reflect some neuroanatomical constraints that allow certain types of cross-activations, and not others (Ramachandran & Hubbard, 2001b; see below).

The sense directionality proposed by the taxonomic approach basically reflects the differential relevance and reliability that most of the western culture has attributed to the knowledge obtained from the sense organs. Unsurprisingly, it almost perfectly mirrors the senses hierarchy of Aristotle that ordered the intellectual relevance of the senses starting from sight, followed by hearing, olfaction, taste, and touch. He regarded touch as the primary sense and sight as the most advanced, with taste as a special type of touch and smell intertwined with taste. The ancient Greek philosophical language "borrowed terms and expressions connected with the act of vision from ordinary language and adapted them to describe acts of knowledge and the original permeation between seeing and knowing" (Napolitano Valditara, 1994, 8). Aristotle put sight among "perfect actions" establishing at the same time a bridge between sight and knowledge and the excellence of vision over the other sensory activities. Also audition and taste, or olfaction and touch, could be used for knowing providing a variety of perceptual information, but the knowledge capacity of sight was by no means reached having a deep and structured similarity with intellectual knowledge (Napolitano Valditara, 1994). Differently, in the Hebraic tradition knowledge has an auditory root, and "Revelation" takes place in a sphere metaphysically related to the auditory dimension (Scholem, 1970).[8]

Functional neuro-cognitive reasons make vision the most typical medium for knowledge, even though one can ignore that Plato, Aristotle, Parmenide, or Senofonte already stated it. The information we derive from the visual system, and from language, in fact sustain the apprehension and architecture of our external and internal world

(Jackendoff, 1987, 1992). As pointed out by Miller and Johnson-Laird in their seminal book on language and perception, our model of "the external world, insofar as we consider it perceptually based, derives primarily from what you see, what you hear, feel, and smell is compatible with such a world" (1976, 618).

### *Cross-Sensory Similarities in Metaphorical Language*

The aim of the psychophysical approach is to investigate the perceptual correspondences between sensory experiences and linguistic metaphors. A consistent body of evidence exists showing that sensory metaphorical transfers are not at random but are motivated by the perceptual characteristics of the event metaphorically matched with another perceptual event (i.e., the brightness of a light with the pitch or loudness of a sound, and so forth; e.g., Marks, 1982, 1996; Marks & Bornstein, 1987).

According to Marks (1982), if you ask several people "which is brighter, a cough or a sneeze?" (p. 177), the vast majority responds that a sneeze is brighter, higher in pitch than coughs, and that high-pitched sounds are like bright lights. Sneezes and coughs are examples of acoustic events that can be easily described in visual terms. What Marks elegantly demonstrated is that such descriptions are systematic and based on the psychophysical characteristics of the mapped perceptual events due to a "metaphorical consanguinity" (1982, p. 192) between pitch and brightness and between loudness and brightness. This produced a "suprasensory attribute – brightness – that is common to the auditory and visual domains" rooted in "some fundamental phenomenological property of the makeup of sensory experience" (1982, p. 192).

Marks (1978) and Marks and Bornstein (1987) showed that many French and English synaesthetic metaphors rest on just a few cross-modal resemblances anchored to the general properties of perceptual responses. Sensory metaphors such as "the murmur of the gray twilight" of Poe or the "bright sound of battle, loud light of thunder" of Swinburne are based on the sensory equivalence of the softness of a sound and the dimness of a light, that is of loudness and brightness. The ease of comprehension of these lines of poetry reflects the structure of semantic memory where "a 'murmur' is coded as prototypically soft, and 'twilight' is coded as prototypically dim" (Marks & Bornstein, 1987, 54), a viewpoint consistent with a recent perceptually based model of knowledge (Barsalou, 1999) and with cognitive neuroscience findings. Comprehension is not so effortless in metaphors such as "the sound of coming darkness" or "dawn comes up like thunder" (Marks & Bornstein, 1987) since there fairly different and unaligned values of auditory and visual intensity are matched. The softness of the sound has to be computed via its metaphorical equivalence with the dim light of the coming darkness, and the decrease in light brightness with an abrupt burst of sounds. Both cases go beyond, and must be independently computed from, the psychophysical characteristics of the events. Specifically, in Kipling's metaphor dawn "does not reach especially high on the scale of brightness. Thunder, on the other hand, is loud" (Mark & Bornstein, 1987, p. 60).

Many other types of cross-sensory correspondences were investigated in the literature. Zellner and Kautz (1990) observed that odor perception is influenced by the color of the to-be-perceived substance for both traditional odor–color associations (e.g., orange-flavored drinks with an intense orange color) and for newly created ones (Rouby et al., 2002). Usually, if a substance has no specific color, it is also expected to be odorless, while colored substances are supposed to be odorous. Another interesting case is the color–temperature correspondence (e.g., yellow/orange to warmness, and blue/green to coldness) whose metonymic structure, according to Marks and Bornstein (1987), reflects a range of universal experiences "with fire and flames, with the warmth of the sun, with the cool lakes and rivers and so forth. Throughout the world, the sun appears yellow, whereas large bodies of water appear blue and green, and these associations transcend specific cultures" (p. 57).

### *Five Separate Senses?*

Generally, we speak of the five senses as if they were distinct specialized entities, although we are ordinarily exposed to an array of stimuli that reaches and simultaneously activates more than one sensory modality at a time. Human perceptual experience involves in fact simultaneous stimulation through multiple sensory channels whose information is integrated by the brain in multisensory integration sites (Callan et al., 2004). Experientially, the boundary between sensory modalities can easily be broken when we infer, for instance, the haptic quality of a surface (e.g., its roughness) from seeing it, or in the case of the taste of a food that is influenced by its texture, smell, visual properties, and temperature (a mélange perfectly known by chefs and sommeliers). Can we have any experience of taste without being able to perceive the corresponding smell?[9] Hardly not, as suggested by the neural structures subserving taste and smell (see below), and even by the experience of having a cold, or closing our nose. Therefore, it is not surprising that the criteria mainly proposed by philosophers for separating each sense from the other are far from being clear-cut and independent (cf. Cacciari & Levorato, 2003; Leon, 1988; Nelkin, 1990; Stoffregen & Bardy, 2001). We might summarize them as follows:

1. The experiential criterion: the senses can be differentiated using the experiences associated with their operations (Leon, 1988; Nelkin, 1990). For instance, there is a qualitative difference between seeing an object as square and feeling an object as square. This would lead to distinguish between a visual shape and a tactile shape which is hardly convincing.
2. The property criterion: the senses can be distinguished based on the properties detected by means of them. For instance, sight would be specialized for perceiving shape and color. But many properties exist that can be detected by more than one sense (for instance, shape, extension, and position by both vision and touch). We also develop sensory expectations so that if we see a rose bush we also expect it to have a rose perfume. Furthermore, the operation of one sense can even interfere with that of another one as demonstrated by the McGurk effect (McGurk & MacDonald, 1976) where the perception of an auditorily presented phoneme was affected by an incongruent co-occurrent visual cue (i.e., lip movements).
3. The activating mechanism criterion: The senses can be differentiated based on the mechanisms that activate them, those on which they depend for their operations (e.g., light in the case of sight). But we can infer, for instance, tactile information from seeing a surface.
4. The sense-organ criterion: the senses would differ according to the different parts of the body involved, namely, according to the sense organs involved (e.g., the eyes for visual perception, the ears for hearing). But the eyes are both visually and tactually sensitive, and the neural basis of the sensory system is much more cross-modal than posited by this criterion;
5. The belief criterion: since certain kinds of sensations are perceived as correlating with what we take to be stimulation of a particular part of the body, we construct belief systems concerning the correlations between sensation and sense-organ. But, as Nelkin put it, do we have five senses because "there is a systematic correlation between our sorts of sensations and our beliefs about their organic origin or because of a systematic correlation between our sorts of beliefs and our beliefs about their organic origin, or a combination of the two?" (1990, 164). It is hard to tell.

None of these criteria suffices for dividing perception into the visual, auditory, gustatory, olfactory, and tactile senses. As Stoffregen and Bardy (2001) put it, the assumption of separate senses may seem to be so self-evident as to be atheoretical, instead it carries profound theoretical implications for theories of perception. Stoffregen and Bardy propose to consider perception as driven by a single system whose parts operate as a unit to pick up information that is available only to that unit and not accomplished by a set of distinct perceptual systems working in parallel (and often in conflict).

Whether or not sensory specialization indeed exists is still an open question that goes beyond the aim of this chapter. In any case, the similarities and commonalities, as well as the differences, among touch, hearing, vision, taste, and smell suggest that the senses are better conceptualized as interrelated modalities than as separate independent channels (Marks, 1978).

### *Synaesthesia: The Relationship between Linguistic Description and Perceptual Experience*

The synaesthetic use of language must be distinguished from perceiving the world synaesthetically, a fairly infrequent experience, as we will see. What cross-modal similarities and synaesthesia share is that properties belonging to different modalities are systematically realigned in both cases (Marks, 1996), suggesting that, despite important dissimilarities, they might draw on similar underlying mechanisms (see the distinction between strong and weak forms of synaesthesia proposed by Martino & Marks, 2001).

The fact that ordinary language has plenty of synaesthetic metaphors raised a fascinating and complex question: what is, if any, the relationship between perceptual metaphors and synaesthesia? Ramachandran and Hubbard suggested that the types of cross-sensorial induction typical of synaesthetic perceptions and the directionality expressed in sensory metaphors are not arbitrarily established but based on "constraints imposed by evolution and by neural hardware" (2003, 51). Consider the smell of nail polish: usually it is described as "sweet, even though we have never tasted it. This might involve close neural links and cross-activations between smell and taste (. . .). This would not only make sense functionally – e.g., fruits are sweet and also smell 'sweet' like acetone – but also structurally: the brain pathways for smell and taste are closely intermingled and project to the same parts of the frontal cortex" (Ramachandran & Hubbard, 2003, 52). Hence, the cross-sensory correspondences experienced in synaesthesia and many of those described at a metaphorical language level would both reflect, at different levels, "hard-wired properties of perceptual systems" (Marks, 1996, 43) that surface in perceptual experiences for synaesthetes, and in linguistic events for non-synaesthetes.

To assess whether the mental processes that underlie cross-modal associations in real synaesthesia (that they term strong synaesthesia) apply to cross-modal processing as well, Martino and Marks (1999, 2001) designed a cross-modal selective attention task: a person is requested to respond to a stimulus in one modality (e.g., classifying a tone as high or low) while she or he is presented with concurrent input from a different, unattended modality (e.g., a black or white square). If the unattended stimulus affects the response to the attended one, in that the intrusion of unattended stimuli into the elaboration of attended ones decreases the processing efficiency, then the two can be considered to interact. This happened to be the case. Furthermore, the nature of attended–unattended stimuli (i.e., their cross-modal similarity) affected the nature and intensity of the intrusion: participants were in fact faster at classifying high-pitched tones when matched with white squares than with black squares, and faster with low-pitched tones when accompanied by black (vs. white) squares.

The "congruence effect" found in the cross-modal matches of attended and unattended stimuli can be accounted for by two hypotheses (Martino & Marks, 1999, 2000, 2001):

1. A "*sensory hypothesis* according to which congruence effects involve absolute correspondences processed within low-level sensory mechanisms (. . .) /that/ may arise from common properties in underlying neural codes" (2001, p. 64). Hence, cross-modal interactions would take place at an early perceptual stage prior to the engagement of linguistic or semantic mechanisms.
2. A "*semantic coding hypothesis*," endorsed by the authors (and by Marks in previous works), based on high-level post-sensory (semantic) mechanisms that develop over childhood from experience with percepts and language (Marks, Hammeal, & Bornstein, 1987). The experienced relationships between sensory percepts and language would produce an abstract semantic network that captures the synaesthetic correspondence common to dimensions of both modalities, and where sensory representations and cross-sensory similarities are amodally recoded (Martino & Marks, 1999).

Differently from Martino and Marks (and from traditional theories of knowledge) that propose that sensory and linguistic stimuli are post-perceptually recoded into amodal representations, an alternative hypothesis can be proposed: such cross-modal matches might be produced by simultaneous activation of low-level sensory mechanisms and of high-level post-sensory ones. Evidence suggesting that this might be the case comes from several sources (e.g., Barsalou et al., 2003; Cacciari, Massironi, & Corradini, 2004; Gentilucci et al., 2000; Stanfield & Zwaan, 2001). For instance, integration between chromatic and linguistic information was recently shown in a study on the metaphorical use of color names in complex literary metaphors (Cacciari et al., 2004). Participants were asked to read short literary excerpts containing a color name metaphorically used to describe a character's mental state. These brief texts were presented on a computer screen together with five shades of the appropriate color (e.g., yellow). Several tasks were employed: for instance, participants were asked to choose the shade expressively most appropriate to the narrative content or to rank the expressive fitness of each of the five shades of color metaphorically used in the narrative. The color name–mental state correspondences did not correspond to any conventionalized association, and hence had to be computed afresh. We hypothesized that if the mental model readers formed exploited chromatic information, together with linguistic/conceptual information, then a consistent agreement in participants' choices of the shade of color was to be expected. On the contrary, if the mental model was predominantly amodal, then a lower agreement if not a mere chance choice was predicted. Indeed, the first happened to the case in that a very high and significant consistency in the participants' choices and rankings were obtained suggesting that participants indeed looked for the shade of color whose perceptual properties had the best expressive correspondence with the story content (see the article text for further details). This suggests that readers formed a complex mental model that took advantage of several sources of information integrating modal perceptual information with amodal linguistic-conceptual information (Cacciari et al., 2004). This evidence converges with that provided by Stanfield and Zwaan (2001) in suggesting activation of perceptual information in language-related tasks. Stanfield and Zwaan in fact showed that the mental representations of expressions such as *He put the pencil into the cup* and *He put the pencil on the table* included the pencil's orientation, that is, vertical in the former and horizontal in the latter, even though this perceptual information was not explicitly available in the linguistic input.

We now turn to consider real synaesthetic perceptions.

## SYNAESTHETIC PERCEPTION

In synaesthesia, the stimulation of a sensory modality automatically triggers a perceptual experience generally in a different modality that has not been directly stimulated (Baron-Cohen & Harrison, 1997;

Baron-Cohen, Wyke, & Binnie, 1987; Baron-Cohen et al., 1993; Cytowic, 1989, 1997; Cytowic & Wood, 1982a, 1982b; Ramachandran & Hubbard, 2001a, 2001b, 2003). In its most diffuse version – colored-hearing, often referred to as *photism* – listening to particular sounds (e.g., a phoneme, a word) induces vivid perception of a given color. Other types of across-modalities or within-modality synaesthetic perceptions have been observed as well (e.g., phonemes with a specific taste, geometrical forms with a smell or a taste; see Cytowic, 1999). As Cytowic pointed out, "Synaesthesia is not just a more intense form of cross-modal metaphor (. . .) being a vivid cross-modal association, synaesthesia is obviously a higher cortical function" (1989, 849).

Many people can use cross-modal similarity statements to describe events or emotions but only synaesthetes "experience a real percept" (Cytowic & Wood, 1982a, 23). Synaesthesia generally has a childhood onset and can be rarely acquired later in life as a result of brain injury or of a sensory deafferentiation (Grossenabacher & Lovelace, 2001). A case of acquired synaesthesia is described by Armel and Ramachandran (1999): a person developed retinitis pigmentosa in childhood and progressively lost his vision becoming completely blind at 40. Two years after, he started experiencing vivid synaesthesia in that tactile stimuli on the hand (Braille letters) evoked a vivid sensation of movement. Synaesthetic experiences must be also differentiated from those reported during ingestion of hallucinogenic drugs (e.g., LSD, mescaline), or resulting from neurological pathologies.

The first medical reference to synaesthesia was located at the beginning of the eighteenth century, when an English ophthalmologist, Thomas Woolhouse, described a blind patient who perceived sound-induced colored visions (Cytowic, 1989, 1997, 1999). At the end of the seventeenth century, John Locke wrote of a man who had strange word–sound associations. Some years earlier (1704), sounds to color mathematical connections were at the core of Newton's work and based the invention of a "clavecin oculaire" (a clavichord simultaneously playing sound and light). Although the phenomenon has been long known and has fascinated physicians, psychologists (e.g., Galton and Luria; see Osgood, 1980), artists (e.g., Kandinsky, Hockney), and writers (e.g., Goethe, Verlaine, Baudelaire, Maupassant, Nabokov), a full-fledged definition of synaesthesia has been proposed only recently thanks to the development of brain imaging techniques and to the impressive amount of knowledge brought about by cognitive neuroscience (cf. Baron-Cohen & Harrison, 1997; Harrison & Baron-Cohen, 1997). Despite this, we still are far from a full understanding of the neural basis of synaesthesia.

Four lines of experimental evidence converge to show the perceptual nature of synaesthesia that Ramachandran and Hubbard (2001a) summarized with respect to its most diffuse form, grapheme-color induction, as follows: "(1) Synaesthetically induced colors can lead to perceptual grouping, segregation, and pop-out. (2) Synaesthetic colors are not seen with eccentric viewing even if numbers are scaled in size to make them clearly visible. (3) A crowded grapheme that is not consciously perceived can nevertheless evoke the corresponding color. (4) A color-blind synaesthete sees colors in numbers that he cannot otherwise see in real-life visual scenes" (p. 27).

Despite attempts to formulate a unified approach to synaesthesia, there still is little evidence that a common underlying mechanism can account for the heterogeneity of synaesthetic perceptions (Rich & Mattingly, 2002). Chances are that, as for many other neuro-cognitive phenomena, different cognitive mechanisms and markers will be identified for each type of synaesthetic experience. Some authors suggested that working intensively on the most diffuse forms of synaesthesia (e.g., colored perceptions arising from orthographic or phonological processing of digits and letters) can be the right track for revealing the basic cognitive and neurophysiological underpinnings of other forms of synaesthetic experiences as well (Rich & Mattingly, 2002).

The most important parameters used for describing synaesthesia in the neuroscience literature can be schematized as follows (Cytowic, 1989; Frith & Paulesu, 1997; Grossenbacher & Lovelace, 2001; Harrison & Baron-Cohen, 1997; Paulesu et al., 1995; Ramachandran & Hubbard, 2001a, 2001b, 2003; Rich & Mattingly, 2002):

1. Origin: it generally initiates during childhood.
2. Automaticity: it is involuntary, characterized by awareness, and it can be suppressed only in highly specific conditions.
3. Realism: the sensations do not appear in the mind, but usually are perceived as real and discrete.
4. Specificity: the attributes of the associated modality (the concurrent one, see below) are highly specific and memorable.
5. Prevalence: synaesthesia concerns at least 1 out of 2,000 persons (but there also are higher and lower estimates, depending on the classification criteria);
6. Age: it is more frequent among children than adults.
7. Gender: it is six times more frequent among women than men.
8. Familiarity: there is a high prevalence among biological relatives, presumably due to a genetic predisposition transmitted by an X-linked autosomal dominant gene (Bailey & Johnson, 1997).

Although synaesthetic perception is unitary, usually two interrelated components were identified (Grossenbacher & Lovelace, 2001): an inducing event (the "inducer" event) and the synaesthetically induced sensory attributes ("concurrent event"). For instance, in the case of a person reporting that the sound of her crying baby had an unpleasant yellow color, the sounds were the inducers that were experienced as having a concurrent color, together with their normal auditory features [an induction usually schematized as (sound) → (color)].

For instance, consider the (digit) → (color) induction: one might wonder whether when shown the digit, the concurrent color (or concurrent photism) is experienced in the synaesthete's "mind's eye" or externally projected on the inducer. For instance, Dixon et al. (2000) and Smilek et al. (2001) reported a case in which the color of the photism induced by a digit was externally projected: if shown a "4," the synaesthete described a blue photism being seen "out there, on the page, overlaid on the top of the 4" and covering it. But a remarkable perceptual heterogeneity exists.

For the vast majority of individuals, synaesthesia is unidirectional in that if a sound induces a color experience, the same color does not typically trigger the experience of a sound, but "the relationship between inducers and concurrents is systematic in that each specific concurrent is typically induced by only one inducer" (Grossenbacher & Lovelace, 2001, 36). Not all forms of synaesthesia span across two sensory modalities (cross-modal synaesthesia); some forms in fact exist in which the inducer and concurrent share a same modality, for instance, vision, as in the reading of visual letters of the alphabet that triggers the perception of colors (intramodal synaesthesia).

It still is controversial the degree of processing of the inducer necessary for triggering a synaesthetic perception: according to some authors (e.g., Mattingly et al., 2001; for an overview see Rich & Mattingly, 2002), the [(letter) → (color)] induction would take place at a relatively late stage of perceptual processing, after selective attention is allocated, that is, following overt recognition of the inducing stimulus. Hence, synaesthetic colors would typically arise only for inducers that are represented at a conscious level of visual processing (that might include meaning activation, if appropriate), being absent when a grapheme is visually masked, for instance. On the contrary, other researchers (e.g., Ramachandran & Hubbard, 2001a, 2001b) found a perceptual link between inducer and concurrent even at a relatively early stage of perceptual analysis, namely, before explicit identification of the inducer stimulus. A related and still controversial issue is whether synaesthetic experience arises automatically or under voluntary control. The evidence collected using variants of the Stroop task[10] converges to show that synaesthetic colors are automatically elicited by graphemic forms and are difficult to suppress, although inhibitory effects were observed under specific experimental conditions.

We now turn to examine separately the characteristics of inducer and concurrent stimuli:

1. The inducers: many of them have a meaningful symbolic nature, as we already saw. Generally, inducers are systematically associated with the same concurrent, but while the form of the inducer can change, the concurrent remains stable. If, for instance, seeing the letter "B" induces the perception of a particular shade of red, such color remains constant despite different handwriting styles, font, or case. If listening to a voice reading aloud an alphabetic letter induces seeing it colored, it is irrelevant whether the voice is feminine or masculine (Grossenbacher & Lovelace, 2001). Concurrent synaesthetic experiences can be induced through voluntary imagery of the inducer as well, that is, without direct exposure to the stimulus. It is well known that imagery involves many parts of the brain that are active also during visual perception. Since no physical stimulus is available and no afferent signals enter the cortex while imaging, this implies that synaesthesia can take place even with incomplete activation of the cascade of perceptual signaling propagated during visual perception.
2. The concurrents: it is quite rare to find two people sharing a same color triggered by the same set of alphabetic letter. There is in fact a high inter-individual heterogeneity in concurrent stimuli.[11] Despite this, given individual concurrent stimuli are highly specific and constant in time. They also are extremely memorable, as shown by a study where the consistency with which synaesthetes and non-synaesthetes assigned color names to letters and words was investigated (Baron-Cohen et al., 1993). After one week, the control group remembered the color names only in 38% of the cases, while synaesthetes in 92% even a year later. Concurrent stimuli usually comprise simple features (e.g., a color) or combination of simple features much more than complex configurations (e.g., a face).

Two main types of synaesthesia have been distinguished depending on the sensory or conceptual nature of the inducer (Grossenbacher & Lovelace, 2001): while in "synaesthetic perception," the concurrent events are induced by experiencing specific sensory stimuli; in "synaesthetic conception," the concurrent events are triggered by thinking about specific concepts, as shown by a synaesthete for whom each of the 12 months of a year was located in a spatially organized colored configuration. Symbolic levels of representation can in any case influence synaesthetic experiences, as shown in a case of "lexical–gustatory synaesthesia," where specific learned combinations of phonemes, but not environmental sounds, induced involuntary sensations of taste (Ward & Simner, 2003). Synaesthesia can even by triggered by the concept that underlies the inducer: Dixon et al. (2000) reported a case of a person for which the digit 7 elicited a yellow photism. Such color was automatically induced also when she was not presented with the digit but simply asked to calculate "5+2." Hence, photism can also be concept driven, as shown by this case of arithmetic calculation.

When considering the sense directionality of perceptual metaphors, I anticipated that also synaesthetic inductions are not equally distributed among the senses. As noted by Cytowic (1995), the five senses can have many but finite possible pairings; yet, some of them (e.g., sight and sound) are much more frequent than others. It is rare for smell and taste to be either the inducer or the concurrent (see Cytowic, 1993, for "The man who tasted shapes"). Day (2006) analyzed 621 cases of synaesthesia reported in the literature and found that 427 of them (68.8%) were (graphemes) → (color) inductions versus only one case of (smell) → (taste).

So far no unified account of the neural-cognitive basis of synaesthesia exists and different, although not necessarily alternative, hypotheses have been proposed. They can be summarized as follows:

1. Synaesthesia derives from anomalous cross-wiring between brain areas that subserve the sensory modalities involved (e.g., between area V4 and the number area in the fusiform gyrus; Ramachandran & Hubbard, 2001a, 2001b). This could be due to the survival of links among cortical sensory systems that used to be connected at birth in human infants (as in other species) but are normally disconnected after the neonatal stage (Baron-Cohen, 1996; Maurer, 1997): the neonatal synaesthesia hypothesis (Maurer, 1997) in fact posits that all babies are synaesthetic up to some point of their early life (approximately, up to about four months of age) in that they experience sensory inputs in an undifferentiated way. Alternatively, synaesthesia would result either from a partial failure in the normal pruning process that eliminates these cross-modal connections, or from the sprouting of additional synaptic connections resulting in a cross-wiring among areas (Baron-Cohen et al., 1993; Ramachandran & Hubbard, 2001a, 2001b). In any case, adult synaesthesia would represent a breakdown in the process of modularization (Baron-Cohen et al., 1993).
2. The close anatomic proximity of visual and auditory pathways might be at the origin of "leaks" among pathways, so that auditory information leaks into pathways and areas that ordinarily deal with visual information.
3. Synaesthesia might result from abnormal feedback in existing neural pathways (Grossenbacher, 1997; Grossenbacher & Lovelace, 2001; Smilek et al., 2001). More specifically, it could be due to a process of neural communication, of cross-talk of brain regions, that has its origin in feed-forward signals in the inducer neural representation and culminates in activation of the otherwise independent concurrent representation via feedback signals (based on pathways convergence).
4. Synaesthesia is subserved by areas located in the left-brain hemisphere and "is accompanied by large metabolic shifts away from the neocortex that result in relatively enhanced limbic expression. The hippocampus is an important and probably obligate node in whatever neural structures generates the synaesthetic experience" (Cytowic, 1995, 8; see also Cytowic, 1989, 1997).

As Ramachandran and Hubbard (2001a, 2001b) noted, in the past synaesthesia was often dismissed as childhood memories or confused with a "mere metaphor," "an example of the classic fallacy of trying to explain an enigma (synaesthesia) with a mystery (metaphor)" (2001a, 982). On the contrary, "understanding synaesthesia (a concrete perceptual effect the anatomical locus of which can be potentially pinned down) can provide an experimental level for understanding the neural basis of metaphors" (Ramachandran & Hubbard, 2001a, 982).

## Beyond Synaesthesia

The general view underlying this chapter is that metaphorical language is pervaded by cross-modality references that mirror, at a linguistic level, our neural architecture (Marks, 1996; Ramachandran & Hubbard, 2001a, 2001b). To provide further evidence, let us consider some additional examples of multimodal processing in the brain.

The human brain, together with that of other non-human primates, can form many types of cross-sensory integrations aside from synaesthesia: one is related to the integration of visual–tactile representations of a specific portion of the visual space that surrounds the body, the peripersonal space (for an overview, see Ladavas, 2002). Neuropsychological studies showed that an integrated system exists that controls both visual and tactile inputs within the peripersonal space around the face and the hand. Such a system is functionally separated from the one that controls visual information in the extrapersonal space. This implies that our visual experience of a body part is intrinsically linked with the experience of touch, as it had been described for arm amputees who reported vivid tactile sensations in the phantom arm when they saw the experimenter touching the mirror image of their normal arm (Ramachandran & Rogers-Ramachandran, 1996).

A specific case of sensory integration between language and actions has been extensively investigated by Rizzolati and colleagues (for an overview, see Rizzolati & Arbib, 1998; Arbib & Rizzolati, 1996). These authors showed that the human motor system becomes active during observation of gestures made by others and that Broca's area and the left temporal lobe are consistently activated during action observation. This finding originates from a set of previous studies showing that a specific part of ventral premotor cortex (area F5) in monkeys contains neurons that discharge both when the monkey grasps an object and when she or he observes the experimenter making a similar gesture. The neurons endowed with this property were called "mirror neurons" and were considered to provide representations used for both imitating and comprehending actions. Such a mirror system for gesture recognition was found in human brain close to Broca's area and considered as the human homologue of the F5 area in monkeys. The motor properties of human Broca's areas were observed in a set of PET studies that showed that such areas became active during the execution of hand or arm movements, during mental imagery of hand grasping movements, and during mental rotations of the hand (for an overview, see Rizzolatti & Arbib, 1998).

Gentilucci et al. (2000) showed that the motor program relative to grasping an object was modified by the presence of a written linguistic label located on the to-be-grasped object specifying an extrinsic or intrinsic property (e.g., "near," "far," "big," "small"): the kinematics of the initial phase of reaching and grasping an object were affected by the word meaning suggesting that a cognitive function, word processing, can intervene in visuo-motor transformations. That motor-related concepts can be conceived of as multisensory memories was recently argued by Oliveri et al. (2004) and Pulvermüller, Lutzenberger, & Preissl (1999) who showed that the motor schemata associated with a given action word are "embedded within its cortical representation, and are activated automatically whenever that word is retrieved" (Oliveri et al., 2004, 377). Using a brain stimulation technique (TMS or transcranial magnetic stimulation), Oliveri et al. observed that the left primary motor cortex was maximally and much more activated during the retrieval of action verbs and action-related nouns (e.g., "to throw," "the key") than of non-action-related words (e.g., "to belong," "the cloud"), even when the participants were not in any way instructed to consider the meaning of the words. Hence, the cortical regions activated by words referring to actions were shown to comprise regions encoding information that is not purely linguistic or conceptual but reflect the sensorimotor properties associated with the concept underlying them.

## To Conclude: On Language Conventionality and "Hard-Wired" Motivation

Many cross-sensory expressions are so common in language that one might doubt that they still are perceived as non-literal. For instance, saying of a pain that it is sharp seems as literal as saying that it is intense, since "double-function" adjectives (Asch, 1958) like "sharp" are commonly used to modify a variety of dimensions, as already noted by Aristotle in the De Anima. As

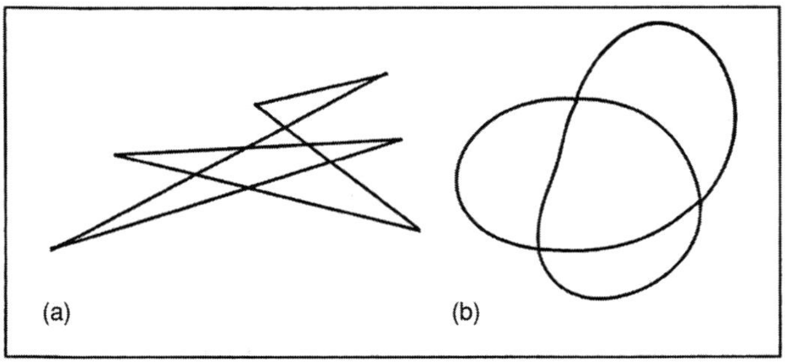


**Figure 24.2.** "Takete" (a) and "Maluma" (b) (Koehler, 1947).

Miller and Johnson-Laird stated, "Perhaps it is a mistake to think that the concept expressed by a word like 'sharp', which can describe touch, taste, sound, intelligence, terrain, strictness, eagerness, and objects is legitimately applicable only to touch and must be generalized for other applications" (1976, 360). A sharp mind "may be as good an instance of SHARP as a sharp pain; a warm person may be as good an instance of WARM as a warm tactual experience" (Miller & Johnson-Laird, 1976, p. 360).

But polysemy mostly originates from metaphorical language. As several authors noted (e.g., Nunberg, 1979; Sweetser, 1991), generally words do not acquire new senses randomly but according to a "cognitive structuring" that relates them in a motivate fashion: "linguistic categorization depends not just on our naming distinctions that exist in the world, but also on our metaphorical and metonymical structuring of our perceptions of the world" (Sweetser, 1991, 9).

An example of a cross-modal correspondence not conventional at all was provided by Koehler (1947; see also Lindauer, 1990, 1991; Werner, 1963) that presented participants with two meaningless visual shapes (see Figure 24.2) and asked them to pair each shape with either the linguistic label *Takete* or with *Maluma*. The participants unambiguously associated the one with sharp changes in the visual directions of the lines (a) with *Takete* and the rounded one (b) with *Maluma* even though they had never seen these stimuli before. Since then, many studies replicated such effect with variants of the original visual shapes of Koehler.

One of the most credited interpretations of this form-to-sound match is based on the link between phonemic and perceptual–geometrical properties (see Bozzi & Flores d'Arcais, 1967): as also recently argued by Ramachandran and Hubbard (2001b), the sharp changes in the visual directions of the lines in the angular figure mimic the sharp inflections of the sound as well as the movements of the tongue on the palate.[12] The two visual forms and labels act via diverse sensory systems (sight and audition) but are treated as similar and put into correspondence on the basis of one or more shared cross-modal properties.

According to Gestalt psychologists, the visual forms and the phonemes forming the linguistic labels share an evocative trait, namely, a "tertiary" property (or "physiognomic"; see Werner, 1963). According to Gestalt psychologists, in fact, objects possess three different kinds of property:

1. Primary properties that are objective, measurable, and independent from the perceiver (e.g., form, extension). It is the world described by natural sciences.
2. Secondary properties that are perceptually tied to an observer's activity and are mediated by sense organs (e.g., color, sound).
3. Tertiary or expressive properties that belong to the object although they are perceived by the individual as part of his/her experience: they are not "occasional emotional vibrations, but the contribution of emotion to the cognitive side of perception" (Massironi, 2000, 12).

In this vein, the expressive properties of the sharp sound of *Takete* and of the angular shape had a better fit than those of *Maluma* with the same geometrical form (Bozzi, 1990; Marks, 1996).

Expressive properties span all over the perceptual world for Gestalt psychologists and are as real as shape or color. Likewise, Gibson's affordances (1979) were not seen as emotional projections or experience-based associations but as real, objective, and physical properties contained in the optical array: "a postbox 'invites' the mailing of a letter, the handle 'wants to be grasped' and things 'tell us what to do with them'" (Gibson, 1979, 77).

As Marks (1996) argued, many, if not all, cross-modal similarities expressed in metaphorical language might reflect "natural correspondences between experiences in different sense modalities (. . .) that seem to be nothing less than 'hard-wired'" (Marks, 1996, 61). This is one of the reasons why trying to explain these linguistic metaphors as assertions of similarity between sensory events would prove useless: what in fact motivates the existence, and systematicity, of some metaphorical correspondences and excludes others? Once again, confusing metaphors with similes, transforming metaphors into "is-like" statements, leaves the problem unexplained (Glucksberg, 2001, and in this volume; Glucksberg & Keysar, 1990).

Language, be it literal or metaphorical, can construct a perceptual scenario that might even substitute the corresponding perceptual reality. As shown in Landau and Gleitman's study (1985) on the acquisition of visual verbs by sighted and blind children, the verbs "look" and "see" are acquired as if "the meaning component 'visual' is never encoded in the syntax of these verbs, which is observable by both the blind and the sighted children, but rather is learned from extralinguistic observation alone, which varies for the blind and sighted children" (Fisher, Gleitman, & Gleitman, 1992, 377). On a literary ground, the capacity of linguistic descriptions to construct, better replace, perceptual reality gave raise to the fortune of a literary genre, of the seventeenth to the nineteenth centuries, "le récit de voyage" (travel narrative). Famous writers (e.g., Goethe, Stendhal) mostly traveling in Italy described still untouched Italian landscapes to their contemporaries contributing with painters to create an imaginary country of Roman and Greek ruins, old palaces, and volcanoes. When we see Turner's drawing of the Canal Grande in Venice, or read Ruskin's description of the palaces lining along it, we are aware that these are (gorgeous) representations of a perceptual scenario, Venice, that might or might not resemble the real Venice. Many, maybe not all, sensory-based metaphors go beyond this illusory effect being something different from an "intrusion" of language into the perceptual world since they indeed reflect the structure of perceptual experience, of semantic memory, and of the neural circuits subserving them.

At the beginning of this chapter, I stated my working hypothesis as follows: metaphorical language expressing sensory experiences does not reflect an abstract–amodal combination of word senses, but rather the neural endowment necessary for treating sensory information. I tried to show that this might be the case examining direct as well as indirect sources of evidence (synaesthesia and multisensory experience). Neurosciences offer an extraordinary opportunity to investigate metaphors for what they might concretely be, linguistic bridges between the mind and the brain.

## Notes

1 This chapter is dedicated to Paolo Bozzi (1933–2003). Part of the ideas illustrated in this chapter was first presented in Cacciari (1998, 2004).

2 I will refer to sensory and perceptual metaphors as if the two adjectives were synonymous. I only consider linguistic metaphors, but, of course, there also are cases of nonlinguistic perceptual metaphors (e.g., caricatures).

3 *The Physiology of Taste. Or, Meditations on Transcendental Gastronomy.*
4 I owe this definition to Paolo Bozzi.
5 This applies to other senses as well (e.g., the taste of a peach, the sound of a bell) that nonetheless have a variety of generic terms (Boisson, 1997).
6 Many other instances of the reduced ability of language to name perceptual experiences are offered by spatial language. Landau and Jackendoff (1993) extensively investigated it showing that language filters out representations of spatial properties and relationships. For instance, dimensional adjectives (e.g., big/small, thick/thin) refer to continuous dimensions, but the linguistic expressions bifurcate them into binary contrasts.
7 Other forms of figurative language as well can exploit perceptual language, for instance, idiomatic expressions, proverbs, and oxymora, but I will mostly consider metaphors.
8 I thank Umberto Eco for this observation.
9 I thank Sam Glucksberg for this observation.
10 In the standard Stroop task, participants must name the color of the ink in which words are written.
11 The inter-synaesthetes heterogeneity led Ramachandran and Hubbard (2001a) to differentiate between higher and lower forms of synaesthesia based on the attentional–cognitive triggers of synaesthetic perceptions (e.g., required focused attention), and on the neuroanatomical loci of cross-activation observed in the brain of higher and lower synesthetes.
12 This raises an interesting question concerning sound symbolism that goes beyond the aim of the chapter.

## References


Ackerman, D. (1990). *A natural history of the senses*. New York: Random House.

Arbib, M. A., & Rizzolatti, G. (1996). Neural expectations: A possible evolutionary path from manual skills to language. *Communication & Cognition*, 29(3–4), 393–424.

Armel, K. C., & Ramachandran, V. S. (1999). Acquired synaesthesia in retinitis pigmentosa. *Neurocase*, 5, 293–296.

Asch, S. (1958). The metaphor: A psychological inquiry. In R. Tagiuri & L. Petrullo (Eds.), *Person perception and interpersonal behavior* (pp. 86–94). Stanford, CA: Stanford University Press.

Bailey, M. E., & Johnson, K. (1997). Synaesthesia: Is a genetic analysis feasible? In S. Baron-Cohen & J. E. Harrison (Eds.), *Synaesthesia: Classic and contemporary readings* (pp. 182–210). Cambridge, MA: Blackwell.

Baron-Cohen, S. (1996). Is there a normal phase of synaesthesia in development? *Psyche*, 2(27).

Baron-Cohen, S., & Harrison, J. E. (Eds.). (1997). *Synaesthesia: Classic and contemporary readings*. Cambridge, MA: Blackwell.

Baron-Cohen, S. Harrison, J. E., Goldstein, L. H., & Wyke, M. (1993). Coloured speech perception: Is synaesthesia what happens when modularity breaks down? *Perception*, 22(4), 419–426.

Baron-Cohen, S., Wyke, M. A., & Binnie, C. (1987). Hearing words and seeing colors: An experimental investigation of a case of synesthesia. *Perception*, 16, 761–767.

Barsalou, L. W. (1999). Perceptual symbol systems. *Behavioral and Brain Sciences*, 22, 577–660.

Barsalou, L. W., Kyle Simmons, W., Barbey, A. K., & Wilson, C. D. (2003). Grounding conceptual knowledge in modality-specific systems. *Trends in Cognitive Sciences*, 7(2), 84–91.

Beck, B. (1978). The metaphor as a mediator between semantic and analogical modes of thought. *Current Anthropology*, 19, 83–94.

Beck, B. (1987). Metaphor, cognition and artificial intelligence. In R. S. Haskell (Ed.), *Cognition and symbolic structure: The psychology of metaphoric transformation* (pp. 9–30). Norwood, NJ: Ablex.

Boisson, C. (1997). La dénomination des odeurs: variations et régularités linguistiques. *Intellectica*, 1(24), 29–49.

Bozzi, P. (1990). *Fisica Ingenua*. Milano: Garzanti.

Bozzi, P., & D'Arcais, G. B. (1967/1993). Ricerca sperimentale sui rapporti intermodali fra qualità espressive. In P. Bozzi (Ed.), *Experimenta in visu. Ricerche sulle percezione* (pp. 93–122). Milano: Guerini Editore.

Brillat-Savarin, A. J. (1825). *La physiologie du goût. Or méditations de gastronomie trascendente*. (Italian translation). Milano: Rizzoli.

Cacciari, C. (1998). Why do we speak metaphorically? Reflections on the functions of metaphor in discourse and reasoning. In A. Katz, C. Cacciari, R. W. Gibbs Jr., & M. Turner (Eds.), *Figurative language and thought* (pp. 119–157). Oxford: Oxford University Press.

Cacciari, C., & Levorato, M. C. (2003). "Res accendent lumina rebus": La descrizione dell'esperienza sensoriale, ovvero dei rapporti fra percezione e linguaggio. In U. Savardi & A. Mazzocco (a cura di), *Figura e sfondo. Temi e variazioni per Paolo Bozzi* (pp. 179–200). Padova: CLEUP.

Cacciari, C., Massironi, M., & Corradini, P. (2004). When color names are used metaphorically: The role of linguistic and chromatic information. *Metaphor & Symbol*, 19(3), 169–190.

Callan, D. E., Jones, J. A., Shapiro, K., Munhall, K., Kroos, C., Callan, A. M., et al. (2004). Multisensory integration sites identified by perception of spatial wavelet filtered visual speech gesture information. *Journal of Cognitive Neuroscience*, 16(5), 805–816.

Callejas Bretones, C. (2001). *Synaesthetic metaphors in English. Technical Reports* (TR 01-008). Berkeley, CA: International Computer Science Institute.

Cazeaux, C. (2002). Metaphor and the categorization of senses. *Metaphor & Symbol*, 11(1), 3–26.

Classen, C. (1993). *Worlds of senses: Exploring the senses in history and across cultures*. London: Routledge.

Cytowic, R. E. (1989). *Synesthesia: A union of the senses*. New York: Springer Verlag.

Cytowic, R. E. (1995). Synesthesia: Phenomenology and neuropsychology. *Psyche*, 2, 10.

Cytowic, R. E. (1997). Synesthesia: Phenomenology and neuropsychology. In S. Baron-Cohen & J. E. Harrison (Eds.), *Synaesthesia: Classic and contemporary readings* (pp. 17–42). Cambridge, MA: Blackwell.

Cytowic, R. E. (1999). *The man who tasted shapes*. Cambridge, MA: MIT Press.

Cytowic, R. E., & Wood, F. B. (1982a). Synesthesia: I. Review of major theories and their brain basis. *Brain and Cognition*, 1, 23–35.

Cytowic, R. E., & Wood, F. B. (1982b). Synesthesia: II. Psychophysical relations in the synaesthesia of geometrically shaped taste and colored hearing. *Brain and Cognition*, 1, 36–49.

David, S., Dubois, D., Rouby, C., & Schaal, B. (1997). L'expression des odeurs en Français: analyse lexicale et représentation cognitive. *Intellectica*, 1(24), 51–83.

Day, S. (1996). Synaesthesia and synaesthetic metaphors. *Psyche*, 2, 32.

Derrig, S. (1978). Metaphor in the color lexicon. In D. Farkas, W. M. Jacobsen, & K. W. Todyris (Eds.), *Papers from the parasession on the lexicon* (pp. 85–96). Chicago: Chicago Linguistic Society.

Dixon, M. J., Smilek, D., Cudahy, & Merikle, P. M. (2000). Five plus two equals yellow. *Nature*, 406, 365.

Fisher, C., Gleitman, H., & Gleitman, R. L. (1992). On the semantic content of subcategorization frames. *Cognitive Psychology*, 23, 331–392.

Frith, C. D., & Paulesu, E. (1997). The physiological basis of synaesthesia. In S. Baron-Cohen & J. E. Harrison (Eds.), *Synaesthesia: Classic and contemporary readings* (pp. 123–147). Cambridge, MA: Blackwell.

Gentilucci, G., Benuzzi, F., Bertolani, L. Daprati, E., & Gangitano, M. (2000). Language and motor control. *Experimental Brain Research*, 133, 468–490.

Gibbs, R. W. (2003). Embodied experience and linguistic meaning. *Brain and Language*, 84, 1–15.

Gibson, J. J. (1979). *The ecological approach to visual perception*. Boston: Houghton Mifflin.

Glucksberg, S. (2001). *Understanding figurative language: From metaphors to idioms*. Oxford: Oxford University Press.

Glucksberg, S., & Keysar, B. (1990). Understanding metaphorical comparisons: Beyond similarity. *Psychological Review*, 97(1), 3–18.

Grossenbacher, P. G. (1997). Perception and sensory information in synaesthetic experience. In S. Baron-Cohen, & J. E. Harrison (Eds.), *Synaesthesia: classic and contemporary readings*. Oxford: Blackwell.

Grossenbacher, P., & Lovelace, C. T. (2001). Mechanisms of synesthesia: Cognitive and physiological constraints. *Trends in Cognitive Sciences*, 5(1), 36–41.

Harrison, J. E., & Baron-Cohen, S. (1997). Synaesthesia: A review of psychological theories. In S. Baron-Cohen & J. E. Harrison (Eds.), *Synaesthesia: Classic and contemporary readings* (pp. 109–122). Cambridge, MA: Blackwell.

Howes, D. (2002). Nose-wise: Olfactory metaphors in mind. In C. Rouby, B. Schaal, D. Dubois, R. Gervais, & A. Hollet (Eds.), *Olfaction, taste, and cognition* (pp. 67–81). Cambridge: Cambridge University Press.

Jackendoff, R. (1987). On beyond zebra: The relation of linguistic and visual information. *Cognition*, 26, 89–114.

Jackendoff, R. (1992). *Languages of the mind: Essays on mental representation*. Cambridge, MA: MIT Press.

Jha, R. (1999). *Smell*. New York: Soho Press.

Koehler, W. (1947). *Gestalt psychology* (6th ed.). New York: Mentor Book.

Ladavas, E. (2002). Functional and dynamic properties of visual peripersonal space. *Trends in Cognitive Sciences*, 6(1) 17–22.

Landau, B., & Gleitman, L. (1985). *Language and experience: Evidence from the blind child*. Cambridge, MA: Harvard University Press.

Landau, B., & Jackendoff, R. (1993). "What" and "where" in spatial language and spatial cognition. *Behavioral and Brain Sciences*, 16, 217–265.

Leon, M. (1988). Characterizing the senses. *Mind and Language*, 3(4), 243–270.

Lindauer, M. (1990). The meanings of the physiognomic stimuli *Taketa* and *Maluma*. *Bulletin of the Psychonomic Society*, 28, 47–50.

Lindauer, M. (1991). Physiognomy and verbal synaesthesia compared: Affective and intersensory descriptors of nouns with drawings and art. *Metaphor and Symbolic Activity*, 6, 183–202.

Marks, L. E. (1978). *The unity of senses*. New York: Academic Press.

Marks, L. E. (1982). Bright sneezes and dark coughs, loud sunlight and soft moonlight. *Journal of Experimental Psychology: Human Perception and Performance*, 8(2), 177–193.

Marks, L. E. (1996). On perceptual metaphors. *Metaphor and Symbolic Activity*, 1(1), 36–96.

Marks, L. E., & Bornstein, M. H. (1987). Sensory similarities: Classes, characteristics and cognitive consequences. In R. S. Haskell (Ed.), *Cognition and symbolic structure: The psychology of metaphoric transformation* (pp. 49–65). Norwood, NJ: Ablex.

Marks, L. E., Hammeal, R. J., & Bornstein, M. H. (1987). Perceiving similarity and comprehending metaphor. *Monographs of the Society for Research in Child Development*, 52(1), 215.

Martino, G., & Marks, L. E. (1999). Perceptual and linguistic interactions in speeded classification: Tests of the semantic coding hypothesis. *Perception*, 28, 903–923.

Martino, G. and Marks, L. E. (2000). Cross-modal interactions between vision and touch: the role of synaesthetic correspondence. *Perception*, 29, 745–754.

Martino, G. and Marks, L. E. (2001). Synaesthesia: Strong and weak. *Current Directions in Psychological Science*, 10(2), 61–65.

Massironi, M. (2000). *L'osteria dei dadi truccati. Arte, Psicologia e dintorni*. Bologna: il Mulino.

Mattingly, J. B., Rich, A. N., Yelland, G., & Bradshaw, J. L. (2001). Unconscious priming eliminates automatic binding of colour and alphanumeric form in synaesthesia. *Nature*, 410, 580–582.

Maurer, D. (1997). Neonatal synaesthesia: Implications for processing of speech and faces. In S. Baron-Cohen & J. E. Harrison (Eds.), *Synaesthesia: Classic and contemporary readings* (pp. 224–242). Cambridge, MA: Blackwell.

McGurk, H., & MacDonald, J. (1976). Hearing lips and seeing voices. *Nature*, 264, 747–748.

Miller, G., & Johnson-Laird, P. (1976). *Language and perception*. Cambridge, MA: Harvard University Press.

Napolitano Valditara, L. (1994). *Lo sguardo nel buio. Metafore visive e forme grecoantiche della razionalità*. Bari: Laterza.

Nelkin, N. (1990). Categorizing senses. *Mind and Language*, 5, 2, 149–165.

Nunberg, G. (1979). The non-uniqueness of semantic solutions: Polysemy. *Linguistics and Philosophy*, 3, 143–184.

Oliveri, M., Finocchiaro, C., Shapiro, K., Gangitano, M., Caramazza, A., & Pascual-Leone, A. (2004). All talk and no action: A transcranial magnetic stimulation study of motor cortex activation during action word production. *Journal of Cognitive Neuroscience*, 16(3), 374–381.

Osgood, C. E. (1980). The cognitive dynamics of synesthesia and metaphor. In R. P. Honeck, & R. R. Hoffman, (Eds.), *Cognition and figurative language* (pp. 203–238). Hillsdale, NJ: Lawrence Erlbaum Associates.

Paulesu, E., Harrison, J., Baron-Cohen, S., Watson, J. D. G., Goldstein, L., Heather, J., et al. (1995). The physiology of coloured hearing: A PET activation study of colour-word synaesthesia. *Brain*, 118, 661–676.

Pelamatti, A., & Savardi, U. (2003). I sensi della conoscenza. In U. Savardi & A. Mazzocco (a cura di), *Figura e sfondo. Temi e variazioni per Paolo Bozzi* (pp. 201–224). Padova: CLEUP.

Pulvermüller, F., Lutzenberger, W., & Preissl, H. (1999). Nouns and verbs in the intact brain: Evidence from event-related potentials and high-frequency cortical responses. *Cerebral Cortex*, 9, 497–506.

Ramachandran, V. S., & Hubbard, E. M. (2001a). Psychophysical investigations into the neural basis of synesthesia. *Proceedings of the Royal Society of London B, Biological Sciences*, 268, 979–983.

Ramachandran, V. S., & Hubbard, E. M. (2001b). Synesthesia: A window into perception, thought, and language. *Journal of Consciousness Studies*, 8(1), 3–34.

Ramachandran, V. S., & Hubbard, E. M. (2003). The phenomenology of synesthesia. *Journal of Consciousness Studies*, 10(8), 49–57.

Ramachandran, V. S., & Rogers-Ramachandran, D. (1996). Synesthesia in phantom limbs induced by mirrors. *Proceedings of the Royal Society of London B, Biological Sciences*, 263, 377–386.

Rich, A. N., & Mattingly, J. B. (2002). Anomalous perception in synaesthesia: A cognitive neuroscience perspective. *Nature Reviews: Neuroscience*, 3, 43–52.

Rizzolatti, G., & Arbib, M. A. (1998). Language within our grasp. *Trends in Neurosciences*, 21(5), 188–194.

Rouby, C., Schaal, B., Dubois, D., Gervais, R., & Hollet, A. (2002). (Eds.) *Olfaction, taste, and cognition*. Cambridge: Cambridge University Press.

Schab, F. (1990). Odors and the remembrance of things past. *Journal of Experimental Psychology: Learning, Memory, and Cognition*, 16(4), 648–655.

Scholem, G. (1970). *Il Nome di Dio e la teoria cabalistica del linguaggio*. Milano: Bompiani.

Shen, Y. (1997). Cognitive constraints on poetic figures. *Cognitive Linguistics*, 8(1), 33–72.

Shen, Y. (1998). How come silence is sweet but sweetness is not silent: A cognitive account of directionality in poetic synaesthesia. *Language and Literature*, 7(2), 123–140.

Smilek, D., Dixon, M. J., Cudahy, C., & Merikle, O. M. (2001). Synaesthetic photism influence visual perception. *Journal of Cognitive Neuroscience*, 13, 930–936.

Stanfield, R. A., & Zwaan, R. A. (2001). The effect of implied orientation derived from verbal context on picture recognition. *Psychological Science*, 12, 153–156.

Stoffregen, T. A., & Bardy, B. G. (2001). On specification and the senses. *Behavioral and Brain Sciences*, 24, 2, 195–261.

Sweetser, E. (1991). *From etymology to pragmatics. Metaphorical and cultural aspects of semantic structure*. Cambridge: Cambridge University Press.

Ullmann, S. (1945). Romanticism and synaesthesia. *Publications of the Modern Language Association of America*, 60, 811–827.

Ullmann, S. (1962). *Semantics: An introduction to the study of meaning*. Oxford: Basil Blackwell & Mott.

Ward, J., & Simner, K. (2003). Lexical-gustatory synaesthesia: Linguistic and conceptual factors. *Cognition*, 80, 237–261.

Werner, H. (1963). On expressive language. In G. Kepes (Ed.), *The new landscape in art and sciences* (pp. 280–282). Chicago: Theobald.

Williams, J. M. (1976). Synaesthetic adjectives: A possible law of semantic change. *Language*, 32(2), 461–478.

Zellner, D. A., & Kautz, M. A. (1990). Color affects perceived odor intensity. *Journal of Experimental Psychology: Human Perception and Performance*, 16, 391–397.

# Part VI

# METAPHOR IN NONVERBAL EXPRESSION

CHAPTER 25

# Metaphor and Art

*John M. Kennedy*

Ron Eady is a Canadian encaustic painter with a studio in the hamlet of Rosseau, Ontario, two hours drive north of Toronto. With a friend, Frances, to whom I had been describing Eady's noir work, I walked by and pointed out the single poster outside the studio. It showed one of Eady's paintings (Figure 25.1). Frances immediately said, "I see what you mean."

In the picture, a thin man has turned to face us, arms by his sides. A sharp-nosed face with dark eye sockets stares directly at us. His heavily textured body sheds elements into the surrounds. The result is disquieting, odd.

How does this unnerving poster do its work? It did not have the picture's title – "Lost (Stickman)." The picture alone was enough. A shedding textured figure is not made of ordinary flesh and blood. Alive, confronting us, it may be nearly dead. Eady's pictures have incomplete buildings, mounds of twigs, dark-blue water, dense forest, shadowy figures glimpsed through windows, and mirrors reflecting impassive faces over taps and washbasins. They are sinister and compelling at first glance.

Eady's pictures conjure metaphor from objects, geometries, lines, and contours. Indeed, as will become clear, art's devices cut broadly across cognition and the senses, in ways likely to be remarkably universal. I will contend pictures are prototypical art objects, and pictures have to use perceptual tactics that are realistic, so violations of realism in art are readily taken to be metaphors. The general principle at work here is that metaphor violates standard representational practice. However, the limits on pictures as representations are stricter than those on words. The result is that metaphors can fail in one and succeed in the other. Indeed, the differences in the limits are so marked that ultimately I will claim on the one hand that "art objects can be metaphors" is a metaphor, and on the other that it is an enormously successful one, as true as any metaphor can be. Helpfully, arguments leading to this result reveal in plain fashion how representations indicate features of objects in language and pictures, in metaphors and in mental imagery.

A discussion of metaphor in art can set a good example. Much colorful, intriguing talk

**Figure 25.1.** Ron Eady's "Lost (Stickman)."

about metaphor, and art, is dearly in need of being uncloaked to the point where the literal features supporting metaphors become evident. The base machinery of comprehension is not found by tracing one metaphor to another or by reference to conventional or familiar sayings. Comprehension occurs when we know what features are attributed to a topic. Just so, as a case in point, my goal here is to use art to show what must be literal in metaphor.

## Clear Examples of Violations of Realism

The core argument for this chapter is basically this. "The guard's heart is a stone" violates the standard, literal use of stone. It relies on features stone has in common with the villain (Chiappe, Kennedy, & Smykowski, 2003). Likewise, art's metaphors rely on features in common to devices and their referent. Often the use runs counter to standard uses of the devices, as, for example, Figure 25.2 has shapes of straight spokes of a wheel playfully altered.

Five wheels are shown. One suggests a wheel in steady spinning motion, one shows a static wheel, one a wobbly wheel, one a wheel in jerky motion, one a wheel spinning too fast to make out, and one a wheel with its brakes on. Of interest, the wheels are identified in similar fashion by blind adults using raised line pictures and the sighted using printed pictures (Kennedy & Gabias, 1985). Steady spin is suggested to both groups of subjects by curved spokes, static by straight spokes, wobbly by wavy spokes, jerky by bent spokes, too fast to make out by dashed spokes, and brakes-on by spokes extended beyond the wheel's perimeter. These are not pictorial onomatopoeia, in the fashion of murmuring sounding like its referent, for they do not give the impression of motion, but each form and motion have a useful feature in common. For example, wobbly motion is relatively smooth and varies in direction, while jerky motion changes abruptly.

Not only are the meanings of the wheels the same for the blind and the sighted, when blind and sighted subjects were asked to order the wheels from most to least successful in terms of which suggest steady spin, both groups put curved first, bent second, wavy third, dashed next, and extended spokes last. This is impressive for both groups were unfamiliar with the particular devices, and the blind were unfamiliar with depictions of any kind. It seems unrealistic representations can be effective by sharing relevant features (Vervaeke & Kennedy, 2004). What is salient in them seems highly reliable (Giora, 2003).

Gombrich (1963, 1972) commented that there can be no question of realism or naturalistic representation in these devices. There are intuitions to be uncovered here

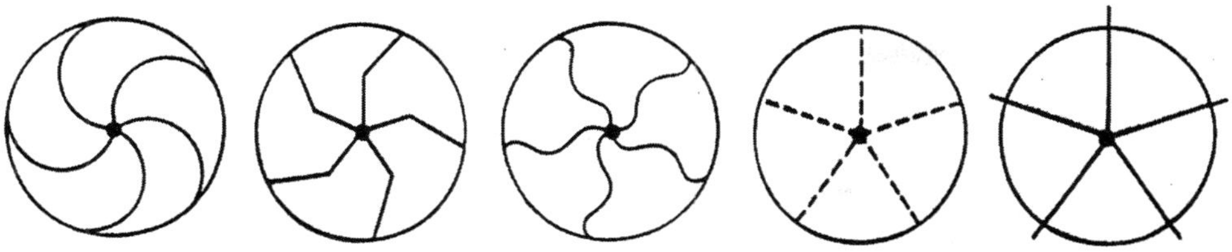

**Figure 25.2.** Wheels suggesting motions – spinning, wobbly, jerky, too fast to make out, and brakes on. Reprinted with permission from Kennedy and Gabias (1985).

about pictures, what their standard use should be and what might be pertinent in an unrealistic picture (Arnheim, 1974).

Behind a serious-faced man in a business suit, a picture might have his reflection be that of a naked prancing devil, revealing two sides of his nature. An obese religious leader can be shown tucking into a banquet while half-hidden, dwarfed in his giant shadow, gaunt children huddle round begging bowls. We are meant to take these pictures as metaphoric comments on states of affairs.

In Jean-Honore Fragonard's "The Bolt" (ca. 1778), a strong bare-legged man holds his inamorata fast while stretching out to slide home a bolt locking a bedroom door. She is yielding while protesting. In the folds of the drapes of the four-poster bed, the careful Louvre viewer can discern massive and bold sexual imagery, anticipating events of the near future. Fragonard's intention is entirely undeniable. The shapes are there for all to see, though many see cloth and nothing more. The picture is proleptic, meaning it anticipates the future. It is a double entendre, or perhaps in this case one should say a double voir.

Expression in Eady's "Lost," comic-book wheels, political caricatures of business and religious leaders and disguised eroticism are grist for theory of metaphor and art. Here we try to define the population these pictures sample and their rules. What must be defended is that perception of the natural world is in some sense realistic (Gibson, 1979), and therefore pictures can be realistic or metaphoric. Finally, how metaphoric pictures relate to cognition – concepts, examples, and claims – needs to be described.

A word on vocabulary: metaphor in ordinary English, as in "I was speaking metaphorically," covers many figurative expressions, including exaggeration, understatement, and irony. The technical term for all figures of speech is trope, but it is odd to say, "I spoke tropely." Using metaphor (a type of trope) to stand for trope is catachresis, the use of a term to stand in for one that does not exist in many people's everyday lexicon. A popular catachresis is "he fell in love" because we have no simple verb for becoming in love. In metonymy, a part (such as metaphor) stands for the whole (in this case, trope). Technically, this chapter could be entitled "trope in art" or "trope in pictures." It is about figures of representation, tropes not restricted to language.

"My job is a jail" uses jail as a typical member of the category "unpleasantly confining situations" (Gentner & Bowdle, 2001; Glucksberg, 2001), much as metaphor can stand for trope. If pictures convey messages metaphorically, representational dance, sculpture, mime, design, and movies can be metaphoric. Pictures are prototypical examples of art, much as metaphors are of tropes.

## Literal Pictures Are Realistic

A literal picture shows a scene and uses devices as they are in standard practice. Literal pictures must conform to standards. However, since pictures vary all over the map in style, the standards could be mere conventions (Kennedy, 2002; Sacks, 2002). That pictures are not purely conventional will have to become clear in what follows, or the notion of a metaphoric picture violating significant standards would be suspect.

Pictures can be realistic even when they depict an imaginary scene, for example, the Toronto CN Tower as beside Niagara Falls. This is simply wrong, not metaphoric, like the statement, "Mounties ride camels." Metaphor requires a claim that has two meanings, one a standard use of terms and another making a point via features of the standard referent of the terms. The second meaning is not meant to correct the standard one, as "DNA uses a double helix" did when it first appeared. Metaphor is a play on expression itself, pro tem, like a quotation. Similarly, metaphoric pictures play on picturing itself, in effect alluding to another way of using a pictorial device, to make a point about the topic. A metaphoric illustration for a Freudian text may show a man made of sexual imagery to make a point about unconscious drives. The topic is man, and the vehicle the sexual pictures. A picture of a man made of fruit or animals may be cleverly done but have no point to make about the man. It is not metaphoric.

## Natural Laws Are Standards That Can Be Transgressed

If a rule is violated, there is a standard. Literal pictures follow discoveries from the dawn of picturing. A mere thousand generations ago, a tick on evolution's time scale, cave pictures arrived. They capitalize on preexisting, eons-old ways of perceiving the world. The visual system Darwin evolved for us over millennia is used in part by pictures.

To see the world, vision uses optic input from surfaces, edges, shadows, shapes of objects, and perspectives dictated by the observer's vantage points. Pictures use contours, lines, and patches on surfaces to re-create the key features of this highly informative optic input. Vision is largely the servant of rich, physical optic laws. Pictures piggyback on these laws.

Typically, what metaphors do in pictures is violate two kinds of laws. One kind governs what confronts us every day. Fragonard violates the rules of bed drapery by painting two huge organic sexual forms in their folds. The bedroom is an apt place, but what is present as cloth is a physical anomaly. The second kind governs surfaces and edges. For example, spokes of wheels are not bent by jerky motion. The shape is another physical anomaly.

In literal pictures, contours, lines, and patches depict in surprisingly few ways. We see because of surfaces reflecting light to us. Surfaces enclose matter, and so fronts face a vantage point and rears face away, with edges between fronts and backs. Contours depict the edges, and the region bounded by contours stands for the surface. Contours depict occluding edges of flat surfaces like a roofline, occluding bounds of curved surfaces like brows of hills, and the edge of one surface meeting another at a corner (Figure 25.3).

Lines depict the same surface layouts. A line has two contours and so in addition it can depict a wire (two occluding surface edges close together) or a crack (two surface edges on either side of a gap).

Lines and contours give us vivid impressions of the scene surfaces – so realistic at times even a line drawing can deceive the observer into thinking the real thing is present (Kennedy, 1974; Kubovy, 1986). The strong affinity between contours and surface edges allows any other use of line and contour to be distinct, and plausibly nonliteral, as in Figure 25.4 by Esref, a congenitally, totally blind man, drawing wheels in motion (Kennedy & Merkas, 2000), for his first time.

Esref deploys lines for wirelike forms and other referents. Esref's lines in air behind a wheel depict its path of motion, or its wind. His incomplete wheel perimeters on either side of a braking wheel aptly suggest shuddering, but there are no incomplete rims flanking braking wheels. Spokes do not become circles when the wheel rotates fast. The ground is not wavy under a wobbly wheel. The shapes of wobbly wheels do not become elliptical in keeping with the arc of the ground. The ground does not become dashed under a jerky wheel, shown twice, once turning and once still.

Each astonishingly creative picture takes a property such as line length, number of wheels, orientation, location, and shape and

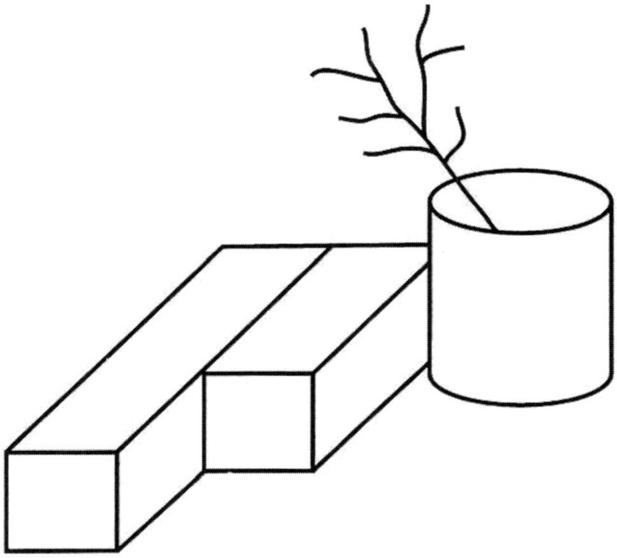

**Figure 25.3.** Surface edges depicted by lines.

pairs it with a motion property. Lines to one side of a wheel suggest a direction of motion. Line length suggests speed of motion, and line shape a path of motion.

Asked about such devices, blind people judge them to be imaginary and not realistic. When pressed to decide if they are literal or metaphoric they plump for metaphoric (Kennedy, 1993).

## Theory That Edge Depiction by Contours and Lines Gives Universal Impressions

In convention theory, pictures are entirely arbitrary. But lines trigger impressions of edges. To understand how, it is helpful to note that lines do not convey impressions of any visual borders, for example, line fails to

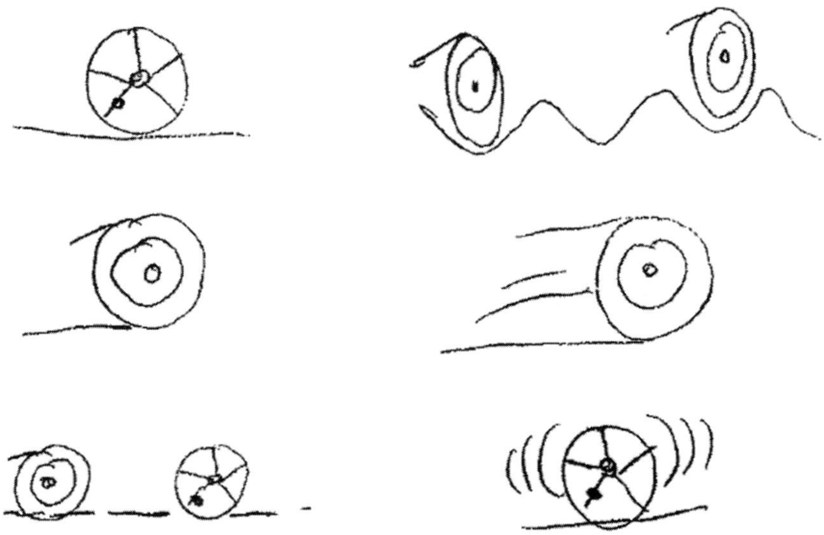

**Figure 25.4.** Wheels drawn by Esref. Reprinted with permission from Kennedy and Merkas (2000).

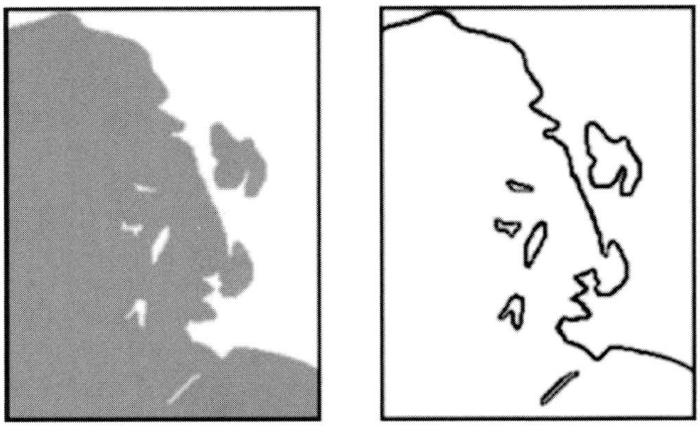

**Figure 25.5.** Head in shape-from-shadow, shown via a contour and copied as a line. Reprinted with permission from Kennedy and Bai (2004).

give impressions of color and shadow borders.

To come to grips with this point, consider borders on surfaces as opposed to borders of surfaces.

The striped flanks of a zebra vary in reflectance. A stripe's borders can be copied in an outline drawing but the interior of the stripe will not look dark. The zebra may cast a shadow on the ground, and its flanks curve downward away from the sun to bear attached shadows. Line copies of borders of the shadows on the ground and flank will not produce percepts of shaded regions.

In contrast, contours of dark regions can depict zebra stripes with excellent visual mimicry, and copy margins of the shadows to give rise to percepts of extended shadows and the complex surfaces on which they lie. A face in partial shadow in Figure 25.5 is perceived because the contours trigger adroit shape-from-shadow analysis in vision. Outlining the shadow patches does not trigger the analysis, as Figure 25.5 shows. One reason: the line has two contours, a positive and a negative, and the negative blocks the analysis the positive might otherwise support (Kennedy & Bai, 2004).

Contours look like surface edges for obvious reasons. A dark surface against a bright background has a continuous border, and a continuous contour on a picture surface has too. Explanation cannot stop there for a dotted line can also depict a continuous surface edge, in vision or touch. Perception groups dots as continuous, like stitching revealing the presence of a continuous thread. Dots can be seen as lying on a continuous surface like freckles on a forehead. A cloud of gnats (or a school of fish or a flock of birds) swarming can seem like one writhing snake-like body.

Continuous edges are suggested by the stitching at a border, the freckles aligned at the border of the forehead, and the gnats at the cloud's perimeter. That is, dotted lines on a page and texture at a surface edge trigger the same perceptual alignments.

Perceptual functions triggered by dots, lines, and contours help the perceiver detect real surfaces. Taking advantage of these natural laws, lines, and contours in pictures trigger perceived surfaces. Metaphors for motion violate the laws. What goes for motion goes for smell, taste, surprise, pain, heat, and the like in comic-book devices originating in the 19th century (Kennedy, 1993). Wavy lines above garbage stand for smells. Spiky lines around a swollen thumb stand for pain.

About representing motion, Cutting (2002) noted "the purpose of these representations is not to trick the visual system into seeing motion; instead it is merely to suggest to an observer, sometimes a well-informed one, that motion has occurred" (p. 1190). The devices share a pertinent feature with the referent. Cutting writes that they often use what Arnheim (1974) called dynamic balance (objects are depicted with asymmetry), multiple images (as in Esref's device for jerky motion, and Marcel Duchamps' famed "Nude Descending a Staircase, No. 2," of the Philadelphia Museum of Art's Annenberg Collection), affine shear (the object leans forward), photographic blur, and Figure 25.3's action lines. Motion is not balance, multiplication, leaning, blur, or trailing lines, but these suggest motion, that is, are metaphors for it.

Cutting's list is not exhaustive. Devices have many features, and if the desired referent changes what part of a device is useful changes in its wake.

All of this is customary, but none of it is due to custom. That lines and contours show surface edges was discovered by cave artists (Kennedy & Silver, 1974). The Songe of Papua/New Guinea, a small tribe of about 300 people, do not have pictures in their culture, but they recognize outline drawings of trees, houses, birds, and people on first exposure to them (Kennedy & Ross, 1975). It follows that other uses of line and contour could be meant to communicate in a nonliteral fashion.

## Form Symbolism Relies on Matching Features of a Form and the Referent

As motion-representation tests metaphorical use of lines, forms such as circles and squares can test symbolic functions.

Ping and pong can be matched with sweet (ping) and sour (pong), or high and low, or cat and elephant (Gombrich, 1996). A similar game can be played with circle and square (Liu & Kennedy, 1996). One is soft and one is hard. Overwhelmingly, people match circle with soft and square with hard (100% agreement from Toronto undergraduates). Similarly, most match circle with good and square with evil (89%). Most pair strong with square and weak with circle (79%). Gombrich (1996, p. 140) wrote:

> When my father, hard and square
> Met me with a frosty stare
> What a comfort I then found
> In my mother, soft and round.

Levels of agreement vary from unanimous to random. That circle is summer and square winter is somewhat unsure (81% agreement). That circle is cat and square is dog is questioned by many (only 74%). Quiet (circle) and loud (square) are at just 62%. Near and far are randomly assigned to circle and square (53%), like deep and shallow (51%).

Correlation of the levels of agreement is highly significant when English speakers are compared with Japanese, Danish, and Slovene speakers (Kennedy et al., 2003). The informants assigned circle on its own to either soft and hard, happy or sad, love or hate, bright or dark, alive or dead, and so on, and square on its own to the same referents to show circle on its own being selected frequently, for one of the options, predicted square being selected for the opposite, in each language group.

In no two languages did circle and square have the same slang referents, for example, "my father is a real square" is not found in Danish and "en firkant" in Danish is a demanding person, who does not fall in line and agree with us, declined as I am well-informed, you have opinions, but he is "saa firkant."

A telling finding is that the highest levels of agreement were across language. Selections for square by the Japanese and Slovenes were correlated .9. Danes selecting options for circle did not always select the opposite for square (correlation –.62) but selections for circle by Japanese and square by Danes correlated –.77.

Theory of metaphor as feature matching accounts for the results as follows. The form symbolizes the referent by means of features such as smooth, continuous, sharp-cornered, and stable (Arnheim, 1974; Liu & Kennedy, 1997). For example, sharp corners are dangerous and so is evil. Squares are stable, and circles easily rolled, offering weak resistance to sideways pressure. If a salient feature is in common to the form and its referent, there is a high level of agreement. If a nonsalient feature has to be sought, the subject is slow and unsure, rivalrous features are entertained, and deciding between them is fairly slow and effortful (Giora, 2003).

## Few Geometries Are General but Objects Have Many Features, Some Apocryphal

Perspective is general in perception because we have to perceive shadow from somewhere, because to see we need illumination.

Being general, any special use will be quite evident. For example, once linear perspective was mastered, the vanishing point was frequently used for emphasis. It is convenient to put a major figure there and to arrange others on either side like supports. This was common in Italy in the 16th century (Kubovy, 1986). Shadow can be used to similar effect, to surround a central source of light. In the 1600s, paintings of interiors often depicted faces in memorable fashion around a single candle, in close-up, one face youthful, shadowy regions surrounding the lit center. Lighting a single candle against the night is not to be gainsaid. Youth is a candle, figuratively. Despair is the night, metaphorically.

A few principles govern perspective and shadow, but the objects to which they apply are numberless. Like Lego toys, objects are combinations of elements (surfaces), and the elements can be added or taken away ad infinitum. For example, we can invent a new alphabet. Perception is open to new objects and new uses of old objects, some adamantly related to the properties of the object and some purely conventional.

Vicari (1993) has given an excellent account of an art movement stemming from the early 1500s that invested depicted objects such as labyrinths with metaphoric significance. A labyrinth meant voluptuousness in one picture, accompanied by an explanation in an epigram. Pipe and tobacco in a Dutch book by Daniel Heinsius, printed in 1615, had a Latin exposition to the effect that love is but a fume and lovers live on air.

The title for the movement is Emblematica. As it spread, it became learned and instructional. As a sign of being educated, it became important to know the proper meanings of emblems. Falcons, in one tradition, meant eternity. A goose meant a son. A vulture stood for mother. The principle behind the movement was that everything in nature had significance. Everything meant something else, but often it did so for spurious reasons. Vulture meant mother because of a belief that there were no male vultures.

Goose meant son in Emblematica because it was thought that the Egyptian words for goose and son had the same sound. This was not a metaphoric link. But many other uses of a character such as a lion had a metaphoric character. A lion can mean the king because traditionally it is the king of beasts or gold because gold is the king of metals. It can also mean a heretical blasphemer because of its evil-smelling mouth. A motto accompanying the picture in a given publication picked out properties from our ideas about lions.

Vicari reports that in 1522 Alciati, the writer of Emblematica's first major volume, noted the movement could take something from history or nature after which painters and goldsmiths could fashion badges and insignia. These could be worn in hats for example and be accompanied by precepts. He noted the design of a dolphin twined around an anchor meaning both speed and stability would be a hieroglyph for "make haste slowly." In 1548, Vicari recounts, emblems were recommended for walls of a house, window glass, wall hangings, curtains, tableware, seals for documents, signet rings, personal attire, parts of furniture such as bedposts, and weapons. A modern would find this obsessional.

Vicari offers an interpretation of a painting by Dossi entitled "Portrait of an Unknown Young Man." A man points outside a window where an ass is eating thistles. The little scene is an emblem that refers to Aesop's fable in which an ass loaded with a sack of the best oats and barley eats thistles as if nothing better was available. This fable is about a miser who starves himself amid plenty, too mean to spend. But surely, what his money symbolizes is his talents, his unwillingness to dream, to hope, to bring about a great future. Ultimately, the emblem is about an inability to love and care wisely for self and others.

Emblematica is an elaborate tissue of literary allusions. Rich and rewarding, it was largely to do with what is arbitrary, though it had an idea that the divine put meaning into nature coded. It was partly inspired by texts on Egyptian lore, which were eventually discovered to be clever fictions. Overburdened by dictionaries of arbitrary meanings, such as a crocodile is hypocritical (shedding crocodile tears), it fell gradually into disfavor. Its raison d'être is also still present in eagles, beavers, kangaroos, and kiwis standing for countries and sports teams – handy summaries, indispensable in a visual age. Political cartoons still use these along with cornucopias and hourglasses, lions, and labyrinths. Greeting cards still use cupids and darts.

The pictures of Emblematica are "encoded allusions to literary sources . . . the interpreter must know to what discourses they allude" (Vicari, 1993, p. 162). The text accompanying emblems was often itself enigmatic. "An emblematic image, therefore, is indirectly a visual metaphor by way of an allusion to a literary source, or perhaps we might say a metaphor for a text which in itself is already figural – metaphoric or metonymic. It is a metalepsis – a metaphor for a metaphor" (p. 162).

## Awkward Metaphors in Pictures Despite Success in Words

Besides being apt or arbitrary, metaphoric pictures may fail. For example, love's emblems can be gauche in pictures. It is a fine thing in language to have a burning passion. The loved one can stoke the fires with one brief glance, words might have us believe. A letter, a brief message, a hurried call can inflame desire, a story might have it. Hearts are warmed by attention from the one we care for, we might think. This is all very well in language, but surely, a picture of an actual person in flames is something to be rejected outright. Certainly, greeting card racks do not show the object of affection holding out smoking brands or putting burning coals to the adoring one's chest. Language inside the card may allow what a concrete image on the front would not, being just too dismaying. Hence, the pictures on the fronts show aerobatic cherubs, floating symbolic hearts, and skeins of flowers, not flames. The hot words giveth, but the pictures avoid. One moral is that thought does not use the images that would most directly illustrate the thought. Often, additional physical details are extraneous, gauche, and distracting: a faux pas.

The moral is also plain in theological illustrations. Egyptians believed our heart was weighed in the afterlife, to judge our character. A picture of this as bleeding muscles on a scale, veins and arteries dangling, is an off-putting version of this attractive conceit. Some celebrate the idea that God is three in one. But most images of this God show three entirely distinct entities, not a hydra-headed body. Indeed, God the Spirit is shown as a dove, not a person, despite rumors about God being in three persons. Perception disallows what cognition names in this instance. A sack with three heads is a sad version of what is a light and charming paradox in language.

What is metaphoric in religious concepts is not clear to many scholars who care about such things and may not cross the mind of congregants. It may be that depicting a vivid concept can help distinguish the message from the treatment. A drawing to show "God is your father," taken literally, would be as plainly odd as the three-in-one sack, one to be treated scurvily even by saintly folk.

Failings in transfer go from images to words too. We will make little headway referring to a jerky wheel as one with bent spokes, a wobbly wheel as oval-shaped, and a spinning wheel as one with curved spokes. Language specifies the motion and does not need the circumlocution to nonsalient features (Giora, 2003).

More upbeat for the case for metaphoric pictures is the evident success of some genres. Metaphoric badges and coats of arms are old-fashioned. But schematic logos are accepted without question, and their designs carry implications: CN railways has a continuous line making the C and N.

In the 19th century, stained-glass windows offered emblems and portrayals of stock characters. Justice with a balance, Wisdom with a book, Art with an easel, and Democracy with a speech were presented as women in Greek robes carrying objects indicating their role. (Alas no caryatid for Doubt, Argue, Test, and Prove!)

Public buildings are now rather spare. Any principle on view is via architecture, and implicit. Judicious shape, texture, material, lighting, and function take the place of solid maidens and explicit ideals. The result is considerable debate on the meaning of a building, if any. The affordances of a public space for assembly may be quite evident or hidden. A V-shaped roof may be taken to indicate flight, as if the V stood for wings. The flight in turn can stand for ambition, progress, or optimism. Linz Cathedral, Austria, has unique postwar stained-glass windows with the forms and colors of modern scientific and technical imagery. This act of imagination deserves applause. The metaphor may be "value accepts knowledge." Westminster Abbey is filling its niches with celebrated figures such as Nelson Mandela. They are not ciphers. They are known as expressive people because of close-up, informal news pictures in our living rooms. Perhaps as informality grew, formal imagery standing for values has shrunk.

The absence of exhortation and statements of principle, the loss of formality and the absence of mottos, epigrams, and labels of Emblematica, means implicit messages from pictures in the media and styles of building may now be especially important. In practice, the result may be that skill in reading metaphors in public constructions may be taken for granted by some onlookers and may be something to which others are oblivious.

As with public buildings, highly public pictures now often try to be suitably metaphoric. Advertisements do more than just show the latest style of shoe, for example they compress a forthcoming movie into a single image. Henri Cartier-Bresson made a career from photographing a moment that summarized a story – a man frozen at the instant he leaped a puddle in Paris, delighted to be alive, it seemed, in a great city emerging from a blanket of war, or an irrepressible urchin grinning as he carried home bread and wine in a family shopping basket. Great photographs offer sensuous pleasure and metaphoric claims about lifestyles. In this, they are reminiscent of emblems. Vicari (1993, p. 167) wrote that "emblems were believed to be good teaching devices, because they combined sensuous appeal with a precept in such a way as to make the precept more memorable. The initial puzzle posed by the motto and picture would arrest the mind, driving the meaning into memory." Likewise, in an advertisement, a pretty model beside a car or the scene around it are thought to hold attention while the character and personality the maker wants the car to seem to have is communicated, reinforced by the person or landscape in the picture.

Cigarettes used to be shown being consumed by rugged cowpokes and radiant athletes. As if. . . . But what exactly did the ad specify? That cigarettes were medically fine? A generous interpretation is that the actors were not harmed by the products and made only occasional, pleasurable use of them. But even in past days child actors were off limits. The idea that children would be deliberately targeted by a picture with a message that cigarettes are glamorous is clearly of legal interest. The intellectual stumbling block of the law is that there are no pat ways to establish a picture conveys a given metaphoric message. That a few people get the message can be set against many others taking the image other ways. The upshot is that to err on the side of caution only metaphoric warning pictures are fully legal. Cigarettes can be shown as made of white skulls, implying "cigarettes kill," or sadly limp to suggest they cause impotency.

A weakness of emblems is they require explanation, for example, soccer followers have scarves and baseball fans have caps. Communicative power today often lies in staying relatively close to the standard meaning of objects while using them imaginatively. Arnheim (1974) said that a heap of objects is just that unless a theme unites them. An advertisement from Holland shows a low wall, constructed from ordinary crates of bottles of a famous beer, snaking across a Dutch field, with the motto, "They have the Great Wall but we have our beer," an advertisement that does not take itself too seriously (Forceville, 1996). The theme explains the crates unrealistically receding into the distance across a farmer's field. In an amusing ad about fitness, each slot in a parking lot has no car, just a pair of running shoes, offering a theme to do with active exercise versus sit-down commuting.

## Degrees of Realism as Apparent Naturalism

If realistic features are what are violated in many metaphors, pictures need to appear more or less realistic. Apparent realism was a topic of concern a century after the discovery of perspective in the Renaissance. One response was that pictures would look more natural if they included incidentals. In the result, a precursor of 19th-century Naturalism (a term invented by Emile Zola), the depicted setting for, say, a saint's trial was deemed more realistic if it included accidental objects such as dogs sniffing around a corner, a restless baby off to one side, a servant busy about his business, a bluebottle on a sleeve. Similarly, movies are full of off-topic extras, little to do with the gist of the story. In *Good Will Hunting* (Van Sant, 1997), a barfly (Pat O'Donnell) opens a scene. (Pat says, "Bullshit! You never said that!") The action then moves to the back of the bar, where Will's psychologist has a conversation with his teacher. The barfly only helped set the scene.

## What Tropes These Pictures Be

Besides failing as versions of particular sayings, shortcomings of pictures may tell us a great deal more about art and metaphor than Emblematica simply falling out of fashion has done. Indeed, pictures may fail whole classes of metaphors. Only some tropes suit pictures (Kennedy, 1982). Let us consider several kinds, some succeeding, some not, and the principles that divide them.

Hendiadys is one by means of two, as in "I want you to give a really big hand to a great member of Parliament and a wonderful family woman." It could be two people, but it is just one. Esref's drawing of a wheel in jerky motion uses hendiadys, showing the wheel twice.

Euphemisms cover what it is rude to say bluntly as in "WC" for toilet and "passed-on" for dead. Fig leaves are painted in unrealistic places, and long hair tresses just happen to cover sex parts too, too conveniently.

Hyperbole is exaggeration. Exaggerated features make faces more recognizable and more rapidly recognized (Rhodes, 1996).

Synecdoche uses a part to represent the whole. "Sail hoy" means a ship is near, not just its sail. Walls are often sketched as top and bottom and a few representative bricks. A few cows drawn fairly fully and a few parts of the head and horns of the rest of the cattle can suggest a herd. Caricaturists sometimes draw a distinctive object carried by their subject – Churchill's cigar, Franklin D. Roosevelt's cigarette holder, Napoleon's hand in his jacket. Wellington has no such legacy, not even his boots.

Personification attributes human characteristics to inanimate objects. Common in children's books, it is not just child's play. It can depict social conflicts, with unions and companies as characters. Poverty, science, and progress are personified at times. Someone can be presented as a personification of evil, with the danger that they lose their humanity, their capacity for missteps and anguish. In their picture, they will appear as a cipher, dehumanized. The strange man with a hat, moustache, and gun is pictured expressionless. He is taken to be incapable of rational negotiation, his affirmations and denials irrelevant. Conversely, Harpur (2004) writes, great religious figures many take to be real are often just personifications of character traits, desires, dealings with birth and death and social values, once portrayed as Amun Re or Zoroaster or Osiris. New personifications can be major contributions to civilization, such as the United States's Santa Claus figure, and the refreshingly touching Danish figure of Christ, which portrays a sweet man with his arms held low and open toward the viewer in a comforting gesture.

Pictures spread personified images. With time, the image can take over, so white robes on a slim man with long hair, beard, clear smooth skin is a prototype prophet. Though God may be female, there are no widely accepted images of Her. Or of the God who plays dice.

In the reverse of personification, people are portrayed with characteristics of objects, arms as missiles, fingers as barrels of guns, hair as flowers, or arms as wings. Lopes (1996) writes, Picasso's painting "Francoise Gilot, 'Femme Fleur'" (1946) showed her as a flower. There were more flower properties than Gilot on display. Lopes suggests the painting could be metaphorically true, and it may be Gilot had a flowery disposition.

In the Van Eyck brother's altarpiece at St. Bavo's in Ghent, the painting is of a lamb standing on an altar. In Lopes's words, "the picture represents Christ, whose innocence is being compared to a lamb's, yet none of the properties it ascribes to him is literally true" (1996, p. 96). Lopes's phrasing suggests a simile "Christ is like a lamb."

In the Van Eyck, there is no overt contradiction, and the picture works like a proverb. "Too many cooks spoil the broth" is meant to tell us about situations far removed from cooking. So too a metaphoric picture can operate by analogy (Gentner & Bowdle, 2001) its message directed very generally, not at the situations in the painted scene.

Some tropes transfer not at all well to pictures. Meiosis (understatement) is a good case. Just as facial features can be exaggerated, they can also be diminished. But recognition is impaired. No caricaturists work with meiosis as their dominant style (Rhodes, 1996).

Irony in pictures is surely rare (a claim disputed by Giora, 2003, and this volume's gentle editor, I should add, in a personal communication, November 2004). In irony, the opposite is offered, as in "nice catch," after a fumble. Depicting a careful dresser as sloppy or the reverse is not going to improve recognition. Irony emphasizes the difference between two states of affairs, making plain which is true. In language, the irony is often accompanied by a special tone of voice, but alas no manner of portrayal has yet been invented that is the tip-off for pictorial irony. *New Yorker* cartoons are often ironic, but their irony lives in a caption's fit to the picture.

In pictures, metaphor is not readily distinguished from its sibling simile. A simile is a comparison that can be turned into a metaphor without loss of logical status. A literal similarity such as "A Mercedes is like a Volvo" cannot be turned into "A Mercedes is a Volvo," but a metaphor "life is a candle in the wind" can be expressed as a simile, "life is like a candle in the wind." There is no equivalent in pictures for the presence and absence of "like." Hence, this chapter could have been entitled "Simile in Pictures."

To show a Mercedes is literally like a Volvo, the two could be shown side by side. The features of one would not be added to the other. To show "this woman is rooted like a tree" one could well add roots to her image.

"Metaphor in pictures" has only at best subtle advantages over "simile in pictures," but metaphor is the common-talk term for trope and points straightforwardly to an object being treated as something else.

## "Metaphoric Picture" Is a Metaphor

In large measure, tropes in language are not perfectly matched onto pictures because language and pictures are on a different footing (Hopkins, 1998). Pictures use perception, which is far from arbitrary. Hence, violations of perceptual principles are distinctive with little or no prior experience with pictures. The contradictions call for an explanation. If a reason becomes clear, a metaphor may be in play. In contrast, words have arbitrary meanings. Winner means loser, if we wish, with the added factor that, likely, the normal meaning of winner was expected and desired by the protagonist. The reversal game can be extended: I came home expecting to be surprised, but there was no surprise. Therefore, I was surprised.

Perception responds to a contour's value on a dimension such as curvature. At times, it achieves recognition by responding with respect to a mean, for example, a person's nose is a tad longer than the average, hair curlier than the average, eyes more close set than the average. Showing the reverse of each of these does not trigger recognition, since the recognition was not based on an arbitrary direction from a mean. Words are arbitrary, and reversing from taller to tiny is still arbitrary, so a big man may be freely nicknamed "Little John" and become the common reference term, all the while retaining its irony.

In short, pictures use perception that is intuitive and untaught, and words are coinage whose denomination is anything we agree on. Perhaps we want the intuitive format of picturing itself to be transgressed in a good metaphor, and simply adding objects (such as fire in the breast of the would-be lover) seems too nonpictorial a play. Likewise, metaphoric language that simply refers to how someone looks ("he went as red as a beetroot"), without manipulating aspects of language, may seem unsophisticated. We prefer "his embarrassment knew no bounds." Similarly, slogans such as "revenge in the name of the Great Leader" seem apt to unwary minds, literally astray precisely because the gloomy act has to do with the leader, not a purely linguistic device, a name. (Slogans finesse argument. This one assumes greatness would want revenge.)

Words have types, such as "names," with no direct equivalent in pictures. Pictures do not have verbs or nouns. They do not have "to be." They do not have sentence structure. Hence, they cannot make claims. They cannot say A is B or A is not B. Hence, they are only metaphors in a sense of metaphor that needs to be firmly hedged here.

Further still, pictures do not have logical quantifiers. All, some, none, and definite and indefinite articles are missing. They cannot distinguish "all the bunnies on Lancaster lawns" from "some bunnies" or "the bunnies." Hence, they do not offer properties needed for concepts. The mansions in Lennoxvale are examples of the concept "houses." There are more examples such as all the Queen's mansions. All the examples have the proper features of the concept, and some have features of subcategories. The lawns around large Lennoxvale houses help them qualify for the subcategory of mansions. But pictures cannot indicate that the bunnies and the mansions they show are all or some or none of the pertinent examples.

Miss all and some and there is no conceptual hierarchy. Is this a dagger that I see before me? Or a knife? Or a weapon? Or an implement? Or a hand-held object? It is all of these and more. Pictures do not specify the level in a hierarchy at which particular examples should be taken.

Pictures do not say false and "Therefore this dagger is in Sans Souci is false" is not picturable. The "therefore" is not picturable.

A lack of verbs, sentence structure, and defining properties of concepts and arguments means pictures can stimulate thought, but they are not capable of being the actual engines of thought. Imageless thought is what is vital for arriving at conclusions. There is no concrete experience of any image or object whatsoever that specifies any of the necessities of a logical operation.

Finally, metaphors in language work by finding common features, but superficially, they have the form of a claim about a category, as "crime is a disease" mimics "Volvos are cars." Pictures lack the superficial form to be metaphors.

The prosecution rests. The claim that pictures are metaphoric is metaphoric, it seems, having only a metaphoric truth.

## A Metaphoric Picture Is a Successful Metaphor

Perhaps pictures can be parts of claims, elliptical metaphors. They have subjects and treatments and can be understood to have topics and comments. Further, pictures are not self-employed. They are from a person with an intention. Hence, the idea that they are part of a highly successful medium for messages is justified (Gibbs & Gerrig, 1989).

In context, "No, I do not want sugar" may be a legitimate expansion of "No!" So too a picture can be taken to be part of a sentence and a metaphoric sentence to boot. The picture supplies items which can be expanded into a sentence. Picasso's powerful Guernica supplies objects of wartime, defenseless people, an eye in the sky, and more. Many things make it metaphoric, including the eye in the sky. The possible expansion would use all of these objects and possibly more. The form of the sentence could well be "the wartime tragedy is a. . . ." Agreed, the sentence is not in the picture. But the picture is part of a communication, though the structure "the . . . is a . . ." is implicit.

An implicit structure and a picture combined can be metaphoric or literal. If the reader found the examples in this chapter easy to understand, the discussion of particular pictures such as Eady's "Lost" and spinning wheels easy to follow and the claims about emblems defensible, then pictures can be metaphoric. The reason could well be that "the . . . is a . . ." is understood.

Metaphors simply indicate some features of a topic. "Gandhi was a dove" tells us his peaceful tactics are to be entertained. Similarly, pictures have features that are relevant to the message. The devices presenting the features can violate their own literal, standard use, a regular practice in tropes.

As with metaphors in pictures, so with metaphors in language. In both, context combines with the representation to decide whether a metaphor is at work. "Ray is a star" is a metaphor in a context where Ray is a person and a star a point of light. "Your head is cut" only means you are silly in Ulster contexts.

That pictures can be metaphoric is true, and metaphoric. The defense rests, having fully agreed with the prosecution but added to it. Metaphor abounds in art.

## References


Arnheim, R. (1974). *Art and visual perception.* Berkeley: University of California Press.

Chiappe, D., Kennedy, J. M., & Smykowski, T. (2003). Reversibility, aptness and the conventionality of metaphors and similes. *Metaphor and Symbol, 18,* 85–105.

Cutting, J. (2002). Representing motion in a static image: Constraints and parallels in art, science, and popular culture. *Perception, 31,* 1165–1193.

Forceville, C. (1996). *Pictorial metaphor in advertising.* London: Routledge.

Gentner, D., & Bowdle, B. (2001). Convention, form, and figurative language processing. *Metaphor and Symbol, 16,* 223–247.

Gibbs, R. W., & Gerrig, R. J. (1989). How context makes metaphor comprehension seem special. *Metaphor and Symbolic Activity, 3,* 145–158.

Gibson, J. J. (1979). *The ecological approach to visual perception.* Boston: Houghton Mifflin.

Giora, R. (2003). *On our mind.* Oxford: Oxford University Press.

Glucksberg, S. (2001). *Understanding figurative language.* Oxford: Oxford University Press.

Gombrich, E. H. (1963). *Meditations on a hobby horse and other essays on the theory of art.* London: Phaidon Press.

Gombrich, E. H. (1972). *Symbolic images.* London: Phaidon Press.

Gombrich, E. H. (1996). Response from E. H. Gombrich. In R. Woodfield (Ed.), *Gombrich on art and psychology* (p. 140). Manchester: Manchester University Press.

Harpur, T. (2004). *The pagan Christ*. Toronto: Thomas Allen Publishers.
Hopkins, R. (1998). *Picture, image, and experience*. Cambridge: Cambridge University Press.
Kennedy, J. M. (1974). *A psychology of picture perception*. San Francisco: Jossey Bass.
Kennedy, J. M. (1982). Metaphor in pictures. *Perception, 11*, 589–605.
Kennedy, J. M. (1993). *Drawing and the blind*. New Haven, CT: Yale University Press.
Kennedy, J. M. (2002, October 28). Picture this. *New Yorker, 78*, 12.
Kennedy, J. M., & Bai, J. (2004). Line at shape-from-shadow border tested with stereo. *Perception, 33*, 653–665.
Kennedy, J. M., & Gabias, P. (1985). Metaphoric devices in drawings of motion mean the same to the blind and the sighted. *Perception, 14*, 189–195.
Kennedy, J. M., Liu, C. H., Challis, B. H., & Kennedy, V. (2003). Form symbolisim across languages: Danish, Slovene, and Japanese. In C. Zelinsky (Ed.), *Text transfer: Metaphors, translation, and expert-lay communication* (pp. 221–242). Berlin: Mouton de Gruyter.
Kennedy, J. M., & Merkas, C. E. (2000). Depictions of motion devised by a blind person. *Psychonomic Bulletin and Review, 7*, 700–706.
Kennedy, J. M., & Ross A. (1975). Outline picture perception by the Songe of Papua. *Perception, 4*, 391–406.
Kennedy, J. M., & Silver, J. (1974). The surrogate functions of lines in visual perception: Evidence from antipodal rock and cave art sources. *Perception, 3*, 313–322.
Kubovy, M. (1986). *The psychology of perspective and Renaissance art*. Cambridge: Cambridge University Press.
Liu, C. H., & Kennedy, J. M. (1996). Form and its symbolic meaning. In R. Woodfield (Ed.), *Gombrich on art and psychology* (pp. 127–139). Manchester: Manchester University Press.
Liu, C. H., & Kennedy, J. M. (1997). Form symbolism, analogy, and metaphor. *Psychonomic Bulletin and Review, 4*, 546–551.
Lopes, D. (1996). *Understanding pictures*. Oxford: Oxford University Press.
Rhodes, G. (1996). *Superportraits: Caricatures and recognition*. East Sussex, UK: Psychology Press.
Sacks, O. (2002, October 7). The case of Anna H. *New Yorker, 78*, 62–73.
Van Sant, G., director. (1997). *Good Will Hunting* [film].
Vervaeke, J., & Kennedy, J. M. (2004). Conceptual metaphor and abstract thought. *Metaphor and Symbol, 19*, 213–232.
Vicari, P. (1993). Renaissance emblematica. *Metaphor and Symbolic Activity, 8*, 153–168.
Willats, J. (1997). *Art and representation*. Princeton, NJ: Princeton University Press.

CHAPTER 26

# Metaphor in Pictures and Multimodal Representations

*Charles Forceville*

## 1. Introduction

Lakoff and Johnson's characterization of metaphor as "understanding and experiencing one kind of things in terms of another" (1980: 5) strikes a felicitous balance between precision and vagueness. For one thing, it captures Black's (1979) basic idea that a metaphor triggers an interaction between phenomena from two different domains, construable as a target and a source domain, in which features and/or structural relationships of the source are mapped onto the target. This mapping then leads to a transformation of that target. Moreover, Lakoff and Johnson's description emphasizes the dynamic nature of the trope both in the sense that a metaphor requires active uptake by its audience and in the sense that metaphors potentially influence people's perspectives on the world, and the actions they may undertake as a consequence of adopting these perspectives. A third attractive aspect of the formulation is that it does not specify the sign system in which the metaphorical coupling is to be achieved. The authors, of course, deliberately avoid a restriction to the verbal because a crucial tenet of *Metaphors We Live By* is that metaphors are "primarily a matter of thought and action and only derivatively a matter of language" (1980: 5).

Lakoff and Johnson are right that the occurrence of metaphors is not restricted to language. Consider the following film sequences: in a famous scene in *The Gold Rush* (Chaplin, USA 1925) a hungry Charlie Chaplin eats his shoe laces in a manner suggesting that SHOE LACES ARE SPAGHETTI; the Ellen Burstyn character in *Requiem for a Dream* (Aronofsky, USA 2000), stoned on diet pills, sees the fridge containing all the food she cannot eat as a monster (FRIDGE IS MONSTER); and to a 17th-century priest intent on converting the Indians (*Black Robe*, Beresford, Canada/Australia, 1991), the trees in the jungle appear as church pillars (JUNGLE IS CHURCH, see Forceville, 2005a). In none of these scenes, language is necessary for the construal and interpretation of what, in the spirit of Black's interaction theory of creative metaphors, must be called metaphors.

More structurally embedded metaphors, too, can occur in film. Here is a film scene in *Mary Poppins* (Stevenson, USA 1964): Mary, Bert, and the children visit uncle Albert, who whenever he is happy and has fun literally rises to the ceiling and only by thinking of sad things can get himself back on the ground again. The scene exemplifies HAPPY IS UP, evoking connotations that a verbal equivalent (e.g., "Uncle Bert's spirits *rose*," see Lakoff & Johnson, 1980: 15) do not – say, of emphatic humor, and of the inevitability and contagiousness of the effect of laughing (the children join Uncle Albert in his laughing bout and can't help but being lifted to the ceiling, too).

Clearly, if metaphors are essential to thinking (Lakoff & Johnson, 1980, 1999, 2003), it makes sense that they should occur not only in language but also in static and moving pictures, sounds, music, gestures, even in touch and smell – and in their various permutations. It is a shortcoming of conceptual metaphor theory (CMT), however, that it has hitherto largely ignored nonverbal metaphors such as those just mentioned. Studying them is necessary to test and refine CMT, which is currently hampered by the fact that most of the evidence adduced to prove the existence of conceptual metaphors comes from language alone. If the study of metaphor (along with other organizing principles, such as propositional structure, image schemas, and metonymic mapping; Lakoff, 1987: 68) is a key strategy for the delineation of cognitive models (e.g., Kövecses, 2000: 115; Lakoff, 1987: chap. 4), then all possible manifestations of the trope must be studied to avoid the risk that important aspects of its nature are misunderstood because of the concentration on a single mode of expression (Gibbs & Colston, 1995: 354). McLuhan's old adage that the medium is the message holds for metaphorical messages no less than for any other kind.

In this chapter, I will outline the moderately well understood phenomenon of pictorial metaphor and demonstrate the validity of the hitherto untheorized concept "multimodal metaphor." As a first approximation, I will define multimodal metaphors as metaphors in which target, source, and/or mappable features are represented or suggested by at least two different sign systems (one of which may be language) or modes of perception. Multimodal metaphors can be delineated best by first describing pictorial metaphors, the type of nonverbal metaphor that has attracted most scholarly attention. How exactly the construal and impact of pictorial and multimodal metaphors differ from their verbal counterparts is largely unexplored territory, but the following factors seem to play a role. First, the pictorial or multimodal nature of target and source means that they are apprehended differently from their verbal counterparts: pictures, sounds, and gestures have a perceptual immediacy that is lacking in language. One dimension of this perceptual immediacy is a high degree of specificity. Uncle Bert's happiness is not just upward-directed, it is upward-directed in precisely the way depicted in the aforementioned scene, with a certain speed of ascension, a certain instability once the characters are up, and so on. Second, pictorial and multimodal representations have different, medium-determined ways of cueing the similarity between target and source than language has. Third, inasmuch as sounds and pictures are more easily recognized transnationally than (unfamiliar) languages, pictorial and multimodal metaphors allow for greater cross-cultural access than verbal ones. Fourth, pictorial and multimodal source domains probably have a stronger emotional appeal than verbal ones.

The structure of this chapter is as follows. After examining pictorial metaphors in section 2, I analyze in section 3 a number of multimodal metaphors in order to investigate their various dimensions and, where appropriate, suggest possible implications for metaphor theory. The instances presented are all creative, ad hoc specimens of multimodal metaphor. In section 4, I shift to multimodal metaphors of the embedded kind theorized by Lakoff and Johnson (1980) and propose how studying multimodal metaphor can be fruitful for research outside of metaphor scholarship.

Section 5 contains recommendations for further research.

## 2. Pictorial Metaphor

Pictorial metaphor (or visual metaphor) is the most examined nonverbal mode of metaphor (Carroll, 1994, 1996; Cupchik, 2003; Danto, 1993; Dent-Read & Szokolsky, 1993; Forceville, 1988, 1994, 1996, 2000a, 2002; Forceville & Urios-Aparisi, in preparation; Kaplan, 1990, 1992; Kennedy, 1982, 1993; Kennedy & Kennedy, 1993; Maalej, 2001; Moulin, 2002; Rohdin, 2003; Rozik, 1994, 1998; Schuurman, 2003; Simons, 1995; Whittock, 1990), although as yet no unified theory exists. Pictorial metaphors are monomodal: their target and source are entirely rendered in visual terms, just as their verbal sisters have a target and source entirely rendered in language.

For anything to be a metaphor, pictorial or otherwise, the following three questions should be capable of being answered: (1) What are its two domains? (2) What is its target domain, and what its source domain? (3) Which feature or (structured) cluster of features can or must be mapped from source to target? (Forceville, 1996: 108, adapted from Black's 1979 interaction theory). In verbal metaphors, answering the first two questions is often considerably facilitated by language's combination of linearity and syntactical rules, which help distinguish between grammatical subjects ("A") and metaphorical predicates ("is B"). This makes it easy to assess the metaphoricity of, and difference between, say, the evergreens "butchers are surgeons" and "surgeons are butchers" (see Forceville, 1995). In pictures, however, particularly static ones, there is no such linearity, nor grammatical "rules" for disambiguating target and source, so that target and source must be identified as such on other grounds.

A second issue that makes pictorial metaphors different from verbal ones is the *labeling* of target and source. As Lakoff and Johnson's (1980) analyses demonstrate, verbal metaphors of various syntactic forms are manifestations of a conceptual metaphor that can be captured in a paradigmatic A IS B format. But in pictorial metaphors, even if it is clear what entities in an image are to be understood as the target and the source of the metaphor, making it *experienceable*, these entities need to be "translated" into the conceptual (but still verbalized!) A IS B format for them to be academically *discussable*. In fact, this issue is more problematic even in language than Lakoff and Johnson have made it out to be (but cf. Johnson, 2007: 267, passim); for instance, is the verbal metaphor "He *attacked every weak point* in my argument" a manifestation of ARGUMENT IS WAR (Lakoff & Johnson, 1980: 4) or rather of ARGUMENT IS BATTLE, ARGUMENT IS STRUGGLE, or perhaps DISCUSSION IS STRUGGLE? Each verbalization entails a different emphasis (Lakoff & Johnson, 1980, pay some attention to this issue on pp. 83–86; see also Lakoff & Johnson, 2003: 264–265). But however this may be, the *reports* of the "translations" from the verbal to the conceptual and vice versa at least remain within the sign system of language. In order to discuss a certain phenomenon as a specimen of nonverbal metaphor, by contrast, one must perform the mental gymnastics of representing in language that a CONCEPTUAL METAPHOR has a nonlinguistic manifestation, while the choice of label codetermines possible interpretations of the metaphor.

Four types of pictorial metaphor were distinguished in Forceville (1996), one of which ("verbo-pictorial metaphor"), in retrospect, is in fact a subtype of multimodal metaphor. The labels for the types were subsequently (Forceville 2002a) adapted as follows:

### *Contextual Metaphor*

An object is metaphorized because of the visual context in which it is placed. An example is a Dove hair-silk ad from Holland, with the slogan, "Your hair, too, sometimes deserves a treat" (Figure 26.1; translations here and throughout are mine), resulting in the metaphor: HAIR-SILK IS ICECREAM. The spoon in the hair-silk ad is, in this example,

**Figure 26.1.** Dutch advertisement for Dove hair-silk, with the contextual pictorial metaphor HAIR SILK IS ICECREAM.

the most important contextual element that cues the source domain "ice cream" (or a similarly creamy luxury food). The mapped feature is the notion of spoiling oneself with luxury food.

### *Hybrid Metaphor*

Two objects that are normally distinct entities are physically merged into a single "gestalt." An example is an advertisement for the Dutch supermarket chain Albert Heijn, which shows the metaphor CLOGS ARE RUNNING SHOES, with the headline "There's a reason why our spinach is deep-frozen so fast," the body copy specifying that quick deep-freezing best preserves the vitamins (Figure 26.2). The clogs metonymically refer to the farmer who harvests the spinach; the running shoes refer metonymically to a sprinting athlete, and thus cue the mappable feature of "speed." Hybrid metaphor, here regarded as a subtype of pictorial metaphor, appears to be identical with what Carroll considers pictorial (or visual) metaphor par excellence, arguing that it is characterized by both "homospatiality" and "noncompossibility" (1996: 213): Two phenomena are visually represented as occupying the same space in a manner that is physically impossible

**Figure 26.2.** Dutch advertisement for the supermarket chain Albert Heijn, with the hybrid metaphor CLOGS ARE RUNNING SHOES.

(see Forceville, 2002b, for a critical discussion of Carroll's ideas).

### *Pictorial Simile*

Two objects are represented in their entirety in such a way that they are made to look similar. The techniques available to cue this similarity are manifold: similarity in form, position, color, lighting, function, and so on. An example is an advertisement for Nokia mobile phones, featuring a matchstick and a phone against a white background. In between the two pictures there is the text "simply ingenious" (Figure 26.3). The resulting metaphor can be verbalized as MOBILE PHONE IS MATCHSTICK. The features mapped from matchstick to phone are, presumably, the proverbial brilliance associated with its invention and its small size. The body copy confirms this interpretation. While MOBILE PHONE IS MATCHSTICK can be categorized as a monomodal metaphor of the pictorial kind, NOKIA MOBILE PHONE IS MATCHSTICK would strictly speaking be a multimodal metaphor, because the brand name is rendered verbally. Similar reasoning holds for Figure 26.1: the brand name ("Dove") is specified verbally while the source domain is anchored by the headline (particularly the word "treat") and words in the body copy (e.g., "spoil yourself"). Since

**Figure 26.3.** Advertisement for Nokia mobile phones, with the pictorial simile MOBILE PHONE IS (LIKE) MATCHSTICK.

pictorial metaphors in advertisements often have the advertised product (identified by brand name or logo, the latter having a status somewhere in between picture and text; see Koller, in preparation) as their target, they often verge toward the multimodal type (for more on the distinction between types of pictorial metaphors and more examples, see Forceville, 1996, http://www.chass.utoronto.ca/epc/srb/cyber/cforcevilleout.html).

In addition to the types identified in my earlier publications, I now propose to

Figure 26.4. Philips' Senseo coffee machine, with the integrated metaphor COFFEE MACHINE IS SERVANT.

distinguish another subtype of pictorial metaphor, *integrated metaphor*, investigated by Van Rompay (2005): A phenomenon experienced as a unified object or gestalt is represented in its entirety in such a manner that it resembles another object or gestalt even without contextual cues. Philips' Senseo coffee machine suggests, through the curved shape of the reservoir and a plateau on which the cups must be placed, a servant or butler courteously serving coffee (Figure 26.4; I owe the example to Paul Hekkert; see Forceville et al., 2006a).

The types identified can occur in moving images as well as in static ones. Moving images, however, allow considerably more ways to construe metaphors than static pictures (Forceville 1999, 2002b, 2003, 2005a, 2007a, 2007b). Thanks to the dynamics of the camera, the similarity between target and source need not depend on before-camera resemblance but can also be created via identical camera movements, angles, or frame sizes. Moreover, since moving images unfold in time, a target and source need not, as in static images, be represented or suggested simultaneously: A target and a source may be represented seconds, minutes, or hours apart. Finally, a target or source domain can also be cued musically, or via a sound effect, thereby turning the metaphor into a multimodal one (for more discussion on the difference between monomodal and multimodal metaphor, see Forceville 2006a).

Whittock (1990), also drawing on Black's interaction theory, distinguishes 10 types of cinematic metaphor discussed under such labels as "Explicit comparison (epiphor): A is like B"; "Identity asserted: A is B"; "Identity implied by substitution: A replaced by B"; "Juxtaposition (diaphor): A/B." Many of his examples are accompanied by incisive analyses, but from a theoretical viewpoint it is problematic that the types are insufficiently delimitated, as Whittock acknowledges (1990: 68), and that, in some cases, it makes more sense to label the phenomenon under discussion differently (e.g., as a metonym). Similar problems arise in Kennedy (1982; this volume) and Durand (1987). Kennedy deserves credit for alerting metaphor scholars to the possibility of nonliteral visualization and for his rich array of examples, but his analyses suffer from imprecision because he treats "metaphor" as an all-encompassing label synonymous with "trope." The somewhat eclectic list of pictorial specimens in Kennedy (1982), including "allegory," "anti-climax," "hendiadys," and "prolepsis," strongly suggests that pictures can have nonliteral meanings but precludes uniform analysis. Durand, adopting a structuralist framework, places some 30 verbal tropes (only partly overlapping with Kennedy's) in an intricate grid, supposedly governed by the axes of "operation" and "relation," each with various subtypes. Subsequently, he comes up with visual counterparts of these tropes, often supplying no more than a single example for each. Hardly any criteria are given to help distinguish between the tropes (see Forceville, 1996: chap. 3, for more discussion).

However, I *do* support Carroll, Whittock, and Kennedy's emphasis on metaphor producers' intentions. Usually when we interpret something as a metaphor, this something was probably *meant* to be construed as a metaphor – after all, the ascription of intentionality to our fellow humans' communicative acts crucially governs human interaction (e.g., Gibbs, 1999a; Ponech, 1999; Sperber & Wilson, 1995; Tomasello, 1999). I therefore propose to consider intentional metaphors as the default, but not rule out in principle metaphorical analyses of phenomena which their producers did not envisage as metaphors. A distinction can be postulated between explicitly signaled metaphors ("marked metaphors"; Whittock, 1990: 50) and implicitly signaled metaphors (Forceville, 1999: 191–194). These latter pertain to phenomena that can, but need not, be construed as a metaphor to make sense. Such freedom is mostly restricted to metaphors of the pictorial simile variety, where the context may, or may not, make the metaphor salient. For instance, if in a picture close-ups of an open-mouthed businessman and an open-mouthed shark are juxtaposed to warn against businesspeople's unreliability (Teng & Sun, 2002: 302), the simile BUSINESSMAN IS LIKE SHARK is far more strongly suggested than if the same businessman were standing on a beach, shark fins visible in the sea behind him. Sharks' presence in a sea, after all, can be explained very well on nonmetaphorical grounds. Whether viewers will construe a metaphor in the latter case depends on their alertness, awareness of themes in a representation as a whole, extra-textual knowledge, personal experiences, and beliefs.

This leads to a stronger claim: In artistic contexts, a metaphor is sometimes construable even though it was not consciously intended as such by its maker. For instance, a representation may be accessed in a different cultural context, where a source domain has mappable connotations not present in the cultural context in which the metaphor was produced (e.g., a dragon, which in western mythology is a scary creature and in Chinese mythology a lucky one). Or a source domain (O. J. Simpson, the Twin Towers, the Dutch *enfant terrible* filmmaker Theo van Gogh, unexpectedly murdered by an Islamic fundamentalist) may have acquired associations over time that were not pertinent at the time of the metaphor's production. Or a viewer has highly idiosyncratic experiences with a phenomenon such that a particular juxtaposition with another phenomenon makes her construe a metaphor not available to anybody else (the smell of the soap at granny's place, the flowers in her wedding bouquet, the favorite symphony of her ex-husband). In short, the construal and interpretation of such implicitly signaled metaphors depend on the interpreter, while the responsibility for the derivation of explicitly signaled metaphors is the responsibility of the maker (this is commensurate with the relevance-theoretic distinction between strong and weak communication, Sperber & Wilson, 1995: 59 passim).

## 3. Multimodal Metaphor

Multimodality is a complex concept, a mature theory of which needs to take into account sign systems, sensory perception, and the material carriers bridging the two. The material carriers, moreover, involve dimensions of institutional power (Hollywood film, the publishing industry, the advertising business). A full discussion of the interrelationships between all these is far beyond the scope of this chapter. For present purposes, the following will suffice. For a combination of two phenomena to be construable as a multimodal metaphor, three criteria must be met, only the last of which exclusively characterizes the multimodal variety.

1. Given the context in which they occur, the two phenomena belong to different categories.
2. The two phenomena can be slotted as target and source, respectively, and captured in an A IS B format that forces or invites an addressee to map one or more features, connotations, or affordances (Gibson, 1979: chap. 8) from source to target.
3. The two phenomena are cued in more than one sign system, sensory mode, or both.

**Figure 26.5.** Dutch advertisement for TV channel Avante with the multimodal metaphor REMOTE CONTROL PAD IS SWISS ARMY KNIFE.

If the producer wants her metaphor recognized as such, she will help her audience by providing salient clues. The nature of these clues depends on the sign system(s) available to the sort of representation in which the metaphor is conveyed and/or the sensory organs necessary to access the representation. Simultaneity in the presentation of two domains (a picture and a sound, a sound and a smell, a picture and a taste, an inscription and the materiality of the carrier) can play a role, as can similarity in shape or style (a picture of an object and the font of a word; the rhythm in a sequence of shots and the rhythm in a sequence of sounds; the unpleasantness that connects a sound to a smell) or salient positioning (mirroring two objects along an axis; placing an object on the exact spot where another object is expected or where, in a film, that object was earlier positioned) – and any combination of these and, no doubt, other techniques.

A number of multimodal metaphors will now be discussed, chosen both for their hoped-for convincingness and to illustrate issues that surface once one ventures into the complex field of multimodality. In the Dutch science magazine for youngsters *Kijk* (February 2000, an advertisement for the niche TV channel Avante (Figure 26.5) features a hybrid object that is simultaneously a Swiss army knife and a remote control pad with the Avante logo. The accompanying text translates as "Avante. A TV channel to explore. Space travel · espionage · discoveries · science · military forces · submarines · motors · aerospace · expeditions · cars · boats · inventions." The line under the brand name reads "Call your cable provider for more information." In this ad for a TV channel, the metaphor is REMOTE CONTROL PAD IS SWISS ARMY KNIFE. Whereas the target and source are predominantly rendered pictorially, the numbers, symbols, and letters ("progr") help identify the remote control pad part of the metaphor, which qualifies the metaphor as multimodal rather than purely pictorial. What is mapped from the source to the target is presumably the knife's proverbial array of functions and its status as a typical "boy's toy" – and hence the source is likely to appeal to the dominant readership of the magazine, youngsters (mainly boys) with an interest in exploring the world. Note that the target is not itself a representation of the product, a cable provider, but metonymically refers to it, the Avante logo forging the crucial link. The similarity between target and source is suggested by the formal resemblance between a Swiss army knife and a remote control pad, and by the fact that they have been "merged" into a single gestalt. The similarity is *created* (see Black, 1979: 36ff.); outside of the present context we would probably fail to see spontaneously any similarity between a remote control pad and a Swiss army knife.

An ingenious specimen of multimodal metaphor occurs in *La Strada* (Fellini, Italy 1954). Gelsomina (Giulietta Masina), the innocent and simpleminded heroine of the movie, is watching a religious procession in honor of the Virgin Mary. Given the narrative context of the film as a whole, and the cut from Gelsomina to an image of the Virgin Mary carried in the procession, it is possible to construe the metaphor GELSOMINA IS VIRGIN MARY. That Fellini wants us to construe this metaphor is suggested by another cue. While Gelsomina is watching, the camera movement quasi-accidentally makes visible behind her a poster on a wall with the text "Madonna Immacolata" ("Virgin Mother"). This metaphorical construal is not necessary however: Since Gelsomina is, in the story world, admiring a procession in a manner that does not in any sense strike us as impossible or improbable, and since there is no reason why she should not happen to be standing in front of a poster with the text "Madonna Immacolata," we do not *need* to construe a metaphor here. This example teaches us several things. First, if a source domain emanates from the diegesis itself (i.e., the story world as presented at that very moment), the source domain's presence is realistically motivated and hence allows for the construal of a nonmetaphorical meaning. Second, a viewer can miss one of the two cueings of the source domain (the visual cut from Gelsomina to Virgin Mary and the text on the poster) and still construe the metaphor, although an awareness of both will strengthen the idea that Fellini intended the metaphor to be recognized as such. Third, Fellini conveys the metaphor fairly subtly; he could have been more explicit, for instance, by cutting from close-ups of Gelsomina to the Virgin Mary image and the poster, respectively (and, for good measure, cut back once more to a close-up of Gelsomina, or reinforce the similarity by a musical theme or sound effect).

Here is another example of a relatively weakly signaled cinematic metaphor. In a memorable scene from *American Psycho* (Harron, USA 2000), the title's serial killer Patrick Bateman and some of his colleagues are outbidding each other with the stylishness of their business cards. The men carry their cards in a cardholder, which they flick open (this happens twice in close-up), a clicking sound being audible on the soundtrack. When they hand over a card for inspection, the tense silence is only broken by a faint "swooshing" sound, underlining the gesture. One man presents his card with outstretched arm to a colleague, as if threatening him. The scene ends when Patrick, already defeated by the other man's more impressive card, requests to see "Paul Allen's card." When it is given to him, his eyes glaze over, and it drops from his hand on the table.

A colleague asks him, "Something wrong? Patrick? You're sweating!" There is a strong suggestion that the metaphor BUSINESSCARD IS KNIFE is to be construed. Not only the mise-en-scène elements (the sudden drawing of the card, the outstretched arm, the blinking, open-switching of a metallic object, the sweating, the glazing over of the eyes) cue the metaphor; it is also the brevity of the shot of the cardholders that reminds the experienced action film viewer of the way a suddenly drawn knife is represented. Note, incidentally, that even though it is the card*holder* which is silver, blinks, and flicks open, this does not mean that, all of a sudden, the metaphor shifts from CARD IS KNIFE to CARDHOLDER IS KNIFE: We assume that due to the metonymic link between card and cardholder we can construe CARD IS KNIFE.

While it might be argued that this is a pictorial metaphor of the contextual type, the soundtrack aids the construal of the metaphor. The emphatic click of the opening of the cardholder, the brief silence and the "swooshing" sound effect all contribute to the kind of tension that is familiar from imminent knife fights in numerous action films. The *word* "knife" itself is used nowhere: The concept must hence be inferred from the visual clues (mise-en-scène; camera angle, size, and movement; montage) and the sounds. While the metaphor can be verbalized as CARD(HOLDER) IS KNIFE, perhaps a better verbalization is EXCHANGING BUSINESSCARDS IS A KNIFING DUEL. This verbalization does more justice to the important notion that metaphors are used to represent the target domain in a way that suggests (potential) behavior, whether mental or real. That is, it is the affordances attached to the source domain that are mapped to the target – and this is something that the static A IS B format in which a conceptual metaphor is conventionally represented fails to emphasize, as Lakoff and Johnson appear to be aware themselves (1980: 20; for the dangers of the NOUN A IS NOUN B formulation, see also Freriks, 2004). A final point: Construing the metaphor as sketched here does not preclude construing other metaphors instead, or simultaneously. The boyish bragging scene discussed above, for instance, also allows for the metaphor COMPARING BUSINESSCARDS IS COMPARING DICKS. The metaphors could be integrated in Fauconnier and Turner's blending model, with "comparing cards," "comparing dicks," and "knife duel" as the three input spaces, and "male competitive behavior" as the central element in the generic space (see Fauconnier & Turner, 2002, especially the discussion of "The Bypass" on pp. 65–67). Another possible construal is COMPARING BUSINESSCARDS IS PLAYING POKER (personal communication, Antonio Barcelona and Rosario Caballero, Researching and Applying Metaphor conference, University of Leeds, April 2006).

A comparable, but more richly elaborated metaphor occurs in the film *The Showdown* (Garlatti Costa, UK 2000), set in a gym. The humor of this three-minute gem, which contains no spoken language, depends on the exploitation of the metaphor BEHAVIOR IN A GYM IS A WESTERN DUEL. Two muscled men attempt to outperform one another in their workout routines in an atmosphere of intimidation, scaring others away from the climactic confrontation that looms ahead. The source is cued, of course, by the title of the film. In addition, the soundtrack features hooves, nervous violins, triumphant trumpeting, a mouth organ, and ominous silence, while the images include extreme close-ups of eyes such as those in *Once Upon a Time in the West* (Leone, Italy/USA 1968), hands hovering at hip height about to rip away the genital-covering towel as if preparing to draw a gun, and shampoo flacons held as if they were guns. Even without the brief insert of a nondiegetic shot showing a colt being fired, viewers would have deduced that the source domain is that of a Western (rather than a slamming, dancing, or dart-throwing) duel, and that the weapon is a gun (rather than a knife, as in the *American Psycho* scene). It would be reductive to say, drawing on the title, that we here have a manifestation of the verbo-pictorial subtype of multimodal metaphor

BEHAVIOR IN A GYM IS WESTERN DUEL. Neither is it a purely pictorial metaphor. While most viewers would probably be able to identify the metaphor if the sound were switched off, the richness of the mappings would be diminished, since some of the mappable features in the source are enhanced by, or even given exclusively in terms of, the sound track.

For another example, recall the scene of the first killing in *The Texas Chainsaw Massacre* (Hooper, USA 1974). Kirk has entered the house and sees a metal door in the dark corridor. We hear the sound of what seem to be nervously grunting pigs. Kirk walks toward the door, the film's killer, Leatherface, suddenly opens it and quickly butchers Kirk, the grunting sound remaining audible. We could construe this sound as the source of the metaphor KIRK IS A PIG, a pig being a prototypically slaughterable animal. It is not clear whether the grunting is a nondiegetic or a diegetic sound. Even though viewers do not *see* any pigs in the scene, they could well imagine that there are pigs on a Texan farm, and hence that there was a realistically motivated source for the sound. This "naturalizes" the metaphor, which means that the metaphor is probably less salient (and hence more subtle) than when the source domain would have been cued by a transparently nondiegetic sound. Minutes later Kirk's companion Pam is also caught by Leatherface. He carries her inside while she tramples and screams. If the audience construed, consciously or subconsciously, the metaphor KIRK IS A PIG, it may now interpret Pam's trampling and screaming, similarly, as the kicking and squealing of a pig. Indeed, Leatherface proceeds by hanging Pam unceremoniously on a metal hook as if she were an animal, thus reinforcing such a metaphorical construal.

Two examples of a suggestive multimodal metaphor in which there is no diegetic "naturalization" of the sonically conveyed source domain occur in the documentary *Gracious Curves* (Luostarinen, Finland 1997; original title: *Naisenkaari*; thanks to Tarja Laine for drawing my attention to this film), a poetic but disturbing meditation about the pressures on the female body caused by aging and operations, and about how society's models of beauty impinge on women's self-perception. In a brief scene, repeated once, we see the window of a weight scale from above. The pointer in the window goes to and fro before it settles on a number. At the same time, the sound of a spinning roulette ball is audible. A multimodal metaphor of the pictorial-sonic kind is presented here: WEIGHT-WATCHING IS PLAYING ROULETTE. The uncontrollability of the roulette ball's trajectory and end-place could be mapped on the weight scale to suggest that weight-watching is a fickle activity: Sometimes you lose weight, sometimes you gain. Alternatively, the pertinent mapping is that trying to lose weight is an exciting, risky, and/or frustrating gamble. A little later in the same film, we see the feet of a young girl rope-skipping. Whenever the rope touches the ground we hear a whipping sound, suggesting the metaphor ROPE-SKIPPING IS WHIPPING (ONESELF). Given the theme of the film, we could map the notion of self-torture implied by whipping oneself onto the activity of rope-skipping, the latter activity again performed because of weight-losing purposes.

With the exception of the dueling metaphor in *Showdown*, the examples discussed are multimodal metaphors with a local impact: The metaphors, while contributing to overall themes in the narratives in which they occur, do not permeate these narratives as such. But a multimodal metaphor can surface time and again and thereby become a structuring element in a narrative (Forceville, 1999). In this vein, students of mine have investigated metaphors such as MICKEY IS THE DEVIL (*Natural Born Killers*, Stone, USA 1994), ET IS CHRIST (*ET*, Spielberg, USA 1982), and [FILM] FREEWAY IS [FAIRY TALE] LITTLE RED RIDING HOOD (*Freeway*, Bright, USA 1996). Such examples provide the transition to metaphors that are no longer creative in Black's sense (see also Gineste, Indurkhya, & Scart, 2000; Indurkhya, 1991, 1992) but reveal metaphorical relationships

**Figure 26.6.** Still from animation film O (Khurana, India 1994), with the multimodal metaphors LIFE IS A JOURNEY and KNOWLEDGE IS UP.

deeply rooted in our cognitive mental models.

## 4. Embedded Multimodal Metaphor

The examples discussed in sections 2 and 3 all had a target and source domain whose coupling is not conventional and hence are not amenable to such embedded metaphors as are the bread and butter of *Metaphors We Live By*. (I use the encompassing term "embedded" here to include Lakoff and Johnson's structural, ontological, and orientational metaphors; see Lakoff & Johnson, 2003: 264). But if Lakoff and Johnson are correct in their claim that humans impose order on the world via the overarching MIND IS BODY metaphor (1999: chap. 12), one would expect these embedded metaphors to be perceptible in pictorial and multimodal representations no less than in verbal ones. Some work in this area has been embarked upon. Simons (1995) discusses a number of Dutch election broadcasts in terms of multimodal metaphors, such as ACHIEVING A GOAL IS GOING TO A DESTINATION and BUILDING A COALITION IS CROSSING A BRIDGE, exemplifying the "source-path-goal" schema as theorized by metaphor scholars (Johnson, 1993: 166ff.; see also Turner, 1996: chap. 4). In a comparable vein, Forceville (2006b) explores how this schema informs the themes of the journey, the quest, and the story that are central to the first person travel documentary.

The four-and-a-half minute animation film O (Khurana, India 1994) in a surprising and moving manner renders various embedded metaphors in largely nonverbal terms, corroborating conceptual metaphors identified in Lakoff and Johnson (1980). We see a baby growing into an old man, meeting many people, and adding all new insights and experiences garnered from these meetings in the form of pictograms into a balloon over his head (Figure 26.6). The shifting types of pictograms suggest his development, until the balloon becomes, literally, a weight under which he almost collapses (Figure 26.7). The film not only visualizes LIFE IS A JOURNEY but also KNOWLEDGE IS UP, DEVELOPMENT IS UP, and EXPERIENCES ARE A BURDEN (for more discussion of this and other journeys in animated form, see Forceville and Jeulink 2007).

Forceville (2005b) investigates how non-iconic signs in the Asterix comics album *La Zizanie / The Roman Agent* (includingstraight and squiggly lines emanating from a character's mouth, or surrounding its head, called

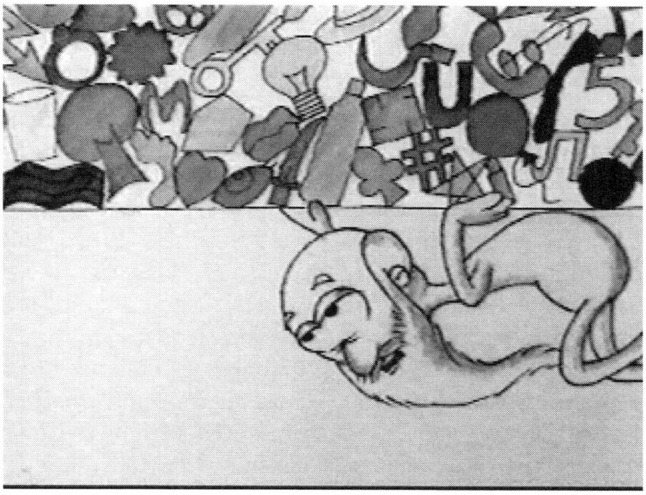

**Figure 26.7.** Still from animation film O (Khurana, India 1994), with the multimodal metaphors DEVELOPMENT IS UP and EXPERIENCES ARE A BURDEN.

"pictorial runes" by Kennedy, 1982) help designate the emotion *anger*. This is done, the argument runs, in a manner commensurate with conceptual metaphors that Kövecses (1986, 2000, 2002) identifies in language, such as ANGER IS A HOT FLUID IN A PRESSURIZED CONTAINER. One of the conclusions is that the marked "eyes," "mouth," and "hand/arm" positions of the angry persons in the Asterix album exemplify comics-specific manifestations of the metaphor. Eerden (2004) extends Forceville's investigations by analyzing another emotion theorized by Kövecses, *romantic love*. His findings demonstrate, among other things, that "eyes" and "hand/arm" positions are important elements in the depiction of enamored people, too, but that passionate love also has pictorial signals not shared with anger, for instance, a petrified body posture and certain symbols around the besotted person's head. In addition, Eerden focuses on anger and love in yet another medium, animation film, showing that an angry character in Asterix animations is often represented by low-angle shots, as if "towering over" others, whereas an enamored person sometimes is represented in slow motion to indicate his mental state (Eerden, in preparation). Shinohara and Matsunaka (in preparation), in turn, show that while most of the runes identified by Forceville also occur in Japanese manga, some runes appear to be culturally specific. This work by Forceville, Eerden, and Shinohara and Matsunaka points toward findings that have important implications for metaphor theory: While the pictorial manifestations of the conceptual metaphors (e.g., ANGER IS HOT FLUID IN A PRESSURIZED CONTAINER, ANGER IS AN AGGRESSIVE ANIMAL, LOVE IS UNITY, LOVE IS PROXIMITY, LOVE IS A PHYSICAL FORCE) appear to be compatible with the verbal examples provided by Kövecses, the media of comics and animation have different ways of representing these metaphors, and hence emphasize different aspects. Moreover, it transpires that the cultural variation in metaphor reported by Kövecses (2005) characterizes non-verbal varieties no less than verbal ones. Mainstream animation is a particularly suitable type of representation for researching embedded metaphors of the multimodal type. Since, unlike in live-action film, literally everything visible and audible in animation is artificially construed, this genre provides excellent opportunities for testing whether conceptual metaphors demonstrate their embodiment on the sound and picture level as well as on the level of language.

Another medium that invites extensive investigations of its multimodal metaphors is computer interfaces. The desktop metaphor, with its documents, folders, and wastebasket, structures our thinking and behavior concerning digital data, as does surfing, hacking, and firewalling. Internet itself is an environment that is largely given structure via metaphors. The Internet theorist Geert Lovink, for instance, reports how, in the early days of the medium, he co-founded an Internet environment on the basis of the multimodal metaphor INTERNET COMMUNITY IS DIGITAL CITY (Lovink, 2002). Steven Johnson, calling infospace a "disordered universe made orderly again by the power of metaphor" (1997: 240), examines the implications of the metaphors propelling graphic interfaces inherent in links, windows, and agents.

Multimodal metaphors can also occur in three dimensions. McNeill (1992: chap. 6 passim), Cienki (1998), and Müller (2004: chap. 3) address embedded metaphors in which the source is conveyed via a gesture. McNeill identifies "metaphorics" as one of the major types of gestures and, among many other things, draws attention to the cultural specificity of metaphoric gestures (1992: 151). Cienki finds that the gestures of students discussing "honesty" reveal conceptual metaphors such as THE PAST IS BEHIND / THE FUTURE IS AHEAD, GOOD IS UP, and UNKNOWN IS UP. Moreover, his results are consonant with the important claim informing the present chapter that "gesture, and other non-verbal means of expression, can serve as independent sources of evidence of the psychological reality of conceptual metaphors" (Cienki, 1998: 190). Müller demonstrates in an illuminating case study that the allegedly "dead metaphor" SAD IS DOWN must be active in a certain speaker's mind, for the speaker accompanies her tale of a sad incident with a downward hand movement (2004: 96). In a very different vein, Van Rompay et al. (2005) show that products and commodities (a vase, a clock) can manifest embodied metaphors by expressing embodied schemas such as INSIDE / OUTSIDE, VERTICALITY, and BALANCE (Johnson, 1987; see also Van Rompay, 2005).

## 5. Avenues for Further Research

Research into pictorial and multimodal metaphor is not only essential for a healthy metaphor theory, then, but can in turn help chart the field that is variously called the "rhetoric of the image" (Barthes 1986), visual rhetoric, visual literacy, and multimodal discourse (e.g., Kress & Van Leeuwen, 1996, 2001). It is illuminating, for instance, to study the kinds of metaphorical source domains that are typically used to promote products in advertising and whether these sources are presented verbally, visually, and/or – more subtly – sonically. It could turn out that the kinds of source domains metaphorically transforming the target domain COMPUTER in print advertisements are often shiny, metallic, toy-like objects, and hence appeal to male rather than female consumers, as I speculate in Forceville (2000). A genre whose examination may also benefit from insights in metaphor theory is the political cartoon, which is full of pictorial and verbo-pictorial metaphors (see El Refaie, 2003, and several contributions in Forceville & Urios-Aparisi, in preparation). This genre contrasts interestingly with advertising, since mappings from sources to targets (typically: politicians) are negative rather than positive, as in advertising. To give another example of potential cross-fertilization: Rick Altman's pioneering *Film/Genre* (1999) has a central thesis that is completely commensurate with the prototype theory popularized by Lakoff (1987) and could have benefited from systematically using it, while in turn the prototype theorists would do well to take into account Altman's emphasis on the pragmatics of institutional categorization. Theorists of the road movie genre (e.g., Cohan & Rae Hark, 1997) could profit from metaphor scholars' work on the source–path–goal schema.

In addition, an awareness of the working of multimodal metaphors can aid their potential deployment in the design and analysis of all types of documents that persuade people to do, or refrain from doing, something, ranging from instruction manuals (see

Westendorp, 2002) and graphic design and mapmaking (see Engelhardt, 2002; Tversky, 2001) to advertising (see McQuarrie & Mick, 1999; McQuarrie & Phillips, 2007; Phillips, 2003).

Further research into multimodal metaphor needs to branch out in various directions and should address, among others, the following questions:

### *How do the various dimensions of a multimodal metaphor affect its potential uptake?*

As we have seen, multimodal metaphors can be distinguished according to, at least, the following dimensions: (1) which sign systems and sensory modes are called upon to cue target and source domains; (2) whether the metaphor occurs in static or in moving representations; (3) by what means the metaphoric similarity is cued; (4) how explicitly or implicitly a metaphor is cued by its producer; (5) whether a metaphor verges toward the creative or the embedded extreme of the continuum. All of these dimensions deserve further theoretical and empirical investigation. This is a huge task, if only because there are so many possible permutations of variables in a multimodal metaphor. Clearly, many more case studies of nonverbal and multimodal metaphor are necessary before generalizations on any of these dimensions are feasible. For the time being, corpus studies of multimodal metaphors comparable to those Charteris-Black (2004) conducts for verbal metaphors are a long way off. But empirical research is greatly facilitated by the opportunities offered by digital treatment, allowing for the manipulation of variables in "real-life texts" (as opposed to invented examples). In representations with a multimodal metaphor, one can, for instance, present conditions with and without music, written text, spoken text, and/or visual context, to test which effect, if any, these factors have on the speed of recognition of a metaphor or on the mappings selected from source to target.

### *How are multimodal metaphors significantly similar to, and different from, verbal metaphors?*

Given CMT's claim that humans, to a considerable extent, think metaphorically, in-depth research is needed to find out whether and how multimodal metaphors convey information or radiate emotion in possibly mode-specific manners not open to their verbal sisters. While we should beware of lumping all types of multimodal metaphors together (various subtypes may well turn out to be as different from one another as from verbal metaphors), for the time being, some hypotheses can be ventured: nonverbal metaphors differ from verbal ones in (1) having a more sensual and emotive impact on viewers; (2) having greater international appeal, since they do not (exclusively) rely on language codes; (3) allowing for subtler ways of being conveyed, hence achieving their rhetorical effects more unobtrusively.

### *How do monomodal metaphors of the nonverbal varieties relate to verbal and multimodal metaphors?*

A complete and balanced theory of multimodal metaphor requires more detailed studies of monomodal metaphors of the nonverbal kind. Whereas the theorizing of the pictorial variety is now well under way, musical metaphors, that is, metaphors whose target *and* source domains are rendered in music, are only beginning to be discussed. Thorau (2003) argues that certain types of themes-and-variations in musical compositions should be understood as metaphors. It is illuminating, and consistent with my own findings in the field of pictorial metaphor, that Thorau points out that while music shares enough similarities with language to warrant the claim that it can manifest metaphors in the first place, the medium also displays idiosyncratic metaphorical behavior. For one thing, the source domain of what is to be construed as a metaphor may, unlike in a verbal A IS B format, become recognizable only gradually, because variations on a theme (the target) *develop* in the course of the musical piece and may at first not be recognizable as source domain. For another, the question of what is target and what is source in musical metaphors may be less easy to answer, and possibly even be irrelevant (for other studies on metaphor involving music and/or sound, see Cook, 1998: chap. 2; Forceville, 2004; Johnson & Larson, 2003; Victor, 2004, Zbikowski, in preparation).

### *What other tropes besides metaphor have nonverbal and multimodal manifestations?*

It has been pointed out (Gibbs, 1993) that if we want to chart the cognitive models that govern human interactions with the world we should not only study metaphor but also investigate other tropes (Barcelona, 2000, has made a start on metonymy). This recommendation must be extended to multimodal representations. Such broadening moreover requires an awareness of which tropes can and which cannot be combined. Perhaps more importantly, theorists should be aware of the danger of routinely adapting a literary model that, while having the advantage of being elaborate and refined, does not *necessarily* have counterparts in the multimodal realm. (Kennedy, this volume, similarly argues against such a complete one-to-one correspondence.) In his study of animation, Wells (1998: chap. 3), for instance, tentatively distinguishes (a suspiciously neat number of) 10 "narrative strategies" that overlap at least partly with what in linguistic–literary studies are called "tropes": metamorphosis, condensation, synecdoche, symbolism and metaphor, fabrication, associative relations, sound, acting and performance, choreography, and penetration. Bensdorp and Vergeer (2004), exploring the types of sound in animation films, arrive at five tropes: metaphor, metonymy, composition, symbolism, hyperbole. Pursuing another line of thought, Teng and Sun (2002) not only elaborate on Forceville's (1996) category of pictorial simile but also propose the new categories of "pictorial oxymoron" and "pictorial grouping." Such endeavors suggest that both nonverbal monomodal (pictorial, auditory, olfactory, tactile, gustatory) and multimodal representations have mode-specific tropes that cannot be predicted or derived from a linguistic–literary model.

### *What impact has the textual genre in which a pictorial metaphor occurs on its construal and interpretation?*

Genre considerations are central in the pragmatics of multimodal metaphor research. Whether something is a metaphor and, if it is, how it should be interpreted, partly depends on whether it occurs in, say, an advertisement, animation film, instruction manual, video installation, or Web site. Indeed, it may matter whether a supposed multimodal metaphor surfaces in a mainstream Hollywood drama, a science fiction film, or a European art movie.

### *Finally, to what extent are multimodal metaphors subject to (sub)cultural variation?*

As in verbal metaphors (Emanatian, 1995; Gibbs, 1999b; Maalej, 2004; Yu, 1998), (sub)cultural connotations evoked by semantic domains may strongly affect the interpretation of a nonverbal or multimodal metaphor (Maalej, 2001; Shinohara & Matsunaka, 2003, in preparation; Shore, 1996; see also McQuarrie & Mick, 1999). Cultural factors, like generic ones, may determine both whether a metaphor can or should be construed in the first place and, if so, what features are to be mapped from source to target.

## Acknowledgments

I am indebted to Ray Gibbs' perceptive comments on an early draft of this chapter and also wish to thank Paul Hekkert and Ed Tan both for their constructive criticisms and our many inspiring talks about metaphor. I owe many examples (and parts of the corresponding analyses) to several generations of students in my Pictorial and Multimodal Metaphor course. Moreover, they often fruitfully challenged my ideas, forcing me to be ever more precise and clear. I specifically want to thank Thomas Bensdorp, Gerthein Boersma, Hans Bouwens, Sigrid Burg, Elena Chatzigrigoriou, Wannes Dirven, Anton Duisters, Bart Eerden, Gunnar Eggertsson, Jantien Ekkes, Josina Freriks, Lidwina van Ginkel, Marloes Jeulink, Marijn de Jong, Anton Kanis, Simone Knetsch, Sarah Knuvelder, Alain Lemaire, Michael Minneboo, Josephine Rietveld, Arjan Vergeer, Paul Victor, Bas Wielenga, and Daisy van der Zande.

## References

Barcelona, A. (Ed.). (2000). *Metaphor and metonymy at the crossroads: A cognitive perspective*. Berlin: Mouton de Gruyter.

Barthes, R. (1986/1964). Rhetoric of the image. In *The responsibility of forms* (R. Howard, Trans., pp. 21–40). Oxford: Blackwell.

Bensdorp, T., & Vergeer, A. (2004). *Geluid en de populaire animatiefilm: Een cognitivistisch onderzoek naar betekenisvorming* [Sound and the popular animation film: a cognitivist approach to meaning formation]. Unpublished master's thesis, Department of Media Studies, University of Amsterdam, The Netherlands.

Black M. (1979). More about metaphor. In A. Ortony (Ed.), *Metaphor and thought* (pp. 19–43). Cambridge: Cambridge University Press.

Carroll, N. (1994). Visual metaphor. In J. Hintikka (Ed.), *Aspects of metaphor* (pp. 189–218). Dordrecht: Kluwer.

Carroll, N. (1996). A note on film metaphor. In *Theorizing the moving image* (pp. 212–223). Cambridge: Cambridge University Press.

Charteris-Black, J. (2004). *Corpus approaches to critical metaphor analysis*. London: Palgrave.

Cienki, A. (1998). Metaphoric gestures and some of their relations to verbal metaphoric expressions. In J.-P. Koenig (Ed.), *Discourse and cognition: Bridging the gap* (pp. 189–204). Stanford, CA: Center for the Study of Language and Information.

Cohan, S., & Rae Hark, I. (1997) *The road movie book*. London: Routledge.

Cook, N. (1998). *Analyzing musical multimedia*. Oxford: Clarendon.

Cupchik, G. D. (2003). The "interanimation" of worlds: Creative metaphors in art and design. *The Design Journal*, 6(2), 14–28.

Danto, A. C. (1993). Metaphor and cognition. In F. R. Ankersmit & J. J. A. Mooij (Eds.), *Metaphor and knowledge* (pp. 21–35). Dordrecht: Kluwer.

Dent-Read, C., & Szokolsky, A. (1993). Where do metaphors come from? *Metaphor and Symbolic Activity*, 8, 227–242.

Durand, J. (1987). Rhetorical figures in the advertising image. In J. Umiker-Sebeok (Ed.), *Marketing and semiotics: New directions in the study of signs for sale* (pp. 295–318). Berlin: Mouton de Gruyter.

Eerden, B. (2004). *Liefde en woede: De metaforische verbeelding van emoties in* ASTERIX. [Love and anger: The metaphorical visualization of emotions in ASTERIX.] Unpublished master's thesis, Department of Media Studies, University of Amsterdam, The Netherlands.

Eerden, B. (in preparation). Anger in *Asterix*: The metaphorical representation of anger in comics and animated films. In C. Forceville & E. Urios-Aparisi (Eds.), *Multimodal metaphor*. Manuscript in preparation, Spring 2008.

El Refaie, E. (2003). Understanding visual metaphors: The example of newspaper cartoons. *Visual Communication*, 2 (1), 75–95.

Emanatian, M. (1995). Metaphor and the expression of emotion: The value of cross-cultural perspectives. *Metaphor and Symbolic Activity*, 10, 163–182.

Engelhardt, Y. (2002). *The language of graphics: A framework for the analysis of syntax and meaning in maps, charts and diagrams*. Amsterdam: University of Amsterdam, Institute for Logic, Language and Computation.

Fauconnier, G., & Turner, M. (2002). *The way we think: Conceptual blending and the mind's hidden complexities*. New York: Basic Books.

Forceville, C. (1988). The case for pictorial metaphor: René Magritte and other Surrealists. In A. Erjavec (Ed.), *Vestnik IMS* (Vol. 9, pp. 150–160). Ljubljana: Inštitut za Marksistične Študije [Slovenia].

Forceville, C. (1994). Pictorial metaphor in advertisements. *Metaphor and Symbolic Activity*, 9, 1–29.

Forceville, C. (1995). (A)symmetry in metaphor: The importance of extended context. *Poetics Today*, 16, 677–708.

Forceville, C. (1996). *Pictorial metaphor in advertising*. London: Routledge.

Forceville, C. (1999). The metaphor COLIN IS A CHILD in Ian McEwan's, Harold Pinter's, and Paul Schrader's *The comfort of strangers*. *Metaphor and Symbol*, 14, 179–198.

Forceville, C. (2000). Compasses, beauty queens and other PCs: Pictorial metaphors in computer advertisements. *Hermes, Journal of Linguistics*, 24, 31–55.

Forceville, C. (2002a). Further thoughts on delimitating pictorial metaphor. *Theoria et Historia Scientiarum*, 6, 213–227 [Torún, Poland].

Forceville, C. (2002b). The identification of target and source in pictorial metaphors. *Journal of Pragmatics*, 34, 1–14.

Forceville, C. (2003) Bildliche und multimodale Metaphern in Werbespots [Trans. from English by D. Schmauks] *Zeitschrift für Semiotik*, 25(1–2), 39–-60.

Forceville, C. (2004). The role of non-verbal sound and music in multimodal metaphor. In H. Aertsen, M. Hannay, & R. Lyall (Eds.), *Words in their places: A festschrift for J. Lachlan Mackenzie* (pp. 65–78). Amsterdam: Faculty of Arts, VU Amsterdam.

Forceville, C. (2005a). Cognitive linguistics and multimodal metaphor. In K. Sachs-Hombach (Ed.), *Bildwissenschaft: Zwischen Reflektion und Anwendung* (pp. 264–284). Cologne: Von Halem.

Forceville, C. (2005b). Visual representations of the Idealized Cognitive Model of *anger* in the Asterix album *La Zizanie*. *Journal of Pragmatics*, 37, 69–88.

Forceville, C. (2006a). Non-verbal and multimodal metaphor in a cognitivist framework: Agendas for research. In G. Kristiansen, M. Achard, R. Dirven, and F. Ruiz de Mendoza Ibàñez (Eds.), *Cognitive Linguistics: Current Applications and Future Perspectives* (pp. 379–402). Berlin: Mouton de Gruyter.

Forceville, C. (2006b). The source-path-goal schema in the autobiographical journey documentary: McElwee, Van der Keuken, Cole. *New Review of Film and Television Studies*, 4, 241–261.

Forceville, C. (2007a). Multimodal metaphor in ten Dutch TV commercials. *Public Journal of Semiotics*, 1, 19–51. http://semiotics.ca/

Forceville, C. (2007b). Pictorial and multimodal metaphor in commercials. In E.F. McQuarrie, & B.J. Phillips (Eds.), *Go figure! New directions in advertising rhetoric* (pp. 272–310). Armonk, NY: ME Sharpe.

Forceville, C., Hekkert, P., & Tan, E. (2006). The adaptive value of metaphors. In U. Klein, K. Mellmann, & S. Metzger (Eds.), *Heuristiken der Literaturwissenschaft: Einladung zu disziplinexternen Perspektiven auf Literatur* (pp. 85–109). Paderborn: Mentis.

Forceville, C., & Jeulink, M. (2007, July). *The source-path-goal schema in animation film*. Paper presented at International Cognitivist Linguistics Conference, Jagiellonian University, Krakow, Poland.

Forceville, C., & Urios-Aparisi, E. (Eds.) *Multimodal metaphor*. Manuscript in preparation, Spring 2008.

Freriks, J. (2004). A pragmatic perspective on metaphor. Unpublished student paper, Department of Media Studies, University of Amsterdam, The Netherlands.

Gibbs, R. W., Jr. (1993). Process and products in making sense of tropes. In A. Ortony (Ed.), *Metaphor and thought* (2nd ed., pp. 252–276). Cambridge: Cambridge University Press.

Gibbs, R. W., Jr. (1999a). *Intentions in the experience of meaning*. Cambridge: Cambridge University Press.

Gibbs, R. W., Jr. (1999b). Taking metaphor out of our heads and putting it into the cultural world. In R. W. Gibbs, Jr., & G. J. Steen (Eds.), *Metaphor in cognitive linguistics* (pp. 145–166). Amsterdam: John Benjamins.

Gibbs, R. W. Jr., & Colston, H. L. (1995). The cognitive psychological reality of image schemas and their transformations. *Cognitive Linguistics*, 6, 347–378.

Gibson, J. J. (1979). *The ecological approach to visual perception*. Boston: Houghton Mifflin.

Gineste, M.-D., Indurkhya, B., & Scart, V. (2000). Emergence of features in metaphor comprehension. *Metaphor and Symbol*, 15, 117–135.

Indurkhya, B. (1991). Modes of metaphor. *Metaphor and Symbolic Activity*, 6, 1–27.

Indurkhya, B. (1992). *Metaphor and cognition: An interactionist approach*. Dordrecht: Kluwer.

Johnson, M. (1987). *The body in the mind: The bodily basis of meaning, imagination, and reason*. Chicago: University of Chicago Press.

Johnson, M. (1993). *Moral imagination: Implications of cognitive science for ethics*. Chicago: University of Chicago Press.

Johnson, M. (2007). *The meaning of the body: Aesthetics of human understanding*. Chicago: University of Chicago Press.

Johnson, M., & Larson, S. (2003). "Something in the way she moves" – metaphors of musical motion. *Metaphor and Symbol, 18*, 63–84.

Johnson, S. (1997). *Interface culture: How new technology transforms the way we create and communicate*. San Francisco: HarperEdge.

Kaplan, S. J. (1990). Visual metaphors in the representation of communication technology. *Critical Studies in Mass Communication, 7*, 37–47.

Kaplan, S. J. (1992). A conceptual analysis of form and content in visual metaphors. *Communication, 13*, 197–209.

Kennedy, J. M. (1982). Metaphor in pictures. *Perception, 11*, 589–605.

Kennedy, J. M. (1993). *Drawing and the blind: Pictures to touch*. New Haven, CT: Yale University Press.

Kennedy, J. M., & Kennedy, V. (Eds.). (1993). *Metaphor and Symbolic Activity, 8*. [Special issue on metaphor and visual rhetoric.]

Koller, V. (in preparation). Brand images: Multimodal metaphor in corporate branding messages. In C. Forceville & E. Urios-Aparisi (Eds.), *Multimodal metaphor*. Manuscript in preparation, Spring 2008.

Kövecses, Z. (1986). *Metaphors of anger, pride, and love*. Amsterdam: John Benjamins.

Kövecses, Z. (2000). *Metaphor and emotion: Language, culture, and body in human feeling*. Cambridge: Cambridge University Press.

Kövecses, Z. (2002). *Metaphor: A practical introduction*. Oxford: Oxford University Press.

Kövecses, Z. (2005). *Metaphor in culture: Universality and variation*. Cambridge: Cambridge University Press.

Kress, G., & Van Leeuwen, T. (1996, revised edition 2006). *Reading images: The grammar of visual design*. London: Routledge.

Kress, G., & Van Leeuwen, T. (2001). *Multimodal discourse: The modes and media of contemporary communication*. London: Arnold.

Lakoff, G. (1987). *Women, fire, and dangerous things: What categories reveal about the mind*. Chicago: University of Chicago Press.

Lakoff, G., & Johnson, M. (1980). *Metaphors we live by*. Chicago: University of Chicago Press.

Lakoff, G., & Johnson, M. (1999). *Philosophy in the flesh: The embodied mind and its challenge to western thought*. New York: Basic Books.

Lakoff, G., & Johnson, M. (2003). Afterword, 2003. In *Metaphors we live by* (pp. 243–276). Chicago: University of Chicago Press.

Lovink, G. (2002). The digital city – metaphor and community. In *Dark fiber: Tracking critical internet culture* (pp. 42–67). Cambridge: MIT Press.

Maalej, Z. (2001). Processing pictorial metaphor in advertising: A cross-cultural perspective. *Academic Research, 1*, 19–42 [Sfax, Tunisia].

Maalej Z. (2004). Figurative language in anger expressions in Tunisian Arabic: An extended view of embodiment. *Metaphor and Symbol, 19*, 51–75.

McNeill, D. (1992). *Hand and mind: What gestures reveal about thought*. Chicago: University of Chicago Press.

McQuarrie, E. F., & Mick, D. G. (1999). Visual rhetoric in advertising: Text-interpretive, experimental, and reader-response analyses. *Journal of Consumer Research, 26*, 37–54.

McQuarrie, E.F., & Phillips, B.J. (Eds). (2007). *Go figure! New directions in advertising rhetoric*. Armonk, NY: ME Sharpe.

Moulin, A. (2002). *Metaphor and visual imagery in advertising*. Unpublished master's thesis, Department of Germanic languages, University of Ghent, Belgium.

Müller, C. (2004). Metaphors, dead and alive, sleeping and waking: A cognitive approach to metaphors in language use Habilitationsschrift, Freie Universität Berlin, Germany.

Phillips, B. J. (2003). Understanding visual metaphor. In L. M. Scott & R. Batra (Eds.), Persuasive imagery: A consumer response perspective (pp. 297–310). Mahwah, NJ: Lawrence Erlbaum Associates.

Ponech, T. (1999). *What is non-fiction cinema? On the very idea of motion picture communication*. Boulder, CO: Westview Press.

Rohdin, M. (2003). Summary in English. In *Vildsvinet I filmens trädgård: Metaforbegreppet inom filmteorin* [The wild boar in the garden of film: The concept of metaphor in film theory] (pp. 318–329). Unpublished PhD dissertation, Stockholm, Edita Norstedts Tryckeri AB.

Rozik, E. (1994). Pictorial metaphor. *Kodikas/Code, 17*, 203–218.

Rozik, E. (1998). Ellipsis and the surface structures of verbal and nonverbal metaphor. *Semiotica, 119*, 77–103.

Schuurman, D. (2003). *Betoverende beelden: Een exploratief onderzoek naar beeldmetaforen in tijdschriftadvertenties*. [Bewitching images: An exploratory investigation into image metaphors in magazine advertisements.] Unpublished master's thesis, Department of

Political and Social Sciences, University of Ghent, Belgium.

Shinohara, K., & Matsunaka, Y. (2003). An analysis of Japanese emotion metaphors. *Kotoba to Ningen: Journal of Yokohama Linguistic Circle, 4*, 1–18.

Shinohara, K., & Matsunaka, Y. (in preparation). Pictorial metaphors of emotion in Japanese comics. In C. Forceville & E. Urios-Aparisi (Eds.), *Multimodal metaphor*. Manuscript in preparation, Spring 2008.

Shore, B. (1996). *Culture in mind: Cognition, culture, and the problem of meaning*. New York: Oxford University Press.

Simons, J. (1995). *Film, language, and conceptual structures: Thinking film in the age of cognitivism*. Unpublished PhD dissertation, Department of Film and TV Studies, University of Amsterdam, The Netherlands.

Sperber, D., & Wilson, D. (1995). *Relevance: Communication and cognition*. (2nd ed.). Oxford: Blackwell.

Teng, N. Y., & Sun, S. (2002). Grouping, simile, and oxymoron in pictures: A design-based cognitive approach. *Metaphor and Symbol, 17*, 295–316.

Thorau, C. (2003). Metapher und Variation: Referenztheoretische Grundlagen musikalischer Metaphorizität. *Zeitschrift für Semiotik*, 25(1–2), 109–124.

Tomasello, M. (1999). *The cultural origins of human cognition*. Cambridge, MA: Harvard University Press.

Turner, M. (1996). *The literary mind*. New York: Oxford University Press.

Tversky, B. (2001). Spatial schemas in depictions. In M. Gattis (Ed.), *Spatial schemas and abstract thought* (pp. 79–112). Cambridge, MA: MIT Press / Bradford Books.

Van Rompay, T. (2005). *Expressions: Embodiment in the experience of design*. Unpublished PhD dissertation, Technische Universiteit Delft, The Netherlands.

Van Rompay, T., Hekkert, P., Saakes, D., & Russo, B. (2005). Grounding abstract object characteristics in embodied interactions. *Acta Psychologica, 119*, 315–351.

Victor, Paul (2004). *The metaphorical use of sound in film*. Unpublished master's thesis, Department of Media Studies, University of Amsterdam, The Netherlands.

Wells, P. (1998). *Understanding animation*. London: Routledge.

Westendorp, P. (2002). *Presentation media for product interaction*. Unpublished PhD thesis, Technische Universiteit Delft, The Netherlands.

Whittock, T. (1990). *Metaphor and film*. Cambridge: Cambridge University Press.

Yu, N. (1998). *The contemporary theory of metaphor: A perspective from Chinese*. Amsterdam: John Benjamins.

Zbikowski, L. (in preparation). Music, language, and multimodal metaphor. In C. Forceville & E. Urios-Aparisi (Eds.), *Multimodal metaphor*. Manuscript in preparation, Spring 2008.

CHAPTER 27

# Metaphor, Gesture, and Thought

*Alan Cienki and Cornelia Müller*

## Introduction

How can a gesture be metaphoric? We will begin to answer the question by considering a gesture that was famously set in stone. The image in Figure 27.1 is that of a statue of Vladimir Lenin, the Russian revolutionary that founded the Soviet Union.

This particular statue stands in Vladivostok and similar statues were located in most major cities throughout the USSR and Eastern Europe in their communist era. On this statue, the right arm is extended, forward, and the hand is also extended pointing forward with the index finger. Other Lenin statues with the outstretched arm have the hand in a different orientation, some thumb up with a vertical palm, some palm down, and others palm facing up with an extended hand. The general image of the Lenin statue as pointing ahead was so prevalent that it became common for foreign tourists to have their picture taken below such statues, mimicking the same forward-pointing gesture. One need only conduct an image search on the Internet for "lenin statue" to get a sense of the many occurrences of this representation of Lenin. But why is Lenin's hand extended forward?

While there are multiple interpretations, including the evocation of religious iconography (Bonnell, 1997: 144), a standard explanation is that Lenin was indicating the "bright future" of communism. As Bonnell (1997: 145) describes a painting of Lenin in the same position, "The position (arm and hand outstretched . . .) suggests forward movement – pointing in the direction of the future." Thus the statue can be seen as frozen in the midst of producing a gesture that metaphorically indicates the future as located ahead. This is a metaphor common to many cultures, as explained below, and has been researched extensively as a conceptual metaphor dating back to Lakoff and Johnson (1980). In the Soviet state, it held special status in connection with the utopian vision of the future. Holz (1993: 74) notes that the Soviet government's Five Year Plans "conceived of contemporary existence – the 'is' – as a permanent progress towards future socialist happiness – the 'will be.'" For the

**Figure 27.1.** Lenin statue pointing toward the "bright future" of communism. *Source*: Wikipedia.org.

same reason, statues of Kim Il-Sung in a similar pose, pointing ahead, can be found in cities throughout North Korea.

The gesture of pointing ahead to indicate the future is not unique to the gestures of human figures in stone; it also occurs in the spontaneous gesturing of living humans while speaking, the kind which will be focused on in this chapter. For example, Calbris (1990: 87) observes that in French and other European cultures, the future can be indicated by "a forward leap of the hand or forefinger (*Two-and-a-half million unemployed * very soon*)," with the timing of the gesture indicated by the asterisk (*). Similarly, postponing an activity to a future time can be indicated gesturally by a movement forward of the hand or forefinger: "*We can't put it off * until next week*" (ibid.; and see Calbris, 1985, for more detail). Such use of gesture spontaneously in these contexts suggests that gesture is another form of human behavior in which we may see (in the multiple senses of that word) the expression of metaphors.

These few examples offer a glimpse of the relevance of studying gesture in relation to thought, both individual thought and ideas shared by cultural groups. More specifically, they indicate the high relevance of gesture research for the study of metaphor in relation to thought. In this chapter, we argue that careful analyses of gestures provide support for the assumption that metaphor is a general cognitive principle and that metaphoric mappings may be processed online. We will report on empirical observations which document moreover that online metaphoric thought is highly creative, flexible, and culturally variable. In a nutshell, we will suggest that metaphoricity is inherently dynamic and – ultimately and unquestionably – a form of embodied cognition.

At the end of this chapter, we will provide a more systematic outline of how the study of gesture is relevant to this topic. But first we need to clarify our understanding of what constitutes a metaphoric gesture, and how metaphoric gestures may relate to speech.

## What Is a Metaphoric Gesture?

Metaphoric gestures have typically been conceived of as movements of the hands that represent or indicate the source domain of a metaphor (e.g., Bouvet, 2001; Calbris, 1990, 2003; Calbris & Porcher, 1989; Cienki, 1998, in press; McNeill, 1992; McNeill, Cassell, & Levy, 1993; McNeill & Levy, 1982; Müller, 1998b, 2004b in press a; Núñez & Sweetser, 2001; Webb, 1997). The first scholar to recognize that gestures may be used metaphorically was, however, the psychologist Wilhelm Wundt. He called gestures that transfer concepts from one domain to another "symbolic gestures," and offered as an example the use of spatial gestures to represent temporal concepts (Wundt, 1922). "Yet the general character of the symbolic gesture consists in transferring the concepts to be expressed from one field to another one, hence for example to indicate time concepts in terms of space, or to represent abstract concepts as perceptual ones."[1] Note that this is exactly what our introductory example illustrates: Pointing ahead in space used to indicate that an abstract object – here "the future" – is situated ahead in time. Space is used to represent time, and the pointing gesture which uses space to refer to time is considered a metaphoric gesture (cf. also Kita, 2003).

This complements the extensive research on metaphors for time as space expressed in numerous languages of the world (e.g., Evans, 2004; Traugott, 1975). In many of these languages, though not in all, the future is talked about as being ahead (e.g., Fleischman, 1982, on Romance languages; Moore, 2000, on the Niger–Congo language Wolof; Shinohara, 1999, on Japanese; Yu, 1998, on Chinese).

Scholars researching metaphoric gestures have often worked with a further specific ontological assumption, namely that the target domain of gestural metaphors is an abstract one. Hence, the gesture would enact or depict the concrete grounds of an abstract concept. Geneviève Calbris (1990: 194–195) who was another one of the first researchers to identify metaphoric gestures, puts it in the following way: "In a way, gesture attests to the metaphor passing from (a) something concrete to (b) the physical representation of something abstract." She gives the example of a gesture where the two palms facing each other are moved apart: in one context the gesture depicts the broadness of a concrete path, "(a) *A path * this wide,*" while in another context it represents the broad range of work which has to be done, "(b) *A fairly * extensive work to be put into images.*" McNeill (1992: 14) argues along similar lines when contrasting metaphoric gestures with iconic ones: "Other gestures are 'metaphoric.' These are like iconic gestures in that they are pictorial, but the pictorial content presents an abstract idea rather than a concrete object or event. The gesture presents an image of the invisible – an image of an abstraction." Müller (1998b) argues that McNeill's iconic and metaphoric gestures are in fact both equally iconic signs, but what distinguishes them is whether they depict aspects of the referent itself (concrete reference) – which could be an entity, action, or relation – or aspects of the entity, action, or relation in terms of which the referent is being characterized (metaphoric [abstract] reference).

It is certainly often the case that metaphoric gestures depict the abstract in terms of the concrete; yet, we would like to point out that metaphoricity is not reduced to conceptualizing the abstract in terms of the concrete. Rather metaphor is a cognitive procedure of understanding one thing in terms of another and hence may also apply to two concrete entities – such as for instance characterizing a woman's body gesturally in terms of an hourglass, or when accounting verbally for all kinds of objects in terms of body parts, as is the case in expressions such as: *the foot of a mountain, the leg of a table,* or *the arm of chair*. Therefore, we are calling metaphoric gestures the ones which have the potential to engage an active cross-domain mapping, that is, the cognitive process of understanding something in terms of something else (cf. Cienki, 1998, in press; Müller, 2004b/in press a).[2]

It is worth a historical aside that the study of human gestures is not restricted to gestural expressions of metaphors. In contrast, the concept of metaphoric gestures has played a minor role in 2,000 years of gesture studies, while the focus was on expressive, regulating, and discursive functions of gestures – from Quintilian to Bulwer to Austin (cf. Kendon, 2004; Müller, 1998b, 2000, 2002, 2004b/in press a). Theorists of rhetorical gesture since Quintilian have explicitly neglected and prohibited (!) the use of iconic gestures – because it was essential for the Roman orator to distinguish himself very clearly from the pantomimes who produced pantomimic performances of the ancient Greek dramas for the lower classes (cf. Quintilian: Inst. orat. XI 3, 89). Another important argument made against using and studying iconic gestures was that people who use too many gestures are unable to use vocal language in an adequate way. In other words, despite a long-standing tradition of gesture studies, gestures which iconically depict something be it concrete or abstract only garnered the attention of gesture scholars in the 20th century.

Because of its primary focus on expressive and regulatory aspects of bodily behavior, research on nonverbal communication has widely ignored the study of gestures as a companion of spoken language. Hence, it is only with the cognitive turn in the eighties and nineties of the 20th century that co-verbal gesturing was considered a valuable phenomenon to study. Although the pioneering work of David Efron (1972/1941), republished by Paul Ekman, made an important point for the study of gestures, it was only with the studies by Adam Kendon (1980) and David McNeill (1985) that gestures came to be widely recognized not only as "illustrators" of speech (as Ekman & Friesen's (1969) terminology suggests) but as intrinsic parts of an utterance. Kendon (1980: 211) characterizes this role of gestures accordingly "[. . .] as if the speech production process is manifested in two forms of activity simultaneously: in the vocal organs and also in bodily movement." It is in the same line of thought that McNeill (1985, 1987, 1989, 1992) then puts forward a radically different theory of language, gesture, and thought, arguing that gestures are verbal, and not nonverbal as implied by the concept of nonverbal communication: "[. . .] that the whole of gesture and speech can be encompassed in a unified conception, with gesture as a part of the psychology of speaking, along with, and not fundamentally different from, speech itslf" (McNeill, 1985: 351). Since the publication of his monograph *Hand and mind: What gestures reveal about thought* (McNeill, 1992) a few years later, the study of human gestures has turned into a vividly expanding field in psychology, psycholinguistics, artificial intelligence, engineering, cognitive and linguistic anthropology, cognitive linguistics, and more recently also in metaphor theory. Gesture is being studied to gain insights into issues such as the relationship between language and thought, embodiment and cognition, metaphor and thought, the structure of mind, linguistic relativity, thinking for speaking, the cognitive and social processes involved in the development of human semiosis, and the origin and nature of the human capacity for language.

Though we will be focusing here on gesture with spoken languages, one can also find examples of manual gesture in signed languages. Since the signs in a signed language are produced using the hands and forearms (in addition to other body parts), gesture has a different character than it does with spoken language. It is important to distinguish what manual forms, positions, and/or movements constitute canonical elements of the signs of the language and which have been optionally added. Liddell (2003b), for example, observes that properties of certain signs which are gradient in nature can be thought of as gestural, namely: the location of the sign (for pointing or depicting) or the orientation of the sign (for certain verbs) which may be overlaid on some signs (see also Okrent, 2002, and Liddell, 2003a). Gestures can also occur interpersed between signs. Emmorey (1999) and Okrent (2002) each give examples in which signers make a questioning gesture in between two signs of an utterance in American Sign Language. In both cases, the gesture is made using two raised open hands (Emmorey glosses the questioning palm-up gesture in her example as "well-what"). While neither author specifically discusses these as metaphoric gestures, one could argue for a metaphorical motivation behind the upward hand position, reflecting the UNKNOWN AS UP. (See Müller, 2004a, on the frequent use of this gesture form to express the fact of not knowing, among other uses.) However, Okrent (2002: 183) discusses these as "gestures that interrupt the sign stream," rather than as gestures co-occurring with sign. Therefore, in contrast with metaphoric gestures with speech, it appears that spontaneous metaphoric gestures do not occur as *independent* forms that are produced simultaneously with signs.

To summarize, we characterize metaphoric gestures, regardless of the context of their occurrence (sign or spoken language), as voluntary movements of the body which use a cross-domain mapping to express certain thoughts or feelings.

## How Metaphoric Gestures May Relate to Speech

The relationship between metaphor and gesture is not always "straightforward." Since the details of how and when metaphors are expressed gesturally can give us new insights into metaphor and thought, we will give some attention to the different kinds of relations that have been found between metaphoric gestures and the co-occurring speech.

### *The Same Metaphor May Be Expressed in Speech and in Gesture*

Perhaps the least surprising use of a metaphoric gesture occurs when it accompanies an utterance with a verbal metaphoric expression. For example, in a data set recorded by Cienki, consisting of videotaped conversations among American students about what it means for them to take an exam honestly, one participant makes the following observation about some students.

(EXAMPLE 1)

*(1a)* *(1b)*
1 [And I think that they're willing to **PUSH**
*(2a)* *(2b)*
their moral **LIMits**,
(. . .)
2 to the exTENT, that they CAN or cannot be LAbelled cheating.][3]

While the speaker made gestures accompanying all of these phrases, let us focus on the two produced with the first transcribed line of speech. In gesture 1a, the speaker forms a fist with her dominant (left) hand, and in 1b she pushes the fist slightly forward. In gesture 2, she changes her left hand shape so that it is half-open with fingers together, making a solid, curved form, palm vertical, facing center space. In 2b, she moves the hand shape outward from herself. The speech and gesture describe a scene in which the possibilities for which behaviors can be considered moral are mapped onto the amount of space in which one can physically move. This correlates with the metaphor which Lakoff (1996/2002) and others have analyzed as MORAL ACTION IS BOUNDED MOVEMENT. This is the model according to which we understand behavior as motion along a path and immoral behavior as straying from the path of what is right. (Evidence of how this metaphor has persisted over time can be found in the origins of the word *deviance*, from the Latin spatial meaning of "away from the road" – *de via*.) Extending the potential for evaluating some behavior as moral or not is described here verbally as *pushing* a moral limit, which is shown with the formation and movement outward of the fist. In addition, the notion of MORAL CONCEPTS AS BOUNDED SPACES is invoked in speech with reference to *moral limits*. This is also depicted in manual form as a curved surface with the hand. The scenario of the moral limits being pushed is shown as the curved hand moves outward from the speaker. Compare the notion that TO CHANGE ONE'S BEHAVIOR IS TO MOVE FROM ONE SPACE TO ANOTHER, as seen in expressions like *overstepping one's bounds*, *sailing into unknown waters*, and *crossing the line* (discussed in Cienki, 1997). In our example, the questionable nature of the ethics involved is expressed in speech and gesture as an alteration being made in the location of the moral boundary.

Also note that here, as in many instances, the formation of the gesture preceded the utterance of its lexical affiliate, the word that relates to it semantically. McNeill and Duncan (2000) argue that the fact that gestures frequently precede their lexical affiliates is evidence in support of the hypothesis that visual and verbal elements are integrated in an idea unit, and then "unpacked" as it is expressed in speech and gesture.

In another example (this one from Müller, 2004b/in press a), a German speaker describes her relationship with her first boyfriend as having been *klebrig* ("clingy"), as he was too dependent on her. The gesture she makes during the quoted example, leading up to using the word *klebrig*, consists of her slowly and repeatedly pressing the palms of her two open hands together.

(EXAMPLE 2)

*open palms touch each other repeatedly*

1 [also da **hab ich schon gemerkt naja** \ **des is: ganz**
"well there I did already realize well \ this is really

*hands clap repeatedly*

2 **schö:n (-) (mh) (-) klebrig** \ **oder heftig**]
pretty (-) (mh) (-) clingy \ or heavy"

Rather than depicting a source domain object mentioned in speech, as in the previous example, this speaker portrays the manner of interacting with a clingy substance, which she likens to the quality of the emotional interaction in this relationship. Once again, the metaphor was expressed gesturally before it was verbalized.

To conclude, gestural metaphors may be semantically co-expressive with speech but temporally detached from the verbal metaphor: they can begin before the co-expressive verbal item is produced, overlap with it and proceed after it is uttered. Gesture and speech therefore appear to share the communicative burden to express one and the same metaphor, which means that metaphor is not limited to the verbal medium of expression. In other words, it can be multi-modal, appearing as a verbo-gestural metaphoric expression (see Müller, 2004b/in press a; Müller & Cienki, to appear).

### *A Metaphor May Be Expressed in Gesture, But Not in the Co-occurring Speech*

Consider the following example (analyzed in Cienki, 1998) from the student conversations about honesty, mentioned earlier. One speaker says, with several restarts,

(EXAMPLE 3)

Like dishonest suggests, like, um, not truthful,
*lh flat OH, PC*
like, [the **TRUTH** is what], like,[4]

On the word "*truth*" (uttered with emphasis, indicated by the capital letters) he makes a flat-hand gesture with his left hand in the vertical plane, fingers pointing away from his body. Though he does not say anything in this context (or in the subsequent utterances), characterizing TRUTH as metaphorically STRAIGHT, that is what appears to be represented in the gesture. The fact that there are linguistic expressions in English which reflect a conceptualization of TRUTH or HONESTY AS STRAIGHT, for example, referring to honest speech as *straight talk*, supports the interpretation that this common metaphor in the culture may have been behind the production of this gesture in this context.

Calbris (1990; Calbris & Porcher, 1989) notes the following context of gesture use in which a metaphor is expressed in the gesture, but not in the co-occurring speech: while uttering a word with an abstract meaning, one sometimes produces a gesture which reflects the concrete origins of the word. Calbris (1990: 196–198) refers to these as etymological gestures. For example, talking about a repetition of an event while making a vertical loop with one hand (in Calbris' notation, an asterisk * indicates the occurrence of the gesture): "*No, paid programs * for retraining.*" In the original French, the speaker used the verb *se recycler*, which is from the Greek *kuklos*, "circle." Another example is cited in Müller (2004b: 95–99) in which a speaker talks about psychological depression with the phrase "*durch dieses depressive*" ('because of this depressiveness') and repeatedly makes a slow, downward movement with her right hand palm down, thumb, and forefinger forming a ring shape. Yet, the origin of German *Depressivität* in the Latin verb *deprimere/depressio* "to press down" is not transparent to the average German speaker of today, for whom this spatial concept would be expressed with a different verb: *drücken*. But the notion that SAD IS DOWN, apparent in the development of the word's abstract meaning, reappears in a gesture with speech. How can this be? Apparently, a conceptual metaphor which motivated the extension of a word to an abstract domain can still be active in a culture and continue to constitute an imagistic way of thinking about the idea, even if it is no longer transparent in the form of the word itself. This may be manifested in a gesture, even if the metaphoric source domain is not explicitly mentioned in the utterance, or ever as a metaphorical expression in the contemporary language. Lakoff and Turner (1989) discuss this issue in the context of rejecting what they term the dead metaphor theory. They argue that metaphors may appear dead on the verbal level but still have the potential to be vital conceptually; in other words, they are no longer used to refer literally; hence, "*comprehend*" is no longer used in the sense of "to grasp" as in Latin, but the conceptual metaphor UNDERSTANDING IS GRASPING is alive and active in contemporary English (as in "*to grasp what someone else is saying*").

McNeill (1992) discusses another category of metaphoric gestures which occur without the utterance of explicit metaphoric expressions. They consist of instances in which mention of a topic of conversation or a question is accompanied by the hands in a position as if holding an object, as in the following example (McNeill, 1992: 148):

(EXAMPLE 4)
*bh OH rise up, PC || bh move outward and down PU as three outer fingers close*
[it **was a Sylves || ter and Tweet**y cartoon]

During the first bracketed phrase, the speaker, who is sitting, has his elbows on the arms of his chair and raises both hands up, palms open and facing each other. During the second phrase in bold type, his hands move apart, forearms rotating outward at the elbows, while three fingers on each hand close (middle, ring, and pinky), leaving the pointers and thumbs extended. Here, the topic being referred to was a specific example of a genre, that of a type of cartoon. McNeill describes the first gesture as one like holding up an object, and the second one like pulling the object open. (The thumbs and forefingers which remain extended could be interpreted as still showing the outer boundaries of the object.) McNeill argues that this and similar gestures are examples of what Reddy (1993/1979) found in his analysis of our language about language, namely, that we often talk (and presumably think) about units of language (words, sentences, whole texts, and even genres) as if they were containers for meaning. Consequently, we often conceptualize, and talk about, communication as if it entailed a simple transfer of language-objects from one person to another. Comprehension should therefore be a simple matter of taking out the meaning that is in the container of language. Although a bit of reflection reveals that effective communication indeed involves more effort than our folk model implies. Reddy refers to this as the conduit metaphor, although as Lakoff and Johnson (1980: 10) note, several conceptual metaphors can come into play, such as LINGUISTIC EXPRESSIONS ARE CONTAINERS, IDEAS ARE OBJECTS, and COMMUNICATION IS SENDING. With the example above, we see that even when no mention is made of the metaphor in the accompanying speech, the metaphor of CARTOON AS

OBJECT appears in the gesture. The gesture shows the metaphoric objectification of the genre referred to in speech. Perhaps because McNeill's (1992) book was the first widely distributed volume in English on gesture studies, this one type of metaphoric gesture (expressing the CONDUIT metaphor) has become frequently cited as *the* kind of gesture that is metaphoric, leading to assumptions that metaphoric gestures can only serve this one function. Although it is a frequently occurring type of metaphoric gesture, it is just one type among many.

Gestures discussed as examples of the conduit metaphor actually fall into several groups. The type discussed above concerns a medium of expression as a container. Another type of conduit metaphoric gestures concern what is in the metaphoric container, namely, the idea(s). These gestures express the metaphor of IDEA AS OBJECT. Müller (2004a) studies uses of the palm-up open-hand gesture, and suggests that its functional core is to present the speaker's idea, as if it were an object on the flat open hand, available for joint inspection. Note the implicit relation to the metaphor of KNOWING IS SEEING here: the gesture proposes a common means of looking at the presented object and metaphorically, it offers knowledge to be shared. We can think of this as a shared perspective, in both senses of the word (a visual point of view, and a particular way of understanding something).

Müller (2004a: 242) provides an example of a Spanish speaker proposing her perspective of what happens to the characters in a particular novel, and it is a perspective which she knows differs from that of her interlocutor. She says,

(EXAMPLE 5)
*PUOH lh* *PUOH lh*
(. . .) [las **pasa bruta (.)**]

*PVOH lh up & down, repeated*
eso si
"they experience brutal things yes indeed"

During the bracketed phrase, the speaker moves her left hand, open with palm up, in a downward motion and then holds it there. The metaphoric reference is not directed to a specific lexical item in the utterance, like in the examples we have seen earlier, but instead the target referent is the fact of presenting an idea. Here, the palm-up open hand is a metaphoric gesture that is serving a different function in that it relates to the meta-narrative level; it reflects the fact that an idea is being presented, rather than reflecting particularities of the idea itself. In this way, it can be considered a pragmatic use of a metaphoric gesture.

McNeill, Cassell, and Levy (1993: 12) discuss another kind of gesture which functions at the meta-narrative level, namely, pointing to spaces in front of the speaker when introducing a new event in a story. In their example, the speaker is retelling the story of a movie to someone who has not seen it. After describing how one scene ends, the speaker says,

(EXAMPLE 6)
*point down right*
and then the next time we see [**anyone**]

and points down to the right. McNeill et al. classify this as a deictic gesture which indicates the position of a new scene. We would argue that this use of abstract deixis could also be considered metaphoric, if the gesture is interpreted as pointing to an EVENT (a new scene) AS AN OBJECT. McNeill et al. contrast this with pointing which relates to elements in the narrative itself, for example, pointing to where characters physically were in the scene when they are first mentioned; we would consider this another form of metaphoric use of pointing gestures.

Another context in which metaphoric gestures occur independent of metaphoric speech is when a logical relation that is being talked about is shown gesturally as a spatial opposition. In the data from students discussing exam-taking practices, one participant talks about factors which determine the amount of effort that one will put into preparing for an exam. She concludes, "*It depends on the student, but it also depends on the teacher.*" While uttering the word "*depends*" the first time, she sets her two hands, palms down, into a space on her right side. She then lifts them and places them back down, but on her left side when she utters "*also*" at the start of the second phrase. The two gestures lay out the two conditions in her argument as separate spaces in front of her. This provides another example of metaphoric gesture at the pragmatic level, here: distinguishing different parts of the argument being made as separate spaces. (See also McNeill's [1992: 155] example of a speaker setting up contrasting spaces for different moral statuses of the characters he is describing – the "good guys" versus the "bad guy.")

Finally, ideas can be indicated not only as points in space but also in an objective way by using parts of the hands as objects to stand for them. Sweetser (1998) notes how even the common gesture of using the index finger of one hand to point to successive fingers of the other hand while listing ideas or making different points of an argument is an example of gesturally manifesting the metaphor of IDEAS AS OBJECTS.

### *Different Metaphors May Be Expressed in Speech and Gesture*

In some instances, one metaphor may be expressed in speech, while at the same time, the target domain for that metaphor is being characterized via a different source domain in a gesture. In example (7) from Cienki (in press), the speaker is talking about moral qualities in two categories, as either black or white.

(EXAMPLE 7)

1 [y'know, there- there is no gradations.

*lh PUOH, rh PV strikes lh* — *repeats slightly to right*

2 Either you're **right** you're **wrong**

*repeats to left* — *repeats to right*

'r **black** 'r **white**, y'know.]

At the same time, she is making a chopping gesture with the side of her right hand against the flat palm of her left hand, as if dividing space; so, we have a "color" metaphor in speech, but a spatial metaphor in gesture. However, the two characterizations of the target domain cohere in that the two source domains can constitute different qualities of the same scene, namely, two spatial areas clearly delimited, with one black and one white.

While in this example the source domain mentioned verbally could not be represented spatially (with a "black" or "white" gesture), it remains to be seen in future research whether different verbal and gestural representations only occur in this circumstance, or whether in some instances a potentially "gesturable" source domain that is verbalized is not used in favor of a different one in order to highlight multiple aspects of a source domain scene. This kind of independence between the content conveyed in gesture and in speech is not restricted to metaphoric gesture and speech: witness the gesture-speech mismatches researched by Goldin-Meadow (2003). Studying children as they tried to solve Piagetian conservation tasks and math problems, she found that children may give gestural evidence of understanding some concept before they can verbally articulate the same idea.

### *A Metaphor May Be Expressed in Gesture Which Is Not One That Is Used in the Language*

In some cases, a metaphoric gesture accompanies non-metaphoric language, and the metaphor structuring the gesture is never used in the language system itself. There is an elaborate example in Cienki (1998) of a student setting up two different events in time: the preparation for an exam, and the taking (writing) of the exam. Ex. (8) is an excerpt.

(EXAMPLE 8)

*bh PD on right* — *rh fingers curl*

1 [**and** you're taking this test,

*bh PD move to left*

2 but you have this **guilt** beforehand,

*bh make rotating motion as they move from left to right*

3 **but it doesn't save** (. . .)]

The speaker explicitly sets up two time frames in separate spaces, prior time to the left and later time to the right. This arrangement of TIME AS SPACE is familiar to speakers of Indo-European languages (among others) and likely relates to the fact that our writing systems have a left-to-right orientation (Calbris, 1990; Müller, 2000). We can also cite the role of this visuo-spatial metaphor in mathematical graphs, in which the "progression" from lower to higher values is to the right, and in time lines, normally oriented with the future to the right. However, one does not say in English that someone did X "to the left of" Y to mean that someone did X *before* Y. Therefore, we see that gesture can be a source of data on (conceptual) metaphors which are employed by members of a culture and which may relate to visuo-spatial thinking, but which may not appear in verbal/linguistic modes of expression.

### *Metaphoric Gestures in Different Cultures*

In the relatively short span of history in which there has been research on metaphoric gestures, there is evidence of their existence from a variety of cultures. As noted earlier, Calbris's study from 1990 is based on French speakers. The research we have cited is based on English, German, and Spanish. Cienki (1999) compares metaphoric gestures produced by Russian speakers talking about "honesty" and "decency." Zalazinska (2001) discusses metaphoric gestures in Polish for abstract concepts such as "nothing," "to want," "to need," and others.

However, these studies all concern languages of European origin. While some research on non-Indo-European languages indicates similarities with the findings previously discussed (such as the use in Georgian of a cup-shaped palm-up hand when presenting an idea [McNeill, 1992: 151–152]), other studies reveal some significant differences.

For example, the metaphor of the FUTURE AS AHEAD does not hold universally: witness the native South American language Aymara, whose speakers talk and gesture about the future as behind oneself, rather than ahead (Núñez & Sweetser, 2001, 2006). Here the motivation is a different experiential basis for the conceptual metaphor. Based on the metaphor that KNOWING IS SEEING, the future is unknown, and thus behind us, where we cannot see. This contrasts with the metaphor in this culture that the PAST IS AHEAD, because it is known, and therefore in the realm in front of us, which we can see.

Some other cross-cultural research, much of it originating at the Max Planck Institute for Psycholinguistics in Nijmegen, The Netherlands, has revealed notable differences in gesture systems which raise questions for the study of metaphoric gestures. One important difference is that in some languages and cultures the default frame of spatial reference is based on the surrounding geography, rather than being relative with respect to the objects in question and the perspective of them that is assumed – for example, saying in English that "the man is standing to the left of the tree." In the Australian language Arrernte, for example, one would say the equivalent of "the man is standing on the east side" of the tree, if that cardinal direction was accurate given the physical positions of the man and tree at the moment (Pederson et al., 1998). This is not just a matter of language but has been shown to be a factor of using what some call an absolute frame of reference in spatial reasoning (see Levinson, 2003, for a survey of the research on cross-cultural diversity regarding space in language and cognition). Spontaneous gestures by speakers of such languages are affected accordingly. Haviland (2000: 13) notes that speakers of another Australian language, Guugu Yimithirr, "assiduously orient pointing gestures in the 'correct' compass directions" when talking about location or motion as part of a story about an event, regardless of the angle at which they are seated when telling the story. Such findings raise questions for future research about how speakers of spatially "absolute" languages gesture metaphorically.

To conclude: metaphoric gestures may indeed relate to speech in a variety of ways, and there is variation as well as consistency across cultures. The specific forms of the interplay between gesture and speech reveals that the issue of metaphor and gesture is not reducible to a mere "illustration" of metaphoric lexemes through a gestural depiction of a source domain. It is also not reducible to metaphoric discursive gestures. Rather gestures appear as an articulatory independent mode of expression which is used flexibly, and not only to illustrate the semantic content expressed verbally, nor only to treat abstract discourse objects metaphorically (see Bohle, 2004).

## The Study of Gesture, Metaphor, and Thought

In this section, we offer an overview of the range and the nature of insights to be gained when studying gesture in relation to metaphor and thought. Although this whole field of research is still in its beginnings, there is already a significant range of observations and findings, some of which carry challenging implications for current theories of metaphor as well as for future research.

### *What Does the Study of Gesture Reveal about Metaphor and Thought?*

#### METAPHOR AS A GENERAL COGNITIVE PRINCIPLE

That metaphors may be realized in gestures as well as in speech adds support to the assumption that the creation of metaphors is based on a general cognitive principle rather than being a property of language only (cf. Cienki, 1998; Johnson, 1987; Lakoff & Johnson, 1980, 1999; Müller, 2004b/in press a). We should therefore be prepared to think about metaphors independently from a specific modality and – as a further consequence – take metaphors as fundamentally multimodal. Metaphors are not only instantiated in gestures, in pictures (Forceville, 1996), in ritual (Shore, 1996; Strauss & Quinn, 1997), and of course in spoken and in written language, but they also appear in combinations: there are verbo-pictorial metaphors (Forceville, 1996), verbo-gestural metaphors (Müller, 2004b/in press a), and combinations of differing verbal and gestural metaphors (Cienki, 1998; see also Forceville & Urios-Aparisi, to appear). Metaphors may also be realized on the verbal level but not on the pictorial or gestural level (Cienki, 1998; Müller, 2004b/in press a), and, as we have documented previously, there are gestural metaphors only – without any metaphoric expression in the co-occuring speech (Cienki, 1998). Finally, gestures drawing upon the source domains of conceptual metaphors may indicate that conceptual metaphors function widely as a vital and productive basis of verbal metaphoric expressions. Metaphoricity is therefore to be conceived of as a general cognitive principle resulting in metaphoric expressions of various modalities as well as in the creation of new conceptual metaphors.

#### METAPHORIC MAPPINGS AND ON-LINE PROCESSING

Gibbs and Colston (1995: 354) note, "Psychologists often contend that cognitive linguistic research suffers from circular reasoning in that it starts with an analysis of language to infer something about the mind and body which in turn motivates different aspects of linguistic structure and behavior." Conceptual metaphor theory, as one of the original areas of cognitive linguistic research, can be considered one of the objects of this critique: the argument is made that metaphoric expressions in language are evidence of certain conceptual metaphors, and that we know this because we find these conceptual metaphors in the language. Gesture, while a co-verbal behavior, involves a different modality of expression than speech and so provides another source of evidence for conceptual metaphors. In particular, gesture data can support arguments about the employment of conceptual metaphors in thought processes while speaking (see below). This provides one response to the criticism that "the linguistic evidence by itself [cited in research on conceptual metaphor theory] is dubious, because it assumes that a certain pattern in speech directly reflects conceptual structure" (Murphy, 1997). Gesture provides another window to understand how we structure concepts, and how we use those structures while speaking.

Gestures can indicate that conceptual metaphors are also cognitively activated when not present in speech. This offers further support for the psychological reality of conceptual metaphors independent from the existing data based of spoken and written examples. Conceptual metaphors can function as active cognitive structures even when they do not trigger verbal metaphoric expressions.

Finally, the analysis of verbo-gestural metaphors shows that seemingly "dead" verbal metaphors (i.e., highly conventionalized metaphors) may still be processed actively as metaphoric expressions. This contrasts with one of the fundamental assumptions of established metaphor theories (in the rhetoric tradition), namely, that a conventionalized verbal metaphor is no metaphor at all because it "no longer has a pregnant metaphorical use" (Black, 1993: 25). Gestures enacting the source of a conventionalized verbal metaphor provide significant evidence that this assumption is false (see Müller, 2004b/in press a).

It appears noteworthy to add that gestures are not just of scholarly interest, as windows onto thought, but they appear to be relevant for language understanding in everyday communication. Beattie and colleagues have shown in multiple experimental studies that recipients take up and use the information encoded gesturally. Both modalities – gesture and speech – appear to share the burden of conveying information; yet, sometimes information given gesturally has a higher impact and is better remembered than information given only verbally (cf., Beattie, 2003; Beattie & Shovelton, 2001). This suggests that metaphoric mappings embodied gesturally may also be understood as metaphors. But, at present, this is a conjecture which remains to be grounded in empirical studies.

### FLEXIBILITY OF ON-LINE METAPHORIC THOUGHT

The study of gesture and metaphor may be taken as a window onto thought in McNeill's terms and offer insights into the dynamic development of processes and forms of imagistic, visuo-spatial, embodied thinking underlying metaphoric expressions. McNeill (1992, 1997), drawing on work by Vygotsky, has given particular attention to how the expression of thought via speech and gesture is not a unidirectional process. Rather, thought, speech, and gesture interact and shape each other as the speaker expresses an idea unit (what McNeill calls a "growth point") in which imagistic and propositional modes of thinking interact. Similarly, Slobin (1987 and elsewhere) has been exploring the dynamic interrelations between thought and speech, and specifically, the "special form of thought that is mobilized for communication," which he calls "thinking for speaking." McNeill and Duncan (2000) integrate these strands of research, arguing that the growth point consists of the imagistic nature of an idea as it is being integrated into the linguistic categories available for its expression in the language. In this regard, metaphoric gestures appear to play an important role for speakers in various ways as they formulate their imagistic understanding of abstract concepts into linguistic expressions. Indeed, there is some evidence to suggest that gestures just produced could even prompt the realization of new images as one is thinking for speaking, and so initiate thinking in terms of new metaphors, giving rise to the use of other verbal metaphoric expressions in the subsequent speech (Cienki, 2000).

Investigations into questions of linguistic relativity and/or universals have profited much from using gesture analyses as windows onto active thought patterns during speaking. This cross-cultural research has once more documented that the study of gestures may provide crucial insights into forms of thought active during speaking, independent of what can be gleaned from spoken language alone. Using the gesture space to perform deictic gestures in an absolute frame of reference, as in Haviland's (1993, 2000) Guugu Yimithirr narration, indicates that the linguistic categories and the semiotics of the gesture system draw on the same cognitive frame of reference. Further research on language and cultures which commonly use absolute spatial reference would provide a more complete picture about which ways of using gestures metaphorically appear to be more universal, and which are more culture specific.

METAPHORICITY IS DYNAMIC AND GRADABLE

So far metaphorictiy has been primarily conceived of as a stable property of words and/or concepts; a verbal expression or a conceptual metaphor tended to be regarded as either vital / productive, or as dead / unproductive. However, a number of researchers (e.g., Cameron, 2003; Fauconnier & Turner, 1998; Grady, Oakley, & Coulson, 1999; Steen, 2002) have pointed out that the salience of metaphors, particularly the recognizability of verbal metaphoric expressions, differs according to various factors, such as grammatical category, semantics, context within the text, and genre. Metaphoricity is thus gradable, and factors such as these influence whether someone will realize an expression as metaphoric.

Looking at the ways in which verbal and gestural metaphors are integrated into ongoing utterances is a way in which we uncover how metaphoricity is gradable and hence a dynamic, not a static, property. The argument is an iconic and an interactive one: the more cues that direct the attention of the interlocutors to the metaphoric quality of a verbal metaphoric expression, the higher the degree of cognitive activation of metaphoricity in the speaker (and also potentially the addressee). One case would be metaphoric gestures which constitute an obligatory part of an utterance in the sense that they contain necessary information and fill a lexical and syntactic gap. If they furthermore receive the speaker's and listener's gaze, and draw upon the same source domain as the verbal metaphoric expression, they must be conceived as foregrounded, as receiving focused attention from both the speaker and the listener, and as displaying a high degree of speaker-internal activation of metaphoricity. When comparing metaphors which receive these attention-getting cues with others that go "unnoticed" (i.e., which are only expressed in one modality and are not accompanied by any cues such as prosodic stress or gaze direction), it is clear that the latter type are not in the focus of interpersonal attention in the same way. Put another way, these clusters of attention-getting cues produce interactive foregrounding of metaphoricity and since what is interactively foregrounded is also intrapersonally foregrounded, metaphoricity should in these cases be highly activated intrapersonally. In short, the close interaction between the modalities and their verbal, bodily, and interactive context indicates that metaphoricity is a dynamic property and not a static one – that is, dynamic not only in gestural motion, but also in cognition (cf. Müller, 2004b/in press a, in press b).

METAPHOR, GESTURE, AND EMBODIED COGNITION

Gestures can spatially depict elements from the source domain of a metaphor, something which is not possible for metaphoric expressions in spoken languages. Many gestures, metaphoric and otherwise, take their form from everyday embodied activities, recreating them iconically. Müller (1998a, 1998b) distinguishes four gestural modes of representation, that is, four forms of practices of gesture "creation." Three of them bear directly upon embodied mundane practices of the hands: (1) hands act as if they would perform an instrumental action (opening a window, holding a steering wheel, presenting an object on the open hand; (2) hands mold short-lived sculptures (the frame of a picture, the shape of a globe, a round object as representation for a love relationship); (3) hands draw routes on a map, the shape of a picture frame, or outline the ups and downs of a love relation as a graph. The interesting point is that the modes of representation are used not only to depict concrete activities or objects or properties of concrete objects but also to represent abstract metaphoric concepts. This fact supports the hypothesis in cognitive linguistics that (many) metaphors are grounded in embodied action. (See Gibbs and Berg, 2002, on the broader questions about mental imagery and embodied activity, as well as the responses to their article in that journal issue. See also Gibbs, 2005, for a summary of different perspectives in the literature on speech and gesture and how these relate to larger questions about embodiment and cognition.) Compare also research on sign languages in which the physical depiction of metaphorical source domains has been shown to play a clear role in the use of metaphor (Taub, 2001; Wilcox, 2000).

## *Implications of Gesture Studies for Future Research into Metaphor and Thought*

Taking the analysis of metaphoric gesture as a serious part of a cognitive linguistic analysis has some important implications for future research. It affects the data as well as the theoretical concepts.

### RECONSIDER DATA AND METHODS OF ANALYSIS USED IN METAPHOR RESEARCH

Lakoff and Johnson (1980) not only laid the groundwork for a new theoretical direction in the study of metaphor; this work also implicitly supported a particular kind of research methodology, one which takes constructed, but intuitively plausible, sentences as data. Only recently has more research appeared which draws on examples from naturally occurring spoken interaction, existing written texts, and/or data from larger corpora. In gesture studies, some research may cite plausible but constructed examples, but the very nature of spontaneous gesture with speech – the fact that it is usually produced unwittingly and that it lacks standards of form (cf. McNeill, 1992) – weighs against the use of constructed data. Particularly, in recent research on metaphor in gesture, the data are almost exclusively video recordings of spontaneously produced co-verbal behavior. This also means that gesture researchers have been confronting the accompanying methodological questions of using natural data in their research on metaphoric gestures. In this way, gesture research cannot only help develop metaphor theories, it might also have an influence on the kinds of data that are studied and the methods by which they are examined. This could include giving greater prominence to spoken language data (and methods for working with it) in metaphor research. The focus on spoken language in the physical setting of its use, inherently part of the video-recorded data used in most gesture studies, could help give greater attention to other questions in the study of metaphor. These include the role of where metaphor occurs in the discourse context, the function of metaphor in the interaction between participants in conversation, and the role of the physical setting (the context of interaction) as a prompt for, or grounding of, the use of specific metaphors.

With greater use of naturally occurring linguistic data in the field of metaphor studies, the methodology or methodologies for identifying metaphoric expressions in spoken discourse and written texts have begun to receive more attention in the research literature. For example, one group of researchers which has devised a reliable procedure for metaphor identification in texts is "Pragglejaz," named after the first initials of the 10 group members (Pragglejaz Group, 2007). Perhaps a similar research group should be formed to develop reliable procedures or guidelines for the identification of metaphoric gestures. However, the scope of what counts as a metaphoric expression, be it in words or gesture, will vary according to the goals of the research project. Some projects may have a broad scope, encompassing any expression with potential metaphoricity, while others may focus more narrowly on expressions which appear to indicate metaphoric processing by the speaker in real time. The important thing is to make one's methodology for metaphor identification clear and appropriate for the goals of one's research.

An additional topic, which can only be touched on briefly here, concerns the method of presenting examples of metaphoric gestures in research presentations and publications. Some, such as the journal *Gesture*, allow video data to be included in publications by providing a CD in each issue with relevant examples. Some studies refer to Web Sites in which the video examples can be seen. Otherwise, we are left with drawings or verbal descriptions, for which there is no standard accepted in the field. Indeed, drawings and verbal descriptions are already interpretations of the data themselves, just as written transcriptions of speech are, and such renderings inherently involve theoretical choices about inclusion and exclusion of detail, which need to be explicitly articulated in presentations of one's research. By way of comparison, research published on metaphor in sign language usually employs written glosses from the dominant language of the country in which the sign language is used, but this is not possible with spontaneous gestures since the relation between form and meaning is not conventionalized.

#### LABELING OF CONCEPTUAL METAPHORS

Gestures range from those with commonly accepted forms and meanings (emblems) to those with spontaneously created forms, whose meanings are hidden in the subconscious of the gesturer. Since spontaneous gesture with speech does not constitute a symbolic system of communication like language itself does, we are confronted not only with challenges in describing the forms of the gestures but also with questions about labeling the conceptual metaphors which they may be expressing. In the framework of conceptual metaphor theory, it has not been seen as problematic to label the proposed cross-domain mappings in terms of words, in the formula TARGET DOMAIN IS SOURCE DOMAIN. However, the examination of gestures and speech makes the potential problems with this method more obvious. To begin with, it entails the interpretation of a gestural form, and of the concept it might represent, in terms of a word or phrase. But it can be very difficult (not to mention inadequate) to capture an embodied action which comprises a source domain in the form of a word or phrase. One solution might be to follow the model of cognitive grammar (Langacker, 1987, 1991) in using diagrams in the mechanics of the analysis, as suggested in Cienki (2005). However, this would require careful motivation for the schematic formation of the diagrams used, as has been observed in cognitive grammar analyses. Since gesture, and embodied concepts, involve motion, this should be incorporated as well in the exposition of the analysis. This is not an unrealistic expectation, given the developing use of computer graphics in the study of gesture. (See, for example, the method of image processing known as vector coherence mapping, employed in McNeill et al., 2001.)

## Conclusion: How the Study of Gesture Advances Our Understanding of the Research into Metaphor and Thought

In this chapter, we have assembled a range of arguments in support of a position that reorients the database of metaphor research from primarily relying on speaker-internal intuitions and dictionary knowledge of verbal metaphors toward the study of (spontaneous) spoken language along with the gestures that speakers produce unwittingly whenever they talk. We have indicated that this new view of metaphors sheds light on fundamental issues of metaphor theory such as the still (after two millennia of scholarly reflection) nontrivial questions: *What is metaphor? How do we find out what metaphor is?* We have argued that this depends strongly upon the empirical sources considered. Looking at gestures and speech shows that metaphor is a general cognitive principle and is not restricted to language alone. In this regard, our findings offer support for a fundamental assumption of conceptual metaphor theory, although, notably, they break the vicious argumentative circle that cognitive linguistics in general has been criticized for. *Yet, what do we find out about metaphor when we look at gesture and speech?* We find that metaphor – or more precisely the establishment of metaphoricity – is a cognitive activity which takes place online during the process of speaking. We find that metaphor is clearly not restricted to language or a specific linguistic or poetic principle. Rather it turns out that metaphor is a way thought is organized, and it is because the products of metaphoric thought have been studied mostly in their verbal forms that metaphor has been traditionally conceived of as a uniquely linguistic and poetic phenomenon. Taking spoken language and gestures into consideration uncovers that metaphors may be instantiated in various modalities, notably without necessarily drawing upon the same conceptual metaphor. Imagistic, embodied, and propositional modes of thinking interact during speaking (witness McNeill's concept of the growth point) and gestures may trigger new verbal metaphoric expressions. Furthermore, the close analysis of the syntactic, semantic, prosodic, and bodily context of verbal and gestural metaphoric expressions reveals that metaphoricity is a dynamic not a static property of linguistic items, which may be more or less foregrounded and so may receive more or less focused attention. Studying metaphor, gesture, and speech in relation to thought opens up a range of new phenomena and facets of metaphor for further investigation – making a strong case for the need to incorporate the study of language use (including gesture) into research on metaphor and thought (see Cienki & Müller, in press).

## Notes

1 [Translation from German CM]: "Der allgemeine Charakter der symbolischen Gebärde besteht aber darin, daß sie die auszudrückenden Vorstellungen aus einem Anschauungsgebiet in ein anderes überträgt, also z.B. zeitliche Vorstellungen räumlich andeutet, oder daß sie abstrakte Begriffe sinnlich veranschaulicht" (Wundt, 1922: 165). Wundt's concept was taken up by Efron's (1972/1941) category of ideographic gestures and McNeill's (1992) concept of metaphoric gestures.

2 Cf. Müller's (2004b/in press a) concept of activation of a triadic structure based on Wittgenstein's concept of "seeing as," Lakoff's and Johnson's "understanding and experiencing one kind of thing in terms of another" (Lakoff & Johnson, 1980: 5), and Richards' cognitive conceptualization of metaphor as having "[. . .] two thoughts of different things active together and supported by a single word, or phrase, whose meaning is a resultant of their interaction." (Richards, 1936: 93)

3 The following conventions are used in this chapter for transcribing speech: capitalization indicates emphasis; "(. . .)" indicates an ellipsis in the transcript; ":" indicates lengthening; "(.)" indicates micropause; '"(-)" indicates a slightly longer pause; "/" indicates rising intonation; " \ " indicates falling intonation. In transcribing gestures, "[ ]" indicates the beginning and end of a gesture phrase, and bold type indicates the main stroke phase of a gesture.

4 Henceforth, the following additional conventions will be used in transcribing gestures: "rh" for right hand; "lh" for left hand; "bh" for both hands; "PU" for palm up; "PV" for palm vertical; "PC" for palm toward center; "PD" for palm down; "OH" for open hand; "||"for change of hand configuration within one gesture phrase.

## References

Beattie, G. (2003). *Visible thought: The new psychology of body language*. Routledge: London.

Beattie, G., & Shovelton, H. (2001). An experimental investigation of the role of different types of iconic gesture in communication: A semantic feature approach. *Gesture, 1*, 129–149.

Black, M. (1993). More about metaphor. In A. Ortony (Ed.), *Metaphor and thought* (2nd ed., pp. 19–41). Cambridge: Cambridge University Press.

Bohle, U. (2004). *Das Wort ergreifen – Das Wort übergeben. Explorative Studie zur Rolle redebegleitender Gesten in der Organisation des Sprecherwechsels*. PhD thesis, Department of Humanities, Freie Universität Berlin.

Bonnell, V. E. (1997). *Iconography of power: Soviet political posters under Lenin and Stalin*. Berkeley: University of California Press.

Bouvet, Danielle. (2001). *La dimension corporelle de la parole: Les marques posturo-mimo-gestuelles de la parole, leurs aspects métonymiques et métaphoriques, et leur rôle au cours d'un récit*. Paris: Peeters.

Calbris, G. (1985). Espace-temps: Expression gestuelle du temps. *Semiotica, 55*, 43–73.

Calbris, G. (1990). *The semiotics of French gestures*. Bloomington: Indiana University Press.

Calbris, G. (2003). *L'expression gestuelle de la pensée d'un homme politique*. Paris: CNRS Éditions, Collection CNRS Communication.

Calbris, G., & Porcher, L. (1989). *Geste et communication*. Paris: Hatier-Crédif.

Cameron, L. (2003). *Metaphor in educational discourse*. London: Continuum.

Cienki, A. (1997). Motion in the metaphorical spaces of morality and reasoning as expressed in language and gesture. *International Journal of Communication, 7*, 85–98.

Cienki, A. (1998). Metaphoric gestures and some of their relations to verbal metaphoric expressions. In J.-P. Koenig (Ed.), *Discourse and cognition: Bridging the gap* (pp. 189–204). Stanford, CA: Center for the Study of Language and Information.

Cienki, A. (1999). Metaphors and cultural models as profiles and bases. In R. W. Gibbs, Jr., & G. J. Steen (Eds.), *Metaphor in cognitive linguistics* (pp. 189–203). Amsterdam: John Benjamins.

Cienki, A. (2000, May). *Gesture, metaphor, and thinking for speaking*. Paper presented at the fifth conference on Conceptual Structure, Discourse, and Language (CSDL-5), Santa Barbara, California.

Cienki, A. (2005). Metaphor in the "Strict Father" and "Nurturant Parent" cognitive models: Theoretical issues raised in an empirical study. *Cognitive Linguistics, 16*, 279–312.

Cienki, A. (in press). Why study metaphor and gesture? In A. Cienki & C. Müller (Eds.), *Metaphor and gesture*. Amsterdam: John Benjamins.

Cienki, A., & Müller, C. (Eds.). (in press). *Metaphor and gesture*. Amsterdam: John Benjamins.

Efron, D. (1972/1941). *Gesture, race, and culture*. The Hague: Mouton.

Ekman, P., & Friesen, W. (1969). The repertoire of nonverbal behavior: Categories, origins, usage and coding. *Semiotica, 1*, 49–98.

Emmorey, K. (1999). Do signers gesture? In L. S. Messing & R. Campbell (Eds.), *Gesture, speech, and sign* (pp. 133–159). Oxford: Oxford University Press.

Evans, V. (2004). *The structure of time: Language, meaning, and temporal cognition*. Amsterdam: John Benjamins.

Fauconnier, G., & Turner, M. (1998). Conceptual integration networks. *Cognitive Science, 22*, 133–187.

Fleischman, S. (1982). *The future in thought and language: Diachronic evidence from romance*. Cambridge: Cambridge University Press.

Forceville, C. (1996). *Pictorial metaphor in advertising*. London: Routledge.

Forceville, C., & Urios-Aparisi, E. (Eds.). (to appear). *Multimodal metaphor*. Berlin/New York: Mouton de Gruyter.

Gibbs, R. W., Jr. (2005). *Embodiment and cognitive science*. Cambridge: Cambridge University Press.

Gibbs, R. W., Jr., & Berg, E. A. (2002). Mental imagery and embodied activity. *Journal of Mental Imagery, 26*, 1–30.

Gibbs, R. W., Jr., & Colston, H. L. (1995). The cognitive psychological reality of image schemas and their transformations. *Cognitive Linguistics, 6*, 347–378.

Goldin-Meadow, S. (2003). *Hearing gesture: How our hands help us think*. Cambridge, MA: Harvard University Press.

Grady, J. E., Oakley, T., & Coulson, S. (1999). Blending and metaphor. In: R. W. Gibbs, Jr., & G. J. Steen (Eds.), *Metaphor in cognitive linguistics* (pp. 101–124). Amsterdam: John Benjamins.

Haviland, J. (1993). Anchoring, iconicity and orientation in Guugu Yimithirr pointing gestures. *Journal of Linguistic Anthropology, 3*(1), 3–45.

Haviland, J. (2000). Pointing, gesture spaces, and mental maps. In D. McNeill (Ed.), *Language and gesture* (pp. 13–46). New York: Cambridge University Press.

Holz, W. (1993). Allegory and iconography in Socialist Realist painting. In M. C. Brown & B. Taylor (Eds.), *Art of the Soviets: Painting, sculpture, and architecture in a one-party state, 1917–1992* (pp. 73–85). Manchester: Manchester University Press.

Johnson, M. (1987). *The body in the mind: The bodily basis of meaning, imagination, and reason*. Chicago: University of Chicago Press.

Kendon, A. (1980). Gesticulation and speech: Two aspects of the process of utterance. In M. Ritchie Key (Ed.), *Nonverbal communication and language* (pp. 207–227). The Hague: Mouton.

Kendon, A. (2004). *Gesture: Visible action as utterance*. Cambridge: Cambridge University Press.

Kita, S. (Ed.). (2003). *Pointing: Where language, culture and cognition meet*. Mahwah, NJ: Lawrence Erlbaum Associates.

Lakoff, G. (1996/2002). *Moral politics: What conservatives know that liberals don't*. Chicago: University of Chicago Press. (Second edition published as *Moral politics: How liberals and conservatives think*.)

Lakoff, G., & Johnson, M. (1980). *Metaphors we live by*. Chicago: University of Chicago Press.

Lakoff, G., & Johnson, M. (1999). *Philosophy in the flesh*. New York: Basic Books.

Lakoff, G., & Turner M. (1989). *More than cool reason: A field guide to poetic metaphor*. Chicago: Chicago University Press.

Langacker, R. W. (1987). *Foundations of cognitive grammar: Vol. 1. Theoretical prerequisites*. Stanford, CA: Stanford University Press.

Langacker, R. W. (1991). *Foundations of cognitive grammar: Vol. 2. Descriptive applications*. Stanford, CA: Stanford University Press.

Levinson, S. C. (2003). *Space in language and cognition: Explorations in cognitive diversity*. Cambridge: Cambridge University Press.

Liddell, S. K. (2003a). *Grammar, gesture, and meaning in American Sign Language*. Cambridge: Cambridge University Press.

Liddell, S. K. (2003b, July). *Spatial mappings, gesture, and metaphor in American Sign Language*. Presented at the Eighth International Cognitive Linguistics Conference, La Rioja, Spain.

McNeill, D. (1985). So you think gestures are nonverbal? *Psychological Review*, 92(3), 350–371.

McNeill, D. (1987). So you do think gestures are nonverbal! A reply to Feyereisen. *Psychological Review*, 94(4), 499–504.

McNeill, D. (1989). A straight path – to where? Reply to Butterworth and Hadar. *Psychological Review*, 96(1), 175–179.

McNeill, D. (1992). *Hand and mind: What gestures reveal about thought*. Chicago: University of Chicago Press.

McNeill, D. (1997). Growth points cross-linguistically. In J. Nuyts & E. Pederson (Eds.), *Language and conceptualization* (pp. 190–212). Cambridge: Cambridge University Press.

McNeill, D. (Ed.). (2000). *Language and gesture*. Cambridge: Cambridge University Press.

McNeill, D., Cassell, J., & Levy, E. T. (1993). Abstract deixis. *Semiotica*, 95, 5–19.

McNeill, D., & Duncan S. (2000). Growth points in thinking-for-speaking. In D. McNeill (Ed.), *Language and gesture* (pp. 141–161). Cambridge: Cambridge University Press.

McNeill, D., & Levy, E. T. (1982). Conceptual representations in language activity and gesture. In R. Jarvella & W. Klein (Eds.), *Speech, place, and action* (pp. 271–295). Chichester, England: Wiley & Sons.

McNeill, D., Quek, F., McCullough, K.-E., Duncan, S., Furuyama, N., Bryll, R., et al. (2001). Catchments, prosody, and discourse. *Gesture*, *1*, 9–33.

Moore, K. E. (2000). *Spatial experience and temporal metaphors in Wolof: Point of view, conceptual mapping and linguistic practice*. Ph.D. dissertation, University of California, Berkeley.

Müller, C. (1998a). Iconicity and gesture. In S. Santi et al. (Eds.), *Oralité et gestualité: Communication multimodale, interaction* (pp. 321–328). Montréal, Paris: L'Harmattan.

Müller, C. (1998b). *Redebegleitende Gesten. Kulturgeschichte – Theorie – Sprachvergleich*. Berlin: Berlin Verlag Arno Spitz.

Müller, C. (2000). Zeit als Raum. Eine kognitiv-semantische Mikroanalyse des sprachlichen und gestischen Ausdrucks von Aktionsarten. In E. W. B. Hess-Lüttich & H. W. Schmitz (Eds.), *Botschaften verstehen. Kommunikationstheorie und Zeichenpraxis. Festschrift für Helmut Richter* (pp. 211–228). Frankfurt/Main: Peter Lang.

Müller, C. (2002). Eine kleine Kulturgeschichte der Gestenbetrachtung. *Psychotherapie und Sozialforschung*, 4(1), 3–29.

Müller, C. (2004a). Forms and uses of the palm up open hand: A case of a gesture family? In C. Müller & R. Posner (Eds.), *The semantics and pragmatics of everyday gestures* (pp. 233–256). Berlin: Weidler.

Müller, C. (2004b/in press a). *Metaphors, dead and alive, sleeping and waking*. Habilitationsschrift, Freie Universität Berlin. In press with the University of Chicago Press.

Müller, C. (in press b). What gestures reveal about the nature of metaphor. In A. Cienki & C. Müller (Eds.), *Metaphor and gesture*. Amsterdam: John Benjamins.

Müller, C., & Cienki, A. (to appear). When speech and gesture come together: Forms of multimodal metaphor in the use of spoken language. In C. Forceville & E. Urios-Aparisi (Eds.). *Multimodal metaphor*. Berlin/New York: Mouton de Gruyter.

Murphy, G. L. (1997). Reasons to doubt the present evidence for metaphoric representation. *Cognition*, 62, 99–108.

Núñez, R., & Sweetser, E. (2001, July). *Spatial embodiment of temporal metaphors in Aymara: Blending source-domain gesture with speech*. Presented at the Seventh International

Cognitive Linguistics Conference, Santa Barbara, California.

Núñez, R., & Sweetser, E. (2006). With the future behind them: Convergent evidence from language and gesture in the crosslinguistic comparison of spatial construals of time, *Cognitive Science* 30, 1–49.

Okrent, A. (2002). A modality-free notion of gesture and how it can help us with the morpheme vs. gesture question in sign language linguistics (or at least give us some criteria to work with). In R. P. Meier, K. Cormier, & D. Quinto-Pozos (Eds.), *Modality and structure in signed and spoken languages* (pp. 175–198). Cambridge: Cambridge University Press.

Pederson, E., Danziger, E., Wilkins, D., Levinson, S., Kita, S., & Senft, G. (1998). Semantic typology and spatial conceptualization. *Language*, 74, 557–589.

Pragglejaz Group (2007). MIP: A method for identifying metaphorically used words in discourse. *Metaphor and Symbol*, 22, 1–39.

Quintilianus, M. F. (1975). *Ausbildung des Redners, Zwölf Bücher, Zweiter Teil, Buch VII–XII. Institutionis oratoriae libri XII, pars posterior, libros VII–XII continens*. (H. Rahn, Ed. and Trans.). Darmstadt: Wissenschaftliche Buchgesellschaft.

Reddy, M. J. (1993/1979). The conduit metaphor: A case of frame conflict in our language about language. In A. Ortony (Ed.), *Metaphor and thought* (pp. 164–201). Cambridge: Cambridge University Press.

Richards, I. A. (1936). *The philosophy of rhetoric*. New York: Oxford University Press.

Shinohara, K. (1999). *Epistemology of space and time*. Kwansei, Japan: Kwansei Gakuin University Press.

Shore, B. (1996). *Culture in mind: Meaning construction and cultural cognition*. New York: Oxford University Press.

Slobin, D. (1987). Thinking for speaking. In *Proceedings of the Thirteenth Annual Meeting of the Berkeley Linguistics Society* (pp. 435–445). Berkeley, CA: Berkeley Linguistics Society.

Steen, G. (2002). Metaphor in Bob Dylan's "Hurricane": Genre, language, and style. In E. Semino & J. Culpeper (Eds.), *Cognitive stylistics: Language and cognition in text analysis* (pp. 183–209). Amsterdam: John Benjamins.

Strauss, C., & Quinn, N. (1997). *A cognitive theory of cultural meaning*. Cambridge: Cambridge University Press.

Sweetser, E. (1998). Regular metaphoricity in gesture: Bodily-based models of speech interaction. *Actes du 16e Congrès International des Linguistes* [CD-ROM]. Elsevier.

Taub, S. (2001). *Language from the body: Iconicity and metaphor in American Sign Language*. Cambridge: Cambridge University Press.

Traugott, E. (1975). Spatial expressions of tense and temporal sequencing: A contribution to the study of semantic fields. *Semiotica*, 15, 207–230.

Webb, R. (1997). *Linguistic features of metaphoric gestures*. Ph.D. dissertation, University of Rochester, New York.

Wilcox, P. P. (2000). *Metaphor in American Sign Language*. Washington, DC: Gallaudet University Press.

Wundt, W. (1922). *Völkerpsychologie. Eine Untersuchung der Entwicklungsgesetze von Sprache, Mythus und Sitte: Vol. 2. Die Sprache*. Leipzig: Alfred Kröner Verlag.

Yu, N. (1998). *The contemporary theory of metaphor: A perspective from Chinese*. Amsterdam: John Benjamins.

Zalazinska, A. (2001). *Schematy mysli wyrazane w gestach*. [Schemas of thought expressed in gestures]. Krakow: Uniwersytet Jagiellonski.

CHAPTER 28

# Metaphor and Music



## *Lawrence M. Zbikowski*



The music in Example 1 is a shorthand version of the string parts and solo bass melody from the opening of the fourth movement of Johann Sebastian Bach's 1714 cantata for the first Sunday of Advent, "Nun komm der Heiden Heiland." The music in the string parts for the passage might be described in one of two contrasting ways. The first is more colorful and more accessible: "The bass obstinately plods along throughout the passage; the chords above are either sour and biting dissonances (as in the first half of measure 1, and all of measures 2–3) or sweet but dark consonances (as in the second half of measure 1, or at the end of the excerpt). The mostly murky sounds of the pizzicato strings, together with the slow tempo, make this a brooding, melancholy piece." The second description is drier, and makes more use of technical jargon: "Above an ostinato tonic bass Bach sounds first a dominant-seventh chord (in the opening portion of measure 1), and then a leading-tone chord with seventh (in measures 2–3). He provides momentary release for the tension created by these dissonances through the introduction of the tonic chord in the second half of measure 1 and then again at the conclusion of the passage."

In analyses of how language is used to characterize music, the first description is typically characterized as metaphorical, the second as literal. The metaphors in the first description are readily apparent:

- the "plodding bass" is nothing more than a repeated note plucked by the cellos
- the consonant harmonies of measures 1 and 4 and dissonant harmonies of measures 1–3 are sounds, and so cannot taste like anything, sweet or sour
- the dissonances in measures 1–3 are simply a consequence of F♯ and D♯ sounding against the E in the bass – no mechanisms for biting are in evidence
- as products of the resonance of a sounding medium the E minor chords of measures 1 and 4 have no particular reflectance and so can be neither dark nor light
- even if we grant that what is meant by the characterization of the piece as "brooding and melancholy" is that it is *expressive* of these feelings, how can a simple sequence

**Example 1.** Measures 1–4 of the fourth movement (Recitativo) from J. S. Bach's cantata "Nun komm der Heiden Heiland" (BWV 61).

of sounds – which is not in any way sentient – express anything?

It would appear that none of the things picked out by the first description could in fact be found in the music – thus the metaphoricality of the description.

The second description does seem to be more literal. The definition of an ostinato is, indeed, a repeated pattern of notes. The pitches B-D♯-F♯-A are those of the dominant-seventh chord of E minor, and D♯-F♯-A-C are those of the leading-tone chord with seventh. With mention of tension and release in the second sentence we are, however, on somewhat shakier ground, for the dissonant chords in the passage require no more or less tension for their production than do the consonant chords. One might argue that such chords give all knowledgeable listeners the sensation of tension and release, but this begs the question: the description is supposedly about a given musical passage, not a listener's reaction to the passage. One solution would be to eliminate the second sentence from the description, but we would then be left with little more than a narrativized rendering of the musical terms that could be applied to this passage. It is the second sentence, with its metaphorical evocation of tension and release, that gives some indication of how the music sounds, rather than what musical elements it comprises. Metaphor seems to be an inescapable part of musical descriptions that aspire to more than a rehearsal of defined terms.

There are, of course, many areas of human experience about which discourse is resolutely metaphorical, emotions being a prominent example. What makes music special is its relationship to language. Both music and language, for instance, are unique to the human species, both unfold over time, both have syntactic properties, and both make use of sound. Indeed, the notion that music is a language is the basis for some of the most prevalent metaphors used to describe music. But music is also *not* like language in at least one important respect: aside from a limited number of exceptional cases when music mimics natural sounds, music makes no reference to the outside world. Music *does* make reference to – or perhaps embody – the interior world of emotions or physiological states, but it is just this world that typically escapes the grasp of nonmetaphorical language.

Given this situation, one could conceivably trace connections between the phenomenon of metaphor and the cultural practice of music back to the earliest written records. (There is, for instance, a brief discussion of metaphors used by Aristoxenus, a fourth-century BCE writer on music, in the introduction to Zbikowski, 2002.) The focus in this chapter, however, is on work that has contributed directly to discussions about metaphor and music and on theoretical frameworks for understanding how the domain of music correlates with other conceptual domains, including that of language. Most of this work dates from the past 50 years, and encompasses a range of disciplines, including philosophy, semiotics, cognitive science, and the critical and analytical study of music. It should be noted that scholars of music are often divided into three subdisciplines, reflecting different intellectual commitments. Although *musicology* is the most comprehensive term, it is currently used to refer to those whose research concentrates on music viewed as a historical practice; *ethnomusicology*, by contrast, tends to focus on the social and cultural contexts of musical practice, with an emphasis on non-western music; *music theory* is concerned, by and large, with developing systematic perspectives on musical organization and on close readings of individual musical works based on these perspectives.

The first part of this chapter is given over to a historical and conceptual survey of music and metaphor (moving through a range of disciplines, including the three subdisciplines of music scholarship), organized around some of the topics adumbrated in the discussion of my opening example. These include the status of knowledge about music, the nature of musical semiotics, the relationship of music to other aspects of human experience (and in particular the expression of emotions), and music as a manifestation of human cognitive capacities. The second part of the chapter will return to the music of example 1 and explore a theoretical framework for analyzing how the domain of music correlates with other conceptual domains, including that of language.

## Research on Metaphor and Music

### *Music and Knowledge*

Perhaps the first extended discussion that connected music with metaphor appeared in the philosopher Nelson Goodman's *Languages of Art* (1968/1976). Goodman was interested in developing a theory of symbols that could apply to works of art as well as to natural language. According to this theory, a painting is a symbol (if of a rather special sort); so are a sequence of musical sounds or a sculpture. One distinctive feature of artistic symbols is that they are typically regarded as expressive: a gray-toned painting with a somber theme is thus described as "sad," as would be a lugubrious melody in a minor key. For Goodman, such sadness is not an attribute of the symbol proper but is instead figurative or metaphorical: in describing the painting or the melody as "sad," we transfer a system of concepts from its typical realm (the emotional states associated with sentient beings) into a new realm (colors and shapes on a canvas or a sequence of sonic events; Goodman, 1976, 72). The expressivity of an art work is, in consequence, not an attribute of the work as such but is simply *attributed* to the work.

Goodman's account of the expressivity of works of art – and in particular, music – was met with two sorts of challenges. The first, and most straightforward, came from philosophers who argued that the expressive character of a work is basic to it: expressivity is an ineliminable property of the musical work. When Goodman relegated the sadness of a melody to the domain of the metaphorical, he simply missed the point, since the purpose of the melody was to be expressive of some emotion (Budd, 1989; Davies, 1994, 150–166).

The second challenge to Goodman came from the philosopher Roger Scruton, who noted that Goodman's approach made no place for human understanding – indeed, for Goodman artistic symbols and the expressive values attributed to them are completely independent of human cognition (Scruton, 1974, 222). Scruton's aesthetic theory, as a whole, sought to place works of art in the intentional realm; in subsequent work on music this strategy led Scruton to argue that to hear various sounds *as music* (as opposed to unconnected if pleasant noises) requires construing such sounds in terms of concepts taken from some other domain. To take a simple example, when the bass sings the first three notes of measure three in Example 1 – C4-A3-F♯3 – we typically describe them as descending.[1] This descent is, however, an illusion: not only does the singer remain where he is, but there is nothing in a scientific account of the sounds themselves that supports the notion that they descend. From Scruton's perspective, this "illusion" is key to understanding the sequence of notes *as music*: the "motion" that we ascribe to the sequence of notes sung by the bass is a consequence of our framing their succession in terms of the motion of physical objects through space from low to high. This sort of metaphorical transfer – taking concepts from one domain (such as that of movement, or space, or concrete objects) and applying them to another – is essential to hearing sounds as music. "If we take away the metaphors of movement, of space, of chords as objects, of melodies as advancing and retreating, as moving up and down – if we take those metaphors away, nothing of music remains, but only sound" (Scruton, 1983, 106).

Scruton took pains here and in later work to emphasize the disjunction between the properties of sounds and the properties of music, for this disjunction pointed directly to the intentionality of art works like music:

> *There lies, in our most basic apprehension of music, a complex system of metaphor, which is the true description of no material fact, not even a fact about sounds, judged as secondary objects. The metaphor cannot be eliminated from the description of music, because it defines the intentional object of the musical experience. Take the metaphor away, and you cease to describe the experience of music. (Scruton, 1997, 92)*

For those who placed little trust in metaphor as a tool for discovering the essential properties of music, however, Scruton's account of musical understanding was just as flawed as Goodman's, if in a different way. Where Goodman isolated the fact of music from its expressivity, Scruton failed to explain how metaphorical statements connected with musical facts (Budd, 1985, 2003). Raising a similar objection, the music theorist Naomi Cumming noted that the sharp distinction between literal and figurative language that Scruton drew was ultimately untenable when the range of language used to describe music was considered (Cumming, 1994, 2000, 49–51).

This difficulty points to a problem common in philosophical writings about music, which tend to treat language as the gold standard for conceptualization and grammar (see, for instance, Dempster, 1998). Against such a standard music comes off rather poorly, for it cannot supply the factuality that is believed to mark language. A somewhat different, albeit related, problem stems from the special status granted instrumental music by some nineteenth-century thinkers. As Lydia Goehr has observed, within German Romanticism "'The purely musical' . . . served as a general metaphor for all that was unknowable by ordinary cognitive or rational means" (Goehr, 1998, 18). For writers who adopt this perspective the impenetrability of music is its raison d'être: "the musical mystery is not 'what cannot be spoken of,' the untellable, but the *ineffable*" (Jankélévitch, 2003, 72; see also Charles, 1995). The metaphors used to describe music – especially to the extent that the mechanisms behind these metaphors remain unexamined – are thus symptomatic of music's ineffability. A final complication is that accounts of metaphor grounded in the philosophy of language may simply be inadequate for music, as can be seen in Steven Krantz's application of Max Black's theory of metaphor to music (Krantz, 1987), and as is demonstrated in Leo Treitler's critique of Goodman (Treitler, 1997).

### Musical Semiotics

The somewhat uncomfortable relationship between language and music evident in philosophical treatments of music and metaphor is also apparent in efforts to adapt semiotic theory to music. Hints that such an adaptation might be possible can be seen as early as Ferdinand de Saussure's *Course in General Linguistics*, where, summing up the possibility of separating out the elements of language for analysis, Saussure comments, "Similarly, a musical series *do, re, mi* can be treated only as a concrete series in time, but if I select one of its irreducible elements, I can study it in the abstract" (Saussure, 1959, 40). A half-century after Saussure the Belgian linguist Nicolas Ruwet, in what proved to be an influential essay, adopted a similar perspective for detailed analyses of four melodies from the middle ages (Ruwet, 1966; reprinted in Ruwet, 1972;

**Example 2.** Two descending melodies from Cooke 1959 (from Cooke's Ex. 58b, p. 134).

for a discussion see Powers, 1980, 10–22). Limitations of the approach, however, soon became evident, especially where meaning was concerned. As the music theorist Kofi Agawu has observed, while it is the case that the basic units of language have a more or less fixed lexical meaning, the basic units of music most typically do not (Agawu, 1999, 144). Related to this, the symbolic structure of language consists of a dense network of mutually interrelated symbols which typically share little if anything with the things to which they refer (Deacon, 1997, chapter 3; 2003). The symbolic structure of music has nothing like this level of complexity: the relationships into which symbols enter are typically more local, and there tends not to be the sort of abstract reference typical of linguistic symbols (see, however, the analyses in Agawu, 1991). Where the perspectives of semiotic theory have reaped the most benefit has not been in showing how music replicates the features of language but through explorations of how meaning specific to music – and in some cases beyond the capacities of language – is possible.

Deryck Cooke, in *The Language of Music*, proposed that certain types of musical materials (with a special focus on the intervals that occur between the notes of a melody) were expressive of certain types of emotions. For instance, Cooke proposed that a descent from the fifth note of a minor scale through the first, of the sort shown in the melodies of Example 2, expresses "acceptance of, or yielding to grief, discouragement and depression; passive suffering, and the despair connected with death" (Cooke, 1959, 133). Cooke's account of the vocabulary of music is much more complex than suggested by this example (for instance, the descent from the fifth through the first note of the scale could be filled in with the fourth and second notes of the scale, or embellished in various ways) and much more detailed. Indeed, the very specificity Cooke offered may have told against him, for this provided fuel for critics who argued that musical meaning was much more various than Cooke seemed to maintain. Nonetheless, Cooke's basic idea – that musical meaning is tied up with the expression of emotion – is not only broadly accepted among musicians (as suggested by the commentary in Agawu, 1999, and the essays in Juslin and Sloboda, 2001) but has recently been the focus of further work. Jan Broeckx, for instance, has argued that musical meaning is a consequence of the direct representation of emotion through musical figures (Broeckx, 1997). While we can certainly *describe* these emotions through language (thus giving rise to the metaphorical descriptions of music's expressivity) such descriptions do not create the meaning that the emotions have. Broeckx, however, does not develop his methodology further, and just how musical figures express emotions remains obscure. Hallgjerd Aksnes, for her part, has made use of current work in cognitive science and metaphor theory to bring clarity to this perspective, proposing that the emotions summoned by passages in the music of the Norwegian composer Geirr Tveitt can be grounded in embodied experience (Aksnes, 2002, chapter 8). Additional methodological support can be found in the composer and semiologist David Lidov's work, recently brought together in Lidov (2005). Although metaphor theory does not figure large in Lidov's theory of musical signification, one can find the integration of an approach sympathetic to Cooke with a general theory of semiotics. The result is a theory of musical meaning based on correlations between emotions, physical gestures, and sequences of musical events.

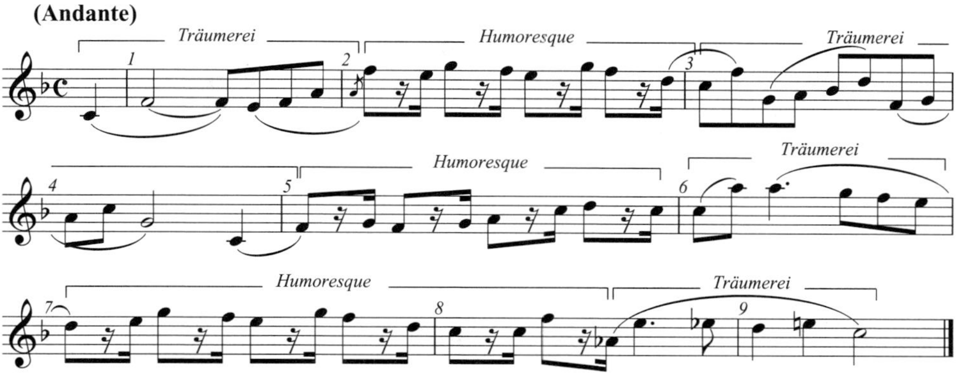


**Example 3.** The melody of Schumann's "Träumerei" combined with the melody of Dvořák's "Humoresque" (adapted from Example 4 from Karbusicky 1987, 436).

Another perspective on musical meaning and its relationship to metaphor was provided by the musicologist Vladimir Karbusicky. Working from a thorough knowledge of the history of semiotic approaches developed by German musicologists under the influence of Ernst Cassirer, Karbusicky made a strenuous argument *against* using semiotic theories formulated for language to explain musical meaning: "The popular definition of music as a kind of language or as auditive communication, which has all too often been taken for granted even in scientific essays, is nothing more than a metaphor" (Karbusicky, 1987, 431). For Karbusicky, "thought in music occurs primarily in asemantical shapes and formulas" (433); any attempt to interpret these shapes and formulas through language or linguistic theory would ultimately fail to capture the substance of musical thought. Karbusicky was, however, willing to entertain the notion that there might be purely musical metaphors (as distinct from linguistic metaphors used to describe music). The example Karbusicky chose to illustrate this idea was inspired by a cabaret pianist who put together the melody of Robert Schumann's "Träumerei" (from *Kinderszenen* op. 15, no. 7) with the melody of Antonin Dvořák's "Humoresque" in G-flat major (op. 101 no. 7; here transposed to F major); see Example 3. (The title "humoresque" makes reference to a term used for literary sketches by German writers during the early nineteenth century. Applied to musical works, it often indicates short occasional pieces with a relaxed – but not necessarily humorous – character.) The opening sections of both Schumann's "Träumerei" and Dvořák's "Humoresque" are eight measures long, and for the most part Karbusicky's example moves back and forth between the two pieces: measure 2 of Example 3 is measure 2 of the "Humoresque"; measures 3–4 of Example 3 are measures 3–4 of "Träumerei." The exception occurs in the second phrase (measures 5–9): while measure 5 replicates measure 5 of the "Humoresque" and measure 6 replicates measure 6 from "Träumerei," measure 7 and the first half of measure 8 are drawn from measures 6–7 of the "Humoresque." This change results in an added measure, with the latter half of measure 8 and all of measure 9 of Example 3 drawn from measures 7–8 of "Träumerei." This minor modification notwithstanding, the free interchangeability of musical materials evident in Example 3 is important for the point Karbusicky wishes to make, for it indicates basic structural similarities between the two melodies that supports their meaningful combination. A closer look at the music of Example 3 suggests that the materials of "Träumerei" – and the image of childhood dreaming that they are meant to evoke – control the musical discourse. These materials frame the beginning and ending of the first phrase (measures 1–4), and, in doing so, help to define its tonal structure. Although the "Humoresque" melody attempts to take control in the second phrase – shoving aside the reprise of the opening of "Träumerei" in measure 5, and running on for nearly two measures in measures 7–8 – the melody of "Träumerei" ultimately wins the day to conclude the second phrase.

In his analysis Karbusicky proposed that both melodies carry a basic semantic charge that might be described as "nostalgia, sentiment" (keeping in mind that each melody projects this charge in a different way). Musical metaphor, as Karbusicky conceived it, comes about because the meaning of "Träumerei" is changed when the unfolding of its languid melody is interrupted by the sprightly gestures of the "Humoresque." The resulting modification of the sentiment of "Träumerei" – pushing it toward cheerfulness – is a consequence of both the introduction of the contrasting semantic content of the "Humoresque" and the common structural features of the two melodies, a commonality that supports associating the sentiment of "Träumerei" with that of the "Humoresque" (Karbusicky, 1987, 436–437).

The basic idea behind Karbusicky's notion of purely musical metaphor, in which disparate musical materials are brought together to generate new meaning, can also be seen in Robert Hatten's work on musical meaning (Hatten, 1994, chapter 7; 1995). Hatten, for his part, proposes that the correlations between musical materials and meaning must be established prior to their being brought together to create new meaning. This process occurs not in the manner of Karbusicky's rather exceptional example (which relies on structural similarities between the two melodies to support their combination) but instead takes advantage of what Hatten calls functional locations, which can be thought of as important structural moments within a musical work (such as the reprise of a significant theme). A functional location may be a consequence of syntactic expectations set up within a particular piece, or may reflect stylistic formal schemas common to any number of pieces. When musical materials with markedly different meanings are subjected to the syntactic pressures that characterize such locations, new meaning emerges. Hatten's general term for this process is musical troping – metaphor is just one type of musical trope that may result. (For a similar perspective, but framed relative to the work of Roman Jakobson and Jacques Derrida, see Ayrey, 1994.) As Hatten readily admits, his approach bears more in common with poetic than with linguistic theory (Hatten, 2004, 297, n. 1); such a perspective is well suited to the interpretive challenges presented by the music of Mozart, Beethoven, and Schubert on which Hatten has focused.

Relationships between similar but structurally (or conceptually) distinct musical entities have long been recognized by musicians, although such relationships are of a sort closer to the pragmatic ones that underlie Karbusicky's analysis than they are to the poetic ones invoked by Hatten. Indeed, one could argue that teaching students how to identify and exploit such relationships is one of the cornerstones of music pedagogy. It is perhaps for this very reason that the framework provided by theories of metaphor or analogy has not generally been used to characterize such relationships. When such frameworks have been applied to relationships among musical materials, it has been as part of a more comprehensive study of correlations between music and other media (Kielian-Gilbert, 1990) or to characterize how idealized musical constructs relate to actual musical practice (Dubiel, 1990, 327; Perlman, 2004, chaps. 6, 8). Again, the topic of metaphor more typically crops up when the issue is how things that are musical relate to things that are not musical.

### *Music and Other Aspects of Human Experience*

The issue of music's connection with other aspects of human experience emerged with force in music scholarship in the period after World War II when, as a consequence of developments in music composition begun a generation before and in keeping with the climate of aggressive positivism that informed a broad range of humanistic studies, there arose the idea that the analysis of music could proceed along the lines of scientific inquiry (see, for instance, Babbitt, 1961/1972). The analyses produced would focus solely on matters of musical structure, on the assumption that a comprehensive account of this structure would explain everything of importance about music. Matters such as what music expressed would either be answered by such an account or regarded as beyond analysis. This perspective was troubling to some; in 1960, Donald Ferguson proposed that "scientific" music theory, in fact, could not provide an adequate account of musical expression. As a corrective he offered a careful and thorough consideration of the basis of expressivity in music. Although the approach had much in common with that of Cooke (as discussed in the appendix to Ferguson, 1960), Ferguson was adamant that expressivity in music had to be connected with human experience. It was because the expressive elements in music were connected to emotional experience that music could serve as a metaphor for the significance of experience (Ferguson, 1960, ix, 185). (For a similar perspective, but one more thoroughly grounded in semiotic theory and more systematically presented, see Coker, 1972, chapter 10.)

Metaphor served as a powerful image for Ferguson but not as an explicit part of his response to analytical practices that ignored music's expressivity. For Marion Guck, it was metaphor itself that suggested an alternative to positivistic descriptions of musical structure. Early in her career Guck became interested in the communicative potential of metaphorical language about music, having noticed that some of her students preferred such language over the formalistic accounts of musical structure that were commonly the focus of instruction in music analysis. Through a series of analytical exercises she and her students explored the use of such language and its relationship to traditional structuralist approaches. She concluded that metaphorical language could put students more directly in touch with those aspects of music upon which traditional analytical techniques were focused, and add richness to their understanding of those aspects.

> *If perceived musical structure is indivisible from physical and emotional response, then metaphors may offer an embryonic structural interpretation reinforced by – explained through – physical-emotional responses. If a structural interpretation is not understood by itself, experiencing the responses may be another avenue to understanding the structure. Equally, metaphors offer a physical-emotional experience reinforced by – explained through – an embryonic structural interpretation.* (Guck, 1981, 42)

Guck eventually came to argue that the whole of analytical discourse was rooted in metaphor (Guck, 1991), although she also strove to connect metaphorical discourse with the "scientific" approach adopted by many music analysts. She concluded that, while the claims for a scientific language about music could not be sustained, statements about music – whether such statements made use of explicit metaphors or whether they were restricted to less colorful technical descriptions – could be organized into consistent and coherent systems correlated with intersubjectively apprehended musical events, and thus able to approach the methodology of scientific inquiry (Guck, 1994).

Although the Anglo-American approach dominated research in music theory and analysis in the latter half of the twentieth century, scientism of the sort to which Ferguson and Guck (among many others) took exception never grabbed hold as firmly on the English side of the equation. When, in 1990, Nicholas Cook described music analysis as metaphorical he was attempting to place it within the context of aesthetic and psychological approaches to music that he viewed not only as viable but as offering key insights into music as a cultural product. Analysis, from this perspective, is a way of imagining music – a metaphor for musical experience rather than any sort of literal record of that experience – much as for Scruton musical understanding itself was fundamentally imaginative (Cook, 1990, 10–43).

As a whole, Anglo-American musicology (as distinct from music theory) was less in thrall to the scientific paradigm during the post–World War II period than were music theory and analysis (although some musicologists aspired to a commensurate positivism; see Kerman, 1985, chapter 2). On the rare occasion when metaphor rose to the surface of musicological inquiry it was in the context of an over-arching pattern of thought that shaped ideas about music. Thus Ruth Solie, in her study of melody, proposed to explore the metaphoric language used to characterize melody to better understand how earlier periods conceived melody.

> *For example, if you are dealing with an "organic structure" or a "melodic curve" or a "universal language," what sorts of behavior will you expect to observe from it, and therefore make note of? What characteristics will you perceive in "the embodied will to motion" that you might not see in a "pitch-time trajectory" or in a "stochastic process with sequential dependencies" – notwithstanding the fact that all three phrases refer to the same melody? (Solie, 1977, 9; see also Solie, 1980)*

Some 20 years later Bennett Zon used a similar approach in his exploration of conceptual models used by nineteenth-century British musicologists, but focused on the metaphorical templates provided by art, religion, and science. These templates provided British musicologists with alternatives to straightforward chronological narratives; Herbert Spencer, for instance, writing in 1857, adopted the framework of evolutionary theory to explain the development of music, and the colloquy that arose around this proposal had a significant impact on the course taken by British musicology in the latter half of the nineteenth century (Zon, 2000, 120–125).

### *Music, Metaphor, and Cognitive Science*

The perspective that guided Solie's work, focusing as much on the language used to describe music as the music itself, was also one that came to prominence in the field of ethnomusicology around the same time. Steven Feld, who had a long-standing interest in how language was used to describe music, noted this trend in a 1981 essay that also made an important contribution to the study of music and metaphor. Drawing on the work of Lakoff and Johnson (1980), David Rumelhart (1979/1993), and Robert Verbrugge (1979), Feld argued that the metaphorical descriptions used by the Kaluli of Papua New Guinea were a reflection of key aspects of their everyday experience. The Kaluli describe melodic intervals – whether in their own music or in the music of others – with the same terms they use to characterize features of waterfalls. For instance, in the language of the Kaluli *sa* means "waterfall," and a *mogan* is a still or lightly swirling waterpool; *sa-mogan* is the flow of a waterfall into a level waterpool beneath it. *Sa-mogan* is also used to describe a melodic line that descends to a repeated note, the contour of which replicates that of a waterfall flowing into a pool (Feld, 1981, 30–31; see also Feld, 1982). The system of metaphorical relationships upon which such characterizations draw offers a rich description of musical events, but one that also has its limitations: for example, the Kaluli do not have specific names for ascending intervals, which nonetheless do occur in their music.

Feld's work pointed toward a new approach to metaphor and music that was based on two important assumptions. The first was that metaphor was not simply a literary device but was instead a basic structure of understanding (Lakoff, 1993). The second was that music constituted a conceptual domain that was, in some measure, independent of language. As a consequence of these two assumptions metaphorical descriptions of music came to be regarded as capable of providing key insights into how the understanding of music was structured. A notion closely associated with the contemporary theory of metaphor, and that would prove important for music scholars, was that of an image schema (Johnson, 1987). Image schemas provided a theoretical basis for metaphorical descriptions of music grounded in embodied experience, an approach that fit with many analysts' intuitions about the nature of musical knowledge and that offered a way to move beyond – or add another dimension to – the abstract formalisms prominent in much music-theoretical work. Subsequent to a special session at the 1996 annual meeting of the Society for Music Theory, an issue of the journal *Theory and Practice* was given over to connections between music theory and embodied knowledge, and included articles by Janna Saslaw on force dynamics in the theoretical writings of Heinrich Schenker and Arnold Schoenberg (Saslaw, 1997–1998), Candace Brower on embodied schemas in Edgard Varèse's *Density 21.5* for solo flute (Brower, 1997–1998), and Steve Larson on how the understanding of tonal melodies is shaped by experience with the forces of gravity, magnetism, and inertia (Larson, 1997–1998).

The cognitive perspective on metaphor and music was, in some instances, part of a broader perspective on the cognitive capacities that shape humans' understanding of music (Spitzer, 2004; Zbikowski, 1991, 1998, 2002) but was often employed in one of two more restricted ways. First, metaphor theory was brought to bear on recognized but not clearly understood conceptual models within music theory, including those pertaining to musical invariance (Saslaw & Walsh, 1996), modulation theory (Saslaw, 1996), hierarchical structures in music (Zbikowski, 1997), and historical conceptions of tonal organization (Gur, 2008). Second, metaphor theory provided a way into novel repertories, including heavy metal (Walser, 1991), musical multimedia (Cook, 1998, chapter 3), the music of the Grateful Dead (O'Donnell, 1999), the music of Neil Young (Echard, 1999, 2005, chapter 4), Javanese Gamelan (Perlman, 2004, chapter 6), and film music (Chattah, 2006).

Recent research on metaphor and music that embodies a cognitive perspective has coalesced around a somewhat broader set of issues, in many cases offering alternatives to previous approaches. Prominent here is work on musical meaning that takes as its starting point the assumption that meaning is grounded in embodied experience (Aksnes, 2002; Borgo, 2004; Chuck, 2004; Cox, 2001; Johnson, 1997–1998; Walker, 2000); an account of the ontology of the musical work framed around the metaphorical notion of a musical object (Butterfield, 2002); and explorations of the bases for and applications of ideas about musical motion and musical space (Adlington, 2003; Cox, 1999; Johnson & Larson, 2003; Johnson, 2007, chapter 11; Spitzer, 2003).

The broad-based approach advocated by Zbikowski (2002, chapter 2), which adopts a generalized view of metaphor as a kind of cross-domain mapping and proposes that music represents a conceptual domain that can be drawn into such mappings, has recently been extended to correlations between patterns in Azerbaijani carpet weaving and musical practice (Naroditskaya, 2005) and to theoretical work on conceptual blending and music. Preliminary work on conceptual blends in which music occupies one of the input spaces was focused on the possibilities for meaning construction created by the correlation of text and music in nineteenth-century art songs (Zbikowski, 1999, 2002, chapter 6) but has since been applied to analyses of the nature of musical meaning (Cook, 2001), analyses of film music, opera, and musical multimedia (Johnson, 2004; Sayrs, 2003; Zbikowski, 2002–2003), the analysis of György Ligeti's *Lontano* (Bauer, 2004), the role of the arabesque in the music of Ravel (Bhogal, 2007), and to the construction of musical meaning as a whole (Chuck, 2004).

Although most applications of the contemporary theory of metaphor to music have been broadly theoretical, recent empirical studies by Zohar Eitan and his colleagues have begun to show in greater detail how metaphor structures our understanding of music (Eitan & Granot, 2006), and how the metaphors used to characterize musical relationships reflect the influence of culuture (Eitan & Timmers, 2006). These studies suggest not only ways to study how metaphor structures our understanding of music, but also ways to investigate how metaphorical processes operate in nonlinguistic domains.

## Metaphor and the Analysis of Music

Although the preceding section provided a historical and conceptual context for the questions asked at the opening of this chapter, it did not provide a methodology for answering these questions. The purpose of this section is to present such a methodology, which takes as its point of departure the contemporary theory of metaphor (as characterized by Lakoff, 1993) and the compositional technique of text painting.

The basic idea of text painting is simple enough. When a particularly strong or compelling image occurs in the text for a musical work, the composer writes the accompanying music to suggest, or "paint," the image. Thus, if the text mentions a galloping horse, the music coincident with the text might imitate the sound and action of a horse proceeding at full speed. While there are limits to what can be represented in this way, composers have found the means to portray descents from heaven, rippling streams, spinning wheels, physical trembling, sexual climax, and a host of other vibrant images (Macy, 1996; Zbikowski, 2002, chapter 2).

The example of text painting I want to consider here involves the portrayal of the act of knocking on a door. It comes to the fore near the beginning of the movement that provided the music for Example 1, which was from Bach's Advent cantata "Nun komm der Heiden Heiland" (BWV 61). Each of the three preceding movements of the cantata explores an aspect of the Advent theme. The first movement is an overture whose text is taken from a chorale by Martin Luther: "Come now, Savior of the gentiles, known to be the child of a Virgin, the whole world marvels that God should have ordained such a birth for Him." The text for the second-movement recitative is by the Hamburg poet, theologian, and pastor Erdmann Neumeister and speaks of the wonder of God made incarnate. The third movement, an aria with a text also by Neumeister, returns to the summons stated by the overture: "Come, Jesu, come to Thy church and grant a blessed New Year!" But with the fourth movement Christ is suddenly before us, speaking words from the third chapter of Revelation: "Behold, I stand at the door, and knock. If any man hear my voice, and open the door, I will come in to him, and will sup with him, and he with me." Bach sets this passage as an accompanied recitative for baritone, with the strings playing pizzicato throughout; the score for the entire movement is given in Example 4.

Bach's text painting is centered on the words "und klopfe an" – that is, "and knock." Bach uses three compositional techniques to paint this activity. First, he summons the repetitions we associate with the act of knocking by repeating the words, and by using three notes to set the first syllable of the initial "klopfe" (a device called a melisma). Second, he uses staccato marks on the three notes of the melisma, which place silences between these notes; these silences are similar to those that fall between knocks on a door. Third, he sets the words with a broken chord (or arpeggio). This places a kind of distance between each successive note but also allows us to hear all as belonging to a single connected gesture.

The conventional explanation for why text painting works relies on the idea of mimesis: the image of knocking is summoned by Bach's setting of "und klopfe an" because the music imitates the sound of knocking. While this is partially true for Bach's text painting, there are certain things that are not quite right. Knocks are usually unpitched, but Bach gives us different pitches for each blow; knocking is not usually accompanied, but here we have pizzicato strings pulsing in the background. A few writers have gone so far as to

**Example 4.** Score for the fourth movement (Recitativo) from J. S. Bach's cantata "Nun komm der Heiden Heiland" (BWV 61).

interpret the steady plucking of the orchestra in this movement as a further embodiment of knocking, but this seems something of a stretch. Not only are the attack points too widely spaced to sound much like knocking but the effect is far too persistent, more like Edgar Allen Poe's telltale heart than a summons from the Savior.

**Example 4.** (*cont.*)

In fact, text painting is not a matter of simple mimesis, in which music, through its resemblance to a natural sound, represents that sound, but of a more complex process through which music represents the image-schematic structure of some event or situation. This sort of representation is somewhat like the iconicity of rhetorical figures discussed by Mark Turner (1998). Turner noted that the form of a rhetorical figure is sometimes matched to the meaning the speaker wishes to convey, connecting the image-schematic structure of the form with the image-schematic structure of the meaning. Thus, a rhetorical figure based on repetition, such as anaphora (which involves the repetition of the same word or group of words at the beginning of successive clauses, sentences, or lines), can be used to summon the image of repeated blows, as in an example attributed to Longinus: "By his manner, his looks, his voice, when he strikes you with insult, when he strikes you like an enemy, when he strikes you with his knuckles, when he strikes you like a slave." The efficacy of such a connection is straightforward enough – Turner remarks, "Involving members of the audience in the image schema of the iconic form automatically involves them in the basic structure of the meaning, thus moving them part way toward accepting the whole" (1998, 50–51). In a similar way, Bach's recitative embodies the image-schematic structure of the act of knocking at the very moment when knocking is mentioned in the text. Bach's music thus moves the listener part of the way toward understanding the force of Christ's act of knocking: where previous movements in the cantata have summoned Christ, Christ is now summoning *us*.

More generally, the connection of music to text in instances such as this relies on structural correlations between the two domains. The specific correlations are between image-schematic structures. In the present example, the text calls up the familiar situation of a person standing before a door with the intent of communicating with people on the other side of the door. A scene of this sort typically involves knocking on the door to establish communication; knocking, in turn, is accomplished through a series of regularly spaced physical gestures that yield a sequence of unpitched sounds of short duration. The conceptual domain set up by the text thus includes the image-schematic structure associated with the act of knocking. The bass melody in the opening measures of this movement does not summon anything as specific as does the text, but it nonetheless participates in establishing a conceptual domain structured in part by image schemata. Features of this conceptual domain include the steadily pulsing strings which contrast with the flowing melody of the bass voice, the dissonances that occur against the pedal E3 in the accompaniment, and the E minor tonality that is projected. The projection of any tonality is a process that unfolds over time – an important part of that process in the case at hand is the bass melody, which is restricted to just those pitches that are necessary for defining E minor. In the course of this melody the distinctive melodic gesture that occupies the beginning of measure 3 stands out: it introduces the largest leap thus far (the minor seventh from D3 to C4), the only melisma, and concludes with another minor-seventh leap (A3 to B2). The passage ends with the shortest notated durations of the passage (the sixteenth notes at the end of measure 3) which serve to further set this measure off from the rest. The image-schematic structure that is relevant here is of a series of discrete events that are evenly spaced and that stand out from their surroundings; this then correlates with the image-schematic structure of the conceptual domain set up by the words to produce an instance of text painting.

One question raised by this example is whether the connection between the image-schematic structure of knocking and the image-schematic structure of this musical passage is necessary. The answer is a qualified "no." It might indeed be possible, without the text, to make a connection between the act of knocking and the music of measure 3. There is enough urgency in the music Bach writes – an urgency that includes both the more rapid durations at the end of the measure and the much smaller registral space they inhabit (contracting from C4 to B2 in the first part of the measure to F♯3 to B4 at its end) – that knocking seems a fairly good description for the music. But the music could be described in other ways as well: the whole of the melody in these opening measures could be characterized in terms of the imagined movements of an actor on a stage who, after a series of relatively constrained gestures (in measures 1–2), suddenly gestures in an exaggerated, expansive way (at the beginning of measure 3) before correcting her excess at the end of the passage. This characterization would draw on the metaphor of musical "space" (and its attendant image-schematic structure) and tend to emphasize the way the pitches of the melody are disposed within this space more than their rhythmic features. The characterization would also provide a perspective that encompasses the whole of the passage rather than focusing on measure 3. The context provided by the text from Revelations is thus key to hearing the music of measure 3 as a representation of knocking and not as a representation of something else. There are, nonetheless, limits to how the passage can be characterized – were someone to describe the passage as an energetic portrayal of religious bliss we would wonder if they had listened to the same music as we had, since there is almost nothing in the musical events of measures 1–4 – or the image-schematic structures through which we might organize our understanding of these events – that would support such a characterization.

Another important factor that shapes correlations between music and other domains is cultural knowledge. Describing musical pitches in terms of their disposition in space (with one pitch "higher" or "lower" than another) has been a commonplace in western traditions since at least the Middle Ages (Cox, 1999; Duchez, 1979; Zbikowski, 2002, chapter 2). Other descriptions are, however, possible: in Bali and Java, for instance, pitches are conceived of not as "high" and "low" but as "small" and "large" (Zanten, 1986, 85), a conception that reflects accurately the norms of acoustic production – small things typically vibrate more rapidly than large things. Thus we would not expect members of a culture that did not practice knocking as a way of announcing an arrival or the initiation of communication to make the connection between the music of measure 3 and the words "und klopfe an" (translated, of course, into the appropriate language for communication).

Text painting is, admittedly, a somewhat rarified compositional technique. It nonetheless points to the basis for metaphorical descriptions of music and gives some sense of how the conceptual domain of music might participate in metaphorical mappings. When we describe a musical passage as "obstinately plodding" or a chord as "sour and biting" we are making connections between one domain of experience (having to do with the ways bodies can move through space, the sense of taste, or the physical actions accomplished by teeth) and the domain of music. The domain of music includes various musical events as well as ways of understanding their relationships to one another; these relationships are in part structured by image schemata. Just how this is accomplished is still being explored empirically, but one of the best theoretical accounts is provided by Lawrence Barsalou's theory of perceptual symbol systems (Barsalou, 1999). According to this theory, sequences of musical events produce brain maps that can be correlated with brain maps produced by other modalities (including vision, taste, and proprioception); these correlations then operate as symbols to form the basis for conceptual knowledge. The array of perceptual symbols (or image schemata) that may be used to structure a given relationship is potentially quite extensive; cultural knowledge provides one constraint on which structures are chosen.

The notion of music as an independent domain with its own properties and relationships – properties and relationships that language attempts to capture through metaphorical descriptions – invites two extensions of the discussion of metaphor and music. First, mappings *within* music (of the sort discussed in Karbusicky, 1987; Kielian-Gilbert, 1990; Perlman, 2004) are a logical entailment of this perspective, and a straightforward example of such a mapping would be between a theme and variations derived from the theme. (For a rich consideration of this topic see Cone, 1987.) These mappings may, however, be closer to those of analogy (and emphasize the alignment of

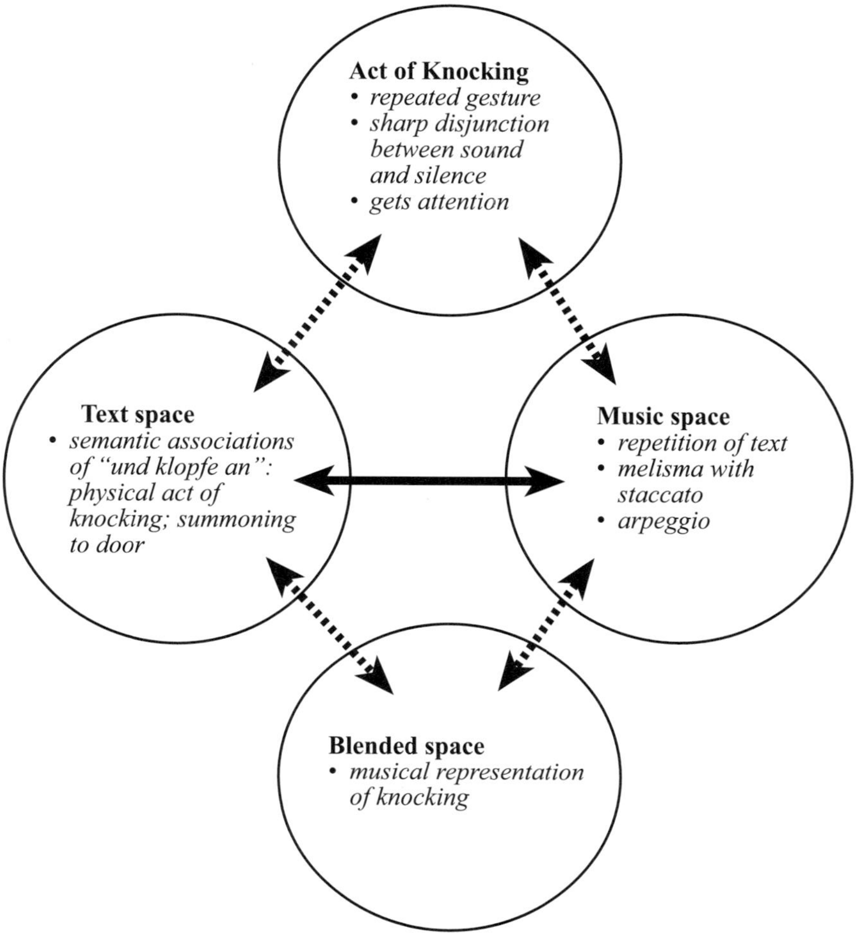


**Example 5.** Basic conceptual integration network for Bach's text painting of "und klopfe an."

structural features) than to metaphor (with its emphasis on the construction of meaning through the correlation of rich networks of knowledge; cf. Gentner, Bowdle, Wolff, & Boronat, 2001). Second, concepts from the musical domain may combine with concepts from another conceptual domain to create a conceptual blend (Fauconnier & Turner, this volume). Two interconnected examples of conceptual blends are provided by the music of Example 4.

The first blend is produced by the text painting that occurs in measure 3; a diagram of the conceptual integration network for the blend is shown in Example 5. The generic space for the blend focuses on physical aspects of the act of knocking: the repeated actions that make up knocking, the sharp disjunction between sound and silence that results, and the way knocking breaks into our attention. The text space is set up by the semantic associations generated by the words "und klopfe an," which not only bring the physical act to mind but also its typical context: a summons of some sort (if only to come to the door and open it). The music space is set up by Bach's text painting: his repetitions of "und klopfe an," the melisma with staccato articulation, and the arpeggio that provides a contextual frame for the notes that set the words. In the blend, musical and linguistic concepts combine to provide a musical representation of someone knocking on a door.

There is more, of course, to the passage from the third chapter of Revelation than simply a description of someone knocking on a door. The image is central to the summons with which this fragment is concerned: Christ is calling us to his church. A simple, everyday act is thus made to resonate with a much more profound meaning: answering this summons is but the beginning of a chain of entailments with profound consequences for all who are concerned. A glimpse at one manifestation of this chain of entailments is provided by a second conceptual blend, which is set up over the course of the movement as a whole.

As noted in my discussion of the first four measures of the movement, Bach makes use of some striking dissonances in the process of establishing E minor. These dissonances – which involve the dominant-seventh and leading-tone chords of E minor – resolve at measure 4, coincident with the second iteration of "und klopfe an." Christ's knocking thus has a real and audible effect on the music.

After the arrival on E minor in measure 4 the bass pedal is abandoned, and the music moves toward G major, which first appears in measures 6 and 7 and then is confirmed with the final cadence in measure 10. The move toward G major is accompanied by a change in the vocal writing, which becomes more lyrical. By the end of this short movement we understand that the opening portion, with its obstinate pedal tone and dissonant harmonies, is meant to lead toward this denouement – it is something we have to leave in order to get to the safe haven of the final cadence. This journey is in fact prepared by Bach's text painting, for it is the musical materials associated with the setting of "und klopfe an" that push us away from the static and dissonant opening materials toward the progress and consonance represented by the G major music. Just as the image of knocking is crucial for the larger story told by the text, the musical representation of knocking is crucial for the larger story told by the music.

This leads us to the conceptual blend shown in Example 6, which takes in the whole of the movement. The generic space for the blend focuses on the notion of redemption. Within the general context of an Advent cantata, redemption is naturally associated with the act of freeing the believer from the consequences of sin. Within the more specific context of the Pietism that influenced Bach's interpretation of the text, redemption means something closer to its etymological roots – that is, to buy something back – and thus requires something of the believer as well. The text space provides the basic elements of the story of redemption: Christ knocking at the door; the believer opening the door; and the act of redemption itself, symbolized by Christ's entrance and the shared meal. Within the music space we get nothing quite as precise as this – indeed, the musical events could be mapped onto a variety of stories or situations – but we do get a tightly organized sequence of events. This sequence involves a number of musical elements and connects with some of our ideas about redemption, including movement from a static and dissonant situation into a progressive and consonant one. In the blend, the narrative from the passage out of Revelation is compressed with syntactic processes proper to music. We begin in a static, dissonant environment with Christ announcing himself and then knocking at the door. This knock is a summons to redemption, and the dissonant environment starts to become more consonant. By the time the opening of the door is mentioned (in measure 6, with the words "und die Tür auftun") we have entered the orbit of G major, and the remainder of the movement fills out the theme of redemption and affirms G major, with one important exception. With the singer's very last word ("mir," in measure 9), Bach returns momentarily to E minor, a move that casts a shadow over the scene and seems to suggest the sacrifices that redemption requires. Although there is little doubt of the promise of redemption at the conclusion of the movement, the musical syntax through which the story is told points to the struggles that are required to achieve redemption. Tonal closure is not assured, but must be won; redemption requires

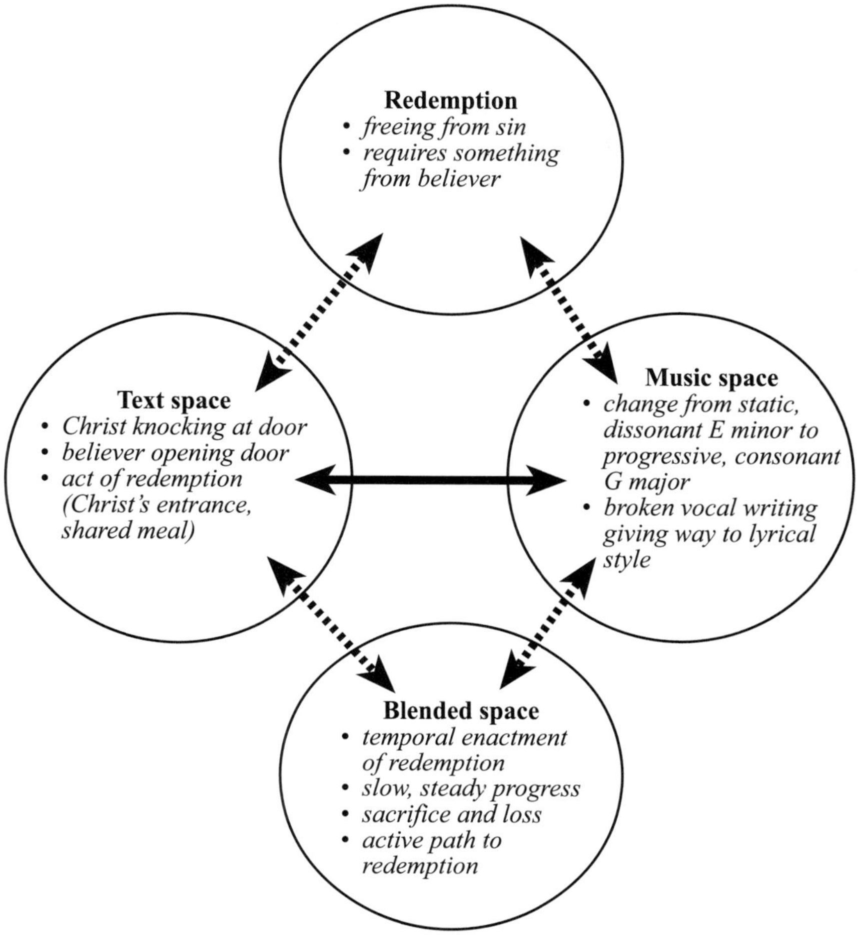


**Example 6.** Conceptual integration network for the fourth movement from J. S. Bach's cantata "Nun komm der Heiden Heiland."

more than simply opening the door to the Savior.

## Conclusion

Music is a rich and complex product of culture – the brief examples discussed here include music that is part of the ritual of religious service (Bach's cantata), music with a programmatic title (Schumann's "Träumerei"), light instrumental music for diversion (Dvořák's "Humoresque"), and even music for the cabaret (which inspired Karbusicky's example). These possibilities barely scratch the surface of musical expression, which is manifested in all known human cultures; includes music for ritual, dance, song, diversion, and a multitude of other activities; and touches on the complete range of human emotion. The cultural practice of music is also largely non-linguistic and non-referential, although both language and reference can play a role in musical practice. Given the range of musical expression and its independence from language, it is not surprising that language *about* music is often metaphorical, nor that the topic of metaphor and music has been touched on by a wide range of scholarly disciplines.

Michael Tomasello (1999, chapter 5) recently proposed that one of the primary functions of language is to manipulate the attention of another person within a shared referential frame. It could be argued that one of the primary functions of music is to manipulate the emotions of others. Although this argument is hardly new (see, for instance, Meyer, 1956), it has often been advanced within the relatively narrow context of instrumental music produced in western Europe during the late eighteenth and nineteenth centuries. The argument could easily be broadened through the recognition that music can also manipulate the emotions through the way it shapes ritual, dance, and the rendering of a text. If it is that case that language and music have different functions within human culture – that they comprise different domains of experience – it follows that mappings between these domains would yield numerous possibilities for the sort of meaning construction associated with metaphor.

According to current theory, mappings between language and music rely on image-schematic structures that are common to the two domains. Music will tend to instantiate such structures dynamically, while language will call them up through reference. When music summons knocking in the fourth movement of Bach's "Nun komm der Heiden Heiland" it does so by replicating features of the act of knocking. The text, by contrast, simply refers to the act, relying on the listener to call up the dynamic schema once the referential frame has been activated. Combinations of music and text such as those created through the compositional technique of text painting thus represent a kind of laboratory for the study of image-schematic structure. Any schema thought to underlie mappings between the two domains will have to be represented in each, and the two different modes of activating schemas – dynamically, and through reference – will give further indications of their relevant properties.

Music, as an expressive medium distinct from that of language, can also offer interesting possibilities for thinking about metaphorical processes. More purely "musical" mappings, such as those between a theme and variation, appear to be closer to analogy. Similar relationships between sonic patterns can also be seen in prose and, more typically, metered poetry, suggesting an exploration of these instances in terms of analogy as well as metaphor. The participation of music in conceptual integration networks, such as the two discussed in connection with the movement from Bach's cantata, offers possibilities for meaning construction that blends concepts from music and other domains. Conceptual blends that involve music and some other domain also provide an opportunity to study the structural features of each domain, given the assumption that blends require a uniform topography between the mental spaces involved in the conceptual integration network.

The question that has often been posed is, "Is music a language?" The composer David Lidov (2005) proposed reversing the terms with his question, "Is language a music?" The exploration of metaphor and music has much to say to both questions, as well as to the constituent features of both of these uniquely human modes of expression.

## Note

1 The pitch designation I use is that of the American Society of Acousticians: middle C is C4; the B below middle C is B3; the octave above middle C is C5.

## References


Adlington, R. (2003). Moving beyond motion: Metaphors for changing sound. *Journal of the Royal Music Association*, 128(2), 297–318.

Agawu, V. K. (1991). *Playing with signs: A semiotic interpretation of classical music*. Princeton, NJ: Princeton University Press.

Agawu, V. K. (1999). The challenge of semiotics. In N. Cook & M. Everist (Eds.), *Rethinking music* (pp. 138–160). Oxford: Oxford University Press.

Aksnes, H. (2002). *Perspectives of musical meaning: A study based on selected works by Geirr Tveitt*. Oslo: Unipub AS.

Ayrey, C. (1994). Debussy's significant connections: Metaphor and metonymy in analytical method. In A. Pople (Ed.), *Theory, analysis and meaning in music* (pp. 127–151). Cambridge: Cambridge University Press.

Babbitt, M. (1972). Past and present concepts of the nature and limits of music. In B. Boretz & E. T. Cone (Eds.), *Perspectives on contemporary music theory* (pp. 3–9). New York: W. W. Norton.

Barsalou, L. W. (1999). Perceptual symbol systems. *Behavioral and Brain Sciences,* 22(November), 577–609.

Bauer, A. (2004). "Tone-color, movement, changing harmonic planes": Cognition, constraints, and conceptual blends in modernist music. In A. Ashby (Ed.), *The pleasure of modernist music: Listening, meaning, intention, ideology* (pp. 121–152). Rochester, NY: University of Rochester Press.

Bhogal, G. (2007). Debussy's Arabesque and Ravel's *Daphnis et Chloé* (1912). *Twentieth-Century Music,* 3(2), 171–199.

Borgo, D. (2004). The play of meaning and the meaning of play in jazz. *Journal of Consciousness Studies,* 11(3–4), 174–190.

Broeckx, J. L. (1997). Beyond metaphor: Musical figures or "Gestalte" as expressive icons. *Journal of New Music Research,* 26, 266–276.

Brower, C. (1997–1998). Pathway, blockage, and containment in *Density* 21.5. *Theory and Practice,* 22–23, 35–54.

Budd, M. (1985). Understanding music. *Proceedings of the Aristotelian Society,* 59(Suppl.), 233–248.

Budd, M. (1989). Music and the communication of emotion. *Journal of Aesthetics and Art Criticism,* 47(2), 129–138.

Budd, M. (2003). Musical movement and aesthetic metaphors. *British Journal of Aesthetics,* 43(3), 209–223.

Butterfield, M. (2002). The musical object revisited. *Music Analysis,* 21(3), 327–380.

Charles, D. (1995). Music and antimetaphor (to Eero Tarasti). In E. Tarasti (Ed.), *Musical signification: Essays in the semiotic theory and analysis of music: Vol. 121. Approaches to semiotics* (pp. 27–42). Berlin: Mouton de Gruyter.

Chattah, J. R. 2006. *Semiotics, pragmatics, and metaphor in film music analysis.* Unpublished PhD dissertation, Florida State University.

Chuck, G. (2004). *Musical meaning and cognitive operations of the embodied mind.* Unpublished PhD dissertation, University of Rochester, Eastman School of Music.

Coker, W. (1972). *Music and meaning: A theoretical introduction to musical aesthetics.* New York: The Free Press.

Cone, E. T. (1987). On derivation: Syntax and rhetoric. *Music Analysis,* 6(3), 237–255.

Cook, N. (1990). *Music, imagination, and culture.* Oxford: Clarendon Press.

Cook, N. (1998). *Analysing musical multimedia.* Oxford: Clarendon Press.

Cook, N. (2001). Theorizing musical meaning. *Music Theory Spectrum,* 23(2), 170–195.

Cooke, D. (1959). *The language of music.* Oxford: Oxford University Press.

Cox, A. W. (1999). *The metaphoric logic of musical motion and space.* Unpublished PhD dissertation, University of Oregon.

Cox, A. W. (2001). The mimetic hypothesis and embodied musical meaning. *Musicæ Scientiæ,* 5(2):195–212.

Cumming, N. (1994). Metaphor in Roger Scruton's aesthetics of music. In A. Pople (Ed.), *Theory, analysis and meaning in music* (pp. 3–28). Cambridge: Cambridge University Press.

Cumming, N. (2000). *The sonic self: Musical subjectivity and signification.* Advances in Semiotics. Bloomington: Indiana University Press.

Davies, S. (1994). *Musical meaning and expression.* Ithaca, NY: Cornell University Press.

Deacon, T. W. (1997). *The symbolic species: The co-evolution of language and the brain.* New York: W. W. Norton.

Deacon, T. W. (2003). Universal grammar and semiotic constraints. In M. H. Christiansen & S. Kirby (Eds.), *Language evolution* (pp. 111–139). Oxford: Oxford University Press.

Dempster, D. (1998). Is there even a grammar of music? *Musicæ Scientiæ,* 2(1), 55–65.

Dubiel, J. (1990). "When you are a Beethoven": Kinds of rules in Schenker's *Counterpoint. Journal of Music Theory,* 34(2), 291–340.

Duchez, M.-E. (1979). La représentation spatio-verticale du caractère musical grave-aigu et l'élaboration de la notion de hauteur de son dans la conscience musicale occidentale. *Acta musicologica,* 51(1), 54–73.

Echard, W. (1999). An analysis of Neil Young's "Powderfinger" based on Mark Johnson's image schemata. *Popular Music,* 18(1), 133–144.

Echard, W. (2005). *Neil Young and the poetics of energy.* Bloomington: Indiana University Press.

Eitan, Z., & R. Y. Granot. (2006). How music moves: Musical parameters and listeners' images of motion. *Music Perception, 23*(3), 221–247.

Eitan, Z., & R. Timmers. (2006). Beethoven's last piano sonata and those who follow crocodiles: Cross-domain mappings of auditory pitch in a musical context. In M. Baroni, A. R. Addessi, R. Caterina, & M. Costa (Eds.) *Proceedings of the 9th International Conference on Music Perception and Cognition, Bologna, Italy, August 22–26 2006* (pp. 875–882). [n.p.]: The Society for Music Perception & Cognition and European Society for the Cognitive Sciences of Music.

Feld, S. (1981). Flow like a waterfall: The metaphors of Kaluli musical theory. *Yearbook for Traditional Music, 13*, 22–47.

Feld, S. (1982). *Sound and sentiment: Birds, weeping, poetics, and song in Kaluli expression*. Philadelphia: University of Pennsylvania Press.

Ferguson, D. N. (1960). *Music as metaphor: The elements of expression*. Minneapolis: University of Minnesota.

Gentner, D., Bowdle, B. F., Wolff, P., & Boronat, C. (2001). Metaphor is like analogy. In D. Gentner, K. J. Holyoak, & B. N. Kokinov (Eds.), *The analogical mind: Perspectives from cognitive science* (pp. 199–253). Cambridge, MA: MIT Press.

Goehr, L. (1998). *The quest for voice: Music, politics, and the limits of philosophy*. Berkeley: University of California Press.

Goodman, N. (1976). *Languages of art: An approach to a theory of symbols* (2nd ed.). Indianapolis: Hackett Publishing.

Guck, M. A. (1981). Musical images as musical thoughts: The contribution of metaphor to analysis. *In Theory Only, 5*(5), 29–43.

Guck, M. A. (1991). Two types of metaphoric transfer. In J. C. Kassler (Ed.), *Metaphor: A musical dimension: Vol. 1: Australian studies in the history, philosophy and social studies of music* (pp. 1–12). Sydney: Currency Press.

Guck, M. A. (1994). Rehabilitating the incorrigible. In A. Pople (Ed.), *Theory, analysis and meaning in music* (pp. 57–73). Cambridge: Cambridge University Press.

Gur, G. (2008). Body, forces, and paths: Metaphor and embodiment in Jean-Philippe Rameau's conceptualization of tonal space. *Music Theory Online* 14(1), March. http://mto.societymusictheory.org/issues/mto.08.14.1/mto.08.14.1.gur.html.

Hatten, R. S. (1994). *Musical meaning in Beethoven: Markedness, correlation, and interpretation*. Bloomington: Indiana University Press.

Hatten, R. S. (1995). Metaphor *in* music. In E. Tarasti (Ed.), *Musical signification: Essays in the semiotic theory and analysis of music: Vol. 121. Approaches to semiotics* (pp. 373–391). Berlin: Mouton de Gruyter.

Hatten, R. S. (2004). *Interpreting musical gestures, topics, and tropes: Mozart, Beethoven, Schubert*. Bloomington: Indiana University Press.

Jankélévitch, V. 2003. *Music and the ineffable* (C. Abbate, Trans.). Princeton, NJ: Princeton University Press.

Johnson, M. L. (1987). *The body in the mind: The bodily basis of meaning, imagination, and reason*. Chicago: University of Chicago Press.

Johnson, M. L. (1997–1998). Embodied musical meaning. *Theory and Practice*, 22–23, 95–102.

Johnson, M. L. (2007). *The meaning of the body: Aesthetics of human understanding.* Chicago: University of Chicago Press.

Johnson, M. L., & S. Larson. (2003). "Something in the way she moves": Metaphors of musical motion. *Metaphor and Symbol*, 18(2), 63–84.

Johnson, S. R. (2004). *Hearing the unvoiceable: Writer's block in Benjamin Britten's "Death in Venice."* Unpublished PhD dissertation, University of Wisconsin–Madison.

Juslin, P. N., & Sloboda, J. A. (Eds.). (2001). *Music and emotion: Theory and research*. New York: Oxford University Press.

Karbusicky, V. (1987). "Signification" in music: A metaphor? In T. A. Sebeok & J. Umiker-Sebeok (Eds.), *The semiotic web* 1986 (pp. 430–444). Berlin: Mouton de Gruyter.

Kerman, J. (1985). *Contemplating music: Challenges to musicology*. Cambridge, MA: Harvard University Press.

Kielian-Gilbert, M. (1990). Interpreting musical analogy: From rhetorical device to perceptual process. *Music Perception*, 8(1), 63–94.

Krantz, S. C. (1987, June). Metaphor in music. *The Journal of Aesthetics and Criticism*, 45(4), 351–360.

Lakoff, G. (1993). The contemporary theory of metaphor. In A. Ortony (Ed.), *Metaphor and thought* (pp. 202–251). Cambridge: Cambridge University Press.

Lakoff, G., & Johnson, M. L. (1980). *Metaphors we live by*. Chicago: University of Chicago Press.

Larson, S. (1997–1998). Musical forces and melodic patterns. *Theory and Practice*, 22–23, 55–71.

Lidov, D. (2005). *Is language a music? Writings on musical form and signification. (Musical meaning and interpretation)*. Bloomington: Indiana University Press.

Macy, L. (1996). Speaking of sex: Metaphor and performance in the Italian madrigal. *The Journal of Musicology, 14*(1), 1–34.

Meyer, L. (1956). *Emotion and meaning in music*. Chicago: University of Chicago Press.

Naroditskaya, I. (2005). Azerbaijani *mugham* and carpet: Cross-domain mapping. *Ethnomusicology Forum, 14*(1), 25–55.

O'Donnell, S. (1999). Space, motion, and other musical metaphors. In R. G. Weiner (Ed.), *Perspectives on the Grateful Dead: Critical writings* (Foreword by R. G. Adams; Afterword by S. Silberman; pp. 127–135). Westport, CT: Greenwood Press.

Perlman, M. (2004). *Unplayed melodies: Javanese gamelan and the genesis of music theory*. Berkeley: University of California Press.

Powers, H. (1980). Language models and musical analysis. *Ethnomusicology, 24*(1), 1–60.

Rumelhart, D. E. (1993). Some problems with the notion of literal meanings. In A. Ortony (Ed.), *Metaphor and thought* (pp. 71–82). Cambridge: Cambridge University Press.

Ruwet, N. (1966). Méthodes d'analyse en musicologie. *Revue Belge de Musicologies*, 20, 65–90.

Ruwet, N. (1972). *Langage, musique, poésie*. Paris: Éditions du Seuil.

Saslaw, J. K. (1996). Forces, containers, and paths: The role of body-derived image schemas in the conceptualization of music. *Journal of Music Theory, 40*(2), 217–243.

Saslaw, J. K. (1997–1998). Life forces: Conceptual structures in Schenker's *Free composition* and Schoenberg's *The musical idea*. *Theory and Practice*, 22–23, 17–33.

Saslaw, J. K., & Walsh, J. P. (1996). Musical invariance as a cognitive structure: "Multiple meaning" in the early nineteenth century. In I. Bent (Ed.), *Music theory in the age of Romanticism* (pp. 211–232). Cambridge: Cambridge University Press.

Saussure, F. D. (1959). *Course in general linguistics*. (C. Rally, A. Sechehaye, & A. Reidlinger, Eds.; W. Baskin, Trans.). New York: Philosophical Library.

Sayrs, E. 2003. Narrative, metaphor, and conceptual blending in "The Hanging Tree." *Music Theory Online*, 9(1), March. http://www.societymusictheory.org/mto/issues/mto.03.9.1/mto.03.9.1.sayrs.html.

Scruton, R. (1974). *Art and imagination: A study in the philosophy of mind*. London: Methuen & Co.

Scruton, R. (1983). Understanding music. *Ratio*, 25(2), 97–120.

Scruton, R. (1997). *The aesthetics of music*. Oxford: Oxford University Press.

Solie, R. A. (1977). *Metaphor and model in the analysis of melody*. Unpublished PhD dissertation, University of Chicago.

Solie, R. A. (1980). The living work: Organicism and musical analysis. *19th-Century Music, 4*(2), 147–156.

Spitzer, M. (2003). The metaphor of musical space. *Musicæ Scientiæ*, 7(1), 101–120.

Spitzer, M. (2004). *Metaphor and musical thought*. Chicago: University of Chicago Press.

Tomasello, M. (1999). *The cultural origins of human cognition*. Cambridge, MA: Harvard University Press.

Treitler, L. (1997). Language and the interpretation of music. In J. Robinson (Ed.), *Music and meaning* (pp. 23–56). Ithaca, NY: Cornell University Press.

Turner, M. (1998). Figure. In A. N. Katz, C. Cacciari, R. W. Gibbs, Jr., & M. Turner (Eds.), *Figurative language and thought. Counterpoints: Cognition, memory, and language* (pp. 44–87). New York: Oxford University Press.

Verbrugge, R. R. (1979). The primacy of metaphor in development. In E. Winner & H. Gardner (Eds.), *Fact, fiction, and fantasy in childhood: Vol. 6. New directions for child development* (pp. 77–84). San Francisco, CA: Jossey-Bass.

Walker, M. E. (2000). Movement and metaphor: Towards an embodied theory of music cognition and hermeneutics. *Bulletin of the Council for Research in Music Education*, 145 (Summer), 27–42.

Walser, R. (1991). The body in music: Epistemology and musical semiotics. *College Music Symposium*, 31, 117–126.

Zanten, W. V. (1986). The tone material of the Kacapi in Tembang Sunda in West Java. *Ethnomusicology*, 30(1), 84–112.

Zbikowski, L. M. (1991). *Large-scale rhythm and systems of grouping*. Unpublished PhD dissertation, Yale University, New Haven, CT.

Zbikowski, L. M. (1997). Conceptual models and cross-domain mapping: New perspectives on theories of music and hierarchy. *Journal of Music Theory, 41*(2), 11–43.

Zbikowski, L. M. (1998). Metaphor and music theory: Reflections from cognitive science. *Music Theory Online*, 4(1), January. (http://smtedu/mto/issues/mto.98.4.1/toc.4.1.html).

Zbikowski, L. M. (1999). The blossoms of 'Trockne Blumen': Music and text in the early nineteenth century. *Music Analysis*, 18(3), 307–345.

Zbikowski, L. M. (2002–2003). Music theory, multimedia, and the construction of meaning. *Intégral*, 16/17, 251–68.

Zbikowski, L. M. (2002). *Conceptualizing music: Cognitive structure, theory, and analysis*. New York: Oxford University Press.

Zon, B. 2000. *Music and metaphor in nineteenth-century British musicology*. Aldershot, England: Ashgate Publishing.

# Author Index

Abrahamson, A. A., 113
Ackerman, D., 425, 426
Adlington, R., 511
Agawu, V. K., 506
Ahrens, K., 69
Aisenman, R. A., 122, 219
Aksnes, H., 506, 511
Albert, J., 154
Albert, N. M., 189
Aleksandrov, A., 343, 346
Alesandrini, K., 216
Alkeslassy Levi, N., 152
Allbritton, D. W., 151
Alston, W. P., 276
Altiti, A., 147
Amira, S. A., 404
Anaki, D., 150, 186, 188
Anderson, D., 216
Anderson, J. R., 117
Andreu, N., 188
Andric, M., 166
Angus, L. E., 403, 404, 405, 406, 407
Ansari, R., 497
Anthony, S., 174
Antos, S. J., 145, 148, 153
Appelt, D. E., 314, 332
Arbib, M. A., 426, 437
Aristotle, 143, 154
Arlow, J. A., 400, 413
Armel, K. C., 433
Arnheim, R., 449, 453, 457
Arvatz, S., 147
Asch, S., 437
Aschersleben, G., 164
Aschkenazi, K., 144–146, 147, 151, 152
Asher, J., 218
Asher, N., 312
Austin, N., 174
Ayrey, C., 508
Azuma, M., 222

Babbitt, M., 509
Babcock, M., 164
Bach, K., 269
Bachman, L. F., 221
Bai, J., 452
Bailey, M. E., 434
Balaban, N., 152
Baldassarri, F., 184
Barbey, A. K., 426, 432
Barcelona, A., 241, 249, 253, 416, 478
Barcelos, A., 212
Bardy, B. G., 430, 431
Barker, P., 401, 402
Barlow, J. M., 200, 398, 404, 405
Barnden, J. A., 319, 320, 322, 325, 326, 327–328, 330, 333
Baron-Cohen, S., 433, 434, 435, 436

Baroti, G., 184
Barsalou, L. W., 175, 426, 429, 432, 516
Bartelt, G., 214
Barthes, R., 476
Bartsch, R., 415, 417
Bates, E., 353
Batori, G., 154, 155, 178, 188, 191
Bauer, A., 511
Bauer, L., 220
Bavelas, J. B., 163
Baxter, L. A., 388
Beardsley, M., 264, 265, 297
Beattie, G., 494
Beck, B., 426
Beeman, M. J., 185, 186
Bensdorp, T., 478
Benuzzi, F., 432, 437
Berg, E. A., 495
Berg, J., 274
Bergmann, M., 262, 274, 276
Bertolani, L., 432, 437
Bertus, E. L., 242
Besson, M., 69
Bever, T. G., 148
Bezuidenhout, A., 269, 274, 277
Biber, D., 241
Bihrle, A., 178, 182, 183, 188
Binkley, T., 264
Binnie, C., 433
Bisiach, E., 190
Black, E., 240
Black, M., 119, 273, 276, 277, 462, 464, 468, 471, 494
Black, T., 163
Blank, G. D., 117
Blasko, D. G., 69, 70, 76, 117, 124, 180, 182, 239
Block, D., 213, 214, 215
Boada, R., 183
Bock, J. K., 300
Boers, F., 217, 218, 219, 224, 226, 253, 289
Boisson, C., 426
Boisson, D., 190
Bonnell, V. E., 483
Bookheimer, S., 187, 188
Bookin, H., 70, 112, 180
Borbely, A., 11, 413, 418
Borgo, D., 511
Bornstein, M. H., 429, 432
Boroditsky, L., 119, 168, 169, 170
Boronat, C. B., 113, 114, 117, 129, 136, 517
Bottini, G., 154, 187, 188
BouJaoude, S., 216
Bowdle, B. F., 7, 67–75, 76, 77, 81, 110, 113, 115, 116, 117, 119, 120, 122, 129, 136, 139, 449, 458, 517
Bower, G. H., 163
Bowles, A. R., 134, 135
Boyd, R., 276
Bozzi, P., 438, 439
Bradshaw, J. L., 434
Braitenberg, V., 189
Brammer, M. J., 69, 154, 188
Branden, J., 10
Bredin, H., 416
Brenner, C., 416
Brillat-Savarin, J. A., 425
Brisard, F., 148
Broca, P. A., 177
Broeckx, J. L., 506
Bromme, R., 216
Brooke-Rose, C., 200, 201
Brower, C., 511
Brown, R., 71, 200
Brown, W., 184
Brownell, H., 178, 182, 183, 186, 188
Brugger, P., 190
Bryll, R., 497
Buchstaller, I., 223
Budd, M., 504, 505
Burke, K., 414
Burns, G. W., 402
Burridge, R. R., 332
Butterfield, M., 511

Cacciari, C., 11, 117, 149, 150, 425, 430, 432, 439
Calbris, G., 484, 485, 488, 492
Callan, A. M., 430
Callan, D. E., 430
Callejas Bretones, C., 427, 428
Cameron, L., 8, 197, 199, 200, 201, 202, 203, 204, 206, 213, 216, 220, 222, 227, 282, 283, 292, 495
Camp, E., 277
Caplan, P. J., 409
Caramazza, A., 437
Carbonell, J. G., 311–312, 322, 327
Carpenter, P. A., 188
Carreti'e, L., 160
Carroll, N., 464
Carroll, P. J., 148
Carston, R., 146, 269, 330
Carter, R., 202, 220, 241
Cassell, J., 485, 490
Cavell, S., 276
Cazeaux, C., 425
Chafe, W., 199
Challis, B. H., 453
Chao, L., 189

Charles, D., 505
Charteris-Black, J., 223, 253, 283, 287, 288, 290, 292, 477
Chernicky, B., 163
Chiappe, D. L., 121, 297, 305, 448
Chiarello, C., 185, 186, 187
Chochon, F., 190
Chuck, G., 511
Cienki, A., 11, 353, 476, 485, 486, 488, 491, 492, 493, 494, 497
Cirillo, L., 399, 402, 407, 410
Clark, A., 163
Clark, H. H., 118, 163, 171
Clark, J. M., 122, 242
Classen, C., 427
Clay, A. L., 399, 402
Clement, C. A., 110, 122
Close, H. T., 400
Cocude, M., 163
Cohen, L., 190
Cohen, M., 302, 303
Cohen, T., 264, 265, 266, 276
Coker, W., 509
Coles, M., 179
Colombo, M., 184
Colston, H. L., 155, 351, 463, 493
Combs, G., 400, 401
Cone, E. T., 516
Connine, C. M., 69, 76, 117, 124
Conrad, S., 241
Consoli, S., 177
Conway, J. B., 406
Cook, N., 478, 510, 511
Cooke, D., 506
Cooper, D., 207
Corcoran, R., 154, 187, 188
Corradini, P., 432
Cortazzi, M., 213
Corts, D. P., 200, 220
Costes, N., 189
Coulson, R., 216
Coulson, S., 8, 65, 155, 177, 178, 181, 182, 189, 495
Courant, R., 344
Cox, A. W., 511, 516
Crider, C., 399, 402, 407, 410
Crisp, P., 238, 239, 242
Croft, W., 415
Csábi, S., 217
Cudahy, C., 434, 435, 436
Cumming, N., 505
Cummings, A. L., 402, 403, 405
Cupchik, G. D., 464
Cutler, A., 117
Cutting, C., 69, 113
Cutting, J., 452
Cytowic, R. E., 428, 433, 434, 435, 436

Dagher, Z., 216
Damasio, A. R., 189
Damasio, H., 189
Dann, K. T., 302
Danto, A. C., 276, 464
Danziger, E., 492
Daprati, E., 432, 437
Dastjerdi, H., 253
David, A. S., 69, 154
David, S., 426
Davidson, D., 46, 262, 263, 266, 276
Davies, M., 276
Davies, S., 504
Day, S., 303, 427, 436
de Guerrero, M. C. M., 214
Deacon, T. W., 506
Deane, P. D., 239
DeBuse, C. J., 154
Decety, J., 189
Dechemeleer, M., 219
Dehaene, S., 190
Deiber, M. P., 189
Deignan, A., 9, 201, 203, 223, 224, 225, 253, 280, 283, 286, 287, 288, 291, 292
Delfino, M., 312–313
Demecheleer, M., 253, 289
Dempster, D., 505
Denes, G., 182
Denham, A., 276
Denis, M., 163
Dennett, D., 416
Dennis, S., 130
Dent-Read, C., 464
Derrig, S., 427
Dessalegn, B., 180, 182
Diamond, S., 186
Dick, F., 353
Dietrich, R., 184
DiGiuseppi, R. A., 400
Dillard J. P., 154
Dirven, R., 119, 224, 249, 330, 331, 412
Dixon, M. J., 434, 435, 436
Dodge, E., 24, 30
Doherty, S., 164
Doughty, C. J., 217
Douglas, D., 221
Downes, W., 240
Drew, P., 205
Du Bois, W. J., 151, 156
Dubiel, J., 508
Dubois, D., 426, 429
Duchez, M.-E., 516

Duit, R., 216, 218
Dumais, S. T., 130
Duncan, S., 488, 494, 497
Durand, J., 468

Echard, W., 511
Edwards, L., 348
Eerden, B., 475
Efron, D., 486
Ekman, P., 486
Elio, R., 117
Elnatan, I., 149, 153, 154, 156
Emanatian, M., 312–313, 392, 478
Emmorey, K., 487
Emmott, C., 239
Engelhardt, Y., 477
Erb, M., 69, 154, 188
Erman, B., 284
Erramouspe, R., 216
Essegbey, J., 352
Estes, Z., 121
Ettinger, Y., 143
Eubanks, P., 407, 409
Evans, C., 205
Evans, V., 65, 485
Eviatar, Z., 154, 155
Eyckmans, J., 253

Fahnestock, J., 416
Fainsilber, L., 312–313
Falkenhainer, B., 111, 315
Fass, D., 312, 317, 318, 319, 331
Fauconnier, G., 6, 53, 57, 65, 109, 115, 181, 241, 291, 305, 327, 342, 415, 472, 495
Faust, M., 150, 154, 186, 188
Fein, O., 144–146, 147, 148, 149, 150, 151, 152, 153, 154, 156
Feld, S., 510
Feldman, J., 17, 18, 189
Fellbaum, C., 137
Feltovitch, P., 216
Ferguson, D. N., 509
Ferguson, R. W., 111, 113
Fernandez-Duque, D., 44
Ferretti, T., 145, 152, 155
Fesmire, S., 44
Fine, B., 416, 419
Fine, H. J., 398, 405
Finocchiaro, C., 437
Fishelov, D., 297
Fisher, C., 439
Fishlov, D., 219
Fleischman, S., 485
Fletcher, P., 187
Flores d'Arcais, G. B., 438
Fodor, J., 48, 49, 50, 69, 144, 146, 147
Fogelin, R., 266
Forbus, K. D., 110, 111, 113, 141, 315
Forceville, C., 11, 457, 462, 464, 466, 467, 468, 473, 474, 476, 478, 493
Forrest, D. V., 400
Foss, M., 296, 297, 298, 305
Fowles, J., 240
Frackowiak, R. S. J., 154, 187
Fracowiak, R. S. J., 434
Frak, V., 189
Francozo, E., 248, 250
Frank, R. J., 189
Franks, H., 205
Freedman, J., 400, 401
Freeman, D. C., 240, 241, 305
Freeman, M. H., 239
French, R. M., 139
Freriks, J., 472
Freud, A., 414
Freud, S., 413, 416
Freyd, J., 164
Friedman, R., 186
Friesen, W., 486
Frisson, S., 146, 148
Frith, C. D., 154, 187, 434
Fuller, J. W., 222–223
Furuyama, N., 497
Fussell, S. R., 312–313

Gabias, P., 448
Gadir, O., 302, 303
Gagnon, L., 183, 184, 188, 191
Gallese, V., 24, 164
Gangitano, M., 432, 437
Ganzi, J., 152
Garcia, R. C., 216
Gardner, H., 154, 178, 182, 183, 184, 188
Geeraerts, D., 394
Gentilucci, G., 432, 437
Gentner, D., 7, 65, 67–68, 71, 75, 76, 77, 81, 109–110, 111, 112, 113, 114, 115, 116, 117, 119, 120, 121, 122, 129, 136, 139, 141, 168, 169, 200, 216, 296, 315, 449, 458, 517
Gergen, K. J., 408
Gernsbacher, M. A., 134, 147, 149, 155
Gerrig, R. J., 122, 151, 178, 316, 460
Gervais, R., 429
Gevaert, C., 394
Giampietro, V., 69, 154
Gibbs, R., 8, 44, 69, 109, 113, 117, 119, 122, 135, 144, 145, 149, 151, 153, 155, 162, 164, 165, 166, 167, 172, 178, 205, 208, 209, 235, 241, 243,

247, 248, 250, 253, 272, 280, 342, 351, 412, 413, 460, 463, 469, 478, 493, 495
Gibbs, Tendahl, 332
Gibbs, W. R., 161, 426
Gibson, J. J., 439, 449, 469
Gick, M. L., 110, 117
Gildea, P., 70, 112, 117, 180
Gineste, M.-D., 473
Giora, R., 7, 69, 70, 80, 117, 143–146, 147, 148, 149, 150, 151, 152, 153, 154, 155, 156, 178, 184, 188, 191, 328, 448, 454, 455, 458
Giroux, F., 183, 184, 188, 191
Glasbey, S. R., 319, 322, 333
Gleitman, H., 439
Gleitman, R. L., 439
Glenberg, A. M., 164
Glicksohn, J., 243
Glucksberg, S., 6, 67, 70, 74, 76, 78, 79, 80, 112, 113, 114, 117, 119, 122, 133, 135, 136, 139, 140, 148, 149, 150, 151, 152, 168, 180, 272, 284, 297, 305, 413, 418, 439, 449
Glynn, S., 216
Goatly, A., 206, 215, 242
Goehr, L., 505
Goldin-Meadow, S., 352, 353, 491
Goldstein, L. H., 433, 434, 435, 436
Goldstone, R. L., 109
Goldvarg, Y., 70, 148, 149
Gombrich, E. H., 448
Goodblatt, C., 243
Goodman, N., 264, 272, 504
Goodnough, A., 72
Goossens, L., 332
Gordon, C., 208
Gordon, R., 164
Gossens, L., 292
Goswami, U., 216
Gould, J., 166
Goulet, P., 178, 183, 184, 188, 191
Grabowski, T. J., 189
Grady, J. E., 26, 41, 46, 218, 219, 248, 495
Grafman, J., 186
Grant, L., 220
Graumann, C., 203
Greenspan, S. L., 163
Grezes, J., 189
Grice, H. P., 67, 143, 144, 145, 153, 178, 266
Grodd, W., 69, 154, 188
Grondelaers, S., 394
Gross, L., 322
Grossenbacher, P., 433, 434, 435, 436
Gruber, H. E., 109
Guck, M. A., 509
Guerin, B., 399, 403, 408, 409
Gwyn, R., 205

Hage, P., 72
Halevy, R., 304
Haley, J., 400
Hall, R. P., 312
Hallberg, E. T., 402, 403, 405
Hallett, M., 189
Hamilton, C., 239
Hammeal, R. J., 432
Hamp-Lyons, L., 218
Hannequin, D., 178, 183
Harding, J. L., 119, 168, 169
Harpur, T., 458
Harrington, C., 212
Harrington, H. L., 214
Harris, P., 164
Harris, R. J., 216
Harrison, J. E., 433, 434, 435, 436
Hasson, U., 148, 149, 151, 152
Hatten, R. S., 508
Haught, C., 76, 78, 79
Haviland, J., 492, 494
Healey, A. F., 122
Heasley, B., 218
Heather, J., 434
Hécaen, H., 177
Hekkert, P., 468
Helmreich, S., 319, 327–328
Hendler, T., 154
Hendley, R. J., 326
Henle, P., 264
Hersh, R., 348
Hesse, M., 216
Heywood, J., 208, 242
Hichwa, R. D., 189
Higginbotham, J., 267
Hill, C. E., 404, 405
Hills, D., 262, 275
Hillyard, S. A., 179
Hinojosa, J. A., 154
Hintikka, J., 312
Hiraga, M. K., 305
Hiraka, M., 239
Ho, D., 252
Hobbs, J. R., 314, 315, 332
Hofstadter, D., 65
Holland, N., 413
Hollet, A., 429
Holme, R., 218
Holt, W., 205
Holyoak, K. J., 65, 109–110, 116, 117, 139, 141, 216
Holz, W., 483

Honda, M., 189
Hopkins, R., 459
Hopper, P. J., 200, 201
Horton, W. S., 284
Howes, D., 427
Huang, S., 394
Hubbard, E. M., 426, 428, 431, 433, 434, 436, 438, 440
Hughes, T., 232
Hummel, J. E., 124, 141
Hwang, K., 252

Ibanez, V., 189
Imai, M., 119, 168, 169
Indurkhya, B., 312, 330, 473
Ingram, J. L., 406
Inhoff, A. W., 148
Iverson, E., 319, 327–328
Iverson, J., 352, 353

Jackendoff, R., 69, 169, 416, 429, 440
Jacquin-Courtois, S., 190
Jankélévitch, V., 505
Janus, R. A., 148
Jaques, J., 353
Jeannerod, M., 189
Jeziorski, M., 109
Jin, L., 213
Joanette, Y., 178, 183, 184, 188, 191
Johnson, A. T., 74
Johnson, B. K., 242
Johnson, C., 26, 219
Johnson, K., 434
Johnson, M. L., 6, 41, 43, 44, 48, 51, 65, 109, 113, 115, 135, 136, 155, 162, 178, 191, 215, 235, 247, 248, 249, 250, 253, 254, 272, 296, 319, 326, 342, 358, 382, 412, 414, 416, 462, 463, 464, 472, 474, 476, 478, 483, 489, 493, 496, 498, 510, 511
Johnson, S. R., 476, 511
Johnson, T., 163
Johnson-Laird, P., 69, 429, 438
Jones, J. A., 430
Jones, L., 296, 297, 298, 305
Jones, L. L., 121
Juslin, P. N., 506
Just, M. A., 154, 155, 188

Kacinik, N. A., 187, 188
Kanwisher, N., 164
Kaplan, D., 263, 268, 269, 277
Kaplan, J., 178
Kaplan, S. J., 464
Kaput, J., 348
Karbusicky, V., 507, 516
Kaschak, M., 164
Kasher, A., 154, 155, 178, 184, 188, 191
Katz, A., 122, 145, 152, 155, 242, 417
Kauffman, S., 421
Kazmerski, V., 180, 182
Keene, M. T., 324
Keil, F. C., 300
Keller, T. A., 188
Keller-Cohen, D., 208
Kellerman, E., 222–223
Kelly, M. H., 300
Kempler, D., 183, 188
Kendon, A., 352, 353, 486
Kennedy, J. M., 11, 119, 121, 208, 297, 305, 448, 449, 450, 451, 452, 453, 457, 464, 468, 475, 478
Kennedy, P. T., 117
Kennedy, V., 453, 464
Kenwood, C., 163
Kerman, J., 510
Keysar, B., 70, 75, 80, 113, 114, 117, 119, 122, 134, 139, 147, 149, 272, 284, 297, 305, 413, 418, 439
Kielian-Gilbert, M., 508, 516
Kiesler, D. J., 406
Kim, H., 152
Kim, I. J., 189
Kimmel, M., 253
King, B., 389, 393
King, J., 267
Kintsch, W., 7, 119, 129, 130, 131, 132, 133, 134, 135, 137
Kircher, T. T. J., 69, 154, 188
Kirmayer, L., 204
Kirsh, D., 163
Kirtner, J. D., 332
Kita, S., 352, 485, 492
Kittay, E. F., 113, 265, 272, 274, 330, 417
Klatzky, R. L., 164
Klein, D. E., 133
Knuf, G., 164
Koehler, W., 438
Kokinov, B. N., 65, 109–116
Koller, V., 200, 220, 222, 292
Kolmogorov, A. N., 343, 346
Kopp, R. R., 400, 401
Korman, Y., 405, 406
Kosslyn, S. M., 186, 189
Kotler, N., 153
Kourtzi, Z., 164
Kövecses, Z., 10, 48, 236, 239, 244, 248, 253, 257, 312–313, 380, 381, 382, 383, 386, 387, 388, 389, 391, 392, 393, 394, 414, 415, 463, 475
Kramer, E., 347

Krantz, S. C., 505
Kravetz, S., 150, 186, 188
Kress, G., 476
Kreuz, R. J., 242, 243
Kroger, R. O., 408
Kronrod, A., 149, 153, 154, 156
Kroos, C., 430
Krouse, K., 81
Krych, M. A., 163
Kubovy, M., 450, 454
Kuiken, D., 295, 304
Kurtz, K., 111
Kutas, M., 179, 188
Kyle Simmons, W., 426, 432

Labbo, L., 212, 214
Ladavas, E., 437
Lakoff, G., 6, 24, 30, 41, 43, 44, 48, 52, 62, 65, 109, 113, 115, 123, 135, 136, 155, 162, 170, 178, 190, 191, 215, 235, 236, 237, 238, 239, 244, 247, 248, 249, 250, 253, 254, 272, 280, 281, 290, 291, 295, 296, 305, 319, 326, 327, 339, 340, 342, 347, 348, 349, 357, 358, 359, 382, 383, 389, 392, 412, 413, 414, 462, 463, 464, 472, 474, 476, 483, 487, 489, 493, 496, 498, 510, 512,
Landau, B., 439, 440
Landauer, T. K., 130
Landis, T., 186
Langacker, R. W., 169, 414, 415, 497
Laplanche, J., 420
Larkey, L. B., 124
Larson, S., 44, 478, 511
Lascarides, A., 312
Lau, I., 225
Lavine, R. Z., 212
Lavrent'ev, M. A., 343, 346
Law, K., 110, 111, 141
Lawson, A., 216
Lazar, G., 226
Le Bihan, D., 190
Leary, T., 406
Lee, C. J., 119
Lee, M. G., 319, 320, 322, 328, 333
Leech, G. N., 234, 235
Leezenberg, M., 274, 328
Lehrer, A., 113, 119
Lenrow, P. B., 398
Leon, M., 430
Lerman, C. L., 221
Leube, D. T., 69, 154, 188
Levin, F., 413
Levin, S. R., 264, 327
Levinson, J., 276
Levinson, S., 492
Levitt, H., 405, 406
Levorato, M. C., 430
Levy, E. T., 485, 490
Levy, G., 152
Lewis, D., 273
Li F-Y, T., 218
Liddell, S. K., 487
Lidov, D., 506, 520
Lima, P., 248, 250
Lima, S. D., 148
Lindamood, T., 179
Lindauer, M., 438
Lindsay, M., 186
Lindstromberg, S., 218, 224
Littlemore, J., 216, 217, 221, 222, 226, 253
Littman, M. L., 137, 138
Liu, C. H., 453
Lodge, D., 238, 239, 240, 242
Loewald, H., 413
Loewenberg, I., 262
Loewenstein, J., 110, 117
Logan, C. G., 189
Long, M. H., 217
Longhini, A., 212
Lopes, D., 458
L'opez-Mart'ýn, S., 154
Louw, B., 203
Love, B. C., 124
Lovelace, C. T., 433, 434, 435, 436
Lovink, G., 476
Low, G. D., 8, 200, 204, 212, 213, 214, 216, 220, 224, 225, 226, 227, 253
Lucchelli, F., 184
Lutzenberger, W., 437
Lyddon, W. J., 399, 402
Lytinen, S. L., 332

Ma, X.-F., 497
Maalej, Z., 253, 464, 478
MacCormac, E., 119
MacDonald, J., 430
MacNealy, M. S., 243
Macy, L., 512
Maglio, P. P., 163
Magnani, L., 44
Makari, G., 413
Malgady, R. G., 296
Manea, S., 312–313
Manfredi, D., 74, 113, 114
Manfredini, D. A., 133, 140
Mangalath, P., 137
Marangolo, P., 184
Margalit, A., 265
Markman, A. B., 71, 109–116, 136
Marks, L. E., 426, 429, 431, 432, 436, 439

Marschark, M., 122, 242
Marsolek, C. J., 186
Marsolek, J. C., 154
Martin, A., 189
Martin, J. H., 312, 315, 402, 403, 405
Martin, J. M., 117
Martin, P., 314, 332
Martinez, A., 188
Martino, G., 431, 432
Mashal, N., 154
Mason, Z. J., 312
Massironi, M., 432, 438
Matlock, T., 8, 161, 163, 169, 170, 171, 181, 189
Matos, J. F., 348
Matsuki, K., 389
Matsumoto, Y., 169
Matsunaka, Y., 478
Matthews, R., 264
Mattingly, J. B., 433, 434
Maurer, D., 436
Mayberry, R., 353
Mbense, T., 391
McCarthy, M., 200, 202, 220
McClone, M. S., 140
McCloskey, B. P., 164
McCullough, K.-E., 497
McDonald, I., 64
McElree, B., 69
McGarry, K., 183
McGlone, M. S., 74, 113, 114, 119, 133, 168, 169
McGuire, P. K., 188
McGurk, H., 430
McKeon, R., 414
McKoon, G., 151
McMahon, M., 409
McMullen, L. M., 10, 397, 404, 406, 409
McNamara, D., 130
McNeil, D., 313
McNeill, D., 352, 353, 476, 485, 486, 488, 489, 490, 491, 492, 494, 496, 497
McQuarrie, E. F., 477, 478
Medford, N. C., 69, 154
Medin, D. L., 109
Medina, J., 117
Melnick, B., 413
Mercado, F., 154
Merikle, P. M., 434, 435, 436
Merkas, C. E., 450, 452
Meyer, L., 520
Meyers, K., 200, 220
Miall, D. S., 295, 304
Michel, C., 190
Michel, D., 178
Mick, D. G., 477, 478
Middleton, J., 216, 217
Miller, G. A., 69, 109, 119, 429, 438
Miller, W. R., 72
Modell, A., 413
Montague, R., 267
Moon, R. E., 282, 288, 293
Moore, B., 416, 419
Moore, K. E., 61, 66, 485
Moran, R., 262, 276
Morgan, P., 248
Morrow, D. G., 163
Moss, M. M., 312–313
Motz, B. A., 168, 169
Moulin, A., 464
Mueller, C., 11
Muggia, S., 184
Mukarowský, J, 233
Müller, C., 476, 485, 486, 487, 488, 489, 490, 492, 493, 494, 495
Munhall, K., 430
Muran, J. C., 400
Murphy, G. L., 123, 133, 351, 493
Musolff, A., 329, 333

Namy, L., 117
Napolitano Valditara, L., 428
Narayanan, S., 24, 26, 189, 323
Naroditskaya, I., 511
Nayak, N. P., 69, 113, 151
Nelkin, N., 430
Nersessian, N. J., 44, 109
Newsome, M. R., 148, 149
Niemeier, S., 218
Nogales, P., 274
Nordlie, J., 69
Norris, J. M., 217, 222
Norvig, P., 311–312, 321
Novick, L. R., 117
Nowottny, W., 234, 239
Nunberg, G., 119, 438
Núñez, R. E., 10, 44, 61, 66, 168, 169, 170, 190, 339, 340, 342, 347, 348, 349, 350, 352, 353, 357, 358, 359, 485, 492

Oakley, T., 65, 495
Oblinger, D., 111
O'Brien, J. E., 117, 166
O'Donnell, S., 511
Ogden, T., 413
Okrent, A., 487
Oliveri, M., 183, 185, 188, 191, 437
Ortega, L., 217, 222
Ortigue, S., 190
Ortony, A., 75, 112, 119, 135, 145, 148, 153, 227, 296, 297, 298, 305, 312–313, 315, 325, 330

Osgood, C. E., 433
Ota, H., 190
Oxford, R., 212, 214, 215
Özcaliskan, S., 253

Paivio, A., 242
Palmer, A. S., 221
Panther, K., 249
Papagno, C., 183, 184, 185, 188, 191
Parani, D., 189
Pascual-Leone, A., 437
Paul, L., 184
Paulesu, E., 154, 187, 188, 434
Pavio, A., 122
Pearce, S. S., 400, 401, 402
Pearl, J., 323
Pederson, E., 492
Pelamatti, A., 427
Peleg, O., 146, 147, 148, 153
Pelligrino, J. W., 164
Perez, E., 186
Perlman, M., 508, 511, 516
Perry, J., 277
Petrov, A. A., 124
Pexman, P. M., 145, 152, 155
Phillips, B. J., 163, 477
Pickering, M., 146
Pilkington, A., 237, 241
Pinel, P., 190
Piquer, A. M., 223
Plath, S., 233
Poli, J., 69
Pollio, H. R., 200, 221, 398, 404, 405
Pollio, M. R., 398, 405
Ponech, T., 469
Pontalis, J.-B., 420
Popova, Y., 240
Porcher, L., 485, 488
Pörings, R., 330, 331
Potter, H., 182, 183, 188
Potter, J., 408
Powelson, J., 178
Powers, H., 505–506
Preissl, H., 437
Priftis, K., 190
Prinz, W., 164
Procyk, E., 189
Pulvermueller, F., 437
Pulvermüller, F., 189
Pynte, J., 69, 179, 180, 182

Quek, F., 497
Quesada, J., 137
Quinn, N., 209, 388, 493
Quintilianus, M. F., 486

Radden, G., 249, 381, 387, 414, 415
Radman, Z., 421
Radvansky, G. A., 164
Ramachandran, V. S., 426, 428, 431, 433, 434, 436, 438, 440
Raman, R., 189
Ramscar, M., 124, 169, 170
Raphaely, D., 163
Rapp, A. M., 69, 154, 188
Raskin, A. H., 177
Rasmussen, B., 403, 405, 407
Rattermann, M. J., 110
Récanati, F., 269
Reddy, M. J., 264, 265, 489
Regan, A. M., 404, 405
Regard, M., 186
Regier, T., 20, 24, 30
Rehak, A., 178
Reider, N., 413
Reinhart, T., 273
Rennie, D. L., 403, 404, 406, 407
Reynolds, R. E., 145, 148, 153
Rhodes, G., 457, 458
Rice, S., 118
Rich, A. N., 433, 434
Rich, S., 217
Richards, I. A., 498
Richardson, D. C., 170, 171
Ricoeur, P., 414, 421
Rinaldi, M., 184
Riviere, D., 190
Rizzo, S., 184
Rizzolatti, G., 426, 437
Robbins, H., 344
Roberts, R. M., 242
Roberts, S., 81
Robertson, R. W., 147, 149
Robichon, F. H., 69
Rode, G., 190
Rodel, M., 186
Rogers-Ramachandran, D., 437
Rohdin, M., 464
Rohrer, T., 417
Romero, L., 183, 185, 188, 191
Roncero, T., 121
Rorty, R., 47, 266
Rosaldo, M., 393
Rosch, E., 412
Rosen, V., 413
Ross, A., 453
Ross, B. H., 116, 117
Rossetti, Y., 190
Rouby, C., 426, 429
Rozik, E., 464
Rubio Fernandez, P., 148, 149, 150, 151

Rugg, M. D., 179
Ruiz de Mendoza Ibáñez, F. J., 327, 332
Rumelhart, D. E., 113, 510
Russell, R. L., 402
Russell, S. W., 311–312, 321
Ruwet, N., 505–506

Sacks, O., 449
Sadato, N., 189
Sakuragi, T., 222–223
Saleh, A., 212
Sandra, D., 118, 148
Sandu, G., 312
Santa Ana, O., 282
Sapir, E., 200
Sarason, S. B., 214
Saslaw, J. K., 511
Saussure, F., 505
Savardi, U., 427
Sayce, R. A., 220
Sayrs, E., 511
Scarpa, P., 154, 187, 188
Scart, V., 473
Schaal, B., 426, 429
Schab, F., 426
Schallert, D. L., 145, 148, 153
Scheffler, I., 274
Scheindlin, R., 272
Schenone, P., 154, 187, 188
Schieffer, B., 184
Schmidt, G. L., 154
Schmitt, N., 227
Scholem, G., 428
Schön, D. A., 212, 213
Schram, D. H., 242, 243
Schuurman, D., 464
Schwartz, D. L., 163
Scribner, S., 214
Scruton, R., 504, 505
Searle, J., 45, 46, 67–68, 75, 135, 143, 144, 145, 153, 178, 266
Seger, C. J., 154
Semino, E., 208, 237, 240, 242, 289
Senft, G., 492
Sereno, M. I., 188
Shalev, H., 298
Shallice, T., 187
Shapiro, K., 430, 437
Shapiro, T., 413
Sharpe, E., 413
Shavit, A., 143, 144
Shen, Y., 9, 119, 149, 242, 284, 296, 297, 298, 299, 300, 301, 302, 303, 428
Shengold, E., 413
Shinohara, K., 478, 485
Shklovsky, V., 295
Shore, B., 478, 493
Short, M. H., 208, 234, 242
Shovelton, H., 494
Shuval, N., 149, 153, 154, 156
Siegelman, E. Y., 400, 401, 402
Silver, J., 453
Simmons, G. F., 347
Simner, K., 435
Simon-Vandenbergen, A. M., 240
Simons, J., 464, 474
Simpkinson, C., 398
Simpson, T., 182, 183, 188
Sinclair, J., 282–283, 284, 285, 288
Skehan, P., 221
Skorczynska, H., 288
Slobin, D., 494
Sloboda, J. A., 506
Smilek, D., 434, 435, 436
Smith, M. K., 221
Smolensky, P., 416
Smykowski, T., 448
Smyth, R., 121
Sobolev, D., 239
Solie, R. A., 510
Sopory, P., 154
Soriano, C., 253
Soroker, N., 154, 155, 178, 184, 188, 191
Sotillo, M., 154
Sparks, C. L., 399, 402
Sperber, D., 7, 146, 155, 237, 266, 269, 330, 469
Spiro, R. T., 216
Spitzer, M., 511
Spivey-Knowlton, M., 166
Squire, L. R., 186
Srinivasan, M., 170
St. George, M., 188
Stahl, E., 216
Stalnaker, R., 267, 273
Stanfield, R. A., 432
Stanley, J., 267, 269
Steen, G. J., 109, 220, 223, 241, 242, 243, 304, 495
Stein, G. C., 319, 327–328
Stelma, J., 199, 200, 203, 213, 220, 222
Stern, J., 9, 262, 263, 265, 267, 272, 273, 275, 276, 277, 328, 329, 333
Sternberg, R. J., 113, 296, 318, 331
Sterzi, R., 154, 187, 188
Stevick, E. W., 227
Stewart, I., 347
Stickel, M. E., 314, 332
Stoffregen, T. A., 430, 431
Strauss, C., 493

Stressler, J., 220
Stringaris, A. K., 69, 154
Strom, L, 166
Stroop, J. R., 69
Stuart, J. J., 405, 406
Stubbs, M., 225
Sun, S., 469, 478
Sunderland, C. C., 402
Sundermeier, A. B., 154
Sutton, C., 216
Swan, J., 236, 238
Sweetser, E., 66, 119, 178, 296, 342, 352, 353, 358, 415, 438, 485, 491, 492
Swindlehurst, K., 240
Swinney, D. A., 117, 147
Szabo, Z., 267
Szoklolsky, A., 464

Tabossi, P., 117, 184
Talebinejad, M., 253
Talmy, L., 20, 169, 342, 350, 383
Tamim, R., 216
Tan, E., 468
Tapia, M., 154
Taub, S., 248, 496
Taylor, J., 391, 415, 418
Taylor, L., 164
Tebbe, M. R., 216
Teng, N. Y., 469, 478
Teuscher, U., 168, 169
Thagard, P., 124, 139, 216
Thelen, E., 352, 353
Thomas, O., 312–313
Thompson, A., 272
Thompson, J. O., 272
Thompson, L., 110, 117
Thompson, S. A., 200, 201
Thompson, W. L., 189
Thomson, E., 412
Tilley, C., 402
Tilo, T. J., 69
Tirrell, L., 119, 272
Tognini-Bonelli, E., 282
Tomasello, M., 469, 520
Tomlinson, S., 212
Tompkins, C., 183
Toupin, C., 216
Tourangeau, R., 113, 296, 318, 331
Trager, G. L., 72
Tranel, D., 189
Traugott, E. C., 118, 485
Travis, C., 269
Treitler, L., 505
Truscott, J., 217, 222
Tsur, R., 234, 235, 236, 237, 239, 302, 305
Tuggy, D., 417
Turner, M., 6, 53, 57, 62, 65, 109, 115, 155, 178, 181, 191, 235, 236, 237, 238, 239, 241, 244, 272, 291, 295, 305, 327, 342, 472, 489, 495, 514
Turney, P. D., 137, 138
Tversky, A., 71, 296
Tversky, B., 163, 477

Ullmann, S., 302, 427, 428
Umilta, C., 190

Vallar, G., 184, 190
Vallee-Tourangeau, F., 174
van de Moortele, P., 190
van den Broek, P., 154
van Dijk, T. A., 327, 333
van Genabith, J., 312
Van Lancker D., 188
Van Leeuwen, T., 476
Van Luncker-Sidtis, D. R., 184
Van Petten, C., 155, 181, 182
Van Rompay, T., 468, 476
Van Sant, G., 457
Van Teeffelen, T., 280
VanLacker, D., 183
Varela, F., 412
Vatikiotis-Bateson, E., 430
Veale, T., 324
Verbrugge, R. R., 510
Vergeer, A., 478
Vervaeke, J., 208, 448
Vicari, P., 454, 455, 456
Vicente, B., 237
Victor, P., 478
Villamil, O. S., 214
Virtue, S., 154
Vivona, J. M., 400
Vogel, C., 312
Vondruska, R., 296, 297, 298, 305
Vosniadou, S., 119
Vuilleumier, P., 190

Walker, M. E., 511
Wallington, A. M., 319, 322, 333
Walser, R., 511
Walsh, C., 239
Walsh, J. P., 511
Wang, J., 320
Ward, J., 435
Warren, B., 284
Watson, J. D. G., 434
Way, E. C., 311–312
Webb, R., 485
Weber, S. H., 311–312

Wechsler, D., 71
Weiner, J., 311–312
Weisper, S., 186, 188
Wells, P., 478
Werner, H., 438
Werner, N. K., 147, 149
Wernicke, C., 177
Werth, P., 240
Westendorp, P., 477
White, R. M., 264, 272
Whittock, T., 464, 468, 469
Wilcox, P. P., 313, 496
Wilcox, S., 313
Wilkins, D., 492
Wilks, Y., 311–312, 317, 320
Williams, J., 118, 150, 151, 426, 427, 428
Williams, S., 188
Willig, C., 408
Wilson, C. D., 426, 432
Wilson, D., 7, 146, 155, 237, 266, 269, 330, 469
Wilson, N., 167
Winner, E., 154, 178, 182, 183, 184, 188, 223
Winston, P. H., 312
Winter, S., 10, 44, 363
Wittrock, M., 216
Wolff, P., 71, 110, 112, 113, 116, 117, 122, 129, 136, 517
Woll, B., 313
Wong, E., 216
Wood, F. B., 433
Wood, L. A., 408
Wray, A., 225, 284
Wright, H. G., 44
Wright, K. J. T., 400
Wundt, W., 485
Wurmser, L., 413
Wyke, M. A., 433, 435, 436

Yan, J., 111
Yarlatt, D., 124
Yelland, G., 434
Yu, N., 9, 223, 250, 253, 256, 257, 258, 303, 305, 312–313, 393, 478, 485

Zaidel, E., 154, 155, 178, 184, 188, 191
Zalazinska, A., 492
Zampetti, P., 184
Zanten, W., 516
Zbikowski, L. M., 12, 502, 503, 511, 512, 516
Zelizer, V. A., 409
Zhang, L., 326
Zharikov, S., 121, 122
Zon, B., 510
Zorzi, M., 190
Zur, A., 149, 153, 154, 156
Zwaan, R. A., 164, 243, 432

# Subject Index


A IS B metaphor format, 215–216, 217–218
abstract concepts, 39–40, 45
  NTL and, 33–34
activation and inhibition, in NTL, 19
AD. *See* Alzheimer's disease
aesthetics, 5, 153–154, 156
Affection is Warmth, 46
agency, time and, 61–62
AI. *See* artificial intelligence
Aleksandrov, A. N., 343
Alzheimer's disease (AD), 184
ambiguity, in law, 364–365, 367
*American Psycho*, 471
American Sign Language, 487
analogy, 139–140, 325. *See also* disanalogies
  AI and, 314, 315
  discover mapping and, 314, 315
  metaphor and, 109–115, 136–139
  metaphor *vs.*, 123
  reasons for, 213
  sample problems, 137
analysis, metaphoric blends, NTL and, 32–33
analytical philosophy, meaning, truth and, 47
anger and love, 381
aptness, 110, 135, 262
  relationality and, 110, 121–122
Aristotle, 48, 67
art, 11. *See also* pictorial metaphors
  artistic symbols, 504
  awkward metaphors in, 455–457
  edge depiction, universal impressions in, 451–453
  Emblematica movement in, 454–455
  euphemisms in, 457
  form geometries *vs.* objects in, 454–455
  form symbolism dependencies in, 453–454
  hendiadys in, 457
  hyperbole in, 457
  irony in, 458
  lines, contours in, 450–451
  literal picture realism in, 449–450
  metaphor limits in, 447
  metaphoric pictures, 459–460
  motion in, 448–449, 452–453
  natural law standards in, 450–451
  personification in, 457–458
  realism as apparent naturalism in, 457
  realism violations in, 448–449
  shortcomings of, 457
  successful metaphors in, 460
  synecdoche in, 457
  tropes, 457–458, 478
artificial intelligence (AI), 10
  aims of, 312–314
  analogy-finding and, 325
  attitude transfer, value judgments and, 333

artificial intelligence (AI) (*cont.*)
ATT-Meta approach to, 319–323, 333–334
Barnden work on, 319–323
belief reasoning and, 333
cognition and, 312
computer science and, 313–314, 334
context/extent and, 328–329
domain distinctions and, 322–323, 330–331
engineering aim of, 312–313, 334
Fass work on, 317–319
general/philosophical aim of, 312
goal-directed reasoning and, 321
gradedness and, 330
Hobbs work on, 314–315
literal meaning and, 332
mapping details and, 326–327
mapping discovery by analogy and, 314, 315
mappings, inference transfer and, 314
map-transcendence, pretense and, 319–323
Martin work on, 315–317
meta5 and, 317–319, 332
Metallel and, 319
metaphor research and, 311–312, 314–334
metaphorical transfers, overall processing and, 328
metonymy and, 331–332
MIDAS and, 315–316, 317
mundaneness and, 326
Narayanan work on, 323–324
non-assertional metaphor and, 326
parallelism, disanalogies and, 327–328
psychological aim of, 312
recent work, 314–326
research products, 313, 334
reversed transfers and, 333–334
Sapper system, 324–326
source-domain, pretense reasoning and, 327
source-domain representation, 323–324
source/target overrides and, 329–330
structure-mapping and, 325
TACITUS system and, 314–315
uncertainty and, 329
unmodified-property usage, 314–315
useful artifacts, 312
Veal work on, 324–326
VNMAs and, 322
attitude transfer/value judgments
AI and, 333
ATT-Meta and, 333
ATT-Meta, 319–323
AI and, 319–323, 333–334
attitude transfer, value judgments and, 333
belief reasoning and, 333
domain distinctions and, 322–323, 330–331
IQ of, 322
reversed transfers and, 333–334
source-domain, pretense reasoning and, 327
source/target overrides and, 329–330
VNMAs aspect of, 322
attributive category theory, 124
automaticity, literal *vs.* metaphorical meaning, 70

Bach, J. S., 502
Barnden, John, 10, 319–323
being, 48
belief reasoning, AI and, 333
best-fit systems, NTL and, 23–24
blended cyclical day (C), 57, 58
blending. *See also* concept blending
integration, 31–32
metaphors and, 30–31, 32–33
metonymic tightening and, 31–32
in NTL, 30, 31–32
topology, 31
unpacking, 31
web, 31
body, emerging metaphors, 249–253
Borbely, Antal, 11
Bowdle, Brian, 7
brain physiology. *See also* event-related brain potentials; neurological correlates
brain hemisphere evidence, 183–184
extension neural circuits, 23
gestalt neural circuits, 21
language deficits and, 178
metaphor comprehension and, 177–179, 182–187, 188
mirror neurons, 19
neural circuit mapping, 22–23
patient studies, 182–184
brain shaping, 18
Bunyan, John, 236

C. *See* blended cyclical day
Cacciari, Cristina, 11
Cameron, Lynne, 8
Canale/Swain/Bachman communication competence model, 222
career of metaphor hypothesis, 7, 115–119, 122–123
categorization, 119
category membership, 139–140
comparison process and, 6–7
comparison *vs.*, 79–80, 123
theory of, 74–75
causal path metaphor, 42–43
causation, 39, 41–42, 44
Chomskian linguistics, 352

Cienki, Alan, 11–12
cinematic metaphor, 468
class-inclusions, 119
CMT. *See* conceptual metaphor theory
cobbling and sculpting, 53–54, 63–64
cognition
  AI and, 312
  efficiency, relevance and, 88, 89
  embodied simulations in, 8
  embodied theories of, 426
  literature as text *vs.*, 241–243
  metaphor, gesture and, 352–356, 495–496
cognitive linguistics, 40, 48
  mathematics and, 342–343
Cognitive Metaphor Theory, 235–236, 239, 244
cognitive science, music, metaphor and, 510–511
Cognitive Science of Mathematics, 341
*Cognitive Science of Mathematics* (Lakoff, Núñez), 340
cognitive theory, law and, 375–376
*The Collector* (Fowles), 240
color of law, 363, 370–371
color of office metaphor, 365–374
  Supreme Court and, 372
communication
  Canale/Swain/Bachman model, 222
  code model view of, 85
  inferential, 87
  language and, 85–87
  relevance principle of, 89–90
comparison, 67–68, 69, 70–74, 110
  categorization *vs.*, 79–80, 123
  dual reference and, 71–73, 74
  outcome, psychotherapy, 404
  theory of, 74–75
  understanding, 70–71
compatible/clashing expressions, 296–297
complex metaphors, 247–249
comprehension, 129
  inferential, 87–88, 90
  of metaphor *vs.* simile, 74–81, 119–120
  neural substrates of, 188–191
  real-time, 179–182
  relevance and, 87–88, 90
  of similes, 298–299
  of synaesthetic metaphors, 303
  of zeugma, 301
compression, 53, 54
computational models, LSA, 130–131
computational theory of metaphor, 7
computer science, AI and, 313–314, 334
concept blending. *See also* blending
  in music, 517, 518–519
  in NTL, 23
  theory of, 6
concepts, 45
  sensorimotor grounding of, 189–190
conceptual integration, 54
conceptual mappings, 53–54. *See also* source-to-target mappings; time-space conceptual mapping
conceptual metaphor theory (CMT), shortcoming of, 463
conceptual metaphors, 5, 236
  abstract thought and, 45
  decomposition account of, 248, 257–258, 259–260
  empirical research on, 45, 248
  force dynamics and, 383–384
  individual minds and, 209
  labeling of, 497
  mathematics and, 349–351, 356
  in NTL, 28–29
  psychological reality of, 351
  talk and, 207–209
constraint-based satisfaction model, 145
*Contact* (Sagan), 339
*The Contemporary Theory of Metaphor* (Lakoff), 25
context, 7, 9, 10–11, 140, 244, 266, 268–274, 287–288, 407–409
  AI and, 328–329
  of homonyms, 74
  inappropriate properties inhibition, 148–149
  incompatible properties retention, 151–153
  incompatible properties suppression, 149–150
  strength of, 98–100
context effects
  direct access view, 145
  inhibition/suppression/retention, 147–148
  temporal priority of, 145
context-dependent hypothesis, 180
contextual metaphor, pictorial metaphor and, 464–465
contrastive metaphors, 152
conventional metaphors, without literal referent, 77
conventionalization, 123
  naturalistic evidence of, 121
Cooke, Deryck, 506
corpus linguistics, 280–282, 283–284, 293
  concordances, intuition based-description, 284
  experimental work linguistic data, 284–287
  FEIs, 282
  introduction to, 280–282
  research, 9, 282–284
Coulson, Seana, 8
Courant, R., 344

*Course in General Linguistics* (Saussure), 505
cross-domain mappings. *See also* domain-mapping; source domains
gestures and, 485–486
mental number line, 190–191
culture, 247, 289. *See also* language and culture
emerging metaphors filter of, 253–256
emotional concepts and, 388–392, 393–394
language acquisition and, 225–226
music and, 516, 519
shared metaphors and, 259

Davidson, Donald, 45, 46
Deignan, Alice, 9
depth psychology theorists, 401
directional asymmetry, 115
directional inference process, 113
directionality principle (DR), 296–297
compatible, clashing expressions and, 296–297
disanalogies, AI and, 327–328
discourse coherence, 153
domain distinctions
AI and, 322–323, 330–331
ATT-Meta and, 322–323, 330–331
domain-mapping
AI and, 326–327
hypothesis, 114
DP. *See* directionality principle
dual reference
comparison and, 71–73, 74
implications of, 73–74
metaphor understanding and, 71–73
duals, 60–61, 65–66

economic policy, metaphoric statements about, 323–324
education, 9
educational change, 213–214
models, metonymy role in, 215
EFL. *See* English as a foreign language
ego, time and, 62
Elliot, T. S., 272
embedded multimodal metaphors, 474–476
Emblematica art movement, 454–455
embodied cognition theory, 426
Embodied Construction Grammar, 36–37
embodied metaphor, pictorial metaphor and, 468
embodied simulation, 8, 162–165, 173–175
fictive motion and, 169–171
in NTL, 18–19
emergence, in NTL, 32
emergent structure, 54, 55
emerging metaphors
body as source for, 249–253
culture filter for, 253–256
emotion
emergence of, 385
figurative language of, 380
force of, 385
master metaphor for, 382–385
musical meaning and, 506
as natural force, 384
as opponent, 383–384
parts of, 380
as physical force, 384–385
emotion concepts
cultural models of, 388–392, 393–394
historical change and, 394–395
metaphors, cognitive construction of, 388–392
universality of, 392–395
emotion metaphors, 10, 380
mentonymies/related concepts, 380–382
relationship metaphors *vs.*, 387–388
uniqueness of, 385–387
universality of, 392–395
empirical studies, 12–13, 248
English as a foreign language (EFL), 214
Erickson, Milton, 401
ERPs. *See* event-related brain potentials
Event Structure Metaphor, 33
event-related brain potentials (ERPs), 179
events, 39
E/X/M blends, 56–61, 62–63
E/X/M/R/S blends, 62–63
explicit metaphors, implicit *vs.*, 469
expression content *vs.* character, 268
extension neural circuits, 23

Fass, Dan, 317–319
Fauconnier, Gilles, 6, 57
FEIs. *See* fixed expressions and idioms
Feldman, Jerome, 17, 18
fictive motion
embodied simulation and, 169–171
mathematics and, 349–351, 356
figurative language
defined, 416
of emotion, 380
interpretation of, 7–8, 184, 363–364
law and, 363–364
literal *vs.*, 69
neurotic defenses *vs.*, 414
in poetic discourse, 305
psycholinguistic study of, 305
psychotherapy and, 398
*The Figure in the Carpet* (James), 240
fixed expressions and idioms (FEIs), 282

fMRI. *See* functional magnetic resonance imaging
Fodor, Jerry, 48–50
force-dynamics of language, 383–384
Forceville, Charles, 11
form geometries *vs.* objects, in art, 454–455
form symbolism dependencies, in art, 453–454
Formal Language metaphor, 50
formal mathematics, 340, 356, 358–359. *See also* mathematics
forward metaphors, 112
Foster, E. M., 240
Fowles, John, 240
Freeman, Donald, 240
*From Molecule to Metaphor* (Feldman), 17
functional magnetic resonance imaging (fMRI), 187–188
functions
  graph of, 344, 348, 349
  limits, continuity of, 343–351

Generative Metaphor, 213–214
  criticism of, 8–9
generic force metaphors, 395
genitive (noun–noun) structures, interpretation generation of, 303–304
genre, 288–289
Gentner, Dedre, 7
gestalt neural circuits, 21
Gestalt psychology, perception and, 438–439
*Gesture*, 496
gesture, metaphor and thought, study of, 493–497
gestures, 11–12
  abstract metaphorical thinking and, 353
  as cognition, 352–356, 495–496
  co-verbal, 486
  cross-domain mapping and, 485–486
  defined, 485–487
  in different cultures, 492–493
  iconic, 485
  interlocutors and, 353
  language, thought and, 486
  Lenin statue and, 483
  parameters of, 353, 355–356
  phases of, 353
  of pointing ahead, 483–484, 485
  sign language and, 486–487
  speech and, 487–493
  speech-gesture co-processing, 353
  speech-gesture complementarity, 353
  speech-gesture development, 353
  speech-gesture synchronicity, 352
  studies of, 352–356
  study relevance of, 484, 497–498
  unconscious production of, 352
  universality of, 352
Gibbs, Raymond, 8, 136
Giora, Rachel, 7–8
Glucksberg, Sam, 6–7
goal-directed reasoning, in AI, 321
*The Gold Rush*, 462
Goodman, Nelson, 504
*Gracious Curves*, 473
graded salience hypothesis, 146–147, 153
gradedness, AI and, 330
Grady, Joe, 26, 46
grammar, 35, 264
  concordance, 119
  form preferences, 120
grasp, grasping concepts, 6
Grice, Paul, 87

*Hand and Mind: What Gestures Reveal about Thought* (McNeil), 486
hemineglect, 190
hendiadys, in art, 457
Hobbs, J. R., 314–315
homonyms, 132
  in context, 74
hybrid metaphor, pictorial metaphor and, 465–466
hyperbole, 94
  in art, 457
hypothetical vehicle properties, 73

idiolects, personal world views, 239–240
  metaphors and, 239–240
idioms. *See* fixed expressions and idioms
image metaphors, 238–239
image schemas
  and cogs in NTL, 24
  preservation in NTL of, 30
implicit metaphors
  construal interpretation of, 469
  explicit metaphors *vs.*, 469
individual studies, 12–13
inference, 48, 54, 413
  about mental states, 87
  AI and, 314
  directional, 113
  in NTL, 19, 29
  relevance and, 87–88, 90
  steps of, 95–98
  transfer, mappings of, 314
inferential communication, 87
inhibition. *See* activation and inhibition
inhibition/suppression/retention, context effects, 147–148

initial target-domain query (IQ), of ATT-Meta, 322
input spaces, intermediate blends, 56–61
integration networks, 53
  compression in, 53, 54
  emergent structure and, 54, 55
  E/X/M blends, 59, 62–63
  time as space, 65–66
intelligence, 312. *See also* artificial intelligence
intent, 374
interdisciplinary studies, 4
interlocutors, gesture and, 353
intermediate blends. *See* input spaces, intermediate blends
International Computer Science Institute, 17
IQ. *See* initial target-domain query
irony, in art, 458

James, Henry, 240
Japanese haiku, 100
Jha, Radhika, 425
Johnson, Christopher, 26, 43, 48, 247
Johnson, Mark, 6, 24, 34
justice, 39

Kennedy, John, 11
Kesey, Ken, 240
*Kijk*, 470
*King Lear* (Shakespeare), 241
Kintsch Construction-Integration model, 131–132
Kintsch Prediction Model, 131, 133–136
Kintsch, Walter, 7
knowledge, 39, 45
  mathematical, 340
  music and, 504–505
Kolmogorov, A., 343
Kövecses, Zoltán, 10

*La Strada*, 471
*La Zizanie/The Roman Agent*, 474
Lakoff, George, 6, 24, 25, 33, 34, 43, 48, 62, 136, 247, 339, 340, 342
language, 206–207, 439. *See also* corpus linguistics; sensory language
  action, sensory integration and, 437
  American Sign Language, 487
  coding, decoding of, 85
  communication and, 85–87
  contemporary philosophy of, 44–48
  creativity of, 140–141
  determinative power of, 402
  EFL, 214
  force-dynamics of, 383–384
  gestures and, 486
  human *vs.* animal, 85
  literal use of, 100
  of mathematics, 339, 344–345
  music and, 12, 502–503, 520
  naturalistic patterns of, 9, 47
  NTL, 189
  ostensive stimuli and, 86–87
  poetic effects and, 100–103
  psychotherapy and, 402
  semantics of, 47
  technical, 206–207
  thought, communication and, 4, 5, 11–12
language acquisition, 212
  culture importance in, 225–226
  EFL, 214
  receptive *vs.* productive skills in, 221–222
  teaching strategies, issues, 219–220
language and culture, metaphor in, 8–10, 11–12
language conventionality
  motivation and, 437–439
  Takete, Maluma, 438
language metaphor, thought as, 49–50
*Language of Art* (Goodman), 504
*The Language of Music* (Cooke), 506
Language of Thought metaphor, 48–50
Latent Semantic Analysis (LSA), 7, 130–131
  Kintsch Construction-Integration model, 131–132
  Kintsch Prediction Model and, 131, 133–136
  semantic representation by, 131
  word senses within, 7
Lavrent'ev, M. A., 343
law, legal theory
  ambiguity in, 364–365, 367
  authority and, 365
  Cognitive Theory of Metaphor and, 375–376
  color of law and, 370–371
  color of office metaphor and, 365–374
  figurative language and, 363–364
  intent and, 374
  *Monroe v. Pape*, 371
  objective criteria and, 365
  objectivist epistemology of, 363
  state action and, 364–365
  Supreme Court, 372
  ultra vires doctrine, 372–373
Lawyer and Shark, cross-categorization of, 71
legal metaphor, 364, 365
Legal Realists, 363
legal reasoning, 10
Lenin, Vladimir, 483
lexical meanings

graded salience hypothesis, 146–147, 153
standard pragmatic model, 145–146
temporal priority of, 145–147
underspecification model, 146
lines/contours, in art, 450–451
linguistic metaphors
conventionalized, deliberate, 202
talk and, 207
tuning of, 202–204
vehicle development, systematicity of, 201–202
linguistic synaesthesia, 427
linguistics. *See also* corpus linguistics
Chomskian, 352
constraints, 275–276
context, 287–288
conventions, 9–10
literal meaning, 143–144. *See also* priority of the literal
AI and, 332
automaticity of, 70
figurative *vs.*, 69
noun–noun combinations and, 70
priority of, 68, 69–70, 80, 145–146
processing of, 68, 69, 70
literal picture realism, 449–450
literalist philosophy. *See* objectivist/literalist philosophy
literal-loose-metaphorical continuum, 93–95
literature
Anglo-American stylists, 233–234
formalistic view of, 233–234
metaphor in, 233–238, 241–243
metaphor uses/functions in, 238–241, 243–244
location-event structure metaphor, 41, 43
logical contradictions, 234
love
anger and, 381
metaphors of, 47–48
*The Love Song of J. Alfred Prufrock* (Eliot), 272
Lovink, Geert, 476
Low, Graham, 8–9
LSA. *See* Latent Semantic Analysis; latent semantic analysis

M1. *See* primary motor cortex
*Macbeth* (Shakespeare), 240
mapping gaps, in NTL, 29–30
Martin, J. H., 315–317
*Mary Poppins*, 463
*Matematika, ee soderzhanie metody i znachenie* (Aleksandrov, Komogorov, Lavernt'ev), 343
Mathematical Idea Analysis, 343
mathematics, 10, 341–343
cognitive linguistics and, 342–343
cognitive science of, 341
conceptual metaphor, fictive motion and, 349–351, 356
constant sequence in, 353–354
dead metaphors and, 351–357
dynamic language of, 344–345
formal, 340, 356, 358–359
functions, limits/continuity of, 343–344, 348, 349–351
human embodied view of, 359–360
knowledge and, 340
language of, 339, 344–345
nature of, 357
number oscillation in, 353–354
ontology, truth and, 357–358
perception and, 341–342
philosophical implications of, 357–360
pure mathematics, numbers, 345–349
romance of, 340–341
social conventions and, 357
source-path-goal schema, 348
teaching of, 341
truth in, 357–358
universal language of, 339
Matlock, Teenie, 8
McMullen, Linda, 10–11
McNeil, D., 486
meaning, 10, 45, 47. *See also* literal meaning; metaphorical meaning
construction of, 90–93
figurative *vs.* literal, 69, 121
literal *vs.* nonliteral, 6
mental stimulation and, 19
nonliteral, 67–68
ostensive stimuli and, 86–87
salient-nonsalient continuum of, 7–8
mental number line. *See* cross-domain mappings, mental number line
mental reenactments, 173
mental spaces, in NTL, 30
mental states
inference about, 87
Language of Thought metaphor and, 48–49
mental stimulation, meaning and, 19
MES. *See* Metaphor Extension System
meta
AI and, 317–319, 332
metonymy and, 318–319
Metallel, 319

metaphor(s). *See also* causal path metaphor; cinematic metaphor; Cognitive Metaphor Theory; color of office metaphor; complex metaphors; conceptual metaphors; contextual metaphor; contrastive metaphors; conventional metaphors; embedded multimodal metaphors; embodied metaphor; emotion metaphors; Event Structure Metaphor; Formal Language metaphor; Generative Metaphor; generic force metaphors; hybrid metaphor; image metaphors; language metaphor; legal metaphor; location-event structure metaphor; metaphor understanding; metaphor-referent metaphors; monomodal metaphors; multimodal metaphors; natural force metaphor; negative metaphors; nominal metaphors; novel metaphors; object-event-structure metaphor; pictorial metaphors; poetic metaphors; pressurized container metaphor; primary metaphors; relationship metaphors; reverse metaphors; synaesthetic metaphors; systematic metaphors; teaching/learning metaphor; verbal metaphor
in abstract concepts, 33–34
aesthetics and, 5, 153–154, 156
affective impact of, 203–204
AI and, 10
AI research on, 311–312, 313, 314–334
analogy and, 109–115, 123, 136–139
analysis methods, 5, 36–37
aptness of, 110, 121–122, 135, 262
in art, 11
from art objects, 447
asymmetry of, 140
*vs.* blends, 30–31
body, culture and, 9
as bridges, 426
categorization, comparison process, 6–7
category-based approaches to, 119
Chinese/English, 250–253, 257
classes of, 129
class-inclusions and, 119
clustering of, 200, 214
cognitive significance of, 276–277
cognitive theories of, 9, 10
computational theory of, 7
conceptual blending theory and, 6
consistent expressions and, 114–115, 214
contextual approach to, 407–409
contextual meanings of, 7
in co-occurring speech, 488
in corpus linguistics research, 9
cosanguinity of, 429
directionality of, 112–113, 115
discourse coherence and, 153
dual reference and, 71–73
as dynamic embodied cognition, 11–12
as dynamic interactions product, 291–293
education and, 8–9
emotion and, 10
emotion concepts, cognitive construction, 388–392
empirical studies of, 3, 12–13, 397–398
explicit training in, 216
expressive, communicative functions of, 398
extended mappings of, 113–114
as falsehood, 363
forward, reverse, 112
as general cognitive principle, 493
gesture, embodied cognition and, 352–356, 495–496
in gesture/language, 491–492
grammar and, 35
grammatical deviance of, 264
historical change and, 394–395
as ideological, 290–291
idiolects, personal world views and, 239–240
implicit *vs.* explicit, 469
in individual plays, 240
individual studies of, 12
inside/outside literature continuity of, 235–238
inside/outside literature discontinuity of, 233–235
interdisciplinary study of, 4, 5
iterative, 223
in language and culture, 8–10, 289
language, thought, communication and, 4, 5, 11–12
Legal Realists and, 363
legal reasoning and, 10
linguistic, conceptual, mental levels of, 416–417
literary studies of, 241, 243–244
in literature, 233–235, 238–241, 243–244
in literature as text *vs.* cognition, 241–243
living/dead, 119, 235, 351–357
logical contradictions in, 234
LSA and, 7
metonymy and, 8–9, 10, 21–22, 31–32, 215, 223, 238, 292–293, 314, 380–382
multimodal, 11
neural theory of, 6, 8, 17, 426
nonlinguistic, 11
non-semantic theory of, 46
in nonverbal expression, 11–12

overidentification of, 212
paradox of, 5
perceptual experience and, 425
poetic appeal of, 100–103
poetic figures and, 9–10
power of, 398–403
problem description, resolution and, 398–399
processing of, 110–111
psychoanalysis, defense and, 417
psychotherapy and, 398
real-time processes, 112
in reasoning and feeling, 10–11
relevance theory perspective on, 7
in religious concepts, 455
research limits, 403–409
research on, 12–13, 283, 293, 496–497
roots of, 6–7
salient-nonsalient meaning continuum and, 7–8
scholarship on, 3–4
semantic theory of, 9
semantics *vs.* pragmatics of, 267–269
as shared discourse space, 205
simile and, 7, 67–69, 74–81, 119–123
speech-act perspective of, 45
in speech/gesture, 487–488, 491
state-of-the-art, 3–6, 12
study scope, 4
successful, 460
syntactical criteria for, 413
teaching, learning and, 8–9
as textual/social phenomenon, 287–291
theoretical approaches to, 312
thought systems, NTL and, 34
total time constraint of, 316
traditional interest in, 4
transference and, 419–420, 427–428
truth-conditions of, 262–263, 268–269, 276
ubiquity of, 4–5, 12–13
understanding, 7–8, 71–73
uniqueness of, 144–145, 156
verbal *vs.* pictorial, 11
*Metaphor and Thought* (Ortony), 3
metaphor comprehension, 68–69, 80, 129
brain hemisphere role in, 182–187, 188
brain physiology and, 177–179
impaired, 184
neural substrate of, 188–191
underspecification model of, 146
Metaphor Extension System (MES), 315–316
metaphor, imagination, simulation. *See also* embodied simulation
bodily imagination, time, 168–169, 171–173
fictive motion, embodied simulation, 169–173
imagining impossible actions, 165–167, 171–173
psycholinguistic evidence, 161–162
real/imagined bodily movement and, 171–173
studies on, 165–173
metaphor interference effect (MIE), 180
Metaphor Interpretation, Denotation, and Acquisition System (MIDAS), 315–317
domain divisions in, 317
MES and, 315–316
metaphor mapping, 139–140
on-line processing and, 493–494
metaphor negotiating/appropriating, in talk, 205–206
metaphor processing, models of, 145
metaphoric competence, 220–222, 223
measuring, 222
metaphoric language
cross-sensory similarities in, 429–430
NTL and, 34–36
metaphoric processes, primary/secondary, 420–421
metaphorical inferences, in NTL, 19, 29
metaphorical meaning, 274–276
automaticity of, 70
processing speed of, 70
temporal priority of, 70
metaphorical sentences, DP effect on, 300–301
metaphorical transfers, AI and, 328
metaphoricity
defined, 417
dynamic, gradable, 495
trauma as loss of, 417–418
metaphor-referent metaphors, 78
*Metaphors We Live By* (Johnson, Lakoff), 24, 247
metaphysics, 45
metonymy, 8–9, 10, 215, 223, 238, 292–293, 314, 380–382
AI and, 331–332
blending and, 31–32
in educational models, 215
emotional, 381–382
linguistic, conceptual, mental levels of, 416–417
linking neural circuits and, 21–22
meta5 and, 318–319
negative defense and, 418–419
psychoanalysis and, 418–419
transference and, 419–420
MIDAS. *See* Metaphor Interpretation, Denotation, and Acquisition System
MIE. *See* metaphor interference effect
mind, 39
conceptual metaphor and, 209
Language of Thought metaphor for, 48–50

mirror neurons, 19
monomodal metaphors, multimodal metaphors
and, 477–478
*Monroe v. Pape*, 371
*More than Cool Reason* (Lakoff, Turner), 62
"Morning Song" (Plath), 237
motion, in art, 448–449, 452–453
Müeller, Cornelia, 11–12
multimodal metaphors, 11, 469–474
dimensions of, 476, 477
monomodal metaphors and, 477–478
uptake of, 477
verbal metaphor *vs.*, 477
mundaneness, 326
music, 12
analysis of, 512–519
concept blending in, 517, 518–519
culture and, 516, 519
function of, 520
human experience and, 508–510
knowledge and, 504–505
language and, 12, 502–503, 520
mappings within, 516–517
meaning, emotion and, 506
metaphor, cognitive science and,
510–511
musical semiotics, 505–508
philosophical writings about, 505
research on, 504–511
scholars of, 503–504
structure of, 510–511
text painting in, 512–515
vocabulary of, 506
mutual inhibition, in NTL, 19

Narayanan, Srini, 26, 323–324
natural force metaphor, 384
natural language, 47
natural law, in art, 450–451
naturalistic language patterns, 9
negative metaphors, 144
networks, 61–63
cobbling, sculpting, 53–54, 63–64
integration networks, 53
neural bindings. *See also* brain physiology
nonce neural, 20
in NTL, 20
permanent obligatory, 20
permanent-ready-but-conditional, 20
neural choreography, in NTL, 20–21
neural circuits, 21–23
extension, 23
gestalt, 21
linking, 21–22
two-way linking, 22
winner-take-all, 21
X-schemas, 23
neural connections, 18
neural maps, in NTL, 20
neural substrates
cross-domain mappings, mental number line,
190–191
of metaphor comprehension, 188–191
sensorimotor concept grounding, 189–190
Neural Theory of Language (NTL), 189
abstract concepts, metaphor and, 33–34
activation and inhibition in, 19
analysis, metaphoric blends and, 32–33
asymmetry in, 28
best-fit systems and, 23–24
blending in, 30, 31–32
brain shaping and, 18
conceptual blends in, 23
conceptual metaphor use in, 28–29
embodiment, simulation semantics in, 18–19
emergence in, 32
image schema preservation in, 30
inferences in, 19, 29
introduction to, 18–37
mapping gaps in, 29–30
mental spaces in, 30
metaphor analysts and, 36–37
metaphorical language and, 34–36
metaphors *vs.* blends in, 30–31
mutual inhibition in, 19
neural binding in, 20
neural choreography in, 20–21
neural circuit types, 21–23
neural maps in, 20
neuron activation spreading in, 19–20
neuronal groups and, 18
old theory of, 24–26
primary metaphors and, 26–28
processing prediction in, 27–28
structural prediction in, 27
thought systems, metaphor and, 34
neural theory of metaphor, 6, 8, 17
neuroimaging, 187–188
neurological correlates. *See also* brain
physiology
fMRI, 187–188
hemineglect, 190
LHD damage, 178
N400 amplitudes, 180–182
PET, 187–188
processing mechanisms and, 154–155
SOA, 183
of synaesthetic perception, 436
visual half-field priming, 185–187
neuron activation spreading, in NTL, 19–20

neuronal groups
NTL and, 18
structured connectionism in, 18
neurotic defenses, figurative language *vs.*, 414
Nietzsche, Friedrich, 39
1984 (Orwell), 240
nominal metaphors, 67
non-assertional metaphor, 326
nonce neural bindings, 20
nonliteral meanings, 67–68
processing priority of, 68
non-semantic theory, 46
nonverbal expression, 11–12
noun–adjective constructions, interpretation generation of, 303
noun–noun combinations, interpretation of, 70
novel metaphors
without literal referent, 78
as simile, 76
NTL. *See* Neural Theory of Language
numbers, in pure mathematics, 345–349
"Nun komm der Heiden Heiland," 502
Núñez, R., 34, 339, 340, 342

O, 474
object-event-structure metaphor, 42, 44
objectivist/literalist philosophy, 39, 44–45, 51
objects *vs.* form symmetries, in art, 454–455
*Once Upon a Time in the West*, 472
*One Flew Over the Cuckoo's Nest* (Kesey), 240
on-line metaphoric thought, flexibility of, 494–495
Optimal Innovation Hypothesis, 154
Ortony, Andrew, 3
Orwell, George, 240
ostensive stimuli, 86–87
meaning and, 87
*ousia*, 48

parallelism, AI and, 327–328
*A Passage to India* (Forster), 240
perception, 425
Gestalt psychologists and, 438–439
mathematics and, 341–342
neurology of, 426
veridical pagelds for, 426
perceptual metaphors, senses directionality of, 435–436
*Perfume* (Süskind), 240
permanent obligatory neural bindings, 20
permanent-ready-but-conditional neural bindings, 20
personal world views. *See* idiolects, personal world views
personification, in art, 457–458
PET. *See* positron magnetic resonance imaging
philosophy, 40–44
history of, 39
of language, 44–48
mathematics and, 357–360
metaphor and, 6, 48–51
metaphorical analysis of, 44
objectivist/literalist, 39, 44–45, 51
perennial questions of, 40
*Philosophy in the Flesh* (Johnson, Lakoff), 34, 43, 48
pictorial metaphor, in pictures, multimodal representations, 464–469
pictorial metaphors, 464–469. *See also* art
contextual metaphor and, 464–465
embodied metaphor and, 468
hybrid metaphor and, 465–466
pictorial simile and, 466–467
target, source pagelding in, 464
textual genre and, 478
types, 464–468
verbal *vs.*, 11, 463
pictorial simile, pictorial metaphor and, 466–467
pictures, multimodal representations
cinematic metaphor and, 468
embedded multimodal metaphors and, 474–476
further research avenues, 476–478
multimodal metaphors and, 469–474
pictorial metaphor in, 464–469
*The Pilgrim's Progress* (Bunyan), 236
Plath, Sylvia, 232–233, 234, 235, 236, 237–238
plays, 240
poetic discourse, 295
cognitive constraints of, 297–298
figurative expressions in, 305
simile distribution in, 297
poetic effects, 100–103, 232–233, 237
poetic figures, 9–10, 295
poetic metaphors, 35, 232–233
poetic structures, cognitive principles and, 305
"Portrait of an Unknown Young Man," 454
positron magnetic resonance imaging (PET), 187–188
pressurized container metaphor, 386
pretense cocoons, 320–321
pretense reasoning, 327
primary metaphors, 46, 247–249
NTL and, 26–28
primary motor cortex (M1), 20
priming techniques, 352
Principle of Relevance, 237

processing predictions, metaphor hypothesis
career, 120–121
psychoanalysis. *See also* psychotherapy
as clinical modality, 412–413
defense, figurativity and, 414–416
hedging equation, 414, 417
history of, 413–414
inference/transference, 413
metaphor, defense and, 417
metaphor in, 11
metaphor theory and, 422
metonymy, negative defense and, 418–419
primary/secondary metaphoric processes
and, 420–421
terminology of, 412
trauma, loss of metaphoricity and, 417–418
psychoanalytical schools, metaphor languages of,
421–422
psychodynamics, 416–417
psycholinguistic evidence, 305
of metaphor, imagination and simulation,
161–162
psychology
AI and, 312
computational models of, 129–130
priming techniques in, 352
*Psychosemantics* (Fodor), 50
psychotherapy, 398
depth psychology theorists and, 401
developmental change processes and, 399
Ericksonian tradition, 401
figurative language and, 398
language and, 402
metaphor in, 10–11, 405
outcome comparisons, 404
therapy-relevant metaphors, 406
pure mathematics. *See also* mathematics
numbers in, 345–349

query-directed reasoning, in AI, 321

realism, in art, 448–449
real-time comprehension, 179–182
real-time processes, 112
reason, 39
reasoning, 48
feeling and, 10–11
recall, of simile, 299
Recall/Space (R/S), 62–63
red herring, 277
relationship metaphors, emotion metaphors *vs.*,
387–388
relevance
cognitive effects and, 88
cognitive principle of, 89
communicative principle of, 89–90
context and, 98–100
degrees of, 88
implications and, 98–100
inferential comprehension and, 87–90
poetic effects and, 100–103
processing effort and, 88
relevance theory, 7, 84–85, 237
inferential comprehension and, 87–88
religious concepts, metaphor in, 455
repetitive transcranial magnetic stimulation
(rTMS), 178, 184–185
*Requiem for a Dream*, 462
retention hypothesis, 151
reverse metaphors, 112
reversed transfers, AI and, 333–334
Robbins, H., 344
"The Romance of Mathematics" (Lakoff,
Núñez), 339
*Romeo and Juliet* (Shakespeare), 241
Rorty, Richard, 45, 46–47
rTMS. *See* repetitive transcranial magnetic
stimulation
Ruwet, Nicholas, 505

Sagan, Carl, 339
salience
salient-nonsalient meaning continuum, 7–8
sentence structure and, 300
Sapper system, 324–326
Saussure, Ferdinand de, 505
Scrouton, Roger, 504–505
Searle, John, 45
semantic relations, 130, 137–138
semantic theory, 9, 262–264
pre-history of, 264–267
skeptical challenges to, 263
sense differentiation
activating mechanism criterion of, 430
belief criterion of, 430
experiential criterion of, 430, 431
property criterion of, 430
sense organ criterion of, 430
senses, 11
five separate, 430–431
metaphorical mapping across, 427–436
sensory language, metaphorical use of, 425–426
sensory metaphors, psychological dimensions of,
427
sentence structure, salience and, 300
Shakespeare, William, 240, 241
shared discourse space, 205
Shen, Yeshaayahu, 9–10
*The Showdown*, 472
similarity models, 140

simile, 7, 67–69, 297–300. *See also* pictorial simile
comprehension of, 298–299
interpretation generation of, 299–300
metaphor and, 74–81, 119–120, 123
novel metaphor as, 76
in poetic discourse, 297
recall of, 299
simulations, 8
SMA. *See* supplementary motor area
SME. *See* Structure-mapping Engine
*Smell* (Jha), 425
SOA. *see* stimulus onset asynchrony
source domains, 11, 49–50, 327, 381
in emotion metaphors, 10
pretense reasoning, ATT-Meta and, 327
source-path-goal schema, 348
source/target overrides
AI and, 329–330
ATT-Meta and, 329–330
source-to-target mappings, 41, 42–43, 47, 49–50, 291–292, 462
counter-examples, 155–156
space, time as, 54–60, 65–66, 485
speech, 487–488
speech-gesture, 487–493
complementarity, 353
co-processing, 353
development, 353
synchronicity, 352
speed, time and, 55
Sperber, Dan, 7
Standard Pragmatic Model, 145–146, 153
Stern, Joseph, 9
stimulus onset asynchrony (SOA), 183
Stroop interference effect, 69–70
Structure-mapping Engine (SME)
appeal of, 112
cascade algorithm, 112
greedy merge algorithm, 110–111
stages, 110–111
structure-mapping theory, 109, 124
supplementary motor area (SMA), 20–21
Süskind, Patrick, 240
symmetric alignment process, 113
synaesthetic metaphors, 11, 302–306, 427
beyond, 436–437
compatible *vs.* clashing, 302
comprehension of, 303
congruence effect and, 431–432
cross-modal associations in, 431–432
directionality and, 428
distribution of, 302–303
genitive (noun–noun) structures, interpretation generation, 303–304
linguistic description/perceptual experience and, 431–432
noun–adjective constructions, interpretation generation, 303
synaesthetic perception, 432–436
age and, 434
automaticity of, 434
concurrent stimuli of, 435
development of, 433
diffuse forms of, 433
experimental evidence, 433
familiarity and, 434
gender and, 434
genetics and, 434
inducers of, 435
medical references, 433
neural-cognitive basis of, 436
in neuroscience literature, 434
origin of, 434
prevalence of, 434
realism of, 434
specificity of, 434
types of, 435
unidirectional, 434
synecdoche, in art, 457
systematic metaphors, talk and, 207–209
systematicity preference, 110

TACITUS system, AI and, 314–315
Takete, Maluma, 438
talk, 8
implicit topics, 201
linguistic, conceptual metaphor and, 207
management of, 204–205
metaphor and, 197–198
metaphor distribution in, 200
metaphor frequency in, 198–200
metaphor grammar in, 200–201
metaphor negotiating/appropriating in, 205–206
metaphor shape in, 198
metaphor use in, 203
research agenda, 209
systematic, conceptual metaphors and, 207–209
teaching/learning metaphor, 8–9, 215–219
basic meaning instruction and, 224–225
classroom/learning management and, 224
culture importance in, 225–226
descriptive *vs.* procedural model, 214–215
EFL and, 214
explicit training, 216
future research directions, 226–227
A IS B metaphor format, 215–216, 217–218
methodological problems, 214–215

teaching/learning metaphor (*cont.*)
receptive *vs.* productive skills, 221–222
strategies, issues, 220–223
TPR learning, 218
technical language, 206–207
*The Texas Chainsaw Massacre*, 473
text painting, music and, 512–515
textual/social phenomenon, 287–291
*Theory and Practice*, 511
Thomas, Dylan, 239
thought, 39
gestures and, 486
as language metaphor, 49–50
Language of Thought metaphor and, 48–50
thought systems and metaphor, NTL and, 34
time, 54–60
agency and, 61–62
duration of, 64
ego and, 62
as money, 53
as space, 54–60, 65–66, 485
speed and, 55
subjective experience of, 64
TIME IS SPACE, 6
time-space conceptual mapping, 54–60
Total Physical Response (TPR) learning, 218
TPR. *See* Total Physical Response learning
transference, 419–420
Trope Form, 76
tropes, in art, 457–458, 478
truth
analytical philosophy, meaning and, 47
conditions, 262–263, 268–269, 276
in mathematics, 357–358
"Tulips" (Plath), 232–233, 236
Turner, Mark, 6, 57, 62
two-way linking neural circuits, 22

ultra vires doctrine, 372–373
uncertainty, AI and, 329
underspecification model, 146
unmodified property usage, AI and, 314

Veal, Tony, 324–326
verbal communication, study of, 84–85
verbal metaphor
multimodal metaphors *vs.*, 477
pictorial *vs.*, 11, 463
view-neutral mapping adjuncts (VNMAs), of ATT-Meta, 322
visual half-field priming, 185–187
VNMAs. *See* view-neutral mapping adjuncts

*The Way We Think* (Fauconnier, Turner), 57
*What Is Mathematics* (Courant, Robbins), 344
*Where Mathematics Comes From* ( Lakoff, Núñez), 34
*Where Mathematics Comes From* (Lakoff, Núñez), 339, 340, 342
*Whose Freedom?* (Lakoff), 33
will, 39
Wilson, Deirdre, 7
winner-take-all neural circuits, 21
Winters, Steven, 10
Woolf, Virginia, 239
words, LSA and, 7
word senses, literal, metaphorical, 131–133
Wundt, Wilhelm, 485

X-schemas, 23

Yu, Ning, 9

Zbikowski, Lawrence, 12
zeugma, 300–301
comprehension of, 301
distribution of, 300–301